Royal
Horticultural
Society
200 YEARS

ROYAL HORTICULTURAL SOCIETY
BICENTENARY
1804 – 2004

MODEST BEGINNINGS

The idea to form a Society for the improvement of horticulture was first proposed by John Wedgwood, of the pottery family. His enthusiasm for the venture was shared by six like-minded fellow founders who, on 7 March 1804, met together in a room over James Hatchard's bookshop in Piccadilly, London. This inaugural meeting was organised by Sir Joseph Banks, President of the Royal Society and scientific mover and shaker of the time. The other five co-founders included two gentlemen amateurs Richard Anthony Salisbury and Charles Greville, two gardeners to George III – William Forsyth and William Townsend Aiton – and the eminent Covent Garden nurseryman James Dickson. With Wedgwood in the chair, rules and regulations were agreed and the object of the Society was set down: "...to collect every information respecting the culture and treatment of all Plants and Trees, as well culinary as ornamental".

From this modest beginning has evolved the Royal Horticultural Society of today with its 300,000 plus members, seasonal flower shows, four landmark gardens, regional centres, advisory services, scientific and educational work, a world-renowned library and an authoritative and extensive range of publications. Although 200 years on the size and scale of the organisation would have astounded its founders, the Society has remained true to their tenets to celebrate gardening in all its many facets.

John Wedgwood
Founder of the RHS and son of the celebrated potter Josiah Wedgwood.

Expanding activities

The Society's range of activities quickly grew as its membership rose. The organisation that began as a repository for factual papers read to sitting members soon expanded. In 1805 the first exhibit – a potato – was shown to Fellows, as the Society's members were known. Books were donated, a library was established and, in 1807, the first volume of the Society's *Transactions,* a lavish publication illustrated with engravings and hand-coloured plates recording those factual papers, was completed. A year later, the Society's first medal was struck. This was awarded not to plants but to individuals for services to the Horticultural Society of London, as it was then known. In 1809 Salisbury negotiated the Society's first royal charter.

A garden was not even considered by the founders, but as increasing numbers of plants were sent in for examination it became essential to have somewhere to house them. A small plot in Kensington was acquired in 1818. Three years later, this was abandoned in favour of 33 acres at Chiswick, leased from the Duke of Devonshire, a President of the Society, to serve as a full-blown experimental garden.

By now the Society was committed to plants, their culture and novelty. But this was not simply through the experiences of its Fellows. Exotics were also shipped to the Society from enthusiasts resident abroad – men like Nathaniel Wallich at the Calcutta Botanic Garden and

Discovering horticultural treasure

Scientist and Horticultural Society founding fellow, Sir Joseph Banks admires the extraordinary flora and fauna of Botany Bay, Australia, with Captain James Cook, 1770, during their circumnavigation of the world on the *Endeavour* (1768–71).

The yellow banksian rose

Rosa banksiae var. *lutea* was brought back from China by John Damper Parks. Its name does not commemorate RHS founder Sir Joseph Banks, but his wife Dorothea.

Stamford Raffles in Singapore. Plant collectors, too, were sent overseas to bring back plants of ornamental promise. The first was John Potts, a member of the Chiswick garden staff, who set off in 1821 for China and the East Indies. The highlight of his collection was 42 chrysanthemum cultivars, which were unfortunately lost on the homeward journey, but seeds of *Primula sinensis*, a *Paeonia lactiflora* var. *pottsii*, hoyas and some camellias were among the precious booty that survived. Other expeditions resulted in the introduction of many plants now familiar in our parks and gardens. From China, John Damper Parks brought back camellias, chrysanthemums, roses and the first aspidistra. David Douglas, one of the best-known plant collectors and an indefatigable

traveller, went to North America where he collected not only conifers, including the famous Douglas fir, but also *Ribes sanguineum*, *Garrya elliptica*, *Mimulus moschatus*, eschscholzia and clarkia. Other notable plant hunters sponsored by the Society included Robert Fortune, who travelled to China, George Don and John Forbes who journeyed to Africa, Carl Theodor Hartweg who hunted for new specimens in North America, and James McRae who travelled to South America. The collected material from these expeditions was grown in the Society's

New ways with glass

Charles Ewing's innovative glass walls, designed for the Horticultural Society's garden at Chiswick. The panels were moveable and used to protect fruit and tender plants.

garden, first at Chiswick and later at Kensington, and exhibited at meetings. When the new introductions flourished and produced seed, this was shared through a plant distribution scheme, initially available only to the Fellows, corresponding members from abroad and botanical gardens in Britain and its colonies. The scheme continues to this day, as excess seed from plants in the various RHS gardens is collected, catalogued and made available to all the Society's members on request.

Floral fêtes and flower shows

A dinner in a local tavern was the usual method of celebration in the early days of the Society, but in 1827 the ruling Council decided to experiment with a public breakfast, soon renamed a "fête", in the garden at Chiswick. This was a paying event organised by a group of aristocratic wives entitled the "Ladies Patronesses". Nearly 3,000 tickets were sold and £500 was raised. Bands played in the garden, a Tyrolean family sang, there was a roped enclosure for dancing, displays of flowers and fine fruits, and marquees for dining. Unfortunately, refreshments were in short supply and only the more determined visitors were able to enjoy the chickens, lamb-tarts, jellies, ices and other fare on offer.

So successful was the venture that it was repeated and became part of the London social season. By the 1830s shows were being held at Chiswick three times a year. In 1861, under the presidency of Prince

Treasures from the East

Many of the plants received by the Society in its early years were brought back by naval captains and in 1820 nine of them were honoured with a medal, including Captain Rawes, who introduced *Primula sinensis*. John Potts, a member of the Chiswick garden staff, collected seeds of this plant during his plant-hunting expedition to China.

Albert, the Society acquired a second garden in Kensington and collaborated in the Second Great Exhibition of 1862, a great success in terms of public acclaim if not financially. This was also the year of the Society's first Great Spring Show. Held initially in Kensington, this event then moved to the Inner Temple, just off the Strand, in 1888, before coming to rest in the grounds of the Royal Hospital, Chelsea, in 1913. Originally the show was accommodated in one tent, but the marquees increased in both number and size until in 1951 the Great Marquee was erected to cover around

three and a half acres of bedding displays and the best of plants from nurseries, growers and parks departments.

In the early years plants were simply grouped on tables according to type: all the orchids together, the fruit, vegetables, and so on. Since the Second World War all grouping has disappeared: cacti jostle with sweet peas, lupins with potatoes and Caribbean exotics with English strawberries. Outside, rock gardens were displayed for decades on the Rock Bank until, in the last years of the 20th century, changing tastes reduced their numbers or

sometimes even eliminated them completely. Instead, visitors now see a wide range of garden styles that reflect contemporary designs and conceptions, and the old canvas marquee has since been replaced by two large floral pavilions. In turn, these will give way in 2004 to a single huge structure to be known as the Great Chelsea Marquee.

Such was the success of the Chiswick fêtes that Prince Albert, as President, urged the Society to organise flower shows in the provinces, too. The first, at Bury St Edmunds in 1867, was greatly enjoyed and profitable in every way, and the second, in Leicester was equally successful. Subsequent shows ran less smoothly, for reasons varying from problems with co-organisers and internal RHS politics, to the weather, which was often

Pleasure palaces and gardens

Victorians attending the Second Great International Exhibition of 1862 at South Kensington. This garden, designed by William Andrews Nesfield and enclosed by Italianate arcades, had two elegant bandstands. When the garden was vacated in 1888 the bandstands were moved to London parks, in Peckham Rye and Southwark.

Horticultural fate

...in consequence of some disappointment in the arrangements...the
refreshments were not attainable until four o'clock, an hour at which
the greater portion of the company had been compelled to seek shelter
from the heavy rain in the most distant tents through oceans of mud,
and under the pelting of one of the heaviest rains of the season...
From a report in *The Times* on the 1829 Horticultural Fête at Chiswick.

too wet, or occasionally too hot. A run of financial
disasters caused the Society to retreat to London after
1886. This remained the venue for its shows for more or
less the next hundred years, until regionalisation was

welcomed again in the 1980s in the wake of the
International Garden Festival in Liverpool.

Scientific interests

The RHS has always involved itself with horticultural
issues of the day and one that caused particular concern
in the late 19th century was atmospheric pollution. This
prompted the Society to hold a Smoke Abatement
Exhibition in 1882 in its garden in Kensington. The
deleterious effects of "urban fog" on cultivated plants
was a growing problem and gardeners noted that not

only were the panes of glasshouses covered in soot but the glass itself showed signs of decay. The RHS Scientific Committee was granted £100 by the Royal Society to investigate the problem. Indeed, it was London's polluted atmosphere that was the principle reason for the Society leaving its Chiswick garden in 1903 for the cleaner air of Wisley.

Citrus sinensis

Plant nutrition also engaged the attention of the Society's Fellows and led to the appointment of a short-lived Chemical Committee, with Edward Solly as RHS Honorary Professor of Chemistry. The programme set in place by the committee resulted in a flurry of activity during the 1840s, when it investigated the chemical composition of plants, soil exhaustion and crop rotation, with experimental trials of lawn fertilisers and manures for the kitchen garden. Lack of funds brought this work to a virtual halt but as the Society's fortunes increased and laboratory facilities became available at Wisley, it was revived in the early years of the 20th century.

In the 1860s the Society set up trials to assess seed quality. The results revealed that the practices of many seed companies were less than honest. In some cases, seed was kept so long it lost its vitality, or it was bulked up with bad or old unviable seed. Also colouring and other

Fruitful pursuits

The Orchard House, as it appeared in the *Gardeners' Chronicle and Agricultural Gazette*, 6 August, 1870. This was one of several glasshouses at Chiswick.

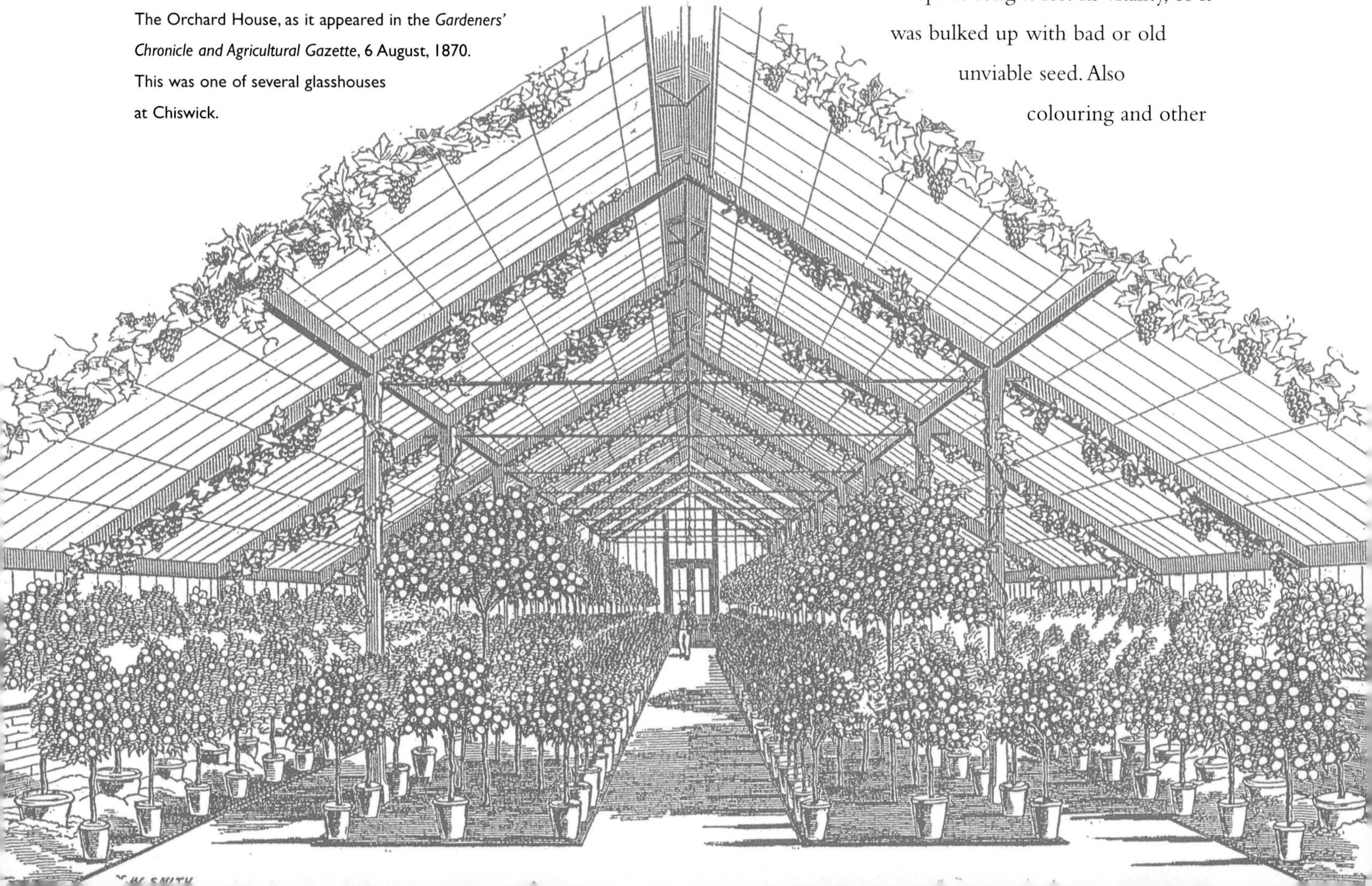

additives were used to disguise inferior seed. Society representatives were called as expert witnesses in a campaign to reform the industry, which later resulted in the passing of the Adulteration of Seeds Act in 1869.

Initiatives in hybridisation and genetics put the Society at the cutting edge of 19th-century science when it organised the First International Conference on Hybridisation in 1899. Gregor Mendel's seminal work on heredity was published for the first time in English in 1900 in the RHS Journal, which rapidly became the vehicle for a lively debate on the application of "Mendel's laws". These were subsequently applied at Wisley to illustrate the history of roses. Other experiments on the genetics of important hybrid groups were carried out, this research culminating after the Second World War with the appointment of the Indian cytologist Dr E.K. Janaki Ammal, the first female scientist on the RHS staff. Her work on the implications of chromosome counts on taxonomy and experiments with colchicine to induce polyploidy – an early form of genetic modification – brought to a close the Society's role at the forefront of plant development. While plant breeding was investigated elsewhere, the RHS instead concentrated its efforts on

Eminent mycologist

The Reverend Miles J. Berkeley was a founder member of the RHS Scientific Committee, along with Charles Darwin.

Rosa 'Ferdinand Pichard'

the study of nomenclature and taxonomy of cultivated plants.

Plant health has also long been of interest to the Society and its Advisory Services currently answer thousands of members' queries each year relating to pests and diseases and methods of cultivation. In the early days of the Society's history, it was the eminent mycologist and Editor of the RHS Journal, the Reverend Miles J. Berkeley, who suggested that potato blight was caused by a fungus, and the Society's Secretary, John Lindley, who stopped the press of the *Gardeners' Chronicle* to announce the devastation of the Irish potato crop and to prophesy the agony of Ireland should the disease spread throughout the country.

As well as its involvement with the diagnosis of plant problems, the RHS held strong views on their treatment. It publicised new chemicals and in 1866 lobbied the government to lift the duty on tobacco imported for horticultural – insecticidal – purposes. But when, after the Second World War, many synthetic chemicals came on the market to kill weeds, pests and diseases, the RHS pathologist, George Fox Wilson, showed great foresight when he warned that "... these preparations [specifically DDT] are toxic to beneficial insects... [which] renders it necessary to time their application with care...". It was also the RHS that spread the good news about biological control in the form of the whitefly parasite *Encarsia formosa*, and became the agent for its production and distribution from the 1930s through to the 1970s.

The Victoria Medal of Honour

In June 1897 Queen Victoria, patron of the RHS, celebrated the 60th anniversary of her accession to the throne. The Society established a new award in her name, their highest honour.

The small gilded medal depicts the Society's symbol of a fruit tree on one side and the goddess Flora kneeling to smell a flower on the reverse. Originally confined to 60 recipients at any one time, the number was increased to 63 in 1901 on the death of Queen Victoria, to commemorate the length of her reign. The first 60 recipients, pictured below, included amateur and professional gardeners, nurserymen, a market gardener, botanists, plant collectors, plant breeders and members of the gardening press. Among them were two women – Gertrude Jekyll and Ellen Willmott – and George Wilson, whose garden at Wisley was presented to the RHS in 1903. Others of note include William Thompson, founder of the seed firm Thompson & Morgan; Harry Turner, who gave us 'Cox's Orange Pippin'; and Frank Rivers, whose fruit breeding successes include the 'Conference' pear we still enjoy today. Among those who made more decorative contributions there is Sir Joseph Hooker, a supporter of Charles Darwin and Director of Kew, who introduced the first of the Himalayan rhododendrons, and Charles Maries, whose collections from Japan included *Hamamelis mollis* and *Primula obconica*.

Wisley glasshouses
This range of glasshouses was built in 1905, two years after the move to Wisley from Chiswick, and occupied the area in front of the laboratory building. After they were demolished in the late 1960s the area was redesigned as a water garden, which is now home to a National Collection of water lilies.

Fruit and vegetables

From the outset, the Society was particularly interested in fruit growing and a reading of the early *Transactions* reveals that the majority of papers relate to fruit cultivation and new varieties, often illustrated by paintings. This interest, no doubt, was encouraged by Thomas Andrew Knight, the Society's dynamic second President. One of his introductions, the cherry 'Waterloo', is still listed in the *RHS Plant Finder*.

Collections of fruit, and to a lesser extent vegetables, including rhubarb, were planted in the Chiswick garden, compared and identified. Through this work it came to light that many were being sold under more than one name, and selection became easier for gardeners when 182 grape varieties were reduced to 99, and 176 nectarines to 19. It was not only hardy fruits that were considered. Pineapples, widely grown in the hothouses of the aristocracy, also attracted the attention of the Society. An extensive collection was assembled at Chiswick, including new varieties brought from Sierra Leone by George Don. Another of the Society's plant collectors, Don had been instructed to gather tropical fruits and obtain information on how they grew in Africa, South America and the West Indies. In 1831 the pineapples were classified and the 450 named varieties were reduced to 52 distinct varieties. The work done, the collection was sold.

Unfortunately this was not the only collection to be sold by the Society. A few years later (1857-59), straitened circumstances led to the sale of the herbarium collections, the auctioning off of the library, a move to

Cherry 'Waterloo'
Introduced by the Society's energetic second president, Thomas Andrew Knight.

Carnation aficionados

The British Carnation Society Show in 1925 held in the Horticultural Hall. In the same year the Hall paid host to the Wireless Exhibition at which John Logie Baird gave the first demonstration of television. Among the other many and varied lettings have been dog, cat and poultry shows, weekly dances between the wars and "Women and their Work" in 1914.

cheaper office premises, and for fruit grown in the Society's gardens to be sold rather than studied.

With reviving fortunes and competition from the Pomological Society, a Fruit Committee was inaugurated in 1858. Renamed the Fruit and Vegetable Committee the following year, it took the Society into the realms of judging and rewarding exhibited produce. Major conferences on apples, pears and potatoes followed; 'Conference', a pear widely enjoyed today, is a reminder

of the National Pear Conference in 1885 when, as an unamed cultivar, it was first exhibited. With the move to Wisley in 1903 came organised vegetable trials and reference collections of fruits. National Fruit Trials began in 1922, but were transferred to Brogdale, in Kent, in 1960, although extensive fruit collections remain at Wisley. RHS trials of vegetables have continued and expanded, and demonstration model gardens show how edible crops of all kinds can be successfully grown, even in small spaces.

Vegetables judged on appearance and size do not necessarily taste good, however, so attempts have been made over the years to assess flavour. One such attempt took the form of a Vegetarian Banquet in 1895. The fare appears to have been simple, with servings of mushroom and potato patties and tomato sandwiches. During a brief period in the 1930s vegetables were cooked before being considered for an award. In more recent years, apple and strawberry tastings have unsurprisingly proved extremely popular.

The Society at war

During the First World War the Society did much to encourage home vegetable growing and set up demonstration allotments in major conurbations. Pamphlets were issued on drying vegetables and bottling fruit, and the Society lobbied the government to exempt sugar from rationing so that fruit could be preserved. In 1919 the RHS organised a grand fête to raise money to help French and Belgian nurserymen re-establish their businesses that had been destroyed by trench warfare.

At the beginning of the Second World War, the Society was engaged by the Ministry of Agriculture to advise the population on how to "Dig for Victory" and cultivate food crops. Again, demonstration allotments were set up and, in true RHS style, a committee was formed to organise lectures, produce pamphlets on how to grow

New machinery on trial

Transplanting a poplar tree at the Society's Chiswick garden in 1853. The ingenious apparatus, invented by a Mr M'Glashan, consisted of two wooden frames screwed around the tree and large iron cutters which were driven into the ground.

and cook vegetables, and ultimately, in 1941, to publish *The Vegetable Garden Displayed*, which sold at one shilling. Extraordinarily influential, it remained in print until 2000. Repeatedly reprinted, it sold around two million copies in all and was even translated into German in 1947 to help re-establish domestic gardening.

Aims and aesthetics

At the Society's foundation, aesthetics were not a prime concern. Instead, the RHS concentrated its efforts on the practicalities of gardening. Early gardens at Chiswick and Kensington were designed for plants that had been donated or collected and for exploring methods of horticulture. Although elegant, the 500ft-long glasshouse range at Chiswick was a highly functional building. Equipment, too, was sometimes trialled. One such piece of machinery was the extraordinary and cumbersome tree-moving apparatus (*see opposite*) demonstrated by its inventor, Mr M'Glashan.

Appearance was of greater importance at the second Kensington garden, where Prince Albert was an influence and W.A. Nesfield contributed to the design. Ornate bandstands were built for entertaining and another notable glasshouse was erected. The appreciation of fine arts was encouraged by the building of arcades in styles summarising the history of Italian architecture and

Royal visitors
King George VI and Queen Elizabeth and the young princesses Elizabeth and Margaret admire a rock garden at the Chelsea Flower Show, 1947.

by the formation of a short-lived Sculpture Committee. Its remit was to purchase works of art for a collection of sculpture and, to help things along, Queen Victoria lent two 16th-century statues by Francavilla. This diversion into fine arts ended with the death of Prince Albert. A proposed memorial to the Great Exhibition was swiftly changed to the Prince Albert Memorial on the request of the Prince of Wales and the resulting statue is now opposite the Royal Albert Hall.

In the decade after the First World War, the Society held a grand conference on garden design with an associated exhibition of modern sculpture featuring pieces by William Reynolds-Stephens and Sergeant Jagger. Fittingly, this was the first exhibition to be held in the Society's new Horticultural Hall, built to a revolutionary Art Deco design.

The importance of plants

This was the only occasion when the Society took an active part in garden design. Through most of its history it has adopted a plant-based role. The Floral Committee was founded in 1859 to examine "all plants submitted to it, with a view to decide upon their respective merit and novelty". As the range of plants increased, so new floral committees were spawned to concentrate on woody plants, glasshouse plants or herbaceous plants. Specialist

groups examined the likes of irises, delphiniums, daffodils, and rock plants and alpines.

Rock and alpine plants demand exacting growing conditions and as their popularity grew so did the fashion for rock gardens. These generally took two forms: one was based on the use of gravel with few actual rocks while the other featured bold, mountain-like rocky structures. Both styles were adopted by the Society, the former at Chiswick and the latter in the large rock garden at Wisley. Rock gardens also dominated the show gardens at Chelsea for decades until their demise in the 1960s. During the late 19th century the tide also started to turn against another gardening style – the rather garish displays of high Victorian tender bedding. Opinion was galvanised by the journalistic attacks of William Robinson and later by Gertrude Jekyll's writings on colour. Her subtle schemes using hardy plants still influence gardening today in much of Europe and North America. But her innovations were recognised by the RHS long ago when it made her one

Training gardeners (above)

The School of Horticulture (pictured in 1959) was based in the laboratory building at Wisley. Although it closed in 1972, the Society's long tradition of training gardeners, which started at Chiswick, continues.

Roses at Hyde Hall (below)

This site in Essex has been cultivated into areas of formal planting with roses and perennials as well as a dry garden mulched with gravel and filled with drought-tolerant plants.

of the first recipients of its premier award, the Victoria Medal of Honour, founded in 1897 (*see page xiii*).

In step with change

After the move to Wisley in 1903, practicality prevailed over design just as it had at Chiswick, with the building of glasshouses and the planting of collections. The emphasis was on teaching gardeners, with the establishment of a School of Horticulture; on scientific research, which included trialling plants for awards of excellence; and on the construction of model gardens to inspire visitors. Changes were made in the 1960s, however, when the glasshouses were moved from in front of the laboratory to a less prominent position and new areas were planted and existing areas redesigned. One of the most dramatic reformations was on Battleston Hill after the trees and rhododendrons had been decimated by the 1987 gales. Wisley continues to evolve, sculpture has

Iris germanica

been introduced and the number of designed elements has increased, with areas planted by Penelope Hobhouse and Piet Oudolf, a redesigned herb garden and a Millennium Mound for fruit.

To Wisley have been added three gardens in widely different localities. Rosemoor was given to the Society in 1987 as an established garden in a Devon valley surrounded by woodland. The gift included an additional area of pastureland, which has now been transformed into a more formal decorative area renowned for its roses as well as a series of outdoor "rooms", each planted in a different style. Another gift of an established garden was Hyde Hall in Essex in 1993. This windswept site, with heavy clay soil, has been further developed to include areas of more formal ornamen1tal planting, including roses and perennials, together with a spectacular gravelled area billowing with grasses and drought-tolerant plants.

The latest acquisition, in 2001, was Harlow Carr in North Yorkshire, its heavy soil threaded with streams, alongside which luxuriate water plants. Associated woodland and wildflower meadows make it a rich and varied habitat for wildlife and visitors to explore. All four RHS gardens set great store on biodiversity and increasingly areas are being managed with wildlife in mind, supported by a policy of recycling and minimal resort to chemicals.

It is through the model gardens each year at Chelsea and at other shows around the country, rather than in its own gardens, that the Society has encouraged modernism in garden design. Ever since the 1990s its judging panels have not fought shy of awarding a Gold Medal to controversial designs. With more people enjoying the shows through the media of television and the internet, their influence has increased.

Under scrutiny

Crowds are very much a part of the Chelsea Flower Show. The many visitors usually make a beeline for the show gardens and can be every bit as critical as the judges in their assessment.

Two hundred years on, what would Wedgwood and friends think of the development of their Society? There are gardens and shows accessible to all. Plants continue to be assessed for their virtues and brought to public notice. Their names are registered and refined. Horticultural research is carried out and sponsored, while horticultural education is supported by bursaries and training, its standards upheld by examinations. The pleasure of horticulture is encouraged through the gardens, shows and publications. What began as an organisation for an enthusiastic few, has expanded to embrace keen gardeners everywhere.

New naturalism

The winner of the coveted Best in Show at the 2003 Chelsea Flower Show, the Laurent-Perrier Harpers & Queen Garden, designed by Tom Stuart-Smith. It perfectly encapsulated the trend for architectural minimalism, naturalistic planting and concern for biodiversity.

TIMELINE

1804 Founding of the Horticultural Society of London. The founder members were John Wedgwood, Sir Joseph Banks, James Dickson, William Forsyth, William Townsend Aiton, R. A. Salisbury and Charles Greville.

1830 First ladies admitted as Fellows of the Society.

1841-6 The Chemical Committee: pioneering researches into plant nutrition and fertilisers.

1827-9 The Society holds its first "fêtes". By 1829 they were an established part of the London season, but in that year were disastrously rained out.

1893 The RHS General Examination instituted.

1882 The Society holds a Smoke Abatement Exhibition at Kensington.

1897 The Victoria Medal of Honour instituted to allow the Society to honour outstanding British horticulturists.

1861 The Society's new garden opened in Kensington. England's first flower arrangement competition held as part of the opening festivities.

1809 The Society receives its first royal charter.

1818 The Society acquires its first garden, in Kensington, as a means of temporarily housing plants it has been sent.

1861 New charter as The Royal Horticultural Society.

1895 Vegetarian banquet held at Chiswick garden.

1821 The Society leases 33 acres of the Duke of Devonshire's estate at Chiswick to serve as an experimental garden.

1866 Publication of *The Journal of the Royal Horticultural Society* begins.

1883 National Apple Conference.

1900 William Bateson makes first public reference in England to "Mendel's laws" in an RHS lecture.

1833 The Society starts holding shows with competitive classes at Chiswick.

1858 Fruit Committee founded. The name was later changed to Fruit & Vegetable Committee.

1858 Awards of excellence for plants introduced in the form of the First- and Second-Class Certificates (the latter later replaced by the Award of Merit).

1885 National Pear Conference, in honour of which a new variety of pear is named 'Conference'.

1900 Publication of Mendel's paper on heredity, translated by Bateson, in the RHS Journal.

1820-46 The Society sends plant collectors overseas: John Potts, John Damper Parks, and Robert Fortune to China, George Don and John Forbes to Africa, David Douglas and Carl Theodor Hartweg to North America, and James McRae to South America.

1867-73 The Society holds a series of annual provincial shows: Bury St Edmunds, Leicester, Manchester, Oxford, Nottingham, Birmingham, Bath.

1822 First garden at Kensington closed. Today the site is occupied by six shop fronts on Kensington High Street, the houses on the east side of St Mary Abbot's Place, and Pembroke Studios at the southern end.

1862 The Second Great Exhibition held in the Society's Kensington garden.

1888 The Great Spring Show is moved to the Temple Gardens, and the fortnightly shows are held in the Westminster Drill Hall.

1857-9 Financial crisis. The Society sells its herbarium, a quantity of plants from its garden, and finally its library.

1836 Examinations for gardeners introduced at Chiswick.

1858-61 Prince Albert is President of the Society.

1903 The late George Fergusson Wilson's garden at Wisley is bought by Sir Thomas Hanbury, who presents it to the Society as a new experimental garden.

1866 International Horticultural Exhibition and Botanical Conference. The proceeds are used to buy the library of the late John Lindley, Secretary of the Society, to replace the one sold in 1859.

1888 The Society vacates its garden at Kensington. Much of the site is now covered by Imperial College.

1862 First Great Spring Show held at Kensington.

1865 Formation of a Committee on the Improved Education of Gardeners results in the first national examinations in gardening.

1899 The Society holds the first International Conference on Hybridisation.

1859 Floral Committee founded.

1868 The Lindley Library Trust founded as a precaution against any future attempt to sell the contents of the Library.

1903-4 Chiswick site abandoned and built over. Marked today by a street name, Horticultural Place, and also by surviving old trees in back gardens.

1868 The RHS sets up a committee to investigate abuses in the seed trade; the result is the Adulteration of Seeds Act, 1869.

1908 Publication of the Society's first register: *Classified List of Daffodil Names.*

1904 New headquarters and exhibition hall built on Vincent Square for the Society's centennial and formally opened by Edward VII.

1911 Work begins on introducing the National Diploma in Horticulture, the first examinations being held in 1915.

1906 The Society holds the third International Conference on Hybridisation, during which William Bateson coins the word "genetics".

1913 The first Chelsea Flower Show as the Great Spring Show is held in the grounds of the Royal Hospital Chelsea.

1914–18 First World War:
RHS provides seeds and plants for allies interned in the Ruhleben civilian camp in Berlin.
RHS publishes pamphlets to encourage domestic food production, and lobbies the government to get sugar rations increased to allow families to make jam.
RHS organises relief fund for Belgian, French and Serbian horticulturists.
Chelsea cancelled after 1916 for duration of war.
RHS Hall seconded for army use 1916-19.
Women gardeners employed at Wisley for the first time in 1917.

1922 National Fruit Trials begun at Wisley (transferred to Brogdale in 1960).

1928 A second exhibition hall (now Lawrence Hall) opened on Greycoat Place, Westminster. More revolutionary in design than the 1904 building, it was constructed of reinforced concrete.

1928 RHS conference on garden planning, which leads to the formation of the Institute of Landscape Architects.

1929–31 Publication of the *Index Londinensis*, the standard bibliography of botanical illustrations, which the Society began compiling in 1909.

1930 Associateship of Honour established to honour professional horticulturists.

1946 First salaried female staff member employed at Wisley, Dr E.K. Janaki Ammal, undertakes investigations of colchicine and its use in inducing polyploidy.

1935 The RHS becomes the supplier of the first biological control agent, *Encarsia formosa*, for the treatment of glasshouse whitefly.

1947 *The Vegetable Garden Displayed* is translated into German to help with reconstruction of the Germany domestic economy.

1939 Publication of the first version of the *Horticultural Colour Chart* to standardise the descriptions of plants.

1939–45 Second World War. RHS collaborates with Ministry of Agriculture on "Dig for Victory" campaign, organising lecture programmes and demonstration allotments around the country to help promote domestic food production.
RHS publishes *The Vegetable Garden Displayed* in 1941.
RHS organises inspections of greenhouse plant collections to determine which are sufficiently important to get extra fuel rations to keep them alive.
Female gardening students accommodated at Wisley after Swanley College is bombed.

1950–2 At the Botanical Congress of 1950, the RHS proposes a *Code of Nomenclature for Cultivated Plants*, and at the 13th International Horticultural Congress in 1952, convened by RHS, the first version is published.

1951 Publication of the *RHS Dictionary of Gardening.*

1951 The RHS publishes *The Fruit Garden Displayed.*

1955 Establishment of International Registration Authorities for plants. The RHS now acts as Registrar for nine categories: daffodils, delphiniums, rhododendrons, lilies, orchids, dahlias, dianthus, conifers, clematis.

1968 Frances Perry becomes the first female member of the RHS Council.

1975 *The Journal of the Royal Horticultural Society* is relaunched as *The Garden.*

1979 *The Plantsman*, a scholarly journal, published quarterly, is launched.

1979 National Council for the Conservation of Plants and Gardens (NCCPG) formed as a result of an RHS conference on conservation. The NCCPG is best known for the National Collections and their protection of cultivated plants.

1984 Institute of Horticulture established to serve the interests of professional horticulturists.

1986 Inauguration of an RHS branch in Japan.

1985 Master of Horticulture (RHS) Award replaces NDH as the premier qualification in horticulture in the UK.

1992 Publication of the *New RHS Encyclopedia of Gardening.*

1990 Schools Gardening Competition instituted, later to become the Greenfingers Challenge and held in association with Britain in Bloom.

1999 First show held at Tatton Park.

2001 Northern Horticultural Society amalgamated with RHS; Harlow Carr becomes the fourth RHS garden.

2002 First Britain in Bloom competition held under RHS management.

1993 Hyde Hall Garden presented to the Society.

1987 Rosemoor Garden presented to the Society.

1995 The Society takes over the administration of *The RHS Plant Finder*, the largest list of plants available in the United Kingdom and authority on cultivated plant nomenclature.

1993 The Society takes over the Hampton Court Palace Flower Show.

1997 RHS Website launched.

2002 RHS hosts conference on biodiversity: "Gardens: Heaven or Hell for Wildlife?" in association with the RSPB and Wildlife Trusts.

Picture credits:

i (fp) Study of flowers painted by Girolami Pini *c*.1614. Musée des Arts Décoratifs   ii (tc) Royal Horticultural Society, Lindley Library   iii (c) Mary Evans Picture Library   iv Royal Horticultural Society, Lindley Library   v (b) Mary Evans Picture Library   vi–vii Royal Horticultural Society, Lindley Library viii–ix (b) Hulton Archive/Getty Images   x (c) Royal Horticultural Society, Lindley Library   xi (tc) *Citrus sinensis*, orange tree, by John Edwards, 1795. Natural History Museum, London   xi (b) Royal Horticultural Society, Lindley Library   xii (bl) *Rosa* 'Ferdinand Pichard' by Sarah Cresswell. Bridgeman Art Library, London/New York   xii (tc) The Wellcome Institute Library, London   xiii (c) Royal Horticultural Society, Lindley Library   xiv (tl) Royal Horticultural Society, Wisley xiv (bc) Cherry 'Waterloo', by William Hooker. Royal Horticultural Society, Lindley Library   xv (b) Corbis/Hulton-Deutsch Collection   xvi (bc) Corbis xvii (tc) Royal Horticultural Society, Lindley Library   xviii (tc) Royal Horticultural Society, Wisley   xviii–xix Steve Wooster   xix (tc) *Iris germanica* by A.H. Church, 1908. Natural History Museum, London   xx (tc) Garden Picture Library   xxii–xxiii Corbis   xxiv (c) Study of flowers painted by Girolami Pini *c*.1614. Musée des Arts Décoratifs

The contents of this section have been drawn from *The Royal Horticultural Society: A History 1804–2004*, published by Phillimore & Co Ltd (2004), with the kind permission of the author Dr Brent Elliott.

THE ROYAL
HORTICULTURAL SOCIETY

encyclopedia of
GARDENING

THE ROYAL HORTICULTURAL SOCIETY

encyclopedia of GARDENING

EDITOR-IN-CHIEF

CHRISTOPHER BRICKELL

LONDON, NEW YORK, MUNICH, MELBOURNE, DELHI

FIRST EDITION 1992

Managing Editor Jane Aspden
Managing Art Editor Ina Stradins
Senior Editor Kate Swainson
Senior Art Editor Lynne Brown
Editors Claire Calman, Alison Copland, Annelise Evans, Helen Partington,
Jane Simmonds; Judith Chambers, Katie John, Teresa Pritlove; Jackie
Bennett, Carolyn Burch, Joanna Chisholm, Allen Coombes, Heather
Dewhurst, Angela Gair, Lin Hawthorne, Jonathan Hilton, Jane Mason,
Ferdie McDonald, Andrew Mikolajski, Christine Murdock, Lesley Riley
Designers Gillian Shaw; Gillian Andrews, Johnny Pau, Vicky Short,
Chris Walker; Rhonda Fisher, Bob Gordon, Sally Powell, Steve Wooster
Photography Peter Anderson (with Steve Gorton and Matthew Ward)
Location Assistants Anne-Marie Dorenbos (with Peter Bainbridge,
Mark Lamey, DK and RHS Wisley staff); Diana Mitchell, Reg Perryman
Picture Research Sue Mennell, assisted by Ginny Fitzgerald
Illustrations Karen Cochrane, Simone End, Will Giles, Vanessa Luff,
Sandra Pond, John Woodcock; Andrew Farmer, Aziz Khan,
Liz Peperall, Barbara Walker, Ann Winterbothom

REVISED EDITION 2002

Senior Editors Louise Abbott, Joanna Chisholm
Senior Art Editor Stephen Josland

Editors Lin Hawthorne, Candida Frith-Macdonald, Lynn Bresler
Editorial Assistants Christine Dyer, Zia Allaway
DTP Designer Louise Waller

Managing Editor Anna Kruger
Managing Art Editor Lee Griffiths

Photography Peter Anderson
Illustrations Rupert Golby, Marian Hill, Karen Cochrane

Picture Research Romaine Werblow, Mariana Sonnenberg
Production Bethan Blase
Index Dorothy Frame

Special thanks to the staff at RHS Wisley and Vincent Square, in particular
Susanne Mitchell, Barbara Haynes, Michael Pollock, Alan Leslie,
Guy Barter, Jim Arbury, Jim England, Andrew Halstead, Chris Prior

First edition published in Great Britain in 1992 by
Dorling Kindersley Limited, London

This revised and expanded edition published in Great Britain
in association with The Royal Horticultural Society by
Dorling Kindersley Limited, 80 Strand, London WC2R 0RL
A Penguin Company

4 6 8 10 9 7 5 3

Copyright © 1992, 2002, 2004 Dorling Kindersley Limited, London

A CIP record for this book is available from the British Library

ISBN 1 4053 0353 0

Colour reproduction by Colourscan, Singapore
Printed and bound by Mohn Media Mohndruck GmbH, Gütersloh Germany

See our complete catalogue at
www.dk.com

CONTENTS

PART ONE: CREATING THE GARDEN

HOW TO APPLY THE PRINCIPLES OF DESIGN, CHOOSE AND CULTIVATE EVERY TYPE OF PLANT, AND CREATE AND PLANT GARDEN FEATURES

PREFACE

IT IS NOW TEN YEARS since the first edition of the *Royal Horticultural Society Encyclopedia of Gardening* was published. During that time it has sold more than 1,000,000 copies and gained a reputation as the definitive guide to all aspects of practical gardening and for meeting the needs of both the home gardener and the student of gardening.

Over the last decade, gardening as a leisure pursuit has been redefined in many TV programmes and in an upsurge of publishing. There have been marked changes to some traditional aspects of the subject and a growing pre-eminence of certain plant groups. This is demonstrated by the use of gravel and other hard landscaping features, growing in containers, as well as an increased interest in water features and conservatory gardening, and in plants such as grasses and bamboos. Two years ago, with the publishers Dorling Kindersley, we decided to put in hand a major revision of the book. In this new edition, more than 100 pages have been added to deal with new topics; in particular, the section on design has been greatly expanded and a new chapter included on containers. Every aspect of the original text and illustrations, including plant recommendations, has been expertly reviewed and updated.

All these improvements have been made to ensure that this book, now published in its second edition, continues to fulfil the Society's commitment to make the best of gardening information readily available to all who seek it. On behalf of the RHS, I would like to thank the Editor-in-Chief, Christopher Brickell, the other contributors, and the publishers for their continuing support in the publication of this book.

Richard Carew Pole

Sir Richard Carew Pole
President, The Royal Horticultural Society
London, September 2002

THE EDITOR-IN-CHIEF

CHRISTOPHER BRICKELL began his career with the Royal Horticultural Society in 1958, becoming Director of Wisley Garden in 1969. From 1985 until his retirement in 1993 he was Director General of the Society, representing its interests all over the world. He has contributed to a number of horticultural and botanical reference works, and is Editor-in-Chief of Dorling Kindersley's *New Encyclopedia of Plants and Flowers* and *A–Z of Garden Plants*, both also published in association with the Royal Horticultural Society. Christopher Brickell has since 1976 held the Society's prestigious Victoria Medal of Honour, and in 1991 was made a CBE for his services to horticulture. He is President of the International Society for Horticultural Science and Chairman of the International Commission for the Nomenclature of Cultivated Plants.

THE CONTRIBUTORS

ROGER AYLETT *DAHLIAS*

BILL BAKER *LILIES*

LARRY BARLOW (WITH **W.B. WADE**) *CHRYSANTHEMUMS*

CAROLINE BOISSET *CLIMBING PLANTS*

DENI BOWN *GROWING HERBS*

ALEC BRISTOW (WITH **WILMA RITTERSHAUSEN**) *ORCHIDS*

ROY CHEEK (WITH **GRAHAM RICE** AND **ISABELLE VAN GROENINGEN**) *PERENNIALS*

TREVOR COLE (WITH **MICHAEL POLLOCK**) *FROST AND WIND PROTECTION*

KATH DRYDEN AND **CHRISTOPHER GREY-WILSON** (WITH **JOHN WARWICK**) *ROCK, SCREE, AND GRAVEL GARDENING; ALPINE HOUSES AND FRAMES*

JACK ELLIOTT *IRISES; BULBOUS PLANTS; TULIPS AND DAFFODILS*

COLIN ELLIS (WITH **MERVYN FEESEY**) *BAMBOOS*

RAYMOND EVISON *CLEMATIS*

JOHN GALBALLY (WITH **EILEEN GALBALLY**) *CARNATIONS AND PINKS*

JIM GARDINER *ORNAMENTAL TREES; DWARF CONIFERS; TOPIARY; HEDGES AND SCREENS; ORNAMENTAL SHRUBS*

MICHAEL GIBSON (WITH **PETER HARKNESS**) *ROSES, ROSES FOR DISPLAY AND EXHIBITION*

GEORGE GILBERT *GROWING FRUIT*

RICHARD GILBERT *HYDROCULTURE*

WILL GILES *HARDY PALMS AND THE EXOTIC LOOK*

RUPERT GOLBY *GARDEN PLANNING AND DESIGN*

DEENAGH GOOLD-ADAMS (WITH **RICHARD GILBERT**) *INDOOR GARDENING*

DIANA GRENFELL *HOSTAS*

JOHN HACKER (WITH **GEOFF STEBBINGS**) *THE LAWN*

ANDREW HALSTEAD AND **PIPPA GREENWOOD** (WITH **CHRIS PRIOR** AND **LUCY HALSALL**) *PLANT PROBLEMS*

LIN HAWTHORNE *MEADOW GARDENING*

ARTHUR HELLYER (WITH **GRAHAM RICE**) *ANNUALS AND BIENNIALS*

CLIVE INNES (WITH **TERRY HEWITT**) *CACTI AND OTHER SUCCULENTS*; (WITH **RICHARD GILBERT**) *BROMELIADS*

DAVID JOYCE *CONTAINER GARDENING, BALCONIES AND ROOF GARDENS, WATER GARDENS IN CONTAINERS*

TONY KENDLE *SOILS AND FERTILIZERS*

HAZEL KEY (WITH **URSULA KEY-DAVIS**) *FERNS, PELARGONIUMS*

JOY LARKCOM (WITH **MICHAEL POLLOCK**) *GROWING VEGETABLES*

KEITH LOACH (WITH **DAVID HIDE**) *PRINCIPLES OF PROPAGATION*; (WITH **MICHAEL POLLOCK**) *BASIC BOTANY*

BILL MAISHMAN (WITH **JEFF BRANDE**) *SWEET PEAS*

PETER MARSTON *CONSERVATORY GARDENING*

PETER MCHOY (WITH **GEOFF STEBBINGS**) *TOOLS AND EQUIPMENT; GREENHOUSES AND FRAMES; STRUCTURES AND SURFACES*

MICHAEL POLLOCK *CLIMATE AND THE GARDEN; THE BED SYSTEM*

DAVID PYCRAFT *WEEDS*

PETER ROBINSON *WATER GARDENING; WATER LILIES; WATER CONSERVATION AND RECYCLING; WATERSIDE DECKING*

DON TINDALL *TENDER VEGETABLES AND FRUITS*

ISABELLE VAN GROENINGEN *PERENNIALS FOR GROUND COVER*

JOHN WRIGHT (WITH **GEORGE BARTLETT**) *FUCHSIAS*

WILLOW WALLS: TEXT AND PICTURES COURTESY OF *THE GARDEN MAGAZINE*

PART TWO:
MAINTAINING
THE GARDEN

PRACTICAL ADVICE ON TOOLS AND EQUIPMENT,
GREENHOUSES, AND BUILDING MATERIALS AND
TECHNIQUES; UNDERSTANDING SOIL TYPE AND
CLIMATE, HOW PLANTS GROW AND REPRODUCE,
AND HOW BEST TO DEAL WITH PROBLEMS

SPECIAL FEATURES

CREATING THE GARDEN

HOW TO APPLY THE PRINCIPLES OF DESIGN, CHOOSE AND CULTIVATE
EVERY TYPE OF PLANT, AND CREATE AND PLANT GARDEN FEATURES

CHAPTER

1

GARDEN PLANNING AND DESIGN

TO NURTURE a garden over a period of time – seeing it develop and mature through the seasons – is a rewarding experience for its creator. For a garden to be successful, however, it needs careful and considered thought from the very beginning. A garden with simple lines and a natural flow, effortlessly summoning up a relaxed charm, may appear to have received little design input, yet it is almost certainly underpinned by intelligent planning. The design process is conspicuous in a garden of geometric formality, but the same input is required for seemingly artless informal plantings if they are to combine the essential qualities of unity, balance, and proportion, and be in sympathy with their surroundings.

Why do we garden?

WHERE does the motivation come from to cultivate a piece of ground, altering its appearance for our own benefit? Perhaps we still have an instinctive need to grow food to survive, or to mark out a territory that defines a specific area as our own, or to raise a defensive boundary around it. Once within the garden gate, we can leave behind our working lives and retreat to the safety of our private space. Whatever the underlying motivation, that first small spark of interest can easily grow into a lifelong passion and a source of real enjoyment.

Climate and surroundings
In the majority of cases a garden will surround a house, creating fundamental practical requirements to tame the environment. The need for entry by foot and by vehicle will mean making clear paths and drives that allow easy access to the house in all weathers throughout the year. Similarly basic is the need for light: plant growth near windows and doors must be kept in check.

At a greater distance, planting a windbreak of trees and shrubs can provide invaluable protection against damaging winds, sheltering both buildings and less robust plantings. Such shelter-belts of trees will also prevent snow drifting into the garden on the prevailing wind. Conversely, in hot climates, trees and shrubs bring shade and coolness to the house and its immediate surround-

ings. Strategic, appropriate plantings of shrubs and trees can also help to preserve soil, by preventing erosion by wind and water.

The garden setting
The garden should never be viewed in isolation, removed from its context and setting. Garden boundaries define and protect our private space, limiting the influence of the outside world on the place we call home. They make it possible to screen, and thus "lose", unsightly features on adjacent land, as well as increasing privacy. Conversely, if your garden backs onto fields, boundaries can be designed to open up the view and bring the countryside into the garden, while still keeping grazing animals at bay. Garden hedges and trees can also baffle noise from a neighbouring property or busy road.

A garden retreat can be used as an extension to the living areas within the home, making an imperceptible transition from house to garden. Paved terraces, plant-covered structures, and open-fronted verandas all blur the hard interface between inside and outdoors. They create safe outdoor play areas for children – especially welcome in a modestly sized house – as well as providing space for enjoying meals *al fresco*.

Enhancing our environment
Beyond the fulfilment of our basic living requirements, there is of course one obvious role that a garden

DEFINING BOUNDARIES
Land adjoining a garden may not need to be screened for privacy, or for protection. Make the most of an attractive rural view and incorporate it visually to blend with and extend your garden.

performs, and that is to improve the appearance of the house, whether for our own private enjoyment or to enhance the street or neighbourhood we live in. Community spirit is not, however, incompatible with a competitive tendency between neighbours, often generating passions and levels of gardening expertise rarely seen in professional horticulture.

To create a beautiful garden around the confines of a house and use the spaces to maximum effect is a challenge that many gardeners relish. Draw inspiration from the period of your house and its construction materials, and let your planting complement the style. The ultimate goal is to achieve a harmonious whole. This may look effortless, but those directly involved can appreciate the hard work, vision, and imagination that went into it.

Planning and designing a garden is a real opportunity to express your creativity, and to allow your personality to come through in the concept, design, colour, and plant combinations. Unlike interior design or painting a picture, a garden is a living thing that constantly changes, and each passing season will present new rewards and challenges. Although hard work, the practical nature of the majority of the tasks and the visual rewards so readily offered, make gardening a great tonic for those who are office-bound in their work.

Home-grown produce
A garden does not have to be large to be productive; even a modest plot can provide vegetables, fruit, and herbs for the kitchen, and flowers for

HARMONIOUS SETTING
This beautifully planted cottage garden is perfectly in keeping with the style of the house. Pleasing colours, textures, and shapes blend delightfully, blurring the boundaries between house and garden.

the home. Traditionally, the garden always incorporated a good-sized vegetable plot for reasons of economy and to guarantee a steady supply of fresh food. Today, despite year-round availability of fruit and vegetables, many people are concerned about the over-use of pesticides and fertilizers and prefer to grow their own produce using organic methods. Although the yield from an organically grown crop may be slightly lower, many consider the taste and

SOFTENING THE LANDSCAPE
Plants in borders, especially flowering herbaceous ones like this yellow Achillea *and blue* Delphinium, *bring intense colours, contrasting forms, and seasonal change, which alleviate built surroundings in harsh urban environments.*

quality to be superior, and there is frequently less waste.

Security and access
The safety and security of your home can be improved by the way the garden is designed and laid out. Open spaces around a house will prevent unseen access, and are particularly important if you have security cameras, which require clear vision around all sides of a building. Footsteps are readily heard on gravel surfaces – a great deterrent to burglars, especially when a dog is alerted by the noise. Impenetrable hedges of prickly and thorny material are also very effective. Climbing plants and wall shrubs that offer easy access to first-floor windows should be avoided. For visitors and deliveries, the everyday accessibility of a house can be greatly improved by the careful planning of the garden, the avoidance of too many level changes, a comfortable width of paths, and the provision of vehicular access to at least one external door of the house.

Environmental concerns
Gardening according to environmentally sound principles is a goal that many today are contemplating. To exclude all harmful chemicals from the garden is a valiant first step towards running a garden in sympathy with the wider natural habitat. There are also many other practices that enhance and protect the environment rather than depleting and

destroying it. Water conservation, recycling organic matter to produce garden compost, using peat-free potting mixtures, and buying nursery stock (particularly bulbs) raised in cultivation rather than collected from the wild are all relatively easy measures to adopt. If you wish to develop your garden further along environmentally sound lines, consider a

A PLANTED OASIS
The smallest of spaces can play host to a treasured collection of flowering plants and also provide a haven for wildlife.

wildlife-friendly garden that includes plant food sources for birds and insects, shrubs and trees for nesting, and water for aquatic creatures. Avoiding the use of chemicals also encourages more pollinating insects, which enrich the garden environment generally and are of particular benefit when growing fruit.

The importance of garden design

The term "garden design" has connotations of formality and, for many, implies the application of rigid rules and formulae. Fortunately, this is not the case, but there is one overrriding principle – adequate thought and consideration of all the alternatives are needed well ahead of any intended works. Many beautiful gardens have been and are created without the implementation of grand planning schemes. They have developed organically from a starting point: a favourite tree planted in an open place; a natural path between road and house; or from a previous owner's layout. Evolving year after year, possibly in a rather haphazard way with much left to chance, a garden of great charm can indeed come about, but opportunities may have been missed and a lack of cohesion is all too often apparent.

Design awareness
We live in a designed society. There is today a great awareness and appreciation of well-designed products, and gardens have not escaped the attentions of designers or the media. Beautifully illustrated books and magazines as well as informative television programmes have created a growing interest in styles, products, and plants, reaching a wider audience than ever before. For the first time, designers have been able to demonstrate visually the advantages

MULTI-DIMENSIONAL PLANTING
This planting combination is a rich mix of complementary colours, textures, and forms. Such a dense, opulent scheme demands a sound knowledge of plants, plus skill and good judgement to restrict the more boisterous specimens and encourage the less robust.

of planning a garden, and then to communicate clearly, using photographs of each stage, the development of a design.

A designer's fresh and experienced eye can realize the potential of a plot, and draw out its strengths, while respecting and taking inspiration

ARCHITECTURAL PLANTS
Clipped evergreens, such as box (Buxus sempervirens), shown here in the confines of a courtyard, take on an architectural role. Their structure and form are in perfect sympathy with the shape of an adjacent building.

from the site. Most importantly, a good designer will not impose his or her own ideas on the garden without also taking the owner's wishes and lifestyle into consideration.

A professional designer can, of course, be engaged to execute the entire project but at some considerable cost. However, a single visit to offer advice, guidance, and an unbiased opinion can be invaluable and is certainly less expensive, with the option of consultations at a later stage as the project progresses.

Garden types and styles

Categorizing gardens into particular types or styles is fraught with difficulties because every garden is different. Many gardens comprise a series of disparate themes loosely linked together, while others do not

fit readily into any single category as they incorporate several styles. All divisions, therefore, are somewhat arbitrary and should be regarded only as very general guidelines.

Developing a style
When starting to make a new garden or reshaping an old one a common theme, even if adapted and personalized, is generally adopted. Plucked from a magazine article, a book, or inspired by a visit to a garden, a particular look can reflect a house interior or evolve from the the style of house and its immediate surroundings. A building and its locality have a great deal to communicate to any receptive garden planner, contributing many simple common-sense details to the scheme.

All gardens should exude a sense of place and of belonging. A garden designed and built in a style that is very alien to the house or landscape may not sit well there, however much

NATURAL SILHOUETTES
A carefully selected combination of trees and shrubs, centred around this fine Cornus controversa *'Variegata' breaking across the lawn edge, gives an impression of elegance and can be maintained with minimum input. A well-tailored lawn and trimmed evergreens flatter beautifully shaped plants, whereas flowering plants might distract the eye.*

not purely decorative; they have an integrity, a personality, and a history, particularly where a botanical collection has been established.

Interestingly, both approaches to gardening can lead to an extended social life. The low-maintenance garden is ideal for outdoor entertaining, while for the plant enthusiast there are opportunities to contact and meet up with like-minded collectors.

Enhancing buildings

The garden presents a wonderful opportunity to manipulate the appearance of a house without running into expensive alterations or major reconstruction. Plants can be used to soften an unsympathetic roof line or to disguise the inappropriate use of ugly and incompatible building materials. An unremarkable structure, too, can be greatly improved by the addition of striking, climbing or architectural plants, which will strengthen the appearance of the building and add character. In both cases, the built structure and planted garden can come together and complement each other. With the exception of very few architecturally significant buildings whose façades are better left unadorned, the majority of houses are greatly improved by allowing plants to stand close by or to clamber part-way across a house frontage – by appearing to bring the garden to the house.

it is desired and however great the resources spent on its creation. Developing and refining a design that reflects the sense of place almost invariably gives more harmonious results, especially where relaxation and calm are desired.

Design variations

Within any broad garden style, you can incorporate variations that reflect a personal interest, a lifestyle, or even the age group using the garden. A desire to attract wildlife into the garden or to grow large quantities of culinary herbs will add another dimension to the design. Or you might want to achieve a purely visual effect by introducing a particular flower colour or luxuriant foliage that blends with the house colours or surrounding vegetation.

Personal preferences and the way in which you use your garden at various times of the year all have a bearing on what is required. A garden that looks particularly striking in midsummer, for example, may be wanted if the space is used mainly for outdoor entertaining. A garden for relaxation that requires minimum upkeep but has appeal throughout the year may be an attractive idea, or you may wish to shut out the world and create a secluded haven where you can cultivate specialist plants in peace.

Planting considerations

The choice of plants growing within the framework of the garden will significantly influence its style. Large-leaved, rich-textured foliage gives depth and luxuriance, while a predominance of fine, silver- and grey-leaved plants will provide a lighter

feel. Of equal influence is the degree of maintenance required in a garden. An efficiently maintained garden with a well-defined layout will look surprisingly different from a garden of similar design that has been poorly or erratically maintained.

High and low maintenance

Generally speaking, it is possible to make a distinction between two different styles of garden in terms of

their function. A garden may have been designed for visual impact, or the creation of a restful ambience may be a priority. A garden for relaxation should be low maintenance, leaving as much time as possible for enjoying the peaceful setting. In contrast, the pleasure for the plant enthusiast with a specialist collection of plants comes from the hours spent nurturing and maintaining the garden. In a prized collection, plants are

THE GARDEN ROOM
On this sunny terrace, hard landscaping materials play a strong role, yet are softened by the surrounding planting. In summer, the garden pool will create lively reflections of the surrounding vegetation and buildings.

Formal garden styles

FORMAL gardens are characteristically well proportioned, usually symmetrical and geometrically balanced in layout, and impart a tangible sense of restraint. They usually derive an inherent strength of line from an underlying backbone in the form of walls, paths, or terracing, around which planting is firmly controlled. Formal planting traditionally contains very few different plants, but these are used in quantity to lend a uniformity of texture and colour. The whole emphasis is one of an overriding sense of control.

Ordered layouts
The underlying philosophy of the formal garden is to present a strong, simple statement of a very obvious control of nature. Intricately clipped parterres that form a filigree of crisply shaped evergreens when set against fine gravel, or a flat, closely mown lawn that is framed by neatly trimmed hedges, are good examples of this philosophy in practice.

Historically, the formal style was chosen to convey a sense of power over the wider landscape and, on a large scale, this achieved an intimidating effect that was an intentional expression of wealth and status. A similar impression was conveyed even on a more modest scale, since such layouts required regular, labour-intensive, and costly maintenance.

Ancient inspiration
The grand formal gardens of seventeenth- and eighteenth-century Italy and France, which influenced garden styles throughout Europe, were themselves inspired by the gardens of ancient Greece and Rome. In these, the strongly defined proportions and scale of the buildings were mirrored by the strong, architectural and symmetrical design of the gardens that surrounded them.

These sumptuous but controlled landscapes were frequently laid out as a series of terraces connected by grand flights of steps, and featured water cascades, canals, and fountains amid hedged and tree-lined walkways, ornamented with classical statuary and potted plants.

Classical gardens
Greek and Roman features that still inspire modern formal gardens include neatly mown and edged lawns, tightly clipped hedges and topiary, and planted borders framed by low, trimmed hedges. Straight paths and a network of vistas that terminate in a view or focal point may be lined by *allées* and avenues of identical, regularly spaced specimen plants. Ornamentation is added with restraint and, where several decorative items are used, they are either designed to form a matching set or a single design is replicated to form a sequence of repeated incidents.

Plants for formal gardens
Whether clipped and trained as hedging or topiary, shaped plants are an important element in the formal garden. The striking profiles of evergreen topiary lend height, form, and dramatic sculptural interest to an otherwise two-dimensional layout. Slow-growing evergreens, such as yew (*Taxus baccata*), box (*Buxus sempervirens*), holly (*Ilex aquifolium*), and holm oak (*Quercus ilex*), all withstand the necessary regular trimming over many years. See also TOPIARY, p.75, and HEDGES AND SCREENS, p.84.

Pleached trees and stilt hedges make attractive internal divisions within a formal garden. Their regimented forms and colonnaded trunks provide a sense of rhythm and order when used to flank walkways and *allées*. Limes (*Tilia* species) and hornbeam (*Carpinus betulus*) are the most frequently used species for this type of feature. Such plantings can also be introduced in a highly functional way. Trained and pleached limes, for example, can be used as a garden boundary to create a living wall that gives privacy and an intimate sense of enclosure. See also "Pleached trees", p.75.

Knots and parterres
Knot gardens and parterres are highly developed types of formal gardening in which control of the planting is absolute. In knot gardens, intricate planting patterns are confined by an edging of dwarf, clipped evergreen shrubs, such as box (*Buxus sempervirens*). Traditional knots were inspired by sixteenth-century needlework designs and decorative plaster ceilings. In parterres, coloured gravels or low plantings fill compartments created by low, trimmed hedging. Both knots and parterres offer year-round structure that is of particular value in winter, especially when located near the house.

Unity and contrast
Elements of naturalistic plantings among otherwise formal layouts create an element of contrast that can sharpen the underlying formality. The lax and free growth of herbs, for example, planted amongst clipped lavender (*Lavandula*), rosemary (*Rosmarinus*), bay laurel (*Laurus nobilis*), or box (*Buxus sempervirens*) can be used to create such contrasts. Similarly, containers on a terrace planted with a set of trimmed Portugal laurel (*Prunus lusitanica*) can bring an element of order and uniformity close to the house that could contrast with less structured planting elsewhere in the garden.

Oriental formality
The gardens of China, which can be traced back over 3,000 years, were created as sublimely peaceful places for contemplation and meditation. They drew inspiration from their dramatic surrounding landscapes, which were replicated in miniature within walled enclosures. Plantings were formal and restrained, often clipped or trained, and usually highly stylized. Each tree or shrub had a symbolic meaning that was intended to stimulate contemplation.

Traditional Japanese gardens borrowed Chinese design ideas more than 1,200 years ago. With a similarly naturalistic inspiration, they used richer, more diverse plantings, symbolically shaped and sited rocks, and raked gravel or sand. Such a garden was based on formal principles of balance, simplicity, and symbolism.

STRUCTURED LAYOUT
The partitioned squares of this box-edged parterre bring order and year-round structure to an otherwise informal medley of planting. Its strong lines lead the eye to a series of focal points beyond the low wall.

TRADITIONAL TOPIARY
Weight and substance are conferred on a design by the imposing forms of mature topiary sculptures, however whimsical the clipped shapes may be. Here, stylized peacocks perch on symmetrically trimmed pediments of yew (Taxus baccata), which flank a broad walkway – the central axis of this formal layout. Their crisp formality is brought into high relief by the informally planted borders around them and the mature trees beyond.

STATUARY
Pleasingly proportioned, well-sited and framed ornaments, used with discretion, can often be a great asset to the general garden scene.

PLEACHED LIMES
High-level screening by a stilted hedge of lime (Tilia) encloses yet does not oppress this small knot garden. In winter when the lime leaves fall, the skilful training of the branch framework offers yet more to be admired.

FORMAL STILL WATER
Mirrored reflections double the impact of a symmetrical design. The random drifting of floating plants on the surface of the dark water adds interest and movement to the serenity of this formal garden.

Informal garden styles

INFORMAL gardens, at their best, often look as though nature has played a part in their design. There is an irregularity and a softness in their lines that, although manufactured, could conceivably have occurred naturally. Even though informal gardens may appear slightly out of control, their success depends on strong design and on the firm hand of the gardener to retain a degree of order amongst what might otherwise become chaos.

Elements of informality

A garden with an air of informality offers a relaxed ambience that can provide a sanctuary from the pressures of modern life. In contrast to the hard-edged geometry of the formal style, an informal garden is created with flowing curves and gentle contours. Hard surfaces are softened by plants that spread over their margins, and borders are stocked with billowing mounds of plants that mingle together, apparently at random. Climbing plants scramble freely over walls or through trees and shrubs. While shrubs may be pruned to ensure good health and productivity, they are allowed to assume natural shapes and are rarely clipped in a restrictive way – as they are in strictly formal situations.

Informal elements within a garden can produce a sense of maturity in a relatively short time-scale, for example, when plantings are used to disguise unsightly features with a mantle of growth. Great charm can be given to the most unpromising site if softening growth disguises the hard angles or harsh colours of a building. Even the most uniform, rectangular garden acquires an element of mystery when its stark outlines are masked by layer upon layer of informal planting.

Informal garden styles

The style and degree of informality of a garden is influenced partly by the nature of the site and partly by individual preference. At one end of the spectrum, it may be possible to augment an existing woodland or meadow area simply by planting more of the natural flora that already grows there. Alternatively, the creation of an informal garden may entail the remodelling of border edges to form curving, sinuous lines, perhaps with a relaxation of the mowing regime and a reduction in border maintenance to permit self-sown plants to thrive. At the other end of the spectrum is a totally new garden, for which there is a range of informal styles from which to choose.

Cottage gardens

The traditional cottage garden was essentially a working garden in which to grow ornamental and edible crops. Fruit, vegetables, herbs, and flowers, such as peonies, delphiniums, and aquilegias, were all combined. The flowers ensured a thriving population of beneficial insects to aid pollination of crop flowers, control harmful insects, and encourage a bird population, all of which helped produce vigorous and healthy crops.

The quaint, homespun appearance of a cottage garden can be created using rustic items such as branch-work arches or woven willow supports for climbers (see WILLOW WALLS, p.87). Brick-patterned or cobbled paths edged with found or reclaimed materials, such as pebbles or tiles, also help define the style.

Wild and woodland gardens

Informal gardens in a more naturalistic style not only provide a beautiful and relaxed type of garden but also offer a lifeline to flora and fauna whose habitats may have become threatened elsewhere.

Areas of turf, for example, where bulbs are naturalized for an early display, can be left uncut so that grasses and meadow flowers can bloom (see MEADOW GARDENING, p.401). An area of water, however small, attracts a range of wildlife into the garden, particularly if edged with waterside plantings to provide safe shelter for birds and amphibians alike. See also "Wildlife ponds", p.284.

Small trees or an area of woodland, especially if underplanted with shrubs and festooned with climbers, provide nesting places for birds and hibernating sites for insects and small mammals. Even in more controlled areas of the garden, seedheads of herbaceous plants, if retained through winter, will provide excellent food for birds when other sources are low.

Controlled chaos

Plants can be ruthlessly competitive and the strongest may smother and eventually kill the weakest. They must be controlled to prevent this. It may be necessary, for example, to divide vigorous herbaceous plants regularly to keep them in check, to thin or reduce over-large shrubs, or to remove colonies of self-sown seedlings. These tasks help to maintain a balance in wild and informal gardens, and will prevent their natural style from degenerating into a wild and unkempt state.

WOODLAND
In the shade of trees, a woodland flora must be selected to tolerate low light levels and the extremes of dry and excessively damp soil conditions.

CULTIVATED AND SELF-SOWN MIXTURE
A shimmering profusion of nectar-rich flowers, in billowing swathes of colour, creates a feature of great beauty and provides an immensely valuable food source in summer for bees, butterflies, and other beneficial insects. Careful management is essential for year-on-year success.

MARGINAL PLANTING (TOP)
Even the smallest pond offers the opportunity to blur the distinction between land and water with a range of garden plants. Native wildlife will benefit greatly from the cool, sheltered conditions.

POTAGER (ABOVE LEFT)
Nasturtiums and pot marigolds jostle with herbs and ornamental cabbages in cottage-garden tradition, where not even the smallest space is wasted.

SELF-SOWN (ABOVE RIGHT)
Melianthus *and Jacob's rod (*Asphodeline*), planted here at the foot of a wall, simulate a self-sown planting. In a mature garden, such combinations may occur naturally – and to great effect.*

RAMBLING ROSES (RIGHT)
Where space permits, an informal regime of pruning and training shrubs and roses allows plants to spill from beds and borders in a generous, relaxed style.

HAND-CRAFTED GATE (ABOVE)
Impromptu, rustic materials and a borrowed view accentuate the theme of a country garden.

MIXED MAINTENANCE (BELOW)
While fruit trees must be well kept for good yields, the relaxation of the mowing regime here gives this small orchard a charming air of informality.

People-orientated gardens

A GARDEN to be enjoyed by a family almost certainly needs to be a multi-purpose space. To ensure that the design serves the needs of all its potential users, spend some time identifying what these might be. They may include a terrace for dining and entertaining, or areas for children to play safely and experiment with growing their own plants. The garden may have to accommodate herb and vegetable patches to provide kitchen produce, or borders for cut flowers to decorate the home.

As well as fulfilling its functional requirements, a garden such as this can also be highly decorative. A pergola clothed with scented climbers, for example, is not only ornamental but it could also provide shade for a favourite place for midsummer dining. By installing outdoor lighting, its usefulness can be extended to include evening entertaining, perhaps with a barbecue. It may also

display ornaments that are highly individual, perhaps presents from friends, or mementoes of anniversaries or holidays abroad.

The style of planting is very much a matter of personal choice, whether highly traditional or more experimental and innovative. Sources of design inspiration have never been more various, from magazines and television programmes to the wealth of gardens, both private and public, that open to visitors.

Gardens for living

Just as the interior of the home is designed to meet the requirements of those living there, so can the garden be tailored to suit the needs and interests of all the household. This often means extending indoor living to outdoors, using the garden as an extra room. If, for example, dining and entertaining are high on the list of priorities, there should be a flat,

clean, all-weather surface near enough to the kitchen to make outdoor dining convenient.

To make access safe and easy, avoid steps, slopes, or changes of level between the house and eating area. On a very sunny terrace, deciduous (rather than evergreen) climbers trained above head height will provide comfortable shade in midsummer, but little or none in spring and autumn, when warmth and light levels are lower.

Where a suitable sheltered, warm site for an outdoor room does not exist, consider creating one by enclosing an area with hedges or scented-leaved shrubs. They will help trap warm air and provide shelter from cool evening breezes.

To maximize use of the space and to create a pleasant ambience, install subtle lighting for the evenings. Bear in mind that the route to and from the dining area should also be well lit.

Special interests

If the garden as a whole is planned with minimal maintenance in mind, this will allow the development of areas for special-interest activities. A simple lawn, for example, surrounded by robust, low-maintenance plantings can offer a games field and camping site for the children, or an oasis of calm for the adults. Around this, areas of more intense activity can evolve. These might include a small kitchen garden to produce unusual vegetables, fruit, and herbs that are difficult to find in shops. If the area is small, tending it will not be a chore; it will give satisfaction to the gardener and it can even be a learning experience if children are encouraged to participate.

Another special-interest area might be a border for cut flowers, to provide material for floral arrangements in the home throughout the year. It might include shrubs such as forsythias and mahonias for early spring and the bright stems of dogwood (*Cornus alba*) for winter decoration. To allow uninhibited cutting during summer and autumn, set aside a patch for perennials, supplementing them with annuals and biennials to supply flowers for many months.

Special needs

For those in the family who are less mobile or who have limited strength, a garden of raised containers or an entire raised bed removes the strain of bending and should satisfy any latent wish to garden. Permanently sited containers can be set at a suitable height and regularly reinvigorated with colourful annuals. A row of outdoor tomatoes planted in pots on top of a sunny wall, or a raised herb garden enjoying a sunny aspect and free-draining soil, will give endless pleasure and produce worthwhile quantities of useful crops.

Looking to the futures

With a little foresight, some areas of the garden can be designed to evolve with a family's changing needs. A timber-built playhouse, for example, could in later years become a tool shed or apple store. An irregularly shaped or formal rectangular sandpit, if positioned carefully when the garden is designed, may be transformed into a small pool once the children are old enough to understand the dangers of water. A climbing frame of smooth timber could, later on, become an interesting support over which climbing plants may scramble to create a dramatic effect.

WELL-DESIGNED TERRACE
This seating area (right) with its all-weather surface, shelter from wind, and overhead shade provision encourages maximum use of the terrace over a long season. Floor-level lantern light and pots of scented plants such as lilies (below) that retain their fragrance into the evening enhance the setting for use later in the day.

GARDENING INTERESTS (RIGHT)
A garden mirrors the particular hobbies of its occupants and its design and general layout are unavoidably dictated by these pursuits. A collection of specialist alpines, for example, is best displayed in stone troughs and a greenhouse, here connected to the house by a path with an all-weather surface.

SAFE WATER FEATURES (BELOW)
Even the smallest and most shallow of pools can pose a danger to small children. This small fountain, however, has a strong metal grid over its concealed reservoir.

PLAY AREA (BELOW RIGHT)
A lawn, surrounded by robust, prickle-free plantings, makes an ideal spot for children to enjoy ball and other types of games.

HIGH-LEVEL GARDENING (ABOVE)
A raised bed makes gardening comfortable for those with limited mobility. An ideal display setting is created where plant detail can be appreciated at close quarters. The use of pots allows those plants in need of attention (here including some developing topiary shapes) to be brought within very easy reach, and for seasonal changes to be made.

DUAL PURPOSE (LEFT)
Here, in late summer, flowers for indoor decoration are grown alongside plants with ripening fruits, to great ornamental effect. This cheerfully haphazard mixture has been planted solely with the needs of the house in mind, yet the result is as decorative as any other type of themed border.

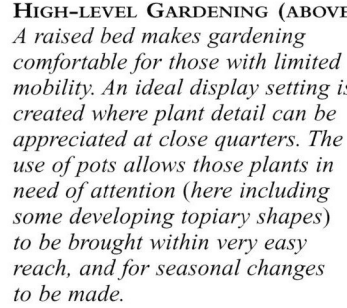

Plant–orientated gardens

I N A PLANT-ORIENTATED garden, the plants take centre stage, rather than being used simply as "soft" design materials. The owner of such a garden can indulge a fascination in collecting and growing a specific range of botanical or exhibition-quality plants. Some plant groups need much more maintenance than others, since they are extremely fussy about their growing conditions. A garden's soil or microclimate might especially suit one specialist group of plants, although more often additional work will be needed to provide the appropriate soil, light, moisture, and shelter.

Pure gardening

The garden that is inspired by plants first and foremost is perhaps the purest form of gardening. There are many and diverse avenues of interest within this type of garden, but all are led by a love and passion for plants.

It is the fascination of collecting, cultivating to perfection, pollination, and propagation that holds the attention and further develops a gardener's interest in horticulture. The search for rare or newly discovered forms can become a life-long occupation. In such a "pure" garden, skill and expertise are obvious at every turn, and demonstrate the gardener's dedication to a wide range of tasks.

Sources for ideas

The site itself may be the inspiration for the plant-orientated garden. Perhaps a dark and damp, north-facing slope will spark an interest in an extensive collection of ferns.

Alternatively, a dry, stony, south-facing bank may encourage the planting of many different Mediterranean natives – such as a collection of *Cistus* species.

Turning what might appear to be a disadvantage into a positive attribute, an area of overgrown woodland may appear lost to cultivation, yet with careful management it can present a wealth of unusual planting possibilities. A collection of shade-loving, woodland-floor natives that is unique to such a site should thrive beneath a deciduous canopy.

Where the conditions provided are substandard, plants will grow poorly, never realizing their full potential. Such poor conditions, however, can often be rectified. Soil conditions can be ameliorated by adding organic matter or improving drainage; shelter can be increased by the use of windbreaks and shelter-belts (see HEDGES AND SCREENS, p.84, and BAMBOOS, p.96); and light levels can be increased by thinning or lifting the canopies of surrounding trees.

Themed collections

An herbaceous border in matching colours, textures, and forms is one way to display a collection that depends solely on good design skills. Many subtly or dramatically different variations are possible. An historical approach may be taken to recreate an early twentieth century border, for example. This would contain tall herbaceous plants that are very dependent on traditional forms of staking with peasticks and hazel wands, for example. Colour-themed

SPECIALIST PLANTS
The display of a very specific plant collection need not be devoid of all aesthetic qualities. Here, many treasured forms of potted auricula primulas are attractively placed on tiered stands.

borders are another possibility for a themed collection (see "Planting for colour and texture", p.45).

A more modern interpretation might be a mixed border, dominated by drifts of shrub roses and self-supporting perennials, self-sown annuals and swathes of ornamental grasses. Alternatively, such a border, particularly in a sheltered situation, might include lush foliage plants and tender bedding perennials in vibrant colours to give a subtropical flavour (see also HARDY PALMS AND THE EXOTIC LOOK, p.60).

Collections with style

The plant-orientated garden may take a very different course from the refinements of the mixed border. A hobby growing plants for exhibition may develop, where perhaps dahlias (see p.234) or pot leeks are grown to perfection, to the exclusion of any aesthetic value their arrangement in the garden might offer. Alternatively, such a well-defined collection could be arranged with every possible

attention paid to aesthetics. A fruit garden, for example, with trees trained in particular forms could provide structural boundaries and internal divisions within the garden as a whole (see GROWING FRUIT, "Trained forms", p.419). Such a display would pay tribute to meticulous, long-term pruning as the trees slowly develop great character, eventually creating an almost timeless ambience.

A collector of trees may be fortunate to have sufficient space to create an arboretum, but this need not be a sterile collection of solitary trees, in serried ranks. Groupings of trees in clumps and copses create a landscape style that is beautiful in its own right (see also ORNAMENTAL TREES, "Trees as design elements", p.54).

To grow a collection of plants indigenous to a particular region may require the controlled conditions of a greenhouse or alpine house. Plants need not be set on gravel-covered, featureless staging. With a little imagination, they can be arranged in a simulation of their native terrain.

NATURAL PLANT COLLECTIONS
An extensive specific collection can readily be incorporated into a garden setting. Here snowdrops (Galanthus) *flourish in this deciduous woodland.*

RESTRICTED COLOUR (ABOVE)
A white border, tiered in height and with every shade of green, white, and silver, is a classic, timeless design theme. The dignified purity of the scheme demands meticulous staking, dead-heading, and weeding.

TROPICAL STYLE (BELOW)
A warm, sheltered area with fertile soil provides an opportunity to experiment with tender exotics through the summer months. Many will need careful lifting and storing over winter, but amply repay such attention.

SINGLE–SEASON DISPLAY (ABOVE)
Some garden designers seek to exploit every plant type, shape, form, and colour so that they perform and peak at the same time – in this case as a colour-coordinated collage.

ALPINE HOUSE (BELOW)
Plants with special needs such as alpines may thrive only in a dedicated greenhouse.

Stylized gardens

A HIGHLY stylized garden can be seen as a refined work of art of purely aesthetic value in which plants fulfil a design function of tight and often strictly limited criteria.

Such a garden might serve as a backdrop to a collection of contemporary sculpture, for example, or might form a calm and unobtrusive setting before an architecturally important house. This style of garden demands a high degree of coordination and pre-planning to distil the essence of the style required.

The colours, textures, and finishes of all the materials are of utmost importance. Here, plants are used as a furnishing – their qualities being assessed and employed for their utility rather than for their individual beauty as living plants.

Dominant themes

When a designer's sole aim is to create a very stylized image, the approach is very similar to that of an artist when painting a picture, or a designer contriving a theatrical stage set. The result can be breathtaking, because all attention has been focused towards maximum visual impact, undiluted by sentiment or an interest in individual plants. Selecting plants only for their colour, form, and texture, and arranging them in an almost abstract, pictorial composition, ensures that the finished arrangement forms a cohesive whole of complementary materials.

While this approach is commonly used by landscape architects in large-

MASS BEDDING
When plants are used as basic building elements to construct an effect, the results can be dramatic. This softly textured landscape has a sculptural quality, which transcends the form of any one individual plant.

scale projects, it might equally well be adapted to smaller, more intimate situations. It avoids the problem of using too many different materials in a confined site, which can prove fussy and distracting. In contrast, minimal materials give an impression of strength and unity. Such essentially sophisticated designs all have at their heart an innate simplicity that is their most telling factor.

Even in gardens of traditional layout, this straightforwardness can underlie the development of an overall concept or theme: for example, a garden based on a restricted colour range, comprising plants only in shades of

green, with black or white flowers. A more radical alternative is a garden that is almost free of plants, consisting only of sweeping grass mounds to be mown in different directions and at varying lengths according to the texture required.

Another alternative that lends style and drama is when a single plant is introduced in great quantity, especially if the plant in question is unusual. Blocks of a hundred or more can be a revelation. A mass planting of peonies, tree poppies (*Romneya coulteri*), or many of the euphorbias can provide a truly spectacular sight. Less radically, gardens

of a practical nature can be given stylistic treatment. A working kitchen garden can be designed as a decorative potager. While still providing edible crops, there is greater emphasis on an attractive display of colour and texture within the strict confines of its highly structured layout.

Coordinated designs

In domestic situations, one of the greatest challenges is to match a highly stylized garden with the house or locality. One way of doing this is to use plants and materials from the area, but in a very different form. For example, locally abundant trees and shrubs (if they withstand clipping) can be used to create trimmed hedges and feature trees that are then arranged in a tightly regimented scheme within the garden (see ORNAMENTAL TREES, "Pleached trees", p.75, and HEDGES AND SCREENS, p.84). Local stone and gravel could form paving and mulches beneath plantings to create a thoroughly modern reinterpretation of the formal garden.

Small town gardens, especially if framed by boundary walls, are ideal for stylized gardens. Since they are frequently viewed from only one aspect – the house windows – they present unusual possibilities. A truly theatrical, almost two-dimensional garden can be created, with an odd or false sense of perspective achieved by the angles of hard surfaces and by the choice of their colours, shapes, and disposition.

PLANTING ARRANGEMENTS
With skill, knowledge, and care a series of well-planned "vignettes" may be constructed. Harmonious colours and contrasting leaf forms and shapes can be positioned with all the accuracy and poise of a staged floral design.

MODERN STYLE
Even the most ordinary plants in a commonplace setting, here against a picket fence, can be used in a stylized way. Their effect is transformed by the use of unexpected and non-traditional galvanized metal containers, which harmonize beautifully with the silver-leaved plants.

MODERN DESIGN (ABOVE)
*Squares of mind-your-own-business (Soleirolia soleirolii),
forming tight, ground-hugging cushions of growth,
alternate with blue glass chips in a contemporary
scheme that plays upon geometry and colour blocks.*

JAPANESE RAKED GARDEN (LEFT)
*In this uncompromisingly simple, abstract arrangement
of rocks and raked gravel, the eye is drawn only to pure
line and the effortless balance of mass and space.*

MODERN SCULPTURE
*A "habitat" created as a setting for a piece of modern
water sculpture enables an otherwise alien artefact to
appear acceptable within the general garden scene.*

SUCCULENTS
*Strongly architectural plants, such as Agave here, form a
dramatic impression in this sunny, dry, terraced bank,
where the plants thrive in the hot sun.*

Assessing the existing garden

Whether you are remodelling your own garden or tackling one inherited from a previous owner, one of the most difficult tasks is to envisage how to transfer all one's ideas and aspirations onto what is already there.

Everything that makes up the existing garden must be scrutinized and assessed, determining those components that positively contribute to the overall effect and those that offer least or are farthest removed from your preferred style and taste. No aspect of the garden should escape this scrutiny, for even those factors that might be considered impossible to change can be influenced and ameliorated by skilful design and planting. Nothing can alter the shape and size of a garden, for example, yet there are any number of design solutions that can make narrow gardens appear wider, open sites become more sheltered, and awkward shapes flow more freely.

A time for reflection

The inspiration for your new design may be held entirely in your imagination – or be the result of visiting other gardens or poring over books and magazines. Before beginning to make even the roughest preliminary sketch, however, a period of time spent in the garden doing nothing more than simply mulling over possibilities will be well repaid. The earli-

DECIDING ON PRIORITIES
An existing garden may contain many elements that meet your own requirements, such as a seating area or raised beds, even if the materials or finishes used are not exactly to your taste. Just as plants can be judiciously retained or reshaped to preserve the structure of borders, so much can be done to adapt and personalize hard materials.

est planning stage of a garden should be a period of calm, cool observation; critical scrutiny of both what exists and what is desired. If insufficient time is given to important decisions, the result will be poor long-term planning.

The garden's development over an extended period of time needs a vision, seeing beyond the clutter of existing features. It should also at this stage be free of the distractions of budgets, labour, and other practical constraints. Defining a goal for the garden, and the means to that goal, can be the realization of a dream that will bestow a style and a personality – your own personality – on the property as a whole. Even if a master plan has to be tackled piecemeal, having such a plan firmly in mind will enable a greater degree of control over the ongoing development of the garden.

Weighing up the elements

As you appraise the existing garden, you will begin to form a broad idea of the scale of remodelling that a new design will involve. It is worth considering at this stage whether you intend to implement the new design in a single operation, or spread the work and expense over several years.

Carry a notebook with you, in which to enter thoughts and ideas about all of the elements the garden contains, set against what you desire. As the wealth of possibilities is distilled into a concept that could work, many ideas will be dispensed with, refining only those thought appropriate to site and scale, period, and local conditions of soil and weather.

A methodical "audit" of structures, surfaces, features, and plantings, with a view to deciding which you will keep, which you will redesign or relocate, and which are redundant, can be tremendously useful. Examples of the kinds of questions that should be asked and factors that should be considered are detailed in the pages that follow.

GET TO KNOW THE GARDEN
Useful information can be gathered just by observing a new garden over an extended period of time. Plants new to you may reveal their value in unexpected seasons.

SEPARATING MATERIALS FROM THEIR CONTEXT
Even if you do not like a feature, or its design makes it awkward to garden around, consider whether its materials might be used elsewhere. If not, items such as these old, good-quality slabs and sink could be sold.

Taking photographs

Difficult decisions can often be simplified and clarified by the use of photographs. A set of pictures portraying the whole garden will help to put all of its features into context, and enable carefully considered conclusions to be drawn. Curiously, a photograph has a focusing and simplifying effect, removing the distractions of a live situation within the garden, and throwing strengths and weaknesses into high relief. The frozen image is easier to analyse, and clearly reveals the underlying composition and workings of the garden. This detachment seems to allow decisions to be made with greater freedom. The dominance of an outsized evergreen shrub, the poorly flowing line of the front of a border, or any weak, muddled plantings are more vividly displayed in static images and these can then be rectified in the new design.

Appraising your own garden

Sentimentality can play a significantly negative role in a garden long established by its owners. Plants that really have no place in a well-designed and practical layout are preserved and overlooked; geriatric, diseased, or inappropriately sized plants are retained, particularly when they commemorate an event or were a gift, a reminder of a dear friend or relative. With the passing of a garden to new owners, such anomalies tend to be addressed more objectively – the horse chestnut tree planted as a conker years ago, for example, which now excludes all light from a terrace, may be removed without so much as a backward glance.

However, individuality – the life-blood of interesting gardens – often stems from quirks of personal sentiment. Although unconventional, it may be these features that give the garden a unique character, so, again, deep thought before action is essential. The clean sweep or makeover approach may have unexpectedly negative consequences. The removal of a conifer simply because it is "unfashionable", for example, may also mean the loss of useful screening from neighbours, or perhaps a well-placed nesting site, visible from the house, to which birds will no longer return in spring.

Appraising a garden new to you

A new owner will almost certainly wish to make changes to an existing garden. A keen gardener will probably waste little time before introducing personal preferences or old friends in the form of plants or ornaments, but if the garden, or parts of it, is not fundamentally to your taste then a broader view is required.

In many ways, the would-be designer tackling a virgin site – for example, on a new housing development – or a completely neglected, featureless plot has an easier task, with a blank canvas on which to project the new vision. To appreciate fully the complexities of an inherited, well-kept garden requires time and patience. The most valuable advice is not to make any hurried changes; an old garden that has evolved over many years may contain features of great worth, which have stood the test of time. To retain and perhaps reinterpret some existing plants and structures is greatly preferable to clearing the site and beginning from a sterile plot.

These existing elements in a garden, laid out by the previous owners, may summon up a certain atmosphere, which it is important to retain. The over-enthusiastic tidying up of such gardens can suddenly remove any charm or mystery. Such a quality is a rare commodity to be nurtured rather than swept aside. A unique richness may be found within a garden cultivated over several generations, layer upon layer of plantings creating microclimates of mutual benefit, evolving beautifully tiered structures of some complexity. With the passing of time, plants and structures can attain a character that takes them beyond mere furnishings.

Watching the garden unfold
The garden should be monitored during as many seasons as possible (ideally, a full year), during which time observations of factors such as shade cast, prevailing wind, areas of warmth, and seasonal value of plant-

CONTEMPLATING EXISTING PLANTS
If at all possible, never discard a beautiful, mature, and healthy plant just because it is in a less than perfect setting. This Trachycarpus *is a fine specimen; it would be well worth rejigging plans to accommodate it; indeed, it could suggest the theme of a new planting scheme.*

ings can be made. Paths and terraces can be used in all seasons, the effectiveness of privacy afforded by screening shrubs can be checked – summer and winter – and the maintenance requirement of the entire garden and its plantings gauged.

Letting plants show their worth
Only within specific seasons may the reason for certain plantings be revealed: an old cherry tree with low sweeping branches, which bursts into flower in spring in partnership with drifts of bulbs beneath it, will immediately justify its existence and unconventional stature.

All too easily, mistakes can be made: a hastily removed "laurel", for some reason planted up against the south-facing wall of a house, may be cut to the ground and discarded only to discover later that this was a fine *Magnolia grandiflora* of considerable age. If you find plants difficult to identify, advice may be sought from a local nursery, gardening club, or botanical garden to avoid the unintentional removal of valuable plants.

Once the identities of all important plants are known, again do not be over-hasty in removing any. To retain some items of obvious age and maturity as a permanent or temporary measure will prevent the complete loss of scale within the reworked garden, offer shelter to young, vulnerable plants, and privacy while other plantings are establishing.

TAKING INSPIRATION FROM SHAPES
This ageing tree cloaked in ivy (far left) may need to be removed, but its overarching low branch creates a pleasing frame for the elements beyond, which might suggest the placement of an arch in its place.

Surfaces, paths, and level changes

Lawns/Grassed areas

Existing Is the lawn level, composed of good-quality grass, and free from weeds? Or is it in poor condition, perhaps shaded by the house or by trees, and becoming mossy because of insufficient light or poor drainage? Will it be large enough to accommodate a tent and be used for games if required? Is it devoid of trees or should it provide a setting for them? If the lawn is very small, in poor condition, muddy, and essentially more trouble than it is worth, would the area be better paved, grav-elled, or incorporated into a planted bed? Alternatively, if a close-mown lawn covers an extensive area, then the far periphery could be mown less frequently to provide a fringe of meadow grass.

Desired A garden without a lawn can seem lacking in serenity. Without a calming area of green it can often feel frenetic and look a little over-worked. Even a broad area of gravel or paving will not have the quieten-ing, soothing effect of grass. There must be adequate access to the lawn for a mower or wheelbarrow, and for pedestrians. The disposal of mow-ings is a further consideration. When a lawn is to replace a hard surface that acts as a thoroughfare through the garden, then it is advisable to retain a hard strip to one side to leave a clear passage for use in bad weath-er. A lawn, even when relatively small, plays a scene-setting role, pro-viding an open foreground to view a scenic background. This role is important enough to justify the removal or reduction of existing planted borders to give an adequate area of grass. For further informa-tion, see THE LAWN, pp.384–400.

Patios and terraces

Existing Is an existing patio area large enough? Is it sunny, or cold and gloomy? Is it at the junction of paths, making it difficult to position perma-nent furniture? A terrace may be sited to catch the last rays of the set-ting sun, but if this is at the far end of the garden, then it may not be practi-cal for frequent outdoor eating and entertainment. Is the surface in good condition, with a slight fall away from the house to remove standing water? Gravel is an uncomfortable surface on which to place chairs and tables. More acceptable is a flat, even surface of paving, or poured concrete with the aggregate exposed to make it non-slip and give texture.

Desired An area of hard standing within the garden is invaluable as a working area and for entertaining outdoors. Its position is critical to achieve maximum benefit from its appearance and usefulness. Ideally there should be separate areas of sun and shade for sitting in at various times of the day and in different sea-sons. Even a small paved area with seating for two or three people will greatly enhance the use of the garden if placed so that it has a good view or sunny aspect. Paving materials often look best when sympathetic to sur-rounding building materials in colour and texture. Decide whether the sur-face should be of one colour and uni-form texture, or highly decorative in design to make a statement in itself. Always ensure clear access between house and terrace – without includ-ing steps, if possible. This minimizes possible accidents when carrying drinks or food. For further informa-tion, see STRUCTURES AND SURFACES, "Patios and terraces", p.585.

Paths

Existing Are paths in good repair and wide enough for easy passage and pushing a wheelbarrow? Broken and uneven surfaces can be haz-ardous and should be repaired or replaced. Do the paths follow natural desire lines through the garden, free of temptations to take short cuts? Paths should be not only a practical network of hard surfaces but also create visual links from one area to another, giving interest and structure to the garden. If some paths are duplicating routes or appear unnec-essary, remove them. Alongside a lawn, paths may also act as mowing edges over which border plants can spill. Grass paths are pleasing yet soft thoroughfares, so will survive without damage only on less fre-quented routes.

Desired Paths should follow the most logical and scenic route. Do not forget that in a private garden beauty should be paramount, so avoid the spaghetti effect of too many paths. Gravel paths are inexpensive and softer on the eye than paved ones, particularly when curves and sweeps are to be negotiated and straight-edged materials are difficult to accommodate. A well-prepared base of compacted hardcore will ensure good drainage and an even surface, which will retain its good line over time. Paths should be broad enough for two people to walk abreast. If appropriate, the width should be suf-ficient to take a small garden vehicle and a loaded trailer. For further infor-mation, see STRUCTURES AND SURFACES, "Paths and steps", p.593.

Steps and slopes

Existing Should any sloping sites within the garden be redesigned to form a series of terraces linked by steps, to overcome logistical problems of land management? Do existing changes of level divide the garden into workable plots? Within the confines of a small garden, would a slight change in level create a different perspective, adding importance to an area or pro-viding an opportunity for a change in materials or theme? Would a flight of steps add a vital link, physically and visually drawing areas together? Do retaining walls and planted or grass banks contribute horizontal divisions, and also do they have the potential to mark a change in style or detail between levels?

Desired However cleverly inter-preted, a flat garden will not possess the drama or liveliness of one that exploits a hillside or the moderate undulation of rolling terrain. A very slight variation in land heights can be exaggerated by the use of retaining walls. Changes in height can be exploited to display plants and water to great effect. A series of pools on different levels, linked by waterfalls, makes a lively composition, full of interest. Consider whether any changes in level would be appropri-ate, especially for the very young and elderly, who may find steps difficult. Steps should be well built and even in rise and tread width throughout their flight. If the sides are planted, a central area of sufficient width must be left uncluttered. For further infor-mation, see STRUCTURES AND SUR-FACES, "Paths and steps", p.593.

Boundaries and structures

Walls and fences

Existing Are existing walls safe? If in doubt, seek expert advice. If work is needed on old garden walls, it is worth contacting an experienced stonemason or builder familiar with local building techniques, in order to effect sympathetic repairs. Check the condition of fencing, in particular inspecting the base of fence posts for rots and fungal growth. Individual panels and posts can often be replaced without renewing the entire structure. The easiest option for an ugly wall or fence is to disguise it with climbers or shrubs. The soil at the base will often be poor and dry; does it need improvement before planting? Where lime has been used in mortars and plasters, especially on an old wall that has shed detritus, note when choosing plants that the soil may have become inhospitable to acid-lovers such as *Camellia*.

Desired Traditional brick or stone walls are among the most challenging and expensive of all garden structures to build. There are cheaper construc-

tion options – for example, a block wall rendered in plaster – but workmanship should never be skimped on if the wall is to be of any height. Remember that height restrictions usually apply to any wall or fence forming the boundary to a neighbouring property. Choose robust fencing for garden boundaries; lighter structures such as screens, trellis, or even woven willow walls (see p.87) make softer, often more pleasing internal garden divisions. For further information, see STRUCTURES AND SURFACES, "Walls", p.596, and "Fences", p.600.

Hedges

Existing Are existing hedges in the right position within the garden, and are they of a suitable type for the site? They may be filtering the wind and sheltering the garden, but at the same time creating excessive shade and possibly obscuring distant views.

Have existing hedges grown too wide or too tall for the garden? Evergreen hedges in particular may prove oppressive and over-dominant. A deciduous hedge could be more suitable, letting more light into the garden on dark winter days. Old hedges can become thin at their base; reducing the height and width of the upper part of the hedge will encourage re-growth lower down.

Desired A hedge need not have the angular rigid lines associated with walls and fences, and can trace a sweeping curve to frame an informal border. The hedging material can also be varied and mixed in different combinations to offer textures and degrees of formality or informality. A hedge of flowering shrubs or those bearing colourful fruits and berries will also give extra interest. Shade cast by overhanging trees will stifle the growth of most hedging plants, a problem that can be overcome by planting a mixed hedge using shade-tolerant species in the reduced light beneath the trees.

A formal hedge can provide structure and definition to a garden design. Closely clipped hedges make living walls for "rooms" containing different garden styles or changes of pace. Windows and archways can also be cut into the hedging to create vistas and entrances from one room to the next. For further information, see HEDGES AND SCREENS, p.84.

Garden buildings

Existing Is the building in good repair? Is it well sited for its purpose? A garden building, whatever its function, should not dominate the garden. If necessary, camouflage it with climbers or shrubs or move the structure to another site. When repairing garden buildings they can be repainted a different colour or be refaced with a more sympathetic material. Would a garden building perhaps be more useful if it were refitted for a different role? A shed or summerhouse could be adapted as a storage area for garden furniture or apples; and a conservatory could double up as a greenhouse for plants.

Desired A garden building, however small, can either form part of the general garden scene, adding a modest architectural element to the area, or else be hidden by climbers and shrubs. The siting of the building is critical. A balance must be struck between its practical use and aesthetic quality in any discreet positioning of a building. A summerhouse, conservatory, or greenhouse requires a position with a favourable aspect for its occupants, whether human or plant. Good light, sun, and shelter are all important, with a pleasing outlook essential for a summerhouse, whereas a garden shed or store can be lost in a shady corner. All structures should be readily accessible, ideally from hard standing, and have adequate foundations. They should also be constructed from strong, easily maintained materials. For further information, see CONSERVATORY GARDENING, p.356, GREENHOUSES AND FRAMES, pp.566–583, and STRUCTURES AND SURFACES, "Garden sheds", p.605.

Pergolas and arches

Existing A metal or wooden pergola, perhaps with brick or stone supports, must be structurally sound. Can it safely carry the combined weight of plants and overhead structure, and withstand the wind resistance offered by the plant canopy? Timber and metalwork structures should be checked, and any weaknesses repaired before replanting; sound surfaces should be cleaned and treated with preservative or other paint. It may be advisable to employ a structural engineer or qualified builder to look over large structures. Plantings that threaten to overwhelm should be drastically cut back, to allow light and air into the canopy. Old, twisted and gnarled specimen climbers should be retained for their character, and carefully pruned.

Desired A pergola or series of arches provides a strong architectural element in a garden. It may be used to define the main axis, so directing the flow of the garden, or to mark a transition from one part of the garden to another. Materials and design may be dictated by those already used in the garden or house. A range of weights can be introduced for different effects, from a skeletal metalwork frame to a heavy brick and timber beam construction. A successfully planted pergola will be draped in plants that obscure most of the construction for much of the year. However, in winter, deciduous plants will reveal their supports, so they do need to be elegant. For further information, see STRUCTURES AND SURFACES, "Pergolas and rustic work", p.603.

Ornamental planting

Trees

Existing Mature or semi-mature trees in a garden are a great asset. Their scale cannot readily be acquired; and the shadows they cast give a special quality to a landscape. Do you wish to add a favourite tree? Small, delicate ones are ideal in confined spaces, while in larger gardens they will, if positioned correctly, enhance the landscape effect of larger "specimen" trees. Conversely, do existing trees dominate? Often gardens are planted heavily for immediate results and this may later require the removal of some trees or at least the reduction of their canopies. If trees have encroached on a view or cut out light, they must be checked with appropriate pruning. The same could apply if leaves from trees near the house are blocking gutters and downpipes, causing damp problems. It is possible to transplant a tree when it is young.

Desired A single carefully selected tree can fulfil many roles. It may have an elegant form, with flowers, fruit, good autumn colour, and perhaps attractive bark, thus providing almost year-round interest. One species or cultivar used in quantity will give continuity to a garden. A mixture of trees can be planted for short- and longer-term effect; part of the enjoyment is watching a tree develop. Tree roots, especially those of fast-growing species, can damage drains and foundations, so take care when positioning trees to give adequate clearance around buildings. For more information, see ORNAMENTAL TREES, pp.52–87.

Shrubs

Existing Do existing shrubs give decorative value over a long period of time? Are they performing well, or are they straggly and undernourished, or perhaps starved of light? Are they overgrown, or too large for the position? Not all shrubs respond well to pruning, and it is important to identify the plants before removing or reducing growth. Shrubs that require regular attention may need to be replaced if a low-maintenance garden is desired. Grafted shrubs may have developed suckers from their rootstock, which if left in place may overpower the chosen plant. These should be removed cleanly at their source. Similarly, if variegated shrubs have produced green-leaved stems, these should also be cut off.

Desired For every month of the year there is a shrub that can provide colour, interest, and scent, even in the darkest days of winter. Their shapes and forms give the garden a soft edge reducing the predictably angular lines of the average plot. Some shrubs are dual-purpose – flowering, then fruiting later in the year. Shrubs are ideal screening plants as they are usually covered with foliage to ground level, with evergreens retaining their leaves throughout winter. Where a hedge or fence would create too strong a division across the garden, a block of free-form shrubs can be a more sympathetic solution. Shrubs can be chosen to provide habitats for nesting birds or a food source for overwintering creatures. Many shrubs are suitable for cutting for indoor arrangements. For more information, see ORNAMENTAL SHRUBS, pp.88–121, and ROSES, pp.146–169.

Climbing plants

Existing Do existing climbers enhance the garden, allowing plant growth to flow up, over, and around buildings and walls, uniting the whole? Or are plants too vigorous for supporting structures, whether a tree, wall, arch, or pergola? A plant that has outgrown its allotted space will require considerable pruning, with the result that flowering and fruiting may be much reduced. Large wall-trained shrubs may damage the foundations of buildings if planted too close. They can also create damp patches if they become too dense, or obscure light from windows if they grow too broad and spreading. Are climbers so overgrown that they are blocking gutters or insinuating their way under roof tiles and weatherboarding? In all these cases the offending plants must be removed or regularly pruned.

Desired When used with thought and intelligence, well-placed climbing plants can redeem the most mundane or ugly building, gently disguising it with a thin veil of foliage, softening lines and construction materials. Some climbers will cling tightly to the angles of walls while others will round and blur the edges, turning corners into curving, flowing forms. The amount of maintenance to which climbing plants are subjected will dictate their appearance. A rampant, trailing climber will, if left unchecked, festoon a building in a few seasons. The same climber, pruned regularly and precisely tied, can offer a neatly tailored, formal layout of well-secured branches. For more information, see "Wall shrubs", p.93, and CLIMBING PLANTS, pp.122–145.

Herbaceous plantings

Existing Is the scale, colouring, and content of an established border to your liking, or does it encompass everything that you dislike? Will the border look spectacular for just one month but depressing for the rest of summer? Have some vigorous plants swamped other more delicate species and spoiled the design and balance? Do some plants need to be rejuvenated by lifting and dividing them, replanting only the young vigorous sections. Is the border overrun with perennial weeds (see p.670) such as ground elder (*Aegopodium podagraria*) or couch grass (*Elymus repens*)? After a year to review the contents, could borders be reduced in size or the planting simplified for easier maintenance?

Desired The main purpose of herbaceous plantings is to provide uplifting colour. If borders of herbaceous plants run parallel to the house, they will be critically observed at close quarters and may fail to please for many months of the year. It is far better to position borders so you look down their length. Then the planting will always appear full, and gaps less noticeable. A new border can adopt a special theme, for example a limited colour range, a particular season, a favourite genus, or a form of foliage that will give a specific look, perhaps to harmonize with the colour or texture of a hedge or material used as an edging, path, or wall. For more information, see PERENNIALS, pp.170–205, ANNUALS AND BIENNIALS, pp.206–223, and BULBOUS PLANTS, pp.224–251.

Garden features

Kitchen garden

Existing Because of the need for an intensive cultivation regime, a vegetable plot demands the best soil in the garden, with a warm, sheltered aspect in good light. Is there a site with more suitable growing conditions than that currently being used? If so, consider relocating vegetable and fruit growing to this area. If you intend to keep an existing kitchen garden area, then before deciding what to grow it is essential that you assess the condition of the soil (see "Soil and its structure", p.616). It may well be in need of improvement, or deep cultivation. Are existing fruit trees and bushes productive, or old and neglected? Old specimens may need careful pruning to restore them to productivity, or they may be better replaced. Take into account, too, the requirements of your household, and any particular likes and dislikes.

Desired Decide on the main requirement, whether growing salad crops, unusual produce unobtainable at the greengrocer, or enough fresh, cheap, possibly organically grown vegetables and fruit to supply the kitchen through the year. Growing good vegetables requires a great deal of time and hard work, and this must be carefully considered before embarking on the cultivation of too large a plot. Where smaller crops are wanted, vegetables and fruit can be integrated throughout the entire garden, benefiting the insect population and looking attractive, too. For further information, see GROWING FRUIT, pp.416–489, and GROWING VEGETABLES, pp.490–548.

Herb garden

Existing Does an inherited herb garden include those plants that are important to you? With such a wide range of possible plants from which to choose, the herb garden and its contents are very much a personal matter. It may be necessary to be ruthless about discarding some of the existing herbs. Replanning and much replanting may be required in order to achieve the desired effect. Have fast-spreading herbs, such as mints, come to dominate and smother less vigorous ones? Such plants should be cut back, but this may not be a permanent solution to the problem; consider growing the more delicate herbs in the safety of containers, or, alternatively, confining the rampant growers to pots.

Desired To grow well, herbs require a free-draining soil, which need not be particularly rich, and a very sunny site, which receives maximum light and warmth. Ideally a herb garden must be located near the house and within easy reach of the kitchen for use throughout the year. However, it is not necessary to group culinary, aromatic, and medicinal plants together. The herb garden theme may be extended throughout the heart of the cultivated areas of the garden. Flowers, fruit, vegetables, and herbs may be combined, using an extended range of fragrances and colour, as well as flower and leaf shapes and textures. Larger quantities of herbs required for culinary or other domestic purposes, such as making pot-pourri, may be grown in specific areas to be harvested and stored for use out of season. For further information, see GROWING HERBS, pp.402–415.

Water features

Existing Are the water features in the garden well maintained or in need of repair or renovation? Before adopting any existing ponds, pools, or canals, their overall condition should be investigated and problems addressed as necessary. Has a pool site become overshadowed by once-small trees, now taking too much light from the water and dropping debris into it? Is the scale of the area of water in relation to the garden as a whole inappropriate, requiring an extension of the water surface and the removal of over-invasive water plants? Ponds and pools require considerable time and effort to keep them in good condition. If this commitment cannot be fulfilled, they may be better removed.

A primary consideration in family gardens must be the safety of the water feature. Is it properly protected? The smallest pond can pose a threat to children – especially those unfamiliar with the garden. The depth of small pools can be dramatically reduced by filling part of them with rounded pebbles while youngsters are small. Ledges around the sides of pools will help older children to scramble out. Sloping pond margins also allow for escape from deeper water, and may save the lives of pets or small garden mammals.

Desired The smallest amount of water brings movement, sound, and life into a garden. A terrace may host a small spout and basin, a garden a modest nature pond of indigenous plantings, and a landscape a series of interconnected pools and water courses, each of an appropriate scale to its setting. For further information, see WATER GARDENING, pp.280–303.

Ornaments and pots

Existing Is there a chance of acquiring long-established decorative garden items? If so, such an opportunity should be seized. To inherit statues and large architectural containers with a house and garden is now, however, a rare occurrence, unless special financial provision for these has been made. In most cases, ornaments will be removed along with the house contents or will be sold. A garden that derives strength from well-positioned ornaments will be weakened by their removal or replacement. Conversely, an over-embellished garden with an excess of decoration, which confuses the eye, needs to be controlled to restore balance and order to the scene.

Desired An extra dimension can be provided by well-placed ornaments, which enhance the style of the garden design. Although seen as a separate entity, the ornament should still comply with local factors, namely scale, style, material, and general appropriateness. Statues and pots can be an indication of and an outlet for personal taste and expression, introducing art – whether traditional or contemporary, representational or abstract. They can also act as signposts within the garden, encouraging the visitor to move through it or pause to admire a view, enhancing certain points and drawing together otherwise disconnected areas. A distinctive individuality can be achieved with the use of commissioned pieces of sculpture or plant containers. For further information, see CONTAINER GARDENING, pp.304–335.

Sketching out a plan

BEFORE measuring a garden accurately and formulating any new design, a preliminary sketch or sketches will help you assess the overall layout of the existing plot. This will form the basis of a detailed scale plan (see p.36), on which you will be able to mark those features and plants that are to be retained, and the elements to be added (see p.38).

These sketches should comprise rough ground plans on which to note the many practical factors that will affect the final layout and choice of plants. With accompanying notes, they should detail elements particular to the site, such as climate, soil type, views to consider, shade cast, and the orientation of plot and house, as well as the shape and size of the area – factors that cannot be changed. They should also include utilities relating to the house as well as to the garden and its maintenance, such as outside taps and garden sheds. Such items may currently be poorly positioned.

Climate and aspect
The climate of the general locality and that found specifically within the garden are key determining factors, influencing its layout and the choice and placing of plants (see CLIMATE AND THE GARDEN, pp.606–615). Information on the general climatic conditions of the locality, annual rainfall, average temperatures, and quantities of sunlight should be sought and studied. These general conditions will be influenced by the particular terrain within the garden.

GARDEN TOPOGRAPHY
An area of water not only increases soil moisture but also the humidity of the surrounding air, to the benefit of many plants. However, water often occupies a low-lying spot, which is very likely to be a frost pocket (see p.607). Plants may need to be selected for their hardiness as well as their suitability for the soil and conditions.

GAINING A PERSPECTIVE
An upstairs window may afford a good view when sketching the boundaries and any irregularities in a garden. It is also an ideal vantage point from which to observe and map changing patterns of sun and shade.

A low-lying garden may be sheltered from strong winds but it may also form a frost pocket, whereas a hilltop site may remain several degrees colder than a neighbouring, protected, south-facing slope. A garden near the sea can also be affected by strong winds, possibly salt laden, but the maritime influence will prevent extreme fluctuations in temperature compared to inland regions.

Within the garden, pockets of particular conditions will exist – forming microclimates of warmth or cold, humidity or dryness, each suiting a different range of plants (see "Microclimate", p.611). The orientation of the garden and the house within it will affect the warmth or coldness of the house walls, and where shadows will create deep or partial shade. These factors will affect not only your choice of plants but also decisions on where seating areas should be positioned.

Assessing your soil type
The soil found within a garden is a crucial factor to take into account. The type, texture, and level of acidity or alkalinity (the pH) of the soil are important to recognize (see "Soil and its structure", p.616). Soils vary greatly from region to region, from a heavy clay to a light sandy loam, or a chalky or limestone soil to an acidic peat. Each variation in soil will suit a different plant range. Those happily accommodated will thrive, while those planted in an inappropriate soil type will struggle to survive. Moisture retention and drainage will vary with soil type, as will ease of cultivation, which can be severely hindered by badly drained, heavy soils.

Poor drainage is a factor that may affect more than plant choice. A soft boggy site will be unsuitable for any substantial building work unless the problem can be alleviated by installing drains and soakaways (see

"Improving drainage", p.623). If large areas of rubble or subsoil have been left from building and construction work, it may be simpler to work with them rather than attempt an overhaul. They may be used successfully to form the foundations of a terraced area, or perhaps a gravel garden; this type of site provides ideal conditions for plants that prefer sharply drained soil (see "Gravel beds and paving", p.256).

Utilities and access
Other fixed details occurring within the garden should be noted on the plan, including drives and pathways that service the house, and important yet irritating features to be worked around, such as manhole covers. There may also be meter inspection points and septic tanks to be marked in. An oil tank or coal bunker is often an ugly but essential component of the garden, especially in rural areas; it may be possible to relocate it, but screening is obviously an easier option. A wood pile, however, can look charming in a garden, and is also an attractive wildlife habitat.

Any overhead power or telephone lines need to be entered onto the site plan, because tall-growing trees must not be planted close to overhead cabling. It is also inadvisable to plant twining climbers on a house wall where cabling enters the building, because the plants will use the wires as a climbing frame. Such points on the house wall are often inaccessible, too, and attempts to prune or pull away growth can be hazardous.

ELEMENTS TO DISGUISE
Inspection covers must be accessible, but can be hidden by low, spreading plants or by using recessed lids with paving set into them (see p.586).

A ROUGH SITE PLAN
Sketch the layout of the garden and the position of the house. Then enter in substantial structural planting such as trees and hedges, the outlines of areas of hard standing and lawns, the route of paths, and any internal garden divisions and buildings such as sheds, screens, and walls. At this point, more generally planted borders and areas may be indicated simply by shading. In this northern hemisphere garden, the diagonal hatching represents shade cast by the sun taking its highest, midsummer route across the sky.

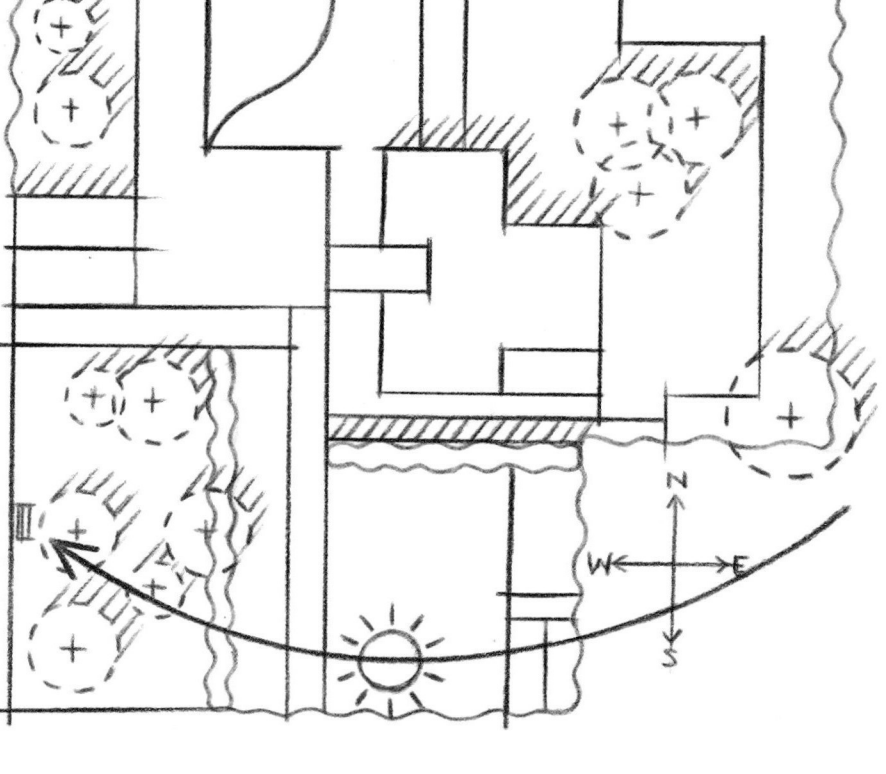

Thinking ahead

While your plans may be at an embryonic stage, ideas for major changes, for example the felling of a tree or construction of a garden building such as a summerhouse, may already be germinating. There are certain legal aspects that will repay investigation right from the start, or you may run the risk of unpleasant surprises thwarting your plans later. These include local building and planning regulations, the possible existence of tree preservation orders, the responsibility for, and delineation between, boundaries separating neighbouring properties, and any statutory environmental protection for your area. Any necessary permissions should be sought as early as possible, even if you eventually do not follow the ideas through, as agreement and clearance, where forthcoming, can take considerable amounts of time.

Other practicalities

There are certain practicalities that few gardens can be without, and a checklist can be compiled to determine whether the existing garden is equipped to suit your needs. Mark the position of outside taps, and consider whether these may need to be moved. To inherit a garden with an established compost heap is a boon, but compost can easily be moved elsewhere, as can other potentially useful structures such as cold frames and incinerators. Draw the current position of these onto the plan, together with sheds and storage bins, and consider whether the capacity these offer is adequate, not only for garden tools but also for general family clutter such as folding chairs, toys, and bicycles.

What lies beyond

Elements quite literally beyond your control should still be noted for consideration on the plan. The immediate surrounds of the garden, where views may be taken advantage of or ugly buildings concealed by carefully positioned trees, will enable an enterprising gardener to exploit the site to the full. Privacy and security at the boundaries of the plot should be examined and noted for their existing effectiveness. Weigh up possible loss of views or sunlight if extra privacy and shelter are required, and ensure that changes will not annoy neighbours in surrounding gardens.

Security can often be improved by opening up the garden, rather than reinforcing enclosure; consider whether driveways and sheds might perhaps be better brought into view.

The impact of a busy road passing the property, perhaps with a junction at which point headlights sweep into the garden, can be reduced or lost if the boundary gaps are filled. Dense, clipped hedges can also act as a useful baffle to noise (see also HEDGES AND SCREENS, p.84).

VIEWS TO OBSCURE
An unwelcome reminder of urban life in the form of a distant car park intrudes onto this otherwise charming plot. Planting a narrow, upright tree, or perhaps raising the height of the rear wall slightly with trellis panels on which a climber could be trained, would restore seclusion. Consider the viewpoint of neighbours before implementing changes that could block light.

LENGTHENING A VISTA
Reshaping this border and introducing more height in the foreground would open up and lengthen a vista towards the well-shaped conifer, and lead on to views of the countryside beyond. Lowering the hedge would also add distance, but its presence, together with the trees behind it, suggests a shelter belt. Prevailing winds should be investigated, as this site could be very exposed.

Making a scale plan

A FINE, dry day is required for compiling a scale plan, with no limitation on time. The assistance of a second person will greatly ease the task, as will a good-sized sketch pad or a clipboard and paper, two 30m (100ft) tape measures, pencil, rubber, a set of compasses, and an ample supply of stout twine and wire pegs with which to pin the twine in place. With a small garden, a single "field plan" can be made of the entire site. Larger gardens can be broken into separate areas, later to be joined on a final plan put together on a larger surface such as a kitchen table or drawing board.

Making a start

The boundaries of the garden should be measured and entered onto the plan with heights of boundary walls, hedges, or fences marked alongside their lengths. Then the house and other buildings must be plotted and fixed within the boundary. This may be achieved by measuring from two known fixed points on the boundary, such as corners, gate posts, or tree trunks, to a corner or fixed point on the house. If three or four such points are established around the house then an accurate location will be found for the building. Surrounding terraces can be relatively easily measured from the house to their edges, checking that they run parallel to the house, and if not, gauging the discrepancy.

Plotting positions

When plotting outlying features that cannot be related easily to a nearby boundary or house wall, you must create an artificial line from which measurements can be taken. A long tape measure pulled straight out between known and pinpointed features in the garden, such as a central door in the house and a fence post on the far boundary, provides a "datum line". From this, use a second tape to identify the position of features, such as a tree, sundial, or manhole cover, by measuring at a right-angle from the first, datum-line tape. Note the measurement on the first tape where the second crosses it, and the distance from this point to the feature.

Once a datum line has been established, any number of items can be measured using coordinates to the left or right of the line. A number of such datum lines may be necessary to plot all features within a large garden. To pinpoint a single, isolated feature, such as a tree in a lawn, the technique known as triangulation (see p.37) may be used. While

(see p.37)

MEASURING FROM A DATUM LINE
Except in the tiniest plots, it is almost impossible to position elements such as trees and small buildings on a plan by taking measurements between them and their nearest boundaries. Using a central datum line makes the job much easier. Here, a line in the paving running parallel to the house has provided a useful starting point for a datum line that will run to a fixed, traceable point at the far end of the garden.

MEASURING THE EXISTING LAYOUT
Using a datum line, or lines, enables you to build up a plotted plan of the garden by making a series of offset measurements to the right and to the left of the line. The running, or incremental, measurements taken along the datum line are also a valuable way of confirming the site's dimensions.

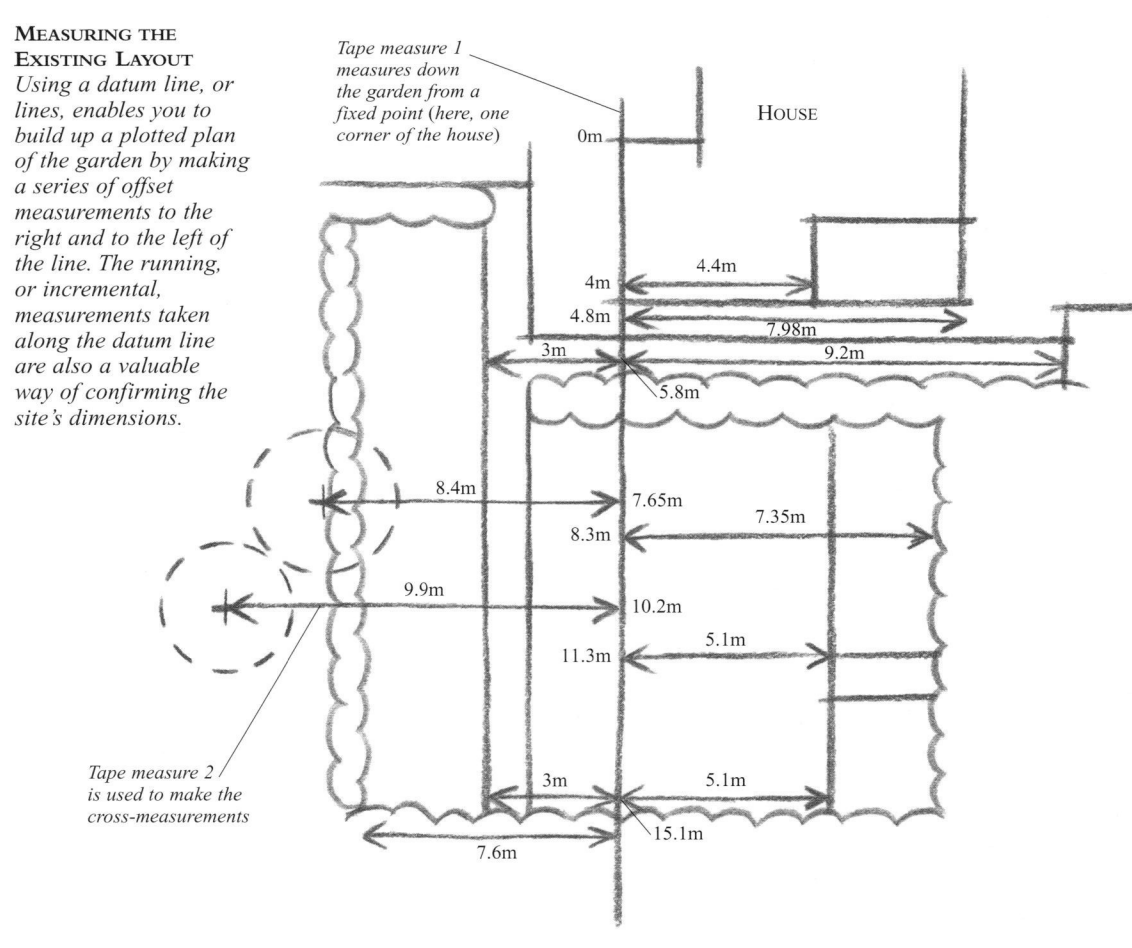

Tape measure 1 measures down the garden from a fixed point (here, one corner of the house)

HOUSE

0m
4m
4.4m
4.8m
7.98m
3m
9.2m
5.8m

8.4m
7.65m
8.3m
7.35m
9.9m
10.2m
11.3m
5.1m

3m
5.1m
15.1m
7.6m

Tape measure 2 is used to make the cross-measurements

TRIANGULATION
Where a feature such as a tree cannot be directly related to existing straight sight lines, measure against two fixed points to establish its position. To transfer to a plan, scale down the two distances appropriately, and use each as the radius of a circle drawn with compasses around the fixed points – here the two corners of the garage. The point at which the circles intersect will be the location of the feature (here a tree). The compasses can also be used to describe the tree's canopy.

Measure distance

Measure distance

GARAGE

Tape measure 2 takes a series of measurements between curved and straight line

Tape measure 1 laid straight between two fixed points

ESTABLISHING AN IRREGULAR CURVE
Two tape measures must be used for this: one to lie straight and flat across the curve (or curves) between two given measured and plotted points, the second to be used to measure the curve at regular intervals from the first tape. For example, at 50cm (18in) intervals along the first tape, the second tape is laid across it at right-angles and the distance to the edge of the curve measured and recorded as a series of coordinates.

straight edges are easy to measure and plot, the curved edge of a drive or generous sweep of a border may take more time to replicate precisely on paper (see above, right).

Adding more dimensions

As linear measurements are taken, other useful information can be gathered. Measure and mark the positions of all gates and entrances on the boundary, and all doors and windows of the house. Heights of internal garden divisions such as screens and hedges should be recorded, together with the height and canopy spread of trees, pergolas, or arches.

Changes in level should also be recorded. These are critical factors that may necessitate terracing, retaining walls, steps, and slopes in future plans for the garden where unsatisfactory level changes prevail. Simple slopes and slight changes can be calculated relatively easily, but an undulating site of various levels and cross-falls will be beyond the capabilities of the average gardener. For this a professional surveyor must be engaged. A large-scale garden, which is more difficult to plot and coordinate than a small one, may also be better left to a professional.

Transferring the field plan

With the "fieldwork" statistics accurately gathered, including a number of extra cross-measurements made as a check to the detail and to the overall plan, the information can be committed to paper. A plan created at too small a scale will be difficult to draw and awkward to read. Where practical, as large a scale as possible should be adopted on which every detail can be recorded. Squared or graph paper will enable the easy

TRANSFERRING THE FIELD PLAN TO SQUARED PAPER

Establish the scale of the plan using the largest dimensions possible on a sheet of paper that will accommodate them; if necessary, stick several sheets together. A general garden plan such as this showing basic outlines and features can be drawn at a scale of 1:100. Mark everything on the plan, including features you may not want to keep. This plan, together with your visual memory of what already exists in each area, will help in both imagining and deciding on the scale of new outlines and features (see p.38).

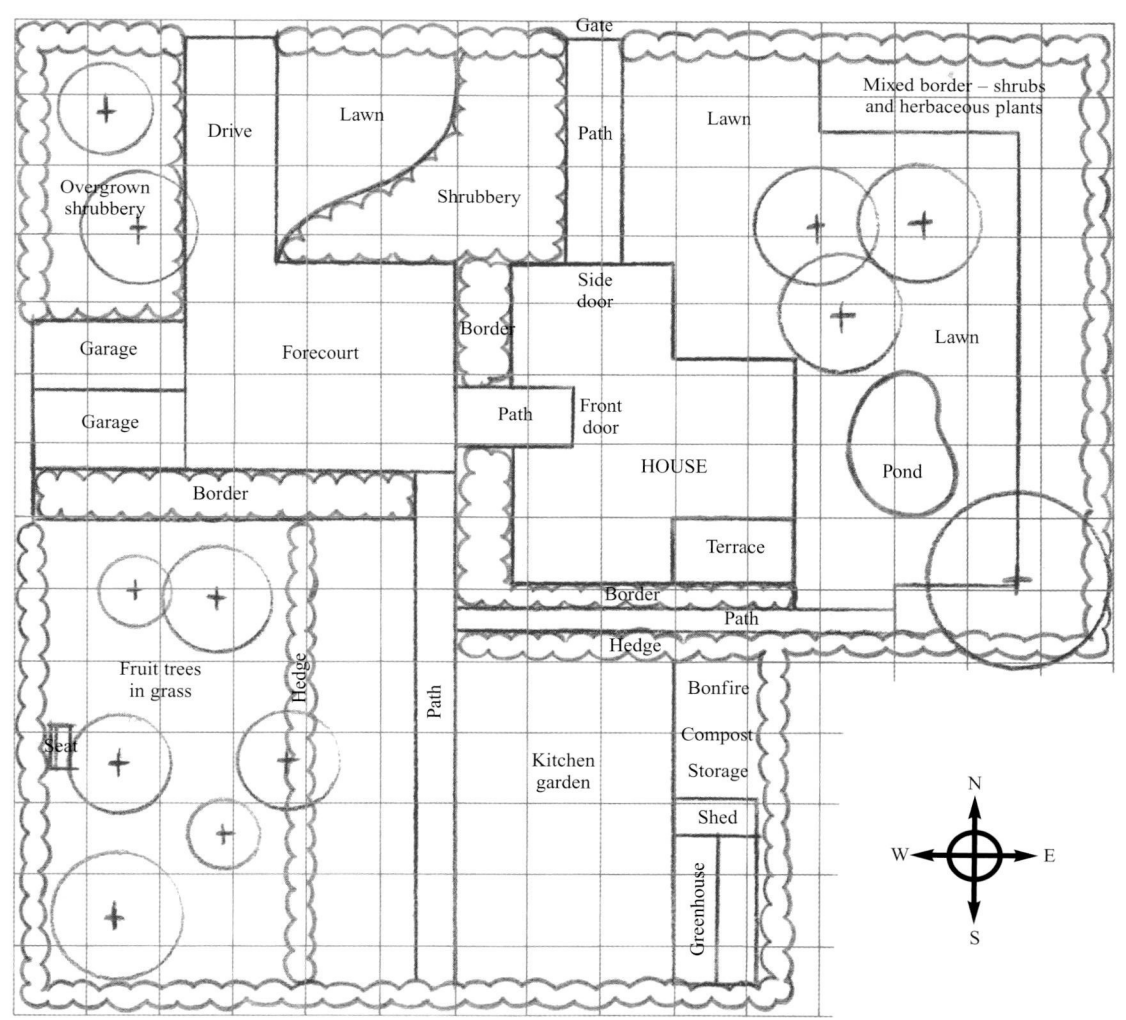

Gate

Mixed border – shrubs and herbaceous plants

Drive

Lawn

Path

Lawn

Overgrown shrubbery

Shrubbery

Side door

Garage

Forecourt

Border

Lawn

Garage

Path

Front door

HOUSE

Pond

Border

Terrace

Border

Path

Hedge

Fruit trees in grass

Hedge

Path

Bonfire

Compost

Kitchen garden

Storage

Seat

Shed

Greenhouse

N

W — E

S

transfer of measurements from field notes to plan, although designs on blank paper using a scale rule, once mastered, will give greater flexibility. A general garden plan detailing all the items and features may be drawn at a scale of 1:100, but a more detailed one of planting within a border (see also p.45) requires a scale of 1:50 or 1:40 for a comfortable depiction of plantings.

When using graph paper, a decision on how many squares are to represent one square metre (square yard) must be made. The biggest scale that the paper can afford should first be calculated by drawing on the greatest measurement, since if this can be accommodated then the entire drawing will fit. Art and design supply stores stock paper in the larger "A" sizes, which may be difficult to find in stationery shops.

Putting pencil to paper

The design novice will almost certainly require several attempts at plotting a scale plan, and even a professional will work only in pencil at this stage. The principal features should be entered onto the plan first, starting with the boundaries and any gateways or openings within them.

From these points, the house with its doorways and windows can be positioned. These openings are important as often a sight line or vista will be revealed from a doorway or window. Once the outer and "inner" perimeters of the garden area are established, small details around the house can be arranged. From here you can draw in paths and driveways, establishing between them areas of lawn, hard standing, and borders. These will facilitate the positioning of more isolated features, such as specimen trees, sheds, and greenhouses.

Omit only those features that will definitely not be retained. At this stage all else must appear on the plan, even elements that may be removed later. The drawing can then be made permanent by inking the lines. A thin line should be used to depict all of the existing detail, to permit the overlay of new ideas and the blocking in or heightening of old features. Thus you will create a new design that includes worthy existing elements enhanced by proposals, suggestions, and experiments new to the site.

Imposing the new design

The original master copy of the plan should remain unmarked. Either take

photocopies on which to work, or use tracing-paper overlays laid across the original. With a known scale and an accurate drawing, there are no limits to the possibilities that can be developed on the plan. Different sizes and positions for terraces, drives, courtyards, and ponds can be considered (see STRUCTURES AND SURFACES, pp.584–605, and WATER GARDENING, pp.280–303). Cutting out shapes representing planting, ornaments, pools, or buildings from card to place and move around the drawing will help to envisage the impact these features will have on the rest of the site.

This preliminary planning period, although rather abstract and divorced from the physical practicalities of making a garden, is an essential one, as all those thoughts, ideas, and dreams of what your personal garden should comprise must be vented, considered, applied to the plan, then adopted or rejected. Many rough drawings should be made to expose all the design possibilities.

Any working drawings that follow the thought process should be kept, as frequently a discarded idea may be resurrected in a different guise. The possibility of two ideas combining and working together when one of

the ideas in isolation would be rejected is sufficient reason for retaining every idea and drawing until the project has been completed.

Rounding out the vision

When a scheme has been rigorously scrutinized, experimented with, and passed such tests as practicality, accessibility, and suitability for the site, then the foundations of a new approach to the garden are beginning to be laid. Areas of the plan could be shaded or coloured to give a more powerful representation of the differing elements, aiding final decisions of proportion and scale.

You will also begin to appreciate the proportions of hard landscaping to "soft" – that is, planting – in your design, and adjust them if needed. You may already have ideas about building materials, and the nature of the main planting elements – even the identities of individual structural plants (see also "Principles of planting", pp.42–51). A scrapbook or collage of photographs, or elements of photographs, culled from magazines and catalogues will add colour and texture to your vision, and serve as a reminder of items to order and buy to complete your design.

BUILDING THE NEW DESIGN ON THE EXISTING PLAN

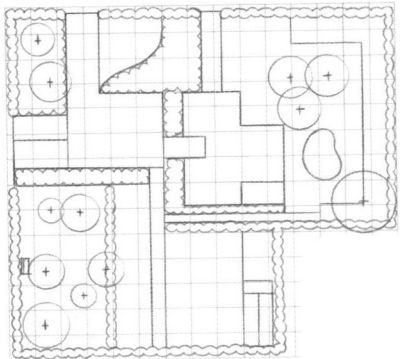

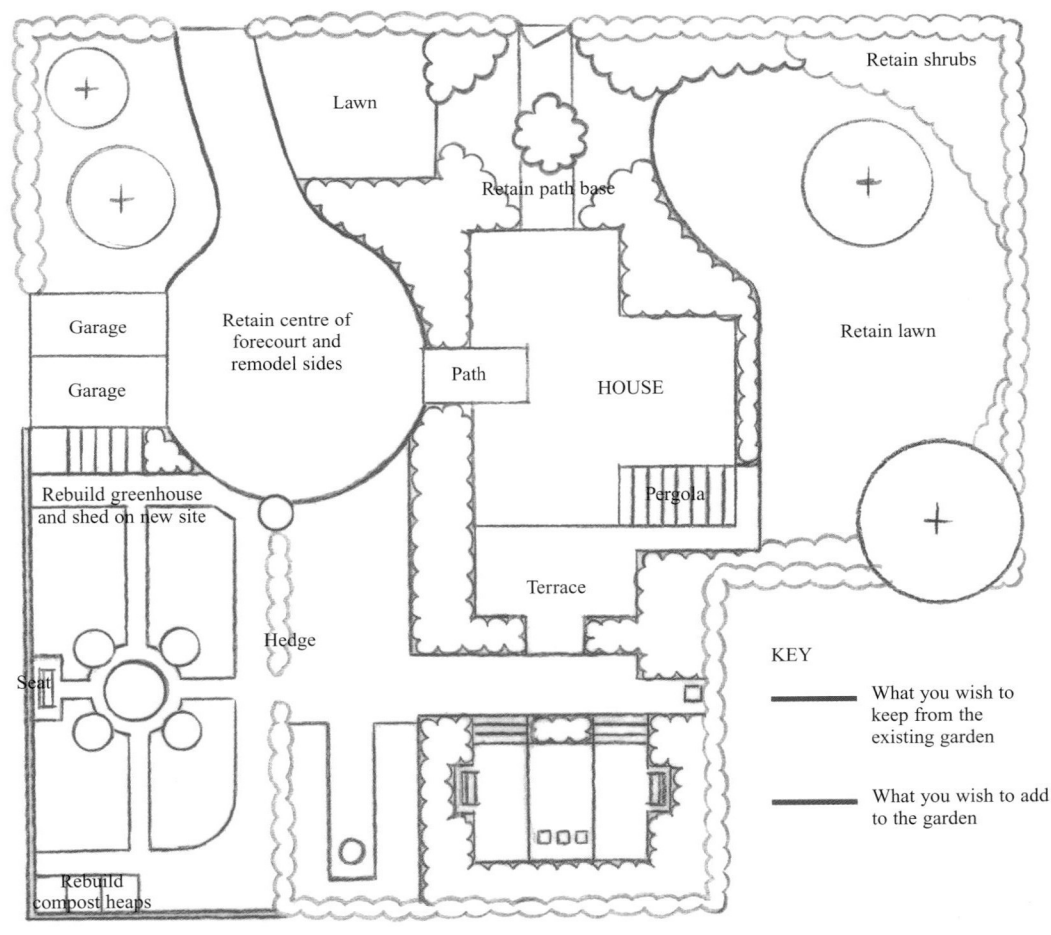

Having created an accurately plotted field plan (see p.37, and above), use copies of it, or tracing paper, to begin experimenting with your new design. The advantage of using tracing paper is that features and outlines that are to be discarded can simply be left out of the drawing, to produce a much cleaner and clearer picture. In the overlay on the right, elements to be retained from the existing garden – including much of the fine mature hedging, and the most desirable of the trees – have been marked in blue. The driveway has been given a softer profile; more space has been allocated to borders; a potager-style kitchen garden replaces a decrepit orchard; and the main reception room of the house now enjoys a serene vista of terracing with a formal pool. See also The Finished Design, opposite.

Labels in plan: Lawn; Retain shrubs; Retain path base; Retain lawn; Garage; Garage; Retain centre of forecourt and remodel sides; Path; HOUSE; Pergola; Retain lawn; Rebuild greenhouse and shed on new site; Terrace; Hedge; Seat; Rebuild compost heaps; KEY; What you wish to keep from the existing garden; What you wish to add to the garden

THE FINISHED DESIGN

This beautifully realized plan has had colour, detail, and texture added, not only in planted areas but also in the choice of hard landscaping materials. An existing garden and house may provide inspiration where materials can be harmoniously linked with those already found on the property. In such a case a seamless flow of materials from the house into the garden will produce a satisfactory design. Even when the identical brick, stone, or concrete cannot be found, a similar colour, texture, and scale of material will be perfectly satisfactory.

A garden devoid of existing materials offers the opportunity to introduce new ones. Local colours and textures should still be respected, yet within the design a particular cobble, sett, brick, or block can be selected. Small-scale, intricately patterned materials are appropriate in small, confined spaces but can look overly complicated and busy on a large scale, whereas bigger units offer a calmer scene.

Timber for pergolas, gates, or fences and gravel for terraces, paths, or a drive must all be chosen for their suitability for the site, aesthetic appeal, and durability. The colour of a fence, whether natural or painted, can alter the appearance of an entire garden, as can the colour and size of gravel and chippings used as loose surfaces.

KEY

1 Evergreen hedge
2 Long grass with bulbs and woodland herbs
3 Gravel drive with timber edging
4 Fine mown lawn
5 Gravel garden with informally placed herbaceous plants
6 Mixed shrub planting
7 Specimen tree
8 Planting with year-round interest
9 Border of shade-loving plants
10 Double garage
11 Potting shed/store
12 Greenhouse
13 Gravel forecourt with enough space for turning
14 Stone-flagged main entrance to house
15 Brick wall with trained fruit
16 Brick paths
17 Vegetables, cut flowers, fruit, and herbs
18 Garden bench
19 Central herb garden
20 Mixed border
21 Stone-flagged terrace
22 Pergola with table and chairs
23 Tree screening neighbouring house
24 Annual colour border
25 Axial vista
26 Sculpture
27 Mown grass path flanked by meadow grass and bulbs
28 Compost heaps and bonfire site
29 Deciduous hedge
30 Urn ornament
31 Formal canal bridged by stepping stones
32 Sunken paved garden with steps

Putting the plan into practice

I N the same way that the existing garden has been recorded on paper, you must now translate your new design onto the site. Often it is during this process of measuring and marking out the proposed plan that problems with the design become apparent. You may have been over-ambitious with the available space, for example, or mistaken about the most practical route for a path. Only by standing at proposed vantage points to contemplate imaginary vistas may an unwelcome eyesore be revealed.

Using props

A scheme can be laid out *in situ* using whatever comes to hand to simulate temporarily the key elements of the design. You must work around features that are probably destined to be removed – however inconvenient this may be – as the experimental layout may show that these are valuable elements that are worthy of retention after all.

Canes, tree stakes, hosepipe, string, pots, cardboard boxes, and dustbins can be used to assume roles such as path and border edges, step treads, specimen trees, ponds, or rows of repeating shrubs across the front of an imaginary terrace. The simplest indicators – heavy wooden tree stakes driven into an open lawn – will readily confirm or condemn a suitable location for a broad, spreading tree, where neighbouring plantings, buildings, and views may all be important considerations.

TRANSFERRING THE DESIGN
Formal, symmetrical designs can be as simple to mark out on the proposed site as they are to plot on paper. A grid may be created using string guides that correspond with the scale on the plan, enabling the entire design to be transferred onto the ground with relative ease. It is important that all of the measurements and angles are correctly taken and then carefully checked.

Where possible, props should be left in place for their impact to be experienced over a few days and at different times of day. Where string guides and stakes indicating the edges of borders may be disturbed, a line of sand run from a bottle or spray paint from an aerosol can be used.

Photographs taken of the garden with its props in place may prove invaluable when determining the eventual placement or removal of features. These final decisions should not be hurried; allow enough time to consider and even reconsider. At this point indecision is a strength,

as holding onto an original concept doggedly in the light of subsequent modifications is foolhardy. Opportunities available now will not present themselves again, and matters of construction are more easily resolved on the drawing board than on site with an impatient contractor.

Order of work

A carefully orchestrated schedule of work is needed to coordinate and implement a newly designed scheme. There are many different elements

and skills involved, and each should be undertaken in a logical sequence to provide a smooth running programme and keep disruption to an absolute minimum.

A fundamental decision must be made as to whether the garden improvements are to be undertaken as a single operation or in stages over a number of weeks, months, or years. Try to have all hard landscaping work completed in a single phase, as this eliminates the need for builders to return and create a second period of dust, noise, and inconvenience (see STRUCTURES AND SURFACES, pp.584–605). Timing the operations is important to enable construction work to be completed in favourable weather in summer or autumn, allowing autumn, winter, or spring for planting, sowing, and turfing.

Remodelling in stages

It is often the case, whether through budgetary constraints, available time, or simply the need to retain a useable outdoor area of some sort at all times, that a reworking of the garden can only be implemented piecemeal. A strategy for change must be drawn up. For some period of time the desired garden will overlay the existing layout, which may perhaps look rather curious, with permanently retained features, temporarily kept items, and newly established plantings and features all present. The evolving hybrid will require intricate planning to ensure a smooth transition to the new design.

To assist with a phased series of changes, the first practical measure must be to label the contents of the

USING PROPS
By arranging and rearranging items gleaned from the house and garden, you can simulate the key features of the proposed design. Here cane wigwams indicate the position of obelisks planted with climbers; inverted tubs stand in for shrubs; and the battens and geotextile fabric form a terraced area flanked by massed plantings of lavender. To complete the effect, a specimen tree in the lawn and an undulating border edging of box plants have been added.

garden with written or colour-coded tags indicating plants and materials to stay, to be moved, to remain temporarily, or to be removed at once. Although decisions have been made, a period of final deliberation is useful, during which the labelled plants may be reassessed to avoid any later confusion and irrevocable errors.

Engaging professionals

Once the scale of operations has been identified then the amount of assistance needed to implement the plans can be gauged. It may be possible over a period of time to make all the changes yourself, or some help may be needed to execute, say, construction work or tree felling. Alternatively, a contract landscaping company may be engaged to create the whole garden. Where assistance is being sought, it is important to state accurately what is required and to obtain a detailed price quotation. Good references or, ideally, personal recommendations for the firm are also highly desirable.

Professional advice may also be sought to assess the condition of trees, walls, and garden buildings. With their good condition confirmed or otherwise, the appropriate action can be taken. Even if some elements are unaffected by the current works, examine their condition early on, as to invite tree surgeons or builders back into the finished garden could be disruptive and damaging.

HARD LANDSCAPING
Because of the inevitable soil compaction involved, built features should always take priority over new planting. Where only part of the garden is being remodelled, as above, clear an area large enough for you to work comfortably. Conduits laid under paving at the construction stage (right) may be useful in the future to carry utilities such as piping and cabling.

Coping with limited access

A terraced house without direct road access into the garden should ideally have its garden works scheduled to coincide with house refurbishments, as materials must be carried through the house itself, creating possible damage to the interior. Materials can be lifted over adjoining walls, but at some cost. Where skips cannot be brought into the garden, you may have to seek permission to site one at the roadside. Waste cannot be burnt where bonfires are prohibited.

Excavations and spoil

When excavations produce large quantities of soil to be taken off-site, remember to discard subsoil, but keep topsoil. Where levels are being reduced, this will involve taking off and reserving the topsoil, digging out and removing subsoil, and then replacing the topsoil, so that the best soil does not leave the garden. When holes are to be dug, first locate any services – water, electricity, or gas pipes – which may be buried in the garden. Carefully excavate to identify their positions precisely before further work is carried out.

Clearing the area

The first stage of the garden's refurbishment is the removal of all unwanted materials and built structures. With the correct permission, trees can be cut down and taken away. Stumps must also be removed; leaving them to rot in the soil increases the danger of honey fungus (see p.661). Quality materials in good condition will have a resale value that justifies taking the trouble to find a reputable dealer. Those materials that are eventually to be reused should be cleaned and carefully stacked in a safe place away from site.

In a large garden the area to be worked on should be fenced off, restricting potential damage and spread of materials to one place. Paving and steps to be retained should also be protected by covering with boarding while heavy materials are being manoeuvred. Turf can be stripped and stacked for a short time before re-use or cleared for new turf to take its place.

Plants left in place

Plants to be left *in situ* can be carefully wrapped in sheets and tied for a brief period if, say, surrounding walls are being repaired. Large shrubs, too big for their locations yet too interesting and attractive to remove, could be thinned or reduced, or even cut hard to the ground to encourage regeneration (see "Renovation", p.110). Before cutting them back, some plants can be propagated as an extra safety measure: in the right season, take cuttings of plants such as roses, hebes, or clematis, to ensure the variant survives (see PRINCIPLES OF PROPAGATION, "Cuttings", p.632).

Clumps of many perennials will tolerate being lifted, divided, and potted up if kept well watered in a sheltered, shady corner (see PERENNIALS, "Lifting and dividing", p.193). Taking cuttings or collecting seed (see "Collecting and storing seed", p.629) is another way of preserving such plants to incorporate into the new garden.

CORRECT TIMING
Never delay the laying of new turf. The timing of delivery is crucial, as if left rolled (as below) for more than a day or two it will swiftly deteriorate. Nothing gives a new lawn an air of maturity like a scattering of bulbs, such as crocuses (left). Turfing in autumn would allow bulbs to be planted simultaneously, to flower in spring.

Creating the landscape

With unwanted materials out of the way, the cleared site should then have any pernicious weeds eradicated (see "Controlling weeds", p.671). At this stage any adjustments to levels can also be made, as well as any excavations for services such as power for garden lighting, or irrigation systems. Wall footings or path bases can now be excavated, and solid foundations built (see "Paths and steps", p.593, and "Walls", p.596). Construction of walls and built structures can then take place (see STRUCTURES AND SURFACES, pp.584–605, and "Erecting the greenhouse", p.571). To add the finishing touches before planting, fences and timber may be treated or painted, and trellising or support wires put up on walls and fences for climbers.

Ready to plant

Where larger plants are being used in a scheme, it may be necessary to plant them as the hard landscape is being constructed, as at a later stage it may not be possible to manoeuvre them into place. However, the task of reintegrating any preserved plant material into new schemes, and introducing new plants, generally begins once the hard construction is completed and services installed.

Before plants are introduced, however, any soil compaction should be remedied, and the soil improved by the addition of organic matter (see "Improving soil structure", p.621).

Any protection given to shrubs and hard surfaces can now be removed, and surfaces cleaned with a high-pressure hose. With the potentially dirty tasks complete, loose surfaces can have their final layers applied, with clean gravel laid on top. After that, new planting plans (see p.42) can begin to take shape.

Principles of planting

Once the general layout of the garden is in place the greatest enjoyment comes with selecting plants. The impact plant choice can make on a garden is extraordinary. Plants give a garden style, charm, character, depth, and warmth – to mention but a few of their qualities. An adjacent street may be enhanced by an overhanging tree, which softens rigid lines and brings seasonal colour and texture to an urban landscape. A sheltered courtyard with high surrounding walls may appear like a prison yard, yet the decorative effect of a climber, such as a wisteria, trained over it will transform the space into a welcoming retreat.

Plants bring calm, clothing severity with flowing form and mellowing tones. As with soft furnishings in a house, they will also help to deaden harsh sounds. It is also increasingly accepted that, allergy sufferers notwithstanding, the presence of plants improves the atmosphere around us, possibly alleviating the effects of pollution, and certainly increasing the oxygen and moisture content of the air as well as adding a pleasing fragrance.

Ensuring plants succeed

Successful plant choice can quite literally make a garden; it might even be said that until plants and flowers are established and growing well a garden does not really exist. The garden's therapeutic powers, which can soothe the mind and alleviate tension, derive mainly from its thriving plants, and perhaps also from the presence of water and the use of sympathetic building materials. The element of quiet combined with charm and style can turn a small plot of planted land into a sanctuary. Even the most elementary of plantings, such as a well-kept lawn that has replaced a hard surface within a built environment, will bring life, colour, and softness to an otherwise harsh and alien site.

Selecting plants for success

The wealth of different plants available can be bewildering, but the choice will never be as limitless as it may seem. Within the categories of trees, shrubs, perennials, and so on, many plants can be dismissed immediately as inappropriate on numerous grounds: for example, incompatible soil type, climate, scale, or growth rate. Once the most suitable plants have been identified, personal preference for certain colours and shapes will limit the choice still further.

The manner and frequency of garden use will dictate the range of plants, too: for example, a garden area that is used only in summer will be planted to perform best in that season. Planting immediately around a house and along an entrance drive will also place greater demands on the choice of plant material, because year-round interest of some description will be expected. A carefully selected combination of plants that will provide a display of flowers in each season is needed. Alternatively, group plants together that combine other attributes – mix evergreens with some fruiting trees or shrubs, add plants with attractive stems or bark, and include bulbs and annuals to inject colour and interest at dull times of the year.

Defining a style of planting

In every garden there are so many variables that each one is unique. So, to talk about a particular or specific planting style may appear to impose false categories and divisions. However, there are two extremes between which all plantings fall. These are the formal and informal styles. Deciding on the degree of formality or informality required will greatly assist the initial selection of plants and the diversity of plant material used. A very formal garden, for example, may have an extremely restricted palette of plants compared to a more informal arrangement.

Formal planting

Great strength and order can be given to a garden by using only a small selection of plants but in quantity. The planting, however, does not necessarily need to be arranged in an angular and regimented fashion, or within precisely designated areas. Some formality can be achieved using sweeps of single plants in broad blocks, creating tranquillity in uniformity. Even relatively informal plants grown en masse can assume an orderly role – an expanse of ornamental grasses planted to create a

CONTRASTING PLANTING STYLES
The style of planting within a garden or area of it can be broadly categorized as either formal or informal. Some plants lend themselves more to one style than the other. The labour involved in maintaining the formal garden (far right) is evident, but an informal planting, such as the border (right), does not necessarily involve less work: a great deal of skill and care is needed to maintain a balance between the needs and vigour of different plants when growing in close proximity.

"EDITING" NATURE
Careful plant choices, to suit the surroundings and compete successfully with less desirable plants, produce a pleasingly naturalistic woodland scene.

AN ARTIFICIAL ENVIRONMENT
Select plants suitable for the conditions: a roof may not be a natural growing site, but these sun-loving, wind-resistant plants are thriving here.

solid platform of texture can impose order and structure, for example.

The strongly architectural quality of the conventional formal garden conveys a powerful image – one of symmetry and balance, precision and accuracy. Plants may be interpreted as structural elements, more closely aligned to walls and other built elements. The sheared, trimmed, and pruned formal garden owes as much of its visual impact to the selection of appropriate plants as it does to their subsequent control and maintenance. Formal plantings will impact on a garden, summer or winter. In winter – with all else laid bare – their angular simplicity in clear bright sunshine can be most appealing. See also TOPIARY, p.76

Formality often requires restraint, which can pose a dilemma for those who would like to design with the widest possible variety of plants. Faced with a spacious driveway approach flanked by mown lawns, for example, some gardeners may find it hard to resist the temptation to choose 20 different species of tree. Yet far greater formal impact would be achieved by repeating a single species, in regular blocks or in a continuous double line, to form a well-designed avenue.

Softening the effect

Strongly formal plantings in a garden can be varied in a number of ways, all with equal effect. Extreme forms of topiary, knot gardens, and parterres, can be planted with or alongside free-flowing informal mixtures of plants to create a marked contrast of styles. This combination changes with the seasons and will reduce the stark impact of the formal plantings. A garden clearly divided into distinct units can also be planted with an area of marked formality to contrast with an adjacent, informal one.

The juxtaposition of styles presents a lively and stimulating garden of surprises at each turn of house corner, hedge, or shrub. Formality can also blend with informality when formal features are allowed to relax towards the informal. A finely clipped hedge of yew (*Taxus baccata*) can be planted in a serpentine line and clipped to simulate clouds, while *Ceanothus*, planted at regular intervals along the whole length of a broad border, will grow to form large mounds of equally spaced and sized yet irregularly shaped forms. Thus, a degree of formality underpins a broadly informal arrangement.

Informal planting

A planting that appears informal may in fact comprise a wealth of different plants – trees, shrubs, herbaceous perennials, and annuals – their diversity, richness, and profusion all skilfully combined to bring the colour, texture, shape, and form of unrelated plants together with dramatic effect.

As with a formal style, there are as many – if not more – variations on the theme of informality. A cottage-style garden of organized chaos, where garden plants are combined in a seemingly haphazard concoction, can rapidly become truly chaotic – an overgrown wilderness in which many plants will not survive the inherent crowding and competition. To preserve and maintain the plant content of such a garden requires expertise and considerable time spent controlling the different plants and keeping their growth in check.

This informality of planting may be taken a few stages further by choosing a combination of plants that will grow together in harmony, whose strengths are well matched and whose climate and soil requirements are met. Herbaceous plants that require little or no support provide a good example. Cultivated garden plants can be combined to create the impression of a wild meadow or indigenous species can be planted to create a "natural" meadow (see MEADOW GARDENING, p.401). Indeed, an entire habitat can be made up of plants that would naturally occur in the locality. Native plants will also attract wildlife to your garden by providing a welcome source of food and nesting sites.

For many people this may be taking informal gardening too far, but by studying the local environment and taking note of which plants thrive in it, the planting scheme can be adapted to cultivated garden plants. Planting a light tree canopy allows sufficient daylight to penetrate for an understorey of shrubs to be grown. Beneath this, shade-tolerant herbaceous plants will thrive after spring bulbs have faded away. This layered community of plants may appear crowded, yet they will all flourish if the chosen plants are given the appropriate light and conditions at each level of the undergrowth, throughout the season.

Planting for structure, shape, and form

ENDURING FORMS

Trees create permanent structure and form in a garden setting. Look for those with interesting leaf shapes, such as Sorbus, with its divided foliage, and the deeply lobed leaves of Japanese maples (Acer palmatum). Both trees have fine autumn tints and beautiful architectural outlines during winter and early spring.

WHEN selecting a plant for a bed or border, its shape, form, and eventual size are often considered of secondary importance to its flowers, fruits, or autumn hues. Yet these colourful qualities are frequently temporary, lasting just a few weeks, unlike the shape of a tree or shrub. To create an enduring planting scheme that will look good throughout the year, select plants that offer beautiful natural forms. The structure of a plant is best appreciated at first hand, and visiting gardens where plants have matured and developed is an ideal way to appreciate their more subtle qualities.

Architectural plants
Plants with bold foliage or a dramatic form are described as architectural or accent plants; they make ideal specimens, creating considerable impact when used on their own as focal points or to contrast with their neighbours. The divided, toothed leaves of *Melianthus major* or the plume-like flowerheads of *Miscanthus sinensis* are examples of structural perennials, while spreading shrubs, such as *Aralia elata*, and *Cornus controversa* also offer exceptional architectural qualities.

Altering outlooks
Planting can be used to highlight garden features or to disguise eyesores. For example, an ugly box-like building will retain its unsightly silhouette if a clinging creeper, such as *Parthenocissus*, is grown over it, but if a more characterful climber, such as wisteria, is used then the outline will be masked beneath its twisted branches and pendulous flowers.

Similarly, a visual barrier, such as a bank that marks a level change, can be lost when a mound-forming or horizontally tiered subject is grown on the lower level. *Viburnum plicatum* or *Euonymus alatus* would work well in this situation.

An area of lawn can be enhanced with a specimen tree. When selecting one, the size of lawn and proximity to the house are important factors to consider, as are soil type and local climate. A specimen tree also needs to look appropriate in its setting. One with a rounded canopy will sit well on a lawn, whereas a tall spire-like form can resemble a rocket on its launch pad in such an open area.

Natural strength
Soothing greens and strong structure can help to create a restful scene. A fernery is a classic example of this style, where beautiful shapes and forms provide interest without the distraction of bright colours (see also FERNS, p.194).

Grasses add a graceful, refined structure, and the sound and movement of their rustling leaves makes them indispensable. Even in winter their skeletal forms play an important role in an otherwise bleak landscape. Planted alongside broadleaved *Macleaya cordata*, the elegant grasses *Stipa gigantea* or *Helictotrichon sempervirens* are very eye-catching.

A backdrop of large evergreens will provide colour and form when all deciduous plants have been left bare in winter. Not only do they present foliage interest and strong shapes throughout the year, but they also protect wildlife in bad weather and can be used to create permanent screens and privacy.

Evergreens that grow into naturally neat shapes resemble topiary, giving the garden a sculptural appearance without the need for trimming. Balls of *Hebe topiaria* or *H. buxifolia* make excellent accent plants along the front of a border, while *Choisya ternata* and *Viburnum x globosum* 'Jermyns Globe' both grow into large orbs of tight foliage.

Pruning into shapes
A plant's natural structure can be enhanced by pruning. When some willows (*Salix*) and dogwoods (*Cornus*) are pruned to the ground, or coppiced, every two years, they produce an explosion of colourful, straight stems. Limes (*Tilia*) and planes (*Platanus*) may be pollarded: if the branches are pruned back to the same point every year or two, they produce swollen "fists" at the pruning points. Both pruning methods create strong architectural forms that can greatly enhance a garden design. See also "Coppicing and pollarding shrubs", p.107.

PLANTS FOR FOCAL POINTS
This variegated Yucca has striking, spiky foliage in contrast to the solid, rounded outline of the giant urn. The Agapanthus in the foreground accentuates the form of the Yucca.

TOPIARY-LIKE SHRUBS (RIGHT)
Plants that have a compact shape, such as this golden Choisya ternata *SUNDANCE, blend well with those of a looser habit, such as that of the purple* Berberis *behind.*

DRIFTS OF PERENNIALS (BELOW)
Perennials and grasses can produce startling shapes when planted in bold drifts. Their loose stems sway in the breeze, creating the impression of rolling sea waves.

FLOWER FORMS (BOTTOM LEFT)
The shape and structure of stems and foliage can be matched by bold flowers. The flat flowerheads of this Achillea filipendulina 'Gold Plate' *are here set off by pompon blooms of* Verbena bonariensis.

CREATING CONTRASTS (BOTTOM CENTRE)
Using a simple colour scheme helps to bring different forms into sharper focus. Here, tall spikes of white lupins are defined by a spreading skirt of Anthemis.

GRACEFUL GRASSES (ABOVE)
A border of mixed ornamental grasses adds structure to the garden throughout the year. Here, fountains of arching flowerheads provide the focal point.

SHAPELY BUILDINGS (BELOW)
Growing a structural climber, such as this wisteria, over a dull shed provides an attractive covering.

Planting for colour and texture

THE use of plant colours and textures in all their infinite variations is of central importance in successful garden design, even though many flowers – for it is the flowers that dazzle and entice – offer such a brief display. The tree peony (*Paeonia suffruticosa*) is a classic example that may bloom for only a few days, yet its huge, tissue-paper flowers make it worthy of a prominent place within a border.

When using colour in the garden personal taste can be allowed to reign almost unhindered. Yet a totally unlimited palette of colours, where every hue and tone are set against a contrasting shade, may produce an indigestible medley that would challenge even the greatest exponent of colour as a tool of garden design. Restraint should be used to limit the range and quantity of colour. For example, a backdrop of muted greens will quieten a busy foreground of mixed colours and allow the vivid shades to shine.

Colour and distance

Bright, light colours such as lemon-yellows and whites are better reflectors of sunlight than darker hues, which from a distance may be lost or appear muted. Such light colours used in the foreground will visually jump forward from their positions. These shades introduced at a distance will also appear closer, foreshortening the perceived length of a garden, usually detrimentally.

Traditionally, colours with depth, such as blues, mauves, purples, and silvers, are used to create a sense of distance at the farther reaches of a garden, with paler shades of yellow, white, cream, and pink occupying the foreground. Reds, oranges, and deep yellows are best planted in the middle of a bed; at a distance they are lost, while close up they dominate.

The influence of light

Location is an important factor to consider when choosing plant colour schemes. In strong direct sunlight, the more powerful yellows, oranges and reds become almost luminous and can produce a vibrant picture. If, however, you wish to cool down a seating area in a hot, sunny corner, silver and grey foliage and blue flowers will create a more restful setting.

A scheme of pastel colours, such as soft blue, pink, creamy-yellow, and silver will create a beautiful composition under low light conditions. A terrace or patio frequented in the evenings for entertaining and planted

with white flowers and pale or white-variegated foliage will, in minimal light, reflect back atmospheric ghostly hues. Equally effective would be a gloomy courtyard enlivened by the use of bright shades.

Combining colours

One of the most challenging areas of garden design is creating effective colour combinations. Blue and white make elegant partners, giving a cool, clean look that is hard to rival, although for sheer purity green and white are unbeatable, especially when on the same flower such as a snowdrop or *Dicentra spectabilis* 'Alba'.

These subtle and refined combinations will be heightened if other plantings display a less restricted palette. Orange and purple, two dominant colours of equal strength, are shockingly brilliant when used together – bright orange calendulas set against the leaden purple foliage

of ornamental cabbages make an eye-catching arrangement. Blue and yellow also create a sharp contrast; the bold intensity of each introdduces a lively juxtaposition of colours. When an acid-yellow tulip or *Fritillaria imperialis* 'Maxima Lutea' is mixed with the clear blue of forget-me-nots (*Myosotis*) or ceanothus, the interplay can be truly electric.

Adding texture

Many plants exhibit rich foliage texture, and interesting effects can be achieved when they are planted in broad swathes. A sweep of lavender (*Lavandula*) or rosemary (*Rosmarinus*), clipped annually, will grow into soft mounds of dense aromatic growth, equal in beauty to any herbaceous flower border.

Even plants of little decorative interest individually can be useful in groups. The shrubby honeysuckle, *Lonicera nitida,* or many of the bam-

BLOCKS OF COLOUR
Masses of flowers in a single bright colour, such as these vermilion roses, will dominate a planting scheme and arrest the attention of all who pass by.

COOL GREENS
There are numerous shades of green within the garden and each plays an important role calming, cooling, and harmonizing the design.

boos provide masses of textural variations, and make excellent hedging (see BAMBOOS, p.96).

A play of different textures creates subtle interest, even within a single plant. A yew (*Taxus*), for example, clipped neatly below but allowed to spread out at the top to form long, loose stems, provides a wonderful textural contrast. A layered look can be achieved with mixed plantings, such as the feathery fronds of shuttlecock fern (*Matteuccia struthiopteris*) set off by the vast flat leaves of *Gunnera manicata*, in turn backed by white-stemmed birch (*Betula*).

Tree stems have tactile qualities that should not be overlooked. Old sweet chestnuts (*Castanea sativa*) develop deep, furrowed bark that contrasts well with smooth, horizontal shapes, while shrubs, such as *Hydrangea aspera* subsp. *sargentiana* and *Euonymus phellomanus* also produce eye-catching barks.

TRADITIONAL PALETTE (ABOVE)
The classic combination of white, pink, and blue is perfect for this romantically planted garden.

FIERY BORDERS (ABOVE RIGHT)
Beds of hot reds, oranges, and rich yellows are energizing and best sited where the sun can illuminate the glowing colours.

SPOT COLOUR (FAR RIGHT)
Buttons of dark red Knautia macedonica *are thrown into sharp focus when grown against the pale hues of the sedum and foxgloves in the background.*

SIMPLE SCHEMES (RIGHT)
Elegant, white daisies and irises edge a tranquil pool, echoing the white window of the house beyond.

PEELING BARK (FAR LEFT)
The beautiful Japanese maple, Acer griseum, *has wonderful chestnut-coloured bark that peels to resemble wood shavings. It is particularly noticeable when used as a specimen tree in a winter garden.*

PLEATED LEAVES (CENTRE LEFT)
The intricately pleated leaves of Veratrum nigrum *provide a strong architectural accent when sited in a sunny or partially shaded spot.*

TEXTURAL CONTRASTS (LEFT)
Complementary textures and shapes heighten interest here, where the wispy, hair-like spikelets of Hordeum jubatum *fall gracefully behind* Echinops ritro, *with its stiff upright stems of spiny blue flowers.*

Planting for seasonal and year-round interest

THE art of planting the well-planned garden is for each season to bring new richness and interest. All too often, from late spring to midsummer, a garden builds up week after week to a peak, but then descends rapidly into a flowerless abyss in autumn and winter. With more than half the year remaining and some late fine weather still to come, it is important to plan for these often-forgotten months.

A garden should contain a well-chosen collection of plants to carry interest throughout these seasons of reduced light and growth. A permanent framework of planting, formed by trees, shrubs, and hedges, will create the basic skeleton onto which a series of overlaying levels – climbers, herbaceous plants, bedding plants, and bulbs – can be used to provide beauty and interest throughout each season.

EXTENDED INTEREST
Crocosmia 'Lucifer' is invaluable for its long-lasting interest. In spring, sword-like, architectural leaves emerge, followed in late summer by sprays of scarlet flowers (right). The seedheads look good, too, when dusted with frost (above).

Spring
Late winter and early spring are not only a time for flowers but also a season for sweet scents. Shrubs, such as Christmas box (*Sarcococca confusa*), the winter honeysuckle (*Lonicera x purpusii*), wintersweet (*Chimonanthus praecox*), and the many beautiful species of *Daphne* fill the air with their powerful perfumes. Bulbs offer early colour, when aconites (*Eranthis hyemalis*) and snowdrops (*Galanthus*) compete to be the first to flower, followed by crocuses, narcissi, and tulips. The bulbs are joined by the earliest flowering perennials, such as hellebores,

and later, as the bulbs die down, other herbaceous plants fill the gaps.

Summer
Early summer heralds an explosion of colour from herbaceous perennials, with every shade, shape, and form working together to create a luxuriance unrivalled throughout the rest of the year. Peonies, delphiniums, campanulas, and lupins give a spectacular display, while roses perform alongside deutzias, mallows (*Lavatera*), and philadelphus in the shrub border. As summer peaks, large-flowered clematis can be used to scramble over spring-flowering

shrubs, such as forsythia. Later on, annuals such as *Nicotiana* and *Cosmos* fill gaps between shrubs, and tender or half-hardy perennials, such as penstemons and diascias, brighten bed or border colour schemes.

Autumn
The well-maintained garden, where regular dead-heading and careful interplanting have been carried out, can often reach a peak in this season. As well as the overspill of summer blooms, late-flowering perennials, such as Japanese anemones, crocosmias, and Michaelmas daisies (*Aster novi-belgii*) perform through the

autumn. As the light pales, clusters of dark pink blooms open on *Clerodendrum bungei*, scenting the cool air with its rich sweet fragrance.

Foliage tints begin to fire up in autumn, with trees such as maples and *Parrotia persica* slowly turning every shade of yellow, orange, purple, and red. The large leaves of *Vitis coignetiae* also provide spectacular colour before they fall. Berries and fruits contribute to the richness of autumn hues, with viburnums and *Euonymus* decorating the garden with their jewelled displays.

Flowering bulbs and corms, such as cyclamen and colchicums, contribute to the autumn display, too.

Winter
The depths of winter are the most testing times in the garden, when colour and interest are most difficult to achieve. It is now that permanent structures take centre stage. The stems of deciduous shrubs and trees, such as silver birch (*Betula*) and colourful dogwoods (*Cornus*), shine out in the weak winter sunlight.

The texture, form, and shape of evergreens furnish the winter garden when all else is bare. A well-trained ceanothus or the rounded clumps of *Euphorbia characias* give substance to otherwise "empty" borders. Meanwhile some evergreen shrubs, such as *Skimmia japonica* and *Viburnum tinus,* put on displays of bead-like flower buds. These are accompanied by the highly scented flowers of *Viburnum x bodnantense*, which will break into bloom at the first hint of milder weather.

SEASONAL SUNLIGHT
Not only planting schemes alter with the seasons; sunlight can also be used throughout the year to highlight evolving shapes and forms. Here, the weak winter sun casts long shadows that stretch over a colourful carpet of Cyclamen coum, *the flowers of which open throughout the winter as light filters through the leafless trees.*

EARLY TO MID-SPRING
Among the first flowers to bloom in early spring are the bulbs. Here, bold swathes of narcissi have been planted to brighten up the borders with their nodding heads of golden-yellow flowers and strap-like foliage. These are accompanied by spikes of spurge (Euphorbia) and emerging perennials, the foliage of which is now pushing its way through the soil.

LATE SPRING
As spring progresses and light levels increase, borders rapidly fill out with lush foliage and early flowers, which help to camouflage the fading blooms and leaves of early bulbs. Here, blue geraniums and wavy-edged, rounded-leaved lady's mantle (Alchemilla mollis) dominate in the foreground, while similarly tinted flowers thrive towards the end of the garden.

HIGH SUMMER
A profusion of flowers, including the blue geraniums that are still in bloom, heralds the height of summer. Pastel blues, soft yellows, and creamy-whites create a cool border that takes the heat out of the summer sun. These colours also give the illusion of extended perspective, making the border look longer and leading the eye to the seating area at the far end.

SUMMER INTO AUTUMN
The pale pastels have given way to splashes of fiery red designed to mirror tree and shrub foliage that will soon be taking on its vibrant autumn tints. This border scheme shows how planting can be used to change the colour and mood, and alter perspectives, in the garden as the seasons progress, building up to a crescendo as summer turns into autumn.

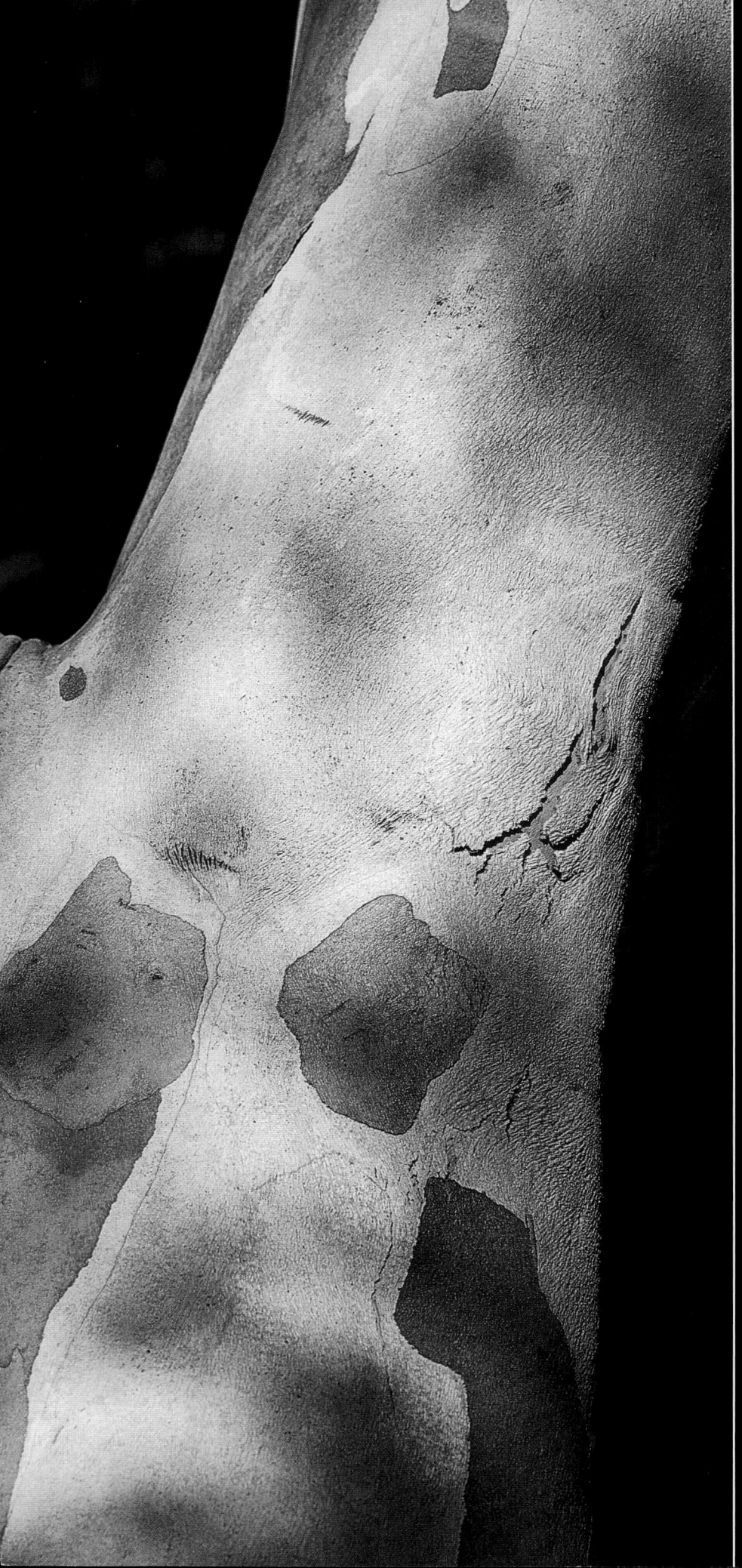

CHAPTER

2

ORNAMENTAL TREES

MORE THAN ANY other plants, trees create a sense of permanence and maturity in a garden. They add height, structure, and sculptural focal points, while their large and distinctive silhouettes form an attractive contrast with the softer lines of other planting. There is an enormous variety of trees, differing in shape and form as well as in the colour and texture of foliage, flowers, and bark. Each has a particular appeal, from the pointed column of a cypress to the blazing autumn colour of a Japanese maple or the patterned trunk of *Eucalyptus*. Trees may be grown in many ways: an informal woodland of hazels and birches, surrounded by bulbs, has naturalistic charm, while an avenue of copper beeches is suitably elegant in a formal setting. Some trees – such as magnolias – are best sited on their own as specimen features.

Trees for the garden

ORNAMENTAL trees are grown for the beauty of their flowers, bark, or decorative fruits, rather than for edible or timber crops. Many fruit trees, however, are graced by beautiful flowers and a few ornamental trees, such as crab apples (*Malus*), bear rich crops of fruits for preserving. The distinction between trees and shrubs is similarly blurred; the former usually, but not always, with a single trunk and the latter, for example lilacs (*Syringa*), multi-stemmed although sometimes reaching tree-like proportions.

Choosing trees

Trees are generally the largest and longest-lived garden plants, and selecting and siting them are major design decisions. The fewer trees a garden can accommodate, the more important careful choice and siting become; in a "one-tree garden" these points are crucial to the success of the design. The general appearance and special features of a tree obviously matter, but its suitability for a garden's soil, climate, and aspect, and its ultimate height, spread, and growth rate, are equally important.

Once a tree is chosen, the design process continues, by deciding where to plant it (see "Choosing a planting site", p.63). Garden centres stock a limited range of the most popular ornamental trees; specialist nurseries, some with a mail-order service, offer a wider choice.

Heights range from about 1m (3ft) for some dwarf conifers to the massive 90m (300ft) of a redwood (*Sequoia*). Growth rates vary from 2.5cm (1in) or less a year for dwarf conifers to 1m (3ft) or more for some poplars (*Populus*). A young tree in a garden centre gives little or no indication of its potential size and some species, particularly conifers, include both miniature and very large cultivars. Select cultivars with care and, if offered substitutes, make sure that they will be equally appropriate for your needs.

TREES IN THE LARGE GARDEN
Trees add structure to a garden and form a long-term part of the design framework. A large garden should include several, varying in height and shape. Group several trees together to create a strong impact of colour and form, as in this informal arrangement of maples (Acer) and other deciduous trees.

Trees as design elements

Trees create a strong visual impact in the same way as do hard landscaping features. They also help to form the permanent framework of a garden, around which the more temporary elements come and go.

Trees may be used as living sculptures (see "Specimen trees", p.55): a simple, contrasting setting is most likely to enhance a tree used in this way. A tree with pale or variegated foliage looks very striking against a hedge of dark green yew (*Taxus*

ENCLOSING SPACE
The arching fronds of palms are used as structural features to enclose and delineate a seating area. They create a lush, cool screen that forms a less rigid division than a wall or fence.

SPECIMEN TREE
Trees that are particularly attractive or well shaped are best sited on their own so that they stand out in the scheme. This double pink hawthorn (Crataegus laevigata 'Rosea Flore Pleno') has a fine show of blossom that may be enjoyed from all viewpoints as well as forming a cornerstone in the design.

baccata), for example, while the bold winter tracery of bare branches stands out well in front of a white-painted wall.

Used structurally, trees can also define or enclose space. A row or informal clump of trees can mark the boundary of a property, separate one part of the garden from another, or emphasize a path. A pair of trees might act as a verdant frame for a distant view or form a living arch through which the garden is entered.

Shape and form
The shape and form of a tree are as important as its size – in setting the mood and style as well as in practical considerations of space. Some trees, such as many ornamental cherries (*Prunus*), are small and charming, while others, such as cedars (*Cedrus*), are grand and monumental. Most can be formal or informal, according to the setting and treatment. *Rhus typhina* has a striking architectural form, which is ideal for a modern, paved garden, while the arching fronds of many palms bring lushness to a courtyard or conservatory. Rowans (*Sorbus aucuparia*) and hollies (*Ilex*) are typical English cottage garden trees; Japanese maples (*Acer palmatum*) and the large *Salix babylonica* var. *pekinensis* 'Tortuosa' are suitable for Oriental gardens; native species are ideal for wild gardens.

Narrow, upright trees, such as *Malus tschonoskii*, are suitable for small gardens but have a formal, almost artificial appearance. Round-headed or wide-spreading trees seem more informal but cast much more shade and rain shadow, making underplanting difficult, while those with an irregular, open-branch framework have a naturalistic appeal. Cone- or pyramid-shaped trees have a sculptural effect, while weeping trees have a softer silhouette.

Consider how long the tree takes to develop its characteristic shape – in some cases, it can be decades. *Prunus* 'Kanzan', for example, has a stiff growth habit when young, with awkwardly angled branches; yet after ten years the branches begin to arch and by 30 years the tree has a graceful, rounded crown.

Where space allows, combining contrasting tree shapes can create a dynamic effect, but planting many differently shaped trees may simply appear fussy and uncoordinated.

Specimen trees

A specimen tree is grown on its own to develop and display its full natural beauty without competition from other trees. Depending on the climate, Chinese dogwood (*Cornus kousa* var. *chinensis*), weeping willow (*Salix* x *sepulcralis* var. *chrysocoma*), various ornamental cherries (*Prunus*), and palms such as *Howea* and *Phoenix* are popular specimen trees. A specimen tree can be effective as a focal point in all scales of surroundings, although you should select a tree that is the right size for its setting – tiny specimen trees look lost in vast gardens and outsized ones

TREE SHAPES

SPREADING
Prunus americana

PYRAMIDAL
Carpinus betulus 'Fastigiata' (Upright common hornbeam)

CONICAL
Pseudotsuga menziesii var. *glauca* (Blue Douglas fir)

COLUMNAR
Acer rubrum 'Columnare' (Red maple)

WEEPING
Salix caprea 'Kilmarnock' (Kilmarnock willow)

ROUND-HEADED
Malus 'Magdeburgensis' (Crab apple)

ARCHING
Archontophoenix alexandrae (King palm)

FOLIAGE COLOUR AND TEXTURE
Here, the autumn foliage of a deciduous tree is offset by the blue-green mass of a conifer, creating a contrasting tableau of colour, texture, and shape.

overbearing in confined spaces. Specimen trees, particularly in formal gardens, are traditionally placed in the centre of a lawn. Siting a specimen tree to one side, however, can add a sense of liveliness and informality to a scheme as well as allowing a view down the garden. Other options include planting a specimen tree next to a gate or garden entrance, or at the bottom or top of a flight of steps, to mark the transition from one space in the garden to another.

Planting in a swathe of gravel or ground-cover plants such as ivy (*Hedera*) or periwinkle (*Vinca*) provides a complementary foil for a specimen tree. In a mixed border, use a tree as the keystone around which to build the colour and form of the surrounding groups of plants. A specimen tree may be reflected in a garden pond or offset by a statue or white-painted bench beneath it, so that each element enhances the other.

COLOUR FROM FLOWERS
The large blooms of Magnolia campbellii *subsp.* mollicomata *stand out against the bare branches.*

Grouping trees

If space allows, consider planting three or more trees together in informal clumps of the same or different species. A group of trees also creates a more substantial, curtain-like frame than a single tree for one or both sides of a view. Clumps of large trees such as oaks (*Quercus*) or beeches (*Fagus*) make focal points on a grand scale, as exemplified in the landscapes of the great 18th-century English landscape gardener, Capability Brown. In warmer climates, stands of tall, bare-trunked palms can be equally impressive on their own in grass or interplanted with lower-growing or multi-stemmed species.

On a smaller scale, a modest group of deciduous trees with light foliage, such as birches (*Betula pendula*) or maples (*Acer*), can form the backbone of a miniature woodland. The dappled shade and leafy soil are perfect for bluebells (*Hyacinthoides non-scriptus*), daffodils, and primroses (*Primula vulgaris*).

Trees in informal groups can be planted closer than the combined potential spread of their crowns. Relatively tall, narrow, or asymmetrical growth may result but the effect can be pleasantly informal, with intermingled branches forming attractive tracery against the sky.

Features of interest

Although trees are most often valued for their architectural qualities, they also provide interest through particular features such as flowers, foliage, berries, and bark. Site a tree so that its attractive characteristics are shown off to advantage (see also "Successional interest", p.57).

Leaves
For sheer mass and duration of display, leaves are by far the most important feature. Their shape, size, and colour offer infinite variation, from the delicate, golden, ferny foliage of *Gleditsia triacanthos* 'Sunburst' to the huge, architectural leaves of palms such as *Phoenix*. Surface texture affects how light is reflected, with glossy leaves adding a bright touch. The density of the canopy ranges from opaque to airy, an important factor if considering underplanting around a tree.

Trees with coloured or variegated foliage, such as the reddish-purple of *Prunus virginiana* 'Schubert' or the yellow-edged leaves of *Ligustrum lucidum* 'Excelsum Superbum', provide a mass of colour that contrasts well with green-leaved trees.

Some leaves, such as those of *Eucalyptus*, are pleasantly aromatic, while others, such as those of an aspen, quiver in the slightest breeze, adding the extra pleasure of sound.

Flowers
Flowers have a fleeting but memorable presence and range from modest to opulent. Autumn, winter, and early spring flowers are especially valuable when there may be less interest from other plants.

Flower colour should complement the larger scheme. Pale flowers stand out against dark leaves, while dark flowers show up best in a pale setting. By training climbers such as clematis or roses up mature trees, you can extend the floral display.

Fragrance is a bonus, ranging from the subtle, winter perfume of *Acacia dealbata* to the heady, summer scent of the Japanese big-leaf magnolia (*Magnolia obovata*) and frangipani (*Plumeria rubra* f. *acutifolia*). For flowers and fragrance a sheltered situation is best.

Fruits, berries, and pods
These can rival or exceed flowers in beauty, ranging from the bright red, strawberry-like fruits of *Arbutus* and the yellow crab apples of *Malus*

INTEREST FROM BARK AND STEMS
*The striking, white skeleton of a silver birch (*Betula utilis *var.* jacquemontii) *brings bright relief to the garden in the gloom of winter, while its bold silhouette forms a strong focal point in the planting design all year round.*

'Golden Hornet' to the sculptural seed pods of magnolias. In warm climates, trees such as lemons and figs may be laden with eye-catching fruits.

Certain trees, such as hollies (*Ilex*), need cross-pollination to fruit; others fruit only when mature or when particular climatic conditions are met. Birds find some ornamental berries such as those of rowan (*Sorbus aucuparia*) tempting and may strip them when barely ripe, but you can choose trees with less appealing berries. Other fruiting trees, such as *Crataegus* x *lavallei* 'Carrierei', ripen late and therefore their fruits persist well into spring. Ask garden centre staff for advice.

Bark and branches

Bark can provide colour and textural interest, especially in winter. Options include the mahogany-red, silky sheen of *Prunus serrula*, the ghostly white bark of *Betula utilis* var. *jacquemontii,* and the exotic-looking *Eucalyptus pauciflora* subsp. *niphophila* with its python-like, green, grey, and creamy-white bark.

The scarlet willow (*Salix alba* subsp. *vitellina* 'Britzensis') bears scarlet-orange young branches, brilliant when lit from behind, and the golden willow (*S. alba* subsp. *vitellina*) has rich yellow shoots. These fast-growing trees are best pruned regularly to produce new shoots as these have the strongest colour. Some trees bear showy bark only when mature; others colour well when young.

Successional interest

Plants that change character with the seasons give a garden a lively tempo. With careful choice and planning, orchestrate their display as foliage, flowers, fruits, berries, and pods come and go against a permanent framework of branches and bark. By planting trees that flower successively, such as a Judas tree (*Cercis siliquastrum*) for spring, *Catalpa bignonioides* for summer, *Eucryphia* x *nymansensis* for early autumn, and *Prunus subhirtella* 'Autumnalis' for winter, ongoing interest is maintained, with the focal point altering as the seasons change. Some trees provide interest all year round, either from their evergreen foliage, or from their fine shape.

Deciduous trees offer the greatest scope to exploit seasonal changes, especially in spring, when many ornamental cherries (*Prunus*) are covered with beautiful blossom, and in autumn, when many maples (*Acer*) have brilliantly coloured foliage. Evergreen trees, on the other

---

TREES WITH ORNAMENTAL BARK

Acer capillipes

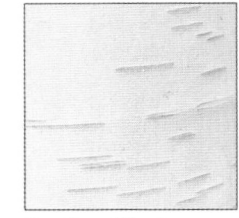
Eucalyptus dalrympleana

Acer griseum

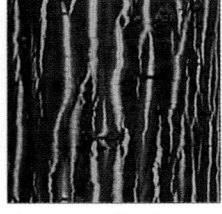
Acer pensylvanicum

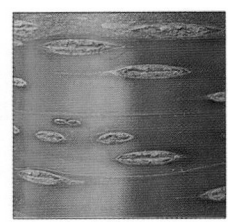
Prunus serrula

Betula utilis var. *jacquemontii*

---

hand, provide a sense of continuity rather than change. Selecting and planting a mixture of deciduous and evergreen trees provides lasting interest in the garden that changes with the seasons to create a dynamic rather than a static effect.

Spring and summer

In spring, emerging leaves and flower buds bring fresh life to the bare branches of deciduous trees. Some – such as the silver-leaved *Sorbus aria* 'Lutescens' – have particularly fine young foliage. As the trees come fully into leaf, they take on their characteristic outlines while the canopies provide striking blocks of colour and texture as well as shade.

In late spring and summer, flowers, ranging in colour and form from the trailing, yellow chains of *Laburnum* to the upright cream or reddish-pink candles of horse chestnuts (*Aesculus*), add extra colour and interest to lighten the dense effect of the massed leaves.

Autumn and winter

When most herbaceous plants die down in autumn, the colour provided by trees is particularly welcome, whether from leaves turning from green through shades of yellow, orange, and red to brown, or from the bright flecks of colour from fruits or berries. Ornamental members of the Rosaceae, especially those from the genera *Cotoneaster*, *Crataegus*, *Malus*, and *Sorbus*, include many species, cultivars, and hybrids that have a handsome display in autumn; in some cases, the fruits will remain on the tree right through the winter months.

In winter, many trees stand out most effectively with little else in the garden to compete with them. Their skeletons or silhouettes become most noticeable and create greater sculptural impact. The colour and texture provided by coniferous and broad-leaved evergreens may be used to complement and soften the architectural, "hard" look of nearby deciduous trees, while patterned, textured, or peeling bark adds an extra point of interest. A few conifers, such as

---

forms of Japanese cedar (*Cryptomeria japonica*), have foliage that takes on attractive russet overtones during winter.

Trees for small gardens

For small gardens, trees that do not reach more than about 6m (20ft) in height are the most suitable. There may only be space for just one tree (see "Specimen trees", p.55), so those that provide more than one season of interest are especially valuable. A Japanese crab apple (*Malus floribunda*), for example, produces masses of crimson buds, then pale pink or white flowers, and finally small red or yellow fruits, on arching branches.

A deciduous tree's appearance when leafless is very important in a small garden, since the tree may be bare for six months each year and visible from every window facing the garden. Good choices include *Rhus typhina*, fig (*Ficus carica*), and *Pyrus salicifolia* 'Pendula'. None has showy flowers but all have handsome foliage and winter silhouettes with character.

Heavily thorned or prickly trees such as hawthorns (*Crataegus*) or hollies (*Ilex*) may be unsuitable in a very small garden as they may restrict access on either side, while

SMALL-GARDEN TREE
The modest stature of this Robinia pseudoacacia *'Frisia' makes it a suitable choice for a small garden. Its airy foliage brightens up the grey stone wall behind and casts only light shade, allowing other plants to grow beneath it.*

Trees for avenues

Primarily used in formal settings, avenues rely on the uniformity of trees and spacing for their grand effect. The longer and straighter the avenue, the more impact the rhythm of the trees and their shadows has on the landscape. Trees should be sited so that they lead the eye to an impressive feature or focal point; large trees are often used on either side of a drive to line the route to the house. Long-term, forest trees such as beeches (*Fagus*) and horse chestnuts (*Aesculus*) are traditionally used for avenues, while the strong shapes of conifers may be more striking in a contemporary design. Trees such as whitebeam (*Sorbus aria*) or the evergreen Chinese privet (*Ligustrum lucidum*) are particularly suitable for smaller gardens.

Informal avenues may also be created, perhaps with the young trees bent and tied over each side to form an arch over a walkway. The spacing may be less rigid than for a formal avenue to avoid a regimented look.

Training for effect

Trees may be pleached to create an elegant formality. The side branches

INFORMAL WALKWAY
Flowering cherries, arching over a path, bring height and structure to a garden with free, informal planting while complementing the character of the setting. The spring display of the arch draws attention up and away from the borders which will in turn fill out and become the centre of interest as the blossom fades.

are trained to meet in horizontal, parallel lines and other growth is cut back or interwoven to form a vertical screen. Beeches, limes (*Tilia*), horn-beams (*Carpinus*), and planes (*Platanus*) are traditional trees for pleaching and, in the fruit garden, espaliered apples and pears provide a variation of this technique.

Pollarding involves regularly lopping back the entire crown to short stumps that produce dense, thin branches and a single, tight ball of

FORMAL, PLEACHED AVENUE
In this large, formal garden, rows of pleached limes lead the eye to the two arches framing the view beyond, linking the garden with the landscape.

foliage. It achieves a formal, if artificial, effect and is useful in urban areas where a natural crown would cast too much shade or impede traffic. Some willows (*Salix*) are often pollarded or coppiced (cut back to ground level) for their colourful young shoots. Coppiced trees look appropriate in a naturalistic or informal setting such as a woodland garden or on the banks of a pond.

Trees for screens and shelter belts

Large-scale tree planting can screen buildings and roads, deaden noise, and provide shelter from wind and frost. A single, straight row of fast-growing Lombardy poplars (*Populus*

nigra 'Italica') is often planted to screen eyesores, but their great height and finger-like shape tend to highlight what they are intended to conceal. Looser, wider stands of mixed deciduous and evergreen trees are usually more natural-looking and effective. Hedges are the most compact and densest form of screening and their size can be controlled (see HEDGES AND SCREENS, pp.84–86).

Trees en masse can filter wind, reducing potential damage more effectively than solid barriers, which often create wind swirl on the leeward side. A shelter belt or group of trees can protect vulnerable plants from frost, especially in spring.

Trees in containers

Growing trees in large pots or tubs greatly extends their design potential. In roof, patio, or courtyard gardens, a collection of containerized trees is the quickest way to create a well-established appearance, adding height and structure to the design. Use trees in large pots or tubs to frame a doorway that is surrounded by hard paving or to flank wide steps; these positions are particularly appropriate for topiary (see TOPIARY, pp.76–77). Trees too tender to over-winter outside may be grown in containers, displayed outdoors in summer, and moved to a frost-free place as cold weather approaches. Annuals and tender plants such as petunias, fuchsias, or trailing nasturtiums (*Tropaeolum*) may be included in the container for seasonal colour and interest, or ivy (*Hedera*) for permanent ground cover.

Containerized trees are long-term features, so use containers that are durable and attractive. A wide range of styles and materials is available (see CONTAINER GARDENING, "Choosing containers", p.320). Make sure that the containers are frost-proof, if they are to be permanent features in an area subject to frost.

CONTAINER-PLANTED TREES
Small trees grown in containers are valuable for bringing colour, vitality, and sculptural interest to a patio, terrace, or balcony. Here, plain paving acts as a stage on which to display a striking Japanese maple (Acer palmatum 'Dissectum Atropurpureum') in an ornamental trough.

Planter's guide to trees

TREES FOR SMALL GARDENS

Those marked ♠ may grow to 6m (20ft) or more

Acer capillipes ♠, *A. griseum* ♠,
 A. palmatum, A. palmatum.
 'Sango-kaku', *A.* 'Silver Vein' ♠,
 A. pseudoplatanus
 'Brilliantissimum' ♠
Aesculus californica ♠
Amelanchier lamarckii
Arbutus x *andrachnoides*
Betula albosinensis var.
 septentrionalis ♠, *B. ermanii* ♠,
 B. pendula ♠, *B. pendula*
 'Dalecarlica' ♠, *B. utilis*
 var. *jacquemontii* ♠
Catalpa bignonioides 'Aurea'
Cercidiphyllum japonicum ♠
Cercis siliquastrum
Cinnamomum camphora ✼
Cornus kousa
Crataegus laciniata ♠, *C. laevigata*
 'Paul's Scarlet', *C.* x *lavallei*
 'Carrierei'
Cydonia oblonga
Eucalyptus pauciflora subsp.
 niphophila ♠
Fagus sylvatica 'Dawyck Gold' ♠
Gleditsia triacanthos 'Sunburst' ♠
Grevillea robusta ✼ ♠
Hoheria lyallii
Laburnum x *watereri* 'Vossii'
Maackia amurensis ♠
Magnolia 'Elizabeth',
 M. 'Galaxy' ♠, *M.* x *loebneri*
 'Merrill' ♠

Pyrus calleryana
'Chanticleer'

Malus 'Dartmouth',
 M. 'Evereste' ♠, *M. floribunda,*
 M. 'Golden Hornet',
 M. tschonoskii ♠
Melia azedarach
Mespilus germanica ♠
Phoenix dactylifera ✼ ♠
Pinus halepensis ♠
Prunus – many including
 P. 'Okame', *P.* 'Pandora',
 P. 'Spire', *P. subhirtella,*
 P. x *yedoensis*
Pyrus calleryana 'Chanticleer',
 P. salicifolia 'Pendula'
Robinia pseudoacacia 'Frisia' ♠
Sorbus aria (some forms),
 S. aucuparia (some forms),
 S. cashmiriana,
 S. commixta 'Embley',
 S. vilmorinii
Stewartia pseudocamellia
Vitex agnus-castus

WINTER INTEREST

Decorative flowers
Acacia dealbata ✼
Magnolia campbellii 'Charles
 Raffill', *M. sprengeri* (and
 hybrids), *M.* 'Star Wars'
Prunus incisa, P. mume,
 P. subhirtella 'Autumnalis',
 P. subhirtella 'Autumnalis
 Rosea'
Salix daphnoides 'Aglaia'

Golden foliage
Alnus glutinosa 'Aurea'
Chamaecyparis lawsoniana
 'Lanei Aurea', *C. lawsoniana*
 'Stewartii', *C. lawsoniana*
 'Winston Churchill'
x *Cupressocyparis leylandii*
 'Castlewellan', x *C. leylandii*
 'Robinson's Gold'
Cupressus arizonica 'Pyramidalis',
 C. sempervirens 'Swane's Gold'
Cupressus macrocarpa 'Goldcrest'
Juniperus chinensis 'Aurea'
Pinus sylvestris 'Aurea'
Salix elaeagnos, S. exigua
Sorbus aria 'Lutescens'
Thuja plicata 'Zebrina'
Tsuga mertensiana f. *argentea*

Grey foliage
Cedrus atlantica f. *glauca*
Chamaecyparis lawsoniana
 'Pembury Blue'
Cupressus glabra 'Pyramidalis'
Eucalyptus coccifera ✼,
 E. pauciflora
Tsuga mertensiana 'Glauca'

Decorative bark
Acer capillipes, A. davidii,
 A. davidii 'Serpentine',
 A. griseum, A. grosseri var. *hersii,*
 A. palmatum 'Sango-kaku',
 A. pensylvanicum (and forms),
 A. 'Silver Vein'
Arbutus x *andrachnoides,*
 A. menziesii
Betula albo-sinensis var.
 septentrionalis, B. dahurica,
 B. 'Jermyns', *B. pendula,*
 B. utilis var. *jacquemontii*
Eucalyptus dalrympleana,
 E. pauciflora, E. pauciflora subsp.
 niphophila
Luma apiculata
Pinus bungeana
Prunus maackii 'Amber Beauty',
 P. serrula
Salix acutifolia 'Blue Streak',
 S. alba subsp. *vitellina*
 'Britzensis', *S. daphnoides,*
 S. 'Erythroflexuosa'
Stewartia pseudocamellia
Tilia cordata 'Winter Orange'

TREES FOR CONTAINERS
Acacia baileyana, A. dealbata ✼
Albizia julibrissin ✼
Araucaria heterophylla ✼
Citrus medica ✼
Cordyline australis ✼
Cupressus macrocarpa 'Goldcrest',
 C. sempervirens
Dracaena draco ✼
Eriobotrya japonica ✼
Ficus benjamina ✼
Grevillea robusta ✼
Jacaranda mimosifolia ✼
Juniperus scopulorum 'Skyrocket'
Lagerstroemia indica ✼
Laurus nobilis
Magnolia grandiflora
 'Galissonnière'

Ficus benjamina
'Variegata'

Olea europaea
Prunus 'Amanogawa',
 P. 'Kiku-shidare-zakura'
Salix caprea 'Kilmarnock'
Taxus baccata 'Standishii'
Trachycarpus fortunei

TWO OR MORE SEASONS OF INTEREST

All year round
Acacia dealbata ✼
Acer capillipes, A. palmatum
 'Sango-kaku'
Arbutus x *andrachnoides,*
 A. menziesii
Betula albo-sinensis var.
 septentrionalis, B. ermanii,
 B. 'Jermyns', *B. utilis* var.
 jacquemontii
Cornus kousa var. *chinensis*
Eucalyptus ficifolia ✼
Ilex x *altaclerensis* 'Golden King'
Magnolia grandiflora

Winter/Spring
Acer negundo
Arbutus x *andrachnoides*
Pyrus pashia

Spring/Autumn
Amelanchier lamarckii
Crataegus x *lavallei* 'Carrierei'
Malus 'Evereste', *M.* 'Golden
 Hornet'
Prunus 'Accolade', *P.* 'Okame',
 P. sargentii
Sorbus cashmiriana, S. commixta
 'Embley'

Summer/Autumn
Catalpa bignonioides
Cladrastis lutea
Cornus kousa,
 C. kousa var. *chinensis*
Eucryphia glutinosa
Fagus sylvatica 'Dawyck Gold'
Liriodendron tulipifera
Stewartia pseudocamellia
Tilia 'Petiolaris'

Autumn/Winter
Acer capillipes, A. davidii,
 A. griseum, A. palmatum
 'Sango-kaku', *A. pensylvanicum*
 'Erythrocladum'
Stewartia pseudocamellia

SPECIMEN TREES
Abies magnifica, A. procera
Acer pensylvanicum,
 A. pseudoplatanus, A. rubrum
Aesculus hippocastanum
Alnus cordata
Betula 'Jermyns',
 B. pendula 'Dalecarlica'
Cedrus
Eucalyptus coccifera ✼,
 E. dalrympleana
Fraxinus oxycarpa 'Raywood'
Liquidambar 'Lane Roberts',
 L. styraciflua
*Liriodendron
 tulipifera*

*Liriodendron
tulipifera*

Livistona ✼
Magnolia campbellii,
 M. campbellii 'Charles
 Raffill'
Metasequoia glyptostroboides
Nothofagus procera
Nyssa sylvatica
Phoenix ✼
Picea breweriana, P. omorika
Pinus nigra, P. radiata,
 P. sylvestris, P. wallichiana
Platanus x *hispanica*
Roystonea ✼
Salix x *sepulcralis* var. *chrysocoma*
Sequoiadendron giganteum
Tilia 'Petiolaris', *T. platyphyllos*
Tsuga heterophylla
Zelkova carpinifolia

KEY
✼ Not hardy

Hardy palms and the exotic look

I N the past, in frost-prone regions, many beautiful tropical and sub-tropical plants were grown for their ornamental effect in the protected environment of heated glasshouses. As the costs of maintenance – particularly heating – soared during the twentieth century, the cultivation of these "exotics" declined. Recently, however, a new style of gardening has emerged that recreates the visual impact of tropical and subtropical plants in sheltered outdoor gardens in temperate regions. This style makes use of hardy, half-hardy, and some tender plants with striking shapes, distinctive textures, handsome, large foliage, and vivid flowers.

In frost-prone climates, most of the plants used should be hardy enough to survive year-round. Planting schemes can then be varied during frost-free months by integrating half-hardy or tender, container-grown exotics into the design (see also p.61). These can be used as focal points, or placed strategically within the overall framework of the planting to create seasonal interest. Such dis-plays require careful planning, of course, as well as the use of a frost-free greenhouse or conservatory in which the plants can be overwintered. Some half-hardy plants may be planted permanently outside in milder areas, although they will need to be swathed in straw, hessian, or other coverings in severe weather, to protect them from cold winds and frosts that would otherwise desiccate evergreen foliage. Equally important

RESISTANCE TO COLD
Frosted fans of a Chusan palm (Trachycarpus fortunei) demonstrate the surprising hardiness of this plant.

is to ensure that such plants are grown in free-draining soil, to avoid root decay, particularly during very cold, frosty spells.

Exotic planting schemes of this type are most likely to succeed in coastal or sheltered city gardens in temperate regions, but variations on this theme may be well worth trying in colder areas.

Key framework plants

Exotic-style plants seldom grow as large in temperate climes as in their native regions, although they can still make handsomely sized, vigorous garden plants for outdoor cultivation in the appropriate situation. Plants to use as tree-like, structural elements in the exotic style of gardening can be divided roughly into three groups: palms and palm-like plants, tree ferns, and bananas. Each contains hardy and half-hardy plants with imposing, attractive foliage, and sometimes flowers. These tropical-looking plants can also be blended with more familiar large, hardy foliage plants, such as elegant bam-boos (see p.96) and *Gunnera*.

Palms and palm-like plants

Several species of palm are grown successfully outdoors in temperate areas – the most familiar being the Chusan or Chinese windmill palm (*Trachycarpus fortunei*) from the Himalayas. This withstands tempera-tures of -15°C (5°F) or below, if grown in a reasonably sheltered posi-tion. The closely related *T. wagneri-anus* has stiffer, more wind-tolerant leaves. Another suitable palm for a garden setting is the Mediterranean dwarf fan palm (*Chamaerops humilis*). Although it originates in hot, dry regions, it will tolerate -10°C (14°F) or below when grown in a sheltered spot. Forms with silvery-blue leaves (*C. humilis* var. *argentea*) are particularly attractive.

Blue hesper palm (*Brahea armata*) from Mexico and California is occa-sionally grown in very sheltered sites outdoors; in cold areas, it is also an excellent container plant for summer garden displays. The jelly palm (*Butia capitata*), although Brazilian and Uruguayan in origin, is also sur-prisingly tough and of similar stature and hardiness to *Brahea*.

Known to survive outdoors and develop to about 5m (15ft) in mild temperate areas, the Chilean wine palm (*Jubaea chilensis*), with its del-icate feathery foliage, is another fine candidate for the exotic style, as is the Canary island date palm (*Phoenix canariensis*). Its delightful dwarf relative, *P. roebelenii*, is better grown in a container in the conserva-tory, and moved outside in summer. Unless large specimens are obtained from specialist nurseries, borderline hardy palms should be grown initially in containers until well established. They can then be planted out in well-drained soil that is reasonably moisture retentive. As the palm stems thicken with age, the plants become more tolerant of lower temperatures, although winter pro-tection is advisable for some years. Palm-like plants, such as cabbage palm (*Cordyline*) and *Yucca* are also

BOLD FOLIAGE CONTRAST
Huge, paddle-shaped banana leaves here contrast strikingly with the palmate foliage of a castor oil plant (Ricinus), to provide a strong focal point.

TREE FERN
A nearby tree offers shade and shelter for this tree fern (Dicksonia). It has been carefully planted just beyond the range of the tree's leafy canopy, beneath which the soil would be too dry for it to flourish.

OLD PALM FRONDS
As a palm tree increases in height, unsightly dead lower fronds can be removed, but do not cut them back too close to the trunk.

valuable constituents of an exotic-style garden. The New Zealand cabbage or Torbay palm (*C. australis*) can be grown outdoors in mild temperate areas, where it reaches 6–12m (20–40ft) in height. Green-leaved *C. australis* grows well without protection in sheltered gardens but in severe winters may lose some or all of its foliage, although it often recovers in spring. Variants with coloured leaves are not always tolerant if the temperature drops below freezing for some days.

Species of *Yucca*, such as Adam's needle (*Y. filamentosa*) and Spanish dagger (*Y. gloriosa*), also provide an exotic feel in a garden and can be

WINTER COVERING
If banana plants, such as Ensete, are left in situ in winter, some of the foliage can be cut back (above). The plant can then be surrounded by wire netting stuffed with straw, and capped with a polythene "hat" (right) to prevent rain from rotting both straw and banana plant.

used as permanent residents within the planting scheme, as both will withstand temperatures down to as low as -15°C (5°F).

Tree ferns

Several species of *Dicksonia* and *Cyathea* are becoming increasingly popular for conservatories and in sheltered gardens. The woolly tree fern (*Dicksonia antarctica*), for example, grows well in humid shade, a habitat that mimics its native temperate rainforests in Australia.

If not already containerized, tree ferns should be planted with the sawn-off "trunk" at least 30cm (1ft) into the ground in a shaded, humid, wind-sheltered site. It is very important, particularly in the first year, to keep the plants moist – they must not be allowed to dry out. A trickle, or drip-feed, system (see p.561) to maintain a high level of humidity around the plants will simulate the natural conditions in which they grow. Sometimes it is better to establish tree ferns in containers, placed in a shaded site, as the developing fronds may burn in bright sun.

Although *D. antarctica* will withstand at least -5°C (23°F), its crown and trunk should be insulated where more severe frosts can be expected (see also "Frost protection", p.613). Slightly more tender are the New Zealand species, *D. fibrosa* and *D. squarrosa*. Both are best grown as container plants, which can be given a summer outing. Another tree fern

Valuable exotics that may be too large to transfer under glass can be given special treatment. Here, a sturdy wooden frame has been built to protect a banana plant during the winter. It is filled with dry straw, while a plastic-coated sloping roof ensures rain and melting snow do not cause the banana to rot.

that requires similar cultivation and sheltered conditions is the spectacular sago fern (*Cyathea medullaris*).

Bananas

The two main genera of bananas grown as ornamentals are *Musa* (including *Musella*) and *Ensete* – a giant African genus with enormous architectural foliage. Both should be grown in moist, fertile soil, and mulched with well-rotted manure. Bananas need sun and a sheltered site, to prevent their large, paddle-like leaves from tearing in the wind, as well as plenty of water and fertilizer during the growing season.

A few *Musa* species, including *M. basjoo*, are reasonably frost hardy and will withstand temperatures down to -8°C (18°F). However, even in sheltered gardens, it is always advisable to provide some winter protection. Young plants should have a deep, straw-filled pot – a chimney pot is ideal – fitted over the crown after the foliage has been cut off. A tile across the pot top will prevent rain from rotting the straw. Older plants can be protected with a 15cm (6in) mulch of straw placed around each trunk. The old foliage will die off in winter, and new shoots should appear in mid-spring.

Given suitable over-wintering conditions, *Musa*, *Ensete*, and many other banana genera are among the best of all foliage plants for inclusion in exotic planting schemes.

OTHER PLANTS WITH A TROPICAL LOOK
Acanthus mollis
Agave americana ❋
Aralia elata, A. elata 'Variegata'
Arundo donax ❋
Astelia chathamica
Beschorneria yuccoides
Blechnum chilense
Brugmansia x *candida* ❋
Canna ❋
Cycas ❋
Dahlia x *coccinea* ❋,
   D. imperialis ❋
Echium candicans ❋,
   E. pininana ❋
Eryngium agavifolium
Euphorbia characias,
   E. mellifera
Fatsia japonica
Gunnera tinctoria
Hedychium ❋
Hibiscus rosa-sinensis ❋
Impatiens tinctoria
Melianthus major
Passiflora caerulea
Phormium
Phyllostachys
Rheum palmatum (and cvs)
Ricinus communis ❋
Solenostemon ❋
Tibouchina urvilleana ❋

KEY
❋ *Needs winter protection in frost-prone areas, or use as summer bedding where appropriate*

Dwarf conifers

DWARF conifers, greatly valued for their ease of maintenance, are particularly suitable for a small, modern garden, whether grown in compact beds or containers. Colours range from rich gold, through brilliant greens to pale blues and silvers, and shapes include globose, pyramidal, and slender, spire-shaped forms. Habits are diverse, with prostrate or mound-forming, erect or weeping types, and the variation in their foliage texture ranges from soft and feathery to dense and spiky. With careful planning, this rich variety of colour, form, and texture can provide interest throughout the year. For details on cultivation, routine care, and propagation, see ORNAMENTAL TREES, pp.63–83.

"dwarf" conifers are simply slower-growing variants of large trees. Conifers can be very difficult to identify when young, since their juvenile foliage often differs widely from that when adult. Check that the plants are correctly named when buying, to avoid introducing plants that will rapidly outgrow their allotted space; if in any doubt seek advice from the retailer.

Selecting the plants

When selecting conifers for a small space, it is important to recognize the true dwarf and slow-growing species and cultivars; sometimes so-called

Designing with dwarf conifers

Dwarf conifers are suitable for a range of situations in a garden. They may be planted individually to form a feature or collectively to create a band of colours; and they may be used either to complement other plants or to provide ground cover. Rock gardens, heather gardens, and ornamental containers are also excellent locations for growing all types of dwarf conifer.

ENHANCING CONIFERS
To display dwarf conifers to the best advantage, add heathers to the planting scheme for bright splashes of year-round colour in the garden.

A RANGE OF DWARF CONIFERS

Pinus sylvestris **'Gold Coin'**

Juniperus squamata **'Blue Star'**

Platycladus orientalis **'Aurea Nana'**

Thuja occidentalis **'Caespitosa'**

Picea pungens **'Montgomery'**

Chamaecyparis obtusa **'Nana Aurea'**

Juniperus scopulorum **'Skyrocket'**

Specimen plants
Some of the slow-growing conifers are suitable for use as specimen plants. Spreading forms, for example, may be used to soften the edges of hard landscaping, while columnar specimens create a focal point.

Group planting
If space allows, a collection of dwarf conifers can make a very attractive feature. The colour spectrum in conifers may also be used to highlight areas at different times of year; blues and silvers, for example, are at their most beautiful in the cool light of winter, while golds and greens appear at their most fresh in spring.

Steep slopes and banks, which often prove difficult to plant effectively, can make striking landscape features when planted with bold drifts of prostrate conifers. Once plants are established, these often problematic areas are easy to maintain and are more or less weed-free.

Associating with other plants
Dwarf conifers associate well with other groups of plants that are similar in character. They are often used as components of heather gardens to extend the season of interest and provide contrast in colour and form with the foliage and colour variants of *Calluna*, *Daboecia*, and *Erica* cultivars. Other complementary plants for dwarf conifers include *Cytisus*, *Genista*, *Cistus*, and the smaller cotoneaster species and cultivars.

Rock gardens
In the rock garden, dwarf conifers provide the framework for other associated but less permanent plants. The

complete repertoire of colours, textures, and shapes can be used, but take care to select plants that will not become too large or dominant. The smaller species and cultivars, such as *Juniperus communis* 'Compressa', are ideal for the miniature landscapes of compact, raised beds as well as troughs, sink gardens, and other ornamental containers.

Ground cover
Many dwarf conifers make excellent weed-smothering ground cover, either by forming dense mats, as with *Juniperus horizontalis* and its cultivars, or by growing taller and spreading to exclude light beneath their canopy. Some Pfitzer junipers are particularly useful for covering manhole covers or concrete paving. See SHRUBS FOR GROUND COVER, p.101.

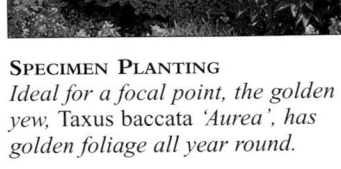

SPECIMEN PLANTING
Ideal for a focal point, the golden yew, Taxus baccata 'Aurea', has golden foliage all year round.

Soil preparation and planting

Once planted, a tree may remain in place for decades or even centuries, so it is essential to provide it with the best possible growing conditions. Climate, soil type, and the amount of light and shelter available all affect a tree's growth, so take these factors into account when deciding on a planting position. Careful preparation and planting as well as aftercare are vital in helping a tree to establish quickly and grow well.

Climate considerations

Before selecting a tree, check that it will flourish in the temperature range, rainfall, and humidity levels of the site. Special local factors, such as strong winds on exposed hilltop sites, should also influence your choice. Even within a species, different cultivars may be more suited to certain conditions, so one plant may thrive while another may not: various cultivars of *Magnolia grandiflora*, for example, tolerate minimum temperatures ranging from -12°C to 6°C (10–43°F).

In areas subject to spring frosts, choose trees that come into leaf late as frost frequently damages young growth. In cold areas, trees that are not fully hardy may be grown outdoors, but they may need protection from frost during winter (see FROST AND WIND PROTECTION, pp.612–613) and should be planted in a sheltered site. If growing tender or tropical species in temperate areas, keep them under cover or grow them in containers so that they may be brought indoors for the winter.

Trees rarely grow well in regions where the annual rainfall is less than 250mm (10in) and most prefer at least four times this amount. Most trees do not require irrigation, however, except when newly planted, as they obtain enough water from rain and, in some areas, from heavy mists condensing on their foliage.

Choosing a planting site

When planting a tree, try to choose the best position for it within the garden because the microclimate may vary considerably from one part of the plot to another. Make sure that the selected site will provide an appropriate amount of light and shel-

ter: many large-leaved trees, for example, will thrive in a sheltered, partially shaded position but may not grow well in an exposed site where the foliage would be subjected to strong winds and high light levels.

In coastal areas, choose a planting site that is sheltered because sea spray and salt-laden winds (even a few miles inland) may scorch foliage and cause damage to the growth buds. Some trees, however, tolerate coastal conditions (see "Trees that tolerate exposed or windy sites", p.67), and may be planted as windbreaks to help screen other, more vulnerable, plants from strong winds. Similarly, if trees are being planted on a slope, bear in mind that tender trees are more likely to succeed halfway down where it is usually more sheltered than at either the top or the bottom (see also "Frost pockets and frost damage", p.607).

It is best not to plant trees very close to walls or buildings, otherwise, when young, the trees may suffer from reduced light and moisture as a result of the "rain shadow" effect

(see *Rain Shadow*, p.610). Ideally they should be planted half their mature height away from any structure. In addition, the strong, fibrous roots of some trees, for example poplars (*Populus*) and willows (*Salix*), may damage drains and the foundations of buildings as they develop (see "Tree roots and buildings", p.70). Tender species may be planted near a warm wall, however; there they will benefit from the wall's retained heat and so may survive in a region where they would fail in more open conditions.

When choosing a site ensure that the trees will not interfere with overhead and underground cables and pipes, which may obstruct trees or be damaged by them.

Selecting a tree

Trees may be bought container-grown, bare-root, or root-balled, although conifers and palms are not usually available bare-root. They may be purchased in a variety of

sizes and stages of maturity, from seedlings through to semi-mature trees. Young trees tend to become established more quickly than older trees, while the latter create a strong and immediate impact in the garden but are more expensive.

Whichever type you choose, check that the tree has healthy, vigorous top-growth and roots with no sign of pests, disease, or damage. Both the branch and root systems should be well developed and evenly balanced around the stem. The top-growth, however, must not be overlarge for the root system, otherwise the roots cannot absorb the nutrients and moisture needed to make new growth, and the tree may fail to establish. The spread of a container-grown tree, for example, should be no more than three or four times the width of its container.

Trees that have been allowed to flower or fruit prematurely, so that they look seemingly impressive to buyers, should also be avoided. Such growth may well have been at the expense of basic root development.

CHOOSING TREES

CONTAINER-GROWN TREE

GOOD EXAMPLE

Well-balanced branch framework

GOOD EXAMPLE

Well-established root system

POOR EXAMPLE

Tightly wound, congested roots

BARE-ROOT TREE

GOOD EXAMPLE

Fibrous "feeder" roots

Evenly distributed, spreading root system

POOR EXAMPLE

Uneven, "hockey stick" roots

POOR EXAMPLE

Tightly coiled roots

ROOT-BALLED TREE

GOOD EXAMPLE

x CUPRESSOCYPARIS LEYLANDII

Firm root ball with the covering intact

Container-grown trees

These are widely available and may be bought and planted at any time of year, except when the soil is very dry or very wet; container-grown trees are usually more expensive than bare-root or root-balled specimens of a comparable size. This is the best method of buying trees that do not establish easily when transplanted, such as magnolias and *Eucalyptus*, because there is less disturbance to the roots. Such difficult-to-establish trees should also be bought and planted when they are still small. Exotic and less common trees are usually sold in pots.

Before buying a tree, remove it from its container, if possible, so that you can see the roots clearly: do not buy a pot-bound tree with a mass of congested roots or one with thick roots protruding through the drainage holes. Such trees may not establish well. Equally, if the compost does not cling to the root ball when the tree is removed from its container, do not buy it as its root system is not sufficiently established. Make sure that the container is large enough in relation to the tree: as a guide, the container's diameter should be at least one sixth of the tree's height. A tall tree growing in a small container will almost certainly be pot-bound.

The potting medium is also important: trees that are container-ized in soil-based potting composts establish more quickly in open ground than those grown in other types of composts, because they have less of an adjustment to make to the surrounding soil.

Bare-root trees

Trees sold bare-root, which are almost always deciduous, are grown in open ground, then lifted with virtually no soil around the roots. As soon as they are exposed to the air, however, the fine feeder roots begin to dry out. A reputable nursery will remove any ragged ends as well as prune away any lopsided, overlong, or damaged roots.

It is essential to buy the bare-root trees when they are dormant, preferably in autumn or early spring; they are unlikely to survive transplanting if purchased and planted when in leaf. Ash (*Fraxinus*), poplars (*Populus*), and many rosaceous trees, such as crab apples (*Malus*), are often sold bare-root from nurseries, while only fruit trees tend to be available bare-root from garden centres.

Make sure that the tree you choose has well-developed roots spreading evenly in all directions. A number of small roots about 2–5mm ($\frac{1}{16}$–$\frac{1}{4}$in)

Staking

As the root system of a newly planted tree will need one or more growing seasons to anchor it firmly in the soil, staking against strong winds may be necessary initially. The stake must be driven in about 60cm (24in) below soil level so that it is completely stable. After two or three years, the tree should be sufficiently established for the stake to be removed. The method of support chosen depends on the tree, the proposed planting site, and personal preference.

Traditionally, a high, vertical stake has been used, placed on the side of the prevailing wind and long enough to reach to just below the crown. A low stake is now generally preferred, as it allows the tree to move naturally in the wind.

With flexible-stemmed trees, such as crab apples, use a high stake in the first year after planting, cut it down to the lower level in the second year, and remove the stake in the third year.

For container-grown and root-balled trees, a low stake angled into the prevailing wind is preferable as it can be driven in clear of the root ball even after the tree has been planted. Alternatively, space two or three vertical, low stakes evenly around the tree outside the area of the root ball.

In windy sites or for trees more than 4m (12ft) tall, insert two vertical stakes when planting, one on either side of the root ball, to provide support. Large trees are often secured by guy-ropes attached to low stakes. Covering the guys with hosepipe or white tape makes them more visible and so helps prevent the risk of people tripping over them.

HIGH STAKE
Drive in a single, high stake before planting. Secure the tree to the stake using two padded or buckle-and-spacer ties.

LOW STAKE
A low stake allows the tree's stem some movement; insert it so that only about 50cm (20in) protrudes above ground level.

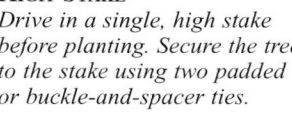
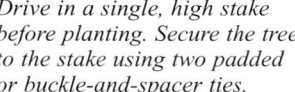
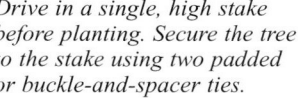

ANGLED STAKE
A low, angled stake may be added after planting. Drive it into the ground at a 45° angle, leaning into the prevailing wind.

TWO STAKES
Insert two stakes so that they are on opposite sides of the tree, and secure them to the tree with heavy-duty rubber ties.

in diameter is a good sign as it indicates that they have been undercut every year or so, a technique that encourages sturdy growth and vigorous root systems. Examine the roots to check that they are free from damage and disease and that there is no sign of dryness that may have been caused by exposure to wind. Do not buy trees with "hockey stick" roots, where all the growth is on one side; these will not establish well.

Root-balled trees

These trees are also grown in open ground but when the trees are lifted the roots and surrounding soil are wrapped in hessian or netting to hold the root ball together and stop the roots from drying out. Deciduous trees of more than 4m (12ft) and many evergreens, especially conifers and palms of more than 1.5m (5ft), are often sold in this way.

Buy and plant root-balled trees when dormant, in autumn or early spring, following the same criteria as for bare-root and container-grown trees. Check that the root ball is firm and its wrapping is intact before purchase: if there is any sign of drying out or root damage, the tree is less likely to establish well and, because the resulting root system is unstable and not well anchored, the tree will be susceptible to wind-rock, especially when mature.

Seedlings, transplants, and whips

Seedlings up to one year old are usually available only from specialist nurseries. Transplants are seedlings or cuttings that have been transplanted in the nursery and are up to four years old. They make sturdy, bushy plants and are usually 60cm–1.2m (2–4ft) tall. The age and treatment may be given by the nursery in shorthand: "1 + 1" denotes a seedling left for one year in the seedbed and then transplanted for a further season; "1 u 1" means that

Tree ties

Tree ties should be secure, long-lasting, and able to accommodate the tree's girth as it grows without cutting into the bark. Various proprietary ties are available, or you can make them from nylon webbing or rubber tubing. To prevent the stake from chafing the bark, use a spacer or form a padded tie into a figure of eight and nail it to the stake. When using two or three stakes, secure the tree to the stakes with heavy-duty rubber or plastic strips. If supporting a large tree with guys, use multistrand wire or nylon rope.

BUCKLE-AND-SPACER TIE
Thread the tie through the spacer, around the tree, and back through the spacer; buckle it so that it is taut but will not damage the bark.

RUBBER TIE
If using a rubber or plastic tie without a buckle, nail it to the stake to prevent bark damage caused by friction.

it was undercut (see "Bare-root trees", p.64) after the first year and remained *in situ* for a further year. Whips are single, whip-like shoots sold by height; they are generally 1–2m (3–6ft) tall and will have been transplanted at least once.

Feathered trees

These trees have a single main leader with a spread of lateral branches, or "feathers", down to ground level. They will have been transplanted at least once and are usually 2–2.5m (6–8ft) tall.

Standards and large trees

Standard trees are approximately 3m (10ft) high and have been pruned to create one single main stem with no lateral branches for about 2m (6ft) above ground level. Central-leader standards are similar to feathered trees but have a clear length of stem at the base, while branched-head standards have been pruned so that they have an open centre. Trees of 2.1m (6½ft) in height, with a clear stem of 1.2–1.5m (4–5ft) are known as half-standards, while trees 3.5m (11ft) tall are selected standards. Larger trees, which are available from specialist nurseries, include extra-heavy standards which are 5m (15ft) tall and semi-mature trees which are 5–12m (15–40ft).

Transportation shock

Many trees, unfortunately, falter or even die of stress and desiccation as a result of being transported on a roof rack, stuck through an opening in a car roof, or exposed on an open truck, where they may be buffeted in the slipstream.

HEELING IN

If planting is delayed, heel in the tree: first prepare a trench, then set the tree in it. Angle the tree so that the trunk is supported. Cover the roots and base of the trunk with moist, friable soil and do not allow the roots to dry out.

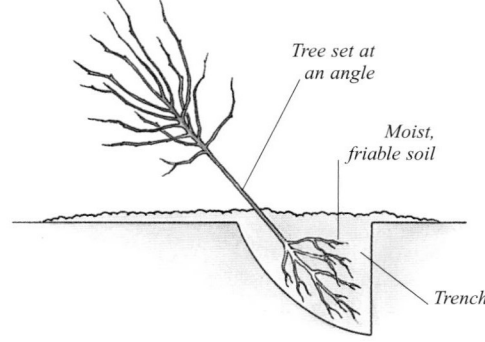

Tree set at an angle

Moist, friable soil

Trench

Trees may also experience a setback in their growth rate because their environment has suddenly changed, from one of protected, close planting in the nursery to isolation and exposure to strong winds, hot sun, or hard frosts within the garden.

When to plant

Container-grown trees may be planted out at any time of year, except during drought, very wet conditions, or frost, while deciduous, bare-root trees should be planted between mid-autumn and mid-spring (avoiding periods of frost and extreme damp). Plant hardy evergreens and hardy, deciduous trees with fleshy roots in mid-autumn or mid- to late spring, and half-hardy trees in mid-spring. Root-balled trees are best planted in early to mid-autumn or mid- to late spring; if deciduous, they may be planted out in winter in mild conditions.

Autumn planting allows a tree's roots to become established before the onset of winter. This helps the tree to withstand any hot, dry spells the following summer. In cold regions, however, planting in spring may allow trees to establish more successfully in the warmer weather. If planting in winter, the ground may be lifted by subsequent spells of frost and, if so, the soil should be re-firmed once it has thawed.

Heeling in

It is best to plant trees as soon as possible after purchase, although container-grown and root-balled trees may be stored in frost-free conditions for a few weeks if kept moist. If a further delay is unavoidable, heel in the trees in a sheltered place, and keep the soil moist.

Soil preparation

Preparing the site in advance allows the soil to settle and minimizes delay between buying and planting a tree. Choose a well-drained site; one that is poorly drained may need to be improved before planting (see "Improving drainage", p.623). Remove turf and all other plant growth, in an area three or four times the tree's root ball, to eliminate competition for nutrients and water in the soil, then dig the soil, incorporating organic matter in the uppermost part.

Most trees require a soil depth of 50cm–1m (20in–3ft) to grow well. Some may grow on soils only 15cm (6in) deep, although they are then less stable and less drought-tolerant.

TREES THAT PREFER ACID SOIL

Abies
Arbutus menziesii
Cercidiphyllum japonicum
Cornus nuttallii
Cryptomeria
Embothrium coccineum
Fagus grandifolia
Magnolia acuminata,
   M. campbellii
   (and cvs)

Magnolia campbellii

Michelia ✤
Oxydendrum arboreum
Picea (most spp.)
Pseudolarix amabilis
Pseudotsuga
Rhodoleia championii ✤
Sciadopitys verticillata
Stewartia
Styrax japonica
Tsuga heterophylla

TREES THAT TOLERATE VERY ALKALINE SOIL

Acer campestre, A. lobelii,
   A. negundo (and cvs),
   A. platanoides (and cvs)
Aesculus
Carpinus betulus
Cedrus libani
Cercis siliquastrum
Chamaecyparis
   lawsoniana (and cvs)
Crataegus
x *Cupressocyparis*
   leylandii (and cvs)
Cupressus glabra
Fagus sylvatica (and cvs)
Fraxinus excelsior, F. ornus
Juniperus
Malus
Morus nigra
Ostrya carpinifolia
Phillyrea latifolia
Pinus nigra
Populus alba
Prunus avium 'Plena',
   P. sargentii

Prunus sargentii

Pyrus
   (spp. and cvs)
Robinia (spp. and cvs)
Sorbus aria (and cvs)
Taxus baccata (and cvs)
Thuja
Tilia tomentosa

KEY
✤ *Not hardy*

Planting trees

Once the site has been prepared, dig the planting hole, between two and four times the width of the tree's root ball, depending on whether the tree is container-grown, bare-root, or root-balled. If doing this in advance, backfill it loosely until ready to plant the tree so that the soil remains warm. Mix the removed soil with well-rotted organic matter and, if planting in spring, about 110g (4oz) of slow-release fertilizer. Fork over the sides and base of the hole to break up the surrounding soil and allow the tree roots to spread into it more easily; this is particularly important in heavy, sticky soils. If you are using a single stake, drive it into the hole just off-centre before planting the tree to ensure that the root ball is not damaged later (see also "Staking", p.64).

Container-grown trees

Thoroughly moisten the compost – if it is very dry, stand the container in water for an hour or two until the compost is moist throughout. Then remove the container, cutting it away if necessary. Gently tease out the roots to encourage them to grow into the surrounding soil; this is essential with a pot-bound plant. Trees with a full but not pot-bound root system could, alternatively, have the outer surface scored with a garden knife, by making two or four shallow vertical cuts, from below, on the root ball before planting. Trim any broken or damaged roots with secateurs.

It is important to check that the planting depth is correct: if a tree is planted too deeply, its roots may not receive enough oxygen and may slow down in growth or even die; if planted too shallowly, the roots may dry out. Place the tree in the hole and

(see also "Staking", p.64).

TREES THAT PREFER SANDY SOIL

Abies grandis
Acacia dealbata ❋
Acer negundo (and cvs)
Agonis flexuosa ❋
Banksia serrata ❋
Betula pendula (and cvs)
Castanea sativa
Celtis australis
Cercis siliquastrum
Cupressus glabra
Eucalyptus ficifolia ❋
Gleditsia triacanthos
Juniperus
Larix decidua
Melia azedarach
Nothofagus obliqua
Phoenix canariensis ❋
Pinus pinaster, P. radiata
Quercus ilex
Schinus molle ❋
Tabebuia chrysotricha ❋
Thuja occidentalis
 (and cvs)

*Tabebuia
chrysotricha*

TREES THAT TOLERATE CLAY SOIL

Acer platanoides (and cvs)
Castanospermum australe ❋
Crataegus laevigata (and cvs)
Fraxinus
Juglans nigra
Malus

*Malus
'Cowichan'*

*Metasequoia
 glyptostroboides*
Populus
Pterocarya fraxinifolia
*Pyrus calleryana
 'Chanticleer'*
Quercus palustris, Q. robur
Salix
Taxodium distichum

KEY
❋ Not hardy

PLANTING A CONTAINER-GROWN TREE

1 *Soak the root ball of the potted tree in a bucket of water for 1–2 hours. Mark out the area of the hole to be dug – about 3 or 4 times the diameter of the tree's root ball. Lift any turf or weeds, then dig out the hole to about 1½ times the depth of the root ball.*

2 *Scarify the sides of the hole with a fork. Mix the removed soil with rotted organic matter.*

3 *If using one stake, hammer it into the hole, just off-centre and on the windward side. Add up to 20% of the organic matter and soil mixture to the pit.*

4 *Lay the tree on its side and slide it out of the pot. Gently tease out the roots without breaking up the root ball and remove any weeds from the compost.*

5 *Hold the tree next to the stake and spread out the roots. Lay a cane across the hole to check the planting depth. Adjust this by adding or removing some soil.*

6 *Backfill around the tree with more of the topsoil and organic matter. Firm around the tree in stages by treading, then fork over lightly and water well.*

7 *Cut back damaged stems, long sideshoots, and lower feathers. Mulch 5–7cm (2–3in) deep around the tree.*

locate the soil mark – a dark mark near the base of the stem indicating the soil level when the tree was growing in the nursery. Place a cane across the hole alongside the stem and add or remove soil from beneath the root ball, if necessary, so that the soil mark is level with the cane. On free-draining soil, a section of 10cm (4in) diameter perforated drainage pipe can be inserted into the planting hole – the top end should be just above ground level while the lower one should rest among the tree's roots. During subsequent hot weather water can be poured down this pipe, direct to the tree's roots.

Backfill the hole, firming the soil in stages to remove any air pockets; take care not to firm too heavily on clay soils as this may compact the ground and impede drainage. On sandy soils, a shallow moat around the tree helps to channel water to the roots. Conversely, on clay soils, a slight mound around the stem drains water away from the root ball.

Lightly prune the top-growth to balance it with the root system (see "Formative pruning", p.72), then secure the tree to the stake with one or more ties (see "Tree ties", p.65).

PLANTING A ROOT-BALLED TREE

1 *Dig a planting hole 2–3 times the diameter of the tree's root ball. Mix the removed soil with well-rotted organic matter, then place the tree in the hole and untie the wrapping.*

2 *Tilt the tree to one side and roll the material up under the root ball, then tilt the tree the other way and carefully pull out the material. Backfill the hole, firm, mulch, and water well.*

Water thoroughly and apply a thick mulch (see "Mulching", p.68).

Bare-root trees
Prepare the site in the same way as for container-grown trees, ensuring that the planting hole is wide enough for the tree's roots to be spread out fully; trim back any damaged roots to healthy growth. If using a single stake, drive it in just off-centre of the planting hole, and spread the tree's roots around it. Adjust the planting depth if necessary, then partly backfill the hole and gently shake the stem to settle the soil. Firm the backfilled soil in stages, taking care not to damage the roots. Finally, water the tree well; mulch the area around it.

Root-balled trees
The method of planting root-balled trees is very similar to that used for container-grown trees. The planting hole should be twice the width of the root ball, however, or, in heavy, clay soils, three times the width. Place the tree in the hole at the correct depth, then remove the hessian or netting surrounding the root ball. If using an angled stake or two stakes, one on either side of the root ball, drive them in; they should rest firmly against the root ball without piercing it.

In heavy, clay soils, it is possible to improve drainage by planting so that the top of the root ball is slightly above soil level, and covering the exposed part with 5–7cm (2–3in) of friable soil, leaving a gap of 2.5–5cm (1–2in) around the stem. Water thoroughly and mulch.

Aftercare
For the first two or three years after planting, it is important to provide trees with plenty of water, particularly in dry spells. Failure to do this may impede establishment, or the tree may even die. Keep the surrounding area clear of grass and weeds, and feed and mulch regularly (see "Routine care", pp.68–70).

Some trees need extra protection from frost and wind; evergreens in an exposed site should be protected initially from drying winds with windbreaks, for example (see FROST AND WIND PROTECTION, pp.612–613).

Protecting the stem

In many regions, it is necessary to protect young trees from damage caused by rabbits or other animals that strip bark. Either surround the tree with a barrier of chicken wire or wire netting secured in place with several canes or stakes, or place a proprietary tree guard around the tree trunk. There are many types of guard available from garden centres and nurseries, including spiral, wrap-around guards made of flexible plastic, as well as those made from heavy-duty plastic or wire mesh. Degradable, plastic-net tree guards are also available in a range of heights from 60cm (2ft) up to 2m (6ft).

In exposed sites, such as on hillsides, tree shelters may be used to assist young transplants and whips to become well established; these degradable plastic structures are up to 1.2m (4ft) long, and between 8cm (3in) and 15cm (6in) across.

A   B   C   D

Protect the bark of newly planted trees from animal damage with a barrier of wire mesh or plastic netting secured to the ground with canes (A), a rigid, plastic tree shelter (B), a heavy-duty rubber or plastic stem guard (C), or a spiral, wrap-around, plastic guard (D).

TREES THAT TOLERATE EXPOSED OR WINDY SITES

Those marked✹ are not suitable for coastal sites
Acer pseudoplatanus
Betula pendula✹,
  B. pubescens✹
Crataegus x *lavallei*,
  C. monogyna
Eucalyptus gunnii,
  E. pauciflora (and subsp.)
Fraxinus excelsior
Ilex altaclerensis (and cvs)
Picea abies✹, *P. sitchensis*✹
Pinus contorta, P. nigra,
  P. radiata, P. sylvestris
Quercus robur
Salix alba
Sorbus aria, S. aucuparia
  (and cvs)

Sorbus aucuparia

TREES THAT TOLERATE POLLUTED AIR

Acer platanoides (and cvs),
  A. pseudoplatanus (and cvs),
  A. saccharinum (and cvs)
Aesculus hippocastanum
Alnus cordata, A. glutinosa
Betula pendula
Carpinus betulus (and cvs)
Catalpa bignonioides
Corylus colurna
Crataegus
x *Cupressocyparis leylandii*
Fraxinus
Ginkgo biloba
Gleditsia
Ilex x *altaclerensis*
Liriodendron
Magnolia grandiflora
Malus
Nyssa
Platanus
Populus

Populus
x *jackii*
'Aurora'

Pyrus
Quercus x *hispanica* (and cvs),
  Q. ilex, Q. x *turneri*
Robinia
Salix
Sophora japonica
Sorbus aria, S. aucuparia,
  S. intermedia
Taxus baccata, T. x *media*
Tilia x *euchlora, T.* x *europaea,*
  T. platyphyllos (and cvs)

Routine care

THE amount of maintenance that a tree needs largely depends on the species, microclimate, soil type, and site. Most trees require watering, feeding, and a clear, weed-free area during the first few years if they are to establish well; container-planted trees should also be regularly top-dressed and occasionally repotted. In addition, other procedures such as removing suckers or controlling pests or diseases are sometimes necessary, while in certain circumstances – for example, if a tree is not thriving – the best solution may be either to remove the tree or to transplant it.

Watering

Most trees need plenty of water to grow well, especially on light, sandy soil or if trees have been planted within the previous two or three years. As a general guide, apply approximately 50–75 litres/sq m (11–15 gallons/sq yd) of water per tree each week in dry weather during the growing season. Once they have become well established, most trees only need to be artificially irrigated during spells of drought.

Fertilizing

All trees benefit from feeding, particularly on soils low in nutrients and during the first few years after planting. Older trees usually require feeding only occasionally. Trees grown for their flowers and fruit require more potash and phosphate than do trees grown for their foliage, which need more nitrogen.

Organic fertilizers such as well-rotted manure or compost are usually applied as a mulch: in autumn, or during any frost-free period in the dormant season, spread the material in a layer 5–8cm (2–3in) deep around the tree, keeping a clear area immediately around the trunk. When feeding a young tree, extend the mulch to the "drip line" – the ground beneath the outer edge of the canopy; an area 3–4m (10–12ft) in diameter is appropriate for a larger tree.

Artificial fertilizers are usually applied in spring. Broadcast the fertilizer around the base of the tree, at a rate of 70g/sq m (2oz/sq yd), or mix it with compost and insert it into small holes dug 2m (6ft) apart around the drip line. Alternatively, apply a proprietary liquid fertilizer around the tree.

Trees planted in grassed areas may need to be fed every year if they are not thriving. The grass between the trunk and the drip line may be removed by hand or with chemicals and a nutrient-rich mulch applied.

Mulching

Mulching around a tree keeps down weeds, reduces the effect of temperature extremes around the roots, and cuts down moisture loss from the soil surface. In general, organic materials such as pulverized bark look attractive, and they can be used to cover a biodegradable mulch mat. Black plastic is also effective, but do not use clear plastic, because heat is rapidly transferred to the soil and may damage surface roots. Mulches that are rich in nutrients are generally used only if a tree needs feeding.

Mulches are best applied in spring but, provided that the soil is moist, they may be spread at any time except during frost. Apply mulch over an area 30–45cm (12–18in) larger than the tree's root system. Top up every year or two under young trees.

Weeding

The area beneath a tree's canopy should be kept clear of weeds and grass as this ensures that the fibrous, feeding roots of the tree do not have to compete for water and nutrients.

Maintaining trees planted in containers

Container-planted trees generally require watering and feeding more frequently than those planted in open ground as the small amount of compost in which they are growing can store only limited reserves of water and nutrients. During hot, dry weather, they may need to be watered at least twice a day. Apply an annual mulch of bark chippings or similar material on top of the compost to help retain moisture. In addition, top-dress the tree each spring before it starts into growth. This involves replacing some of the old compost with fresh compost enriched with fertilizer. At the same time, prune back any dead, damaged, weak, or straggly stems to rejuvenate the tree and ensure that it produces healthy, vigorous growth.

Every three to five years, repot the tree completely either into the same container or, preferably, into a larger one. To do this, first remove the tree carefully from the container, then tease out the roots, cutting back by up to one third any that are large and coarse. Soak the root system well, if dry, then repot the tree into fresh compost (see "Repotting woody plants", p.334). If using the same container, wash it out before adding fresh compost and repotting.

TOP-DRESSING

1 *Using a trowel or your hands, remove any mulch and the top 5cm (2in) of compost.*

2 *Replenish the container with fresh compost mixed with a slow-release fertilizer. Water the compost well, and mulch.*

REPOTTING

1 *Carefully lay the tree on its side and, with one hand supporting the stem and root ball, knock it out of its pot by sharply tapping the base. Remove any top-dressing or mulch material.*

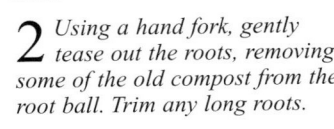

2 *Using a hand fork, gently tease out the roots, removing some of the old compost from the root ball. Trim any long roots.*

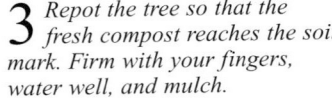

3 *Repot the tree so that the fresh compost reaches the soil mark. Firm with your fingers, water well, and mulch.*

REMOVING SUCKERS

Using secateurs, cut off the suckers as close to the trunk as possible, then pare over the cut surface with a knife; rub out any regrowth as soon as it appears.

REMOVING WATER SHOOTS

Using secateurs, cut back to the base any water shoots that may grow through the bark or sprout at the edges of a wound where a branch has been removed.

If a tree's growth is too rapid, retaining or establishing grass around it will help to reduce its vigour by competing for food and water.

Some weedkillers may be used around trees because they do not affect tree roots. Mulching, however, should make weeding largely unnecessary. For treatment of weeds, see "Weeds", pp.669–674.

Suckers and water shoots

Suckers and water shoots will divert nutrients from the main shoots of the tree if they are left to develop unchecked. Remove them as soon as they appear.

Stem and root suckers

A tree may produce both stem and root suckers: a stem sucker is a shoot that appears just beneath the graft union on the rootstock of a grafted tree; a root sucker is one that develops directly from the roots. Suckers of a grafted plant may quickly grow larger than the top-growth or even replace it within a few years so that the rootstock species predominates rather than the grafted cultivar.

Trees that are particularly vigorous or that have roots near the soil surface, such as poplars (*Populus*) and ornamental cherries (*Prunus*), may form root suckers if the root system is damaged. They may be used for propagation, but are a nuisance if they come up in lawns and paths.

Cut or pull off the suckers as close to the base as possible, digging down to where the sucker joins the root, if necessary. For some genera such as *Prunus*, painting the cuts on the roots with ammonium sulphamate usually prevents regrowth and, in small amounts, does not harm the tree.

Water shoots

Epicormic or water shoots may grow directly out of the trunk, often around pruning wounds. Rub them out with your fingers or thumb as soon as they appear, or cut them back to the base and rub them out as they regrow.

Frost and wind

Trees may be damaged by strong winds, and severe frosts may affect young growth, so provide protection such as windbreaks, particularly in exposed sites. Windbreaks may be artificial, such as fencing, or natural, such as hedges (see also "How a windbreak works", p.611).

The soil around newly planted trees may be lifted by frost; if this occurs, refirm it after thawing so that the roots do not dry out. For further information, see FROST AND WIND PROTECTION, pp.612–613.

Tree problems

Lack of vigour is a reliable indicator that there is a problem with a tree. As well as checking for pests and diseases, make sure that the tree has not been too deeply planted or that the roots and stems have not been damaged, as these are possible causes of poor growth and die-back.

The most common pests are aphids (p.646) and red spider mite (p.646), while honey fungus (p.661) is the most damaging disease, affecting, and often killing, a wide range of trees. To minimize the risk of problems, keep trees properly fed and maintained, and the surrounding area clear of weeds and debris.

Cutting down a tree

Tree felling, which may be undertaken at any time of year, is a skilled and potentially dangerous operation; if the tree is taller than 5m (15ft), it should be tackled by a tree surgeon. Ensure that the tree is not subject to a Tree Preservation Order and, if on a boundary, that it legally belongs to you.

Make sure that there is space for the tree to fall safely and that there is an escape route at right angles to the proposed fall line.

A tree is usually taken down in stages, and you must always wear protective gloves. First remove any large branches in sections (see "Removing a branch", p.71), then cut down the rest of the trunk by taking out a wedge of wood on the side where you want the tree to fall and making another cut on the opposite side of the trunk. The tree can then be pushed over in the required direction. If felling a large tree, tie ropes around the trunk to guide its fall.

It is best to remove the stump but if this is impractical it may be treated with chemicals; if left to rot it could attract honey fungus (p.661), which may then spread. Dig out the stump and any large roots with a spade. Tough roots should be severed with an axe. If the stump is large, you may need to employ a contractor to grind it or winch it out with special tools.

Alternatively, cut the stump flush with the ground and treat the cut surface with a proprietary solution of ammonium sulphamate. Allow at least 12 weeks before planting in the vicinity.

1 *Put on protective gloves. On the side the tree is to fall, make an angled cut just over one third of the trunk diameter and about 1m (3ft) from the ground.*

2 *Cut out a wedge by sawing horizontally to meet the base of the angled cut. Remove the wedge; this ensures that the tree will fall in the right direction.*

3 *On the opposite side of the trunk, make the final cut just above the base of the wedge cut. As the tree starts to fall, push it in the right direction if necessary.*

4 *Remove the remaining stump by digging a wide trench around it, loosening the roots with a fork or spade, and then winching or digging it out.*

Transplanting a tree

It is best to prepare the tree a year in advance before transplanting as this will greatly increase its chances of re-establishing. Unless the tree is quite young, it may be difficult to transplant and may not adjust well; if taller than 2.5m (8ft), the tree may be difficult to establish in its new position. Large trees may need to be transplanted by specialist arborists.

Preparation

In early autumn the year before the planned move, while the soil is still warm and the tree roots are in active growth, mark out the optimum root-ball diameter for the tree – about one third of the tree's height. Dig a trench about 30cm (12in) wide and 60cm (24in) deep just outside the marked area and mix the removed soil with well-rotted organic matter.

Using a sharp spade, undercut the root ball as far as possible to sever any large, coarse roots. This has the effect of stimulating the growth of fibrous "feeder" roots, which will help the tree to develop and grow successfully after transplanting. Then replace the mixture of soil and organic matter in the trench.

Lifting the tree

Transplant the tree the following autumn (see "When to plant", p.65), first pruning out any thin branches and reducing the tree to a well-balanced framework. Then tie in the remaining branches to the central stem to protect them and to increase the working space around the tree.

Dig a trench just outside the one made the previous year and of similar dimensions, and gradually fork away the excess soil until the root ball is of a manageable size and weight; take care not to damage the fibrous roots. On sandy soil, thoroughly soak the ground before starting to dig, to make the root ball firmer. Then cut with a spade through any roots underneath the root ball to separate it completely from the surrounding soil. To hold the root ball together and stop the roots drying out while the tree is removed from the hole, it should be securely wrapped in some hessian or plastic sheeting. This can be tricky to do, but the easiest way is to tilt the tree first one way and then the other, so that each side of the root ball is raised and the hessian slipped under it. Use rope to secure the wrapping around the root ball. Then ma-

noeuvre the tree onto a piece of heavyweight cloth or a wheelbarrow and transport it to its new position.

Replanting

Well before the tree reaches its new site, prepare the planting hole (see *Planting a Root-balled Tree*, p.67). When the tree arrives, lower it into the hole and adjust the planting depth until the dark mark on the tree stem is at soil level. Then undo the root ball ties and, carefully tilting the tree, remove the hessian covering around the root ball. Backfill the hole, working the soil around and over the root ball and firming it in stages, until the soil is level with the dark mark on the tree stem.

It may then be necessary to reduce the crown by a further 25–30 per cent, to minimize water loss and stimulate regrowth the following spring. Until it is well established, support the tree with guy-ropes secured to angled stakes in the ground. Water the tree well, then spread a thick mulch about 10cm (4in) deep on the surrounding soil, to retain moisture and suppress weeds. If it is impossible to replant the tree immediately, give it the same care as you would a newly purchased tree (see *Heeling in*, p.65).

Tree roots and buildings

Many trees, especially large, forest-sized ones in an urban area, grow too large for their surroundings and/or too near buildings, and it is the legal responsibility of the land owner to rectify any damage that their roots or branches may cause.

Tree roots, for example, may crack building foundations, especially if these are less than 50cm (20in) deep and sited on clay soils. Walls are particularly vulnerable in times of drought, because soil shrinks as tree roots absorb the moisture needed to survive. Roots may also block drains, which burst and so cause unstable, wet areas underground.

Roots and suckers may disturb paving slabs on paths and pavements, so they become a hazard to pedestrians, and falling branches may damage roofs, guttering, fences, power lines, or even nearby vehicles.

HOW TO MOVE A YOUNG TREE

1 *Prepare the tree for transplanting (see above). To transplant, start by tying the branches in to the main stem to protect them from damage while working around the tree. Then, keeping outside the area of the root ball, dig a trench about 30cm (12in) wide and 60cm (24in) deep around the tree.*

2 *Carefully fork away the soil from around the root ball, removing a small amount at a time to avoid damaging the roots.*

3 *Undercut the root ball with a spade and cut back with secateurs any awkward roots protruding from the root ball.*

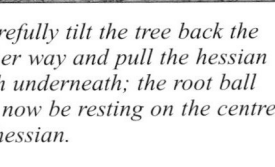

4 *Roll up a length of hessian (or plastic sheeting) and, tilting the tree to raise one side of the root ball, slide the hessian underneath.*

5 *Carefully tilt the tree back the other way and pull the hessian through underneath; the root ball should now be resting on the centre of the hessian.*

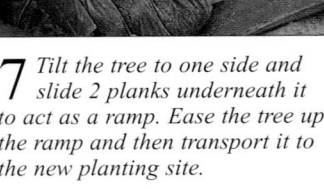
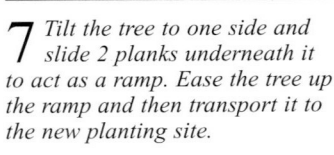

6 *Pull the hessian up around the root ball so that it is completely covered. Tie it securely in place with rope to keep the root ball intact while the tree is being moved.*

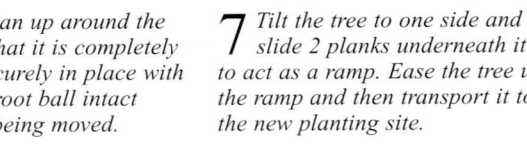

7 *Tilt the tree to one side and slide 2 planks underneath it to act as a ramp. Ease the tree up the ramp and then transport it to the new planting site.*

Pruning and training

CORRECT pruning and training helps to maintain a tree's health and vigour, regulate its shape and size, and, in some instances, improve ornamental qualities. It is important to prune young trees correctly to develop a strong framework of evenly spaced branches.

The degree of pruning and training depends on the type of tree and the desired effect: relatively little is required to produce a well-balanced tree whereas creating a pleached avenue with interwoven branches demands considerably more work and expertise.

When to prune

Most deciduous trees are best pruned when dormant in late autumn or winter; they may also be pruned at other times, except in late winter or early spring when many trees "bleed" (exude sap) if cut. Maples (*Acer*), horse chestnuts (*Aesculus*), birches (*Betula*), walnuts (*Juglans*), and cherries (*Prunus*) all bleed extensively, even towards the end of their dormant season; prune these in mid- to late summer after new growth has matured. Evergreens need little or no pruning except the removal of dead or diseased branches in late summer.

The principles of pruning

Always wear strong protective gloves when pruning. The first stage is to remove any dead, diseased, or damaged wood on the tree, and to cut out weak or straggly shoots. Then assess the remaining framework and decide which branches should be pruned back or removed for well-balanced growth. Take care not to impair the natural growth habit of a tree by pruning unless aiming to produce a certain shape or form, such as an espalier. Hard pruning stimulates vigorous growth, whereas light pruning produces only limited growth.

It is important to make pruning cuts accurately to minimize damage to the tree. If cutting back a stem, cut just above a healthy bud, pair of buds, or sideshoot pointing in the required direction of growth. For example, if thinning out congested stems, cut back to a bud or shoot that is growing outwards so it will not rub against another stem as it grows. Cut neither too far from the bud, which leaves a stub that provides an entry point for disease, nor too close, which could damage the bud itself.

When pruning trees with opposite buds, make a straight cut with sharp secateurs directly above a pair of buds; for trees with alternate buds,

WHERE TO CUT

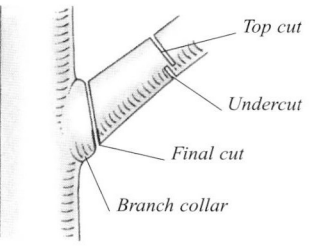

Top cut

Undercut

Final cut

Branch collar

When removing a branch, take care not to damage the branch collar: first remove the bulk of the branch with 2 cuts, then cut off the stub just outside the collar.

CUTTING BACK A STEM

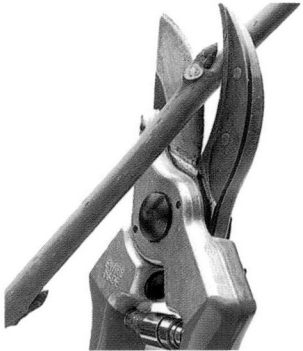

ALTERNATE BUDS
For trees with alternate buds, make a clean, angled cut just above a healthy, outward-facing bud.

OPPOSITE BUDS
For trees with opposite buds, make a clean, straight cut directly above a strong pair of buds.

make a sloping cut 3–5mm ($\frac{1}{8}$–$\frac{1}{4}$in) above a bud so that the base of the cut is just level with the top of the bud, on the opposite side of the stem.

If pruning back a branch completely, cut just outside the branch collar – the slight swelling on the branch where it joins the trunk. This is where the callus is formed that will eventually cover the wound. Never cut flush with the main stem as this damages the tree's natural protective zone, making it more vulnerable to disease. The branch collar on dead branches may extend some way along the branch, but it is still important to make any cut outside it.

Removing a branch

If removing whole branches of less than 2.5cm (1in) diameter, make a single cut with a pruning saw or secateurs. For branches thicker than this, first remove the bulk of the weight: partially undercut the branch at least 30cm (12in) from the trunk, then a little further out saw through from above. If no undercut is made, the branch may break off in mid-cut, ripping the bark back to the trunk so making it vulnerable to infection.

To remove the remaining stub, undercut it just outside the branch collar, then cut through from above. If you find it difficult to locate the branch collar, cut through the stub at a short distance from the trunk, making the cut so that it slopes outwards away from the tree.

If the angle between the branch and the trunk is very acute, it may be easier to cut through the stub from beneath. Do not apply a wound paint or dressing: there is no clear evidence that they speed up the healing process or prevent disease.

CUTTING OFF A BRANCH

1 *Put on protective gloves. Using a pruning saw, undercut the branch 30cm (12in) from the trunk by one quarter of its diameter. This stops the bark tearing.*

2 *Make the second cut about 2.5cm (1in) further away from the trunk, sawing through the branch from above. The undercut will close up, making sawing easier.*

3 *Remove the remaining stub by making a further 2 cuts. First make a small undercut just outside the branch collar.*

4 *Make the final cut just outside the branch collar, angling the saw slightly away from the trunk. Saw through cleanly until the top cut meets the undercut.*

Formative pruning

Young trees benefit from formative pruning to ensure that they develop a strong, well-balanced framework of evenly spaced branches. At its simplest, this involves the removal of dead, damaged, and diseased wood, as well as any weak or crossing branches.

Formative pruning may also be used to determine the tree's shape as it grows: for example, a young feathered tree may be pruned over several years to form a standard, or trained against a wall as an espalier. The extent of the pruning depends on both the type of tree selected and the required shape when mature. As with all types of pruning, care should be taken not to spoil the tree's natural growth characteristics.

It is particularly important to prune young tropical trees as the growth rate is very rapid and the girth of both main stems and branches develops very quickly; provided that they have been pruned correctly during the first few years after planting, they may then be left to grow naturally. Most other evergreens, on the other hand, will develop naturally into well-shaped specimens with little or no attention; pruning is usually restricted to the removal of dead, damaged, or crossing stems, and badly placed laterals.

The formative pruning of ornamental garden trees depends on the type of tree bought or required. Feathered trees have a single, central leader and laterals along the whole length of the stem. Central-leader standards have a clear length of stem at the base, while branched-head standards also have a clear stem but have their central leader removed to encourage the formation of vigorous lateral branches – as commonly seen in many Japanese cherries (*Prunus*).

Feathered trees

Feathered trees may either be simply pruned to enhance their natural shape or more extensively pruned to train them into standards. This process also occurs naturally sometimes. Although many feathered trees retain their lower branches, these die back in some species and the tree becomes a central-leader standard; other trees also lose their central-leader dominance and so become branched-head standards.

Early training is straightforward, however, regardless of the eventual habit of the tree. First remove any competing shoots to leave a single main leader. Then take out any small, weak, and poorly placed laterals, so

PRUNING AND TRAINING YOUNG TREES

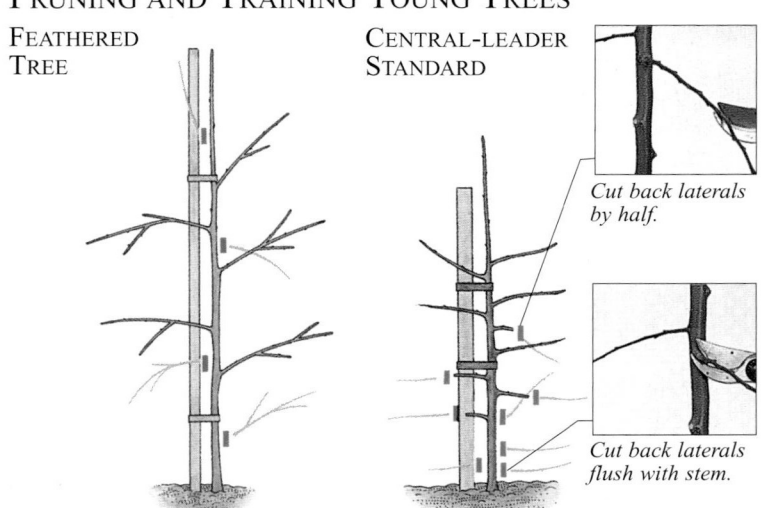

FEATHERED TREE

Remove congested and crossing shoots, then cut out any laterals that are small, spindly, or badly positioned, to achieve a well-balanced framework of branches.

CENTRAL-LEADER STANDARD

Cut back laterals by half.

Cut back laterals flush with stem.

YEAR 1
On the lowest third of the tree, cut back laterals to the main stem; on the middle third, cut back laterals by half. Remove any weak or competing leaders.

YEARS 2 AND 3
Continue the pruning process, removing the lowest laterals completely and cutting back by about half those laterals that are on the middle third of the tree.

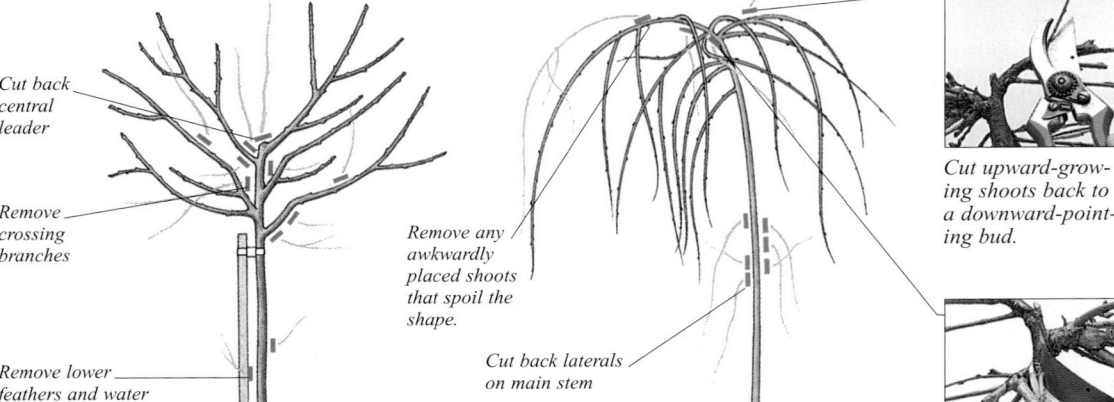

BRANCHED-HEAD STANDARD

Cut back central leader

Remove crossing branches

Remove lower feathers and water shoots

Remove crossing laterals and any growths on the lower third of the tree. Cut back the leader to a healthy bud or shoot.

WEEPING TREE

Remove any awkwardly placed shoots that spoil the shape.

Cut back laterals on main stem

Cut back crossing or vertical branches that spoil the symmetry of the tree. Remove any growths on the main stem.

Cut upward-growing shoots back to a downward-pointing bud.

Cut out crossing, rubbing, or congested growth.

that the framework of branches around the main stem is evenly spaced and well balanced.

Central-leader standard trees

Feathered whips may be pruned over two to three years to form a standard; a technique called "feathering" is often used as it also channels food to the main stem which thickens and becomes sturdier. Initially, prune a feathered whip to remove any competing leaders or weak laterals. Then, on the lowest third of the tree, cut back all the feathers to the main stem; on the middle third, reduce the feathers by about half; leave the top

third unpruned, but remove any vigorous, upright shoots that might form a competing leader.

In late autumn or early winter, cut back the pruned laterals flush with the main stem. Repeat the procedure over the next two or three years to form a tree with approximately 1.8m (6ft) of clear stem.

Branched-head standard trees

To form a branched-head standard, train the tree initially as a central-leader standard to achieve the desired length of clear stem. Then, in mid- to late autumn, cut back the leader to a strong, healthy bud or

shoot to leave a framework of four or five strong, well-placed lateral branches. At this stage, also remove any crossing or congested laterals and any that spoil the balance of the branch framework.

In subsequent years, prune the tree as much as necessary to keep the crown well balanced and with an open centre; remove any vigorous, vertical shoots that may grow into a new leader; and cut back any feathers to the main stem as soon as possible. Some branched-head standards can be formed by top-working (or top-grafting) as for weeping standards (see p.73).

Weeping standards

A weeping standard is formed by grafting one or two scions of a weeping cultivar onto a stock plant with a clear stem of about 1.8m (6ft). This is known as top-working or top-grafting, a technique that is most commonly used for fruit trees (see "Top-working", p.443) but also for weeping ash (*Fraxinus excelsior* 'Pendula'), the Kilmarnock willow (*Salix caprea* 'Kilmarnock'), and a large number of other weeping ornamental trees. Young, pendulous branches start to develop once the grafts have taken.

Pruning is best restricted to the removal of crossing and vertical branches as well as any that spoil the overall symmetry of the framework. Although upward-growing branches are usually removed, leave some semi-upright stems to develop naturally as they often grow downwards later and produce tiers of weeping branches. If growths appear on the main stem, rub or pinch them out as soon as they appear.

Espalier- and fan-trained trees

The aim of both espalier- and fan-training is to form a symmetrical, attractive network of branches in a single plane by pruning and training a young tree over several years. These techniques are occasionally used for growing ornamental trees against fences or walls, but they are more commonly associated with growing fruit trees.

Pruning times vary according to the selected species: for example, *Magnolia grandiflora*, which flowers from mid- to late summer, should be pruned at the start of growth in spring, while the spring-flowering *Acacia dealbata* should be pruned directly after flowering. For full instructions on the pruning techniques, see GROWING FRUIT, "Espalier", p.442, and "Fan", p.441.

Pruning established deciduous trees

Once a deciduous tree is well established, there is little need for further pruning. Major pruning of a mature tree is best carried out by a tree surgeon or arborist, as the work is both skilled and dangerous, and, if poorly executed, may ruin the tree.

Many branched-head trees become overcrowded in the centre as they mature, restricting the amounts of air and light that reach the central branches. Cut out inward-growing shoots and any branches that spoil the balance of the framework.

REMOVING A COMPETING LEADER

Prune out a competing leader by making a clean cut at the base with secateurs or loppers, taking care not to damage the remaining leader.

If a tree is too large for its situation, do not attempt to restrict its size by heading back all new growth each year; this "haircut" pruning produces an unsightly, congested cluster of shoots each season which spoils the tree's natural appearance and reduces flower and fruit production. The correct treatment is as for the renovation of old trees (see p.74).

As a result of hard pruning or the removal of large branches, a tree may produce a mass of epicormic or water shoots; rub or cut these out immediately (see p.69).

If the central leader is damaged, select a strong shoot close to the top of the main stem and train it vertically as a replacement leader. Tie the selected shoot to a cane or stake secured high on the main stem, and prune out any potential competing shoots. Once the shoot has developed into a strong, dominant growth, the cane may be removed.

If a tree develops two or more competing leaders, remove all but the strongest shoot. The very narrow crotch angle between rival leaders is a source of structural weakness and the tree could split open at this point in a high wind.

Vigorous, upright shoots may develop on young, branched-head trees. If left, these will quickly grow into competing leaders and so it is important to remove them entirely as soon as possible.

Pruning established evergreen trees

Broadleaved evergreens need minimal pruning. Provided that the trees have an established leader and that any badly placed laterals have been cut out when young, it is only necessary to remove any dead, damaged, or diseased wood.

Conifers require only basic pruning once established, except when they are grown as a hedge (see HEDGES AND SCREENS, pp.84–85). On some pines (*Pinus*), silver firs (*Abies*), and spruces (*Picea*), the terminal bud on the leader may die; if this occurs, train in the best placed lateral as a replacement leader (see above) and cut out any competing, upright shoots. Established palms require no pruning apart from the removal of dead leaves which should be cut back to the main stem.

Root pruning

If an established tree is growing vigorously, but producing very few flowers or fruit, pruning the roots may help to slow down growth and stimulate better flowering or fruiting performance.

In early spring, dig a trench just outside the extent of the tree canopy. Then prune back any thick roots to the inner edge of the trench, using a pruning saw, secateurs, or loppers. Retain any fibrous roots at the inner edge of the trench, backfill the soil, and firm. For further details, see GROWING FRUIT, "Root pruning", p.430. In some instances, it may be necessary to support the tree with stakes or guy-ropes if it seems unstable afterwards (see "Staking", p.64).

HOW TO COPPICE A TREE

Coppicing may be used to restrict a tree's size, enlarge leaves, or enhance stem colour.

Use pruning loppers to cut back all stems to 7cm (3in); do not cut into the swollen, woody base of the tree.

TRAINING A NEW LEADER

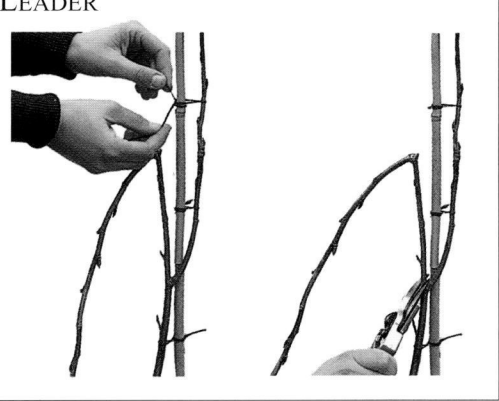

Replace a damaged leader by training in a strong shoot vertically. Attach a cane to the top of the main stem and tie the shoot to the cane. Prune out the old, damaged leader. Remove the cane once the new leader is dominant and growing strongly.

For root pruning of trees in containers, see "Maintaining trees planted in containers", p.68.

Pruning container-planted trees

Container-planted trees should be pruned annually, following the same principles as for other trees, to regulate their shape and size and maintain a strong, balanced framework of evenly spaced branches.

Coppicing and pollarding

Coppicing is the regular pruning of a tree close to the ground to encourage strong, basal shoots to grow. Pollarding is the pruning of a tree back to its main stem or branch framework, stimulating new shoots at this level. Traditionally, both techniques were practised to give a regular supply of firewood or pliable stems for basketwork and fencing. Now they are used in gardens to enhance leaf colour and the size or the colour of ornamental stems, or to restrict tree size.

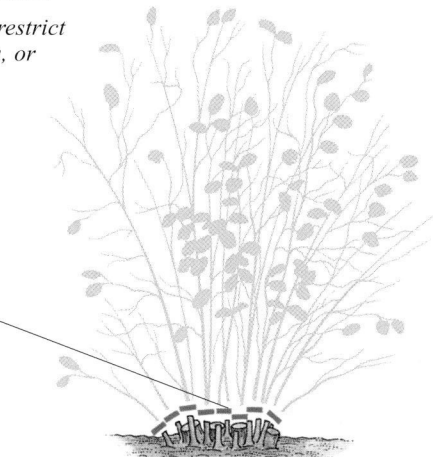

Coppicing

Trees should be coppiced in late winter or early spring; some willows, when grown for their coloured or glaucous stems, may be left until mid-spring, however, and pruned just before or very shortly after bud break. Cut back all stems to the base, leaving the swollen basal wood unpruned as all new growth occurs here. Less vigorous trees should be coppiced over two years, cutting half the stems one year and the remaining old ones the following year.

Pollarding

To form a pollard, plant a young, branched-head standard (see p.72). When its trunk has reached 2m (6ft), or the desired height, prune back the branches to 2.5–5cm (1–2in) from the main stem in late winter or early spring. This results in a mass of shoots developing from the top of the cut stem. Prune back these shoots annually (or every second year) to stimulate further young shoots to grow from the enlarged head of the stem. Thin them if they become congested. Remove shoots that grow on the trunk as soon as they appear.

To produce a pollard with a main branch framework, allow the tree to develop a well-balanced branch system at the desired height. In late winter or early spring, prune back the branches to about 2m (6ft). Cut back the resulting, secondary shoots every two to five years, depending on the species, until the pollard is established. Thereafter, prune every year

TREES FOR COPPICING AND POLLARDING

Corylus avellana 'Contorta' ⅴ
Eucalyptus dalrympleana,
  E. globulus ❀ⅴ,
  *E. gunnii*ⅴ,
  E. pauciflora

Populus x *jackii*
  'Aurora'

Populus x *canadensis*
  'Aurea', *P.* x *jackii*
  'Aurora'
Salix acutifolia 'Blue Streak',
  S. alba var. *sericea*,
  S. alba subsp. *vitellina*,
  S. alba subsp. *vitellina*
  'Britzensis',
  S. daphnoides 'Aglaia',
  S. 'Erythroflexuosa',
  *S. irrorata*ⅴ
Tilia platyphyllos (cvs)
Toona sinensis 'Flamingo'

KEY
❀ Not hardy
ⅴ Coppice only

PRUNING AN ESTABLISHED, POLLARDED TREE

Prune back the shoots every 1–2 years in late winter or early spring to 1–2cm (¹⁄₂–³⁄₄in) from the pollarded head of the main stem. This will stimulate new shoot production the following spring. The new wood of trees such as this Salix alba *var.* vitellina, *grown for its ornamental stems, is particularly highly coloured.*

Using secateurs or pruning loppers, cut back the old stems to the base, taking care not to damage the enlarged head.

or two, and thin the shoots as required. If too many enlarged heads develop close together, cut out some of them entirely.

Renovating old trees

Trees that have outgrown their situation, or that have been neglected, should be either removed and replaced, or renovated to return them to full health and vigour. Renovation requires considerable care and expertise, and it is advisable to consult an experienced tree surgeon. In some cases, a tree may be too old and potentially dangerous to renovate, so it may be better to replace it. In others, such as with old flowering cherries (and other *Prunus*), renovation is rarely successful because of the risk of silver leaf (see p.647).

Renovation may be undertaken at any time of year except at the start of growth in spring; for most trees, however, and particularly those that produce a lot of sap, such as horse chestnuts (*Aesculus*) and birches (*Betula*), late autumn or early winter is the best time.

The first stage is to remove all dead, diseased, and damaged wood. Then prune out any crossing or congested branches and those that spoil the balance of the framework. It is best to carry out extensive renovation over two or three years to allow gradual recovery since drastic pruning may severely weaken or even kill a tree in poor health. If you need to remove any large branches, do this in sections (see "Removing a branch", p.71).

After renovating the tree, feed it by mulching with well-rotted manure and apply fertilizer to the ground

beneath the tree canopy in spring for two to three years. Hard pruning may stimulate the growth of a mass of sideshoots; if congested, thin some of them out to leave a well-balanced framework. Any suckers and water shoots should be removed as soon as they are noticed (see p.69).

Renovating "haircut" pruned trees

Trees that have had all their new growth trimmed back annually produce a congested cluster of shoots every season on knobbly branches, but without the balanced framework of a true pollard. Such "haircut" pruning is unsightly and reduces flowers and fruit. To correct it, first thin out the knobbly stumps at the ends of the main branches. Cut out most of the young shoots on the remaining stumps to leave just one or two and cut these back by about one third; repeat this procedure in the following three or four seasons to develop a more natural growth habit.

Tree surgeons

For pruning, renovation, or removal of large trees, it is advisable to consult a qualified tree surgeon. The nearest horticultural college or arboricultural association may be able to supply a list of approved consultants and contractors, who comply with required standards of safe working practices and technical competence.

Before inviting contractors to tender, decide exactly what work is required, including the disposal of any debris which may be the most expensive part of tree surgery operations. Quotations are normally provided free, but a fee may be charged if advisory work is involved.

RENOVATING A TREE

YEAR 1
Cut out any dead, diseased, and damaged wood, and remove any branches that cross or rub against others and that spoil the balance of the framework.

YEARS 2 AND 3
The following year, thin out the new growth that results from the initial pruning and remove any water shoots. Repeat the next year if necessary.

Pleached trees

Pleached, or plashed, trees are clear-stemmed trees planted in one or more rows with their branches trained horizontally to intertwine, creating a formal, raised "wall" of foliage when in leaf (see "Trees for avenues", p.58). Hornbeams (*Carpinus*) and limes such as *Tilia platyphyllos*, *T. cordata* 'Winter Orange', and *T.* x *euchlora* make excellent pleached avenues, as they can be clipped precisely and, within four or five years, develop an effective, boxed appearance. It is best to use young trees with pliable stems when pleaching.

Constructing the framework

Until the trees are established, they should be trained in to a framework. First, using one stake for each tree to be planted, set up a row of 2.5–3m (8–10ft) high, stout stakes an equal distance apart. Once driven into the ground to a depth of approximately 60cm–1m (2–3ft), they should be at the required height of the lowest branches – about 2m (6ft) or more if they are to allow people to walk underneath. Attach a secondary framework of wooden battens or wires to these stakes to create the desired, overall height.

Initial training

Plant a young tree next to each stake in late autumn or early winter. Choose trees that are sufficiently tall so that their laterals may be trained in to the framework. After planting, tie in the leader and laterals, pruning out any badly placed ones.

Further training

Throughout the growing season, pinch out all new shoots that cannot be trained sideways. Tie in the leader as it extends, and train along the top batten. Tie in a suitably positioned lateral along the top batten on the other side of the main stem.

In winter, shorten any long laterals back to a strong sub-lateral, and cut sub-laterals back to two or three buds, to stimulate new stems to cover the framework. Continue to develop a boxed effect in subsequent seasons by tying in branches and cutting back the laterals to stimulate new shoots and dense growth.

Once the pleached trees are fully established and the branches have intertwined, the framework may be dismantled. Maintain healthy, dense growth by removing any dead, damaged, or diseased wood, and strongly outward-growing laterals; rub out young shoots on main stems as soon as they are noticed.

ESTABLISHING THE FRAMEWORK

YEAR 1

Having constructed a strong framework, plant a three- or four-year-old tree in front of each post, aligning as many laterals as possible parallel to the framework. Tie in the leader, adding extra ties during the subsequent growing season as the tree develops.

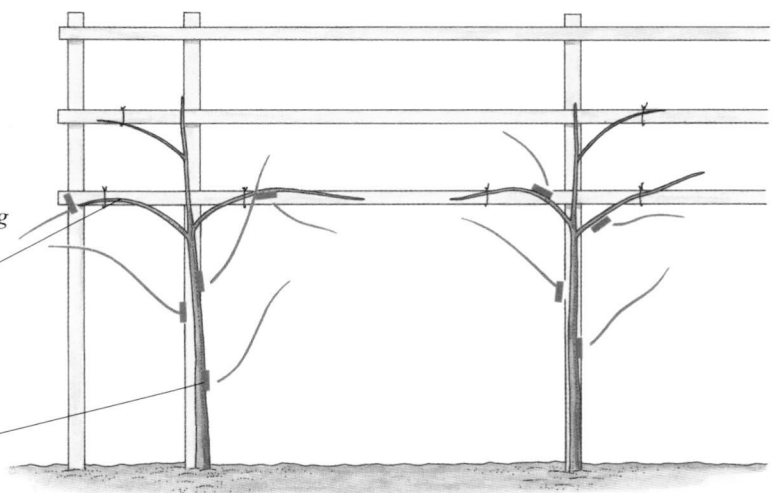

Remove any laterals that cannot readily be secured to a wire or batten. Tie the remaining laterals along an adjacent wire or batten.

Cut back to the main stem any laterals below the bottom wire or batten.

YEAR 2

Intertwine and tie in any untrained branches to the framework to fill in spaces. Pinch or rub out any new growth on the clear trunks.

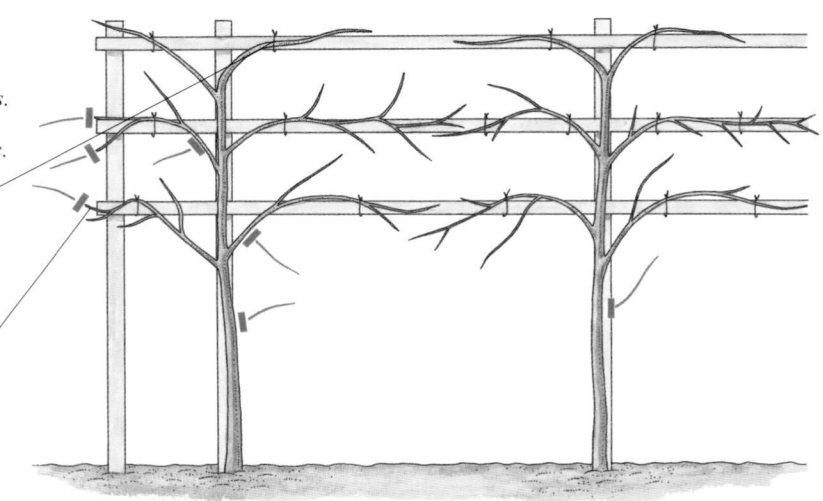

Once the leader is tall enough, bend it over onto the top horizontal of the framework, and tie it in. Train a suitably placed lateral along the top batten on the other side.

In winter, prune back sub-laterals to two or three buds to encourage new growth.

ANNUAL MAINTENANCE

Keep rubbing out shoots on the trunks and remove dead, diseased, or damaged growth. Check old ties and replace them where necessary. Feed the trees well in spring.

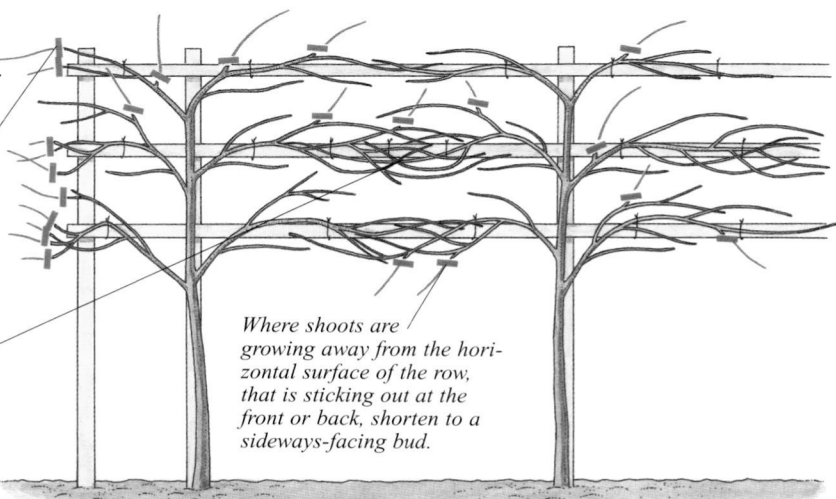

Cut back to one bud all new shoots that extend beyond the limits of the supporting framework.

Continue to weave and tie in suitably placed stems to the framework. As the gaps between the tiers narrow, shoots from above and below can be drawn and tied together.

Where shoots are growing away from the horizontal surface of the row, that is sticking out at the front or back, shorten to a sideways-facing bud.

Topiary

A FORM of training and pruning trees and shrubs to create attractive, boldly artificial shapes, topiary is a garden art that has been popular since Roman times. Traditionally used to produce strongly architectural and geometric shapes in formal gardens, it has been developed to include birds, animals, and unusual, even whimsical features such as giant chess-pieces and full-size trains.

Designing with topiary

Different styles of topiary may be used to create a variety of effects. Imaginative, living sculptures express personal style and add a humorous or bizarre touch. Using topiary for geometric shapes such as cones, obelisks, and columns provides a strong, structural element in a design. This type of topiary may be valuable both in formal gardens, perhaps to frame a vista or form an avenue, and in informal gardens, as a contrasting foil for less structured planting.

In some gardens, it may be appropriate to treat part of the hedge top as topiary, clipping it into one or more birds, spheres, or cubes, for example. Topiary may also be effective in containers; use a single container plant as a centrepiece, a pair to flank a doorway, or several to line a path. It can also be adopted to create eye-catching stem effects, such as twists and spirals, with one or more stems.

HOW TO CREATE A SIMPLE DESIGN

1 If using a young plant (here box) to form a geometric shape, first cut the plant to shape by eye.

2 The following year, make a cutting guide from canes and wire, place over the plant, and cut the plant to shape.

3 When the plant is the desired shape, clip each year with secateurs to retain a crisp outline.

Plants for topiary

Plants to be used for topiary require dense, pliable growth, small leaves, and the ability to recover quickly from clipping. Evergreens such as common box (*Buxus sempervirens*), privet (*Ligustrum ovalifolium*), yew (*Taxus baccata*), *Osmanthus delavayi*, and *Lonicera nitida* are ideal in a temperate climate. *Cupressus sempervirens* can be trained to suit geometric designs, but only thrives in warmer climates. Bay (*Laurus nobilis*), holly (such as non-spiny clones of *Ilex* x *altaclerensis*), and many other evergreens may be used, but are more difficult to train.

Ivies (such as *Hedera helix* 'Ivalace') are very adaptable and may easily be trained to grow up a frame; alternatively, several cuttings can be taken from an existing plant to grow up a moss-padded structure.

Creating a shape

Most topiary designs are best formed with the aid of a guiding framework, although some simple shapes may also be cut freehand.

Simple designs

Using young plants, select the stem or stems that will form the core of the design. The simplest shape to produce is a cone, which needs only guiding canes. For other shapes, attach a framework made from chicken wire or single wires attached to stakes placed in the ground next to the main group of shoots. Tie in the stems to the wire framework and then pinch back the shoots to encourage them to branch and cover the form.

Train new shoots into the framework to fill in any gaps, until they meet around its perimeter. Growth will vary around the plant, depending on the aspect. Shoots trained downwards always grow slowly.

Complex designs

Frameworks for complex designs are now generally available, although you may decide to make your own basic framework from sturdy materials such as heavy-duty fencing wire. Chicken wire or thin-gauge wire may then be intertwined to form a more precise shape. Garden canes are also useful as a temporary aid in developing and shaping a framework. Tarred twine is good for tying shoots onto a framework, since it eventually decays.

SHAPING A TOPIARY BIRD

1 In year 1, insert a fan-shaped cane support at an angle to form the bird tail. Select and tie in well-placed shoots to the canes using soft twine. Tip back weaker shoots, to stimulate branching.

2 During the growing season, shorten the trained-in shoots by up to one third of their length, cutting just above a node. This will encourage dense, compact growth and a solid mass of foliage.

3 In year 2, insert a supporting cane for the bird head and tie three strong shoots to this cane. Trim the tail and tip back shoots on the body. Remove unwanted shoots or wire them to bulk out the tail.

4 In year 3, tie down the strongest shoot at the head to form the beak. Continue trimming to shape the body more precisely; keep the tail growth dense. Once the shape is formed, clip regularly.

CLIPPED BIRD
Traditional shapes are still the most popular for topiary. This delightful bird sits on top of its nest surveying the surrounding gardens.

Training stems

Young stems being trained onto a frame grow quickly and considerable work is thus required to tie in new shoots throughout the growing season. Tie in the shoots while they are young and pliable and check previous ties to make sure that they are not broken, rubbing, or in any way restricting the shoots.

If stakes have been used in the framework, make sure that they are still firm and have not cracked, snapped, or bent. If they are defective, replace them with new ones.

Clipping

Topiary involves much more precise clipping than is required for normal hedge cutting. Take time, particularly when initially forming topiary pieces, to cut the branchlets carefully to the required shape. Do not cut too much in one place as it may spoil the symmetry of a topiary design for a whole season until new replacement growth appears.

Even if you have a good eye for shaping plants, it is sensible to use levels, plumb lines, and any other aids available to check the accuracy of a cut. Always work from the top of the plant downwards and from the centre outwards, cutting both sides together in order to retain a balanced symmetry.

Rounded topiary pieces are easier to produce and maintain than angular, geometric shapes and may often be cut freehand. To produce a spherical shape, first trim the top of the plant and then cut a channel downwards around the circumference to leave a ring. A further ring at 90° should then be cut, leaving four distinct quarters to be trimmed.

Geometric topiary that has precise, flat surfaces and angled or squared edges is difficult to form and maintain successfully and needs to be tackled with confident, accurate clipping for a well-defined shape. Such geometric designs are best cut using guidelines attached to canes to maintain symmetry.

When to clip

Once a topiary feature is established, it will need frequent routine clipping during the growing season. The time between cuts will depend on the rate of growth. An intricate, geometric design in box may need to be cut at four- to six-week intervals. Trim as soon as any new growth begins to appear uneven.

ARCHITECTURAL DESIGNS
Two spiral shapes eye-catchingly enhance the central, cone-shaped topiary along this path as well as complementing the two dome-shaped, side pieces.

If a perfect finish is not required throughout the year, two cuts during the growing season are usually sufficient for a reasonable effect, depending on the plant used. Yew, for example, need be cut only once a year, box (depending on the cultivar) usually needs to be cut twice, and *Lonicera nitida* three times.

Clip plants at the appropriate time of year. Do not clip bushes after early autumn as the young shoots produced after the first clip need to ripen sufficiently to withstand low winter temperatures. In warm climates where growth may be almost continuous, regular trimming will be required throughout the year.

Routine care

Weeding, watering, and mulching is essential in the same way as for free-growing shrubs (see p.100). It is important, however, to apply two or three feeds of a balanced fertilizer at a rate of 60g/sq m (2oz/sq yd) during the growing season.

Winter care

In regions where regular snowfalls occur, netting topiary pieces will help prevent the branches from breaking under the weight of snow. Knock snow off any flat surfaces as it may damage the framework.

Repairs and renovation

If a leader, a section, or a branch of topiary has been damaged or broken, cut it back cleanly with secateurs. Manipulate nearby shoots by tying them in to fill the gap.

If topiary plants have been left unclipped for one or two years, regular clipping should restore the original form within the season. If the topiary has been neglected for years, and the shape has been lost, severe pruning to restore the outline should be carried out the first spring followed by two or three seasons of more precise clipping.

Scorch and die-back

The foliage of some evergreens may be scorched in fierce winters and can die. The damaged foliage will soon be covered by new growth in spring, but cut it back where it is unsightly, taking care to follow the shape of the topiary piece. If shoots do not fill the gap, there may be a root problem, which will need to be treated.

HOW TO MAKE A COMPLEX DESIGN

1 *Make frameworks for large topiary pieces from strong materials as they will be in place for several years. Clip a young plant (here yew) as necessary to keep it within the framework.*

2 *As the plant grows and fills the frame, clip it over once a year, following the outline of the framework and pinching out shoots to encourage bushy growth.*

3 *When mature, the plant will form a dense bush and cover the framework. It needs regular clipping to maintain the precise outline of the design.*

Propagation

TREES may be propagated from cuttings, seed, layering, or grafting. Taking cuttings is probably the most common method of propagation as it is fairly simple and provides new plants relatively quickly, while raising trees from seed or layering is easy but very slow. Grafting is rarely used by amateur gardeners because it requires considerable expertise to grow new plants successfully this way.

Tree species may be propagated from seed but hybrids and cultivars rarely come true to type. Vegetative methods of propagation, such as taking cuttings, layering, and grafting, may be used for hybrids and cultivars as well as species; however, some care in the selection of plant material is required in order to be successful.

Hardwood cuttings

Many deciduous trees may be propagated from hardwood, or dormant, cuttings. In early autumn, prepare the ground for the cuttings while it is still warm. Cuttings can be inserted either outdoors in open ground or, for trees that do not root very easily, in the more stable environment of a cold frame.

Cuttings of trees that root easily, such as willows (*Salix*), may be inserted directly into a trench, while those that are more difficult to root, such as *Metasequoia*, should be inserted in a sand bed, and then transplanted into a trench early the next spring. In either case, make the trench narrow and with one side vertical so that the cuttings are held upright while they root. The depth of the trench will depend on the type of plant required: for multi-stemmed trees, it should be 2.5cm (1in) shallower than the length of the cuttings; for single-stemmed trees, it should be the same depth as the cuttings so that the top bud is barely covered and the lack of light inhibits the growth of all other buds.

For best results, dig the trench in friable, well-drained soil; in heavy, clay soil, add some coarse sand to the base. If preparing a few trenches, space them 30–38cm (12–15in) apart in open ground, or about 10cm (4in) apart in a cold frame.

SLOW-ROOTING HARDWOOD CUTTINGS

1 *For species that do not root easily (here* Metasequoia*), tie cuttings into bundles. Dip the ends in hormone rooting powder.*

2 *Insert the bundles of cuttings in a sand bed and leave in a cold frame over winter. In spring, insert them individually in a trench in a prepared site outside.*

Preparing and inserting the cuttings

Select the cuttings just after leaf fall: choose strong, vigorous shoots of the current season's growth and remove them by cutting just above a bud or pair of buds at the junction between the current and the previous season's growth. Trim down the cuttings as shown and dip the basal cuts in hormone rooting powder to encourage them to root. Place the cuttings against the vertical side of the trench at the correct depth, and backfill with soil. Then firm in gently and water well.

For species that do not root easily, tie the cuttings into bundles of no more than ten and then plunge them in a sand bed (see p.638) in a cold frame for the winter, where they should root before being transplanted.

FAST-ROOTING HARDWOOD CUTTINGS

1 *To prepare the trench, push the spade vertically into the soil, then press it forwards slightly to form a flat-backed trench about 19cm (7in) deep.*

2 *Select strong, straight stems with healthy buds (right); avoid soft, spindly, old, or damaged stems (left). Remove about 30cm (12in) of the stem, cutting just above a bud.*

3 *Remove any leaves. Trim the cuttings to about 20cm (8in): make an angled cut just above the proposed top bud and a horizontal cut below the bottom one.*

4 *Insert the cuttings in the trench 10–15cm (4–6in) apart, and at the correct depth depending on whether a single- or a multi-stemmed tree is required.*

PLANTING DEPTHS

MULTI-STEMMED TREES
For multi-stemmed trees, insert cuttings with the top 2.5–3cm (1–1½in) above the soil surface.

SINGLE-STEMMED TREES
The top bud of each cutting should be just below the soil surface.

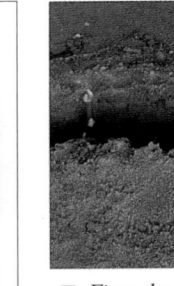

5 *Firm the soil around the cuttings, rake the surface, and label. Space any further rows 30–38cm (12–15in) apart.*

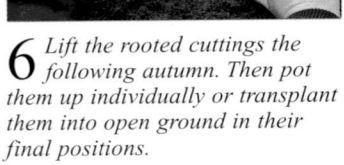

6 *Lift the rooted cuttings the following autumn. Then pot them up individually or transplant them into open ground in their final positions.*

Aftercare

Label the cuttings and leave them until the following autumn. During the winter, the ground may be lifted by frost; refirm the soil around the cuttings if this occurs. By autumn, the cuttings should be well rooted and may then be transplanted individually into open ground or into containers, as required. If they have been kept in a cold frame, harden them off in the first spring, then transplant outside; the following spring, pot them up or move them to their final positions in open ground.

Semi-ripe cuttings

Many conifers, as well as certain broadleaved evergreens such as *Magnolia grandiflora* and *Prunus lusitanica*, may be propagated readily from semi-ripe cuttings. These cuttings are taken in late summer or autumn from stems that have virtually ripened, that is, when they have thickened and become harder (see also ORNAMENTAL SHRUBS, "Semi-ripe cuttings", p.112).

Selecting the cuttings

In a closed case, at 21°C (70°F), or in a cold frame, prepare a suitable rooting medium for the cuttings. For example, this might consist of equal parts of grit and peat substitute or peat (see also "Standard cutting compost", p.565). Using a sharp knife, take heel cuttings from healthy sideshoots, including a sliver of hardened wood from the main stem (see ORNAMENTAL SHRUBS, "Heel cuttings", p.113). Alternatively, take 10–15cm (4–6in) long cuttings from leaders or sideshoots and trim immediately below a node.

For cuttings from conifers, choose leaders or sideshoots that are characteristic of the parent plant, as conifer shoots vary considerably in their growth patterns. It is particularly important to select cutting material carefully from slow-growing (dwarf) conifers; some plants may produce reverted or uncharacteristic shoots, but only use shoots that typify what you want to propagate.

Preparing and inserting the cuttings

With both types of cutting, cut off the lower pair of leaves with a sharp knife and reduce the remaining leaves by one third or a half to minimize the loss of moisture; if the cutting tips are soft, pinch them out. To encourage the cuttings to root, use the tip of the knife to make two shallow, vertical wounds, about 2.5cm (1in) long, on opposite sides of each cutting down to the base. Alternatively, make a longer wound along the side of each cutting with a knife, and remove a sliver of bark as well. In either case, dip the basal cut, including the wound, in hormone rooting powder.

Insert the bottom third of each cutting in the rooting medium, taking care to leave enough space between the cuttings so that they do not overlap; this allows air to circulate freely around them. Then firm the compost, water in thoroughly with a solution containing fungicide, and label.

Aftercare

Check the cuttings periodically, watering them only to keep them from drying out. Remove any fallen leaves as soon as they appear since these may rot and spread disease to the cuttings. In frosty conditions, cold frames should be insulated with hessian or a similar covering.

If the cuttings are being kept in a closed case with basal heat they should root by early spring. Cuttings in a cold frame are usually left until the following autumn, although it is preferable to leave them in the frame for a second winter and pot them up the following spring.

During the summer, mist-spray the cuttings frequently to stop them drying out. If the cuttings are in strong, direct sunlight they risk being scorched and it may be necessary to shade them; apply a greenhouse shading paint or place shading material over the frame (see p.576). Once the cuttings root, lift them out carefully with a hand fork and transplant them into individual pots, then harden them off (see p.637) before potting them on further or planting them out in open ground. Rooted cuttings in a cold frame may be hardened off while still in the frame by raising the frame cover for short then longer periods. Once they are well rooted, pot them up or transplant them outside. If there may be a delay before potting up, give a liquid feed to the rooted cuttings in the interim.

Softwood cuttings

This method of propagation is suitable for birch (*Betula*), *Metasequoia*, some ornamental cherries (*Prunus*), and a few other tree species, although it is more commonly used for shrubs. Softwood cuttings are taken in spring from the fast-growing tips of new shoots and usually root very easily. They wilt rapidly, however, so it is vital to prepare and insert them as quickly as possible after removing them from the parent plant.

Preparing and inserting the cuttings

In spring, before taking the cuttings, prepare containers by filling them with an appropriate compost and then firming to just below the rim. Take the cuttings by removing the new growth from stem tips, cutting just above a bud or leaf joint with secateurs or a sharp knife. To reduce any moisture loss, immerse the cuttings in water straight away or place them in an opaque, plastic bag and seal it. Even a small loss of water will hinder the development of new roots.

Prepare the cuttings by trimming them with a sharp knife to about 6cm (2½in), cutting just below a leaf joint. Remove the lower leaves. The base of each cutting can be dipped in hormone rooting powder to encourage rooting. Insert the cuttings into the prepared pots of compost, label them, and water them with a dilute solution of fungicide.

To encourage rapid rooting, place the containers in a mist unit or closed case at 21–24°C (70–75°F), preferably with basal heat, and water with a fungicide once a week to protect against rotting and disease. Once they are rooted, the cuttings may be hardened off gradually before they are transplanted carefully into individual pots.

PREPARING A SEMI-RIPE CUTTING

Cut a shoot 10–15cm (4–6in) long from a leader or sideshoot and trim immediately below a node. Strip off the lower leaves (here of Chamaecyparis obtusa *'Nana Aurea') and pinch out the tip if it is soft. Make a shallow wound, about 2.5cm (1in) long, down the side of the cutting and dip it in rooting hormone.*

Raising trees from seed

Tree species may be propagated from seed as their seedlings usually retain the distinctive characteristics of the parent plant; hybrids and cultivars rarely come true to type. Raising a tree from seed is a relatively simple process; it is, however, a slow method if a tree is being grown mainly for its flowers, as the tree will take a number of years to reach flowering size.

Extracting seed

The protective covering of some seeds should be removed first. The method for this varies, depending on the type of seed coat. The coating on winged seed may be removed simply by rubbing it between finger and thumb. Some cones disintegrate naturally and the scales may then be separated. Place pine and spruce cones in a paper bag and keep them in a warm, dry place until the cone scales open and shed the seed into the bag; immerse cedar cones in hot water and leave them to soak until the scales open.

The method of extracting seed from fruits or berries depends on the seed size and type of flesh. Large fruits, such as those of crab apples (*Malus*), may be cut open and the seeds extracted. Soak smaller fruits, such as those of *Sorbus*, in warm water for several days. Viable seed will sink in water; discard any floating seed. Pick the remaining flesh off viable fruits so the seed is clean.

Storing

Once the seed has been extracted, dry it if necessary and place it in a sealed and labelled plastic bag. If planning to sow the seed within a few days, store it at room temperature; for longer-term storage, keep it on the top shelf of a refrigerator so that it is cool but not frozen.

1 *Remove the fleshy seed with your fingers. Immerse it in warm water, and soak for 1–2 days. Once the fleshy coating has softened and split, drain off the water.*

2 *Pick off the remaining coating and wipe the seed dry. Sow the seed fresh or store it in a peat/vermiculite mix in a plastic bag in a refrigerator; sow in late winter.*

Breaking seed dormancy

Some seeds have a natural period of dormancy to prevent germination in adverse climatic conditions which would threaten the survival of the seedlings; this has to be overcome before the seed will germinate. Several kinds of dormancy occur, sometimes combined, which vary according to the species: most commonly, dormancy is achieved either by a hard, thick seed coat, which prevents water being taken up, or by a chemical inhibitor, which delays germination until there is a significant temperature change. In most cases, dormancy can be broken artificially by wearing away the seed coat or by chilling the seed.

Scarification

Before sowing seeds with an impermeable coating, scarify them to allow germination to occur: large seeds with a particularly hard covering, such as oaks (*Quercus*), may be nicked with a sharp knife, or a section of the seed coat filed away to let in moisture; smaller seeds that are not easily nicked, such as those of pines, may be shaken in a jar that has been lined with sandpaper or partly filled with sharp grit, or they may be filed individually with an emery board. Seed from legumes (for example *Acacia* and *Robinia*) should simply be left to soak in a container of hot water for approximately 24 hours in a ratio of 3 parts hot water to 1 part seed.

Stratification

Dormancy in seed of trees from temperate climates is commonly overcome by chilling or "stratification". Seed may either be sown outside so that it is chilled naturally during winter or, more reliably, stratified artificially by being stored in a refrigerator.

If refrigerating seed, first mix it with moistened vermiculite, peat substitute, or peat. Place it in a clear plastic bag, then seal the bag and put it in a refrigerator. Check the seed regularly through the unopened bag – it should be sown as soon as there are signs of germination.

The length of chilling time required varies considerably: as a guideline, many deciduous species require about six to eight weeks of chilling at 0.5–1°C (33–4°F), while conifers need only about three weeks. Some seeds only germinate after they have been sown and once chilling has ceased. In such cases, sow batches of seed at intervals – for example after four, eight, and twelve weeks of chilling – as this should ensure that at least some seeds germinate.

Sowing seed in containers

This is a simple way of raising a small number of seedlings. Thoroughly clean any work surfaces and containers to be used before sowing the seed to avoid contamination from soil-borne pests and diseases. First fill the pots, pans, or seed trays with seed compost up to the rim.

Large seeds or those that produce seedlings with long tap roots, such as oaks (*Quercus*), should be sown about 8cm (3in) apart in deep single or multi-celled seed trays, or in individual pots that are about 10cm (4in) deep. Using a presser board, press the seeds into unfirmed compost, then cover them to their own depth with compost and firm to about 5mm (¼in) below the rim (see p.81).

Sow very large seeds, for example those of horse chestnut (*Aesculus*), singly in 10–15cm (4–6in) pots. Insert the seed in firmed compost, so that just the top of the seed is exposed above the surface.

Small seeds, for example those of *Sorbus*, may be either scattered evenly or, if sufficiently large, individually pressed into prepared pots or trays of firmed compost. They should then be barely covered with sieved compost followed by a layer of fine grit 5mm (¼in) deep.

After sowing, thoroughly water all seeds from above, then label. Place the containers in a cold frame or,

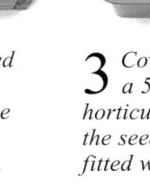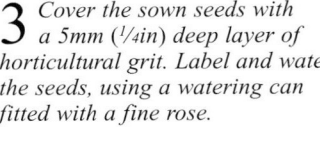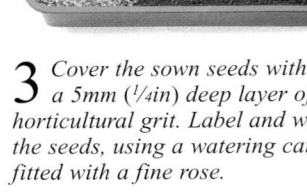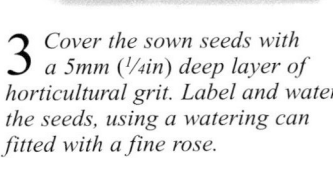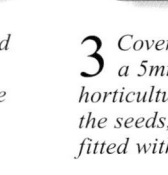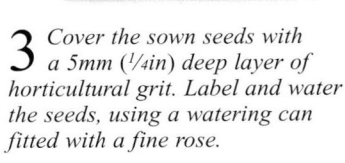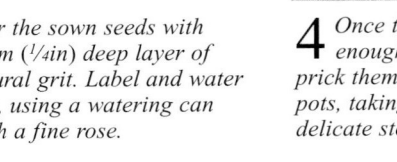

1 *Sow fine seed (here Sorbus) in containers of firmed seed compost, making sure they are scattered evenly; keep your hand low to stop the seeds bouncing.*

2 *Hold a sieve containing seed compost over the tray, then tap the side of the sieve until the seeds are just covered to their own depth with sieved compost.*

3 *Cover the sown seeds with a 5mm (¼in) deep layer of horticultural grit. Label and water the seeds, using a watering can fitted with a fine rose.*

4 *Once the seedlings are large enough to handle, gently prick them out into individual pots, taking care not to crush the delicate stems or roots.*

SOWING LARGE SEED

1 Press large seeds and those of trees with long tap roots into unfirmed compost in individual pots. Cover with compost.

2 Sowing in long Toms – deep pots – allows the tap root (*see inset*) of each seedling (*here* Quercus) *to develop without any restriction.*

within a greenhouse, in a closed propagation case or under a pane of glass. Temperate species are best kept at 12–15°C (54–9°F), and warm-temperate and tropical species at 21°C (70°F) to stimulate germination. Once the seeds have successfully germinated, spray them periodically with a fungicide to discourage damping off (see p.660).

Pricking out

When the seedlings are large enough to be handled by their seed leaves, prick them out so that they have more space to grow. This may be done by knocking the container sides to loosen the compost, and then lifting and transplanting the seedlings into individual pots. Alternatively, remove all the seedlings and compost together from the container so that the seedlings may be separated with minimal root disturbance. After transplanting, firm the compost gently around the seedlings, then level it by gently tapping the pot on the work surface.

Aftercare

Water and label the seedlings, and keep them out of direct sunlight in a temperature similar to that needed for germination until established. Gradually harden them off (see p.637) over a few weeks, feeding them regularly, and spraying them with fungicide. Do not overwater, but make sure that the compost does not dry out. Once hardened off, they may be planted out if there is no danger of frost.

Sowing seed outdoors

If raising a large number of seedlings, seed may be sown in an outdoor seedbed; with this method, the seedlings require less regular attention and their growth is less restricted than if sown in containers, but a special bed must be prepared. If possible, do this a few months before sowing by thoroughly digging the area to a spit deep (see "Single digging", p.619), incorporating organic matter and some coarse grit. Keep the ground clear of weeds.

When ready to sow, rake the soil down to a fine tilth, then broadcast small seeds or station sow larger ones individually. (For depth of sowing, see "Sowing seed in containers", p.80.) Lightly rake over the seeds, cover the bed evenly with a 0.5–1cm (¼–½in) layer of grit, and firm with a presser. If the soil is at all dry, water thoroughly; then label with the plant name and sowing date.

In exposed sites, young seedlings may need to be protected with windbreak netting (see p.613) or with a floating cloche (see p.582). If the seeds are well spaced, disease should not be a problem and the seedlings may be grown on *in situ* for 12 months before being pricked out. Water the seedlings as necessary and check them regularly in case treatment is needed for pests such as greenfly (see "Aphids", p.646) and red spider mite (p.646).

Layering

Layering may be used to propagate hybrids and cultivars as well as species. This method of propagation occurs naturally in some plants, when a low-growing stem roots itself in the ground; once this happens, the stem may be removed from the parent plant and grown on. Air layering, where the shoot remains above ground, may be used for trees without low-growing stems.

The advantage of layering is that the layered stem needs very little attention while the roots become established. It is a slow method, however, because in order to obtain

suitable material the plant must be prepared a year in advance and the layered stem may take a year or more to root.

Simple layering

In this method, a shoot is pegged down into the ground until it has rooted and is then cut off from the parent plant (see also *Propagating a Shrub by Simple Layering*, p.116).

Prepare the parent plant a year before layering is to take place: in late winter or early spring, prune a low branch to stimulate new, young shoots that will root easily. In early spring the following year, select a vigorous shoot and make a small wound 30–45cm (12–18in) from the tip. Brush this with hormone rooting powder to encourage rooting. Add plenty of leaf mould or similar organic matter and sharp grit to the soil where the shoot touches the ground and peg it down into a shallow hole, tying it to a vertical cane.

Backfill the hole and firm the soil well, leaving the shoot tip exposed, then water thoroughly and, if necessary, protect the shoot from rabbits and other animals with wire netting. About 12 months later, check to see whether the shoot has rooted; if it has, sever it from the parent and either plant it in open ground or pot it up; if it has not rooted, leave it in place and check a month later.

Air layering

The principle of air layering is the same as simple layering, except that the layered shoot roots above the ground rather than in it (see also *Air Layering a Shrub*, p.117). In spring, select a strong stem that has ripened in the previous year, and remove any leaves 30–45cm (12–18in) behind the growing tip. Prepare the stem either by cutting a tongue 5cm (2in) long in the bark, 22–30cm (9–12in) behind its tip, or by removing a 6–8mm (¼–⅜in) wide ring of bark from the stem at this point; in either case, brush the wound with hormone rooting powder.

SIMPLE LAYERING

Cut a 5cm (2in) tongue 30–45cm (12–18in) behind the tip of a vigorous shoot, or remove a narrow ring of bark at this point. Brush the wound with hormone rooting powder and peg the shoot into a shallow hole. Tie the shoot to a supporting cane and backfill the hole.

Vigorous shoot

Friable soil

Peg

Tongue

Surround the cut stem with a moist rooting medium and seal it in. To do this, first make a plastic sleeve by cutting off the sealed end of a plastic bag, then slide it along the stem until it surrounds the cut, and secure the lower end with string or tape. Moisten some well-aerated rooting medium (such as sphagnum moss or a mix of equal parts of peat substitute or peat and perlite), then use it to wedge open the tongue; add more medium around the stem inside the sleeve and seal the top.

If the layer has rooted by the next spring, sever the stem from the parent plant, remove the sleeve, and pot on; if not rooted, it should be left in place for another year.

TREE SEED REQUIRING STRATIFICATION

Acer (some)
Betula
Carya
Fagus
Sorbus

TREES TO BE LAYERED

Simple layering
Cercidiphyllum
Chionanthus retusus
Corylus
Davidia
Dipteronia
Eucryphia
Halesia
Hoheria lyallii
Laurus
Magnolia campbellii,
  M. grandiflora,
  M. obovata

Magnolia obovata

Air layering
Ficus ❀
Magnolia grandiflora,
  M. 'Star Wars'

KEY
❀ *Not hardy*

Grafting

Grafted plants, unlike cuttings, have the benefit of a developed root system so they establish relatively quickly. Part of a stem (the scion), taken from the plant to be propagated, is joined to a compatible rootstock of another plant, usually of the same genus. In some cases, the rootstock may confer a desirable characteristic, such as a particular growth habit or high resistance to disease, on the resulting plant.

Grafting methods include spliced side, chip-budding, apical-wedge, whip, and whip-and-tongue. For details of whip and whip-and-tongue grafting, see PRINCIPLES OF PROPAGATION, p.636. Check that the rootstocks and scions are compatible.

Spliced side grafting

This is the most common grafting technique used for ornamental trees; a one-year-old stem is used for the scion and grafted onto the side of the prepared rootstock. It is usually carried out just before leaf break, in mid- to late winter, although for maples (*Acer*) summer-grafting is sometimes more successful.

Prepare the rootstocks a year in advance by potting up one- or two-year-old seedlings in autumn and establishing them in an open frame. About three weeks before grafting, bring them into a cool greenhouse to force them gently into growth. Keep the stocks dry, particularly those from trees that "bleed" sap, such as birches (*Betula*) and conifers, as excessive sap may prevent successful union with the scions.

For the scions, collect strong, one-year-old stems from the tree to be propagated; they should have a similar diameter to the rootstock stems if possible. Trim them down to 15–25cm (6–10in), cutting just above a bud or pair of buds, and place them in a plastic bag in a refrigerator until ready to graft. Either cut back the top-growth of the stocks to about 5–7cm (2–3in) or leave some top-growth above the graft and cut this back in stages later (see "Aftercare", p.83).

Prepare the stocks and scions, one pair at a time, with compatible cuts. It is important to unite the rootstock and scion as soon as they have been cut; if they are allowed to dry out even slightly, this is likely to impede successful union. If the scion is narrower than the stock, align one edge to ensure that at least one side of the cambium layer unites. Tie the scion

TREES TO BE GRAFTED

Chip-budding
Crataegus
Laburnum
Magnolia
Malus
Prunus
Pyrus
Sorbus

Aesculus indica
'Sydney Pearce'

Apical-wedge
Aesculus
Catalpa
Cercis
Fagus

Spliced side
Abies
Acer
Betula
Carpinus
Cedrus
Cupressus
Fagus
Fraxinus
Ginkgo
Gleditsia
Larix
Magnolia
Picea
Pinus
Prunus
Robinia
Sorbus

Robinia
pseudoacacia
'Frisia'

Whip-and-tongue
Fraxinus
Gleditsia
Robinia

PROPAGATING TREES BY SPLICED SIDE GRAFTING

1 *Trim the scion to a length of 15–25cm (6–10in), cutting just above a bud or pair of buds. Place it in a plastic bag and refrigerate until ready to graft.*

2 *Using a sharp knife, make a short, downward, inward nick about 2.5cm (1in) from the top of the rootstock.*

3 *Starting near the top of the stock, make a sloping, slightly inward cut down to meet the inner point of the first cut. Remove the resulting sliver of wood.*

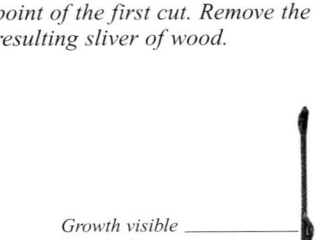

4 *Make the final cut on the stock by slicing straight up with the knife from the first cut below. This leaves a flat cut on one side of the stock (see inset).*

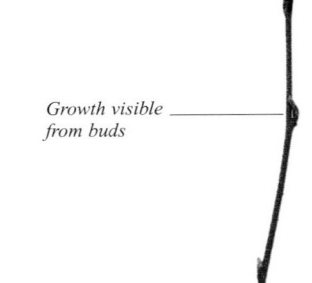

5 *Now prepare the scion: make a shallow, sloping cut about 2.5cm (1in) long down to the base; then make a short, angled cut at the base, on the opposite side (see inset).*

6 *Fit the base of the scion into the cut in the rootstock (see inset). Starting at the top, wrap a length of grafting tape around the union to secure it.*

7 *Brush grafting wax over the external cut surfaces on both the stock and the scion. In addition, wax the top of the scion if it has been trimmed back.*

Growth visible from buds

8 *A few weeks later, if the graft has taken, the buds of the scion will show signs of growth. Remove any suckers that may have appeared on the rootstock or they will divert growth away from the scion.*

in position with clear plastic grafting tape, raffia, or a rubberized strip, then wax over all external cut surfaces to reduce moisture loss. For advice on aftercare, see right.

Chip-budding

Mainly used for fruit trees, this is also a good way to propagate magnolias and plants of the Rosaceae family, for example crab apples (*Malus*). In this method, the scion contains a single bud from which the new growth develops, and the rootstock on which the scion is to be grafted is grown outdoors rather than potted up.

During winter, establish one- or two-year-old seedlings or hardwood cuttings in open ground. These will be used for the rootstocks. In midsummer, remove any lateral branches from the bottom 45cm (18in) of the stem. Select vegetative (non-flowering) shoots as scions (or budsticks) from well-ripened, current season's growth that are of a similar diameter to the rootstock.

The rootstocks and budsticks are then prepared and united (see below). If successful, the graft should unite within a few weeks; the tape or tie may then be removed. For aftercare, see right.

Apical-wedge grafting

This grafting method is similar to spliced side grafting, except that the scion is placed directly on top of the rootstock. In mid-winter, collect some stems of the previous season's growth from the plant to be propagated, and heel them into the ground. In late winter or early spring, lift and wash one-year-old seedlings or vigorous plants for the rootstocks, then cut them back to 5cm (2in) above the roots. Make a vertical cut 2.5–3cm (1–1¼in) down the centre of each rootstock. Cut the base of each scion into a wedge, and insert them into the tops of the stocks; leave the top of the cut on the scion exposed. Bind and pot up the grafted plants, then follow the aftercare guidance given below (see also ORNAMENTAL SHRUBS, "Apical-wedge grafting", p.119).

Aftercare

Deciduous trees should be kept in a greenhouse at 10°C (50°F), while conifers, broadleaved evergreens, and summer-grafted trees should be kept in a closed case in a humid environment at 15°C (59°F). The graft should unite in a few weeks and new growth will be seen on the scion. For even quicker results, place the grafted plants in a hot pipe (see PRINCIPLES OF PROPAGATION, "Hot-air grafts", p.637). Pinch off any suckers below the union as these are growing from the rootstock. After six to ten weeks, harden off the grafted plants. If not cut back at grafting, reduce top-growth of the rootstock to within 10cm (4in) of the union.

Tie the growing bud to the remaining top of the rootstock to ensure that the new shoot grows straight. In mid-summer, cut back the rootstock to just above the union and tie in the new shoot to a supporting cane. Alternatively, the stock may be cut back to just above the union in late spring. Once they are starting to grow vigorously, pot on the grafted trees or transplant them into open ground.

PROPAGATING TREES BY CHIP-BUDDING

1 *Select and cut the budstick (here* Malus*), choosing a long, vigorous shoot of the current season's ripened wood. It should have well-developed buds and be roughly the thickness of a pencil.*

2 *Cut off the soft wood and strip away any leaves at the tip of the shoot.*

3 *Using a sharp knife, make the first cut 2cm (³⁄₄in) below a healthy bud, inserting the blade about 5mm (¹⁄₄in) deep at an angle of approximately 45°.*

4 *Start making a second cut about 4cm (1¹⁄₂in) above the first. Cut down through the wood to meet the first cut, taking care not to damage the bud.*

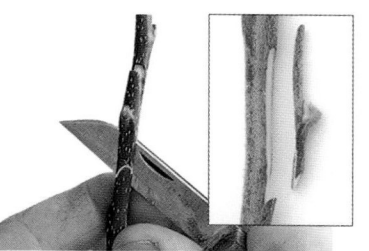

5 *Remove the bud chip, holding it by the bud between finger and thumb to keep the cambium layer clean. Place it in a clean plastic bag to prevent it from drying out.*

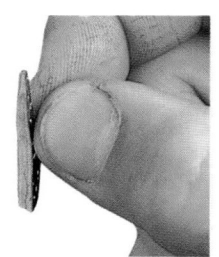

6 *To prepare the rootstock, cut off all the shoots and leaves from the bottom 30cm (12in) of the stem; it is easiest to do this while standing astride the stock.*

7 *Make two cuts in the rootstock to correspond with those on the bud chip so that the stock can be united with the chip. Remove the resulting sliver of wood, taking care not to touch the stem's cut surface (see inset).*

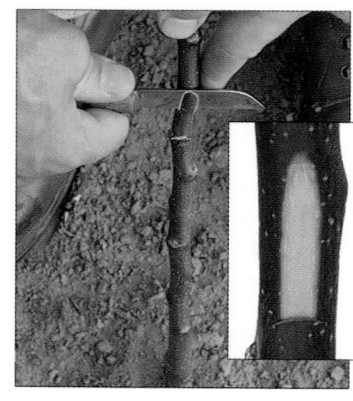

8 *Place the bud chip into the "lip" of the cut rootstock, so that the cambium layers of the chip and stock match as closely as possible (see inset). Bind the join tightly with grafting tape. If the graft takes, the bud will start to swell and develop; the tape can then be removed.*

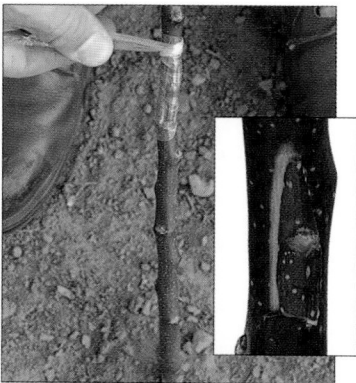

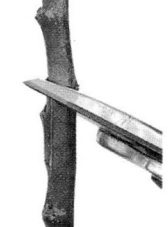

9 *Next spring, cut back the stock just above the union; the bud will develop as the leader.*

Hedges and screens

HEDGES and screens, both formal and informal, can play an important role in the structure and character of a garden as well as having a variety of practical uses.

Practical uses

Most hedges, whether informal, open hedges or formal, solid, clipped ones, are planted for utilitarian purposes, to delineate boundaries, to provide shelter and shade, and to screen the garden. It is possible, however, to combine use with beauty.

Living barriers

As living barriers, hedges may take some years to establish, but, if properly maintained, they are often preferable to fences because they provide texture, colour, and shape. Most plants used for hedging are long-lived and if correctly maintained will provide effective and sometimes virtually impenetrable barriers for many years.

Shelter

Hedges make excellent windbreaks, filtering fast-moving air and reducing the impact caused by turbulence when wind hits a solid object such as a wall or fence. The porosity of a hedge varies between species and times of year; thus a close-clipped, evergreen yew hedge (*Taxus baccata*) will be considerably less porous than a deciduous beech hedge (*Fagus sylvatica*) during winter. At the ideal of 50 per cent porosity it has been calculated that with a 1.5m (5ft) hedge, wind speed is reduced by 50 per cent at a distance of 7.5m (24ft) from the hedge; by 25 per cent at a distance of 15m (50ft); and by 10 per cent at a distance of 30m (100ft). The shelter provided by hedges is invaluable, particularly in windswept gardens where even hardy plants may suffer damage from gales and strong winds.

Noise barriers

Hedges may contribute to noise reduction by screening out unwelcome sounds. One of the most effective types in this respect is a green "environmental barrier", with a solid core of soil. A horizontal weave of osier (*Salix viminalis*) is threaded through vertical stakes and the core is packed with soil to form a wall. The osier roots into the soil core and the top and side growth is pruned back to the woven wall at intervals.

Ornamental hedges

A wealth of plants of diverse shape, size, texture, and colour can be used for hedges, deciduous or evergreen, formal or informal, or with flowers and fruit. Mixing evergreen and deciduous species selected for flower and foliage creates a living mosaic.

Formal

Yew (*Taxus baccata*) makes an excellent hedge, provided that six to ten year's are allowed for establishment, while a hedge of x *Cupressocyparis leylandii* grows extremely rapidly. Low formal hedges are frequently seen in parterres as well as knot gardens and topiary (see TOPIARY, pp.76–77). Various forms of box (*Buxus sempervirens*), especially 'Suffruticosa', are used widely for formal hedges, as are *Santolina* and *Lonicera nitida*. Tapestry or mosaic hedges combine a number of compatible plants within the same hedge line, to provide changing visual effects throughout the year. Species used include *Taxus baccata*, *Ilex aquifolium*, *Carpinus betulus*, and *Fagus sylvatica*.

Mixing evergreen and deciduous species provides an interesting and colourful background throughout the year. Species used must have similar rates of growth if over-vigorous species are not to dominate.

Informal

Informal hedges combine practical and ornamental qualities. Although they are not suitable for creating strictly formal designs, they can still provide effective screening and shelter. Many of the plants used in these informal boundaries produce attractive flowers and fruit, or both, contributing form and colour.

PLANTS FOR INFORMAL HEDGES

Pyracantha 'Golden Charmer'

Fuchsia magellanica

Escallonia 'Langleyensis'

Ilex aquifolium 'Madame Briot'

Rosa 'Roseraie de l'Hay'

Garrya elliptica 'James Roof'

FORMAL, CLIPPED HEDGES

HEDGING	APPROPRIATE PLANTING DISTANCE	HEIGHT	CLIPPING	RESPONDS TO RENOVATION
EVERGREEN				
Buxus sempervirens (box)	30cm (12in)	30–60cm (1–2ft)	Twice/3 times, in growing season	Yes
Chamaecyparis lawsoniana (Lawson cypress) – most cultivars except dwarf types	60cm (24in)	1.2–2.5m (4–8ft), but may be larger	Twice, in spring and early autumn	No
x *Cupressocyparis leylandii* (Leyland cypress)	75cm (30in)	2–4m (6–12ft), but up to 6m (20ft)	Twice/3 times, in growing season	No
Escallonia	45cm (18in)	1.2–2.5m (4–8ft)	Immediately after flowering	Yes
Ilex aquifolium (holly) and cultivars	45cm (18in)	2–4m (6–12ft)	In late summer	Yes
Lavandula (lavender)	30cm (12in)	45–90cm (18–36in)	In spring and after flowering	No
Ligustrum (privet)	30cm (12in)	1.5–3m (5–10ft)	Twice/3 times, in growing season	Yes
Lonicera nitida (honeysuckle)	30cm (12in)	1–1.2m (3–4ft)	Twice/3 times, in growing season	Yes
Taxus baccata (yew)	60cm (24in)	1.2–4m (4–12ft), but up to 6m (20ft)	Twice, in summer and autumn	Yes
Thuja plicata 'Fastigiata'	60cm (24in)	1.5–3m (5–10ft)	In spring and early autumn	No
DECIDUOUS				
Berberis thunbergii	45cm (18in)	60cm–1.2m (2–4ft)	Once, in summer	Yes
Carpinus betulus (hornbeam)	45–60cm (18–24in)	1.5–6m (5–20ft)	Once, in mid- to late summer	Yes
Crataegus monogyna (hawthorn)	30–45cm (12–18in)	1.5–3m (5–10ft)	Twice, in summer and autumn	Yes
Fagus sylvatica (beech)	30–60cm (12–24in)	1.2–6m (4–20ft)	Once, in late summer	Yes

Integrate the different colour backgrounds carefully into the overall design. *Cotoneaster lacteus*, *Berberis darwinii*, or *Forsythia* are often used; hybrid shrub roses and species also make fine informal hedges. Most strong-growing bamboos are suitable for areas where soil moisture is high and a wind filter is needed.

Choosing plants

Before selecting species for hedging consider their eventual height, spread, and speed of development, and ensure that species chosen are hardy within the climatic zone, and suited to the soil type of the garden. Plants for formal hedges must have a dense habit of growth, and be tolerant of close clipping. For informal hedges grown for their flowers or berries, choose plants that need pruning only once a year. The timing of pruning is critical, otherwise the next season's display of flowers or fruit may be spoiled.

The choice of evergreens or deciduous species is partly a matter of taste, but bear in mind that evergreens and conifers provide a dense, wind-proof screen throughout the year, offering protection which may be critical in severe winters.

Soil preparation and planting

Hedges are a permanent feature of a garden. It is therefore important to prepare the site thoroughly before planting, and to top-dress each spring with a well-balanced fertilizer and mulch. Young plants should be planted in a single row in a trench 45–60cm (18–24in) wide, while more mature plants require 60–90cm (24–36in) of prepared ground, depending on the size of the root ball. Double rows, 90cm (3ft) apart, are rarely needed, except possibly for stock-proofing purposes. Young plants are particularly vulnerable to drought, so lay a seep hose along the base of the newly planted hedge and water regularly when the plants are first establishing. Alternatively young hedging plants can be kept moist by planting them through landscape fabric or black plastic sheeting (see "Planting through sheet mulch", p.614). This will also help to discourage competitive weeds.

Aim to prepare the site a month or two before planting to allow the soil to settle. Work well-rotted manure into the bottom of the trench, and mix a general fertilizer with the soil when backfilling the trench.

At planting time, dig a trench rather than individual holes for bundled, bare-root hedging plants, such as mixed native species. For all other hedging plants, soil preparation and planting techniques are the same as for trees and shrubs (see pp.63–67 and pp.97–99).

Spacing for most hedging plants is 30–60cm (12–24in) – see the charts below. If a hedge 90cm (36in) thick or more is required, plant a double, staggered row with spacing of 90cm (36in) within the row, and 45cm (18in) between rows. Plants for dwarf hedges, parterres, and knot gardens should be 10–15cm (4–6in) apart.

Pruning and training

The initial training of a formal hedge is crucial to promote even growth from the base of the hedge to the top. Careful attention to pruning in the first two to three years is essential.

Early pruning and shaping

Most deciduous plants, especially those with a naturally bushy, low-branching habit, need to be cut back by one third on planting, with strong laterals also cut back by one third of their length. In the second winter, cut back again by about one third.

Leyland cypress

Leyland cypress (x *Cupressocyparis leylandii*) is an extremely vigorous evergreen conifer that, if treated correctly, can make an ideal tall screen or windbreak, often growing 45–60cm (18–24in) in a season. It has, however, gained a bad reputation when planted as a garden hedge, because its rapid growth is frequently allowed to continue unchecked. If not clipped back regularly, Leyland cypress will soon deteriorate and then, because it does not renovate well and remains unsightly when cut back hard, it will need replacing.

In spite of its vigour, Leyland cypress can be maintained very successfully as a garden hedge no more than 2–2.5m (6–8ft) high and 60–100cm (2–3ft) thick. In order to do this, in the first year after planting trim the sideshoots back to within 15–20cm (6–8in) of the main stems. In the following season trim back the sideshoots at least three times during the growing season, and if growth is vigorous probably four times. This treatment will produce very dense compact growth.

When the hedge has reached 30cm (1ft) below the height eventually required, cut back the leader shoots. Then prune back the sides and top of the hedge at least twice a year – in early to mid-summer and again in late summer to early autumn. Taper the sides so they slope towards the top of the hedge.

YEAR-ROUND COLOUR
x Cupressocyparis leylandii *cultivars produce contrasting shades of foliage in a mixed conifer hedge.*

INFORMAL AND FLOWERING HEDGES

HEDGING	ORNAMENTAL QUALITIES	PLANTING DISTANCE	APPROPRIATE HEIGHT	WHEN TO PRUNE
EVERGREEN				
Berberis darwinii	Yellow flowers, purple berries	45cm (18in)	1.5–2.5m (5–8ft)	Immediately after flowering
Cotoneaster lacteus	White flowers, red fruits	45–60cm (18–24in)	1.5–2.2m (5–7ft)	After fruiting
Escallonia	White, red, or pink flowers	45cm (18in)	1.2–2.5m (4–8ft)	Immediately after flowering
Garrya elliptica	Grey, green, red, or yellow catkins	45cm (18in)	1.5–2.2m (5–7ft)	Immediately after flowering
Ilex aquifolium	White flowers, berries	45–60cm (18–24in)	2–4m (6–12ft)	In late summer
Lavandula	Purple flowers, grey foliage	30cm (12in)	0.6–1m (2–3ft)	In early to mid-spring
Pyracantha	White flowers, red berries	60cm (24in)	2–3m (6–10ft)	For pruning, see p.109
DECIDUOUS				
Berberis thunbergii	Pale yellow flowers, red fruits, red autumn foliage	30–38cm (12–15in)	1–1.2m (3–4ft)	After flowering, if required to keep in check
Crataegus monogyna	Fragrant white flowers, red berries	45–60cm (18–24in)	3m+ (10ft+)	In winter, remove selected vigorous shoots
Corylus avellana	Yellow catkins	45–60cm (18–24in)	2–5m (6–15ft)	After flowering
Forsythia x *intermedia* 'Spectabilis'	Yellow flowers	45cm (18in)	1.5–2.2m (5–7ft)	After flowering, remove old stems
Fuchsia magellanica	Blue/red flowers, black berries	30–45cm (12–18in)	0.6–1.5m (2–5ft)	In spring, remove old stems
Potentilla fruticosa	Bright yellow flowers	30–45cm (12–18in)	0.6–1.2m (2–4ft)	In spring
Prunus spinosa cultivars	Pale pink or white flowers, red and purple foliage	45–60cm (18–24in)	2.5–4m (8–12ft)	In winter, remove selected vigorous shoots
Rosa 'Nevada'	Fragrant cream flowers	60cm (24in)	1.5–2m (5–6ft)	In spring, remove thin twigs
Rosa 'Roseraie de l'Haÿ'	Fragrant crimson flowers	45cm (18in)	1.5m (5ft)	In spring, remove thin twigs
Ribes sanguineum 'King Edward VII'	Deep pink flowers	30–45cm (12–18in)	1.5–2m (5–6ft)	After flowering, remove selected shoots

FORMATIVE PRUNING

BEFORE PRUNING
Leaders and laterals have grown unrestricted; the hedge (Lonicera nitida) needs formative pruning.

AFTER PRUNING
Cut back the laterals by half and prune the leaders to the required height to encourage bushy growth. Water, feed, and mulch if needed.

To shape strong-growing plants and those with an upright habit of growth, such as privet (*Ligustrum*) and hawthorn (*Crataegus*) cut them back to within 15–30cm (6–12in) above ground level in late spring, followed by a further clipping back of laterals in late summer. During the second winter or early spring, cut hard back, removing at least half of the previous season's growth.

Even from this early stage the hedge sides should be cut at a more or less oblique angle (referred to as the batter), with the base as the widest point. A hedge with a flat-topped "A" shape or a gently curved,

HOW TO SHAPE A HEDGE

1 *Stretch a taut, level string between two upright posts to act as a guideline for the highest point of the hedge, then cut the top of the hedge along this line.*

2 *Cut a template of the shape required. Place the template on the hedge and cut following the line of the template, moving it along as you proceed, then cut the sides.*

3 *Once you reach the end of the hedge, remove the template, posts, and lines of string. Clip the end of the hedge neatly.*

pointed top is less vulnerable to snow and strong winds. Snow will quickly fall away down the sides of a tapered hedge; high winds or gales will be deflected by its sloping sides, causing minimal damage to the plants.

A level top is achieved by cutting to a straight edge or garden line stretched between canes. It is important to use a guide when clipping low hedges too, since discrepancies are just as likely to occur when looking down as when viewing from eye level. Once the size and batter have been achieved, clipping to keep the hedge in shape is all that is required in subsequent seasons.

Conifers and many evergreens are used extensively as hedges. In most cases, laterals only are pruned during the early years, particularly in the formative second year, allowing the apical shoot to grow to the desired height before trimming back.

Maintaining a hedge
A formal hedge needs to be clipped regularly to maintain its shape: in most cases the hedge should be

SHAPING HEDGES

Make hedges narrower at the top to deflect strong winds and snow. In heavy snowfall areas, hedges should have pointed tops to prevent snow settling and causing damage.

 HORNBEAM
 YEW

trimmed twice annually, in spring and late summer (see *Formal, Clipped Hedges*, p.84). Most formal hedges are cut with shears or an electric trimmer. Use a straight edge or a garden line as a guide when trimming the hedge to shape.

Informal hedges also need regular pruning to shape. Remove misplaced growths, and cut back within the required bounds. Flowering or fruiting hedges must be pruned only at the appropriate season (see *Informal and Flowering Hedges*, p.85). Informal hedges and those with large evergreen leaves should, where practical, be pruned with secateurs to avoid unsightly damage to the leaves.

Renovation
A number of hedging species, notably hornbeam (*Carpinus*), honeysuckle (*Lonicera*), and yew (*Taxus baccata*), respond well to renovation even where hedges have been neglected and have become overgrown. For best results, deciduous hedges should be renovated in winter, and evergreen ones in mid-spring.

If drastic pruning is required, alternate sides should be cut back in subsequent seasons. If the renovation is to be successful, it is most important to feed and mulch the plants in the season before pruning, and then again after cutting back to encourage healthy new growth.

TRIMMING HEDGES

TRIMMING WITH SHEARS
To ensure that the top of the hedge is cut level and flat keep the blades of the shears parallel to the line of the hedge at all times.

CUTTING WITH HEDGETRIMMERS
When using an electrical trimmer, keep the blade parallel to the hedge and use a wide, sweeping action.

HOW TO RENOVATE AN OVERGROWN HEDGE

Cut back growth to the main stems on one side only of a neglected, deciduous hedge, trimming the other side as usual (right). A year later, if growth has been vigorous, cut back growth on the other side to the main stems (far right).

Willow walls

WEAVING with willow (*Salix*) stems has a long and distinguished history. Woven hurdles have been used for fencing since prehistoric times, and, when coated with thick layers of mud, clay, and dung, were a major building material in many parts of the world: wattle and daub.

Living willow, used as sculpture, is a new form of horticultural art. The contrast between the lines of the stems and exuberant, fresh young growth gives even functional items such as seats, screens, arbours, and arches an inherent sculptural quality, which many gardeners are becoming keen to incorporate into their own personal landscapes.

Suitable plants
The species or cultivar of willow must be matched to the size and nature of the proposed living structure. Vigour, physical strength, and aesthetic qualities are the main considerations. Most willows are flexible enough for weaving with the exception of the brittle *Salix fragilis*. Cultivars of *S. alba* are especially suitable, as their brightly coloured stems look spectacular in winter.

Preparation

Planting and weaving should be carried out in winter, when the plants are dormant. Willow can be inserted as normal hardwood cuttings of the current year's growth, about 38cm (15in) long and set 30cm (12in) deep, which are then allowed to grow on site, or as long rods that can be woven together immediately. Rods can establish just as successfully as cuttings provided the ground is well prepared, they are freshly cut, and are kept well watered. Another option is to use multi-stemmed plants, which are easy to develop from nursery-grown stock, hard-pruned to encourage the growth of two or more stems.

Plan the shape and height of the screen; it can follow a straight or curved baseline. Mark out the outline before planting, bearing in mind willows need bright light to thrive.

Work out how many rods of what length will be needed. Rods should be planted at least 15cm (6in) apart, and should be more widely spaced for tall screens using more vigorous cultivars. At 15cm (6in) apart, a 12m (40ft) screen would need 80 rods.

Weaving and tying

Once a row of evenly spaced rods has been planted, weaving can begin so an attractive diamond pattern is created. It is best to try and weave to the desired height in one go to keep the main lines straight. New shoots can be used to continue the structure upwards, but will not follow the original rods exactly. The weaving itself will hold the stems together to some extent, but crossing points should be tied firmly with tarred twine. For simple screens, tie only every third or fourth crossing point.

The twine will biodegrade over about two years, but grafts may form more quickly than this. Check the tied crossing points regularly, and, if the stems have united, remove the tie.

Where long rods have been planted, remove sideshoots as they appear, so growth is restricted to the stem tips. This will encourage extension growth and the formation of the pressure grafts. Once the stems have united, allow sideshoots to develop and use them to fill in as required, again weaving them over and under the main stems. When structures are established, trim back or weave in new shoots regularly.

Weaving horizontal and vertical stems to form a screen of squares is more difficult. Horizontal living stems cannot be established initially, as they would have to be bent through 90 degrees. Dead stems can be woven in as horizontals until the verticals produce sideshoots which can take their place, but the screen will take longer to establish. Training shoots horizontally also lowers their sap flow and reduces vigour.

More complex structures
The other main weaving technique, which is used to form arches and tunnels, is to bend and twist the stems around each other. The twisted stems need to be tied to hold them together. Extra stability is also provided by planting large rods deeper than 30cm (12in); this does not affect their ability to root successfully.

REGULAR MAINTENANCE
Although different willow cultivars vary in vigour, all living willow structures need pruning every winter and new shoots woven in. In summer shoots should be trimmed, but weaving should be avoided, because soft, new shoots are easily broken.

HOW TO SHAPE A LIVING WILLOW WALL

1 *Plant a row of evenly spaced rods. Then weave together by angling them at 45 degrees from the vertical and alternately crisscrossing over and under each rod.*

2 *Tie the crossing points securely with tarred twine. This will force the stems together as they expand and so unite their cambium layers, forming pressure grafts to hold the structure.*

3 *At the top of a screen, join the last row of crossing points with rubber plant ties. These allow the rods to move slightly in the wind and prevent their tops breaking.*

GREEN TRELLIS
Screens of living willow make excellent garden sculptures. They have even been employed on a scale large enough to shield whole villages from the sights and sounds of heavy traffic.

CHAPTER

3

ORNAMENTAL SHRUBS

VALUED BY GARDENERS for their architectural quality and long-term interest, shrubs play an important role in forming the skeleton of a planting design. In a mixed border, they provide solidity and substance, balancing the softer, more transitory herbaceous plants, while grouping evergreen and deciduous shrubs allows you to create an effective, low maintenance display all year round. As well as a diversity of shapes and forms, shrubs possess a magnificent variety of features: from the shiny, palmate leaves of *Fatsia japonica* or the heavily perfumed plumes of lilacs, to the bead-like berries of pyracanthas or the icy white stems of *Rubus biflorus*. Whatever the size or situation, there is a shrub to suit every garden.

Shrubs for the garden

SHRUBS are woody-stemmed plants that typically produce a framework of branches from the base, unlike the single trunk characteristic of most trees. The division between shrubs and trees is not a rigid one, however, as some shrubs (such as fuchsias) may be trained as standards with a single trunk and a number of trees are multi-stemmed. Similarly, the difference in scale is not a clear demarcation, as some shrubs grow larger than some trees.

Whether the term "shrub" is used very strictly or rather more loosely, it covers an enormous choice of plants suitable for gardens of any size and style. Species have been collected from many parts of the world and these have given rise to numerous cultivars and hybrids of ornamental value.

Choosing shrubs

Shrubs are invaluable in the garden for many reasons; perhaps most important of all, they impart shape, structure, and substance to a design, and provide a framework. They are far from being purely functional keystones, however, for they are also endowed with a variety of ornamental qualities, including fragrant and colourful flowers, evergreen or variegated foliage, attractive fruits, and coloured or shapely stems.

These decorative attributes exert great influence on your choice of plants. There are, however, important practical considerations to be taken into account when deciding which shrubs to grow.

INFORMAL PLANTING
In this garden, an informal grouping of shrubs, including a variegated holly (Ilex aquifolium)*, the fiery* Euonymus alatus, *and a tall* Aesculus parviflora, *provide an effective display of contrasting colours and shapes.*

Compatibility with the given or adapted growing conditions is essential (see "Selecting shrubs for site conditions", p.91), while a shrub's growth rate, habit, and eventual height and spread also determine whether it is suitable for a garden or not and where it is best sited.

Form and size
In size, shrubs range from dwarfs, such as the mat-forming *Cotoneaster salicifolius* 'Gnom' at only 20–30cm (8–12in) tall, which are suitable for the rock garden, to much more substantial plants that are 5–6m (15–20ft) tall, such as some of the handsome, evergreen rhododendrons.

Shrubs have many different forms and habits, including rounded, arching, and vertical. Some – for example *Yucca gloriosa*, with its explosive spray of sword-like leaves and erect panicles of flowers – are worth growing for their form alone. Others, such as *Chaenomeles japonica*, have a sprawling habit that often looks better if wall-trained. Most are

invaluable in low-maintenance gardening, especially low-growing shrubs used as ground cover, surrounded by bark or gravel mulches.

Shrubs as design features

When selecting shrubs, consider how they will associate with the other planting as well as any structural elements nearby, such as the house or patio. If they are to form part of the design framework, shrubs with distinctive, sculptural silhouettes are usually most suitable – for example the spreading, wave-like form of *Juniperus squamata* 'Blue Carpet' or the bold, upright mass of *Mahonia* x *media*. Think of them as abstract shapes that may be used singly or in combination to create a balanced scheme of contrasting and complementary forms.

Foundation planting
Shrubs are often used as foundation planting to link the house with the garden, forming a transition between the rigid lines of the building and the softer shapes and textures of border plants and lawn.

This type of planting is effective when used to mark the entrance to the house; symmetrical groups or rows of shrubs could flank the drive or the doorway, for example, or an informal curved bed might border a winding path to the door.

Design the planting so that it complements the style, colour, and scale of the building. Evergreen shrubs are often chosen because of their continuous display but, in an informal setting especially, including deciduous plants as well creates a greater variety of interest while still providing mass and structure.

Selecting shrubs for site conditions

To ensure that shrubs flourish and give pleasure for a long time, it is essential to invest in plants that will thrive in the particular conditions of your garden. Even within a small garden, these growing conditions often vary considerably. Since there are so many shrubs from which to make a selection, there is no need to grow plants that are unsuited to the chosen site.

Soil types
The character of the soil should be the first consideration; in many cases, it may be improved to widen the range of plants that can be grown satisfactorily. It is particularly important to make heavy soils more open and free-draining and light soils more moisture-retentive, as well as to

moderate any excessive acidity or alkalinity that may be a problem.

Successful planting must take into account the soil's underlying character, however. Even for relatively extreme conditions, there is a number of plants from which to choose: dogwoods (*Cornus*) and willows (*Salix*) like moist soils, for example, while broom (*Cytisus/ Genista*), lavender (*Lavandula*), and *Phlomis* thrive on well-drained soils. Rhododendrons and other ericaceous plants generally require acidic conditions; but many shrubs do well on alkaline soils, including *Deutzia*, *Hypericum*, and *Philadelphus*.

If a chosen planting site has only recently been cleared of weeds, plant the shrubs through holes in geotextile or black plastic sheeting, which will keep down competitive weeds until the shrubs are established (see "Planting through sheet mulch", p.614).

Aspect and microclimate
A plant's preference for sun or shade should also be borne in mind. Sunlovers such as *Cistus* will become drawn and straggly if not planted in full sun, but many shrubs tolerate or even prefer some shade. The latter

GROWING PLANTS IN THE RIGHT CONDITIONS
Light shade from the overhead tree canopy and acid soil are ideal for these impressive banks of rhododendrons lining an informal grass path. Clashing shades have been boldly mixed to create a spectacular avenue of colour.

are often ideal for town gardens, where instead of dappled light filtering through the tree canopy there tend to be sharp contrasts between full sun and deep shade cast by surrounding buildings.

The hardiness of shrubs is another factor to consider. The temperature range, altitude, degree of shelter, aspect, and distance from the sea all affect the range that may be grown. The sea has a moderating influence on temperature, but salt-laden winds can damage many plants in gardens near the coast. There are, however, shrubs (such as most *Escallonia* and *Genista*) that benefit from the mild conditions and tolerate salt spray. Plants of borderline hardiness for the area that might well succumb if grown in the open garden are more likely to thrive as wall-trained specimens in a sheltered position.

Successional interest

When selecting shrubs, take account of the seasonal interest that they provide and whether it is continuous, as from evergreen foliage, or transitory, as from a burst of summer blooms. A shrub with a brief period of splendour is often best sited near one that reaches its peak shortly afterwards to create a changing but unbroken display.

Spring
As well as new, emerging leaves, shrubs bearing spring flowers are valued for the colour and vitality that they bring early in the year. Combine them to provide interest throughout the season – from the early *Salix hastata* 'Wehrhahnii',

with its bud-like, silver-grey catkins borne on deep purple stems, to the fragrant, white and pink flower clusters of *Daphne* x *burkwoodii* 'Somerset' in late spring.

Summer
The choice of summer-flowering shrubs is immense and, again, they are best combined to form a continuous display. Invaluable shrubs such as *Potentilla* 'Elizabeth' and *Syringa microphylla* 'Superba' deserve to be widely grown, since their flowering period often extends from late spring until early autumn.

Autumn
This is the season when many deciduous shrubs really come to the fore, with colourful foliage providing an eye-catching spectacle. Shrubs for autumn interest include *Euonymus alatus*, with its intense red leaves, and the various cultivars of *Cotinus coggygria*, with yellow, red, or purple foliage. Colour from berries, such as the yellow clusters of *Pyracantha* 'Golden Dome' or the shiny red fruits of *Cotoneaster* 'Cornubia', is also valuable.

Winter
Shrubs are vital elements in the winter garden, with a rich variety of features. Evergreen foliage probably makes the greatest contribution, providing bold masses of colour and texture. Flowers also play their part, however, with a choice ranging from the sculptural *Mahonia japonica*, with its spreading, yellow sprays, to the spidery, red flowers borne by *Hamamelis* x *intermedia* 'Diane', while other fragrant shrubs such as *Viburnum* x *bodnantense* may be

---

RECOMMENDED SHRUBS FOR ACID SOIL

Rhododendron 'Homebush'

Camellia x *williamsii* 'Donation'

Erica x *williamsii* 'P.D. Williams'

Eucryphia milliganii

Gaultheria shallon

Vaccinium parvifolium

Rhododendron wardii

Gaultheria mucronata 'Wintertime'

Zenobia pulverulenta

welcome. Less common are shrubs with ornamental stems, such as *Cornus sericea* 'Flaviramea', which has vivid, lime-green shoots.

Shrub borders

One of the most satisfactory ways of using shrubs in the garden is to grow them in a border on their own. From the large range available that will be suitable for the soil, climate, and site, a selection may be made that will give a succession of colour and interest throughout the year. The aim is to create a balanced design, taking into account the shape, form, height, and spread of each shrub, as well as its ornamental qualities and any seasonal changes in appearance.

The planting may rely almost entirely on a blend of foliage textures and colours, but other features may also play their part. Include shrubs with interesting shapes, for example, and others with colourful berries or stems to maintain interest throughout the year. Resist the temptation to rely on flowers, since their display may be impressive but transitory. By careful selection, however, it is possible to sustain a long succession of flowers in the shrub border.

Some shrubs may be regarded as long-term plants while others tend to mature and fade quickly. When planning a border, space out the long-term shrubs so that they will not need thinning or drastic pruning to keep them in check once mature. Fast-growing shrubs may also be included but they should be thinned as soon as they threaten to crowd out the core planting of shrubs.

Herbaceous perennials, annuals, and other plants may be interplanted initially, so that in the short term the shrub border might have similar components to a mixed border. Dense planting, including ground cover, may help to keep down weeds although mulching is advisable to reduce weeds and water loss while the plants are becoming established.

Mixed borders

The idea of a mixed border is to combine a framework planting of shrubs with a variety of herbaceous plants to reap the benefits of both. Its main advantage is that the shrubs provide long-term, sometimes year-round, interest and a background to a succession of other plants. As the shrubs provide height and structure, there is less need to grow tall perennials that require staking than in a traditional herbaceous border.

The mixed border may be designed to suit various settings. If it is situated next to a wall, the planting may include a combination of wall-trained and other shrubs at the back as well as climbers, other plants being introduced in loosely shaped niches between shrubs in the foreground. In an island bed, shrubs are normally used to form an irregular core at the centre, surrounded by other plants in clumps or drifts.

Managing a mixed border is sometimes more complex than caring for a shrub one, because the various plants have diverse needs. It is, however, one of the most effective ways of bringing together the wide-ranging qualities of different plant groups.

Specimen shrubs

Shrubs that are particularly attractive – perhaps because of their fine shape or a characteristic such as exquisite flowers or striking foliage – may be best planted as individual specimens, sited so that they can be seen from a number of viewpoints.

Suitable shrubs

Since a shrub grown in this way clearly stands out in the garden, it is important that its appearance warrants

RESTRICTED COLOUR BORDER
Here, a restricted colour scheme with a predominance of yellow, gold, and bright green creates a sunny, cheerful effect, with evergreen and deciduous shrubs including elders (Sambucus), *golden conifers, and* Euphorbia.

its prominent position. Shrubs with very shapely silhouettes are especially suitable, such as the dense, symmetrical cone of *Pittosporum* 'Garnettii', although a flowering shrub such as *Camellia* x *williamsii* 'Donation' would also be an impressive focal point.

When selecting a plant to be grown as a specimen, its long-term interest is an important consideration. In a large garden, a relatively short but magnificent display may be sufficient. A shrub occupying a prime spot in a small garden, on the other hand, needs to justify itself by contributing colour and form throughout the year or by having more than one interesting phase – flowers and good autumn foliage, for example.

Siting a specimen shrub

When deciding where to site a specimen shrub, ensure its size will be in keeping with its position in the garden and that it relates well to the overall design. Often the best location is as the focal point of a view from a main window of the house or at the meeting point of two vistas. The background is as important as the shrub itself; usually, a uniform texture and colour, as provided by a dense, evergreen hedge or the green swathe of a lawn, forms the most complementary foil.

There is, however, scope for experimenting with the positioning of specimen shrubs, particularly in combination with other garden features, such as a pool that creates appealing reflections. Before planting, roughly assess the effect of the shrub's scale and position in the design by substituting bamboo canes of the same height and width.

SPECIMEN SHRUB
In late spring and early summer, the spreading tiers of Viburnum plicatum 'Mariesii' are richly clothed with blooms but its unusual shape ensures its value as a strong feature throughout the year.

WALL-TRAINED SHRUBS
Growing a shrub such as this pyracantha against a wall enhances its display of ornamental, bright orange-red berries.

Wall shrubs

A border at the foot of a warm, sheltered wall is a prime site for many plants; although it frequently tends to be somewhat dry, if the plants are adequately watered, the conditions are suitable for various shrubs that might otherwise be too tender to grow elsewhere in the garden.

Training shrubs against a wall is often the best option for lax shrubs such as *Ribes speciosum* and *Forsythia suspensa* that make tangled growth unless supported. For a number of shrubs, it is the best way of displaying their ornamental features, such as the orange or red berries of pyracanthas. Some hardy shrubs, such as *Chaenomeles*, that may also be grown free-standing, look attractive wall-trained, and complement the unfussy background.

Sometimes no training is needed: shrubs such as myrtle (*Myrtus*) may simply be planted close to the foot of a wall for them to benefit from the warmth and shelter. Other shrubs such as *Buddleja crispa* do need training to flower well.

Dwarf and ground-cover shrubs

Planting low shrubs, such as many *Hebe* cultivars or *Daphne* 'Bramdean', in raised beds or containers makes it easy to enjoy them at close quarters, as well as providing structure and long-term interest in the planting scheme. On a large scale, use low-growing shrubs to balance against contrasting, rounded, or upright forms in beds and borders.

These shrubs are also excellent where interest is needed at ground level; *Helianthemum* cultivars and a vast array of colourful heathers (*Calluna*, *Daboecia*, and *Erica*) brighten up the front of a mixed border or soften the hard edges of a path.

Some spread into an attractive carpet that forms a fine foil for other planting. Those that are relatively fast-growing may be used as ground cover (see p.101). Ground-cover shrubs present one of the best solutions for sites such as steep banks that are difficult to cultivate; even in the unpromising, shady areas directly beneath trees, shrubs such as *Mahonia repens* and cultivars of *Euonymus fortunei* grow well.

Foliage

The substance and seasonal continuity of a garden depend to a large extent on foliage. Evergreen shrubs, in particular, hold the garden together all through the year. The leaves of deciduous shrubs – from spring growth to autumn leaf – also give a longer period of interest than most flowers.

COLOURFUL GROUND COVER
To create a colourful patchwork effect use harmonizing and contrasting low-growing shrubs. Here, massed heathers make a fine display.

Colour

Much may be made of foliage colour, which includes not only every shade of green but also silvers and greys, reds, and purples, as well as yellow, gold, and variegated forms. The boldest leaf colour effects, such as the yellow of *Choisya ternata* 'Sundance', the red of the young growth of some *Pieris*, or the white-splashed green of *Euonymus fortunei* 'Silver Queen', may be used in much the same way as flower colour.

Shape and texture

There are many other attributes of shrub foliage that are worth exploiting in an ornamental display. Large or distinctively shaped leaves such as those of *Fatsia japonica* are particularly striking, and changes of texture, from smooth and glossy to matt and felted, also provide satisfying contrasts.

Flowers

Ranging from the tiny, pea-like flowers of many brooms (*Cytisus/ Genista*) to the large, heavy panicles of lilacs (*Syringa*), there is an impressive diversity of shrub flowers.

Colour and form

Shrubs have flowers in every colour, with endless variations of each; for example, shades of pink range from the pale pinkish-white blooms of *Magnolia* 'Pinkie' to the crimson of *Rhododendron* 'Hinodegiri'.

Sometimes it is the sheer mass of flowers that appeals, as with the dense blue clusters of *Ceanothus* or the sprays of star-like, yellow flowers of forsythias, while other shrubs – such as the exquisite but short-lived flowers of *Paeonia suffruticosa* – seduce by the sumptuous beauty of their individual blooms.

In a large garden it does not much matter that a plant's star turn is only brief; in a small garden, this may be

ORNAMENTAL STEMS *An informal group of red-barked dogwoods (Cornus alba) forms a striking blaze of colour rising from a spreading mass of variegated Euonymus fortunei.*

FLOWERS FOR SCENT *Fragrant shrubs such as Euphorbia mellifera here are often best grown next to a path or patio so that their scent may be easily enjoyed. This white-flowered Carpenteria californica also benefits from the warmth and shelter of the wall behind it.*

a serious drawback, so consider a plant's form and foliage, too, if its floral display is very short.

Scent

While the appeal of some flowers lies largely in their colour and form, those that are scented give the garden another dimension. The flowers may be showy and also deliciously fragrant, as are many *Philadelphus*, or, like the minute flowers of *Sarcococca*, more muted in appearance but casting their fragrance through the garden in midwinter.

Berries

Berrying shrubs are valuable for sustaining colour from late summer into winter, and also for attracting birds. On evergreens such as pyracanthas, bright berries framed by green foliage make an attractive contrast, while those on deciduous shrubs such as *Viburnum opulus* are seen against a changing backdrop of autumn foliage followed by bare

winter stems. Orange and red berries are common, but there are other colours – from yellow *Cotoneaster* 'Rothschildianus' to pretty pink *Gaultheria mucronata* 'Sea Shell'.

Bear in mind that with some species of shrubs male and female flowers are borne on separate plants. Thus, satisfactory fruiting is only achieved when male and female plants are grown in proximity.

Bark and stems

In winter, the silhouettes of bare stems may be very striking. As well as their sculptural simplicity, some, such as dogwoods (*Cornus*), are strongly coloured while others, for example *Salix irrorata*, are overlaid with an attractive, glaucous bloom.

Group a few shrubs of the same type together to reap the benefit of their massed stems, or site a single fine specimen against a simple background. Imagine the brilliant red stems of *Cornus alba* 'Sibirica' offset by a plain, white wall, or the chalk-white skeleton of *Rubus biflorus* by a dark one.

The delicate tracery of fine stems is often overlooked unless it is highlighted by vivid colouring, but unusual shapes and heavily thorned or contorted shoots provide added interest. The bizarrely twisted stems of *Corylus avellana* 'Contorta' and *Salix* 'Erythroflexuosa' make them interesting curiosities to set against a plain wall or plants of more familiar growth pattern.

Many shrubs grown for their stems require regular pruning, because it is the new wood that is most effective (see "Coppicing and pollarding shrubs", p.107).

Shrubs in containers

Provided that they are watered and fed regularly, many shrubs adapt happily to life in containers: grown in this way, they make versatile as well as ornamental features. Use them as living sculptures to provide strong shapes and a framework to offset other planting. An evergreen shrub or dwarf conifer forms a fine centrepiece in a planter all year round, which may be complemented by bulbs in spring and colourful and trailing annuals in summer.

A container-grown shrub is particularly valuable in a small, paved garden, patio, or balcony. It may be used alone as an isolated specimen or combined with a changing display of other plants in containers. In a larger garden, a single, handsomely potted shrub may make a more striking focal point than a piece of garden statuary, for example. Container-grown shrubs may introduce a formal note simply, as a pair flanking a flight of steps or an archway, or, more elaborately, making a symmetrical framework or an avenue in grander schemes.

Selecting plants

The most suitable shrubs are those with a long season of interest. Good examples for containers include evergreen camellias and rhododendrons, which remain attractive even after their flowers have faded. For valuable foliage effects, consider the tender *Chamaerops humilis*, which has huge, palm-like, glossy fans, and conifers with their wide range of colours and textures.

Deciduous foliage can change from spring to autumn and, in the case of Japanese maples (*Acer palmatum*), an intricate pattern of delicate stems remains when all the leaves have fallen. Shrubs such as *Spiraea japonica* 'Goldflame', with its strikingly coloured leaves and heads of rose-pink flowers, often look particularly fine grown in an ornamental container.

Practical advantages

An advantage of growing shrubs in containers is that tender plants, such as *Nerium oleander* and palms, may be used to give the garden a Mediterranean or subtropical look in the summer, and then be moved to a protected site for winter. It is also an excellent way of including shrubs that would not otherwise tolerate the soil of the open garden: for example, given lime-free water and ericaceous compost, camellias and rhododendrons may be grown in pots or other containers even in chalky areas.

Planter's guide to shrubs

EXPOSED SITES

Shrubs that tolerate exposed or windy sites; those marked ✿ are not suitable for coastal sites

Arctostaphylos uva-ursi
Bupleurum fruticosum
Calluna vulgaris (and cvs)
Cassinia fulvida
Cistus, some ❀
Cordyline ❀
Cotoneaster (dwarf spp.),
    C. horizontalis
Elaeagnus angustifolia
Erica carnea (and cvs)✿
Escallonia
Euonymus fortunei
    (and cvs)
Fuchsia magellanica
    (and cvs)

*Fuchsia
magellanica*

Gaultheria shallon✿
Genista, some ❀
Griselinia, some ❀
Halimodendron halodendron
Hebe, some ❀
Hippophäe rhamnoides
Ilex aquifolium
Lavatera
Olearia, some ❀
Ozothamnus, some ❀
Phormium
Prunus spinosa
Pyracantha
Rhamnus alaternus
Rhododendron ponticum✿
Salix
Senecio, some ❀
Spartium
Spiraea
Tamarix
Ulex
Yucca, some ❀

SHELTERED SITES

Shrubs that prefer sheltered sites

Abelia floribunda ❀
Abutilon, some ❀
Acer palmatum (cvs)
Ardisia ❀
Banksia ❀
Beschorneria ❀
Bouvardia ❀
Brachyglottis ❀
Citrus ❀
Coprosma ❀
Datura ❀
Dendromecon rigida ❀
Euryops pectinatus ❀
Musa basjoo ❀
Nerium ❀
Rhododendron maddenii,
    R. Section Vireya ❀

WALL SHRUBS

Abelia, some ❀
Abutilon, some ❀
Acacia dealbata ❀
Azara, some ❀
Buddleja crispa
Callistemon, some ❀
Camellia, some ❀
Ceanothus, some ❀
Cestrum, some ❀
Chaenomeles
Colquhounia
Daphne bholua
Fremontodendron
Itea ilicifolia
Pyracantha
Solanum crispum 'Glasnevin',
    S. jasminoides ❀

AIR POLLUTION

Shrubs that tolerate polluted air

Aucuba
Berberis
Buddleja davidii
Camellia japonica (and cvs)
Cornus stolonifera
Cotoneaster
Elaeagnus
Euonymus japonicus
Fatsia japonica
Fuchsia magellanica (and cvs)
Garrya
Ilex x altaclerensis, I. aquifolium
Leycesteria, some ❀
Ligustrum
Lonicera pileata
Magnolia grandiflora
Mahonia aquifolium
Osmanthus
Philadelphus
Salix
Spiraea
Viburnum

DRY SHADE

Shrubs that tolerate dry shade

Aucuba
Cornus canadensis
Daphne laureola
Euonymus fortunei, E. japonicus
Fatsia japonica
Hedera, some ❀
Ilex aquifolium
Pachysandra

MOIST SHADE

Shrubs that prefer moist shade

Aucuba
Buxus sempervirens
Camellia japonica
Cornus canadensis
Daphne laureola
Euonymus fortunei, E. japonicus
Fatsia japonica

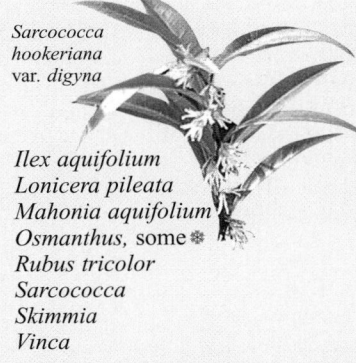

*Sarcococca
hookeriana
var. digyna*

Ilex aquifolium
Lonicera pileata
Mahonia aquifolium
Osmanthus, some ❀
Rubus tricolor
Sarcococca
Skimmia
Vinca

TWO OR MORE SEASONS OF INTEREST

All year round

Acacia baileyana ❀
Ardisia japonica ❀
Convolvulus cneorum
Elaeagnus x ebbingei 'Gilt Edge'
Euryops acraeus
Lavandula stoechas
Ozothamnus ledifolius

Winter/Spring

Berberis temolaica
Corylus avellana 'Contorta'
Salix irrorata

Spring/Summer

Calycanthus occidentalis
Pieris 'Forest Flame'

Spring/Autumn

Cornus 'Eddie's White Wonder'

Summer/Autumn

Citrus 'Meyer's Lemon' ❀
Cornus mas 'Variegata'
Cotinus coggygria 'Flame'
Cotoneaster conspicuus
Dipelta yunnanensis
Hydrangea quercifolia
    'Snowflake'
Lonicera korolkowii
Myrtus communis,
    M. communis
    var. tarentina

*Myrtus
communis*

Neillia thibetica
Phlomis chrysophylla
Pyracantha
Rosa 'Fru Dagmar Hastrup',
    R. moyesii 'Geranium'

Autumn/Winter

Arbutus unedo
Berberis temolaica
Cornus mas 'Variegata'

FRAGRANT FLOWERS

Abeliophyllum distichum
Buddleja alternifolia
Camellia sasanqua
Chimonanthus praecox 'Luteus'
Choisya 'Aztec Pearl', C. ternata
Clethra alnifolia 'Paniculata'
Colletia armata 'Rosea'
Cytisus battandieri
Daphne bholua, D. blagayana,
    D. cneorum, D. odora
Elaeagnus
Erica lusitanica
Hamamelis mollis 'Pallida'
Lonicera x purpusii 'Winter
    Beauty', L. standishii
Luculia gratissima ❀
Magnolia sieboldii,
    M. x thompsoniana
Mahonia japonica
Osmanthus delavayi
Philadelphus, many
Pittosporum tobira
Rhododendron auriculatum,
    R. edgeworthii ❀,
    R. 'Fragrantissima' ❀, R., Ghent
    hybrids, R., Loderi Group,
    R. luteum, R. occidentale (and
    hybrids), R. 'Polar Bear',
    R., Rustica hybrids, R. viscosum
Sarcococca
Viburnum (many)

*Rhododendron
luteum*

AROMATIC FOLIAGE

Caryopteris
Prostanthera ❀
Ruta graveolens
Santolina
Skimmia x confusa

ARCHITECTURAL SHRUBS

Agave ❀
Aralia elata 'Aureovariegata'
Chamaerops ❀
Cocos ❀
Cordyline ❀
Cycas revoluta ❀
Dracaena ❀
Eriobotrya japonica
Howea ❀
Jubaea ❀
Pandanus ❀
Phoenix ❀
Phormium
Sabal ❀
Yucca, some ❀

KEY
❀ Not hardy

Bamboos

BAMBOOS are evergreen, woody members of the grass family and have delicately handsome foliage and a graceful habit. They store their food in underground stems (rhizomes), from which both woody stems (culms or canes) and roots develop. The culms grow to their full height in one season, but usually take three years to mature fully. Culms produce new leaves each growing season, thus maintaining a fresh look. Most species grow without flowering for 20 years or more. After they have eventually flowered, however, they may be so weakened that they need replacing or cutting back to ground level.

Many bamboos are tropical but a considerable number are hardy in temperate regions. Some will grow 7m (22ft) tall, while others reach less than 50cm (20in). Their great diversity makes them invaluable in the garden: some bamboos make good specimen plants, others useful screens, hedges, or windbreaks; most will grow happily in containers. Some bamboos are reasonably docile and clump forming, others invasive.

General cultivation

Most bamboos will grow in sun or shade, and prefer humus-rich, moist but well-drained soil. The pH is not important. As bamboos are shallow rooted, their planting hole should be no deeper than 40cm (16in). Dig the site thoroughly and add bone meal and well-rotted manure, before planting the bamboo.

Never let bamboos dry out, especially when young, nor allow their roots to freeze. Container-grown ones should be kept frost free. Even hardy bamboos may occasionally be slightly frost damaged but they usually recover quickly in spring, provided there is sufficient water.

In spring, give an annual application of balanced fertilizer, at a rate of 50g/sq m (2oz/sq yd), a mulch of well-rotted manure, and a dressing of calcium silicate.

Restricting bamboo growth
Some of the best-looking bamboos are highly invasive. To keep them in their allotted space, insert a physical barrier into the soil, at least 40cm (16in) deep, around the root ball, and seal well at the join(s); then keep a careful watch and cut off any rhizomes that spread across the top of the barrier. Alternatively, a couple of times a year, insert a sharp spade right around the clump, then pull out any rhizomes that have strayed outside that cut line.

To reduce the vigour of low-growing bamboos, cut them to the ground in early spring. Such pruning will also make the plants look even more attractive as they will display only fresh new culms each summer.

Pests and diseases

Bamboos are particularly vulnerable to the bamboo spider mite – a sap-sucking insect that lives on the underside of leaves covered by a fine web. New plants should be inspected for dots and dashes (like Morse code) of longitudinal, yellow variegations on the leaves. To eradicate bamboo spider mite, remove and burn infected leaves; if necessary, spray with an acaricide that will kill these mites. Whiteflies (p.646) and red spider mite (p.646) will attack bamboo under glass but are not a problem outdoors. Aphids (p.646) are a nuisance on some species, and rabbits (p.666) and squirrels (p.659) may eat the new growth.

Pruning

Dead, damaged, or spindly culms and all those more than five years old should be removed at or very close to the base, in spring. Never partially shorten culms as this ruins their appearance. Loppers or a saw, and stout protective clothing, are often essential when pruning.

If a clump has become too dense and overwhelming for its position, it can be thinned in spring or late summer to let air and light into the centre. Thinning also displays well those species that have coloured stems, or those in which the young culms are the most attractive.

Propagation

Bamboo roots are sensitive to drought so choose a cool, overcast day for propagation to stop the roots drying out.

Tightly clumped bamboos can be increased by simple division in spring, when new growth is visible (see "Division", p.118). Spray water on divided plants regularly and liberally until they are established.

All bamboos can be propagated in spring by dividing their rhizomes. Lift a clump or part of one, and cut one or more rhizomes into pieces, ensuring that each has at least one growing shoot. Take care not to damage the fine roots. Insert the pieces into individual pots of a free-draining compost and cover the rhizomes to their original depth. Keep them cool and moist, and in good but not strong light until the plants are established.

PROPAGATING BAMBOOS BY DIVIDING RHIZOMES

1 *Dig around the clump to expose the outer rhizomes with new shoots. Separate these from the parent plant.*

2 *Cut the rhizomes, each with at least one shoot, into pieces. Dust the cut surfaces with fungicidal powder (see inset).*

3 *Pot up each piece with the rhizome just below the surface of the compost and the shoots exposed. Firm in and water.*

RESTRICTING THE SPREAD OF BAMBOO

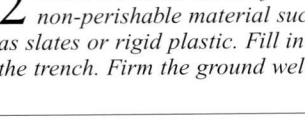

1 *Dig a narrow trench, deeper than the plant's root, all round the clump. Chop through and remove peripheral roots.*

2 *Insert a barrier made of non-perishable material such as slates or rigid plastic. Fill in the trench. Firm the ground well.*

THINNING ESTABLISHED CLUMPS OF BAMBOO

Wearing thick gloves and using loppers, remove weak, dead, and damaged culms, then cut out the oldest ones at the base until the desired effect is achieved. Then, without damaging new shoots, clear away debris at the base to relieve congestion further, let in light and air, and allow young culms to grow unchecked.

Soil preparation and planting

A wide range of shrubs can be grown in most gardens, even if the soil falls short of ideal – which is a fertile, well-drained but moisture-retentive loam. Improving the drainage of wet soils and, by the addition of humus, the structure and moisture-holding properties of dry soils greatly increases the range of shrubs that may be grown. The soil acidity or alkalinity, another factor limiting the range of plants that can be grown, may also be modified.

Important though these improvements may be, garden soil will still naturally tend towards being moist or dry, heavy or light, and acidic or alkaline. The best shrubs for your garden are those suitable for the growing conditions available.

Selecting shrubs

Shrubs may be bought direct from garden centres, nurseries, and non-specialist outlets such as supermarkets. Some nurseries also sell shrubs by mail order; plants are normally dispatched during their dormant period. They are sold in containers, root-balled, or bare-root.

Shrubs on sale should be accurately labelled, healthy, undamaged, and free of pests and diseases. When buying direct, inspect the plants thoroughly and select a specimen with evenly distributed branches close to ground level or, with standard shrubs, at the head of a clear stem of the desired height. Shrubs sold in the warm, dry atmosphere of a supermarket have a short shelf life. Reliable suppliers may give a year's guarantee to replace the shrub if it is not true to name or if it dies within the first year, provided that it has been given reasonable care.

Shrubs in containers
Shrubs are most commonly sold as container-grown specimens, the containers ranging from rigid pots to plastic bags. Most shrubs sold in this way have been container-grown throughout their lives. Some are field-grown and potted up (containerized) in the season before sale to prolong their sale life. The two are difficult to distinguish, although container-grown shrubs normally have better-established root systems (often visible through the drainage holes of the pot).

If possible, slide the shrub out of its container; the roots should show healthy, white tips and the root system, if well established, will retain all or most of the compost from

SELECTING A SHRUB
CONTAINER-GROWN SHRUBS
GOOD EXAMPLE

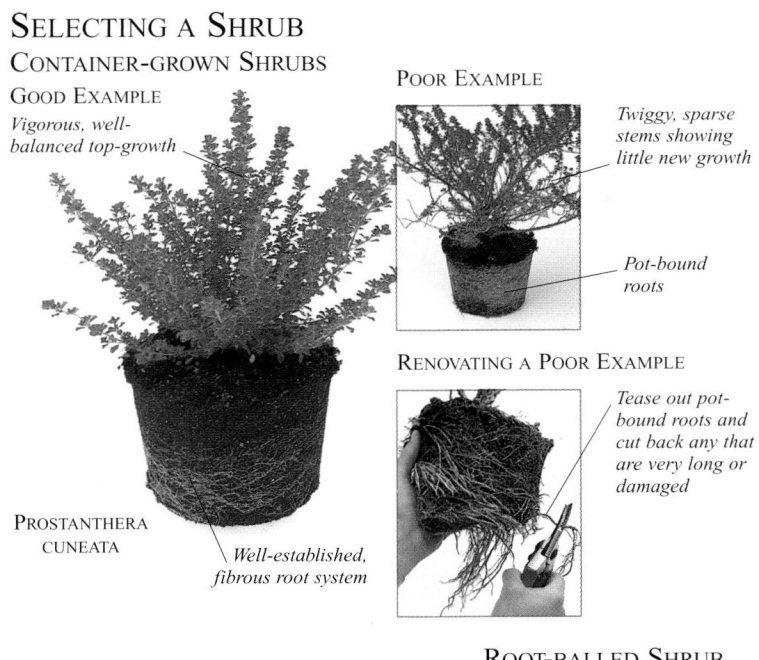

Vigorous, well-balanced top-growth

POOR EXAMPLE

Twiggy, sparse stems showing little new growth

Pot-bound roots

RENOVATING A POOR EXAMPLE

Tease out pot-bound roots and cut back any that are very long or damaged

PROSTANTHERA CUNEATA

Well-established, fibrous root system

GOOD EXAMPLE

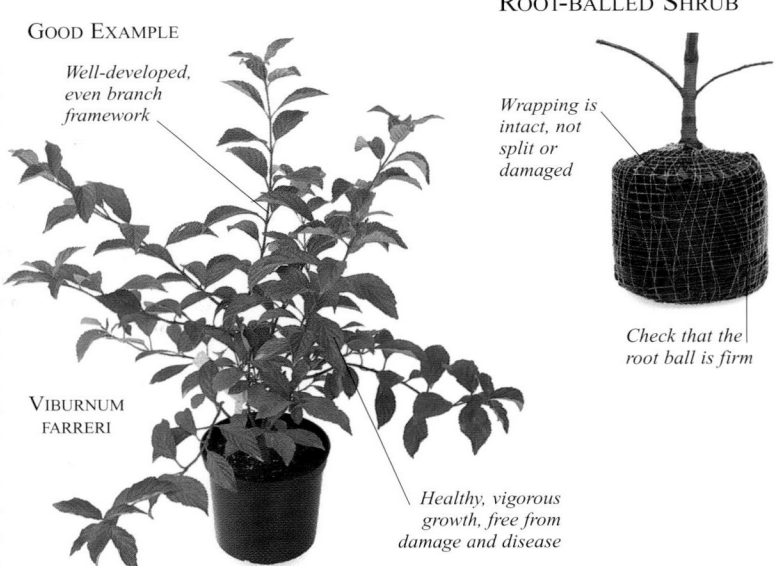

Well-developed, even branch framework

VIBURNUM FARRERI

Healthy, vigorous growth, free from damage and disease

ROOT-BALLED SHRUB

Wrapping is intact, not split or damaged

Check that the root ball is firm

the pot. Reject plants with poorly developed root systems and those that are pot-bound (with roots protruding from the container), since these rarely grow well.

A major advantage of container-grown shrubs is that they may be bought and planted out at any time, except when there are extremes of temperature or drought. Containerized shrubs can be safely planted out in winter, but at other times may be slow to establish unless they have a well-developed root system.

Bare-root shrubs
Deciduous shrubs that are easily propagated are sometimes lifted from the open ground during their dormant season and sold with their roots

bare of soil. The buying season for these bare-root shrubs is from autumn to spring. To prevent desiccation, they are normally heeled into the ground until they are sold. Before purchasing, check that bare-root shrubs have an evenly developed, fibrous root system.

Root-balled shrubs
These shrubs, usually available in autumn or early spring, have been grown in open ground, then lifted with soil around their root balls; the root balls are wrapped in hessian or netting. Conifers are often sold in this way. Always check that the wrapping is intact, as otherwise the roots may have been exposed to drying wind, and that the root ball is firm.

SHRUBS THAT PREFER SANDY SOIL

Berberis empetrifolia
Calluna vulgaris (and cvs)
Ceanothus thyrsiflorus
Cistus x *cyprius*
Clethra alnifolia ◆
Cytisus scoparius

Cistus x *cyprius*

Erica arborea, E. cinerea
Fuchsia magellanica (and cvs)
Genista tinctoria
Hakea lissosperma
Halimodendron halodendron
Helianthemum
Helichrysum, some ✳
Hippophäe
Lavandula, some ✳
Olearia, some ✳
Ozothamnus, some ✳
Phlomis
Phormium
Spartium junceum
Tamarix
Ulex europaeus
Yucca gloriosa

SHRUBS THAT TOLERATE WELL-DRAINED, CLAY SOIL

Amelanchier
Aralia
Aronia arbutifolia
Aucuba
Berberis

Chaenomeles x *superba* 'Nicoline'

Chaenomeles x *superba* (and cvs)
Cornus alba 'Sibirica'
Cotinus
Cotoneaster
Deutzia
Forsythia
Garrya
Hippophäe
Kalmia latifolia
Lonicera, some ✳
Mahonia x *media*
Philadelphus
Potentilla
Pyracantha
Salix caprea
Sambucus racemosa
Spiraea
Taxus
Viburnum opulus
Weigela

KEY
✳ *Not hardy*

When to plant

Autumn to spring is the planting season for bare-root and root-balled shrubs, and the optimum time for container-grown shrubs; however, those of borderline hardiness should be planted in spring. Autumn planting allows the roots to establish while the ground is still warm, so the shrub should be growing vigorously before dry weather the next summer.

Planting may be carried out during mild weather in winter, but not when the ground is frozen. Roots will not grow away in very cold soil, and there is a risk that they may freeze and be killed.

The major disadvantage of spring planting is that top-growth is likely to develop before the roots establish and, if there is an early spell of dry weather, watering may be required to help the plants survive.

Soil preparation

Many shrubs are potentially long-lived, so the ground needs to be thoroughly prepared before planting. The aim should be to cultivate an area well beyond the planting site for an individual shrub and, preferably, the entire bed.

The best seasons for cultivation are late summer and autumn. Remove or kill all weeds first, taking care to eradicate perennials (see "Weeds", pp.669–673). Double dig (see p.620), incorporating an 8–10cm (3–4in) layer of well-rotted organic matter into the lower trench. If this is impractical, work large quantities of organic matter into the top 30–45cm (12–18in) of soil. Add fertilizer if appropriate (see "Soil nutrients and fertilizers", pp.624–625).

How to plant

The planting hole for a shrub must be wide enough to accommodate the shrub's root ball. For container-grown or root-balled plants, make the hole twice the width of the contained root mass, or as much as three times the width if planting in clay soils. For bare-root shrubs, the hole must be large enough to allow the plant's roots to be spread out fully. The hole must also be sufficiently deep to allow the shrub to be planted at the same level as it was in its container or in the open ground. This is indicated by the soil mark – a dark mark near the base of the stem. A cane laid across the top of the planting hole provides a useful guide to the depth of planting. Treatment of a containerized shrub depends on how developed the root system is when removed from the pot. If the compost falls away, plant as for a bare-root shrub; if it does not, treat as if container-grown. Tease out the root system if at all rootbound. Remove the hessian or netting surrounding a root-balled shrub after it is in the hole. When backfilling the hole, shake a bare-root plant gently to settle the soil. Firm the soil in stages but do not compact clay soils.

PLANTING A WALL SHRUB

1 Dig a hole at least 22cm (9in) away from the wall. Plant the shrub (here a pyracantha) and tie in the supporting cane to a wire.

2 Firm back the soil. Secure lateral bamboo canes to the central cane and to the wires, so that the sideshoots can be supported and tied in (see inset).

PLANTING A CONTAINER-GROWN SHRUB

1 Dig a hole about twice the width of the shrub's root ball (here a Viburnum). Mix the removed soil with organic matter. Fork over the base and sides of the hole.

2 Placing one hand on top of the compost and around the shrub to support it, carefully ease the plant out of its container. Place the shrub in the prepared hole.

3 Lay a cane alongside to check that the soil level is the same as before. Adjust the planting depth, if necessary, by adding or removing topsoil beneath the shrub.

4 Backfill around the shrub with the removed soil and organic matter mixture, firming the soil in stages to prevent air pockets from forming.

5 Once the hole has been filled with the planting mixture, carefully firm the soil around the shrub with your heel or hands.

6 Prune any diseased or damaged wood back to healthy growth and cut back any inward-growing or crossing stems to an outward-growing shoot or bud. You should also remove any very long, weak, or straggly stems, or those that spoil the overall balance of the shrub's framework.

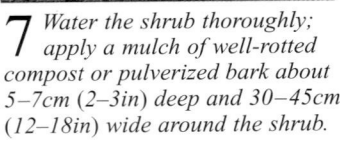
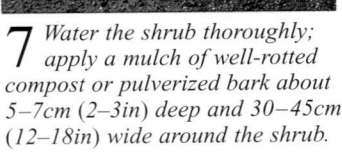
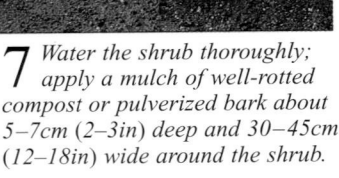
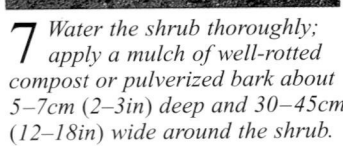

7 Water the shrub thoroughly; apply a mulch of well-rotted compost or pulverized bark about 5–7cm (2–3in) deep and 30–45cm (12–18in) wide around the shrub.

To improve drainage around shrubs to be grown in clay soils, plant the shrub slightly proud of the soil level and mound soil around the exposed section of the root ball up to the level of the soil mark. On sandy soils, plant the shrub in a slight dip to channel water around the plant's roots. Water the shrub and mulch.

Planting wall shrubs

Some shrubs may be trained on wires fixed to a wall or fence. Plant these at least 22cm (9in) from the wall, leaning the plant in towards the wall. Support the main stem and laterals of the shrub with canes, which are then tied into the wires (see also "Wall shrubs", p.108).

Staking

Shrubs do not normally need staking, except for large, root-bound specimens and standards. The former, which ideally should not be selected, will almost certainly need some support in their first year or two at least, until their roots begin to spread out and they become stable.

The best method for any shrub that branches from near ground level is to brace the shrub with guys fixed to three stakes spaced evenly around a circle with a radius of about 1m (3ft) centred on the shrub. To prevent bark damage, cover the guys where they touch the branches with rubber or similar material (see also ORNAMENTAL TREES, "Staking", p.64).

For standards, insert the stake in the planting hole before planting to avoid damaging the root system. The top of the stake should be just below the first branches. Secure the stem to the stake, using a proprietary tie with a spacer or a homemade figure-of-eight tie to prevent chafing.

STAKING A STANDARD SHRUB

1 *Drive a stake into the hole just off-centre; the top of the stake should be just below the head of the shrub after planting. Plant the shrub next to the stake.*

2 *If the depth is correct, backfill and firm in. On free-draining soil, form a dip around the shrub to retain moisture. Secure the stem with a suitable tie (see inset).*

Protecting newly planted shrubs

Newly planted shrubs may suffer from desiccation or cold if not protected. Broadleaved evergreens and conifers in exposed positions are particularly vulnerable.

A screen of hessian or mesh significantly reduces the drying force of cold winds. Erect a strong, wooden framework 30cm (12in) away from the windward side of the shrub needing protection. Tack the hessian or the mesh to the frame, which should extend at least 30cm (12in) above and either side of the shrub. More complete protection is given by surrounding individual plants with a four-sided framework to which hessian or mesh is tacked.

Another measure, which may be used either alone or in addition to screening, is to spray the plants with an anti-desiccant product, to reduce water loss. Apply a thin film of spray to both sides of the leaves.

A mulch spread around the base of the shrub will help to protect the roots from ground frost. It is best to spread the mulch during periods of mild weather, preferably when the ground is reasonably warm and damp.

In areas of heavy snow, particularly vulnerable, evergreen shrubs may need additional protection. This is best provided by a timber and chicken wire cage. Dislodge any heavy accumulations of snow promptly. More extreme measures may be needed to protect half-hardy and tender shrubs (see FROST AND WIND PROTECTION, pp.612–613).

When removing the insulation in spring, check for pests and diseases that may have benefited from the winter protection.

Planting shrubs in containers

Late summer to autumn is the main period for planting shrubs in containers (see also CONTAINER GARDENING, "Shrubs", p.316). When transplanting a shrub, the new container should be 5cm (2in) larger in depth and diameter than the previous one. If using an old container, scrub its inside surface thoroughly before filling.

Heavy containers should be placed in position before planting. Stand the container on bricks or blocks to allow free drainage. Place broken crocks over the drainage holes and then add a 2.5cm (1in) layer of drainage material, such as coarse gravel.

A loam-based compost, which is nutrient-rich, is preferable to a peat-based one, which contains only limited, added nutrients and dries out more rapidly. Shrubs grown in peat-based composts will therefore require frequent feeding. Use an ericaceous compost for rhododendrons and other lime-haters, or to obtain blue flowers on hydrangeas. After placing the plant in the pot, spread its roots out evenly and work compost round them. Ensure that the soil mark is level with the compost surface. Top-dressing the compost with a covering of grit or bark chippings ensures the compost does not form a crust. Such a mulch also looks decorative.

With container planting, ensure that the compost is at least 4cm (1¹/₂in) below the rim to allow room for mulching and watering.

SHRUBS THAT REQUIRE ACID SOIL

Andromeda
Arbutus (most spp.)
Arctostaphylos, some ❀ (some spp.)
Calluna
Camellia, some ❀

Camellia x *williamsii*
'Wilber Foss'

Clethra, some ❀
Cornus canadensis
Corylopsis (most spp.)
Desfontainia spinosa
Enkianthus
Erica (most spp.)
Fothergilla
Gaultheria
Hakea, some ❀
Kalmia
Leucothöe
Menziesia
Philesia magellanica ❀
Pieris
Rhododendron, some ❀ (most spp.)
Styrax officinalis
Telopea speciosissima ❀
Vaccinium
Zenobia pulverulenta

SHRUBS THAT TOLERATE VERY ALKALINE SOIL

Aucuba japonica (and cvs)
Berberis darwinii
Buddleja davidii (and cvs)
Buxus
Chamaerops ❀
Choisya ternata
Cistus, some ❀
Cotoneaster
Cytisus, some ❀
Deutzia
Euonymus
Forsythia
Hebe, some ❀
Hibiscus, some ❀
Hypericum, some ❀
Ligustrum
Lonicera, some ❀
Nerium oleander ❀
Philadelphus
Phlomis fruticosa
Photinia

Philadelphus
'Dame Blanche'

Potentilla
(all shrubby spp.)
Rosa rugosa
Rosmarinus
Senecio
Syringa
Viburnum tinus
Vitex agnus-castus
Weigela
Yucca aloifolia ❀

KEY
❀ *Not hardy*

Routine care

THE following guidelines for maintenance are generally applicable, although not all shrubs have the same requirements. Newly planted shrubs usually need watering and feeding, while those planted in containers should also be periodically top-dressed or repotted. In addition, dead-heading, removing suckers, weeding, and controlling pests and diseases may all be necessary.

Feeding

Most shrubs benefit from regular applications of organic or inorganic fertilizers, especially if pruned regularly. A wide range of organic-based fertilizers is now available as well as fast-acting and slow-release ones. They are best applied in early spring. Some slow-release fertilizers discharge their nutrients only when temperatures are high enough for plants to use them. A standard rate of application is 60g/sq m (2oz/sq yd) (see also SOILS AND FERTILIZERS, "Types of fertilizer", p.624).

Quick-release powder fertilizers are useful to boost growth as it commences in spring. Liquid fertilizers work even faster than powders, and these should be applied once the shrub is in growth.

Fertilizers in granular or powder form should be worked into the soil over an area slightly wider than the spread of the top-growth of the shrub. With surface-rooting shrubs, allow the fertilizer to leach in naturally or water it in to avoid the risk of the roots being injured by forking. The application of fertilizers may affect the soil's pH level; most inorganic, nitrogenous fertilizers, for example, make the soil more acidic (see also SOILS AND FERTILIZERS, "Soil nutrients and fertilizers", pp.624–625).

Watering

Established shrubs require watering only in periods of prolonged drought, but young specimens may need regular watering. Apply the water to the ground around the shrub, soaking the soil. Do not water often and lightly, since this encourages root growth close to the surface. Shallow roots make shrubs vulnerable in drought conditions. The best time to water is in the evening, when evaporation is minimal.

Mulching

Mulching with well-rotted, bulky manures helps soil conserve moisture and, if nutrient-rich, improves soil fertility. It also moderates extremes of temperature around the roots and inhibits weeds.

Apply the mulch around newly planted shrubs over an area about 45cm (18in) wider in diameter than the plant's root system. The mulch around established shrubs should extend beyond the area of top-growth by 15–30cm (6–12in). A mulch of bark chippings, wood chips, or manure should be 5–10cm (2–4in) deep but kept clear of the stems of the shrub. Do not apply any mulch in cold weather or when the soil is dry.

Weeding

Weeds compete for nutrients and moisture, so it is essential to clear the ground of all weeds before planting. The area around newly planted ground-cover shrubs needs weeding until the plants form dense growth that suppresses competition. For treatment, see "Weeds", pp.669–673.

Removing suckers

Some grafted shrubs, including rhododendrons, are prone to producing growths, or suckers, beneath the graft union, from either stems or roots. Rub out suckers between finger and thumb as soon as they are noticed: if too large to treat in this way, cut them off as close as possible to the stems or roots from which they are growing. Pulling them off helps to remove any dormant growth buds, but take care not to damage the stem or root. Watch for further growth.

Reversion and mutation

Many variegated shrubs are propagated from green-leaved plants that have produced mutated branches, known as sports. From time to time, branches of variegated shrubs revert to the original foliage of the parent plant or mutate to plain cream or yellow leaves. Since these branches are usually more vigorous, they eventually crowd out those showing variegation, and should be cut out.

Dead-heading

Some shrubs, including rhododendrons, lilacs (*Syringa*), and *Kalmia*, benefit if their faded flowerheads are promptly removed, where practical, before seed sets. Removing old flowers diverts energy into growth, improving the flowering potential for the following season, but it is not essential for the health of a shrub.

DEAD-HEADING A RHODODENDRON

Before new buds have fully developed, snap each dead flowerhead off at the base of its stem. Take care not to damage any young growth.

To avoid damage to new buds, dead-head as soon as the flowers fade, using fingers and thumb to pick off each one where it joins the stem. Most flowerheads come away cleanly but trim any snags with secateurs.

Shrubs in containers

Container-grown shrubs need more care than those grown in the ground, since they have less access to moisture and nutrients. Until shrubs reach maturity, repot them every year or two in spring, then top-dress. When mature, just replace the top 5–10cm (2–4in) of potting compost each spring. (See also CONTAINER GARDENING, "Maintaining shrubs and trees in containers", p.334.)

HOW TO REMOVE SUCKERS

SUCKER REMOVAL
Pull or cut off the sucker (here on a Hamamelis) at the base; if it is pulled off, pare over the wound to leave a clean cut (see inset).

RECOGNIZING SUCKERS
A sucker may usually be distinguished by its leaves: a normal stem from the top-growth, left; a sucker from the root, right.

REMOVING NON-VARIEGATED AND REVERTED SHOOTS

NON-VARIEGATED SHOOT
With variegated shrubs (here Euonymus fortunei 'Emerald 'n' Gold'), cut any plain shoots back to the variegated growth.

REVERTED SHOOT
Cut back reverted shoots (here on E. fortunei 'Emerald Gaiety') to the main stem. If necessary, remove the entire stem.

Shrubs for ground cover

COVERING the ground with a dense carpet of flowering or foliage plants is a planting technique designed primarily to minimize weeding among ornamental plants. Ground cover can also reduce evaporation from exposed, freely draining soils. A dense planting of drought-resistant evergreens, such as *Cistus* x *hybridus* or the pink-flowered *C.* x *skanbergii*, and most cultivars of rosemary (*Rosmarinus*) and lavender (*Lavandula*), will shade the soil and keep it cool, and their slowly decomposing leaf litter also acts as a mulch.

Steep banks, subject to erosion by rain and wind, may be planted with ground-cover shrubs such as *Juniperus squamata* 'Blue Carpet' or *Cotoneaster dammeri*. Their low, spreading habit, evergreen foliage, and vigorous rooted layers combine to form a stable cover that prevents erosion of topsoil.

In a wildlife garden, ground cover can be used to attract bees and butterflies: the low, creeping thymes, such as *Thymus praecox* and its cultivars, for example, are extremely attractive to bees.

Once established, ground-cover plants will smother most weed seedlings that attempt to grow beneath their canopy, by depriving them of light, as well as by competing with them for water and nutrients. In the wild, this is frequently a natural

TEXTURAL CARPET
A vigorous dwarf juniper, Juniperus squamata *'Blue Carpet', provides a spreading mat of colour and texture up to 3m (10ft) wide.*

process; nature may be imitated in the garden to create attractive, integrated planting schemes requiring very little aftercare.

In open gardens, evergreen ground-cover shrubs can act as low boundary markers. They also trap wind-blown rubbish beneath their branches which can be raked out readily and removed.

Selecting plants

Choose attractive, vigorous plants that will quickly cover their allotted space with close, dense growth. Low-growing shrubs with a spread-

ing habit are among the most useful. Evergreens are a good choice for year-round visual interest, especially if, like *Euonymus fortunei* 'Gold Spot' with its golden-variegated, dark green leaves, they will brighten a dark corner.

Plants should be selected to suit the location, for example wet or dry, shady, or hot and sunny situations. They should be easy to care for, routinely requiring either no pruning or perhaps an annual clipping and feed. Choose long-term plants that should remain healthy for five to ten years or more. Finally, look for species, cultivars, and forms that will provide attractive foliage and habit, with flowers and fruits as a bonus.

Combining plants

Massed groupings of a single plant give a unified "carpeting" effect, but plants can be combined provided that they are of similar vigour. Ground-cover plants with various colours, textures, and forms may be mixed to make garden features in their own right, or may provide an attractive linking element in a design. A low carpet of shrubs can also make an excellent, low-maintenance background for naturalized bulbs such as daffodils, and, unlike grass, will not need mowing as the bulb foliage fades.

Some shrubs are particularly useful in providing medium-height cover, or as an under-canopy below trees. *Cotoneaster conspicuus*, with bright scarlet berries, *Prunus laurocerasus* 'Otto Luyken', with glossy, dark green leaves, and also *Fatsia japonica* 'Variegata', with deeply lobed leaves edged with white, cover the ground well and provide interest, even in winter.

General cultivation

Once the ground has been thoroughly prepared, there are several ways of planting ground-cover shrubs to ensure quick cover: plant them at spacings recommended for the species or cultivar concerned and cover the soil with a loose mulch; plant them at recommended spacings through a weed-resistant, black plastic sheet mulch; or plant them more densely than would be usual to provide cover more quickly.

The choice of method will depend on the type and cost of plants used, the climate and soil conditions, and how long you are willing to wait for the final effect. Fast-growing plants in favourable conditions and at recommended spacings will generally fill in within two to three years.

Once established, many shrubby plants benefit from an occasional trim, to keep them compact, as well as the removal of dead or damaged shoots. A few need more intrusive, annual pruning: for example, shrubs such as *Vinca* and *Hypericum calycinum* that, after a few years, become rather straggly, and those such as *Santolina* that tend to open out, revealing their centre.

PRUNING GROUND COVER

SANTOLINA
Some bushy plants need hard pruning. In spring, cut back to just above where new growth is breaking on the main stems.

HYPERICUM CALYCINUM
In spring, cut the previous season's shoots hard back.

Mulching ground cover

When ground-cover plants have been newly planted at the correct distance, the ground between them will still be bare. Until the plants have begun to spread over the surrounding area, it is advisable to apply a mulch in the gaps around them. This will help to retain moisture in the soil, and will also discourage the growth of weeds. A loose mulch, for example bark chippings, is ideal for the purpose, and should be applied to a depth of about 5cm (2in).

To preserve moisture between new plants (here Erica carnea*), apply a loose mulch 5cm (2in) deep. Every spring, renew the mulch around established plants.*

Moving an established shrub

Careful selection and siting of a shrub should make transplanting unnecessary, although sometimes it may be desirable or unavoidable. Before moving evergreens, spray the foliage with an anti-desiccant. With deciduous shrubs, thin out growth by up to one third, to compensate for root disturbance.

When to transplant

Most deciduous young shrubs may be lifted bare-root when dormant. Established shrubs that have large root systems should be lifted with a ball of soil around the roots before being moved. Autumn is the best time to do this. Evergreens should be transplanted in spring, just before new growth occurs, carefully digging up the whole root ball.

Root-balling a shrub

Most often, it is best to root-ball a shrub so that root damage is kept to a minimum. Prepare the new planting position before lifting the shrub.

Dig a trench around the shrub just beyond the spread of its branches. Cut through woody roots but leave fibrous ones intact. If necessary, use a fork to loosen the soil around the root ball and reduce its size. Then undercut it with a spade; use secateurs to sever any woody tap roots.

Once the root ball is free, work a sheet of hessian or similar material underneath it. Tie the hessian firmly around the ball, lift the shrub from the hole, and transplant it. Remove the hessian before replanting.

Transplanted shrubs require the same treatment as those that have been planted for the first time, although they may take longer to re-establish (see p.99).

Shrub problems

Plants are less likely to succumb to pest attack or disease if they are given good growing conditions and care. Many problems originate from poor drainage, lack of moisture, planting too deeply, compaction of the soil, or exposure to temperature extremes in an unsuitable site.

Physical damage

Wounds caused by a jagged pruning cut, a badly placed cut, or pruning at the wrong time may allow disease fungi to establish. This may also cause die-back. Mechanical wounding, for example by lawnmowers grazing a stem, also provides a convenient entry point for disease.

Pests and diseases

Maintaining good garden hygiene minimizes the chance of pests and diseases establishing a foothold. As shrubs age, however, they lose vigour and become more prone to pests and diseases. Old or diseased shrubs that have lost their vigour are rarely worth saving and should be replaced.

Pests and diseases most likely to affect shrubs are aphids (p.646), red spider mite (p.646), fireblight (p.649), honey fungus (p.661), *Phytophthora* stem rots (see "*Phytophthora* root rots", p.654), and powdery mildew (p.646). Be alert to the signs of a problem, which include streaking and changes of foliage colour, drooping leaves, loss of leaves, distorted growth, and the development of fungi.

Frost and wind

When selecting and siting shrubs it is vital to take account of the general weather pattern of the area as well as the garden's own individual microclimate; it is almost impossible, however, to take precautions against freak extremes of temperature or exceptional winds.

There is a wide range of hardy shrubs available and many gardeners choose to rely on these rather than risk the loss of more tender specimens. If growing shrubs that are of borderline hardiness for the area, then it is worth using the appropriate frost and wind protection methods (see pp.612–613).

Container-grown shrubs are more vulnerable to extremes of weather than those grown in the open garden. In areas where temperatures fall only occasionally below freezing, most container-grown hardy shrubs may be overwintered outdoors (except those, such as camellias, that are root-tender). In colder areas, however, move shrubs indoors to where the ambient daytime temperature is about 7–13°C (45–55°F) or higher, according to the species.

TRANSPLANTING A SHRUB

1 *Before moving a large shrub, it may be helpful to thin out growth. This will make handling easier and help it to re-establish. Then, using a spade, mark out a circle around the extent of the shrub's branches (here Ilex aquifolium 'Golden Milkboy'). Tie in any trailing stems or wrap the shrub in hessian, to prevent damage.*

2 *Dig a trench around the circle, then use a fork to loosen the soil around the root ball. Take care not to damage any fibrous roots.*

3 *Continue carefully to fork away soil from around the shrub's root ball to reduce its size and weight.*

4 *Undercut the root ball with a spade, cutting through woody roots if necessary to separate them from the surrounding soil.*

5 *Roll up a length of hessian. Tilt the shrub to one side and unroll the hessian beneath the root ball. Tilt the root ball the other way, and unroll the rest of the hessian.*

6 *Pull the hessian up around the root ball and tie it securely. Remove the shrub from its hole and transport it to its new position.*

7 *Remove the hessian and replant the shrub in the new, prepared hole with the soil mark at the same level as before. Firm, water well, and mulch.*

Pruning and training

SOME shrubs, particularly ever-greens of naturally compact habit such as *Sarcococca*, make attractive plants with little or no pruning or training. They may require no more than the removal of dead, damaged, and diseased wood. If left untreated, this will be unsightly and, more seriously, may put the health of the whole shrub in jeopardy. Many shrubs, however, need pruning or a combination of pruning and training in order to realize their full ornamental potential.

Aims and effects of pruning and training

The most common requirement is for formative pruning that creates a vigorous and well-shaped shrub. Many shrubs also require a regular regime of pruning to maintain or enhance the ornamental quality of their flowers, fruit, foliage, or stems. The timing of this pruning, which may often be critical, varies depending on the growth pattern of the shrub and the effect desired.

Pruning can also be a way of bringing neglected and overgrown plants back to healthy, manageable growth. It is a matter of judgment whether a shrub warrants being rescued. Replacement is often the best course when a shrub requires regular cutting back because it is too large for the space available.

Shrubs grown as topiary or hedges require specialized pruning from their formative stage. For further information see TOPIARY, pp.76–77, and HEDGES AND SCREENS, pp.84–86.

In training, the gardener plays an active role in directing the growth of plants. Most shrubs grown in the open require no training at all. Shrubs grown against supports, however, normally need a combination of pruning and training to form a well-spaced framework of branches.

Principles of pruning and training

Pruning normally stimulates growth. The terminal shoot or growth bud of a stem is often dominant, inhibiting by chemical means the growth of buds or shoots below it. Pruning that removes the ends of stems affects the control mechanism, resulting in more vigorous development of lower shoots or growth buds.

WHERE TO CUT

OPPOSITE SHOOTS
Prune stems with opposite buds to just above a strong pair of buds or shoots, using a clean, straight cut.

ALTERNATE SHOOTS
For shrubs with alternate buds, prune to just above a bud or shoot, using a clean, angled cut.

AN ANGLED CUT
Angle the cut so that its lowest point is opposite the base of the bud and the top just clears the bud.

Hard or light pruning

Hard pruning promotes more vigorous growth than light pruning; this needs to be borne in mind when correcting the shape of an unbalanced shrub. Hard cutting back of vigorous growth often encourages even stronger growth. Prune weak growth hard but strong growth only lightly.

How to prune

Pruning wounds, like other injuries that a shrub might suffer, are possible entry points for disease. The risk is reduced by making well-placed, clean cuts with sharp tools.

Stems with alternate or whorled arrangements of growth buds should be cut just above a bud pointing in the desired direction of growth – for example, an outward-facing bud that will not cross another shoot as its growth develops. Use an angled cut, starting opposite a healthy growth bud, and slant the cut so that it finishes slightly above the bud. If the cut is too close, the bud may die; if too far, the stem itself may die back.

With shrubs that have buds in opposite pairs, cut straight across the shoot just above a pair of healthy buds. Both buds will develop, resulting in a forked branch system.

In the past, gardeners have often been advised to use a wound paint on pruning cuts, but research now suggests that wound paints are not generally an effective way of controlling diseases and in some cases may even encourage them.

Pruning alone will not promote vigorous new growth. Shrubs that are renovated or regularly cut back benefit from feeding and mulching. Apply a general-purpose fertilizer at the beginning of the growing season at a rate of 120g/sq m (4oz/sq yd) and mulch to a depth of 5–10cm (2–4in) with well-rotted organic material in spring, when the ground has warmed up a little.

Training

The growth of lower buds or shoots on a stem may also be modified by training. When a stem is allowed to grow upright, the lower shoots on the stem usually grow weakly. With stems that are trained more horizontally, however, the lower shoots and buds grow more vigorously. Training branches near the horizontal can substantially increase the amount of flower and fruit that a shrub is able to produce. Wall-trained shrubs should be tied in to supports as growth develops. As stems ripen and turn woody they become far less flexible and are therefore more difficult to train successfully.

Formative pruning

The aim of formative pruning is to ensure that a shrub has a framework of well-spaced branches so that it will develop according to its natural habit. The amount of formative pruning required depends very much on the type of shrub and on the quality of the plants available. When

FORMATIVE PRUNING

After planting a young shrub (here Philadelphus), *cut out any dead, damaged, and weak stems, and remove crossing and congested stems to form a well-balanced framework with an open centre.*

Prune back crossing or congested shoots to an outward-facing bud or, if necessary, right back to the base.

Prune out any very weak and spindly, or long and straggly stems, cutting them right back to the base.

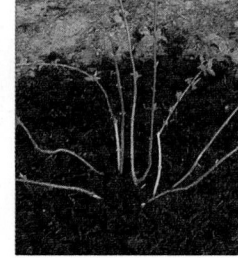
Also remove any very awkward stems that spoil the shape of the shrub to leave an evenly branching framework.

103

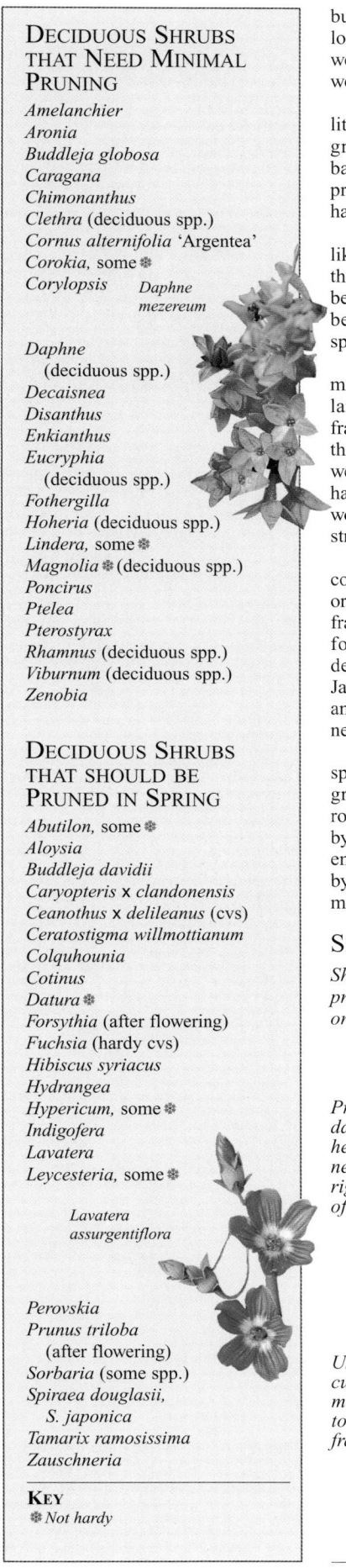

DECIDUOUS SHRUBS THAT NEED MINIMAL PRUNING

Amelanchier
Aronia
Buddleja globosa
Caragana
Chimonanthus
Clethra (deciduous spp.)
Cornus alternifolia 'Argentea'
Corokia, some ❁

Corylopsis

Daphne mezereum

Daphne
   (deciduous spp.)
Decaisnea
Disanthus
Enkianthus
Eucryphia
   (deciduous spp.)
Fothergilla
Hoheria (deciduous spp.)
Lindera, some ❁
Magnolia ❁ (deciduous spp.)
Poncirus
Ptelea
Pterostyrax
Rhamnus (deciduous spp.)
Viburnum (deciduous spp.)
Zenobia

DECIDUOUS SHRUBS THAT SHOULD BE PRUNED IN SPRING

Abutilon, some ❁
Aloysia
Buddleja davidii
Caryopteris x *clandonensis*
Ceanothus x *delileanus* (cvs)
Ceratostigma willmottianum
Colquhounia
Cotinus
Datura ❁
Forsythia (after flowering)
Fuchsia (hardy cvs)
Hibiscus syriacus
Hydrangea
Hypericum, some ❁
Indigofera
Lavatera
Leycesteria, some ❁

Lavatera assurgentiflora

Perovskia
Prunus triloba
   (after flowering)
Sorbaria (some spp.)
Spiraea douglasii,
   S. japonica
Tamarix ramosissima
Zauschneria

KEY
❁ Not hardy

buying shrubs, therefore, you should look for sturdy specimens with a well-balanced branch formation, as well as healthy roots.

Evergreen shrubs generally need little formative pruning. Excessive growth resulting in a lopsided, un-balanced shape should be lightly pruned in mid-spring, after the shrub has been planted.

Deciduous shrubs are much more likely to require formative pruning than evergreen shrubs. This should be carried out in the dormant season, between mid-autumn and mid-spring, at or after planting.

The following guidelines apply to most deciduous shrubs. If a particularly vigorous shoot distorts the framework, cut it back lightly rather than severely, to encourage relatively weak growth. If the shrub does not have a well-spaced, branch frame-work, cut it back hard to promote strong growth.

In the case of most shrubs, remove completely any spindly and crossing or rubbing branches that clutter the framework. An exception is made for a handful of slow-growing deciduous shrubs, in particular Japanese maples (*Acer japonicum* and *A. palmatum*), which generally need no pruning at all.

Sometimes an apparently good specimen will make too much top-growth in relation to the size of its roots. Reducing the number of stems by up to one third, and then short-ening those stems that remain, also by one third, will help to create a more stable plant.

MINIMAL PRUNING OF ESTABLISHED DECIDUOUS SHRUBS

If pruning is needed, which may not be every year, do it immediately after flowering, taking out any dead wood, weak stems, and congested growth to maintain a balanced, open-centred framework on shrubs such as Hamamelis.

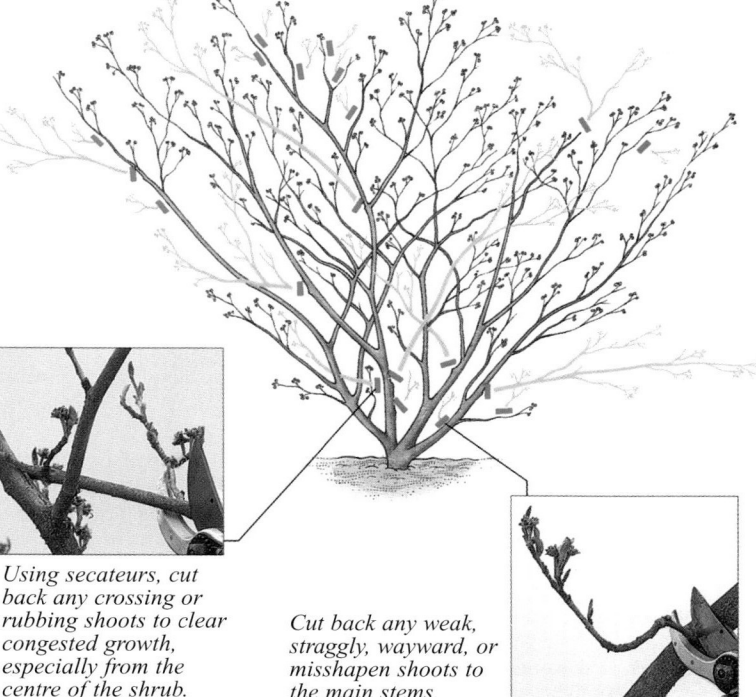

Using secateurs, cut back any crossing or rubbing shoots to clear congested growth, especially from the centre of the shrub.

Cut back any weak, straggly, wayward, or misshapen shoots to the main stems.

Deciduous shrubs

These may be divided into four groups: those that require minimal pruning; those that are pruned in spring and usually flower on the cur-rent season's growth; those that are pruned after flowering in summer, and usually flower on the previous season's wood; and those of sucker-ing habit. Two important factors are the degree to which shrubs produce replacement growths and the age of the flower-bearing wood.

SHRUBS THAT ARE PRUNED IN SPRING

Shrubs (here Spiraea japonica *'Bumalda') that flower on wood produced in the current season should be pruned in spring in order to encourage the growth of new, flowering stems.*

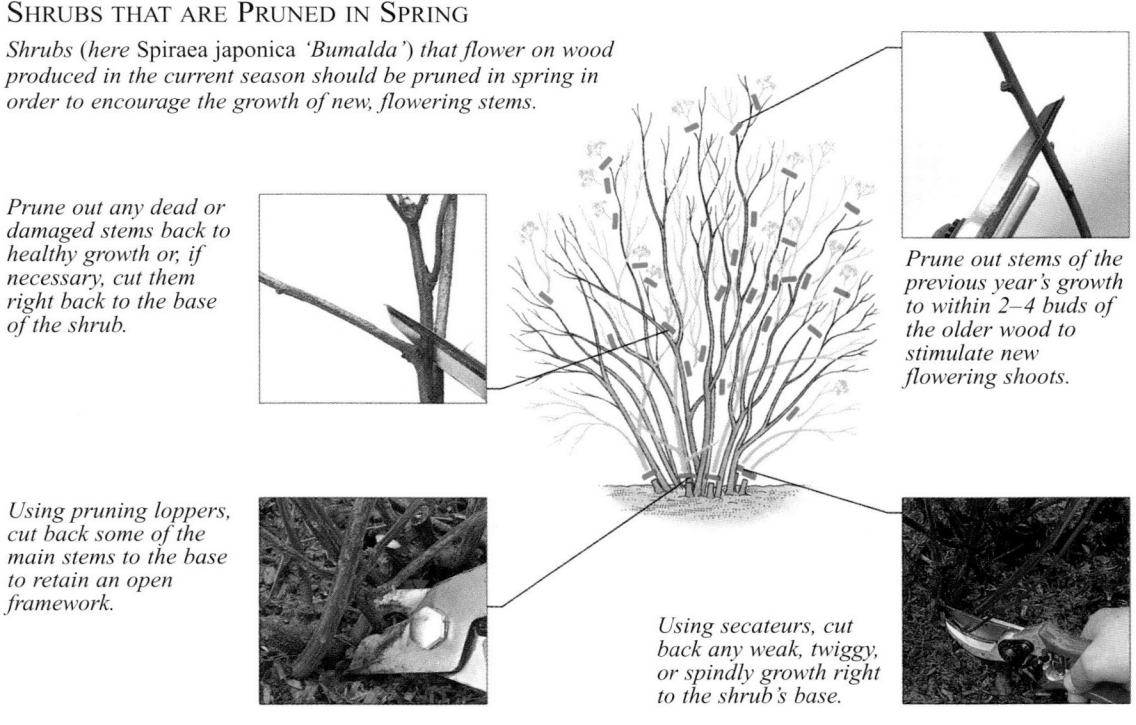

Prune out any dead or damaged stems back to healthy growth or, if necessary, cut them right back to the base of the shrub.

Prune out stems of the previous year's growth to within 2–4 buds of the older wood to stimulate new flowering shoots.

Using pruning loppers, cut back some of the main stems to the base to retain an open framework.

Using secateurs, cut back any weak, twiggy, or spindly growth right to the shrub's base.

Minimal pruning

Once established, shrubs that do not regularly produce vigorous growths from the base or lower branches need little or, often, no pruning at all; the chief need is to remove dead, diseased, and damaged wood and to cut out crossing or weak growth. Do this just after flowering. Feed and mulch in spring. Japanese maples and other shrubs prone to heavy bleeding if pruned in spring should be pruned in mid- to late summer, when their sap is least active.

Pruning in spring

Left unpruned, deciduous shrubs that bear flowers on the current season's growth tend to become congested and flower quality deteriorates. When pruned in spring, these shrubs generally produce vigorous shoots that carry flowers in summer or early autumn. Shorten flowered stems in autumn, as well, to minimize the risk of wind-rock.

Some large shrubs, such as deciduous *Ceanothus*, develop a woody framework. In their first spring, lightly prune the main stems of less vigorous shrubs and, in the second spring, reduce the previous season's growth by half. In late winter or early spring of subsequent years, prune hard to leave only one to three pairs of buds of the previous season's growth. Prune framework branches to slightly different heights to encourage flower production at all levels. On mature specimens, cut out some of the oldest wood as part of the annual pruning operation to prevent congestion. For pruning *Buddleja davidii*, see above.

Some subshrubs, for example *Perovskia*, may form a woody base that allows them to be pruned hard back to a 15–30cm (6–12in) high framework. Cut back the previous season's growth annually in spring, leaving one or two buds.

A few shrubs, such as *Prunus triloba*, that flower in late winter or early spring on wood produced in the previous season are best pruned hard in spring after flowering, and so may be treated as other shrubs in this group. In the first spring after planting, shorten the main stems by about half to form a basal framework. After flowering in subsequent years, cut back all growth to two to three buds of the framework stems. In areas where annual growth is limited by cool summers, cut back only one third of shoots near to ground level, and the others to 15–30cm (6–12in).

For all shrubs in this group, apply fertilizer just after pruning. In mid-spring, mulch the area matching the spread of the shrub before pruning.

Pruning *Buddleja davidii*

As it is very vigorous, *Buddleja davidii* needs more drastic formative pruning than most other shrubs that flower on new wood. At the back of a border, where a tall plant is required, prune to leave a woody framework 90–120cm (3–4ft) high. In another position, however, this may be no more than 60cm (2ft) high.

In the first spring after planting, shorten main stems by a half to three quarters, pruning to pairs of shoots or buds. Cut out growths other than main stems. In early to mid-spring of subsequent years, cut back the previous season's growth and shorten new growth from the base. To stop congestion, cut out one or two of the oldest branches as part of the annual pruning.

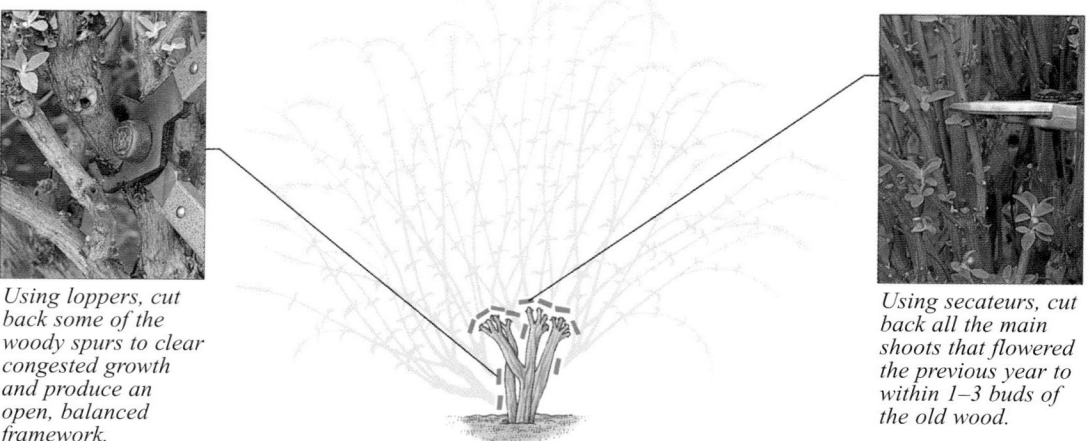

Using loppers, cut back some of the woody spurs to clear congested growth and produce an open, balanced framework.

Using secateurs, cut back all the main shoots that flowered the previous year to within 1–3 buds of the old wood.

Hydrangeas

For pruning purposes, hydrangeas (excluding climbing species such as *Hydrangea anomala* subsp. *petiolaris*) fall into three groups.

The first group (for example *H. paniculata*) flowers from midsummer onwards on the current season's growth, and these plants should be treated in the same way as other shrubs that require hard pruning in spring (see facing page).

In early spring of the first year after planting, cut out all but two or three strong stems, pruning these back to a healthy pair of buds about 45cm (18in) from ground level. If the shrub is planted in an exposed position, and where summer temperatures will not ripen the stems sufficiently to withstand very cold winters, prune to just above ground level. Apply a quick-release fertilizer at a rate of about 120g/sq m (4oz/sq yd) and a 10cm (4in) deep mulch in a 60cm (24in) circle around the shrub. In early spring of subsequent years, cut back the previous year's growth to leave one or two strong pairs of growth buds. Then feed and mulch.

The second group, comprising mophead and lacecap hydrangeas (*H. macrophylla*), also flowers from midsummer but on shoots made during the previous growing season. Lightly prune young plants in early spring, cutting out thin, twiggy growth and any old flowerheads. Once the plant is established and about three or four years old, remove some of the oldest wood annually in early spring. Cut out stems that are more than three years old and shorten the other stems that flowered in the previous season, cutting back to a strong pair of buds 15–30cm (6–12in) from the base. Then feed and mulch.

Other species, such as *H. aspera*, and related forms constitute a third group and need only minimal pruning in spring.

In spring, prune back all flowered stems, also damaged and weak growth, and cut back some older wood to the base.

H. MACROPHYLLA

Cut back any dead wood to healthy growth or right back to the base, if necessary.

Prune out all flowered stems, making a straight cut above a strong pair of growth buds.

Shrubs pruned in summer after flowering

Many deciduous shrubs that flower in spring or early summer carry their flowers on wood produced in the previous growing season. Sometimes, the flowers are formed on last year's wood, as with *Chaenomeles*, for example. Other shrubs bear their flowers on short lateral growths produced from last year's wood – for example *Deutzia*, *Philadelphus*, *Syringa*, and *Weigela*.

Without regular pruning to encourage development of vigorous, young growths from close to ground level, many shrubs in this group tend to become densely twiggy, often top-heavy, and the quantity and quality of flowers deteriorate. The removal of spent flowerheads also prevents shrubs from expending energy in seed production.

When planting any shrub in this group, cut out all weak or damaged growth and trim back the main shoots to a healthy bud or pair of buds, to encourage the development of a strong framework. If any flowers are produced in the first year, prune again immediately after flowering. Cut back flowered shoots to a strong bud or pair of buds and remove any spindly growth. After pruning, lightly work in fertilizer and apply a mulch around the shrub.

Carry out the same procedure immediately after flowering in subsequent years. Although it is desirable to cut back flowered wood to the strongest buds, do not adhere to this rigidly since it is also important to maintain a well-balanced shape. Feed and mulch as a matter of course after pruning.

As plants mature, more drastic pruning may be required to encourage growth. After the third year, up to one fifth of the oldest stems may be cut back annually to within 5–8cm (2–3in) of the ground.

Use your discretion when following these guidelines, since harsh pruning of young specimens of some shrubs in this group, for example forsythias, may result in an awkward and unnatural shape.

Other shrubs in this group, especially when grown as freestanding rather than as wall shrubs, require very little pruning. *Chaenomeles*, for example, has a naturally twiggy habit, with numerous crossing branches, and mature specimens need little pruning. Spur pruning will, however, encourage heavier flowering (see GROWING FRUIT, "Winter pruning", p.438); shorten spurs and sideshoots to three to five leaves in midsummer.

Particular care must be taken in pruning shrubs such as lilacs (*Syringa*) that come into growth during flowering. The new shoots that form below the flowers may be easily damaged when the old flowerheads are cut, and this reduces flowering in the next year.

Flowering shrubs of suckering habit

A few shrubs that are grown for their flowers produce flowers on wood of the previous year but make most of their new growth from ground level. These shrubs spread by suckers and are pruned in a different way from shrubs that form a permanent woody framework.

After planting, prune suckering shrubs by cutting out weak growth but retain vigorous stems and their sideshoots. The following year, immediately after flowering, remove any weak, dead, or damaged stems, then cut back flowered stems hard to a strong bud or pair of buds.

From the third year, annually cut back a quarter to a half of all flowered stems to 5–8cm (2–3in) above ground level and prune others by about half to vigorous, replacement shoots. After pruning, feed and mulch.

SHRUBS PRUNED IN SUMMER AFTER FLOWERING

Buddleja alternifolia
Deutzia
Dipelta
Exochorda
Holodiscus discolor
Jasminum humile
Kolkwitzia
Neillia
Philadelphus
Photinia villosa
Ribes sanguineum
Rubus deliciosus,
  R. 'Tridel'

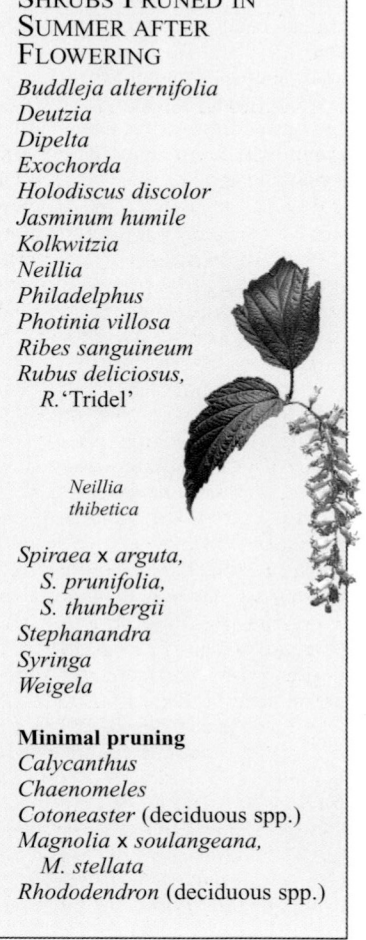

*Neillia
thibetica*

Spiraea x *arguta*,
  S. *prunifolia*,
  S. *thunbergii*
Stephanandra
Syringa
Weigela

Minimal pruning
Calycanthus
Chaenomeles
Cotoneaster (deciduous spp.)
Magnolia x *soulangeana*,
  M. *stellata*
Rhododendron (deciduous spp.)

PRUNING SHRUBS IN SUMMER

After shrubs such as Weigela *have flowered, cut back flowered shoots and remove dead and spindly stems. Also prune out some old, main stems.*

Using secateurs, cut any dead wood back to healthy growth.

BEFORE AFTER

Cut out up to one fifth of the oldest wood to within 5–8 cm (2–3in) of the ground.

Cut out any very weak, twiggy, or straggly stems back to the base just above soil level.

Continue cutting out weak or crossing stems to form an open-centred, well-balanced shrub.

PRUNING A DECIDUOUS SUCKERING SHRUB

After flowering, prune back all flowered stems on deciduous suckering shrubs (here Kerria*), most by about half, the remainder almost to the ground. Cut out any weak, dead, or damaged growth.*

Prune the flowered stems by about half their length, cutting back to strongly growing, new shoots.

Cut back up to half of the flowered stems to within 5–8cm (2–3in) of the ground. Also cut to the ground any dead or damaged shoots.

Coppicing and pollarding shrubs

A number of deciduous shrubs grown for the ornamental value of their stems or leaves require severe pruning in spring. Most of these shrubs flower on shoots formed the previous season but, when grown for their stems or leaves, their flowers are sacrificed. The method of hard pruning used on these shrubs is essentially an adaptation of traditional methods of managing trees and shrubs to give a constant and renewable supply of wood for canework, firewood, and fencing materials. In coppicing, shrubs and trees are cut back regularly to near ground level. In pollarding, growth is cut back each year to a permanent framework of a single stem or several stems.

Coppicing shrubs such as *Cornus alba* ensures a regular supply of young growths, which are more strikingly coloured than older wood and effective in winter. On shrubs such as *Sambucus racemosa* 'Plumosa Aurea' that are grown for their foliage, hard pruning generally results in larger leaves. Just before growth commences in early to mid-spring, coppice vigorous shrubs such as *Salix alba* subsp. *vitellina* 'Britzensis' (syn. *S. alba* 'Chermesina') by pruning all shoots to within about 5–8cm (2–3in) of ground level. It may be preferable to vary the height to which stems are cut back to avoid a rigid, uniform effect. Weaker shrubs such as *Cornus alba* 'Sibirica' may be cut back less severely by coppicing only about one third to one half of the stems. Then apply a quick-release fertilizer and mulch liberally, covering a circle of 60cm (24in) radius around the shrub.

Shrubs that have been trained so that they have one or more clean, main stems are pruned back – or

POLLARDING A EUCALYPTUS

Establish a framework by cutting back a young shrub to one or more main stems (below). Each subsequent spring, cut the previous year's growth hard back either to within 5–8cm (2–3in) of the framework or to the base, as Eucalyptus can regenerate from ground level (right).

pollarded – to this stem framework each season. The aim of pruning in the first year is to establish the framework; after planting, before growth commences in spring, cut back a young plant to form a standard with a single stem of 30–90cm (1–3ft). Alternatively, leave three, five, or seven stems, depending on the size of plant required and the space available in the garden. Apply a quick-release fertilizer and mulch around the stem (or stems), as for shrubs that are coppiced.

During the plant's first growing season, restrict the number of shoots growing from below the cut to only four or five, rubbing out all others that are superfluous and any that develop low down on the main stem. Continue this process for the next year or two; this will allow the main stem to thicken so that it will be able

to support heavier top-growth. In spring of the second and subsequent years, reduce the previous season's growths to above a bud within 5–8cm (2–3in) of the framework (see also *Pollarding a Eucalyptus*, above). If a larger specimen is needed, prune only a half or one third of the stems. Feed and mulch.

Evergreen shrubs

The appropriate method for pruning and training most evergreen shrubs depends on the size they are expected to reach when mature. All evergreens that show signs of die-back after a particularly hard winter, however, should be treated in the same way, regardless of size.

In mid-spring, prune out all dead wood to where the shrub has started to regenerate and thin out the new shoots if they are overcrowded or crossing. If a shrub shows no sign of life by mid-spring, nick the bark to see if there is any live, green wood beneath. Some shrubs may remain dormant for a whole growing season.

Small shrubs up to 90cm (3ft)
Low-growing, evergreen shrubs may be divided into two main groups, each requiring a different pruning technique. The first group includes a number of relatively short-lived shrubs that flower profusely, provided that they are trimmed each year and are not over-mature. Examples of these shrubs include lavender (*Lavandula*), cotton lavender

(*Santolina chamaecyparissus*), and most heathers (*Calluna*, *Daboecia*, and *Erica*, but not tree heaths). These shrubs are generally best replaced every 5–10 years. Also replace plants that have been left unpruned for several years since they become weak and leggy and seldom flower or regenerate successfully.

In mid-spring, use secateurs or garden shears to cut out any weak growth or flowering shoots on newly planted shrubs. This ensures that new growth is generated from basal shoots in the centre of the plant. Each subsequent year in mid-spring, remove the old flowerheads, as well as any dead, diseased, or damaged shoots. Some heathers have attractive winter foliage and these, as well as other evergreens, are sometimes dead-headed in autumn. In very cold areas there is, however, a risk of die-back after autumn dead-heading and for this reason pruning is normally delayed until mid-spring. After pruning, apply slow-release fertilizer at a rate of 60g/sq m (2oz/sq yd) and apply a mulch to a depth of 5cm (2in).

COPPICING A SHRUB FOR WINTER STEM EFFECT

With shrubs that have coloured stems (here a Cornus sericea *cultivar) cut back hard all the shrub's stems to about 5–8cm (2–3in) from the base before growth begins in spring (see inset). Apply fertilizer around the shrub to promote new growth, and then mulch. Coppicing stimulates the growth of new, vigorous stems whose colour is especially strong.*

The second group comprises slow-growing shrubs, such as dwarf cotoneasters and hebes. These require less pruning than those in the first group, the main purpose in pruning them being to remove dead, diseased, or damaged shoots in mid-spring. Dead-heading, however, is not necessary.

Medium-sized, evergreen shrubs up to 3m (10ft) tall

Most medium-sized evergreen shrubs require little pruning once a well-balanced framework has been established. This principle applies to *Berberis darwinii*, camellias, *Escallonia*, *Hibiscus rosa-sinensis*, and many rhododendrons.

In mid-spring, just before growth is about to commence, remove any weak or crossing shoots as well as any that may affect the overall symmetry and balance of the shrub. Feed and mulch. Subsequent pruning is normally limited to cutting out straggly growth, restricting size, and shaping the plant to suit its position in the garden. Use secateurs or long-handled loppers to remove all or part of selected branches.

Winter- or spring-flowering shrubs, such as *Berberis darwinii* and *Viburnum tinus*, should be pruned immediately after flowering. Prune others that flower from midsummer onwards, such as *Escallonia*, by removing older wood at the start of growth in mid-spring or by cutting

out flowered stems in midsummer. *Hibiscus rosa-sinensis*, with its flowering season from spring to autumn, is best pruned in mid-spring. Feed and mulch spring-pruned shrubs after pruning, while those pruned in late summer should not be fed or mulched until the following spring, to minimize damage from frosts.

Large, evergreen shrubs more than 3m (10ft) tall

Large rhododendrons and other tall evergreens require little pruning but may need shaping as young plants to create a well-balanced framework. Prune young plants before they start into growth or else wait until the flowers have faded.

The aim of pruning here is to encourage an open-centred bush with well-spaced branches. Cut out all weak and crossing branches, and feed and mulch after pruning. Regular pruning is generally limited to the removal of dead, damaged, and diseased wood. Some large evergreens such as laurels (*Prunus laurocerasus*) may also be used for hedging (see pp.84–86).

Palm-like shrubs

The palm-like *Cordyline* and *Yucca* need pruning only if they have suffered frost-damage or if a bushy, multi-stemmed specimen is required. In spring, once new growth has started to appear, cut damaged branches back to just above newly formed shoots. Feed and apply a mulch. To create a multi-branched specimen, remove the growing point before growth commences in spring then feed and mulch. Both genera also respond well to hard pruning and renovation: cut back to suitable sideshoots or basal shoots.

Other palm-like succulents such as *Agave* and *Phormium* require only their dead leaves to be removed or faded flower stems cut out.

Wall shrubs

There are three reasons for growing shrubs against walls. First, some are too tender for the open garden in frost-prone areas, but will thrive if sheltered against a warm wall. Second, training shrubs, including hardy shrubs such as pyracanthas, against a wall makes it possible to accommodate plants for which there might not otherwise be space. Third, some shrubs are natural scramblers (for example *Cestrum elegans*) and will therefore need support of some kind.

It is important to train and prune all wall shrubs from an early stage so that they present a compact and

"well-tailored" appearance and produce plenty of flowering shoots regularly. When training wall shrubs, provide a framework to which growth can be tied. Trellis, netting, or regularly spaced, horizontal wires as used for wall-trained fruit trees (see p.424) may be used. Plant hardy shrubs in autumn, half-hardy or tender shrubs in spring.

Recommendations for pruning freestanding shrubs also apply to wall-trained specimens, but more care is needed for formative training and pruning. It is vital to tie in shoots as they grow and cut back sub-laterals growing strongly away from the wall.

Formative training and pruning

During the first growing season, train in the leader and main laterals to form a framework; prune back any outward-growing laterals to encourage short sideshoots to develop close to the framework. Remove completely any laterals growing towards the wall or fence, and any shoots that are growing outwards in the wrong

direction. The aim should be to create a neat, vertical "carpet" of foliage to cover the allotted space.

Routine pruning

In the second and subsequent seasons, flowering laterals should be formed. After flowering, cut back the flowered shoots to within 7–10cm (3–4in) of the main framework. This encourages new flowering laterals to develop that will provide next season's display. Continue tying in framework shoots; trim outward-pointing laterals and remove inward-growing and other wrongly aligned shoots. Do not trim wall shrubs after midsummer as this may reduce the following year's flowering shoots; this is particularly important with *Ceanothus* and many half-hardy evergreen shrubs which might otherwise produce soft growth liable to frost damage. Feed and mulch wall-trained shrubs annually in spring to maintain strong, healthy growth.

Shrubs such as pyracantha that are grown both for flowers and fruits or berries need slightly modified pruning. The shoots that have flowered are not

EVERGREEN SHRUBS THAT TOLERATE SEVERE PRUNING

Aucuba
Berberis darwinii
Buxus
Choisya ternata
Citrus ❀
Escallonia 'Donard Seedling'
Euonymus fortunei,
  E. japonicus
Hibiscus rosa-sinensis ❀
Ilex x *altaclerensis,*
  I. aquifolium
Ligustrum japonicum
Lonicera nitida, L. pileata
Nerium oleander ❀
Osmanthus
Phillyrea
Prunus laurocerasus,
  P. lusitanica
Rhododendron ponticum,
  R. Subsection Triflora
Santolina
Sarcococca humilis
Taxus
Viburnum tinus

KEY
❀ Not hardy

PRUNING EVERGREEN SHRUBS

After flowering, prune evergreen shrubs (here Prunus lusitanica) *by removing damaged or dead wood and cutting back flowered stems and any awkward or straggly stems that mar the shape.*

Cut back flowered stems to a main stem. Cut out thickly congested and crossing stems.

Cut back awkwardly growing stems to well-placed, healthy, outward-growing shoots.

Cut out any dead or damaged wood back to healthy growth or, if necessary, to the base.

PRUNING AND TRAINING A YOUNG WALL SHRUB

In the first year, prune the shrub (here a pyracantha) to build up a balanced framework, tying in main stems. In subsequent years, tie in new growth in spring; in midsummer, cut back inward- and outward-growing shoots to form a vertical "carpet"; remove entirely dead, damaged, or spindly growth.

Using secateurs, cut back any weak, spindly stems as well as any dead or damaged wood.

Trim back any outward-growing stems to 7–10cm (3–4in) from the framework in midsummer.

Check and replace any broken ties. Use garden twine tied in a figure-of-eight to re-secure the stem to the wire.

PRUNING AN ESTABLISHED WALL SHRUB

Prune mature plants to maintain a well-balanced framework of stems and, on berrying shrubs, to expose the berries. In late summer, remove outward-growing shoots and, with the exception of shrubs grown for their fruits or berries, cut back flowered shoots to promote dense growth. The shrub shown here is a pyracantha.

Cut back young shoots to 2–3 leaves from their base to expose the ripening berries.

In late summer, check and replace ties where necessary; in spring, tie in new shoots.

Using secateurs, cut back any damaged or dead wood to healthy growth.

cut back but are left to develop fruits. Trim back any laterals that develop to two to three leaves from their base as the fruits swell, so that they are exposed to more light and ripen well. Old fruit trusses may be cut out in spring as young growths develop.

Summer- and autumn-flowering wall shrubs, including some *Ceanothus*, should be trained as described earlier but pruned according to whether they flower on the previous season's wood (see "Shrubs pruned in summer after flowering", p.106) or that of the current season (see "Pruning in spring", p.105). Some half-hardy or tender shrubs, particularly *Ceanothus*, do not break readily from old wood and are difficult to renovate once neglected.

Scrambling shrubs

These also require careful training to contain their flexuous shoots. On some, such as the half-hardy *Cestrum elegans*, that produce flowers in late summer on terminal shoots or short laterals, the flowered shoots may be cut out entirely or cut back to strong, low, lateral growths in spring. Others flower in summer mainly on lateral growths, which should be cut back after flowering to 7–10cm (3–4in) and will often produce further sub-laterals that flower the same season. In spring, these laterals are pruned back again to 7–10cm (3–4in) and will flower in summer.

Fan-training ornamental shrubs

A few shrubs, such as ornamental peaches (for example *Prunus persica* 'Klara Meyer'), are suitable for fan-training like fruit trees. In the first spring after planting, cut back the plant 38–45cm (15–18in) above the graft union, retaining three or four strong shoots. Train the shoots on canes tied to horizontal wires. Towards the end of the growing season, remove the central shoot if three strong shoots were retained; if four shoots were kept, space these out to form a fan. In winter, reduce all shoots by half their length.

The following growing season, select two or four new shoots on each stem; attach each of these to a cane tied to the wires. Then, in midsummer, remove all other shoots. In the third year, immediately after flowering, cut back all framework shoots by a quarter to one third. Tie in two or three new shoots on each framework stem. Remove unwanted shoots in midsummer. If there are gaps in the fan, prune back adjacent shoots by one third after flowering has finished to encourage new growth. Cut back all other extension growths to 5–8cm (2–3in) to encourage flowering on one-year-old spurs. For full details, see GROWING FRUIT, "Fan", p.453.

PRUNING CEANOTHUS

Immediately after flowering, cut back new shoots of spring-flowering Ceanothus *to 2–3 leaves. Tie in new shoots and trim back outward-growing shoots to keep growth trained close to the wall or fence.*

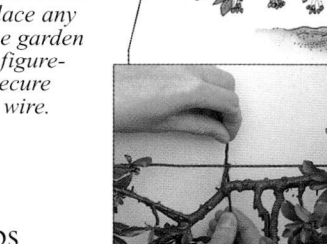

FAN-TRAINING A SHRUB

This fan (Prunus mume 'Beni-chidori') has been trained to develop an evenly spaced branch framework, in the same way as pruning fan-trained fruit trees.

Training and pruning standard shrubs

Some shrubs, for example, fuchsias and *Buddleja alternifolia*, may be grown as standards. The height of the stem varies according to the vigour of the plant and the effect wanted. For details on training a standard fuchsia, see p.121; for pruning a standard rose, see p.162.

To train a shrub such as *Buddleja alternifolia* as a standard, tie a strong stem to a cane in the first growing season. Pinch all sideshoots back to two or three leaves, leaving a few growing near the stem tip. As the stem grows, continue to pinch out. When the clear stem is at the desired height, stop the terminal shoot to encourage shoots to form the head. In early spring of the following year, shorten the branches of the head to about 15cm (6in). Retain two or three of the shoots that each produces. Feed and mulch. Prune subsequently as for other shrubs pruned in summer after flowering (see p.106).

Some pendulous cultivars are grafted onto the clear stem of a rootstock. Remove any suckers (see p.100) from the stock and treat as for roses (see "Suckers and how to deal with them", p.159).

Root pruning

Root pruning is sometimes used to control the top-growth of vigorous shrubs and to make them flower more freely; grafted specimens that are making prolific leaf growth but producing few flowers or fruits usually benefit from root pruning.

In early spring, dig a trench around the shrub to a depth of 30–60cm (12–24in) with a circumference just beyond the spread of the top-growth. Use pruning loppers or a saw to cut back the thick, woody roots; as a guideline, shorten them to about half the radius of the trench. Leave fibrous roots unpruned. Control further spreading of the roots by inserting a barrier of slates or polycarbonate sheets around the circumference of the trench (see *Restricting the Spread of Bamboo*, p.96). After backfilling, mulch the area within the trench.

Root pruning is often used to control container-grown shrubs. This is best carried out when repotting the shrub. Shorten up to one fifth of woody roots by a quarter and cut back others so that they fit comfortably in the container. Repot, using fresh compost with a slow-release fertilizer added, and water thoroughly.

Renovation

Old, tangled, or overgrown shrubs may sometimes be renovated by extensive pruning. Shrubs that respond well usually produce young growth from the base. It is not worth trying to salvage a shrub that is badly diseased. Some shrubs do not tolerate drastic pruning; if in any doubt about a particular shrub, stagger a programme of heavy pruning over a period of two or three years.

Renovate deciduous shrubs, such as lilacs, after flowering or when dormant; for evergreens, such as *Viburnum tinus*, delay renovation until mid-spring, after flowering.

Renovating old or overgrown shrubs

Cut out all weak and crossing stems and shorten main stems to 30–45cm (12–18in) above ground level, ensuring that a balanced framework is left. Apply a slow-release fertilizer at 120g/sq m (4oz/sq yd), and mulch the area around the shrub to a depth of 5–10cm (2–4in). Keep the shrub well watered throughout summer.

During the following growing season, a mass of shoots should grow from below the cuts on the main stems. Retain only two to four of the strongest on each stem to provide the new branch framework. On deciduous shrubs, cut out superfluous shoots during the dormant season. On evergreen shrubs, do this in mid-spring.

In the following growing season, some secondary growth may occur where shoots have been cut. Rub out these growths.

Staggered renovation

An alternative, less drastic method is to spread the pruning over two or three years. Prune deciduous shrubs after flowering, evergreens in mid-spring. Prune half of the oldest stems to 5–8cm (2–3in) from the ground. Where possible cut back the remaining stems by about half to new, vigorous, replacement shoots. Apply a slow-release fertilizer, water well, and mulch. At the same time the following year, repeat the process on the remaining old stems. Thereafter, prune the shrub according to its growth and flowering characteristics.

GRADUAL RENOVATION

Renovate deciduous shrubs after flowering and evergreens in mid-spring. Cut back a third to a half of the oldest main stems (here on a Deutzia*) almost to the ground and remove dead, twiggy stems. Over the next year or two cut back remaining old, main stems.*

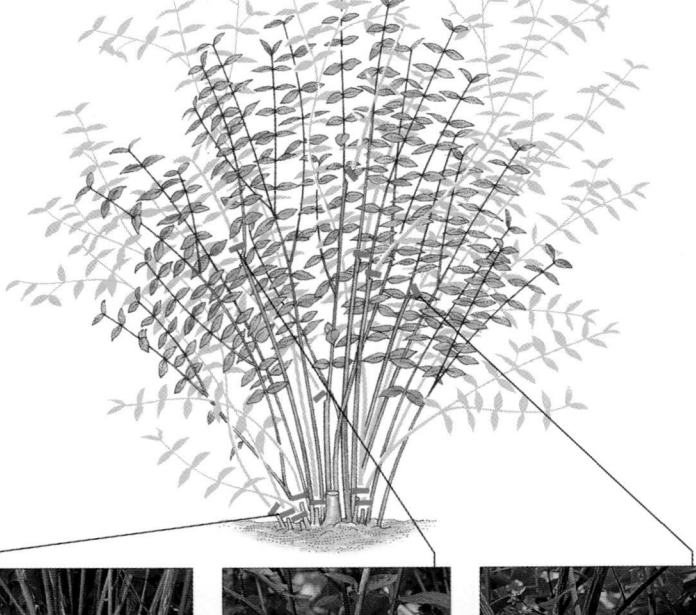

DRASTIC RENOVATION

A shrub that produces new growth from the base (here lilac) can be renovated when dormant if it is deciduous or in mid-spring if evergreen. Cut back all main stems to within 30–45cm (12–18in) of the ground. Remove suckers by cutting them off at the base.

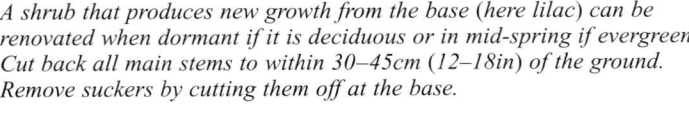

Cut back about half of the stems to within 5–8cm (2–3in) of the base. Remove the oldest stems and any that spoil the shrub's shape.

Cut back older stems by half to new, vigorous shoots, and remove any weak, twiggy growth or dead wood.

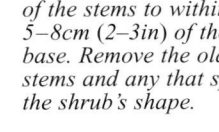

Prune back any crossing, rubbing, or congested stems to a bud or stem that will not cause another crossing shoot to develop.

Propagation

THERE are many ways to propagate shrubs to raise new plants, including taking cuttings, sowing seed, layering, division, and grafting.

Taking cuttings is a simple way of propagating many shrubs and, unlike seed, which may produce variable offspring, it may be used for cultivars, hybrids, and sports.

Sowing seed is simple and inexpensive but it is relatively slow to produce plants of flowering size. Some shrubs may be divided, while others may be layered.

Grafting involves uniting a stem from the plant to be propagated with the rootstock of a compatible plant. It is not commonly used outside commerce, since it requires more expertise and skill than other methods, but it is the most suitable method for some shrubs.

Softwood cuttings

This technique is suitable for raising several, mainly deciduous, shrubs, for example *Fuchsia* and *Perovskia*. Softwood cuttings are taken in spring from fast-growing stem tips when these are about 6–8cm (2½–3in) long. The cuttings have a soft base and a higher capacity to root than cuttings of more mature wood.

Preparing the cuttings

Take the cuttings early in the morning. Select healthy, pliable, single-stemmed shoots and seal them in an opaque, plastic bag. Prepare the cuttings as soon as possible after collection: trim the cuttings just below a node and remove the lower leaves. The soft tip is generally pinched out as it is vulnerable to rotting; its removal also encourages the cutting, once rooted, to form a bushy plant. Use a cutting compost of equal parts peat substitute (or peat) and either perlite or sharp sand. With a dibber, insert them into the compost. Water them in, applying a fungicide to minimize rot, label, and place in a mist unit or propagator.

Aftercare

Softwood cuttings wilt quickly if not kept in a humid atmosphere and aftercare is very important; remove dropped leaves daily, if possible, and apply a fungicidal spray every week. Once rooted, harden off the cuttings and transplant them into individual pots or retain them in the container. If kept in the cutting medium, give a supplementary feed every two weeks during the growing season and pot up the rooted cuttings individually the following spring.

Greenwood cuttings

Almost all the shrubs that may be propagated by softwood cuttings may also be propagated by greenwood cuttings. Take greenwood cuttings, either nodal or heel cuttings (see p.113), from vigorous shoots in late spring or early summer, when these are firm and slightly woody at the base. Follow the method for softwood cuttings.

Remove the soft tips if the cuttings are more than 8–10cm (3–4in) long and trim off the bottom leaves. On a nodal cutting, make a straight cut with a sharp blade directly below the node. Trim off the tail on a heel cut-

Select and prepare greenwood cuttings (here of Philadelphus*) in late spring when growth has slowed and the new stems are firmer.*

ting. Dip the cuttings in a rooting hormone and insert them into the compost. Water the cuttings with a fungicidal solution before placing them in a mist unit or propagator. Remove any fallen leaves daily and apply a fungicide once a week.

Once rooted, harden off the cuttings and transplant them or grow them on in the original container.

PROPAGATING SHRUBS BY SOFTWOOD CUTTINGS

1 *In spring, cut off young, non-flowering shoots (here from a hydrangea) with 3–5 pairs of leaves. Seal them in an opaque plastic bag and keep shaded until they can be prepared.*

2 *Reduce each cutting to 8–10cm (3–4in) in length, making a straight cut just below a node (see inset). Trim off the lower leaves and pinch out the growing tip.*

3 *Insert the cuttings into prepared pots of cutting compost, ensuring that the leaves do not touch each other.*

4 *Water the cuttings with a fungicidal solution, then label and place them in a propagator. Maintain a temperature of 18–21°C (64–70°F).*

5 *Once the cuttings have rooted, harden them off, then remove them from the pot and carefully tease them apart.*

6 *Transplant the separated cuttings into individual pots and firm in. Water, label, and keep the cuttings in a shaded position until well established.*

SHRUBS TO PROPAGATE BY SOFT/GREENWOOD CUTTINGS

Abelia, some ❀
Abutilon, some ❀
Aloysia, most ❀, ❦
Calluna
Caryopteris
Ceanothus, some ❀ (deciduous spp.)
Ceratostigma, some ❀, ❦
Cestrum ❀ ❦
Cotoneaster (deciduous spp.)
Cytisus, some ❀
Daboecia
Daphne x *burkwoodii*
Deutzia (some spp.)
Enkianthus
Erica
Forsythia
Fuchsia, some ❀
Genista, some ❀
Halesia
Hydrangea ❦
Kolkwitzia
Lagerstroemia, some ❀, ❦
Lantana ❀ ❦
Lavatera ❦
Perovskia
Philadelphus
Potentilla
Viburnum (deciduous spp.)
Weigela (some spp.)

KEY
❀ *Not hardy*
❦ *Softwood cuttings only*

PROPAGATING BY SEMI-RIPE CUTTINGS

1 *In mid- to late summer, select healthy shoots of the current season's growth for the cuttings. Sever them from the parent plant (here* Ilex x altaclerensis *'Golden King') just above a node. They should be semi-ripe: still soft at the top but firm at the base.*

2 *Remove the sideshoots from the main stem. Trim each sideshoot to 10–15cm (4–6in) long, cutting just below a node.*

3 *Trim off the soft tip of each cutting and then remove the lowest pair of leaves, cutting flush with the stem.*

4 *Stimulate rooting by wounding the cutting: carefully cut away a piece of bark about 2.5–4cm (1–1½in) long from one side of the base.*

5 *Dip the base of each cutting in hormone rooting powder, then insert it into cutting compost in a propagator or in pots in a cold frame.*

6 *Once they are well rooted, carefully lift the cuttings and plant them individually. Gradually harden them off before growing them on in their pots or transplanting them outside.*

If the latter, feed them regularly during the growing season and transplant them the following spring.

Semi-ripe cuttings

Many evergreen as well as some deciduous shrubs may be propagated from semi-ripe cuttings.

Suitable cuttings

The cuttings are normally taken from mid- to late summer and sometimes into the early autumn. Select shoots from the current season's growth that are firm and woody near the base but still soft at the tip. Unlike softwood cuttings, they should offer some resistance when bent. Some shrubs are propagated by variations of this semi-ripe cuttings technique, such as mallet cuttings (see p.113) or leaf-bud cuttings (see p.113).

Preparing the rooting medium

Before collecting the cutting material from the parent shrub, fill sufficient containers of appropriate size, or a propagator (equipped with basal heating) with a suitable rooting medium: use fine-grade pine bark or a mixture of equal parts of peat substitute (or peat) and either grit or perlite.

Preparing the cuttings

Cuttings may be taken with a heel (see p.113) or as nodal cuttings. Heel cuttings should be 5–7cm (2–3in) long, trimmed at the heel; nodal cuttings should be 10–15cm (4–6in) long, taken from leaders or sideshoots, and cut with a sharp knife or secateurs just below a node.

Remove the soft tips of nodal and heel cuttings. In both cases, remove the lowest pair of leaves and with large-leaved plants reduce the size of the remaining leaves by about a half to minimize moisture loss.

An optional step is to prepare the base of the cuttings by making a shallow wound at one side; on plants that are difficult to root, such as *Daphne sericea*, this cut should be made deeper so that a sliver of bark is also removed.

Potting up

Dip the bases of the cuttings, including the entire wound on wounded cuttings, in a rooting hormone before using a dibber to insert them in the prepared compost, either directly in a propagator, or in containers.

Space the cuttings approximately 8–10cm (3–4in) apart, and make certain that their leaves do not overlap, since this may create stagnant conditions in which rot fungi thrive.

Firm the compost mixture around the cuttings. Label each container and water the cuttings thoroughly with a fungicidal solution to protect them against damping off diseases (see p.660).

Correct temperature

Overwinter cuttings in containers in a cold frame or greenhouse. Those that have been inserted directly in a propagator should have basal heat maintained at 21°C (70°F).

Aftercare

Inspect the cuttings periodically during the winter period, removing any fallen leaves promptly. Water the containers if the compost mixture shows any signs of drying out. If the cuttings are being overwintered in a cold frame, this may need some form of insulation, such as a hessian cover or a piece of old carpet, to protect the cuttings from damage by frost.

Cuttings kept in a cold frame or unheated greenhouse will almost certainly need a further growing season in their containers before rooting satisfactorily. Keep the frame closed, except on very mild days. The glass should be kept clean and free of any condensation, since the high moisture content of the air inside the frame provides ideal conditions for fungal infection to occur. In late spring and early summer, gradually open the cover for longer and longer periods to harden off the rooted cuttings. If necessary, protect the cuttings from strong, direct sunlight by covering the glass with suitable shading material.

Throughout the growing season, apply a liquid feed every two weeks to all semi-ripe cuttings. Check them regularly, and remove any that are weak or showing signs of disease.

Transplanting

Cuttings overwintered in a propagator should have rooted by early spring, since the basal heat helps to speed up root development. Check that there is strong root growth before transplanting the cuttings. Ease them from their containers, separate each cutting carefully, and either pot up individually or plant, clearly labelled, in the open ground. If some cuttings have not rooted but have formed a callus, scrape off some of the callus to stimulate rooting and re-insert the cuttings in the compost mixture.

Cuttings grown in a cold frame may be planted out in autumn, if well developed, or kept in a sheltered position outside or in the cold frame until spring. They are then potted up individually or planted out.

Heel cuttings

Heel cuttings, which may be taken from greenwood, semi-ripe, or hardwood stems, are vigorous sideshoots of the current season's growth. Each cutting is taken with a "heel" of old wood at its base, in which the growth hormones that assist the rooting process are concentrated.

Heel cuttings are particularly suitable for a number of evergreen shrubs such as *Pieris* and some azaleas (*Rhododendron*), deciduous shrubs that have pithy or hollow stems such as *Berberis* and *Sambucus*, and those shrubs that have greenwood stems such as broom (*Cytisus/Genista*).

Select as cuttings healthy sideshoots that are characteristic of the parent plant. Pull the shoot away from the main stem so that a small strip of bark from the parent shoot comes away with it. Avoid tearing too much bark off the main shoot as this may expose it to infection. Trim the heel with a sharp blade and then follow the technique for greenwood (see p.111), semi-ripe (see p.112), or hardwood cuttings (see right), according to the particular stem's maturity.

1 *Pull away healthy sideshoots of the current season's growth (here on* Prunus laurocerasus *'Schipkaensis') with a heel of bark.*

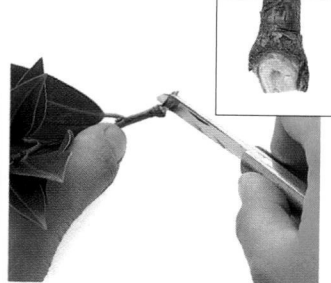

2 *Using a sharp knife, trim off the "tail" at the base of the heel before inserting it in cutting compost.*

Mallet cuttings

A mallet cutting, which is taken from semi-ripe stems, is a ripened shoot of the current season's growth attached to a piece of wood from the previous season, forming a mallet-shaped plug at its base. Mallet cuttings are often used to propagate shrubs with pithy or hollow stems, because rot fungi are less likely to affect older wood. It is particularly suitable for many *Spiraea* and deciduous *Berberis*, which produce short sideshoots on main branches.

In late summer, remove a stem of the last season's growth from the parent and cut it into sections, each containing a vigorous sideshoot of new growth. If the mallet is more than 5mm (¼in) in diameter, slit it lengthwise. Then treat as for semi-ripe cuttings (see p.112).

MALLET CUTTINGS

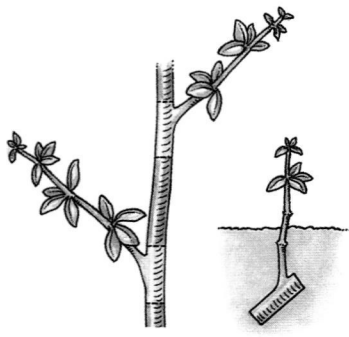

Remove a stem produced the previous year and cut it above each sideshoot and about 2.5cm (1in) below. Reduce it to 10–13cm (4–5in) and trim off lower leaves.

Leaf-bud cuttings

A leaf-bud cutting is taken from semi-ripe stems and comprises a short piece of stem bearing a leaf and a leaf bud. In comparison with stem cuttings, leaf-bud cuttings make much more economical use of the material from the parent plant. This method of propagation is most commonly used for camellias and mahonia.

In late summer or early autumn, select a vigorous shoot of the current season's growth, bearing healthy leaves and well-developed buds. Using a sharp knife or secateurs, cut the stem just above each leaf, then make a cut about 2cm (¾in) below the petiole so that the shoot is divided into several sections.

Leaf-bud cuttings do not need to be treated with hormone rooting powder before potting up, but may be wounded at the base to hasten rooting. Insert them in containers of cutting compost and treat as for semi-ripe cuttings (see p.112).

To save space in the cold frame or propagator, roll up any large leaves and secure them with elastic bands; a cane inserted down the middle of a rolled-up leaf will help to anchor it firmly in the compost. Trim compound leaves on shrubs such as mahonia by a half.

Hardwood cuttings

An easy way to raise many deciduous and some evergreen shrubs is from hardwood cuttings. Use fully ripe, vigorous growths of the current season, taken from late autumn to midwinter. Take cuttings of deciduous shrubs just after leaf fall, or just before bud burst, in spring.

Preparing the ground
Cuttings are best rooted in a prepared bed or containers kept in a

PROPAGATING BY LEAF-BUD CUTTINGS

1 *Select semi-ripe shoots (here of* Camellia japonica). *Make a straight cut 2cm (¾in) below each leaf and a further cut just above.*

2 *Remove a 5mm (¼in) sliver of bark at the base of each cutting (see inset). Insert the cuttings in the compost so that the leaf axils are just visible above the surface.*

SHRUBS TO PROPAGATE BY SEMI-RIPE CUTTINGS

Andromeda
Arctostaphylos
Aucuba▽
Azara, some ❋,▽
Berberis, some ❋,▽
Boronia ❋ ▽
Brachyglottis ❋
Bupleurum▽
Buxus
Callistemon ❋ ▽
Camellia, some ❋
Cantua ❋ ▽
Carmichaelia, some ❋,▽
Carpenteria▽
Cassinia▽
Cassiope▽
Ceanothus, some ❋,▽
Choisya
Colletia▽
Coprosma ❋ ▽
Corokia, some ❋,▽

Cotoneaster 'Firebird'

Cotoneaster▽
Cytisus, some ❋,▽
Daphne
Deutzia (some spp.)
Drimys
Elaeagnus▽
Erica
Escallonia▽
Garrya▽
Gordonia ❋ ▽
Grevillea, some ❋ ▽
Griselinia, some ❋,▽
Hibiscus rosa-sinensis ❋
Ilex, some ❋
Itea ilicifolia▽
Lavandula, some ❋
Leptospermum, some ❋ ▽
Leucothöe▽
Magnolia grandiflora▽
Mahonia
Nerium ❋ ▽
Olearia, some ❋,▽

Olearia phlogopappa

Philadelphus
Photinia▽
Pieris▽
Pittosporum, some ❋
Prunus (evergreen spp.)▽
Pyracantha
Rhododendron▽
Skimmia▽
Viburnum
Weigela

KEY
❋ Not hardy
▽ With a heel

113

Atriplex halimus
Aucuba (some spp.)
Buddleja
Buxus (some spp.)
Cornus alba, C. sericea
Cotoneaster x *watereri*
Deutzia x *elegantissima*
  'Rosealind', *D. longifolia,*
  D. x *rosea, D. scabra*
Forsythia
Hypericum x *moserianum*
Ligustrum ovalifolium
Philadelphus

*Deutzia
longifolia
'Veitchii'*

Ribes
Rosa rugosa
Rubus
Ruta graveolens
Salix
Sambucus
Spiraea
Symphoricarpos
Tamarix
Viburnum (deciduous spp.)
Weigela

cold frame but they may also be inserted in a bed in open ground.

Prepare the bed in late summer or early autumn, first working the soil until it is friable, and then digging out a flat-backed trench 12–15cm (5–6in) deep. To encourage rooting, put a 2.5–5cm (1–2in) layer of coarse sand in the base of the trench; this is essential on heavy soils. Space the trenches 38cm (15in) apart.

Preparing the cuttings

Take cuttings that are about pencil thickness, cutting at the junction of the current and the previous season's growth.

Trim deciduous cuttings into 15–22cms (6–9in) lengths, cutting at the top just above a bud or pair of buds and, at the bottom, below a bud or pair of buds; make evergreen cuttings 15cm (6in) long, cutting above and below leaves. Take heel cuttings of pithy stems (see p.113). Remove all leaves on the bottom two thirds of evergreen cuttings and cut large leaves in half. Treat the basal cut with a rooting hormone. Removing a sliver of bark near the base may encourage difficult cuttings to root.

Insert the cuttings in containers of cutting compost. Alternatively, place deciduous cuttings against the vertical side of a prepared trench, 15cm (6in) apart in open ground, or in a cold frame, 10cm (4in) apart. Leave 2.5–5cm (1–2in) of the cuttings above ground. Backfill the trench and firm in the cuttings.

Aftercare

If the ground is lifted by frost, firm it down around the cuttings. Keep the bed weed-free and well watered during the growing season. Cuttings in a cold frame will normally root by the following spring. Harden them off (see p.637) before potting up or planting out. Those in the open ground should be left in place until the following autumn and then transplanted to their permanent position.

Root cuttings

Shrubs that may be propagated from root cuttings include *Aesculus parviflora, Aralia, Clerodendrum, Myrica, Rhus,* and *Xanthorhiza simplicissima.* Lift a young plant prior to regrowth, in mid- to late winter, and tease the soil from its roots. If this is not practical, expose part of the shrub's root system. Cut off young roots – 5mm (¼in) in diameter or more – close to the main stem. Keep them in moist sacking or a plastic bag until they can be prepared.

Preparing the cuttings

First remove and discard fibrous, lateral roots. Then make a straight cut on an undamaged root at the end where it was severed from the plant. At the opposite end of the root, make a slanting cut. Cuttings should be 5–15cm (2–6in) long – thinner cuttings should be longer – and several cuttings may be prepared from the same root. The colder the rooting environment and the thinner the root, the longer the cutting needs to be; cuttings to be rooted outdoors need to be at least 10cm (4in) long. Dust each cutting with fungicide but do not treat with a rooting powder, since this will tend to discourage the production of shoots.

Inserting the cuttings

Aralia and other shrubs that reproduce readily from root cuttings may be inserted in open ground. For shrubs that root less readily, a controlled environment is preferable. Prepare containers of cuttings compost large enough for several cuttings. Firm the compost lightly and insert each cutting vertically 5cm (2in) apart with the slanted end down. Thinner, longer cuttings can be laid horizontally. Firm the compost so that the flat end of each cutting is just visible. Cover with 3mm (⅛in) of grit (or vermiculite for those laid horizontally), and water. This watering may be sufficient to last until the shoots develop; excessive moisture may lead to rotting.

Aftercare

Cuttings will root in ten weeks outdoors, eight weeks in a cold frame or cool greenhouse. Under glass, cuttings will produce shoots in four to six weeks if they are kept at 18–24°C (64–75°F). Cuttings from shrubs that make rapid growth should be repotted as soon as they have rooted. Other root cuttings may be left in their pots for a further 12 months; apply a liquid feed once or twice a month. Then pot up or plant out.

Raising shrubs from seed

Growing shrubs from seed is simple and economical. In genera whose species hybridize readily, only use seed produced by controlled pollination. Garden-raised hybrids, however, can produce interesting new plants when open-pollinated seed is used.

EXTRACTING SEED FROM BERRIES

1 *Squash berries (here pyracantha) between finger and thumb, removing most of the outer flesh. Wash seeds by rubbing them in warm water.*

2 *Dry the seeds with tissue and place them in a clear plastic bag with a little coarse sand or moist vermiculite; refrigerate until ready to sow.*

PROPAGATING SHRUBS BY HARDWOOD CUTTINGS

1 *Select strong, healthy, ripened shoots from this year's growth for the cuttings (see inset, left); avoid weak, thin stems (centre) and older wood (right).*

Healthy   Weak   Old wood

2 *Remove any deciduous leaves and trim off the soft tip. Cut the stem into 15–20cm (6–8in) lengths, dipping the bases into hormone rooting powder.*

3 *Insert the cuttings into prepared pots of cutting compost so that approximately 2.5–5cm (1–2in) of each is visible. Label the pots and place in a cold frame.*

Collecting and cleaning seed

Gather the seed capsules or fruits when ripe. Extract the seed, then clean and dry it before sowing or storing. Soak fleshy fruits in warm water or squash them so that the seed may be picked out more easily. Collect fine seed by gathering whole capsules, preferably when they have already turned brown. Place the capsules in a paper bag and keep at room temperature until they split open.

Storing seed

The length of time seed is viable depends on the species and storage conditions. Daphne, *Kalmia*, and rhododendrons, for example, should be sown when fresh. Oily seeds do not store well and should be sown soon after collection. The viability of seed may be prolonged if it is stored at 3–5°C (37–41°F).

Breaking seed dormancy

The seeds of some shrubs have a form of dormancy to stop them germinating in adverse conditions. This dormancy may be broken artificially by scarification or stratification (see also PRINCIPLES OF PROPAGATION, "How to overcome dormancy", p.629).

To allow air and moisture to penetrate large seeds with hard coats, such as camellia and peonies (*Paeonia*), scarify them by nicking the seed coat with a knife or filing away a small section before sowing. Hard-coated seeds that are too small to be nicked may be rubbed with glasspaper. Germination of some seeds may be aided by soaking the seed in either cold water (for example camellia and *Pittosporum*) or hot but not boiling water (for example *Arbutus*, *Caragana*, *Coronilla*, and *Cytisus*) for a few hours. This softens the hard seed coat allowing water to enter and germination to begin.

Seeds that need a period of chilling are stratified – *Acer palmatum*, *Amelanchier*, cotoneaster, *Euonymus*, *Hippophäe*, and viburnum producing seeds that need such treatment. As soon as the seed is gathered, place a layer of crocks in the base of a container that has drainage holes, and scatter the seed between two layers of a sand and peat substitute (or peat) mix. Plunge the container in the open garden or place in a cold frame.

The next spring, by when some of the seed may have germinated, it may be separated out and space sown. Seed of certain hardy shrubs, such as some *Viburnum*, may need further chilling in a refrigerator.

Refrigerating hardy seed may produce more reliable results. Mix the seed with moist vermiculite, peat substitute, or peat, then seal it in a clear plastic bag and refrigerate. The chilling period varies from species to species and it is best to try and sow the seed before it starts germinating in the fridge, that is in mid- to late winter. For safety, keep a few extra seeds in the fridge, checking them each week until germination has started, then remove and sow them.

Sowing seed in containers

Seeds of hardy shrubs are sown in a cold frame in autumn, or placed in a fridge and sown in mid- to late winter, while seeds of temperate and tender shrubs are sown in spring, in pots. Most fine, ericaceous seed is stored in the fridge until mid- to late winter, when it is germinated under mist at a temperature of 15°C (59°F).

Clean all containers, implements, and surfaces. Use a standard seed compost, but for lime-haters use an ericaceous compost. Many large seeds are sown individually into their own module or root trainer. Overfill a pot or tray with compost and gently firm before scraping off the surplus. Firm again with a presser board so that the level is 1cm (½in) below the rim of the pot or tray. Sow the seeds 5cm (2in) apart, then firm them evenly into the compost. Cover with a 5mm (¼in) layer of sieved compost and a 5mm (¼in) layer of clean grit. Label and date each container and water the seeds.

Many medium-sized seeds may also be sown in this way, but the gap between the rim and compost should be 5–8mm (¼–⅜in). Cover seeds with sieved compost and then 5mm (¼in) of clean grit. Place wire netting over the container to protect the seedlings from small animals. When sowing fine seed, firm the compost to within 5mm (¼in) of the container rim. Water and allow the compost to drain before sowing, carefully shaking the seed out over the surface. Do not cover the seed or water it from above.

Aftercare for seedlings in containers

After sowing, place the containers in a propagator, greenhouse, or cold frame. Temperate species need a temperature of 12–15°C (54–9°F); warm-temperate and tropical species prefer 21°C (70°F). For seed sown in spring under glass, a temperature of 12–15°C (54–9°F) should be maintained. Inspect containers of seed regularly and water as necessary. Never water fine seed from above; place the container in a shallow water tank for a short time so that water is taken up by capillary action. When the seeds have germinated, spray occasionally with fungicide.

SOWING SEED IN CONTAINERS

1 *Sow seeds evenly onto a prepared tray of sieved seed compost by tapping them from a folded piece of paper.*

2 *Cover the seeds with a fine layer of compost, then add a 5mm (¼in) layer of grit. Label and place in a cold frame until the seeds have germinated.*

3 *When the seedlings are large enough to handle, prick them out, lifting them carefully with a widger and holding them gently by their leaves.*

4 *Transfer the seedlings into individual pots or insert 3 in a 13cm (5in) pot. After the second pair of leaves has formed, pot them up individually.*

Pricking out

Once large enough to handle, prick out the seedlings. Knock the sides of the container gently against, for example, the greenhouse bench to loosen the compost or remove the seedlings and compost together and separate the seedlings, disturbing their roots as little as possible.

Transfer the seedlings into clean pots or seed trays of cutting compost, levelled but not firmed. Make a hole in the compost using a widger and insert the seedling. Level the compost by tapping the top of the container and firm in, then label and water. Until the seedlings are established, place the pots out of direct sunlight in a temperature similar to that needed for germination.

Sowing seed outdoors

Open-ground seedbeds are useful for sowing large batches of seed that do not require daily attention. Such beds are generally 90–100cm (36–39in) wide and raised 15–20cm (6–8in) above the surrounding ground, to improve drainage. Prepare the bed between six months and a year before sowing.

In autumn, rake the soil to a fine tilth. Fine seed is broadcast sown over the area, while medium or large seed is sown up to 10–15cm (4–6in) apart, in rows 45cm (18in) apart. Large seeds may be sown at greater distances apart, if required.

Cover large and medium seeds to a depth of 0.5–1cm (¼–½in) but leave fine seed uncovered. Then place a 0.5–1cm (¼–½in) layer of grit over the seedbed. Firm the grit with a presser board, and label the rows.

Aftercare for seedlings outdoors

Protect seedlings from wind damage by covering them with 50 per cent permeable netting, and from frosts by using firmly secured horticultural fleece. If the seeds are well spaced, they should not be troubled by disease, but greenfly (see "Aphids", p.646), red spider mite (p.646), and mice (p.662) may be a problem.

If the spacing is adequate, the seedlings may be left in the seedbed until the following autumn; they should then be either potted up or transplanted into a separate nursery bed.

Propagation by layering

Layering is a method of propagating shrubs whereby a stem is encouraged to develop roots before being removed from the parent plant. Dropping and stooling, techniques often used commercially, are variations of layering.

Simple layering

Many deciduous and evergreen shrubs may be propagated by this method. In autumn or spring, about 12 months before layering is to take place, prune a low branch on the parent plant to encourage vigorous shoots, which have a greater capacity to root. Between the following late autumn and early spring, prepare the soil around the stem to be layered so that it is friable. Add grit and humus if the ground is heavy.

Retain any leaves at the tip of the selected shoot but strip off others and any sideshoots. Bring the stem down to ground level and mark the ground about 22–30cm (9–12in) behind its tip. Dig a shallow hole or trench at this point for the stem. Wound the stem at the point where it will be pegged into the hole, that is about 30cm (12in) behind its tip, either with an angled cut or by removing a ring of bark. Dust the cut with a rooting hormone, then peg the stem in the hole with bent wire, turning up the tip and securing it to a cane. Infill the trench and firm the soil, leaving the tip exposed.

Throughout the growing season keep the area around the layer moist. The layer should have rooted by autumn. In the following spring, check that there is a good root system before severing the layer from the parent plant and potting it up or planting it out in the open garden. If it has not rooted or there are only a few roots, keep it attached and in place for another growing season.

Air layering

This technique is particularly suitable for shrubs with branches that are difficult to lower to ground level. It is also good for plants growing in high humidity and rainfall and in warm-temperate situations.

In spring, choose a strong, healthy, one-year-old stem that has ripened. Trim the sideshoots or leaves to leave a clear length of stem behind the tip. Wound the stem with an angled cut and dust the cut surface with a rooting hormone.

Cut off the sealed end of a black or opaque plastic bag, about 22 x 18cm (9 x 7in). Slip it over the stem and secure the end farthest from the growing tip, using tape, raffia, or string.

Moisten a well-aerated rooting medium of sphagnum moss or equal parts of perlite and peat substitute or peat so that it is wet but not sodden. Pack the moist medium into the bag around the stem's cut surface and seal the top end. Keep the bag in position for a complete season.

The following spring, check that the layer has rooted. If so, sever it immediately below the point of layering. Remove the bag and tease out the roots. Prune back any new growth on the layered stem to a leaf or bud close to the old wood. Pot up using a standard or ericaceous potting compost, as appropriate. Label and place the layer in a cool greenhouse or cold frame until well established. If only a few (or no) roots have developed when the bag is removed, reseal it and leave it in place for several months more. Then follow the process described above.

Tip layering

A few shrubs, mainly species and hybrids of the genus *Rubus*, root readily from the tips of stems and may be propagated in this way. In spring, select a vigorous, one-year-old shoot and pinch out the growing point to promote sideshoots. In late spring, cultivate the soil around the shoot. Work in organic matter and grit, if the soil is heavy.

In midsummer, when the tip growth has firmed slightly, bring the stem down to ground level and mark the position of the tip. At that point, dig a trench about 7–10cm (3–4in) deep, with one side vertical and the other sloping towards the parent plant. Using inverted, "U"-shaped, wire staples, peg the growing tip at the bottom of the trench close to the vertical side. Infill the trench, firm lightly, and water.

By late autumn, well-rooted plants should have developed. Sever these at the point where the arched stem enters the trench. Lift the rooted layers and pot on or replant outdoors. (See also *Tip Layering*, p.471.)

Dropping

With this technique a plant is almost buried. It is used to raise dwarf shrubs, such as low-growing rhododendrons and heathers (*Erica*, *Daboecia*, *Calluna*), from parent plants that have become straggly.

In the dormant season, thin out branches of plants that have a mass of congested stems, to allow the remaining stems sufficient contact

PROPAGATING A SHRUB BY SIMPLE LAYERING

1 *Select a young, pliable, low-growing stem. Bring it down to the soil and mark its position with a cane about 22–30cm (9–12in) behind the tip.*

2 *At the marked point, dig a hole in the prepared soil about 8cm (3in) deep, with a shallow slope on the side where the stem joins the parent plant.*

3 *Trim off sideshoots and leaves on the selected stem. On the underside of the stem, at a point where it touches the ground, cut a tongue or ring of bark.*

4 *Apply a rooting hormone to the wound on the stem. Peg down the stem with bent wire so that the stem's cut surface is held in contact with the soil.*

5 *Gently bend up the stem's tip vertically and secure it to the cane with a tie. Fill in the hole with more soil. Lightly firm with your fingers and water in.*

6 *Once rooted (see inset), lift the layered stem and cut it off the parent plant, severing it close to the new, young roots. Pot up the layer or plant it out.*

AIR LAYERING A SHRUB

1 Select a healthy, horizontal stem from the previous year's growth. Trim off any leaves and sideshoots to provide a 22–30cm (9–12in) section of clear stem.

2 Slide a plastic sleeve over and along the stem; seal and secure the lower end of the sleeve to the stem with adhesive tape.

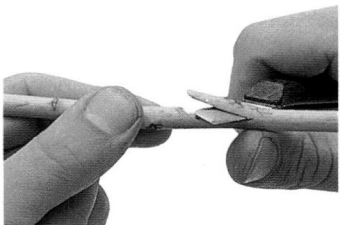

3 Fold back the plastic. Make a 4cm (1¹/₂in) diagonal cut 5mm (¹/₄in) into the stem in the direction of growth, away from the shrub. Apply a rooting hormone.

4 Soak about 2 handfuls of sphagnum moss in water, then gently squeeze it out. With the back of the knife, pack the cut with moss, wedging it open.

5 Pull back the plastic sleeve over the cut. Carefully pack the sleeve with more moistened moss so that the moss is all around the stem.

6 Continue to pack the sleeve until the moss is about 5cm (2in) from the open end. Close the end and secure it firmly in place with adhesive tape.

7 The sealed sleeve encourages rooting by retaining moisture. Leave it in place for at least a growing season to allow new roots to develop.

8 Once the layer has rooted, remove the sleeve and cut off the layer below the roots. Pot up or plant out the new shrub (here a rhododendron) in the open ground.

STOOLING

Cover shoots with free-draining soil, adding more as they grow. The shoots will root down and can be separated in autumn and potted on.

with the soil to develop roots once buried. Before growth starts, but after the risk of penetrating frosts has passed, dig a pit large enough to bury the plant with only the branch tips visible. If the soil is heavy, add grit and organic material.

Lift the parent plant with the root ball as complete as possible and "drop" it into the prepared hole. Work the soil around each stem, leaving 2.5–5cm (1–2in) of each tip exposed. Firm the soil and label the plant. In summer, keep the soil moist and, in autumn, carefully tease away the soil around the plant to check for rooting. Sever any rooted shoots from the parent plant, and pot up or plant out, clearly labelled. If rooting has not occurred, replace the soil and leave for a further 12 months.

Stooling
Although primarily used to raise fruit tree rootstocks, stooling may also be used to propagate deciduous ornamental shrubs such as dogwoods (Cornus) and lilacs (Syringa) from ungrafted plants.

Plant a rooted layer or other young plant in spring, label, and grow on for a season. The next spring, cut back the stem to within 8cm (3in) of the ground and apply a balanced fertilizer at 120g/sq m (4oz/sq yd). When the resulting shoots from this stem (or stool) are 15cm (6in) long, work friable soil enriched with organic matter between the shoots and bury them. Add grit if the ground is heavy. As the shoots grow, continue mounding up soil until about 22cm (9in) of each shoot is buried. Keep the soil moist in dry weather.

In autumn, gently fork away the soil to ground level straight after leaf fall, leaving the rooted shoots exposed. Cut them off and pot them up or plant them out. Provided that the stools are kept fertilized, the process may be repeated annually and the same stool used for propagation in subsequent years.

French layering
This method is a form of stooling and is used to increase the stock of deciduous shrubs such as dogwoods (Cornus alba, C. sericea) and Cotinus coggygria.

In spring, plant a rooted layer or young plant, label it, and grow it on for a season. Then, in the dormant season, cut back the stool to within 8cm (3in) of the ground. In the following spring, apply a balanced fertilizer at the rate of 60–120g/sq m (2–4oz/sq yd).

The following autumn, cut out all but about the ten best stems; shorten the tips of these so that they are all about the same length. With "U"-shaped, wire staples, pin each stem to the ground, spreading the stems evenly around the parent stool. Each bud along the length of the stem should break evenly in spring.

When the new shoots on the pegged-down stems are approximately 5–8cm (2–3in) long, take out the pegs and cultivate the ground around the parent stool, incorporating a balanced fertilizer at a rate of 60–120g/sq m (2–4oz/sq yd). Space the stems evenly again, dropping each into a 5cm (2in) deep trench. Peg down each stem in the bottom of the trench and cover with soil, leaving the shoot tips exposed. Earth up all but 5–8cm (2–3in) of the new shoots as they develop, until the mound is 15cm (6in) high. Water the area well in dry weather.

After leaf fall, carefully fork away the soil from around the new shoots until the stems that were laid horizontally are exposed. Cut these flush with the central stool. Then cut the stems to separate the rooted sections. Pot these up or plant them out in the open garden, and label them. The same stool may be used again.

Division

Division is a simple way of increasing shrubs that produce suckers. Suitable shrubs include *Ruscus*, *Kerria*, *Gaultheria*, and *Sarcococca*. Shrubs must be growing on their own roots not grafted onto another rootstock.

Before growth starts in spring, lift the plant. Break the clump into sections, retaining those with vigorous shoots and well-developed roots. Prune any damaged roots, and cut back the top-growth by one third to a half to reduce water loss. Replant the divisions in the open and water in dry weather. Alternatively, simply lift a suckering root, severing it from the parent plant, and then replant it in the open.

With a few shrubs, including *Rhus*, suckering may be encouraged by digging deeply around the parent plant in summer or autumn. This damages the roots and stimulates adventitious buds to develop suckers in spring. These rooted suckers may then be lifted and potted up or planted out.

Grafting

This technique is used to unite two plants so that they grow together as one. One part, known as the scion, is taken from the plant to be propagated and provides the top-growth of the new plant, while the other part, known as the rootstock or stock, provides the root system. The rootstock and scion must be compatible and they are normally of the same or closely related species.

Grafting is an important way of propagating shrubs that are difficult to root or that are unlikely to come true from seed. By using selected rootstocks, it is possible to improve a plant's vigour, disease-resistance, or tolerance to specific growing conditions, or sometimes to control its basic growth pattern.

Among the many variations of this particular technique, three that are widely used are saddle, spliced side-veneer, and apical-wedge grafting. In all cases, the stocks and scions should be joined immediately after they have been cut and the cut surfaces of each should be kept clean. All types of graft respond well to hot-pipe callusing, which speeds the formation of the callus (see *Hot-pipe Callusing of Grafts*, p.637)

Saddle grafting

This grafting technique is predominantly used to propagate evergreen rhododendron species and hybrids, with *Rhododendron ponticum* or *R.* 'Cunningham's White' generally serving as the rootstock. About one month before grafting is to commence, in late winter or early spring, bring the rootstock into a greenhouse maintained at a temperature of 10–12°C (50–54°F).

In late winter or very early spring, select the scion material so that it is ready for grafting. The scions selected should be about 5–13cm (2–5in) long, and taken from vigorous, non-flowering, one-year-old shoots on the plant to be propagated. If only shoots with flower buds are available, pinch these out. The scions should be labelled and stored in a plastic bag in a refrigerator.

Select a straight-stemmed rootstock of about pencil thickness and cut it back to within 5cm (2in) of the base, making a straight cut across the stem with secateurs. Then, using a knife, make two slanting cuts to make an upside-down "V" wound on the top of the stock. Prepare the scion by making two corresponding angled cuts so that its base – the saddle – will fit snugly onto the apex of the rootstock.

Ensure that the two sections of the graft fit well together, and then bind the stock and scion together with a length of clear grafting tape. Cut back any very large leaves by half to reduce moisture loss. Label clearly, and then place the grafted plant in a propagator and shade it from direct sunlight. Check the plant daily for watering and hygiene, and spray it once a week with a fungicide solution. Union normally takes place within four to five weeks.

Once the scion is growing away freely, remove the tape and gradually harden off the grafted plant – opening the propagator for longer periods each day. If the grafted plant is kept in the original pot for a season, give it a liquid feed once a month.

Spliced side-veneer grafting

This grafting technique is used to propagate a variety of both evergreen and deciduous shrubs. Most spliced side-veneer grafting is carried out in midwinter, but deciduous shrubs, such as *Viburnum* x *burkwoodii*, may also be grafted during the summer.

For the appropriate rootstocks, choose one- to three-year-old seedlings that are compatible with the plant to be propagated. The stems should be of pencil thickness. About three weeks before grafting, bring the rootstock into the greenhouse. Water it sparingly so that the rootstock does not break dormancy too quickly, since vigorous sap movement may prevent successful grafting. If grafting in summer, use two-year-old seedlings for the rootstocks and keep them fairly dry for a month in advance.

For both summer and winter grafting, prepare and unite the stocks and scions in the same way.

Just before grafting takes place, collect vigorous, one-year-old shoots that have some mature wood to be used as scions. They should be of a similar thickness to the rootstocks onto which they will be grafted. If there is any delay, label the scions and place them in a plastic bag in a refrigerator.

When grafting, first trim the scion to a length of 15–20cm (5–8in), or 10–12cm (4–5in) for magnolias. Make a sloping cut at the base of the scion, 2.5–4cm (1–1½in) long then

---

SUCKERING SHRUBS TO DIVIDE

Amelanchier canadensis
Andromeda
Aronia
Aster albescens
Berberis buxifolia
Buxus sempervirens
Cassiope hypnoides
Ceratostigma plumbaginoides
Clerodendrum bungei
Cornus alba,
   C. *canadensis*,
   C. *stolonifera*
Cornus canadensis

Danäe racemosa
Diervilla lonicera
Erica
Euonymus fortunei
Gaultheria, some ✳
Itea virginica
Kerria
Mahonia repens
Menziesia ciliicalyx
Paxistima
Pernettya
Polygala, some ✳
Rhus, some ✳
Ruscus aculeatus
Sarcococca
Spiraea japonica (cvs)

KEY
✳ Not hardy

PROPAGATING SUCKERING SHRUBS BY DIVISION

1 *Lift a root with suckers on it, without disturbing the parent plant. Check that there are fibrous roots at the base of the suckers.*

2 *Remove the long, suckering root by cutting it off close to the parent plant. Firm back the soil around the parent plant.*

3 *Cut the main root back to the fibrous roots, then divide the suckers so that each has its own roots. Cut back the top growth by about half.*

4 *Replant the suckers in open ground in prepared planting holes. Firm the soil around the suckers and water in. (The plant used here is* Gaultheria shallon.)

SADDLE GRAFTING

1 Select vigorous, non-flowering shoots of the previous year's growth from the plant to be propagated (here a rhododendron) as scions.

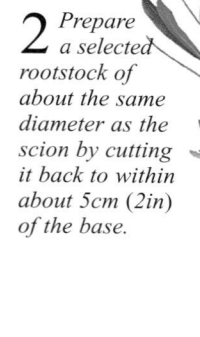

2 Prepare a selected rootstock of about the same diameter as the scion by cutting it back to within about 5cm (2in) of the base.

3 Using a sharp knife, cut the stock with two upward-angled cuts so that its apex is shaped like a slightly rounded, upside-down "V".

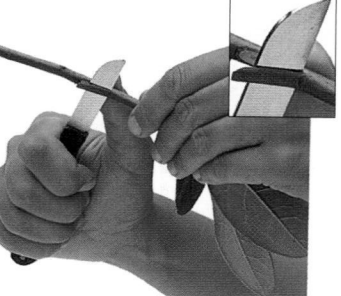

4 Make compatible, angled cuts on the scion (see inset), trimming its length to about 5–13cm (2–5in).

5 Place the cut scion (see inset) on top of the stock so that they fit together. If the scion is too narrow, place it so one side of the cambium layer meets that of the stock.

6 Bind the scion in place with plastic grafting tape or raffia. Cut back very large leaves by half. Leave the grafted plant in a propagator until union occurs.

SHRUBS TO GRAFT

Saddle
Rhododendron, some ❀ (many hybrids and species)

Spliced side-veneer
Acer palmatum (cvs)
Aralia elata 'Aureovariegata'
Arbutus unedo (cvs)
Camellia reticulata, C. sasanqua
Caragana arborescens
Cotoneaster 'Hybridus Pendulus'
Daphne bholua, D. petraea
Hamamelis
Magnolia
Pittosporum eugenioides 'Variegatum' ❀
Prunus glandulosa
Rhaphiolepis

Apical-wedge
Caragana arborescens 'Walker'

Hibiscus sinosyriacus 'Lilac Queen'

Daphne arbuscula
Hibiscus, some ❀
Syringa

KEY
❀ Not hardy

---

turn it over and make a small wedge-shaped cut on the other side.

Reduce the rootstock stem to about 30cm (12in). Make two cuts in the stock, starting 8cm (3in) above soil level, to take out a sliver of wood, leaving a cut that roughly matches that on the scion.

Place the rootstock and scion together so that the cambium layers match as closely as possible, and if necessary on one side only for stocks and scions of differing widths; tie them securely in position with grafting tape. Label the grafted plant and place it in a propagator at an even temperature of 10–15°C (50–59°F). Water the plant regularly and, once a week, spray with a fungicide.

Union should occur in four to five weeks. Harden off the grafted plant over the next four weeks, then remove it from the propagator and grow it on in a cool greenhouse.

As the scion starts to grow, gradually cut back the stem of the stock; by the end of the first growing season, all the stock above the graft union should have been cut back. During the first season, remove the initial tie and, if growth is rapid, replace it with a single, raffia tie.

On plants that have been grafted in summer, cut back the stock to just above the union before growth starts in spring. Replace the old tie with a small one around the union, since there is a tendency for the scion to be pushed off the stock. After repotting, support the leader with a cane.

Apical-wedge grafting

Apical-wedge grafting, or cleft grafting, is a comparatively straightforward technique and is suitable for the propagation of a number of shrubs, including *Caragana*, *Hibiscus*, and lilac (*Syringa*).

During midwinter, collect vigorous, one-year-old stems for use as scions. Place these in a clearly labelled plastic bag and store them in a refrigerator in order to retard their development.

Also in midwinter, select one-year-old seedlings of compatible shrubs as rootstocks. Stock and scion should both be about the thickness of a pencil. Immediately prior to grafting, lift the rootstock and wash it.

Cut its stem horizontally, about 2.5cm (1in) above the roots. With a sharp knife, make a 2.5cm (1in), vertical cut down the centre of the rootstock stem.

Remove the scions from the refrigerator and select one with healthy buds that is of similar diameter to the rootstock. Trim it down by making a horizontal cut just above a healthy bud or buds and a similar cut 15cm (6in) below. To form the wedge, make a 2.5–4cm (1–1½in) long, sloping cut down towards the middle of the scion base, and a similar cut on the other side.

Push the scion into the prepared cut on the stock. If the scion is narrower than the stock, align one edge of the scion so that it is flush with one edge of the stock. Bind them with grafting tape or moist raffia. If raffia is used, coat the union edges with grafting wax to stop moisture loss and to seal the top of the scion.

Either pot up the grafted plants or insert them in potting compost in a seed tray. Label and then, to provide basal heat, place them in a propagator at 10–15°C (50–59°F).

The union of the stock and scion should take place within about five to six weeks. Remove the tape or raffia when there is a firm union. Pot up the plants that are in seed trays and harden them off gradually. Grow the plants on for a further year in a cold frame before planting them out.

APICAL-WEDGE GRAFTING

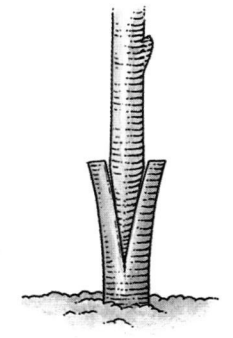

Make a simple, vertical cut down into the stock. Cut the base of the scion with 2 downward cuts into a "V" and push the base into the stock. Bind them together, pot up, and place in a propagator.

Fuchsias

Fuchsias are extremely adaptable plants, cultivated for their very attractive, pendent flowers, which range from modest, slender tubes to fully double, bicoloured blooms with distinctive, swept-back sepals. All the species and cultivars may be used in summer bedding schemes or grown in containers (see CONTAINER GARDENING, "Shrubs", p.316), and many are hardy enough to be used in permanent plantings. Those of upright habit may be trained as standards or as other formal shapes, while lax or trailing cultivars look very attractive when planted in hanging baskets and windowboxes.

Most fuchsias cannot tolerate intense sun or warm greenhouse conditions; in cold areas, many may need frost protection in winter.

Routine care

Water sufficiently to keep the soil moist but not waterlogged – at least once a day for fuchsias growing in hanging baskets, and every few days for those in plastic pots. Never leave containers standing in water.

Fuchsias in hanging baskets benefit from a balanced liquid feed in late summer. Hardy garden fuchsias need a dressing of general fertilizer after pruning in spring and again during summer. Mature plants benefit from an occasional balanced feed in early spring and a high-potash liquid feed when flowering begins.

Vine weevil (p.645), greenfly (see "Aphids", p.646), whiteflies (p.646), red spider mite (p.646), and grey mould (*Botrytis*) (p.646) can be

CUTTINGS

STEM SECTION

Stem trimmed just above and below one set of leaves

TIP CUTTING

SINGLE-LEAF CUTTING

Stem split vertically to retain only one leaf

Cuttings may be taken at any time of the year from growing tips, when stopping the plant.

troublesome. At the first signs of rusts (p.648) remove infected leaves and spray with a systemic fungicide.

Propagation

Fuchsias grow easily from cuttings, and plants propagated in this way are almost always superior to those raised from seed. Cuttings may be taken at any time of year when plants have suitable, non-flowering shoots. If taken in early spring, they can make exhibition plants by late summer; if taken in late summer, cuttings may be overwintered in a greenhouse for late spring flowering. The tips removed when pinching out, or stopping, will also root. Hardwood cuttings are also successful.

Softwood cuttings

Cut the stem below a node, with the tip and three sets of leaves. Remove the lowest two sets and proceed as for other shrubs (see p.111). To produce several cuttings, cut a young shoot into sections, each with a group of leaves and approximately 1cm ($\frac{1}{2}$in) of stem above and below the leaves. These may be split to form single-leaf cuttings if the bud in the leaf axil is undamaged. Provide bottom heat to accelerate rooting, especially early in the year. Maintain a moist atmosphere, but allow air to circulate freely so that the cuttings do not damp off.

Once rooted, transplant them into 7cm (3in) pots of potting compost, and feed them weekly with a high-nitrogen

HARDY AND TENDER FUCHSIAS

F. 'Celia Smedley'
Upright habit. Suitable for training as a standard. Half hardy.

F. 'Lady Thumb'
Lax habit. Suitable for training as a miniature standard. Frost hardy.

F. 'Thalia'
Upright habit. Suitable for summer bedding schemes. Frost tender.

F. 'Estelle Marie'
Upright habit. Suitable for summer bedding. Half hardy.

F. 'Heidi Weiss'
Upright habit. Suitable for training as a standard. Half hardy.

F. fulgens
Upright habit. Edible but acid fruits. Frost tender.

HOW TO TRAIN A BUSH FUCHSIA

1 *When the fuchsia cutting has developed 3 sets of leaves, pinch out the growing point. This will stimulate the production of sideshoots lower down the stem.*

2 *A few weeks later, when several sideshoots have developed, pinch out the top set of leaves from each sideshoot to encourage further branching.*

3 *Continue to pinch out the growing points of new sideshoots as they develop.*

4 *Stop pinching out sideshoots when the plant has a symmetrical shape with evenly spaced shoots. Lax plants may need staking.*

HOW TO TRAIN A STANDARD FUCHSIA

1 *When the cutting is about 15cm (6in) high, pinch out any sideshoots as they appear in the leaf axils.*

2 *Continue to do this to produce a long, straight stem. Tie the plant to a cane.*

3 *When the standard reaches the required height, leave it to produce 3 more sets of leaves, then pinch out the growing tip.*

4 *Pinch out the tips of the sideshoots that form at the top of the stem so that they will branch further.*

5 *Once the head has filled out, the leaves on the stem will usually drop off naturally, or they may be carefully removed.*

liquid fertilizer. In the early stages, do not use feeds that are high in phosphate and potash.

Pot on into 13cm (5in) pots when the roots reach the outside of the soil ball. Use peat-substitute- or peat-based compost with good drainage. Plant out after the last frost.

Hardwood cuttings

In late autumn, before severe frosts occur, cut the stem just below a node, 22cm (9in) long; remove all the leaves and soft tip. Wound the base of the cutting and dip it into hormone rooting powder or (preferably) liquid. Insert three or four cuttings in a 9cm (3½in) pot of cutting compost, and set in a cold frame. Ensure the compost remains just moist throughout winter. Once the cuttings have rooted, in early spring, pot on or use the young shoots as softwood cuttings.

Training

Fuchsias are most commonly trained into bushes or standards. Fans and espaliers may be created in the same way as fruit trees (see pp.441–442, and "Peaches", p.453).

Bush fuchsias

Begin training bushes as soon as the young plants have developed three sets of leaves. To form a bush, pinch out (stop) the growing tip to stimulate two to four sideshoots to grow. When these have each developed two sets of leaves, stop the shoots until the plant is as bushy as needed.

Pinching out increases the potential number of blooms but delays actual flowering. To time flowering for exhibition purposes, stop for the last time 60 days before the show for single cultivars (four petals), 70 days for semi-doubles (five to seven petals), and 80 days for doubles (eight or more petals).

Standard fuchsias

To train a standard, leave the tip of the young plant to grow and wait until sideshoots appear. Then pinch out all the sideshoots, but do not remove the leaves on the main stem. Tie the stem at intervals to a cane to provide support for the plant.

Continue until the required length of stem has been reached. The recognized stem lengths for a standard are: "mini standard" 15–25cm (6–10in); "quarter standard" 25–45cm (10–18in); "half standard" 45–75cm (18–30in); and "full standard" reaching 75–107cm (30–42in). Now allow a further three sets of leaves to develop, then pinch out the tip. After this, training involves the same stopping procedures as for a bush.

It will take 18 months to achieve a full standard and about six months for a quarter or mini standard.

Growing fuchsias in containers

Fuchsias grow well in pots and hanging baskets and if well cared for will remain in flower from soon after planting until the first frosts. Position them where they will receive some shade for part of the day. For baskets, choose just one cultivar per container, since different cultivars grow at different rates. Mixing fuchsias with other trailing plants makes a very successful basket display. In large patio pots or containers it is possible to use a mixture of fuchsias, such as *F.* 'Checkerboard' or *F.* 'Royal Velvet', with other plants.

Planting

Use three good plants for a 24cm (10in) diameter basket or half basket, a minimum of four for a 30cm (12in) basket, and more for a larger one. For a trailing effect, select young, bushy plants that have been stopped several times.

Use either a standard or a proprietary potting compost, both of which incorporate slow-release fertilizers to reduce the need for regular extra feeding and also water-retaining gels to reduce the frequency of watering.

Overwintering

Some fuchsias are hardier than is thought and often bedded-out plants, such as *F.* 'Mrs Popple', can be left *in situ*, although it is a good idea to take cuttings in early autumn as an insurance against frost damage. Standards should always be brought under cover in winter.

Hardy fuchsias

In areas that are cold in autumn, mulch fuchsias with straw, bracken, or bark over the crowns. Even if the plants are cut back by frost, they will shoot from the crown like an herbaceous plant. Deep planting (see below) is also very useful. Do not prune until regrowth starts in spring, then cut back to ground level.

Non-hardy fuchsias

In late autumn, move frost-tender fuchsias into frost-free conditions. If a minimum temperature of 8°C (46°F) is maintained, they may continue flowering through the winter.

If there is no greenhouse available, place tender bedding fuchsias, standards, and other trained fuchsias in frost-free conditions. Lift and pot up plants that have been bedded out. Remove the green tips and leaves. Keep plants dormant through the winter – cool and not quite dry. In spring, repot the plants into slightly smaller pots, and prune hard back. Water them and encourage fresh growth by lightly spraying the wood.

OVERWINTERING

Place a frost-hardy fuchsia in a hole 8cm (3in) deeper than the root ball. A combination of such deep planting and a straw mulch protects most borderline fuchsias from cold damage.

CHAPTER

4

CLIMBING PLANTS

WOODY AND HERBACEOUS CLIMBERS make up one of the most versatile plant groups, providing enormous scope for imaginative designs. Whether grown against a house wall or up pillars and over pergolas, climbers bring a strong vertical element to planting schemes. If unsupported, their stems spread luxuriantly, adding colour, texture, and horizontal lines, while some also function as weed-smothering ground cover. When allowed to scramble through other tall plants, climbers can extend the season of interest, and may be used to weave together other colourful and textural elements in the garden. One of their greatest uses is for clothing unsightly garden features, such as fences or walls, tree stumps, sheds, and other garden buildings. Many popular climbers are also fragrant, bearing abundant strongly scented flowers.

Designing with climbing plants

GARDENS of every size and aspect may be enhanced by climbing plants. Some, such as *Lapageria* and *Passiflora* species, are grown primarily for the exquisite beauty of their flowers; others – *Lonicera periclymenum*, for example – are equally valued for their fragrance. Many are appreciated for their handsome foliage, which can give year-round interest in the case of evergreens, or provide rich and spectacular autumn colour, as with *Parthenocissus* and *Vitis coignetiae*. Even when leafless, their elegant habit and often strong architectural form enhance the stark, winter outlines of hard landscape features. A significant number of climbers bear fruits or berries that are attractive both to the gardener and to wildlife.

In their natural habitats, climbers use various techniques to climb through host plants to gain access to the light. In gardens, natural and purpose-built supports may be exploited to suit the particular mode of growth used by the plant selected.

A FLORAL ENTRANCE
Bougainvillea naturally links a series of archways in this elegant courtyard setting. The brilliant spectacle of its showy, pink bracts harmonizes well with the sun-baked supporting wall. In frost-free gardens, it is one of the most vigorous and luxuriant of all climbers.

Climbing methods and supports

Some climbers are self-clinging, attaching themselves to their supports either by aerial roots (adventitious rootlets), as do ivies (*Hedera*), or by adhesive tendril tips, as does Virginia creeper (*Parthenocissus quinquefolia*). These cling to any surface offering sufficient purchase, including walls and tree trunks, and need no additional support except during the early stages, when they require the guidance of a cane, string, or wire until they are able to establish secure contact. Climbers with aerial roots are also particularly well-suited for use as ground cover.

Twining species coil their stems in a spiralling motion around their support – clockwise or anticlockwise depending on their anatomical and morphological characteristics. Both *Lonicera periclymenum* and *Manettia inflata*, for instance, twine clockwise, whereas *Ceropegia sandersonii* and *Wisteria sinensis* twine anticlockwise. All twining species need permanent support, usually provided by trellis or wire. They may also be grown up the stems and branches of a sturdy host plant (see also "Growing climbers through other plants", p.126).

A few climbers such as clematis and some nasturtiums (*Tropaeolum*) attach themselves to supports by means of curling leaf stalks. Many others are tendril climbers that twine around their supports by means of contact-sensitive tendrils, which are often modified leaves or leaflets as in

GARDEN DESIGN
Framing a formal piece of statuary during summer, the herbaceous climber Humulus lupulus *'Aureus' helps to reinforce a striking focal point in this garden. Its fresh, lime-green leaves have a distinctive charm of their own.*

Bignonia capreolata and sweet peas (*Lathyrus odoratus*); axillary shoots as in *Passiflora*; or terminal shoots as in vines. In *Parthenocissus*, the tendrils develop adhesive discs at the tips once they come into contact with a support.

Scandent, scrambling, and trailing climbers, such as bougainvillea, *Quisqualis indica*, and winter jasmine (*Jasminum nudiflorum*) produce long, arching stems that attach themselves only loosely, if at all, to their supports. These plants need to be tied in to a wire framework or trellis. Alternatively, they may be left to spread over walls and banks for a less formal effect. Plants in this group are also sometimes used as ground cover.

Some species, including climbing roses and certain *Rubus* species, are equipped with hooked thorns that help them to scramble naturally through host plants. If not grown through other plants, these need to be tied in to sturdy supports.

Site and aspect

To achieve their full potential, a number of climbers prefer a sunny position with their roots in shade, although some need a cooler spot. Others are less demanding and, while preferring a sunny aspect, may still tolerate shade – *Parthenocissus* and *Schizophragma* are just two examples.

Tender climbers will require the protection of a south-facing wall in cool climates. There are numerous hardy climbers, however, that will perform perfectly well without any protection at all.

Sunny or sheltered sites
In temperate areas, a sheltered wall provides a suitable microclimate for growing tender or exotic-flowering climbers. *Lapageria rosea* and the common passion flower (*Passiflora caerulea*) both thrive with winter protection in such a position; the heat reflected by the wall helps to ripen the wood so that the plants are better able to withstand cold winter temperatures.

The wall itself also gives protection against several degrees of frost. If frost is likely to occur at flowering time, avoid planting such climbers in positions where the flower buds are exposed to early-morning sun, since the buds will often be damaged as a result of rapid thawing. Sun-loving herbaceous plants and bulbs may be planted near the base of the climbers to help keep their roots cool.

Cool or exposed sites
For shady, north-facing walls and those exposed to cold winds, vigorous, hardy climbers – some honeysuckles and many ivies, in particular – are the most suitable plants. In a heavily shaded site, use green-leaved ivies; those with variegated or yellow leaves prefer more light and may be prone to frost damage.

Climbers on walls, buildings, and fences

Whether complementing or camouflaging their support, climbing plants make an immediate visual impact when trained against walls and buildings. Many provide strong colour, while others give a more diffuse and subtle backdrop to the whole garden design. Most buildings may be enhanced by the softening effect of a climber grown against them. In the same way, garden walls and fences become decorative features when clothed with plants bearing blossom and foliage.

Enhancing a building
Before planting, assess the architectural merits of a building and use the plants to emphasize its good points. A well-designed building may be complemented by climbers that have a strong visual impact with, for example, distinctively shaped or coloured foliage or outstanding flowers. *Actinidia kolomikta*, with its pink- or white-tipped leaves and cup-shaped white flowers in summer, is one of the most spectacular climbers for this purpose.

A less visually pleasing building may also be made more attractive by using climbers. Regular panels of plants may be used to break up long stretches of blank wall, and may also serve to exaggerate or mitigate strong vertical or horizontal lines. Narrow panels of foliage that extend upwards can make a building seem taller than it is. On the other hand, wider panels of plants allowed to grow only as high as the first floor will make a tall, narrow building appear broader. The most suitable plants for this purpose include most species of ivy and other self-clinging root climbers, such as *Hydrangea anomala* subsp. *petiolaris* and *Schizophragma integrifolium*; these form rich panels of foliage that may be pruned into the desired shape.

In a more relaxed, informal setting, vigorous climbing plants may be combined for a profusion of flowers and fragrance: the dark green foliage and white flowers of *Clematis armandii*, or the strongly fragrant red and yellow flowers of *Lonicera* x *americana*, combine well with many species of climbing rose, perhaps with annual sweet peas (*Lathyrus odoratus*) grown through them. This year-long combination is particularly effective around a window or doorway, where the flowers and scents may be best appreciated.

Screening with climbers
The more vigorous climbing plants may be used to camouflage an unattractive outhouse, wall, or fence

FLORAL BOUNTY
Climbers such as these roses are displayed at their best when wound around a vertical support, so they are stimulated into producing numerous flowers.

remarkably quickly. Use plants such as *Clematis montana*, for its considerable mass of creamy-white or pink flowers in late spring, or Russian vine (*Fallopia baldschuanica*, syn. *Polygonum aubertii*, *P. baldschuanicum*), which soon produces dense cover combined with panicles of tiny white flowers in late summer. It is known as mile-a-minute vine for a good reason – it is extremely rampant and must therefore be sited with great care, since it will swamp even reasonably vigorous neighbours. It also needs regular and severe pruning to keep it within bounds.

Where all-year cover is required, ivies may be more appropriate. Alternatively, use a combination of evergreen and deciduous plants; the finely cut, evergreen leaves of *Clematis cirrhosa*, for instance, provide the perfect foil in summer for the soft-pink blooms of the climbing rose 'New Dawn'.

Climbers on pergolas and pillars

Pergolas, pillars, and other purpose-made structures enable climbers to be viewed from all sides and, in addition, contribute strong stylistic elements to the garden design. They may be used to add height to an otherwise flat garden. Depending on materials used, they may be formal and elegant, or informal and rustic. If well designed, they can be at their most attractive when only partially covered with plants. They must, however, be strong enough to bear the often considerable weight of stems

and foliage and should also be durable, as the plants will need their support for many years.

Pergolas

Pergolas or arbours festooned with climbers not only provide a cool, shady sitting area in the garden but also bring a sense of seclusion and privacy to an otherwise open site. The most suitable plants to choose are those that put on their best display at the time of day or during the particular season when the structure is most often used.

If an arbour is to be used often on summer evenings, suitable plants might include common jasmine (*Jasminum officinale*), *Lonicera periclymenum* 'Graham Thomas', or the climbing rose 'Madame Alfred Carrière', all with beautifully fragrant blooms in pale colours that show up well in the fading light. For summer shade, use large-leaved climbers such as *Vitis coignetiae* (which also gives splendid autumn colour) or *V. vinifera* 'Purpurea', whose claret-coloured young leaves turn dusky purple as they mature. Alternatively, use the massed floral display of *Wisteria sinensis* 'Alba' as a summer canopy. The flowers of this plant look very effective if it is grown up a pergola flanking a walkway. Ensure that the crossbeams are high enough, however, so there is no need to stoop to avoid the flowers.

For winter interest, plant evergreens, such as ivy or, in mild areas, tender *Lardizabala biternata*. Alternatively, use deciduous plants such as *Celastrus* or wisteria, whose bare stems take on beautiful sculptural qualities in winter.

GROWING ON PERGOLAS
Wisteria sinensis 'Alba' is the ideal choice for a pergola over a walkway. It produces a mass of fragrant white blooms in early summer that hang down in garlands, releasing their welcome scent at just the right height to be appreciated.

Pillars

To add a strong vertical element to a mixed or herbaceous border, climbers such as clematis or *Passiflora* may be grown up and around pillars. Also consider using pillars to mark an axis or focal point, perhaps at the corner of a border or at a point where the garden level changes. A series of pillars at the back of a flower bed or along a path may also be linked by rope or chain swags, and climbers trained along them.

For an evergreen climber, or as a temporary feature, a stout post with mesh panels wrapped around it will provide adequate support. If growing a deciduous plant, which means that the pillar will be visible in winter, buy a ready-made trellis obelisk or column, which will be attractive when it is bare of flowers.

Growing climbers through other plants

In the wild, many climbers grow naturally through other plants, which is a habit that may be copied to great advantage in the garden – although

NATURAL SUPPORT
The scarlet flowers of Tropaeolum speciosum *are made yet more intense by the rich, deep-green backcloth provided by a hedge of yew* (Taxus baccata).

PLANT ASSOCIATION
The heart-shaped leaves of Vitis coignetiae *make a striking contrast in shape and texture with those of* Euonymus fortunei *'Silver Queen'.*

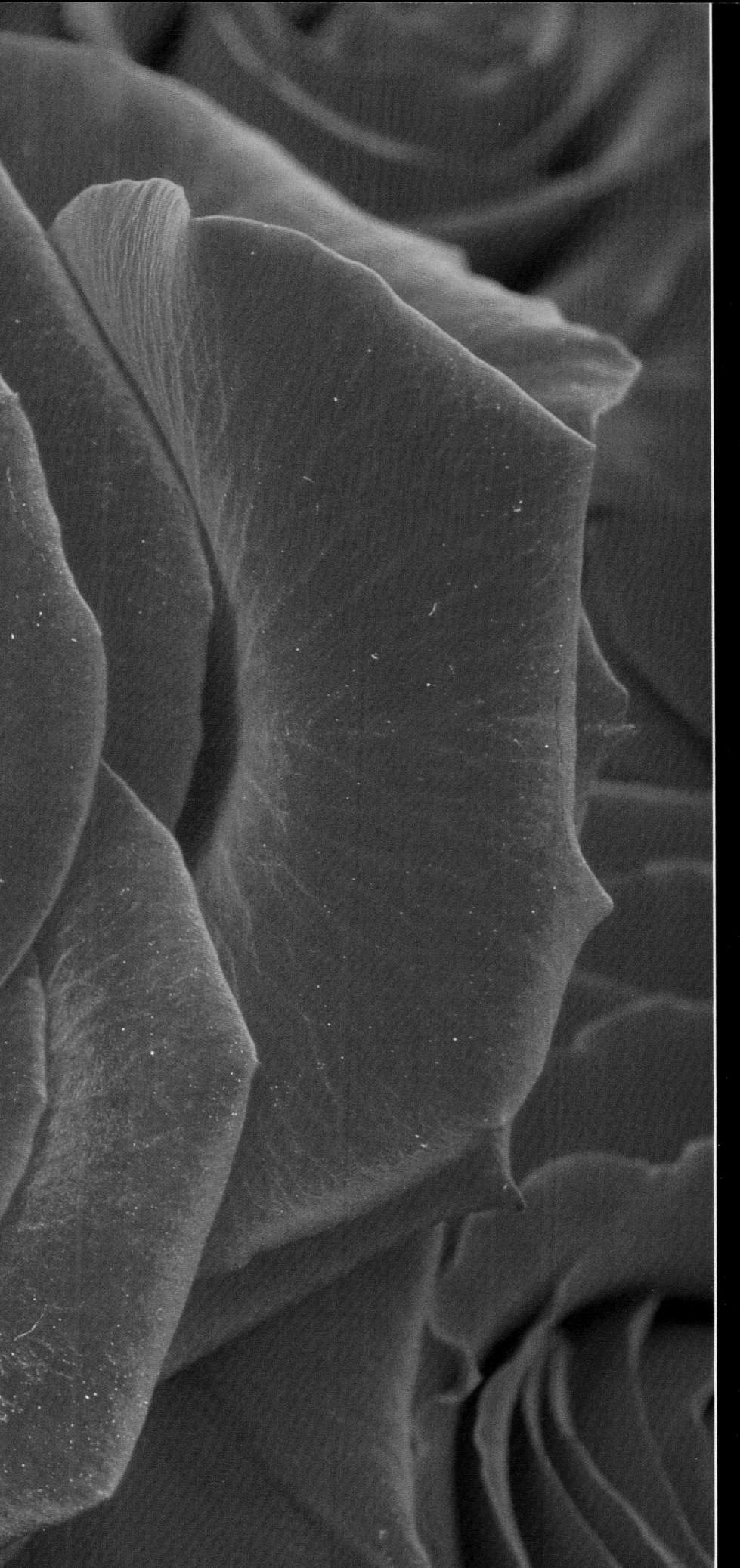

CHAPTER

5

ROSES

GARDENERS AND POETS since before Roman times have revered the rose as the queen of flowering plants for the extraordinary beauty of its blooms. The rose family offers an enormous range of flower colour, shape, and scent, from the simple purity of the wild rose to the pastel charm of an old garden rose, or the jewel-like brilliance of a modern hybrid.

Few plants are so varied as the rose in its growth habit, height, foliage, and form; it is possible to clothe the whole garden in rose blooms, from the delicacy of a tiny pot rose to the foaming mass of a huge rambler. Whether grown alone in the splendour of a formal garden or used to heighten a mixed planting, roses epitomize the glory of a summer's day.

Designing with roses

WHETHER you choose to grow old garden roses for their grace of habit, foliage, and scent, or modern roses for their long flowering season and showy blooms, the diversity of roses (*Rosa*) makes it possible to find a plant for almost every part of the garden, and to create any style or mood of planting, whether restrained classicism or luxuriant informality.

Roses are adaptable plants that grow happily in almost all parts of the world. They are most vigorous in warm, temperate regions, although some adapt well to subtropical or cold regions. In hot climates, they may flower virtually continuously throughout the year.

Choosing roses

The number of rose cultivars available is bewildering, with many new ones each year. Before choosing, it is well worth visiting some established gardens to observe as many different roses as possible growing in garden conditions. Do this over a period of time to assess the plants' habit, eventual height, health, vigour, fragrance, fastness of flower colour in strong sun, and all the other desirable features of a good rose. Note, too, whether a rose produces a single flush of blooms or if it is a remontant rose, which, being a repeat- or perpetual flowering plant, will have a greatly extended flowering period.

Most national rose associations publish listings that give details of where species roses and cultivars stocked by member nurseries may be purchased; these are often invaluable in locating suppliers of more unusual roses. In addition to their selling name, many roses now have coded cultivar names – for example the rose sold as CASINO has the coded cultivar name 'Macca' – so you can be sure that you are buying the correct plant (see also "Plant names", p.677).

Flower shapes
The genus *Rosa* comprises many flower forms, from the simple, single flowers of species roses to the elegantly furled blooms of the modern rose and the cabbage-like complexity of many old rose flowers.

The main flower shapes illustrated right give a general indication of the flower shape when in its perfect state (which in some cases may be before it has fully opened). The flowers may be single (4–7 petals), semi-double (8–14 petals), double (15–20 petals), or fully double (over 30 petals).

Fragrance
Roses have long been prized for their scent; most old garden species and some modern roses possess enchanting and diverse perfumes with hints of clove, musk, honey, lemon, spice, and even tea, as well as the "true rose" fragrance. It is not easy to be specific about rose scent as its character and intensity may vary greatly with the time of day, the air humidity, the age of the bloom, and the "nose" of individual gardeners; some will find a particular cultivar fragrant, while others will not.

OLD WORLD CHARM
The open blooms and sprawling habit of shrub roses, including 'Constance Spry', 'Céleste', and 'Cerise Bouquet', blend with perennials in a subtle colour theme to create a mood of informal and restful abundance. The proximity of the beds and the grass walk provides a secluded setting in which to enjoy the heady rose scents.

FLOWER SHAPES

Flat *Open, usually single or semi-double, with petals that are almost flat.*

Cupped *Open, single to fully double, with petals curving outwards from the centre.*

Pointed *Semi-double to fully double Hybrid Tea type, with high, tight centres.*

Urn-shaped *Classic, curved, and flat-topped, semi- to fully double, Hybrid Tea type.*

Rounded *Double or fully double, with even-sized, over-lapping petals forming a bowl-shaped outline.*

Rosette *Flattish, double or fully double, with many confused, slightly overlap-ping petals of uneven size.*

Quartered-rosette *Flattish, double or fully double, with con-fused, uneven petals in a quar-tered pattern.*

Pompon *Small, rounded, double or fully double, with masses of small petals; blooms are usually borne in clusters.*

The different rose types

More than a hundred wild (or species) roses exist, and all 13,000 cultivated roses now commercially available descend from them. The ancestry of almost all of them is so mixed, after many centuries of casual and indiscriminate breeding before cross-pollination was understood and proper records of parentage kept, that it is impos-sible to classify them precisely. For example, the hybridizing of miniature roses with Floribunda roses has led to dwarf Floribunda bush roses, intermediate in stature between the parents.

Because roses are continually evolving, the categories (or class-es) that rose lovers devise are sub-ject to change and they should be regarded as convenient signposts for guidance, rather than inflexible definitions. The following is based on recommendations of The World Federation of Rose Societies and The Royal National Rose Society.

Species roses (also known as wild and near–wild roses)

Species, or wild, roses and species hybrids (which share most charac-teristics of both parent species) are generally large, arching shrubs or climbers bearing one flush of sin-gle, five-petalled flowers during spring or midsummer and then decorative hips in autumn.

Old garden roses

This category is so large that it is divided into two groups, depend-ing mainly on their ancestry.

GROUP A

Mostly of European origin, freely bearing clusters of fragrant blooms in summer on matt-foliaged, shrubby plants. Alba, Damask, and Gallica were origi-nally grown for their scent. Two Damasks and one Scots rose flower in autumn.

Alba ("white") Large shrubs with plentiful, greyish-green foliage and white, cream, or blush, scented flow-ers. Ancient.

Centifolia ("hundred-petalled") Also called Provence roses. Dense, leafy, prickly, rather lax shrubs, including pink, white, and purplish forms, usu-ally well scented. 1450s onwards.

Damask (possibly "from Damas-cus") A varied group of leafy, often lax shrubs. Most are pink flowered (some are white) and fragrant. Ancient.

Gallica ("French") Generally dense and leafy, with a compact, shrubby, suckering habit. There are pink, maroon, purple and striped forms, many with good fragrance. Ancient.

Moss These shrubs bear unusual, "moss-like" growth on stems and calyx, otherwise generally similar to Centifolia. 1720s onwards.

Scots (or Scotch) Briar Prickly, usually low-growing shrubs bearing white, pink, purple, yellow, or striped flowers. Selections or hybrids of *R. pimpinellifolia.* 1790s onwards.

Sweet Briar Hybrids derived from *R. rubiginosa* (syn. *R. eglanteria*), which is noted for its apple-scented leaves. Large, twiggy, prickly shrubs in pink, fawn-yellow, or purple. 1890s onwards.

GROUP B

Hybrids between Oriental and European roses. Almost all produce flowers in autumn as well as summer.

Bourbon (from an island group) Leafy shrubs and climbers of rather lax, open habit. Flowers, often fra-grant, include pink, white, purplish, and striped forms. 1817 onwards.

Boursault Generally smooth-stemmed, dark-wooded shrubs with early flowers; may need protection from disease. 1820s onwards.

China Hybrids with *R. chinensis* in their parentage. Shrub, bush, and climbing roses, with shiny, pointed leaflets and twiggy, sometimes sparse growth. Diverse flower forms and colours include pink, white, red, buff, and yellow. Minimal scent. 1750s onwards.

Hybrid Musk Vigorous, remontant shrubs with abundant foliage and often fragrant, mainly double blooms borne in trusses. 1910 onwards.

Hybrid Perpetual Vigorous shrub, bush, and climbing roses of upright, leafy habit, with large, full-petalled, often fragrant flowers in red, pink, white, or purple. 1830s onwards.

Noisette (named after a French grower) Silky-petalled, cream, yel-low, or buff flowers in clusters on vigorous shrubs or climbers with shiny leaves. Spicy scent. Developed from *R. moschata*, Chinas and Teas. 1805 onwards.

Portland/Damask Portland Leafy, stiff-growing shrubs bearing size-able, fragrant flowers in white, pink, purple, or carmine, raised from earli-er roses interbred with Chinas. Autumn flowering not dependable. 1780s onwards.

Tea (possibly from the delicate "tea" aroma) Bushes and climbing roses noted for the elegance and beauty of their silky-petalled, spicy-scented flowers, most of which are coloured yellow, buff, pink, white, or carmine. 1810 onwards.

Sempervirens ("evergreen") White or pink, cluster-flowered, summer-blooming climbers, with shiny leaves. 1820s onwards.

Modern garden roses

Most modern roses produce excel-lent repeat flowers throughout sum-mer and autumn and have glossy foliage, both characteristics showing the influence of Oriental roses.

Climber Vigorous, stiff-stemmed climbing roses of varied character and available in many colours, suit-able for training on solid supports. 1870s onwards.

Climbing Miniature Remontant climbers with small leaves and flowers, some fragrant, in many colours. 1990s onwards.

Floribunda Cluster-flowered bushes, providing excellent conti-nuity of blooms, some fragrant, in many colours. Garnette roses do well under glass, for the cutflower market. 1909 onwards.

Ground cover Shrub roses with a markedly creeping or spreading habit, in many colours. Some are fragrant. 1919 onwards.

Hybrid Tea Bush roses with large, high-centred flowers in many colours, usually full-petalled, often fragrant, borne singly or in threes. 1860s onwards.

Miniature Tiny counterparts of Hybrid Tea and Floribunda roses, rarely fragrant. 1920s onwards.

Patio Resembling Floribunda, shrub, or ground-cover roses but with smaller, neater appearance, giving a scaled-down effect. Little scent. 1980s onwards.

Polyantha ("many flowers") Bush, shrub, and climbing roses bearing big clusters of small blooms, mostly in white, pink, or red. Slight scent. Derived from *R. multiflora.* 1870s onwards.

Rambler Vigorous climbing roses in many colours, having lax growth and long, flexible shoots, easy to train on supports. Some are fragrant and most bear clusters of small flowers freely but in summer only. 1890s onwards.

Rugosa ("wrinkled") Vigorous, hardy shrubs related to *R. rugosa*, many recognizable by their wrin-kled leaves and showy hips, with scented flowers mostly in white, pink, or purple. 1790s onwards.

Shrub Roses of ampler and leafi-er growth than bush roses, very varied in character, colour range, blooming period, and fragrance. 1890s onwards.

DESIGN FOR A FORMAL ROSE GARDEN

Here, all is symmetry and order, with clean lines and colour laid out in patterns of geometric simplicity. This design creates a restrained setting in which to enjoy the classic beauty of roses. Formal yew hedges enclose beds of massed bush roses in pale and deep golds and white, which in turn focus on a graceful, trailing rose in the centre. Red standard roses lift the planting with a bold contrast of colour and form.

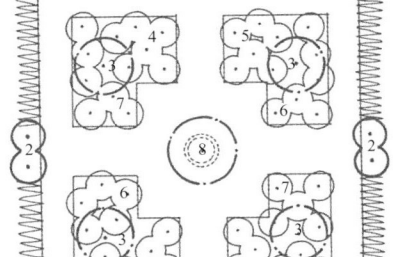

1 *Yew* (Taxus baccata)
2 *Rosa* 'Golden Showers'
3 *R.* SUFFOLK ('Kormixal')
4 *R.* 'Korresia'
5 *R.* AMBER QUEEN ('Harroony')
6 *R.* 'Hakuun'
7 *R.* MARGARET MERRIL ('Harkuly')
8 *R.* SWANY ('Meiburenac')

With most roses one must be quite close to smell them; they are best enjoyed by planting them near a door or a window where their scent may drift into the house on summer evenings, around the patio or along a path, or in a sheltered position in the garden. Other roses, particularly many of the tree-climbing ramblers, are so freely scented that they can perfume the whole garden.

Flower colour

Modern roses embrace virtually every colour of the spectrum, from pale pastels to bold, bright reds and yellows. The blue rose remains the stuff of legend, despite the use of the word "blue" in such cultivars as 'Blue Parfum', which is actually mauve. The old garden roses range in hue from white, through the palest of blush pinks, deep pink, crimson, and violet, to purple; many are striped pink and white or purple and white. Most roses look good together and with other plants, but combining too many brilliant colours, for example bright vermilion with cerise pink, may create a discordant effect. Plant white roses or those with softer, pastel hues between groups of strongly toned roses to cool them down and prevent them from clashing.

Foliage colour

As well as producing a fine flowering display, some groups of roses provide colour in other ways to extend the season of interest. The Alba roses and many of the species roses have pleasing foliage, from a soft grey-green to a deep, glossy blue-green, making them attractive even when the bush is not in flower. The bright-green foliage of Rugosa roses has an interesting wrinkled (or rugose) texture and, if the roses are planted as a hedge, it makes a good background for other plantings. The leaves of some species are a dusky plum-purple, as in *R. glauca*, while the foliage of some, such as *R. virginiana*, turns in colour to vivid sunset tints in autumn.

Ornamental rosehips or thorns

Rugosa roses with single or semi-double flowers also develop bright red, decorative hips at the end of the flowering season. Some of the species roses too, such as *R. moyesii* and its hybrids, produce ornamental hips in autumn that range in colour from yellow and orange, through all the shades of red, to a blackish-purple.

R. sericea subsp. *omeiensis* f. *pteracantha* has huge, flat thorns which, when young, glow ruby red if the sun is behind them.

The garden setting

One of the best settings for the beds of a rose garden is a smooth, green lawn, but the subtle grey and honey tones of stone paving can be just as attractive. A mellow brick path may complement a rose planting alongside it, especially one of soft, pale tones. Whatever the material, avoid multi-coloured patterns that may compete with the roses. Gravel, although pleasant in appearance and texture, can be troublesome to look after as weeds soon appear and the stones may gradually spread or disappear into the soil.

Edging plants may be used to frame a rosebed. A traditional box hedge makes a formal boundary but many other plants may be used more informally, particularly those that possess grey-green or silver-grey foliage. *Anaphalis nepalensis* var. *monocephala* (syn. *A. nubigena*), with woolly, lance-shaped leaves, or the more dwarf forms of lavender are suitable, as is catmint (*Nepeta*) if there is room for it to sprawl over the path.

Many of the more restrained hardy geraniums, in particular those with blue flowers, are similarly appealing, and even miniature roses, in contrasting or complementary colours, may be grown on the sunny side of a bed.

Formal rose gardens

The most popular way to grow roses is in a formal rose garden, devoted to displaying the glories of the rose in beds shaped to reflect the plant's classic elegance. Generally, Hybrid Tea or Floribunda bushes and standards are used as permanent bedding plants, grouped in blocks of colour. The rather stiff and upright growth of many such bushes lends itself to the formality of bedding and tends not to blend so well with other plants, although roses may be attractively underplanted (see p.151).

Rosebeds may be designed in any shape or size – square, oblong, triangular, or round; at the edges of paths or drives they may be narrow and ribbon-like. Before creating new rosebeds, draw a plan on paper and experiment with different shapes and layouts of beds in order to decide which is the best design for the site that has been chosen. Do not make the beds so wide that access to the roses for spraying, mulching, and pruning becomes difficult.

If mixing rose cultivars in the same bed, plant no less than five or six plants of the same cultivar together in a regular formation for substantial clumps of colour; not all cultivars reach their peak of flowering at exactly the same time. A garden planted with variations on a colour theme, for instance pale and deep pinks with a touch of white, creates a harmonious effect that is more pleasing than mixed, bright colours.

When planting, bear in mind the variations in eventual height of different cultivars. For a bed in an open area, choose cultivars of a more or less uniform height. A rosebed that is backed by a wall or hedge is more attractive if the roses at the front are shorter than those behind.

Standard roses may be used to give height to any bedding scheme. Placing a single standard in the centre of a round bed that echoes the shape of the rose creates a graceful symmetry, while several standards placed at intervals of about 1.5m (5ft) along the middle of a long bed help to break up its uniformity.

Informal plantings

The charm of roses may be exploited in a wide range of informal planting schemes, particularly with herbaceous plants or other shrubs. Roses suitable for virtually any site in the garden may be chosen from the multitude of shrub, miniature, climbing, and ground-cover roses of varied stature and habit now available.

Roses combine happily with other plantings; for example miniature roses give both summer colour and height to a planting of rock plants that are mainly spring-flowering, and a ground-cover rose may clothe a bank with fragrant flowers.

The belief that roses do not mix with other plants probably dates from the days when many commonly used cultivars were large and ungainly and did not suit the Edwardian and Victorian bedding schemes. They were grown in separate walled gardens simply to provide cut blooms for the house. It has, however, long been recognized that roses need not be grown in isolation.

Roses with herbaceous plants

Growing roses in beds or borders with herbaceous plants both highlights the beauties of the rose in flower and provides interest when the rose itself is dormant. The growth habit of many shrub roses, such as the light and airy China roses or the lax and open Damasks, perfectly suits the casual profusion of an informal planting.

Muted drifts of flower or foliage, for example the haze of tiny, white *Crambe cordifolia* flowers, best com-

INFORMAL STYLE
Large roses, including 'Penelope' in the foreground, clothe the background walls with a fragrant mass of summer colour and provide a magnificent foil for the tall spikes of plants such as campanulas and delphiniums and the low mounds of the other perennial plants in an informal mixed border of cool blues and whites.

plement the showy flowers of roses in the summer. At other times of the year, use more flamboyant flowering plants or some with evergreen foliage to extend the season and conceal the bare rose stems.

Many plants may enhance a planting dominated by roses. The tall spikes of purple foxgloves (*Digitalis purpurea*), white *Lilium regale*, or other white and pink lilies pushing up through a planting of lush, old garden roses, for example, make for a striking contrast, both in habit of growth and flower form.

Roses with other shrubs

Both shrub and species roses combine well with other shrubs, as long as they receive enough sunlight. They provide abundant, beautiful,

often fragrant flowers to set against the foliage of other spring-flowering shrubs, sometimes right through the summer. Many such roses have almost evergreen foliage and coloured hips in the autumn (see "Ornamental rosehips or thorns", p.150). Smaller shrub roses as well as the Gallicas, most of the Damasks, the Portland roses, and many modern cultivars of similar stature make an excellent ornamental foreground to any planting of shrubs.

Roses that have long, questing branches, such as the freely flowering 'Scharlachglut' or 'Complicata' with its deep pink blooms, may scramble through and enliven a dull, evergreen shrub. Ramblers may adorn a tree's foliage with their blooms or transform a dead tree.

The soft colours of old roses are particularly attractive when planted with subshrubs that combine greygreen leaves with blue flowers, such as the free-flowering *Caryopteris* x *clandonensis*, the ethereal fronds of *Perovskia atriplicifolia*, certain hebes, and most lavenders.

Underplanting a rosebed

The display in a rosebed may be enhanced and extended beyond the rose flowering season by growing low, shallow-rooted plants between the roses. A wide range of plants may clothe the ground and provide the roses with a background of contrasting colour, texture, and form. Violets (*Viola*) are a favourite choice: the white, soft blue, and mauve cultivars complement roses well. All such ground-cover plants make mulching difficult, however. Take care not to

tread on the ground-cover planting when spraying the roses in a particularly wide bed.

When planting between roses, take account of the eventual heights of the various companion plants, and place them so that they will not obscure each other or the roses when they are mature.

The yellow-green of *Alchemilla mollis*, pink and white heads of *Armeria maritima*, and spreading, hardy geraniums also make a fine display under roses.

Spring bulbs brighten up bare rosebeds early in the year: try planting blue or white *Chionodoxa*, daffodils, snowdrops (*Galanthus*), and white, starry *Tulipa turkestanica* to create a gay patchwork of colour. Their only drawback is their dying foliage, which looks untidy until it is removed and may make it difficult to maintain the bed for the roses.

FLOWERS AND FOLIAGE
Richly coloured rose blooms are set like jewels against an underplanting of herbs with elegant, grey-green foliage, and the golden tones of gravel.

SINGULAR SPLENDOUR
A standard rose, 'Little White Pet', provides a handsome focal point.

Many fragrant, evergreen herbs are good companions for roses: use cotton lavender (*Santolina chamaecyparissus*), various thymes (*Thymus*), or sages (*Salvia*) – either the culinary kind or any that have attractive, variegated leaves. Roses always look well when they are contrasted with the silver foliage of perennial plants such as the fern-leaved *Artemisia ludoviciana* and *A. frigida*, or the grey, woolly-leaved, mat-forming *Stachys byzantina* (syn. *S. lanata*).

Terraces

On a steep hillside, terraces may be used to transform a difficult site into a striking showcase for roses. They provide areas sufficiently level for planting and retain moisture which the roses need while creating eye-catching graduations of height and perspective. The terrace walls look best if made of weathered brick or mellow stone. Bush roses may be grown in the terrace beds, and ramblers or ground-cover roses planted to tumble over the retaining walls, creating curtains of bloom.

Smaller terraced beds are ideal, too, for growing miniature roses. It is much easier to savour the beauty and scent of their tiny, individual flowers if they are raised some way above ground level. Each bed for miniature roses should be approximately

SUMMER RETREAT
A mature rambler rose in full, glorious bloom transforms this trelliswork arbour into an eye-catching feature that is at once intimate and airy. The floral canopy fills the air within the arbour with its delicious perfume, and provides a cool, leafy shelter from which to enjoy the views of the surrounding garden.

45–60cm (1½–2ft) wide. Place miniature standards along the top bed of the terrace to draw the eye and use some of the smaller and more dainty ground-cover roses to tumble over the walls. This kind of terracing also makes an excellent surround for a sunken rose garden.

Specimen planting

A large shrub rose on its own makes a handsome specimen plant, perhaps in a lawn or to mark a focal point in

AN ORNAMENTAL ARCH
The old-fashioned, rich pink flowers of Rosa *'Bantry Bay' festoon this rustic arch to form an enticing and decorative frame to the view beyond.*

a garden, as long as it is an outstanding rose of its type; any defects in a specimen are immediately obvious. Used in this way, weeping standard roses can be especially striking. These are formed by grafting rambler cultivars onto a 1.5m or 2m (5ft or 6ft) stem, so that their long, flexible shoots, laden with blossom in summer, hang down all round, right to the ground. They usually flower for a limited period, unless a standard grafted from a remontant, ground-cover rose is chosen.

Climbing roses grown as standards may provide a profusion of blooms throughout the entire summer, but their stiff growth does not produce the same, dramatic waterfall effect as weeping standards.

Many of the larger shrub roses, with their graceful, arching habit, almost evergreen foliage, and abundant flowers, are natural choices for planting as specimens in larger gardens. 'Nevada', for example, which can reach 2 x 2m (6 x 6ft) or even more, is smothered with large, cream blooms in early summer, and again in late summer. Other roses, particularly species roses and their hybrids, such as 'Frühlingsgold', have no second blooming.

For a small garden where space for flowering plants is limited, use remontant roses that earn their space in the garden by blooming all summer and well into the autumn, such as the strongly scented 'Roseraie de l'Haÿ'. Smaller shrub roses, such as 'Chinatown' which has masses of gold blooms tinged with pink, and 'Sally Holmes' with large, white flowers clustered above the foliage, are not quite large enough to justify being planted on their own, but are very handsome if planted in specimen groups of three.

Walls, arbours, and pergolas

Most ramblers and climbing species roses are very vigorous, and produce an exuberance of bloom in midsummer. They may clothe structures such as arbours, walls, and fences, disguise unsightly features, or give height to the summer display in the garden. Be sure to choose a rose with an eventual height that will cover the intended area well without outgrowing it.

Ramblers and climbing roses may be trained on a range of plastic-coated metal bowers, tunnels, arches, and tripod pillars now on the market. Although metal supports may not look so attractive initially as ones made from rustic poles, they have a much longer life and are soon concealed once the roses trained on them become well established. Rustic arches, even if treated, eventually rot at soil level.

Other climbing plants, such as clematis, or wall shrubs may be planted to grow through the rose, to complement the rose blooms as well as to extend the flowering season; climbers with blue flowers are particularly effective. Some of the more vigorous shrub roses, particularly Bourbons, also make excellent short climbers for a pillar or small wall.

Ramblers
Ramblers have more flexible shoots than climbers and are easier to train along complex structures such as pergolas, arches, and trellises. When grown against walls, however, their mass of shoots may become mildewed as a result of the poor air circulation.

AUTUMN TINTS
The brilliant scarlet hips of this species rose contrast vividly with its yellowing foliage.

DECORATIVE HEDGING
Rosa gallica 'Versicolor', also known as 'Rosa Mundi', is one of the oldest roses available and has unusually striped petals. It forms an attractive informal hedge that bursts into a riot of flower in the summer to create an enchanting ribbon of colour. Here, the line of the rose hedge provides a pleasing contrast of height and perspective with the tall spikes of hollyhocks (Alcea). *The deep pink flowers in the rose hedge show reversion to its parent,* R. gallica *var.* officinalis.

To cover a long pergola, use one of the vigorous, small-flowered, white ramblers such as 'Bobbie James', but remember that they can grow to 10m (30ft) or more and will overwhelm a small structure.

For a picturesque effect, try training roses along chains or ropes that are suspended between uprights to create great swags of bloom.

Climbers

The stiffer shoots of climbing roses are easier to prune than those of ramblers and happily grace walls and fences. Many of the less robust modern climbers may be grown on pillars or as freestanding shrubs with great effect. Pink ALOHA ('Kormarcus') is beautifully scented but is too stiff and upright in habit for an arch, although it would be suitable for the pillar supports of a tall pergola.

The Bourbon rose 'Zéphirine Drouhin', which has pink flowers and repeats well, is an old favourite for growing on arches and pergolas, as it is the only currently available climber that is both thornless and fragrant. It is, however, prone to mildew.

Rose hedges and screens

Roses may, if carefully chosen, provide some of the most colourful and attractive plants for an informal hedge or screen. A few, for example *R. rugosa* and its hybrids, may be shaped to some extent by gentle clipping in winter to make dense hedges while maintaining the natural outline of the shrub. No rose is fully evergreen, so few provide a screen that gives privacy all year, although the thorns make the hedge virtually impenetrable. For further details, see HEDGES AND SCREENS, pp.84–86.

The Hybrid Musk roses, such as the apricot 'Buff Beauty', grow into a thick, thorny screen up to 2m (6ft) in height covered in fragrant flowers all summer long – if their natural unpredictability of growth is curbed by training on horizontal wires or chain-link fencing. If a rose hedge is to line a path, use upright cultivars since those of unpredictable growth may impede the pathway.

For a small garden, a hedge of tall, Floribunda roses is preferable. These are generally upright plants with little spread and, if planted in two staggered rows (see *Planting Distances for a Rose Hedge*, p.157), cultivars such as the apricot-yellow ANNE HARKNESS ('Harkaramel') rapidly form a pretty screen about 1.2m (4ft) tall. Some shorter-growing old garden roses, such as 'Charles de Mills', have attractive foliage and form hedges of similar height but flower only at midsummer. Their vulnerability to mildew is, however, increased by close planting.

A delightful way of dividing one part of a garden from another is to train climbing roses or ramblers on decorative screens formed by constructing open, wooden frameworks of the desired height. Ready-made wooden and plastic trellis is available but make sure that it is sturdy, since it has to support a considerable weight and to last for years.

Ground-cover roses

Some low-growing roses readily spread along the ground to form a dense and floriferous carpet. These may be used to continue the theme of a rosebed, or as a prettily spreading edging to a cottage border, as well as to disguise an unsightly feature such as a manhole cover, or scramble down a steep bank that is otherwise difficult to plant.

A CARPET OF BLOOM
This ground-cover rose, SURREY, *attractively masks an expanse of bare earth with a succession of double flowers from summer to autumn.*

Some more recently introduced cultivars, such as NIPPER ('Hareco'), cover the soil very well although, at 1–1.2m (3–4ft), they grow too tall for true ground cover. Other roses that are suitable for a small space are 'Flower Carpet' or those named after English counties.

Ramblers such as PHEASANT ('Kordapt') and GROUSE ('Korimro'), which both have small, pink flowers and glossy foliage, make marvellous ground-cover roses, but their vigour makes them unsuitable for a small garden. They grow naturally along the ground, rooting as they go and covering it very closely, but need strict control to stop them from spreading too far.

If you have a sunken rose garden with fairly low walls, roses such as AVON ('Poulmulti') or SUMA ('Harsuma') have the right kind of low, spreading growth, if planted along the top, to form waterfalls of flowers over the walls.

Much attention has been given to developing ground-cover roses, but some cultivars that are sold as such are simply low-growing but fairly wide-spreading bushes. They are seldom dense enough in growth to be very effective weed-smotherers, and in winter they shed their leaves, so allowing in air and light which enable weeds to germinate.

Roses in containers

Roses are invaluable for their summer colour and fragrance in patio gardens where the surface is mostly paved and there are few or no beds. Containers of many sorts, including hanging baskets, are suitable as long as they are in a position that receives sun for at least half the day (see also CONTAINER GARDENING, pp.304–335). Select bushy and compact modern cultivars (see CONTAINER GARDENING, p.317), as leggy roses with bare stems at the base look unsightly. If grouping roses in a container, ensure that it is large enough for the plants to be spaced out to allow for future growth.

Even quite vigorous climbers may, given the support of a wall, be grown in tubs or half-barrels. They should be planted and trained as other climbing roses but as the nutrients in the containers will be quickly exhausted (and the roses difficult to repot), they will require regular feeding.

Roses grown in containers do not have to be confined to a patio garden. They may bring colour to other paved areas, such as the centre of a herb garden, the surrounds of a pool, or even a roof garden.

Roses for display and exhibition

ENTERING roses in a local flower show and, with experience, in a town or county horticultural show, can be very rewarding. Higher levels of competition than this require much more dedication and time than the average gardener can give.

Rules for exhibiting roses vary from country to country, depending on the requirements of national, and local, rose associations. It is as important for serious exhibitors as it is for judges to be familiar with the details of such rules, so always study the schedule before entering a show.

Cultivating roses for exhibition

Grow several bushes of the same cultivar to ensure a wide choice of blooms. Ordinary garden bush roses can be used for exhibition purposes, provided that they are well looked after in the garden and the foliage is kept free from disease. Prune

DISBUDDING ROSES

Terminal bud left to develop

Pinch out sidebuds

HYBRID TEA ROSES
As soon as they are large enough to handle easily, pinch out all the sidebuds, leaving the main, central bud to grow on.

Pinch out terminal bud

Sidebuds left to develop

FLORIBUNDA ROSES
Pinch out the young, central bud of each smaller spray in the truss for uniform flowering.

CHINESE HATS

To protect a show bloom from rain damage, insert a stake or cane with a "Chinese hat" by the rose stem and tie the stem in to the stake.

cultivars severely to produce a limited number of strong shoots with only eight or nine blooms a season from which to choose exhibition blooms. Maintain vigorous growth with extra fertilizer. Roses are often disbudded to produce exhibition quality blooms. Remove the newly formed sidebuds from Hybrid Tea roses so that the main bud develops strongly. Disbudding the central bloom of Floribunda roses ensures that all the other buds open at roughly the same time.

Some blooms are easily damaged by rain, and showing rules permit the use of individual bloom protectors, or "Chinese hats", in the form of plastic cones fixed to canes. They are by no means essential, however, and are not easy to use on the large trusses of Floribunda bushes.

Selecting blooms

Timing is crucial in exhibiting. A Hybrid Tea bloom should, at the moment of judging, be only three quarters open, and a Floribunda truss should have the maximum number of blooms open, although the stamens should not yet have blackened. Blooms should be of average size for the cultivar. Good, healthy foliage is also important.

Preparing for a show

It is better for the novice exhibitor to restrict entries in any one show to a maximum of three classes at first, until they have gained experience. They should cut about double the number of roses to be entered, with

stems at least 30cm (12in) long, on the evening before the show. Remove the lower leaves and thorns from the cut stems; plunge the stems into buckets of cold water, right up to the necks of the flowers. Keep the containers overnight in a cool place.

Do not be put off if your blooms suffer weather damage. Others are in the same position. If the blooms must be transported any distance, keep each bloom or truss separated, using tissue paper, so that they are not bruised or otherwise damaged.

Staging the blooms

Once at the show, collect your class entry cards from the show secretary and carry your roses straight to the staging table. Use vases or bowls that are as plain as possible. Staging the blooms always takes longer than expected, but greater speed and skill will come with experience.

Arrange the roses symmetrically, placing any larger bloom in the front so it is less noticeable. The blooms should be close, but not touching; a good blend of colours may win an extra point. Cut out faded Floribunda blooms if this does not leave obvious cut stems or gaps. Use a water-colour brush to remove insects or dust specks and sponge off any traces of insecticide deposit with cotton wool. If needed, "dress" Hybrid Tea blooms by gently teasing any petals that are slightly out of place into the correct position. Do not reposition the petals too much, since overdressed blooms may lose points.

When arranging the blooms, check that they conform to the schedule,

EXHIBITION STANDARD BLOOMS

A HYBRID TEA ROSE 'DREAM TIME'

High, conical centre

Circular outline

Firm, unblemished petals

Bloom ¾ open

Clean, undamaged leaves of good size

Outer petals evenly reflexed

A FLORIBUNDA ROSE HANNAH GORDON ('Korweiso')

Firm, unblemished petals

Pleasing outline

Blooms fully open

Unfaded stamens

Clean, undamaged leaves of good size

Good, fresh colour

for example "One bloom each of three cultivars of a Hybrid Tea rose in a vase"; if there is any deviation, the arrangement will be judged as N.A.S. (Not According to Schedule). Place the class card, and one listing the cultivars, in front of the vase. Tidy away the debris and top up the vases with water.

EQUIPMENT FOR EXHIBITING ROSES

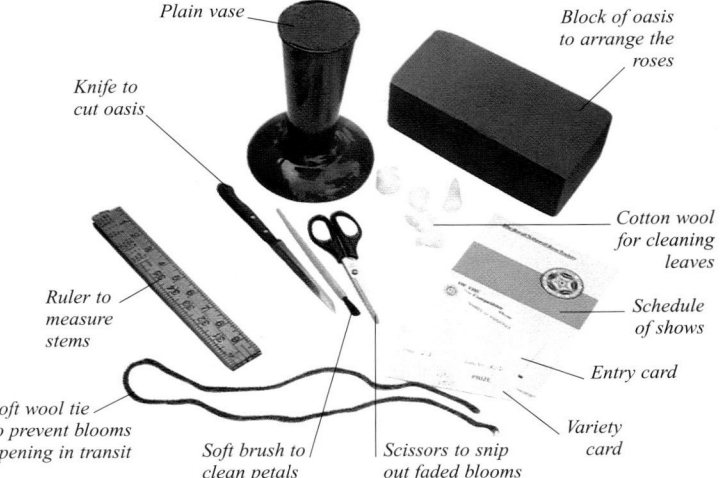

Plain vase

Block of oasis to arrange the roses

Knife to cut oasis

Cotton wool for cleaning leaves

Ruler to measure stems

Schedule of shows

Entry card

Soft wool tie to prevent blooms opening in transit

Soft brush to clean petals

Scissors to snip out faded blooms

Variety card

Planter's guide to roses

MOST FRAGRANT FLOWERS

Combining excellent scent with reliable garden performance
Rosa ALEC'S RED ('Cored')
Rosa 'Arthur Bell'
Rosa x *centifolia* cultivars
Rosa 'Climbing Etoile de Hollande'
Rosa 'Compassion'
Rosa DOUBLE DELIGHT ('Andeli')
Rosa FRAGRANT CLOUD ('Tanellis')
Rosa GERTRUDE JEKYLL ('Ausbord')
Rosa 'Korresia'

Rosa FRAGRANT CLOUD

Rosa L'AIMANT ('Harzola')
Rosa 'Madame Hardy'
Rosa 'Madame Isaac Pereire'
Rosa MARGARET MERRIL ('Harkuly')
Rosa NEW ZEALAND ('Macgenev')
Rosa PERCEPTION ('Harzippee')
Rosa 'Prima Ballerina'
Rosa 'Rose de Resht'
Rosa ROSEMARY HARKNESS ('Harrowbond')
Rosa 'Roseraie de l'Haÿ'
Rosa SCEPTRE'D ISLE ('Ausland')
Rosa 'Wendy Cussons'

DECORATIVE HIPS

Rosa 'Fru Dagmar Hastrup'
Rosa 'Geranium'
Rosa *glauca*
Rosa *rugosa* 'Alba', R. *rugosa* 'Rubra'
Rosa 'Scabrosa'
Rosa 'Sealing Wax'

HEALTHIER ROSES

Garden roses with good resistance to and/or tolerance of disease
Rosa ALEXANDER ('Harlex')
Rosa ANNE HARKNESS ('Harkaramel')
Rosa ARMADA ('Haruseful')
Rosa 'Arthur Bell'
Rosa 'Ballerina'
Rosa CHATSWORTH ('Tanotax')
Rosa 'Dortmund'
Rosa ELINA ('Dicjana')
Rosa ESCAPADE ('Harpade')
Rosa FELLOWSHIP ('Harwelcome')
Rosa GORDON'S COLLEGE ('Cocjabby')
Rosa HERTFORDSHIRE ('Kortenay')
Rosa LOVELY LADY ('Dicjubell')

Rosa MARJORIE FAIR ('Harhero')
Rosa MISTRESS QUICKLY ('Ausky')
Rosa OPEN ARMS ('Chewpixcel')
Rosa PINK FLOWER CARPET ('Noatraum')
Rosa PRETTY LADY ('Scrivo')
Rosa QUEEN MOTHER ('Korquemu')
Rosa ROSE GAUJARD ('Gaumo')
Rosa *rugosa* hybrids
Rosa SAVOY HOTEL ('Harvintage')
Rosa SURREY ('Korlanum')
Rosa 'The Fairy'
Rosa WINE AND DINE ('Dicuncle')

MIXED FLOWER BORDERS

Front of border
Rosa AVON ('Poulmulti')
Rosa BABY LOVE ('Scrivluv')
Rosa BERKSHIRE ('Korpinka')
Rosa HERTFORDSHIRE ('Kortenay')
Rosa KENT ('Poulcov')
Rosa 'Mevrouw Nathalie Nypels'
Rosa PRINCESS OF WALES ('Hardinkum')
Rosa 'The Fairy'
Rosa THE TIMES ROSE ('Korpeahn')
Rosa VALENTINE HEART ('Dicogle')

Middle ground
Rosa ANNA LIVIA ('Kormetter')
Rosa ARMADA ('Haruseful')
Rosa 'Ballerina'
Rosa BETTY HARKNESS ('Harette')
Rosa BONICA ('Meidomonac')
Rosa 'Buff Beauty'
Rosa ESCAPADE ('Harpade')
Rosa FRIEND FOR LIFE ('Cocnanne')
Rosa 'Fru Dagmar Hastrup'
Rosa *gallica* 'Versicolor'
Rosa HERITAGE ('Ausblush')
Rosa ICEBERG ('Korbin')
Rosa JACQUELINE DU PRÉ ('Harwanna')
Rosa MARJORIE FAIR ('Harhero')
Rosa 'Penelope'
Rosa ROSY CUSHION ('Interall')

Rosa GERTRUDE JEKYLL

Middle to rear
Rosa 'Cornelia'
Rosa 'Fantin-Latour'
Rosa 'Felicia'
Rosa GERTRUDE JEKYLL ('Ausbord')
Rosa 'Golden Wings'
Rosa GRAHAM THOMAS ('Ausmas')
Rosa 'Marguerite Hilling'
Rosa 'Nevada'

Rosa 'Roseraie de l'Haÿ'
Rosa 'Sally Holmes'
Rosa WESTERLAND ('Korwest')

SOUTH- AND WEST-FACING WALLS AND FENCES

Rosa ALTISSIMO ('Delmur')
Rosa ANTIQUE ('Kordalen')
Rosa BREATH OF LIFE ('Harquanne')
Rosa CLAIR MATIN ('Meimont')
Rosa 'Compassion'
Rosa CRIMSON CASCADE ('Fryclimbdown')
Rosa 'Danse du Feu'
Rosa 'Dreaming Spires'
Rosa DUBLIN BAY ('Macdub')
Rosa GOOD AS GOLD ('Chewsunbeam')
Rosa HIGH HOPES ('Haryup')
Rosa 'Madame Alfred Carrière'
Rosa 'New Dawn'
Rosa PENNY LANE ('Hardwell')
Rosa SUMMER WINE ('Korizont')
Rosa 'White Cockade'

NORTH- AND EAST-FACING FENCES AND WALLS

For structures over 2m (6ft)
Rosa 'Albéric Barbier'
Rosa 'Compassion'
Rosa 'Dortmund'
Rosa 'Morning Jewel'
Rosa 'New Dawn'

For areas up to 2m (6ft)
Rosa ARMADA ('Haruseful')
Rosa 'Chinatown'
Rosa 'Cornelia'
Rosa 'Penelope'
Rosa 'Prosperity'

ATTRACTIVE FOLIAGE

Rosa *fedtschenkoana*
Rosa *glauca*
Rosa *gymnocarpa* var. *willmottiae*
Rosa *nitida*
Rosa *primula*
Rosa *sericea* subsp. *omeiensis* f. *pteracantha*
Rosa *virginiana*

GROUND-COVER ROSES

Rosa AVON ('Poulmulti')
Rosa BERKSHIRE ('Korpinka')
Rosa HERTFORDSHIRE ('Kortenay')
Rosa RED BLANKET ('Intercell')
Rosa ROSY CUSHION ('Interall')
Rosa SURREY ('Korlanum')
Rosa SWANY ('Meiburenac')

SPECIMEN SHRUB ROSES

Rosa 'Cerise Bouquet'
Rosa 'Complicata'
Rosa 'Felicia'
Rosa 'Fritz Nobis'

Rosa 'Marguerite Hilling'
Rosa 'Nevada'
Rosa 'Scabrosa'
Rosa *xanthina* 'Canary Bird'

ARCHES AND PILLARS

Rosa ALOHA ('Kormarcus')
Rosa ALTISSIMO ('Delmur')
Rosa 'Bantry Bay'
Rosa BRIDGE OF SIGHS ('Harglow')
Rosa CITY GIRL ('Harzorba')
Rosa 'Compassion'
Rosa 'Dortmund'
Rosa 'Dreaming Spires'
Rosa DUBLIN BAY ('Macdub')
Rosa 'Golden Showers'
Rosa 'Goldfinch'
Rosa LAURA FORD ('Chewarvel')

Rosa CITY GIRL

Rosa 'Leverkusen'
Rosa 'New Dawn'
Rosa 'Phyllis Bide'
Rosa ROSALIE CORAL ('Chewallop')
Rosa 'Veilchenblau'
Rosa WARM WELCOME ('Chewizz')

PERGOLAS

Rosa 'Albéric Barbier'
Rosa 'Albertine'
Rosa 'Alister Stella Gray'
Rosa 'Climbing Cécile Brunner'
Rosa 'Easlea's Golden Rambler'
Rosa 'Emily Gray'
Rosa 'Félicité Perpétue'
Rosa 'François Juranville'
Rosa HIGH HOPES ('Haryup')
Rosa 'Madame Alfred Carrière'
Rosa 'Madame Grégoire Staechelin'
Rosa 'Maigold'
Rosa 'Sander's White Rambler'
Rosa 'Sympathie'

ROSES TO GROW INTO TREES

Rosa 'Bobbie James'
Rosa 'Blush Rambler'
Rosa 'Emily Gray'
Rosa *filipes* 'Kiftsgate'
Rosa *mulliganii*
Rosa 'Paul's Himalayan Musk'
Rosa 'Rambling Rector'
Rosa 'Seagull'
Rosa *soulieana*
Rosa 'Treasure Trove'

Soil preparation and planting

GROWING roses in the garden is not difficult if their basic needs are satisfied. They are relatively long-lived flowering plants, so it is worth investing time and effort in choosing a suitable site, properly preparing the soil, selecting cultivars appropriate to the conditions, and planting the roses correctly.

Site and aspect

All roses need a site that is open to the sun and sheltered from strong winds, with good air circulation and a fertile soil. They do not thrive in deep shade, under trees, if crowded by other plants, or in "rose-sick" (see right) or waterlogged soil. Most sites may be improved to meet these needs, for example by erecting wind-breaks or by draining heavy, wet soils (see SOILS AND FERTILIZERS, "Improving drainage", p.623). Planting roses in an appropriate compost in raised beds or containers may solve the problem of unsuitable soil.

Evaluate the planting site carefully before choosing a cultivar: the enormous variety of the rose family provides plants that tolerate a range of conditions. Most modern roses do not flourish on chalk, but almost all the old garden roses grow well in alkaline conditions if given large quantities of organic material when being planted and mulched. *Rosa rugosa* and *R. pimpinellifolia* groups do well on sandy soil. These are generalizations since even among modern roses there may be great differences between cultivars: for example, on poor soils 'Just Joey' and FULTON MACKAY ('Cocdana') suffer but SAVOY HOTEL ('Harvintage'), THE TIMES ROSE ('Korpeahn'), and others thrive if given extra food and moisture. Certain rootstocks may help in some circumstances: for example *R. canina* tolerates and often grows well in heavy, cold soils.

Soil quality

Roses grow in most types of soil, but prefer slightly acid conditions, about pH 6.5. A water-retentive yet well-drained soil is best of all. Always clear weeds when preparing the soil to avoid the young roses having to compete with them for light, moisture, and nutrients.

Improving the soil
The drainage of clay soils, water-retentiveness of light, sandy soils, and pH level of alkaline soils may be improved by incorporating plenty of organic matter. If, on chalk, the topsoil is very shallow, excavate it to about 60cm (24in) when planting, and replace some of the chalk with extra organic matter. For further information on how to influence the soil acidity, and on general soil preparation, see "Soil cultivation", pp.618–621. If possible, prepare the soil approximately three months before planting to allow it to settle.

Rose-sick soil
New roses do not thrive if planted in a rosebed where roses have been grown for two years or more, as they will almost always succumb to "rose sickness" (see "Replant disease/soil sickness", p.665): it seems that the fine feeding roots of new roses are more prone to attack than are the older, tougher roots of roses that are already growing in the bed.

If replacing only one or two roses in an established bed, dig a hole at least 45cm (18in) deep by 60cm (24in) across and exchange the soil with some from a part of the garden where roses have not grown for several years. As this is a daunting task to carry out for an entire rosebed, either locate the bed on a different site, or have the soil chemically sterilized by a qualified contractor.

Choosing roses

Where and how you buy roses will depend to some extent on the particular cultivars that you wish to buy.

Many old roses are obtainable only from specialist nurseries, by mail-order if they are not situated locally. Bear in mind that catalogue photographs may not always accurately represent the colour of the flower, nor is it possible to assess the quality of the plant before it arrives, although with a reputable nursery this should not be a problem. Beware of special "bargains", often advertised in the press, that offer bedding or hedging roses cheaply as the plants may be of poor quality.

Nurseries in the UK now generally use *R.* 'Laxa' as a stock, since it is comparatively sucker-free and does well on most soils. Rootstocks may be purchased by those wishing to bud their own roses (see also "Hybridizing", pp.168–169).

Bare-root roses
Mail-order suppliers, stores, and supermarkets sell roses with bare roots, sometimes packaged in plastic. The bare-root roses are in a semi-dormant or dormant state and their roots are virtually clean of soil. Provided that they have not dried out in transit and are planted as soon as possible after arrival, they should establish perfectly satisfactorily.

When buying a bare-root rose in a store, examine it carefully. If the environment in which the rose has been kept is too warm, the rose either dries out or starts growing prematurely, producing blanched, thin shoots that usually die after planting. Do not purchase any roses that display such symptoms.

Container-grown roses
Roses grown in containers may be planted at any time, except during periods of prolonged drought or when the ground is frozen. Many garden centres and suppliers trim the roots of unsold bare-root roses and pot them into containers for convenience of sale; before buying a rose in a container, check that it has not been recently potted up by holding the plant by its main shoot and gently shaking it. If the rose is not firmly rooted and moves about in the compost, it probably has not been grown in its container.

Suppliers whose priority is quick, convenient production tend to select roses that fit into standard-sized containers rather than picking the largest and best plants. These roses are acceptable provided that they are in general good health and do not have spindly, weak growth. Treat them as bare-root roses where

SELECTING HEALTHY ROSES

A BARE-ROOT BUSH ROSE
GOOD EXAMPLE

Strong bud union

Good network of fibrous roots

BAD EXAMPLE

Spindly, damaged shoots

Stunted root system

A CONTAINER-GROWN ROSE
GOOD EXAMPLE

Vigorous, foliage of a good colour

Healthy root system

BAD EXAMPLE

Spindly shoots

Black spot

Dead or dying leaves

Weeds

A STANDARD ROSE
GOOD EXAMPLE

Strong, healthy shoots, evenly distributed

Sturdy, well-balanced top-growth

Moist compost

Stem has been securely staked by grower

Straight stem

BAD EXAMPLE

Dead wood

Unbalanced, one-sided head

PLANTING DISTANCES FOR A ROSE HEDGE

TALL HEDGING ROSES
Plant the roses in a line 1–1.2m (3–4ft) apart, so that, when mature, the branches intermingle to form an effective screen.

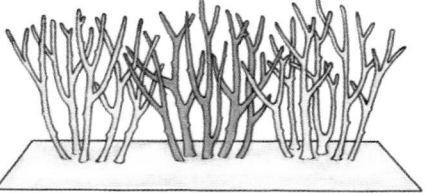

MODERN BUSH ROSES
For a denser hedge, plant roses in a staggered formation in 2 rows that are 45–60cm (18–24in) apart.

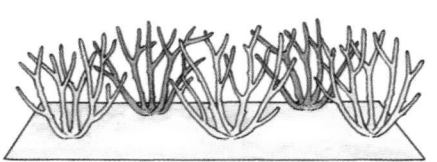

storage and planting are concerned. If any roots are growing through the drainage holes in the container, knock the plant out of its pot and check that its roots are not thickly coiled around the root ball – a sign that the rose is pot-bound and has been in the container for too long.

Selecting a healthy rose

Whether bare-root or container-grown, the plant should have at least two or three strong, firm shoots and a healthy network of roots in good proportion to the top-growth. Any foliage on container-grown roses should be vigorous. If buying a climbing rose, check that the shoots are healthy and at least 30cm (12in) long. Choose a standard rose with a balanced head since it is likely to be viewed from all sides; a straight stem is best, although a slightly crooked stem is acceptable.

Preparing to plant

Following a few simple principles at the planting stage, such as observing correct planting distances and depths, handling the roots carefully, and providing proper support where necessary, avoids problems with routine care later on. Delay planting for a few days if the ground is too wet, frozen, or too dry for roots to adjust easily to the soil.

When to plant bare-root roses

Bare-root roses are best planted just before or at the beginning of their dormant period, in late autumn or early winter, to lessen the shock of transplanting. Early spring may be better in areas that suffer from bad winters. Plant the roses as soon as possible after purchase. If there is any delay, perhaps because of unsuitable weather, it is best to heel them into a spare piece of ground, with the

roots buried in a shallow trench (see ORNAMENTAL TREES, *Heeling in*, p.65). Alternatively, store the roses in a cool and frost-free place, and keep the roots moist.

When to plant container-grown roses

These may be planted at any time of the year in suitable weather conditions. Container-grown roses, unlike bare-root roses, may be left outdoors in their containers for three weeks or more while awaiting planting, as long as they are kept properly watered. Even though they are frost hardy, do not risk exposing them to prolonged frost as the roots in the containers may suffer some damage in very cold conditions.

Spacing bedding roses

The growth habit determines the planting distances between bedding roses. Over-close planting makes mulching, spraying, and pruning more difficult and may create stagnant air conditions which allow rapid spread of mildew and black spot. A narrow, upright cultivar needs less space for healthy growth than a lax, spreading one and so tolerates closer planting. Plant the bushes 45–60cm (18–24in) apart and about 30cm (12in) from the edge of the rosebed.

If underplanting modern roses or very large species roses, allow more space, about 75–120cm (2½–4ft), depending on their ultimate size and growth habit. Space miniature roses roughly 30cm (12in) apart, according to the varying spread and final height of the plants.

Spacing roses for a hedge

The size and growth habit of the chosen cultivar governs the position of roses in forming a hedge. To gain uniformly dense growth, plant tall, hedging roses such as 'Penelope' and 'Golden Wings', which reach

1.2m (4ft) or more across, in a single line, and modern bush roses such as ALEXANDER ('Harlex') in two rows in a staggered formation.

Planting a bush rose

The first stage in planting a rose is to prepare the plant. If the roots of a bare-root rose look dry, soak the plant in a bucket of water for an hour or two until thoroughly moist. Place a container-grown rose in a bucket of water until the compost surface appears moist. If the root ball is wrapped in plastic or hessian, cut away the wrapping carefully. Remove any loose compost, gently tease out the roots, and prune any damaged or diseased roots or shoots; on bare-root roses, remove any buds or hips and most remaining leaves.

Make a planting hole that is wide enough to accommodate the roots or root ball, and deep enough so that, when planted, the bud union of the rose is about 2.5cm (1in) below

ground level or 1cm (½in) for miniature roses. The bud union is easily recognizable as a bulge at the base of the shoots where the cultivar has been grafted onto the rootstock.

Add a planting mixture of garden compost, soil, and a little general fertilizer to the base of the planting hole. Position the rose in the centre of the hole and check that the planting depth is correct. If the roots of a bare-root rose all point in one direction, place the rose close to one side of the hole and fan the roots out as widely as possible. Then fill the rest of the hole with the soil that was removed from it, shaking the rose a little to allow the soil to settle around the roots or root ball.

Tread the rose in firmly, but not too hard. Use the toe rather than the heel to apply the right amount of pressure, especially on heavy soil that might easily become compacted. Take care not to damage the shoots. Label and water well, but do not mulch until the following spring (see "Mulching roses", p.159).

HOW TO PLANT A BARE-ROOT BUSH ROSE

1 *Remove diseased or damaged growth. Cut out any crossing shoots and thin or straggly stems at the base to produce a balanced shape. Trim any thick roots by about one third.*

2 *Dig the planting hole in a prepared bed and fork half a bucketful of organic compost, mixed with a small handful of general fertilizer, into the bottom of the hole.*

3 *Place the rose in the centre of the hole and spread out the roots evenly. Lay a cane across the hole to check that the bud union will be 2.5cm (1in) below soil level when the rose is planted.*

4 *Fill in the hole with soil, firming with your hands in stages to ensure that there are no air pockets among the roots. Lightly tread down the surrounding soil. Rake over the soil and water well.*

HOW TO PLANT A CLIMBING ROSE

1 *Place the rose in the planting hole, leaning it towards the wall at an angle of about 45° so that the shoots reach the lowest support wire. Place a cane across the hole to check the planting depth.*

2 *Use canes to guide the shorter shoots towards the wires. Tie all the shoots to the canes or wires with plastic straps (see inset).*

Planting a climbing rose or a rambler

Train climbers grown against a wall or fence along horizontal wires that are about 45cm (18in) apart and held in place by tapered vine eyes or strong nails driven into the surface. If the brickwork or masonry of a wall is very hard, drill holes for the vine eyes with a 4.7mm (³⁄₁₆in) bit. Keep the wires 7cm (3in) away from the wall to allow air circulation and discourage diseases.

The ground next to a wall is likely to be dry, since it is in a rain shadow and the masonry absorbs moisture from the soil. Plant about 45cm (18in) from the wall where the soil is less dry and water from any eaves will not constantly drip on the rose.

Prepare the soil and planting hole, and trim the rose as for bush roses. Position the plant, leaning it towards the wall at 45°, and fan out its roots towards moist ground. If necessary, train the shoots along canes pushed into the ground, but keep each cane far enough from the roots to avoid damaging them.

After filling in and firming, as for a bush rose, attach the shoots to the support wires with the small, readymade, plastic straps that are designed for tying in roses. Take care not to tighten the straps too much around the rose's stems as room must be left for the shoots to grow.

Do not prune the main shoots of a climber at this stage: wait until the beginning of the next growing season before lightly pruning, and be prepared to wait a year or two before the rose begins to climb. In the first year, keep the roots thoroughly watered and uncrowded by other plants to help them establish.

Planting a rambler by a tree
It is essential to match the vigour of the rose to that of the tree in which it is to grow, as the considerable weight of some ramblers is quite capable of pulling over a small or weak tree.

Plant a rose that is to scramble up a tree on the windward side of the tree so that the rose's young, flexible shoots blow towards and around the tree, rather than away from it. Dig a planting hole at least 1m (3ft) away from the trunk to increase the amount of rain that reaches the roots of the rose. Train all the new shoots towards the tree along sloping canes, carefully but securely tied at their upper ends to the trunk, the other ends inserted just behind the rose. If planting in this way on a boundary, bear in mind that the blooms grow towards, and are visible from, the direction of the strongest sunlight.

Planting a standard rose

Most nurseries bud their standard roses on *Rosa rugosa* stocks which have a tendency to sucker, although a few nurseries are experimenting with other rootstocks. To keep suckering to a minimum, plant the rose no deeper than the soil mark: deeper planting will increase sucker growths. If necessary, trim off the top layer of roots so that the bottom layer does not sit too deeply in the soil.

A standard rose needs a stake, placed on the side of the prevailing wind, to support it. Paint the whole stake with a preservative that is not toxic to plants and allow it to dry. Insert the stake very firmly near the centre of the planting hole before positioning the rose, so as to avoid damaging the roots and thereby encouraging suckers. Position the rose next to the stake and check that it just reaches the base of the lowest branches; if necessary, adjust the height of the stake. Use a cane or rake handle to make sure the soil mark and soil surface are level.

Fill in and firm the soil as for a bush rose. Secure the stem to the stake with two rose ties – these should incorporate a buffer to prevent the stake from rubbing the stem – but do not tighten them fully until the rose has settled in the soil. The ties will need to be loosened at least once during the growing season as the diameter of the stem increases.

Planting roses in containers

The container should be at least 30–45cm (12–18in) deep for bush roses or 23–35cm (9–14in) deep for miniatures to allow for root growth. Place a layer of crocks over the drainage holes and fill the container with a standard, loam-based potting compost. Plant in the same way, and at the correct depth, as for bush roses (see p.157). See also "Planting large and long-term plants", pp.324–326.

HOW TO PLANT A STANDARD ROSE

1 *Position the stake in the hole so that the rose stem will be in the centre. Drive the stake into the ground and check that the top is just below the head of the rose.*

2 *Place a cane across the hole to check the planting depth. Use the old soil mark on the stem as a guide and plant at the same depth. Fill in the hole and firm.*

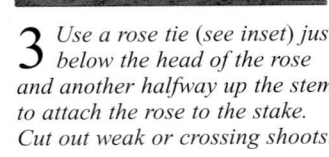

3 *Use a rose tie (see inset) just below the head of the rose and another halfway up the stem to attach the rose to the stake. Cut out weak or crossing shoots.*

Routine care

Roses need regular care to produce healthy, vigorous plants that are resistant to pests and diseases. Attention paid to fertilizing, watering, mulching, and general maintenance will be rewarded with a fine display throughout the season.

Fertilizing

Roses are gross feeders and quickly exhaust even a well-prepared rose-bed that is rich in nutrients. Many essential mineral salts rapidly leach out in the rain, especially from light soils. If the roses are to flourish, they require regular feeds in a balanced formulation of essential nutrients (nitrogen, phosphates, and potassium) and trace elements. Many suitable proprietary compound rose fertilizers are available, mostly in powder or granular form. For information on how to deal with particular nutrient deficiencies, see PLANT PROBLEMS, pp.639–673.

After pruning in the spring, and when the soil is moist, sprinkle a small handful or 25–50g (1–2oz) of fertilizer around each rose. Hoe or rake it in lightly and evenly, keeping it clear of the stems. Repeat the application about a month after midsummer, when the roses are developing a second flush of bloom. Do not apply a general feed later in the year, because this encourages soft autumn growth that may suffer frost damage. A dressing of sulphate of potash, however, applied at a rate of 60g/sq m (2oz/sq yd) in early autumn, protects late shoots by helping them to ripen.

Foliar feeding (spraying a liquid feed on the leaves and bypassing the roots) is usually only needed to obtain extra-large blooms and leaves on exhibition roses. It may help, however, in a prolonged drought or on chalky soils: in both instances, roses may have difficulty in taking in nourishment through the roots.

Fertilizing roses in containers
Roses in containers soon use up the compost nutrients. Compensate for this loss by top-dressing annually with a balanced fertilizer and foliar feeding once or twice in the growing season to maintain vigorous growth.

Watering

Roses need plenty of water for healthy growth, especially if they are newly planted. Watering too

Suckers and how to deal with them

Suckers are shoots that grow below the bud union, directly from the rootstock onto which a cultivar has been grafted. They are usually narrower and a much lighter green than those of the cultivar, often with thorns of a different shape or colour, and paler green leaves may have seven or more leaflets.

Remove any suckering shoots as soon as they appear. This prevents the rootstock from wasting energy on the sucker's growth at the expense of the cultivar. Some rootstocks produce suckers more readily than others, especially if they have been planted at the wrong depth. Damage to the roots, caused by severe frosts or any accidental nicks from hoes, other implements, or a stake, may also stimulate the production of suckers.

Pull the sucker to detach it from the rootstock: this removes any dormant buds that may be present at the point where it joins the roots. Do not cut it as this is the equivalent of pruning it and only encourages more vigorous sucker growth. It may, however, sometimes be necessary to cut a sucker if it originates from beneath the rose and if pulling it off would mean damaging or lifting the rose.

Shoots on the stem of a standard rose are also suckers, since the stem is part of the rootstock. They normally have the dull, dark green leaves that are typical of *Rosa rugosa* rootstocks. Snap them off or pare them from the stem with a knife.

REMOVING A SUCKER FROM A STANDARD ROSE
Pull away any suckers growing from the rose stem (see inset), taking care not to rip the bark.

REMOVING A SUCKER FROM A BUSH ROSE

1 *With a trowel, carefully scrape away the soil to expose the top of the rootstock. Check that the suspect shoot arises from below the bud union.*

2 *Using a glove to protect your hand, pull the sucker away from the rootstock. Refill the hole and gently firm the soil.*

HOW A SUCKER GROWS

Sucker

The sucker (right) grows directly from the rootstock. If only cut back at ground level it will shoot again and divert further energy from the rose.

little and too often can be counterproductive since it encourages the roots to grow towards the surface and compete for water and light; give the roses a good bucketful of water to soak the soil thoroughly around their roots instead.

Roses are deep-rooted plants and can flourish even in long, dry summers and near-drought conditions, particularly if they are well established. In such conditions, the flowers may be smaller than usual and may open very quickly. The petals may also be vulnerable to scorching by the sun. During the flowering season, do not water roses in strong light as the blooms may spoil. Water roses in containers every other day, or even daily if the weather is exceptionally hot and dry.

Eradicating weeds

When weeding, the soil around the bases of roses should not be disturbed too deeply to avoid damaging the roots. Control annual weeds by hand pulling them or with light use of a hoe and eliminate persistent, perennial weeds (see PLANT PROBLEMS, "Weeds", pp.669–673). Mulching roses (see right) or underplanting them with shallow-rooted ground cover also suppresses weeds.

Hygiene

The uncollected fallen leaves, prunings, and any other debris from afflicted plants can spread diseases among roses. Gather up and destroy such material regularly, if possible by burning it; never put it on a compost heap as any diseases present may survive to infect other plants.

Mulching roses

An 8cm (3in) layer of mulch applied in early spring after pruning and feeding helps to smother any weed seeds, and maintain high moisture levels and even temperatures in the soil. Well-rotted stable manure is an ideal mulch, providing many of the nutrients that roses need, but if this proves difficult to obtain, bark chips or cocoa shells are both satisfactory alternatives. For further details, see also SOILS AND FERTILIZERS, "Top-dressings and mulches", p.626.

Dead-heading

The purpose of dead-heading, that is removing faded flowers, is to stimulate the earliest possible development of new, young shoots and further blooms throughout the flowering season. Once a rose flower has been fertilized, it soon fades, and, if left on the plant, may delay the production of new shoots below the old flower cluster.

In some roses, a seed pod or hip forms, and this diverts energy from further flower production; remove the dead flowers regularly unless you require the hips for ornamental purposes. In autumn, even if some roses continue to bloom, stop dead-heading to avoid encouraging new, soft growth which would be damaged by the first frosts.

Moving roses

A rose may be moved at almost any age, but the older it is the greater is the risk that it may resettle badly. The roots of older roses are thick and spread deeply, and also have fewer of the fine feeding roots that are essential for re-establishing the plant. It is not difficult to move roses that are up to three or four years old, but do not risk planting in old rosebeds (see "Rose-sick soil", p.156).

If circumstances allow, move a rose only when it is dormant and always into a well-prepared bed. First loosen the soil by cutting down on all sides with a spade at least 25cm (10in) out from the root ball.

Blind shoots

These are shoots that develop without a terminal flower bud. They divert the plant's energy in the same way as a sucker (see "Suckers and how to deal with them", p.159), so prune any out as soon as they appear.

Cut the blind shoot by about a half to an outward-facing bud to encourage it to grow away and flower. If no bud is visible, cut back to the main stem.

1 FLORIBUNDA ROSES *The central bloom of a truss fades first and should be cut out to maintain the display.*

2 *When all the flowers have faded, remove the whole truss by cutting back to an emerging bud or a fully formed shoot.*

HYBRID TEA ROSES
Cut back stems bearing faded flowers to an outward-facing bud (see inset) or fully formed shoot.

Insert a fork well away from the centre of the plant and lift it, taking a good ball of soil with it and disturbing the roots as little as possible; on light soils, use a spade as the soil is likely to fall away from the roots. Trim off any coarse roots and wrap the root ball in plastic or hessian to prevent the roots from drying out before transferring the plant to its new position. Water immediately after replanting and regularly until the rose is established.

Autumn cut-back

Strong winter winds may loosen the roots of roses, making them vulnerable to frost damage. In heavy soils, the compacted earth may form into a small funnel around the base of the stem and fill up with water that later freezes. The expansion of the water as it freezes may damage the bud union – the most vulnerable part of the rose. To prevent this, shorten tall Hybrid Tea or Floribunda bushes in autumn.

Winter protection

In temperate climates, roses need protection only in a very bad winter. In very extreme climates, severe winters can kill roses outright if they are not protected; any plants that do survive have to make completely new growth each year and will have a very short flowering season.

Hybrid Tea and Floribunda roses may tolerate temperatures as low as -10° to -12°C (10–14°F) for a week

---

or so if soil is mounded over the crown. Pack the crowns of standard roses with straw or bracken, loosely tied in place with twine. At colder temperatures, provide greater protection or choose roses that tolerate extreme cold. Roses that are hardy between -20°C and -23°C (-4°F to -10°F) include Bourbon, China, and Centifolia roses, *Rosa californica*, and *R. wichurana*. Grow Alba, Damask, and Gallica roses, and some of the species roses, such as *R. foetida* and *R. palustris*, in areas where the temperature falls to -30°C (-22°F). A few roses, such as *R. virginiana*, *R. blanda*, *R. canina*, *R. glauca*, and

---

R. rugosa, survive cold as severe as -37°C (-35°F). For full instructions on protecting roses, see FROST AND WIND PROTECTION, pp.612–613.

Pests and diseases

Aphids (p.646), black spot (see "Bacterial leaf spots and blotches", p.648), rose die-back (p.665), powdery mildew (p.646), and rusts (pp.648 and 653) are common problems; spray as a precaution if necessary. Inspect roses regularly and control diseases or pests as soon as any symptom is noticed.

CUTTING BACK IN THE AUTUMN

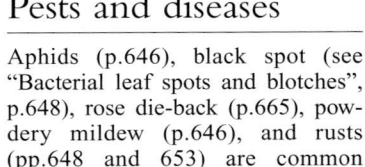

BEFORE (*left*)
In mid- to late autumn, cut back Hybrid Tea and Floribunda roses that are over 75cm (2¹⁄₂ft) in height (left) to avoid the effects of wind-rock.

AFTER (*below*)
Reduce the entire bush by a half to one third of its height, cutting all shoots above a bud.

Pruning and training

THE purpose of pruning is to speed up the natural process of new, vigorous, disease-free shoots developing to replace the old, weakened ones, and so produce an attractive shape and the optimum display of blooms. Training a plant on supports stimulates the production of flowering sideshoots and directs new growth into the given space. The severity of pruning depends on the rose type; certain principles of pruning, however, apply to all roses.

Basic principles of pruning roses

A pair of sharp, high-quality secateurs is essential; long-handled pruners and a fine-toothed pruning saw are also useful for removing gnarled, woody stumps and thicker shoots. Wear strong, protective gloves for all pruning tasks.

How to prune

Always make a clean, angled cut above a bud that faces in the direction in which the resultant new shoot should develop. This is usually an outward-facing bud, but it may face inwards on a lax, spreading rose if the centre of the bush needs filling out. Cut to the appropriate height if a dormant bud is not visible, and cut out any stubs that develop later.

Remove dead and dying shoots, cutting back to disease-free, white pith, even if this means pruning almost to ground level; also cut out crossing growths that might prevent the free circulation of light and air into the centre of the plants.

Opinions differ as to whether to prune bush roses further. The Royal National Rose Society has been conducting pruning trials to assess the merits of different pruning methods. Whereas the traditional practice is to remove all thin, twiggy growths that seem incapable of producing flowering shoots, the trial results indicate that it can be beneficial to leave them on the plant, because they tend to come into leaf early, and thus provide a source of energy to the rose at the start of the growing season.

When to prune

Prune roses when they are dormant or semi-dormant, that is between autumn leaf-fall and when the buds are just beginning to break in the spring. Pruning a rose in active growth is sometimes necessary but severely checks growth. Do not

MAKING A PRUNING CUT

Position the thin blade of the secateurs just above the bud. Take care not to make the cut too far from the bud, or leave a snag, because disease may enter the stem and cause die-back. If this happens, cut back the shoot as far as is necessary to reach good, healthy wood.

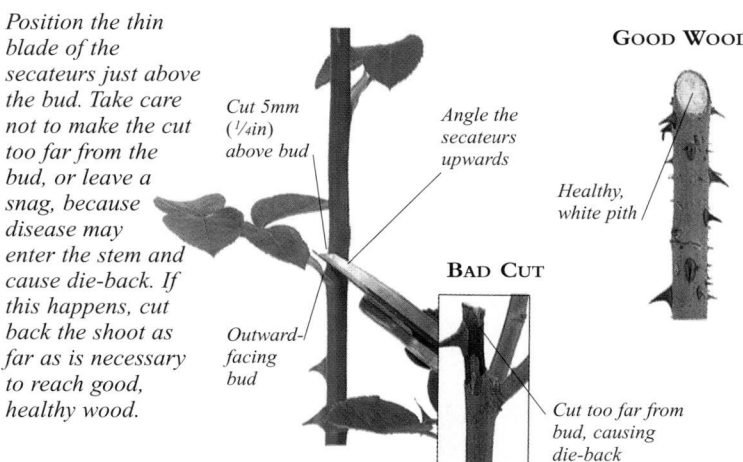

Cut 5mm (¼in) above bud

Angle the secateurs upwards

Outward-facing bud

GOOD WOOD

Healthy, white pith

BAD CUT

Cut too far from bud, causing die-back

prune in frosty conditions as the growth bud below the cut may be damaged and the shoot may die back. Following a very severe winter, cut back frost-damaged shoots in spring to a healthy bud; if the winters are always severe, prune roses in spring, immediately after removing any winter protection material. Conversely, in a climate so warm that the roses flower almost continuously, prune them in the cooler months to induce dormancy and give them an artificial period of rest.

HOW TO PRUNE A HYBRID TEA ROSE

Prune the rose fairly hard, in autumn or spring, by trimming off any unproductive growth and then reducing the main shoots to form a strong, balanced framework.

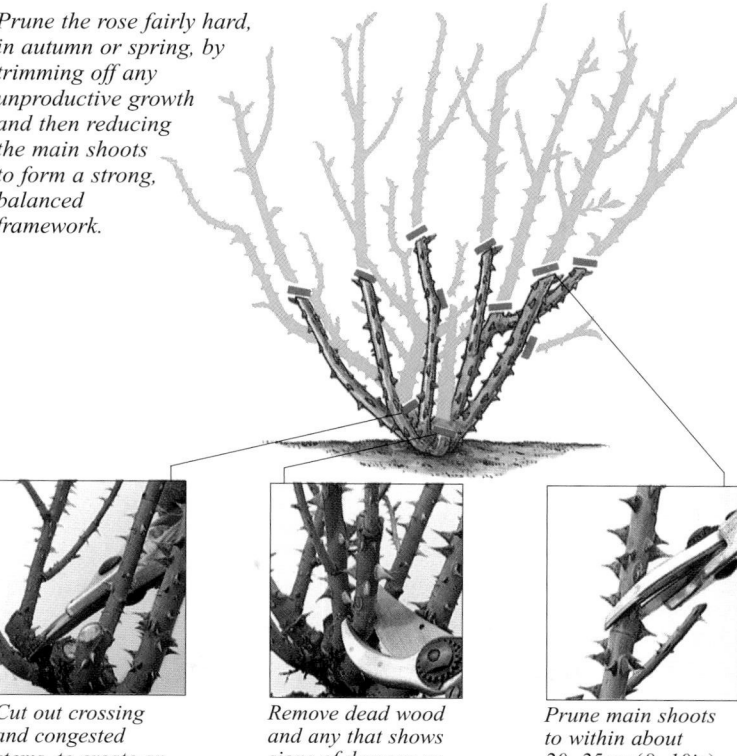

Cut out crossing and congested stems, to create an open-centred plant.

Remove dead wood and any that shows signs of damage or disease.

Prune main shoots to within about 20–25cm (8–10in) of ground level.

Pruning roses after planting

Almost all newly planted roses should be pruned hard to encourage the development of vigorous shoot and root systems. Climbing roses are the exception to this rule – give them only a light, cosmetic pruning in the first year to remove any weak, dead, or damaged shoots. Remove any weak, dead, or crossing growth from standard roses. Less severe pruning

Prune a newly planted bush rose to about 8cm (3in) above ground level. Cut back to outward-facing buds and remove any frost-damaged growth.

and regular fertilizing are preferable for roses grown in soils that are deficient in nutrients.

Pruning modern garden bush roses

Modern roses flower on new or the current season's growth, so they are pruned fairly severely to stimulate vigorous, new shoots and to produce a good display of blooms.

Hybrid Tea roses

Remove dead, damaged, and diseased shoots, cutting to healthy growth. Twiggy shoots may be left on the plant, if desired (see "How to prune", left). Use long-handled pruners or loppers to cut away stumps from previous prunings that, although healthy, have not produced any worthwhile new growth.

Thin out any weak or crossing shoots from the centre of the bush to leave a well-balanced framework and allow free air circulation. It is not as important to produce a balanced framework with bedding roses planted close together as with one that is grown as a specimen, and is seen from all sides.

In temperate climates, the main shoots should then be pruned back to between 20–25cm (8–10in) for general display purposes, but in extremely mild areas, the shoots may be cut down less severely to about 45–60cm (18–24in). To achieve blooms that are of exhibition quality, cut the main shoots hard back to leave only two or three buds.

Floribunda and Polyantha roses

When pruning these types of rose, cut out any unproductive wood as for Hybrid Tea roses (see p.161). Reduce any sideshoots by about one third on smaller cultivars and by two thirds on taller-growing cultivars, such as 'Sally Holmes'. Cut back the main shoots to 30–38cm (12–15in), but reduce the shoots of taller cultivars by about one third of their length. Do not prune them any harder, unless growing the roses for exhibition, since this reduces the number of blooms that will be produced in the following season.

Patio roses

These are smaller versions of the Floribunda roses, and should be pruned in autumn or spring following the same principles.

Miniature roses

There are two distinct methods of pruning miniature roses. The simpler of the two is to give them only the minimum of attention: remove shoots that have died back, thin out occasionally the shoots of those cultivars that produce a dense tangle of twiggy growth, and shorten any over-vigorous shoots that may throw the whole plant out of balance.

The second method is to treat the plants as if they were miniature Hybrid Tea or Floribunda roses. Cut back all growth except the strongest shoots, and then shorten these by about one third. This method is used satisfactorily for cultivars introduced from the USA to the UK that do not adapt easily to their new conditions. Such plants benefit from the extra stimulus of a severe pruning and produce strong, new growth. It can also improve poor shape (see below).

HOW TO PRUNE A FLORIBUNDA OR POLYANTHA ROSE

In autumn or spring, cut out unproductive growth and prune the sideshoots. Reduce the main shoots by a proportion suitable to the height of the cultivar.

Remove crossing or congested wood back to the main stem.

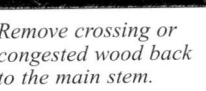

Prune out all dead, damaged, or diseased wood to a healthy bud.

Prune main shoots to 30–38cm (12–15in) from ground level.

Reduce sideshoots by one to two thirds, cutting to a bud.

Pruning standard roses

The majority of standards are formed from Hybrid Tea or Floribunda bush cultivars or from small shrub roses budded onto a straight, unbranched stem, usually 1.1–1.2m (3½–4ft) high. Prune as for the bush or shrub rose equivalents, cutting back the shoots by about one third, so that the shoots are all roughly equal in length. It is especially important to achieve a balanced head that will look pleasing from all sides. If the head is unbalanced, prune the shoots on the thicker side less hard so that they do not produce as much new growth as those on the thinner side.

Weeping standards

These roses are usually formed from cultivars of small-flowered ramblers grafted onto especially tall standard stems of about 1.5m (5ft). The flexible shoots are pendent and require only limited pruning: remove the old, flowered wood when the blooms have faded, leaving growth from the current season intact.

Pruning shrub and old garden roses

Although these vary enormously in their growth habit, most modern and old garden shrub roses, and all the species roses, flower on wood that is two or more years old. They should be pruned fairly lightly to leave the flowering wood intact. Many flower freely for years without any formal pruning if allowed to develop naturally. It is necessary only to cut out any dead, damaged, diseased, or weak wood to keep the roses really healthy. Despite this, some pruning may help to increase the number and quality of the blooms.

Give mature, remontant shrub roses a light renewal pruning each winter by cutting down some of the older, main growths to the base. This encourages the production of vigorous, new basal shoots that will flower the following summer. Over a four-year period of renewal pruning, all the shoots are replaced and, with regular fertilizing, the bushes will remain free-flowering and healthy for many years. Treat non-remontant roses similarly but prune them immediately after flowering.

Rugosa and China roses may be given similar, annual, renewal pruning to keep them in good health.

HOW TO RESHAPE A MINIATURE ROSE

BEFORE
Miniature roses often produce a mass of twiggy growth (left). The shape of this plant is unbalanced by over-vigorous shoots growing from the base.

AFTER
Twiggy growth and damaged wood have been removed, and vigorous shoots cut back by half (below).

HOW TO PRUNE A STANDARD ROSE

BEFORE
In the spring, prune a standard rose to prevent the plant from becoming too top-heavy and to retain an evenly shaped, floriferous head.

AFTER
All dead and damaged wood, and any crossing stems, have been removed to leave healthy shoots. The main shoots have been reduced to 20–25cm (8–10in) and the sideshoots by about one third.

PRUNING A GALLICA ROSE

Throughout the flowering season, thin out the rose to keep it healthy. The annual pruning after flowering involves cutting back sideshoots, unproductive wood, and some older shoots to encourage new growth.

Thin out twiggy growth regularly, and remove spent blooms by cutting back to the main shoot.

Every 3–4 years, cut out up to one quarter of old main shoots at the base.

Shorten sideshoots, but not the main shoots, by about two thirds. Cut out any dead, diseased, or weak wood.

PRUNING ALBA, CENTIFOLIA, DAMASK, MOSS, AND PORTLAND ROSES

Prune after flowering, cutting back both main shoots and sideshoots. If necessary, prune again in late summer to remove any overlong shoots that have developed.

Reduce main shoots that are old and woody by one quarter to one third.

LATE SUMMER

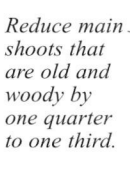

Cut back any overlong, whippy shoots by about one third.

Prune sideshoots to about two thirds of their length.

Gallica roses

Many of these produce a twiggy tangle of shoots that should be regularly thinned out. After flowering, shorten the sideshoots only and remove any dead or diseased wood. Gently clip over Gallica roses used for hedging to maintain a tidy shape. Do not attempt to shape them into a formal hedge as this would remove many of the sideshoots on which flowers are borne the following year.

Species, Noisette, Scots, Sempervirens, and Sweet Briar roses

Much of the charm of these roses lies in their arching shoots which, in the second and subsequent years, carry flowers all along their length, often on short sideshoots. Formative pruning is needed to establish a balanced framework of strong, new growth. Thereafter these roses need no further pruning other than the removal of dead and diseased wood, unless they become too dense or produce few flowers, in which case renewal prune them in the same way as non-remontant shrub roses.

Severe pruning encourages strong vegetative growth but produces few, if any, flowers until the second year. If the bush becomes lopsided, re-shape it after flowering and trim back all the overlong shoots.

Alba, Centifolia, Damask, Moss, and Portland roses

After flowering, reduce both main shoots and sideshoots. At the end of the summer, cut back any vigorous,

Pruning ground-cover roses

The majority are low-growing, spreading, modern shrub roses, so renewal-prune them as for shrub roses. Some, mostly related to *Rosa wichurana* (a rambler), creep over the ground. Prune these only to stop them spreading beyond the space available (see also below).

Prune shoots to well within the intended area of spread, cutting to an upward-facing bud.

overlong shoots that might whip about in the wind and cause wind-rock damage to the roots.

Bourbon and Hybrid Perpetual roses

These are usually remontant, so prune them, and all hybrids derived from *Rosa rugosa*, in early spring as for Hybrid Tea roses (see p.161), but much more lightly.

Pegging down roses

This technique is an effective, although time-consuming, way of increasing flower production on Bourbon and Hybrid Perpetual roses that tend to send up long, ungainly shoots with flowers only at the tips. Instead of pruning the shoots in late summer or autumn, bend them over gently, taking great care not to snap them. Peg the shoots firmly into the ground. Alternatively, tie the tips to pegs in the ground, to wires strung between pegs, or to a low wire frame placed around the plant. Prune sideshoots on the pegged shoot to 10–15cm (4–6in).

This has much the same effect as horizontally training the shoots of climbing and rambler roses (see p.164) and produces an arching mound covered with a large number of flowering sideshoots in the following season.

Select long, non-flowering shoots and prune the soft tips. Gently bend each shoot over and fasten it to the soil with sturdy wire hoops (see inset).

Climbing roses and ramblers

These roses require minor pruning but regular annual training. Neither climbing nor rambler roses are self-supporting and, if trained incorrectly, may not flower freely and may become bare at their base. Some bush roses that send out large shoots at awkward angles, such as some of the Hybrid Musks, may also be trained against walls, fences, or other supports for an effective display.

Climbing roses

In their first year, and in their second unless they have made exceptional growth, do not prune climbing roses except to remove any dead, diseased, or weak, twiggy growth. Never prune climbing sports of bush roses (roses with the word "climbing" before the cultivar name, for example 'Climbing Shot Silk') in the first two years, since they may revert to the bush form if cut back hard too soon.

Begin training, however, as soon as the new shoots are long enough to reach the supports; train them sideways along horizontal supports to encourage flowering. Where this is not possible, such as on a narrow area between a door and a window, choose a cultivar that is halfway between a tall shrub and a climbing rose. Many of these flower well from the plant base without special training: examples are 'Golden Showers', 'Joseph's Coat', and some of the more vigorous Bourbon roses.

Many climbing roses flower well for years with little pruning, except the removal of dead, diseased, or

HOW TO PRUNE AND TRAIN A CLIMBING ROSE

In the first two years after planting, restrict pruning to cutting out unproductive growth. From the third year, prune in autumn after flowering.

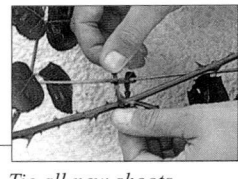

Reduce the sideshoots by about two thirds or about 15cm (6in), cutting above an outward-facing bud.

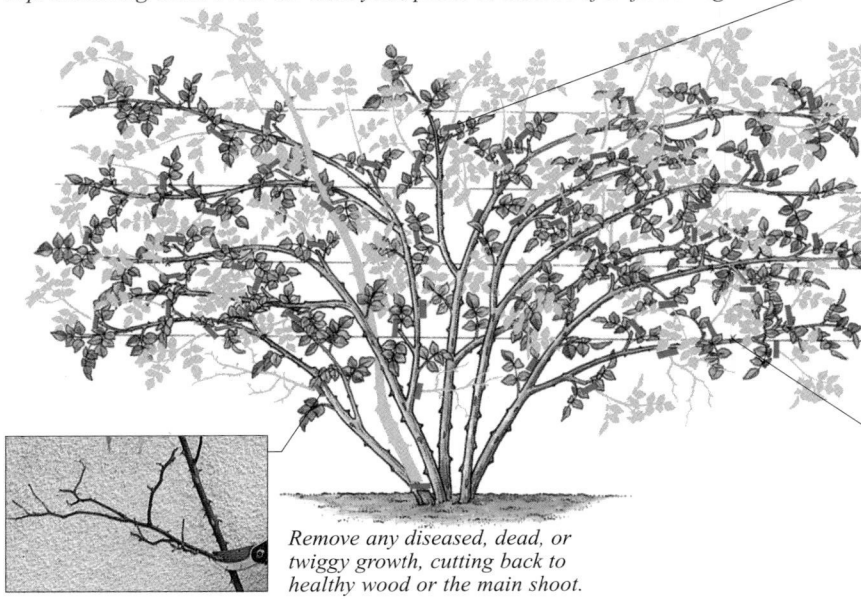

Remove any diseased, dead, or twiggy growth, cutting back to healthy wood or the main shoot.

Tie all new shoots into horizontal wires 15–20cm (6–8in) apart: the shoots should not cross each other.

twiggy growth. Prune them in the autumn, after flowering. Leave unpruned the strong main shoots unless they are exceeding their allotted space, in which case shorten them as appropriate. Otherwise simply shorten the sideshoots. Train in all the new season's growth to the supports while it is still flexible.

Occasional renewal pruning may be necessary if the base of a climbing rose becomes very bare. Cut back one or two of the older, main shoots to within 30cm (12in) or so above ground level to encourage vigorous new shoots to develop and replace the older growths. Repeat this as required in subsequent years.

Rambler roses

Like climbing roses, ramblers flower satisfactorily for a good many years without any formal pruning. They produce much more growth from the base than most climbers and, if not carefully trained, grow into a tangle of unmanageable shoots. This results in poor air circulation, which encourages the incidence of disease, and makes it extremely difficult to spray the plants thoroughly.

Prune ramblers in late summer. In the first two years, restrict pruning to cutting back all the sideshoots by about 7.5cm (3in) to a vigorous shoot; also remove dead or diseased wood. In later years, prune the rose

more heavily to maintain its framework. Untie all the shoots from their supports and, if possible, lay them on the ground. Cut no more than a quarter to one third of the oldest, spent shoots to ground level, leaving the new shoots and some older, but still vigorous, shoots for tying in to form a well-balanced framework.

Remove any unripe wood from the tips of the main shoots and cut back any sideshoots. Cut back any wayward shoots that are outgrowing the available space or spoiling the overall shape of the rose. Train in the shoots, as close to the horizontal as possible, to encourage flowering on new, short sideshoots that will develop all along the main shoots.

Training on arches, pergolas, pillars, and trees

Climbing roses or ramblers may be trained up pillars, arches, or pergolas. Twist the main shoots around the uprights to encourage flowering shoots to form low down. Carefully train the shoots in the direction of their natural growth before they have matured and hardened. This is vital for climbers that have stiff, semi-rigid shoots. Tie them in using twine or plastic rose ties; these are easy to undo when pruning or to loosen as the shoots develop. Once the main shoots reach the top of the support, regularly prune them to keep the rose within bounds.

An excess of overlong sideshoots may spoil the appearance of a pillar rose but a little additional pruning soon remedies this. Cut sideshoots back to three or four buds or by about 15cm (6in) in the spring.

HOW TO PRUNE AND TRAIN A MATURE RAMBLER ROSE

After the first two years, prune in late summer as soon as flowering is over, cutting out any dead, diseased, or weak wood. Then train in the new shoots.

Cut sideshoots down to leave between 2 and 4 healthy buds or shoots.

Cut back any old, spent shoots to ground level, using loppers.

Tie all shoots into the wires as close to the horizontal as possible. Secure any loose wires.

Propagation

Roses may be propagated in three main ways: by taking cuttings, by budding onto a rootstock, or from seed. Taking cuttings is the easiest method but it involves the longest wait: it takes about three years, except for miniature roses, for the new plant to become established. Budding needs rootstocks that have grown on in advance, but usually produces stronger and more vigorous plants. Many species roses (*Rosa glauca*, for example) readily breed true from seed. Cross hybrid roses with other hybrids, or sometimes with species, to produce new cultivars.

Hardwood cuttings

Most roses may be propagated from hardwood cuttings, in particular some cultivars that are related quite closely to wild species, such as rambler roses. Cuttings taken from miniature roses root so easily and develop so quickly that they are propagated in this way commercially. Hybrid Tea roses of complex parentage do not root so readily and may not be of sufficient size to sell commercially for two or three years, so they are seldom available on their own roots.

One advantage of roses grown from cuttings is that they do not have a different rootstock and so do not produce suckers. The disadvantages include a loss of vigour with some cultivars (although this may be useful with miniatures), and a tendency towards vigorous but non-flowering growth in the first few years, particularly with species roses.

In many climates, roses from hardwood cuttings are the most reliable, but success in rooting them is variable; it is therefore sensible to take a good number of cuttings to allow for possible failures.

Preparing the cuttings

In early autumn, select material for cuttings from the current season's growth. Trim any old flowerheads from the chosen shoots and put the shoots into a transparent plastic bag to stop them from drying out. Prepare the cuttings by trimming off their leaves and shortening them to 23cm (9in). Breaking off the thorns will make the cuttings easier to handle. Moisten the base of each cutting, dip it into hormone rooting powder, and shake off the surplus.

Take shorter lengths of stem for miniature rose cuttings, which need be only 5–10cm (2–4in) long.

Preparing the cutting bed

Choose an open site for the cutting bed, preferably one that is sheltered from the midday sun. Single dig the area required, firm, and rake it to produce an even surface.

Inserting the cuttings

Make a series of planting holes, 15cm (6in) deep, with a cane or dibber, and trickle a little coarse sand into the bottom of each one to improve the drainage. Alternatively, dig a narrow, slit-like trench to the same depth and trickle sand along the base. On light, sandy soil, it is sufficient to push a spade vertically into the earth along a centre line, working it backwards and forwards to widen the slit.

Insert the cuttings vertically into the holes or trench, leaving about one third of their length above ground. They should be inserted far enough apart so that, once rooted, they may be lifted individually without disturbing adjacent cuttings. Firm and water the soil around the cuttings. In any dry spells that follow, water them again; after frost, which may loosen the roots in the ground, refirm the soil.

Another option is to root hardwood cuttings in deep pots of light, sandy soil. Plunge the pots in soil or sand in a shady outdoor site, and water them as needed. Growing bags or pots in a cold frame or cool greenhouse may be more convenient for miniature rose cuttings.

Development of the cuttings

During the autumn a callus should develop at the base of each cutting, from which the roots will be produced in spring. Once rooted, the young plants should develop strongly, but if flower buds form during the summer, remove them so that the plants can concentrate their energy on the production of new, strong, vegetative growth. The following autumn, if they are large enough, that is about 23–30cm (9–12in), transplant the young roses to their permanent positions; if they are not yet large enough, leave them to grow on for another year.

Semi-ripe cuttings

Semi-ripe cuttings may be more successful than hardwood cuttings in areas that are subject to severe winters. In the late summer after flowering, select mature sideshoots that are still green. Take 15cm (6in) lengths, cutting above a bud where the shoot is beginning to turn woody, and trim off the soft tips. Prepare cuttings about 10cm (4in) long, following the same procedure as for hardwood cuttings.

Insert them into deep pots of sandy compost (equal parts peat substitute, or peat, and sand). Cover the pots with plastic bags, or put them in a propagator, to prevent the cuttings from losing moisture, in a cool, frost-free place. In spring, plant out the rooted cuttings in a nursery bed.

HOW TO PROPAGATE ROSES FROM HARDWOOD CUTTINGS

1 *Select a healthy, well-ripened shoot of roughly pencil thickness (here 'Dreaming Spires'), that has flowered in the summer and is about 30–60cm (12–24in) long. Remove it, cutting at an angle, just above an outward-facing bud. Prepare the cuttings by removing the leaves and soft tip wood.*

2 *Cut into 23cm (9in) lengths, making an angled cut above the top bud and a straight cut below the bottom bud. Dust the base with hormone rooting powder.*

3 *Make a row of planting holes 15cm (6in) deep and the same distance apart. In heavy soil, put a little coarse sand to a depth of about 2.5cm (1in) in each hole.*

4 *Insert a cutting into each hole: make sure that it reaches the bottom and that about 15cm (6in) of the cutting is buried. Firm the soil, water, and label the cuttings.*

5 *A year later, lift each rooted cutting with a hand fork, taking care not to damage the roots. Plant them in a bed or put them in a cold frame to grow on.*

Bud-grafting

The budding process involves uniting plant material taken from two different roses in order to combine the virtues of both. A dormant bud (the scion) from the top-growth of one plant, usually chosen for its display, is inserted under the bark just above the roots of a rootstock, normally a rose species or a specific clone that is selected for its vigour and hardiness. Different rootstocks may be used to suit the soil conditions or climate or to promote the vigorous growth of the scion.

Choosing a suitable rootstock

Many stocks are used to suit varying conditions: the hardy and vigorous *Rosa multiflora* is widely used as a rootstock, particularly where the winters are cold; it is also suitable for use on poor soils although plants budded onto this stock are not long-lived. *R. canina* produces hardy plants and is popular where winters are severe or on heavy soils, but it suckers freely; the crimson climber 'Dr Huey' (at one time known as 'Shafter' when used as a stock) is more often used where the dormancy period is shorter. The selected clone 'Laxa' has now largely replaced most other commercial stocks, as it performs reliably in most soils and climatic conditions, is almost thornless, easy to use for budding, and rarely produces suckers. Any commercial supplier of rootstocks, or a local nursery, should be able to provide information on the best stock to use for local growing conditions. Stocks may be obtained from wild hedgerow roses, but their quality is unreliable and it is better to use stocks with more uniform growth characteristics.

Planting the rootstocks

Plant the rootstocks in autumn in a nursery bed, about 30cm (12in) apart and with 75cm (30in) between the rows. For bush roses, the scions are inserted at the point where the shoots and roots join (the "neck"), so for ease of budding, plant the rootstocks at an angle of 45°, with the top of the roots just at soil level. Mound soil up to the base of the shoots to keep the bark moist and supple at the point where the scion is to be inserted. Standard rootstocks must be grown on to about 2–2.2m (6–7ft), and any buds rubbed off before they develop to create a straight, bare stem.

When to bud-graft

Budding should be carried out from mid- to late summer, preferably in cool, showery conditions. If the

T-BUDDING ONTO A STANDARD ROOTSTOCK

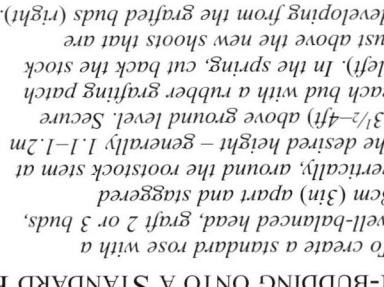

To create a standard rose with a well-balanced head, graft 2 or 3 buds, 8cm (3in) apart and staggered vertically, around the rootstock stem at the desired height – generally 1.1–1.2m (3½–4ft) above ground level. Secure each bud with a rubber grafting patch (left). In the spring, cut back the stock just above the new shoots that are developing from the grafted buds (right).

HOW TO BUD-GRAFT A ROSE

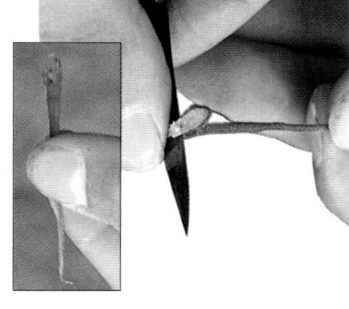

1 Select a flowered shoot about 30cm (12in) long, with 3–4 growth buds. Remove it, making an angled cut above an outward-facing bud on the parent plant.

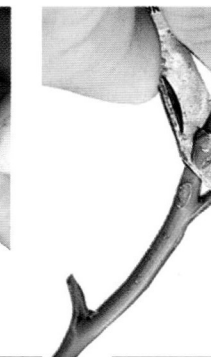

2 Hold the budwood so that the buds point downwards. Insert the knife 5mm (¼in) from a bud. With a scooping action, remove the bud with a 2.5cm (1in) "tail".

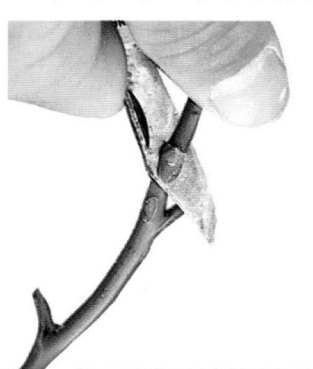

3 Holding the scion by the tail, peel away the coarse wood from the green bark. Discard the wood. Trim off the tail, to leave a scion about 1cm (½in) long.

4 Clean the bark on the stem of the rootstock, by gently using a soft, dry cloth. This will remove any soil or grit, which could blunt the blade of the budding knife.

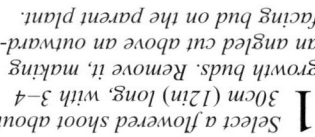
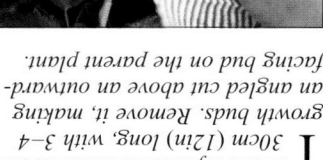

5 Make a 5mm (¼in) horizontal cut into the rootstock bark, 5–10cm (2–4in) above ground level. Then make a vertical cut upwards, to join the horizontal cut.

6 Using the reverse blade of the knife, gently prise open the flaps of bark created by the two cuts. The thin, green cambium will be revealed underneath.

7 Hold the scion by the leaf stalk and slip the tapered end under the bark flaps in the rootstock. Sit the bud neatly under the flaps; if needed, trim the scion across the top so it fits the T-cut.

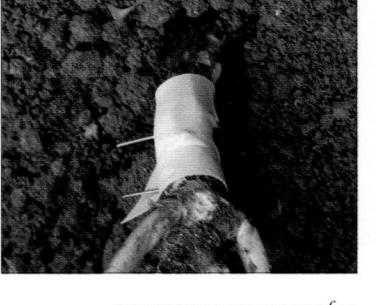

8 To ensure close contact between scion and rootstock, secure a rubber grafting patch around the graft, pinning it on the side opposite the bud. The rubber patch will gradually rot away.

THE FOLLOWING SPRING In early spring, cut off the top of the rootstock, just above the top of the bud. For a multi-stemmed plant, cut back to 8cm (3in) the shoot emerging from the bud, in late spring.

weather is very dry in the months that precede budding, water the rootstocks regularly and thoroughly. This ensures a free flow of sap that prevents the wood from drying out, so that it is possible to lift the bark from the wood without bruising the wood underneath. Speed is also important to prevent the wood of both bud and rootstock from drying out before they have been grafted together.

A budding knife, with a single, specially formed blade and a sharp, tapered end (see "Garden knives", p.555) may be used but an ordinary horticultural knife is also suitable. Any knife used for budding must be kept scrupulously clean and sharp.

Selecting the budwood
Prepare scions from well-ripened shoots that have fat, dormant growth buds in their leaf axils. These shoots are known as the budwood. Cut off the leaves and leaf stalks; alternatively, leave the stalks as "handles" for inserting the buds later. Place the budwood in a plastic bag to prevent it from drying out before it is used.

Preparing the scion
Hold a piece of budwood upside down and, from just above the base of a bud, use the budding knife to scoop out the bud together with a thin tail. This shield-like piece of bark, about 2.5cm (1in) long, within which the growth bud is contained, is known as the scion. Remove the woody material behind the bud, and shorten the tail so the scion is about 1cm (½in) long. If retained, the wood will prevent the bud from uniting with the rootstock or "taking". The base of the bud should then be visible as a small, circular growth. It is difficult to do this without damaging the bud if the shield has been cut too deeply from the shoot.

Preparing the rootstock
For a bush rose, clear the soil from the rootstock neck, take off the thorns, and wipe the neck clean. Using the blade of the budding knife, make a "T"-shaped cut in the neck, penetrating the bark without cutting into the wood, as this causes damage.

Grafting the bud onto the rootstock
Carefully peel back the cut bark of the rootstock with the blunt side of the knife blade, taking care not to tear the bark or the wood beneath. Gently push the scion into position in the "T" so that the bud faces upwards. Trim off any of the tail that may still be visible and, if necessary, the leaf stalk. Use a rubber grafting patch to hold the bud securely in

place and keep the flaps of bark tightly closed to avoid moisture loss. The patch is easily pinned in place and does not inhibit the growth of the bud as it soon rots away. Inserting two scions, opposite one another on the rootstock, is sometimes recommended to produce balanced shoot growth more rapidly but is seldom practised commercially except on standard roses.

Cutting back the rootstock
If the scion takes successfully, the bud will quickly swell and will then produce a shoot, generally by the following spring. Once the shoot develops, cut off the growth of the rootstock above the scion. If the shoot needs support, tie it to a cane, but this is not usually necessary.

Bud-grafting a standard rose
Budding onto a standard rootstock is performed near the top of the stem at the desired height, usually about 1.1–1.2m (3½–4ft); weeping standards are usually budded a little higher, at about 1.5m (5ft). Insert two or three buds around the stem to achieve an evenly balanced head. If using *Rosa canina* rootstocks, insert the buds into equally spaced lateral growths, close to the main stem. It is more usual to place three buds around the main stem of *R. rugosa* stock, staggered vertically.

Layering roses

Any rose which possesses shoots that are long and flexible enough to be bent over and pegged into the ground may be successfully propagated by simple layering.

In late summer after flowering, choose a shoot of healthy, mature wood and trim some of the leaves to create a clear length of stem. Work some peat substitute or peat into the ground where the shoot is to be layered and peg the shoot down into the prepared ground to encourage it to root. The next spring, separate the rooted layer from the parent by cutting the shoot just behind the roots, and plant it out into its destined position to grow on.

Ramblers and climbing roses are ideal for layering, although if they are planted in narrow beds along the base of a wall there may not be a large enough area of exposed soil to peg down the shoots, particularly if other plants are growing around the base of the rose. Many shrub roses, such as Damask, Centifolia, Bourbon, and most Alba and species roses, are suitable for layering as they have a lax growth habit and are

likely to have more exposed soil around the base into which the selected shoots may be inserted.

Modern shrub roses such as 'Chinatown', which are in fact very tall-growing Floribunda roses, have fairly stiff shoots, so train these shoots horizontally while they are still young and flexible to prepare for layering. Cultivars of groundcover roses lend themselves to this method of propagation. The shoots of some, such as PHEASANT ('Kordapt') or GROUSE ('Korimro'), root naturally into the soil; simply separate them from the parent and plant them out.

The modern Hybrid Tea and Floribunda roses found in the majority of gardens are mostly too stiff and upright in their habit of growth for successful layering and should be increased by taking cuttings. Only a few which are lax, wide-spreading growers, such as QUEEN MOTHER ('Korquemu'), are easily increased by layering.

HOW TO LAYER ROSES

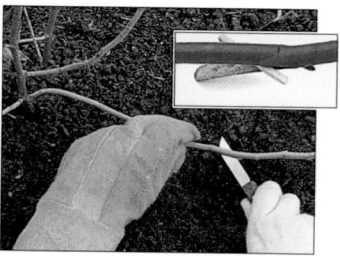

1 Make a 2.5cm (1in) slit on the lower side of a long, ripe, but flexible shoot. Dust the cut with hormone rooting powder and then wedge it open with a match (see inset).

2 Position the shoot in a small depression in prepared soil and peg it down firmly with a wire hoop. Cover it with soil, firm, and tie in the tip of the layered shoot to a short cane.

Propagation by division

If a rose is growing on its own roots, taking rooted suckers and planting them out is an easy method of propagation. Most roses from nurseries are grafted onto rootstocks, however, so suckers will be from the stock and the plant is therefore not suitable for propagation by division.

Some species grown from seed and other roses grown from cuttings sucker naturally. In the dormant period, detach the rooted suckers or shoots from the parent and plant them out, either in a nursery bed or into permanent positions. Deep planting of budded shrub roses sometimes stimulates the cultivar shoots to produce roots. Treat such rooted shoots as rooted suckers.

Roses that sucker freely such as the cultivars of *Rosa pimpinellifolia*, *R. rugosa* and some Gallica roses are readily propagated in this way.

PROPAGATING ROSES BY DIVISION

1 In late autumn or early spring, select a well-developed sucker. Scrape away the soil to expose its base. Sever it from the rootstock, with as many roots as possible.

2 Prepare a hole, wide and deep enough for the roots. Plant the sucker immediately and water and firm the soil (see inset). Trim shoots to 23–30cm (9–12in).

Propagating roses from seed

Species roses, unlike cultivars, are self-fertile and may be raised from seed in the same way as other shrubs. Although seeds are not generally available from commercial sources, it is easy to extract them from mature roses in the garden. Hybrid roses do not breed true to type from seed so they are usually propagated by bud-grafting (see p.166).

Extracting and sowing seed

In the autumn, when the rose hips are swollen and ripe, extract the seeds and stratify them in a refrigerator before sowing (see "How to overcome dormancy", p.629). Stratification – the simulation of natural temperature changes – is necessary for all seed of species roses.

Sow the rose seed into seed trays, packs, or into individual pots, which should be at least 6cm (2½in) deep. If using a seed tray, place the seeds on the compost about 5cm (2in) apart, and cover them to their own depth with sand or grit. Then leave the tray or pack in a cold frame to protect it from mice and other animals. The seed may take up to a year to germinate. Prick out the seedlings into individual containers as soon as the first true rose leaves have formed; the first pair, the seed leaves, are oval, unlike typical rose leaves. Care is needed in handling the seedlings as they are very fragile at this stage in their development.

Grow on the young seedlings in the cold frame until they have become established in their pots. Then harden them off by moving them out of the cold frame during the day. Once acclimatized, the seedlings may be kept in the open, and potted on as necessary until they are large enough to be planted out.

Hybridizing

New rose cultivars are created by hybridizing, a process by which one cultivar or species is cross-pollinated with another and the new seed sown and grown on. The aim is to create a new rose that inherits the best characteristics of both parents.

Selecting the parents

Most roses are of mixed ancestry, so it is impossible to predict the results of hybridization, and the chances of producing a quality cultivar, with distinct characteristics, are small. Knowledge of the parent roses' genetic characteristics, in particular their chromosomal number and structure, is important in breeding.

The chromosomes are the parts of plant cells that control the inheritance of characteristics through the genes. Roses may have different chromosome numbers, although the total number per cell in each case is always a multiple of seven. Most of the species roses have 14 (diploid), 28 (tetraploid), 42 (hexaploid), or 56 (octoploid) chromosome numbers. When two roses have been cross-pollinated, equivalent chromosomes from the parents arrange themselves in pairs, which then fuse and count as one in the chromosome number of the new cultivar. Most garden roses are tetraploids and two tetraploids brought together in this fusion

HOW TO HYBRIDIZE ROSES

PREPARING THE SEED PARENT

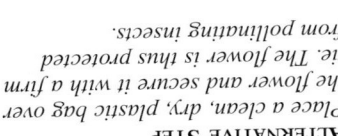
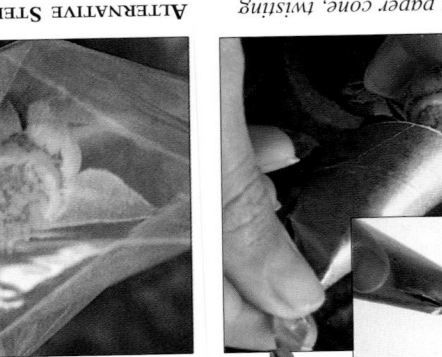

1 Select an unblemished bloom (here PRINCESS MICHAEL OF KENT) that has not fully unfolded its petals and should therefore not yet have been pollinated.

2 Remove the petals, taking off the outer ones first. Work gradually towards the centre, taking care not to damage the stigmas as they become exposed.

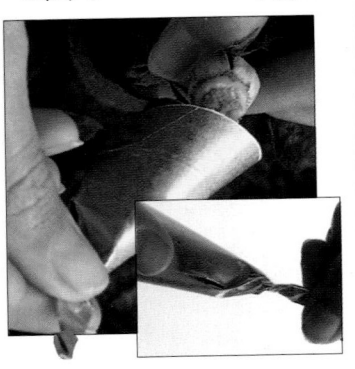
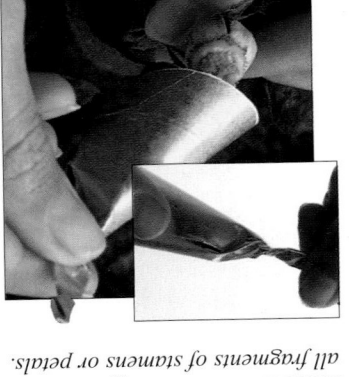

3 Using tweezers or a small pair of scissors, remove the stamens around the stigmas and all fragments of stamens or petals.

4 Use a magnifying glass to inspect the rose and make sure that no fragments remain. If left they may decay and allow rot or fungi to enter the rosehip.

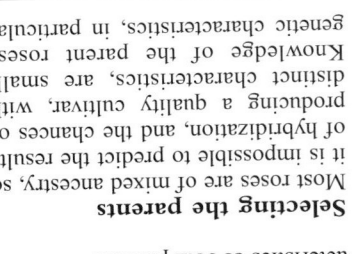

5 Make a paper cone, twisting its point firmly closed (see inset). Holding back the sepals, cover the flower with the cone, and tie securely around the stem.

ALTERNATIVE STEP

Place a clean, dry, plastic bag over the flower and secure it with a firm tie. The flower is thus protected from pollinating insects.

RAISING ROSES FROM SEED

SEED

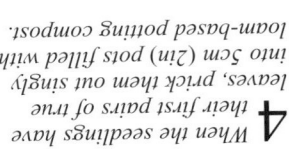

1 Slit open a ripe hip (see inset), taken from the parent plant, with a clean, sharp knife. Take out individual seeds carefully with the back of the knife blade.

2 Place the seed in a plastic bag of moist peat substitute or peat and keep it for 2–3 days at room temperature. Then put it in a refrigerator for 3–4 weeks.

3 Sow the seeds singly onto the surface of a sandy compost (1 part sand:1 part peat substitute). Cover with grit, label, and put in a cold frame.

4 When the seedlings have their first pairs of true leaves, prick them out singly into 5cm (2in) pots filled with loam-based potting compost.

produce another tetraploid rose. A diploid (14) crossed with a tetraploid (28), however, results in 7 + 14 chromosomes, or a total of 21 (triploid) in the new rose. As this is not an even number there are seven chromosomes left without comparable chromosomes with which to pair. Triploids are often sterile and of little or no use in breeding.

Where the chromosome count is known, it is given in the most recent edition of *Modern Roses* (American Rose Society for the International Registration Authority for Roses). This publication also details the pedigree of large numbers of roses.

Heredity is not the only factor influencing the selection of parent plants. Some hybrid roses make good pollen (male) parents, but poor seed (female) parents, and vice versa. Some are completely infertile and others almost so, and in a rose with a very large number of petals, such as a Centifolia, a proportion of these may have taken the place of the stamens, so that little pollen is available for hybridizing. Crossing a non-remontant rose with a remontant one may be a problem if remontancy is one of the desired characteristics, as the first generation from such a cross is always non-remontant. At least one more cross is needed before remontancy reappears in the offspring.

This is a simplification of a very complex subject and there is a good deal of chance involved in rose breeding. However scientific an approach is taken, the result is still largely unpredictable. As a general principle, choose the healthiest cultivars available as parents, and start with what is perhaps the easiest cross of all, that between two different cultivars of Floribunda roses.

Controlling the growing environment

Except in a frost-free climate, use pot-grown roses in a greenhouse, as this allows greater control of temperature, humidity, insect pests, and diseases, and gives the hips a better chance of ripening properly. Precise record-keeping is essential: after crosses have been made, carefully identify all the flower stems with a dated label on which is written the names of both parent plants, giving the seed parent first, for example ANNE HARKNESS ('Harkaramel') x MEMENTO ('Dicbar').

Preparing the seed parent

First select a bloom of the rose you have chosen for the seed parent, at the stage where it is starting to unfold but before insects could have reached the stamens in the centre and contaminated them with alien pollen. Carefully remove the petals and the stamens (emasculation), and make sure that no tissue is left that could later lead to rot in the hip. Tie a paper cone or plastic bag over the emasculated flower and leave it for one to two days to allow the stigmas to mature.

Preparing the pollen parent

Cut the flower that is to be the pollen parent, which should be at about the same stage as the seed parent. Stand the pollen parent in a vase of water and protect it from insects until the anthers release the tiny, orange pollen grains, usually on the day after being cut. The stigmas of the seed parent should begin to exude a sticky secretion, indicating that they are ready to receive the pollen. Pull off the petals from the pollen parent, leaving the anthers intact.

Pollinating the seed parent

Remove the protective covers and brush the stamens of the pollen parent against the stigmas of the seed parent; their sticky secretion helps the pollen adhere to the stigmas. Replace the cover on the pollinated flower and label the stem.

An alternative method is to cut off the pollen parent's anthers, place them in a small, clean container, such as a plastic pill-box, labelled with the name of the rose, and store it in cool, dry conditions until the released pollen grains are visible in the box. Using a fine brush, dust pollen from the box onto the stigmas of the seed parent. If carrying out more than one cross with different roses, make sure that the brush has been thoroughly cleaned between each operation, preferably with methylated or surgical spirit.

If the cross has not taken successfully, the newly forming hip will shrivel quickly. If it has been successful, the sepals will begin to lift and the hip to swell; once this is evident, remove the protective cone or bag to allow the hip to grow.

The hip will continue to swell; it normally takes about two and a half months to ripen, according to the climate. As it ripens, the hip changes its colour from green to red, to yellow, or possibly maroon, depending on the individual rose.

Harvesting and sowing

Remove the ripened hip from the plant and carefully extract the seeds. Sow and raise the seed (see "Extracting and sowing seed", p.168). Seed resulting from hybridization, however, may be sown fresh without a stratification period.

Selection

The seedlings are likely to flower in the first year – often within a few weeks of germination in a greenhouse – but it is only in the second year that the blooms will be more or less typical of the new hybrid and it is possible to judge whether it should be kept and developed or discarded.

Promising new seedlings can be budded onto rootstocks (see "Budgrafting", p.166) when they have stems of sufficient thickness, that is about 5mm (¼in). Even experienced hybridists, however, find judging the potential challenging, as it is not easy to detect faults until a selection has been grown in trials for a few years.

PREPARING THE POLLEN PARENT

6 *Select an unblemished bloom that is not yet fully open (here* ELINA*). Cut the stem of the flower at an angle just above a bud.*

7 *Place the chosen flower in water and keep it indoors, free from insects, until it opens fully (usually overnight).*

8 *When the flower is open and the anthers split, revealing the pollen, gently remove all the petals.*

9 *The exposed anthers are now ready to release their tiny pollen grains.*

POLLINATING THE SEED PARENT

10 *Uncover the seed parent and brush the anthers of the pollinator across its stigmas. The pollen grains will adhere to the sticky stigmas of the seed parent.*

11 *Replace the protective cone over the seed parent and tie securely. Label the rose with the names of the seed parent and pollen parent, and leave it to ripen.*

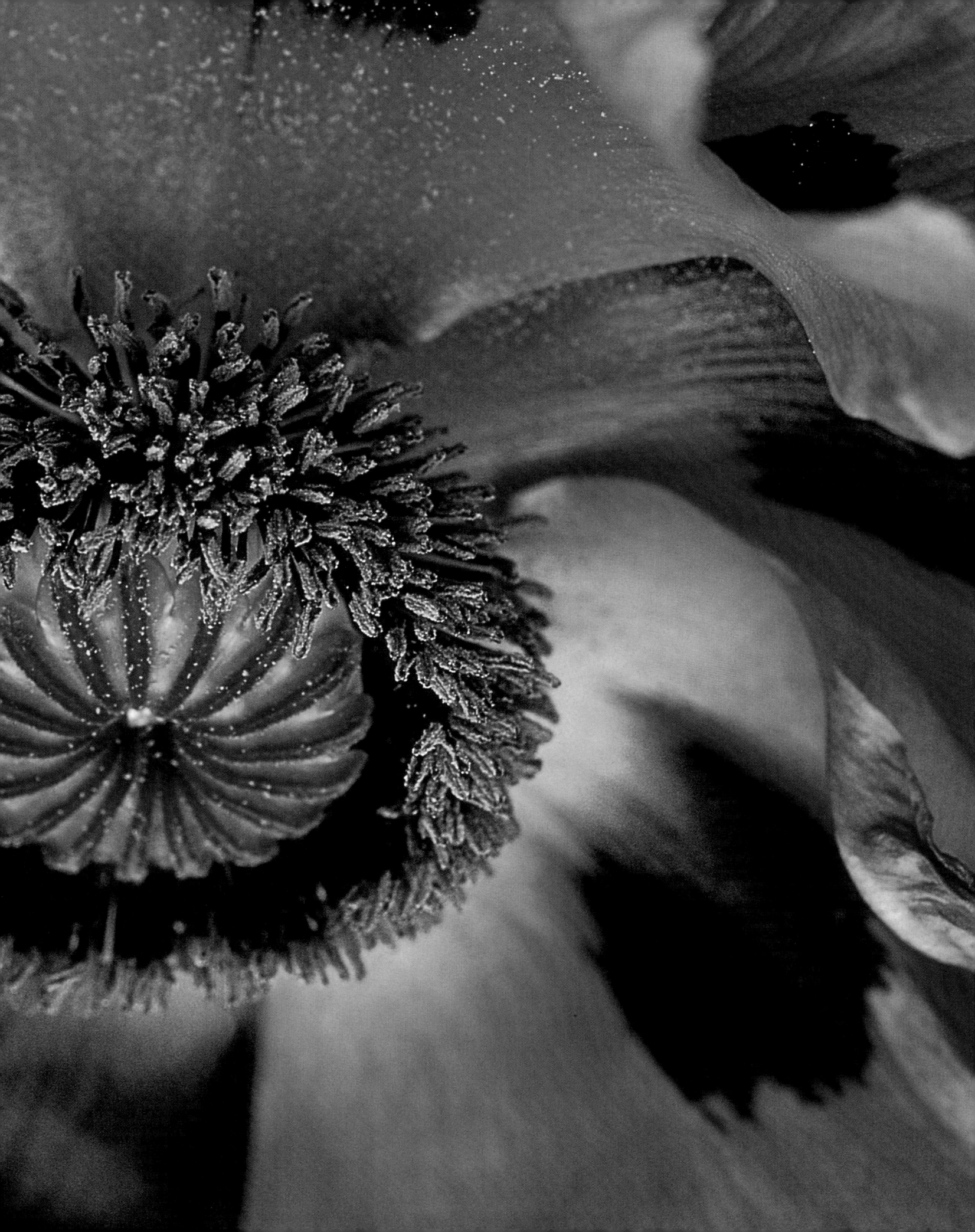

CHAPTER

6

PERENNIALS

WITH FLOWERS IN every colour of the rainbow, a breathtaking range of shapes and textures, and often fine scents, perennials richly deserve their popularity. Their diversity makes them suitable for most gardens, while their reliability makes them a lasting source of pleasure. For many people, a traditional herbaceous border is the epitome of garden beauty, but perennials can be equally effective in mixed borders, interplanted with shrubs, annuals, bulbs, and vegetables, or grown in containers or as ground cover. Foliage ranges from lacy fern fronds to the strap-like leaves of crocosmias; and there are flowers to suit all tastes, from delicate *Gypsophila* to sumptuous peonies. Some, like many sedums, are followed by pretty seedheads. Against a more static background of woody plants, perennials provide an almost unlimited, changing planting palette.

Designing with perennials

ALTHOUGH botanically speaking these plants should be referred to as herbaceous perennials, they are usually known as just "perennials". "Herbaceous" explains the fact that the part above ground dies down each year, while "perennial" refers to the fact that the root system lives for three or more years. A few perennials, such as *Helleborus foetidus*, are evergreen, and so have a valuable winter presence.

Most perennials will flower, set seed, and then die back to ground level by autumn, going dormant for the winter season. Some retain a woody base, such as *Achillea filipendulina*, or fleshy shoots, such as *Sedum telephium*, while others disappear completely underground. Some perennials, such as *Doronicum orientale*, go completely dormant during the heat of summer, instead of during the cold of winter. Most perennials flower during summer, though some, such as *Liriope muscari* and *Iris unguicularis*, enliven the garden in autumn and winter, while *Helleborus orientalis* and *Pulmonaria* welcome in early spring.

Choosing perennials

More than any other group of plants, perennials have an immense variety of shape, form, colour, texture, and scent. Mostly valued for their flowers, many also have attractive foliage – from ribbed, unfurling hosta leaves, or sword-like straps of iris, to transparent tracery of fennel (*Foeniculum vulgare*). Particularly in a small garden, some perennials should have ornamental leaves, to extend the season of interest – the foliage usually outlasting the flowers.

Perennials range in height from the *Acaena* at just 5cm (2in) tall to the statuesque *Helianthus salicifolius*, whose feathered stems reach 2.5m (8ft) or more. Low-growing perennials are ideal for the front of borders or in between shrubs, while tall, plants belong at the back of a border to give height and structure to the planting design. Perennials with an attractive structure, such as the African lily (*Agapanthus*) or some grasses such as *Chionochloa rubra* and *Carex comans* 'Frosted Curls', are good specimen plants in a border or container.

Some perennials, such as many carnations and pinks (*Dianthus*) and highly perfumed lily-of-the-valley (*Convallaria majalis*), are worth growing for their fragrance alone. Carnations and pinks are ideal for raised beds or windowboxes, while ground-covering lily-of-the-valley thrives in shady shrubberies. Other perennials, such as *Sedum spectabile* and many of the daisy and umbel family, such as asters and *Angelica*, bear flowers that attract beneficial insects such as bees and butterflies.

It is also possible to prolong the season of interest into autumn and winter by selecting plants with interesting seedheads and winter silhouettes. Fennels, *Iris sibirica*, and *Achillea* are a few examples of flowers that will surprise you at a time of

PERENNIAL BORDER
The addition of the elegant ornamental grasses and Achillea 'Terracotta' *gives this scheme a contemporary feel that fits well with the traditional, hot-coloured flowers, such as* Crocosmia *and the poker-headed* Kniphofia.

FORMAL BORDERS
In this formal garden, a traditional grass path divides a pair of wide, straight borders. The plants are arranged by height, with low plants such as Sedum spectabile *at the front so that all can be clearly seen. While the planting in each border is not a rigid mirror-image of the other, a number of plants are repeated on both sides to provide a balanced, harmonious effect.*

year when you least expect it. Birds will gain twofold from these seedheads: they enjoy eating the seeds, and benefit from the insects that overwinter in the cavities created by hollow stems and seedheads.

As with all plants, when choosing perennials for a planting scheme, make sure that they are appropriate for the growing conditions, such as soil, micro-climate, and aspect of the bed or border. Given the correct environment, plants are much more likely to flourish, and require less maintenance than those struggling in an unsuitable position (see also "Site and aspect", p.183).

Herbaceous and mixed borders

Perennials are traditionally used in borders: these are long, rectangular beds, fronted by lawn or a path and backed by a hedge or wall, either as a single border or as double, facing borders. Popularized in the late 19th century, herbaceous borders were planted only with perennials, in groups or drifts, the shortest plants at the front, grading up with lupins, phlox, and the like, to the taller ones such as delphiniums at the rear. Their season of interest was restricted to the summer months, as in many gardens the borders were but one of many areas of interest, each with a different seasonal highlight. As gardens reduced in size during the 20th century, and space became more restricted, the flowering season and plant range of borders were forced to extend. As a result, mixed borders have become increasingly popular; they now contain a variety of plants including bedding plants, shrubs, climbers, and even small flowering trees, as well as perennials. The

advantage of a mixed border is that it can be less labour-intensive than an herbaceous one, because larger areas may be filled with less-demanding woody plants (see "Designing beds and borders", p.174)

A successful border requires regular maintenance. Careful staking is needed, as the perennials may grow long and lanky as they compete for the somewhat reduced light levels caused by the close planting, and the presence of a wall or hedge in the background. Water and nutrient levels also need monitoring regularly in any such dense planting scheme.

Additional chores generated by a mixed border involve bedding out early bulbs and wallflowers, followed by dahlias, cannas, and other tender plants, to extend the length of interest into early spring and autumn. Plants also need to be dead-headed and kept tidy over the longer flowering period.

Island beds

Surrounded by lawn or paving, island beds can be seen and accessed from all sides, so the planting design should

be effective from all viewpoints. As with borders, beds that are dedicated solely to herbaceous plants are at their most impressive in summer. For a more enduring display, interplant the perennials with a variety of bulbs and perhaps one or two shrubs.

Because access to the centre of the bed may be difficult, plants should be sturdy, dwarf, or compact, to reduce the need for staking, though generally there will be less requirement for support as higher light levels and better air circulation promote sturdier plant growth than within borders.

Geometrical, round, square, or rectangular island beds suit a formal setting; in an informal garden or one with gently undulating ground, loosely curved island beds are more appropriate. Avoid intricate shapes and tight curves, since they are awkward to maintain and may detract from the planting itself. To gain space, small gardens can be filled with island beds.

Raised island beds can provide improved growing conditions for demanding perennials, tougher alpines, and Mediterranean plants in gardens where the soil is poor or waterlogged. The increased bed height also enables plants to be tended with minimal stooping – which is an important factor for less-able or elderly gardeners.

RAISED PLANTING
Easily accessible beds such as this raised wooden one are not only at a convenient height for watering, deadheading, and other maintenance but can also be used to provide different soil conditions from those in the rest of the garden. Acid-loving plants, for example, can be grown or those that prefer very well-drained soil.

Designing beds and borders

When designing a planting scheme, the principles are broadly similar whether planning an herbaceous or mixed border or an island bed. Considerations of height, mass, scale, texture, sequential interest, form, and colour are all variable factors that influence the design. Planting is a very individual issue.

Everybody has favourite plants and colours as well as set ideas as to which plants look good together. Imagination and personal taste will inevitably influence your planting schemes, but there are a few basic guidelines to follow.

General principles

Herbaceous borders may be designed and planted in various styles so that they set or strengthen the character and tone of the garden. Crisply edged, straight-lined borders backed by well-trimmed hedges create a dominant structure, which will be attractive in winter, but which can be softened by planting island beds. Irregularly shaped island beds, weaving their way through the garden, are much more relaxed, but will do little for the garden during winter. Self-contained, stately plants such as lupins, delphiniums, and veronicas, arranged according to a restricted colour scheme and planted in a rhythmical pattern look somewhat formal. For a more relaxed approach, introduce plants with a loose, less ordered habit, such as baby's breath (*Gypsophila*) and lady's mantle (*Alchemilla mollis*), and then add key feature plants such as *Sedum* 'Herbstfreude' at random rather than at strict intervals.

Before starting a planting plan, prepare a comprehensive list of plants you want to use. This should contain any existing plants you would like to retain, as well as a thoroughly researched list of others that will cover all seasons, and are well suited to your garden. It may be easier to compile this list with the help of a good local nursery catalogue, as you will know where to obtain the plants.

Allow sufficient room for the plants to spread as they mature, taking account of the different rates at which they develop. Slow-growing plants can be surrounded by shade-tolerant ground cover (see PERENNIALS FOR GROUND COVER, p.180) to fill the area while waiting for the main plant to achieve its desired size. Start by placing the key plants, such as shrubs, roses, and any imposing perennials and grasses, as well as the important feature plants, which you may wish to repeat at regular intervals to create a symmetric rhythm to the border. Position the smaller plants last. Set out the plants according to your planting plan and make any adjustments to the scheme at this stage, before planting them. However carefully the scheme has

MASSED FORM AND COLOUR
Large drifts of perennials and grasses create a generous sense of space within a garden. The vertical spires distract the eye from the horizontal bands of colour created by the wide-scale plantings. Even after flowering is over, such a display will look effective until the flowerheads are cut off in late winter.

MIXED BORDERS
Colourful tulips provide spring interest, while shrubs such as a golden-leaved Spiraea japonica 'Goldflame' and the sculptural mass of Euphorbia characias subsp. wulfenii add colour and form from spring through to autumn, extending the period of interest beyond the summer burst of colour offered by the hardy Geranium species and other perennials.

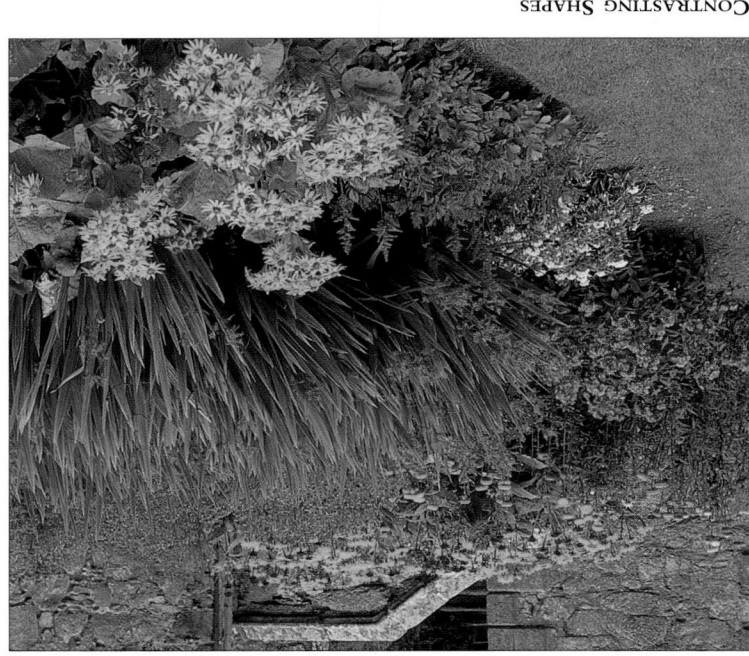

CONTRASTING SHAPES
The pointed swords of red Crocosmia here create a strong vertical accent behind the rounded Ligularia leaves in this large border.

HARMONIZING TEXTURES

A mixture of moisture-loving plants with airy and feathery flowers, such as Astilbe, Lythrum virgatum, Filipendula palmata, *and tall, yellow* Ligularia stenocephala *forms a satisfying pattern of textures. The fluffy outline of the Filipendula flowerheads successfully breaks up the general mass of vertical heads on the other plants.*

CONTRASTING FORMS

This grouping of foliage plants gives prominence to differences in form and texture. The impressive, jagged foliage of Rheum palmatum *at the rear contrasts with the heart-shaped leaves of* Ligularia dentata *and the softly arching straps of an ornamental grass. The* Rodgersia *adds a distinct colour and texture accent with its large, ribbed, dark red foliage.*

been planned, minor adjustments are inevitable, as no two gardens are alike, and plants react differently, however well you know them.

Scale of planting

Although the size of beds and borders is usually dictated by the surrounding space, the scale of planting should take account of the scale of the garden and adjacent buildings.

The extent of a border or bed will vary but, as a rough guide, the larger the garden setting, the more generous the border or bed can be. Two large beds are better than three or four little ones; they will enhance the

feeling of space, and will prevent the garden from looking too bitty.

A border should be no less than 1.5m (5ft) deep, and preferably 3–5m (10ft–15ft), depending on a path's length and width. This will give a good planting width and create a layered, well-balanced effect.

Large borders, seen from a great distance, and flanked by a wide path, should be planted with bold groups of plants, to create sufficient visual impact. The smaller the viewing distance, the smaller the planting scale should be, so that the border remains interesting as you stroll along it (see also "Planting in groups", right).

Varying plant height

Traditionally, tall plants are placed at the back of a front-facing border, grading down the heights as they approach the front, to create a tiered effect in which no flowering plant is hidden behind another. In an island bed, the tallest plants are placed in the centre, with the smallest round the outer edge. This planting rule will create quite a formal, rigid scheme. Mystery and contrast can be added by introducing the occasional taller but translucent plant near the front; this will give a stronger undulation to the overall scheme. Particularly transparent plants such as

Verbena bonariensis or many grasses such as *Stipa gigantea* provide extra height, while allowing the eye to wander past them. Plant textural perennials, such as *Molinia caerulea* subsp. *arundinacea* 'Transparent' with its soft flower panicles, so they are close enough to touch from the edge of the bed.

As a rule, later-flowering perennials tend to be the tallest, as they have the longest growing period. This can result in late summer flowers towering over the dead flower stalks of earlier plants. To hide gaps where earlier flowerers such as Oriental poppies have vanished, plant some of the lower late flowers such as *Aster* x *pringlei* 'Monte Cassino' near to the front of the bed.

Generally, the wider the bed or border, the taller the plants may be; very tall plants in narrow borders may look awkward and the angle from the tallest to the shortest, uncomfortably steep.

Planting in groups

Several plants of the same cultivar can successfully be massed together to create larger groups. Particularly towards the rear of a border, or the centre of a bed, large clumps of one plant will create a good impact, whereas near the front smaller clumps will increase variety and interest. Depending on the scale of the scheme, always aim to plant in groups of three or more, up to a dozen or so. For a fluid, informal style, plant in odd numbers – even numbers creating a formal rigidity to a bed or border.

Groups of varying sizes should also be introduced. If in doubt, create an "outline" of the plants – using

ISLAND BED

A flower bed often looks best when shaped to reflect the contours of its surroundings. It should also have most of the tallest plants in the middle of the bed, and the lowest ones at the edge. Here eye-catching height is provided by Astilbe, Lobelia, *and* Filipendula, *which are planted with lower-growing variegated Solomon's seal* (Polygonatum), Blechnum, *and hellebores among other perennials.*

bamboo canes, brooms, or other more bulky props – to see what would fit the space.

Small-leaved perennials are more impressive when planted in large groups: small-leaved London pride (*Saxifraga* x *urbium*), for example, is best planted in groups of seven or more, while large-leaved *Bergenia* species and hybrids look effective in threes. The huge *Gunnera manicata*, however, is striking enough to be planted singly (see "Specimen planting", p.179).

Plants that have strong outlines, such as *Kniphofia caulescens* with its upright, pokerhead flowers, are more dramatic when planted in smaller groups than those of less distinct forms such as the loose-flowered *Geranium phaeum*.

Forms and outlines

Perennials have widely differing forms and silhouettes, including upright, rounded, arching, as well as horizontally spreading outlines. Juxtapose groups of plants with contrasting forms to create a series of vignettes, which build up within a bed or border. The slim spikes of delphiniums or *Eremurus*, for example, act like giant, colourful exclamation marks, when seen against the foaming, cloud-like cushions of *Gypsophila paniculata* or *Crambe cordifolia*. Contrast is introduced when the vertical lines of irises and other strap-leaved plants contrast with the horizontal planes of the flowerheads of *Achillea* 'Moonshine' or *Sedum telephium* 'Matrona'.

Some plants are two tiered, and have their own contrasting form: a fine example is *Rheum palmatum* 'Atrosanguineum', which makes a lower layer of reddish-purple leaves 1m (3ft) tall, over which tower smoky-pink plumes of tiny flowers.

Understanding plant textures

Although flowers, and to a lesser extent stems, contribute to the overall texture of a planting scheme, it is

LONG-LASTING DISPLAY
The rich brown seedheads of Sedum spectabile *may be left uncut to provide interest in late autumn and winter long after the succulent leaves have died back.*

foliage that provides the strongest impact, because it is present for a much longer period of time during the year. Even when seen from a distance, it can create striking contrasts and subtle harmonies. The dainty leaves of *Coreopsis verticillata* or the filigree fronds of fennel (*Foeniculum vulgare*) are very delicate, whereas large, individual leaves such as those of *Hosta sieboldiana* var. *elegans* create a bold, textural effect.

Grasses, particularly, can add a wide range of textural variety to a garden. The narrow flowering stems and strap-shaped leaves tend to be very supple, yet strong, waving in the wind, bringing flowing movement into a garden, as well as a gentle rustling sound of the foliage. Many, such as *Miscanthus sinensis* 'Malepartus' or *Calamagrostis* x *acutiflora* 'Karl Foerster', are so strong that their dried flower stems will remain standing well into autumn, or even throughout the winter.

Texture is also affected by a leaf's surface, whether it is the matt, waxy foliage of *Sedum spectabile*, the glossy, leathery leaves of *Bergenia purpurascens*, or the woolly texture of *Lychnis coronaria*. It is important to understand how a leaf's texture will affect your planting scheme: glossy surfaces, for example, reflect light, adding sparkle on a sunny day, while matt ones absorb light, creating a more sombre effect.

As with form, juxtaposing groups of plants with contrasting textures increases interest; for example, the downy, pleated leaves of lady's mantle (*Alchemilla mollis*) contrast well with the spiny stems and jagged foliage of sea holly (*Eryngium*). Ground-cover perennials such as hardy *Geranium* species and cultivars and *Ajuga reptans* are especially useful to grow as a low foil for other plants, and to fill a gap in a planting scheme, and so complete the textural tapestry (see also PERENNIALS FOR GROUND COVER, p.180).

A "WHITE" GARDEN
Contrasting flowers and leaves in white, silver, and green here help to build up the tension in this monochrome planting of delphiniums, valerian (Centranthus ruber *'Albus'*), Anthericum liliago, *aquilegias, and artemisia.*

Colour blends and contrasts

Choosing colours is a very personal affair. Everyone has preferences as well as dislikes. It is important to select hues that you feel comfortable with, regardless of their current fashion status, or your best friend's opinion. A restricted colour palette can be wonderful, but may be hard to adhere to in a small garden.

For the widest plant choice, opt for an extensive range of colours that will either appear at the same time or follow on in a seasonal succession. If you are concerned about creating too dramatic clashes, try using all but one of the colours. The most awkward ones to combine are oranges and pinks. Using one or other with yellows, violets, blues, and reds can look very attractive. Alternatively you could opt for complementary colours – those opposite each other in the colour wheel – such as oranges and blues, yellows, and violets, or greens and reds. Another possibility is to use adjacent hues in the wheel,

combining all the hot colours such as yellows, oranges, and reds, or the cool pinks, blues, purples, and mauves. Such combinations were frequently used by the doyenne of colour schemes, Gertrude Jekyll.

In a monochrome planting design, foliage plays as important a role as flowers. Such a one-colour scheme, however, not only restricts the plant range but can also prove visually boring unless there is considerable contrast and variety within the design. When creating a white garden, for example, it is important to include different types of white, such as cream, pinkish white, and blueish white, as well as shades of green. Introducing contrasting leaf tones, shapes, and textures help to bring tension to a scheme. Thus, in a white garden, use silver, grey, and glaucous leaves as well as light, mid-, and dark green ones.

Unusually tinted foliage plants will emphasize a colour scheme, particularly in a mixed border, where golden-, silver-, or red-leaved shrubs can help to enhance flowers. They should be used as small accents, and not become the main features.

Colour intensities can also play an important part in garden design. Light colours such as white, pale pink, and pale yellow reflect higher levels of light than do darker shades – blue, red, and violet – and will be seen from further away. They also start shimmering at dusk when light levels have dropped – causing some flowers seemingly to disappear, while others develop an almost luminous character. The latter can be used near an area where you are likely to sit in the evenings. Light colours also help to enliven dark corners, or can be employed to draw attention to a focal point. Dark colours, on the other hand, are better used in the foreground, nearest to the viewpoint.

Seasonal interest

Although, in a mixed border, it is possible to plan a succession of colour schemes that change with the course of the seasons, to do so involves coordinating the timing of each plant's display, so that one feature smoothly follows another and fading flowers pass unnoticed, eclipsed by nearby plants coming into bloom. A scheme that manages to maintain a succession of interest requires forethought, yet mistakes are easily corrected by re-siting the offenders the following autumn.

The spring season may be announced as early as midwinter, when the first snowdrops (*Galanthus*) and winter aconites (*Eranthis hyemalis*) reveal their petals, soon followed by hellebores. Some winter-flowering shrubs and climbers, such as wintersweet (*Chimonanthus praecox*) and honeysuckle (*Lonicera* x *purpusii*) at the rear of mixed borders will help to increase the early show. Later in the season such woody plants can support not-too-vigorous herbaceous climbers such as the flame creeper (*Tropaeolum speciosum*) or *Clematis viticella* hybrids. In late winter and early spring, yellow is predominant, from primroses (*Primula vulgaris*), daffodils, and *Doronicum*, and pale blue, from irises and *Pulmonaria*, interspersed with grape hyacinths (*Muscari*). With tulips, spring comes to an end.

By early summer, most of the bulbs have finished their performance, and the real season for perennials starts. There are showstoppers such as Oriental poppies, with their short-lived but showy flowers, and the wonderfully baroque peonies as well as dainty, long-spurred *Aquilegia chrysantha* and the numerous

RIMED IN FROST
By retaining attractive seedheads, such as those of Cynara *and* roses *(here) and other eye-catching perennials, the season of interest in the garden can be extended well into winter. After a heavy frost, this border, with its columnar conifers and yew hedge in the foreground, is transformed into a glimmering wonderland.*

hardy geraniums. Once there is little risk of frost, the remainder of the tender plants will gradually vie for attention, including dahlias, argyranthemums, osteospermums, and cannas. These all flower over a long period, and are invaluable for providing colour until the first frosts arrive in autumn. There are hundreds of plants to choose from, including lupins, old-fashioned scabious, fluffy meadow rue (*Thalictrum*), strongly scented phlox, red hot pokers (*Kniphofia*), and numerous daisy family members such as fleabanes (*Erigeron*), *Helenium*, coneflowers (*Echinacea purpurea*), sunflowers (*Helianthus*), *Rudbeckia*, chrysanthemums, and

asters – the last two being vital for autumn flowers.

It is sometimes possible to extend the effect of a particular plant or group by growing next to it a plant that gives a similar impression. The deep blue flower spikes of *Delphinium* 'Blue Nile', for example, could be followed by those of *Aconitum carmichaelii*, and, if the latter is planted in front, the yellowing delphinium foliage will be hidden. Plant perennials such as lupins (*Lupinus*) that die back early in front of plants such as *Physostegia* that develop later in the season, to hide awkward gaps or fading leaves.

In mixed borders, bulbs are particularly useful for providing colour in late winter and spring when perennials are starting into growth. Similarly, the new growth of the latter masks the fading foliage of the bulbs once their flowers have finished. For example, the black-purple leaves of the evergreen *Ophiopogon planiscapus* 'Nigrescens', the soft grey-blue foliage of *Acaena saccaticupula* 'Blue Haze', or the copper variants of *A. microphylla* make excellent foils for snowdrops (*Galanthus*) and continue to provide interest after the snowdrops are past their best. Daffodils and tulips, planted towards the rear of a border, will have finished flowering by the time perennials come into growth, and so hide the dying foliage.

Particularly in small gardens, shrubs are invaluable to maintain the shape and structure of the design in

NATURALISTIC PLANTING
The bronze inflorescences of reed grass Calamagrostis x acutiflora *'Karl Foerster' provide vertical interest behind a sizeable, horizontal drift of* Helenium *'Moerheim Beauty' and* Hordeum jubatum. *The dark evergreen background brings the ornamental grasses and other perennials further into focus.*

177

SPRING SHOW *Most woodland perennials, such as aquilegias and peonies here, flower early in the growing season, while light levels are still relatively high. Many become dormant once the trees burst into foliage, and remain so until leaf fall. In summer in a woodland garden, attention switches to foliage shape and colours such as on Bowles' golden grass (Milium effusum 'Aureum') here.*

Naturalistic planting styles

Particularly in a large area, sizeable drifts of perennials look good when planted in naturalistic settings. Plants should be chosen to match the given habitat – such as woodland plants for woodland conditions, and waterside plants for boggy margins – and the planting pattern should reflect each plant's natural regeneration habits. Such planting schemes should be allowed to evolve gradually. Plants that increase by self-seeding in the immediate vicinity should be dotted about singly, while those with spreading rootstocks, such as asters, are best planted in drifts. All soil should be covered, either by plants or with a mulch.

In creating a matrix of vegetation, a much more natural and relaxed effect is obtained, one in which plants can evolve and change. Looking after such a scheme becomes more an issue of vegetation management than gardening in the conventional way, as you need to control vegetation groups, occasionally reducing a species or cultivar if it is getting out of hand. Ideally such a scheme is looked after by somebody who understands its aims and who knows which seedlings to leave and which ones are likely to become a threat. Maintenance is minimal, as there is little or no need for staking or dead-heading, because plants are usually selected with their autumn and winter appearance in mind and are allowed to retain their seedheads. Grasses play an important part in naturalistic plantings. They bring movement and are likely to remain looking good into autumn and winter, especially on a frosty morning.

late autumn and winter, as well as contributing colour and texture. The inclusion of deciduous shrubs with attractive autumn foliage (such as *Cotinus coggygria* 'Royal Purple') and those with bright fruits (such as many shrub roses) will also help to distract attention from perennials with dying foliage.

Cottage gardens

Traditional cottage gardens are a glorious mixture of herbs, roses, climbers, annuals, fruits, and vegetables, as well as perennials. They are noted for their simplicity in form, maximizing the space for production, with little money invested in elaborate structures. Planting areas are intersected by narrow paths and adorned with simple structures such as arches supporting climbers. In the past, cottagers bred plants themselves and produced enchanting perennials such as pansies (*Viola x wittrockiana*), auriculas (*Primula auricula*), and scented pinks (*Dianthus*). Plants were exchanged or passed on to other gardeners, as there were few plant nurseries until the late 19th century. Many of these old cultivars have now been lost, or have been superseded by stronger or more reliable ones.

Other typical cottage plants are peonies (*Paeonia*), lupins (*Lupinus*), Madonna lilies (*Lilium candidum*), Oriental poppies, delphiniums, and phlox, while wild flowers with fragrant, double, extra-large, or unusually coloured blooms, such as primulas and daisies (*Bellis perennis*), are also very appropriate.

Perennials in woodland gardens

Deciduous woodland provides conditions of shelter, light shade, and humus-rich soil suitable for many perennials. A small grove of birches (*Betula*) and other light-foliaged, deciduous trees may provide a suitable setting for a number of shade-loving plants; site the perennials

MOIST WOODLAND *Where there is a permanent source of water from a pond or stream, a wide range of moisture-loving perennials such as candelabra primulas and skunk cabbage (Lysichiton) can be grown for a prolonged, spring and early summer display. The fresh green fronds on the ferns here add a luxuriant touch to this wooded setting.*

where they will not face too much competition from tree roots. If such roots are unavoidable, make sure the planting area is generously mulched with a medium- to low-fertility mulch, such as leaf mould, each year, to give the shallow-rooted perennials a moist rooting zone.

Woodland gardens are normally rather informal, imitating nature in their layout, structure, and planting. Therefore straight lines and sharply defined planting groups should be avoided by intermingling plant communities at the edges and scattering individual plants such as foxgloves through the area. Many ferns thrive in the low light levels of a woodland setting and add architectural interest, whether planted in bold swathes or scattered through other planting.

Some of the most enchanting perennials are the small woodland plants that usher in spring. In order to grow, they make use of the light and rain that penetrate through to the woodland floor during autumn, winter, and spring, and then lie dormant during dry, dark summer, having adapted to the low light levels and

dry conditions that prevail in the summer months. For colour and interest in spring, while the overhead canopy is still leafless, plant perennials such as cyclamen, snowdrops (*Galanthus*), primroses (*Primula vulgaris*), wood anemones (*Anemone nemorosa*), and dog's-tooth violet (*Erythronium*). Combine them with woodland bulbs and shade-loving shrubs. In cool, dry woodland shade, grow ground-cover perennials such as lily-of-the-valley (*Convallaria majalis*), Solomon's seal (*Polygonatum*) with its pearly-white flowers, and *Pulmonaria*, some of which have attractively marked foliage.

Among the few shade-tolerant, summer-flowering perennials are *Kirengeshoma palmata*, with its waxy, soft yellow, tubular bells, and *Aster divaricatus*, which bears white, starry flowers on lax, wiry stems.

Specimen planting

In large areas of lawn or gravel, stately perennials with an architectural form or sculptural foliage, such

PERENNIALS IN CONTAINERS
A clump of one type of perennial in a large pot can perform the role of a specimen plant in a paved area. Those with fine flowers or foliage, for example Chionochloa rubra, *left, are particularly attractive in appropriate containers and may be left for years to increase in size.*

as *Acanthus spinosus*, may be sited on their own as specimen plants to create a striking effect. In smaller gardens, a specimen perennial, surrounded by low ground cover, could be used to provide a focal point where a border projects onto a lawn or hard paving, or in a corner of a garden where two borders meet. The jutting, sword-shaped leaves and arching, fiery-red flower stems of *Crocosmia* 'Lucifer', for example, look spectacular rising above the frothy, lime-green mass of lady's mantle (*Alchemilla mollis*) or a neatly cropped blanket of *Acaena microphylla* 'Kupferteppich'.

For year-round interest, evergreen perennials such as *Phormium tenax* and *Euphorbia characias* subsp. *wulfenii* are excellent. In sheltered areas, try *Melianthus major* with its neatly serrated, grey-green foliage. Many of the grasses will provide a long show. Especially well behaved and elegant are *Molinia caerulea* subsp. *arundinacea* 'Karl Foerster', with its slender flower spikes that arch elegantly in the rain, the tall, light panicles of *Stipa gigantea*, and the airy, silky plumes of *Miscanthus sinensis* 'Grosse Fontäne', which will be especially eye-catching through autumn and well into winter, if left uncut.

Other perennials that provide a briefer display may also make spectacular accent plants because of their form, flowers, or foliage. These range from the towering, felty stems of *Verbascum olympicum* to the massive leaves of the moisture-loving *Gunnera manicata* or the glorious, pink blooms of *Paeonia lactiflora*

'Sarah Bernhardt'. As these are all plants that die down in winter, it may be desirable to place another feature, such as a pot-grown plant, nearby, to create interest during their dormant period.

Specimen plants are best offset by a plain backdrop, such as a hedge, wall, or stretch of lawn, so that nothing detracts from their impact.

Growing perennials in containers

Perennials are as welcome in containers on a paved patio, courtyard, balcony, or roof garden as they are in open beds and borders (see also CONTAINER GARDENING, p.315). Growing them in this way also makes it possible to include plants that must be brought under cover for winter, as well as those that require a different soil type or moisture levels from the garden soil, such as the ornamental rhubarb *Rheum palmatum* 'Atrosanguineum', which does best when it has its feet moist. Pots are also ideal for plants that might otherwise invade a garden, such as variegated ground elder (*Aegopodium podagraria* 'Variegatum') or *Houttuynia cordata* 'Chameleon'.

Container-grown evergreen perennials such as *Bergenia purpurascens* and *Liriope muscari* can be on display all year round, while herbaceous perennials may be better planted with an evergreen shrub or winter-flowering bulbs such as winter aconites (*Eranthis hyemalis*), to extend the season of interest.

ACCENT PLANTING
*A few well-chosen plants with particularly eye-catching texture, shape, or size of leaves or flowers, such as mullein (*Verbascum bombyciferum 'Polarsommer'*) here, look stunning when introduced selectively in a border.*

Perennials for ground cover

GROUND-COVER planting is particularly suitable for areas of minimal maintenance, such as woodlands and shrubberies, or on embankments, which need stabilizing with plants. It is also important in areas that would otherwise have bare soil, as ground cover not only prevents topsoil erosion and nutrients leaching out but also reduces evaporation and weed growth.

Many ground-cover perennials will cope with shady conditions, as their natural habitat is the understorey in woodlands. They are therefore ideal when planted among taller perennials, shrub roses, or other shrubs, especially when such plants are young and will take several years to bulk out. The ground can be covered with shade-tolerant, early-flowering perennials such as *Viola odorata*, *Pulmonaria* 'Sissinghurst White', or *Doronicum orientale*. These can be removed and planted elsewhere when the shade becomes too dense for healthy growth.

Plants to use

A variety of perennials can be used as ground cover. Some, such as the day lily (*Hemerocallis*) or the mouse-tail plant (*Arisarum proboscideum*), develop through underground tuberous growths, which gradually form large, dense clumps. Some of these die back quite early, so they are suitable under spreading, late perennials or deciduous shrubs and trees.

Carpeting plants produce surface runners that root where they touch the soil. Alpine strawberries, the purple-leaved *Ajuga reptans* 'Catlins Giant', or the silver-variegated *Lamium maculatum* 'Beacon Silver' are good colonizers, often covering large areas within a few years.

The most effective type of ground-cover plants produce underground roots, which send up new shoots. Good examples of these are the stately *Acanthus mollis*, goose-necked *Lysimachia clethroides*, or *Euphorbia cyparissias* 'Fens Ruby' with its fine, needle-like, glaucous foliage and dark red buds in spring. Such persistent spreaders can become problematic if they are too invasive.

Some ground-cover perennials are better weed suppressants than others. The most valuable establish quickly, have dense foliage that blocks out light to prevent weed germination, and retain their leaves during the dormant season. Good examples are *Bergenia cordifolia* and *B.* 'Abendglut', with its red foliage in winter, *Epimedium*, and some of the geraniums, particularly *Geranium* 'Tiny Monster' and *G. macrorrhizum* cultivars, which flower over a long period, have scented foliage, and provide

LEAFY CARPET
Many perennials make excellent woodland ground cover, as they carpet the floor with dense foliage, which excludes sunlight and prevents weed growth.

some autumn colour. Clump-forming plants that bear low, spreading stems, such as *Euphorbia myrsinites*, also quickly and extensively cover the surrounding soil.

Mixing plants

To create a more naturalistic effect and extend the season of interest, drifts of one plant can be interspersed with key specimens of another species, flowering at a different time. Ground cover that flowers later in summer can be interplanted with bulbs: medium-height perennials can be mixed with daffodils and bluebells, while low-growing ones look good interspersed with crocus and snowdrops. Low-growing, early-flowering species that are not too rampant can be planted with summer- and autumn-flowering, sturdy perennials, such as *Persicaria polymorpha* or *Kirengeshoma palmata*, as well as a wide variety of ferns.

General cultivation

Particularly in areas where established trees and shrubs create competition for light and moisture, it is important to plant in early autumn, soon after leaf fall, giving the ground cover plenty of time to become established before the trees produce new growth and leaves.

Plant ground-cover perennials in well-prepared soil and water them well, especially in areas where there is considerable competition from tree roots. Additional mulching will help to keep the area weed-free, increase fertility, and retain moisture.

Most ground-cover perennials need only little routine care (see pp.191–193). *Epimedium* foliage, however, should be cut back in late winter, enabling flowering stems to come up before the new leaves.

ORNAMENTAL GROUND-COVER PLANTS

Hosta fortunei var. **aureomarginata**
Plant 30–45cm (12–18in) apart.

Houttuynia cordata 'Chameleon'
Plant 30–45cm (12–18in) apart.

Lamium maculatum 'Beacon Silver'
Plant 20–30cm (8–12in) apart.

Tanacetum densum
Plant 15–20cm (6–8in) apart.

Tiarella cordifolia
Plant 30cm (12in) apart.

Epimedium x youngianum 'Niveum'
Plant 30cm (12in) apart.

MORE PERENNIALS FOR GROUND COVER

Ajuga reptans
Anaphalis triplinervis
Asarum europaeum
Cornus canadensis
Epilobium angustifolium var. *album*
Epimedium
Euphorbia cyparissias, *E. griffithii*
Fragaria vesca
Geranium
Heuchera
Luzula sylvatica
Lysimachia clethroides
Persicaria
Prunella
Pulmonaria
Sedum cauticola, *S. spathulifolium*, *S. spurium*
Stachys
Symphytum
Tellima
Tiarella
Viola odorata, *V. riviniana* 'Purpurea'

Planter's guide to perennials

EXPOSED SITES

Perennials that tolerate exposed or windy sites

Achillea
Anaphalis
Armeria maritima
Artemisia absinthium
Calamagrostis x acutiflora 'Karl Foerster'
Centaurea dealbata, C. hypoleuca
Centranthus ruber
Crambe maritima
Eryngium variifolium
Euphorbia characias
Festuca glauca
Lavatera maritima, L. thuringiaca
Limonium latifolium
Nepeta
Phlomis russeliana
Sedum spectabile, S. telephium
Stachys byzantina
Yucca filamentosa, Y. flaccida

MOIST SHADE

Perennials that prefer moist shade

Ajuga reptans
Astilbe simplicifolia

Hemerocallis 'Marion Vaughn'

Astrantia major
Brunnera macrophylla
Carex (except C. buchananii and C. comans)
Convallaria majalis
Geranium sylvaticum
Hemerocallis
Hosta
Kirengeshoma palmata
Ligularia przewalskii
Milium effusum 'Aureum'
Molinia
Myrrhis odorata
Peltiphyllum peltatum
Persicaria bistorta 'Superba'
Primula bulleyana, P. florindae, P. japonica, P. pulverulenta
Rodgersia aesculifolia, R. pinnata
Thalictrum
Trillium grandiflorum, T. sessile

DRY SHADE

Perennials that tolerate dry shade

Acanthus mollis
Aconitum carmichaelii, A. napellus
Adiantum pedatum
Anemone hupehensis, A. x hybrida
Aquilegia vulgaris
Asarum europaeum
Asplenium
Campanula trachelium
Dicentra
Digitalis grandiflora, D. lutea

Epimedium
Geranium
Helleborus foetidus, H. orientalis
Iris foetidissima
Lathyrus vernus
Luzula sylvatica 'Marginata'
Matteuccia
Ophiopogon
Saxifraga umbrosa, S. x urbium
Symphytum grandiflorum
Tellima grandiflora 'Purpurea'
Vinca minor
Viola odorata, V. riviniana

WINTER AND EARLY SPRING INTEREST

Decorative flowers

Bergenia 'Ballawley', B. cordifolia
Doronicum
Epimedium
Euphorbia amygdaloides var. robbiae, E. characias
Helleborus
Iris lazica, I. unguicularis
Lathyrus vernus
Pulmonaria

Decorative leaves

Arum italicum 'Marmoratum'
Carex comans bronze
Festuca glauca
Heuchera 'Chocolate Ruffles', H. 'Pewter Moon'
Iris foetidissima 'Variegata'
Lamium maculatum 'Beacon Silver', L. DELLAM ('Golden Anniversary'), L. 'White Nancy'
Liriope muscari 'Variegata'
Ophiopogon planiscapus 'Nigrescens'
Phormium (cvs)
Stachys byzantina 'Silver Carpet'
Tiarella polyphylla
Vinca (variegated cvs)

FRAGRANT FLOWERS

Convallaria majalis
Cosmos atrosanguineus ❀
Dianthus, many'
Dictamnus albus
Filipendula ulmaria
Galium odoratum
Hemerocallis
Hesperis matronalis
Hosta plantaginea var. grandiflora
Iris graminea
Oenothera odorata
Paeonia lactiflora
Phlox paniculata
Viola cornuta, V. odorata

FLOWERS FOR CUTTING

Alchemilla mollis
Allium
Alstroemeria

Aquilegia
Aster
Astrantia
Centaurea
Cephalaria
Crocosmia
Dahlia ❀
Delphinium, some ❀
Dianthus
Dicentra
Doronicum
Erigeron
Gypsophila
Helenium
Kniphofia, some ❀
Monarda
Paeonia
Phlomis tuberosa 'Amazone'
Phlox
Rudbeckia
Scabiosa
Sedum spectabile, S. telephium
Solidago
Veronica

FLOWERS FOR DRYING

Achillea
Alchemilla mollis
Anaphalis
Aruncus dioicus
Astilbe
Catananche
Centaurea
Cynara ❀
Echinops bannaticus, E. ritro
Gypsophila
Limonium, some ❀
Persicaria amplexicaulis 'Firetail'
Rodgersia
Sedum spectabile, S. telephium
Solidago

Cynara cardunculus

ARCHITECTURAL PLANTS

Acanthus hungaricus, A. mollis
Angelica archangelica, A. gigas
Arundo donax 'Variegata' ❀
Cortaderia selloana
Crambe cordifolia
Cynara ❀
Eupatorium purpureum subsp. maculatum 'Atropurpureum'
Foeniculum vulgare
Gunnera manicata ❀
Helianthus salicifolius
Helleborus argutifolius
Hosta sieboldiana var. elegans
Inula magnifica
Ligularia dentata 'Othello'
Lysichiton americanus
Macleaya
Melianthus major ❀

Miscanthus sinensis
Persicaria polymorpha
Rheum palmatum 'Atrosanguineum'
Rodgersia
Sedum telephium 'Matrona'
Stipa gigantea
Verbascum olympicum

DECORATIVE SEEDHEADS

Acanthus
Achillea
Eryngium
Foeniculum vulgare
Hosta
Inula magnifica
Iris
Lunaria rediviva
Miscanthus
Molinia
Papaver orientale
Physalis alkekengi
Sedum

ATTRACTIVE TO INSECTS

Aster
Digitalis
Echinacea purpurea
Foeniculum vulgare
Helenium
Inula
Nepeta
Oenothera
Salvia
Sedum
Verbascum

FAST-GROWING PERENNIALS

Achillea filipendulina 'Gold Plate', A. grandifolia
Artemisia lactiflora Guizhou Group
Arundo donax 'Macrophylla' ❀
Centaurea macrocephala
Cephalaria gigantea
Crambe cordifolia
Eupatorium purpureum subsp. maculatum 'Atropurpureum'
Ferula communis
Gunnera manicata ❀
Macleaya cordata
Malva alcea var. fastigiata
Persicaria polymorpha
Phormium tenax ❀
Rheum palmatum 'Atrosanguineum'
Romneya coulteri
Rudbeckia 'Goldquelle'
Salvia uliginosa ❀
Solidago canadensis
Stipa gigantea
Thalictrum rochebruneanum
Vernonia crinita
Veronicastrum virginicum

KEY
❀ Not hardy

Irises

THE genus *Iris* includes some of the loveliest of flowering plants. Their intricate blooms offer a rich spectrum of colours as well as satin or velvet textures. Species can be selected for diverse situations, ranging from woodland and rock garden, waterside and bog, to herbaceous borders. Botanically, *Iris* is divided into Subgenera, Sections, and Series; these divisions vary in their cultural needs and form a convenient horticultural classification.

Routine care and propagation

Species may be propagated in the autumn or spring by division of offsets or rhizomes, or by seed in autumn (named cultivars by division only). For further information, see PERENNIALS, "Routine care", pp.191–193; BULBOUS PLANTS, "Routine care", pp.242–244, and also "Propagation", pp.245–250.

Rhizomatous irises

Irises in this group have rhizomes as rootstocks, with sword-shaped leaves arranged in a basal fan. Botanically, they are divided into several Subgenera and Series but for horticultural purposes the main groups are bearded, crested, and beardless irises.

Bearded irises

Characterized by a "beard" of numerous hairs along the centre of the falls, this group includes the common irises that are grown in gardens, with many cultivars and hybrids, most flowering in early summer. Suitable for herbaceous and mixed borders, they are easy to grow in rich, well-drained, alkaline soil in sun; many also tolerate poorer soils and partial shade.

Oncocyclus irises are natives of areas with little summer rainfall and need the protection of an alpine house or frame in climates that are subject to summer rains. They have large, beautiful, and sometimes bizarre blooms but are exacting in their requirements and are not easy to grow. They need a fertile, sharply drained soil and full sun, with a dry, dormant period after flowering. If they are grown in pots, the compost must be nutrient-rich, well drained, and preferably alkaline.

Repot before growth begins in early spring, if required. When the foliage dies down after flowering, stop watering, and keep the rhizomes dry while they are dormant. Resume watering in spring.

Regelia irises, with their bearded standards and falls, are related to the Oncocyclus irises and have similar cultural requirements although they are easier to grow. Some species, such as *I. hoogiana*, may be grown outside, given good drainage and a hot, dry site in the summer. The Regeliocyclus group (Regelia x Oncocyclus hybrids) is more easily grown in the open.

Crested irises

These have ridges, or cockscomb-like crests, instead of beards.
Evansia irises are usually found in damp woodland. Larger species, such as *I. confusa* and *I. japonica*, are not fully hardy and need a sheltered position in humus-rich soils, with some shade provided in warm climates. Smaller species, such as *I. cristata* and *I. gracilipes*, are ideal for planting in peaty pockets in a shaded rock garden.

Beardless irises

Irises in this group do not have bearded falls, but usually have crests. Most have similar cultural requirements to bearded irises, but some prefer heavier soil.
Pacific Coast irises, a group that includes *I. innominata* and *I. tenax*, are useful for cutting. Many good, free-flowering hybrids have been produced which are excellent for humus-rich, acid soils, in sun in cool regions or in shade in warmer climates. Others from groups that need similar conditions include: *I. missouriensis*, which is more tolerant of alkaline soils; *I. verna* and *I. prismatica*; and *I. setosa*, which is more tolerant of sun.
Water irises are a group of elegant, moisture-loving plants that thrive in pond margins, bog gardens, or rich, permanently damp soils. They include *I. laevigata*, *I. pseudacorus*, *I. ensata* (syn. *I. kaempferi*), *I. fulva*, *I. versicolor*, and *I.* 'Fulvala'. All need similar damp conditions but can be difficult to establish.
Siberian irises have slender leaves and beautifully formed, delicately marked flowers. This group includes *I. chrysographes*, *I. clarkei*, *I. forrestii*, and *I. sibirica*. They are easily grown in borders in rich soil that does not dry out, and are particularly suited to very moist, waterside soil. The flowers last well when cut.
Spuria irises have narrow, reed-like foliage and elegant blooms. Spurias – *I. orientalis*, *I. graminea*, and *I. spuria* – are suited to sunny herbaceous borders, in well-drained soil; they tolerate drier conditions than the Siberian irises.

Bulbous irises

The storage organs of these irises are bulbs, sometimes with thick, fleshy roots. Subgenera include Reticulata, Juno, and Xiphium irises.

Reticulata irises

Dwarf, hardy bulbs, which flower early. They prefer a sunny position in well-drained, acid or alkaline soil, or may be grown in pots in the bulb frame.

Juno irises

Junos need similar conditions to the Oncocyclus irises and are also difficult to grow. Vigorous species, such as *I. bucharica* and *I. magnifica*, grow well in warm, outdoor sites.

Xiphium irises

These include the brightly coloured Dutch, English, and Spanish irises, often grown for cut flowers. Any alkaline, well-drained soil in full sun is suitable. In cold areas, lift the bulbs in autumn to overwinter in a frost-free place. Replant in spring.

RHIZOMATOUS AND BULBOUS IRISES

I. 'Bold Print'
(bearded)

I. 'Carnaby'
(bearded)

I. innominata
(Pacific Coast)

I. 'Geisha Gown'
(Japanese)

I. bucharica
(Juno)

I. 'Joyce'
(Reticulata)

INFORMAL ELEGANCE
The colourful blooms of Siberian irises (blue and white) and
I. pseudacorus (yellow) *provide a focal point by a garden pond.*

Soil preparation and planting

Herbaceous perennials originate from many regions, which have widely varying climatic and soil conditions, so whether the proposed site is sheltered or exposed, fertile or stony, there is always a number of plants that will thrive. It is better to select plants that will flourish in the given growing conditions rather than struggle against nature.

Site and aspect

When deciding which plants to grow, take into account climate, aspect, and soil type, as well as the amount of sun, shade, and shelter the site receives at different times of day and from season to season. For example, the shade cast by deciduous trees is most dense in late spring and summer when the trees are in leaf.

Different areas of the garden may provide varying growing conditions: for example, a south-facing border would be ideal for plants that thrive in sun, such as sedums, while a north-facing site or a position beneath a tree would be better for shade-loving species, such as hostas, provided that they can be kept moist.

The ground next to a wall, fence, or hedge is usually fairly dry due to the effect of rain shadow, but since it also tends to be warm and sheltered, it may be a good position for plants that are not fully hardy.

Altering conditions

In small gardens especially, it may be necessary to adapt some elements to create growing conditions that suit a wide range of plants. Heavy, waterlogged soils may be drained or the plants grown in raised beds or containers, while lighter soils may benefit from the addition of organic matter. Shade from trees may be reduced by judicious pruning, and shelter provided by shrubs, hedges, or windbreaks (see also FROST AND WIND PROTECTION, pp.612–613, and HEDGES AND SCREENS, pp.84–86).

Soil preparation

The ideal soil for the majority of perennial plants is a fertile loam that is well drained but retains adequate moisture. Use a proprietary soil-testing kit to find out the degree of acidity or alkalinity of the soil, because this partly determines which plants will thrive there.

It is also important to check soil drainage; if much of the ground

remains waterlogged in wet weather, then it will be necessary to install soakaways or drains (see "Improving drainage", p.623).

Clearing the site

All weeds should be cleared from the site prior to planting because, once other plants are established, perennial weeds, in particular, are difficult to eradicate. If the ground is infested with weeds, treat the whole area with an appropriate weedkiller during the season before planting. If there are only a few perennial weeds, however, they may be forked out when preparing the soil in winter.

During the first growing season, any remaining perennial weeds should be carefully removed with a hand fork as soon as they are noticed, or spot-treated with a systemic weedkiller, taking care not to harm the newly planted perennials. Annual weeds may be either sprayed or forked out before the site is planted.

Improving the soil

All soils may be enhanced by the addition of humus or well-rotted organic matter or by proprietary soil improvers (see SOILS AND FERTILIZERS, "Soil nutrients and fertilizers", pp.624–625); this increases the water retention of light, free-draining soils and helps to open up the texture of heavy, clay soils. It also improves the soil's fertility. Before planting (preferably a few weeks in advance), apply a 5–10cm (2–4in) layer of well-rotted organic matter over the site, then fork or dig it into the top spit of the soil. Allow the soil to settle before planting. If the soil is sufficiently fertile and rich in humus, it may be unnecessary to use fertilizer when planting perennials, although they may require feeding in subsequent seasons (see "Fertilizing", p.191).

LUPIN

Strong, healthy top-growth

Moist compost

Established, vigorous roots

Weak, woody top-growth

Under-developed root system

Dry compost

Moss and weeds growing on the compost

Pot-bound roots

Selecting plants

Most perennials are sold container-grown, but bare-root plants are also sometimes available from autumn to early spring, when they are dormant. When selecting plants, look for healthy, vigorous specimens with no sign of dieback or abnormally coloured leaves that may indicate a lack of nutrients. If buying herbaceous plants at the beginning of the growing season, check that there are strong, emerging shoots: plants that have a few fat, healthy looking buds are better than those that have a large number of weaker ones.

One or two annual weeds growing in the compost may be removed easily enough, but do not buy any container-grown plants with perennial weeds, moss, or liverworts.

These often indicate that the plant has been in its container for too long and may be starved of nutrients or that the compost is poorly drained, in which case the plant's roots may have rotted or died back.

When possible, remove the plant from its container and inspect the roots: do not choose a plant with a mass of tightly coiling roots or one that has large roots pushing through the drainage holes. The roots should, however, be sufficiently established to retain most of the compost when the plant is removed from its container. For plants growing in flexible plastic bags, check that there is good root growth by feeling them through the bag.

If buying bare-root plants, ensure that the root systems are strong and have not dried out, and that the young shoots are not wilting. Plant them as soon as possible after purchase, protecting them against moisture loss by wrapping them in plastic or wet newspaper until ready to plant.

Dividing large plants

When buying fibrous-rooted plants, choose large examples with a number of healthy shoots that may be divided before planting, rather than a few smaller, cheaper specimens. Divide the plant by prising it apart with your hands or two hand forks used back-to-back, taking care that each division has its own root system and retains as much soil around the roots as possible (see also "Dividing perennials", p.200).

DIVIDING LARGE PLANTS

1 When buying easily divided perennials, look for a large plant with several strong shoots (here Aster tongolensis).

2 Gently pull the plant apart to make several small sections, each with its own roots. Keep plenty of soil around the roots.

Perennials that Thrive in Sandy Soil

Acanthus spinosus
Achillea
Alchemilla
Armeria
Asphodeline lutea
Centranthus ruber
Dianthus, some ❄

Echinops ritro 'Veitch's Blue'

Echinops
Eryngium tripartitum
Gaillardia x *grandiflora* (cvs)
Globularia
Limonium latifolium
Nepeta x *faassenii*
Origanum vulgare 'Aureum'
Papaver orientale
Romneya coulteri
Sedum, some ❄
Sempervivum
Sisyrinchium, some ❄

Perennials that Tolerate Clay Soil

Aruncus dioicus
Astilbe
Butomus ♦
Caltha ♦
Cardamine pratensis
Dodecatheon
Eomecon
Filipendula ulmaria 'Aurea'
Gunnera manicata ♦
Hemerocallis
Hosta
Houttuynia
Lobelia cardinalis, L. fulgens ❄
Lysichiton ♦
Lysimachia, some ❄
Lythrum
Mimulus guttatus ♦
Myosotis scorpioides ♦
Peltiphyllum peltatum
Phormium
Polygonum
Pontederia ♦

Primula bulleyana

Primula bulleyana,
P. florindae, P. rosea
Ranunculus ficaria cultivars,
R. flammula ♦
Rheum
Rodgersia
Sagittaria, some ❄
Scrophularia auriculata
Trollius

Key
❄ *Not hardy*
♦ *Tolerates waterlogged soil*

When to plant

Perennials grown in containers may be planted out at any time of year when the soil is workable, but the best seasons are spring and autumn. Planting in autumn helps the plants to establish quickly before the onset of winter since the soil is still warm enough to promote root growth yet is unlikely to dry out. Spring planting is preferable for late-flowering perennials, and in cold areas is also better for perennials that are not entirely hardy or that dislike wet conditions, such as *Kniphofia, Schizostylis, Lobelia cardinalis*, and *Scabiosa caucasica*. It should ensure that they are fully established before their first winter.

Bare-root specimens should generally be planted in spring or autumn, although a few, such as hostas, may be transplanted successfully during the growing season.

Planting perennials

Plant perennials in prepared ground, taking care to position them at the right depth (see below): for example, those prone to rotting at the base are best planted proud of the soil so that excess water may drain away.

Container-grown plants
Water the plant thoroughly, preferably the night before it is to be planted. Then dig a planting hole, then remove

How to Plant a Container-grown Perennial

1 *In a prepared bed, dig a hole 1½ times wider and deeper than the plant's root ball.*

2 *Soak the compost in the pot before sliding out the plant (here an* Aster*).*

3 *Gently scrape off the top 3cm (1½in) of compost to remove weeds and weed seeds. Carefully tease out the roots around the sides and base of the root ball.*

4 *Check that the plant crown is at the correct depth when planted and fill in around the root ball. Firm in around the plant and water thoroughly.*

Planting depths

While most perennials are best planted out at the same soil level as they were in their pots, a number grow better if planted higher or deeper, depending on their individual requirements. Some prefer a raised, well-drained site while others thrive in deeper, moist conditions.

Aster

Ground-level Planting
The majority of perennials should be planted so that the crown of the plant is level with the surrounding soil.

Sisyrinchium striatum 'Aunt May'

Raised Planting
Set plants that are prone to rot at the base, and variegated plants that tend to revert, with their crowns slightly above the ground.

Hosta

Shallow Planting
Plant perennials that require a moist environment with their crowns about 2.5cm (1in) below ground level.

Polygonatum

Deep Planting
Plant perennials with tuberous root systems so that their crowns are about 10cm (4in) below the soil surface.

the plant from its container, taking care not to damage the roots. To help the plant to establish quickly, carefully loosen the sides and base of the root ball, particularly if root-bound, by teasing out the roots with your fingers or a hand fork. Place the plant at the appropriate depth in the prepared hole, backfill with soil, and firm. Loosen the surface of the soil with a hand fork and water in thoroughly.

Bare-root plants

To prevent dehydration, plant bare-root perennials as soon as possible after purchase. Prepare a hole as for container-grown plants, spread out the roots evenly, work in soil between the roots, then water well.

Transplanting self-sown seedlings

A number of perennials, for example *Aquilegia* and foxgloves (*Digitalis*), regularly produce self-sown seedlings that may be moved to another position in the garden or nursery bed.

Before lifting the seedlings, prepare suitable planting holes, spacing them to allow room for the plants to develop. Then gently lift each seedling with a trowel, taking care to retain as much soil around the roots as possible, and replant it immediately. Firm it in well and water it thoroughly. Shade the plants in sunny weather, and water them regularly until they are established.

Raised beds

These beds are often used for growing acid-loving plants in a garden with alkaline soil or for providing a free-draining bed on heavy, clay soil. Plants that will only thrive in acid soil are best planted in a raised bed filled with an ericaceous compost (see also THE ROCK GARDEN, "Raised beds", p.257, and "Ericaceous plants", p.257).

Raised beds may be constructed from a variety of materials including wood, bricks, stone, and logs (see also STRUCTURES AND SURFACES, "Raised beds", p.599). Include a deep layer of coarse drainage material (such as broken bricks) in the base – about one third of the depth of the bed is ideal. Cover this with a layer of fibrous material and fill in with topsoil before planting.

Containers

As well as being a highly attractive way of displaying a number of plants, growing perennials in containers provides an opportunity to include plants that would not flourish in the open garden, either because they are too tender, or because the soil type is not suitable. If growing different plants together in one container, take care to choose those that thrive in similar conditions.

When choosing a container, make sure that it is sufficiently deep and wide to allow room for the plants' roots to develop properly. Consider how the selected plants will look when in full growth in relation to the container to achieve a pleasing balance between them. Tall plants in deep, narrow containers and small plants in large, wide ones may seem out of proportion.

TRANSPLANTING SEEDLINGS

Lift seedlings with soil around their roots so as not to break up the root ball. Plant out and water well.

Planting in containers

If using a heavy container such as a stone urn, lead trough, wooden half-barrel, or large terracotta pot, place it in position before filling and planting since it will be very cumbersome to move afterwards; plastic containers are, of course, considerably lighter, but they are less stable and may be blown over in strong winds. Set the container on a support of blocks or bricks to allow free drainage.

Make sure that the container has drainage holes in the base or low on the sides to prevent waterlogging. Cover the holes with 5–8cm (2–3in) of broken crocks or stones and add a layer of fibrous material, for example upside-down turves or coir fibre; this allows water to filter through freely yet prevents compost from being washed down into the base and blocking the drainage holes.

Most potting composts are suitable, although acid-loving plants must be planted in an ericaceous compost. A prepared, general compost with a slow-release fertilizer added (see p.323) suits most plants; those that need extra drainage (such as *Sedum* or *Achillea*) prefer a compost containing extra grit or sharp sand.

Before planting, arrange the plants on the compost to ensure that they have enough room to develop freely. Plant as for perennials in open ground and keep well watered until established.

Heuchera micrantha var. *diversifolia* 'Palace Purple'

Penstemon 'Rich Ruby'

Geranium sanguineum var. *striatum*

Artemisia 'Powis Castle'

1 *When planting in a container, group the plants while still in their pots to determine the spacing and arrangement. Then plant, firm in, and water well.*

2 *A few months later, the plants will have grown and developed to form a well-balanced, attractive display.*

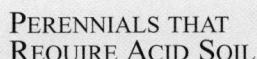

Hostas

GROWN primarily for their bold, sculptural foliage, many hosta species and cultivars also produce attractive white, lilac, or purple flowers. Easy to maintain and long-lived, hostas make a valuable addition to any garden.

Although there are more than 2,000 registered cultivars, there is no agreed formal classification system for hostas. Many nurseries, however, follow the American Hosta Society sizing, which is based on the foliage height of the clump when mature: dwarf hostas are less than 10cm (4in) tall; miniatures are 10–15cm (4–6in) tall; small 15–25cm (6–10in) tall; medium 25–45cm (10–18in) tall; large 45–70cm (18–28in) tall; and extra large taller than 70cm (28in).

Using hostas in the garden

Hostas are highly sought after as foliage plants for light to moderately shaded areas, and make eye-catching displays in pots or beside ponds. The range of colours, textures, and shapes of their foliage is stunning: modern hybrids may have leaves patterned in shades of green, white, and gold, or edged in a different, contrasting colour. Their texture may be rich and glossy or soft and velvety. Leaves may be narrow and ribbon-like, heart-shaped or almost circular. There are hostas suitable for most degrees of shade, from light or dappled, to moderate. In general, the blue-leaved hostas flourish in light shade all day, while yellow-leaved cultivars prefer some sun.

Hostas for shady places
Hostas make excellent companion plants for other shade-loving perennials. They act as a foil for bright flowers such as those of *Astilbe*, while their large leaves make a counterpoint to the finer foliage of other plants including Japanese painted fern (*Athyrium niponicum* var. *pictum*) and sedges (*Carex*). For shady places in the rock garden, choose miniature hostas such as *H. venusta* and *H.* 'Shining Tot'.

Consider planting a hosta to enliven a shady entrance. Choose a variety with striking foliage such as the plate-like *H.* 'Blue Angel' or white-margined *H.* 'Patriot', both of which have showy flowers in midsummer. Fragrant hostas ideal for planting close to the house include *H.* 'Sugar and Cream', *H.* 'So Sweet', and *H. plantaginea*, which is one of the last to flower.

On a shaded patio, grow hostas in containers to contrast with more flamboyant annuals. Golden-yellow *H.* 'Richland Gold' or the yellow-centred *H.* 'June' are excellent plants for pots or other containers.

MIXED BORDER
Hostas blend well with other shade plants, acting as a foil for summer flowers, and providing interest after the flowers have finished.

Ground cover
Hostas make particularly striking ground cover when planted as a mass. Choose cultivars carefully for continuous interest from both foliage and flowers. For example, a combination of *H.* 'Green Piecrust', *H.* 'Krossa Regal', *H.* 'Honeybells', and *H. plantaginea* makes an exotic planting that will flower for several months in succession. A more subtle effect is achieved by restricting the design to a few hostas within a limited spectrum of leaf colours. For a fast-growing, low ground cover, choose cultivars such as *H.* 'Pearl Lake' and *H.* 'Ground Master'.

Hostas in other positions
Several hostas planted together may be used as a low summer hedge that needs no clipping. The lance-leaved hosta (*H. lancifolia*) is ideal for this and will take full sun in all but the hottest regions; it gives a display of slender purple bells in late summer.

HOSTAS FOR DIFFERENT SITUATIONS

H. tokudama f. aureonebulosa
Medium-size, for medium shade

H. decorata
Medium-size, for light to moderate shade

H. 'Gold Standard'
Medium-size, prefers light shade

H. 'Halcyon'
Medium-size, for light shade

H. plantaginea
Large, likes full sun and a little light shade. Scented flowers

H. ventricosa var. aureomaculata
Large, prefers light to medium shade

H. montana 'Aureomarginata'
Extra-large hosta, for light to medium shade

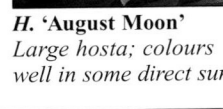

H. lancifolia
Medium-size, tolerating full sun

H. 'August Moon'
Large hosta; colours well in some direct sun

H. sieboldiana var. elegans
Extra-large; light shade

H. ventricosa
Large, for light to moderate shade

Most hostas grow well in sites that are close to water; *H.* 'Sum and Substance', *H. undulata* var. *erromena*, and *H. undulata* var. *albomarginata* are especially good in soils that are moist.

Cultivation

Hostas tolerate a wide range of soils, except for unimproved heavy clay or pure sand. They grow best in good, moist loam, rich in organic matter, with a pH from 6.5 to 7.3. Prepare the soil well before planting, particularly if it is lacking in nutrients (see "Soil preparation", p.183).

Planting hostas
Bare-root hostas can be planted in spring or autumn. Container-grown hostas can be planted at any time, but do not disturb the roots if planting while they are in active growth (see "Planting perennials", p.184). In spring or autumn, however, unless the container is full of roots, it is better to shake off much of the compost and treat as a bare-root hosta.

Plant with the crown at ground level (see "Planting depths", p.184). Do not allow any manure to come into contact with the roots at planting, as it may cause discoloured foliage in the first year. Leave a slight depression around the plant at

first so that, when you water, the moisture soaks directly down to the roots of the plant.

Routine care
Hostas take about five years to reach maturity and can then be left undisturbed for many years. Hostas do best if the soil is moist at all times.

To produce lush foliage of a good colour, top-dress hostas with well-rotted manure or compost as these increase the soil humus and nutrient content. Apply a well-balanced fertilizer to hostas in poor soil, in spring.

Mulching
Apply a spring mulch while the soil is moist. Use only well-rotted materials in order to discourage slugs. In regions with very cold winters, apply a mulch of straw or leaves around each hosta before the ground has frozen; take care not to cover the crown of the plant. On new, shallow-rooted plants the mulch prevents them from lifting after a severe frost, while on established plants it often reduces crown rot. If very coarse material is used as a mulch, it should be removed in the spring.

Pests and diseases
Slugs and snails (p.644) may devastate hostas, sometimes reducing leaves to tatters by the end of the season; earwigs (p.644) will also chew

holes in the foliage. Crown rot (p.665) may cause problems, especially on heavy soils or in climates that are relatively humid.

Propagation

Hostas are easily increased by division (see "Dividing hostas", p.200) or cutting a slice out of a crown with a sharp spade. Although the offspring only rarely come true to type, hostas may be raised from seed collected when the capsules turn brown. Sow in autumn or winter (see p.198).

Division by "topping"
A practical method of propagating hostas is to "top" them: small cuts are made in the rootstock in spring to stimulate new buds and roots. This method is useful for hostas that are slow to increase.

By autumn, the cuts will have callused and developed new roots and dormant buds. The entire plant can then be lifted in autumn or the following spring and divided into pieces, each with its own bud. After transplanting, the new plants should be allowed to grow on for at least a year before this process is repeated.

GROUND COVER
In a border with dappled shade, hostas make ideal ground cover. Select leaf colours to go with the varying degrees of shade.

PROPAGATING HOSTAS BY "TOPPING"

1 *In spring when the buds have started to grow, carefully scrape away the soil from around the base of a young plant to expose the crown.*

2 *Carefully wipe the surface of the rootstock clean with a soft, moistened cloth, taking care not to disturb the roots.*

3 *With a sharp knife, make a vertical cut through the crown. Unless the plant is very small, make a second cut at right angles to the first.*

4 *Dust each cut with hormone rooting powder and insert a toothpick to hold the cut open.*

5 *Pack the surrounding soil back around the crown of the plant, firm it well, and water thoroughly. By autumn, dormant buds will develop.*

6 *Lift and divide the clump the following spring when new shoots emerge. Alternatively, divide the previous autumn.*

Chrysanthemums

THE rich colours and luxuriant shapes of their long-lasting flowerheads make the florists' chrysanthemum popular for providing displays in the garden, cutting for the house, and for exhibiting.

Classifying chrysanthemums

The florists' chrysanthemum is derived from a number of species from eastern Asia and is of complex hybrid origin. A range of different flower types has been developed, and these are grouped according to the shape and arrangement of the petals and florets within the flowerheads, as well as by the flowering season.

Chrysanthemums will naturally form a number of flowerheads on the same stem; these are known as "sprays". "Disbudded" chrysanthemums are formed by removing the lateral buds of spray types at an early stage; this leaves a single, terminal bud that produces a much larger flowerhead.

Early-flowering chrysanthemums bloom from late summer to early autumn, and are grown outdoors. Late-flowering ones are grown in pots outdoors in summer and are brought into a greenhouse, where they flower from autumn until late winter. Cultivation is similar for early- and late-flowering types, but plants grown for exhibition are given more time and attention. Early charms are dwarf chrysanthemums, which flower from late summer to mid-autumn and are grown outdoors in beds or on a patio.

Early-flowering chrysanthemums

Early-flowering cultivars may be ordered from a specialist for delivery in spring. To be sure of selecting the desired colours, it is best to see the plants at flowering time, or to choose them from an illustrated catalogue.

Once established in the garden, plants that are growing vigorously and that are producing good, healthy

DISBUDDED CHRYSANTHEMUMS
These (here C. 'George Griffiths') are formed by removing all but one of the flower buds on each lateral, producing large, individual blooms.

blooms should be marked so that they can be used for propagating new plants from cuttings.

Soil preparation and planting
Early-flowering chrysanthemums require a fairly sunny, sheltered site. They prefer a well-drained, slightly acid soil with a pH value of 6.5. For most soils, the ground should be prepared in late autumn or early winter, incorporating plenty of organic

matter. Light soils need not be prepared until early spring, with the organic matter applied as a mulch in early summer.

Prior to planting out in late spring, insert 1.2m (4ft) canes about 45cm (18in) apart (a split cane may be tied to the top to support a tall cultivar, if necessary). Plant each chrysanthemum next to a cane, with the root ball just covered with soil. Tie the stem of each plant to the cane.

TYPES OF CHRYSANTHEMUM FLOWERHEAD

INCURVED
C. 'Yellow John Hughes'
Fully double flowerheads with incurved petals closing tightly over the crown.

FULLY REFLEXED
C. 'Primrose West Bromwich'
Fully double flowerheads with curved petals reflexing back to touch the stem.

REFLEXED
C. 'Brietner'
Fully double flowerheads with partly reflexed petals and a spiky outline.

INTERMEDIATE
C. 'Beacon'
Fully double flowerheads with loosely incurving petals and a regular shape.

SPIDER
C. 'Muxton Plume'
Fully double flowerheads with pendent, long, fine florets with hooked or coiled tips.

QUILL
C. 'Honeycomb'
Fully double flowerheads with straight, tubular florets that open at the tips to form spoon shapes.

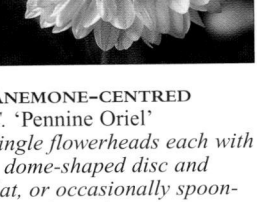

ANEMONE-CENTRED
C. 'Pennine Oriel'
Single flowerheads each with a dome-shaped disc and flat, or occasionally spoon-shaped, petals.

POMPON
C. 'Salmon Fairie'
Fully double, dense flowerheads bearing tubular florets with flat, rounded petals.

SINGLE
C. 'Golden Woodman's Glory'
Flowerheads with prominent central discs and 5 rows of flat-petalled florets.

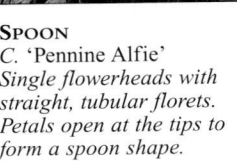

SPOON
C. 'Pennine Alfie'
Single flowerheads with straight, tubular florets. Petals open at the tips to form a spoon shape.

Stopping

Soon after planting (refer to a growers' catalogue or specialist publication for precise timing), the plants need to be "stopped". This consists of pinching out the growing tips to encourage flower-bearing laterals.

When the laterals are about 8cm (3in) long, reduce them to the number required: four laterals to each main stem should be sufficient for a general display on cultivars grown as sprays, whereas four to six are needed for disbudded plants and two or three for those grown for exhibition.

About one month after stopping, hoe and water in a balanced fertilizer, at a rate of 70g/sq m (2oz/sq yd). Repeat this feed about one month later, to encourage strong growth. Remove any sideshoots that develop from the laterals as soon as possible so that all the plant's energy is concentrated on the laterals.

Disbudding

Seven or eight weeks after stopping, a main, or apical, bud, surrounded by

STOPPING AND REMOVING LATERALS

STOPPING
When the cutting is 15–20cm (6–8in) high, pinch out 1cm (½in) at the tip to encourage laterals.

REMOVING EXCESS LATERALS
About 2 months later, select 3 or 4 healthy, evenly spaced laterals and remove any others.

DISBUDDING

For disbuds, once the side buds around each apical bud have tiny stalks, pinch them out so that only the central bud develops.

sideshoots, should be visible at the end of each lateral.

If only one flower per stem is required, snap off all the sideshoots from each lateral. The apical buds can then develop unhindered and each lateral will bear a single bloom (the "disbud"). To produce a spray of small, even-sized flowerheads, pinch out the apical bud only; this allows all the sideshoots to develop and produce a spray of flowers.

Routine care

Water plants regularly, and apply a balanced liquid feed at weekly or 10-day intervals while the buds are developing. Feeding must be discontinued just before the buds show colour, so that the blooms do not become soft and prone to damage.

Overwintering

Early-flowering chrysanthemums may be overwintered in the ground in mild climates that are frost-free, and their stems cut down only in spring. In temperate climates, however, plants are best lifted and stored. After flowering and before the first frosts, cut the stems to about 22cm (9in) and remove all shoots. Keep the plants labelled while in store to identify them the following year.

Lift the plants, wash the roots, and store the stools (rootstocks) in batches of six or eight in a shallow box of loam-based potting compost. Make sure that the compost is slightly moist and that the stocks are not buried too deeply. Do not water them in: keep them almost dry to minimize the risk of rot. Place the containers in a frost-free cold frame or cold greenhouse for two months.

Bring the boxed stools into a greenhouse in mid-winter, water them, and keep them at a temperature

OVERWINTERING

1 *After flowering, cut back the stems, lift the plant (here a young plant is used), and wash the roots. Trim any straggly roots to leave the root ball about the size of a tennis ball.*

2 *Line a 10cm (4in) deep box with paper and place the plants with stems upright on a 2.5cm (1in) layer of damp compost. Fill around them with more compost and firm; store the box in a cool, light place.*

of about 7°C (45°F). They will soon produce young shoots.

Taking cuttings

Take cuttings four to six weeks after new shoots have appeared and discard the parent plant. Select close-jointed shoots near the base of the stem, with soft but firm growth, and remove them with a knife or snap them off. Trim them to about 4cm (1½in), cutting just under a leaf node. Dip the base of each cutting in a rooting hormone, insert them in standard cutting compost, and then place the pots in a propagator, preferably with gentle bottom heat at 10°C (50°F). Rooting occurs in two to three weeks (see also *How to Propagate by Basal Stem Cuttings*, p.202).

Aftercare

Once rooted, move the cuttings from the propagator to slightly cooler conditions for about a week, then plant them in batches of six to eight to a pot or box, filled with moist loam-based or loamless potting compost. If there are just a few cuttings, pot them up individually. Keep them slightly dry for a few weeks, in frost-free conditions. Check regularly for pests and diseases, and treat them accordingly (see PLANT PROBLEMS, pp.639–668). After a month or so, transfer the plants to a cold frame and gradually harden them off; protect them from severe frost and provide ample ventilation.

Late-flowering chrysanthemums

Indoor or "late" chrysanthemums are grown in containers and are brought into a house or a temperate or warm

greenhouse to flower. Their cultivation requirements are similar to early-flowering chrysanthemums.

Planting

Plants may be potted up using moist loam-based or loamless potting compost in late spring and staked as for early-flowering cultivars. The stakes may be tied between support wires to hold them upright in windy weather. Stand the pots outdoors throughout the summer, in a sunny, sheltered position. Water when necessary, never allowing the compost to dry out completely.

LATE-FLOWERING SPRAY
Allow indoor spray chrysanthemums (here C. 'Pin Nu Rosemary') grown without daylength regulation to bear 6–7 flowerheads per stem.

Stopping and disbudding

Stop the plants in midsummer; they will produce their flower buds 10–12 weeks later. Disbud and remove sideshoots in the same way as for early-flowering chrysanthemums.

Routine care

In early autumn, move the pots to a cool greenhouse with the temperature kept to about 10°C (50°F). The greenhouse should be shaded, if necessary, so that the temperature is kept low. Continue feeding with a balanced liquid fertilizer until the flower colour just begins to show. Bring them into a warmer place to flower.

Overwintering

Cut back the plants after flowering to about 22cm (9in). It is not necessary to lift the stools; keep them in their pots in a cool greenhouse or frame at about 5°C (41°F) and in good light for about a month. Then bring them into growth at about 7°C (45°F) to produce shoots for cuttings in late winter, about four to six weeks later.

Taking cuttings

Take cuttings and root them in a propagator, as for early-flowering chrysanthemums. Cuttings of late-flowering spray cultivars do not need to be rooted until early or midsummer.

Once rooted, treat the cuttings as for early-flowering cultivars. In late spring, when the plants' roots have filled their pots, pot them on into their final containers. Use 24cm (9in) or 25cm (10in) pots, depending on root vigour. Use a moist loam-based potting compost, with additional slow-release fertilizer. Stake tall cultivars, as well as those with large flowerheads, before final potting.

Early charms

Sometimes known as garden 'mums or cushion 'mums, these dwarf chrysanthemums have become very popular. They are planted direct in garden beds or borders or in pots or tubs on the patio.

Their cultivation requirements are similar to early-flowering chrysanthemums when grown outside and to late-flowering ones when container-grown, except that charms should not be disbudded.

Plant out in late spring, setting the plants 30–38cm (12–15in) apart in a bed, or insert three plants in a 30cm (12in) pot. Stop the growing points

CHARM CHRYSANTHEMUMS
These are dwarf plants, bearing a mass of single flowers, each with a diameter of about 2.5cm (1in). The star-shaped blooms (here of C. 'Morning Star') densely cover each plant to form a rounded head.

immediately, and again when lateral shoots reach 5cm (2in) long. Continue to stop container-grown early charms, to encourage a large, well-shaped plant. Early charms are self-supporting, so do not need to be staked. Apply a balanced fertilizer regularly (see p.191).

Early charms can be grown in open ground year-round in mild climates that are frost-free. Elsewhere, in mid-autumn dig up the plants, place them in a loam-based potting compost in a box, and store dry in a frost-free greenhouse overwinter. At the same time bring container-grown plants into the greenhouse for winter.

Taking cuttings

In late winter or early spring take cuttings for container-grown early charms and root them in a propagator. Take cuttings in mid-spring for charms to be planted in a garden bed. Once rooted, harden off the cuttings and pot on or plant out.

Growing blooms for exhibition

Blooms grown outdoors for exhibition require protection from the elements. White and yellow blooms may be covered satisfactorily with special greaseproof bags of various sizes. Spray or dust the buds to remove any pests before covering them. The developed blooms are heavy, and care must be taken to support the stems so that the heads do not snap off in high winds.

Blooms of other colours, and any particularly large reflexes, sprays, and plants grown in rows, are better protected by a specially prepared structure, like a small greenhouse with unglazed sides.

It is possible to advance or retard the flowering time of indoor cultivars by regulating the periods of light and darkness. Bud-forming (which usually requires 10 hours of continuous darkness) can be advanced by excluding daylight or, conversely, delayed by extending the period of daylight with artificial light.

Late-flowering spray chrysanthemums intended for exhibition may be subjected to extended hours of darkness for a period of three weeks to encourage bud initiation on the required date. This is achieved by completely blacking out the greenhouse for at least 14 hours a night, or, if only a small number of plants is being grown, by placing black plastic bags over individual plants.

Preparing for exhibition

Blooms for exhibition are cut when fully or virtually fully open; the stems are then plunged immediately in deep water for 24 hours.

Exhibition classes will usually be for sprays with one, three, or five blooms in a vase. A single bloom is staged in the centre and at the top of the vase and held upright with paper. A group of three is staged with either two blooms at the back and the third slightly lower in front, or one at the back and two slightly lower in front. Five blooms are always staged with three flowerheads in an arc at the back and two slightly lower in front.

All the blooms in a vase should match as closely as possible in size and form. If there is any variation between the blooms, stage those with the best outline at the back, and place those with the best developed centres at the front.

There is also a class for charms (dwarf plants that produce hundreds of star-shaped flowers), which are shown in a 30cm (12in) pot, or larger.

PROTECTING BLOOMS FOR EXHIBITION

1 *When the blooms are just beginning to open, enclose each one in a 15 x 15cm (6 x 6in) greaseproof bag fastened with a twist-tie. Leave this on for 7–10 days.*

2 *The bud should then be at the "paintbrush" stage with the colour just showing. Remove the bag and replace it with a 30 x 33cm (12 x 13in) bag.*

PROTECTING A ROW OF BLOOMS

Construct a temporary "greenhouse" of wooden supports with a clear plastic roof (do not enclose the sides). The structure should be 2.2m (7ft) at the ridge and 2m (6ft) at the eaves. The slope allows rain to run off, so it is important to keep the soil around the plants moist.

Routine care

ALTHOUGH most perennials will thrive with only little maintenance, certain routine tasks help to keep them looking attractive and healthy. Occasional watering and feeding is necessary and the surrounding ground should be kept clear of weeds. In addition to this, many perennials produce further growth and flowers if dead-headed or cut back, while dividing the plants renews vigour. Tall, fragile perennials, or those with top-heavy flowerheads, may also require staking, particularly in exposed gardens.

Watering

The amount of water that plants require depends on the site, climate, and the individual species; provided that they are grown in appropriate conditions, established perennials often need little or no additional irrigation. If there are prolonged dry spells during the growing season, give extra water to the plants. If they wilt or die back from lack of water they will normally recover fully after heavy rainfall or will become dormant until the following season. The most efficient way to provide extra water is using drip or trickle irrigation, rather than an overhead spray (see also TOOLS AND EQUIPMENT, "Watering aids", pp.560–561).

Young plants need to have sufficient water to become established but they should not be watered once they are growing satisfactorily, except in very dry weather. Irrigation, if necessary, is best applied in the evening, when water evaporates less quickly from the soil surface.

Fertilizing

In soil that has been thoroughly prepared before planting, few perennials require more than an annual top-dressing of bone meal or a balanced slow-release fertilizer, preferably applied in early spring after rain.

If conditions are dry, first water the soil thoroughly, then work the fertilizer into the soil surface with a hand fork. Do not let the fertilizer touch the leaves since it may scorch them. Plants that are grown primarily for their ornamental foliage, for example *Rheum* and hostas, benefit from an occasional liquid feed during the growing season.

If a plant is not growing well, in spite of being in a suitable site, look carefully to see if it has been attacked by pests or disease and treat accordingly. Foliage that is yellowing prematurely may indicate problems with soil drainage or a lack of certain nutrients. If appropriate drainage or feeding does not seem to improve the condition of the plant, sending a soil sample for analysis by a laboratory will determine which elements are lacking (see also "Soil nutrients and fertilizers", pp.624–625).

Mulching

An annual mulch of organic matter, such as proprietary mulch or bark chippings, helps to suppress weed growth, reduce soil moisture loss, and improve the structure of the soil. Apply mulch when the ground is moist during spring or autumn by spreading a 5–10cm (2–4in) deep layer around the crowns of the plants (see also SOILS AND FERTILIZERS, "Mulches", p.626).

Weeding

Keep beds and borders free from weeds at all times, if practical, as they compete with the ornamental plants for moisture and nutrients in the soil. Underplanting with suitable ground-cover plants (see p.180) or mulching in spring helps to reduce problems with annual weeds. Any weed seedlings that do appear from wind-blown seed or seeds that have been dormant in the soil should be removed by hand before they become established.

If perennial weeds appear in the ground after initial cultivation, carefully dig them out with a hand fork. It is usually impractical to apply systemic weedkillers at this time because, to be effective, they must be applied when the weeds are in full growth, usually as they reach the flowering stage. At this point it is virtually impossible to avoid spraying the ornamental plants accidentally at the same time.

If the roots of a perennial weed have grown into those of a border plant, dig up the plant in early spring, wash the roots, and carefully pull out the weed. Then replant the border plant, ensuring that no part of the weed is left in the original site. Do not hoe around perennials since this may cause damage to any surface roots and emerging shoots. For further information on controlling weed growth, see PLANT PROBLEMS, "Weeds", pp.669–673.

APPLYING MULCH

Clear any weeds, and apply a 5–10cm (2–4in) layer of mulch to moist soil; do not damage the young shoots of the plant (here a peony).

Improving flowering

Certain perennial plants may be cut back during growth in one of two ways to improve the number or size of their flowers or to extend the flowering season.

Thinning

Although most herbaceous plants produce numerous vigorous shoots in spring, some of these may be spindly and thin; if these weak shoots are removed at an early stage of growth, the plant then goes on to develop fewer, sturdier shoots that usually produce larger flowers. When the plant is about a quarter to a third of its eventual height, pinch out or cut back the weakest shoots. This thinning technique may be used successfully with, for example, delphiniums, phlox, and Michaelmas daisies (*Aster*).

Stopping

It is possible to increase the number of flowers on perennial plants that readily produce sideshoots, such as *Helenium* and *Rudbeckia* species and cultivars, by removing or "stopping" the growing tip of each stem; this also produces sturdier growth and stops the plant becoming too tall and straggly. Stopping should generally be carried out when the plant is about one third of its ultimate height, and in this case 2.5–5cm (1–2in) of each shoot is pinched off with the fingers or cut back with secateurs just above a node. This encourages the buds in the uppermost leaf axils of the shoot to develop.

Individual plants in a group may be stopped a few days apart; this has the added effect of producing a longer flowering season overall. For further information on how to produce fewer but larger blooms, see DAHLIAS, "Stopping and disbudding", p.235.

Dead-heading

Unless decorative seedheads are required or the seed is to be collected to raise further plants, remove the

HOW TO THIN AND STOP PERENNIALS

THINNING
Thin young shoots (here of a phlox) when no more than a third of their final height. Remove about 1 shoot in 3 by cutting or pinching out weaker shoots at the base.

STOPPING
When the shoots (here of an Aster) are one third of their final height, "stop" them by pinching out the top 2.5–5cm (1–2in) to promote bushier growth.

CUTTING BACK TO EXTEND FLOWERING

DELPHINIUM
After flowering, when new basal shoots are visible, cut back old stems to ground level.

PHLOX
Cut back the central part of the flowerhead as the blooms fade to encourage the sideshoots to flower.

flowers as they begin to fade. Further flowering sideshoots may then develop on the plant and extend the flowering season.

With a number of perennials, for example delphiniums and lupins (*Lupinus*), cutting back the old stems to their base when the first flowers have faded may encourage new shoots to develop that will produce a second display of flowers later in the season.

Cutting back

Woody-based perennials, for example penstemons, should be pruned back annually in early spring. Cut the overwintering stems with secateurs close to the base, where young shoots will develop; or shorten the stems by about half to three quarters, removing twiggy, weak, or unproductive growth. This will encourage vigorous shoots to develop, which will produce flowers throughout summer and autumn.

Autumn clearance
Once perennial plants have finished flowering in autumn, cut down the shoots to the base and remove all dead or faded stems and leaves, as well as any weed growth, so that the beds or borders are tidy. The top-growth of plants that are not fully hardy, however, may be left over winter to provide the crown with some protection from frost; the dead top-growth is then removed in spring. Some perennial plants, such as *Sedum spectabile* and many grasses, have foliage or flowerheads that

remain attractive even when brown, and these may be left on the plant to provide winter decoration if required until early spring.

Transplanting established perennials

Most perennials may be transplanted easily if you wish to change the planting scheme. If possible, move them when dormant in late autumn, or when just coming into growth in spring. Plants that dislike cold, wet conditions, such as *Kniphofia*, and those that are not fully hardy should be moved in spring once the soil has warmed to encourage rapid growth. A few long-lived plants, notably

CUTTING DOWN IN THE AUTUMN

In autumn or early winter, cut dead stems (here of Rudbeckia) *to ground level, or to just above new growth.*

Staking

Tall and fragile perennials may need stakes to support them, particularly in windy situations. Insert stakes early in the season, since staking is harder to do and more likely to damage the plant when growth is more developed. Push the stakes deep into the ground so that they can be raised in stages as the plant grows.

For delphiniums and other tall, single-stemmed perennials, use sturdy canes that are two-thirds of the stem's eventual height: push a cane firmly into the ground near the base of each shoot, taking care not to damage the roots. Secure the stem to the cane with figure-of-eight twine ties as it grows.

To support plants with many stems, it may be easier to use a number of canes placed at intervals in a circle around the plant.

Loop twine around the canes at about one-third and two-thirds of the plant's height. Clump-forming plants, such as peonies (*Paeonia*), may also be supported with proprietary devices such as ring stakes and link stakes, or similar home-made supports constructed from large-gauge wire mesh fixed to stakes. Stems grow through the support and eventually hide it.

There are two fairly unobtrusive methods of staking. Push several twiggy hazel stems, or peasticks, into the soil next to the young shoots and bend them inwards at right-angles to form an effective "cage" that is soon covered by the plant as it grows. Alternatively, insert one stout stake in the centre of a small group of plants or stems and radiate ties out to each stem.

RING STAKE
Stake low, clump-forming plants (here peony) early in the season. Raise the stake as the plant grows.

LINK STAKES
For taller plants such as this Aster, *push link stakes deep into the soil, then raise them as the plant grows.*

SINGLE CANE
Stake single-stemmed plants (here delphinium) *when 20–25cm (8–10in) high. Tie in the stem loosely.*

RING OF CANES
Encircle weak-stemmed plants (here Centaurea) *with twine, looped around split canes to secure it.*

peonies (*Paeonia*) and hellebores (*Helleborus*), resent disturbance and take two or more years to establish after transplanting. They should be lifted only if it is necessary to propagate them.

Prepare the new site as for planting, and dig a hole of suitable size. Lift the plant, keeping as much soil around the root ball as possible. It is best to divide the plant at this stage (see "Lifting and dividing", below). Remove any weeds from the clump by hand, then replant the divisions as for container-grown perennials (p.184), firming in and watering well.

Moving plants during the growing season

Occasionally, it may be necessary to move a plant while in full growth; mature plants may not transplant successfully, however, and should be treated carefully if transplanting is essential at this time. To minimize the stress caused to the plant, soak it in a bucket of water for several hours after lifting it. Then cut back the top-growth to within 8–12cm (3–5in) of the base and pot up the plant into a good potting compost. Keep the plant in a cool, shaded position, spraying daily but lightly until there are signs of healthy, fresh growth, then replant it in its new, prepared position.

Storing plants

Perennials may be lifted and stored over winter or if replanting is to be delayed – if transplanting them to a new garden when moving house, for example. The plants should be lifted when dormant and carefully packed in boxes or crates of moist compost or bark so that they do not dry out. Store in a cool, frost-free place.

Lifting and dividing

Where practical, perennials in a bed or border should be lifted, divided, and replanted every three to five years. Fast-growing, vigorous species, particularly those that have a mat-forming habit, such as *Ajuga* and *Stachys*, may need to be divided every other year. Plants that have become woody, with signs of dieback at the centre, or that look congested and flower less freely than in previous years, are in need of being divided.

Lifting plants makes it possible to clear the site of any weeds, and dig over and incorporate well-rotted organic matter or fertilizer as required. Dividing a plant rejuvenates it, keeps it healthy, and checks over-vigorous growth.

In late autumn or early spring, lift the plant, taking care not to damage its roots, and divide it into several portions by gently pulling them away from the main plant. Discard the old, woody centre; each division should contain a number of healthy, young shoots and its own root system (see also "Dividing perennials", p.200). Then dig over and fertilize the original site as necessary and replant the divisions, leaving enough space between each for the plants to develop. Alternatively, replant the divisions in prepared ground in a new position as required.

Pests and diseases

Perennial plants, if grown in fertile soil, are not usually seriously troubled by fungal diseases, insects, or other pests. Damage by slugs and snails (p.644), attack by vine weevil

PREPARING PLANTS FOR TEMPORARY STORAGE

Lift the plants in winter when they are dormant and place them in a box half-filled with moist bark or compost. Cover the roots with more bark or compost to keep them from drying out.

(p.645), aphids (p.646), and thrips (p.647) and, with certain plants (such as cultivars of *Aster novi-belgii*), infestations of powdery and downy mildew (p.646) do occur but seldom give cause for concern. In the growing season, check the plants regularly for any signs of attack, and treat them with an appropriate fungicide as necessary.

Maintaining perennials in containers

Perennials planted in containers require more care than those in open ground as they have limited reserves of food and water. Ensure that the compost does not dry out during the growing season: daily watering may be necessary in hot, dry weather. Plant roots should always remain moist but not wet. Water-retaining granules can be added to compost (see CONTAINER GARDENING, p.323), to help conserve soil moisture for longer.

Mulching helps to reduce soil water evaporation as well as suppressing weeds; if using an organic mulch, replace it periodically.

Every year or two in spring or autumn, divide the plants and replant the most vigorous portions using fresh compost, otherwise they soon exhaust the available nutrients and become too large for the container. If using the same container, wash the inside well before replanting, or pot up into a larger container (see "Repotting woody plants", p.334). Cut back the roots of shrubby perennials by about a quarter before repotting.

In cold areas, bring in half-hardy and tender plants in the autumn, and protect them until all danger of frost has passed (see FROST AND WIND PROTECTION, pp.612–613).

1 *In early spring or autumn, rejuvenate perennials in containers by thinning out plants and renewing the compost.*

2 *Lift out the plants, separating them carefully, and shake the old compost from their roots. Discard half of the old compost.*

3 *Refill with fresh compost, mixed with slow-release fertilizer, to within 10cm (4in) of the rim. Divide overgrown plants.*

4 *Plant up the container, fill in with more fresh compost to which slow-release fertilizer has been added, and firm in well.*

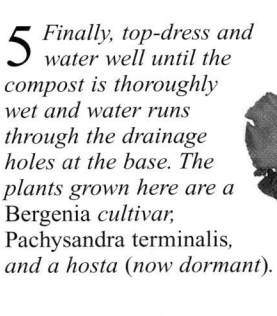

5 *Finally, top-dress and water well until the compost is thoroughly wet and water runs through the drainage holes at the base. The plants grown here are a* Bergenia *cultivar,* Pachysandra terminalis, *and a hosta (now dormant).*

Ferns

AMONG the most popular of the foliage plants, ferns add texture and atmosphere to the house or garden, where they are particularly effective in settings by streams or in damp, shady corners.

Cultivation

Hardy ferns are suitable for growing in the open garden, whereas tender tropical ferns are best cultivated indoors in a greenhouse or conservatory, or as house plants.

Hardy ferns

Most hardy ferns are easily grown and are suitable for shaded, moist conditions. Being very tough, they require the minimum of cultivation and upkeep once they have become established. With the exception of *Thelypteris* and all the *Blechnum* and *Cryptogramma* species, which require acid soil, ferns prefer neutral to alkaline conditions. Well-dug garden soil, with added humus, will suit most species.

Planting may be carried out at any time if container-grown plants are used. In dry weather water them regularly until established. Always plant in full or dappled shade; some genera, such as *Dryopteris*, will tolerate dry conditions if they are well shaded, but almost all require damp conditions to thrive.

Many ferns, such as *Athyrium*, *Cryptogramma*, and *Osmunda*, die down at the first touch of frost, but some of the *Dryopteris* retain their fronds well into winter. Leaving the old fronds on the plant until early spring protects the crowns, but these should be removed as the young ones start to uncurl. All species and cultivars of *Asplenium*, *Cyrtomium*, *Polystichum*, and *Polypodium* make good plants for the cold greenhouse, flourishing in the coldest weather under glass without the need for any artificial heat.

Tender tropical ferns

Ferns that will not withstand frost make excellent greenhouse or conservatory foliage plants, grown also in pots or hanging baskets. Some also make good house plants. Most require a winter minimum temperature of 10–15°C (50–59°F) but do not like hot, dry conditions and should be shaded from direct sunlight; a north-facing position on a bed of gravel that can be damped down in hot weather is ideal.

Tender ferns are usually sold in very small pots and should then be potted up into 13cm (5in) or 15cm (6in) pots using a soil-less potting compost. For this, use 3 parts peat-substitute- or peat-based potting mixture to 2 parts coarse sand or medium-grade perlite. Add a cupful of charcoal granules to every litre (1¾ pints) of mixture and, following the pack instructions, a balanced granular or powdered fertilizer.

The root ball should not dry out completely; keep the plant in its pot inside a watertight outer container with about 2.5cm (1in) of sand or gravel permanently kept damp at its base. Ferns, particularly *Adiantum* species, do not like to be sprayed or overwatered, and *Nephrolepis*, which are probably the easiest to keep as house plants, should be nearly dry before watering. Feed the ferns occasionally with a house plant liquid fertilizer.

Propagation

Ferns are mainly raised from spores, but may be propagated by division or, in some species, by bulbils.

WATER SETTING
Matteuccia *thrives in damp conditions by a stream and provides a striking contrast of form and texture with the* Rodgersia *in the foreground.*

ROCK CREVICE
The lance-shaped fronds of the semi-evergreen Ceterach officinarum *contrast well with the rock behind that provides shade and shelter.*

PROPAGATION BY BULBILS

1 *Select a frond that is drooping under the weight of bulbils. The bulbils may have tiny green fronds emerging from them. Cut off the parent frond close to the base. The plant shown here is* Asplenium bulbiferum.

2 *Peg down the frond onto prepared compost. Make sure the frond's ribs are flat.*

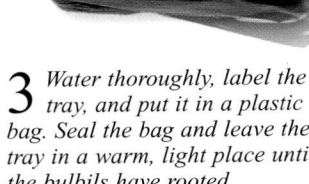

3 *Water thoroughly, label the tray, and put it in a plastic bag. Seal the bag and leave the tray in a warm, light place until the bulbils have rooted.*

4 *Remove the wire pegs and lift each rooted bulbil with a widger or knife; if necessary, cut it away from the parent frond.*

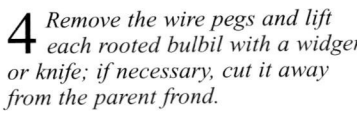

5 *Put each rooted bulbil into a 7cm (3in) pot of moist, soil-less compost. Keep moist in a warm, light place until the plants are large enough to replant.*

Bulbils

Asplenium bulbiferum and some of the hardy *Polystichum* species produce bulbils or small plantlets along the fronds. These may be used for propagation by pegging down that part of the frond with bulbils onto a tray of seed or cutting compost. The bulbils soon produce rooted plantlets which can then be separated and potted up. During the dormant season, it may take up to six months before the new plants are ready for planting out or potting on.

Spores

Ferns produce neither flowers nor seeds, and have a unique way of reproducing. Fronds carry on their undersurfaces very small capsules (sporangia), which release large numbers of powdery spores, which, when sown on damp compost, produce small growths (prothalli). Each prothallus carries both the male and female organs: the male organ (antheridium) produces spermatozoids which swim across the surface moisture of the prothallus to fertilize the "egg cell" lying within the female organ (archegonium). After fertilization, a zygote is formed which eventually develops into a tiny new fern. In this way the normal cycle of growth is continued.

Growing ferns from spores may take 18 to 24 months from sowing the spores to planting out the mature ferns. Collect the spores by removing from the parent plant fronds that are almost ready to shed their spores. Ripe sporangia are plump and vary in colour between species; many are dark brown, some blue-grey, others orange. Immature sporangia are flat and green or pale yellow. If the sporangia are dark brown and rough,

they will probably already have shed their spores. Lay the fronds on a sheet of clean paper and leave them in a warm room. In a day or so the spores will be shed onto the paper, looking like brown dust. Transfer them to a labelled seed envelope.

Fill a 7cm (3in) pot with standard seed compost; firm and smooth the surface. Sterilize the compost by carefully pouring boiling water through a piece of paper towel laid on the surface until water comes through the drainage holes. When the compost has cooled, remove the paper towel and sow spores very thinly over the surface. Cover the pot, or put it in a propagator, and leave it in a warm, light place out of direct sunlight. To keep the surface constantly moist, mist-spray it regularly with previously boiled, lukewarm water. Remove the cover when the top of the pot is covered with a green, velvet-like "moss"; if the compost seems dry, moisten it by standing the pot in a saucer of water for a short time.

Depending on the species, it takes from six to twelve weeks for the young prothalli to cover the compost surface. Prick them out by lifting small pieces of the "moss". Space them evenly, green side up, on the surface of other pots of sterilized seed compost, press them down, and spray with lukewarm water that has been boiled. Cover the pots with clingfilm or return them to the propagator. As the prothalli develop, spray them daily with lukewarm water until tiny plantlets appear. When they are large enough to handle, transplant them separately into pots of soil-less compost and grow them on, potting up as necessary, until they are large enough to plant out.

FORMAL PLANTINGS
The clean, horizontal line of the golden box (foreground) provides a perfect foundation for the striking, shuttlecock shapes of Matteuccia struthiopteris.

PROPAGATION BY SPORES

1 *Examine the undersides of the fronds to find one with sporangia that are ready to release their spores. Cut off the selected frond with a clean, sharp knife and place it carefully on clean, white paper to collect the spores. The plant shown here is* Adiantum raddianum *'Fritz Lüthi'.*

NOT READY   **READY**   **TOO LATE**

2 *Sow a few of the collected spores onto a pot of prepared sterile compost by tapping them from a piece of folded paper. Cover with some clingfilm or place the pot in a propagator.*

3 *Mist-spray twice a week until the surface is covered with a bumpy green "moss". Lift small clumps with a widger or a knife.*

4 *Divide the clumps into small pieces and gently firm them down onto sterile compost. Spray with water and then return them to the propagator.*

5 *When leaf-like plantlets appear, lift them carefully. Firm into packs or small pots of moist compost. Pot on when they have developed small fronds.*

Carnations and pinks

CARNATIONS and pinks belong to the genus *Dianthus*. They have attractive, usually fragrant flowers and grey-green, evergreen foliage. They are grouped according to their growth habit, flower characteristics, and hardiness: the upright, bushy border carnations and low, spreading pinks are both hardy and prolific.

Modern pinks are repeat-flowering and more vigorous than the old-fashioned cultivars. (For dwarf pinks see ROCK, SCREE, AND GRAVEL GARDENING, "Choosing plants", p.255.) Border carnations and pinks will provide an increasing supply of flowers over three or four years. Perpetual-flowering carnations and spray carnations grow much taller than border carnations, are not frost hardy, and can flower throughout the year. The old-fashioned Malmaison carnations have large, double, very fragrant blooms and should be grown in a conservatory or cool greenhouse. They flower sporadically throughout the year. Annual and biennial carnations and pinks (*Dianthus chinensis* and its hybrids as well as *D. barbatus*, sweet William) are treated as other hardy or half-hardy annuals (see ANNUALS AND BIENNIALS, "Sowing and planting", pp.261–221).

Carnation flowers may be in one colour ("self"), in two or more colours ("fancy"), or edged in a contrasting colour ("picotee"). Pinks flowers may be in one colour ("self"), with a central zone or eye of a second colour ("bicolour"), in two or more colours ("fancy"), or marked with a different colour just inside the edge of every petal, and usually with a central eye of the same colour ("laced"). All carnations and pinks provide long-lasting cut flowers.

General cultivation

Border carnations and pinks prefer a sunny, open site and a free-draining soil with a pH of 6.5–8. Perpetual-flowering carnations should be grown in a greenhouse, and will bloom in minimum temperatures of 10–12°C (50–54°F); at 5°C (41°F), only a few flowers are borne in winter.

In winter, clear away any dead leaves or other debris from around the plants, and firm any young plants growing outdoors that have been lifted by frost.

Border carnations
For best results, obtain these from specialist growers as rooted layers in autumn or pot-grown plants in spring.

To prepare the bed for planting, single dig in autumn, incorporating humus-forming material, and the following spring fork in a balanced fertilizer at the manufacturer's suggested rate. Water the young plants before planting them out 38–45cm (15–18in) apart in moist soil. Firm them, making sure that the lowest leaves are clear of the soil surface. Water only if dry conditions persist during the first month after planting; once established, the plants need watering only in very dry weather. Stake plants with twigs or canes.

Border carnations are bushy, so they do not need pinching out. If grown for garden display, it is not necessary to disbud one-year-old plants. To produce larger blooms on two-year-old plants, remove surplus buds. Hold the brittle main stem by the node at the base of the bud stalk, and sharply pull the stalk sideways to remove it, leaving two or three buds per stem. Leave the crown bud only on three- and four-year-old plants.

Pinks
Buy pinks as rooted cuttings in autumn or as pot-grown plants in spring. Plant them as for border carnations, but space them 22–30cm (9–12in) apart. When growing modern, repeat-flowering pinks from cuttings, pinch out the growing tips of the young plants to leave five or six pairs of leaves. Old-fashioned pinks do not usually need pinching out.

Perpetual-flowering carnations
These are best obtained as rooted cuttings or pot plants in spring and early summer. If growing rooted cuttings, break off their growing tips a week or two after potting them up to induce axillary growths (breaks); the plant is then described as "stopped and broken". Such plants with three to five sideshoots may be purchased in spring and are ready for potting on into 14cm (5½in) pots of standard potting compost. Water thoroughly, and support them with 1.2m (4ft) canes.

A month or so after repotting, stop a few sideshoots a second time, to extend the flowering season. (Do not "second-stop" spray carnations.) Disbud plants gradually over several days so that the calyx (the green petal casing) does not split. Leave only the crown bud and place a calyx band over the bud. With spray carnations, remove only the crown bud. Pick flower stems with seven nodes on their stems to induce strong sideshoots to develop lower down.

Water the plants only when the compost begins to dry out, preferably early in the day. Feed with a balanced liquid fertilizer, at first fortnightly, then weekly by midsummer for a good flowering display. In late autumn, change to a monthly, high-potash feed for sturdy foliage, and continue with it throughout winter.

During spring, repot one-year-old plants into 21cm (8in) pots. Then sprinkle one level teaspoonful of ground limestone on the surface to prevent the compost becoming sour through constant watering. A month later, resume feeding the plants as usual for the growing season. Discard plants at the end of the second year, replacing with young stock.

TYPES OF CARNATION AND PINK

PERPETUAL
D. 'Clara'
Repeat flowers usually unscented; half hardy.

BORDER CARNATION
D. 'Bookham Fancy'
Flowers often scented; frost hardy.

OLD-FASHIONED PINK
D. 'Musgrave's Pink'
Scented; frost hardy.

MODERN PINK
D. 'Doris'
Scented flowers in 2 or 3 flushes; frost hardy.

SPRAY
D. 'Cartouche'
Five or more flowers per stem; half hardy.

MALMAISON
D. 'Souvenir de la Malmaison' *Fragrant flowers; half hardy.*

STOPPING AND BREAKING

1 *When a rooted cutting of a perpetual-flowering carnation has 8 or 9 pairs of leaves, snap or pinch out the top 3 or 4 pairs. A month or so later again remove the tops of a few sideshoots, leaving 5 or 6 nodes on each sideshoot.*

DISBUDDING

To produce one large bloom on each flower stem of perpetual-flowering carnations, support the stem with one hand and pinch off each bud except the crown bud (left). For spray cultivars, pinch off the crown bud of each flower stem as the colour begins to show (right).

Pests and diseases

Carnations and pinks may be attacked by aphids (p.646), caterpillars (p.645), thrips (p.647), fungal leaf spots (p.648), and rusts (p.648). Greenhouse-grown carnations are most prone to infestation by red spider mite (p.646). In hot, dry summer conditions, frequent spraying with clear water acts as a deterrent. In winter, use insecticidal and fungicidal smokes and dusts, rather than sprays, to discourage fungal diseases.

Propagation

All carnations and pinks can be raised from cuttings, but for best results border carnations are layered. All *Dianthus* may be grown from seed (see ANNUALS AND BIENNIALS, "Sowing", p.216, and PERENNIALS, "Seed", p.198). Most perennial *Dianthus* do not breed true, and most do not flower in the first year.

Exhibition plants are normally discarded after one year. With successful plants, take cuttings or propagate by layering (as appropriate), before throwing them away.

Cuttings
Take cuttings from pinks in the summer. Choose healthy shoots with four or five pairs of leaves and break them off cleanly. Trim off the bottom pair of leaves just below a joint. Insert the cuttings about 4cm (1½in) apart into trays or pots of clean, sharp sand, or a mixture of standard cuttings compost and sand in equal parts; keep the leaves clear of the rooting medium. Cover them with a plastic bag or put in a propagator or mist unit and treat as for stem tip

PREPARING CUTTINGS

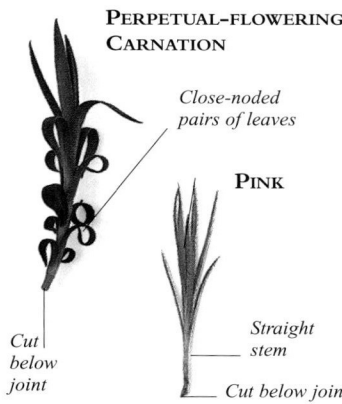

PERPETUAL-FLOWERING CARNATION

Close-noded pairs of leaves

PINK

Straight stem

Cut below joint

Cut below joint

Select non-flowering, closely jointed shoots. Remove the bottom pairs of leaves to create small stems and trim them. Any hook on a stem should be cut out, below a joint.

cuttings (see p.202). The cuttings should root after two to three weeks; pot them singly in 7cm (3in) pots of standard potting compost to grow on in a cold frame or greenhouse.

Perpetual-flowering and spray carnation cuttings may be taken at any season, if bottom heat of 20°C (68°F) is provided. Choose strong, axillary shoots that have developed after the flowers have been picked, and prepare them as for pinks. Dip the base of each cutting into water and then into hormone rooting powder, after which they should be treated in the same way as pinks.

Layering
Propagate border carnations after they have flowered by layering the one-year-old plants. Dig in equal parts of sharp sand and either damp cuttings compost, sieved garden compost, or peat substitute, to a depth of 7cm (3in) around the parent plant, and firm. Select a few well-spaced, non-flowering sideshoots and remove all but the top four or five pairs of leaves on each shoot. Just below the node with the lowest leaves, cut downwards through the next node, forming a tongue. Pin the shoot so the tongue is held in the prepared soil. When the layered shoots have rooted, detach them from the parent and plant them out to flower the following year.

To propagate exhibition plants in their pots, remove a ring of compost about 2.5cm (1in) wide and 7cm (3in) deep from the surface around the plant. Replace it with equal parts of standard cuttings compost and sharp sand, then layer the plants around the pot rim. In six weeks, when the layers have rooted, pot them singly into 7cm (3in) pots of standard potting compost.

When the roots reach the edge of the compost, pot them on into 15cm

LAYERING BORDER CARNATIONS

1 *Slit the stems of non-flowering sideshoots to encourage new roots to form; then pin the shoots into the soil surrounding the plants. Gently push the tongue of each shoot into the soil, and pin it down securely with a layering pin.*

2 *Ensure the layered shoot is held almost vertical, with the slit kept fully open in the soil. Stake the leafy tip, if necessary. Spray the rooting area lightly to keep it moist. After 5 or 6 weeks, separate and lift the rooted layers. Pot them on or plant them out.*

(6in) pots with the top of the root ball flush with the compost surface. Firm the compost to about 2.5cm (1in) below the pot rim. Alternatively, insert two plants in a 21cm (8in) pot. Stake them with 1m (3ft) canes and water thoroughly; then water only when the compost is drying out.

Exhibiting blooms

Carnations and pinks have been grown as exhibition plants for centuries. Pinks and perpetual-flowering carnations are grown as in "General cultivation" (see opposite), but border carnations are usually grown in a light, airy greenhouse to protect the blooms. In summer, the greenhouse must be well ventilated, lightly shaded, and mist-sprayed frequently.

Preparing for a show
When the buds on pinks or carnations begin to form, feed at ten-day intervals with a balanced, liquid fertilizer until they show colour, then give just one high-potash feed. As soon as their buds are large enough to handle, carnations should be disbudded; do this over several days. Slip calyx

bands over the remaining buds to prevent their calyces from splitting. Pinks, on the other hand, are never disbudded, although exhibitors may remove any spent blooms.

Select blooms for exhibition from well-watered plants in the early morning or late evening, if possible 48 hours before a show. Trim the stems with a sloping cut just above a node and place them up to their necks in water in a cool, dark place, free from draughts, until needed.

CALYX BANDS

Calyx band

Split calyx

When a bud shows colour, put a soft wire ring or a rubber band around it (left) to stop it splitting and forming an untidy bloom (right).

BLOOMS FOR EXHIBITION

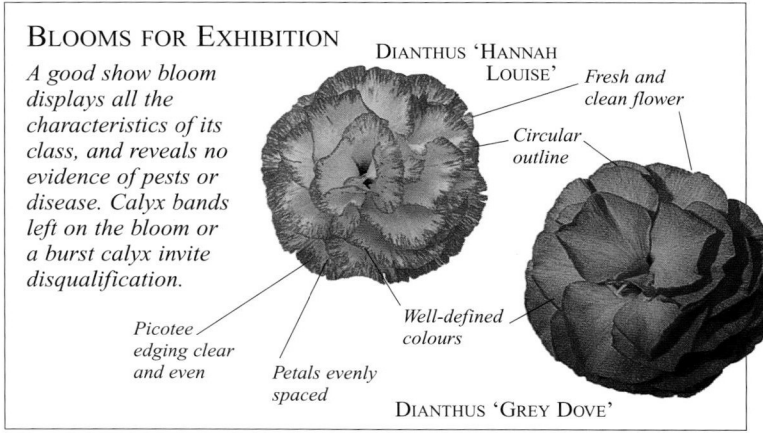

A good show bloom displays all the characteristics of its class, and reveals no evidence of pests or disease. Calyx bands left on the bloom or a burst calyx invite disqualification.

DIANTHUS 'HANNAH LOUISE'

Fresh and clean flower

Circular outline

Well-defined colours

Picotee edging clear and even

Petals evenly spaced

DIANTHUS 'GREY DOVE'

Propagation

THERE are several ways of propagating herbaceous perennials. Growing them from seed is ideal where a large number of new plants is required. Little experience or expertise is needed to raise the seedlings successfully, but this method is generally only suitable for propagating species rather than cultivars.

For many perennials, the simplest and commonest method of propagation is to lift them and divide clumps into separate plants, but others are better raised from seed or by vegetative means, such as cuttings or, more rarely, grafting. Vegetative methods should be used for propagating almost all named cultivars.

Seed

Raising plants from seed is a simple and inexpensive way to propagate many perennials but, apart from a few named cultivars (for example, *Lathyrus latifolius* 'Blushing Bride'), most cultivars do not come true from seed. Most species also show some variation in habit and flower colour so, if collecting seed yourself, always gather it from plants with the best flower and growth characteristics.

Seed of early-flowering perennials, which ripens on the plant in early to mid-summer, usually germinates quickly if sown as soon as it is ripe, producing young plants that may be overwintered successfully in open ground or in a cold frame. For most perennials, however, sow the seed immediately after it has been gathered in autumn so that it germinates early the following spring. If stored in cool, dry conditions, most seed also germinates well when sown in spring.

Seed of some herbaceous plants , however, such as peonies (*Paeonia*) and hellebores (*Helleborus*) usually remains dormant for a considerable period – peonies for up to 18 months – unless suitable conditions are provided or occur naturally to break dormancy and induce germination. Some require a period of exposure to cold or light, while others have hard seed coats that should be weakened by scarification or softened by soaking before sowing (see also PRINCIPLES OF PROPAGATION, "How to overcome dormancy", p.629).

Pre-germination treatment of seeds
Seeds that need to be subjected to a cold period to break dormancy may either be sown outside in autumn or winter (see also *Sowing Seed that Requires Chilling*, p.199) or chilled in a refrigerator for a few weeks before sowing in spring. This method of breaking dormancy is suitable for many genera, including *Aconitum, Adonis, Campanula*, and *Primula*. Seeds of a few plants, such as those of *Gentiana asclepiadea*, require a period of exposure to light for successful germination.

Scarifying and soaking
A number of perennials, particularly those of the pea family Leguminosae, have seeds with hard coats that impede rapid and even germination. Just before sowing the seeds, scarify them either by rubbing them with an emery board or sandpaper or by chipping them slightly with a sharp blade to allow water to be taken up and then germination to occur.

Alternatively, many seeds may have their hard coats softened by being soaked in hot, but not boiling, water for 12–24 hours; this allows the seed to absorb water and germination to take place. Soaking is suitable for a number of perennials, for example *Arum, Baptisia*, and *Euphorbia*. Once soaked, the seed should be sown immediately.

Double dormancy
Peony and *Trillium* seeds usually require two periods of cold to trigger germination of both roots and shoots. Root development from the germinating seed occurs during the first season but the shoots do not normally start to appear until the seeds have received a second period of cold, usually during the following winter. Sow the seeds in containers in autumn in the normal way.

Sowing seed in containers

Unless a very large number of plants is required, it is easiest to sow seed in containers. A plastic half-tray accommodates as many as two or three hundred seeds, while even a large square pot is adequate for sowing up to 50 seeds, depending on their size. Square pots fit closely in rows and provide a greater area of compost than round pots of the same width.

Fill the pot or tray with an appropriate seed compost. Loam-based composts are often preferred to peat-based ones if the young seedlings are to be kept in them for more than a short period after germination. Gently press the compost around the edges of the pot or tray, then roughly level the surface and firm it with a presser board or the base of another pot, so that the soil is about 1cm (½in) below the container rim.

Sowing
The seeds should always be sown thinly – about 0.5cm (¼in) apart; sowing too densely may result in thin, spindly plants that are prone to damping off (see p.664). Fine seeds, and those that require light to germinate, for example some gentians (*Gentiana*), may be left

Collecting seed

Collect the seed as it ripens: shake it from the pods or tie the seedheads into small bunches, enclosed in paper bags, and hang them upside-down so that the seeds fall into the bags. Make sure that the seed is completely dry before storing it in clean paper bags or envelopes labelled with the plant name and harvesting date.

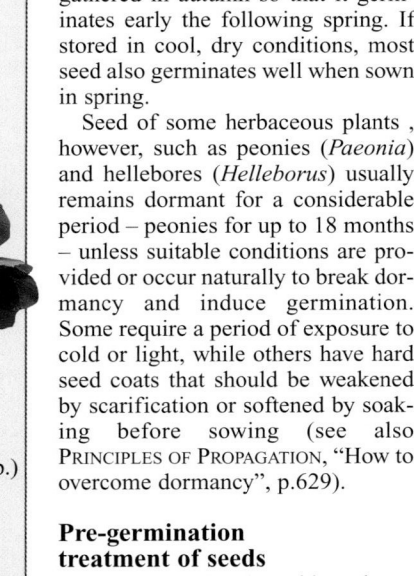

Collect ripened seed pods (here of Meconopsis) *when they have turned brown. Shake the seeds out of each pod onto a piece of paper and store in a cool, dry place until ready to sow.*

uncovered or sprinkled with a shallow layer of fine, sieved compost, perlite, or vermiculite and then gently firmed with a presser board. Larger seeds, such as those of peonies, should be covered with a 0.5cm (¼in) layer of sieved compost.

Aftercare

Label the containers with the seed name and sowing date, then water them using a can with a fine rose, taking care not to dislodge the seeds. Alternatively, if small seeds are being sown, stand the containers in a bowl or tray of water for a short time until they have absorbed enough to moisten the compost throughout; this method prevents the seeds from being washed away. Minimize evaporation by covering the containers with glass, a plastic sheet, or plastic film, and place them in a cold frame or greenhouse. In sunny weather, provide some shade with newspaper or shade netting. Once the seeds have started to germinate, remove the cover and reduce any shading.

Plunging the containers in an outdoor bed

If the containers are to be placed outside unprotected from the weather during autumn and winter to break seed dormancy, add a covering of grit over the sown seeds. This prevents them from being washed out of the containers by heavy rain and, to some extent, deters mosses and liverworts from growing on the compost surface. Cover the containers with fine-mesh chicken wire to protect the seed if rodents or birds are likely to be a problem.

Plunge the pots in an open sand bed as this provides stable, even conditions for germination. Once the seed has germinated and the seedlings are visible, place the containers in a cold frame and care for the seedlings as for those raised under cover.

Pricking out

Once the seedlings are large enough to handle, that is when the first or second pair of true leaves has formed, they may be pricked out. Either space them evenly in seed trays with about 30–40 in each tray or prick them out into individual containers. The latter is advisable for seedlings that do not tolerate much root disturbance. Alternatively, prick out the seedlings into modules (compartmentalized trays). In all cases, a good, loam-based potting compost should be used.

Water the seedlings thoroughly, label them, and then place them in a cold frame or cool greenhouse until they are established. They may then be potted on individually or planted out in their permanent site in open ground when they are large enough.

RAISING PLANTS FROM SEED

1 *Fill a 13cm (5in) pot with moist seed compost. Firm the compost to about 1cm (½in) below the rim of the container.*

2 *Using a clean, folded piece of paper, scatter the seeds (here* Chrysanthemum x superbum) *sparingly over the compost.*

3 *Cover the seeds with a shallow layer of fine, sieved compost. Label and then water without displacing the seeds.*

4 *Cover with a clear plastic sheet or clear film to retain moisture. Place the pot in a cold frame until the seedlings develop 2 pairs of leaves.*

5 *Prick out the seedlings into pots; degradable pots (inset) allow planting out direct. Handle the seedlings by the leaves since the stems are easily damaged.*

6 *When the seedlings have developed into small plants with a good root system, plant them out or pot them up, as appropriate.*

SOWING SEED THAT REQUIRES CHILLING

2 *Label the pots with the seed name and date of sowing, and water thoroughly. Then plunge the pots in an open sand bed outside to encourage the seeds to germinate.*

1 *In autumn, sow the seed thinly in pots of compost, then cover with a thin layer of fine compost and top-dress with fine grit.*

Sowing outside in open ground

If large numbers of plants are needed, it may be more convenient to sow seed outside. Prepare an area in fertile, well-drained soil by clearing any weeds and cultivating the soil to a fine tilth. Using a line or a straight-edged board as a guide, make a seed drill using a draw hoe, onion hoe, or the point of a large label.

The depth of the drill depends on the size of the seed to be sown: about 0.5cm (¼in) deep is adequate for small seeds, while large seeds require a drill at least 1cm (½in) deep. If the seedlings are to be transplanted when young, set the drills 10–15cm (4–6in) apart; if, however, they are to be grown on in rows, allow about 15–22cm (6–9in) between them. Sow small seeds thinly so that they are about 0.5cm (¼in) apart, large seeds such as peonies at intervals of 2.5cm (1in) or more.

After sowing, cover the drills by raking soil lightly over them, then label each drill with the name of the seed and the date. Water carefully, without washing away the soil. For further details, see ANNUALS AND BIENNIALS, *Sowing in Drills*, p.217.

Dividing perennials

This method is suitable for propagating many perennials that have a spreading rootstock and produce plenty of shoots from the base. As well as being a way of increasing stocks, in many cases division rejuvenates the plants and keeps them vigorous, because old or unproductive parts may be discarded (see also "Lifting and dividing", p.193).

Some perennial plants can be divided simply by pulling sections apart by hand, or by using two forks back-to-back; other plants that have fleshy roots are best split apart by using a spade or knife.

When to divide

Most plants should be divided when they are dormant, between late autumn and early spring, but not in extremely cold, wet, or dry weather since these conditions may make it difficult for the divided plants to re-establish successfully.

Fleshy-rooted perennials are usually best left until the end of their dormant season, in spring, before being divided. At this time their buds will be starting to shoot, which will indicate the most vigorous areas of growth, and therefore the best way of dividing up the plant.

Preparation

First lift the plant to be divided by loosening the surrounding soil, taking care not to damage the roots, then levering it up gently with a fork. Shake off as much loose soil from the roots as possible and remove any dead leaves and stems to make it easier to see the best points for division. This also enables you to see which are the healthy parts of the plant to be retained and which are the old, unproductive parts that can be discarded.

Wash most of the soil off the roots and crowns of fleshy-rooted plants, so that all the buds are clearly visible and therefore do not become damaged inadvertently when you are dividing the plant.

Fibrous-rooted plants

Insert two border or hand forks back-to-back near the centre of each plant so that the tines are close together and the handles apart; then push the handles gently backwards and forwards so that the prongs gradually tease the plant apart and separate the clumps into two smaller portions. Repeat this process with each portion to divide the plant into more sections, each with some new shoots.

Plants that tend to form woody clumps or that have thick, solid roots should be cut into portions with a spade or sharp knife; make sure that there are at least two growth buds or shoots on each piece. Discard the old, weak, and often woody growth from the centre of the plant; the sections containing vigorous, young shoots and healthy roots tend to grow at the perimeter of the plant.

Perennial plants that have loose, spreading crowns and numerous shoots, for example Michaelmas daisies (*Aster*), are easy to pull apart by hand or with two hand forks. Simply separate off single stems growing at the edges of the crown so that each has its own root system.

Fleshy-rooted plants

Plants that have bulky, almost solid, fleshy roots, such as *Rheum*, may need to be divided with a spade as it would be difficult to separate the crowns using back-to-back forks. After cleaning the plant so that the developing buds are clearly visible, slice through between them with a spade, taking care to leave two or more buds on each piece. Then trim each division neatly with a knife, discarding any old, woody material and any damaged or rotting roots.

Plants with numerous, intertwined crowns, such as *Arthropodium* and tufted ornamental grasses, may also be divided with two forks.

Replanting and aftercare

After dividing a plant, dust any cut surfaces with an appropriate fungicide (see PRINCIPLES OF PROPAGATION, "How roots form", p.632). Replant the divisions as soon as possible.

Dividing hostas

Large hostas with tough rootstocks should be divided using a spade. Include several buds on each division and trim any damaged parts with a knife. Hostas that have looser, fleshy rootstocks may be separated by hand or with back-to-back forks; each division should have at least one "eye" or shoot.

TOUGH, FIBROUS ROOTS
Divide the crown with a spade; each section should include several developing buds.

LOOSE, FLESHY ROOTS
Divide small plants and those with a loose rootstock by pulling the clump apart by hand.

HOW TO PROPAGATE PERENNIALS BY DIVISION

1 *Lift the plant to be divided, taking care to insert the fork far enough away from the plant so that the roots are not damaged. Shake off surplus soil. The plant shown here is a* Helianthus.

2 *Separate plants with a woody centre by chopping through the crown with a spade.*

3 *Divide the plant into smaller pieces by hand, retaining only healthy, vigorous sections, each with several new shoots.*

4 *Cut back the old top-growth and replant the divided sections to the same depth as before. Firm in and water thoroughly.*

ALTERNATIVE METHOD

Divide fibrous-rooted, herbaceous plants (here Hemerocallis) *using 2 forks back-to-back.*

It is important that they do not dry out, so if replanting is unavoidably delayed for a couple of hours, dip the plants briefly in water and keep them in a sealed plastic bag in a cool, shady place until you are ready to replant them.

Large divisions, if replanted immediately, may still provide a good show of flowers in the same season although the stems are often slightly shorter than those of more established plants. Very small divisions, however, are best grown on for a season in a nursery bed or in pots in order to become established. In general, the divisions should be replanted at the same depth as the original plant, but those that are prone to rotting at the base are best set slightly proud of the surrounding soil level to keep the crowns of the plants free of excess water (see also "Planting depths", p.184).

When replanting, ensure that the roots are well spread out in the planting hole and the plant firmed in. Water newly planted divisions thoroughly; take care not to expose the roots by washing away any soil.

Division of rhizomatous plants

Divide plants with thick rhizomes, such as *Bergenia* and rhizomatous irises, by splitting the clump into pieces by hand, then cutting the rhizomes into sections, each with one or more buds (see right). Bamboos have tough rootstocks that either form dense clumps with short rhizomes or have long, spreading rhizomes; divide the former with a spade or use two back-to-back forks; use secateurs to cut the latter into sections, each of which should have three nodes or joints (see also BAMBOOS, p.96).

1 *Lift the plant to be divided (here an iris), inserting the fork well away from the rhizomes to avoid damaging them.*

2 *Shake the clump to remove any loose soil. Using your hands or a hand fork, split the clump into manageable pieces.*

3 *Discard any old rhizomes, then detach the new, young rhizomes from the clump and neatly trim off their ends.*

4 *Dust the cut areas with fungicide. Trim long roots by one third. For irises, shorten the leaves to about 15cm (6in) long, to prevent wind rock.*

5 *Plant the rhizomes about 12cm (5in) apart. The rhizomes should be half buried, with their leaves and buds upright. Firm in well and water.*

Dividing peonies

Peonies should be divided with particular care as they dislike being transplanted and tend to re-establish slowly. For best results, lift and divide the plants towards the end of the dormant season in early spring, when the swelling, red growth buds are clearly visible. Cut the crown into sections, each with a few buds, taking care not to damage the thick, fleshy roots.

1 *Lift the plant in early spring, when healthy growth buds are visible on the crown. Cut it into sections, each one with several buds.*

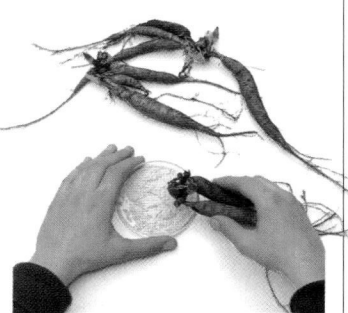

2 *Dust all the cut surfaces of the divided sections with fungicide to discourage infection and rot.*

3 *Plant out the divided sections approximately 20cm (8in) apart. The buds should just be visible at the surface. Firm the soil well.*

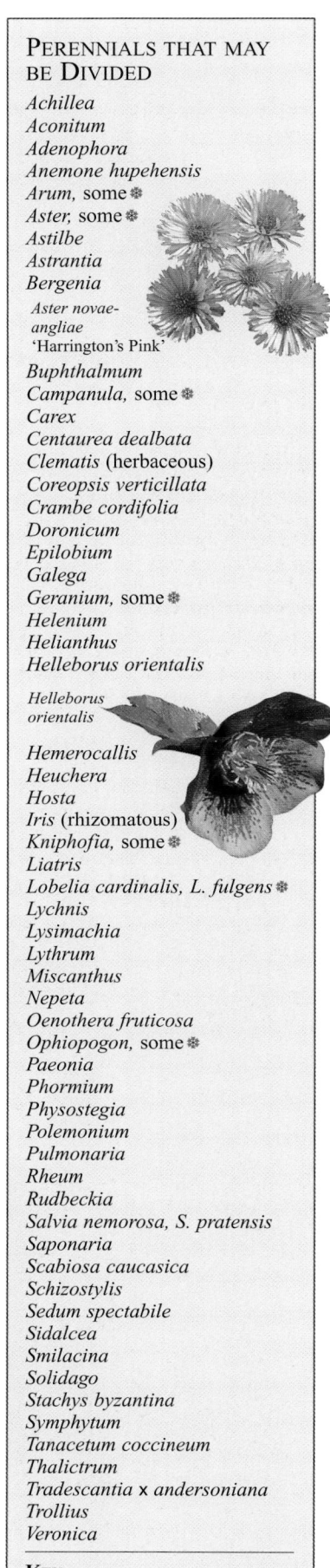

PERENNIALS THAT MAY BE DIVIDED

Achillea
Aconitum
Adenophora
Anemone hupehensis
Arum, some ❀
Aster, some ❀
Astilbe
Astrantia
Bergenia

Aster novae-angliae 'Harrington's Pink'

Buphthalmum
Campanula, some ❀
Carex
Centaurea dealbata
Clematis (herbaceous)
Coreopsis verticillata
Crambe cordifolia
Doronicum
Epilobium
Galega
Geranium, some ❀
Helenium
Helianthus
Helleborus orientalis

Helleborus orientalis

Hemerocallis
Heuchera
Hosta
Iris (rhizomatous)
Kniphofia, some ❀
Liatris
Lobelia cardinalis, *L. fulgens* ❀
Lychnis
Lysimachia
Lythrum
Miscanthus
Nepeta
Oenothera fruticosa
Ophiopogon, some ❀
Paeonia
Phormium
Physostegia
Polemonium
Pulmonaria
Rheum
Rudbeckia
Salvia nemorosa, *S. pratensis*
Saponaria
Scabiosa caucasica
Schizostylis
Sedum spectabile
Sidalcea
Smilacina
Solidago
Stachys byzantina
Symphytum
Tanacetum coccineum
Thalictrum
Tradescantia x *andersoniana*
Trollius
Veronica

KEY
❀ *Not hardy*

PROPAGATING PERENNIALS BY STEM TIP CUTTINGS

1 *Select short lengths of soft wood about 7–12cm (3–5in) long from the tips of strong, healthy shoots. The plant shown here is a* Penstemon *cultivar.*

2 *Trim the lower end of each cutting just below a node, with a straight cut, reducing the length to 5–7cm (2–3in). Remove the lower pairs of leaves.*

3 *Insert the cuttings around the edge of a 15cm (6in) pot of cuttings compost and water in. Cover with a plastic bag, held away from the cuttings by canes.*

4 *When the cuttings have rooted, gently lift them and pot them up individually into 10cm (4in) pots.*

PERENNIALS TO PROPAGATE BY STEM CUTTINGS

Tip
Arctotis ❄
Argyranthemum ❄
Calceolaria integrifolia ❄
Cuphea ❄
Dianthus, some ❄
Diascia
Erysimum
Felicia, some ❄
Lobelia cardinalis
Lotus berthelotii ❄
Oenothera macrocarpa
Osteospermum, some ❄
Parahebe
Penstemon, some ❄
Salvia, some ❄
Scrophularia auriculata
Sphaeralcea ❄
Tradescantia, some ❄
Trifolium pratense
Verbena ❄

Osteospermum 'Buttermilk'

Viola, some ❄
Zauschneria californicum subsp. *cana*

Basal
Anthemis tinctoria
Aster, some ❄
Chrysanthemum, some ❄
Delphinium, some ❄
Lupinus
Monarda
Phlox paniculata (variegated cvs only)
Physostegia
Sedum, some ❄

Anthemis tinctoria 'E.C. Buxton'

KEY
❄ *Not hardy*

Stem tip cuttings

This method of propagation is used most commonly for herbaceous perennials that are difficult to divide successfully and for cultivars that do not come true from seed. Cuttings may be taken at any time during the growing season provided that suitable shoots are available.

Select strong growing tips without flower buds, rejecting any that are thin, weak and leggy, or damaged. If there is likely to be any delay before inserting the cuttings, place them in a sealed plastic bag to protect them from dehydration.

Preparing and inserting the cuttings

Take cuttings with secateurs or a sharp knife, cutting across the stem immediately above a node. Remove the leaves from the lowest third of each cutting, then trim the cuttings to just below a node or to 5cm (2in) long. Dip each base into hormone rooting powder or gel. Then insert the cuttings into prepared pots or trays of an appropriate cuttings compost and firm in with your fingers. Leave sufficient space between the cuttings so that the leaves do not touch each other and air can circulate freely. This inhibits the spread of damping off diseases (see p.664).

Aftercare

Water the cuttings using a watering can with a fine rose and treat them with a fungicide to reduce the risk of infection and rot. It is important that the cuttings are maintained at a high humidity level otherwise they will wilt, so, if possible, keep them in a mist unit or propagator. Alternatively, cover the cuttings with a plastic tent or bag; this should be supported on canes or hooped wires to prevent the plastic from touching the leaves since any condensation forming on the foliage could encourage fungal infection. In hot weather, shade the cuttings with newspaper, proprietary shade netting, or other semi-translucent material to prevent the leaves from scorching or wilting. The shading should be removed as soon as possible to allow the cuttings plenty of light.

Inspect the plants daily, removing any fallen and dead leaves and any material that is infected. Water the compost as necessary to keep it moist but not wet. After about two to three weeks, the cuttings should produce roots and may be potted on into individual pots. Any healthy cuttings that have not developed roots by this stage should be re-inserted and cared for as before until they have rooted.

Basal stem cuttings

This type of cutting is suitable for a number of herbaceous plants that produce clusters of new shoots at the base in spring. Short, basal cuttings of plants with hollow or pithy stems,

HOW TO PROPAGATE BY BASAL STEM CUTTINGS

1 *Take cuttings when the shoots (here of* Chrysanthemum*) are 7–10cm (3–4in) high, slicing at the junction with the woody tissue.*

2 *Remove the basal leaves from each cutting. Make a straight cut just below a node, if visible, or so the cuttings are 5cm (2in) long.*

3 *Dip the cuttings in hormone rooting powder or gel, then insert into a prepared pot of moist cuttings compost. Place the pots in a propagator or plastic bag.*

4 *When the cuttings have rooted, separate them, retaining as much compost as possible around the roots. Pot up the cuttings individually.*

such as lupins (*Lupinus*) and delphiniums, as well as those that have soft tissues, may be rooted successfully from sturdy shoots that are taken from plants in mid-spring.

If required, the plants to be propagated may be lifted and grown in pots or trays in a warm greenhouse to encourage the production of basal shoots earlier than if the plants were growing in the open ground. The cuttings should then be rooted, and young plants established, earlier in the season. The plants from which cuttings have been taken may then be replanted in the garden.

Preparing and inserting the cuttings

Select strong, sturdy shoots whose first leaves have just unfolded and, using a sharp knife, remove them as close to the base as possible; include part of the woody, basal tissue in the cutting. Do not use any shoots that are hollow or damaged.

Trim off the lower leaves of the cuttings, dip them in hormone rooting powder, and insert them in cuttings compost, either individually or several to a pot, or in trays. Firm in the cuttings, water thoroughly, and place in a cold frame or propagator. Alternatively, cover each of the containers with a clear, plastic bag supported on wire hoops firmly inserted into the compost. Shade the cuttings from direct sunlight to prevent the leaves from scorching or wilting.

Aftercare

Check the cuttings every few days, removing any dead or decaying foliage as soon as possible to prevent the spread of rot. Ensure that the compost is moist, but not wet, at all times, and wipe away excess water and condensation from the glass or plastic covers. The cuttings should normally be well rooted within a month and they may then be potted on into individual pots filled with equal parts of loam, sand, and peat substitute or peat.

Root cuttings

This is a useful method of propagating perennials that have fairly thick, fleshy roots, such as *Verbascum* and *Papaver orientale* cultivars. It is also the only way of raising new, healthy plants from border phlox cultivars that are affected by eelworm. As the eelworms occur in the top-growth of affected phlox, but not in the roots, taking root cuttings makes it possible to produce healthy, eelworm-free plants. This method cannot be used for those phlox cultivars with variegated foliage, however, because the resulting plants produce only plain green leaves.

Take care to minimize damage to the parent plant when cutting its roots, and replant it straight after taking the cuttings. Root cuttings are most successful when they are taken during the plant's dormant period, usually in winter.

Preparation

Lift a strong, healthy plant and wash off the soil so that all the roots can be clearly seen. Select roots that are young, vigorous, and relatively thick, as these are more likely to provide successful new plants than those that are weak and thin or old, gnarled, and woody. Cut off the young roots close to the crown and replant the parent plant.

When propagating plants with thick roots, for example *Acanthus, Anchusa, Romneya*, and *Verbascum*, choose roots that are about the thickness of a pencil and cut them into sections 5–10cm (2–4in) long. With thin-rooted perennials, cut the roots into 7–13cm (3–5in) lengths so there is sufficient food-storage for the developing cuttings.

Cut each section so that the top end (that nearest the plant's stem) is cut straight across and the bottom end (nearest the root tip) is cut at an angle; this makes it easy to insert the cuttings the correct way up. Shoots will develop from the top end of the cutting and roots from the lower end. Trim off any fibrous roots before inserting the cuttings.

Inserting the cuttings

After preparing the cuttings, dust them with fungicide to protect against rot. Then insert them vertically, straight ends at the top, in prepared pots or trays of cuttings compost about one and a half times their depth; the tops of the cuttings should be level with the surface. Cover the pots with a thin layer of fine sand or grit, label, and place them in a propagator or cold frame. Do not water the cuttings until they begin to root. Once young shoots have developed, pot them up singly into an appropriate compost.

Plants with thinner roots, such as *Anemone hupehensis, A.* x *hybrida, Campanula*, phlox, and *Primula denticulata*, are often treated slightly differently as their roots may be too fine to insert vertically. Lay the root cuttings flat on the surface of pots or trays of firmed compost, then cover with more compost. Then treat as for standard root cuttings.

HOW TO PROPAGATE PERENNIALS BY ROOT CUTTINGS

1 *Lift the plant (here Acanthus) when dormant and wash the roots. Select roots of pencil thickness and cut them off with a knife, cutting close to the crown.*

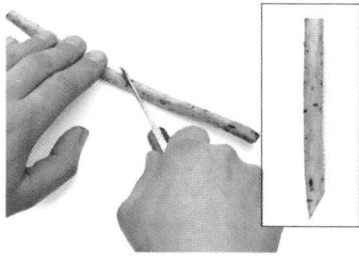

2 *Trim the roots and cut each into lengths of 5–10cm (2–4in). Make a straight cut at the upper end of each cutting and an angled cut at the lower end (see inset).*

3 *Insert the cuttings into holes made in pots of moist cuttings compost, and firm. The top end of each cutting should be flush with the compost surface.*

4 *Top-dress the pots of cuttings with coarse grit, label them, and place them in a cold frame until the cuttings root.*

5 *When the cuttings have developed young shoots, pot them up into individual pots filled with loam-based potting compost. Water and label the pots (see inset).*

ALTERNATIVE METHOD FOR THIN ROOTS

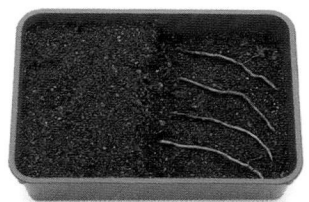

Place the trimmed cuttings horizontally on moist, firmed compost. Cover with compost and firm lightly.

PERENNIALS THAT MAY BE PROPAGATED BY ROOT CUTTINGS

Acanthus
Anchusa azurea
Anemone hupehensis,
   A. x *hybrida*
Arnebia
Campanula, some ✿
Catananche caerulea
Echinops

Catananche caerulea 'Major'

Erodium,
   some ✿
Eryngium,
   some ✿
Gaillardia
Geranium, some ✿
Gypsophila
Limonium latifolium
Mertensia
Morisia
Papaver orientale
Phlox paniculata, P. subulata
Primula denticulata
Pulsatilla vulgaris
Romneya
Trollius
Verbascum

KEY
✿ *Not hardy*

Pelargoniums

PELARGONIUMS are almost all tender, evergreen, perennial plants of South African origin. When introduced to Britain, they were given the common name geranium because of their botanical similarity to the hardy, herbaceous species of the genus *Geranium*, which was commonly cultivated in Europe at that time. This common name still remains in widespread use today, although almost all the plants usually referred to as geraniums belong to the genus *Pelargonium*.

Types of pelargonium

Pelargoniums may broadly be divided into five groups, according to the main characteristics of the plants. The groups are: zonal, dwarf and miniature zonal, regal, ivy-leaved, and scented-leaved.

Zonal

These pelargoniums have rounded leaves, usually marked with a distinct, dark zone, and single, semi-double, or double flowers. Some cultivars, however, do not have a zone and others have gold- or silver-variegated, or tricoloured leaves.

In temperate climates, they grow well in the open garden and are ideal for summer bedding as they bloom continuously from early summer until late autumn. They also thrive in windowboxes, hanging baskets, and containers. Zonals will happily adapt to the growing conditions in a greenhouse or conservatory.

TYPES OF PELARGONIUM

ZONAL
P. 'Dolly Varden'
Rounded leaves, with a darker zone, and single to double flowers.

REGAL
P. 'Purple Emperor'
Deeply serrated leaves and broadly trumpet-shaped flowers.

IVY-LEAVED
P. AMETHYST ('Fisdel')
Trailing plants with lobed leaves and single to double flowers.

SCENTED-LEAVED
P. 'Royal Oak'
Plants with small, often irregularly star-shaped flowers, grown for their fragrant leaves.

DWARF ZONAL
P. 'Timothy Clifford'
Bushy, free-flowering plants, similar to zonals, 13–20cm (5–8in) tall.

Dwarf and miniature zonal

Dwarf zonal pelargoniums should be 13–20cm (5–8in) tall, measured from soil level to the top of the plant, not including stem length and flower. They make excellent windowbox plants and pot plants for displaying in greenhouses and conservatories. Miniature zonals should be 7–13cm (3–5in) tall, as measured in the same way as dwarfs. These very floriferous plants bear double and single blooms in a wide range of colours, and have green to greenish-black leaves.

In recent years, F1 and F2 hybrid zonal pelargoniums have been developed. These are grown from seed and are used mainly for bedding. They are single-flowered and are available in the same range of colours as the cultivars that have been propagated vegetatively.

Regal

These pelargoniums are small shrubby plants with rounded, deeply serrated leaves and wide, trumpet-shaped flowers, often in exotic colours.

They may be grown in the open garden but, in temperate countries, they are much more extensively used as greenhouse, conservatory, and house plants, since the flowers are quickly spoilt by rain. In warmer climates, where they may be planted out permanently, they make splendid flowering shrubs, almost continuously in bloom year round.

Ivy-leaved

These trailing pelargoniums have rounded, lobed, ivy-like leaves, and flowers similar to those of zonals, available in a rich assortment of colours. They are used mainly in hanging baskets and other containers, where their flowers on trailing stems can be displayed to best advantage. They may also be planted so that they spill over the edge of a raised bed or a wall.

Scented-leaved

Scented-leaved pelargoniums have small, delicate flowers with five petals, and fragrant foliage for which they are chiefly grown. They make excellent house and greenhouse plants, and in temperate climates may be grown outside during the summer and autumn, in containers or as bedding plants.

General cultivation

Pelargoniums may be grown in all types of well-drained compost – loam-based, peat substitute, or peat – provided it is fresh and has been stored away from direct sunlight. Care needs to be taken with watering, however, as some composts drain more freely than others and pelargoniums must be kept on the dry side until well established. They then may need plenty of water during the growing season.

Give pelargoniums a weekly application of a high-potash feed such as tomato fertilizer. Start these feeds three weeks from potting up and use throughout the summer. This helps the plants to continue producing a mass of good-quality blooms without becoming too leafy.

Overwintering

Pelargoniums must be kept frost-free, except for *P. endlicherianum*, a hardy species from Turkey, which survives in a raised outdoor bed. In temperate climates, plants grown outside may be saved for the following season by moving them under cover before the first frost is expected. Remove the plants from the ground or container, and shake as much compost from the roots as possible. Then trim the stems by half and remove any remaining leaves. Using fresh potting compost, repot the prepared plants into a box or small pots, to make the best use of storage space. (Old or badly stored compost may be a reason for losses during winter.) Then water the compost well and leave the box or pots in an airy position

P. 'Dolly Varden'

P. 'Frank Headley'

P. 'Mrs Quilter'

P. 'Lady Plymouth'

PELARGONIUMS IN CONTAINERS
Planting a combination of zonal and scented-leaved types provides attractive foliage as well as a long-lasting display of decorative blooms.

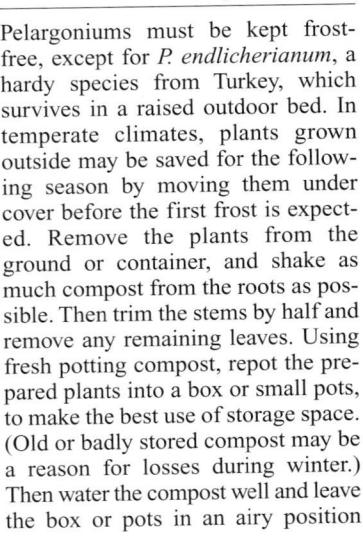

CONTRASTING HABITS
Use trailing, ivy-leaved pelargoniums to spill over the edge of a container. These will make an attractive contrast with upright forms in the centre.

for two to three days, while the cut stems seal and so prevent black-leg disease (see p.664). Then store in good light in a frost-free place.

Shoots will soon appear. Water only on a fine day, when the foliage will dry more quickly, and feed every six weeks during winter with a well-balanced fertilizer. During very cold weather, keep the plants dry and add extra protection, such as horticultural fleece, which lets through light.

By spring the shoots will be large enough to use as cuttings. Alternatively, the stools may be potted up separately and grown on for planting out in early summer.

Propagation from cuttings

Pelargoniums are easily propagated from cuttings, and the method used is the same for all types. Taking cuttings is an inexpensive way of producing new plants and allows the old plant to remain flowering outside in the garden until the first frosts, thus prolonging the display.

Selecting the cuttings
Although it is possible to take cuttings from spring onwards, the best time is late summer, when light

conditions are good and the weather is still warm. Select strong, healthy shoots (non-flowering ones if from a regal or scented-leaved pelargonium), cutting just above the third joint below the growing tip. Trim each cutting just below the lowest joint and remove the lower leaves.

Inserting the cuttings
Choose the pot size according to the number of cuttings: a 13cm (5in) pot will take up to five cuttings. Fill the pot with standard seed or cutting compost, press down firmly, and place the pot in a container of water until the compost surface becomes moist. Remove the pot and allow it to drain. Insert the cuttings, pressing them down gently to eliminate any air pockets beneath the bases of the cuttings. Do not water them yet.

Aftercare
Place the pot in a light, warm position, but not in full sun. One week after insertion, water the cuttings from below (as above). Water again a week or ten days later, by which time the cuttings should be rooting. If watered from above, the cuttings may suffer from grey mould/*Botrytis* or other damping off diseases. Do not use propagators or cover them with plastic sheeting, for the same reason. Always allow free circulation of air around them. As soon as the cuttings have rooted (when fresh leaves appear) pot them up singly into 7cm (3in) pots.

Growing F1 and F2 hybrids from seed

Seed-sown F1 and F2 hybrids are difficult for the amateur to produce as they require a specialized environment. In hot countries they will flower from seed in six months, but in colder countries it can take 15 months. To shorten this time, commercial nurseries grow on seedlings at high temperatures in artificial light for 14 hours a day over five winter months. They also treat the plants with dwarfing compounds in order to maintain a compact habit and to achieve early flowering.

Sowing the seed
Sow seed in early summer (see ANNUALS AND BIENNIALS, "Sowing in pots or trays", p.218). When the seedlings are 15cm (6in) high, pinch out the growing tips to encourage bushy growth. Grow on as cool greenhouse plants throughout the winter and spring, to flower the following summer.

TAKING CUTTINGS

1 *Choose a healthy shoot and cut straight across the stem just above the third joint below the growing tip.*

2 *Using a sharp knife, remove leaves from each cutting, leaving two at the top. Pinch out any flowers or buds.*

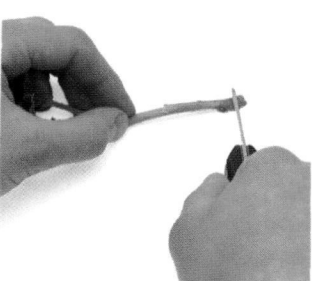

3 *Carefully trim the base of each cutting to just below the lowest joint with a straight cut.*

4 *Make holes 2.5cm (1in) deep in pots of moist, firmed seed or cuttings compost. Insert the cuttings and firm.*

OVERWINTERING

1 *Lift the plants before the first frosts and shake off any loose soil. Cut down the stems to about 10cm (4in) and remove the leaves.*

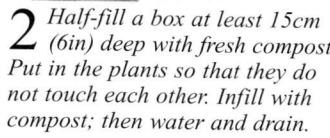

2 *Half-fill a box at least 15cm (6in) deep with fresh compost. Put in the plants so that they do not touch each other. Infill with compost; then water and drain.*

3 *Store in a well-lit, frost-free place. In spring pot up the plants, or use the new shoots to take cuttings from, as necessary, when they are sufficiently large.*

CHAPTER

7

ANNUALS
AND BIENNIALS

ANNUALS AND BIENNIALS are traditionally regarded as a quick and inexpensive means of achieving colour in the garden. To restrict their use in this way, however, is to overlook the vast range of foliage, fragrance, texture, and stature they have to offer. Their uses are as varied as their attributes: in just a few months they can enliven a garden or, as cut or dried flowers, add a splash of colour indoors. Although short-lived, a large number of these plants flower freely over many weeks and even months. The gardener can use this profusion of colour to create infinite patterns of bedding with plants that are planned to flower in succession. While annuals and biennials are most often used to fill beds and containers, some varieties with a trailing or climbing habit are particularly striking grown up a support or when allowed to sprawl luxuriantly over a bank.

Designing with annuals and biennials

THE term "annual" describes a plant whose entire life cycle, from germination to seed production through to death, takes place within one year. Those that are able to withstand frost are known as hardy annuals; those that are not are known as half hardy and must be raised under glass and planted out only after all danger of frost has passed.

"Biennials", however, require two growing seasons. In their first season after sowing they produce leaf and root growth; they then overwinter and flower in the following year.

Many plants used for annual bedding are in fact shrubby in their natural habitats, for example pelargoniums, snapdragons (*Antirrhinum majus*), or even the castor oil plant (*Ricinus communis*). In temperate climates they prove more vigorous and free-flowering if grown from seed as annuals. They are then discarded at the end of the growing season, although many can be overwintered under glass or as cuttings, protected from frost.

Annual borders

Whole borders or beds devoted to annuals produce colourful effects. Ideal in a new garden where they quickly provide a vibrant show, annuals may also be used as features in established gardens. The plants may be changed several times in a season to create different displays.

Colour effects

The most effective annual borders are often those that exploit a limited range of colours – dazzling oranges and reds, muted pinks and purples, soft blues and mauves. Plan the planting with a broad sweep of colour, selecting tones that, when adjacent, blend together harmoniously. Greys, greens, and whites are particularly useful for providing a respite from some of the more vibrant reds and blues. Many annuals, such as antirrhinums, pansies and violas (*Viola* x *wittrockiana*), and petunias, are available in a very wide range of colours, making it possible to select a particular plant whatever the colour range required. A bed devoted to pure white flowers looks fresh and crisp, but plain green-foliaged plants prevent the planting looking cold. Creams should not be substituted for the cleaner whites or mixed with them.

Form and texture

Border compositions are often enhanced by the leaf texture or the overall plant shape as much as by colour alone. Place plants with contrasting textures of either leaf or flower in adjacent groupings. Their differing characteristics will then be better appreciated. Form and texture

SUMMER-FLOWERING ANNUALS AND BEDDING PLANTS
Frost-tender perennials grown as annuals bring exotic colour to gardens in temperate climate zones. Although they only last a season, high-impact schemes like these can be designed and implemented in a matter of weeks.

of annuals are often overlooked but they add greatly to the character of a planting, whether it be with the wispy foliage of *Nigella*, the bold spikes of *Salvia splendens*, or the spreading informality of the poached-egg flower (*Limnanthes douglasii*) to provide contrast. Consider adding annual vegetables with attractive foliage to provide boldness and solidity to annual flower plantings; purple-leaved cabbage and Brussels sprouts, and various kales are especially suitable.

Including a variety of shapes and sizes adds interest to the scheme. Select from, for example, the daisy-like shapes of *Gaillardia*, the golden discs of sunflowers (*Helianthus annuus*), the large bells of petunias, the feathery plumes of *Celosia cristata* 'Childsii' (*C. plumosa*), the cylindrical spikes of *C. cristata*, or the tiny pompons of double daisies (*Bellis perennis*) or double-flowered feverfew (*Tanacetum parthenium* 'Virgo').

Grouping the plants

Most annuals look their best when planted in large groups of one cultivar to give a bold block of colour. Single plants can otherwise easily become isolated and weaken the structure of the planting. Sow in irregular patches so that the effect as the plants mature is similar to the interlocking drifts of flowers made by perennials in a traditional herbaceous border. The shapes and sizes of the groups should be varied to create a natural, free-flowing look.

When a border is to be viewed mainly from one direction, perhaps from a path or lawn, or is backed by a fence or hedge, graduate plants according to height. Plant the tallest plants, such as hollyhocks (*Alcea*), the taller *Amaranthus*, and tall sunflowers, at the back, and naturally low-growing species such as *Ageratum*, sweet alyssum (*Lobularia maritima*), and *Phlox drummondii* to clothe the front of the border. For those that are intermediate in height, juxtapose groups of slightly different heights to achieve variation. This creates a billowing, undulating informality.

Combine plants that flourish in similar conditions. For instance, species or cultivars of *Nicotiana*, which have loose clusters of scented tubular flowers on tall stems, combine well with the low-growing, flower-covered, compact shapes of busy Lizzie (*Impatiens* cvs), since both generally prefer cool and shady sites.

Foliage plants

There are several annuals grown chiefly for their foliage to harmonize or contrast with bright flower colour, and to add to the range of textures in a bed or border.

Senecio cineraria with its silver-grey leaves is easily cultivated from seed. Although frequently treated as a half-hardy annual, it is in fact a perennial, and may be kept for years if it is protected from frost. Similar in its requirements, but much more upright in its habit, *Tanacetum ptarmiciflorum* has upright, flat sprays of silvery dark grey foliage. A clump of castor oil plants (*Ricinus communis*), an evergreen shrub that flourishes in cooler climates when treated as a half-hardy annual, provides an eye-catching feature, with its green or purplish-bronze leaves. The bushy, bright green, cypress-like columns of the annual *Bassia scoparia* f. *trichophylla* (syn. *Kochia*) contrast well with colourful planting schemes, while selected cultivars of coleus (*Solenostemon*) and *Amaranthus* provide a range of foliage colour: reds and purples, yellows and greens, and two or three colours often combined in one leaf. The foliage of golden feverfew (*Tanacetum parthenium* cvs) remains sunny all summer, while some fibrous-rooted begonias are as well worth growing for their attractive bronze leaves.

Some ornamental vegetables also make excellent foliage plants to use with annuals. Cultivars of *Beta vulgaris* such as 'Ruby Chard', with its vivid red, upright stalks, 'Bright Yellow', with its dazzling, buttercup-yellow stems, or the mixed 'Bright Lights', which contains six different colours, are especially vivid. The ornamental cabbages and kales (*Brassica oleracea* forms) provide low-growing, muted foliage in purples, pinks, greens, and white late in the season and some edible curly kales such as the purple-leaved 'Redbor' are also very effective together with red cabbage and purple-leaved Brussels sprouts.

Annual grasses

One of the most impressive foliage plants is a grass – the variegated maize, or Indian corn (*Zea mays* 'Quadricolor'), which has broad, strap-like, green leaves striped white, cream, and pink. For a lighter, more delicate touch, other annual grasses make delightful additions to the summer border. Hare's tail (*Lagurus ovatus*) produces soft grey-green heads on wiry, upright stems and also dries exceptionally well. The rustling, heart-shaped flowers of quaking grass (*Briza maxima*) open green then turn straw-coloured and will usually self-sow; this is very suitable for Mediterranean-style

A TAPESTRY OF SUMMER COLOUR
These beautiful drifts of half-hardy and hardy annuals are attractively offset by the mellow tones of the mature wall in the background.

AN ANNUAL BORDER

A complete border may be devoted to annuals, biennials, and other short-lived plants. In this design, good use has been made of the different heights and growth habits of a wide variety of plants. Newer cultivars of sunflower (Helianthus), of medium height and with robust, self-supporting stems, lend valuable stature and focus.

SEMI-PERMANENT BEDDING SCHEME
Perfect for colouring in a pre-existing pattern of box (Buxus), *lavender, and* Santolina, *here forget-me-nots* (Myosotis) *make vivid monochrome panels.*

A MIXED BORDER
Annuals and biennials create a rich tapestry effect when planted among perennials. Tall, yellow spires of biennial Verbascum, *golden sunflowers, and marigolds are interwoven with blue cornflowers and pink* Cosmos.

plantings on dry soil. Taller and more imposing in stature, foxtails (*Setaria italica*) produces fat green heads like hairy caterpillars.

Seasonal display
Plan the planting so that the flowering periods of the annuals coincide as much as possible as this should avoid gaps appearing in the scheme. To provide interest over a long period, use annuals that bloom in succession; for specific colour combinations, make sure that the chosen plants bloom at the same time.

For a spring display choose wallflowers (*Erysimum*), forget-me-nots (*Myosotis*), daisies (*Bellis*), pansies and violas (*Viola* x *wittrockiana*), primroses (*Primula vulgaris*), and polyanthus. For summer and early autumn, the range of plants coming into flower is much greater, and the possible combinations are seemingly limitless.

Petunias have been diversified so greatly that elaborate colour schemes may be created using them alone. Choose from the boldly contrasting, striped blooms, the bright, single colours, or the subtly shaded ones, using them either singly or in combination. Where possible, select hybrids that are not spoiled by rain.

Tagetes also offer a wide range of colours, from cream to deep orange to mahogany-red, and the flowerheads vary from the single daisies of *Tagetes tenuifolia* to the great globes of the African cultivars. Easy-to-grow French marigolds, derived from *Tagetes patula*, with single and double flowerheads, display colouring in the full range from lemon, through gold and orange to chestnut and mahogany. Their bushy growth may be used to provide an effective display of colourful ground cover.

Formal bedding schemes
The wide variation of colour, shape, and size, as well as the uniformity of growth obtainable in many modern cultivars of annuals, provides opportunities to create long-lasting displays from spring to autumn. One of the glories of annuals is the intensity of colour achieved when a single cultivar of one of the low-growing, floriferous kinds is massed in a bed so that individual plants merge together. A scarlet carpet of pelargoniums or of *Salvia splendens*, for example, makes a vivid display when set into a fresh, green lawn. Patterned designs, using annuals of different colours, may produce similarly bold effects.

The dense growth habit and continuous flowering of many annuals make them ideal candidates for these complex, formal patterns. There is a wide range of dwarf and intermediate cultivars available.

Plants may be used to add colour to designs that have been delineated with bricks, gravel, or other architectural materials.

Annuals are excellent for knots and parterres, where small evergreen plants, such as box (*Buxus*), thyme (*Thymus*), or lavender (*Lavandula*), are clipped to create permanent outlines. Vary colour schemes with

ANNUALS IN MIXED BORDERS

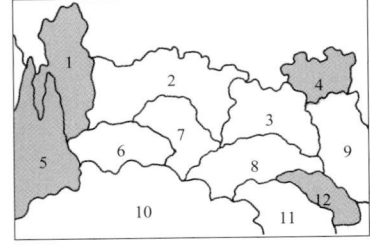

1 *Onopordum acanthium*
2 *Papaver orientale*
3 *Paeonia* 'Sarah Bernhardt'
4 *Papaver somniferum*
5 *Digitalis purpurea* cvs
6 *Bergenia cordifolia* 'Purpurea'
7 *Monarda didyma* 'Croftway Pink'
8 *Ornithogalum narbonense*
9 *Dianthus* 'Mrs Sinkins'
10 *Allium giganteum*
11 *Dicentra formosa*
12 *Viola tricolor*

In this bed, annuals and biennials (represented by grey areas on the diagram) have been planted between the perennials and bulbs to provide splashes of colour throughout the summer months. The sculptural, silvery-grey Scotch thistle (Onopordum acanthium) *and the tall, purple and white spikes of foxgloves* (Digitalis purpurea cvs) *appear majestically above the clumps of perennials.*

Bright red opium poppies (Papaver somniferum) *punctuate the planting and, at the front of the border, the delicate* Viola tricolor *spreads over the path. The pinkish-purple of the* Viola *complements the pink peony* (Paeonia 'Sarah Bernhardt'), *the rich purple foxgloves, and the profuse blooms of the bergamot* (Monarda didyma 'Croftway Pink'), *helping to create an integrated planting scheme.*

the seasons: a winter planting of pansies that continues into spring may be followed by a summer one of dwarf zinnias, for example.

Alternatively, annuals, biennials, and other temporary plants can be used alone to create designs that are expressed in the use of contrasting colours and form. An outline of low, mound-forming plants in a single colour will help to define a pattern and contain the infilling plants. White always makes a crisp, clear edging – double daisies (*Bellis perennis*) in spring, sweet alyssum (*Lobularia maritima*) or white *Lobelia erinus* cvs in summer. The fillers may be flowers with a looser, more irregular shape, such as antirrhinums.

Mixed borders

A mixed border, containing shrubs, perennials, bulbs, and annuals, is one of the delights of the garden. With such a diversity of plants, it offers the greatest possible variety in terms of colour, texture, season of interest, and design. Annuals and biennials warrant a place in any permanent planting scheme, in which they can be sown each year or left to self-seed. If allowed to self-sow, they will produce a random effect and a profusion of flowers reminiscent of the traditional cottage garden, where all manner of plants, including salad and vegetable crops, happily jostle for space in the same informal plot.

Used as colour highlights among perennials and shrubs, annuals and

biennials bring life to established borders. Possible effects range from cheerful mixtures of *Clarkia* (syn. *Godetia*), *Cosmos*, *Eschscholzia*, and corn poppies (*Papaver rhoeas*) to carefully co-ordinated toning schemes. For example, flowering annuals such as crimson *Amaranthus caudatus* and white *Nicotiana x sanderae*, or scarlet begonias, pelargoniums, and *Verbena* cultivars will add highlights to a "red" border with a framework of purplish foliage.

Self-sown annuals and biennials may soon become a permanent feature in a mixed border, helping to unify the planting and introducing a pleasing unpredictability. In early summer *Nigella damascena* makes a hazy web of colour, filling gaps and weaving together neighbouring blooms and the young leaves of later-flowering plants. The spire-like stems of certain biennials such as *Verbascum* and foxgloves (*Digitalis*) add an invaluable vertical accent to plants growing lower down.

Architectural plants
Handsome leaves, eye-catching flower shapes, and striking habits of growth make certain plants stand out from their companions. Annuals or biennials with such architectural qualities can be key features in a mixed bed or border, enhancing the composition. These plants create the greatest impact when they complement – rather than dominate – the other plants in the vicinity. The large, spiny, grey leaves and tall, widely branched flower stems of the Scotch thistle (*Onopordum*

TRAILING TREASURE
With its tumbling form, shapely leaves, and long-lasting, attractive double flowers, this scarlet nasturtium, Tropaeolum *'Hermine Grashoff', needs no companion plants to make a vivid and striking focal point in a decorative terracotta container. Although a short-lived perennial, this nasturtium is raised from cuttings each year.*

acanthium), for instance, make a statuesque centrepiece in a border that features other types of silver-foliaged plants. The flower spikes of the Excelsior Series foxgloves and Imperial Series and Sublime Series larkspur (*Consolida*) rise gracefully above all the neighbouring plants. Shapely blooms, such as those of *Cleome* and floss flower (*Ageratum*), will also command attention.

Plants grown primarily for their foliage also play an architectural role. In large borders the green or purple, palmate leaves of castor oil plants (*Ricinus communis*) add a strong textural quality, as do the bold leaves of the ornamental cabbages (*Brassica oleracea* forms).

Annuals and biennials as fillers

As they grow rapidly and are relatively cheap to raise, use annuals and biennials to fill gaps that occur, either through failure of a plant or between immature perennials and recently planted shrubs in a new border. Sow seed where the plants are to flower, choosing cultivars in a height and colour range to suit the permanent planting scheme.

At the end of the season, plant wallflowers (*Cheiranthus*) in the same gaps for their winter foliage and spring flowers. Multi-coloured carpets of winter-flowering pansies and violas (*Viola x wittrockiana*), primroses (*Primula vulgaris*), or polyanthus may be interplanted with spring-flowering bulbs, such as daffodils, hyacinths, or late-flowering tulips.

Until alpines become established, gaps in the rock garden may be filled

by sun-loving annuals that enjoy the same conditions. To avoid overwhelming their delicate colours and modest stature, however, choose annuals that are on a similar scale, such as *Viola tricolor, Lobelia erinus,* and *Portulaca.*

Annuals and biennials for ground cover

Some annuals and biennials may be used as temporary ground cover, creating pools of colour in an otherwise bare space. There are annuals to suit shade as well as sun, poor soil as well as rich. Single-colour cultivars of sweet alyssum (*Lobularia maritima*) or annual candytufts (*Iberis*) may be used to provide dense cover in a sunny spot or busy Lizzies (*Impatiens* cvs) in shade, where their spreading growth and colourful, continuous blooms will quickly cover the ground. For a more textured quality as well as lively colour, sow corn poppies (*Papaver rhoeas*) or *Eschscholzia*; both spread quickly. Attractive ground cover is also swiftly created by using cultivars of *Convolvulus tricolor* in blue, purple, or rose, or the bushier nasturtiums in red, orange, and yellow, some with variegated leaves.

Climbers and trailers

Vigorous annuals and biennials that climb and trail quickly may transform an expanse of wall or fence with a colourful curtain of foliage and flower, weaving a screen to provide privacy, or embellishing an existing structure. Many annuals have attractive leaves as well as

GROUND-COVER ANNUALS
Busy Lizzies (Impatiens *cvs) in contrasting tones form a carpet of intense colour in the cool shade under trees or shrubs.*

211

beautiful flowers, and a few, for example sweet peas (*Lathyrus odoratus*), offer the additional pleasure of scent (see SWEET PEAS, pp.214–215).

Plants with a climbing or trailing habit are particularly valuable in restricted spaces such as patios and balconies, where they make use of the vertical space as well as the ground area. Moreover, many annual climbers can be grown in pots, and are ideal for furnishing new gardens, softening surfaces, and disguising or distracting from an unsightly view.

In addition to favourites such as sweet peas and morning glory (*Ipomoea*), an increasing range of half-hardy and tender climbers is now more widely available as seeds or young plants. Exuberant plants such as the climbing cultivars of nasturtium or *Thunbergia alata* (black-eyed Susan) may be used to provide an abundance of summer flowers in company with more permanent perennial climbers. Particularly striking and effective, if slower to grow away initially, are *Cobaea scandens* with its large bell-shaped flowers in purple or greenish-white, and *Rhodochiton atrosanguineus*, an intriguing plant with curious, deep purple, tubular flowers in dusky maroon calyces.

Climbing annuals are also effective when grown through host plants, such as ivy (*Hedera*) or conifers. Use the climbing annual canary creeper (*Tropaeolum peregrinum*), which has pale green, dissected leaves and bright yellow, fringed flowers. Another good choice is the half-hardy *Eccremocarpus scaber*, the fiery Chilean glory flower, which climbs by means of tendrils and has a long flowering season, with clusters of tubular flowers that glow yellow, orange, or red among small, tooth-

WINDOWBOX COMPOSITIONS
This restrained cream, blue, and green colouring mixes begonias and pansies with trailing Lobelia, *ivy, and* Lysimachia nummularia.

shaped, pinnate leaves. For a dense, leafy screen, plant scarlet runner beans (*Phaseolus coccineus*), which have delicate, scarlet flowers, and the bonus of edible pods. For a more exotic look, try the purple lablab bean (*Lablab purpureus* 'Ruby Moon') with purplish-green foliage, bright purple flowers, and deep shining purple pods.

Annuals for cutting and drying

Many annuals can provide excellent cut flowers for the house. If space is available in your garden, it is worth growing flowers especially for cutting. They may be either integrated into borders or sown in a separate area. Taller cultivars may be particularly suitable; choose from antirrhinums, cornflowers (*Centaurea cyanus*), stocks (*Matthiola*), and *Gypsophila*. Sweet peas (*Lathyrus odoratus*) are particularly good as cut flowers and fill the house with their heady fragrance; if the flowers are cut regularly the plants will continue to bloom for many weeks. Larkspur (*Consolida*) is also useful for cutting and is equally attractive whether fresh or dried.

Many annuals may be dried as "everlasting" flowers for decoration indoors; they include helichrysum (*Bracteantha*), *Limonium*, and *Amaranthus caudatus*. Others such as honesty (*Lunaria*) and *Nigella* are grown for their decorative seedheads. Annual grasses, such as *Aira elegantissima* and *Pennisetum setaceum*, are also worth cultivating for their dried seedheads.

Annuals in containers

Whether it is a pot, tub, or windowbox, any container is a potential focal point in the garden, and the plants grown in it can make an eye-catching feature. F1 and F2 hybrid annuals, with their even growth habit and consistent flower colours, are specifically bred to provide uniform, long-lasting displays. Most annuals, however, may be used in containers, either on their own or to complement other plants (see also CONTAINER GARDENING, p.315).

Annuals are available for a year-round display. In spring and early summer, winter-flowering pansies and violas, dwarf wallflowers, primroses, and polyanthus cultivars will continue to thrive in sheltered spots. Protected but sunny sites on patios are also ideal for petunias, calibrachoas, gazanias, zinnias, and busy Lizzies (*Impatiens* cvs), which maintain their colour throughout summer.

Hanging baskets and windowboxes

Plants with a trailing habit are ideal for growing in windowboxes and hanging baskets, and effective displays may be created by a mass of foliage and flower. Reliable performers include sprawling petunias, trailing *Lobelia erinus*, such as the Cascade and Regatta Series, and some *Verbena* x *hybrida* cultivars, which are available in a wide range of colours, including pure reds and scarlets as well as deep purples, crimsons, and whites. Trailing violas and trailing F1 pelargoniums, renewed annually from seed, are also good value (see also PELARGONIUMS, pp.204–205).

PLANTING IN THE VERTICAL PLANE
Hanging baskets and windowboxes transform a bare wall. Trailing plants such as ivy-leaved pelargoniums reach down to meet upright, bushy annuals, making a continuous curtain of colour.

Planter's guide to annuals and biennials

EXPOSED SITES

Annuals and biennials that tolerate exposed or windy sites (may require support)

Borago officinalis
Calendula
Centaurea cyanus
Clarkia
Dianthus barbatus, D. chinensis
Echium vulgare
Erysimum
Eschscholzia
Glaucium flavum
Iberis amara, I. umbellata
Lavatera trimestris
Limnanthes
Linum grandiflorum
Lobularia maritima
Lunaria
Malcolmia
Malope trifida
Oenothera biennis
Papaver rhoeas, P. somniferum
Petunia ❉
Rudbeckia hirta (hybrids)

*Rudbeckia
hirta*

Salvia horminum
Tagetes tenuifolia ❉
Vaccaria hispanica
Xanthophthalmum carinatum,
* X. coronarium, X. segetum*

DRY SHADE

Annuals and biennials that tolerate dry shade

Digitalis purpurea
Matthiola bicornis

MOIST SHADE

Annuals and biennials that enjoy moist shade

Impatiens walleriana ❉
Matthiola bicornis
Mimulus Calypso Series ❉,
* M.* Magic Series ❉,
* M.* Malibu Series ❉
Oenothera biennis
Primula Polyanthus Group
Viola x *wittrockiana*

FRAGRANT FLOWERS

Amberboa moschata
Calomeria amaranthoides ❉
Centaurea moschata
Dianthus Giant Chabaud Series,
* D. chinensis*
Exacum affine ❉

Heliotropium, some ❉
Lathyrus odoratus
Lobularia maritima
Matthiola Brompton Series,
* M.* East Lothian Series,
* M.* Ten-week Series
Nicotiana alata ❉, *N.* x *sanderae* ❉
* (some cvs)*
Primula, some ❉
Reseda odorata
Viola x *wittrockiana*

TRAILING PLANTS FOR CONTAINERS

Antirrhinum 'Lampion' ❉
Arctotis venusta ❉
Begonia Panorama Series ❉
Bidens ferulifolia ❉
Brachyscome iberidifolia
Calibrachoa
Convolvulus tricolor
Heliotropium, some ❉
Impatiens walleriana ❉
Lathyrus odoratus Sweetie Series
Lobelia erinus Cascade Series ❉,
* L. erinus* Fountain Series ❉,
* L. erinus* Regatta Series ❉
Lobularia maritima Trailing Series,
* L. maritima* 'Wandering Star'
Pelargonium Multibloom Series ❉,
* P.* Summer Showers Series ❉ (and
* suitable other F1 and F2 Series)*
Petunia ❉
Sanvitalia procumbens
Tropaeolum majus semi-trailing cvs
* including T. majus* 'Empress of
* India', T. majus* Gleam Series,
* T. majus* Whirlybird Series
Verbena x *hybrida* ❉ (trailing types)
Viola x *wittrockiana* Splendid Series

FLOWERS FOR DRYING

Ageratum ❉
Amaranthus ❉
Ammobium alatum
Avena sterilis
Briza maxima, B. minor
Calendula
Celosia ❉
Centaurea cyanus
Clarkia
Consolida ambigua
Gomphrena globosa ❉
Helipterum ❉
Hordeum jubatum
Lagurus ovatus
Limonium sinuatum ❉
Lonas ❉
Moluccella laevis ❉
Nigella
Panicum violaceum
Pennisetum villosum
Salvia horminum
Setaria glauca
Stipa pennata

ANNUAL CLIMBERS
See list on p.129.

ARCHITECTURAL PLANTS

Alcea rosea, syn. *Althaea rosea*
Amaranthus caudatus ❉,
* A. tricolor* ❉
Bassia scoparia f. *trichophylla* ❉
Brassica oleracea Osaka Series,
* B. oleracea* 'Tokyo'
Campanula medium (tall cvs)
Canna
Cleome hassleriana ❉
Consolida
Digitalis purpurea 'Excelsior',
* D. purpurea* 'Glittering Prizes'
Helianthus annuus

*Helianthus
annuus*

Onopordum acanthium,
* O. arabicum*
Ricinus communis ❉
Salvia sclarea var. *sclarea*
Silybum marianum
Tagetes erecta (tall cvs)
Verbascum bombyciferum,
* V. densiflorum*
Zea mays 'Quadricolor' ❉

POT PLANTS
Annuals suitable for growing from seed as (greenhouse) pot plants

Antirrhinum, some ❉
Begonia semperflorens ❉
Calomeria amaranthoides ❉
Campanula pyramidalis
Capsicum ❉ (ornamental fruit cvs)
Centaurea moschata
Coleus ❉
Datura (dwarf cvs)
Exacum affine ❉
Impatiens walleriana ❉ (tall cvs)
Osteospermum ❉
Pelargonium ❉ (F1 and F2 hybrids)
Pericallis x *hybridus* ❉ (cvs)
Petunia ❉
Primula malacoides ❉,
* P. obconica* ❉, *P. sinensis* ❉
Psylliostachys suworowii ❉
Salpiglossis ❉
Schizanthus ❉
Thunbergia alata ❉
Torenia fournieri ❉
Trachelium caeruleum ❉
Trachymene coerulea, syn.
* Didiscus coeruleus* ❉

PERENNIALS THAT MAY BE GROWN AS ANNUALS

Achillea 'Summer Pastels'
Agastache 'Fragrant Delight'
Alcea 'Majorette', *A.* 'Summer
* Carnival'*
Coreopsis 'Early Sunrise'
Delphinium Centurion Series
Dianthus 'Champion', *D.* 'Floristan'
Leucanthemum 'Snow Lady'
Linaria purpurea cvs
Lobelia Fan Series, *L.* Kompliment
* Series*
Penstemon Tubular Bells Series
Prunella 'Pagoda'
Veronica 'Sightseeing'

FLOWERS FOR CUTTING

Agrostemma githago 'Milas'
Antirrhinum ❉ (tall cvs)
Calendula
Callistephus ❉ (tall cvs)
Centaurea cyanus
Erysimum cheiri
Consolida ambigua
Coreopsis 'Early Sunrise'
Cosmos ❉
Dianthus barbatus,
* D.* Giant Chabaud Series,
* D.* Knight Series
Gaillardia pulchella
Gilia capitata
Gomphrena globosa ❉
Gypsophila elegans

Antirrhinum majus
Princess Series

Helianthus annuus,
* H.* Colour Fashion Series
Helipterum ❉
Lathyrus odoratus
Limonium sinuatum ❉
Lunaria annua
Matthiola Brompton Series,
* M.* East Lothian Series,
* M. incana, M.* Ten-week Series
Moluccella laevis ❉
Nigella damascena
Papaver nudicaule, P. Summer
* Breeze Series*
Psylliostachys suworowii ❉
Rudbeckia hirta (hybrids)
Salvia horminum
Xanthophthalmum carinatum,
* X. coronarium, X. segetum*
Xeranthemum annuum ❉
Zinnia ❉

KEY
❉ *Not hardy*

Sweet peas

SWEET peas (*Lathyrus odoratus*) have been dubbed "the queen of annuals" for their beautiful flowers, marvellous scent, and long flowering period. Trained up wigwams, pillars, or canes, they provide long and colourful displays. Grow them among perennials or shrubs or as a decorative contribution to the vegetable garden or potager.

Types of sweet pea

Most familiar are the Spencer and Grandiflora cultivars, which climb a supporting framework by means of leaf tendrils. The large-flowered Spencer cultivars may grow 2–3m (6–10ft) high depending on growing conditions; Grandiflora cultivars have smaller, "old-fashioned" flowers but they are more highly scented.

OLD-FASHIONED SWEET PEAS

![Old-fashioned sweet peas]

Old-fashioned sweet peas are closer to the species than most of the modern cultivars. They have delicately coloured, small, highly scented flowers.

DWARF SWEET PEAS

Dwarf sweet peas grow to about 45cm (18in) high and need little or no support. They grow well when planted in tubs, windowboxes, and hanging baskets.

Intermediate sweet peas, such as 'Knee-Hi' and 'Snoopea', reach about 1m (3ft) tall if supported but 'Snoopea' especially will make good ground cover if not supported. Dwarf types include 'Pink Cupid', 'Bijou', and 'Patio Mixed'.

Growing sweet peas from seed

Seeds may be sown in mid-autumn in fairly mild districts, or in late winter or early spring where winters are colder. The process is identical in both cases. Protect seedlings and plants from being eaten by mice.

Sowing

Sweet pea seeds vary in colour from pale buff to black. To help them germinate, nick the darker seeds with a sharp penknife, removing a small piece of seed coat opposite the eye. Sweet pea seeds may be soaked to achieve fast germination, although there may be a problem with rotting.

Sow in seed trays, root trainers, pots (one, two, or three seeds per pot), or in special sweet pea tubes, 5cm (2in) in diameter and 15cm (6in) deep. Use a loamless potting compost with 20 per cent grit added or a standard seed compost.

Dark seeds germinate well in fairly damp compost, but pale ones require a compost that is only just moist. Cover the containers with glass and keep them at about 15°C (59°F). When the seedlings appear, transfer them to a cold frame.

Potting on

Prick out seedlings from trays and then pot them on individually when plants are about 3.5cm (1½in) high. Fill 6cm (3in) pots, or sweet pea tubes, with a similar compost to that used for sowing. Pinch out the root tips and then repot.

Autumn-sown sweet peas (Spencers) should be pinched out only if they have not produced sideshoots by midwinter. Stop spring-sown seedlings at the second pair of leaves.

Overwintering seedlings

Keep the cold frame open as much as possible, during slight frosts, to harden off the plants. In frosts below -2°C (28°F) close and insulate the frame. In heavy rain, prop open the lights on the frame, for ventilation. Control aphids (p.646) and give a dilute liquid feed in late winter.

BUSH SWEET PEAS

PEASTICK SUPPORTS
Peasticks are the traditional means of supporting sweet peas. Insert the peasticks when the seedlings are planted out, leaning the sticks in towards the centre of the clump for extra stability.

WIRE RINGS
Bush sweet peas may be grown up wire rings anchored with several bamboo canes. The plants will grow through the wire, hiding their supports.

WIGWAM
A wigwam of canes secured near the top also provides a sturdy support. One seedling beside each cane is usually enough to provide a dense mass of flowers.

Hardening off spring-sown plants

This demands more care as the plants are smaller and growth is softer than on autumn-sown plants. Keep the cold frame well ventilated, but close the lights if frost threatens and protect well with polystyrene sheets or fleece during any very hard frosts.

Planting

Sweet peas thrive in sunny, open sites and well-drained, humus-rich soil (see "Soil structure and water content", p.620). Three weeks prior to planting, carefully rake in a balanced fertilizer at a rate of 85g/sq m (3oz/sq yd). For the best results, trench or double dig the ground in autumn (see "Double digging", p.620). Add well-rotted manure to the lower spit.

Plant out autumn-sown sweet peas in mid-spring, spring-sown ones in late spring. Set plants 23cm (9in) apart just behind and to one side of their support, with the bottom shoot level with the soil. Water during dry spells and when flower buds appear. Apply liquid feed two or three times at fortnightly intervals from midsummer onwards. Dead-head plants to encourage continuous flowering.

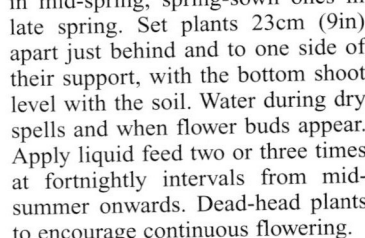

INITIAL TRAINING OF CORDONS

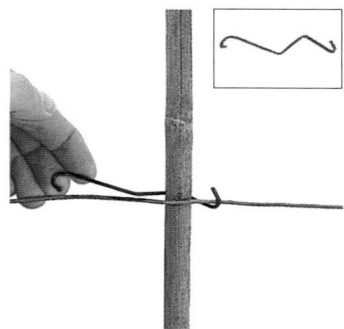

1 *After fixing the wires and posts, insert 2.5m (8ft) tall canes 23cm (9in) apart at a slight angle along the row and attach them to the wires using "V" clips.*

2 *About 2 weeks after planting the young sweet peas, select the strongest shoot of each plant and attach it to the cane with a wire ring loosely fastened beneath a leaf node.*

3 *At the same time, pinch or cut out all the other sideshoots to concentrate the vigour into the main shoot.*

4 *Keep pinching out any sideshoots or tendrils that form and any flower stems carrying less than 4 buds.*

LAYERING CORDONS

1 *In early summer, when the sweet peas have reached a height of 1.2m (4ft), they are ready to be layered. This will give them more space to continue growing and flowering.*

2 *Carefully untie the plants from their canes and lay them on the ground to their full length. If the plants are in double rows, do this for one row at a time.*

3 *Attach the shoot tip to a new cane further along the row, so that it reaches 30cm (1ft) up the cane. Work along the row until all the plants are fixed to new canes.*

4 *Repeat for the second row of plants, if required. Flowers will then continue to be produced on the new growth stimulated by the layering method. Sweet peas can be layered again later in the season, provided the plants remain healthy and disease free. Once they reach the top wire, untie each stem and attach the tip to a new cane further up the row.*

Bush sweet peas

Sweet peas are usually allowed to develop naturally into bushes. Support the plants with peasticks, canes, trellis, or rigid plastic netting. Canes and sticks may be grouped in circles, wigwam-style, or arranged in rows. A double row of peasticks and canes must be well supported, preferably with a post at each end and a strainer wire. Tie young plants to their supports with plastic ties; thereafter they need little tying in. Sideshoots are left to develop, producing more flowers on short stems.

Cordon sweet peas

Sweet peas trained into cordons produce top-quality flowers so are usually grown in this way by exhibitors.

Providing supports

At each end of a row, drive in a post with a 45cm (18in) cross-piece near the top, set at 2m (6ft) above ground level. Stretch two parallel wires between the cross-pieces. Place 2.5m (8ft) canes, spaced 23cm (9in) apart, at a slight angle against the wires and secure them with "V" clips. Rows should run north to south to expose plants evenly to sunlight.

Initial training

Leave plants to establish for two weeks. Then pinch out the weaker shoots to leave the strongest shoot on each plant as well as the shoot immediately below the growing point in case the main leader is damaged by, for example, birds. Train the shoots up the cane, tying them with raffia, tape, or rings at each node. Remove sideshoots and tendrils as they grow. When flower stems form, remove any with fewer than four buds.

Layering

When plants are 1.2m (4ft) tall, they should be untied and trained up a new cane further along the row (see *Layering Cordons*). Do this on a warm day when plants are not too sappy. They will then continue to grow and flower for several weeks.

Sowing and planting

ANNUALS AND BIENNIALS THAT ENJOY SANDY SOIL

Anchusa capensis
Argemone mexicana ✽
Brachyscome iberidifolia
Calendula officinalis
Camissonia cheiranthifolia
Centaurea cyanus
Clarkia amoena
Coreopsis tinctoria
Dianthus
Eschscholzia californica
Glaucium flavum
Helichrysum bracteatum ✽
Lavatera trimestris
Limnanthes douglasii
Limonium sinuatum ✽
Linaria maroccana
Lobularia maritima
Mentzelia lindleyi

Papaver rhoeas
Shirley Series

Oenothera biennis
Papaver rhoeas,
  P. somniferum
Platystemon californicus
Portulaca grandiflora ✽
Rudbeckia hirta
Schizanthus ✽
Tagetes ✽
Verbascum bombyciferum

ANNUALS AND BIENNIALS THAT TOLERATE VERY ALKALINE SOIL

Ageratum houstonianum ✽
Antirrhinum majus ✽
Calendula officinalis
Callistephus chinensis ✽
Calomeria amaranthoides ✽
Cosmos
Dianthus, some ✽
Erysimum cheiri
Gomphrena globosa ✽
Lavatera trimestris
Limonium sinuatum ✽

*Lavatera
trimestris
'Silver Cup'*

Lobularia maritima
Matthiola Brompton
  Series, *M. incana*
Primula
Salvia horminum
Tagetes ✽
Tropaeolum, some ✽
Ursinia anthemoides ✽
Xeranthemum annuum ✽
Zinnia ✽

KEY
✽ Not hardy

ANNUALS and biennials are among the easiest of plants to raise from seed. They may also be obtained as seedlings or young plants from nurseries or garden centres, and will provide an instant display of colour in a garden border or container placed indoors or outside.

Buying seeds

Always buy fresh seeds that have been stored in cool conditions. The viability of seeds of different species varies greatly; while some, such as peas and beans, may remain viable for a few years if kept cool and dry, most start to deteriorate after a year, especially if they are stored in damp, warm conditions. Seeds in sealed foil packets last for several years; once the packets are opened, however, the seed viability deteriorates.

F1 and F2 hybrid seeds are available for many annuals and some biennials; these produce plants that are vigorous and true to type with even growth and flower characteristics. These seeds are ideal for the gardener seeking uniformity, but for most ordinary garden purposes well-produced, open-pollinated seeds are equally satisfactory.

Pelleted and primed seeds

Seeds may be individually coated with a paste, or pelleted, to form a smooth ball. This enables them to be handled separately, so that they may be more easily spaced in containers or the open ground. If pelleted seeds are space-sown at the correct distance for the cultivar concerned they need not be thinned so, although they cost more, fewer are required. The seeds should be watered thoroughly after sowing to ensure that the moisture needed for germination to occur penetrates the seed coat as quickly as possible. Pelleted seeds are normally available in a number of hybrids and species, especially where the seed is small, as well as in some open-pollinated genera, such as *Lobelia* and *Alyssum*.

Primed seeds have been treated so that they are ready to germinate as soon as they are sown. They are particularly useful for species and cultivars that do not germinate easily.

Seed tapes and gels

Seed tapes are tissue-like, soluble strips with evenly spaced seeds embedded within them. The tapes are laid at the base of a drill, then covered with a thin layer of soil. Gel kits may be purchased for fluid sowing – seeds are added to a paste so that they are suspended and therefore evenly spaced throughout. The mixture is then squeezed along a pre-prepared drill. It is important not to allow the mixture to dry out. Both these methods distribute the seeds evenly so that less thinning is required than for hand-sown seeds.

Buying seedlings

Seeds of some plants that germinate less readily are available from some seed firms at the chitting stage – when the seed coat has burst open and roots and seed leaves are starting to emerge. The seeds are usually sown on agar jelly and despatched in a sealed plastic container. Healthy seedlings should have fresh, moist roots and seed leaves; reject any that have pale green leaves or are overcrowded. The jelly contains sufficient food and moisture to sustain them for a few days but the germinating seeds should be transferred to the required growing conditions as soon as possible so that the seedlings have sufficient light to develop.

Seedlings of selected cultivars may be purchased as plug plants, when they have developed at least one pair of true leaves and are ready for pricking out (see p.219). This is useful for plants with very small seeds, such as begonias, which are

MAIL-ORDER PLUG PLANTS

A rigid moulded plastic container separates and protects the tiny plants when these are sent by post.

Hardy and half-hardy annuals and biennials

Annuals complete their life cycle in a year, while biennials require two years. Horticulturally, annuals and biennials are termed hardy or half hardy. Hardy annuals are resistant to frosts and so may be sown early in open ground and will be established before more frost-prone annuals. Half-hardy annuals withstand only a limited amount of cold and are killed or badly damaged at freezing temperatures; they need to be maintained in frost-free conditions of 13–21°C (55–70°F) in order to germinate and establish.

Hardy biennials should be sown by midsummer to allow the plants to become well established by the winter. Overwinter half-hardy biennials in a cool greenhouse or insulated cold frame.

difficult for many gardeners to germinate successfully. The plugs are sent out in a rigid transparent plastic container to keep them as fresh as possible. If pricked out within 24 hours of arrival and kept in a protected environment they will usually grow as well as plants from home-germinated seeds.

Small seedlings already well established in wedges or plugs of compost are also readily available. Depending on size, they can be grown on in their module trays or be potted up individually in small pots or hanging baskets. They should be grown on in a greenhouse or cold frame, or on a sunny windowsill, until they are ready to be hardened off and planted out. They are much cheaper than bedding plants.

Sowing

When and where to sow annuals and biennials depends on when they are required to flower and the temperature they need for germination.

Hardy annuals

Sow hardy annuals where they are to flower when the soil has warmed up to at least 7°C (45°F) in the spring. If sown in successive batches until midsummer, hardy annuals provide a long summer display.

Some hardy annuals, if sown *in situ* in the autumn, germinate to produce small plants that overwinter satisfactorily outdoors and flower in late spring or early summer the following year. Love-in-a-mist (*Nigella*), cornflower (*Centaurea cyanus*), and poppies (*Papaver*) are some examples.

Seeds of hardy annuals may also be sown in pots or seed trays and either planted out in their final flowering positions in late autumn or overwintered in a cold frame to be planted out in spring. This is a useful practice in gardens with clay soil that is slow to warm up in spring.

Hardy biennials

Most hardy biennials may be sown outdoors from late spring until midsummer. The optimum time varies according to what is being grown: forget-me-nots (*Myosotis*) grow rapidly so should not be sown until midsummer, while Canterbury bells (*Campanula medium*) need longer to develop and should be sown in late spring or early summer.

The young plants may be transplanted to their final flowering position in autumn or, if they are not crowded, the following spring. Premature flowering reduces the spring display, so pinch out any buds that form in the first season.

Half-hardy annuals and biennials and bedding plants

In warm climates, sow seed directly outside once the soil temperature reaches the optimum for germination. In colder regions, sow half-hardy annuals in containers in spring at 13–21°C (55–70°F), according to the particular genus. Half-hardy biennials may be sown under the same conditions in midsummer. Frost-tender perennials, for example busy Lizzies (*Impatiens* cvs), gazanias, and some *Lobelia* species, may be raised from seed in the same way as half-hardy annuals.

Many tender perennials (including *Argyranthemum* and *Osteospermum*) may be propagated by cuttings taken in autumn (see PERENNIALS, "Stem tip cuttings", p.202) and be overwintered in frost-free conditions for planting out in late spring.

Sowing in open ground

There are two main methods of sowing outdoors *in situ*: broadcast and in drills. For both, a seedbed in a sunny place should be prepared. Dig over the soil to one spade's depth, then rake and firm it by treading gently on the surface. Do not sow in soil that is too rich, as this encourages leaf rather than flower production. In soils lacking nutrients, however, a dressing of 70g/sq m (2oz/sq yd) of a balanced fertilizer may be added before sowing (see "Soil nutrients and fertilizers", pp.624–625).

Before sowing a border, prepare a plan showing the position of each cultivar, using any areas likely to be shaded to grow those that are shade-tolerant. Mark the area for each cultivar with grit or a cane so that it is easy to check the balance of colours, heights, and habits of the different plants before sowing the seed.

Open ground sowing is particularly suitable for annuals that produce deep tap roots such as *Clarkia*, *Gypsophila*, and poppies (*Papaver*), because they are best sown where they are to flower since they do not transplant readily.

Sowing broadcast

Sprinkle seeds thinly and evenly on the surface of the prepared seedbed and rake them in lightly. Label, then water the area with a watering can fitted with a fine rose.

Sowing in drills

Seeds sown in drills produce seedlings growing in straight rows at regular intervals so they are readily distinguished from weed seedlings, which are randomly distributed. The seedlings initially look regimented but, once thinned, will form a dense and informal planting, and the rows

MARKING OUT ANNUAL BORDERS

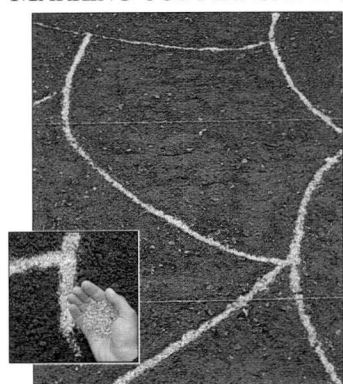 

1 Sprinkle grit or sand on the soil or score the soil with a stick to mark out interlocking areas for sowing seeds.

2 The seedlings may appear too sparse at first but will blend together as they grow.

SOWING IN DRILLS

1 Using a line of string as a guide, make a furrow about 2.5cm (1in) deep with a hoe.

2 Holding the seeds in one hand, pick up several at a time and scatter them evenly along the drill.

ALTERNATIVE STEP

If the seeds are pelleted, place them individually in the base of the drill.

3 Rake the soil back over the drill without dislodging the seeds. After labelling the row, water the soil using a fine rose.

SOWING SEED BROADCAST

1 Prepare the soil by raking to produce a fine tilth. Scatter the seeds thinly over the prepared area by hand or from the packet.

2 Rake over the area lightly at right angles to cover the seeds so that they are disturbed as little as possible.

Tanacetum parthenium

Tropaeolum majus
Vaccaria hispanica
Verbascum
Viola (many spp.)
Xanthophthalmum segetum

THINNING SEEDLINGS

INDIVIDUAL SEEDLINGS
Press on either side of the seedling to be retained (here larkspur, Consolida ambigua) while pulling out the unwanted ones around it. Refirm and water.

SEEDLING GROUPS
Lift groups of seedlings (here sweet William, Dianthus barbatus) with plenty of soil around the roots if they are to be replanted. Firm in and water the remaining seedlings.

in adjoining areas can be arranged at different angles.

Using either a trowel tip or the corner of a hoe, mark out shallow drills 8–15cm (3–6in) apart depending on the ultimate size of the plants. Sow seeds thinly and evenly by sprinkling or placing them along each drill at the appropriate depth for the annuals being sown, then carefully draw back the displaced soil with a rake or hoe to cover them. Label each row and water well with a watering can fitted with a fine rose.

Thinning

To prevent overcrowding, the seedlings usually need to be thinned. Do this when the soil is moist and the weather mild, taking care to retain the sturdier seedlings where possible and achieve an even spacing. To minimize disturbance to a seedling being retained, press the soil around it with your fingers as the surplus seedlings are extracted.

If seedlings are very dense, dig them up in clumps, retaining plenty of soil around the roots; disturb as little as possible the other seedlings in the ground. Some biennials such as forget-me-nots (*Myosotis*) and honesty (*Lunaria*) germinate readily and if sown where they are to flower should be thinned appropriately – forget-me-nots to 15cm (6in) and honesty to 30cm (12in), for example.

The thinnings may be used to fill sparse areas caused by uneven sowing or irregular germination, or may be transplanted for use elsewhere in the garden. For transplanting,

select the strongest and healthiest among the thinned seedlings, then replant them where needed at the appropriate spacings and water them lightly to settle their roots.

Many annuals and biennials scatter their seeds freely, often producing dense clumps of seedlings; these need to be thinned carefully to the appropriate distances apart, so that the young plants retained may develop without competition.

Sowing in pots or trays

Half-hardy annuals are usually sown in containers so that they may develop under cover and be planted out as young plants when conditions are favourable. Hardy annuals may also be sown in containers left outside, and the seedlings transplanted to their flowering positions when there is sufficient room.

Pots, seed pans, seed trays, and module trays are all suitable containers, depending on the number of seeds to be sown and the space they require. Degradable pots are also useful for seedlings that do not transplant well, because the whole pot may be planted out without disturbing the roots.

Sowing the seeds

Fill the chosen container to its rim with standard seed compost and press in lightly around the edges with the fingertips to make sure that there are no air pockets. To settle the compost, tap the container against a hard surface and then gently firm the compost level so that the top of the compost is just below the rim of the container. Water with a fine rose and leave for an hour or so to drain.

Sow the seeds thinly on the surface of the compost, tapping them from the seed packet or from V-shaped paper to achieve an even spread. Large or pelleted seeds may be sown individually in compartmented packs or spaced out in trays or pans. Very small seeds are easier to sow if they are mixed first with the same bulk of fine sand; this produces a more even distribution.

Cover the seeds to about their own depth with sieved compost, perlite, or vermiculite; then water lightly, so as not to disturb the seeds or the surface of the compost. Dust-like seeds, such as those of begonia, should be left uncovered and watered from below: place each container within 2.5cm (1in) of its rim in water until the surface of the compost is moist. Do not leave them soaking for too

Protecting and supporting seedlings

Support is required for slender-stemmed or tall annuals. Carefully insert peasticks or thin twigs into the soil around young plants; the supports should be slightly shorter than the ultimate height of the plants so that they will be concealed when the plants reach their mature size. These supports may also help protect the seedlings from possible rodent and bird damage.

Alternatively, stretch wire netting, with a mesh no greater than 2.5cm (1in), over the seedbed, bending it down at the edges so it does not touch the seedlings. Secure firmly in the soil, using sticks or wire pins. The plants grow up through the mesh and cover the netting when fully grown.

SUPPORTING WITH TWIGS
Peasticks or thin twigs may be pushed into the soil among the seedlings. Tall annuals (here larkspur, Consolida ambigua) grow to hide the support.

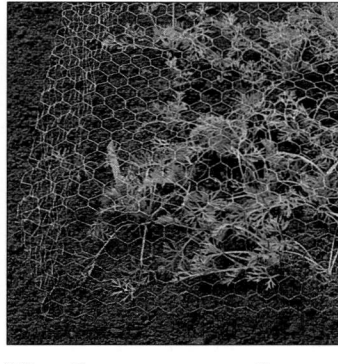

WIRE PROTECTION AND SUPPORT
Protect seedlings (here Eschscholzia) with mesh wire netting bent to form a cage. The netting will support the seedlings as they grow through.

SOWING IN A TRAY

3 *Cover the seeds with a layer of sieved moist compost, perlite, or vermiculite to about the same thickness as the seeds themselves. Water the seeds in lightly.*

1 *Fill the seed tray with a standard seed compost and level with a presser board to 1cm (¹/₂in) below the rim.*

2 *Using a V-shaped piece of paper, sprinkle the seeds thinly over the compost surface, to achieve an even covering.*

4 *Place a piece of glass or clear plastic sheeting over the tray to maintain even humidity.*

5 *Shade the tray with netting if the tray is in direct sunlight. Remove both glass and netting as soon as germination starts.*

Seeds with special requirements

A few seeds need special conditions in order to germinate successfully. Coleus (*Solenostemon*), begonia, and busy Lizzie (*Impatiens*) seeds require light and prefer a constant temperature of 21°C (70°F). Primulas prefer light, but need temperatures of no more than 20°C (68°F). Some seeds including *Phacelia*, pansies (*Viola* x *wittrockiana*), and other *Viola* should be germinated in the dark. Seeds of *Thunbergia alata* and pelargoniums require scarifying, sowing, and 21–24°C (70–75°F) to germinate. Seeds of *Moluccella* should be stratified: the seed pan is set in a refrigerator for a couple of weeks before bringing it into a temperature of 18–21°C (64–70°F) for a further two or three weeks.

---

long since waterlogging may cause the seeds to rot before germination or encourage seedling diseases (see "Damping off", p.660).

To maintain even humidity place a piece of glass or clear plastic sheeting over the container; do not let it touch the compost surface as this may disturb the seeds. Place the container on a heated mat (see GREENHOUSES AND FRAMES, "Propagation aids", p.580), in a propagator or on a greenhouse bench, and shade with fine netting or newspaper if it receives direct sunlight. As soon as the first seedlings germinate, the cover should be removed. Keep them in good light and the compost moist until they are ready for pricking out.

Pricking out
Seedlings raised in trays or pans need to be transplanted into larger containers before they become overcrowded, as they quickly become weak and spindly if deprived of sufficient space or light. This is known as pricking off or pricking out. It enables the seedlings to continue to develop until they are ready for planting out in the garden.

Fill the new containers with potting compost and firm gently. Small pots, no more than 7cm (3in) in diameter, or module trays, are ideal for individual seedlings; larger pots, pans, or trays may be used for several seedlings.

To prick out, first knock the container of seedlings against a table top or bench to loosen the compost slightly and remove it intact from the container. Then hold each plant gently by the small seed leaves to avoid bruising the stems or growing tips and loosen it with a widger or other small implement. Then carefully lift each plant from the soil, retaining some of the moist seed compost around the roots to ensure that there will be little or no check to growth when the seedlings are replanted.

Use a dibber to make holes in the compost and insert a seedling into each hole. Make sure that all the roots are covered with compost, then gently firm in each seedling using fingers or a dibber, and level the compost. As each container is filled, water it from a can fitted with a fine rose to settle the compost around the roots. Cover the containers with clear plastic for a few days while the seedlings re-establish, but make sure that the plastic does not touch the leaves because this may encourage rotting. Then return the seedlings to their previous growing conditions to develop further.

If seedlings are ready for planting out, but this is delayed because of a late frost, pot them on into a larger container and give a liquid feed, to ensure that growth is not checked.

Seeds that have been sown singly in packs or space-sown will not need pricking out and may be hardened off before planting out.

Hardening off
All half-hardy annuals that have been raised either under glass or in any other controlled environment before being planted outdoors need to be acclimatized gradually to the natural conditions outdoors. The aim

PRICKING OUT INTO MODULES

1 *When the seedlings (here Tagetes) are large enough to handle, tap the tray on a hard surface to loosen the compost.*

2 *Carefully separate the seedlings, handling them by their seed leaves. Keep plenty of compost around the roots.*

3 *Transplant each seedling into a separate cell of a module tray. Firm the soil around each one with fingers or a dibber, and water.*

Annuals in pots

Many annuals make excellent pot plants. Prick out young seedlings into divided trays or individual pots and, when the roots have just filled the container, transfer each seedling to a larger pot prepared with loam-based potting compost. The pot size will vary according to the species or cultivar and time of sowing. Put plants sown in late summer into 9cm (3½in) pots over the winter when growth is slow, and transfer them later to their final pots – either 13cm (5in), or 19cm (7in), or much larger pots for groups of three or five plants per container. Transplant spring-sown annuals directly into their final pots or containers.

Many annuals (here Schizanthus) are very useful for providing an early, colourful display in a cool greenhouse in spring.

of this is to harden the plants, reducing their dependence on artificial heat and protection without exposing them to sudden environmental changes that might cause damage.

Hardening off is most easily done using a greenhouse and a cold frame. Six or seven weeks before planting the seedlings outdoors, move them to a cooler part of the greenhouse for about a week. Then transfer them to a closed cold frame; increase the ventilation little by little, eventually dispensing with the frame light (the lid) entirely for the last few days unless frost is forecast.

Keep a close watch on the plants for any indication that the change in temperature is too great or too swift: there may be a check in growth, for example, or the leaves may yellow.

Other equipment ideal for hardening off includes glazed frames, the covers of which may be removed completely when conditions are favourable, and cloches, which may be lifted off and replaced as necessary.

Alternatively, the young plants may be placed outdoors in sheltered positions and protected (normally only necessary at night) with horticultural fleece, plastic, or other coverings on temporary wood or bamboo frames. Unless the weather conditions are poor, the covers should be removed during the day to ensure that the plants always receive sufficient light and adequate ventilation.

Planting out

Plant out half-hardy seedlings once all danger of frost has passed. This is particularly important in the case of the more tender plants, such as begonias and *Salvia splendens*. Provided that they have been hardened off, some half-hardy annuals will, however, tolerate cool, but not frosty, conditions for short periods.

Before planting out, prepare the bed (see "Sowing in open ground", p.217), water the young plants thoroughly, and then leave them to drain for an hour or so. To remove a

plant from its pot, invert it, supporting the stem with a finger on either side. Then tap the rim against a hard surface to loosen the root ball from the pot. Break apart packs or divided trays to remove each seedling with its root ball undisturbed.

If plants are in trays without divisions, hold the tray firmly with both hands, and tap one side sharply on the ground to loosen the compost. Then gently slide out the contents in one piece. Separate individual plants carefully with the fingers, keeping as much soil as possible around the roots. Alternatively, remove each plant gently using a widger or other small tool, taking care not to damage the young roots.

Make a hole sufficiently large to accommodate the root ball readily. Space the plants so that the leaves will just touch when the plants are fully developed. Normal planting distances range from 15 to 45cm (6 to 18in) depending on the habit of the species or cultivar being grown.

Check that the plants are at the same depth as in the container, then firm the soil around the base of the stem, without compacting the soil too much. After planting, gently break up the soil surface between the plants with a hand fork. To settle them in, water the plants thoroughly using a watering can fitted with a fine rose so that the soil is not washed off the roots.

Stopping or pinching out

As young annuals develop, some may require stopping or pinching out in order to encourage the plants to produce sideshoots and develop a bushy habit.

Stopping is done by nipping the growing tip off a young plant. Even with annuals that branch naturally it may be necessary when a few plants in a bed produce stronger shoots than others. If an even growth habit

of plants is required, stop tall plants when they have reached five or six joints by removing the tip of each long shoot back to the required height.

Stopping delays flower production and so should not be carried out if an early display is preferred. Nor should it be done on plants such as antirrhinums or stocks (*Matthiola*) that have strong terminal shoots, as these develop the main flower spikes and will also produce lateral growths naturally during the summer to continue the flowering display.

PLANTING OUT INTO OPEN GROUND

1 *Break the pack apart and carefully remove each seedling (here* Tagetes) *with its root ball intact.*

2 *Place each plant in a hole large enough to take its root ball, ensuring that the plant is at the same level as it was in its container.*

3 *Return the soil around the roots and gently firm so that there are no air pockets. Water the area.*

HARDENING OFF

TUNNEL CLOCHE
Place half-hardy annuals (here Tagetes) *in a tunnel cloche. Lift the sides for ventilation.*

COLD FRAME
Seedlings may also be placed in a cold frame left open for progressively longer intervals.

FIRST-YEAR GROWTH

Biennials such as Canterbury bells make only vegetative (leafy) growth in their first year. Flowers develop the following summer.

HOW TO BUY PLANTS

BEDDING PLANTS

GOOD EXAMPLE

Compact, vigorous growth

POOR EXAMPLE

Healthy, green foliage

PETUNIAS

Leggy, bare stems

Dead leaves

POT-GROWN ANNUALS

GOOD EXAMPLE

POOR EXAMPLE

Bushy, sturdy growth

Healthy buds developing

Moist compost

BUSY LIZZIE
(IMPATIENS CV)

Yellowing, discoloured leaves

Bedding plants

Buying more mature annuals and biennials to plant out directly into beds, borders, or containers can save time and may be necessary if no greenhouse is available to grow half-hardy annuals from seed. In addition, whereas seeds of many annuals may be bought only as mixtures, commercial growers are usually able to obtain colours separately, providing gardeners with a much wider range of plant materials with which to plan their bedding schemes.

Judging the quality of bedding plants

Sturdy young plants with evenly balanced, short-noded shoots and healthy foliage are most likely to establish well and give the best results. The plants should have well-developed root systems but must not be pot-bound. Do not purchase plants in dry compost or with yellowing or diseased foliage because they do not always establish well and often produce few flowers.

Half-hardy bedding plants are sold at various stages from seedling to flowering plant, frequently well ahead of the date at which it is safe to plant them outdoors. Make sure that you have appropriate conditions under cover to grow them on properly if this is necessary. Check also that they have been hardened off if they are for immediate planting outside. Acclimatize the seedlings slowly until the danger of frost is past; sudden exposure to frost or even cold wind may kill them since they may have been produced in heated greenhouses. They may then be planted outdoors.

Annual climbers

Climbing annuals should be planted where they are able to grow naturally through a shrub or tree or be trained against a fence, wall, or some other support. If a twining annual is to climb through a shrub, position the plant on the side where it will receive the most sunlight. Where the climber is intended to be grown up a wall or fence, provide a support that will suit its habit of growth (see CLIMBING PLANTS, "Types of support", p.130); then plant it 30cm (12in) from the base of the wall or fence.

Planting bedding plants to a design

Before starting to plant up a bed or border, assemble all the bedding plants to be used and check them off against the plan. Place the plants, still in their containers, roughly in position on top of the prepared soil to ensure that the bed will be neither too crowded nor too sparsely planted. Now is the time to make any final adjustments to plant positioning – it will be too late once they are in the ground. Keep a few plants in reserve to replace any that may die.

1 *Mark out the design of the whole bed before starting to plant. Work from the centre outwards, or from the back of the bed to the front. Use a plank or kneeler for kneeling on so that the soil does not become compacted, making it difficult to work and inhibiting drainage.*

2 *Plant the seedlings carefully, handling the plants as little as possible. Firm the soil around each. Complete one section of planting before moving on to the next.*

3 *As each section of planting is completed, trim off any damaged, uneven, or straggly shoots to make the patches of plants more compact. Water thoroughly section by section so that the seedlings planted first do not dry out while the others are being planted.*

Routine care

SINCE they have a relatively short life, annuals generally require little maintenance unless they are grown in a container (see CONTAINER GARDENING, "Routine care", p.332). They do need to be watered regularly during drought, however, especially if they are grown in containers, and dead-headed to prolong flowering. Continue to pinch out the growing tips (see p.220). Tall annuals may require staking when or soon after planting to prevent them from blowing over or toppling under their own weight. When the foliage starts to die down after flowering or at the end of the season, the plants should be cleared away.

Watering, feeding, and weeding

Young annuals and biennials that are planted in open ground should be watered regularly with a sprinkler or watering can, soaking the bed thoroughly. Once the plants have become established, water only during prolonged dry weather. Those planted against a wall or fence may need extra attention to watering, because they may naturally receive less water (see *Rain Shadow*, p.610).

Annuals rarely need extra feeding if the soil has been well prepared. A liquid fertilizer may be applied on very poor soils as flower buds develop. Biennials may benefit from a little food, but only those grown for show purposes need regular feeding. Over-rich conditions produce vigorous vegetative growth at the expense of flowers. Plants in containers may benefit from the addition of slow-release fertilizers and the application of foliar feeds (see CONTAINER GARDENING, "Fertilizing", p.332.

Keep annuals and biennials free from weeds as these compete for light, water, and soil nutrients. Pull out any weeds by hand while they are still small and remove self-sown seedlings in the same way if they are not required or are too numerous.

Providing supports

Many annuals and biennials have rather slender stems, which benefit from some support. Use small, bushy branches, or peasticks, for plants with a mature height of up to 1m (3ft). When the plants are only a few centimetres high, insert the sticks in the soil around them so that they can grow up through the sticks, which will quickly be covered and hidden. Take particular care not to damage the plants, especially their young roots, when pushing in the sticks.

Taller annuals will flourish and flower more freely if artificially supported by a wigwam, tripod, obelisk, pergola, trellis, fence, wall, or strong tree or shrub, or on wires or trellis between pillars. Such supports should be positioned before the annuals are planted.

Annuals as dried or cut flowers

Dried or fresh flowers of many annuals and biennials are decorative indoors. Harvest "everlasting" flowers, such as *Xeranthemum*, *Helipterum*, and *Limonium*, when they are about half open, then hang them upside-down in a warm, well-ventilated area. Cut *Helichrysum* flowerheads before they show colour to help keep their shape when dried. Cut fresh flowers as the buds show colour. Dip Iceland poppy (*Papaver nudicaule*) stems into boiling water for a few seconds, to seal them and avoid air locks that prevent water uptake.

1 *Cut flowers for drying (here statice, Limonium sinuatum) as the heads start to open. The best time of day to do this is when the weather is cool, in early morning or in the evening.*

2 *Many everlasting flowers may be dried upside-down in bunches fastened with soft string or raffia. Once they have dried, any excess stem may be cut off to suit the flower arrangement.*

Although twining annuals and those that have tendrils such as sweet peas are all self-supporting, their stems or tendrils may need to be guided towards their support. Attach the leading shoots with soft string, which is then tied to the support. Some scrambling annuals that do not twine or have tendrils will also need to be tied in to their support.

Supporting tall and climbing annuals

Many annual climbers reach 2–3m (6–10ft) during their short life, and these are best guided to their support with plastic ties or soft twine until they take hold. The twine should be tied loosely around the stem and support using a figure-of-eight knot, to prevent chafing against any hard surfaces and to allow for stem expansion.

Very tall plants, such as hollyhocks (*Alcea*) or sunflowers (*Helianthus*), may need to be individually staked. Push the cane into the soil where it will be least visible and, as the plant develops, tie in the stem at intervals as required.

Tall annuals in containers may be supported by inserting a few canes around the edge of the pot and tying soft string around the canes – the supports are hidden by the plants as they develop.

SUPPORTING WITH CANES
A tripod, or wigwam of 3 canes tied together at the top, securely inserted into the ground provides support for twining annuals (here Thunbergia alata). Tie a seedling loosely to each of the canes, while its stem is still young and supple.

SUPPORTING WITH WIRE
When planting climbers (here Eccremocarpus scaber) near a wall or fence, tie them onto strong wire or a wooden trellis.

POT-GROWN ANNUALS
Support tall annuals such as Salpiglossis by pushing canes into the potting compost and tying string around the canes.

DEAD-HEADING

To prolong the flowering period, remove flowerheads as they fade, cutting near the base of the stalk. The plants (here pansies) will produce new blooms for some time.

Dead-heading

In many cases, the flowering season of plants may be extended and their appearance improved by promptly removing any flowerheads that are fading or dead; this prevents a plant from setting seed, and its energy is used to produce additional flowers. Snap off any faded flowers between the fingers and thumb, breaking the stems cleanly; use a pair of sharp scissors or secateurs for tougher stems or where there is a danger of disturbing the plant as the dead flowerheads are removed.

Do not dead-head if the seeds or fruits form part of the ornamental characteristic of the annual or biennial – as they do with honesty (*Lunaria*), *Hibiscus trionum*, and ornamental maize (*Zea mays*), for example. Nor should plants be dead-headed if their seeds are required for growing the plant again during the following season.

A few annuals and biennials, such as poppies (*Papaver*), do not produce any more flowers after dead-heading.

Saving seeds

Seeds may be easily collected from many annuals for sowing the following year. It is, however, often worth saving seeds only from those annuals and biennials that stay true to type, such as *Nigella* or honesty, as seeds saved from most garden-grown cultivars and all F1 hybrids will not produce plants that possess flower or habit characteristics similar to those of their parents.

Dead-head those plants that have poor flowers so that no seeds are formed and later collected for sowing the following season. Such seeds are unlikely to produce plants with good-quality flowers.

Self-sown seedlings are likely to vary to some extent in character and quality but may nevertheless produce quite acceptable plants. Distinct cultivars of *Eschscholzia*, Excelsior Series foxgloves (*Digitalis*), sweet alyssum (*Lobularia maritima*), marigolds (*Calendula*), forget-me-nots (*Myosotis*), and many other annuals and biennials usually vary in flower colour and other characteristics from the original plant.

When seed capsules turn brown and begin to split, cut them off and spread them on paper-lined trays in a warm, sunny place until they are fully dry. Extract the seeds and clean away any debris. Packet, label, and store them in dry, cool conditions until they are required for sowing.

Clearing the bed

In autumn, once the flower display is over, lift and compost all dying plants after any seeds required have been gathered. Burn any diseased plants so that they do not spread infection elsewhere in the garden. Perennials grown as annuals or

AUTUMN CLEARANCE

When annuals have finished flowering, carefully loosen the soil around their roots with a fork and then rake up and compost or burn the old plants.

biennials, such as pansies (*Viola* x *wittrockiana*) and polyanthus, may be lifted and replanted elsewhere, where they may grow and flower satisfactorily for several years. Others, for example wallflowers (*Erysimum*) and antirrhinums, seldom grow as well after their first year, so they are usually not worth retaining for future use.

Tender perennials such as begonias and busy Lizzies (*Impatiens* cvs) may be lifted and potted up in late summer to continue flowering in the house, conservatory, or greenhouse. Hollyhocks (*Alcea*) and other short-lived perennials may be cut down in autumn and retained since they sometimes survive for several seasons, although the quality and vigour of the plants will deteriorate. Retain a few plants of the new F1 and F2 strains of pelargonium in a frost-proof greenhouse or conservatory since they will usually survive, if kept quite dry, and flower again the following year. *Eccremocarpus scaber*, too, will survive for years in protected positions outside.

Pests and diseases

The pests most likely to be troublesome to annuals and biennials when they are seedlings, as well as when they are more mature, are slugs and snails (p.644), aphids (p.646), and caterpillars (p.645); plants may also be attacked by rusts (pp.648 and 653) and other fungal problems (see "Fungal leaf spots", p.648). Fungicides may prevent or check these diseases but often little can be done beyond pulling out and burning badly affected plants. Young seedlings growing under cover may suffer from damping off (p.664) – a group of soil-borne diseases that causes the plants to rot and collapse.

(p.644), aphids (p.646), and caterpillars (p.645); plants may also be attacked by rusts (pp.648 and 653) and other fungal problems (see "Fungal leaf spots", p.648).

CUTTING DOWN SHORT-LIVED PERENNIALS

1 *Not all seedheads ripen at the same time. To prevent self-seeding, remove flowered stems before any seedheads ripen fully.*

2 *Short-lived perennials such as hollyhocks may flower for several seasons if cut down immediately after flowering.*

3 *Carefully cut each stem at its base, ensuring that the new growth that has been produced during the growing season is not damaged in the process.*

SAVING SEEDS

1 *Seeds may be collected when the capsules or seedheads (here* Nigella*) have been dried on blotting paper or newspaper and release their seeds.*

2 *Once the seedhead has dried, shake the seeds out and separate them from any other debris. Store them in a labelled envelope in a dry place in a constant, cool temperature.*

CHAPTER

8

BULBOUS PLANTS

FROM THE CHEERFUL, golden daffodil trumpeting the arrival of spring to the cyclamen, herald of autumn, bulbous plants ring the seasonal changes throughout the year with glorious flower displays. Some possess handsome foliage, and others are valued for their fragrance, but it is their blooms that make bulbs essential. They offer a wide variety of colour and form, from bright, primary shades to delicate, pastel hues, and the tall grandeur of gladiolus spikes to the dainty bells of tiny fritillaries. Whether they form bold patterns in a formal bed, fill in the detail in a mixed border, provide a splash of colour in containers, or create highlights beneath trees or in grass, bulbs bring vitality to the permanent plantings of the garden.

Designing with bulbs

GROWING bulbs is an easy way of brightening up the garden with decorative, often flamboyant, and sometimes fragrant displays. The bulbs that are grown in the garden are dominated by hardy favourites, for example crocuses, cyclamen, daffodils, hyacinths, and tulips, of which there is an immense variety of both species and cultivars. Many tender bulbs also deserve a place in the garden, including the starry *Ixia*, *Sparaxis* with its loose, gaudy spikes, and the fiery *Tigridia*.

The key characteristic of bulbs is that they provide visual interest for only one season, remaining dormant and unnoticed for the remainder of the year. This can be an asset with careful planning, making bulbs invaluable as border plants as well as ideal for naturalizing in grass or growing in containers.

In many gardens, bulbs may be left to increase naturally from year to year while their dying foliage is hidden by the developing growth of herbaceous plants or shrubs that provide a succession of interest. Many bulbs, including the popular crocuses, daffodils (*Narcissus*), and snowdrops (*Galanthus*), increase very rapidly in most sites. Bulbs may also be lifted after flowering and replanted each year to provide room for other seasonal plants, making them especially convenient for small gardens or restricted areas.

Seasons of interest
The main bulb season is from early spring to early summer, but many other bulbs flower outdoors or under cover at other times of the year. For colour in winter when most of the garden is dormant, early bulbs such as the pink *Cyclamen coum*, the tiny, deep blue *Iris histrioides* 'Major', and snowdrops may be grown outdoors, and other bulbs forced indoors. Bulbs that flower in summer or autumn are often larger, and of more exotic shapes and hues, than spring bulbs.

Where to grow bulbs
If given the well-drained soil that they need to grow and flower well, bulbs are among the easiest of all garden plants to cultivate. There are numerous cultivars and species now available that thrive in all aspects except deep shade.

Many bulbs in cultivation come from areas with a Mediterranean climate, so need to be grown in sunny sites and prefer hot, dry summers – although a huge range of bulbs flourishes in the open garden in regions with summer rainfall.

Bulbs that would normally grow in woodland thrive in moist, light shade. Many others, including some bulbs described as "sun-loving", are happy in light shade cast by nearby shrubs, walls, or trellises. Even dry shade is tolerated by most hardy cyclamen. Bulbs with white or pale flowers appear almost luminous in dusky light, so look very effective when planted in a shaded site.

Whatever the setting, bulbs look best planted in groups of the same species or cultivar, whether jostling shoulders with other plants or forming a single, swaying sea of colour in a formal bed or in grass.

EFFECTIVE USE OF BULBS IN A MIXED BORDER
The dusky, purple-pink globes of Allium sphaerocephalon *pick up the colour theme of this mixed border, providing a strong accent of colour and form amid the softer silhouettes of herbaceous perennials and shrubs.*

The different types of bulbous plant

BULB (*Hyacinthoides* x *massartiana*)

CORM (*Gladiolus callianthus*)

In this book, the term "bulb" refers to all bulbous plants, including corms, tubers, and rhizomes as well as true bulbs. The terms "corm", "tuber", and "rhizome" are used only in their specific sense throughout. With all bulbous plants, a portion of the plant is swollen into a food storage organ that enables the plant to survive when dormant or when conditions are unsuitable for growth.

Bulbs
True bulbs are formed from fleshy leaves or leaf bases, and frequently consist of concentric rings of scales attached to a basal plate. The outer scales often form a dry, protective skin or tunic, as found in daffodils, Reticulata irises, and tulips. With some lilies (*Lilium*) and *Fritillaria* species, the scales are separate and no tunic is formed. Juno irises are unusual in having swollen storage roots beneath the bulbs.

Corms
Corms are formed from the swollen bases of stems and are replaced by new corms every year. They are common in the family Iridaceae, which

TUBER (*Dahlia* 'Monk Marc')

RHIZOME (*Iris* 'White City')

includes crocuses, gladioli, *Romulea*, and *Watsonia*; usually they have a tunic that has been formed from the previous year's leaf bases. In the Liliaceae and related families, they are found in such genera as *Brodiaea* and *Colchicum*.

Tubers
Tuberous is a term applied to many plants with swollen, often irregularly shaped stems or roots used for food storage. It is often misapplied, for example to the tuber-like roots – actually rhizomes – of *Anemone blanda* and the long, thin rhizomes of *A. nemorosa* (for convenience, both are included here as "bulbous plants"). True tubers of various kinds are found in *Dahlia*, *Corydalis*, some orchids, such as *Dactylorrhiza*, cyclamen species (although these are often called "corms"), and in plants such as *Ranunculus asiaticus* where they are lobed or clustered together.

Rhizomes
Rhizomes are swollen, usually more or less horizontal, underground stems, found in the Iridaceae, notably in irises, and in Liliaceae.

Formal beds

Bulbs make a valuable contribution to formal bedding displays. Spring-flowering bulbs are excellent for planting en masse in a bed to be occupied by bedding annuals later in summer, since they may be lifted and stored during their dormant season. Classic bedding bulbs are

A PAGEANT OF COLOUR
Serried ranks of tulips parade along these formal beds in bold, bright blocks of contrasting colour, creating an energetic counterpoint to the quiet orderliness of the formal garden. White tulips intersperse those of stronger hue to prevent the colour combinations from appearing too strident.

hyacinths and tulips because of their strong, sculptural forms; in general, the larger, showy flowers of hybrid bulbs are best grown in a formal position in the garden. Plant in blocks of colour, each of one type of bulb, or in mixed groups that flower at different times to provide a long display of colour during the spring. Bulbs may completely fill the bed or

be combined with companion plants with flowers in complementary or contrasting colours, such as deep blue forget-me-nots (*Myosotis*) or fiery wallflowers (*Erysimum*).

There is also scope for effective formal planting with summer- or autumn-flowering bulbs: *Galtonia*, with its elegant, white or green spikes, or the more compact cultivars of gladioli, especially the Primulinus or Butterfly groups, look impressive when planted in large blocks bordered by purple-blue violas, or any similar, low-growing ground cover. *Agapanthus* Headbourne Hybrids, with their large, rounded flower-heads of blue or white, combine well with the graceful, pink blooms of *Nerine bowdenii*.

Mixed herbaceous and shrub borders

Bulbs fill in the permanent planting of a border with a lively variety of seasonal colour. Loose drifts may blend in with the general scheme or draw the eye with splashes of colour. Architectural bulbs, such as *Crinum* x *powellii*, with its huge, pink or white trumpets, punctuate the flow of a border with an arresting contrast

of height and form. Grow some bulbs through low ground-cover plants so that their blooms appear to float above the mat of foliage. For a more informal cottage border, choose species bulbs since florid hybrids may sometimes look out of place.

Mixed plantings for spring flowering
Planting bulbs in a mixed border extends the flowering season, and provides an array of fresh, bright colour from late winter through to early summer. Before the herbaceous perennials and deciduous shrubs in the border begin to grow and spread, bring the front of the border to life with the smaller daffodil species, pale or dark blue Reticulata irises, snowdrops, and the golden cups of winter aconites (*Eranthis hyemalis*).

Plant starry carpets of pink and blue *Anemone blanda*, *Chionodoxa*, and *Scilla bifolia*, or pale yellow drifts of the more freely increasing dwarf daffodil species and hybrids beneath such early-flowering shrubs as *Corylopsis*, forsythia, and witch hazel (*Hamamelis*) to complement their display.

For later in spring, a much wider range of bulbs is available and larger plants, such as the tall daffodils, *Fritillaria* species (for example the purple-black *F. persica* and the regal *F. imperialis*) or tulips, may be used in casual groups to give height among the shrubs and perennials.

Mixed plantings for summer and autumn flowering

A number of bulbs add greatly to the beauty of the garden in summer. Although they are often regarded as only of secondary importance, in fact many summer- and autumn-flowering bulbs are tall and robust enough to hold their own among the surrounding flowering perennials and they offer a dazzling range of colours and flower forms.

Early in the season, try *Camassia leichtlinii* with its creamy-white flower plumes, vivid gladioli, *Triteleia laxa* (syn. *Brodiaea laxa*) for its loose, purple-blue clusters of bloom, and the bold, scarlet goblets of *Tulipa sprengeri*.

Follow them in mid- to late summer with the huge, purple globes of *Allium aflatunense*, arching sprays of blazing red or yellow *Crocosmia*, sun-loving lilies (*Lilium*) and, later, slim pink, red, or white spires of *Schizostylis*. In warmer gardens, greenish-white *Eucomis* with its pineapple-like flowerheads brings an exotic touch to the border planting.

In autumn, continue the display with the fragrant, pink trumpets of *Amaryllis belladonna*, the brilliant yellow funnels of *Sternbergia lutea* or *S. sicula*, and blue to white forms of autumn-flowering crocuses.

Naturalizing bulbs

When left undisturbed, many bulbs readily increase to form flowing drifts of colour. Allowing them to

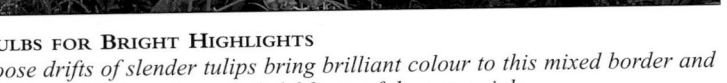

BULBS FOR BRIGHT HIGHLIGHTS
Loose drifts of slender tulips bring brilliant colour to this mixed border and contrast with the soft, mounded foliage of the perennials.

naturalize in this way gives interest to areas of the garden that otherwise might not be given over to flowering plants. Species, which are more delicate in hue and form than most cultivars, create a natural effect when planted in large, informal groups.

Planting with specimen trees

Bulbs make perfect partners for specimen trees with deep roots and light, deciduous canopies. Use bulbs that flower mostly in spring or autumn to form a decorative ground cover when the tree has few leaves to deepen the shade. In spring the soil beneath the tree is moist and sunlit, ideal for anemones, crocuses, daffodils, or *Scilla*. Hardy, autumn-flowering cyclamen, with mottled, silvery foliage and softly folded petals, tolerate the dry summer conditions, and enjoy partial shade.

The flowers of bulbs can complement a tree's habit effectively. White-flowered bulbs, for example, mirror the white blossom of ornamental cherries (*Prunus*), the crisp shape of crocuses echo the chalice form of magnolia blooms, and bulbs with pendent flowers imitate the habit of a weeping tree.

Use dwarf cultivars to naturalize the area around a newly planted tree or shrub, since rapidly increasing bulbs such as daffodils reduce the available food.

Woodland settings

Bulbs are invaluable planted in large, informal pools of colour to enhance the natural beauty of deciduous woodland and any mossy ground cover. Many relish woodland conditions, blending well with other woodland plants, such as ferns, hellebores (*Helleborus*), and primulas.

Plant bulbs for a succession of flower, and contrast of form and height, with subtle variations on a colour theme to reflect the tranquil mood of woodland. Snowdrops

(*Galanthus*) and cyclamen species in pinks and purples make a striking combination, while drifts of *Scilla* and *Chionodoxa* add shades of blue. Spanish bluebells (*Hyacinthoides* x *massartiana*, syn. *H. hispanica* of gardens) or many of the more rampant grape hyacinths (*Muscari*) provide swathes of blue, pink, and white, together with tiny, white sprays of lily-of-the-valley (*Convallaria majalis*). These can all colonize considerable areas once established. English bluebells (*Hyacinthoides non-scriptus*) should only be planted on their own because they will rapidly invade other plantings.

Planting in grass

Bulbs can transform grass, whether a bank, a section of a lawn, or an entire meadow, into a gay carpet of spring or autumn colour that spreads more thickly year by year. The bulbs must be robust species that can withstand competition from grass roots. Many of the larger bulbs look best in grass where after flowering their fading foliage is less obtrusive.

Plant earlier-flowering bulbs in grass that is to be mown from spring onwards so that their leaves have time to die down before the grass is cut. Later-flowering bulbs, such as terrestrial orchids (*Dactylorrhiza*), may be grown with grass and wild flowers in "meadows" that are not cut until mid- or late summer. Bulbs that bloom in autumn start into growth and flower before the end of the usual mowing season so the grass must be left unmown after late summer. Alternatively, plant bulbs in irregular but defined areas so that it is possible to mow around them.

Daffodils are the classic choice for grass and a remarkable range – especially the more robust species and hybrids – may be grown in this way. Many crocuses grow well in grass. A more delicate effect may be achieved with the pendent bells of the summer snowflake (*Leucojum aestivum*) and the snake's-head fritillary (*Fritillaria meleagris*) that shiver softly in the breeze.

Where the grass is less vigorous, particularly in partly shaded areas, some of the dwarf bulbs do well: the purple flowered *Crocus tommasinianus*, *Chionodoxa*, some daffodils (for example, *Narcissus cyclamineus*), *Scilla*, and snowdrops all flourish in these conditions.

An area that is naturalized with bulbs on the outskirts of a garden provides a harmonious transition between the flowerbeds of a formal garden and the grassy fields of the surrounding countryside by combining elements of both.

WOODLAND CHARM
Hardy Cyclamen coum *and crocuses in deep and pale shades of pink, lilac, and violet colonize a woodland, clustering prettily around the feet of the trees to provide a show of colour when the trees are bare.*

SPRING SPECTACLE
Naturalized crocuses in bloom cover this lawn with vivid pinks, purples, and yellows. The bulbs are planted in great swathes of a single hue, that merge with each other to create a sea of colour. Snowdrops (Galanthus) planted among the crocuses provide highlights of white.

Bulbs with alpines

Using bulbs in the rock garden, trough, or raised bed prolongs the season as most alpines flower in late spring. The erect habit, upright flowers, and spear-like leaves of bulbs contrast well with the low, mounded, or spreading habit of most alpine plants, as well as introducing a greater variety of form. Choose dwarf bulbs with dainty blooms to complement the character of the alpines, and plant some bulbs to grow through and lift the alpine planting. Avoid mat-forming alpines that exhaust the soil around the bulbs and so deprive them of food.

In the rock garden
Many smaller bulbs, especially the more temperamental species for which sharp drainage is essential,

AN ALPINE SETTING
The strange beauty of the bell-like flowers of Fritillaria acmopetala *is best shown off in the small-scale planting of an alpine garden.*

thrive in rock gardens, in sun or partial shade. Dwarf bulbs look attractive when planted in pockets of rock or offset against the grit top-dressing of the bed, which also stops their delicate flowers from being muddied during wet weather. If planting very small alpines in the bed, do not use the taller bulb species, which would appear out of proportion to their neighbours.

Bulbs in troughs
Old stone troughs make an attractive setting for a collection of dwarf bulbs and smaller alpine plants where their tiny charms may be appreciated at close hand. The bulbs benefit from the gritty, well-drained soil, and may easily be given the careful watering that they need.

To keep the display in proportion, grow the smallest species and their less robust hybrids; rapidly increasing bulbs may swamp neighbouring alpines. Grow the smaller *Fritillaria* species for their intriguing flowers, whether the purplish-brown and yellow *F. michailovskyi* or the chequered green *F. whittallii*.

Rhodohypoxis are excellent for troughs, producing pink, red, or white starry flowers through most of the summer. Keep the bulbs moist during the growing season, and give them an occasional liquid feed. The genus *Cyclamen* includes species that are suitable for troughs in spring and autumn, ranging in hue from pure white to deepest purple-pink.

In a leaf-mould bed
A shady raised bed filled with leaf mould and well-rotted garden compost provides perfect conditions for the dwarfer "woodland" bulbs, whether planted on their own or with

ericaceous shrubs or alpines. Try erythroniums, with their dainty, reflexed flowers in shades of pink, white, or yellow, which you can then view from underneath, or plant any of the trilliums in a leaf-mould bed.

Bulbs to associate with water gardens

A few bulbs flourish in damp, poorly drained conditions and provide some of the most striking flowering plants to grow around water. Their strong shapes and colours create pleasing reflections; plant them in clumps to contrast with the flat, open surface of the water. Several handsome rhizomatous irises and the arum lily (*Zantedeschia aethiopica*), with large, white spathes above broad, arrow-shaped leaves, thrive in pond margins. Both the snake's-head fritillary and summer snowflake (*Leucojum aestivum*) grow naturally in water meadows, so enjoy a moist site or damp beds around ponds.

Other bulbs that enhance water gardens are the magnificent, purple-red *Iris ensata* (syn. *I. kaempferi*), white-flowered *I.* 'Geisha Gown', with its deep pinkish-purple veins, and *Dierama pendulum*, with its wand-like flower sprays, although all of these prefer a soil that is well drained as well as moist.

BULBS IN POTS
Larger bulbs are naturals for use in containers. Here, Lilium regale *provides the focus of interest in this grouping of pots, which have been arranged on different levels and in gradations of size to draw the eye upwards. The huge, white lily trumpets combine with white pelargoniums and terracotta tones to form an attractive composition that is in harmony with the natural stone wall and greenery behind it.*

Bulbs in containers

Growing bulbs in ornamental pots, windowboxes, and other containers provides a varied and spectacular display, which can be extended throughout the season by moving containers into view as they come into flower (see also "Changes in focus", p.306). Careful choice of bulbs may lengthen the season to include late winter as well as spring and summer. Plant a single species or cultivar in each container to provide a uniform, even effect and then group the containers together for a mass of colour.

Place pots of bulbs with fragrant flowers (e.g. hyacinths or Tazetta daffodils) near the house entrance where they may be fully appreciated. Pots used for spring bulbs may be used for summer-flowering plants later: when the bulbs die down, lift and replant them in the garden (or store them) and replace them with annuals or tender perennials.

Some larger bulbs are sufficiently striking to be planted on their own in containers. Tall lilies (*Lilium*) or *Crinum* x *powellii*, in pink or white forms, are particularly effective. Any *Agapanthus* species or hybrid provides a long season of showy flower. Alternatively, group several bulbs of varying heights and colours in a large container such as a half-barrel to provide a feature on a patio.

Windowboxes

When planting in windowboxes, choose smaller bulbs that are in proportion to the size of the container. They are excellent for planting in layers below other plants to make best use of limited space; the bulbs thrust through the surface planting to create a pleasing contrast of height and form. Blending the plants with winter-flowering pansies (*Viola* x *wittrockiana*) and ivy (*Hedera*), followed by trailing tender perennials and annuals, gives a prolonged display of colour.

Bulbs under cover

Growing bulbs under cover extends the range that may be cultivated to include many rare species that need particular care. In temperate or cold regions, tender bulbs may be grown that would not survive unprotected in the garden. In regions with summer rainfall, it is the most practical way of growing many of the species bulbs currently in cultivation because they need a dry, summer resting period in order to flourish and flower well. Bulbs may be planted in pots or in a greenhouse bed or bulb frame. This allows easier control of the local environment to accommodate the individual needs of a wide range of bulbs, be it a summer drying-off period or protection from excessive winter wet, cold, or frost.

Bulbs in pots

Growing bulbs in pots allows each plant to be grown in conditions that best suit its individual requirements, especially when cultivating small stocks of uncommon bulbs. The pots are easily transferred from outdoors to the shelter of frames or greenhouses when required, or from the greenhouse to the conservatory to enjoy them when in full flower.

Pot cultivation in an unheated greenhouse enables many bulb species that are otherwise of borderline hardiness in temperate climates to be grown. Many are South African and South American bulbs with an exciting diversity of richly coloured blooms, such as *Watsonia* with its dense spikes of deep pink, white, and red. To enjoy tender bulbs, such as *Gloriosa*, and winter-flowering *Veltheimia*, the shelter of a frost-free greenhouse is needed. Overwinter other tender species or cultivars of such genera as begonias, *Canna*, or *Crinum* in a cool greenhouse and bring them out when in bloom to enhance the summer display in the open garden.

If desired, bulbs may be grown in shade and the compost adjusted accordingly to grow small "woodland" bulbs, including *Trillium rivale*, which has finely spotted petals in pink or white, or tender, terrestrial orchids such as the free-flowering *Calanthe* species.

Gardeners with an alpine house may add a little height and splashes of colour to the display by interspersing the plants with pots of dwarf spring bulbs. The alpine house environment is especially suitable for rare or tender bulbs (for example, ice-white *Narcissus cantabricus* or bright blue *Tecophilaea cyanocrocus*).

Greenhouse beds

Tender bulbs may be planted out directly in prepared greenhouse beds, rather than in pots, for a more natural and vigorous display. The bulbs may be combined in a mixed bed with other plants that flower in summer when the bulbs are dormant. Choose companion plants that tolerate a dry period coinciding with that needed by the bulbs, or that can be plunged in plastic pots and watered without the moisture reaching the bulbs around them.

Spreading, heat-loving plants, such as *Osteospermum* or gazanias, and many silver-foliaged plants could be used in this way, and then removed or cut back hard at the end of summer when the bulbs start into growth. Late-flowering *Brodiaea*, *Calochortus*, and *Triteleia* prolong the flowering season still further: group them together and water them separately. Summer-growing bulbs, such as *Eucomis*, some *Gladiolus* species, and the tender *Nerine* species do not need interplanting.

Bulb frames and raised beds

The term "bulb frame" usually refers to a raised bed devoted solely to bulbs; it is covered with a cold frame or Dutch lights during the natural resting period of the bulbs in summer, and also in winter to protect them from excessive rainfall which could cause them to rot. Alternatively, a frame may simply cover bulbs in pots plunged in a sand bed. Such frames may be made more attractive by using stone for the sides.

Bulb frames are the best alternative to the alpine house as a place to grow tender or demanding bulb species without the root restriction of pots, and are used mainly by enthusiasts or collectors. This method of cultivation is suitable for most bulbs, other than those used to some summer rainfall, such as "woodland" and high mountain species. Some crocus,

Bulbs for cut flowers

Many bulbs have flowers that can be cut for the house since their shapely, often solitary, flowers on long stems make them especially suitable for floral arrangements. A few have powerful scents that can fill a room and most are long-lasting if picked before the blooms reach maturity. Some, such as daffodils, are so vigorous and prolific that they may be cut without leaving a gap in the garden display. Alternatively, set aside a separate area to grow bulbs especially for cutting.

Gladioli make fine cut flowers and are often used in this way, since the taller cultivars are difficult to place satisfactorily in an open border.

The pretty, wonderfully fragrant freesias are the only tender or half-hardy bulbs that are commonly grown under cover to provide cut flowers. They have a long flowering season during the winter but make somewhat straggly pot plants that need staking, so they are best cut for display indoors where they will last well.

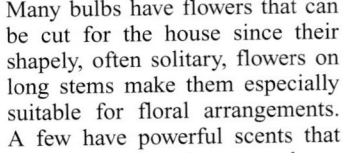

Schizostylis coccinea 'Sunrise'

Crocosmia 'Lucifer'

Narcissus 'Cheerfulness'

Dahlia 'Zorro'

Freesia 'Everett'

Gladiolus 'Tesoro'

Zantedeschia aethiopica 'Crowborough'

Nerine bowdenii

Alstroemeria Ligtu Hybrids

Tulipa 'Clara Butt'

Allium giganteum

Lilium 'Enchantment'

daffodil, *Fritillaria*, and tulip species, Juno and Reticulata irises, and the more difficult *Brodiaea* and *Zigadenus* species tend to be less successful in temperate climates as open garden plants; they may not survive unless they are protected from excess moisture in bulb frames or seasonally covered raised beds throughout the dormant season.

Forcing bulbs

A good way of bringing colour and fragrance indoors during the winter and early spring is to force bulbs in pots. The bulbs are kept in a cool, dark place for a few months before bringing them into the light to encourage them to flower earlier than they do naturally. *Hippeastrum* with its giant, exotic blooms, scented hyacinths, and daffodils, especially *Narcissus papyraceus*, or the 'Paper White' narcissi, are all suitable and are often offered for sale as "prepared" bulbs. These have been given an artificial cold period in imitation of winter cold to speed up the natural flowering cycle. Many hardy spring bulbs, such as tulips, can be forced for early flowers, but some, such as crocuses, may abort their flowers if forced too quickly. A gentler method is to grow bulbs under cover in pots and bring them indoors when the flowers begin to show colour, a week or two before they would normally bloom in the open garden, so that the warmth stimulates them into bloom.

Planter's guide to bulbous plants

EXPOSED SITES

Bulbs that tolerate exposed or windy sites

Anemone
Chionodoxa
Colchicum
Crocus
Cyclamen, some ❋
Fritillaria (dwarf spp.)
Galanthus
Ipheion
Iris reticulata (cvs)
Muscari, some ❋
Narcissus (dwarf spp. and cvs)
Ornithogalum, some ❋
Oxalis, some ❋

*Oxalis
depressa*

Scilla, some ❋
Sternbergia lutea
Triteleia
Tulipa (dwarf spp.)

WALL PROTECTION

Bulbs that prefer the protection of a wall

Agapanthus, some ❋ (most spp.)
Alstroemeria (except Ligtu
    Hybrids)
Amaryllis belladonna
Anomatheca laxa
Belamcanda chinensis
Bloomeria crocea
Eucomis
Fritillaria persica
Gladiolus ❋ (tender spp.)
Gynandriris sisyrinchium
Habranthus, some ❋ (some spp.)
Hippeastrum advenum
Ixia
Lycoris squamigera
Moraea spathulata
Nerine bowdenii
Scilla peruviana
Sparaxis ❋
Sternbergia lutea, S. sicula
Tulbaghia, some ❋
Watsonia ❋
Zephyranthes candida

DRY SHADE

Bulbs that tolerate dry shade

Anemone nemorosa
Arum italicum 'Marmoratum'
Cyclamen coum,
    C. hederifolium, C. repandum
Galanthus nivalis (forms)
Hyacinthoides non-scriptus
Ranunculus ficaria (cvs)

MOIST SHADE

Bulbs that prefer moist shade

Anemone apennina, A. blanda,
    A. ranunculoides
Arisaema, some ❋ (most spp.)
Arum italicum
Cardiocrinum
Corydalis (some spp.)
Eranthis
Erythronium
Fritillaria camschatcensis,
    F. cirrhosa
Galanthus
Ipheion uniflorum
Leucojum aestivum, L. vernum
Lilium (some spp.)

*Lilium
hansonii*

Narcissus cyclamineus,
    N. triandrus
Nomocharis
Notholirion
Scilla bifolia
Trillium
Tulipa sylvestris

FLOWERS FOR CUTTING

Agapanthus, some ❋
Allium (some spp.)
Alstroemeria (taller spp. and cvs)
Amaryllis belladonna
Anemone De Caen Series,
    A. St Brigid Series
Camassia
Clivia ❋
Crinum, some ❋
Crocosmia

Dierama, some ❋
Freesia ❋
Galtonia
Gladiolus, some ❋
Iris, Dutch Hybrids,
    I. latifolia, I. xiphium
Ixia ❋
Lilium
Narcissus
Nerine, some ❋
Ornithogalum, some ❋
    (tall spp.)
Ranunculus asiaticus ❋ (forms)
Sparaxis ❋
Tulipa
Watsonia ❋
Zantedeschia, some ❋

ARCHITECTURAL PLANTS

Allium cristophii,
    A. giganteum
Canna ❋
Cardiocrinum giganteum
Crinum x *powellii*
Fritillaria imperialis
Lilium (most spp. and cvs)

ROCK GARDENS

Bulbs suitable for planting in rock gardens

Albuca humilis ❋
Allium (dwarf spp.)
Anemone (some spp.)
Bellevalia (some spp.)
Brodiaea (smallest spp.)
Bulbocodium vernum
Colchicum (small spp.)
Corydalis (some spp.)
Crocus
Cyclamen (hardy spp.)
Fritillaria (many spp.)
Gagea, some ❋ (some spp.)
Galanthus
Ipheion
Iris (dwarf spp.)
Leucojum (some spp.)
Merendera
Muscari, some ❋ (non-invasive spp.)
Narcissus (dwarf spp. and hybrids)
Ornithogalum, some ❋ (dwarf spp.)
Oxalis, some ❋ (some spp.)
Puschkinia

Rhodohypoxis
Romulea, some ❋ (some spp.)
Scilla, some ❋
Sternbergia lutea, S. sicula
Tulipa (dwarf spp.)
Zephyranthes candida
Zigadenus

BULBS FOR ALPINE HOUSES

Albuca ❋
Anemone (some spp.)
Anomatheca
Arum, some ❋ (some spp.)
Babiana ❋
Bellevalia
Biarum
Bongardia chrysogonum
Bulbocodium vernum
Calochortus
Colchicum (small spp.)
Crocus
Cyclamen, some ❋
Fritillaria (most spp.)
Gagea, some ❋
Galanthus
Habranthus, some ❋
Hippeastrum, some ❋ (dwarf spp.)

Moraea huttonii

Iris (dwarf spp.)
Leontice
Leucocoryne ❋
Leucojum (some spp.)
Merendera
Moraea, some ❋ (some spp.)
Muscari, some ❋ (some spp.)
Narcissus (dwarf spp.)
Ornithogalum, some ❋ (dwarf spp.)
Oxalis, some ❋ (some spp.)
Pancratium, some ❋
Pinellia
Rhodohypoxis
Romulea, some ❋
Scilla, some ❋
Sternbergia
Tecophilaea
Tulipa (dwarf spp.)
Zephyranthes, some ❋
Zigadenus

KEY
❋ *Not hardy*

231

Tulips and daffodils

TULIPS (*Tulipa*) and daffodils (*Narcissus*) are highly valued for the bold splashes of colour they bring in spring. Grow them together to extend the flowering season in a mixed border: some daffodils bloom very early in the year, while many tulips last well into late spring. Tulips are excellent for beds or borders, while many daffodils are especially suitable for naturalizing in grass. Dwarf forms are ideal for rock gardens, alpine houses, or containers, where they may be seen at close range.

Tulips

This diverse, versatile genus is horticulturally classified in 15 divisions based on flower form, but may conveniently be grouped by flowering season and garden use.

Early tulips
Single, early tulips have classic, goblet-shaped blooms, some with striped, flushed, or margined petals. Early doubles have long-lasting, open bowl-shaped flowers, often flecked or margined in toning colours. Traditionally used for cutting, in formal bedding, or as border edgings, many can also be grown in pots indoors. In informal schemes their elegant outlines contrast well with spreading or prostrate plants.

Mid-season tulips
This grouping includes Triumph tulips, with their simple, conical blooms, and the Darwin hybrids, with rich and intensely coloured flowers, often with a satiny, basal blotch and dark, velvety anthers. Both types are sturdy, robust, and noted for their weather resistance.

Late tulips
Some of the most vibrant colours and intricate forms are seen in late-flowering tulips. They include the graceful lily-flowered types, vivid and extravagant Parrot tulips, green-tinged Viridifloras, and exuberantly striped and feathered Rembrandts. Peony-flowered forms are suited to informal cottage gardens. All are effective used informally with dark green or grey ground cover or in formal bedding schemes.

Dwarf species and hybrids
The compact Kaufmanniana hybrids produce their brightly coloured blooms very early in the spring while the slightly taller Fosteriana and Greigii tulips usually flower a little later. Many have very attractively marked foliage. The dwarf species are ideal for containers, raised beds, or rock gardens. *Tulipa sprengeri* and *T. sylvestris* tolerate light shade and will naturalize in fine grass.

Cultivation and propagation
Most tulips thrive in fertile, well-drained, humus-rich soils, in sun and with shelter, and in ideal conditions some robust cultivars persist from year to year. Many, however, are best regarded as annual bedding plants, being lifted after flowering and either discarded (if diseased) or replanted until they have died down. The bulbs seldom flower well in the

TULIPS IN A SPRING BORDER
The strong, vertical stems and neat flower-cups of tulips provide height and structure, as well as vivid colour, in an informal spring border.

GROWING IN CONTAINERS
The lily-flowered tulip 'West Point' here displays its ornate blooms.

Types of tulip

Tulips include an impressive range of flower forms, from the simple, upright goblets of single-flowered tulips to the frilled and twisted petals of Parrot tulips and the open, double blooms of peony-flowered forms. They are available in most colours, except blue, from the purest white to the deepest purple, with many glorious shades of yellow, red, and crimson in between. Many of the dwarf tulips also have attractively marked leaves.

SINGLE

***Tulipa* 'Dawnglow'**
Darwin hybrid

T. 'Queen of Night'
Single, late

T. 'Spring Green'
Viridiflora

DOUBLE AND PARROT

T. 'Peach Blossom'
Double, early

T. 'Estella Rijnveld'
Parrot

DWARF SPECIES AND HYBRIDS

T. tarda
Dwarf species

T. 'Dreamboat'
Greigii hybrid

T. 'Giuseppe Verdi'
Kaufmanniana hybrid

T. 'Greuze'
Single, late

EXTENDING THE FLOWERING SEASON
Growing tulips and daffodils together provides a continuous display of colour from early spring until well into summer.

Daffodils

Grown for their cheerful spring blooms, daffodils (*Narcissus*) are among the easiest and most rewarding of bulbs to grow. They are horticulturally divided into 13 groups, based on the form of the flowers.

Daffodils in containers

Most daffodils can be grown in pots, if they are deep enough to allow the bulbs to be covered to 1½ times their own depth. Tazettas, with clusters of up to 12 scented blooms, are often grown under glass or as pot plants to bloom from late autumn to spring. The richly fragrant jonquil hybrids are also useful as container plants for house decoration. Small species, such as *N. cantabricus* and *N. romieuxii*, produce blooms early in the year in the alpine house; they may also then be brought indoors.

Daffodils in the garden

Valuable for formal spring bedding and to give early interest in the mixed border, daffodils are among the most reliable of bulbs for naturalizing: they rarely need lifting in borders or grass. Even tiny species, such as *N. cyclamineus* and *N. minor*, will thrive in fine turf. Dwarf daffodils are ideal for rock gardens and raised beds, some, such as *N. romieuxii*, *N.* 'Tête-à-tête', and *N. asturiensis*, flowering early in the year.

Cultivation and propagation

Daffodils will grow in almost any soil type, but prefer well-drained, moist, slightly alkaline conditions.

NATURALIZING DAFFODILS IN GRASS
In an informal or wild garden, daffodils may be grown in grass, bringing welcome colour to a dark corner or the ground beneath a tree.

second year but if replanted in autumn may reach flowering size again within two years.

Dwarf tulips generally prefer open, gritty soils, and full sun; lift and replant them only when overcrowded. Propagate by offsets (see p.245) or, for species, by seed (see p.246). Tulips are prone to tulip fire (see p.649) and other bulb problems (see p.244).

They thrive in sun or light, dappled shade. Plant the bulbs 12–15cm (5–6in) deep in late summer or early autumn. When bulbs are naturalized in grass, do not cut the old foliage until at least six weeks after they have flowered. Bulbs in containers must be grown in cool conditions, with plenty of fresh air. Temperatures above 7–10°C (45–50°F) usually cause flowers to abort. Place the pots in a cold frame after planting, and

bring them into a cold greenhouse about 12–16 weeks later. Once flower buds have formed, blooming can be advanced by raising the temperature gently although not exceeding 13°C (55°F).

Propagate by offsets (see p.245), or by chipping (see p.249); new hybrids and species may also be raised from seed (see p.246). Daffodils may be affected by both narcissus eelworm (p.663) and bulb flies (p.663).

Types of daffodil

Daffodils provide a wide variety of shapes and forms, from the tiny, exquisite Cyclamineus hybrids, with their swept-back petals, to the tall, trumpet daffodils and the showy double forms. Modern developments include the split corona and collarette types. In addition to the characteristic bright yellow flowers, cultivars include those with pale butter-yellow blooms or brilliant white petals and fiery orange cups.

DWARF SPECIES AND HYBRIDS

Narcissus triandrus
Dwarf species

N. romieuxii
Dwarf species

N. 'Jumblie'
Cyclamineus hybrid

N. 'Pride of Cornwall'
Tazetta

SINGLE

N. 'Passionale'
Large-cupped

N. 'Fortune'
Large-cupped

N. 'Ambergate'
Large-cupped

DOUBLE

N. 'Irene Copeland'
Double

N. 'Tahiti'
Double

Dahlias

DAHLIAS flower from the middle of summer to the first frosts in autumn, providing bright colour in the garden for several months. All are frost tender. They can be grown in various soil types, providing that they are fertile and well drained. Dahlias make an excellent border plant as well as being ideal plants for summer display in containers (see also CONTAINER GARDENING, "Bulbs", p.316).

If grown for exhibition or for cut flowers, they are best planted in rows in specially prepared beds. Dwarf bedding dahlias are grown in two ways: either by vegetative propagation, that is by cutting or division of tubers of named cultivars, or by growing annually from seed (see ANNUALS AND BIENNIALS, "Sowing in pots or trays", p.218). These dwarf dahlias are suitable for planting in containers. Dahlia flowerheads have

a diversity of petal forms in a wide colour range, from white to rich yellow through pinks and reds to purples.

Dahlias are classified into ten groups: single-flowered; anemone-flowered; collerette; waterlily; decorative; ball; pompon; cactus; semi-cactus; and miscellaneous. Four of these groups have been subdivided by the size of their blooms. For waterlily dahlias, there are miniature, usually under 102mm (4in) in diameter; small-flowered, usually 102–152mm (4–6in) in diameter; and medium-flowered ones, usually 152–203mm (6–8in) in diameter. Decorative, cactus, and semi-cactus dahlias have two additional subdivisions: large-flowered, usually 203–254mm (8–10in) in diameter; and giant-flowered ones, usually over 254mm (10in) in diameter. Ball dahlias are subdivided into: miniature ball, usually with flowers 52–102mm (2–4in) in diameter; and small ball, usually 102–152mm (4–6in) in diameter. Pompon dahlia flowers should be under 52mm (2in).

DAHLIA FLOWER GROUPS

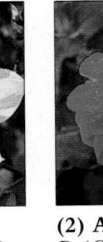

(1) SINGLE
D. 'Yellow Hammer'
Flowerheads with 8–10 broad florets surrounding an open, central disc.

(2) ANEMONE
D. 'Comet'
Fully double flowerheads with one or more rings of flattened ray florets surrounding a group of shorter, tubular florets.

(3) COLLERETTE
D. 'Easter Sunday'
A single yellow disc of stamens in the centre, with a collar of small florets lying between the stamens and the large, outer florets.

(4) WATERLILY
D. 'Pearl of Heemstede'
As their name implies, these flowerheads look like water lilies, and have broad, flat florets.

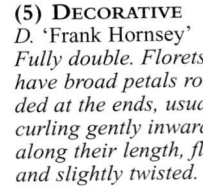

(5) DECORATIVE
D. 'Frank Hornsey'
Fully double. Florets have broad petals rounded at the ends, usually curling gently inwards along their length, flat, and slightly twisted.

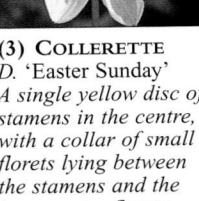
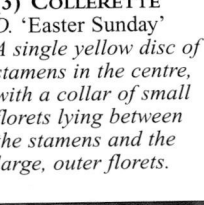

(6) BALL
D. 'Wootton Cupid'
Rounded flowerheads with spirally arranged florets. The petals are rolled for over half their length.

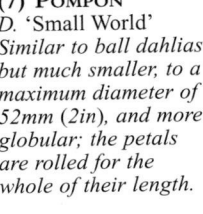

(7) POMPON
D. 'Small World'
Similar to ball dahlias but much smaller, to a maximum diameter of 52mm (2in), and more globular; the petals are rolled for the whole of their length.

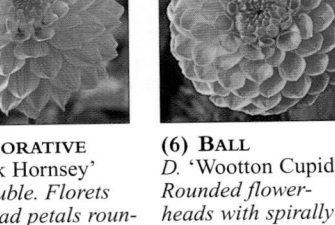
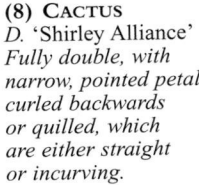

(8) CACTUS
D. 'Shirley Alliance'
Fully double, with narrow, pointed petals curled backwards or quilled, which are either straight or incurving.

(9) SEMI-CACTUS
D. 'So Dainty'
Fully double. The ray florets have pointed, straight or incurving, broad-based petals that curve backwards.

Cultivation

Dahlias thrive in well-drained, fertile soils of about pH7. Prepare the soil early in the year. They are gross feeders, so dig in a heavy dressing of manure or garden compost; then add bone meal at 125g/sq m (4oz/sq yd), leaving the bed roughly dug so that frost can break up the soil.

Where and when to plant

Dahlias may be planted as pot-grown plants, as dormant tubers, or as rooted cuttings taken from tubers. Plants in leaf may be preferable to tubers, as they are often more vigorous. Dormant tubers, however, may be planted directly, about six weeks before the last frosts, whereas plants in leaf should not be planted until all danger of frost has passed.

Choose an open, sheltered site that is not overshadowed. Immediately before planting, top-dress with a blood, fish and bone at 125g/sq m (4oz/sq yd) worked well into the soil. Tie young plants into their stakes to support them as they develop.

Planting pot-grown dahlias

When planting pot-grown dahlias, canes should be positioned at the appropriate spacings. Plants that are 120–50cm (4–5ft) tall are planted 60–90cm (2–3ft) apart, and those that are 75cm–1.1m (2½–3½ft) tall

PLANTING TUBERS

Insert a 1m (3ft) stake in a planting hole. Place soil around the tuber so that the base of the new shoots is 2.5–5cm (1–2in) below soil level.

60cm (2ft) apart. Bedding dahlias growing less than 60cm (2ft) tall are planted 45cm (18in) apart. Water the plants in their pots and leave to drain. Plant with care, to avoid disturbing the root ball, and firm gently, leaving a slight depression at the base of the stem. Water thoroughly. The plants will make a tuber by late autumn; this may be lifted and stored for replanting in spring.

Planting tubers

Dormant tubers may be planted directly in the border about six weeks before the last frosts are expected. The ground is prepared as for pot-grown plants. Prepare a planting hole about 22cm (9in) across and about 15cm (6in) deep, place the tuber in the hole, and cover over. Mark the position of the tuber with a labelled split cane placed just to the side; this will indicate the exact position of the tuber when inserting its support stake. The tuber takes about six weeks to develop a shoot above ground. If the shoot emerges above ground level while there is still a risk of frost, cover the shoot for protection.

Planting rooted cuttings

Established tubers may be grown on in the cold frame or greenhouse, to provide cuttings (see "Propagation", facing page). Plant out rooted cuttings after all danger of frost has passed. As growth develops, water the plants moderately; to retain moisture, mulch when the plants reach 30–38cm (12–15in) tall with well-rotted compost or manure. Do not place the mulch close to the base of the plants since this may encourage stem rot. If composted grass cuttings are used, ensure that they are not treated with selective weedkiller.

STOPPING

1 *When the plant is about 38cm (15in) high, pinch out the central shoot to encourage the development of sideshoots.*

2 *When the plant has 6–8 sideshoots, pinch out the top pair of buds. Tie in the stems to stakes.*

Stopping and disbudding

When the dahlias have grown to about 38cm (15in), stop the plants by removing each growing point to encourage sideshoots. Insert two more canes and tie the shoots in.

The number of shoots allowed to develop should depend on the size of the blooms required. For giant or large blooms, restrict each plant to 4–6 shoots; for medium and small blooms, allow 7–10 shoots. To produce high-quality blooms, disbud some from each shoot (see below).

DISBUDDING

To encourage show-quality flowers, pinch out the side (wing) bud and 1 or 2 pairs of sideshoots below the terminal bud.

Summer feeding

Four to six weeks after planting, feed with a high nitrogen and potash fertilizer, either in granular form, or by weekly applications of liquid fertilizer as a root or foliar feed. As flower buds develop, extra potash in the liquid fertilizer gives strong stems and good flower colour, especially in pinks and lilacs; this is important when growing for exhibition.

The tuber's development during late summer and early autumn is stimulated by the shortening day length. During this period, apply a split application of sulphate of potash and superphosphates at the manufacturer's recommended rate. Avoid contact with leaves or stems as this may cause scorch.

Pests and diseases

Dahlias are affected particularly by aphids (p.646), thrips (p.647), red spider mite (p.646), and earwigs (p.644). These may be controlled by spraying regularly. Lift and burn any plants infected with viruses (p.649).

Lifting and storing tubers

When the foliage has been blackened by the first frosts in autumn, trim back the stems to about 15cm (6in). Carefully lift and clean the soil from the tubers, trim off any fine roots, and treat the tubers with fungicide. Place them upside down for a few weeks to ensure that no moisture remains in the stems and leaves.

Label the tubers and pack them in wooden boxes in vermiculite, coir, or a similar medium. Store in a dry, cool, frost-proof place. Inspect the tubers regularly in winter; if any mildew or rot has developed, cut it out with a clean, sharp knife and dust the cut surfaces with sulphur.

LIFTING AND STORING

1 *Cut the stems to about 15cm (6in) above ground level. Loosen the soil and ease the tubers out. Remove excess soil.*

2 *Store the tubers upside-down for about 3 weeks in a frost-free place so that the stems dry out thoroughly.*

3 *When the stems have dried out, place the tubers in a wooden box and cover them with coir, vermiculite, or a similar medium. Set the box in a cool, frost-free place. Keep the tubers and stems dry until spring.*

Propagation

Divide established tubers in spring. First bring them into growth in a cold frame or greenhouse. Press the tubers gently onto the top of a tray of compost, spray with water, and keep warm and damp. As shoots develop, divide the tuber into sections with a sharp knife, ensuring that each piece has at least one growing shoot. Pot up each section separately using a general-purpose compost.

Alternatively, in late winter, force tubers at 15–18°C (59–64°F). When shoots each have a growing point and two or three pairs of leaves, take basal cuttings, trim at a node, and root in a propagating case with bottom heat. Grow on under glass and harden off before planting out.

Showing dahlias

Cut blooms with a sharp knife in the morning or evening, making sure that the stem length is in proportion to the bloom. When exhibiting, blooms should always be well developed with undamaged petals. Read the schedule and present the correct number of stems staged in the vase, with the blooms facing the front.

HOW TO PROPAGATE BY BASAL CUTTINGS

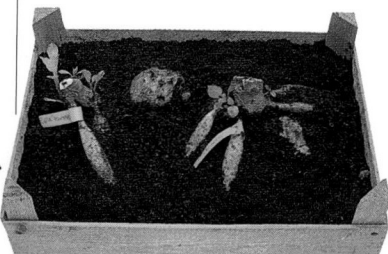

1 *In late winter, force the tubers in a greenhouse. Take cuttings when the young shoots are 7.5cm (3in) long.*

2 *Cut each shoot with a growing point and 2–3 pairs of leaves from the parent tuber. Trim at a node. Remove bottom pair of leaves.*

3 *Insert the cuttings in a pot of moist compost. Place in a propagator or plastic bag to root. Then pot up singly to grow on.*

Soil preparation and planting

Most bulbous plants have long, dormant periods underground after flowering and require relatively little attention for much of the year. The initial stages of selecting good stock, preparing the soil, and planting bulbs correctly do, however, contribute significantly to long-term success in cultivating bulbs.

Buying bulbs

There is considerable variation in the quality and size of bulbs available commercially, so examine any bulbs carefully before buying them. Different types of bulb are sold at various times of the year; always buy them when they are as fresh as possible. Select bulbs that are appropriate to the planting site: most enjoy sun, some prefer shade, and others will naturalize in grass.

Conservation

Conservation of bulbs in the wild is of the utmost importance and there are strict rules governing their importation. Wherever possible, check that the bulb stocks on sale at nurseries and garden centres have been obtained from sources of cultivated bulbs, rather than from stocks that have been collected in the wild.

Dry bulbs

Most bulbs are sold in a dry state during their dormant period. Buy these as early as possible before they

HOW TO SELECT BULBS

GOOD EXAMPLES

TULIP

HYACINTH

DAFFODIL (SINGLE-NOSED)

DAFFODIL (TWIN-NOSED)

POOR EXAMPLES

Split tunic

Signs of disease

Diseased tissue

Damaged outer scales

No tunic

Deterioration of bulb tissue

Soft nose

Offset too small to flower

start into growth; most daffodils, for example, normally start producing roots in late summer, and most other spring-flowering bulbs will begin to grow by early autumn. Autumn-flowering crocuses and *Colchicum* species and hybrids especially benefit from early planting: specialist nurseries sell them in midsummer.

All autumn-flowering bulbs are best bought and planted by late summer. Bulbs tend to deteriorate if kept dry too long; they will have a shorter growing period and will take some time to recover and flower satisfactorily, so buy and plant them as soon as they are available. Some dry bulbs, usually those that have a summer

growing season, such as *Galtonia*, gladioli, and *Tigridia*, are available for purchase in spring.

When buying bulbs, make sure that they are healthy and firm with strong growing points, and no soft or diseased areas or any signs of insect damage. Bulbs that are much smaller than average for their type, and bulb offsets, will not produce flowers in their first season.

Juno irises are unusual in having permanent storage roots beneath the bulb; if these have broken off, do not buy the bulb since it will not develop satisfactorily. Tulips should have intact skins, or tunics, otherwise they will be vulnerable to disease.

Moist bulbs

Although most bulbs may be stored dry, a few are better kept in slightly moist bark, peat substitute, or some similar material. This particularly applies to some of the shade-loving bulb species, such as *Erythronium*, *Anemone nemorosa*, and *Trillium*, that are normally found growing in damp woodland.

When buying cyclamen tubers, look for those with fibrous roots that are stored in moist bark or that are in root growth in pots. Cyclamen that have healthy roots establish much more effectively than dry tubers and so, although more expensive, are a much better buy.

Pot-grown bulbs

Pots of bulbs in active growth, and frequently in flower, are often sold in nurseries and garden centres. These are usually bulbs that were not sold when dormant and have been potted up. They grow satisfactorily and may be planted at once, without disturbing the roots. Alternatively, they may be kept in pots until they have flowered and planted as dry bulbs after they have died down. They are more expensive, however, than dry bulbs.

CHOOSING CORMS, TUBERS, AND OTHER BULBOUS PLANTS

ANEMONE RANUNCULOIDES

Firm, plump tubers

ERYTHRONIUM OREGONUM

IRIS AUCHERI (JUNO GROUP)

Fleshy, storage roots intact

CYCLAMEN HEDERIFOLIUM

Good root growth

Fresh, plump tubers

Moist, peat-substitute or peat packing

CORYDALIS SOLIDA

Distinct growing point on corm

Transplanting or buying snowdrops

Dry snowdrop (*Galanthus*) bulbs often fail to establish so some gardeners transplant or buy snowdrops "in the green", ie after flowering but still in leaf.

As leaves and roots remain active for some time after the flowers fade, transplanting at this stage causes nutrient loss. It is therefore advisable to delay transplanting until the foliage starts to turn yellow at the tips. This allows the bulbs to develop fully and avoids loss of bulb weight that occurs if snowdrops are dug up in full growth.

Snowdrop bulbs should never be allowed to dry out. If there has to be a delay in planting, put the bulbs in a slightly damp loam-based compost and keep in cool conditions until needed.

The influence of different soil types

Bulbs grow in a range of soil types, habitats, and climates throughout the world; the conditions in which they occur naturally indicate their needs in cultivation. Most hardy bulbs are from Mediterranean-type climates and thrive in a warm, sunny site, in freely draining soils that warm up quickly in spring, and become dry in summer. Some species tolerate heavy soils that are moist during the growing season, as long as they are baked dry in summer. If the soil is moderately fertile and humus-rich, many bulbs increase steadily from year to year by seed or vegetative means. Most prefer a near-neutral or slightly alkaline soil.

Good drainage is vital since most bulbs are prone to rot while dormant if the soil is wet and poorly aerated. A few occur in the wild in riverside or swampland habitats; these thrive in moist (or even permanently wet) soils that do not dry out in summer.

Light soils

Sandy or light soils usually warm up rapidly in spring and provide the good drainage that most bulbs need, although they are often deficient in humus and nutrients. Dig in plenty of well-rotted garden compost or manure before planting and, in early spring, top-dress with a balanced fertilizer applied at the manufacturer's recommended rate. Always incorporate manure below the level at which the bulbs are planted to avoid the risk of disease or chemical damage. If using fresh manure, dig it in at least three months before planting. More fertile, sandy soils and loams benefit from extra organic matter, but fertilizer dressing is unnecessary in the first year. In rock gardens, dig in coarse grit to make up at least one third of the top 30cm (12in) of soil for the extra drainage that most dwarf bulbs need.

Heavy soils

Heavy clay soils often need a lot of work to improve their drainage; on very poorly drained soils, a drainage system must first be installed to grow bulbs successfully. Coarse sand or grit at a rate of at least 1½–2 buckets/sq m (sq yd) dug into the whole planting area will be required to make a significant difference. Heavy applications of well-rotted organic matter also improve the soil structure and therefore the drainage. For further information, see "Soil structure and water content", p.620.

Shady areas

Shade-loving bulbs most often occur naturally in woodland habitats, but grow well in any shady situation, as long as the soil is properly prepared: it should be rich in nutrients and humus and also retain moisture. Incorporate plenty of leaf mould or some other organic matter, such as well-rotted manure or garden compost, before planting. Acid-loving "woodland" bulbs thrive in the peat garden where at least half the soil is leaf mould, peat substitute, or peat.

Planting time

Dry bulbs should be planted as soon as possible after purchase. If the bulbs have been stored over winter (see "Lifting, drying, and storing", p.243), plant them at the end of their dormant period before they start growing. Pot-grown bulbs may be planted after purchase throughout the season, or kept in their pots until after they die down and treated as dry bulbs. Plant summer-flowering bulbs, including those that bloom in late summer under cover, and bulbs in the green, in early to mid-spring.

Planting in the open

Bulbs are usually best planted several to a large hole dug out with a spade. Alternatively, they may be planted singly. Do not make the outline of the planting area or the spacing of the bulbs symmetrical as this will look unnatural and if one or two bulbs fail they leave unsightly gaps.

In a rock garden, remove any top-dressing before planting bulbs and replace it afterwards.

Planting depths and spacing

Plant bulbs with two to three times their own depth of soil above them (deeper in light than in heavy soils) and two to three bulb widths apart. Remove soil to the correct depth, fork some bone meal into the bottom of the hole, and insert the bulbs.

Occasionally it is difficult to identify the "top" of a bulb, especially with rootless cyclamen tubers. The upper surface is usually flatter than the lower, or sometimes concave. *Corydalis* tubers can be almost globular, but there is usually some sign of shoot growth on the top. If it is impossible to be sure, plant the bulb on its side.

Replace the soil, breaking down any clods. Firm gently so that there are no air spaces around the bulbs.

Bulbs in the green

It may be necessary to plant bulbs in the green if transferring them from another garden, if space is restricted and bulbs are lifted each year (see right) to make way for other plants, or if planting snowdrops that have been sold in this state.

Use a trowel or a widger to create randomly spaced holes sufficiently wide to spread out the roots, and plant each bulb individually, at the same level as it was planted before. This is indicated by the colour change between the green top-growth and the chlorotic, yellow-green leaf bases that were underground. Water thoroughly after planting.

CORRECT PLANTING DEPTHS

The planting depth depends on the size of the bulb. Use the length of the bulb as a rough guide and plant the bulb 2–3 times deeper than that length.

PLANTING BULBS IN THE OPEN

1 *Dig out a large hole in well-prepared ground and plant the bulbs (here tulips), with growing points uppermost, at least twice their own depth and width apart.*

2 *For a natural effect, space the bulbs randomly. Once they are in position, gently draw the soil over them with your hand to avoid displacing or damaging them.*

3 *Tamp down the soil over the planted area with the back of a rake. Avoid treading on the soil surface, as this might damage the growing points.*

PLANTING BULBS SINGLY

Plant each bulb in a separate hole at the appropriate depth. Draw back the prepared soil with a trowel and firm it down gently afterwards.

Pot-grown bulbs

Bulbs that have been purchased as pot-grown plants may be planted as dry bulbs after they have died down. When planting them, make a hole large enough to accommodate the whole pot, so that the contents may be planted without disturbance.

LIFTING BULBS

These bulbs (here planted in a lattice pot for convenience) have been left until the leaf tips start to turn yellow before being dug up and replanted elsewhere in the garden.

HOW TO PLANT CYCLAMEN IN ROOT GROWTH

1 *Select a planting site where the soil is rich in leaf mould or humus, or prepare the soil as necessary, working in organic matter well below the depth of the planting hole to encourage the roots to grow into the soil after planting. Leave it to settle for a day or two, then make a hole that is deep enough to plant the tuber with its roots spread out below it.*

2 *Plant the tuber so that it will lie with its upper surface just visible at soil level. Fill in around the roots with soil, taking care not to damage the roots.*

3 *Gently firm the soil around the tuber with your fingers, leaving the growing point just exposed. Lightly cover it with a loose mulch.*

If the bulbs become pot-bound, gently tease out the roots at the base before planting to encourage them to grow out into the soil. If they are growing in a peat-based compost, keep the bulbs under cover in winter. Otherwise the peat acts as a sponge and the dormant bulbs rot in the waterlogged compost.

Planting tubers and corms in root growth

A number of "woodland" species, such as cyclamen, are best planted when they are in root growth, rather than as dry bulbs, as they will then become established more quickly.

They are also more likely to flower in their first season after planting; dry corms or tubers are much less reliable in this respect. Planting in root growth also eliminates any problems in distinguishing between the bottoms and tops of tubers or corms. Work plenty of leaf mould or well-rotted, organic matter into the

soil before planting to create the moist, humus-rich conditions that "woodland" bulbs require, otherwise the bulbs will not thrive.

Planting depth and spacing
Calculate the spacing and planting depth for corms and tubers in the same way as for dry bulbs (see "Planting in the open" and *Correct Planting Depths*, p.237), but allow additional space for the roots.

Cyclamen are unusual in that they grow near the soil surface in the wild, so do not plant the tubers too deeply or they may not flower. Make sure that their tips are at about the same level as the surrounding soil. They may be planted more closely than other bulbs, but they should be spaced at least their own width apart.

Planting
Plant the corms or tubers singly or as a group. It is important for the planting hole to be sufficiently deep and wide to accommodate the roots properly. Spread them out in the hole as this helps the plants to establish more quickly. Fill in the hole and firm it well to remove any air spaces.

The tips of cyclamen tubers may be left exposed or, if preferred, lightly covered with a loose mulch. Use leaf mould or, if the bed already has a top-dressing, coarse grit.

PLANTING LARGE BULBS IN GRASS

1 *Clean the bulbs (here daffodils), removing any loose, outer coatings and old roots. Scatter the bulbs randomly over the planting area, then make sure that they are at least their own width apart.*

2 *Make a hole for each bulb, using a long- or short-handled bulb planter to remove a core of turf and soil to a depth of about 10–15cm (4–6in).*

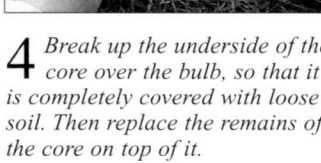

3 *Place a balanced fertilizer, mixed with a little of the soil from the core, into each hole and put in a bulb, making sure that the growing point is uppermost.*

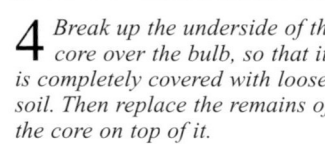

4 *Break up the underside of the core over the bulb, so that it is completely covered with loose soil. Then replace the remains of the core on top of it.*

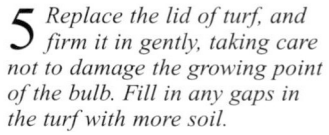

5 *Replace the lid of turf, and firm it in gently, taking care not to damage the growing point of the bulb. Fill in any gaps in the turf with more soil.*

Naturalizing in grass

When planting bulbs for naturalizing in grass, first cut the grass as short as possible. Random rather than regimented planting achieves a more natural effect; scatter the bulbs by hand over the chosen area and plant them where they have fallen,

PLANTING SMALL BULBS IN GRASS

1 *Using a half-moon edger (or spade), cut an "H" shape in the turf. Cut to the full depth of the half-moon blade to make sure that it penetrates the soil below.*

2 *Undercut the turf and fold back the flaps to expose the area of bare soil beneath. Take care not to crack or tear the turf unduly.*

3 *Using a hand fork, loosen the soil beneath to a depth of at least 7cm (3in), mixing in a little bone meal at a rate of about 15g/sq m (½oz/sq yd).*

4 *Press the bulbs (here crocuses) gently into the soil, taking care not to damage the growing points. Space the bulbs randomly but at least 2.5cm (1in) apart.*

5 *Score the underneath of the turf with a hand fork to loosen the soil, so that the bulbs will be able to penetrate the turf easily.*

6 *Roll the turf flaps back into position, taking care not to dislodge the bulbs or to damage the turf. Firm down the turf, particularly along the joins.*

USING A FORK TO PLANT SMALL BULBS

1 *Push a garden fork into the grass to the appropriate depth and rock it back and forth. Repeat at random over the rest of the planting area.*

2 *Thoroughly mix a little fertilizer with some garden soil. Trickle a small amount of this mix into the bottom of each hole, using a widger or a small spoon.*

3 *Place a single bulb in each hole, growing point uppermost, ensuring that it is buried at twice its own depth. Then cover all the planted bulbs with soil.*

making sure that they are at least one bulb's width apart. Dig planting holes with a trowel or use a bulb planter; this useful implement cuts out neat plugs of turf and soil to a depth of about 10–15cm (4–6in) and is most suitable for larger bulbs.

Check that all the holes are at the correct depth and that the bulbs are the right way up, before inserting them and replacing the turf.

Planting large groups of small bulbs in grass

It is easier and less time-consuming to plant large numbers of very small bulbs, such as crocuses, by lifting a section of turf and planting a whole group of bulbs in the soil beneath rather than planting each bulb individually. Loosen the soil beneath the turf since it may be compacted; fork in a little balanced fertilizer or

some bone meal. Position the bulbs randomly, at least their own width apart. Replace the turf over the bulbs and firm it by hand or by tamping it down gently with the back of a rake.

Alternatively, use a broad-tined garden fork or a spade to make holes in the turf, and rock the tool back and forth in the ground to enlarge the holes slightly so that they easily accommodate the bulbs. The tines

should be inserted to three times the depth of the bulb, for example 7cm (3in) for crocuses. Repeat this at random for the entire planting area, so that the final arrangement of holes, in straight but criss-crossing lines, gives a natural effect. Mix a little bone meal with soil and place some in each hole before planting the bulbs singly, then top-dress the whole area with more prepared soil.

BULBS THAT REQUIRE A RESTING PERIOD

Anemone biflora,
  A. tschernjaewii
Bellevalia (some spp.)
Bongardia
Calochortus

Calochortus luteus

Colchicum (most spp.)
Corydalis (some spp.)
Crocus (some spp.)
Cyclamen, some ❋ (some spp.)
Gladiolus, some ❋
Iris, Onocyclus group
Leontice
Leucocoryne ❋
Merendera (most spp.)
Moraea ❋ (winter-growing spp.)
Narcissus atlanticus,
  N. cantabricus, N. romieuxii,
  N. rupicola, N. rupicola subsp.
  marvieri, N. rupicola subsp.
  watieri
Pancratium, some ❋
Ranunculus
  asiaticus ❋

Narcissus rupicola subsp. *watieri*

Romulea, some ❋
  (some spp.)
Tecophilaea cyanocrocus
Tigridia ❋

HOW TO PLANT BULBS IN POTS

Growing tip uppermost

1 Plant the bulbs (here daffodils) at twice their own depth, and one bulb's width apart.

2 Cover the bulbs with compost to 1cm (½in) below the rim. Top-dress with grit (see inset), and label.

PREPARING CLAY POTS

Before planting bulbs in a clay pot, place a single crock – or several, according to the drainage requirements of the plant – over the drainage hole in the base before adding compost.

Composts for bulbs under cover

A good compost mixture with the required humus content and drainage for use in bulb frames and greenhouse beds may be prepared as follows: mix together 2 parts peat substitute or peat, 3 parts coarse grit, and 4 parts loam; then add a base fertilizer or some bone meal at a rate of 25g/5 litres (1oz/1 gallon) and (except for lime-hating plants) garden lime at a rate of 25g/18 litres (1oz/4 gallons).

Make up sufficient compost to prepare a bulb bed that is at least 30cm (12in) in depth, with a layer, 5cm (2in) deep, of well-rotted garden compost or manure beneath it.

A similar compost is suitable for most bulbs, whether in pots or other containers. If using a proprietary potting compost, mix in some grit or coarse sand – at least one third, by bulk – because these composts are often not sufficiently well-drained for use with bulbs.

"Woodland" bulbs grown in pots or containers require a well-drained compost with additional organic matter that is rich in nutrients, for example a mixture of 3 parts leaf mould, 2 parts loam, and 2 parts grit.

Planting in pots and under cover

It is easy to grow most bulbs under cover in pots because the growing conditions can be precisely tailored to the particular needs of the plant. Suitable composts may be used for different types of bulb, and plants can be given the correct seasonal care, such as a summer drying-off period, restricted winter watering, or plunging in a bed.

Similar control is possible when cultivating bulbs that are planted directly into a greenhouse bed or bulb frame; the planting method is the same under cover as for bulbs grown in the open (see "Planting in the open", p.227).

Choosing clay or plastic pots
Bulbs may be planted in either clay or plastic pots. Clay pots are not so readily available but they are more suitable for bulbs that are unable to tolerate excessive moisture, because the compost dries out more quickly after watering than in plastic pots. Plastic pots are now extensively used and are perfectly satisfactory as long as they are filled with a freely draining compost; water the compost less frequently than with clay pots. For plants that need moist conditions, such as "woodland" bulbs, the greater water retentiveness of plastic pots is particularly valuable.

If using clay pots, place one or more crocks over the drainage hole; no "crocking" is necessary for plastic pots as long as the compost itself is well drained. A piece of perforated zinc placed over the drainage hole prevents worms entering the pot.

Planting bulbs in pots
Bulbs should be planted in pots at the same depths as bulbs grown outdoors (see "Planting depths and spacing", p.237). This may not be possible with larger bulbs, in which case make sure that each bulb has at least 2.5cm (1in) of moist compost beneath it in the pot. Plant bulbs of flowering size at a distance of one bulb's width apart. If planting a mixture of larger bulbs with smaller offsets, space the flowering-sized bulbs a little more widely, and scatter the small offsets between them.

Cover the bulbs with moist compost, leaving sufficient room below the pot rim for a top-dressing, and firm it well. Top-dress the pot with a generous layer of horticultural grit, which helps to retain moisture and improves the appearance of the pot. Label with the plant name, the date of planting, and source. No watering is necessary until the compost is almost dry. When the roots start into growth, begin watering again.

Lattice pots

Bulbs grown in beds under cover are often planted in pots with open-meshed, or latticed, sides, which allow different types of bulb to be closely planted without mixing them up or restricting their roots. Plant the bulbs in the pots, label them, and plunge them in a bulb bed containing the same compost as the pots. The pots may be lifted from the bed without disturbing their neighbours later. Alternatively, but less conveniently, groups of bulbs in beds may be separated by tiles or pieces of slate sunk into the bed between them.

PLANTING IN LATTICE POTS
Plant up the lattice pots with bulbs in the usual way. Sink the labelled pots up to their rims in a bulb bed so that the compost just covers them. Stagger the rows for economical use of space.

Lilies

LILIES (*Lilium*) are among the most graceful of summer-flowering plants – their tall, slim stems bear flowers with an enormous variety of dazzling colours and exotic shapes. There are a great many to choose from – more than 80 species of lilies and thousands of hybrids, which are more tolerant of different conditions and so are often easier to grow.

Lily classification

Lilies are classified into nine different divisions based on their origin, parentage, and flowers. It is now possible to cross lilies between different Divisions, using embryo-culture.

Div.I Hybrids of Asiatic species such as *L. cernuum* and *L. davidii*.
Div.II Hybrids of *L. martagon* and *L. hansonii*.
Div.III Hybrids of *L. candidum* and *L. chalcedonicum*.
Div.IV Hybrids of American species lilies such as *L. parryi*.
Div.V Hybrids of *L. longiflorum* and *L. formosanum*.
Div.VI (Aurelian hybrids): Trumpet lilies and *L. henryi* crosses.
Div.VII (Oriental hybrids): From Far Eastern species.
Div.VIII All other hybrids.
Div.IX All species and cultivars.

Where to grow lilies

Lilies need a well-drained position and are excellent woodland plants and superb companions for roses. They often do not survive the competition experienced in herbaceous borders but can be grown in pots and placed where needed when in flower. Div.V lilies are not fully hardy, but make excellent pot plants for the cold greenhouse and conservatory.

Planting and care

Always buy fresh bulbs and plant them immediately. Do not buy any shrivelled bulbs. Most lilies grow well in a range of soils, but if grown in pots need slow-release fertilizer. Div.III lilies prefer alkaline soils and full sun; Div.VII hybrids must be grown in lime-free soil or ericaceous compost in containers; Div.IV hybrids are best suited to damp, woodland conditions. Plant lilies in autumn at two and a half times the depth of the bulb in well-prepared, free-draining soil; *L.candidum* needs only 2.5cm (1in) of soil above the bulb and should be planted in late summer. The routine care of lilies is similar to that of most bulbs (see pp.242–244); stake the plants well so that their flowering stems do not snap.

Propagation

Lilies may be propagated easily by stem bulbils, scaling, seed, or by simple division for *L. pardalinum* and Div.IV hybrids. Always propagate from healthy stock.

Bulbils and bulblets
Species such as *L. lancifolium* (syn. *L. tigrinum*), *L. bulbiferum*, and their hybrids produce stem bulbils in the leaf axils and bulblets at the base of the old flowering stem. Remove these and pot them up to grow on. The following autumn, plant them out together, or pot up individually.

Seed, scaling, and division
Seed sowing produces vigorous, virus-free bulbs (see "Growing lilies from seed", p.247), but is slow; Div.V lilies are easy to propagate in this way. For details of division and scaling, see pp.245 and 248.

LILY FLOWERS

Lilium martagon (long-lived and useful for shady areas)

***L.* Oriental hybrids** (very scented; need acid soil)

***L.* 'Bright Star'** (an Aurelian hybrid; likes lime)

***L.* 'Connecticut King'** (an old Div.I hybrid; now in pink, red, and white forms)

L. regale (fragrant trumpets; easy to grow)

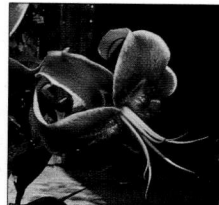
***L.* 'Scheherezade'** (hybrid cross Aurelian x Oriental)

Pests and diseases

Lilies are particularly vulnerable to several viruses (p.649) transmitted by aphids. *L. lancifolium* and some of its hybrids are carriers but show no symptoms; keep them away from other lilies to minimize infection. Grey mould (*Botrytis*) (p.646) may cause problems in damp, windless conditions, and poorly drained positions may encourage basal rot. Red lily beetle (p.644) destroys the foliage and flowers.

PROPAGATING FROM STEM BULBILS

1 *Throughout late summer, as soon as the bulbils loosen and are ripe, collect them from the leaf axils of the lily stems by carefully picking them off.*

2 *Insert the bulbils in pans of moist, loam-based potting compost, pressing them gently into the surface. Cover with grit, and label (see inset). Place in a cold frame until young bulbs develop.*

RAISING LILIES FROM BULBLETS

1 *After flowering, lift the bulb and dead stem, pick off the bulblets, and replant the main bulb. Alternatively, leave the bulb in the ground, cutting the stem above it to remove the bulblets.*

2 *Plant the bulblets, at twice their own depth, into 13cm (5in) pots of moist, loam-based potting compost. Cover with a layer of grit, label, and place in a cold frame until the spring.*

CHAPTER

9

ROCK, SCREE, AND GRAVEL GARDENING

CLIMATE CHANGE AND a growing interest in hard landscaping are inspiring many gardeners to create planting environments with rock and stone products – features that mimic high alpine habitats, or the sun-baked, stony soil of Mediterranean and desert environments. With this has come a growing appreciation of the often diminutive beauty and resilience of plants adapted to grow in such regions. Whether a traditional rock garden, or a simple gravelled bed or paved area studded with aromatic creeping plants and succulents, such features bring many rewards to the plant enthusiast.

Designing with rock and rock plants

ALPINES are plants that grow at high altitudes above the tree line, although the term is often loosely used to include a vast range of low-growing rock garden plants, including many bulbs, that may be grown successfully at relatively low altitudes. Their diminutive form and graceful habit make them suitable for grouping together in fascinating, brilliantly coloured collections.

True alpines

Alpines may be deciduous or evergreen woody plants, or they may be herbaceous, or grow from bulbs, corms, or tubers – there are very few annual alpines. They are characteristically hardy, adapted to survive in extremes of climate, and compact, with few over 15cm (6in) tall. In their native mountain habitat, the dwarf or creeping habit of alpines reduces their wind resistance, and helps them to resist the crushing weight of heavy snow in winter.

In alpine regions, plants experience very high sunshine and fresh, constantly moving air during their growing season. Their cushion- or mat-forming habit and their small, fleshy, hairy, or leathery leaves protect them from water loss in high winds and hot sun. Edelweiss (*Leontopodium alpinum*), for example, has its entire surface covered in woolly hairs, which help to conserve moisture, while the leaves of houseleeks (*Sempervivum*) have fleshy, water-retaining tissue.

Although most alpines are adapted to extremes of temperature, few withstand constant wetness at the roots in winter or warm, humid, summer conditions. In their native habitats, they often grow in thin, poor soil that lacks nutrients and has a low organic content but which allows rapid drainage. Most develop extensive, spreading root systems to seek out nutrients and moisture.

Rock garden plants

Rock plants are simply those slow-growing plants of relatively small stature that are suitable in scale for growing in rock gardens. They include dwarf trees and shrubs, which are particularly useful for framework (background) plantings, architectural plants, which give focus to a planting scheme, and many other plants that are not necessarily from alpine regions. Some, such as *Armeria maritima*, occur in coastal habitats, while many miniature bulbs are native to sunny, Mediterranean hillsides. In common with true alpines, they share the need for a free-draining soil and are therefore suitable for planting among alpines. Small perennials and dwarf drought-tolerant plants can be used to set the framework in a rock garden; they are also useful in a low-maintenance, gravel or scree garden.

A WELL-FURNISHED ROCK GARDEN
This gently sloping rock garden is studded with a diverse range of alpine plants, from low-growing Dianthus *and saxifrages in the foreground to the dwarf shrubs* Genista lydia, Helianthemum, *and* Potentilla *at the rear.*

Since many true alpines bloom in the spring and early summer, rock garden plants are especially valuable if they are late blooming, when they may be used to extend the season of interest.

Alpines and rock plants in the garden

The usually restricted size of alpines and rock garden plants fits particularly well into the confines of the small, modern garden. Few other types of plant are so characteristically neat and compact and this allows a substantial collection of species and hybrids to be grown in a relatively small space.

Easily grown alpines
Many alpine species, and their more showy cultivars, are undemanding in their cultural requirements and may be grown easily in the open garden. They present a wealth of habit and form, from tiny, cushion-forming plants to spreading mound- and mat-formers; some of the easier alpines bloom well into summer, almost invariably producing a profusion of flowers. The low-growing cultivars of *Aubrieta*, *Dianthus*, *Phlox*, and *Veronica* form mats of clear, bright colour when in bloom,

PLANTING IN THE OPEN GARDEN
Daphne x burkwoodii '*Somerset*' bears a profusion of scented pink flowers that spill over the edge of a border and drift into the plants on either side.

and may be used to edge beds, their informal, spreading habit gently softening straight lines.

Specialist alpines
Other alpine genera, such as the Aretian *Androsace* and the tight cushion-forming saxifrages, have special requirements, in particular a need for extremely free-draining soil and protection from excessive winter wet. Most also require plenty of sun but their roots need to be cool; lower-altitude, woodland species often prefer dappled shade and may need moist, acid soil.

The rich and varied colours and diverse forms of many specialist plants may still be enjoyed in the garden, however, as long as well-drained conditions and a suitable aspect are provided. The best way to fulfil these requirements is to raise the plants in some way from the underlying garden soil by planting them in specially constructed or carefully controlled environments and using prepared, gritty, free-draining soil or composts.

Some alpine plants need a cool root run and shelter, and rock gardens and pockets within stone or brick walls are an ideal way to grow such plants and display them to their best advantage in natural-looking surroundings. In more formal garden settings or if space is limited, raised beds or troughs and sinks are attractive alternatives, especially when they are constructed from materials that complement any existing hard landscape features. Free-standing troughs and sinks also allow colour to be introduced at a variety of heights and on hard surfaces such as patios and paths.

The rock garden

A sunny, south- or south-west-facing slope makes an ideal site for the stony outcrops of a rock garden. Well-constructed rock gardens emulate natural rock formations and make strikingly attractive features. They replicate, as nearly as possible, the natural habitat of alpine plants, creating the conditions in which they thrive – the soil beneath the rocks provides the cool, moist, but freely draining root run that they particularly enjoy.

Planning a rock garden
For the greatest visual impact, a rock garden should be constructed on as generous a scale as the site allows. Where possible, choose a naturally sloping, open site that will provide good drainage. A series of rocky outcrops with gullies running in between is highly effective, especially if streams and pools are also included in the design.

A sunny aspect will suit most rock plants, although those that prefer shade may be grown in cooler, shady pockets on the north side of large rocks. Careful placing of the rocks at the construction stage (see p.263) will provide a wide range of planting areas and rock niches to meet the needs of many different alpine plants.

Choosing plants
Several alpine species, such as *Gentiana verna*, with its flowers of intense blue in spring, prefer deep pockets of well-drained, gritty soil, while the mat-forming *Persicaria affine* 'Donald Lowndes', for example, thrives in broader terraces between rock strata. Both *Lewisia* Cotyledon Hybrids and *Saxifraga* 'Tumbling Waters', which have cascades of white flowers over rosettes

A BLAZE OF SUMMER COLOUR
The brilliant red flowers of Sedum spurium *and* Helianthemum *cascading down the rocky outcrop make a striking contrast with the grey-green stems and leaves of both* Dianthus *and* Hebe pinguifolia '*Pagei*' *just behind them. The fresh green foliage of the surrounding plants provides a bright but cool counterpoint.*

SCREE ROCK GARDEN
Many rock plants retain the charm of wild flowers but selected forms and hybrids often display greater numbers of attractive, sometimes larger flowers in a range of clear colours. Some need a specialized environment, such as this scree bed, but many more are amenable plants that grow in any well-prepared site.

of lime-encrusted foliage, are most at home in the narrow crevices between vertical stone faces. Alpine or dwarf pinks such as *Dianthus alpinus* and *D.* 'Mars' provide evergreen, grey or green mats or cushions of neat foliage and masses of often clove-scented, single to double, red, pink, or white blooms throughout the summer and into autumn; they are at home in any well-drained site.

Plan the planting scheme to include as much seasonal variation as possible. Alpine bulbs such as *Crocus laevigatus* and *Iris histrioides* 'Major' help to bring the garden to life in winter or early spring, and *Cyclamen hederifolium* and *Sternbergia lutea* add interest in autumn. For year-round colour, include a few evergreens, such as the dwarf *Chamaecyparis obtusa* 'Nana Pyramidalis' and *Juniperus communis* 'Compressa', and dwarf shrubs such as *Hebe buchananii* 'Minor'.

Add texture and structure to the planting by using species with unusual leaves or stems and variation in height and form. Contrasting leaf texture can be particularly striking:

bold, fleshy, rosette-forming plants may be used to offset the delicate, feathery leaves and flowers of *Pulsatilla* species, for instance, and a combination of spreading, cushion-forming, and trailing alpines with several dwarf shrubs or trees provides great visual interest. The sword-shaped, silver leaves of *Celmisia coriacea* contrast well with mat-forming plants such as *Polygala calcarea* Bulley's form, with deep blue flowers in late spring and early summer, and *Campanula cochleariifolia*, with clusters of pale blue or white bells in summer.

Scree formations

On mountain slopes, the natural weathering of rock outcrops produces a mass of small, broken rocks and stones. These loose, stony slopes, known as screes, are home to many plants that need plenty of moisture at their roots during the growing season, but grow best through an apparently dry 15cm (6in) surface layer of stones. Scree dwellers are

among the most beautiful and jewel-like of alpine plants and well worth the extra care needed to grow them.

The scree bed

The scree bed attempts to re-create the highly specialized habitat of natural scree dwellers. A scree is a deep, preferably gently sloping bed of loose rock fragments of varying size, into which is mixed a suitable compost (see p.262). Screes may also be constructed on flat sites, raised from ground level to assist drainage, becoming, in effect, a specialized form of raised bed (see p.257).

Scree dwellers usually form low mats or cushions of dense foliage, and many bear their small, brilliantly coloured blooms in such profusion that the flowers almost completely obscure the leaves. The neutral background of small stones offers an ideal foil for the rich textures and colours of this type of planting.

Specialist plants, for example *Vitaliana primuliflora*, *Anchusa cespitosa*, and *Myosotis alpestris*, thrive in screes. Other rock garden plants which are easier to grow also

appreciate the conditions created in a scree bed. Some species, such as *Achillea clavennae* and *Artemisia glacialis*, are grown primarily for their silver foliage, which provides a cool contrast for stronger colours. A number of species, including *Androsace carnea* subsp. *laggeri*, which bears a mass of pink blooms in early summer, naturally self seed. The tiny, blue, bell-shaped flowers of *Campanula cochleariifolia* also spring up around the garden but may become a nuisance if they begin to compete with less robust species.

Integrating the scree bed

Where space is available, one or more scree beds may be integrated with a rock garden on one site to form a bold, unified design and provide a broad range of habitats. A backing of large rocks skirted by scree beds is particularly effective.

Alternatively, pockets of scree mixture may be included in a rock garden to accommodate specialized scree dwellers that need particularly good drainage around their necks. *Dianthus haematocalyx*, for example, is a tightly tufted pink whose deep rose petals have an unusual buff underside; it benefits from a soil surface of loose, dry stones.

The visual effect of a scree bed is enhanced by incorporating just a few carefully positioned, larger rocks. Plants may then be allowed to skirt their base or to grow over them to soften their outlines.

Gravel beds and paving

Areas of gravel or shingle and paving are becoming increasingly popular alternatives to traditional, labour-intensive and water-hungry garden features such as herbaceous borders and lawns. Conservation concerns about the sourcing of hard materials have been partially allayed by the increasing range of manufactured stone products, many utilizing by-products of the quarrying industry. In appearance these are far more naturalistic than previous offerings, and hence much more attractive and easy to blend in to the garden.

These hard landscaping features must be planted if they are not to appear harsh and sterile. However, in order to use successfully the rock garden and drought-tolerant plants that will visually complement such materials, it is esssential that the underlying soil has the free drainage that they need. It may be necessary to improve the drainage of the site, by adding grit to the soil or even installing a rubble sub-base to act as a soakaway for excess water (see p.623). Incorporating a slope will also assist drainage. A gently sloping site facing the sun, with free-draining soil top-dressed with gravel or pebbles, is an ideal environment for a Mediterranean-style mixed planting. Coastal plants such as sea pinks (*Armeria*), sea lavender (*Limonium*), and horned poppies (*Glaucium flavum*) will also thrive. Instead of dwarf conifers as accent plants, small grey-leaved shrubs such as *Convolvulus cneorum* and spiky perennials such as *Phormium* could be used.

On a sunny patio, crevices and planting spaces between pavers filled with free-draining soil provide ideal conditions for low-growing, sun-loving plants. Both gravelled and paved areas also make attractive settings for containers planted with rock plants (see also "Troughs, sinks, and other containers", p.258).

Ericaceous plants

Alpine plants that require an acid soil or a woodland environment are not always easily accommodated in a rock garden. Acid-loving plants such as *Arctostaphylos*, *Cassiope*, gentians, and most *Vaccinium* species will only thrive in soil with a low pH, and woodland plants prefer moist, shady conditions and leafy, humus-rich soil. Specially constructed beds containing ericaceous compost provide a moist, acidic growing medium and, when sited in dappled shade, closely imitate woodland conditions.

Site and materials

Such acidic-humus beds may be constructed either as individual garden features or as extensions to a rock garden. The shady, north-facing side of a rock garden provides ideal conditions. Do not place an acidic-humus bed directly beneath trees since the drip from the leaves after rain may damage plants. For best results, the site should be in sun for part of the day.

Traditionally, such beds were filled with moss peat, which has a naturally low pH, good aeration, and excellent water retention. In view of current anxieties about conserving existing peat reserves, alternative composts based on leaf mould, bark, or coconut fibre, which have similar characteristics, should be used. Bark and coconut fibre often have large amounts of nitrogen added, mostly in the form of urea. These are suitable for fast-growing plants but too overpowering both for ericaceous ones and most rock garden plants.

Raised beds

In small gardens, raised beds make highly economical use of limited space. In larger gardens, narrow raised beds may make a useful and attractive boundary feature. The formal appearance of raised beds blends in well with the design and layout of many modern gardens and, in areas where suitable rock is not easily

A LOW RAISED BED
Here, a raised alpine bed flanks one side of a narrow stone path. The plants draw the eye along the path and entice the visitor to the open lawn beyond.

available, or is prohibitively expensive, a raised bed provides a good substitute for a rock garden.

Since drainage in raised beds is entirely independent of the underlying soil, these structures are especially useful in gardens with poorly drained soils (such as wet, heavy clay) that are otherwise unsuitable for the cultivation of alpines. In addition, the dimensions of a raised bed may be planned so that the bed will easily accommodate a frame light to allow cultivation of choice species that require protection from too much winter wet, without restricting airflow around the plants.

Various materials may be used for the construction of a raised bed, including traditional bricks or dry stones and wooden railway sleepers. For further information, see STRUCTURES AND SURFACES, "Raised beds", p.599.

Planting in raised beds

Large raised beds may be divided into separate areas or compartments, and different composts used in each to suit the specific requirements of different plant groups. Rocks may be introduced to the surface of the compost and bedded in to provide textural contrast and vertical niches and crevices for those plants that demand them.

Rectangular raised beds present several aspects so that plants with different requirements may be planted in niches on their sunny or shady side. In addition to growing plants in the bed itself, the walls may be designed to incorporate planting niches, in the same way as walls that are used for trailing species.

Choose plants that will give successional interest as the seasons progress. The dense, evergreen rosettes of *Haberlea rhodopensis* send

A TAPESTRY OF COLOUR
A vivid display in which the rich colours and varied forms of the alpines blend with the evergreen shrubs *and dwarf conifers, which form the framework of this attractive rock garden.*

up sprays of funnel-shaped flowers in spring, and may be succeeded in summer by *Aquilegia flabellata*, a clump-forming alpine that produces bell-shaped, soft blue flowers, each with fluted petals and a short spur. Both of these plants prefer semi-shade and are small enough to be planted in a raised bed without over-crowding it.

For a sunnier aspect, choose compact species of *Dianthus*, such as *D. alpinus* and *D.* 'Bombardier', with *Erinus alpinus* 'Dr Hähnle' trailing from the retaining wall.

Walls

Garden walls may be modified, if required, to provide excellent sites for alpines and rock garden plants. The walls of raised beds and those used to retain banks of earth on a terraced slope may be modified in the same way. If possible, however, leave spaces, crevices, or cracks between the stones or brickwork during the construction of such walls so that these may be planted up when building is complete.

Choosing plants
The most suitable plants to choose are cushion- or mat-forming plants such as *Acantholimon glumaceum*, which forms evergreen cushions that are clothed in pink flowers during summer, or *Dianthus deltoides* and other alpine pinks. Plants that are prone to rotting at the collar, such as *Lewisia* and *Ramonda* species, are well suited to being grown in walls, since the roots enjoy the cool conditions and extra drainage provided by the crevices. The trailing, semi-evergreen *Asarina procumbens*, with its creamy-white, snapdragon-like flowers, and the shrubby *Penstemon newberryi* f. *humilior*, bearing a profusion of flowers on gently arching branches, are also ideal for walls.

Dry-stone walls
These provide ample room for the root systems of many rock garden plants to penetrate, and also allow sharp drainage. Free-standing, single or double dry-stone walls with careful choice of suitable plants make extremely attractive features. The well-drained tops of dry-stone walls provide an ideal home for mat-forming plants, such as *Gypsophila repens* or *Saponaria ocymoides*, both of which cascade attractively over the edge of the wall. The neat, spreading rosettes of lime-encrusted saxifrages and houseleeks (*Sempervivum*) may be dotted at intervals across the surface, and

AN ALPINE TROUGH COLLECTION
A collection of troughs makes an appealing feature. Large troughs accommodate dwarf trees and shrubs as well as smaller alpine plants.

using both vertical faces of a wall will allow both sun and shade-loving plants to be grown.

Troughs, sinks, and other containers

Containers provide an opportunity to grow alpines in a small garden, and may also be used to flank pathways or steps. Old stone sinks and troughs make handsome containers for rock plants, although both are scarce and expensive. However, troughs made of reconstituted stone or hypertufa, and glazed sinks coated with this material (see p.266) are inexpensive alternatives. Troughs and sinks can be used as features for patios and courtyards, or on terraces and gravelled areas in larger gardens (see also CONTAINER GARDENING, "Designing with containers", pp.306–318).

Planting in troughs
The smallest alpine species are often the most intricate. *Antennaria dioica* 'Minima' and other compact alpines and rock plants should be used. By careful selection, a plant community of dwarf and slow-growing species may be planted to make up a rock garden in miniature.

Try to introduce some variation in height. Use small conifers, such as *Chamaecyparis obtusa* 'Nana Pyramidalis' or *Juniperus communis* 'Compressa', and dwarf trees such as *Ulmus parvifolia* 'Geisha' as framework plants, choosing from others such as *Campanula zoysii*, *Dianthus alpinus*, or *D. microlepis* for the middle and foreground of the trough. Miniature shrubs may be added to provide contrasting form and colour throughout the year.

Other containers
If an appropriate compost is used and the plants are well maintained, almost any container may be used to good effect, provided that it has adequate drainage. Large flower pots and tubs are suitable for small collections of the tiniest alpines, especially those that trail over edges, such as *Silene schafta*. Small containers suit compact, slow-growing alpines such as *Androsace chamaejasme* and *Sempervivum arachnoideum*. Old chimney pots make beautiful features planted with *Sedum* or *Sempervivum* species.

The alpine house

In the wild, many alpines spend their winter dormancy insulated by a deep snow blanket that shields them from

AN UNUSUAL CONTAINER
Many different types of container may be used for rock plants and alpine species. Here, part of a hollowed-out tree trunk has been planted with Sedum spathulifolium *'Cape Blanco', valued for its small clusters of tiny, yellow flowers above the rosettes of silvery-green leaves.*

excess water, cold drying winds, and severe frosts; temperatures under the snow cover hover at, or just below, freezing point. In gardens at lower altitudes, where conditions are very different, the more exacting alpines need the protection of glass.

A simple, open cloche may be sufficient protection for some plants but a specially designed greenhouse, or alpine house (see GREENHOUSES AND FRAMES, "Alpine house", p.569), greatly extends the range that may be grown, and allows the enthusiastic gardener to try growing some of the most challenging plants. Containers are especially suitable for cultivating miniature species, and allow plants such as the tiny *Primula scotica*, with its golden-eyed purple flowers, to be appreciated and grown in a situation where they will not be swamped by larger and more vigorous neighbours. Ranging several containers together provides a good opportunity to build up collections devoted to plants of one genus that flourish under similar environmental conditions.

Using an alpine house
An alpine house will accommodate a huge range of the choicest alpines in carefully controlled conditions. The season of interest in the alpine house may be maintained throughout the early winter months, when colour in the open garden is scarce. Interest increases rapidly in early spring, when the majority of true alpines flower. Where dwarf shrubs, bulbs, conifers, and ferns are also included in the collection, there will be something to attract attention throughout the year (see also ALPINE HOUSES AND FRAMES, pp.277–279).

Planter's guide to rock plants

EXPOSED SITES

Rock plants that tolerate exposed or windy sites

Antennaria dioica
Campanula portenschlagiana
Carlina acaulis
Chiastophyllum oppositifolium
Crepis incana
Dryas octopetala
Erigeron karvinskianus
Eryngium, some ❀, ◭
Euphorbia myrsinites
Hebe, some ❀, ◭
Helianthemum
Limonium bellidifolium
Pterocephalus perennis
Sedum, some ❀, ◭
Sempervivum
Silene uniflora
Veronica spicata

AIR POLLUTION

Rock plants that tolerate polluted air

Aubrieta
Aurinia saxatilis
Campanula garganica,
    C. poscharskyana
Erinus alpinus
Euphorbia, some ❀, ◭
Sedum, some ❀, ◭
Sempervivum

DRY SHADE

Rock plants that tolerate dry shade

Ajuga pyramidalis, A. reptans
Dianthus carthusianorum,
    D. deltoides
Diascia barberae 'Fisher's Flora',
    D. 'Ruby Field'
Erodium guttatum
Genista sagittalis
Gypsophila repens
Helleborus, some ❀
Lamium maculatum
Saponaria ocymoides
Waldsteinia
    ternata

Waldsteinia
ternata

MOIST SHADE

Rock plants that prefer moist shade

Adonis amurensis
Cassiope
Cyclamen hederifolium,
    C. purpurascens
Daphne blagayana

Galax aphylla
Hepatica nobilis,
    H. transsilvanica
Hylomecon japonicum
Iris cristata
Meconopsis cambrica
Primula, some ❀ (many spp.
    and cvs)
Sanguinaria canadensis
Shortia uniflora
Stylophorum diphyllum
Trillium

SCREE GARDENS

Acantholimon glumaceum
Aethionema grandiflorum,
    A. 'Warley Rose'

Androsace
lanuginosa

Alyssum montanum
Androsace lanuginosa,
    A. sarmentosa,
    A. sempervivoides
Dianthus alpinus, D. anatolicus,
    D. echiniformis
Erinus alpinus
Gypsophila aretioides
Linaria alpina
Papaver burseri,
    P. miyabeanum,
    P. rhaeticum
Pritzelago alpina
Sempervivum
Silene acaulis
Viola cornuta 'Minor', V. jooi

CREVICES AND PAVING

Aubrieta deltoidea (many cvs)
Aurinia saxatilis
Campanula cochleariifolia,
    C. portenschlagiana
Erinus alpinus
Erodium reichardii, syn.
    E. chamaedryoides
Geranium sanguineum var. striatum
Globularia cordifolia
Mentha requienii
Onosma alborosea, O. echioides
Pratia pedunculata
Scabiosa graminifolia
Thymus, some ❀

WALL CREVICES

Antirrhinum hispanicum, A. molle
Aurinia saxatilis 'Citrina'
Campanula portenschlagiana

Erinus alpinus
Globularia cordifolia
Haberlea rhodopensis (shade)
Lewisia Cotyledon Hybrids,
Onosma taurica
Polemonium pulcherrimum
Ramonda myconi (shade)
Saxifraga callosa, S. cochlearis,
    S. longifolia, S. paniculata
Silene uniflora 'Robin Whitebreast'

PLANTING IN TROUGHS

Anchusa cespitosa
Androsace (small spp. and cvs)
Antennaria dioica 'Minima'
Arenaria purpurascens
Asperula suberosa
Daphne (some)
Dianthus alpinus, D. freynii,
Dryas octopetala 'Minor'
Edraianthus pumilio
Gentiana saxosa, G. verna
    subsp. angulosa
Helianthemum oelandicum
Linum suffruticosum subsp.
    salsoloides 'Nanum'
Myosotis alpestris
Omphalodes luciliae ❀
Oxalis enneaphylla
Paraquilegia anemonoides
Petrophytum hendersonii
Phlox subulata
Primula farinosa,
    P. marginata

Saxifraga
sancta

Saxifraga, some ❀ (many spp.
    and cvs)
Sedum cauticola
Soldanella alpina, S. montana
Thymus serpyllum 'Minus'
Vitaliana primuliflora

PLANTING IN TUFA

Androsace (small spp. and cvs)
Campanula piperi, C. zoysii
Draba mollissima, D. polytricha
Edraianthus pumilio
Paraquilegia anemonoides
Physoplexis comosa
Potentilla nitida
Saxifraga, some ❀ (many types,
    especially the Kabschias)
Viola cazorlensis, V. delphinantha

RAISED BEDS

Aethionema 'Warley Rose'
Androsace
Antirrhinum molle, A. sempervirens
Aquilegia discolor, A. flabellata

Armeria juniperifolia
Bolax gummifera
Callianthemum anemonoides
Campanula raineri, C. zoysii
Daphne arbuscula, D. cneorum,
    D. petraea 'Grandiflora',
    D. x susannae 'Cheriton'
    D. x whiteorum 'Beauworth'
Dianthus, some ❀
Draba rigida var. bryoides,
Edraianthus dinaricus,
    E. graminifolius
Erinacea anthyllis
Gentiana acaulis,
    G. verna subsp. angulosa
Globularia meridionalis, G. repens
Haberlea rhodopensis
Leontopodium alpinum, L. nivale
Lewisia (some spp. and hybrids)
Origanum (some spp. and hybrids)
Oxalis adenophylla,
    O. enneaphylla, O. 'Ione Hecker'
Papaver burseri, P. miyabeanum
Paraquilegia anemonoides
Primula auricula, P. marginata
Ramonda myconi
Saxifraga cotyledon, S. longifolia,
    S. 'Tumbling Waters'
Sempervivum
Silene acaulis
Verbascum 'Letitia'

DWARF SHRUBS

Berberis x stenophylla 'Corallina
    Compacta'
Betula nana
Chamaecyparis obtusa 'Intermedia'
Cryptomeria japonica 'Vilmoriniana'
Daphne cneorum, D. retusa,
    D. sericea
Erinacea anthyllis
Euryops acraeus
Genista delphinensis
Hebe buchananii
    'Minor'
Ilex crenata 'Mariesii'
Juniperus communis '
Compressa'

Ozothamnus
coralloides

Lotus hirsutum,
    syn. Dorycnium
    hirsutum
Ozothamnus coralloides,
    syn. Helichrysum coralloides
Picea abies 'Clanbrassiliana',
    P. abies 'Gregoryana', P. glauca
    var. albertiana 'Conica'
Potentilla 'Nana Argentea'
Salix x boydii
Sorbus reducta

KEY

❀ *Not hardy*
◭ *Rock garden species only*

Construction, soil preparation, and planting

VARIOUS methods may be used to grow alpine plants in gardens. Planting them in a rock garden is perhaps the best-known method, although this can take up a great deal of space. For a smaller display, screes, raised and peat beds, and the crevices of walls can make very attractive features. Where space is more limited, troughs, sinks, and other containers may also be used for a fine alpine display.

ROCK PLANTS THAT REQUIRE ACID SOIL

Arctostaphylos alpina
Cassiope
Corydalis cashmeriana,
 C. flexuosa
Cyananthus
Epigaea gaultherioides,
 E. repens
Galax urceolata
Gaultheria
Gentiana sino-ornata
Glaucidium palmatum
Haberlea rhodopensis
Kalmia angustifolia,
 K. polifolia 'Microphylla'
Leiophyllum buxifolium
Leucopogon fraseri
Leucothöe keiskei
Linnaea borealis
Lithodora diffusa
Menziesia ciliicalyx
Mitchella repens
Ourisia caespitosa,
 O. coccinea, O. 'Loch Ewe'
Paris polyphylla

Phyllodoce
caerulea

Phyllodoce caerulea,
 P. aleutica subsp. *glanduliflora,*
 P. nipponica
Pieris nana
Polygala chamaebuxus,
 P. vayredae
Primula boothii alba,
 P. gracilipes,
 P. nana,
 P. sonchifolia
Pyrola rotundifolia
Rhododendron (dwarf spp. and cvs)
Sanguinaria canadensis
 f. *multiplex*
Shortia soldanelloides
Soldanella villosa
Tanakaea radicans
Vaccinium delavayi,
 V. myrtillus, V. uliginosum

Buying plants

The rock garden should be regarded as a feature that will provide, with careful choice of plants, interest all year round.

Before buying any plants, refer to standard texts to find out the likely range of plants that is suitable for a particular type of locality in terms of climate, soil, and general situation. Visit established rock gardens in parks and botanic gardens, as well as specialist nurseries, to assess the relative merits of various plants for your own requirements. The shape, form, and colour of foliage, fruits, stems, and the overall growth habit are often as important as flowers.

Where to buy plants

Plants are available from a wide range of sources, including garden centres and specialist nurseries. Non-specialist outlets often sell a limited range of colourful cultivars and easily grown species; these may form large, spreading clumps that quickly overwhelm more delicate plants in the rock garden.

The experienced nurseryman is able to advise on the most suitable choice of plants for a particular situation, and often has display beds of mature plants. These give a good indication of the ultimate size, spread, and habit of different plants, and are invaluable at the planning stage. Such specialist outlets may also be consulted for information on composts and suppliers of rock.

A much wider range of plants will be offered by the specialist grower, who is also able to provide detailed advice on cultivation – this is particularly useful for the beginner. Demand for rare or unfamiliar plants sometimes means that general suppliers may carry stocks of plants that are best left to the specialist, since they are often unsuitable for the average rock garden. Such plants may be attractive but are often expensive and may be difficult to cultivate. They offer a rewarding challenge, but only purchase them after obtaining advice on growing them.

Selecting alpine plants

Choose plants that have healthy, compact foliage, and no sign of pests and diseases or water deprivation. Do not buy plants with yellowing or weak growth, since this indicates that they have been kept in poor light. Labels should bear the name of the plant as well as details of flowering times and brief cultivation

HOW TO SELECT ALPINE PLANTS

GOOD EXAMPLE   SAXIFRAGA   **POOR EXAMPLES**

Healthy looking, compact growth

Weed-free compost

Unbalanced, weak growth

Weeds in compost

Roots curled around inside of pot

requirements. Plants should not be pot-bound and the roots should either not be visible, or only just, through the hole in the base of the pot. Do not purchase any plants that have rooted into the material on the surface of the display area, since these are almost certain to be pot-bound.

The top-growth of a plant may remain healthy for some time after the root system has been damaged or has actually died, so check that the plant has a healthy root system by sliding it out of its pot and inspecting the root ball carefully.

Large specimens are sometimes available but unless they are grown on correctly, with careful attention to watering, they may take much longer to become established than smaller, vigorous ones.

Select plants that are as weed-free as possible. Before planting, gently scrape off the grit or surface compost so that any weed seeds are removed. Introducing weeds such as pearlwort (*Sagina procumbens*) and hairy bittercress (*Cardamine hirsuta*), causes problems as, once established, they are difficult to eradicate.

A number of plants that are sold for growing in the rock garden, such as some of the ornamental onions (*Allium*), are over-prolific seeders. Choose plants carefully to avoid introducing such problem plants.

Siting a rock garden or scree bed

Good siting is critical for a rock garden or scree bed, because alpine plants require good light and well-drained conditions to thrive. The rock garden or scree should also blend in with the rest of the garden. Before starting construction, draw a rough plan on paper showing the rock garden or scree bed in relation to other garden features. A scree may be integrated into a rock garden or built as a separate feature.

SITING A ROCK GARDEN

Limit of afternoon shade from nearby plants

Sloping ground

Limit of morning shade from hedge

Build a rock garden on sloping ground, if possible, to ensure sharp drainage. Choose an open site that receives full sun, away from the roots and overhanging branches of trees and large shrubs.

Choosing the site

Choose an open, sunny site away from overhanging trees; trees drip water onto plants beneath, and leaves shed in autumn may also smother plants or create a damp atmosphere that rots them. Tree roots may also compete with the plants for moisture and nutrients. Do not site a rock garden or scree in a frost pocket or on a site exposed to cold, drying winds. A sloping site is ideal for a rock garden; it will have excellent drainage, and artificial outcrops of rock may be made to look more natural, and provide different pockets and aspects to suit a variety of plants. Scree beds (see p.264) or raised beds (see p.269) are usually better for level sites.

A rock garden or scree is best sited where it will blend into an informally planted area of the garden, on a slope, by a terrace, or as a natural-looking outcrop from an area of shrubs. Plan any water features, such as a pond or stream, into the scheme from an early stage. If the rock garden or scree is to be next to a lawn, ensure that it does not interfere with cutting and edging. It is unlikely to look natural next to herbaceous borders, bedding displays, or any other formally planted areas, such as the vegetable or fruit garden. If the main garden is formal, it may be better to grow alpines in a rectangular raised bed (see p.269) rather than trying to integrate the informality of a rock garden into the design.

Choosing stone

Buy salvaged or second-hand natural stone for rock garden construction wherever possible; otherwise try local quarries to inspect the rock and

Natural strata

Sedimentary rock, such as chalk and limestone, occurs naturally in distinct layers, or stratum lines, that are clearly visible to the eye. Rocks of this type may easily be split along the stratum lines for use in rock gardens.

Sedimentary rocks that occur in nature always have stratum lines following the same direction; it is important to place the stones in a rock garden to simulate the same kind of effect, otherwise they will look too obviously artificial.

NATURAL STRATUM LINES

choose suitable pieces that are not too large to handle after being delivered. Choose stone in a range of different sizes to construct a natural-looking outcrop. Garden centres may offer a range of stone, although there is sometimes a limited choice of size and shape. Reconstituted stone products may also be available.

Natural stone

Some types of rock, especially water-washed limestones, are now under great threat in their native surroundings and, for conservation reasons, should not be used. Occasionally, long-quarried, weathered limestone is available second-hand, but do not purchase freshly quarried limestone or rock that has been collected from its natural surroundings or removed from stone walls.

Do not use soft, quick-weathering rock, such as shales and chalk, or hard, featureless, igneous rocks without strata, such as granite and basalt. Hard stone with no clear strata may be inexpensive but is difficult to

use, takes several years to acquire a weathered appearance, and seldom looks natural. Other materials, such as slate, are also used but are sometimes difficult to blend in.

The most suitable rocks are the various sandstones, in which the natural strata or layers are clearly visible. One great advantage of using rocks with stratum lines is that they may easily be split. Alternatively, you may be lucky enough to find a source of tufa, also known as "old horse bone" – a porous, limy rock filled with numerous air pockets. Its light weight makes it easy to transport and handle. Cavities for plants may be dug or drilled out of its relatively soft surface. It provides ideal conditions for many plants that require free drainage.

Artificial rocks

Reconstituted rocks made from quarry waste and even fibreglass "rocks" can also be obtained; they may be more or less convincing in appearance and certainly need careful blending in with suitable top-dressings (see p.265) and planting in order to appear natural. It is possible to produce artificial rocks on a garden scale from a mix of 2 parts sharp sand, 2 parts coir, and 1 part Portland cement, to which colouring powders may be added. The mix is worked into moulds formed from polythene-lined holes excavated in the soil.

Soils and soil mixes

In nature, many alpines and rock garden plants grow in "soil" that is largely made up of rock fragments and gravel, usually with some accumulations of humus-rich detritus, which retains moisture. Such a growing medium is extremely well drained and it is important to simulate this as closely as possible in a rock garden or scree bed. Ordinary

Types of stone

Tufa is an excellent choice for the rock garden because its soft, porous nature means that plants may be grown in cavities on its surface as well as in crevices between the stones. Natural-looking, weather-worn sandstone is also a good choice, as is limestone (if available second-hand).

TUFA

SANDSTONE

LIMESTONE (KENTISH RAG)

CREATING A ROCK GARDEN FRAMEWORK

1 *Place a 15cm (6in) layer of coarse rubble, such as broken bricks, on the proposed site to form a mound and improve drainage in the rock garden.*

2 *Cover the mound with inverted turves to prevent soil from being washed down to the layer of rubble at the base.*

3 *Firm down the turves and cover them with a 23–30cm (9–12in) layer of sharply drained topsoil. Before beginning to lay the stones, use pegs and a length of rope to mark out roughly the shape of each main rock outcrop.*

4 *Using a spade, dig out hollows for each large piece of stone to make them more stable when placed in position.*

5 *Use a crowbar to manoeuvre large stones into their final positions. Ensure that the stones are well supported by wedging smaller stones or bricks underneath.*

6 *Infill underneath and in between the stones with garden soil, making sure that each stone is firmly in place.*

7 *Build each outcrop in the same way. Tread down the soil gently around the stones (see inset) to make sure that each stone is firmly seated. Once all stones are in place, add more soil around each stone, up to a third of its depth. Do not compact the soil between the stones.*

8 *Mix equal parts loam, garden compost or leaf mould, and sharp sand or grit. Then add a layer of this specially prepared compost to the surface of the rock garden and around each of the stones. Create planting pockets in which to grow different types of plants.*

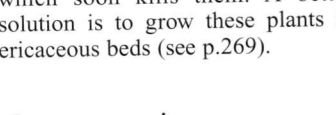

garden soils may be adapted, to some extent, for cultivating most rock garden plants and alpines by adding peat substitute (or peat) and/or grit, but large quantities of grit are required to provide the rapid drainage needed for the more moisture-sensitive species, such as those grown in scree beds.

Standard mix

A mix of 1 part sterilized garden soil, 1 part peat substitute (or peat), and 1 part sharp sand or coarse grit is suitable for most rock garden plants. The humus-rich materials ensure moisture retention, while the sand or grit maintains good drainage.

Scree mixture

Scree plants will require a very free-draining compost. Make up a soil mixture using the same ingredients as for the standard mix, but in different proportions: 3 parts coarse grit or stone chippings (not sand) instead of 1 part. In order to produce an even freer-draining compost, increase the proportion of stony material included in the mix. In dry areas, this proportion of stone chippings may have to be reduced to 2 parts; alternatively, use a more water-retentive mix consisting of 2 parts loam, 2 parts leaf mould, 1 part sharp sand, and 4 parts stone chippings.

Special mixes

Some choice alpines, such as the tiny, cushion-forming *Androsace* species and saxifrages, need very free-draining compost. These plants usually come from high altitudes where soil nutrient levels are low. Use a mix of 2 or 3 parts chippings or gravel, to 1 part loam or leaf mould (or peat substitute or peat).

For acid-lovers use a mix of 4 parts lime-free leaf mould, peat substitute (or peat), composted bark, or bracken litter with 1 part coarse sand. On an alkaline soil, however, growing plants in pockets of acid mixture is only effective in the short term, due

to the inevitable percolation of lime, which soon kills them. A better solution is to grow these plants in ericaceous beds (see p.269).

Constructing a rock garden

Never attempt to construct rock gardens when the soil is wet, since heavy rocks may compact the soil and severely damage its structure; this interferes with drainage and causes problems with the establishment and growth of the plants. If the site is grassed, cut the turf carefully and remove it for later use when constructing the rock garden.

Clearing weeds

Remove all perennial weeds from the site and, if siting the rock garden near trees or shrubs, remove any suckers that these may have produced. Perennial weeds are very difficult to eradicate from an established rock garden, so it is essential to dig them out or kill them (see PLANT PROBLEMS, "Weeds", pp.669–673).

Drainage

Make sure that the site, particularly if level, is well drained, and if necessary install a soakaway or other drainage system (see SOILS AND FERTILIZERS, "Improving drainage", p.623). This is important on heavy clay soils. Do not simply dig deep holes – these act as sumps in which the water remains, unless they are connected to a drainage ditch. Raising the rock garden above the level of the surrounding ground helps to improve drainage. On naturally sloping sites drainage is not usually a problem, although a drainage ditch may be needed at the lowest point.

If the underlying drainage is good, just dig the soil over and remove any perennial weeds. Then consolidate the soil by treading gently to avoid subsequent sinking; fork over the surface of the soil to maintain good soil structure.

Building the base

Put down a 15cm (6in) layer of coarse rubble, broken bricks, stones, ballast, angular gravel, or pea shingle. Spread over this a layer of inverted turves, if available; these prevent compost from the rock garden clogging the free-draining layer at the base, without inhibiting normal drainage. If turves are not available, use a polypropylene sheet, with holes punctured at regular intervals to allow water to drain through.

Purchase topsoil or bring in good soil from elsewhere in the garden, ensuring that it is as weed-free as possible; use this for the top layer of the rock garden. Specially prepared, sharply drained compost (see p.265) should be used for filling in between stones where plants are to be grown.

Placing the stone

Rock is heavy and rough on the hands, so wear gloves and protective footwear. Use rollers to move large rocks, and arrange for the consignment to be delivered as close to the site of the rock garden as possible. To manoeuvre large rocks into their final positions, it may be necessary

to use a block and tackle, with a steel crowbar as a lever for final adjustments. Mark the approximate positions of larger rocks first, to avoid unnecessary labour.

Select first the large stones that will act as "keystones". These are the dominant rocks from which each outcrop is developed. Position the largest of the keystones first, and then arrange the remaining ones so that the strata flow naturally from them to form outcrops. Further large stones acting as subsidiary keystones

may then be used to extend the outcrops. Use enough rock to make the outcrops realistic, while leaving sufficient room for planting. Check progress visually as construction proceeds. If the rocks being used have stratum lines, en-sure that these all run in the same direction and at the same angle.

The rocks should be placed to provide the widest range of opportunities for planting. For example, butting rocks together serves to create the narrow crevices in which a

variety of plants may thrive. Where space allows, a carefully planned, tiered rock garden may produce a number of useful, broad planting pockets between the rocks.

Bury the rocks to a third of their volume and tip them backwards slightly. This ensures stability and allows water to run back off the rock into the bed rather than onto the plants beneath. Stand on the rocks to make sure that they are stable.

As rocks are positioned, infill planting spaces with prepared com-

PLANTING AND TOP-DRESSING

1 *Before starting to plant, water all the plants and allow them to drain. To check the planting arrangement, set out the pots on the surface of the bed, taking account of the eventual height and spread of the plants.*

2 *Carefully remove each plant from its pot and loosen the root ball a little to encourage the roots to spread. Remove any moss and weeds before planting.*

3 *Using a trowel, dig a hole large enough to accommodate the root ball. Ease the plant into the hole, and label.*

4 *Fill in around the plant with compost and firm gently, making sure that there are no air pockets between the root ball and the compost.*

5 *Top-dress the compost with a layer of grit or gravel, easing a little around the collars of the plants.*

6 *Continue to plant in the same way until the rock garden is complete. Check that the whole area is properly top-dressed and water in the plants well.*

THE FINISHED ROCK GARDEN *The plants will soon grow away to produce an attractive and mature-looking rock garden.*

post and firm it in. Any obvious unconformities in the rocks may then be masked by careful planting.

To provide a cool, well-drained cavity for alpines and rock plants, plant them between two layers of stone as the rock garden is constructed. Position the plants in the soil close to a stone that has already been firmed in and add a little compost around the roots, firming gently. Use small rocks to protect the plants as the next stone is positioned against the first to form a planting pocket. The small rocks can then be removed and the second stone firmed in place. Add more compost around the plants and infill with soil between the stones before top-dressing.

Planting a rock garden

Alpines and rock garden plants are almost always purchased as pot plants and may be planted at any time of the year, although it is better not to plant them when the ground is either wet or frozen, or during very warm or dry periods.

Water all the plants thoroughly before planting and allow them to drain. Set the plants out in the planned positions while still in their pots to give an idea of the finished planting. Make any rearrangements at this stage and adjust planting distances, allowing for the vigorous and rapid growth of some types. Slide each plant carefully out of its pot and remove any weeds from the compost. Inspect the roots and top-growth for pests and diseases and treat, as necessary, before planting (see PLANT PROBLEMS, pp.639–673).

Make a planting hole with a trowel or hand fork, ensuring that the hole is big enough to accommodate the roots. Loosen the root ball, position the plant in the hole, and firm in the compost. The plant should sit with the collar slightly above the surface of the compost to leave room for a top-dressing of gravel or chippings.

When all the plants are in place, water them in thoroughly. Keep them moist until they are established and starting to make new growth. If planting is followed by a dry period, water the plants at approximately weekly intervals until the roots have penetrated the surrounding compost. Thereafter, there should be no need to water except during a drought.

Planting in crevices

Crevices between rocks are ideal for alpines and rock plants that enjoy cool, well-drained sites, but they may be difficult to establish and so need extra care when planting. It is preferable to plant them at the construction stage, although this is not always possible. To avoid the danger of a rock slipping when planting horizontal crevices, support the upper rock with small stones and plant between them. When planting in vertical crevices, small stones can also be used to retain the compost (see "Planting in vertical crevices", p.268). If planting in the crevices of an established rock garden, use a small tool, such as a widger, to make a planting hole.

Use young, rooted cuttings with vigorous root systems. If only pot-grown plants are available, trim the root balls and top-growth to the appropriate size before planting. Put a small stone in the crevice and place a little compost on top, then ease in the roots with a widger so that the plant faces outwards. Add more compost around the plant and firm in; place a small stone on top of the root ball for extra support.

Aftercare

Use netting or other deterrents to protect newly planted alpines from birds. Periodically refirm any plants that may have worked loose, adding new compost if necessary. Label the plants or maintain a planting plan to record their names at the time of planting; update planting plans and labelling as plants are added, replaced, or relocated.

Constructing a scree bed

Prepare the site in a similar way to a rock garden, installing artificial drainage, if necessary (see SOILS AND FERTILIZERS, "Improving drainage", p.623). Sloping sites have naturally good drainage but on flat ground screes are best raised slightly above the ground to assist drainage, and retained within low walls, logs, or old railway sleepers in the same way as raised beds (see p.269).

Scree beds should be 30–40cm (12–16in) deep; about half the depth should be composed of coarse rubble, as for rock gardens, and the upper layer of scree mixture (see p.265). Mark out the site with a rope or hosepipe and on previously grassed areas remove the turf. Lay the rubble foundation and line with thinly cut, inverted turves or a polypropylene sheet, pierced at regular intervals for good drainage.

Finish off the bed with a 15–20cm (6–8in) layer of scree mixture, and firm by gently treading over the whole area. Water the bed and allow it to settle, then top up with scree mixture any areas that may have sunk before pricking over the surface with a hand fork.

Planting in a scree bed

It may be more difficult to establish plants in a scree bed than in a rock garden, since the freely draining compost tends to dry out before the plants are established. Care during planting and conscientious watering

MEDITERRANEAN-STYLE PLANTING ON AN INCLINE

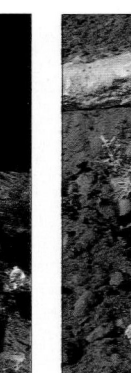

1 *If necessary, work sharp sand or grit into the soil to improve drainage. Dig and firm in larger stones. Arrange the plants in their pots (here a selection of herbs).*

2 *Plant the large and then the small plants at the same depth as they were in their containers, and water well. Let the soil surface dry a little before top-dressing.*

3 *Add smaller stones and then a thick layer of stone chippings or shingle. Use a trowel or your hands to spread it carefully between and around the plants.*

THE FINISHED "MEDITERRANEAN" BANK
Such a drought-tolerant garden provides an attractive low-maintenance area that should need little watering once the plants are established. The surface layer of chippings or shingle will help to conserve moisture in the soil, reflect heat onto the sun-loving plants, and keep down weeds. Remove any weeds that do appear by hand as soon as you spot them.

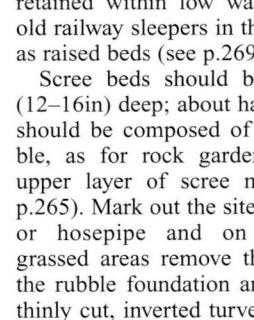

IMPROVING SOIL DRAINAGE BENEATH A GRAVEL BED

1 *On heavy soil, remove and reserve the top layer of soil to a depth of 60cm (24in), fork over the ground, and spread a 15cm (6in) layer of rubble or hardcore.*

2 *Cap the rubble with a layer of inverted turves, in order to prevent the top layer of lighter soil being washed down through the layer of rubble.*

3 *Mix the reserved soil with plenty of sharp sand or gravel, and spread it over the turf layer. Tamp the soil with the head of a rake or tread on it lightly to firm.*

4 *After firming, water the area to settle the soil, and top up to fill any voids. Top-dress with a 10cm (4in) layer of gravel or shingle and rake it level.*

---

are the keys to success. The well-developed root systems of pot-grown alpines do not readily penetrate the gritty scree compost, so gently shake off most of the compost (especially if peat-based) from the roots. Keep the bare roots moist. Place the plant in a planting hole with its roots spread out, and infill carefully with scree mixture. Top-dress around the plant with rock chippings and water immediately and thoroughly.

Scree mixes are fast-draining, so water young plants regularly until they are established. Try to minimize wetting the foliage. In their natural habitats, scree dwellers have deep and extensive root systems to seek out water and nutrients, so when established they will survive for long periods without watering.

Top-dressings, gravels, and pebbles

After planting is completed, a rock garden or scree bed may then be top-dressed with stone chippings, grit, or gravel. This material should match as closely as possible the rock used at the construction stage.

Top-dressing has a number of advantages: it provides an attractive and natural setting for the plants and blends in better with the rocks than bare soil, creates especially good drainage around the collars of the plants, inhibits weed growth, conserves moisture, and protects the soil surface from compaction during heavy rain or watering. The layer of top-dressing on a rock garden should

be at least 2.5cm (1in) deep; on a scree bed it may be 2–15cm (¾–6in) deep, depending on the plants grown; for most screes, a 2–3cm (¾–1¼in) layer is sufficient.

On gravel beds and gardens, a water-permeable geotextile fabric may be used beneath the layer of gravel to further assist in weed suppression and to extend the life of the top-dressing by preventing it gradually working into the soil (see "Using weed-suppressant geotextile fabric", left). Such fabrics also largely prevent ornamental plants from self-seeding, and are ideal where a very low-maintenance feature is required, although they do prevent plants from spreading in a natural fashion.

Stone chippings and gravels with which to dress areas of planting in gravel are offered by garden centres and builders' merchants in a variety of grades and colours. If the surface is to be walked upon regularly, or used as a patio area on which to set garden furniture and containers, a fine grade of gravel, often referred to as "pea shingle", is recommended as it provides a smooth, more easily

PLANTING IN A GRAVEL BED
Large plants are more conveniently planted before the gravel is spread, but small plants can be added later. Draw the gravel aside and scoop out a hole; if necessary, mound the spoil on a plastic sheet to keep the gravel clean. Water well.

negotiable surface. Small pavers may be set unobtrusively in the gravel layer to provide strategic support points where stability is important – for example, beneath table legs.

Choose a colour that blends in with local stone for the most natural look. Striking, modernistic effects may be created using contrasting tones – for example, "rivers" of dark slate chippings flowing between outcrops of paler rock – although such features need considerable skill in their design and planting to avoid a clumsy impression.

Cobbles and pebbles

Never collect any quantity of cobbles or pebbles from beaches, where they may form important defences against erosion; in areas with statutory environmental protection or where man-made sea-defences exist, it may actually be against the law to do so. Good garden centres should offer responsibly sourced, washed pebbles. You may find them in aquatic departments now that they have become popular decorative items with which to dress small fountain features.

Using weed-suppressant geotextile fabric

These fabrics, now widely available, may also be referred to as mulching membranes or landscape sheeting. They are easily pegged down using wire hoops. Soak plant root balls thoroughly before planting them through

cross-cuts in the fabric (see WATER CONSERVATION AND RECYCLING, p.614). Water them regularly until they are established. The fabric should help retain more moisture in the soil than a surface layer of shingle or gravel alone.

HIDING THE FABRIC
Once the fabric is secured over the entire area, the top layer of shingle or gravel can be added. The layer must be thick enough to prevent any fabric being visible, as black or white are the only colours generally available.

 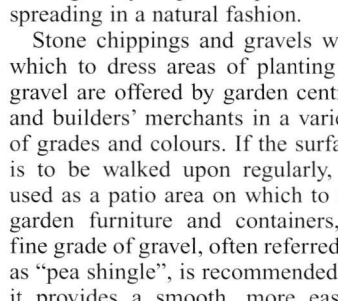

Troughs, sinks, and other containers

Alpines and rock plants look particularly attractive grown in troughs and sinks, although most frost-proof containers with good drainage are suitable. Choose the correct site at the outset as, once filled, they are difficult to move. Rocks may be placed in the containers to create the effect of a miniature rock garden; do this before planting up the container.

Types of container

Old, stone animal troughs and sinks, traditionally used to grow alpines, are now scarce and expensive. Glazed sinks coated in hypertufa, or troughs made entirely of hypertufa or reconstituted stone are now often used, as are large pottery and terracotta pots and tubs. All should have drainage holes to ensure that there is a free flow of water through the compost. If extra drainage holes are needed, they should be at least 2.5cm (1in) in diameter; if the base of the container is not flat, make the drainage holes at the lowest point. Plants in glazed sinks do not need nearly as much water as those in stone or hypertufa troughs, so, to prevent waterlogging in all but dry areas, an extra drainage layer should be added under the compost.

Covering glazed sinks

Deep, glazed, flat-bottomed sinks may easily be made to resemble stone containers by coating them with hypertufa. Ensure that the sink is clean and dry then score the surface with a tile- or glass-cutter to help the hypertufa adhere to the sink. To aid adhesion further, paint the surface with a bonding agent before applying the hypertufa.

Make hypertufa from 1–2 parts sifted peat substitute (or sphagnum peat), 1 part coarse sand or fine grit, and 1 part cement. Add sufficient water to form a thick paste. Apply this to the outside of the sink and also inside, down to well below the final level of the compost. Put the hypertufa on by hand (wear gloves); it should be 1–2cm (½–¾in) thick. Roughen the surface so that it resem-

GLAZED SINK WITH HYPERTUFA COATING

Glazed sinks covered with hypertufa make fine containers for alpines.

bles stone. When the hypertufa is fully dry, after about a week, scrub the surface with a wire brush and coat with a weak solution – about 3tsp to a litre (2tsp to a pint) of water – of permanganate of potash or liquid manure to discourage algae and encourage moss and lichen.

Hypertufa troughs

Troughs may be made entirely from hypertufa, if required. Prepare the mixture as for coating but increase the proportion of sand and grit to three parts to make a stiffer mix.

Use two wooden boxes that fit inside one another, with a cavity of 5–7cm (2–3in) between them. Stand the larger box on blocks so that it may be lifted once finished; pour two thin layers of the hypertufa mix into the base, with strong wire netting between the layers and parallel to the vertical sides. Press thick dowels or pegs through the hypertufa to make drainage holes. Fit the smaller box inside the larger, with netting between the two, and fill the space with the mix, tamping it down to remove air pockets.

When the cavity is full, cover the trough with a sheet of plastic for at least a week while the mix sets and protect the trough from frost, if necessary. When the mix has set hard, remove the boxes and dowels. If the boxes do not slide off easily, ease them off carefully with a fine chisel and a small hammer. Roughen the surface of the trough with a wire brush and paint on a coat of liquid manure or permanganate of potash to encourage growth.

HOW TO MAKE A HYPERTUFA TROUGH

1 *You will need two boxes to make the trough, one slightly larger than the other. Coat the surfaces of the boxes with oil to prevent the hypertufa sticking.*

2 *Place a 2.5cm (1in) layer of hypertufa mix in the base of the larger box and put wire netting on top of this layer and around the sides to reinforce the trough. Then add another layer of hypertufa.*

3 *Press several thick, wooden dowels into the wire and hypertufa base to make the drainage holes for the bottom of the trough.*

4 *Put the smaller box centrally on top of the hypertufa base, making sure the vertical netting is between the two boxes. Fill the cavity with the hypertufa mix, tamping down well as you fill.*

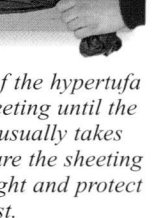

5 *Cover the top of the hypertufa with plastic sheeting until the mix has set (which usually takes about a week). Secure the sheeting in place with a weight and protect the trough from frost.*

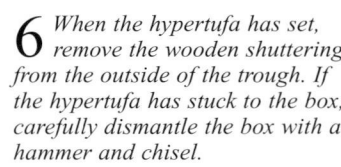

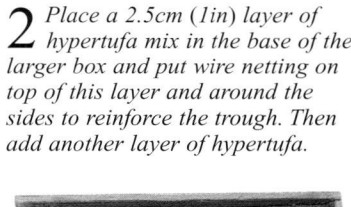

6 *When the hypertufa has set, remove the wooden shuttering from the outside of the trough. If the hypertufa has stuck to the box, carefully dismantle the box with a hammer and chisel.*

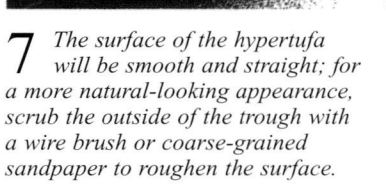

7 *The surface of the hypertufa will be smooth and straight; for a more natural-looking appearance, scrub the outside of the trough with a wire brush or coarse-grained sandpaper to roughen the surface.*

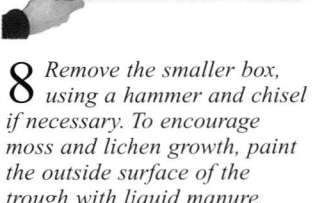

8 *Remove the smaller box, using a hammer and chisel if necessary. To encourage moss and lichen growth, paint the outside surface of the trough with liquid manure.*

Siting containers

An open position, with sun for at least part of the day, is ideal for most plants. Do not place containers in windy sites, unless tough plants are being grown, or on lawns, since it is difficult to maintain the surrounding grass. Avoid slopes, which cause instability, and put containers as close as possible to a tap or hosepipe.

Raise troughs and sinks off the ground, up to a height of about 45cm (18in); the plants may then be viewed comfortably and water will drain away readily. Stone or brick pillars at the corners of a container provide sturdy, stable supports. These must bear the weight of the container without danger of tipping, and should not block the drainage holes. Sinks with single drainage holes should be tilted so that excess water drains off.

Placing rocks and tufa

Virtually any type of rock may be used in troughs and sinks. Rocks give height, and allow a greater depth of compost. A few large rocks are better than many small ones. Niches and crevices in the rocks may also be used to support plants, especially if hard tufa is used. Tufa's light weight and the ease with which planting holes can be excavated in it make it ideal. Roots spread into the porous rock, which is well aerated but also retains water.

Whatever type of rock is used, bury from one third to one half of each stone in the compost to ensure that it is firmly seated.

Filling the container

Rock garden plants need a loam-based potting compost, with some additional drainage material, in order to extract the nutrients they need to thrive. Add about one third by volume of perlite or 6–9mm ($\frac{1}{4}$–$\frac{3}{8}$in) stone chippings, and mix in some slow-release fertilizer to the compost. Acid-loving plants need a lime-free compost, with added granite or sandstone chippings.

Cover the drainage holes with broken crocks or wire gauze and fill the bottom quarter to one third of the container with coarse aggregate, gravel, or stone chippings. Fill up with slightly moist compost, and firm it gently.

Position pieces of rock or tufa on the compost, and bed them in as the container is filled. Place rocks to form crevices and niches, providing both shaded and sunny faces to suit different plants, and add randomly placed smaller pieces of stone to simulate a small-scale rock garden. Water thoroughly and leave to drain completely before planting.

Planting

Choose slow-growing plants that will not swamp their neighbours and quickly exhaust the available nutrients. Do not overplant the container, and replant as soon as it becomes overcrowded (see "Replanting an alpine trough", p.271).

Position container-grown plants, still in their pots, on the compost or make a plan on paper of the planting scheme. Make planting holes, carefully slide the plants out of their pots, and loosen the root balls. Place the plants in the holes, fill in with compost, and firm. When complete, water thoroughly. Then add a top-dressing of chippings or gravel to help ensure sharp drainage.

Planting in tufa

If plants are to be grown in tufa rock, use a drill or a hammer and chisel, and make holes 10–12cm (4–5in) apart. They should be about 2.5cm (1in) in diameter and 5–7cm (2–3in) deep, angled at 30–45° on vertical or sloping surfaces, or straight down on horizontal planes. Soak the tufa, then put a little sharp sand in each hole, and add some compost. Use young, rooted cuttings or small plants, since they establish easily. Wash the roots before planting; ease them into the holes with a small dibber or a pencil and sprinkle in compost until the hole is full. Ensure that the neck of the plant is bedded in and not standing proud of the hole. Firm the compost and wedge small pieces of tufa around the plants to hold them in place. Water thoroughly and keep the tufa moist until the plants are established. In hot, dry weather, soak the tufa regularly.

HOW TO PLANT UP AN ALPINE TROUGH

1 *If planting in tufa, first drill holes in it about 2.5cm (1in) wide, 7cm (3in) deep, and no less than 10cm (4in) apart. Immerse the tufa in water overnight.*

2 *Lay fine-mesh netting over the trough base or cover the holes with crocks, and add 7–10cm (3–4in) of coarse grit.*

3 *Partly fill the trough with a gritty, moist compost, firming it in stages. Set the tufa in place so that at least $\frac{1}{3}$–$\frac{1}{2}$ of it is buried to keep it stable.*

4 *Continue to fill with compost and firm well to allow about 5cm (2in) for top-dressing and watering. Insert a little compost into the tufa holes for planting.*

5 *Wash the roots of the plants to go in the tufa, and ease them into the planting holes. Dribble compost into the holes, firm, and put small rock pieces around the plants.*

6 *Set the plants, still in their pots, on the compost to check that the arrangement and spacing are satisfactory, then plant and firm them in.*

7 *Water the compost thoroughly, then top-dress the trough with a 2.5–5cm (1–2in) deep layer of coarse gravel or stone chippings.*

THE FINISHED TROUGH

Helianthemum oelandicum subsp. alpestre

Androsace pubescens

Sisyrinchium 'E.K. Balls'

Penstemon pinifolius

Saxifraga cotyledon

Sempervivum arachnoideum

Oxalis 'Ione Hecker'

Draba aizoides

Saxifraga cochlearis 'Minor'

Talinum okanoganense

Phlox douglasii cv.

Saxifraga paniculata

Oxalis enneaphylla 'Minutifolia'

Rhodohypoxis baurii

Dianthus 'La Bourboule'

267

Walls

Alpines and rock garden plants may be grown in the crevices of dry-stone walls, including the retaining walls of raised beds and sloping banks. Trailing plants are especially effective when grown in this way. For details on constructing a wall, see "Dry-stone walls", p.598.

If possible, plan for any planting in walls before construction work starts. The most practical approach is to leave planting niches at intervals in the wall and plant them up when the building work is finished.

It is also possible to position the plants as construction proceeds. This produces excellent results, since the plants may be placed at the desired level, and ensures good contact between the roots of the plants and any soil behind the wall. Planting during construction also makes it easier to eliminate air pockets in the compost and firm around the roots.

Planting in existing walls is another option but some of the soil will need to be removed first with a widger or teaspoon before planting. Use young plants or rooted cuttings, since these fit easily in the crevices.

HOW TO BUILD A DRY-STONE RETAINING WALL

MAKING THE FOOTINGS
Dig a trench 38cm (15in) deep; fill it with 25cm (10in) of rubble with a large, sturdy stone on top.

PLACING THE STONES
Slope the stones backwards and downwards for stability and so that water is carried into the compost.

FILLING BETWEEN STONES
As you build, fill crevices between the stones with a compost of loam, leaf mould, and sand or grit.

Planting

Use the following compost mix for filling the planting crevices in walls: 3 parts loam (or good sterilized garden soil), 2 parts coarse peat substitute or peat, and 1–2 parts sharp sand or grit. Use extra grit, sand, or stone chippings for plants that are to be grown in the wall itself, since this will help to ensure good drainage. Choose plants that grow well in the aspect and conditions available in the wall. Carefully remove old compost from the roots and ease them into the hole, using a widger, small dibber, or pencil. Do not try to cram roots into too small a space as this damages the plants. Holding the plant in position with one hand, trickle in fresh, moist compost, then firm it with the widger to remove any air pockets. It may also be helpful to wedge small stones around the collars of the plants to hold them in place and prevent the compost from becoming dislodged.

Water thoroughly from the top of the wall and spray the plants regularly until established. After several days, top up any sunken areas with spare compost. Periodically check the plants and firm any that have worked loose.

HOW TO PLANT IN A DRY-STONE WALL

1 *If planting in an existing wall, check that there is an adequate amount of compost in the crevices to support the plants.*

2 *Use seedlings or small rooted cuttings. Place them on the flat of a stone and, using a widger, ease the roots into the crevices. The plant shown here is a* Sempervivum.

3 *Bed the plants down into compost and pack more compost into the crevices to hold the plants in position. Firm the plants in with your fingers.*

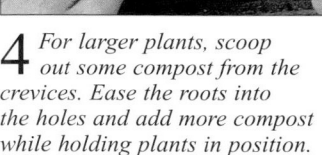

4 *For larger plants, scoop out some compost from the crevices. Ease the roots into the holes and add more compost while holding plants in position.*

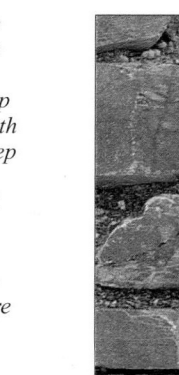

5 *When all the plants are in position, water them from the top of the wall or with a mist spray. Keep the plants moist until established and refirm any that work loose. Planted with the* Sempervivum *are two saxifrages.*

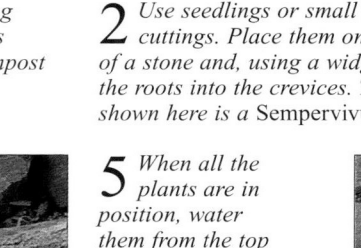

PLANTING IN VERTICAL CREVICES

1 *Fill the crevice with a gritty compost. Carefully ease in the roots of the plant (here* Campanula).

2 *Cover the roots with compost, then wedge in a small stone, sloping it down the rock-face. Firm further compost into the crevice.*

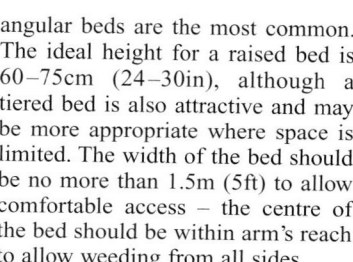

SOFTENING SURFACES
Soften the edges of steps, retaining walls and paving by inserting low, spreading plants in gaps and crevices. Fill in any gaps around them with gritty compost. Take care that growth does not obscure steps and render them hazardous.

Raised beds

A wide range of alpine plants may be grown in raised beds, both in the beds themselves and in crevices in the supporting walls. The bed's design should harmonize with the house and garden. Depending on the needs of the chosen plants, a raised bed may be positioned in either sun or shade. Fill the bed with well-drained compost to suit the plants (see "Soil for raised beds", below). If necessary, plants may be protected in winter with glass or plastic covers placed over the bed.

Siting
For most alpines and rock garden plants, raised beds should be sited in an open, sunny position away from the shade cast by overhanging trees or nearby buildings and fences. Place a raised bed in shade only if woodland or other plants requiring cooler, shadier conditions are to be grown.

To aid mowing, a raised bed that is positioned on a lawn should have a surround of paving slabs or bricks set just below the level of the grass. Raised beds that are constructed for elderly or disabled gardeners may need to be built with wheelchair access, and the beds should be of a height and width to allow plants to be tended easily from a seated position. On sites where the construction of a ground-based scree bed is not possible because of poor drainage, a scree may be placed on the surface of a raised bed instead (see p.264).

Materials and design
Raised beds may be made from stone, brick, old wooden railway sleepers, or any other suitable and attractive material. Stone is the dearest; new or second-hand bricks and sleepers are cheaper and easier to use.

The bed may be almost any shape but it should harmonize with the general design of the garden. Rect-angular beds are the most common. The ideal height for a raised bed is 60–75cm (24–30in), although a tiered bed is also attractive and may be more appropriate where space is limited. The width of the bed should be no more than 1.5m (5ft) to allow comfortable access – the centre of the bed should be within arm's reach to allow weeding from all sides.

Large beds may need an irrigation system; install water pipes and inlets before filling the beds with compost.

Construction
Retaining brick walls for raised beds should be vertical; the thickness of one brick is usually adequate. They are built in the same way as a conventional wall and may be mortared but small gaps should be left between bricks at intervals for plants to be inserted. There should also be gaps at the base for drainage. For further information, see STRUCTURES AND SURFACES, "Raised beds", p.599.

Raised beds may also have stone retaining walls. If they are built without mortar they need a slight inward slope for stability (see "Dry-stone walls", p.598). Dry-stone walls are time-consuming to build, since each stone needs to be chosen and positioned carefully. Large crevices may be left between the stones to be planted up with alpines. If wooden sleepers are used, crevice-planting is not possible.

Soil for raised beds
Use a mix of 3 parts loam (or good sterilized garden soil), 2 parts coarse fibrous peat substitute (such as acidic leaf mould or garden compost) or peat, and 1–2 parts grit or sharp sand. For plants that need acid conditions, use lime-free loam and grit. To grow plants that need different soil types in a large bed, divide it into sections with plastic sheeting to keep the sections apart, and fill each with appropriate compost (see p.322).

Preparing the raised bed
Fill the bottom third of the bed with coarse gravel, stones, or rubble, then place a layer of inverted turves or fibrous peat substitute (or peat) over the top to prevent the drainage material from becoming clogged. Fill the bed with prepared compost, which should be well worked into all the corners and firmed as filling proceeds. Incorporate a slow-release fertilizer. Some settling always occurs, so water the bed thoroughly and leave it for two or three weeks. Top up any sunken areas with spare compost before planting.

Adding rocks gives the effect of a rock garden in miniature and enhances the appearance of raised beds. Set pieces of rock of varying sizes into the compost to provide suitable sites for a range of different plants. Several large pieces of rock arranged together as outcrops are more effective than scattered rocks.

Planting and top-dressing
Make a planting plan or set out the plants on the surface of the bed to see how they will look. Dwarf conifers and small shrubs, tufted and cushion-forming alpines, trailing alpines at the edges of the bed, and smaller bulbs are ideal. Select plants for year-round interest. Plant as for rock gardens (see p.264); crevices in the retaining walls may also be planted up as for dry-stone walls (see p.268).

After planting, top-dress the bed with stone chippings or coarse grit, to match any rocks. Work a 1cm (½in) deep layer of the top-dressing carefully around the plants and beneath their collars. This looks attractive, suppresses weeds, and reduces evaporation. Water the bed regularly until the plants are established.

Winter protection
Many alpines dislike excessive winter moisture, even in the well-drained conditions of a raised bed. The alpine beds can be protected with cloches or sheets of glass or plastic, supported with bricks or a wire frame. Fasten down the covering, so that it does not blow away. Such protection should be put in place in late autumn and removed the following spring. If the whole bed needs protection, build a wooden framework for a glass or plastic roof. Plenty of air must circulate around the plants to ensure that they remain as dry as possible, so do not cover the sides of the protective frame.

Beds for ericaceous plants

Acidic-humus or peat beds provide ideal conditions for a wide range of acid-loving and woodland plants. In gardens with alkaline soils, such beds should always be isolated from the ground with a plastic or butyl rubber liner so that lime cannot enter. Surround each bed with logs or old railway sleepers.

Consider the needs of the plants when deciding where to place an acidic-humus bed, and construct the bed so that it blends in well with the rest of the garden. It is not necessary to use pure peat in the bed, since acidic peat substitutes are widely available. A wide range of acid-loving plants may be grown both in the bed and in wall crevices to produce an attractive display.

Siting
Choose a site that receives sun and dappled shade, ideally facing away from direct sun. An area next to a rock garden, on a slope, or by the side of a building is appropriate. Acidic-humus beds on exposed sites in full sun lose moisture rapidly, and need frequent watering. Dense shade of trees is unsuitable, and the tree roots nearby soon exhaust the moisture and nutrients. Water-logged sites and frost pockets are not suitable either.

A FINISHED BED
Plant up acidic-humus beds with acid-loving rock garden plants for a fine display. Water often to keep the soil moist, especially in the first year. Top-dress the bed with bark chippings to conserve moisture and suppress weeds. Feed the plants regularly with a balanced fertilizer.

Routine care of rock plants

EVEN when alpines and rock plants are established in the garden, it is essential to care for them regularly. Beds, troughs, and sinks must be kept clean and free of weeds. Although the plants do not usually need nutrient-rich soil, they should be fed at intervals and watered whenever the soil becomes dry. Top-dressings, which improve drainage around the collars of the plants, suppress weed growth, and reduce evaporation of water from the soil, should be replenished occasionally.

Alpines and rock garden plants benefit from periodic removal of dead wood, leaves and flowers, and should be kept trimmed. Troughs, sinks, and other containers should be replanted as soon as they become overcrowded. Check plants routinely for signs of pest infestation and disease, and treat them as necessary. In cold or wet weather, some plants may need winter protection.

Weeding

The use of sterilized compost when planting should minimize problems with weeds, at least for the first years. Always try to remove all weeds as soon as they appear, certainly before they flower and set seed. If perennial weeds do become established and are difficult to remove, paint the foliage carefully with a translocated weed-killer, which is transmitted to the roots and kills them. For further information, see PLANT PROBLEMS, "Controlling weeds", p.669.

When weeding, use a three-pronged hand cultivator to loosen and aerate compacted soil around young plants, if necessary, taking care not to disturb the plant roots.

Feeding

Newly planted areas should not normally need feeding for some years if the original compost has been correctly prepared and includes slow-release fertilizer. After some time, however, the growth of the plants may begin to slow down and flowering become sparser. This may be remedied by applying a dressing of slow-release fertilizer around the plants each spring.

Alternatively, carefully remove any top-dressing and a layer of about 1cm (½in) of compost from the surface of the bed and replace it with fresh compost and a further top-dressing of grit.

Top-dressing

The type of top-dressing used for alpines and rock garden plants depends on the plants that are grown, although it should match any of the rocks and stones that feature in beds and rock gardens as closely as possible. Top-dressings used in troughs, sinks, or raised beds should also harmonize with the pot or retaining walls.

Coarse grit or stone chippings are suitable for most situations, but limestone chippings should never be used around lime-hating plants. For plants grown in peat beds, a top-dressing of bark chippings will complement the plantings.

Renewing top-dressings

Top-dressings may need to be renewed from time to time, since grit or stone chippings gradually wash away, especially on slopes, and bark tends to decompose and mix in with the underlying compost. Watch for bare patches throughout the season and top up as necessary. Pay close attention to top-dressings in the autumn, to ensure good soil coverage in winter and avoid compaction by heavy rain. Check again in spring and top up, as necessary. A slow-release fertilizer may be applied at the same time.

Watering

Established plants growing in rock gardens and screes root deeply into the soil and do not usually need more water than is supplied by rainfall. In droughts, however, the area should be thoroughly soaked. Do not water in very frosty conditions or during the heat of the day – early mornings or late evenings are the best times; soak occasionally rather than giving small amounts of water frequently. If the compost is dry at a depth of 3–5cm (1¼–2in), water thoroughly until the water has penetrated to the full depth of the roots. During an average summer this should only be needed two or three times but in very dry summers may be required more frequently.

Watering in containers, raised beds, and under cover

Alpines and rock garden plants that are grown in raised beds, sinks and troughs, under frames, and in the alpine house will need more regular watering, since the soil dries out more quickly than in rock gardens and scree beds.

It is preferable to hand-water troughs and sinks if specialist collections of plants are being grown, so that each plant may be provided with the correct amount of water. This is time-consuming, however, particularly where there are several containers to be watered.

Plants grown in pots in alpine houses and frames should be watered individually. If the pots are plunged in gravel or stone chippings, water both the pots and the surrounding material. Some alpine plants have water-sensitive foliage and therefore dislike overhead watering; if this is the case, regularly soaking only the plunge material should provide sufficient moisture.

1 *Remove the old top-dressing and some compost (see inset). Fill in around the plants with fresh compost (see p.262).*

2 *Top-dress the bed with a fresh layer of coarse grit or gravel, adding some around and beneath the collars of the plants.*

Trimming and pruning

Alpines and rock garden plants need to be cut back periodically to maintain a natural, compact shape and healthy growth, and to restrict them within their allotted space.

Pruning woody plants

To keep rock garden shrubs and woody perennials healthy, any dead, diseased, or damaged wood should be removed. Check the plants regularly and prune them cleanly, using secateurs or sharp scissors.

Severe pruning is unnecessary because most dwarf shrubs are slow-growing and do not outgrow their

REMOVING DEAD GROWTH

In spring, after all danger of frost has passed, cut out any dieback from plants, trimming carefully to healthy growth with sharp scissors or secateurs.

WEEDING

Weed around young plants with a 3-pronged cultivator, which also loosens and aerates the soil. Remove any top-dressing first and replace it after weeding.

REMOVING DEAD ROSETTES

1 *To remove dead rosettes from plants such as saxifrages, cut out the rosettes with a sharp knife without disturbing the rest of the plant.*

2 *Top-dress the exposed soil to prevent weeds growing through the gaps until the plant produces fresh growth.*

CUTTING BACK AFTER FLOWERING

1 *After flowering, cut back stems (here Helianthemum) to half their length to encourage healthy, new growth.*

2 *The plants will remain compact and produce a good crop of flowers the following year.*

RENOVATING AN ALPINE BED

1 *Plants that spread rapidly (here Paronychia kapela* subsp. *chionaea) may eventually smother less vigorous plants nearby. Cut them back in spring.*

2 *Dig up or pull out clumps of encroaching plants. Straggly plants should be cut back severely. Make sure that plants nearby have plenty of room to grow.*

3 *Add a dressing of balanced fertilizer to the bed, before placing a fresh layer of top-dressing on the surface of the compost around the plants.*

positions for many years. When pruning, aim to maintain the natural shape of the plant, especially in the case of dwarf conifers.

Removing dead flowers and foliage

Regularly remove all dead flowers and leaves, and any unwanted seed-heads, with a sharp knife, secateurs, or scissors. Pick over small alpine plants by hand, using tweezers, if necessary, to remove dead leaves and flowers. Carefully cut out dead rosettes from plants such as saxifrages; do not pull them off by hand, as this may loosen healthy rosettes.

Helianthemum species and cultivars, in particular, need clipping with shears annually after flowering, cutting back the stems by about half their length to encourage growth for

flowering the following year. Genera such as *Arabis*, *Aubrieta*, and *Aurinia* also benefit from hard annual pruning (after flowering), which helps to keep them compact and free-flowering. Plants may produce a second flush of flowers if cut back before they set seed.

Encroaching plants

Over-vigorous plants and old, straggly plants that are beginning to encroach on their neighbours should be cut back in early spring. Mat-forming plants may simply be pulled out by hand, others may need to be lifted with a hand fork. Support nearby plants and refirm any that are accidentally lifted. Remove or cut back plants to allow a clear area of bed around all the remaining plants so that they can grow unimpeded.

Hard-pruned plants should be top-dressed with a balanced fertilizer in order to promote strong, new growth.

Winter protection

Plants in troughs, sinks, or raised beds, and some alpine bulbs, may need protection from winter wet. Use a single, propped pane of glass, an open cloche, or, for large areas, a frame light, which will give overhead protection without inhibiting air circulation. Ensure that covers are firmly secured. Some protection from severe cold may be provided by placing a layer of evergreen branches or pine boughs over the plants.

Controlling pests and diseases

Few serious problems affect alpines and rock garden plants, but some of the more common pests and diseases may need to be controlled. Regular, basic garden hygiene is often sufficient to control most problems encountered. Aphids (p.646) are likely to be troublesome if alpines are grown in too rich a soil, which induces soft, lank growth.

Coarse top-dressings around plants tend to deter slugs and snails but some control is still necessary, particularly for choice alpines, such as *Campanula zoysii*, which are susceptible to attack from these pests. Control insects such as ants (p.666), which will excavate under cushion-forming plants. Prevent birds from disturbing newly planted specimens by covering them with wigwams of sticks or wire pushed into the soil.

Fungal diseases may quickly become established in alpine houses and frames (see pp.277–279).

Replanting an alpine trough

Plants in containers eventually need replanting when nutrients in the compost are exhausted. Water thoroughly before carefully removing the plants. Discard the compost and replace it with a fresh, suitable mix (see p.262), containing a slow-release fertilizer. Trim roots and top-growth before returning plants to the container; allow for their eventual spread and top-dress with gravel.

Helianthemum sp.

Iris cristata

Ramonda myconi

Helianthemum sp.

Propagation

MANY alpines and rock garden plants may be propagated from seed, although some plants are sterile and do not produce seed. In addition, cultivars seldom come true from seed and must be increased in other ways. Alternative methods include cuttings (of various types) and division.

Seed

Propagation from seed is the best way to produce large numbers of plants. Since many alpines flower in early spring, ripe seed is often available from midsummer, and may be sown straight away. Germination will usually occur rapidly and strong seedlings will be produced before winter. Autumn-sown seeds may remain dormant until spring; if germination occurs, overwinter the seedlings in frames. It may sometimes be better to store seed over winter and sow in early spring, although short-lived seed should be sown as soon as it is ripe.

Seed collection and storage
Collect seed as the seedheads become ripe. Remove them while still attached to the stems and place them in paper (not plastic) bags to dry out. Enclose in envelopes any that might split open on drying. Store seeds in a cool, dry, well-ventilated place. Most alpines have seed capsules from which seed may be extracted by rubbing between the fingers. Fleshy fruits may need to be squashed and left on paper to dry.

Separate the seed from the debris by sieving or hand-picking when dry. Put it in sealed, labelled envelopes, and place these in an airtight container in a cool place.

Pre-sowing treatment
Seeds with hard coats need special treatment to allow them to absorb water. Scarify by chipping the seed coat with a sharp knife or rubbing with a file or fine abrasive paper. In some cases, soaking the seed for 12–24 hours will accelerate the take-up of water.

Hard-cased seeds of woody rock garden plants do not respond to scarification alone; they also need exposure to cold (stratification). Store the seeds in boxes of moist sand outdoors for two or three months during winter, and sow in spring; alternatively, sow the seed in pots of seed compost and keep these in the freezer or refrigerator, sealed in plastic bags, for several

weeks before plunging the pots in the ground outside until the seed germinates. Some seeds, such as *Trillium* and peonies (*Paeonia*), need alternating periods of cold and warmth to germinate successfully.

Sowing the seed
Use clean clay or plastic pots, and place broken crocks over the drainage holes. A compost of equal parts sieved peat substitute (or peat) and perlite is suitable, or use loam-based seed compost, mixed with an equal amount of perlite or sharp sand. Fill the pots and firm the compost. Tap out small seeds thinly and evenly and space large seeds by hand, covering them with their own depth of compost. Mix fine seeds with fine, dry, silver sand before sowing but do not cover with more compost.

After sowing, cover all but fine seeds with a 5–10mm (¼–½in) layer of 5mm (¼in) diameter grit or pea shingle, to deter mosses and liverworts and protect the seed from heavy rain or watering. Label the pots and stand them in water to half their depth, removing them when the compost surface becomes moist. Keep the compost moist at all times.

Germination
Speed of germination depends on the type and age of the seed, and when it is sown. Some seed takes months or even years to germinate.

A cool, sheltered site outdoors is ideal for the seeds of most alpines. Plunge pots in moist sand to maintain an even temperature and reduce the need for watering. When seedlings appear, move the pots to a cold frame. Germination may be speeded up by placing the pots in gentle heat in early spring, but do not expose the seeds to high temperatures.

Pricking out and potting up
Prick out seedlings when they are 5–10mm (¼–½in) tall and when two true leaves have formed. Knock out the compost and separate the seedlings. Handle only by the leaves or cotyledons to avoid damage to stems and roots. Pot up seedlings individually in small clay pots or plastic pots, or in module packs using low-fertility loam-based potting compost mixed with an equal amount of grit. Fill the container, settle the compost, and make a hole for the roots. Put the seedling in the hole, fill with compost, and firm lightly.

Top-dress seedlings in individual pots with a 5–10mm (¼–½in) layer of grit. Water them thoroughly with a

fine-rosed watering can and place the containers in a lightly shaded position, until the seedlings are established. Water as required. When the roots are visible through the drainage holes, pot them on.

Seeds that are slow to germinate often do so erratically, and if only a few seedlings appear prick them out as soon as they are large enough to handle. Disturb the rest of the compost as little as possible, and cover it with fresh top-dressing. Put the pot back into the frame in case more seeds germinate.

ROCK PLANT SEED TO SOW FRESH
Anemone
Codonopsis
Corydalis
Cyclamen (alpine spp.)
Dodecatheon
Hepatica
Meconopsis
Primula
Pulsatilla
Ranunculus

SOWING SEED

1 *Prepare a pot by filling it with equal parts of seed compost and horticultural sand. Firm the compost gently to level the surface and eliminate air pockets.*

2 *Small seed (here* Lewisia*) should be tapped out evenly over the surface of the compost. Space larger seed by hand.*

3 *Cover the seeds with a fine layer of compost, then topdress with grit to protect the seeds and prevent the growth of mosses. Water in and label.*

4 *Prick out seedlings when they have 2 true leaves (see inset). Lift the seedlings carefully, handling them by the leaves only.*

5 *Fill pots with equal parts of loam-based potting compost and grit. Pot up the seedlings singly, firming with a dibber.*

6 *Top-dress with grit, water, and place the seedlings in light shade. Pot on the seedlings when the roots fill the pot.*

Softwood and greenwood cuttings

Softwood cuttings are taken from the non-flowering, leafy shoots of a plant during periods of active growth, usually in spring.

Greenwood cuttings are taken in early summer when growth has slowed down; although slightly riper than softwood cuttings, they require the same treatment.

Taking the cuttings

Take the cuttings early in the morning, when the shoots are fully turgid. For softwood cuttings select strong, young shoots that are soft and pliable, with no trace of woodiness or hardening; greenwood cuttings may be just beginning to harden at the base. Cuttings should be about 2.5–7cm (1–3in) long and taken with a sharp knife. Place them immediately in a plastic bag to conserve moisture and prevent them from wilting.

Inserting the cuttings

Trim the base of each cutting cleanly with a sharp knife just below a node (leaf joint) and remove the lower leaves. Pinch off any shoot tips that are soft, particularly if these are showing signs of wilting.

Fill pots with standard cutting compost and make holes for the cuttings with a small dibber. Insert each cutting into the compost by up to half its length so that the lowest leaf is just above the surface.

Label the cuttings and water with a fungicide solution, then place them in a closed propagator with gentle bottom heat, or in a mist propagation unit. Alternatively, seal the pots in plastic bags. Keep the cuttings in good light but out of direct sun, as otherwise the air and soil temperature may become too hot and the cuttings wilt.

Remove with tweezers dead and diseased cuttings, since these may infect their healthy neighbours. Watering is seldom required until after rooting. Look for signs of new growth, and check for rooting by gently pulling at the cuttings. Once they are well rooted, pot them up.

Potting up

Water the rooted cuttings well, and gently slide them out of the pot. Carefully separate them before potting them up individually, using equal parts of potting compost and grit.

Top-dress with a 1cm (½in) layer of sharp grit. Water the cuttings thoroughly and return them to the propagator, keeping them out of direct sun. Keep the cuttings well watered. Once fresh growth appears, place the cuttings in a cold frame and harden them off carefully before planting them out.

Semi-ripe and ripewood cuttings

Semi-ripe cuttings are taken in mid- to late summer from non-flowering shoots of the current season's growth; the shoots offer distinct resistance to pressure when bent gently and should be beginning to harden at the base. Ripewood cuttings are taken from evergreen plants during late summer and autumn when the wood has fully ripened.

Taking the cuttings

The cuttings will vary in length with the plant concerned from 1 to 4cm (½ to 1½in) or more. Cut them from the parent plant using a sharp knife or secateurs. Make a clean cut below a node and remove soft tissue at the tips. Remove the lower leaves and dip the ends into hormone rooting powder. Alternatively, take cuttings with a "heel" and trim the heel with a sharp knife to remove any snags.

Potting up

Small cuttings root best in pots of cutting compost, topped with a 1cm (½in) layer of fine sand. Make holes in the sand and insert the cuttings by one third to one half of their length. Label, water with a fungicide, and place in a propagator in a cool greenhouse. Check regularly for disease. Water sparingly and, as growth begins, apply a dilute liquid feed.

If a large number of cuttings is taken, they may be inserted into a cold frame with drainage at the base. Fork over the soil in the frame and then add a mixture of 1 part peat substitute (or peat) and 1 part grit; top with a 2.5cm (1in) layer of sand. After inserting the cuttings, water them and close the frame. Open the frame in mild weather. If there is a danger of frost, insulate the frame.

The following spring, when the cuttings have rooted, repot or pot up those in frames in equal parts potting compost and grit, or plant out in a nursery bed but only after danger of frost is passed. Water well.

Grow on, keeping the rooted cuttings moist and sheltered from direct sun. Give a liquid feed in the growing season. Transplant into their permanent positions in autumn.

SOFTWOOD CUTTINGS

1 *In spring, choose young, non-flowering shoots (here, from* Gypsophila repens) *and take cuttings 2.5–7cm (1–3in) long. Put the cuttings in a plastic bag.*

2 *Trim off the base of the cuttings, and the lower leaves and soft tips (see inset). Fill a pot with moist compost, inserting the cuttings by up to half their length.*

3 *Water and label the cuttings. Place the pot in a sealed plastic bag, keeping it in good light but out of direct sun.*

4 *When rooted, pot up the cuttings singly, holding them by the leaves only. Top-dress the pots, water well, and label.*

Leaf cuttings

This method is suitable for plants with fleshy leaves, such as *Haberlea*, *Ramonda*, and *Sedum*.

Using a sharp knife, cut healthy, strong, and relatively young leaves from the stem at their base. Prepare pots with a mixture of equal parts of standard cutting compost and sand; insert each cutting at a 45° angle, so that it is just held in place by the compost. Enclose each pot in a plastic bag and, when the plantlets appear, pot them up individually.

Basal cuttings

Some plants, such as *Primula marginata* and its cultivars, may be propagated from basal cuttings. These are taken from young shoots at the base of the plant at, or just above, soil level. Basal cuttings are usually taken in spring, but may also be taken in summer or autumn.

Use a well-drained, proprietary cutting compost, or a mix of equal parts of loam and peat substitute (or peat) with 2 parts grit. Fill pots with compost, and firm.

Trim the base of each cutting cleanly just below a node. Make sure that the cutting is not hollow at the base. Remove the lower leaves and dip the base in hormone powder.

Insert one third to one half of each stem into the compost, keeping the leaves clear of the soil. Water well and place the pots in a shaded, closed propagator or cold frame. Rooting takes three to six weeks, after which the cuttings may be potted up individually or lined out in nursery beds or a cold frame to grow on.

BASAL CUTTINGS

Primula marginata

In spring, take cuttings 5–7cm (2–3in) long with new leaves and a short stem. Trim the base and remove the lower leaves, inserting the cuttings to the depth indicated.

Selecting cutting material

For all types of cutting, always choose strong, healthy stems or leaves that show no sign of pests or diseases. Non-flowering shoots that are in active growth should be used. Except for basal cuttings, do not take the cuttings from the base of any plant because this part may be weaker than elsewhere. Do not take all the cuttings from the same area on the parent plant since this may make it look lop-sided.

After taking the cuttings, immediately place them in a clean, plastic bag to prevent any moisture loss. Many cuttings will root readily if they are inserted into pots of cutting compost with added grit. Alternatively, simply use horticultural sand. Insert the cuttings at the depths indicated.

SEMI-RIPE
(Phlox)
In mid- to late summer, select shoots that are just hardening but not woody. Remove 3cm (1¼in) lengths, trimming to about 1cm (½in).

GREENWOOD
(Erodium)
Take cuttings from the soft tips of new shoots in early summer. Remove 2.5–7cm (1–3in) lengths and trim them to about 1cm (½in).

ROSETTE
(Saxifraga)
In early to midsummer, select new rosettes. Cut the rosettes about 1cm (½in) below the leaves. Trim each cleanly across the base.

RIPEWOOD
(Dryas)
In late summer and autumn, select new shoots and take cuttings about 2.5cm (1in) long. Trim to about 1cm (½in) below the base of the leaves.

LEAF
(Sedum)
Throughout the growing season, select mature leaves that are undamaged, cutting off selected leaves. Trim each cleanly across the base.

Division

Many alpines and rock garden plants may be successfully propagated by division, and in some cases division is the only practicable method of increasing the stock if seed is rarely produced or the plant is sterile.

Plants that are particularly suitable for division include mat-forming species, which produce a mass of fibrous roots, and clump-forming plants that produce clusters of shoots that are readily separated.

ROCK PLANTS TO PROPAGATE BY "IRISHMAN'S" CUTTINGS

Achillea ageratifolia
Arenaria montana,
   A. purpurascens
Gentiana acaulis, G. verna
Primula auricula (and cvs),
   P. marginata (and cvs)
Silene
Veronica peduncularis
Viola cornuta (and cvs)

ROCK PLANTS TO DIVIDE

Achillea ageratifolia
Alchemilla alpina,
   A. ellenbeckii
Allium sikkimense
Antennaria dioica
Arenaria montana
Artemisia schmidtiana 'Nana'
Campanula carpatica,
   C. cochleariifolia
Chiastophyllum oppositifolium
Gentiana acaulis,
   G. sino-ornata
Primula allionii

Gentiana
sino-ornata

Sagina subulata 'Aurea'
Viola cornuta

ROCK PLANTS TO PROPAGATE BY ROOT CUTTINGS

Anacyclus pyrethrum
   var. *depressus*
Carduncellus rhaponticoides
Centaurea pindicola
Gentiana lutea
Meconopsis delavayi
Morisia monanthos
Papaver lateritium
Phlox mesoleuca
Primula denticulata
Pulsatilla
Roscoea cautleoides
Weldenia candida ❋

KEY
❋ *Not hardy*

A number of clump-forming plants have a tendency to die out at the centre. These may be divided to rejuvenate them by replanting only the youngest, most vigorous pieces.

When to divide

Most plants are best divided in early spring, when new growth is just beginning; do not divide plants in cold and frosty weather, or when the ground is frozen or waterlogged.

Plants may also be divided in early autumn, which allows new roots to be made while the soil is still warm. Where hard winters are expected, spring division may be safer, since this allows a full growing season for establishment. Some plants, for example primulas and *Meconopsis*, should be divided immediately after flowering, when they enter a period of strong, vegetative growth. They must be well watered after replanting until they are fully re-established.

How to divide

Lift plants and shake off the soil. For large clumps, insert the tines of two garden forks back-to-back into the centre of the clump; lever the plant into two halves. Tease these smaller clumps apart by hand or cut them

with a sharp knife to produce a number of small pieces with healthy roots and growth buds. The older, woody, central part of the plant should be discarded.

If not replanting or potting up the divisions immediately, wrap them in plastic bags or moist sacking and store them out of direct sun. Divisions of most hardy plants may

HOW TO PROPAGATE BY DIVISION

1 *Plants with fibrous roots (here* Gentiana acaulis) *may be divided and replanted to provide new plants. Lift a clump of the parent plant and shake off the soil.*

2 *Using hand forks back-to-back, loosen the root mass and divide the clump into pieces. If necessary, cut away sections from the clump with a knife.*

3 *The plants should have a good root system. Replant them outdoors into their permanent positions, firming around the roots. Add top-dressing around the plants and water thoroughly with a fine-rosed watering can.*

"IRISHMAN'S" CUTTINGS

1 *Lift the rooted shoots close to the base of the plant (here* Veronica) *and remove them with a sharp knife. Trim off sideshoots and straggly roots (see inset).*

2 *Pot up the cuttings individually. Place a little gritty compost in a pot, insert the cutting, then add more compost. Firm gently, water, and top-dress.*

be replanted immediately into their permanent positions. If, however, plants are particularly precious, or the divisions are quite small, it may be safer to pot them up and place them in a cold frame until they are established before planting them out. Use 1 part low-fertility, loam-based potting compost and 1 part grit or a lime-free mix for acid-lovers. If replanting in the open ground, make holes large enough to allow the roots to be spread out fully. Firm in and water well. Keep the soil moist until the plants are established.

"Irishman's" cuttings

These are essentially sideshoots that have already rooted. Thymes and other creeping rock plants produce this sort of cutting. The technique is particularly useful for plants with woody rootstocks that are not easily divided, or for those that naturally produce offsets or runners.

Before taking the cuttings, brush away surface soil from the base of the parent plant. Cut rooted pieces from the plant with a sharp knife and pot them up in equal parts of low-fertility, loam-based potting compost and grit. Alternatively, plant them out in a cool, sheltered spot in the garden until well established.

Root cuttings

A limited number of alpines and rock garden plants, such as *Morisia monanthos* and *Primula denticulata*, may be propagated from root cuttings. Take root cuttings from the healthiest-looking roots in either late autumn or winter, when the plants are dormant.

Selecting material

Choose a strong, healthy plant and lift it from the soil. Select young, vigorous roots and cut them from the parent plant. The cuttings should be about 5cm (2in) long. Cut the roots straight across at the top end (nearest the plant's stem) and use sloping cuts at the lower end (nearest the root tips). Wash the cuttings in tepid water and replant the parent stock immediately or, if old and straggly and no longer required, discard it.

Inserting the cuttings

Use pots at least 10cm (4in) deep. Put broken crocks over the drainage holes and place over these a 2.5cm (1in) layer of low-fertility loam-based potting compost. Fill the pots with washed sand, then firm. Make several planting holes in each pot around the edges.

Insert the cuttings into the holes, with the straight ends uppermost and the tops level with the surface of the sand. Cuttings of plants with thin, wiry roots may be laid flat on the surface of the compost. Top-dress with fine grit. Label the pots, water thoroughly, and place them in a cold frame on a layer of grit or gravel or in a propagator. Close the frames in cold weather; otherwise they should be ventilated freely.

Water the pots when new growth appears. When the new shoots are growing strongly, check that the cuttings have rooted before potting them up: gently knock them out of their pots to inspect their roots.

Potting up rooted cuttings

Slide the cuttings out of their pots and separate them carefully. Pot them up singly, using low-fertility, loam-based potting compost mixed with an equal amount of sand. Instead of sand, a mix of peat substitute (or peat) and sand may be used.

HOW TO PROPAGATE BY ROOT CUTTINGS

1 *In late autumn or winter, using a hand fork, carefully lift a healthy plant (here* Primula denticulata) *with a well-developed root system.*

2 *Wash the roots clean of earth, then select thick, healthy roots for the cuttings. Using a sharp knife, cut off selected roots close to the crown of the plant.*

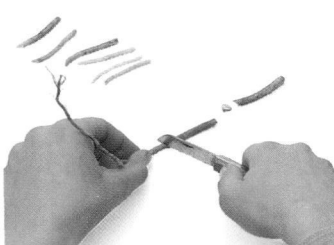

3 *Prepare 5cm (2in) lengths of root, cutting each one straight at the thicker end (closest to the parent plant) and angled at the lower end.*

4 *Place a layer of compost in the base of a pot, then fill almost to the brim with sharp sand. Insert the cuttings so that straight ends are just level with the sand surface.*

5 *Cover the sand with a 1cm (½in) layer of grit. Water and label the cuttings, then place the pot in a propagator or on the greenhouse bench.*

Top-dress the pots with 1cm (½in) of sharp sand or grit. Water and then place outside, out of direct sun. Leave until the new plants are established, watering as required.

Scooping rosettes

Plants that grow quickly or form rosettes, for example *Primula denticulata*, may be propagated *in situ* in midwinter from root cuttings by scooping out the rosettes with a sharp knife, to expose the top of the rootstock. Select strong-growing rosettes and brush the tops of the roots with fungicidal powder to prevent grey mould/*Botrytis* (see p.646); cover the pots with a thin layer of horticultural sharp sand.

Shoots should soon appear on each root apex. When the shoots are about 2.5–5cm (1–2in) tall, they are ready to be lifted. Separate the clumps into individual, small plants that have healthy-looking, vigorous shoots and roots, pulling them apart by hand or dividing them with a sharp knife.

Pot up the young plants to grow on, using equal parts of potting compost and horticultural sand. Water thoroughly, and place outside in a shady site. Keep moist and plant out the young plants when their roots have filled the pots.

HOW TO SCOOP ROSETTES

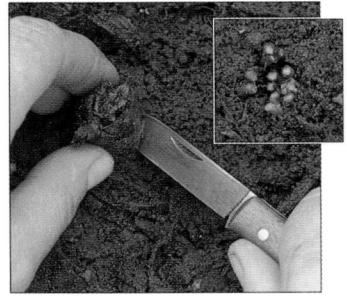

1 *Scoop out the live crowns of rosette-forming plants (here* Primula denticulata) *with a sharp knife, so that the tops of the roots are visible (see inset).*

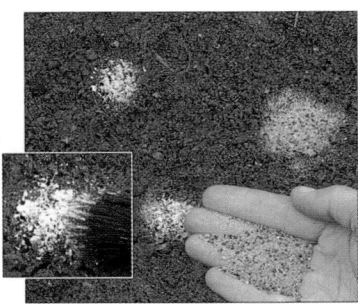

2 *Dust the exposed roots with fungicidal powder (see inset) to protect them from moulds and fungi. Lightly cover with sharp, horticultural sand.*

3 *When new shoots appear from the roots, lift the whole clump, using a hand fork or trowel. Take care not to damage the new roots.*

4 *Divide the clump into individual plants, each with one shoot and well-developed roots. Pot them up using equal parts potting compost and sand.*

Alpine houses and frames

A<small>LTHOUGH</small> some high-altitude alpines grow well in the open garden in temperate climates, provided that their specific requirements of situation and soil are satisfied, most will perform considerably better if they are grown under cover. Many alpines bloom in late winter and very early spring when, if left in the open, their delicate flowers may be damaged by inclement weather, eaten by slugs or snails, or pecked by birds.

In an alpine house, plants are protected from winter wet, cold, drying winds, and sudden sharp frosts, as well as from the attentions of most pests. This enables a far wider range of alpines and rock plants to be grown, either in pots or in ground-level or raised beds, to provide an eye-catching and lasting display.

USING AN ALPINE HOUSE
Part of the house may be used to grow on young plants (foreground) in beds supported by brick pillars.

Using an alpine house

An alpine house is an unheated greenhouse, usually with raised benches, designed for growing and displaying alpines and rock plants under controlled conditions. Often, half of the house is used for growing the plants, and the other half for displaying them. Alternatively, the plants may be grown in cold frames (either attached to or sited very near the alpine house) and brought temporarily into the house for display when they are at their best.

Displaying the plants
Displays may be of plants in pots simply standing on the staging or, more commonly, plunged up to their rims in a layer of sand. Plunging keeps roots cool and moist and reduces temperature fluctuations, while allowing easy irrigation of plants that dislike overhead watering. Specially built display beds are an attractive option. Create miniature rock gardens in the alpine house, either waist-high where staging is strong enough to support the weight, or at ground level. These may have some permanent planting as well as areas of sand or sandy compost into which different plants may be plunged, according to season. Lightweight tufa rocks may be incorporated and planted up to enhance this type of display.

Siting the alpine house
Choose a firm, level site away from the shade of trees, fences, walls, and tall buildings if possible. Siting the alpine house on a north–south axis is ideal but any open, sunny position is

AN ALPINE HOUSE DISPLAY
A wide range of rock plants may be grown in pots and attractively displayed in raised sand beds in an alpine house.

acceptable. Always avoid hollows where cold air forms frost pockets and do not site it in exposed, windy situations. Try to position the alpine house where it will harmonize with other garden features, perhaps even using it as a focal point. For further information on greenhouses, ventilation, shading, and staging, see G<small>REENHOUSES AND</small> F<small>RAMES</small>, pp.575, 576, and 579.

Using frames

Frames should be sited near the alpine house, where they may be used to protect a range of choice plants from climatic extremes, as an "overspill" area, or for storage when plants are not in flower. They are very useful for bulbs which need to be kept dry when dormant, or for plants that will not tolerate the very hot conditions that may arise in summer. Frames incorporate a top light that must be opened as required to provide good ventilation; a standard Dutch light frame is suitable but other types are available. The lights may be removed in summer if required, but they should be kept on if the frame contains dormant bulbs. Those plants that do not tolerate direct summer sun can be protected by covering the frame with mesh shading (see G<small>REENHOUSES AND</small> F<small>RAMES</small>, "Meshes and fabrics", p.576). Pots in a frame are usually plunged in a material such as washed builder's sand over a layer of rubble to give them good drainage.

CARE OF ALPINES AND DWARF BULBS AFTER FLOWERING

ALPINES INDOORS
After flowering, pots of alpines needing a careful watering regime (here Dionysia spp.) should be plunged in sand under cover.

ALPINES OUTDOORS
Alpines that tolerate variable summer weather conditions, such as saxifrages, may be plunged in open cold frames after flowering.

BULBS INDOORS
Pots of dwarf bulbs (here irises) that have finished flowering may be kept dry by plunging in sand or gravel under staging.

PROTECTING FLOWERING ALPINES
Alpines coming into flower may be grown in outdoor frames before bringing them into the alpine house for display.

Alpines in pots

Growing alpines in pots ensures that special watering, compost, or feeding requirements can be provided for individual plants.

Plastic and clay pots

Although plastic pots are suitable for growing alpines and retain moisture well, clay pots are more attractive – important if the plants are to be exhibited. The compost in plastic pots dries out more slowly than in clay pots so take care not to over-water the plants. Clean and sterilize all pots before use: sterilants based on dilute solutions of sodium hyperchlorite are suitable, but do not use tar-based disinfectants.

Composts

All alpines need a freely draining compost and benefit from a layer of broken crocks in the bottom of clay pots, or grit in plastic pots, since even moisture-loving plants will not tolerate stagnant conditions.

Most species grow well in loam-based potting compost, mixed with an equal amount of grit. Those from high, alpine habitats of scree and rock-face crevices, such as the Aretian *Androsace* species and other cushion-forming plants, need a less fertile and more freely draining mix if they are to retain their neat, natural habit. In rich composts, they quickly become soft and lush and are then more prone to attack by pests and diseases. For these plants use a mix of up to 3 parts grit to 1 part loam-based compost. Introduce plants to these "lean mixes" when they are young, since they may not adapt easily if they have been potted on from a more fertile medium.

A number of species, usually ones from woodland habitats, or those which occur in humus-rich pockets in rocky habitats, such as *Haberlea* and *Ramonda*, prefer well-drained composts that are rich in organic matter. For these, a mix of 1 part each of loam-based compost and grit, with 2 parts leaf mould, peat substitute, or peat will be suitable. Take care to check on the individual needs of each plant before selecting an appropriate compost, and ensure that for lime-hating plants all ingredients are lime-free.

Top-dressings

After planting up the pots (see right), top-dress them with a layer of grit or stone chippings to enhance the plant's appearance, to keep the neck of the plant well drained, and to prevent the growth of mosses and liverworts. Use a top-dressing that is appropriate to the pH requirements of the plant, for example limestone chippings for lime-loving species or granitic grit for lime-hating plants.

Some small, cushion-forming alpines are very sensitive to the presence of water around their necks, so, as well as top-dressing with grit, prop small wedges of rock beneath their cushions in order to keep them clear of the surface.

Repotting

When a plant has outgrown its pot, transfer it carefully into a slightly larger pot, disturbing the root ball as little as possible. Pot on herbaceous and shrubby plants in spring and summer, when they are growing strongly; bulbs should be potted on when they are dormant. Plant to the same level as in the previous pot, firm in fresh compost, and then add a new layer of top-dressing.

Water well after potting by standing the pot in at least 2.5–5cm (1–2in) of water until the top of the compost becomes moist. Then remove the pot to avoid the risk of root rot.

Planting in beds

The beds may be at ground level or raised some 1m (3ft) high. A raised bed allows plants to be tended and

REPOTTING A SAXIFRAGE

1 *The roots of this saxifrage can be seen growing through the drainage hole at the bottom of the pot. The plant is pot-bound and should be repotted.*

2 *Choose a pot that is one size bigger than the one that the plant is growing in. Use crocks and gravel to provide drainage at the base of the pot.*

3 *Arrange the crocks carefully over the drainage hole. The crocks should then be covered with a layer of gravel.*

4 *Remove the plant from its pot by tapping gently on the base to loosen the root ball; tease out the roots to encourage fresh roots to penetrate the new compost.*

5 *Cover the crocks in the larger pot with a little compost; position the plant so that the neck is at the same level as in the original pot, and fill in with compost.*

6 *Spread the gravel top-dressing over the surface of the compost, taking care to tuck it under the collar of the plant to keep it sharply drained.*

7 *Place the pot in a bowl of water and leave it until the surface of the compost and gravel appears damp.*

8 *Then remove the pot and place it on a layer of sand in a cold frame, where any excess moisture can easily drain off. This will prevent any risk of root rot.*

9 *The repotted plant may then be plunged in sand in a cold frame or bed to grow on.*

REMOVING DEAD LEAVES

Tweezers should be used regularly to remove any brown or withered leaves from alpine plants such as this Campanula chamissonis.

viewed more easily and is especially useful for elderly or disabled gardeners. The staging must drain well and be solidly constructed to bear the weight of the bed (see also GREENHOUSES AND FRAMES, "Raised beds", p.578).

Use a compost of 3 parts loam (or good sterilized garden soil), 2 parts coarse fibrous peat substitute (or peat), and 2 parts sharp sand or grit. Add rocks to the bed to create a miniature rock garden. Tufa is particularly useful because it is lightweight, very moisture-retentive, and as plants can be grown in the rock itself. Plant out alpines in the bed, avoiding species that are invasive and free-seeding, but leave some gaps for plunging a succession of seasonal, pot-grown specimens. Grow ferns and other shade-loving species under a raised bed.

Routine maintenance

As alpines have quite specialized growing requirements, they need considerable attention through the growing season. Plants that are regularly repotted rarely need additional feeding, but where fertilizers are used be sure that they are low in nitrogen – high-nitrogen feed will lead to soft, lush growth that is uncharacteristic of alpines and more prone to pests and diseases.

Ventilation

Ventilating surfaces must occupy at least 25 per cent of the glass area, as the aim is to provide the maximum possible air circulation at all times. In spring and summer, the vents and the greenhouse door can remain open permanently, unless there is strong wind or heavy rain. Use a screen of small-diameter mesh over vents and doors to keep out cats and birds. During heavy rain and windy weather, close the vents on the receiving side to avoid drip on the foliage and reduce strong draughts that may damage foliage and flowers. In severe winds, it is safest to close all vents and doors.

In winter, open the vents fully (unless it is windy, raining, or snowing) but close them before nightfall to retain any residual warmth. In very cold weather, allow temperatures in the alpine house to rise gradually before ventilating; on bright, sunny days, however, open the vents as soon as possible to prevent the temperature from rising too rapidly. In damp, foggy weather, especially in areas with high levels of atmospheric pollution, close down the house completely to keep out cold, damp air, and use a cool air fan to maintain air circulation.

Temperature

Shading will be necessary during sunny weather, from late spring to autumn, to avoid scorching tender, new growth, and to help reduce temperatures. Do not use heavy shading as this might cause etiolation or lop-sided "drawing" of plants towards the available light source. In very hot weather, damp down the house floor to reduce temperatures and maintain atmospheric humidity; plants may be gently misted over with cool water in the evenings.

Heating should be used to stop the pots freezing in severe weather, and a method of heating that does not produce excessive fumes or moisture is best (see GREENHOUSES AND FRAMES, "Heating", p.574).

Hygiene

Remove dead foliage and faded flowers regularly to reduce the risk of fungal attack. Check the plants for pests and diseases and treat any outbreaks promptly (see PLANT PROBLEMS, pp.639–673). Always keep the floor of the house clean to minimize the risk of diseases, and make sure that the glass is clean so that plants receive maximum light.

Watering

Water regularly throughout the season, especially on sunny spring and summer days, when water loss is rapid. If plants are allowed to dry out between waterings, growth may be severely checked, and flower buds may shrivel. For pots standing on staging, water from above but avoid splashing the foliage. Plunged pots derive moisture from the surrounding material but may need additional watering in warm periods. For plants that are sensitive to moisture on their foliage, water the plunge medium around the pots. As autumn approaches, reduce watering as plants prepare for dormancy. During winter, alpines need to be kept dry but not dust dry (for plunged pots, the plunge medium should be just damp to the touch).

Winter maintenance

A spell of clear, dry weather during late winter is a good time to store the plants in a frame and clean the alpine house (see GREENHOUSES AND FRAMES, "Routine maintenance", p.583). Clean and top up the sand or grit on beds and renew labels. Then transfer pots back from the frame.

Exhibiting

Alpines for showing should be in the best possible condition on exhibition day. No matter how perfect the plant, it will lose marks if poorly presented in a less than scrupulously clean pot, or if top-dressings are thin or show evidence of algal growth. Remove all evidence of weeds, pests, and diseases. Check plants for dead, discoloured, or misshapen leaves and faded flowers, and remove these carefully with tweezers.

Clay pots should be scrubbed clean with a wire brush or scourer. Alternatively they may be double-potted: insert the specimen in its pot into a larger, new pot, covering the inner rim with top-dressing. Renew all top-dressings with materials appropriate to the plant's natural habitat, then relabel. Support tall, fragile plants during transport with tripods of split canes. Water plants thoroughly the day before the show and allow to drain before packing for transportation. Carry spare top-dressing to renew any lost in transit.

TRANSPORTING PLANTS

When transporting fragile plants (here Fritillaria uva-vulpis)*, make a tripod from split canes bound at the top with twine, and tie in stems.*

PREPARING PLANTS FOR EXHIBITION

1 *Use fine sand together with a wire brush or scouring pad to clean the outside of clay pots. This will remove any algae or limescale that may be present.*

2 *Replenish the top-dressing. For this* Dionysia aretioides *the medium is coarse gravel; but stone chippings, grit, or pine needles may be used, depending on the plant.*

3 *Add new, clearly written labels. Pack the pots carefully in a tray using newspaper to hold them steady, and carry extra top-dressing for last-minute renewal.*

CHAPTER

10

WATER GARDENING

A WATER FEATURE is an irresistible attraction in any garden. Whether it is a formal pool graced by water lilies and the bright gleam of goldfish, a trickling stream bordered by ferns, or a simple pond reflecting the sculptural silhouette of a clump of irises, there is a style suitable for every setting. Creating a water garden provides habitats for a specific range of plants as well as attracting a host of wildlife, including newts, frogs, toads, dragonflies, and perhaps even water birds. Water may be either restful or exciting: still water is valued for its properties of reflection and tranquillity, while moving water – whether a classical fountain or a rushing waterfall – adds a delightful sound and a dynamic vitality to the garden.

Designing a water feature

UNLIKE any other element in the garden, water brings an ever-changing pattern of reflections, sound, and movement that is particularly appealing. Even when frozen, its surface provides contrasts of colour and texture. A pond is a popular form of water feature but there are others: a waterfall, fountain, or watercourse, for instance.

A garden water feature allows you to grow many plants that do not thrive in any other conditions, from the floating frogbit (*Hydrocharis morsus-ranae*) and water hyacinth (*Eichhornia crassipes*) to the bog garden candelabra primulas.

When deciding which type of water feature to create, bear in mind the size and style of the garden. If large and informal, a meandering watercourse may be effective, while in an enclosed town garden, a raised formal pool might be appropriate. Water may even be included in a garden for children in the form of an attractive "bubble fountain" – in which the water splashes over stones and is recirculated without forming an area of any depth.

A NATURALISTIC WATER GARDEN
In an informal or semi-wild garden, a gently meandering stream provides a lush, cool area by which to sit and relax. Clouds of pink rhododendrons add both height and colour to the scheme, while marginal plantings of bright yellow Iris pseudacorus, *ferns, and rushes form a transition between the stream and the garden.*

Siting a pond

Exploit the reflective quality of water by siting a pond where it mirrors an eye-catching feature – a specimen plant or statue, perhaps. It may help to lay a reflective sheet on the proposed site to give an idea of reflections to be seen during the day and evening; check it from major viewpoints such as the house and patio.

An open, sunny position, away from overhanging trees, provides the best conditions in which to grow most water plants.

If planning to create a pond on wet land that is prone to flooding, check that there is no danger of fertilizer or pesticide residues leaching into the water from an adjacent vegetable garden or farmland. These substances invariably affect pond life adversely. Direct potential overflows to a suitable drainage system. Land with a high water table may cause problems because, in very wet periods, water pressure from below may push a pond liner out of shape.

Do not site a pond in a frost pocket or in a very exposed position, since this restricts the range of plants that may be grown and protection may have to be provided in winter.

Informal ponds

In an informal garden, a natural, sunken pond may look most effective. Usually, this is in an irregular, curved shape, bordered with natural materials such as turf or stones to link it with the garden. The water surface is, however, only part of the total scheme: the inclusion of marginal and moisture-loving plants

A FORMAL POOL
Water lilies (Nymphaea) *bring elegance and colour to a rectangular pond.
A sundial links the informality of the plants to the pool's formal margins.*

A water spout is usually fixed to a wall, with a pump and pipe similar to those used for a watercourse; the pump circulates water from a pool or reservoir to the rear of the spout and out through the "mouth".

Streams, watercourses, and waterfalls

Few gardens have a natural stream or waterfall, but it is possible to create a circulating watercourse spilling out into a pool or underground reservoir. Making a watercourse or waterfall is an attractive way of exploiting a change of level in the garden. It may be used to link parts of the garden as well as providing points of interest between levels.

In an informal garden, a watercourse may be made to look more natural by being edged with rocks or stones and moisture-loving plants such as ferns and irises. Ornamentals that have large leaves, for example *Rheum palmatum*, are particularly valuable for watercourses made from liners or preformed units since they help to disguise the edges.

Bog and wildlife areas

In an informal or naturalistic design, a bog garden makes an attractive and unconventional feature. Usually most appropriate next to ponds, bog gardens provide a gradual and

TRADITIONAL WATER SPOUT
A water spout is attractive even in a tiny garden. Here, mellow stone complements this traditional spout.

natural transition from aquatic to moisture-loving plants and ideal conditions for wildlife.

Bog gardens
Creating a bog garden is a better way of using waterlogged land than struggling against nature by trying to drain it. While the ground next to a man-made pool is unlikely to be wet enough to provide suitable conditions for growing bog plants, using a liner under the soil will retain sufficient moisture.

Bog gardens bring a freshness of growth in late summer when many other plants are showing the effects of drought; most bog plants, however, die back naturally after frost, so they do not provide great interest in winter months.

around the pond, to soften or hide its outline completely, helps to create a lush and refreshing effect.

As when planting in a border or bed, consider how the plants will combine to create complementary and contrasting associations of colour, texture, and form.

Formal ponds

In contrast to the natural effect of an informal pond, a formal pool makes a much bolder feature. It may be raised or sunken and is usually of a regular, geometric design. As a rule, less space is devoted to planting than in an informal pond, although plants with floating leaves and flowers (eg water lilies) are often included; sculptural plants such as certain ferns, grown next to the pool, provide attractive reflections. A fountain or water spout to complement the style of the pond can be an ornamental and dramatic addition.

Far from being disguised, the edge of the pond may form an important feature, perhaps made of attractive paving or, if the pool is raised, wide enough to form a seat; this type of design is particularly suitable for elderly or disabled people.

In many cases formal ponds are sited so that they form a striking focal point in the garden, at the main axis of paths, for example, or where they may be conveniently viewed and enjoyed from the windows or terrace of the house.

Fountains

The style and size of a fountain should be considered in the context of the surrounding pool and the overall design of the garden. Often used in a formal garden as a focal point, a fountain is also invaluable for adding height to a design, and for its dynamic contribution of sound and movement and the scattering of light. In addition, a fountain is particularly effective if lit at night.

A cobble or bubble fountain, in which water bubbles over stones into a small underground reservoir, looks more informal than a standard fountain and is ideal in a garden that is used by children.

As well as being ornamental, fountains also provide a practical function: the splashing action introduces oxygen into the water and this is beneficial to any fish. Most water plants do not flourish in disturbed water, however, so they should not be grown close to a fountain.

Water spouts

While a fountain or waterfall might be too large in an average garden, a water spout provides all the pleasure of running water scaled down for the smallest garden or even a conservatory. There are many styles, from the classical lion's head or gargoyle above a pool to the simplicity of an oriental bamboo pipe trickling water over stones.

AN INFORMAL WATERCOURSE
A terrace of weirs formed from thick slabs of stone creates cascades of water that spill into a shallow, cobble-lined pool. Overhanging plants such as ivies (Hedera), *Japanese maple* (Acer palmatum), *and primulas help to break up the rigid line of the stone, while the meandering path of the watercourse gives the scheme an appealing informality and charm.*

FLUID ATTRACTION
Reservoir features such as this textured fibreglass millstone fountain create a source of movement and sound. Such simple, child-safe water features work well not only in a small garden but also as a surprise element in a larger one.

Wildlife ponds

A water feature increases diversity in a wildlife garden, providing a habitat for waterfowl, frogs, newts, and an enormous range of insects. Limiting the planting to native species only will attract more wildlife, although many native plants can prove invasive; the inclusion of some exotic ornamentals creates a greater opportunity to make the pond a highly decorative feature as well. Informal ponds with muddy bottoms and shallowly sloping edges interspersed with large, flat stones are particularly suitable, providing ideal conditions for amphibians.

Water in small gardens

In a small garden or patio, or where major construction work is impractical, it is still possible to have a water feature. The most suitable one might be a small quantity of water being continually recirculated by a small pump, which fills a basin or other container, or a "bubble" fountain, which conceals a reservoir. Such "covered" features are particularly suitable in family gardens, where safety is a concern.

Wall fountains are available in many styles, both formal and informal, in a range of materials such as stonework, pottery, or metal. A miniature pool could also be introduced by using an appropriate ornamental container, such as a sealed and lined half-barrel or terracotta pot (see also WATER GARDENS IN CONTAINERS, p.331). Larger containers could also include a simple fountain or Japanese water feature.

Plants are usually incidental within a small feature, but if it includes moving water, any surrounding plants must be able to tolerate the high humidity caused by the fine spray.

Water garden plants

In any water garden, plants are vital to the scheme. Lush foliage and flowers enhance the pool and link it with the rest of the garden, while certain plants help to maintain clear water and, in the case of oxygenators, good conditions for fish.

Plants suitable for a water garden range from those that thrive in deep water to those requiring moist soil only around their root tips. They are usually grouped into six categories: oxygenators, deep-water plants, surface floaters, marginals, bog plants, and moisture-loving plants.

Oxygenators

Lagarosiphon major (syn. *Elodea crispa*) and *Myriophyllum* are examples of oxygenators: submerged, fast-growing plants that will help to clean and oxygenate the water. In sunny weather, submerged algae may turn a new pond completely green within a week or two of installation. Oxygenating plants, however, compete for the dissolved mineral salts on which algae thrive and starve them out so that the water eventually becomes clear once more. Such oxygenators are essential if you are planning to keep fish in the pool.

Deep-water plants

These flourish in a depth range of 30–90cm (12–36in). This category includes plants such as *Aponogeton* and *Orontium*, with water lilies (*Nymphaea*) forming the largest group (see pp.286–287). Apart from their ornamental value, their floating leaves also help to reduce algae by cutting down the amount of light allowed to reach the water.

Surface floaters

Floating plants, such as *Trapa natans* and *Azolla caroliniana*, perform a similar function to the deep-water plants, especially during the establishment phase. It is vital not to let them cover too much water, however, since oxygenators may suffer if there is not enough light.

Marginals

Marginal plants grow in shallow water usually about 7–15cm (3–6in) deep. Many of these plants are extremely attractive, such as *Iris laevigata* 'Variegata' with fans of green- and cream-striped leaves and lavender-blue flowers, and they are valuable in an informal pond for breaking up the outline. In a wildlife pool, marginal plants provide cover for wildfowl and other small creatures. Some species such as *Mentha aquatica* and *Veronica beccabunga* also help to oxygenate the water.

Bog plants

Bog-loving plants such as *Lysichiton* or some *Caltha* species thrive in waterlogged soil and can withstand occasional flooding. Under a bog-plant heading, nursery catalogues may include plants that grow in moist or even wet soil but do not tolerate a waterlogged soil; when ordering, ensure that any plants chosen tolerate high water levels around the roots.

Moisture-loving plants

These thrive in soils that contain extra moisture without being waterlogged. Moisture-lovers include many herbaceous perennials, such as *Astilbe*, *Ligularia*, and *Primula florindae*. They all associate well with marginal plants in the areas surrounding natural, informal pools where growing conditions are ideal.

Planting associations

Create a varied and attractive display by mixing plants with different heights and growth habits around the pool. Similar design principles should be applied as for planting in the rest of the garden to develop a successful scheme with a diversity of shapes and forms (see also "Principles of planting", pp.42–51). Site *Gunnera manicata*, for example, so that its immense, platter-like leaves tower over the jutting swords of *Acorus calamus*. Use plants at the edge of the pond to act as a foil for floating plants or deep marginals – an island of water lilies such as *Nymphaea alba* with its pure white blooms would be beautifully offset by a drift of ostrich-feather ferns (*Matteuccia struthiopteris*).

BOG GARDEN
The boggy ground next to a pond is ideal for plants such as Primula bulleyana *and* Iris laevigata, *which thrive in such an environment.*

CHAPTER

11

CONTAINER GARDENING

GROWING PLANTS IN containers is an exceptionally versatile way of gardening. An enormous range of plants adapt well to these essentially artificial conditions, whether they be short-lived bedding plants, which make colourful summer displays in pots, hanging baskets, or windowboxes, or relatively large shrubs and trees, which can live for many years in large containers. With such a diversity of plants to choose from, container gardens can be created almost anywhere, from spaces as confined as a patio, roof garden, balcony, or windowbox to areas in the larger garden.

Designing with containers

GROWING plants in containers is one of the most flexible of gardening techniques. For many modern gardeners, who are aiming to create a pleasing environment in a limited space, container gardening is practical and appealing. For centuries plants have been grown in containers to allow them to be sited where there is no garden soil, for example in a paved courtyard, on a balcony (see p.312), or under cover in the home (see INDOOR GARDENING, pp.352–383), greenhouse, or conservatory (see CONSERVATORY GARDENING, p.356). Plants are also pot-grown to give them prominence in a display – their unique qualities being easier to appreciate when they are placed in an inconspicuous pot – or to enhance them in a container that is attractive in its own right.

Growing plants in containers also allows the cultivation of genera that may not thrive in a particular garden's soil, by using tailored formulations of growing mixes. These include lime-free (ericaceous) mixes for lime-hating plants, such as rhododendrons and azaleas, or very gritty mixes for alpine plants or succulents, which need sharp drainage.

Changes in focus
In a conventional garden, plants are grown in the open ground and displays are relatively static because the components cannot easily be moved about. In such gardens, containers can play a role as focal points, for specimen planting, and for filling gaps in beds and borders. In the container garden, pot-grown plants are easily regrouped: with subtractions and additions, a planting scheme can be quickly rejuvenated or even completely transformed. Container gardening, therefore, is ideal for the experimental gardener wishing to create stimulating arrangements that can be changed when they have outlived their initial appeal.

Formal and informal styles
These two broad approaches to garden design are as relevant to container gardening as they are to gardening in open ground. The formal style is based on geometric order, with a division of space into balanced, often symmetrical units, and the repetition of elements at regular intervals. The informal approach has little or no geometry and the elements are arranged without obvious symmetry. At their most effective, informal arrangements take their cue from the irregularity of natural landscapes, although there is usually a carefully thought out, underlying balance of mass, form, and space.

Many popular manufactured containers are of a regular outline that is perfectly suitable for formal arrangements. Most plants, however, naturally grow in an informal way and so can be used to obscure the lines of the container. When arranging container-grown plants, it is just as easy to create an informal style – with soft, "freestyle" planting – as it is to ensure formality by planting to emphasize and echo the regularity of the container's shape.

An alternative approach to the informal style is to use "found" or reclaimed containers, such as chimney pots, old sinks, or drinking troughs, whose original purpose was quite other than for growing plants.

CONTRASTING SHAPES
The strong lines of this formal terracotta pot are softened and enhanced by an exuberant and informal planting of mound-formers and trailers.

Selecting a container

The choice of container is a matter of personal taste and aesthetics. Whether the container is manufactured or improvised, however, it must satisfy key practical requirements to make it suitable for the cultivation of plants. The most fundamental elements are that a container holds sufficient growing mix to sustain the plants and has provision for excess water to drain away.

The materials of which containers are made will also affect the final choice. These include unglazed and glazed terracotta, natural or reconstituted stone, concrete, metal, wood, fibreglass, and plastic. No material has a longer history of use than unglazed terracotta and its warm, earthy colour and matt-textured surface provide one of the most sympathetic foils for foliage and flowers. Terracotta lends itself to decoration with incised or relief patterns that are pleasing, but not distracting. It also blends in well with most architectural features, whether they are of stone, wood, or metal.

More opulent effects can be achieved with containers of marble, or more austere ones in other types of stone. The severity of concrete containers, or the strong lines of light-reflecting, galvanized zinc ones, lend themselves particularly well to an ultra-modern style, while wooden ones can be used to create more rustic atmosphere. Containers in fibreglass and plastic can look inconspicuous, but both materials have practical virtues, in terms of moisture retention, for example; and

COORDINATED CONTAINER
A large earthenware tub is an ideal container for an elegant bamboo; its subtle, earth-toned glaze echoes the bamboo fence behind, the whole lending a distinctly appropriate and stylish note to an Oriental-style garden.

the best successfully imitate much more expensive materials.

Plants and their containers should complement rather than compete with each other, and the texture, colour, and surface finish of a container are considerations as important as the material itself. To a large extent, this is a matter of individual preference, but it is worth bearing in mind that containers of a strong, assertive colour, a bold, high-gloss finish, or with conspicuous decoration will demand an equally strong planting scheme.

Size, shape, and scale

The size and shape of a container are governed by practical considerations as well those of visual appeal. The container must be large enough to accommodate the plant or plants to be grown. It is equally important to match the size of the pot to the visual mass of the planting it will hold. A small stone trough, for example, would be in scale with diminutive alpines; an Ali Baba jar would suit a vigorous trailing specimen, and a Versailles tub is ideal in both style and capacity for a topiary specimen. For a packed and colourful display of upright and trailing summer plants, a generously proportioned copper vessel (as once used for boiling or washing) might be appropriate.

As a general rule, the larger the pot the better, and larger pots need less frequent watering. One advantage of smaller pots, however, is that they can be dropped into arrangements as plants reach their prime,

and removed when past their best. This technique works best in conjunction with a holding area, such as a cold frame, in which plants are brought to near perfection, and to which they are returned to recover when their display is over.

Single specimens in containers

Growing single plants in individual containers is very practical: the growing mix, watering, and feeding regime can be geared to the plant, which is also freed of competition for moisture and nutrients. It can also work well in design terms, particularly if the plant has a strong architectural shape. The spiky New Zealand cabbage palm (*Cordyline australis*) and yuccas make fine specimens, as do plants of softer, weeping form, such as cultivars of the Japanese maple (*Acer palmatum*). Arching and mound-forming grasses, such as the green-and-gold variegated *Hakonechloa macra* 'Aureola', also look good alone in containers, as do species that are formally trained, such as a frame-grown common ivy (*Hedera helix*) or a clipped topiary specimen, such as box (*Buxus sempervirens*). Clematis and other moderately vigorous climbers can be allowed to trail from tall containers, or be trained upwards

CORRECT PROPORTIONS
This arrangement of beautifully contrasting foliage textures with hosta, fringe cups (Tellima grandiflora), and slender grasses, is perfectly in scale with the broad, shallow container. The proportions of plants to pot are about two thirds planting mass to one third pot, an old architectural trick that gives a well-balanced and visually pleasing effect.

MIXED PLANTING
Magenta petunias form a harmonious fringe beneath rich violet heliotropes, their intensity offset by copper and soft pinks and white highlights.

on a simple obelisk. Lax shrubs, such as ground-cover roses, look perfect when trailing their stems over the container's edge, and many other quite modest plants – heathers, primulas, and violas – radiate a special charm when given the luxury of their own pot.

Mixed planting

Individual plants in their own containers can be grouped to give the impression of a mixed planting. But a greater challenge is to bring together a number of plants that complement each other and give a sustained display for several weeks or even months. The keys to success are to select plants that share the same or similar cultural needs, and to create arrangements of compatible colours and contrasting forms and textures in foliage and flowers. Mixed displays are most effective with a strong structure, for example where a vertical or domed centrepiece is surrounded by lesser "uprights", with trailing plants breaking over the edge of the container to form an irregular "skirt".

A spring mixture, for example, might contrast upright dwarf irises and crocuses with a mat of small-leaved thyme (*Thymus serpyllum*); richly coloured polyanthus among mounds of sky-blue forget-me-nots (*Myosotis sylvatica*); or daisies (*Bellis perennis*) with tulips as strong verticals. In summer, the choice is almost endless – by selecting long-flowering bedding and foliage plants, it is possible to assemble rich arrangements to provide many months of colour.

Colour themes

When packing several plants close together, colour clashes become much more conspicuous than in the less condensed conditions of the open garden. In containers, it is perhaps more important to devise combinations of plants based on colour harmonies or contrasts. The harmonies of closely related colours can be quiet and subtle, as in a warm scheme based on cream, soft yellow, and pale apricot, while more heavily saturated colours – rich purples with violets and blues – create more vibrant harmonies. Contrasts are based on complementary colours: red with green, blue with orange,

or yellow with violet. The eye is comfortable with these opposites, which tone well with one another.

Alternatively, more shocking combinations can be tried, for example orange with magenta-pink. Colour clashes can be stimulating, but, in a small space, it is often helpful to ease the tension by using pale flower colours – creams or near-whites – or foliage as a buffer. Grey-leaved plants, such as *Helichrysum petiolare*, are invaluable in this respect, as are white- or cream-variegated plants, such as small-leaved cultivars of common ivy (*Hedera helix*).

Siting containers

Planted containers can be used simply as isolated features, but are often most effective in the garden when used as an integral part of a wider design. In the formal garden, for example, containers can provide accents that reinforce a sense of geometry. Similarly, looser arrangements can underline the more subtle rhythms of a more naturalistic theme.

The position of containers should be based on practical as well as aesthetic considerations. Container-grown plants need frequent watering in summer, so easy access to a water supply is vital, especially in sunny sites where plants may need attention at least once daily during spells of hot, dry weather.

It is worth bearing in mind, too, that thieves target gardens as well as houses, and a valuable urn or antique jar is safer placed in full view of the house, rather than in a more secluded position, and may even be best fixed or bolted to the ground.

AVENUE DESIGN
A broad walk flanked by an avenue of citrus trees in terracotta pots achieves formality through repetition of simple elements. Such a design demands discipline, but the elegant effect becomes its own reward.

Defining accents

Placing containers to create a succession of accents is a useful technique for delineating areas of the garden, or marking boundaries. At its simplest, a row of containers may mark a boundary, perhaps in conjunction with a wall or fence. Try lining pots along the base of a fence or along the top of a wall, provided they are secure and will not topple, or even suspend them from it. The effect can be achieved at little cost – perhaps with brightly painted, recycled tins planted with long-flowering and colourful pelargoniums. Containers can also be used to define compartments within a garden, for example when set singly or in clusters at the corners of a rectangular paved area.

Container accents are invaluable for enhancing other features. A squared arrangement around a circular pool, for example, forms a very effective contrast; alternatively place pots in the curved quadrants to emphasize the line of the pool's edge. Accents such as this can fulfil a dual role: they can define a shape while also softening a hard outline. This is especially useful in integrating the severe geometry of a rectangular pool into the wider garden: containers arranged around the pool echo its shape, yet, if filled with loose arrangements of plants, they soften the effect. It is best to set containers back from the water's edge so that they are not a hazard, and to reduce the risk of dead leaves and flowers fouling the water.

Containers as focal points

The main lines of a small, modern garden in a formal style rarely terminate in a natural view of a landscape

or an architectural landmark, but, even on a small scale, a vista that does not lead to a natural conclusion can seem unsatisfying. Features that are traditionally introduced to terminate vistas include trees and statuary, but on a smaller scale an urn, or large pot or tub, can fulfil the role equally well. Such focal points give an almost instant effect and, in comparison with statuary, are generally much less costly. Even an empty container can make an effective eye-catcher, provided that the scale is right; but when planted with an upright plant or group of plants, surrounded by a fringe of trailers, the design is far more handsome.

There is no simple rule of thumb for ensuring the correct scale; it is often most satisfactory to do it "by eye". Make a preliminary test by positioning a cane where the container is to stand, and then check its position from various points along the vista. In some cases, it may be necessary to raise the container on a plinth to achieve the desired effect. This can be a ready-made, architectural plinth or can be improvised, for example, with a stack of unmortared bricks, or wooden blocks, depending on the desired style.

In garden compartments, a central focal point is usually a good idea. A planted container is often a much simpler and cheaper option than a statue, sundial, or fountain. A formal herb garden divided into quarters, for example, may include a central paved or gravelled area – an ideal spot for a large pot planted with an architectural specimen, such as angelica (*Angelica archangelica*). Alternatively, to maximize the growing area, the container could stand on

a plinth in the middle of the bed, but ensure that access for watering and maintenance is provided for, perhaps by means of stepping stones.

Containers may also be used as focal points to direct the eye through the garden, for example by placing a large container at a turning point on a path, or to act as a distant feature that leads the observer on to another view or vista. In gardens where one mass of planting deliberately masks another, the unexpected has special value. A carefully placed container can introduce such an element of surprise, and an empty container of architectural quality – erect or on its side – can be just as dramatic as one full of plants.

Emphatic arrangements

Containers, especially if arranged in pairs, are an ideal way of marking a transition in the garden. This can be as simple and low-key as a one-step change of level, for example by using clipped balls of box (*Buxus sempervirens*) in terracotta pots to flank the step, emphasize the change, and warn people against tripping. Grander flights of steps can be treated in a more lavish way, with paired containers at top and base and others at different landings, to create a dramatic setting. But when using containers on steps in this way, they must be carefully placed so as not to present a hazard.

Paired containers can also play a supporting role to another feature, such as a garden bench, that may not have sufficient impact to terminate a vista by itself. Setting matched containers on either side strengthens the central feature, which assumes greater visual weight. For strictly

TRANSITIONAL ARRANGEMENTS
Simple urns mark changes of level, with a cleverly placed verbascum that lends emphasis with its strong vertical line; the whole scheme is enhanced by a marriage of complementary colours – yellows and mauves.

formal, long-term designs, pots could be planted with a topiary or, to ring the seasonal changes, a spring display of tulips could be followed with summer bedding plants that will bloom continuously for several months.

Paired containers can lend particular emphasis when positioned to form an "avenue". This formal pattern can work well on a relatively small scale: even in confined spaces, the effect can be monumental, for example when citrus trees in large terracotta pots or urns are placed in bays along a broad walk. On a more modest scale, pots of evergreens or seasonal flowers can be introduced to mark the main axis of a tiny garden.

Containers in beds and borders

Containerized plants, when rising above plantings in open ground, can be used to create contrast or to reinforce a colour theme in beds and borders: for example, violet-purple flowers such as heliotrope (*Heliotropium arborescens*) or petunias could oppose a border theme of oranges, creams, and yellows. Alternatively, subtle harmonies can

be created, like the pale pink of the double tulip 'Angélique' in pots beside beds of wallflowers, such as *Erysimum cheiri* Fair Lady Series, in shades of pink, yellow, and cream.

Container-grown plants are particularly valuable when the rest of the garden is relatively empty. Winter-flowering pansies, such as *Viola* x *wittrockiana* Universal Series, brighten dull days for many weeks in winter and early spring and can gradually be supplemented with a succession of bulbs, such as daffodils and tulips. In the autumn garden, container-grown shrubby plants such as *Argyranthemum*, fuchsias, and *Phygelius* will perform well until the first frosts.

Another approach is to boost beds and borders with pot-grown plants plunged into the ground. This is a particularly useful way to fill gaps in a border when the foliage of summer perennials, such as the Oriental poppies (*Papaver orientale* cultivars), has died back. It can also be used to supplement the display when newly planted perennials and shrubs have yet to attain their full size in a bed.

AN INFORMAL INVITATION
Planted containers here have many purposes: informality masks the severe lines of hard landscaping and draws the eye to a dramatic focal point, which, in turn, suggests an invitation to explore unseen vistas.

In some cases, the proximity of buildings and walls means that a paved garden receives little or no direct sun for all or part of the day. While painting walls white helps to make such shady areas brighter, the plants that really thrive in these conditions are committed shade lovers, such as hostas and ferns. These plants grow more lush and look beautiful for much longer periods in cool shade, providing the possibilities of sumptuous arrangements of foliage colour and texture.

Where direct light penetrates for several hours a day, many more plants will thrive, especially those that occur naturally in the dappled shade of a woodland setting, such as camellias and rhododendrons. When light levels are low, try moving the plants around from time to time, so that they have more exposure to sunlight; it helps promote balanced growth and encourages them to flower more freely.

Two other features of a paved environment affect the choice of plants: the weight of a pot and the watering regime. Solid walls often create turbulence as they deflect wind, and unstable pots may be toppled by sudden downdraughts; the growing mix also dries more rapidly in windy conditions. Containers close to walls may also stand in a rain shadow, where natural rainfall does not penetrate (see *Rain Shadow*, p.610). Even after heavy rain, plants may not receive sufficient water, so provision must be made for adequate watering.

Choosing containers

There are no hard-and-fast aesthetic rules when choosing containers for paved areas. They can be matched closely in texture and material to architecture and hard surfaces – terracotta pots are ideal against brick, for example. An equally valid approach is to use containers that stand out in a paved setting. Glazed jars, painted wooden tubs, and galvanized metal cubes and containers are just some of the choices that can help to define a distinctive style.

Arranging containers

Any arrangement of containers must take account of practicalities. For example, it is important to leave some clear space for access and to allow enough room for the unrestricted use of furniture. But from autumn to spring, when many paved areas are less heavily used, containers can be rearranged to provide displays that are visible from indoors. Stacked arrangements of pots loaded with bulbs, evergreens, or winter-flowering pansies (*Viola* x *wittrockiana* cultivars),

CORNERPIECE
Billowing foliage and a restricted colour scheme create a beautiful cornerpiece; the red blooms pick up and echo a warm-toned brick wall.

placed in view of French windows, allow the display to be enjoyed in warmth and comfort.

The most difficult aspect of managing changing displays is finding a place for plants before and after their most decorative season – only a limited number of those past their best can be hidden among plants in their prime. In the absence of a holding area, one solution is to rely heavily on annuals and biennials that are discarded when their season is over, leaving containers available for a succession of seasonal displays. Another option is to use containers that are ornamental in their own right; if carefully selected, they can be attractive even when empty. And if more permanent plantings of bulbs, perennials, and shrubs should outlive their usefulness, they are often gratefully received by friends with more space in their gardens.

Formal arrangements

The most usual formal arrangements in paved areas are paired containers flanking doors, benches, or other furniture set against walls. Where there is room, the symmetry can be expanded to include matching clusters of containers, with additions and subtractions as the seasons advance. At times of the year when the paved area is much used, arrangements – formal or otherwise – are best kept to the perimeter, but this does not preclude using them as a focal point, perhaps where they can be viewed from a door or window.

Although space may be limited, there is no need to restrict containers

---

UNITY AND DIVERSITY
A variety of unglazed terracotta pots creates a sense of unity within a group and forms a warm but neutral foil for this colourful and attractive arrangement.

Containers in paved gardens

The pleasures of gardening, and the contribution that plants make in enhancing the living environment, are being appreciated by more and more people. At the same time, gardens are increasingly being thought of as outdoor rooms, to be used for relaxing and entertaining, dining, and cooking. In the summer months, an outdoor room may even be much busier than living rooms indoors.

For many people, particularly in urban areas, the garden is a small paved space bounded by walls or fences: a courtyard, patio, or terrace. There are also other areas of hard landscaping in gardens, such as paths

and forecourts, and while the range of surfaces includes a huge variety of stone, tile, gravel, or concrete, or even wooden decking, open soil is often at a premium. The only way to include plants in such sites, where soil and space are so limited, is to grow them in containers.

Plants for paved areas

A large number of plants is suitable for containers in paved areas. In enclosed gardens, especially near sunny walls, there is often a very favourable, warm, and sheltered microclimate (see p.611). Tender plants, such as the fragrant-leaved lemon verbena (*Aloysia triphylla*) or myrtle (*Myrtus communis*), often succeed here when they may not thrive in a more open garden.

to small pots with flowers just above ground level. Such arrangements can appear mean in scale; fewer but larger plants will have much more impact. If there is no room for loose, rounded shapes, such as those of *Fatsia japonica* or the mophead *Hydrangea macrophylla* cultivars, consider naturally narrow, upright plants, such as a slow-growing conifer like *Juniperus communis* 'Sentinel', or plants such as yew (*Taxus baccata*) and box (*Buxus sempervirens*), which can be clipped to form a narrow cone or column.

To bring colour to the scheme, use flowering plants, such as clematis and miniature climbing roses, or variegated foliage plants, such as cultivars of common ivy (*Hedera helix*), and train them onto upright obelisks or narrow, willow-wand pyramids.

Many urban gardens have a paved path between a wall or fence and the house. Without plants, these passageways can appear bleak, but there is seldom enough room at ground level for pots or tubs. One solution is to place deep, narrow troughs at the foot of the wall. They can be filled with free-standing arrangements, or even with climbing plants that will cover the wall if given support. Another option is to fix containers securely to the wall top, so that plants can cascade down the wall's face. There is also a wide range of flat-backed, half-round containers available that are specifically designed to be mounted on the vertical surface of a wall or stout fence.

FORMAL ENTRANCE
An elegant façade is enhanced by tightly clipped lollipop trees (here privet); pink pelargoniums bring this quietly understated colour scheme to life.

Stands for containers

A plant stand with shelves at different heights provides a support for a neat and attractive display of container-grown plants and has the advantage that a diverse display can be created within a relatively small area. The most suitable and durable are usually made of aluminium and are of simple design with stepped and slatted shelves. The slats allow water to drain away freely and the "rake" of the shelves means that plants on the top shelf do not over-shadow those lower down. Most stands can be fixed against a wall or placed in a more open position, but some are specifically designed to fill corners, and these make good use of a potentially awkward space. An alternative to proprietary stands are those made from stacked bricks, clay drainpipes, or upturned flower-pots as uprights, and plain wooden planks as a standing surface. Such improvised structures have the advantage of being easily dismantled and reassembled as the need arises.

The position of a stand is frequently a matter of compromise, especially in the summer when the area is most heavily used. A good position for viewing from the house is against a wall opposite a door or window overlooking a courtyard or patio. In winter, when the patio is less often used, a staged display can be placed more centrally. Wherever the stand is put, the best results are usually achieved with a balanced combination of flowering and foliage plants. Even quite ordinary plants can make a striking display when skilfully arranged.

Informal clusters

Stray containers, unless carefully placed, can be both a nuisance and a hazard in paved gardens, but informal clusters can be a very effective way of displaying plants and their pots. An interesting range of plants in containers of different heights and sizes can, to some extent, mimic the layered effect of plants in the open garden. This can be enhanced by standing some containers on bricks or upturned pots to give additional prominence and by varying the height of their contents.

Any irregularly shaped cluster is a useful way of filling a corner, and informally planted containers along the borders of a patio or terrace can help mitigate the formal severity of paving. Very pleasing, unifying effects can be achieved by using differently shaped containers in the same material – unglazed terracotta pots, for example, are available in a wide range of shapes and sizes.

Keep it clean

The main disadvantage of clustered containers is that, inevitably, dust, dead leaves, and other detritus accumulate around their bases, which can be difficult to sweep away. A power hose is useful for keeping the surfaces clean, but it is also worth considering investing in wheeled bases for pots. These not only make it easier to sweep detritus away but are also an invaluable aid when moving heavy pots to re-create displays as plants fade at the end of their season.

TIERED CONTAINER DISPLAY
A banked mass of brilliant colour is achieved here by using pots of various sizes, with additional height gained by means of upturned empty pots – an inexpensive alternative to staging. The range of bronze-tinted greens found in the pelargonium leaves forms a linking element and is a complementary foil for the brilliant reds.

Balconies and roof gardens

BALCONIES and areas of flat roof can be converted to architecturally pleasing spaces in which container-grown plants can be used with extraordinary effect to create gardens in the air. Large-scale roof gardens can incorporate many of the features of a garden at ground level, including seating for relaxing and entertaining, barbecues, ornamental pools, and trees and climbers on supports. But even the smallest balcony, without room for furniture, can be transformed into a green and flower-filled outdoor room – a valuable extension of the living space indoors and a beautiful frame for the world beyond.

Special challenges

Almost any balcony or flat roof area has garden potential, but such spaces do present special challenges and safety is a major consideration. Plants, moist growing mix, containers,

and all the other features that make up a garden constitute a considerable load, which must be within the structure's load-bearing capacity. In addition, flooring must be waterproof and adequately drained. It is always advisable to consult an architect or structural engineer before planning a roof or balcony garden, and a check that local by-laws permit such structures must be made. Expert advice should include suggestions for fortifying structural support, or on how to site heavy elements to use the existing load-bearing capacity of walls or cross-beams. With careful choice of materials, the accumulated weight of garden components can be minimized. For example, consider wooden decking rather than tiling as a flooring material. Select plastic or fibreglass containers rather than those made of very heavy materials, such as stone and concrete; and use loamless rather

PARTIAL SCREENING
A see-through screen helps to create an intimate, sheltered atmosphere in this roof garden. New Zealand flax (Phormium) stands up well to windy conditions and is used here to make an impressive focal feature in a large but lightweight urn.

than loam-based growing mix to reduce the load further.

Balconies and roof gardens need barriers to protect those using the space: consult relevant building regulations governing minimum standards and heights for railings and walls. Balconies and roof gardens are much more likely to be affected by turbulence and strong winds than gardens at ground level, so all containers must be firmly secured. It is important, too, that none of the contents of a balcony or roof garden falls off, so putting at risk people and property below. Even within a roof garden or balcony, falling pots and large plants can cause damage, for instance, to windows. Lightweight containers may need ballast to prevent their being blown over or be fixed in positon. Bear in mind that

tall, narrow-based pots are much less stable than squat, broad-based ones.

The blustery winds that are a typical feature of balconies and roof gardens may damage fragile growth and wither tender foliage on plants such as Japanese maples (*Acer palmatum* cultivars). Drying winds combined with full sun create testing growing conditions. The most successful plants are tough and drought-tolerant; however, a wide range of plants will grow well provided they receive an adequate and regular water supply. On a large roof garden, an automated irrigation system can be the most efficient way to maintain satisfactory moisture levels, provided that provision is made for dealing with excess water. It is important that the structure incorporates drainage channels so that water does not form

SHADE IN SUMMER
This lightweight bamboo screening provides invaluable shade from fierce overhead summer sun on a roof or balcony garden.

WELL-MANAGED SPACE
On this wood-decked, first-floor terrace, container-grown plants are carefully grouped so that they do not impede access to the steps.

PLANTING FOR AN EXPOSED POSITION
Flowers and foliage plants, including grey-leaved Senecio maritima *and spreading* Scaevola *with fan-shaped flowers, make a wind-tolerant mixture.*

MINIMALIST FORMALITY
Strip decking, squared-up layout, and rounded topiary all contribute to the formality of a roof garden that includes planted and empty containers.

pools, for example, after a storm. Wooden decking can be laid to disguise any drainage systems required.

Planting on balconies

Plants for balconies can be grown in pots and troughs that stand on the balcony floor, in wall-mounted containers, or in those that are securely fixed to railings. When a balcony forms a garden extension to a room, the appearance of the containers and plants is most often judged from inside. Use planting to frame rather than obscure a good view, perhaps by grouping containers at either side of a clear central area. If, on the other hand, the view is dull or mediocre, use container-grown plants to block it out. In a similar way, trailing plants, spilling from pots or troughs mounted at the top of railings, can ensure privacy by screening the room within from view.

Balcony plantings can be just as attractive from within as from outside a building. Balconies, like windowboxes, may be planted to complement the architecture, perhaps with schemes that coordinate with plantings at ground level and on the floors above. Good trailing plants for sunny balconies include ivy-leaved pelargoniums; these are reasonably drought-tolerant and flower freely through summer and into autumn. Many bushy and upright plants also adapt well to life on sunny balconies, including aromatic herbs, such as hyssop (*Hyssopus officinalis*) and long-flowering annuals, such as the kingfisher daisy (*Felicia bergeriana*). While the choice for shady balconies is more limited, elegant schemes can be created using cultivars of common

ivy (*Hedera helix*) and evergreens, such as box (*Buxus sempervirens*), which provide year-round interest. Add extra colour with compact, shade-tolerant annuals and biennials, for example winter- and summer-flowering pansies (*Viola x wittrockiana*) or busy Lizzies (*Impatiens walleriana*), which bloom for several months during summer.

Planting in roof gardens

Large balconies and roof gardens often provide viewing platforms for dramatic cityscapes. If this is the case, capitalize on the view and use planting to frame it. Whether the

CAREFULLY PLACED PLANTS
Even though plants play a subdued role on this balcony, they soften the hard lines of the essential safety barrier. While they have been chosen and placed carefully so as not obscure the impressive long vista, the smaller plants do help to block out the near and least attractive part of the view. Taller plants to the rear create a partial screen for shelter and privacy from neighbours.

design is formal or informal, try to group containers so that the revelation of a view is gradual. Alternatively, create frames for a series of different vistas, which will ensure that the grandest one of all does not lose its novelty.

Perhaps more common than a beautiful prospect is a dreary view from a draughty and overlooked space. In this case, the best option is to create a more inward-looking garden. A climbing plant, barrier, or trellis not only helps to block out ugly views but also establishes an intimate atmosphere and helps reduce wind turbulence. Within the defined space, the design could be strictly formal, using relatively few shrubs trimmed to simple geometric shapes, or you could assemble plants to suggest the medley of a traditional cottage garden. For colourful, long-lasting displays, massed bedding plants are a good option, but there is also scope to experiment with vegetables and herbs, or subtropical and tropical plants. By creating compartments with screens, or even a pergola, variety is increased and intimacy enhanced.

Whatever the chosen style, arrange containers so as not to clutter areas used for seating or entertaining. For the most wind-resistant results, choose bushy and compact plants; they are less likely to be damaged or desiccated by strong winds. Compact cultivars of most popular bedding plants are readily available and there are many bushy shrubs to choose in preference to those that are tall and top-heavy.

Hanging containers

A variety of manufactured and improvised containers can be suspended or mounted to create a planted environment above ground level. They are particularly useful where space is limited, but even in conventional gardens there are many opportunities to use aerial displays of plants. They are invaluable for softening architectural environments; helping to lift the eye above other planting; and can be integrated into ambitious schemes in which plants are arranged on several levels.

Hanging baskets

The traditional hanging basket is a simple suspended container consisting of a wire frame in which a liner holds sufficient growing mix to sustain one or, more usually, several plants. A number of other suspended containers – either ready-made or improvised – serve the same purpose and are planted and displayed in a similar way to hanging baskets.

Wire-framed baskets and other suspended containers are best planted so that the container itself is concealed by full and trailing growth. This may be achieved with a single vigorous trailer, such as *Tradescantia zebrina*, a popular house or conservatory plant that can also be moved outdoors in summer.

In general, however, it is much easier to create a floating cloud of foliage and flowers with a mixture of several different, less tender plants. The aim is to achieve a loosely rounded shape, using plants of different habit, so that growth hides the container. One approach is to use upright and rounded plants to form a crown above an irregular, hanging fringe of trailing or spreading plants. This could be achieved by including erect cultivars of pelargoniums and *Verbena* x *hybrida*, flanked by trailing fuchsias, lobelias, and petunias. Another option is to use containers that are in themselves ornamental, so that, even when the display is at its peak, some of the container is visible.

Hanging baskets are often hung as isolated features, perhaps to take advantage of an existing support. This might be an arch or the cross-piece of a pergola, for example. Another approach is to fit specially made supports for single or multiple hanging baskets. Brackets can be simple and inconspicuous, or can be ornamental and in a style that suits the surroundings. A hanging basket can make a dramatic focal point to enliven a blank wall, especially if it can be seen from a window or door. They can also be eye-catching when

ELEVATED EYE-CATCHER
A reliance on foliage colours and textures ensures a long season of interest. Here, it masks the basket, but the ornamental bracket can still be seen.

suspended from the corner of a building, but for safety they must be well above the height of passers-by.

The most obvious of the multiple arrangements are pairs of baskets, mounted, for example, either side of a door or combined with other containers. A handsome design can be created by using a large container, such as an urn, at ground level against a wall, with hanging baskets mounted above it and on either side. The plants in the hanging baskets may match or contrast with those in the large container. For a more ambitious scheme, hanging baskets can be hung in rows, for example, on a series of arches, or on brackets along a wall. Carefully coordinated or contrasting plantings can be dramatically staged by using a cast of smaller baskets either side of a large one, or by introducing variations in the

height at which the containers are suspended. Using the cross-pieces of a pergola, a sequence of paired hanging baskets either side of a path makes an impressive avenue, although it is worth bearing in mind that such features will be time-consuming to water.

Windowboxes

These containers are available in a wide range of materials, including wood, terracotta, concrete, and plastic. They are sometimes designed to be ornamental on their own account, with painted or relief decoration. Plain wooden windowboxes can be painted to match other architectural details, but for more adventurous effects consider painting windowboxes on the front of a building in a bold colour to make them stand out. The planting style and content of a

windowbox depends to some extent on the position from which it is viewed. For some apartment-dwellers, for example, their whole garden may amount to one or two windowboxes, so the view from inside matters more than that from ground level. The greatest pleasure may be had from choosing plants of refined beauty, good scent, or aromatic foliage. If windowboxes form an integral part of the decoration of a house front, on the other hand, the view from outside is what really counts. The most valuable plants in this sort of display will be those that perform reliably over a long season, and might include evergreens such as box (*Buxus sempervirens*) or hebes.

If windowboxes are in windy, exposed positions, they may not be suitable for tall plants, which will be battered by wind; they may also block out the light. But to avoid a dull, uniformly low display, position compact but rounded plants, such as pelargoniums, in the centre, with lower plants on either side and trailing plants cascading from the front. There are many variations to play on this theme, using a wide range of plants, including evergreens for winter or year-round effect.

Wall-mounted containers

The types of containers that can be wall-mounted include semi-circular wire or strip-metal baskets, metal-frame mangers, and plastic or terracotta half-pots. Brackets can also be fixed to walls to hold standard pots of small or medium size, and more solid brackets can be used to support troughs – but be sure that they are fixed securely. Wall-mounted containers filled with plants are invaluable in breaking up the blankness of bare walls, whether used on their own or in conjunction with other planting. They are equally useful where windows open outwards or lack a sill. The best alternative to a windowbox can be a trough mounted on brackets below the window. Wall-mounted containers are perhaps of greatest value in narrow spaces, or where a courtyard or passage is partly shaded. In a raised position, plants have greater access to light, and will often thrive better when elevated than they would at ground level.

In general, stone or brick walls make a beautiful backdrop to plantings, but, to take full advantage of their possibilities, it is important to choose containers that tone or contrast with the background colour. Full planting and generous use of trailing plants is generally the best option but, if the container itself is decorative, it should obviously be

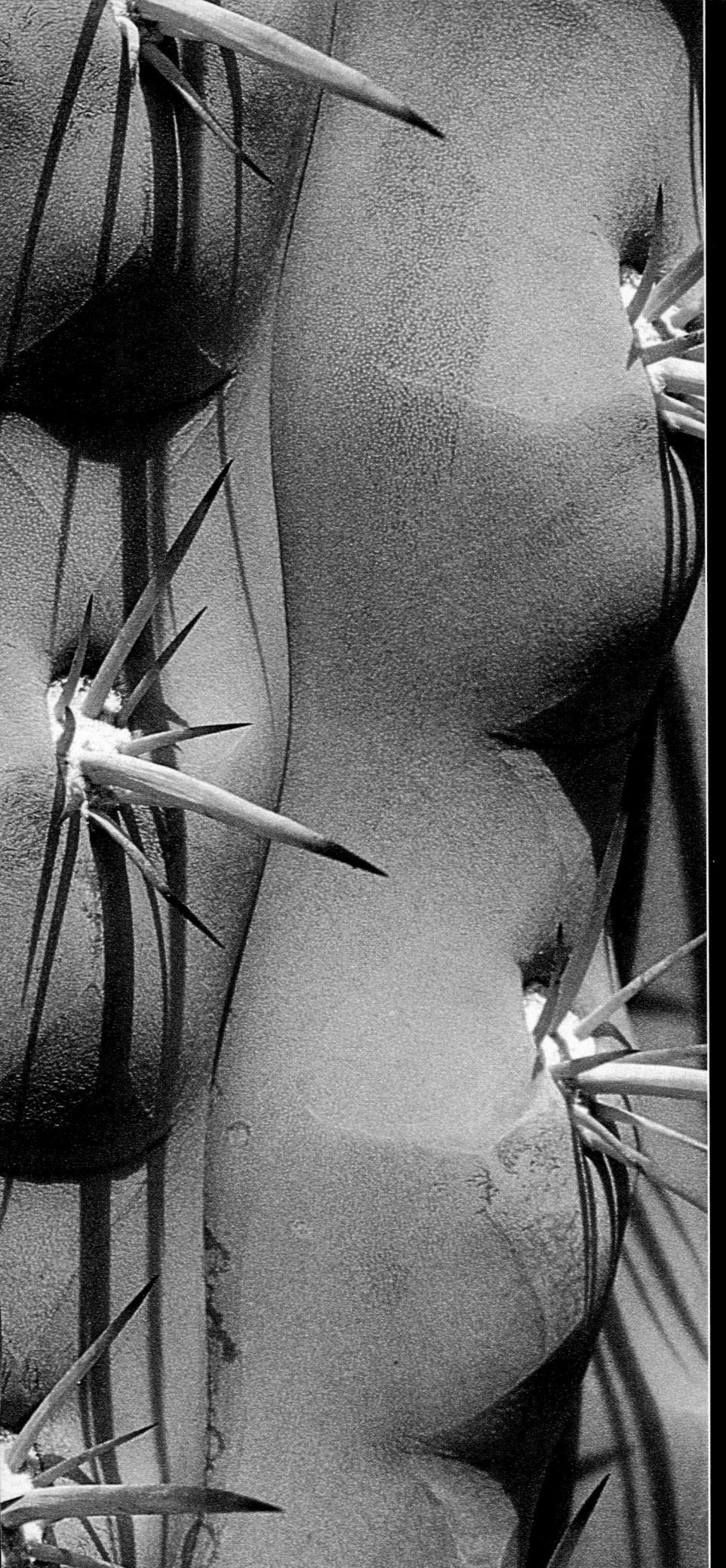

CHAPTER

12

CACTI AND OTHER SUCCULENTS

WITH A UNIQUE variety of sizes and shapes, and a wealth of colour and texture, cacti and other succulents can make spectacular displays. Their forms range from the symmetrical rosettes of *Echeveria* to the squat, globular *Echinocactus* and the fluted columns and candelabra of some desert cacti. Many bloom only briefly and bear large, brightly coloured flowers, while others flower for longer periods, producing a profusion of exquisite blooms. In cool-temperate climates, most cacti and succulents are grown in the greenhouse or as house plants, but hardier species also make beautiful garden specimens. In warmer climates, they offer scope to create an outdoor desert garden. Whether grown as focal plants or grouped for contrast of form and texture, cacti and other succulents are ideal for containers, both indoors and out.

Designing with cacti and other succulents

MANY cacti are native to the desert regions of the southern USA, Mexico, and South America, where rainfall is low and intermittent, and there are great extremes of temperature. In contrast, some of the most floriferous cacti originate in the warm, humid rainforests of Central and South America. These plants are usually epiphytic, which means that they grow on other plants, either weaving through host trees or lodging in niches in their branches.

Other succulent plants occur in a far greater range of habitats than cacti, and, since they are found in at least 20 different plant families, show a wide diversity of characteristics. Their natural habitats include the semi-arid regions of Central America, Africa, and Australasia, as well as the more temperate and cold climates of Asia, and northern parts of Europe and America.

Characteristics of succulents

Cacti and other succulents show a number of adaptations, such as reduced leaf size and loss of leaves in very dry weather, that are designed to conserve water by reducing transpiration. The distinguishing feature that is common to all, however, is the presence of water-storing, fleshy tissue in the stems, leaves, or roots. It is this tissue that allows succulent plants to withstand long periods of drought.

Cacti are easily distinguished from other succulents by structures called areoles – the cushion-like growths on their stems from which the spines, hairs, flowers, and shoots develop.

Succulent plants may be loosely divided into three groups, depending on which part of the plant contains the moisture-retaining tissue. Some genera, for example *Euphorbia*, may be represented in more than one group. Most cacti are stem succulents, as are some succulent plants from the Asclepiadaceae and Euphorbiaceae families. Others, including *Aloe*, *Echeveria*, *Lithops*, and *Sedum*, are leafy succulents. Plants in the third group are known as caudiciform succulents and have the water-storing tissue in a swollen rootstock (the caudex), although this often extends into the stem, as in *Adenium obesum*. Plants that belong to this group are mostly found in the families Apocynaceae, Cucurbitaceae, and Convolvulaceae.

Form and habit

The diverse forms and growth characteristics of cacti and other succulent plants may be used to create a range of effects. The tall

A NATURAL GROUPING
Collections of succulent plants make an impressive sight. Here Euphorbia canariensis *towers above* Agave americana *'Marginata' and* A. attenuata.

VARIETY OF FORM
The strong, architectural leaves of Agave americana (*centre*) *make a fine contrast with the orange flower spikes of the* Aloe (*left*) *and the prostrate, blue-grey leaves of a* Senecio *cultivar in the foreground.*

FLOWERING CACTI AND SUCCULENTS

Thelocactus setispinus

Oroya peruviana

Parodia chrysacanthion

Strombocactus disciformis

Lithops pseudotruncatella* var. *pulmonuncula

Rebutia fiebrigii

columns of *Cleistocactus strausii*, for example, make strong, vertical lines that contrast with foreground plantings of smaller, spherical forms, such as *Echinocactus grusonii*, or the characteristically flattened segments of some *Opuntia*.

Several species have a creeping habit that adds a horizontal element to the garden design. *Carpobrotus edulis*, for instance, as well as *Lampranthus* and *Ruschia*, make dense carpets of growth that provide excellent ground cover.

Trailing succulents, for example *Ceropegia linearis* subsp. *woodii*, *Schlumbergera* and *Rhipsalis*, produce cascades of slender stems or leaves that are seen to best effect in hanging baskets. Several are scrambling climbers: *Aloe ciliaris* and *Selenicereus* add height to mixed plantings if given the support of trellis or the branch of a tree. In warm, frost-free climates, the jointed and climbing stems of *Hylocereus* are most effective when allowed to spread over walls.

Flowering cacti and other succulents

Cacti and other succulents often produce exquisite blooms and will flower regularly once they reach maturity, although this may take between one and 40 years. Most are day-blooming, with individual blossoms sometimes lasting for several days. Some epiphytic cacti are winter-flowering and have blooms that are carried in succession over long periods.

Others bloom only briefly, however, the flowers sometimes appearing soon after sunset and fading as evening advances. Many of the large, columnar cacti produce buds that gradually unfold during the evening and then fade in the early morning hours.

The flowers, often of delicate appearance and silken texture, are usually exceptionally large in comparison with the size of the plant, and their colour range is mainly at the warm end of the spectrum with a profusion of rich yellows, hot scarlets, and vivid carmines. A number of genera, often those of the family Mesembryanthemaceae, and some of the epiphytes, have sweetly scented blooms. Some species, especially members of the Agavaceae, are monocarpic, that is they die after flowering and setting seed. A number of small, non-flowering offsets are often formed around the flowering rosette, however, and these flower in subsequent years, when mature.

Outdoor display

With careful selection and skilful arrangement, attractive collections of cacti and other succulents may be grown outdoors even in relatively cool conditions. Few succulents, however, tolerate excess moisture; even the hardy species require good drainage – these grow well in raised beds where water drains away freely. Among the hardiest are *Opuntia humifusa*, *Sedum*, and houseleeks (*Sempervivum*), along with some *Crassula* and *Umbilicus*.

With sharp drainage and a good baking in summer, a number of desert plants, particularly some *Echinocereus* and *Opuntia*, withstand surprisingly low temperatures – although not the combination of cold and wet.

In mild areas that have few frosts, the range of plants is extended to include the spectacular rosettes of *Agave americana* and its cultivars, *A. filifera*, and *Beschorneria yuccoides*. Half-hardy species need a freely draining site with the shelter of a warm, sunny wall for additional protection. Where temperatures are unlikely to fall much below 7–10°C (45–50°F), such as in the southern and south-western USA and the more southerly parts of Europe, there are few restrictions when choosing succulents for outdoors.

Mixed plantings
When growing non-succulent and succulent plants together, it is important to choose plants that have similar needs for light, soil type, and watering regime. In frost-free gardens, compatible non-succulents include *Fuchsia*, *Nerium*, *Gazania*, and *Rehmannia*, all of which provide additional colour and variety. Bulbous plants such as *Clivia*, *Cyrtanthus*, and *Sprekelia* are also

HARDY AND HALF-HARDY CACTI AND SUCCULENTS

Beschorneria yuccoides (half hardy)

Maihuenia poeppigii (hardy)

***Sedum spectabile* 'Brilliant'** (hardy)

Agave filifera (half hardy)

Opuntia compressa (hardy)

Sempervivum montanum (hardy)

good choices in mixed plantings in the appropriate climates.

In cooler regions, slow-growing and compact annual species as well as plants that are grown as annuals, such as *Lampranthus* and *Portulaca grandiflora*, are suitable for planting outdoors among groups of perennial cacti and succulents.

Desert gardens

In arid climates where temperatures seldom fall below 10°C (50°F), the complete range of cacti and other succulents may be grown in a desert garden to create a fine landscape feature. Where the subsoil is particularly heavy, collections of plants may be grown in raised beds to ensure the excellent drainage that these plants require.

Use smaller species at the front of the bed, so that their delicate beauty is not obscured by taller plants. Allow clump-forming plants, such as *Echeveria*, *Haworthia*, and *Mammillaria*, sufficient space to develop fully. These low-growing, cluster-forming species flower at different periods from spring to autumn, to give colour during the warmer months.

For background planting, erect, columnar cacti and other succulents are ideal. Choose plants such as the tall, single-stemmed *Cephalocereus senilis*, the branching *Cleistocactus strausii*, or the towering, tree-like form of *Euphorbia candelabrum*.

Containers outdoors

Most cacti and succulents have shallow roots and respond well to being grown in containers. Select

A DESERT GARDEN
The branching arms of Euphorbia candelabrum *balance the surrounding globular and columnar cacti to complete this striking collection.*

containers that enhance the shape and form of the plants – a wide, shallow bowl, for example, is the natural choice for displaying low-growing and creeping species, whereas those with stronger form, such as *Agave attenuata*, are much more suitable for large pots or urns.

Troughs are particularly useful for creating imaginative combinations of plants of quite different sizes and habits, and hanging baskets are suitable for displaying trailing and pendent species.

Choosing and siting the plants

In cool regions, but where temperatures seldom fall below freezing, many species will thrive outdoors in

troughs and pots, provided that these are raised above the ground to allow water to drain away freely. A warm, sheltered position such as a corner of a covered patio or balcony, where the plants can more easily be protected from rain, will provide the ideal environment.

The foliage shapes of *Sedum* and neat rosettes of *Sempervivum* may be used to form a contrast with the leafy forms and brilliant blooms of *Lewisia* species and cultivars, or with the green-flowered *Echinocereus viridiflorus* and the scarlet, early summer blooms of *Echinopsis chamaecereus* (syn. *Lobivia silvestrii*). Other species, such as *Agave parryi*, which has

symmetrical rosettes of plump, grey-green leaves, or *Opuntia polyacantha*, with its brilliant display of yellow flowers, make striking focal points if they are planted on their own in large bowls.

In warmer climates, there is much greater scope for growing cacti and other succulents outdoors in containers. In large pots, group plants that flower at different periods and have striking foliage forms: the purple-leaved *Aeonium* 'Zwartkop', *Aloe vera*, which has yellow flowers, and the red-flowered *Crassula falcata* will provide structural interest all year round, and give a succession of attractive blooms throughout the warmer months.

Where temperatures do not consistently fall below 13°C (55°F), many dwarf cacti, such as *Gymnocalycium*, *Mammillaria*, and *Rebutia*, make fascinating displays of form and texture in outdoor bowls and troughs in the garden. These dwarf, cluster-forming species also give a magnificent display of vibrant colour that will last for many weeks on end during the summer.

Indoor display

The protected environment of the greenhouse or conservatory, which allows almost complete control of light, temperature, humidity, and water, provides ideal conditions for an extensive range of cacti and other succulents – most of the plants recommended for outdoor cultivation in warm climates will thrive under cover in cooler regions. The adaptations these plants have made to help them to survive in harsh, arid

MIXED PLANTING
The neat rosettes and delicate, nodding flowerheads of Echeveria *provide a dainty contrast with the strap-like leaves of* Agave filifera (centre), *the focal point of this attractive arrangement.*

AN OUTDOOR CONTAINER
This varied collection of tall, spreading, and pendent cacti and other succulents creates a highly decorative and unusual feature on a balcony outdoors.

AN INDOOR BED
The bright foliage of Agave americana *'Mediopicta', offset by the rosettes of* Orostachys chanetii, *is a fine centrepiece in this greenhouse bed.*

environments in the wild also make them very suitable for the warm, dry conditions of a centrally heated home, where many other plants may fail to thrive.

The variation in shape and habit, and their beautiful flowers, ensure that these plants provide interest throughout the year, and, since different species are adapted to a variety of environmental conditions, they may be selected for a number of situations in the home.

Providing the right conditions
The great majority of cacti and other succulents need high light levels, warmth, and good ventilation to thrive, although some, the leafy succulents in particular, may need protection from direct sun in summer to avoid leaf scorch.

There is an important group, however, that requires shady conditions, or at least filtered light: these are epiphytes that come mainly from the humid and shaded rainforests of Central and South America.

Epiphytic plants are among the most floriferous of cacti and other succulents, and they can be used to great effect to add bold splashes of colour and interest to shady corners of the home or garden. The best known of this group are the Christmas cactus (*Schlumbergera* x *buckleyi*), *Hatiora gaertneri*, and *H. rosea*. Some of the loveliest are the magnificent hybrids created by crossing *Epiphyllum* with species or hybrids of *Echinopsis*, *Heliocereus*, *Hylocereus*, and *Nopalxochia*. These hybrids produce extraordinarily beautiful, and sometimes fragrant, flowers in spring and summer, in colours ranging from pure white, through cream, yellow, and orange to red and deepest purple.

Plants for the greenhouse and conservatory
Plants in a greenhouse or conservatory may be grown in pots or open beds, either at floor level or raised on benches. Planting in open beds offers potential for growing larger species and even for creating a miniature desert garden.

When in growth, many species from warm habitats need bright light, a fairly dry atmosphere, and a temperature of 18°C (64°F) if they are to develop to their full potential and bear flowers. These conditions are more easily provided under glass than in a home environment, and many cacti grow and flower most successfully in a greenhouse.

Some, notably *Rhipsalis*, require fairly high levels of humidity (80 per cent) to thrive, and nearly always perform best in the humid atmosphere of a conservatory. Other groups that are very suitable for the conservatory and greenhouse are those that need space to flower well.

GREENHOUSE DISPLAY
The rich colour and diverse forms of, among others, Crassula, Echeveria, Echinocactus, *and* Mammillaria *provide a sumptuous collection of plants for the greenhouse bench.*

These include the clambering *Selenicereus* (the most outstanding species is Queen-of-the-night, *S. grandiflorus*) and several *Hylocereus*, all preferring filtered light.

When drawing up planting plans for a greenhouse or conservatory, combine groups of cacti and other succulents that have similar cultural needs, to make maintenance easier.

Container-growing indoors

If provided with warm, bright, and draught-free conditions, many cacti and other succulents will thrive in indoor containers. Use small pots for displaying individual plants, or large bowls for planting a variety of compatible species together.

Wear thick, leather gloves when handling spiny plants such as *Agave*, *Aloe*, and *Opuntia*, because their sharp spines may easily become embedded in your fingers if you brush against them, causing a painful injury.

Bowl gardens
If planted with different species that have the same cultural requirements, bowl gardens are particularly effective for growing succulent plants indoors. One or two plants with an erect habit, for example young specimens of *Cephalocereus*, *Cleistocactus*, or other columnar genera, may provide the focal point of the bowl. Alternatively, use a leafy succulent such as *Crassula ovata* as the main plant. Fill the rest of the bowl with smaller plants, such as *Echeveria* and *Haworthia*. Free-flowering cacti such as *Mammillaria*, *Parodia*, and other globular cacti are also good choices for planting in a bowl garden indoors.

A HANGING BASKET
The graceful stems and flowers of Kalanchoe manginii *cascade like a waterfall against the house wall.*

Hanging baskets
Cacti and succulents in hanging baskets make colourful displays in the home or conservatory. Pendent cacti such as *Aporocactus flagelliformis*, and trailing succulent plants such as *Kalanchoe*, *Hatiora gaertneri*, and *Schlumbergera* are the most suitable plants to choose, since they will trail attractively over the edge of the basket. *Sedum morganianum* and other semi-trailing species are also very effective in hanging baskets (see also "Planters guide to cacti and other succulents", p.342).

Plant hanging baskets with just one specimen, or use several species for a harmonious but varied arrangement. In general, non-epiphytic plantings require bright light, but epiphytes need partly shaded conditions or bright but filtered light, so position the baskets accordingly.

Planter's guide to cacti and other succulents

DAMP CONDITIONS

Succulents that tolerate damp conditions
Crithmum maritimum
Salicornia europaea
Suaeda fruticosa, S. maritima
Umbilicus intermedius, U. rupestris

SHADE

Succulents that tolerate light shade
Lewisia Cotyledon Hybrids,
 L. leeana
Orostachys chanetii ✱, O. spinosus ✱
Rhodiola wallichiana
Sedum dasyphyllum, S. sediforme,
 S. spectabile, S. ternatum,
 S. villosum
Sempervivum arachnoideum,
 S. ruthenicum

BOWLS AND TROUGHS

Sun
Adenium obesum ✱
Aeonium arboreum ✱,
 A. nobile ✱
Agave filifera ✱, A. stricta ✱,
 A. victoriae-reginae ✱
Aloe humilis ✱, A. longistyla ✱,
 A. rauhii ✱
Astrophytum myriostigma ✱,
 A. ornatum ✱
Cephalocereus senilis ✱
Cereus uruguayanus ✱, C. validus ✱
Cleistocactus strausii ✱
Cotyledon campanulata ✱,
 C. orbiculata var. undata ✱
Crassula ovata ✱,
 C. perfoliata var. minor ✱,
 C. rupestris ✱, C. socialis ✱
Echeveria agavoides ✱,
 E. derenbergii ✱, E. pilosa ✱
Echinocactus grusonii ✱
Echinocereus berlandieri ✱,
 E. pentalophus ✱

Echinocereus
pentalophus

Echinopsis chamaecereus ✱,
 E. eyriesii ✱, E. kuehnrichii ✱,
 E. marsoneri ✱, E. oxygona ✱,
 E. pachanoi ✱, E. pasacana ✱,
 E. pentlandii ✱, E. spachiana ✱
Espostoa lanata ✱
Euphorbia flanaganii, E. milii ✱,
 E. obesa ✱
Faucaria felina ✱
Ferocactus cylindraceus ✱,
 F. latispinus ✱
Gasteria batesiana ✱,
 G. bicolor var. liliputana ✱

Glottiphyllum linguiforme ✱
Gymnocalycium baldianum ✱,
 G. gibbosum ✱, G. mihanovichii ✱
Haworthia cooperi ✱,
 H. limifolia ✱, H. reinwardtii ✱
Jatropha podagrica ✱
Kalanchoe blossfeldiana ✱
Lithops dorotheae ✱,
 L. karasmantana subsp. bella ✱
Mammillaria bocasana ✱,
 M. compressa ✱, M. gracilis ✱,
 M. hahniana ✱, M. mystax ✱,
 M. rhodantha ✱,
 M. spinosissima ✱,
 M. zeilmanniana ✱
Opuntia microdasys ✱
Orbea variegata ✱
Pachypodium geayi ✱, P. lamerei ✱
Parodia leninghausii ✱,
 P. mutabilis ✱
Rebutia albiflora ✱, R. aureiflora ✱,
 R. glomeriseta ✱, R. heliosa ✱,
 R. marsoneri ✱, R. minuscula ✱,
 R. senilis ✱, R. steinbachii ✱
Sansevieria trifasciata 'Hahnii' ✱,
 S. trifasciata 'Laurentii' ✱
Thelocactus bicolor ✱,
 T. rinconensis ✱

Thelocactus
bicolor

Partial shade
Epiphyllum oxypetalum ✱
 (and hybrids)
Hatiora gaertneri ✱, H. rosea ✱
Hoya australis ✱, H. carnosa ✱
Schlumbergera x buckleyi ✱,
 S. truncata ✱ (and hybrids)

HANGING BASKETS

Aporocactus flagelliformis ✱
Ceropegia haygarthii ✱, C. linearis
 subsp. woodii ✱
Disocactus ✱
Epiphyllum oxypetalum ✱
 (and hybrids)
Hatiora gaertneri ✱, H. rosea ✱,
 H. salicornioides ✱
Heliocereus ✱ (most spp.)
Hoya lanceolata subsp. bella ✱,
 H. linearis ✱, H. polyneura ✱
Kalanchoe jongsmanii ✱,
 K. manginii ✱, K. pumila ✱
Rhipsalis cereuscula ✱,
 R. mesembryanthemoides ✱,
 R. pachyptera ✱
Schlumbergera x buckleyi ✱,
 S. truncata ✱ (and hybrids)
Sedum morganianum ✱
Selenicereus ✱

SUCCULENTS THAT TOLERATE TEMPERATURES DOWN TO 0°C (32°F)

Agave americana ✱, A. lophantha ✱,
 A. parryi ✱, A. utahensis ✱
Echinocereus viridiflorus ✱
Echinopsis chamaecereus ✱
Opuntia compressa, O. erinacea ✱
Sedum anglicum, S. cyaneum ✱,
 S. dasyphyllum, S. formosanum ✱,
 S. hispanicum, S. lanceolatum,
 S. rupestre, S. spectabile
Sempervivum (most spp.)
Umbilicus (spp. only)

SUCCULENTS THAT TOLERATE TEMPERATURES DOWN TO 7°C (45°F)

Agave attenuata ✱, A. parviflora ✱
Aloe arborescens ✱, A. aristata ✱,
 A. brevifolia ✱, A. distans ✱,
 A. variegata ✱, A. vera ✱
Bulbine frutescens ✱, B. latifolia ✱,
 B. mesembryanthemoides ✱
Caralluma europaea ✱
Carpobrotus acinaciformis ✱,
 C. edulis ✱
Cereus chalybaeus ✱, C. jamacaru ✱
 (and other columnar spp.)
Crassula sarcocaulis ✱,
 C. sarmentosa ✱
Delosperma ✱ (most spp.)
Echeveria cuspidata ✱,
 E. coccinea ✱, E. elegans ✱,
 E. gibbiflora ✱
Echinocereus chloranthus ✱,
 E. enneacanthus ✱,
 E. pentalophus ✱
Echinopsis chamaecereus ✱
Gasteria carinata ✱, G. carinata
 var. verrucosa ✱, G. disticha ✱
Gibbaeum album ✱

Kalanchoe
delagoensis

Kalanchoe delagoensis ✱,
 K. marmorata ✱
Lampranthus falcatus ✱,
 L. roseus ✱
Lewisia Cotyledon Hybrids
Maihuenia poeppigii ✱
Opuntia exaltata ✱, O. fragilis ✱,
 O. polyacantha ✱, O. robusta ✱,
 O. subulata ✱
Orostachys chanetii ✱, O. spinosus ✱
Pelargonium acetosum ✱,
 P. echinatum ✱, P. tetragonum ✱
Senecio haworthii ✱,
 S. macroglossus ✱

FLOWERING CACTI

Day-flowering
Aporocactus flagelliformis ✱
Astrophytum myriostigma ✱

Astrophytum
myriostigma

Bergerocactus emoryi ✱
Cleistocactus strausii ✱
Echinocereus engelmannii ✱,
 E. triglochidiatus ✱
Echinopsis aurea ✱, E. mamillosa
 var. kermesina ✱, E. oxygona ✱
Epiphyllum anguliger ✱,
 E. crenatum ✱
Gymnocalycium bruchii ✱
Hatiora gaertneri ✱, H. rosea ✱,
 H. salicornioides ✱
Heliocereus speciosus
 var. superbus ✱
Lobivia famatinensis ✱,
Mammillaria blossfeldiana ✱,
 M. bocasana ✱, M. hahniana ✱,
 M. milleri ✱, M. spinosissima ✱,
 M. zeilmanniana ✱
Matucana aureiflora ✱
Nopalxochia phyllanthoides ✱
Opuntia lanceolata ✱,
 O. paraguayensis ✱
Parodia brevihamata ✱,
 P. graessneri ✱, P. haselbergii ✱,
 P. leninghausii ✱,
 P. mammulosa ✱, P. mutabilis ✱
Rebutia aureiflora ✱,
 R. glomeriseta ✱, R. marsoneri ✱,
 R. neocumingii ✱, R. senilis ✱
Schlumbergera x buckleyi ✱,
 S. truncata ✱
Thelocactus bicolor ✱

Night-flowering
Cephalocereus senilis ✱
Cryptocereus anthonyanus ✱
Echinopsis deserticola ✱,
 E. mirabilis ✱, E. spachiana ✱,
 E. terscheckii ✱
Epiphyllum cartagense ✱
Espostoa lanata ✱, E. melanostele ✱
Haageocereus limensis ✱,
 H. setosus ✱, H. versicolor ✱
Harrisia bonplandii ✱,
 H. gracilis ✱
Hylocereus ocamponis ✱
Pachycereus pringlei ✱
Rebutia eyriesii ✱
Selenicereus grandiflorus ✱,
 S. macdonaldiae ✱
Stenocereus ✱ (most spp.)

Soil preparation and planting

Many cacti and other succulents grow naturally only in desert or jungle conditions, but they also make striking displays out of doors in cooler climates. Whether grown indoors or outside, specially prepared, well-drained soil or compost is essential. A sunny site with adequate protection from frost is also required for most species.

Buying cacti and other succulents

When buying cacti and other succulents, choose healthy, unblemished plants that show new growth or have flower buds forming. Do not buy damaged or slightly shrivelled specimens, or any with dull, dry, or flaccid segments. Also reject plants that have outgrown their pots.

Planting in a raised bed or desert garden

Cacti and other succulents require well-drained conditions, so they benefit from being planted in a bed

RAISED BED CONSTRUCTION

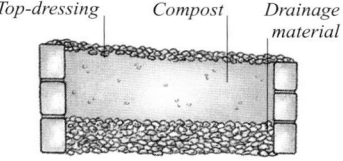

Top-dressing   Compost   Drainage material

A raised bed has a deep gravel base and free-draining compost.

SELECTING CACTI AND SUCCULENTS

GOOD EXAMPLE

REBUTIA

New buds forming

POOR EXAMPLE

Healthy growth

Damaged growth

GOOD EXAMPLE

Plump, fleshy leaves

Healthy, new growth

POOR EXAMPLE

CRASSULA OVATA

Shrivelled leaves

that is raised at least 25cm (10in) above ground level. To ensure good drainage make the bed slightly sloping and provide a thick base of gravel or crocks that is at least one third of the total height of the bed.

Never construct the bed on a concrete or other impermeable base as this impedes drainage. Choose a bright, sunny site with a minimum temperature of 5°C (41°F). In cooler areas, provide adequate protection for tender species (see FROST AND WIND PROTECTION, pp.612–613).

Preparing the soil and compost mix

Cacti and other succulents do not usually thrive in ordinary garden soil, because it is not sufficiently

well drained; it needs to be replaced by, or supplemented with, a carefully prepared growing medium. Good garden loam that has a pH level of 4–5.5 may be used as the basis of a homemade compost. It must be sterilized first, however, to kill pests or weed seeds that might be present, and to eliminate diseases.

To prepare the compost, mix 2 parts sterilized garden loam with 1 part peat substitute or fine shredded sphagnum or sedge peat, 1 part sharp sand or washed grit, and a little slow-release fertilizer.

If the garden loam is alkaline, use a loam-based proprietary compost mixed with sharp sand or grit in a ratio of 1 part sand or grit to 3 parts compost.

Handling cacti

Most cacti have sharp spines. When moving or planting them, either wear leather gloves or take other protective measures.

When handling spiny cacti, such as this Ferocactus, *wrap a loop of folded paper around the plant.*

Placing the plant in the bed

Remove the plant from its pot. Carefully tease out the roots, checking them for disease or pest infestation (see also p.345), and treat any infections before planting.

Dig a hole of appropriate size and place the plant so that its base is at the same level in the soil as it was in its container. Fill in around the roots with compost, and firm, making sure that the stems and leaves are above soil level. Top-dress with grit, to protect the plants from excess moisture and reduce soil water evaporation. Allow the plants to settle, then water, lightly at first, gradually increasing the amount until the plants are well established and producing new growth.

PLANTING IN A BED OUTDOORS

1 *To plant out a cactus (*here Espostoa lanata*), dig a hole large enough to accommodate the root ball in a prepared, well-drained bed. Allow space for the development of the plant and those around it. Then remove the cactus from the pot.*

2 *Gently tease out the roots and place the cactus in the hole at the same depth as it was in the pot. Firm the compost around the roots.*

3 *Top-dress with a 5mm (¼in) layer of clean 3mm (⅛in) grit. Water after 2–3 days when the plant has settled.*

Succulents in containers

A collection of cacti and other succulents grown in pots, bowls, or troughs provides an attractive focal point on a patio or windowsill.

Preparing the potting compost

The compost used should be well-drained and preferably slightly acid with a pH of 5.5–6.5. Use 1 part sand or grit to either 3 parts loam-based compost or 2 parts loamless compost.

A slightly more acid potting compost may be required for epiphytic succulents, such as certain *Hoya*, and cacti – *Rhipsalis* and *Schlumbergera* in particular – native to forest areas. Mix 1 part humus (such as peat substitute, sphagnum peat, or leaf mould) with 2 parts standard potting compost; add sufficient sand or grit to ensure adequate drainage.

Choosing the container

Both clay and plastic containers are suitable for growing cacti and other succulents. Potting compost in plastic pots retains moisture longer than that in clay ones, which means that the plants need less frequent watering, but clay pots provide better aeration around the roots. Choose containers that have one or more holes in the base to ensure that water drains away quickly. The size of pot or container should always be proportionate to the size of the plant but never less than 10cm (4in) deep; for tuberous-rooted species such as *Echinocereus*, a pot with a depth of at least 15cm (6in) is preferable.

Planting in containers

Always wash thoroughly all containers before use to remove possible sources of infection. Place a layer of drainage material (washed gravel or broken crocks) in the base, to approximately one third of the depth of the container; large troughs as well as deep bell- or urn-shaped pots need at least an 8cm (3in) base of gravel or crocks to ensure sufficiently sharp drainage. Fill the container with compost to within 1cm (½in) of the rim.

Carefully remove the plant from its pot, discarding any top-dressing and loosening the root ball. Insert it into the new container so that the plant is at the same level in the compost as it was in the original pot. Firm it into the compost, and top-dress with coarse gravel or with grit.

When planting several cacti or other succulents in one container, space the plants so that there is room for them to develop. To create a more natural effect, decorative pieces of rock or pebbles may be added to the composition.

Allow the plants to settle for a few days before watering; water routinely (see p.345) only when the plants are well established.

Hanging baskets

To create an attractive and slightly unusual feature, plant trailing succulent species in a hanging basket. Make sure that the basket is completely clean. Wire baskets should be lined with a proprietary liner or a layer of sphagnum moss. Do not line the basket with plastic sheeting, since this restricts drainage. If using a plastic basket that has a fixed drainage tray, place a layer of small pebbles or gravel in the base instead of sphagnum moss.

Fill the basket with an appropriate potting compost, without disturbing the moss or pebbles, then insert the plants in the same way as for other containers. Do not overcrowd the basket, as most suitable species have a naturally spreading or pendent habit; one plant is often sufficient to fill an average-sized basket. Top-dress with gravel or grit if extra drainage is required; allow to settle for a few days before watering. Once the plant is established and showing new growth, routine watering may be applied (see p.345).

PLANTING IN A BOWL

Crassula ovata
Cereus peruvianus
Mammillaria muehlenpfordtii
Aloe 'Black Gem'
Mammillaria polythele

1 *Select a group of plants that have similar cultivation requirements. Arrange the group by positioning the pots in the container, placing the taller plants at the back or in the centre of the planting.*

2 *Prepare the container, placing a shallow layer of drainage material – gravel or crocks – in the base and covering this with a layer of compost (1 part sharp sand, 3 parts loam-based potting compost).*

3 *Remove the plants from their pots, place them in the container, and infill with compost.*

4 *Top-dress the planted container with a 5mm (¼in) layer of 3mm (⅛in) gravel.*

PLANTING IN A HANGING BASKET

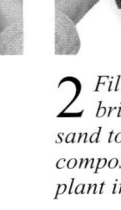
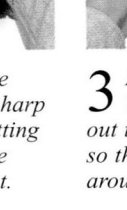
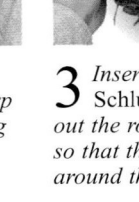

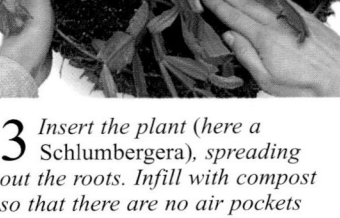
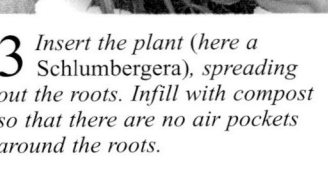
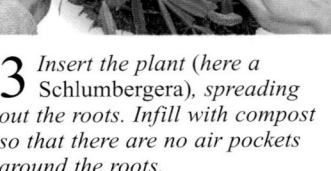

1 *Line a wire hanging basket with a layer of moist sphagnum moss. The layer should be 3cm (1¼in) thick when compressed.*

2 *Fill the basket almost to the brim with a mix of 1 part sharp sand to 3 parts loam-based potting compost. Prepare a hole for the plant in the centre of the basket.*

3 *Insert the plant (here a Schlumbergera), spreading out the roots. Infill with compost so that there are no air pockets around the roots.*

4 *Wait for 2–3 days after planting before watering the finished basket.*

Routine care

CACTI and other succulents need little maintenance in order to thrive, but they must have adequate light, warmth, and ventilation. Feed and water as appropriate for the particular species, and check regularly for signs of diseases or pests. Repot plants in containers as soon as they outgrow them, to prevent them from becoming pot-bound.

The right environment

Place cacti and other succulents in a position appropriate to their cultural needs. Most species need full sun, although some prefer dappled shade. The maximum daytime temperature in spring and summer should be 27–30°C (81–6°F), and the night-time temperature 13–19°C (55–66°F). During the dormant season, most plants should be kept at a temperature of at least 7–10°C (45–50°F), although species from the tropics and equatorial regions may require a warmer environment, with a minimum temperature range of 13–19°C (55–66°F).

Ventilation

Good ventilation is essential, although cacti and other succulents should not be exposed to draughts. For plants grown in a greenhouse it may become necessary to use blinds or to apply proprietary shading paint to the outside of the glass, if ventilation is insufficient to keep the temperature below 27–30°C (81–6°F) (see "Shading", p.576). In exceptionally hot weather, watering the greenhouse floor will help to reduce the temperature. Occasionally, plants grown in the open may need some shade to protect them in conditions of extreme heat.

Watering and feeding

Water only when the plants are in active growth (not during their resting period). For most cacti and other succulents this is in summer, but epiphytes and succulents from forested areas bloom principally between late autumn and early spring. In the dormant season, do not water unless temperatures remain high, and then only enough to prevent complete dehydration.

Watering

During the growing season, moisten the soil or potting compost thoroughly with water, allowing it almost to dry out before watering again. Provided that the plants are grown in a free-draining medium, surplus moisture drains away quickly.

Water early in the day or in the late evening, as the plants may scorch if they are covered in water droplets in bright sunshine. Alternatively, plants that are grown in pots may be watered by placing the container in a shallow pan of water, so that the water permeates the compost but does not touch the stems or leaves. Remove the container from the water to drain as soon as the surface of the compost appears moist; the plants will rot if left standing in water.

Epiphytic plants and those that need shaded conditions should be kept moist but not wet: an occasional, light mist-spray maintains a reasonable level of humidity.

Feeding

During the growing season, feed cacti and other succulents to help maintain healthy, vigorous growth and to encourage flowering. Several proprietary fertilizers are available but a standard, well-balanced liquid fertilizer containing all the major nutrients is satisfactory. Apply every two to three weeks during the growing season. Never apply fertilizer when a plant is dormant or the soil is dry, because this may damage the stems and foliage.

Hygiene

Cacti and other succulents may need occasional cleaning, as dust sometimes accumulates on the leaves or between the spines. During the growing season, house plants may be sprayed lightly with water; succulents in the greenhouse or garden may be hosed down carefully, provided that they are not in direct sun.

Pests and diseases

Check cacti and other succulents routinely for pests and diseases. The most prevalent pests are mealybugs (p.646), scale insects (p.648), red spider mite (p.646), root mealybugs (see "Mealybugs", p.646), and sciarid flies (see "Fungus gnats or sciarid flies", p.666).

Diseases of cacti and succulents are rare, although poor cultural conditions or excess nitrogen in the soil may encourage the development of black rot, which principally affects epiphytic cacti and *Stapelia*. The plants become disfigured and may die. There is no treatment, so, if it appears that a plant is likely to die as a result of infection, take healthy shoots or sections as cuttings and grow them on to replace the diseased plant.

Repotting

Cacti and other succulents should be repotted as soon as the roots reach the sides of their pot – usually every two to three years for fast-growing species. Repot slower-growing plants every three to four years, even if they have not yet outgrown their pot.

Carefully remove the plant from its original container. Inspect the roots, looking for signs of pests or disease, and treat if appropriate. Cut out any roots that are dehydrated or dead, and dust the remainder with fungicide. Choose a new container one size larger than the original, and repot in fresh compost, ensuring the planting depth is the same.

REPOTTING SUCCULENTS

1 *When a succulent (here Aloe arborescens) has outgrown its container, repot it, selecting a container that is at least one size larger than the current one. Carefully slide the plant out of its pot.*

2 *Gently tease out any roots that have become coiled or compressed.*

3 *Place some crocks and a little compost in the new pot. Position the plant at the same depth as it was in the previous container.*

4 *Carefully infill around the root ball with more compost. As you add the compost, firm it in stages to eliminate any air pockets between the roots. Wait until the plant is settled in the new pot before watering.*

Propagation

Cacti and other succulents may be propagated from seed, from leaf or stem cuttings, by division, or by grafting. Division and cuttings are the easiest methods. Raising plants from seed is slower and more difficult but provides the opportunity to obtain selected variants from within species, and to raise new hybrids by hand pollination. Grafting is useful for rare species and hybrids, and for those slow-growing succulents that are difficult to propagate by other methods.

Propagating plants from seed

Seeds of cacti and other succulents vary widely in shape and size, and some have special requirements. Some fine seeds are slow to germinate, while some of the larger ones have a thick coating (eg those of several *Opuntia* species) and seldom germinate unless they have been stratified – they should be placed in a refrigerator for 48 hours.

Sowing

Sow seed under cover between late winter and late spring. Place a layer of coarse gravel, combined with a sprinkling of charcoal chippings, in the base of a seed tray or pot. Fill to the top with seed compost, then level and firm lightly.

Sprinkle fine seeds evenly over the surface, barely cover with sterilized, sharp sand or a sand and grit mix, then water lightly. Larger seeds should be pressed into the compost, allowing ample space between them, and covered with coarse sand or grit. Stand pots or trays of larger seeds in tepid water and leave them until the

upper surface of the soil is moist, then remove the containers and let the surplus moisture drain.

Place the containers in a propagator, maintaining a temperature of 21°C (70°F). Alternatively, seeds in pots may be sealed in a clear plastic bag. Keep the seeds in partial shade until they have germinated.

Care of seedlings

When the seedlings appear, remove the pots from the plastic bags or the propagator and provide additional ventilation. Spray the seedlings with fungicide to discourage damping off (see p.664). Maintain a temperature of 21°C (70°F), giving further light and air as the seedlings develop.

Pricking out

After six to twelve months (depending on the species), when the seedlings are at least thumbnail-sized, prick them out into a seed tray or, if substantial (as below), singly into small pots. Prepare the pot with a layer of crocks and fill almost to the brim with compost, then firm gently.

PROPAGATION FROM SEED

1 *Cover the base of the pot with crocks, then add at least 1cm (1/2in) of coarse gravel mixed with a little charcoal.*

2 *Fill the container to the brim with fresh seed compost, then level with a suitably shaped presser board to 1cm (1/2in) below the rim.*

3 *Sprinkle fine seeds evenly over the surface of the potting compost, tapping the seed packet side with a finger.*

4 *Cover the seeds with a top-dressing of sterilized, fine gritty sand – only a very thin layer is required. Water lightly.*

5 *Label and place the pot in a plastic bag. Keep in partial shade, at a minimum temperature of 21°C (70°F).*

SOWING LARGE SEED

Press each seed into the compost, sowing at twice the seed's own depth. Space seeds about 1cm (1/2in) apart, so that they have room to develop.

PRICKING OUT SEEDLINGS INTO INDIVIDUAL POTS

1 *When the seedlings are thumbnail-sized or larger, lift a clump from the pot, taking care not to damage the roots.*

2 *Divide the clump into individual small plants, retaining as much compost as possible around the roots (see inset).*

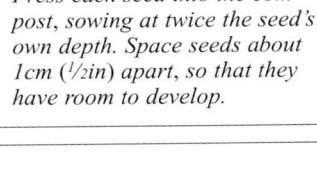

3 *Insert each seedling into a tray or pot containing 3 parts cactus compost to 1 part gritty sand. Keep the top-growth clear of the compost.*

4 *Top-dress with a 5mm (1/4in) layer of 3mm (1/8in) gravel, and label. Do not water the seedlings for 3 or 4 days.*

Remove a group of seedlings and separate them out carefully. Plant out the seedlings singly, top-dress them with a thin layer of gravel, and then label each pot. Keep the young plants at a minimum temperature of 15°C (59°F). After a few days, water them, sparingly at first, but then gradually increasing the amount until, after three weeks, the normal watering routine may be followed (see p.345).

Leaf cuttings

Some succulent plants, for example many species of *Crassula* and *Echeveria*, may be propagated from leaf cuttings. These should be taken from the parent plant in spring or early summer when there is plenty of new growth.

Choose firm, fleshy leaves and remove them carefully from the parent plant. Sever them with a sharp knife or pull them gently downwards, ensuring that a small piece of stem remains attached to the base of each. Put the severed cuttings on a clean piece of paper and place them in partial shade at a minimum temperature of 10°C (50°F). Leave them for a day or two until each one has formed a noticeable callus.

Fill pots almost to the brim with equal parts of fine peat substitute (or peat) and sharp grit or sand. Each cutting should be inserted in an upright position in a pot so that the stem of the leaf is just held in place in the top of the compost. Firm the compost around the cuttings with your fingers.

Cover the surface with a light top-dressing of gravel or grit to help keep the cuttings in position. Label the pot, and place it in dappled shade,

making sure that you maintain a regular temperature of 21°C (70°F). Keep the young cuttings moist by watering them every day with tepid water. Use a fine mist-spray to cause least disturbance to the cuttings.

Rooting does not take long, and normally occurs within a few days. Approximately two weeks after new growth appears, pot up the rooted cuttings into suitably sized pots, filling them with standard, loam-based potting compost.

PROPAGATION FROM LEAF CUTTINGS

1 *Remove a healthy leaf by carefully pulling it away from the parent plant. It should break off at the base, with a small piece of stem attached.*

2 *Allow 24–48 hours for the wound to callus (see inset). Fill a pot with equal parts fine peat substitute (or peat) and sand. Insert the cutting so that the base is just held in the compost.*

3 *Top-dress with gravel or grit, and label. When new growth has been developing for about two weeks (see inset), the rooted cutting is ready to pot up into loam-based potting compost.*

Producing hybrids

When growing cacti and other succulents in a mixed collection, cross-pollination may occur, i.e. pollen from the flowers of one species or cultivar may pollinate those of another to produce hybrid offspring. Sometimes these hybrids are improvements on other types raised and may be worth propagating. More frequently, however, they are not worth keeping.

To be sure of raising plants with the desired characteristics, it is

To produce a batch of hybrid seed (here from a Schlumbergera), *dust pollen from the anthers of one of the selected parent flowers onto the stigmas of the other parent, using a fine-haired brush.*

necessary to control the pollination process. Controlled pollination may be used to produce further plants of the same species, which retain the parental characteristics, or purposely to produce hybrid offspring from different species (which combine the characteristics of the parent plants).

To produce a new hybrid, choose the parent plants (usually species of the same genus) in an attempt to combine the best characteristics (eg leaf shape or flower colour) of both

parents. To prevent open pollination by insects occurring, just before the stigma appears receptive or the anthers are ready to dehisce, tie a small paper bag loosely over the flowers that are to be used. Transfer the pollen from the anthers of one parent flower to the stigma of the second parent by hand, using a soft, fine brush. Then re-cover the hand-pollinated flower with a paper bag.

Many cacti and other succulents are not self-fertile, and it is essential to cross-pollinate in order to obtain seed. If a species is self-fertile, however, cover the flowers with a bag, as above, to prevent cross-pollination by insects. A gentle tap on the bag is usually sufficient to spread pollen onto the stigmas within the flower and effect self-pollination.

As the fruits ripen they become soft and fleshy and may release seed. If not, slice the fruits open and leave them for two or three days in a partially shaded but warm position so that the pulp dries out. Then wash the seed to remove the pulp and dry it on blotting paper before sowing.

CACTI AND SUCCULENTS TO PROPAGATE BY LEAF CUTTINGS

Adromischus cooperi ❋
Aeonium arboreum ❋
Begonia peltata ❋,
  B. venosa ❋
Cotyledon ladismithiensis ❋,
  C. orbiculata var. *oblonga* ❋
Crassula, many including
  C. arborescens ❋,
  C. ovata ❋, *C. perfoliata* ❋,
  C. socialis ❋
Dudleya, most ❋
Echeveria, many including
  E. agavoides ❋,
  E. elegans ❋
Gasteria batesiana ❋
Graptopetalum ❋
Kalanchoe, many including
  K. beharensis ❋,
  K. daigremontiana ❋,
  K. tomentosa ❋
Lenophyllum pusillum ❋,
  L. texanum ❋

Pachyphytum oviferum

Orostachys chanetii
Othonna dentata
Pachyphytum ❋
Peperomia dolabriformis ❋
Sedum, many including
  S. hintonii,
  S. sempervivoides ❋
Streptocarpus saxorum ❋
Thompsonella platyphylla ❋
Umbilicus chloranthus ❋

KEY
❋ *Not hardy*

Kalanchoe 'Wendy'

Stem cuttings and stem sections

Stem cuttings may be used to propagate many species of succulent, including *Euphorbia*, *Stapelia*, and most columnar cacti.

Take stem cuttings or sections in early to mid-spring. The amount and type of stem material that is removed depends on the plant. Some cacti, such as *Opuntia*, consist of a series of rounded pads or sections that may be severed with a sharp knife at the joint or base for propagation. For plants that have flattened, leaf-like stems, for example *Epiphyllum*, make a cut across a stem to produce a section 15–22cm (6–9in) long. To avoid disfiguring the plant, remove a complete "leaf" at the point where it joins the main stem, and treat this as the cutting or cut it into several sections (see below). Most columnar cacti, and some *Euphorbia* species, may have sections of stem removed to provide cuttings (see below).

All *Euphorbia* species and some asclepiads produce a milky latex when cut; to stop the flow, dip the cutting into tepid water for a few seconds. Seal the cut on the parent plant by holding a damp cloth against the wound. Avoid getting the sap on your skin, because it can cause irritation.

Leave stem cuttings in a warm, dry place for anything between two days to two months to allow a callus to form, before potting them up in suitable compost.

Inserting the cuttings
Insert one stem cutting centrally into a prepared pot, or place several small ones around the edge of the container. The cuttings should be inserted just deep enough to stay upright but not too deeply, as otherwise the base of the cuttings may rot before they have rooted. Stem cuttings from succulents that bear true leaves, such as *Pereskia*, need to have the lower leaves removed before they are inserted, in the same way as non-succulent plants. Apply a mist-spray of tepid water occasionally, but do not overwater, as this may cause the cuttings to rot. Rooting normally takes place after approximately two weeks, although cuttings from some genera such as *Selenicereus* may take a month or more.

STEM CUTTINGS

2 *Trim the stem (see inset) below a node. Remove the lowest pair of leaves, if necessary.*

1 *Choose a healthy, vigorous stem (here from* Kalanchoe *'Wendy'). Make a straight cut, severing the stem as close to the base as possible.*

3 *Insert each cutting into a compost of equal parts fine peat substitute (or peat) and sharp grit or sand. The leaves should be just clear of the compost surface.*

PROPAGATION FROM PAD SECTIONS

1 *Sever a pad, making a straight cut across the joint, and leave it in a warm, dry place for about 48 hours to allow the wound to callus (see inset).*

2 *Insert the cutting into a pot containing equal parts fine peat substitute (or peat) and sharp grit or sand, and label. Once rooted, pot on into standard potting compost.*

Propagation from stem sections

Many cacti and other succulents may be propagated from a small section of stem rather than using a complete one. Use lengths of about 15–22cm (6–9in), depending on the species. For columnar cacti, remove a section of stem (below), cutting it off at the appropriate point; for cacti with flattened, leaf-like stems, cut the stem laterally into pieces (right). Then treat each section as a stem cutting.

COLUMNAR STEM SECTION
Sections of stem taken from some columnar cacti may be treated as cuttings.

LEAF-LIKE STEM SECTION
Stems (here of Epiphyllum *'Oakwood') cut it into sections and inserted with the end nearest the parent stem in the compost.*

Division of offsets

A large number of clump-forming cacti and other succulents, such as *Conophytum*, *Mammillaria*, and *Sedum*, may be propagated from offsets early in the growing season.

Clump-forming offsets

Scrape away the top layer of soil from around the parent plant to reveal the base of the offsets, and carefully detach one or more from the parent plant, as required, with a sharp knife. Treat any wounds on the offsets with fungicide, leaving them to dry for two to three days to allow a callus to form. Pot up undamaged offsets immediately.

Rootless offsets should be inserted into compost made up of equal parts fine peat substitute (or peat) and sand. If the offsets have already developed roots, use a standard potting compost. Use appropriately sized containers with a layer of crocks at the bottom. Pot up offsets separately and water them in lightly.

Keep the potted offsets in semi-shade for about two weeks at a minimum temperature of 15°C (59°F), and water them again after the first week. Once new growth appears, the plants should be potted on into a standard potting compost and the normal watering routine applied (see p.345).

Offset tubers

Some tuberous-rooted succulents, such as *Ceropegia*, produce small, offset tubers around the main tuber of the parent plant. These may be treated as divisions and grown on to produce new plants. During the dormant season, remove some compost to reveal the offsets and separate them from the parent plant using a clean, sharp knife. Treat the cut surfaces of rootless offsets with fungicide and

DIVISION OF CLUMP-FORMING OFFSETS

1 *Gently scrape away the top surface of compost around an offset. Cut straight across the joint and allow the wound to callus (see inset).*

2 *Using a compost mix of equal parts coarse sand and peat substitute (or peat), insert the offset just below the surface of the compost.*

3 *Top-dress with 5mm (¼in) of grit, label, and place in semi-shade. Water after 3–4 days.*

4 *When new growth appears pot on into standard potting compost, top-dressing as before.*

allow a callus to form. Insert each offset tuber in a clean pot that contains a mix of equal parts peat substitute (or peat) and coarse sand.

If the offsets have roots, place them directly into a standard potting compost. Top-dress with a thin layer of washed, sharp grit, and label. Place the pots in semi-shade and maintain a temperature of 18°C (64°F).

Allow the tubers to settle for three or four days and then water them regularly with a fine mist-spray. As soon as growth starts and some young shoots begin to appear, follow the normal watering routine (see p.345). Pot on into a standard potting compost as soon as the young plants have several shoots and have become well established.

DIVISION OF OFFSET TUBERS

1 *Scrape away some compost from around the main tuber and carefully detach offset tubers. Lift them without damaging the roots, if present (see inset).*

2 *Treat wounds with fungicide, and allow to callus. If roots are present, insert into potting compost, otherwise use equal parts of fine peat substitute (or peat) and sand.*

3 *Top-dress with a 5mm (¼in) layer of 3mm (⅛in) sharp grit. Label the pot but do not water for several days.*

Division of rootstock

Many species of Aizoaceae such as *Delosperma* and *Frithia*, some clump-forming cacti, and genera such as *Aloe* are readily propagated by division. For some cultivars of *Sansevieria*, division is the most reliable method of retaining the variegation, as leaf cuttings may produce plants that revert. Divide clump-forming cacti and other succulents in the early stages of the growing season.

Lift the whole plant from its pot, and carefully pull apart or cut the rootstock into a number of smaller pieces, each with a healthy bud or shoot and well-formed roots. Treat all cut areas with fungicide and pot up each section separately into standard potting compost. Label, water, and place in a semi-shaded position until well established.

Alternatively, cut away a piece of the rootstock without lifting the plant, and ease a section out of the soil with a hand fork. Dust the cut surfaces with fungicide and pot up as for offset tubers (see p.349). Fill any gaps that are left around the parent plant, using a standard compost, and water lightly.

DIVISION OF ROOTSTOCK

1 Lift the plant (*here* Sansevieria trifasciata). *Divide it into sections by cutting straight through the rootstock.*

2 *Discard old, woody material and any soft or damaged roots before replanting each new section.*

Grafting

Some cacti and other succulents, notably certain members of the Asclepiadaceae, such as *Edithcolea* and *Pseudolithos*, are slow to mature and flower when grown on their own roots. By grafting them onto established specimens of related species that are quicker to mature, they can be induced to flower in a comparatively short space of time. During the growing season the top-growth, or scion, of the required plant is grafted

APICAL-WEDGE GRAFTING

1 *Prepare the rootstock by trimming off the tip, making a straight cut through the stem with a clean, sharp knife.*

2 *Make a slender "V"-shaped cleft (see inset) in the stock, to a depth of about 2cm (³⁄₄in).*

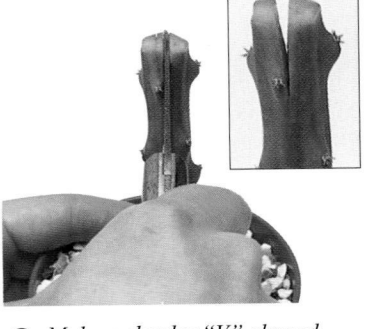

3 *Select the scion material and remove from the parent plant (here a* Schlumbergera), *cutting straight through at a node with a sharp knife.*

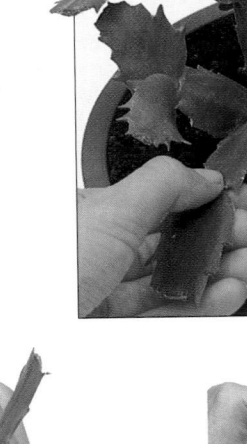

4 *Trim the lower end of the scion to a narrow wedge shape to match the "V"-shaped cleft in the stock plant.*

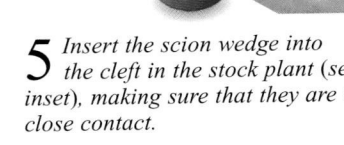

5 *Insert the scion wedge into the cleft in the stock plant (see inset), making sure that they are in close contact.*

6 *To secure the scion in place in the clefted stock, insert a cactus spine through the grafted area.*

ALTERNATIVE METHOD
Bind the graft firmly, but not tightly, with raffia or a weak clothes peg.

onto the rootstock of one of the more vigorous species. Three grafting methods may be used: apical-wedge grafting, flat grafting, and side grafting.

Apical-wedge grafting

Epiphytic cacti are often propagated by apical-wedge grafting in order to create an erect "standard" or tree-like plant. Use *Pereskiopsis* or *Selenicereus*, which are sturdy but of slender growth, as the rootstock.

To produce the rootstock, take a stem cutting (see p.348) of the selected plant. When this has rooted and shows evidence of new growth, it is ready to be used for grafting. Slice off the tip and then make two slanted, downward cuts into the top of the rootstock stem to produce a narrow, vertical, "V"-shaped slit approximately 2cm (¾in) long.

Select a healthy shoot from the scion plant and prepare it by trimming the lower end into a wedge shape to match the cleft in the stock. Insert the prepared scion "wedge" into the cleft so that the cut surfaces match as closely as possible. Secure the stock and scion firmly in position either by pushing a cactus spine horizontally through the graft or,

alternatively, by binding with raffia or a weak clothes peg.

Place the grafted plant in partial shade at a temperature of 21°C (70°F). The stock and scion should unite within a few days; once this has happened, remove the spine or raffia, dusting any holes made by the spine with fungicide. When fresh growth appears, water and feed as for established plants (see p.345).

Flat grafting

This method is used to propagate crested variants (succulents with atypical, often contorted, growth), certain other succulents with tufts of hair, and *Gymnocalycium mihanovichii* and *Echinopsis chamaecereus* as their seedlings may lack chlorophyll. Genera for use as rootstocks include *Echinopsis*, *Harrisia*, and *Hylocereus*.

Make a straight, horizontal cut through the stem of the rootstock at the required height. Then remove the rib margins with a sharp knife to form a bevelled edge, and trim off any spines near the cut.

Prepare the scion in a similar way, and position its base on the cut surface of the stock plant. Place elastic

bands over the top of the scion and under the base of the pot to keep the scion securely in place; make sure that the bands are not too tight.

Leave the grafted plant in a well-lit position, but not in full sun. Keep the compost barely moist until the scion and the stock have united (normally in one to two weeks), when the elastic bands may be removed. Thereafter, water and feed as for established plants.

When grafting asclepiads, the fleshy tubers of *Ceropegia* or the robust stems of *Stapelia* may be used as rootstocks. The former, in particular, make excellent stock plants for some of the Madagascan and Arabian asclepiads, which may otherwise be difficult to propagate.

Side grafting

This method is useful if the scion is too slender to be grafted onto the top of the stock. It is very similar to spliced side grafting, used for woody plants. Prepare the stock by slicing off the top at an oblique angle, then trim the base of the scion to match the stock as closely as possible. Secure them together with a spine or raffia and treat as for flat grafting.

FLAT GRAFTING

1 *Slice off the top of the rootstock with a sharp knife, to produce a flat surface.*

2 *Trim the cut surface to produce a slightly bevelled edge; hold the stem without touching the wounded area.*

3 *Cut the scion material, slicing through at the base. Bevel the edge of the scion (inset) so that it will fit closely onto the stock.*

4 *Place the scion on the stock and secure firmly, but not tightly, with elastic bands. Label with the name of the scion plant.*

5 *Place the pot in good light at a minimum temperature of 16°C (61°F). Remove the elastic bands when new growth appears.*

SIDE GRAFTING

If the scion plant is slender it may be grafted onto the side of the stock. Make a slanted cut in both stock and scion, place the cut surfaces together, and fasten with a cactus spine and raffia. Leave in good light at 16°C (61°F) until new growth appears.

CACTI AND SUCCULENTS TO GRAFT

Flat grafting
Alluaudiopsis ✹
Astrophytum ✹
Austrocactus ✹
Aztekium ✹
Blossfeldia ✹
Coleocephalocereus ✹
Decabelone ✹
Discocactus ✹
Duvalia ✹
Echinopsis
Edithcolea ✹
Epithelantha ✹
Frailea ✹
Gymnocalycium mihanovichii (and cvs) ✹

Gymnocalycium mihanovichii 'Red Head'

Hoodia ✹
x *Hoodiapelia* ✹
Lophophora ✹
Maihuenia ✹
Mammillaria ✹
Mila ✹
Nopalxochia ✹
Orbea ✹
Parodia ✹
Pediocactus ✹
Pelecyphora ✹
Pseudolithos ✹
Pygmaeocereus ✹
Rebutia ✹
Trichocaulon ✹ (most spp.)
Neolloydia ✹
Uebelmannia ✹

Aporocactus flagelliformis

Side grafting
Aporocactus flagelliformis ✹
Disocactus ✹
Echinocereus ✹
Haageocereus ✹
Hatiora ✹
Lepismium ✹ (flat-stemmed spp.)
Rhipsalis ✹ (spp. with rounded or angled stems)
Selenicereus ✹
Weberocereus ✹ (spp. with rounded stems)

Schlumbergera 'Gold Charm'

Apical-wedge grafting
Disocactus ✹
Hatiora ✹
Schlumbergera ✹
Selenicereus ✹

KEY
✹ Not hardy

CHAPTER

13

INDOOR GARDENING

THE GARDEN MAY be enjoyed in comfort, whatever the season, by bringing it indoors, with tender plants offering leaf and flower colours and forms as rich as those of outdoor varieties. Gardening under cover also opens up opportunities for creating different effects, from ornamental table displays of flowering pot plants, to leafy terrariums or bottle gardens. In regions subject to frost, a conservatory can be transformed into a small-scale jungle with the lush foliage and exotic flowers of tropical plants, guaranteed to brighten up even the dullest of winter days. Indoor plants are also highly versatile, and some require little maintenance when bought as design accessories that are displayed, enjoyed, and then discarded. Alternatively, the enthusiast may choose to grow collections of rare plants that demand more regular care and attention.

Displaying plants indoors

THE range of plants that may be grown in a home and a greenhouse offers a wealth of form, colour, and texture. Plants may be chosen for their handsome foliage or the beauty of their blooms, from the exuberant hues of bougainvillea to the cool elegance of *Zantedeschia aethiopica*. Others, such as *Solanum pseudocapsicum*, are valued for their brightly coloured fruits.

The choice of plants depends on whether the display is to be permanent, when plants with interesting form and foliage are the best choice for a year-round display, or temporary, when the seasonal interest of plants such as *Cyclamen persicum* may be used to give spots of colour.

Plants may reinforce or contrast with the style of the indoor setting, whether it is a rustic cottage kitchen or a formal and sophisticated urban living room. The plants may dominate the scene and give a room its essential character, create pockets of interest, or simply add to the detail. Whatever effect is desired, select plants that will both thrive in and enhance their intended position.

Foliage and form

Plants that have attractive foliage are invaluable for long-term indoor display. They may have huge leaves, as does *Fatsia japonica*, or a mass of dainty ones, such as those of *Soleirolia soleirolii*, syn. *Helxine soleirolii*. Leaves may have subtle or striking patterns and colours, as do *Calathea* species, or interesting shapes, for example the Swiss-cheese plant (*Monstera deliciosa*).

Foliage also has different textures, from the high gloss of the rubber plant (*Ficus elastica*) to the corrugated surfaces of *Pilea involucrata*, and the soft velvet of *Gynura aurantiaca*. Some plants are chosen for their strong forms, whether they are spiky bromeliads, graceful palms and ferns, or pebble-like *Lithops*.

Grouping plants

When planning an arrangement, choose plants with strongly coloured flowers or patterned leaves carefully, so that they do not detract from each other. Experiment with contrasts by placing plants together in shops, nurseries, and garden centres before making a purchase.

Architectural plants such as palms make very fine specimen plants or striking focal points in a group. Smaller plants have impact when arranged together on a tiered stand, but may be used singly as a dainty finishing touch. A tight group of identical plants, for example a bowl of white hyacinths, makes a strong yet simple statement.

A GARDEN ROOM
Yellow Abutilon, *blue* Agapanthus, *purple and white* Streptocarpus, *and lush foliage create a garden-like setting in which to relax.*

A CONTRAST OF STRONG SHAPES
Variegated ivy (Hedera), Dieffenbachia, Fatsia japonica, *and the sculptural fronds of* Platycerium bifurcatum *complement the very pale blue* Plumbago.

The indoor environment

The specific temperature and light requirements of plants are the most important factors in deciding where to position them indoors (see "Planter's guide to indoor plants", p.361). If the conditions are incompatible with the plants' needs, they will soon become stressed and unhealthy. Newly purchased plants that have just come from controlled conditions are especially vulnerable.

Temperature
Although most modern houses are kept warm during the day in winter, the temperature is often allowed to drop markedly at night – a problem for many house plants of tropical origin. Place these plants where they are protected from draughts and are not subject to wide fluctuations in temperature. Do not leave tender plants on windowsills at night, especially if the drawn curtains close off residual warmth from the room, or place plants directly above radiators or heaters that are in use. To flower, indoor plants need warmth, but if the temperature is too high for the individual species, the blooms quickly fade and die.

Light
Most plants thrive in bright, filtered sunlight or in a well-lit position that is not in direct sun. Plants that have variegated leaves need more light than those with plain, green leaves, but over-strong sunlight will damage the foliage. Flowering plants such as *Hippeastrum* need good light if they are to flower well, but excessive light can shorten the life of the blooms. Indeed, few indoor plants can tolerate direct sunlight.

Insufficient light results in plants with pale, stunted new leaves, and drawn-out, or etiolated, growth with long, thin, weak stems. Some variegated plants may begin to produce plain leaves. In time, the mature leaves will turn yellow and fall. A plant thus weakened is especially vulnerable to pests and diseases.

The amount of natural light in a room depends on the number, size, height, and aspect of the windows. Light levels fall quickly as the distance from the window increases. In winter, there is far less natural light than in summer, and some plants may need to be moved in response to the seasonal light variation – a plant trolley is ideal for this purpose.

If plants start to grow lopsidedly towards a source of light, turn them slightly when watering them. If light levels are too low for healthy growth (most plants need 12–14 hours of daylight per day) supplementary growing lamps are effective (see *A Growing Lamp*, p.577). These are particularly valuable when growing African violets (*Saintpaulia*), which need a long daylength if they are to flower continuously.

Positioning the plants

With a little forethought and planning, it is possible to find a handsome house plant that flourishes in almost every site indoors, from a brilliantly lit room to a dim passage or alcove.

The indoor setting
Give careful consideration to the impact of plants within a room. Are they in proportion to the room? A tiny pot plant is lost in a large space. Is the background suitable? Plain, pale walls show flowering plants to advantage. Does the flower or foliage colour blend with the decor?

High-level hanging baskets and shelves suit trailing plants, while eye-level positions are best for plants with delicate flowers or foliage. Train climbing plants, such as *Cissus antarctica*, *Philodendron scandens*, and ivy (*Hedera*), on a trellis or freestanding support to create a screen.

Use plants to enliven empty corners or space, such as an unused fireplace, which provides an instant frame for a display. Large plants or groups may play an architectural role as room dividers or as a link between the house and the garden.

Plants for various light levels
Bright, sunny conditions suit succulent plants as well as plants with woolly, waxy, or grey leaves. *Hoya carnosa*, pelargoniums, and *Ananas comosus* var. *variegatus* will also appreciate direct sunlight. In positions with indirect or filtered light, grow foliage begonias such as *Begonia rex*, epiphytic orchids such as *Phalaenopsis*, and *Spathiphyllum* with their striking, white spathes.

For corners that are remote from a window, choose ferns and tough-leaved plants such as *Chamaedorea*, *Fatsia japonica*, and ivy. Expose the plants to slightly brighter light occasionally, if only for a few days.

Kitchens and bathrooms
Temperatures and humidity in kitchens and bathrooms, especially small ones, can fluctuate, so choose plants that can tolerate extremes. Smooth, hard bathroom surfaces contrast well with the soft, feathery forms of ferns and grasses, and some *Cyperus* species. Bathrooms often have low levels of light, ideal for *Episcia*, *Nephrolepis*, or *Pilea*. Fill high-level bathroom space with trailing plants such as *Philodendron scandens*. Do not put trailing plants on top of kitchen cabinets since they may interfere with the cupboard doors; also the light levels high up are likely to be extremely low, so plants will become thin and straggly. In brightly lit positions, use hanging baskets to grow a selection of herbs or tiny tomato cultivars. Herbs are also ideal for growing on a sunny kitchen windowsill.

Tolerant plants
Attractive foliage plants that tolerate a wide range of conditions include *Aspidistra*, *Chlorophytum*, *Cissus antarctica*, and *Sansevieria*. Flowering plants are more exacting, but chrysanthemums (see pp.188–190) or forced bulbs (see p.231) may give short-term floral colour.

HAZARDS OF A WINDOWSILL

Too much sunlight, excessive heat from radiators, and draughts through the frame can weaken or kill house plants that are placed on a windowsill.

VARIATION OF LIGHT LEVELS WITHIN A ROOM

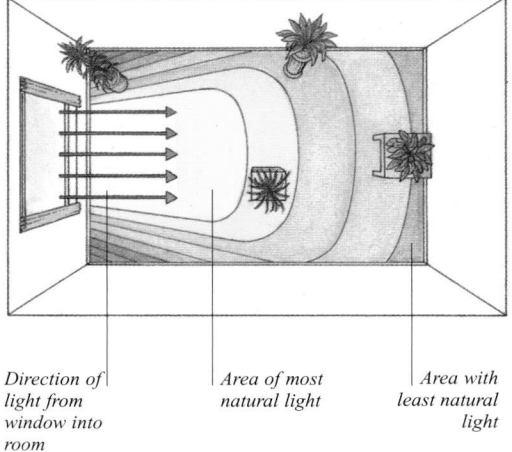

Direction of light from window into room

Area of most natural light

Area with least natural light

The farther away from a window a plant is sited, the less natural light it will receive. If the plant is 2m (6ft) away, the light level may be as little as 20 per cent of that by the window. Plants that are placed close to a window but to one side of it derive little benefit from the position, especially if the windowsills are very deep.

Conservatory gardening

A CONSERVATORY is often treated solely as an additional interior living room, comfortably furnished and usually ornamented with potted plants. However, plant enthusiasts may instead want their conservatory to be an enclosed extension to the garden; a protected environment that will meet the needs of more unusual plants. Incompatibilities exist between the two approaches – for example, the warm, humid conditions required by subtropical plants will quickly rot soft furnishings, books, and magazines – and many keen gardeners opt for a greenhouse (see GREENHOUSES AND FRAMES, pp.566–583) which can be tailored more exactly to meet the needs of plants. But there is no doubt that a conservatory is often preferred, and when a new conservatory is intended primarily as a place in which plants will thrive, it is worth spending time at the design stage to ensure that the end result is practical and successful in its aim.

Siting and orientation

With a greenhouse, the orientation and site can usually be chosen for maximum light and best growing conditions, but with a conservatory the priorities are usually where it looks best attached to the house, while at the same time conveniently connecting with a kitchen, passageway, or other living area. A conservatory in full sun all day needs generous through-ventilation; large roof ventilators, windows that open

A PLACE FOR PLANTS
The keen gardener will find that plants and potting activity soon come to dominate space in the conservatory. Make sure flooring and furniture are practical and resilient – popular conservatory materials such as wicker, rattan, and natural fibre matting of seagrass are particularly unforgiving of compost spills.

and doors that can be folded back in summer, coupled with effective roof shading. One oriented to receive only morning or evening sun, in shade during the hottest parts of the day, will suit plants tolerant of a wide range of conditions. If the best site is relatively sunless, this should not automatically be considered a disadvantage. The shade will encourage foliage growth and the conservatory will have a relatively even temperature, ideal for shade-tolerant plants.

Basic materials

Most conservatories have brick or timber base walls supporting a glazed timber or metal framework and a ridged roof. Shelves or staging may be needed to raise small plants to the light. Wide interior windowsills can be useful for pots. Unlike most greenhouses, conservatories are normally double-glazed, to retain heat from within the house. Because of its more robust structure, a conservatory will never allow in as much light as does a greenhouse, which should be borne in mind when selecting plants, especially if the conservatory receives little sun – tomatoes may crop better in a greenhouse, for example, or an oleander be more likely to flower on a south-facing terrace.

The most practical flooring materials are slatted and oiled hardwood, tiles, or stone, which are easy to keep clean yet tolerate the humid atmosphere generated by plants, and also water when damping down.

Ventilation

Ample roof ventilation is essential for successful conservatory cultivation. There are no precise formulae for calculating the amount of ventilation required, as it depends on aspect and the design of the building.

Roof ventilators allow upward convection of warm air into the roof to escape, and through ventilation works best when at least one-third of the glazed area can be opened. Greenhouse ventilators, hinged from the roof ridge, modified to take the weight of double-glazing, and watertight when closed, are effective if

ENSURING A THROUGH DRAFT
If the building is in full sun, double doors that open out and can be hooked back will considerably aid ventilation. As many windows as possible should be openable.

ROOF AND SIDE BLINDS
The traditional fabric, pinoleum, is made from woven pine "reeds" and provides 70–75 per cent shading. Satisfactory alternatives are stiffened cotton, foil-backed plastic to reflect the sun, and fibreglass mesh.

large enough. Electric or mechanical screw-jack openers should be used to operate the ventilators unless the roof is unusually low, in which case wax-operated greenhouse openers are suitable. See also GREENHOUSES AND FRAMES, "Ventilation", p.575.

Shading
Unless the conservatory receives no direct sunlight, shading will be needed to protect plants from scorching. Roller or concertina blinds are the most usual solution, fitted from the roof and supported by fine taut wires to prevent sagging. Internal roof blinds can be problematic if climbers are being grown, but while external blinds, as used on greenhouses, are practical they may not look appropriate. Side blinds fitted to windows and doors are used more for privacy than shading. See also GREENHOUSES AND FRAMES, "Shading", p.576.

Heating
Because a conservatory is sheltered against the house, it is relatively easy to keep warm and can often be connected to the domestic central heating. It should ideally have separate pipework and controls to maintain minimum nocturnal temperatures for plants, which may be greater than that desired in the house. If a domestic connection is not feasible, use a thermostatic convector heater. All types of heater are best positioned in a corner on the external, colder sides of the room, as are thermostats.

Underfloor heating, of which there are two types, is another possibility. The first uses electric cable or a small hot-water pipe snaking back and forth over insulation, beneath the

floor screed. These heat up the floor slab to provide even, continuous heating and are best used in a north-facing conservatory where there will be little direct sunshine. The second type of underfloor heating is trench heating, which consists of central heating pipes, usually finned to give greater output, set in a channel 30cm (12in) wide, placed around the perimeter of the conservatory and covered with a grille of plain or decorative cast-metal. Trench heating is more expensive to install than electric cables, but is more quickly adjusted; it is also easier to raise humidity simply by pouring water through the grille to create steam.

Humidity
Conservatories can become very dry, which will not suit many plants and will also encourage pests and diseases. Grouping plants together will help, as transpiration from their leaves will produce a miniature, moist climate. Trays of gravel or shallow dishes kept filled with water will increase humidity. On hot days, damping down – splashing water on the floor – will be necessary, especially as doors and windows will need to be open simultaneously to provide ventilation. Another reliable source of humidity is a wall fountain or, if there is sufficient space, an indoor pool. See also GREENHOUSES AND FRAMES, "Humidity", p.576.

Watering
Irrigation systems, although effective, are often difficult to disguise in a conservatory. Most gardeners rely on hand watering. The water used should be at the same temperature as

the plants and their compost. Traditional conservatories often had storage tanks inside, set in the floor. Water drawn from the mains or from an outdoor butt or tank should be left in watering cans or buckets for a couple of hours before use.

In a hard water area, watering will leave deposits of scale and gradually increase the alkalinity of the soil, which for many conservatory plants such as citrus, camellias, and gardenias will cause chlorosis and poor growth. This can be overcome by installing a water softener or by using rainwater collected from the conservatory's guttering into a water butt (see also p.614). Ideally a pipe should be fitted just above its base leading to a tap in the conservatory, and the butt raised high enough for the tap to be fed by gravity, or use an electric pressure-release pump.

PURPOSE-BUILT BEDS
This raised planting bed sits on an watertight, edged gravel base which can be topped up with water, increasing the humidity levels for plants such as bromeliads (here Neoregelia) *that enjoy such conditions.*

Displaying plants
Some plants are better grown in soil beds than in pots. Beds in the floor are rarely practical as they will interfere with damp courses, are difficult to keep clean (especially if pets have access to the room), and are permanent, making it inconvenient to alter the layout. Raised brick or block beds are preferable, and make gardening particularly convenient for the elderly or less able. Raised beds should be as deep as practical to allow ample root growth and have a waterproof lining, with a gravel base layer for drainage (see also "Raised beds", p.269).

Climbers can be grown on wall trellis or wires fixed to the wall and roof. Container-grown plants may be also trained on freestanding supports such as tapering wire frames (see also CONTAINER GARDENING, p.325). In a timber roof, fit long-stemmed screw eyes to keep training wires 15cm (6in) or more away from the glass. With a metal or plastic roof, self-tapping screws and specially made brackets are generally available. Make sure that climbers are kept well clear of light fittings.

Plant health
Conservatories have the same range of problems as a greenhouse (see p.375), but, because of the proximity to the house and the fact that a conservatory is used for people, the methods of control will vary. Biological control is effective for many pests if used at the right time (see PLANT PROBLEMS, "Biological control", p.642). Routine fumigation will be out of the question in most cases, as will the regular use of sprays. If these are needed, it is best to take the plants outside on a mild day, cleaning them thoroughly before treating. Allow the spray to dry before bringing plants indoors again.

A HANGING GARDEN
This temporary planting creates an instantly attractive, high-level feature.

Stephanotis floribunda

Ficus benjamina 'Starlight'

Solenostemon blumei

Gardenia augusta

Parthenocissus quinquefolia

Containers

Choose a container whose material, colour, and shape blends with the decor and shows the individual plant or group to its best advantage. The choice is enormous, both in style and materials, allowing a range of effects from rustic to ultramodern. The most unlikely household objects, such as birdcages, coal scuttles, cooking utensils, kettles, and urns, can be introduced to provide unusual and striking plant holders.

Hanging baskets

Hanging baskets are popular features on porches, balconies, patios, and terraces, but may also be an attractive way of growing indoor plants. Hang them in stairwells, from rafters, by windows, or from free-standing supports for an economical and colourful use of space (see also CONTAINER GARDENING, "Hanging baskets", p.314).

Arching fern fronds, the rosettes of epiphytes, and cascading habit of many foliage plants lend themselves perfectly to hanging baskets. Vary the planting during the year to take advantage of seasonal displays. In a winter arrangement, Christmas cactus (*Schlumbergera bridgesii*) provides a mass of bright colour as do fuchsias in summer. Temporary arrangements may be created by planting up a basket with pot plants, but they will need replanting each year. Permanently planted baskets are easier to manage, especially if devoted to a single, large plant.

Choosing a hanging container
Hanging baskets are available in various materials and designs. When choosing and positioning them, take into account the fact that most plants require frequent watering. Plastic-coated wire hanging baskets are practical indoors only in rooms that have water-resistant floors; some rigid, plastic baskets have in-built drip saucers which provide a practical solution. Also available are attractive, although heavy, pottery and terracotta hanging pots, and wrought iron, wooden, or wicker baskets.

A planted basket is heavy, especially when just watered, so it must be supported by strong rope or chain from a hook or bracket fixed securely to a ceiling joist or a solid wall.

Terrariums and bottle gardens

Terrariums are enclosed glass containers, often decorative in their own right, used to display small plants in the home. They were popular in the 19th century as a way of providing a suitable microclimate for ferns, but any slow-growing ornamental plants that need a humid atmosphere thrive in a terrarium. A selection of plants with contrasting leaf textures and colours is the most effective – avoid flowering plants because the dead blooms rot in the moist conditions. Terrariums may be built permanently into a window to house a lush arrangement of larger plants.

Bottles may also be used to create a diminutive landscape of foliage plants. As long as the neck is sufficiently wide to allow the insertion of the plants and routine aftercare, any shape or colour of bottle may be used, but bear in mind that tinted glass cuts out some of the light.

Indoor lighting

A display may be enhanced by ordinary floodlights or spotlights, or given dramatic contrasts of light and shade with uplighting or downlighting. Do not place plants too close to the light source, since the heat may damage them. Ordinary, incandescent bulbs do not significantly improve food production (photosynthesis) or growth.

Plants for the office

Introducing plants into an office not only brightens it visually, but may help to deaden noise, refresh the air, and create a less stressful ambience. In a modern, open-plan office that is air-conditioned and fully glazed, temperatures are constant, air pollution is minimized, and space and light are plentiful – almost ideal growing conditions. Older buildings with smaller windows and little climatic control present more challenging conditions.

Use self-watering containers, especially if the plants are sited near electrical equipment, or plunge several plants into a large container. Unless maintenance contractors are employed, ensure that responsibility for care is clearly assigned.

Suitable plants
Evergreen, shiny-leaved plants are as tough and tolerant in an office as they are in the home. The popular genus *Ficus* includes plants of every shape and size, from the lustrous, huge-leaved *F. lyrata* (stand it in solitary splendour in a large space) to *F. deltoidea* with its small, leathery-textured leaves.

Another large and impressive genus with handsome leaves is *Philodendron*, which includes climbers and trailers. The tenacious, long-lived Swiss-cheese plant (*Monstera deliciosa*) climbs slowly but will eventually reach several metres in height and spread.

Sun rooms and conservatories

The garden may be brought indoors, either into a sun room, which is a living space furnished with container plants, or into a conservatory, which is devoted principally to planting. In temperate climates, both may be used to give winter shelter to container-grown plants that spend the summer months outdoors; a conservatory may also provide the warm, humid environment needed by tropical and subtropical plants (see also CONSERVATORY GARDENING, p.356–357).

The high light levels usually found in conservatories encourage coloured leaves to assume intense hues, and plants to flower well. Scented flowering plants, for example *Jasminum polyanthum*, are especially welcome in a confined space, where fragrance lingers in the air.

Select plants that suit the conservatory's aspect and temperature, bearing in mind that glass structures can be costly to heat in winter and very hot in summer.

Create a lush profusion of planting by taking full advantage of all the available space: grow plants at different levels in raised and ground-level soil beds, in pots on the floor,

SEASONAL COLOUR
In this room, a white poinsettia (Euphorbia pulcherrima)*, carmine azalea* (Rhododendron)*, and Calamondin orange* (x Citrofortunella microcarpa) *add winter interest to a permanent framework of evergreen foliage plants.*

COOL CONSERVATORY

The foliage and flowering plants shown here are among the many that thrive in the cool, but frost-free, conditions of a lean-to conservatory to create a fine display.

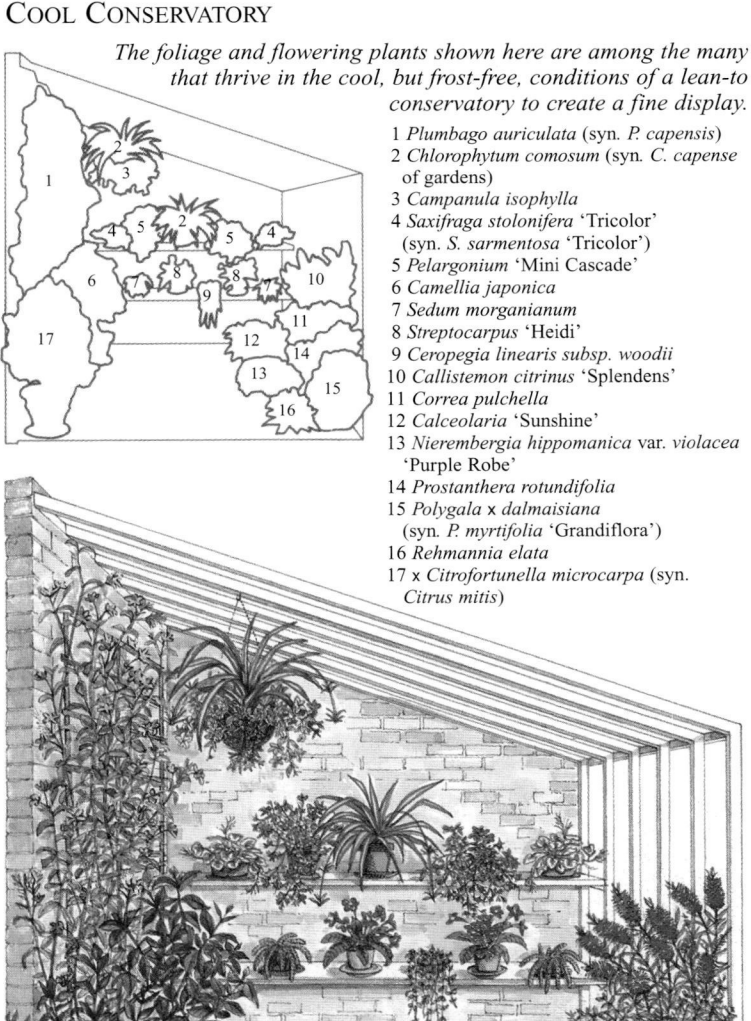

1 *Plumbago auriculata* (syn. *P. capensis*)
2 *Chlorophytum comosum* (syn. *C. capense* of gardens)
3 *Campanula isophylla*
4 *Saxifraga stolonifera* 'Tricolor' (syn. *S. sarmentosa* 'Tricolor')
5 *Pelargonium* 'Mini Cascade'
6 *Camellia japonica*
7 *Sedum morganianum*
8 *Streptocarpus* 'Heidi'
9 *Ceropegia linearis subsp. woodii*
10 *Callistemon citrinus* 'Splendens'
11 *Correa pulchella*
12 *Calceolaria* 'Sunshine'
13 *Nierembergia hippomanica* var. *violacea* 'Purple Robe'
14 *Prostanthera rotundifolia*
15 *Polygala* x *dalmaisiana* (syn. *P. myrtifolia* 'Grandiflora')
16 *Rehmannia elata*
17 x *Citrofortunella microcarpa* (syn. *Citrus mitis*)

MULTI-LEVEL DISPLAY
Staging, shelves, and floor space are used to maximum advantage in this cool greenhouse. Busy lizzie (Impatiens cultivars), Plumbago, and Streptocarpus flowers are complemented by a variety of foliage plants, including ivy (Hedera), scented-leaved pelargoniums, Hypoestes, Pellaea, and Tolmiea.

on windowsills and shelves, and in hanging baskets. Large tropical or subtropical plants and climbers that are free-standing are useful for training on trellis or wires affixed to the walls and roof. Use plants in the conservatory that complement those in the open garden; this will create a visual link between the two as well as a sense of space.

Indoor water features

A sunken or raised pool or a half-barrel may accommodate tropical water lilies or other tender aquatic and marginal plants. A simple and elegant water spout will provide the restful murmur of falling water and help to maintain humidity (see also WATER GARDENING, pp.280–303).

Growing plants in a greenhouse

The control of light, temperature, and humidity in a greenhouse will allow a much wider range of plants to be grown than in a garden that is subject to frost. It also extends the season of display and cropping from early spring until late autumn, or even all year round if desired.

Uses of a greenhouse

A greenhouse is very useful in cool temperate climates, where there is frost, strong winds, or excessive rain: it may be used for propagation; raising and growing tender plants or flowers for cutting; or for crops such as salads, early vegetables, and even fruit. Many plants grow faster under cover and fruit or flower more profusely than they would outdoors. Half-hardy plants may be grown in containers outdoors and transferred to temporary shelter in the greenhouse when needed.

Some gardeners grow specific plants in the greenhouse, such as auriculas or fuchsias (see pp.120–121), while others may hold a specialized collection of plants, such as alpines (see pp.277–279), orchids (see pp.368–369), cacti (see pp.338–351), ferns (see pp.194–195), or carnivorous plants.

The greenhouse layout

The traditional, free-standing greenhouse interior comprises a central path with waist-high staging at the sides and far end; wider greenhouses may also have staging in the centre. Staging (see also p.579) is essential; even if removed in summer for border crops, it may be used at other times of the year for raising seedlings, propagating cuttings, and displaying pot plants. Slatted or meshed staging is used for pot plants, to avoid pools of standing water and ensure that air circulates freely, particularly in winter.

For extra display space, use tiered staging, bench beds, or soil borders. If the glass begins at ground level, ferns and other shade-loving plants, and dormant plants, may be grown or rested under the staging. Raised beds are useful for displaying small plants, such as alpines and cacti, that are planted directly in the beds or in pots plunged into gravel or sand.

The ornamental greenhouse

Although a greenhouse is often used more for practical purposes than a conservatory, part or all of it may be devoted to ornamental displays. Groups are usually more attractive than widely spaced plants. Feature a single genus, for example *Streptocarpus*, or mixed plants and display them in a random pattern or as a landscape in miniature. Try to include contrasts of leaf form, size, and texture and control the use of colour, whether from flowers or foliage, to create a harmonious arrangement.

A lean-to greenhouse against a house wall may double as a conservatory. Make the most of the back wall by growing climbers, which need only a 30cm (12in) wide bed or pot. Paint the wall white to help to reflect light and provide a contrasting background for the plants.

The greenhouse environment

Essential requirements for success are adequate ventilation and heat, as well as shading in summer; piped water and electricity are also useful.

The temperature range of a greenhouse depends on its purpose, but there are four basic types of greenhouse: cold or unheated, cool or

The temperate greenhouse
Raising the temperature to 10–13°C (50–55°F), with a night-time minimum of 7°C (45°F), widens the scope still further. If kept in a temperate greenhouse, plants associated with the essentially frost-free climates of California, the Mediterranean, South Africa, and parts of Australia and South America may be enjoyed in harsher climates than they could normally bear. These include genera such as *Brunfelsia*, *Jacaranda*, and *Strelitzia*, and orchids such as *Cymbidium* species and hybrids. If zonal pelargoniums are kept at 9°C (48°F) they will flower all the year round.

The warm greenhouse
A minimum temperature of 13°C (55°F) to 18°C (64°F) in a warm greenhouse allows cultivation of subtropical and tropical plants, as well as year-round propagation or flower displays. Tender plants, for example many bromeliads (see pp.362–363) and a number of orchids (see pp.368–370), may be grown to bring indoors when at their best.

The warm greenhouse needs controllable heating throughout the year, even in summer in cooler climates. This incurs considerable heating costs in temperate zones. Equipment such as thermostats, double glazing, fans, and automatic ventilation, an automated watering and damping-down system, and shading help to control conditions and facilitate routine care. A warm section in a cool greenhouse is a useful, cheaper option; a warm conservatory, or plant room, is another possibility.

AN INTERIOR GARDEN
Where space allows, a naturalistic landscape may be created within a greenhouse. Here, foliage plants, including Cordyline, Eucomis, Justicia, *and* Phormium, *provide a lush framework that is offset by the colourful blooms of flowering plants such as blue* Agapanthus, *pink fuchsias, and white and salmon pelargoniums.*

frost-free, temperate, and warm. For further information, see GREEN-HOUSES AND FRAMES, "Creating the right environment", pp.573–577; see also "Planter's guide to indoor plants", p.361.

The cold greenhouse
An unheated greenhouse protects against extremes of wind and rain and is significantly warmer, even in summer, than outdoors. It extends the growing season by providing the plants with an artificially early spring and late autumn.

Most hardy annuals, biennials, and shrubs may be overwintered in an unheated greenhouse, and half-hardy annuals, bulbous plants, and shrubs grown on to plant out in summer, when the garden soil has warmed up and danger of frost is past. A cold greenhouse is also useful for raising seed and enabling an early start to be made with fruit or vegetables. As an alpine house, it may be used to provide the specialized conditions needed for growing alpines and rock plants in pots (see ALPINE HOUSES AND FRAMES, pp.277–279).

An unheated greenhouse does not exclude frost for more than an hour or two, so it is not suitable for overwintering plants that are not frost hardy. Sunlight, or even bright light, raises the temperature during the day, but night temperatures can drop almost as low as those in the open garden. In temperate climates, most greenhouses built against a warm house wall give conditions similar to those in a cool greenhouse (see below), but this will not prevent tender plants from being killed by a few days of really sharp frosts.

The cool greenhouse
Freedom from frost increases the range of plants that may be grown. A frost-free greenhouse is also easier to manage, since protective measures become unnecessary. Daytime temperatures of 5–10°C (41–50°F) and a minimum at night of 2°C (36°F) allow ornamentals to be enjoyed throughout the year.

In a cool greenhouse, hardy bulbous plants, particularly those with delicate blooms that are not noticed in an open garden, flower earlier, providing colour in late winter and early spring. Here tender patio plants may be raised and overwintered; house plants may be revived and propagated in warmer months; and winter-flowering plants such as the aromatic *Prostanthera* may be grown in bench beds or in pots. Grown under cover, chrysanthemums and perpetual-flowering carnations (*Dianthus*) provide a good supply of cut flowers, while hardy annuals raised from seed sown in late summer sowings give early flowers.

The cool greenhouse requires heating capable of excluding frost and maintaining a minimum temperature in all weathers (see GREENHOUSES AND FRAMES, "Heating", p.574). Even if the entire greenhouse is not heated, an electrically heated propagator, or a propagating bench, will enable an early start to be made on raising new plants in the spring.

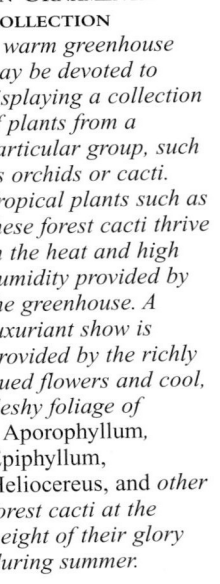

AN ORNAMENTAL COLLECTION
A warm greenhouse may be devoted to displaying a collection of plants from a particular group, such as orchids or cacti. Tropical plants such as these forest cacti thrive in the heat and high humidity provided by the greenhouse. A luxuriant show is provided by the richly hued flowers and cool, fleshy foliage of x Aporophyllum, Epiphyllum, Heliocereus, *and other forest cacti at the height of their glory during summer.*

Planter's guide to indoor plants

WARM GREENHOUSE

(Minimum 13–18°C/55–64°F)

Flowering plants
Aeschynanthus ❀ ◎
Anthurium ❀ ◎
Aphelandra ❀ ◎
Brunfelsia ❀ ◎
Columnea ❀ ◎
Euphorbia fulgens ❀ ,
    E. pulcherrima ❀
Hibiscus rosa-sinensis ❀
Hoya lanceolata ❀
Justicia ❀
Kohleria ❀ ◎
Medinilla ❀ ◎
Pachystachys ❀
Ruellia ❀ ◎
Saintpaulia ❀ ◎

Sinningia
'Red
Flicker'

Sinningia ❀ ◎
Smithiantha ❀ ◎
Spathiphyllum ❀ ◎

Foliage plants
Aechmea ❀ ◎ (and most bromeliads)
Aglaonema ❀ ◎
Begonia rex ❀ ◎ (and other spp.)
Calathea ❀ ◎
Chamaedorea ❀ ◎ (and most palms)
Codiaeum ❀ ◎
Dieffenbachia ❀ ◎
Dracaena ❀ ◎
Ficus, some ❀
Fittonia ❀ ◎
Maranta ❀ ◎
Peperomia ❀ ◎
Philodendron ❀ ◎
Tradescantia, some ❀ , ◎

TEMPERATE GREENHOUSE

(Daytime 10–13°C/50–55°F; night minimum 7°C/45°F)

Flowering plants
Achimenes ❀
Begonia ❀ ◎
Catharanthus ❀
Cyclamen, some ❀ , ◎
Exacum ❀ ◎
Haemanthus ❀
Impatiens, some ❀ , ◎

Impatiens,
Novette Series
'Red Star'

Schlumbergera ❀ ◎
Strelitzia ❀
Streptocarpus ❀ ◎

Foliage plants
Asparagus, some ❀
Jacaranda ❀
Solenostemon (syn. *Coleus*) ❀ ◎

COOL GREENHOUSE

(Daytime 5–10°C/41–50°F; night minimum 2°C/36°F)

Flowering plants
Abutilon, some ❀
Bougainvillea ❀
Browallia ❀
Brugmansia, some ❀
Calceolaria, some ❀ , ◎
Callistemon, some ❀
Cestrum, some ❀
Chrysanthemum, some ❀ , ◎
x *Citrofortunella* ❀
Cuphea ❀
Freesia ❀
Fuchsia, some ❀
Gerbera ❀
Hippeastrum, some ❀
Hoya ❀
Jasminum, some ❀
Lachenalia ❀
Lantana ❀
Lapageria ❀
Nerium ❀
Passiflora ❀
Pelargonium ❀
Plumbago, some ❀
Primula, some ❀
Schizanthus ❀
Senecio, some ❀

Senecio articulatus
'Variegatus'

Sprekelia ❀
Streptosolen ❀
Tibouchina ❀ ◎
Veltheimia ❀
Zantedeschia, some ❀
Zephyranthes, some ❀

Foliage plants
Aspidistra ❀
Chlorophytum ❀
Cissus rhombifolia ❀
Rhoicissus ❀
Ricinus ❀

COLD GREENHOUSE

Flowering plants
Agapanthus (hardy spp.)
Anemone
Antirrhinum (hardy spp.)
Camellia (hardy spp.)
Crocus
Cyclamen (hardy miniature spp.)
Dicentra
Erica
Erysimum (syn. *Cheiranthus*)
    (hardy spp.)
Hyacinthus
Jasminum (hardy spp.)
Narcissus
Rhododendron (hardy azaleas in
    shady greenhouse)

Foliage plants
Adiantum ◎ (hardy spp.)
Euonymus
Fatsia ◎
Hedera ◎ (hardy spp.)
Laurus nobilis
Phormium
Tolmiea

PLANTS THAT PREFER DIRECT LIGHT INDOORS

Warm room (18°C/64°F and over)
Ananas ❀ ◎
Bougainvillea ❀
Euphorbia pulcherrima ❀
Hibiscus rosa-sinensis ❀
Hippeastrum, some ❀
Justicia ❀
Opuntia, some ❀
Senecio, some ❀
Solanum capsicastrum ❀ ◎

Cool room (5–18°C/40–64°F)
Billbergia ❀
Browallia ❀
Campanula isophylla ❀ ◎
Capsicum ❀ ◎
Chlorophytum ❀
Clivia ❀
Crassula, some ❀
Cyclamen, some ❀ , ◎
Cyrtanthus ❀
Echeveria ❀
Gerbera ❀
Hyacinthus
Jasminum, some ❀
Kalanchoe ❀
Nerine, some ❀

Pelargonium
'Caligula'

Pelargonium ❀
Solenostemon
    (syn. *Coleus*) ❀ ◎
Streptocarpus ❀ ◎
Veltheimia ❀

PLANTS THAT PREFER INDIRECT LIGHT INDOORS

Warm room – medium light (18°C/64°F and over)
Adiantum, some ❀ , ◎
Aechmea ❀ ◎ (and all bromeliads)
Caladium ❀
Codiaeum ❀ ◎
Cryptanthus ❀ ◎
Dieffenbachia ❀ ◎
Exacum ❀ ◎
Howea ❀
Hypoestes ❀
Kohleria ❀ ◎
Mandevilla ❀ ◎
Maranta ❀ ◎
Neoregelia ❀ ◎

Peperomia ❀ ◎
Pilea ❀ ◎
Saintpaulia ❀ ◎
    (needs direct light
    in winter)
Sansevieria ❀
Schefflera ❀
Sinningia ❀ ◎
Spathiphyllum ❀ ◎
Stephanotis ❀ ◎
Streptocarpus ❀ ◎
Syngonium ❀ ◎
Thunbergia ❀
Tradescantia, some ❀ , ◎

Pilea
cadierei

Warm room – poor light (18°C/64°F and over)
Asplenium, some ❀ ◎
Calathea ❀ ◎
Chamaedorea ❀ ◎
Cissus ❀
Dracaena ❀ ◎
Episcia ❀ ◎
Fittonia ❀ ◎
Philodendron ❀

Cool room – medium light (5–18°C/41–64°F)
Epiphyllum ❀ ◎
Epipremnum ❀
Fatsia ◎
Grevillea ❀ ◎
Monstera ❀
Platycerium ❀
Primula malacoides ❀ , *P. obconica* ❀
Schefflera ❀ ◎
Sparmannia ❀ ◎

Cool room – poor light (5–18°C/41–64°F)
Aspidistra ❀
x *Fatshedera* ◎
Hedera, some ❀ , ◎
Pteris ❀ ◎
Rhoicissus ❀

HYDROCULTURE

Anthurium ❀
Chamaedorea ❀ ◎
Cissus ❀
Codiaeum ❀ ◎
Dieffenbachia ❀ ◎
Dracaena ❀ ◎
Euphorbia milii ❀
Ficus benjamina ❀
Hedera, some ❀ , ◎
Monstera ❀
Nephrolepis ❀ ◎
Saintpaulia ❀ ◎
Schefflera ❀
Spathiphyllum ❀ ◎
Streptocarpus ❀ ◎

KEY
❀ Not hardy
◎ Requires high humidity

361

Bromeliads

BROMELIADS, the 2,000 or so members of one of the most diverse and exotic families, the Bromeliaceae, are a fascinating group of plants that can make curiously beautiful specimens for the home, the warm greenhouse, or conservatory. Most are tropical epiphytes growing naturally on tree branches and rock faces, clinging by means of anchorage roots. These plants obtain moisture and nutrients via their leaves directly from the atmosphere, often from mists and low, moisture-laden cloud. Others are terrestrial, growing in the earth.

Almost all bromeliads are rosette-forming, frequently with strikingly coloured or variegated foliage, and many produce flamboyant blooms. Their forms range from the long and graceful, silvery strands of Spanish moss (*Tillandsia usneoides*) to the imposing *Puya alpestris*, which holds its massive spike of tubular, metallic-blue flowers above a rosette of arching, spiny foliage.

Displaying epiphytes

Most epiphytes are displayed to their best advantage if attached to a section of tree or branch, simulating the way that they grow in nature. This method also avoids the risk of root and basal rot, which may occur if plants are grown in compost. Old, branched sections of trees cut to size

WRAPPING WITH MOSS

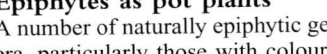

Position moistened sphagnum moss around the roots of a plant (here a cultivar of Tillandsia latifolia) *and attach them to the mount by binding the root ball to it with wire, string, or raffia. The moss must be kept moist at all times.*

are ideal. Attractive pieces of driftwood can also be used.

When attaching the plant to its display mount, it is usually easiest to start working from the bottom of the root ball. Move upwards, gradually firming moss around the roots and keeping it in position with wire, string, or raffia.

Bromeliad trees

If using an upright branch, secure it firmly in a deep container with cement or, if small, a strong adhesive. Alternatively, an artificial tree or branch may be constructed from a metal or wire framework covered in bark. There is a wide range of epiphytes suitable for displaying in this way, including many species from the genera *Aechmea*, *Cryptanthus*, *Guzmania*, *Neoregelia*, *Nidularium*, *Tillandsia*, and *Vriesea*. Use young plants if possible because they are easier to mount and tend to become established more quickly.

Prepare the plants by removing any loose compost from around the roots, then wrap the roots in moistened sphagnum moss and bind them to the support. Soon the plants will root onto their support and the binding may be removed. Some small plants may be lodged securely in crevices without being bound, as described for *Tillandsia*, below.

Displaying *Tillandsia*

Tillandsia species may be mounted individually or in groups on pieces of driftwood or cork bark, on rocks, or even on natural crystal. Lodge the plant in a crevice or press it onto the mount and secure with twine. Such airplants should never be glued.

Epiphytes as pot plants

A number of naturally epiphytic genera, particularly those with coloured foliage and the usually epiphytic species and cultivars of *Aechmea*, *Billbergia*, *Neoregelia*, *Nidularium*, and *Vriesea*, may also be grown as pot plants, provided that an appropriate compost is used. It must be an extremely open, porous mixture, high in humus and almost lime-free. For this, use half coarse sand or perlite, and half peat substitute (or peat). To ensure that any extra moisture drains away swiftly, add pieces of partly composted tree bark to the potting medium.

Growing terrestrials

There are several hundred terrestrial bromeliads belonging to the genera *Abromeitiella*, *Ananas*, *Dyckia*, *Hechtia*, *Portea*, and *Puya*, but one of the best known is pineapple (*Ananas comosus*). In regions where temperatures never fall below 7–10°C (45–50°F), a wide variety of terrestrials may be grown outdoors. *Fascicularia bicolor* may even be grown without protection in temperatures as low as 0°C (32°F).

Terrestrial bromeliads often have stiff, spiny leaves and a spreading habit. While they may be grown in pots as house plants, they perform much better if given more space in a greenhouse or conservatory border or, where conditions permit, out of doors. With their eye-catching foliage and strong outlines, they make a

---

BROMELIADS SUITABLE FOR GROWING INDOORS

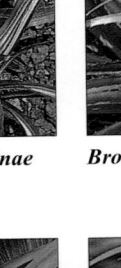
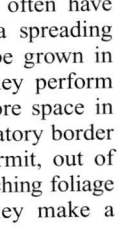
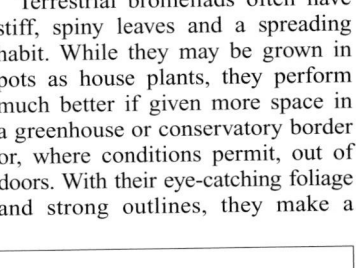

Tillandsia stricta

Tillandsia caput-medusae

Neoregelia carolinae 'Tricolor'

Bromelia balansae

Ananas bracteatus 'Tricolor'

Aechmea fasciata

Cryptanthus bivittatus

Nidularium regelioides

Guzmania lingulata var. minor

Vriesea splendens

distinctive addition to the garden, particularly if combined in schemes either with cacti and other succulents or with subtropical plants.

Bright filtered light is preferred by epiphytic bromeliads during the summer, while bright light with several hours of direct sunlight will keep leaf colour high and encourage flowering in winter and spring. Terrestrials prefer bright light throughout the year. Low levels of light and short day-lengths will usually induce a period of rest.

Routine care

As most bromeliads originate from tropical rainforests, they need warm, humid conditions in order to thrive; most need a minimum temperature of 10°C (50°F). In the right conditions they require little maintenance but, indoors, attention is needed to maintain the necessary humidity.

Watering
As epiphytes draw moisture from the air, they should be mist-sprayed once every day rather than watered conventionally; use soft water or rainwater when possible, particularly for genera that do not tolerate lime, such as *Aechmea, Neoregelia, Nidularium, Tillandsia,* and *Vriesea.* In spring and summer, add a dilute quarter-strength liquid feed of an orchid fertilizer to the spray every four to five weeks to keep the plants healthy and vigorous (see ORCHIDS, "Feeding", p.370). Provided they have adequate humidity, plants grown in cool temperatures can be encouraged to take a winter rest by reducing the frequency of watering.

Where plants are growing with sphagnum moss around their roots, the moss must be kept constantly moist by regularly spraying it with tepid water and also mist-spraying the foliage occasionally.

Bromeliads whose rosettes form a natural well or "urn" in the centre should be kept filled with water, particularly in hot, dry conditions. Change the water and apply a dilute foliar feed to the leaves occasionally Stop watering the "urn" as soon as a developing flower spike becomes obvious; this prevents detritus in the "urn" possibly causing blemishes to the flowerhead.

Propagation

Bromeliads may be propagated by vegetative methods or by seed. Most epiphytic plants produce offsets that may be removed and grown on sepa-

DIVIDING ROOTSTOCKS

Gently tease or cut the offset away from the parent plant (here Billbergia nutans) so that the root system remains undamaged.

rately, while stoloniferous terrestrial kinds may be divided at the start of the growing season.

Offsets of epiphytes
Many epiphytic bromeliads are monocarpic, meaning that the rosettes flower only once and then die. Before they flower, however, they form offsets around the base of the mature rosette. The offsets should be left in place until they are about one third the size of the parent plant. (If they are removed earlier than this, the offsets will take longer to become established on their own.) In many cases, the offsets may be removed by hand, but some will have to be cut off with a sharp knife, as close to the parent plant as possible. If the offsets have already developed any roots, these should be carefully retained. Replant the parent plant, so that it can produce more offsets.

Once removed, the offsets should be transferred immediately into prepared pots of free-draining compost, comprising equal parts peat, well-rotted leaf mould, and sharp, gritty sand, with their bases just held firm in the compost (see "Epiphytes as pot plants", p.362). Keep the young plants slightly shaded at about 21°C (70°F), and lightly mist-spray them with tepid water daily.

Offsets of the non-monocarpic species may be detached from the parent plant and attached to mounts in the same way as for adult plants. The offsets may have no roots, but these will soon develop if the plants are regularly mist-sprayed and if a few strands of moist sphagnum moss are fixed at the base of the rosettes to retain moisture.

Offsets of terrestrials
Some terrestrial bromeliads, for example some *Ananas* and *Hechtia,* have stoloniferous rootstocks that also produce offsets. At the start of the growing season, lift the parent plant from the ground, or remove it from its container, so that the offsets may be cut off without injuring the parent plant. Very often the offsets will have some roots growing from them and as many of these should be retained as possible. Replant the parent and pot up the young offsets in a compost of 1 part shredded peat substitute (or peat), 1 part leaf mould, and 3 parts coarse sand.

Raising plants from seed
Most bromeliad seeds are sown like other seeds, although it is important to sow them when they are fresh because, with a few exceptions, they do not remain viable for long.

A less conventional method is used for *Tillandsia* seeds, which are

generally "winged" for easy dispersal – much like dandelion "clocks". Sow the seeds on bundles of conifer twigs, such as *Thuja,* that are packed with well-moistened sphagnum moss and then bound together. Hang the bundles in a slightly shaded position, mist-spray them regularly, and ensure that there is free air circulation but no draughts. If kept in a temperature of about 27°C (81°F), seeds will germinate in around three to four weeks. Young plants may then be transferred to branches or other types of support and grown on.

PROPAGATING TILLANDSIA BY SEED

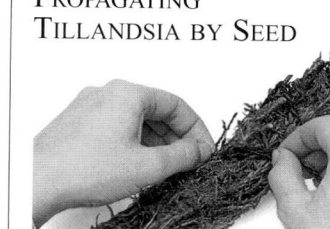

1 *Make a bundle of Thuja twigs interspersed with moist sphagnum moss, binding it with string, raffia, or wire.*

2 *Sprinkle the seed evenly over the prepared bundle; it will adhere readily to the moist moss.*

3 *Water the seeds with a light mist-spray and then hang up the bundle in position (see inset). Continue to mist-spray on a regular basis.*

PROPAGATING BY DIVISION OF OFFSETS

1 *When the offsets are about one third of the size of the parent plant (here Aechmea), sever them at the base with a knife. Retain any roots that they may have.*

2 *Pot each offset into a mix of equal parts shredded peat, decomposed leaf mould, and sharp, gritty sand, inserting it so that the base stays on the surface.*

Soil preparation and planting

STRONG, healthy plants, suitable for an indoor environment, are vital for success. Since pot plants grow in a limited amount of soil, it is important to use appropriate composts and to maintain nutrient levels in the compost with correct feeding.

Choosing plants

Most indoor plants are container-grown. If possible, check their date of delivery at the point of sale and buy those that have recently arrived. Each plant should be labelled with its full name and cultivation details.

Look for sturdy plants with strong stems, healthy foliage, and vigorous growing points; reject any that have weak growth, dieback, or dis-coloured, wilting, or brown-edged leaves. Choose younger plants, which should adapt more easily than larger specimens to new conditions. Do not buy pot-bound plants or those with dry, weedy, or moss-covered compost – they have been starved of nutrients and seldom recover fully. Make sure that the growing tips and leaves are free of pests and diseases.

Flowering plants should have plenty of buds that are just starting to colour. Climbing plants should be correctly pruned and trained. Do not

SELECTING A HOUSE PLANT

GOOD EXAMPLE

Vigorous, healthy top-growth

Strong stems

Leaves of good colour

Moist, weed-free compost

SOLENOSTEMON (COLEUS)

Label

POOR EXAMPLE

Spindly, unbalanced top-growth

Pallid leaves

Dry or weed-infested compost

buy tropical plants in winter, since sudden fluctuations in temperature may have damaged them. If transporting plants in cold weather, wrap them in plastic for insulation.

Positioning a plant

Place each plant in a room that provides the levels of temperature, humidity, and light that it requires.

Flowering house plants that are of subtropical or tropical origin flower poorly or not at all if kept too cool or in poor light, whereas many foliage plants tolerate cool and shady areas. Cacti and other dry-atmosphere plants need light, airy, and dry conditions; plants such as *Begonia rex* require more humidity. If conditions in your home are not ideal for a particular plant, a different cultivar of the same genus may be more suitable.

Potting mixtures

Always use good-quality, prepared potting composts for indoor plants. Loam-based composts are generally most suitable, because they contain and retain more nutrients, dry out less quickly, and are easier to re-wet than peat-substitute- or peat-based mixes. They are also heavier, providing stability for big pot plants.

Composts based on peat substitute or peat are often used for short-lived plants, for example *Primula malacoides*. They have little inherent fertility compared with loam-based mixes, and plants grown in them require careful, regular feeding. These composts tend to lose their structure in time, causing poor aeration and watering difficulties.

Lime-haters such as camellias need special lime-free or ericaceous composts. Other groups of plants such as orchids (see pp.368–370) need specialized composts. For further information, see "Composts for containers", pp.322–323.

Grouping plants

For ease of management, group together plants with similar needs for water, humidity, temperature, and

Plant supports

Various supports are available for house plants. Choose one that is suitable for the growth habit of the plant, taking into account its speed of growth and eventual size.

Plants with aerial roots grow well up a moss pillar; tie in the shoots until the roots penetrate it; keep the pillar damp by misting. Trailing or climbing plants with several stems may be trained onto wire hoops. Use a single hoop or several, depending on the plant's vigour. A balloon shape of up to eight wires is attractive, allowing good air circulation and access to light for plants with many stems.

Many climbers support themselves by means of twining stems, leaf stalks, or tendrils, and grow readily up bamboo tripods; they may need tying in at first. Single-stemmed plants need only a bamboo cane for support; insert the cane before planting to avoid damaging the roots. For details of support aids, see TOOLS AND EQUIPMENT, "Ties and supports", p.564.

PHILODENDRON SCANDENS

Moist moss

Natural direction of growth

Shoot pinned to moss pillar

MOSS PILLAR
Twine stems with aerial roots round a pillar, tying them in so that they are in contact with the moss.

Wire hoops tied together at the top

JASMINUM OFFICINALE

WIRE HOOP
Train trailing plants around wire hoops inserted into the potting compost. Tie them in regularly as they grow, adding extra hoops if necessary.

FICUS BENJAMINA 'VARIEGATA'

Cane

Plastic twist-tie

STAKE
Insert a cane into the compost before planting. Tie in the stem of the young plant.

TRACHELOSPERMUM JASMINOIDES

Tripod formed by tying 3 canes together with twine

BAMBOO TRIPOD
Encourage stems or tendrils of climbing plants to twine around the canes by tying them in.

light. If planting into the same container, ensure the potting compost is suitable for all the plants. In permanent arrangements, use plants with similar growth rates, otherwise vigorous specimens may swamp their more delicate neighbours.

To increase the humidity level in a dry, centrally heated building, group individually potted plants on wet gravel in shallow bowls or trays. Alternatively, place plants on upturned pots in a tray of water, with their roots above water level.

Plunging pot plants

Plants arranged in large containers may be plunged in their individual pots in water-retentive material, such as clay pellets, to reduce water loss and improve the local humidity. Clay can absorb up to 40 per cent of its own weight in water, so use a watertight outer container. Any plant that is past its best or too big may then be easily removed. Alternatively, divide (see "Propagation by division", p.378) and replant it.

Coconut fibre, bark, and peat are used as plunge materials, but plants may root into the medium, making them difficult to remove. Overwatering peat may result in waterlogging, which can rot the roots. Moisture indicators are useful in gauging when the plants need water.

Planting a hanging basket or box

Conventional wire baskets, with a 5cm (2in) mesh, make versatile hanging containers for a balcony, conservatory, or greenhouse (see CONTAINER GARDENING, "Hanging containers", p.314). A traditional, slatted, wooden orchid box is an attractive alternative; this can be purchased or easily built (see right). Where dripping water would cause damage, use solid or plastic-lined baskets or boxes, with integral drip trays or an outer container that has no drainage holes. Water these with care to avoid waterlogging.

While planting a hanging container, place it on a bucket or large pot to keep it stable and clear of the ground. Line an open-sided container with green florist's foam or plastic sheeting, to reduce moisture loss. Alternatively, use sphagnum moss; a plant saucer placed between the moss and the compost forms a small reservoir of moisture. Multi-purpose composts based on loam, peat substitute, or peat are suitable, although loam-based composts are easier to re-wet.

Plant the container in stages from the base. If necessary, cut the plastic to insert plants through the sides of the hanging basket or box.

SINKING PLANTS INTO A LARGE CONTAINER

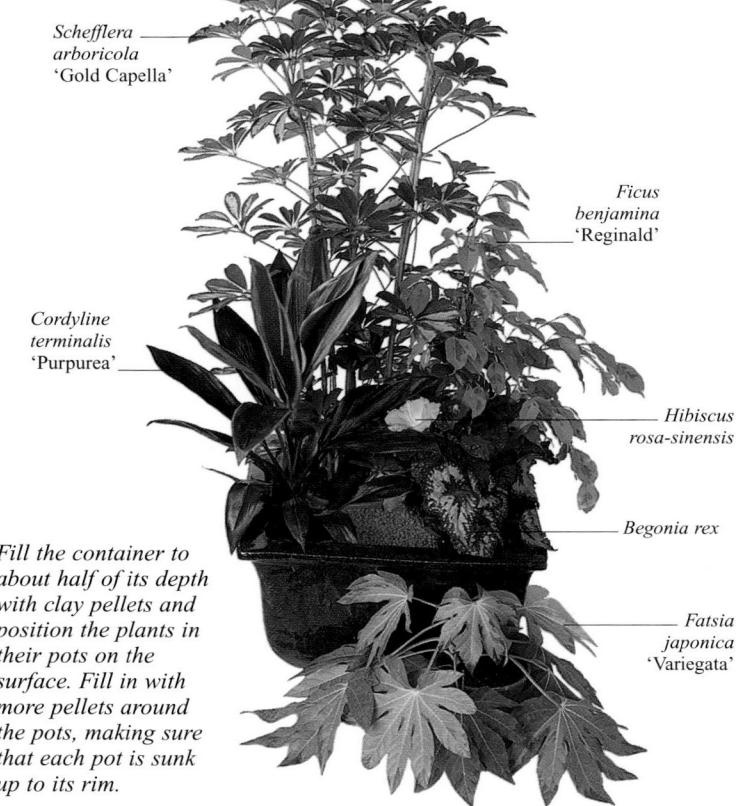

Schefflera arboricola 'Gold Capella'

Cordyline terminalis 'Purpurea'

Ficus benjamina 'Reginald'

Hibiscus rosa-sinensis

Begonia rex

Fatsia japonica 'Variegata'

Fill the container to about half of its depth with clay pellets and position the plants in their pots on the surface. Fill in with more pellets around the pots, making sure that each pot is sunk up to its rim.

HOW TO MAKE A SLATTED WOODEN BOX

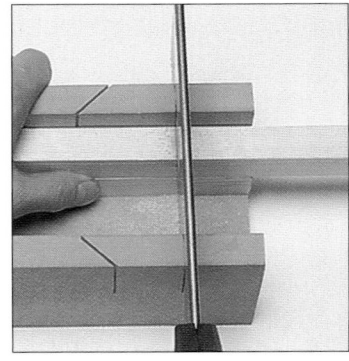

1 *Measure and mark 20 x 20mm (¾ x ¾in) timber into 14 side pieces, each 25cm (10in) long. To ensure a straight edge use a panel saw and mitre box to cut the lengths. Place one of the side pieces over an offcut of wood and secure to the workbench.*

2 *Mark drilling holes on one face of the side piece, centred on the width and 1.5cm (½in) in from each end. Drill the holes using a 3mm (⅛in) wood bit. Mark and drill similarly placed holes on the other side pieces, always drilling with the offcut underneath.*

3 *Cut out a 25cm (10in) square of plywood board. Mark and drill holes 1.5cm (½in) in from each side at the corners of the square, using the 3mm (⅛in) wood bit. Mark and drill 7–9 evenly spaced holes for drainage, using a 8mm (⅜in) wood bit.*

4 *Use pliers to cut 2 lengths of strong, plastic-coated wire, at least 30cm (12in) long. Working from the same side, thread each length of wire through 2 corner holes in the plywood board, then pull flush with the board.*

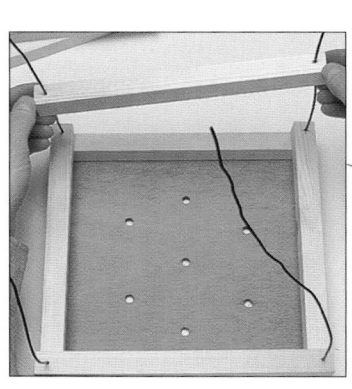

Creeping fig (Ficus pumila 'Variegata')

Blechnum chilense

5 *Make sure that there are 4 equal lengths of wire above the board, then build up the sides of the box. After threading the final side piece, twist each wire end around a pencil to make a secure loop. Cut off excess wire. Finish with a non-toxic paint.*

RECOMMENDED PLANTS FOR TERRARIUMS

Acorus gramineus 'Pusillus'
Adiantum raddianum ❀
Asparagus densiflorus
  'Sprengeri' ❀
Asplenium nidus ❀
Begonia 'Tiger Paws' ❀
Callisia ❀
Chamaedorea elegans ❀
Cissus discolor ❀
Codiaeum ❀
Cryptanthus acaulis ❀,
  C. bivittatus ❀,
  C. bromelioides ❀, *C. zonatus* ❀
Dracaena sanderiana ❀
Episcia ❀
Ficus pumila ❀
Fittonia verschaffeltii ❀
Hedera (miniatures) ❀
Hypoestes phyllostachya ❀
Nertera granadensis ❀
Pellaea rotundifolia ❀
Pellionia daveauana ❀
Peperomia caperata ❀

Pilea cadierei ❀, *P. spruceana* ❀
Plectranthus oertendahlii ❀
Pteris cretica ❀
Saintpaulia (miniatures) ❀
Sansevieria trifasciata 'Hahnii' ❀
Schefflera elegantissima
  (seedlings) ❀
Selaginella ❀
Soleirolia soleirolii
Stromanthe amabilis ❀

Fittonia verschaffeltii

Strobilanthes dyerianus ❀
Syngonium hoffmannii ❀
Tradescantia cerinthoides ❀,
  T. fluminensis ❀, *T. spathacea* ❀

Planted hanging baskets and boxes are heavy, so ensure that supporting chains and fixings are sound. A universal hook fixing allows the container to be rotated to receive an even amount of light.

Planting in a terrarium

Before planting, clean the terrarium thoroughly to avoid contamination with algae and fungal diseases which thrive in enclosed and humid environments. Choose a mixture of tall, upright plants and smaller, creeping ones and decide how to arrange them before starting to plant.

Since a terrarium is self-contained, it must have a layer of drainage material, such as clay pellets, gravel, or pebbles, as well as some horticultural charcoal, which absorbs any gaseous by-products and helps keep the compost fresh. A lightweight, free-draining, but moisture-retentive potting compost is the most suitable planting medium. Extra peat substitute or peat may be added to keep the soil well aerated.

Use young plants with root systems that are sufficiently small to establish easily in shallow compost. Soak them thoroughly before planting, and remove dead foliage. Insert the plants into the compost, allowing space for them to spread. If the terrarium is too small to accommodate a hand easily, attach a split cane to a widger to assist planting, and a cork or cotton reel to another cane to make a firming implement. Cover bare areas with moss or pebbles to stop the compost drying out, and water lightly before replacing the lid.

Once established, terrariums require very little or no watering (see "Maintaining terrariums and bottle gardens", p.373). If excess condensation appears on the glass, ventilate it a little until there is only a slight misting of the glass in the morning.

PLANTING A TERRARIUM

1 Plan the arrangement with taller plants either at the back (as here) or in the centre, depending on whether the terrarium will be viewed from the front only or from all sides. The plants used here are:

Asparagus densiflorus 'Sprengeri'
Stromanthe amabilis
Ficus pumila 'Variegata'
Selaginella martensii
Soleirolia soleirolii
Selaginella kraussiana 'Aurea'

2 Cover the terrarium base with a 2.5–5cm (1–2in) deep layer of pebbles and a few pieces of horticultural charcoal. Add 2.5cm (1in) of moist potting compost.

3 Remove each plant from its pot and shake off any loose compost. Gently tease out the roots, reducing the size of the root ball, to help the plant establish.

4 Use a widger or other small implement to make hollows for the plants, and insert them carefully, allowing space between them for further growth.

5 Fill in around the plants with more moist compost and firm the surface. A cork fixed to the end of a split cane provides a tamper of suitable size.

6 Using tweezers, place a layer of moss (or pebbles) over any bare areas of compost between the plants. This will prevent the compost from drying out.

7 Spray the plants and the moss lightly with a fine mist of water and replace the lid. The terrarium is now ready for display.

GROWING PLANTS IN A SOIL BENCH

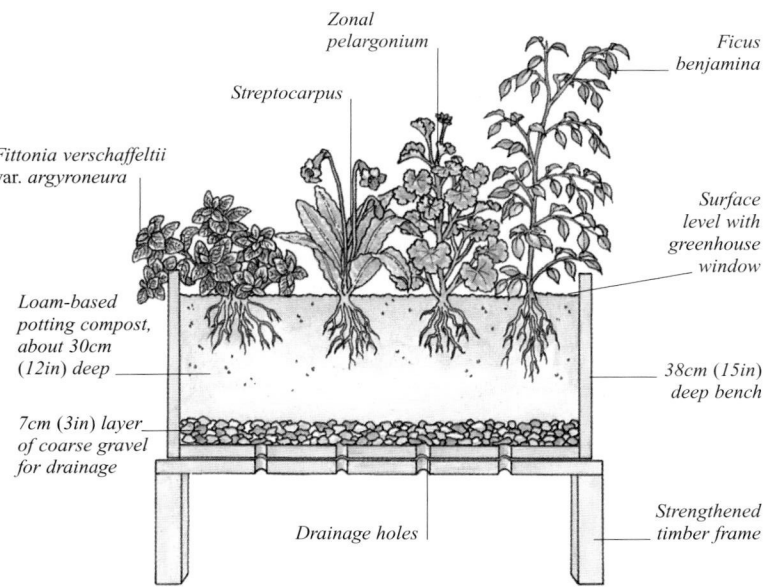

Zonal pelargonium

Streptocarpus

Ficus benjamina

Fittonia verschaffeltii var. argyroneura

Surface level with greenhouse window

Loam-based potting compost, about 30cm (12in) deep

38cm (15in) deep bench

7cm (3in) layer of coarse gravel for drainage

Drainage holes

Strengthened timber frame

Prepare the soil bench for planting by placing a layer of drainage material in the bottom and then filling the bench with loam-based potting compost. Plant a selection of ornamentals for a fine display in the greenhouse.

Soil preparation and planting under cover

Conservatories and greenhouses allow control of the environment, and extend the range of plants that can be grown in temperate or cool climates.

Soil beds and bed benches

Although conservatory and greenhouse ornamentals may be grown in pots, a large number, particularly climbers and woody shrubs, may be planted permanently in soil borders. For a new conservatory, consider at the planning stage if soil borders are needed. Raised and well-drained soil beds provide a good method of display. Prepare soil beds well, since ornamentals will be in place for some years. Make the beds about four weeks before planting to allow the soil to settle, and at least 30–45cm (12–18in) deep, with 7–15cm (3–6in) of drainage material at the base.

A bench bed is useful for propagating and raising different plants, and for specialized plant collections. Bench beds are shallow raised beds, usually at waist height, on supporting frames or pillars. They are ideal for small plants and for use with soil-warming cables (see p.580), mist units (see p.580), and automated watering systems (see p.577). Site the bench to make maximum use of available light.

Bench beds are usually built from aluminium or wood, lined with wire mesh or perforated plastic. They should be at least 15–22cm (6–9in)

deep and no more than 1m (3ft) wide for easy access. A 7cm (3in) layer of drainage material is sufficient.

Composts under cover

For soil beds, use a well-drained, loam-based compost enriched with organic matter at a rate of about 10 litres/sq m (2¼ gallons/10 sq ft). Do not use unsterilized garden soil as it can harbour pests, diseases, and weeds. No safe chemical soil sterilization methods are readily available to amateurs, and heat-sterilizing units, although effective, are expensive.

In general, use loam-based composts under cover. They contain their own nutrients and trace elements that do not leach out as readily as in less rich peat-substitute- or peat-based composts; loam-based composts are also easier to re-wet.

It is important to select the appropriate compost for specific purposes and for groups of plants with special needs. Most container-grown plants require a good-quality, loam-based compost that is free-draining and of approximately neutral pH. Tropical plants prefer more humus-rich, leafy soils, so incorporate additional leaf mould in the compost before filling containers or soil beds. Most ferns, heathers, and many lilies (*Lilium*) need an ericaceous compost, as do hydrangeas in order to produce blue flowers rather than pink ones.

Ornamental plants grown in borders need a dressing every year of 50–85g/sq m (2–3oz/sq yd) of a balanced fertilizer with a mulch of well-rotted compost in spring. If the

Planting a bottle garden

Bottle gardens provide an attractive way of growing very small, slow-growing plants in an enclosed microclimate. Many of the smaller plants grown in terrariums are suitable (see *Recommended Plants for Terrariums*, p.366).

Use any clean, plain, or slightly coloured, glass bottle, as long as the neck is wide enough to allow plants to be inserted easily. If the neck is too narrow to take a hand, make special tools, from split canes, loops of wire, and common household utensils such as a dessert fork and teaspoon, to help with planting and routine care.

With the aid of a wide funnel or cardboard tube, pour clay pellets into the bottle to provide a 3cm (1¼in) layer of drainage material and add a handful of horticultural charcoal to keep the compost sweet. Cover it with a 5–7cm (2–3in) layer of dampened, peat-substitute-based potting compost.

If the bottle is to be viewed from the front, use a widger to bank up the compost at the back. Level the compost if the bottle is to be viewed from all sides.

Begin planting at the sides of the bottle and work in towards the centre. Remove the plants from their pots, and shake off any excess compost. Carefully lower each plant into a planting hole, using tweezers, tongs, or a length of wire twisted into a noose. Space the plants at least 3cm (1¼in) apart to allow room for growth. Cover the roots with compost, and use a cork tamper to firm it gently.

Trickle a cupful of water down the sides of the bottle interior to dampen the compost, and cover bare areas with sphagnum moss to keep it moist. Clean the inside of the glass with a sponge fixed to a length of cane or stiff wire. If the bottle garden is not sealed after planting, water occasionally.

Hypoestes phyllostachya 'Purpuriana'

Asplenium nidus

Dracaena sanderiana

Saintpaulia cv

Hedera helix 'Eva'

Selaginella kraussiana

Hypoestes phyllostachya 'Splash'

Sphagnum moss

planting needs renewal after several years, remove and dispose of the plants, having propagated them first. Then dig in some well-rotted compost or manure and incorporate a slow-release fertilizer or base dressing prior to replanting.

In beds of ornamental plants, there is seldom such a build-up of pests and diseases that it is necessary to change or sterilize the soil. With crop plants grown in borders where pests and diseases may increase rapidly, the soil usually has to be replaced annually or sterilized if a suitable method is available. Crop plants are better cultivated in growing bags or containers, where the compost can be disposed of if problems occur. Always ensure that the bases of

containers with drainage holes do not come into contact with the border soil. This avoids cross-contamination by pests and diseases.

Planting

Always select plants that grow well in the range of temperatures provided (see "Planter's guide to indoor plants", p.361). Make sure that ornamentals or crop plants are planted at spacings that allow free air circulation and so inhibit the spread of pests and diseases. Position the plants to receive optimum light and ventilation for their growing requirements. Make full use of temperature, light intensity, humidity, and air-circulation controls that are provided in a well-built and fitted-out greenhouse.

Orchids

INCLUDED in the orchid family are some 750 genera, nearly 25,000 species, and more than 100,000 hybrids. Their exotic blooms and intriguing habit make them very desirable ornamental plants, mostly for indoor display, although some terrestrial species are hardy.

Terrestrial orchids

As the name suggests, these orchids grow in the ground, in widely varying habitats. Most of those that inhabit temperate to cold regions die down after flowering and exist in a resting state as tubers or similar underground storage organs during the winter. These hardy and near-hardy terrestrials often have flowers that, although individually small, are borne in dense spikes. Many are attractive plants for the rock garden or alpine house (see pp.277–279).

Some terrestrials, such as the slipper orchids (*Paphiopedilum*) come from warmer regions, where they inhabit sheltered sites, such as the forest floor. These remain evergreen throughout the year, but – because they are delicate – they need to be cultivated in a greenhouse.

Epiphytic orchids

Epiphytic orchids, which form a very large proportion of those grown by enthusiasts, are fundamentally different in their structure and habit of growth. As implied by their name (derived from the Greek *epi*, upon, and *phyton*, plant), they make their homes in the branches of trees.

They are not parasites (as they do not feed off the tree) but "lodgers": they take their nourishment from substances dissolved in the rainwater and from debris accumulated around their roots. A few orchids known as lithophytes live in a similar manner on rocks. In temperate climates, epiphytes need to be grown under glass.

Sympodial and monopodial
Epiphytes have two methods of growth: sympodial and monopodial. Sympodial orchids, such as *Cattleya* and *Odontoglossum* species and hybrids, have creeping rhizomes. Each season new growths arise from growing points on the rhizomes, and these develop into swollen stem structures known botanically as pseudobulbs. Flowers of the different sympodial species vary greatly, and

may appear from the top, base, or side of the pseudobulbs.

Monopodial orchids grow in an indeterminate manner. The stem elongates indefinitely, growing taller as new leaves are produced at the apex. Monopodials include many of the most spectacular orchid genera, such as *Dendrobium* and *Vanda*. These occur wild in warmer regions of the world, climbing towards the light through dense, jungle foliage. Most monopodials bear their flowers in branched, often gracefully arching, sprays from axillary points along their stems, from which aerial roots are also often produced.

Where to grow orchids

Some orchids demand fairly rigorous growing conditions, but many hybrids are bred for ease of cultivation, and can be successfully grown in the home. Before choosing which to grow from the vast range of types available, consider the conditions and care that you are able to provide. Many indoor plants need a slightly humid environment out of a draught.

While the hardy terrestrials (notably *Cypripedium*) do well in a rock garden or alpine house, others (usually described as half hardy) may also be grown in unheated conditions in mild areas. They include the cool-growing genera *Pleione* and *Bletilla*, which need only enough heat to ensure frost-free conditions.

A cool greenhouse, with a minimum night temperature in winter of 10°C (50°F), is suitable for a large number of different orchids,

including some *Brassia*, *Coelogyne*, *Cymbidium*, *Dendrobium*, *Laelia*, *Odontoglossum*, *Oncidium*, and *Paphiopedilum* species and hybrids.

An intermediate house, with a minimum winter night temperature of 13–15°C (55–59°F) will greatly extend the range of possibilities, to include species and hybrids of *Cattleya* and its relatives, and a wider selection of the *Odontoglossum* group and of *Paphiopedilum* species and hybrids.

A warm house, with a minimum night temperature of at least 18°C (64°F), provides the necessary conditions for species and hybrids of *Phalaenopsis* and *Vanda* and their many relatives, as well as the heat-

loving species and hybrids of *Dendrobium*, and many orchids from the hot and humid lowlands of the tropics and subtropics.

Choosing plants

It is best to obtain plants from a specialist orchid nursery, which can also provide valuable advice on suitable species for the conditions you have at home. Hybrid orchids are generally the easiest to grow, being themselves bred partly for vigour and ease of care. The species thrive best in environments similar to those in which they grow naturally, and these conditions are not always easy to re-create.

Owing to commercial techniques of mass production, orchids are no longer prohibitively expensive. For a modest price, plants that are attractive but have not yet won an award may be bought when you visit specialist nurseries and see them in flower. Least expensive of all are the unflowered seedlings that may take several years to come into bloom; the result is uncertain, but there is always the exciting possibility that one of the seedlings may be a future award-winner.

Cultivation

The unusual structure and growth habit of epiphytic orchids give them a reputation for being delicate and

RECOMMENDED ORCHIDS

Dendrobium nobile

Cymbidium Strath Kanaid

Vanda Rothschildiana

Paphiopedilum callosum

Cattleya bowringiana

Miltonia candida

COMPOST FOR EPIPHYTIC ORCHIDS

FIBROUS PEAT

The different components combine to provide the perfect growing medium: bark and peat substitute or peat retain moisture, grit aids drainage, and charcoal prevents the compost from becoming too acid.

CRUSHED CHARCOAL

COARSE GRIT

MEDIUM BARK

ORCHID COMPOST

difficult to grow. With a little knowledge, however, most of the difficulties are easily remedied or avoided.

Compost

Although most epiphytes can be grown in pots, their roots are specially adapted to open conditions on trees or rocks (lithophytes), so they cannot endure the close-textured composts suitable for most other plants. Orchid composts must drain very freely after watering; if they remain wet for long the roots are likely to rot. Chopped pine or fir bark makes an excellent potting medium, with some additions to keep the mixture open and prevent it from becoming sour. A suitable compost mix is as follows: 3 parts medium-grade bark (dust-free), 1 part coarse grit or perlite, 1 part charcoal pieces, and 1 part broken dry leaves or fibrous peat substitute or peat. A popular inorganic alternative to bark is rockwool, which is made from molten mineral rock fibres. Its porous structure provides the precise water:air ratio needed for healthy orchid growth. Specialist mixes can usually be obtained from orchid nurseries.

Terrestrial orchids also require a much more free-draining potting mixture than most plants. A suitable compost can be made up of 3 parts fibrous peat substitute or peat, 3 parts coarse grit, and 1 part perlite, with the addition of 1 part charcoal.

Potting

When a plant has filled its container, it should be transferred to a new pot a size or two larger to provide space for further growth. Choose a pot that will accommodate the roots and allow for one or two years' growth but no more; a pot that is too large for the root system is likely to lead to stagnant conditions in the compost. To assist drainage, many growers fill the bottom quarter of the pot with broken crocks, pieces of polystyrene, or large grit. This also adds extra weight to plastic pots, making them less likely to be knocked over.

Hold the plant with one hand so that the crown is just below the rim of the pot and place the compost around the roots, tapping the pot sharply in order to settle the compost. Use relatively dry compost, which should be thoroughly watered after repotting. The plant, especially the roots, should be disturbed as little as possible.

Some epiphytes do well in containers that allow more air to reach the roots, such as hanging baskets made of wire or wooden slats. Such containers are essential for species of *Stanhopea*, because their flowers grow down through the compost to emerge on the underside.

When potting on sympodials, old pseudobulbs of two to three seasons' growth that have lost their leaves (usually called "back-bulbs") may be removed and used for propagating (see p.371). Place the rear of the plant against one side of the pot, leaving space on the opposite side for the new growth to develop.

Support

Many flower spikes are sturdy enough not to need support. Others, however, require careful staking to look their best, particularly long flowering stems that carry many heavy blooms. Use upright canes or stout wires, to which the stems may be tied as unobtrusively as possible. Do this as the stems are growing and before the flower buds open. Avoid changing the position of the plants or the effect will be spoilt because the flowers will face in different directions.

Growing on bark

Some orchids that do not grow successfully in containers will thrive if mounted on pieces of either bark or tree-fern with moss at their roots, although they do then require a constantly humid atmosphere. Initially they must be tied firmly to the slab; nylon thread is ideal for this purpose. New roots will gradually appear, which will adhere to the slab and thus secure the plant.

Routine care

For successful cultivation, it is vital to provide orchids with their particular care requirements.

Watering and humidity

These are perhaps the most important factors in orchid cultivation. Watering should be frequent enough to avoid drying, but not so frequent that the compost becomes soggy – once or twice a week for most of the year is usually sufficient. In the summer months, plants may need watering every day, while during the period of short winter days this task may require doing only once every two or three weeks.

Rainwater is usually recommended, but drinkable tapwater is quite safe. Water plants in the early morning. Do not let water remain too long on

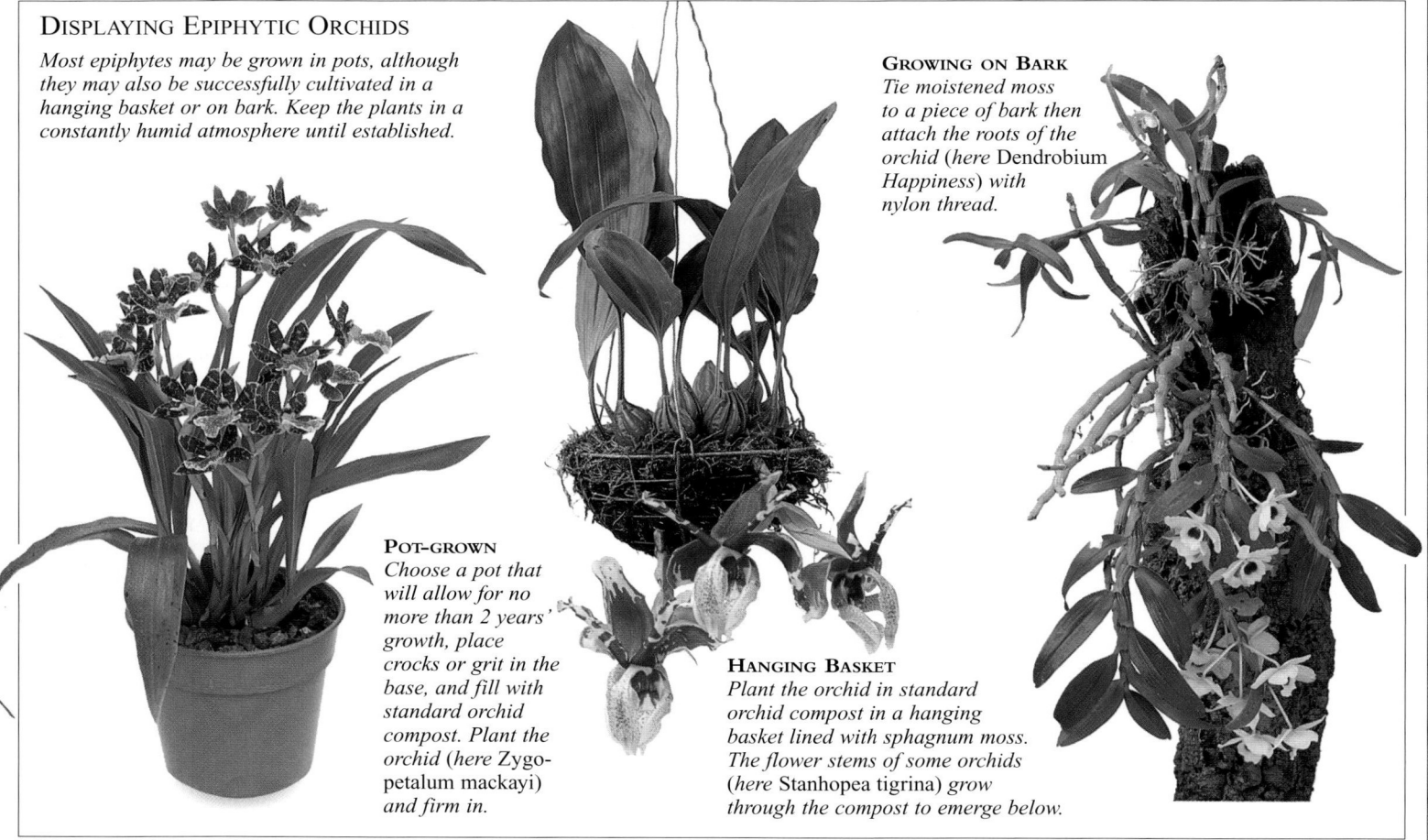

DISPLAYING EPIPHYTIC ORCHIDS

Most epiphytes may be grown in pots, although they may also be successfully cultivated in a hanging basket or on bark. Keep the plants in a constantly humid atmosphere until established.

GROWING ON BARK
Tie moistened moss to a piece of bark then attach the roots of the orchid (here Dendrobium Happiness) *with nylon thread.*

POT-GROWN
Choose a pot that will allow for no more than 2 years' growth, place crocks or grit in the base, and fill with standard orchid compost. Plant the orchid (here Zygopetalum mackayi) and firm in.

HANGING BASKET
Plant the orchid in standard orchid compost in a hanging basket lined with sphagnum moss. The flower stems of some orchids (here Stanhopea tigrina) *grow through the compost to emerge below.*

the foliage, or it may cause leaf scorch if the plants are exposed to hot sun. Overwatering must be avoided, but water thoroughly, so that the compost is evenly moist. Allow the compost to become nearly – but not quite – dry before watering again; if in doubt, delay watering.

During the growing season, orchids need a high level of humidity. This may be achieved by damping down the orchid house by spraying water over the paths and earth and on the staging between plants. Do this early in the morning; as the day progresses, the water will be drawn up as vapour. This daily damping down may be discontinued when natural conditions are cold and damp. Be careful, however, because in extremely cold weather the heating system may make the air very dry, and the greenhouse may need to be damped down more often.

Orchids grown in the home as windowsill plants must be chosen from those that do not demand very high humidity. Even these may benefit from additional local humidity by standing them on a layer of moist gravel or expanded clay aggregate in a tray or deep saucer.

Feeding
Since modern orchid composts contain little nourishment, orchids will need feeding during their growing period. Liquid fertilizers are the most convenient and these can be added during watering. Any proprietary, general-purpose brands sold for pot plants may be used. Orchids are not heavy feeders, so it will be necessary to dilute the fertilizer to half the strength recommended for other pot plants. Feed the orchids once every three weeks from spring to autumn, and only every six weeks (if at all) during the winter.

Ventilation
Most orchids, especially the popular cool-greenhouse kinds, require free-moving air conditions. They dislike cold draughts, however, which can cause flower buds to drop and slow down growth. Ventilators should be only partially opened in spring, when sunny days may be accompanied by chill winds, and closed well before the temperature starts to drop in the late afternoon. As days become warm, ventilators may be opened wider and for a longer time. Remember, however, that water vapour is quickly lost through open ventilators and humidity is reduced, so that extra damping down is needed. A small electric fan, inexpensive both to buy and run, will keep the air moving without letting out humidity or letting in draughts.

Shading
Although different orchids may have different light requirements, from the shade-loving *Paphiopedilum* orchids to the sun-loving *Laelia* species and hybrids, some form of shading is needed to protect new growth from being scorched by the sun and to prevent the greenhouse from overheating. The cheapest method is to use a greenhouse shading compound. White is more efficient than green in reflecting back the sun's rays, and it becomes almost transparent in rain, letting in more light on dull days. More effective, but more expensive, are manual or automatic roller blinds, made either of wood slats or plastic mesh.

Resting
An important and integral part of an orchid's lifecycle is the resting period, when growth is halted. During this time, which in the case of some orchids may last only a few weeks and in others several months, they need very little water, if any, in order to survive.

Although plants' requirements vary, the general rule is that those orchids that lose their leaves when resting should not be watered until new growth begins. Water sparingly at first, then normally (taking care not to overwater). Plants that keep their leaves will need to be given only a little water during the resting period to avoid dehydration.

Propagation

Vegetative propagation methods are the easiest for the amateur to learn. They also have the advantage of

---

PROPAGATING BY ADVENTITIOUS GROWTHS

1 *When a new plantlet with aerial roots has formed from a leaf node, cut it away carefully from the parent plant with a sharp knife.*

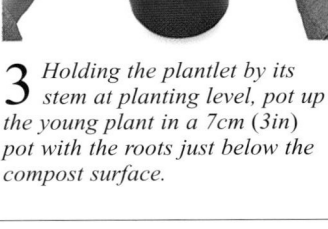
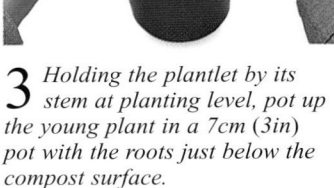

2 *The selected cutting should have healthy leaves and an evenly developed root system.*

3 *Holding the plantlet by its stem at planting level, pot up the young plant in a 7cm (3in) pot with the roots just below the compost surface.*

PROPAGATING BY STEM CUTTINGS

1 *Cut off a section of stem at least 25cm (10in) long, just above a leaf node or at the base of the plant (here* Dendrobium*).*

2 *Divide this into lengths of about 7cm (3in), cutting midway between leaf nodes. Each cutting should have at least 1 node.*

3 *Lay the cuttings in a tray on a layer of moist sphagnum moss and store in a humid place out of direct sunlight.*

4 *After several weeks, the dormant buds will have developed into plantlets, which will then be ready to pot up.*

producing offspring which are identical to the parent plant, so that the results are predictable.

Adventitious growths

The simplest cuttings, which are known as "keikis", are small plantlets that appear adventitiously (that is, atypically) from the nodes on stems of monopodial orchids, such as some *Dendrobium* and reed-type *Epidendrum*, also *Phalaenopsis* occasionally. As soon as these plantlets have developed a few vigorous roots, they should be severed from the parent plant with a sharp knife, and then potted into a standard orchid compost. Water them sparingly at first, but remember to spray the leaves with a fine mist until the roots have established and the plants have had a chance to become accustomed to their new environment.

Stem cuttings

Cuttings may also be made from the stems (often called canes) of many *Dendrobium* orchids. With a sharp knife, cut off sections up to 30cm (12in) in length. Divide these into cuttings 7–10cm (3–4in) long, each with at least one dormant bud. Lay the cuttings on damp sphagnum moss or a similar moist material, and keep them in a humid, shaded place. When the buds have produced plantlets, detach these and pot them up separately.

Division

The usual method of propagating sympodial orchids such as *Cattleya*, *Cymbidium*, and *Odontoglossum* is by division. Simply cut through the rhizome between pseudobulbs and pot up the pieces separately. Each piece should have at least three healthy pseudobulbs and a healthy dormant bud to produce new growth.

Back-bulbs offer another way of propagating sympodials such as *Cymbidium*. Remove a back-bulb, preferably one with roots, by pulling or cutting the rhizome just beyond it. Insert the back-bulb at one side of a pot of grit, sharp sand, or standard orchid compost. Position the cut surface of the bulb nearest the edge as the bulb will shoot from the other side. Place in a cool, shady spot, and keep moist. Shoots should appear in two or three months. When the bulbs have developed roots, pot them on.

Commercial techniques

Growing orchids from seed is difficult and requires specialized knowledge and skills. Orchids raised commercially from seed are germinated in flasks of nutrient jelly in a controlled laboratory environment. They are sometimes also propagated by meristem culture: microscopic pieces of plant tissue are grown on under laboratory conditions to mass-produce replicas of the original plant. As a result, first-class cultivars may now be purchased at a reasonable price. Both are, however, highly specialized techniques seldom practised by the amateur gardener.

PROPAGATING BY DIVISION

1 *When the orchid has grown too large for its pot and has several leafless bulbs, it may be divided. The plant shown here is a* Cymbidium.

2 *Remove the orchid from its pot, then divide the plant by separating or cutting it into 2 sections; each section should have at least 3 healthy pseudobulbs.*

3 *When dividing the orchid, any leafless back-bulbs may be pulled away. Discard shrivelled ones, and retain those that are firm for potting up separately.*

4 *Trim each section of the divided plant by removing surplus compost and cutting off any dead roots with secateurs.*

5 *To replant each section, hold the plant with the oldest pseudobulbs at the back of the pot and at planting level, and place the compost around it. New growth will develop in front of the plant.*

PROPAGATING WITH BACK-BULBS

1 *Plant selected back-bulbs singly in 7cm (3in) pots. Insert each bulb with the cut side nearest the edge of the pot.*

2 *Within 2 or 3 months the old back-bulb will produce a healthy new shoot.*

PROPAGATING IN FLASKS

Meristem culture takes place under sterile conditions. Microscopic pieces of plant tissue are placed in a flask on a special nutrient medium such as agar-agar jelly; they then develop into young orchid plants.

Routine care

Unlike plants grown outdoors, indoor plants are not subject to the extremes of the seasonal cycle so need relatively little attention. They require only watering and fertilizing, and an annual potting on, to perform at their best.

Watering and humidity

A common problem in the care of indoor plants is overwatering. In general, water when the compost is nearly dry. Take special care with coconut fibre composts, because the surface is inclined to dry out while the rest stays moist.

Water plants frequently while they are in active growth, less in winter when they are dormant – twice a month or even less may be enough. Wet the compost thoroughly, but do not leave the pot standing in water. Some plants, such as cyclamen, are susceptible to root rot; to water them, stand the pots in a little water until the compost is dark and damp. If tap water is hard, use distilled water or rainwater for lime-hating plants.

Buildings are often poorly ventilated and the atmosphere dry and unsuitable for many indoor plants. Maintain humidity by grouping pot plants on wet gravel in trays or in containers (see "Grouping plants", p.364), or on capillary matting (see "Care of house plants before going away", p.374).

Electric and ceramic humidifiers are readily available; bowls containing water placed in a room so that the water evaporates are also effective. Plants that need high humidity benefit from being mist sprayed with soft water. Use sprays sparingly on plants with hairy leaves, and avoid sunlight, since spots of water on the leaves can cause scorch.

Cleanliness

Always remove dead leaves and flowers promptly since they may harbour diseases or pests. Do not allow dust or grime to build up and block the leaf pores; dust the foliage with a soft brush. Thoroughly spray the plants occasionally to keep them clean and fresh, but do not spray cacti or plants with hairy leaves unless it is warm enough for any excess moisture to evaporate rapidly, or the leaves may rot. Only use leaf shine on glossy-leaved plants and check that it is compatible with individual species.

Fertilizing

Pot plants grow in relatively small volumes of compost and soon use up the available nutrients. Frequent watering also leaches out nutrients and the plants could starve without regular feeding throughout the growing season.

Balanced fertilizers are available in various forms: water-soluble or liquid (most convenient for indoor plants), granular, and solid. Always be careful to follow the manufacturers' instructions and never apply fertilizer to dry compost because it will not soak through evenly and may damage the roots.

Stopping

The appearance of many pot plants, especially trailing plants, may be improved by pinching out growing tips on young plants to encourage production of more sideshoots. This keeps the foliage bushy and increases the number of flower buds. Only stop plants that are in active growth.

CLEANING SMOOTH-LEAVED PLANTS
Gently wipe each leaf (here variegated Ficus elastica) *with a clean, moist, soft, and lint-free cloth.*

REMOVING DEAD LEAVES
Pinch out dead leaves and stems at the base of the plant (here Nephrolepis exaltata) *or cut them out.*

Neglected plants

With the exception of orchids and palms, most plants that have weak, leggy, or damaged growth produce new, vigorous growth if cut hard back to a healthy bud or joint in early spring. Cut back a neglected fern to the crown; keep the root ball moist and in medium light to induce growth.

Plants that root readily are best renewed from cuttings, while some plants are rejuvenated by air layering (see p.383). Revive exhausted plants by repotting or with a rest in a shaded greenhouse. To rescue an overwatered plant, remove all the sodden compost from the root ball, trim off rotting foliage and roots, and repot it in fresh compost. Refresh an underwatered plant by immersing the pot in water until the bubbles stop rising; then let the pot drain.

Potting on and top-dressing

Indoor plants also need periodic potting on to accommodate their growth and to replenish the compost. A potbound plant has retarded growth, fails to thrive, and water rinses clean through its pot. Pot on before this stage so that the plant's development is unimpeded. A few plants, such as *Hippeastrum*, enjoy confined roots, so do not pot them on; instead they should be top-dressed.

The best time to pot on is at the start of the growing season, although fast-growing plants may need potting on several times in one season. The process may delay flowering because the plant initially concentrates its energy on new root growth. Never pot on a dormant plant.

Potting on
Ensure that the root ball is completely moist so that it comes easily out of its pot without damaging the roots. Turn the pot upside down and slide the plant out into your hand. If the pot is too big to lift easily, run a knife around the inside; then lay the pot on its side. Support the plant

RENEWING TOP-DRESSING

HIPPEASTRUM

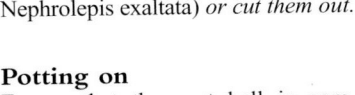

1 *Use a widger to remove the top 2½–5cm (1–2in) of the old compost, taking care not to damage the plant's roots.*

2 *Replace it with fresh, moist compost to which a small amount of fertilizer has been added. Firm the compost well around the crown and water.*

Create suitably humid conditions for indoor plants by providing them with their own microclimate. Loosely pack a shallow tray with clay pellets or gravel and fill it with water. Group several pot plants on the tray. Keep the water topped up so that the gravel or pellets remain wet.

Pilea cadierei

African violet (*Saintpaulia*)

Begonia

Streptocarpus

with one hand and rotate the pot, gently tapping the sides with a wood block to loosen the compost fully before removing the plant.

Put fresh potting compost in the new pot until the plant is positioned at the same depth as before, with space allowed for watering. Check that the roots are spread out and the plant centred, fill in with more compost, and firm gently. Water, but do not feed the plant for four to six weeks so that it will send out new roots into the compost in search of food. Keep the plant out of direct sun for a few days to recover.

Repotting

If a plant is in the largest available container, has grown to its full size, or is very slow-growing, repot it into the same size pot to renew the compost. Take the plant out of its pot, removing as much of the old compost as possible. Prune out damaged or diseased roots before repotting the plant in fresh compost.

Top-dressing

With plants that react badly to root disturbance, or enjoy confined roots, do not repot, but at the start of each growing season replace the old, surface compost with fresh compost of the same type and enrich it with balanced fertilizer.

Hanging baskets

Hanging baskets need regular care. Never allow the compost in a basket to dry out. Water it thoroughly; in very warm weather, this will need to be done both morning and evening. If the plants wilt, soak the basket in a bowl filled with water.

Feed plants in a basket regularly with a balanced liquid feed, and control any pests. Dead-head flowering plants, clip back over-long trailing plants, and thin out any untidy or tangled growth. Remove and replace any dead plants.

Maintaining terrariums and bottle gardens

A closed container rarely needs water; but if required use a long-necked watering can to trickle water against the glass inside to avoid disturbing the compost. Use just enough water to clean the glass and moisten the surface. If the glass is continuously obscured by mist, the compost is too wet – remove the cover or cork until it clears. To get rid of condensation or algae inside the glass, use a small

POTTING ON AN INDOOR PLANT

1 *Before potting on a plant (here* Dracaena fragrans *'Warneckei'), make sure that its root ball is moist by watering it thoroughly an hour beforehand. Select a pot that is one or two sizes larger than the old one. Make sure the pot is clean (whether washed, disinfected, or new) to avoid spreading diseases. The fresh potting compost should be of the same type as that in the old pot.*

2 *Remove the plant by inverting the pot and sharply tapping the rim on a hard surface to loosen the root ball. Support the plant as it slides out of the pot.*

3 *Gently tease out the root ball with a hand fork or fingers. Put some moist potting compost in the base of the new pot.*

4 *Insert the plant so that its soil mark is level with the rim base. Fill in with compost to within 1.5cm (¹/₂in) of the rim, firm, water, and place in position (right).*

Keeping plants from year to year

When all danger of frost is past, flowering plants grown for winter colour should be plunged in outdoor beds in their pots to "rest" during the warmer months. Choose a cool place, with indirect light, and keep them watered with soft (lime-free) water. At the end of summer, repot or top-dress them, bring them indoors, and feed them regularly once flower buds appear. To keep a cyclamen after flowering, do not water it until new growth starts, then remove old roots, and repot in loam-based potting compost so that the corm is level with the surface. Put it in a cool, well-lit place, and water regularly.

WINTER-FLOWERING POT PLANTS
In late spring, transfer the plants, here azaleas (Rhododendron), to a plunge bed in semi-shade outdoors. Sink each pot up to its rim in weed-free soil or another suitable plunge material, allowing space for the plants to grow. Bring them in before frost threatens, and keep them cool until the buds open.

CYCLAMEN
Let the leaves die down naturally after flowering. Place the plant on its side, in its pot, under a greenhouse bench or in a cold frame.

REPLANTING A TERRARIUM

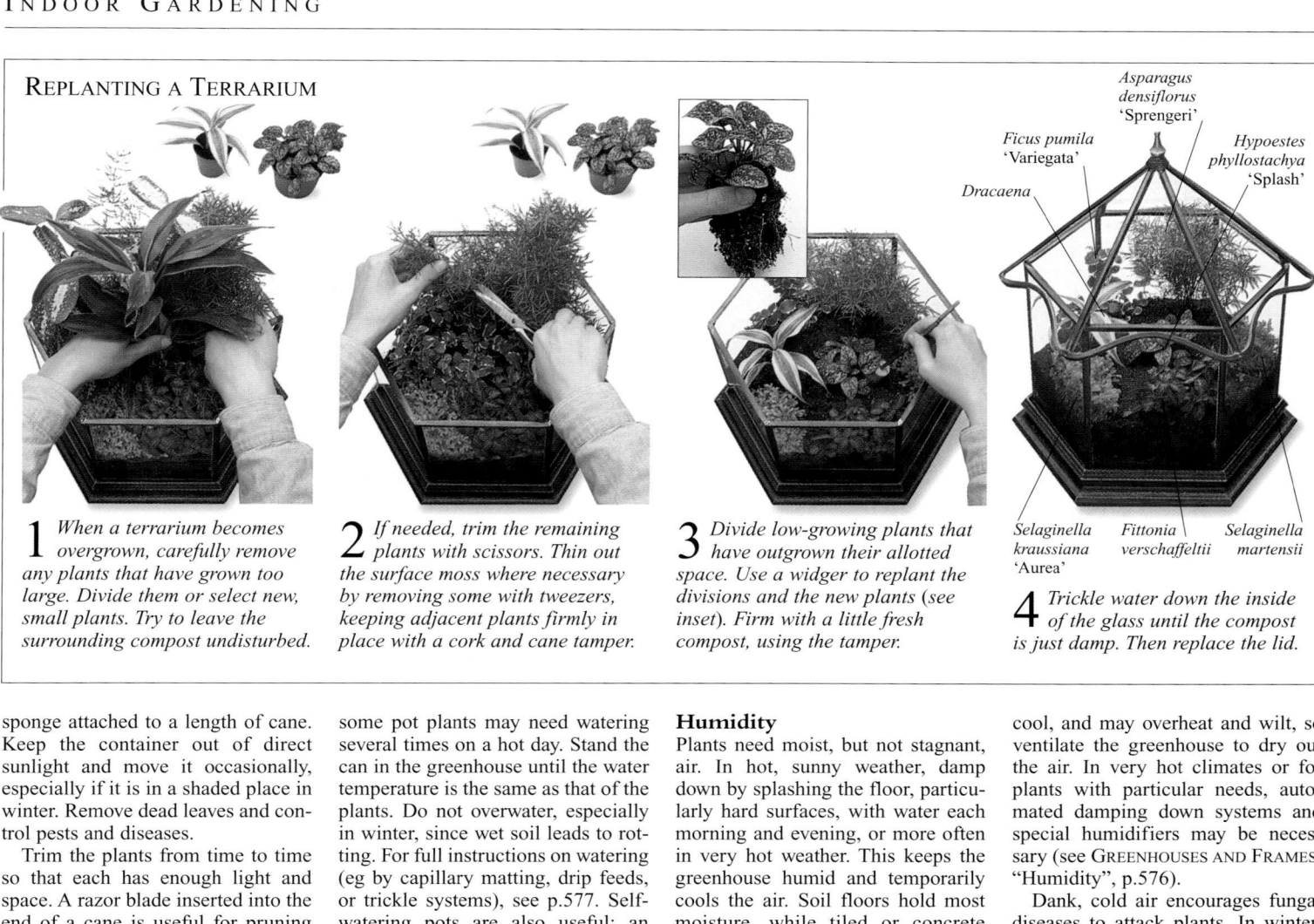

Asparagus densiflorus 'Sprengeri'
Ficus pumila 'Variegata'
Hypoestes phyllostachya 'Splash'
Dracaena
Selaginella kraussiana 'Aurea'
Fittonia verschaffeltii
Selaginella martensii

1 *When a terrarium becomes overgrown, carefully remove any plants that have grown too large. Divide them or select new, small plants. Try to leave the surrounding compost undisturbed.*

2 *If needed, trim the remaining plants with scissors. Thin out the surface moss where necessary by removing some with tweezers, keeping adjacent plants firmly in place with a cork and cane tamper.*

3 *Divide low-growing plants that have outgrown their allotted space. Use a widger to replant the divisions and the new plants (see inset). Firm with a little fresh compost, using the tamper.*

4 *Trickle water down the inside of the glass until the compost is just damp. Then replace the lid.*

---

sponge attached to a length of cane. Keep the container out of direct sunlight and move it occasionally, especially if it is in a shaded place in winter. Remove dead leaves and control pests and diseases.

Trim the plants from time to time so that each has enough light and space. A razor blade inserted into the end of a cane is useful for pruning plants in small-necked bottle gardens. If any plants encroach upon others, either replace them with smaller plants or replant the entire container (see above).

Plants in greenhouses

These need regular, sometimes daily, attention, even if the greenhouse is equipped with automatic systems. Watering, ventilation, misting, and feeding are especially important in summer, as is heating in winter and proper hygiene at all times. Routine care of pot plants, including feeding and potting (see pp.372–373), is similar to that of indoor plants.

Watering

In the enclosed greenhouse environment, correct watering is crucial. The amount needed varies with the season and the weather. In summer, water more on sunny than on cloudy days. Use a hose in a big greenhouse, with a low water pressure to avoid washing surface compost away from the roots. A watering can is best in a small or mixed greenhouse, where plants have differing water needs:

some pot plants may need watering several times on a hot day. Stand the can in the greenhouse until the water temperature is the same as that of the plants. Do not overwater, especially in winter, since wet soil leads to rotting. For full instructions on watering (eg by capillary matting, drip feeds, or trickle systems), see p.577. Self-watering pots are also useful; an outer pot holds water that is borne by capillary action along a wick to the compost in an inner pot.

Humidity

Plants need moist, but not stagnant, air. In hot, sunny weather, damp down by splashing the floor, particularly hard surfaces, with water each morning and evening, or more often in very hot weather. This keeps the greenhouse humid and temporarily cools the air. Soil floors hold most moisture, while tiled or concrete floors dry most quickly. If the air is too humid, plants cannot transpire water vapour from the leaves to keep

cool, and may overheat and wilt, so ventilate the greenhouse to dry out the air. In very hot climates or for plants with particular needs, automated damping down systems and special humidifiers may be necessary (see GREENHOUSES AND FRAMES, "Humidity", p.576).

Dank, cold air encourages fungal diseases to attack plants. In winter, keep the air dry by ventilating when weather permits or install a fan or a de-humidifier.

Care of indoor plants before going away

When going away, it is possible to ensure that indoor plants do not dry out. To keep water loss to a minimum, move plants into the shade and use one of the following watering methods. To use a capillary mat, group pot plants on an upturned tray, draining board, or shelf. Let the mat trail into another tray, the sink, or bath that is filled with water to supply the plants. Holes in plastic pots allow water through,

and clay pots are as good if saturated beforehand. Stand large or single pots on wick waterers, which draw water into the compost from a reservoir by means of a wick. Alternatively, water

Guzmania lingulata
Syngonium podophyllum 'Albolineatum'
Aglaonema

the plant thoroughly, allow it to drain, and place it in a sealed, plastic bag to avoid moisture loss. Check for and control any pests or diseases before going away.

CAPILLARY MATTING
Adiantum capillus-veneris
Place pot plants on one end of a piece of wet matting. Leave the other end submerged in a water reservoir. The plants must be above the water so that they can draw it up as they need it.

Ficus pumila 'Variegata'

PLASTIC BAG
Hold a clear, plastic bag away from the foliage with split canes. Seal with a plastic twist-tie or fold the neck of the bag under the pot.

Temperature regulation

Use ventilation to control temperatures in the greenhouse and avoid severe fluctuations that can harm plants. Too much ventilation slows growth; too little leads to high temperatures. On windy days, ventilate the greenhouse on the leeward side to avoid harmful draughts. For further information, see GREENHOUSES AND FRAMES, "Ventilation" (p.575) and "Shading" (p.576).

Hygiene

Keep the greenhouse clear of all debris that may harbour pests, and remove dead leaves and flowers before they rot. Wash or renew the aggregates on benches if they are infested with tiny snails or clogged with soil. Each autumn, take the plants outside and clean the greenhouse. Choose a still, warm day when the change in their environment is least likely to affect the plants. A thorough scrub-down is preferable, otherwise give the greenhouse a good sweeping and hosing down (see GREENHOUSES AND FRAMES, "Routine maintenance", p.583).

Frost protection

In unheated greenhouses, stop plant roots freezing in cold weather by keeping them nearly dry. Cover plants with a layer of plastic sheeting, fibre fleece, or newspaper, and beds with bracken or straw. Lag the base of shrubs and climbers with insulating material, secured with netting or twine. Plunge small pots in sand.

Pests and diseases

Regularly check buds, growing points, and the backs of leaves, and take early remedial action. Destroy badly infested plants, and isolate less affected specimens until they are clear of trouble. Isolate newly purchased plants for two weeks and control pests and diseases before placing them with other plants. Particular problems may be caused by vine weevil grubs (p.666) and red spider mite (p.646), especially in dry, centrally heated air in winter.

In warm, moist, greenhouse conditions, pests and diseases, such as grey mould/*Botrytis* (p.646) and powdery mildew (p.646), aphids (p.646) and hence viruses (p.649), and whiteflies (p.646), can spread rapidly. During the annual clean-up, (see "Routine maintenance", p.583) remove plants likely to be harmed by chemicals; fumigate the greenhouse and control any pests or diseases before replacing the plants. See also PLANT PROBLEMS (pp.639–673).

Hydroculture

This system has developed from hydroponics, which is a technique for growing plants in water to which all necessary nutrients are added. In hydroculture, "water roots" (which are slightly different from plant roots growing in soil) are supported by inert growing media – water and nutrients being added as necessary. Plant roots need oxygen to thrive and this method allows considerably more air to the roots than in traditional potting composts.

Hydroculture has several advantages: it is easy to provide the plants with a precise amount of water and nutrients; the growing medium is clean, well drained, odourless, not too acid, and free from clogging, which discourages weeds, pests, and diseases; and growth is often faster and stronger than in soil. Bulbs, cacti, indoor bonsai, orchids, and many plants that are commonly grown in offices flourish under hydroculture; see also the "Planter's guide to indoor plants", p.361.

A recent development in hydroculture growing media involves very porous clay pellets or granules that absorb more than their own weight in water and nutrients, which are taken up by the plant as required. Thus less frequent watering is necessary, and the medium does not shrink or compact like ordinary compost. The terracotta granules are clean and easy to use, and reasonably attractive. A window in a water indicator changes colour when the root ball is dry, and suitable nutrients are added at every watering, so container-grown plants are kept well nourished. Two types of liquid food have been specially formulated: one for foliage plants and the other for flowering ones.

All earlier methods of hydroculture involved buying a special, two-part container – an aggregate one and a watertight one – but the new method can be used with any container. Another great advantage is that, when transplanting, it is not necessary to wash all the old potting compost off the plant roots.

Setting up the system

Choose a watertight container at least twice the size of the pot in which the plant is currently growing. Measure and note down how much water it holds. In all future waterings, use one quarter of that volume, to avoid waterlogging.

A TABLE-TOP DISPLAY

Chamaedorea elegans

Euphorbia milii

Syngonium podophyllum

Aucuba japonica 'Variegata'

Pilea 'Norfolk'

Fill the container about one third full of granules. If the plant has previously been growing in a potting compost, very gently wash any soil or other debris off the roots Carefully protecting the roots of the plant being moved, place the root ball on the granules and infill around the root ball with more granules. Push the tip of the watering indicator carefully down into the centre of the root ball, leaving the gauge window clearly visible. Pour a measured amount of water (one quarter of the pot's capacity) containing a suitable liquid feed over the granules. The gauge window will then turn from red (dry) to blue (wet). Set the newly potted container in a suitably lit position in the house or conservatory.

Routine maintenance

Wait until the gauge window turns completely red again before watering with the same volume of water mixed with the same liquid feed. The water indicator should be replaced about once a year.

Foliage and flowering house plants should be watered and fed year-round. Actively growing plants use more water than those that are resting (semi-dormant) and the red-window signal will appear more often.

While in active growth, cacti, succulents, and orchids should be fed at half strength. During the winter rest period, keep cacti and succulents in a brightly lit position; give no feed to succulents but water them with half the normal volume. Cacti should be much drier – just water them sparingly to prevent dehydration but add no fertilizer. Give orchids a quarter-strength feed every four to six weeks if some growth is being made or flower spikes start to appear during a rest period.

Plants should be repotted into slightly larger containers as required. Clay granules do not deteriorate, so can be re-used: just wash them thoroughly, break up any lumps, and dry.

Propagation from cuttings

Cuttings of all types root very quickly in moist granules, because of the good aeration. Prepare cuttings in the normal way (see p.380). Insert them to one third of their length in a watertight container filled with granules. Treat as for rooted plants except that the liquid feed should be at half the recommended rate. In a greenhouse, free-draining containers may be used but high humidity levels must be maintained by covering with a plastic bag or cut-down clear plastic bottle, in order to guard against excessive water transpiration and quicker drying. Keep cuttings in bright, indirect light while they form roots. As soon as new growth appears, remove the cover. After a while, repot the new plants and start normal watering and feeding.

Seeds will germinate and seedlings grow on successfully in clay granules, using watertight or free-draining containers. After sowing or planting, moisten the granules using the one-quarter water measure and half-strength feed, then cover with plastic film or a plastic bag. Place in a shaded position until the new growth appears, when the cover can be taken off and the container moved into bright but not direct light. Start normal watering and feeding for plants in watertight pots, but allow the granules to dry out a little between applications for those in free-draining pots.

Training and pruning plants grown under cover

THE basic principles of training and pruning under cover are much the same as for outdoors, although it may be necessary to adapt these to accommodate extended flowering periods and limited space. Climbing plants that are too tender to be grown in the open may be readily cultivated under cover. If properly trained and pruned, they make efficient use of confined space and provide shade for other plants.

Plant supports

Plants that need support when grown under cover include ornamental climbers, some shrubs, annuals, fruiting vegetables, fruit trees, and vines (*Vitis*). True climbers find their own way up supports (see "Climbing methods and supports", p.124), while shrubs grown as climbers against a wall need tying in.

Some climbers require a permanent, rigid support securely attached to the framework of a wooden greenhouse or to the glazing bars of an alloy-framed one. Wires, stretched horizontally along the walls of the greenhouse, are useful for training all climbers. In lean-to greenhouses,

CLIMBING PLANTS FOR GROWING UNDER COVER

Prune after flowering
Allamanda cathartica 'Hendersonii' ❀ ◉
Bougainvillea ❀
Clerodendrum thomsoniae ❀ ◉
Distictis buccinatoria ❀
Jasminum, some ❀
Kennedia rubicunda ❀
Mandevilla splendens ❀ ◉

Mandevilla splendens

Pandorea jasminoides ❀
Passiflora, most ❀
Senecio, some ❀
Solanum wendlandii ❀ ◉
Stephanotis floribunda ❀ ◉
Thunbergia ❀

Prune as required
Agapetes macrantha ❀
Cissus ❀
Cobaea scandens ❀
Gynura aurantiaca ❀ ◉
Hoya ❀
Ipomoea horsfalliae ❀
Lophospermum erubescens ❀

KEY
❀ Not hardy
◉ Requires high humidity

ESTABLISHING THE SUPPORT FRAMEWORK

Stretch wires tightly between vine eyes (see inset). Tie in the stronger shoots and prune them to downward-growing buds to encourage horizontal growth.

stretch the wires between vine eyes attached to the rear wall to avoid cutting out light. Alternatively, attach the wire to drilled and bolted, vertical wall battens. Keep the wires taut by using a straining bolt at the end of each wire. Space the wires at equal intervals: vines require a 25cm (10in) spacing; fruit trees 38–45cm (15–18in). Tie in the stems of climbers with soft string to horizontal or vertical support wires.

Netting may be attached to the framework of the greenhouse and used to support plants. Plastic netting perishes and needs replacing after one or two seasons, so it is not suitable for perennials. Instead, use plastic-coated wire netting.

There are also some useful purpose-made, wire-mesh frameworks and various forms of wooden trellis available: fix them securely to battens attached to the greenhouse wall. Train the plants gently along netting or mesh as they grow, and tie them in with soft string.

Annual ornamental climbers, or fruiting vegetables such as tomatoes, may be tied with soft string to bamboo canes placed vertically at 15–30cm (6–12in) intervals. Alternatively, drop lengths of strong string from secure fixings in the roof to the base of the plants. Tie the string loosely below the plant's first true leaf, then wind it around the stems and run it back to the frame. Never let the string become too tight around the stem of the plant. For details of the treatment you should give to particular plants, see the pruning and training sections in the relevant chapters.

Pruning plants grown indoors

Like plants that are grown outdoors, many indoor plants require regular pruning to maintain their vigour and encourage flowering. Others simply become too big for the available space, or need cutting back to maintain an attractive and balanced framework. With pruning, cutting back, or pinching out, most plants may be trained and shaped. Drastic pruning is required only to remove old, weakened sections or to renovate a neglected plant.

Pinching out
To improve the shape and increase the number of flowering shoots that are produced on young, scandent, or trained shrubs, pinch out the tips of new shoots during the growing season. Shrubs that respond well include fuchsias, *Abutilon, Brunfelsia, Centradenia, Hibiscus, Reinwardtia*, and *Tibouchina*. Repeated "pinch pruning" (see p.377) can also be used to form certain plants into novel shapes for display.

When and what to prune
The best time for pruning depends on the flowering season of the plant and on the age of wood on which plants bloom. Some plants flower only on the new season's growth, and on these the old growth may be safely cut back in the spring without harming production of the next season's flowers. Others flower on older wood, so should be cut back only

CUTTING BACK AFTER FLOWERING

Cut back the flowered shoots to leave two or three buds. This encourages the production of next season's flowering shoots, which should be tied horizontally onto the wires.

after flowering. See pruning guides for shrubs (pp.103–110), climbers (pp.134–137), and on pruning to produce fruit on vines (pp.461–466) and tree fruits (pp.435–460).

Pruning to restrict growth
Under glass, space for shrubs and climbers is always limited. Although major problems may be avoided by choosing the most suitable plant for the size of the greenhouse, it may be necessary to stop growth to stop plants blocking the light. Climbers growing in the ground have a freer root run and so have to be rigorously controlled when they have filled their allotted space since they may overwhelm other plants.

Few shrubs and ornamental climbers grown under glass flower on old wood (but do check first), so pruning back fairly hard after flowering is generally advisable and safe. Cut back over-long stems in autumn; remove unwanted shoots whenever they appear.

Some plants flower for much of the year under glass, yet must be pruned to control them. In early spring, cut out the previous season's growth on mature *Abutilon* hybrids, and cut back *Coronilla* and *Hibiscus*. The flowers of *Hoya* are produced on short, woody spurs on both new and old growth; retain as many of these spurs as possible. Each can produce flowers over several years. *Agapetes* also flowers on old wood, but may need cutting back to induce bushiness.

The stems of some plants – particularly figs, such as the rubber plant (*Ficus elastica*), and euphorbias, such as poinsettia (*Euphorbia pulcherima*) – exude sap profusely when cut. The flow can be staunched by wetting the wound.

AUTUMN PRUNING TO RESTRICT GROWTH

In the autumn, cut out the weaker shoots and reduce dense growth; this allows plenty of light to penetrate the foliage and encourages the development of strong shoots to form a sturdy framework.

Pinch pruning

ALSO known as "finger-and-thumb pruning", the technique of repeated pinch pruning as a plant develops can be used to produce decorative shapes in a range of tender subshrubby plants, such as coleus (*Solenostemon*), fuchsias, *Helichrysum*, and *Pelargonium*. Simple shapes such as fans and cones are well within the grasp of a novice gardener, with experience, all manner of forms are possible – favourites being a ball, pillar, and pinch-pruned standard. Pinching, though in itself a simple technique, must be repeated at frequent, regular intervals during the growing season. No tools are generally required.

Shaping the plant

Plants must be healthy in order to respond well to this technique. Site plants growing under glass in a well-lit, well-ventilated position. Always pinch prune young plants right from the start, encouraging them to form bushy mounds before beginning to form a more specific shape.

With finger and thumb, pinch out the tip of the shoot just above an opened leaf. Remove only the very tip to stimulate the maximum number of buds into producing sideshoots. Side buds will then break and develop into shoots. When these have developed two to four leaves (or two pairs), repeat the process.

Pot young plants on regularly, while they are maturing. For some shapes, such as a fan, two or more specimens should be planted in the same pot. Do not pinch prune a week or so before or after potting to enable root systems to re-establish well. After that, start pinching the growing tips out of young plants regularly once again, to encourage dense growth and a compact form.

FINISHED COLEUS FAN

Training frames and supports

Once plants are in their final pot, a supporting framework may be erected around them to assist training to the desired shape. Bamboo canes, wire and wire netting, both large- and small-gauge, can be used to create a variety of interesting forms, such as cones, pillars, and fans. If a large framework is needed, ensure that the pot is also sufficiently large to give the trained plant stability. The head of a pinch-pruned standard needs no frame, but is formed entirely by bushy growth, pinch pruned to create and maintain an even shape (see also *How to Train a Standard Fuchsia*, p.121). However, no subshrub can, in one season, produce a stem sturdy enough to support the head, so staking with a cane is required initially.

Routine care

Pick off discoloured leaves as seen. Feed young plants with a fertilizer high in nitrogen to stimulate growth, then, when pinching stops, switch to a high-potash feed to stimulate flower development or, in coleus, to allow the leaf colour to develop fully.

With flowering plants, such as fuchsias, once the shape is formed to your satisfaction, stop pinching about two months before flowers are desired, to give the terminal flower bud time to develop. Flowering should be simultaneous – and dramatic. With foliage plants, where flowers are not wanted (such as coleus and *Helichrysum*), continued pinching will prevent the formation of flower buds.

In cool climates, plants can be moved out of doors after the danger of frost has passed, either onto a patio or planted out as summer bedding, then if desired brought back under glass to overwinter. In spring, trimming and pinching are resumed as new growth begins.

Do not feed flowering plants while they are overwintering.

PINCH-PRUNING A COLEUS FAN

1 *Pinch out all shoots as they develop until the plants are 25cm (10in) tall. Then pinch only on two opposite sides, developing a flattened shape to the plants.*

SUPPORTING FRAMEWORK
When the plants are 50cm (20in) tall (see left), they will need the support of a framework, made from canes arranged and tied as a fan.

2 *Carefully insert the canes that form the fan's ribs into the pot, along the flattened outline of the plants, and tie in cross-bars to brace them.*

3 *Using figure-of-eight knots and soft twine, tie in stems to the canes wherever possible, gently drawing some growth down to the horizontal.*

SIDE VIEW OF FAN
Once the frame is covered, the fan shape can be maintained by pinching all growth. This will also stimulate fresh, bright young leaves.

4 *Allow all shoots that extends towards the perimeter of the fan to grow on, tying them in at regular intervals to the cane framework. Continue pinching all shoots on the flat faces of the fan.*

Propagation

PROPAGATING indoor plants is an economical way to increase your stock and to replace old plants with younger, more vigorous specimens. Successful propagation requires clean conditions, warmth, light, and sufficient humidity.

The easiest method of propagation is by division, which produces only a few plants at one time. The majority of new plants for growing indoors or under cover are grown from seed or cuttings, however, since these methods usually yield a greater number of new plants. Some plants may be increased by layering.

Propagation by division

Division is a quick way of propagating plants. Many plants produce plantlets, runners, offsets, or bulbils, which root themselves and may be severed from the parent and potted up.

Dividing the rootstock

Before dividing a pot plant, water the root ball thoroughly and allow it to drain. Herbaceous and clump-forming plants may be gently pulled apart or cut into separate pieces, each with its own root system, and repotted. Use a sharp knife to separate the fleshy roots of rhizomatous plants; retain vigorous sections with young growth and fibrous, feeding roots. Prune any long, thick roots, and any that are damaged. Dust the wounds with fungicide. Replant each division in a clean pot using a similar compost to that used for the parent plant. Water the plants and keep them in good light, but out of direct sun, until they are established. See also "Potting on and top-dressing", p.372.

Dividing plantlets

Plantlets are small versions of the parent plant that grow on its leaves, stolons, stems, or inflorescences. Once they are large enough to handle, detach them with about 3cm (1¼in) of the leaf stalk or stolon, where appropriate. Insert the plantlet stalk in a pot of peat-substitute- or peat-based potting compost so that the plantlet rests on the surface. Water the pot and cover it with a plastic bag to preserve the humidity. Roots should form in about three weeks. After this, the plantlet takes up to five weeks to resume growth, at which point it is ready to pot on.

Dividing rooting runners

Some plants, such as *Saxifraga stolonifera* (syn. *S. sarmentosa*) and *Episcia*, spread by runners. If these are rooted individually in pots of compost, they may then be severed from the parent to make new plants.

Dividing offsets and bulbils

Offsets are small plants that develop around the base of plants. Choose a well-developed one with some roots; cut or break it off cleanly from the main stem and insert it in a pot of

---

INDOOR PLANTS TO DIVIDE

Plantlets/runners
Chlorophytum ✽
Cryptanthus ✽ ◎
Haworthia ✽
Saxifraga stolonifera ✽ ◎
Maranta leuconeura var. *kerchoviana*

Rootstock
Adiantum ✽ ◎
Anthurium ✽
Aspidistra ✽
Calathea ✽ ◎
Cyperus ✽
Maranta leuconeura ✽ ◎
Microlepia strigosa ✽
Phlebodium aureum ✽ ◎
Pteris cretica ✽ ◎
Sansevieria ✽
Stromanthe ✽ ◎

KEY
✽ *Not hardy*
◎ *Requires high humidity*

PROPAGATING POT PLANTS BY DIVISION

1 *Thoroughly water the plant (here* Calathea*) an hour before dividing it. Support the plant, then invert the pot and tap its rim on a hard surface. Slide out the plant.*

2 *Remove surplus compost, either by gently shaking the plant or by teasing some of the compost away with your fingers, so that the roots are accessible.*

3 *Use hands or a hand fork to prise the root ball into sections, each with a portion of roots. Take care not to damage the stems or fibrous roots.*

4 *Using a clean, sharp knife, trim back any thick roots so that the divisions will fit into their new pots, but take care to leave the delicate, fibrous roots intact.*

5 *Select sections with healthy, young shoots (see inset) for replanting. Insert each section in a pot of moist, loam-based potting compost. Gently firm the compost and water well to encourage the roots to establish. Label the pot.*

PROPAGATING BY ROOTING RUNNERS

1 *Peg down runners (here* Saxifraga stolonifera*) in individual 7cm (3in) pots of moist, standard cutting compost. Keep them well watered.*

2 *After a few weeks, separate each rooted plantlet, in its pot, from the parent by cutting the runner close to the young plant. Label the pot.*

moist potting compost. Cover the pot with a plastic bag until new growth is produced.

Some plants produce bulbils on the fronds or in the leaf axils. Detach these and root them in moist, loam-based potting compost. For further information, see LILIES, *Propagating from Stem Bulbils*, p.251.

Growing indoor plants from seed

The seed of pure species breeds true but that of many hybrid indoor plants does not. Uniform results may be obtained, however, from selections, or first generation (F1) hybrids of bien-nials, annuals, and a few perennials, such as cyclamen and pelargoniums.

Seed composts and containers
Use a compost prepared specifically for seed (see TOOLS AND EQUIPMENT, "Standard seed compost", p.565). It should be a free-draining and open-textured mix, which holds moisture without becoming sodden or forming a hard crust on the top.

A variety of containers may be used, such as half-pots, pans, and half or quarter seed trays. Always use a size of container that is appropriate to the number of plants required. Special cellular trays that allow each seed to grow in its own individual plug of soil are also readily available.

When to sow
Most seeds are spring-sown, but seeds of early spring-flowering species are usually sown in autumn. Annuals may be sown in several batches from spring to early summer for a succes-sion of blooms. Seeds of many exotic species are spring-sown but often germinate freely if sown as soon as they are ripe. It may be difficult, however, to keep the young seedlings alive in winter.

Preparing the seed
Some seeds need special treatment to help them germinate. Seeds with hard coats often need pre-sowing treat-ment, such as soaking in warm water; the time required varies from about 10 minutes for *Cordyline australis* to about 72 hours for banana seed. Other hard-coated seeds, such as *Caesalpinia pulcherrima*, will not ger-minate unless the seed coat is chip-ped with a knife or file. If the seed is too small to handle, gently abrade it between two sheets of fine sandpa-per. Follow the supplier's instructions on the seed packet to ensure success.

Sowing the seed
Overfill the container with standard seed compost and tap it on the bench; scrape off the surplus so that the compost is level with the container rim. Firm the compost to within 1cm (½in) of the rim.

Water the compost before sowing the seed, and allow the container to drain well. Watering with a watering can after sowing may "bunch" the seed or wash it together, leading to problems with overcrowding and damping off later.

Sow all seed thinly and evenly. Tiny seed is easier to sow if it is first mixed with horticultural sand. Place large seeds far enough apart to allow the seedlings to grow without being thinned later on. Alternatively, sow the seeds singly into small pots, cellular trays, or soil blocks.

As a general rule, cover seeds with compost to the depth of their small-est diameter. Very tiny seeds, how-ever, or seeds that require light to germinate, should be left uncovered on the surface of the compost. Cover the container with a sheet of glass, a plastic bag, or a propagator lid to maintain humidity and stop the com-post drying out. Place the container in the correct temperature, in good light but out of direct sunlight, and leave the seed to germinate.

Germination temperatures
Seeds usually germinate at 5°C (10°F) higher than the minimum needed by the same plant in growth. As a gen-eral rule, a temperature of 15–18°C (59–64°F) is suitable. The correct temperature varies for different seed, so follow the instructions given on the seed packets. Plants that are raised under cover for growing outside ger-minate at 10°C (50°F) or less. Many tropical or subtropical plants need 24–26°C (75–79°F) to germinate. If it is hard to maintain such temperatures indoors, consider using a heated propagating case. Although there are many different types and sizes, most have thermostats that allow a specific temperature to be maintained.

Aftercare of sown seed
Wipe off any condensation on covers to discourage fungal diseases. After seven to ten days, check the con-tainers daily for signs of germin-ation and remove the covers as soon as the seedlings appear. Germ-ination times vary greatly, however, so some larger seeds may take sev-eral months to germinate. Keep the compost moist; use either a watering can or, for very delicate seedlings, a mist-sprayer.

Feeding should not be necessary if seed was sown in compost con-taining a small amount of nutrient, although seedlings that are to stay in their container for some time may benefit from a liquid feed as they grow. If the seedlings start to bend towards light, turn them daily and shade with cardboard or shade net-ting if there is danger of sun scorch.

Pricking out the seedlings
When the seedlings are 1cm (½in) high, they may be pricked out into larger pots or packs. Water them first, allow them to drain for an hour, then loosen them by tapping the side of the container. Lift the seedlings out of the container using a small, flat implement. If the seedlings are clumped together, use a dibber or pencil to tease them apart. Handle the seedlings carefully by the leaves since the stems are easily damaged.

Use a dibber to make holes in some fresh compost in a container. Lower each seedling into place so that it is at the same depth as before. Place more compost around the roots and lightly firm in each seedling. Small seed-lings should be set about 2.5cm (1in)

INDOOR FLOWERING PLANTS TO RAISE FROM SEED

Alonsoa ❋
Begonia (fibrous-rooted and tuberous kinds) ❋ ◎
Browallia ❋
Caesalpinia pulcherrima ❋
Campanula ❋ ◎
Clitoria ❋
Cobaea ❋
Cuphea ❋
Cyclamen, some ❋ ◎
Exacum affine ❋ ◎
Impatiens ❋ ◎
Jacaranda mimosifolia ❋
Pelargonium (modern multi-bloom hybrids) ❋
Pericallis x *hybrida* ❋
Primula kewensis ❋ ◎,
  P. malacoides ❋ ◎,
  P. obconica ❋ ◎,
  P. sinensis ❋ ◎

Primula malacoides

Salpiglossis ❋
Schizanthus ❋
Sinningia ❋ ◎
Thunbergia ❋
Torenia ❋

KEY
❋ Not hardy
◎ Requires high humidity

RAISING INDOOR PLANTS FROM SEED

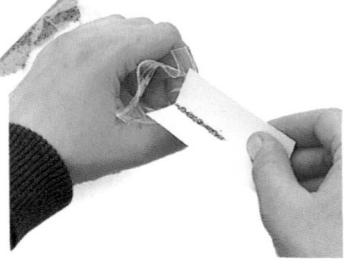

1 *Mix very fine, dust-like seed (here* Campanula*) with dry, fine sand in a bag; this makes it possible to sow the seed more evenly. Sow larger seed by hand.*

2 *Sow the mixture thinly onto a pot of moist, seed compost, using a small funnel of paper held close to the compost surface. Label, and place in a propagator.*

3 *When the seedlings are large enough to handle by their leaves, use a dibber to prick them out into a container of moist potting compost.*

4 *Once the seedlings have become established, pot them on singly into individual pots or modules to grow on. Water, and label each pot.*

apart, and larger ones about 5cm (2in). Water the seedlings with a fine-rosed watering can. For seedlings sown individually in a cellular tray, lift the seedling with its plug of compost, and pot it up.

Potting on

Once the roots of plants have filled the containers, they need potting on (see p.372). The new pot should be large enough to allow for a 2.5cm (1in) gap all around the root ball. Insert the plant so that the base of its stem is level with the surface of the compost. Settle the compost by tapping the pot on a bench, firm it lightly, and water it using a fine rose.

Once potted on in normal compost, the new plants can be treated as mature specimens. Ensure that the correct conditions are maintained; different indoor plants have widely varying requirements.

Propagation from cuttings

Most tender, indoor plants may be readily propagated from softwood (tip) cuttings (rooted in compost or in water), leaf-bud or leaf cuttings. Semi-ripe or woody cuttings may be taken from indoor shrubs. The important factors for success with cuttings are timing, hygiene, warmth, and humidity.

Semi-ripe cuttings

Take cuttings of semi-ripe wood from the current season's growth, in summer after the main flush of fast, spring growth but before the wood is fully ripe; suitable material is firm, but flexible, and offers some resistance if bent. Plants grown under cover may reach maturity before mid-summer, so check new shoots carefully from early summer onwards. For details of the technique, see ORNAMENTAL SHRUBS, "Semi-ripe cuttings", p.112.

Leaf-bud cuttings

Genera such as *Ficus* and *Hoya* may be increased by leaf-bud cuttings, a type of semi-ripe cutting. Cut stems into 2.5–5cm (1–2in) lengths, each with a single leaf and leaf axil bud. Then insert them into pots of cutting compost and place the pots in a propagator at a temperature of 15–18°C (59–64°F). For further details, see ORNAMENTAL SHRUBS, "Leaf-bud cuttings", p.113.

Softwood cuttings

These are taken in early spring. Select new, short-noded sideshoots and remove them with a clean, sharp knife. When preparing cuttings, make clean, precise cuts so that no snags are left on the stems. Dip the base of each stem in hormone rooting powder, and, using a dibber or a pencil, insert several cuttings into a pot of standard cutting compost. The cuttings may be close together in a pot or placed around the edges as long as their leaves do not touch.

Place the pot in a propagator or cover it with a plastic bag to reduce water loss – make sure that the bag does not touch the cuttings, however. Leave the pot in a warm, light position but out of direct sunlight. Check the cuttings each day or two and, if necessary, clear any condensation by opening the propagator or bag for a while.

It should take about four to six weeks for new roots to form. At this stage, when young growth may be seen, transfer the cuttings to individual pots of peat-substitute- or loam-based compost to grow on. Keep the young plants in a warm, lightly shaded place until they are well established.

PROPAGATING FROM SOFTWOOD CUTTINGS

1 *Fill a 13cm (5in) pot with moist cutting compost and tamp it down until it is level.*

2 *Using secateurs or a clean, sharp knife, cut off, just above a node, some new, short-noded shoots 10–15cm (4–6in) long. The plant shown here is Gynura aurantiaca.*

3 *Trim each cutting just below a node, removing the lower leaves to create a length of clean stem at the base (see inset). Do not leave snags, which might rot.*

4 *Dip the base of the cuttings into hormone rooting powder. Insert them in the pot so that the leaves are just above the compost.*

5 *Water and label the cuttings. Place the pot in a propagator in a warm, light place and maintain a soil temperature of 18–21°C (64–70°F) until the cuttings are rooted and ready to pot on.*

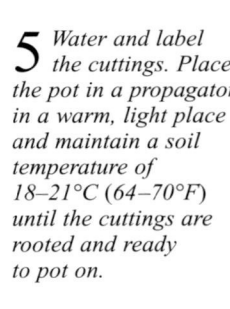

Rooting softwood cuttings in water

The simplest method of rooting softwood cuttings is to place them in a glass or jar of water in a light, warm position. Prepare each cutting as for a normal softwood cutting, ensuring that the lower leaves are cleanly removed. Support the cutting on netting placed over the glass so that the stem is suspended in the water. When the roots develop and there is fresh growth, pot up the cuttings. Prepare pots with drainage material and 2.5cm (1in) of compost. Hold each cutting in a pot with its roots spread and fill in with compost until the roots are covered. Firm and water the cuttings thoroughly.

Propagating from leaves

Some plants may be propagated easily from whole leaves or leaf sections. In some cases, the leaves are inserted in compost (or water), while in others they are scored or cut up before being inserted in or secured flat onto the compost. Each leaf should produce a number of small plantlets where the leaf veins have been cut.

Whole leaves

Certain plants, often those with fleshy leaves growing in rosettes such as African violets (*Saintpaulia*) and gloxinias (*Sinningia speciosa*), as well as Rex and rhizomatous begonias, and some succulents (see p.347) may be increased from leaf cuttings.

For the cuttings, choose healthy, undamaged, fully grown leaves and cut them off close to the base of the leaf stalks. Trim each stalk with a straight cut 3cm (1¼in) below the leaf blade; insert the cuttings individually into prepared pots of cutting compost (1 part sand and 1 part peat substitute or peat), label, and water. Place the pots in a propagator or cover each one with a clear plastic bag or improvised cloche (see below). As soon as each cutting produces plantlets, remove its cover. Grow on the cuttings until the plantlets are large enough to be teased apart and potted on individually. Alternatively, leaves with long stalks (especially African violets) may be rooted in water, although rooting tends to take longer than in compost.

Scored or cut leaves

The leaves of plants with prominent veins, such as Rex begonias and

PROPAGATING SOFTWOOD CUTTINGS IN WATER

1 *Using a sharp, clean knife, remove healthy, short-noded cuttings, 10–15cm (4–6in) long, from a healthy, vigorous plant (here Solenostemon). Cut each stem carefully just above a node.*

2 *Trim each cutting below a node and remove the lower leaves to create a length of clean stem at the base (see inset).*

3 *Insert the stems through a piece of wire netting over the top of a jar of water. Ensure that the stems are in the water.*

4 *Keep the water topped up so that the lower end of each cutting is always below the surface. A network of roots should develop.*

5 *When the cuttings are well rooted, carefully plant each one into a 7cm (3in) pot of sandy potting compost.*

HALF-LEAF SECTIONS

1 *Divide the leaf (here Streptocarpus) by cutting out the midrib and exposing the veins.*

2 *Insert the sections, cut edges down, in shallow trenches. Gently firm them in.*

PROPAGATING INDOOR PLANTS FROM LEAF CUTTINGS

1 *Cut healthy leaves from the parent plant (here Saintpaulia). Insert each stalk in a small pot of cutting compost so that the leaf blade is just clear of the compost.*

2 *Water, label, and cover the pots. Small cloches made from the bases of plastic drinks bottles are suitable. Leave them in a warm, light place out of direct sunlight.*

3 *Each leaf should produce several plantlets. When these develop, remove the covers, and grow them on until they are large enough to pot up individually.*

various members of the family Gesneriaceae, for example *Streptocarpus*, will produce small plantlets if they are scored or cut up and the cut veins are then kept in contact with moist compost; the leaves may be divided either in half or into small sections, or they may be scored through.

Whichever method is used, keep the container in a propagator or in a clear plastic bag in a light place but out of direct sunlight; inflate the bag so that it does not touch the leaf sections, and seal it. The leaves being propagated should be kept at 18–24°C (64–75°F).

When clumps of plantlets develop from the cut veins, carefully lift and separate them, retaining a little compost around the roots of each one, and pot them up individually into 7cm (3in) pots of cutting compost.

Some succulent plants, including *Sansevieria* and those that have flattened, leaf-like stems such as *Epiphyllum*, may also be propagated from "leaf" sections although these are treated slightly differently. For details, see CACTI AND OTHER SUCCULENTS, "Propagation from stem sections", p.348.

PROPAGATING FROM CUT LEAVES

1 Select a young, healthy leaf (*here* Begonia rex) and make a 1cm (½in) long incision with a sharp knife straight across each of the strongest veins on the underside of the leaf (see inset).

2 Place the leaf, cut side downwards, on a tray of cutting compost. Pin its veins to the compost. Label, and place the tray in a propagator or a plastic bag.

3 Leave the tray in a warm place out of direct sunlight. When the plantlets have developed, carefully separate them from the leaf (see inset) and pot them on singly.

LEAF SQUARES

1 Cut 4 or 5 square sections the size of a postage stamp from a healthy leaf. Each piece should include a strong vein.

2 Place the sections, veins downwards, on moist compost. Pin with wire hoops, then treat as other leaf sections.

Propagation of tuberous begonias

When begonia tubers die back naturally in autumn, store them in their pots at 5–10°C (41–50°F) in a dry place over winter. Alternatively, lift and clean the tubers, dust their crowns with fungicide, and store them in boxes of dry sand, peat substitute, or peat.

At the beginning of the growing season, place the tubers in a tray of moist, sandy compost (1 part sharp sand, 1 part peat-substitute- or peat-based compost). Store them at a minimum temperature of 13–16°C (55–61°F). When new buds are clearly visible, cut the tubers into sections, making sure that each has at least one bud and some roots. Dust the sections with fungicide and leave them to dry for a few hours in a warm place. When the cut surfaces have formed calluses, pot up the sections in loam-based compost. Do not firm the compost heavily or water it, since this encourages fungal attack.

Alternatively, allow new shoots to develop on the tubers, and use these as basal cuttings. Take the cuttings so that each retains an eye. Dip the base of each cutting in hormone rooting powder and insert them, 2cm (¾in) deep, around the edge of a pot or pan of loam-based potting compost.

1 In autumn, lift the dormant tubers and clean them. Dust the crowns with fungicide and overwinter them in a dry place.

2 In spring, place the tubers, concave side upwards, 5cm (2in) apart and 2.5cm (1in) deep, in a tray of moist, sandy compost.

3 When shoots appear, cut the tubers into sections, each with a bud and some roots. Dust cut surfaces with fungicide and allow to dry.

4 Pot up the sections singly in 13cm (5in) pots, with the top of each level with the compost surface. Label each container.

5 Keep the pots in a propagator in a warm, frost-free place until the sections are established, then pot them on singly.

BASAL CUTTINGS

Remove 5cm (2in) shoots from the tuber, each with a eye of the tuber at the base. Pot them up and treat as divided tubers.

Propagation by layering

Layering involves wounding the stem of a plant, inducing it to produce roots, and then separating the rooted stem. This method has a high success rate since the layered stem receives nutrients from the parent plant while it is developing.

Some indoor plants may be propagated by layering – either in air or in the soil. Air layering produces a fairly large, new plant from an older specimen but it may take some considerable time. Simple layering in soil provides new stock quite quickly.

Air layering

This is an excellent method for replacing old or damaged house plants, for example the rubber plant (*Ficus elastica*) and its relatives. The top of the plant, or tip of a branch, may be encouraged to form new roots, and is then severed from the parent.

Choose a section of stem of new growth that is straight, about 10cm (4in) long, and of at least pencil thickness. Cut the bottom off a clear, plastic bag to create a transparent sleeve and slip it over the stem or, if the leaves are too large to permit this, fold a clear, plastic sheet around the stem and tape up the seam. Secure the sleeve below the selected area of the stem.

Using a sharp knife, make a shallow, upward-slanting cut in the side of the stem, then wedge this tongue open with moist sphagnum moss. Alternatively, on woody plants, score two rings 1–2cm (½–¾in) apart below a healthy leaf joint on the selected area of the stem; the scores should be just deep enough to penetrate the bark without harming the wood. Peel off the bark between the rings, leaving the cambium undisturbed.

In both cases, dust the cut area with rooting powder. Pack the sleeve with damp moss, and seal it so that the area is tightly enclosed to prevent it from drying out. If the stem is heavy, provide cane support.

It may be many months before the roots show. If the moss begins to dry out, open up the plastic, add a little water, and reseal. When roots appear, sever the layered stem from the parent and pot it up into a loam-based potting compost. Water the young plant sparingly until it is established.

Simple layering

Climbing or trailing shoots may be layered into soil while they are still attached to the parent plant.

Choose a long, vigorous shoot and peg it down into a small pot of moist cutting compost. After three to four weeks, roots should start to grow into the compost and new shoots begin to form; the rooted layer may then be detached from the parent plant. If required, several shoots may be layered at the same time, each in its own pot.

When severing the new plants, always take care not to spoil the shape of the parent plant. For further information, see CLIMBING PLANTS, p.145.

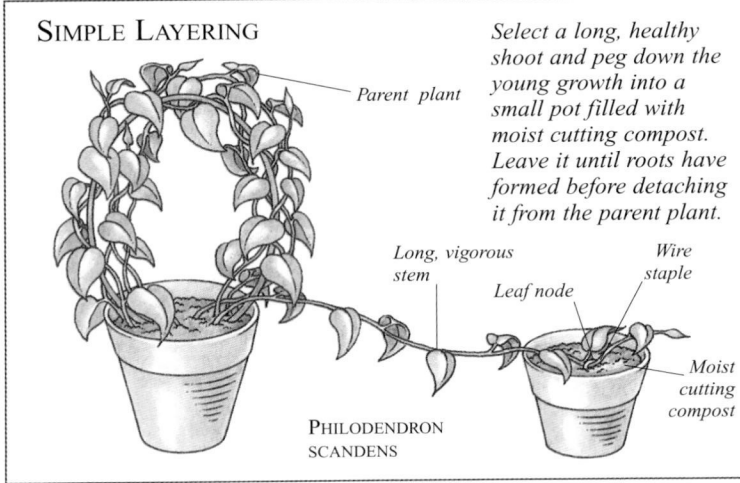

SIMPLE LAYERING

Select a long, healthy shoot and peg down the young growth into a small pot filled with moist cutting compost. Leave it until roots have formed before detaching it from the parent plant.

Parent plant

Long, vigorous stem

Leaf node

Wire staple

Moist cutting compost

PHILODENDRON SCANDENS

PROPAGATING BY AIR LAYERING

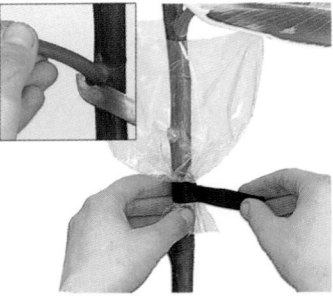

1 *Trim the leaves (here Ficus elastica) from a straight length of stem (see inset). Slide a plastic sleeve over the stem and fix the lower end with adhesive tape.*

2 *Fold down the sleeve. Hold the stem firmly and cut a "tongue" in it, making a slanted, upwards incision 5mm (¼in) deep and 2.5cm (1in) long.*

3 *Apply hormone rooting powder to the wound and push moist sphagnum moss into the incision, using a split stake or the back of a knife blade.*

4 *Roll the sleeve back into position around the packed incision. Fill the sleeve with more moist sphagnum moss.*

5 *When the sleeve is tightly packed with moss, secure the upper end to the stem with adhesive tape.*

6 *When the new roots are visible through the sleeve, cut through the stem just below the root ball with secateurs. Remove the plastic sleeve.*

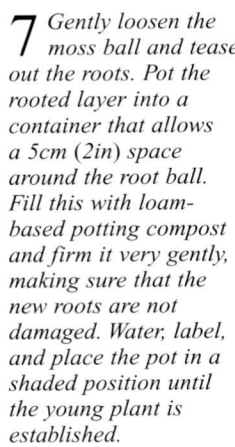

7 *Gently loosen the moss ball and tease out the roots. Pot the rooted layer into a container that allows a 5cm (2in) space around the root ball. Fill this with loam-based potting compost and firm it very gently, making sure that the new roots are not damaged. Water, label, and place the pot in a shaded position until the young plant is established.*

CHAPTER

14

THE LAWN

FROM THE STRIPED green sward in a formal garden to the closely mown turf of a sports area or rough grassland under a grove of trees, there is a lawn to suit all situations. Whether it is a showpiece in its own right, a foil for colourful borders, a playing surface for children, or simply a relaxing haven, the lawn can be both functional and a design feature. Frequently undervalued as merely a flat surface underfoot, the lawn can make a much more important contribution to the garden, softening hard surfaces, helping to define distinctive features, and unifying the garden as a whole. For centuries, grass has been used to create lawns because it is visually appealing, tolerates wear, and may be cut very low without being damaged, although chamomile and other low-growing herbs make wonderful scented alternatives for ornamental use.

Creating lawns

A HEALTHY, well-maintained lawn is an attractive feature that also provides a clear area in which to walk, play, and relax. In addition to such ornamental and utility lawns, grass may be used to cover the ground in other areas such as sports or games lawns, in orchards and wild gardens, for wide paths and gently sloping banks.

Some broadleaved plants, for example chamomile (*Chamaemelum nobile*), may also be used to form lawns; they should, however, be considered primarily as ornamental, to be admired rather than extensively used, because they are less tolerant of wear than grass (see "Non-grass lawns", p.389).

When deciding on the type and shape of the lawn as well as where to site it, consider how it will link to the rest of the garden – to other plants, features, and the overall layout – so that it forms a congruous, unifying part of the design.

Grass

Grass is most commonly chosen for a lawn because it is hard-wearing and usually attractive all year. It may also be repeatedly cut low without damage as the growing points are at the base of the plants.

Mown lawns

Mown areas of grass include high-quality lawns, utility lawns, and sports lawns. A primarily ornamental, high-quality lawn is suitable where a perfect, even appearance is paramount; it stands some wear but requires a considerable amount of maintenance to keep it in pristine condition. If the grass is likely to be subject to heavier wear – by being used as a play area, for example – opt for a utility lawn; this should also be attractive but may contain minor imperfections and requires less maintenance.

Sports areas, such as for lawn tennis or bowls, demand a particularly hard-wearing surface that can be cut very low. To stop unnecessary additional wear, they are best sited separately from the main lawn.

Long grass and grassland

As part of a wild garden or orchard, unmown grass or flower-rich grassland is very attractive, but as the grass is relatively long, it is not practical for a utility lawn. It needs very little maintenance, however, so may be suitable for an area such as a slope or a stream bank where mowing is difficult. Flower-rich grasslands often thrive on impoverished soils, so this may be a good way of using a part of the garden where little else grows.

Mixing long and short grass

Using different grasses in various parts of the garden, or varying the height of cut, helps to define separate areas and adds textural contrast. For example, a closely mown path running through long, flower-rich grassland provides an eye-catching

A FORMAL LAWN
Here, the close-clipped, pristine expanse of a high-quality, formal lawn provides a uniform, fine-textured foil for an elegant planting of white Agapanthus, *silver-grey* Senecio, *and other complementary plants, and a platform to offset an ornamental garden seat and pots of marguerites (*Argyranthemum frutescens*).*

CONTRASTING TEXTURES
Create low-relief, geometric patterns and provide definition or interesting textures in an area of lawn by altering the height of cut.

shift in height, colour, and texture, and also encourages people to walk only on the path.

In large gardens, consider having a low-cut lawn sited near the house where its fine appearance may be easily enjoyed; a path or steps could then lead to a utility lawn farther away; while an area of long grass and wild flowers could lie at the far end of the garden. Mixing grass height in this way provides contrasting but complementary ornamental, wild-life, and play areas; mowing time is also reduced as part of the area requires cutting only infrequently.

Position and form

The lawn may well be the largest single area in the garden, so plan its position and shape carefully within

GRASS PATHS
Including a closely mown grass path through the garden allows a clear view of adjacent plants; here, a broad, straight path contrasts with the informal planting of daffodils and shrubs and clearly indicates where people are expected to walk.

the context of the overall design. Take into account both practical and aesthetic considerations so that the lawn will be pleasurable to use, convenient to maintain, and an enhancing, integral part of the garden plan.

Siting a lawn
A lawn is best positioned in an open sunny area, as grass requires good light, well-drained, nutrient-rich soil, and regular moisture to thrive. A partially shaded spot can be used, provided it is laid with shade-tolerant turf or sown with a seed mixture that is suitable for shade (see "Choosing the right mixtures", p.389). Alternatively it might be better to introduce a non-grass lawn of shade-tolerant plants that tolerate some wear (see "Non-grass lawns", p.389). A chamomile or other herb lawn may also suit a garden where there is no space in which to store a mower, as these plants do not need mowing to keep them tidy.

If the proposed lawn is to surround a tree, an area the width of the tree's canopy should preferably be left ungrassed around it, because the grass cannot compete with the tree for nutrients and moisture. Alternatively plant difficult areas with shade-tolerant grass (see "Problem areas", p.389) or other ground cover.

Shape
The shape of the lawn may harmonize with the garden style or be used to dictate it. A symmetrical layout of geometrically shaped lawns bordered by paths would be appropriate in a highly stylized, formal garden. In a small garden, a simple shape such as a circle could be visually striking and might be echoed imaginatively by the introduction of a cir-

INFORMAL LAWN
The bold, curving sweep of an informal lawn is echoed by a winding, gravel path beyond and a ribbon of gold-leaved plants in an adjacent border.

cular pool or patio and containers packed with ornamental plants.

A curved, irregular design lends the garden fluidity, linking the different elements with a sweeping plane of even colour. Broad, flowing curves can be created to set off the planting in a border, and to lead the eye to a focal point. Steer clear of fussy, scalloped edges or awkward angles, however, as they may detract from the impact of any planting and make mowing difficult.

Space permitting, it may be more effective to have more than one lawn; perhaps two or more similar or complementary shapes linked by paths or archways. The farther lawn could be partially screened to provide a half-glimpsed reflection of the nearer one.

Design functions
As well as being attractive in its own right, the lawn may fulfil different

design criteria for both plants and hard features. Uniform areas of grass create a natural bond between otherwise disparate elements, leading the eye from one part of the garden to another. A statue or specimen tree sited in a lawn has maximum impact since the surrounding sea of plain colour separates it from other, more distracting elements. In a large lawn, one or two flower beds or trees may be effective if they are positioned so that they break up the green expanse, but do not dot the entire lawn: as well as making maintenance more time-consuming, the overall effect may be cluttered and disjointed.

The uniform texture and colour of grass form a neutral background that enhances other planting particularly well. The level surface acts as a foil for more sculptural plants – the strong silhouette of a columnar tree, the jutting spread of a prostrate shrub – as well as the variety of shapes, colours, and textures found in a mixed or herbaceous border.

Paths and access
Narrow areas of grass are usually subject to heavy wear and are difficult to mow; for these reasons, paths narrower than about 1m (3ft) may be impractical. For a frequently used route across a lawn, a hard path or stepping stones helps to prevent uneven wear.

If possible, leave at least one side of the lawn open for access; if there are only one or two narrow openings, the grass may become damaged at these points and need constant repair.

Edging
Edging the lawn with paving stones or bricks helps to define its shape and that of the borders, and also has practical advantages. It makes it easier to cut the lawn right to its edge

while avoiding the risk of damaging other plants. Trailing plants may be allowed to overhang the edge, breaking up any effect of rigidity, but without depriving the grass beneath of light. In addition, ornamental containers may be set on the hard edging as focal points or to provide an interesting change of level. Alternatively, a narrow "mowing strip" of bare earth may be left at the edge of a lawn; this is particularly useful if the lawn is adjacent to a wall or fence.

Climatic considerations

Turf grasses are often divided into two main groups depending on their temperature tolerance. Cool-season grasses that grow mainly in a temperate climate prefer temperatures of 15–24°C (59–75°F); those that grow best in subtropical or tropical climates, thriving in temperatures of 26–35°C (79–95°F), are known as warm-season grasses.

In large countries that cover a number of climatic zones, local advice can be sought on the best grass species to use. In temperate regions, warm-season grasses are not normally used for lawns because they turn brown during winter as they become dormant, although some can be grown satisfactorily.

Cool-season grasses
Temperate or cool-season grasses are widely used for lawns throughout the UK, Northern Europe, North America, and other regions with similar climates (see "Climate zones", p.606). The grasses that are most commonly found in cool-season lawns are bents (*Agrostis*), fescues (*Festuca*), meadow grasses (*Poa*, also known as blue grasses), and perennial ryegrass (*Lolium perenne*).

Bents are low-growing and the most tolerant of close mowing. Fescues are fine-leaved and may be cut low; they are quite hard-wearing and some species tolerate poor soils. Meadow grasses are more resistant to wear but do not withstand low mowing, and some have quite coarse leaves. Ryegrass is very hard-wearing and tolerates most soils, including heavy clay, but is coarse-textured and should not be closely mown. Annual meadow grass (*Poa annua*) is also found in many lawns, but is often considered a weed grass as it quickly runs to seed and forms coarse patches of grass.

Cool-season grasses are usually sown as mixtures of more than one species, although in some areas of

temperate North America, smooth-stalked meadow grass, which is also known as Kentucky blue grass (*Poa pratensis*), is grown on its own. If sowing a single species lawn, however, it is common to mix several cultivars together as this improves the lawn's disease resistance and the overall colour (see also "Choosing the right mixtures", p.389).

Warm-season grasses
These occur naturally in tropical and subtropical regions of South America, Africa, and Asia, especially southern China; they are therefore adapted to growing successfully in a wide range of warm climatic zones.

The major warm-season grasses that are planted in lawns and other areas of intensive use are the various species and cultivars of Bermuda grasses (*Cynodon*), St Augustine grass (*Stenotaphrum secundatum*), and zoysia grasses (*Zoysia*).

The Bermuda grasses include common Bermuda grass (*Cynodon dactylon*), African Bermuda grass (*C. transvaalensis*), Bradley Bermuda grass (*C. incompletus* var. *hirsutus*), and Magennis Bermuda grass (*C.* x *magennisii*).

Three species of zoysia grasses are appropriate for use as lawns: Japanese lawn grass (*Zoysia japonica*), Manila grass or Japanese carpet grass (*Z. matrella*), and also Mascarene grass (*Z. tenuifolia*). Zoysia grasses grow particularly well in areas that have very warm summers combined with cool winters.

Warm-season grasses are usually grown as a single species turf as they have a strong, creeping habit and do not mix well together. If other grasses are included, they tend to form unsightly, distinct patches of differing colour and texture. Warm-season species become dormant and lose their colour at temperatures below 10°C (50°F), which can be problematic where conditions are ideal only during summer. In these areas, cool-season grasses, such as ryegrasses and fescues, may be oversown in autumn to improve the colour of the lawn in winter.

Selecting the right grass

Before selecting seed or turf, assess the relative importance of the lawn's appearance, wearability, and maintenance needs. Of the many different grass mixtures available, some are particularly good for areas of heavy use while others may give attractive colour and texture. The grass seed should also be suitable for the growing conditions such as the soil type and drainage, and the degree of shade.

High-quality lawns
To create formal, high-quality lawns, where a perfect appearance is the prime consideration and very heavy wear is not anticipated, select mixtures of grass species that create an attractive, uniform texture and colour.
Cool season For the highest quality lawns, a grass mixture of fine-leaved bents and fescues is used. Browntop and highland bent (*Agrostis tenuis* and *A. castellana*) are mixed with Chewing's fescue and slender, creeping red fescue (*Festuca rubra* var. *commutata* and *F. rubra* var. *rubra*).
Warm season Cultivars of the common Bermuda grass are excellent for high-quality lawns. There are several

PLAY AREAS
If the lawn is to include an area for games or play, as in this garden, use a particularly hard-wearing grass mixture in order to prevent the lawn from becoming patchy.

improved cultivars that tolerate heat, drought, and heavy wear. Zoysia grasses also form a high-quality, slow-growing turf.

Utility lawns
Lawns that are primarily functional, perhaps providing a play area for children or a space for outdoor entertaining, need to be relatively hard-wearing but they must still provide an attractive, even surface; grasses for this purpose do not usually create the perfect texture and colour of a high-quality lawn, as this is inevitably of secondary importance.
Cool season For hard-wearing lawns, the major grass is perennial ryegrass; it is usually mixed with red fescue (*Festuca rubra* var. *rubra*), smooth-stalked meadow grass (*Poa pratensis*), and browntop or highland bent (*Agrostis tenuis*, *A. castellana*). Lawns of only smooth-stalked meadow grass are quite widely planted in temperate regions of North America.
Warm season The Bermuda grasses (see "High-quality lawns", left) are tough enough for most utility lawns but need frequent mowing. St Augustine grass has a less fine texture but is also suitable, particularly for shady areas. For a low-maintenance lawn, choose bahia grass (*Paspalum notatum*), carpet grass (*Axonopus*), or centipede grass (*Eremochloa ophiuroides*). These require less frequent mowing, but have coarse-textured leaves. They do not provide a fine finish.

Games and sports areas
Areas of grass used for ball games or sports need particularly wear-tolerant species and selected cultivars. In addition, some sports lawns must be able to tolerate a very low cut in order to minimize the effect of the grass on the run of the ball.

Cool season A mixture of bents and fescues as for high-quality lawns (see p.388) is suitable for areas such as croquet lawns, bowling greens, and golf putting greens; very heavy use, however, soon damages the grasses. If a more hard-wearing surface is needed, such as for lawn tennis, it is better to opt for a mixture containing perennial ryegrass (see "Utility lawns", p.388).

Warm season The Bermuda grasses (see "High-quality lawns", p.388) should provide a reasonably hard-wearing, attractive surface. Some cultivars are more tolerant of wear than others, so take care to select those recommended as suitable for games areas.

Flower-rich grassland

For flower-rich areas, whenever possible use grass species that are native to the area: as well as being more likely to flourish, they do not look incongruous or artificial (see also MEADOW GARDENING, p.401). Usually a flower-rich seed mixture consists of slow-growing grasses and various native, broad-leaved flowering species. As well as climate, soil type, soil moisture, and aspect may affect the choice of species sown; some prefer extremely dry, well-drained conditions, while others grow well on marshy ground.

Cool season Bents and fescues are usually included, while a short-lived grass, such as Italian ryegrass (*Lolium multiflorum*), may be added for initial, fast ground cover. If mown, Italian ryegrass will die out within two years, leaving behind the fine-leaved grasses and broadleaved flowering plants. Some species need a cold period before they will germinate, and so may not appear in the first year after sowing.

Warm season In areas where warm-season grasses are grown, it is rare for flower-rich grassland to be cultivated: as warm-season grasses grow vigorously they tend to smother the flowering plants.

Problem areas

For lawns in difficult sites, such as shady, wet, or dry areas, choose a grass mixture that is specially designed for such conditions. In extreme cases, it may be better to grow ground-cover shrubs or perennials instead (see pp.101 and 180).

Cool season In wet, shady areas, grass does not readily grow into a dense, vigorous sward, and regular mowing will compact the soil and reduce grass growth. Some species, however, are more tolerant than others: wood meadow grass (*Poa nemoralis*) is often sown with rough-stalked meadow grass (*P. trivialis*), although neither survives close mowing or heavy wear. Fescues may also be included; they grow reasonably well in these conditions and take a lower height of cut when mowing. Turf timothy (*Phleum pratensis* subsp. *bertolonii*) is sometimes used in place of perennial ryegrass in moist, not too shady areas.

In very dry regions, use grasses native to such areas, such as western wheatgrass (*Agropyron smithii*) which grows naturally on the great plains of North America, or fairway crested wheatgrass (*A. cristatum*) which is native to the dry, cold plains of Russia and Siberia. The wheatgrasses generally produce medium- to low-quality lawns; couch grass or quackgrass (*Elymus repens*) may become a weed in lawns that are left to grow over 2.5cm (1in).

Warm season For shady areas, St Augustine grass is a good choice; it is also salt-tolerant and so is valuable for coastal gardens. It is coarser than the various forms of either Bermuda grasses or zoysia grasses, however, so is generally only used where finer species do not thrive.

Choosing the right mixtures

Many modern grass mixtures have been specially produced to provide qualities particularly valued in lawns, such as even colour, disease resistance, wear and shade tolerance, and compact growth. Shade-tolerant mixtures, for example, may include fescues and bents such as Chewings fescues, hard fescues, and brown top bent. When selecting grass seed or the type of turf best suited to your site, make sure that the mixture includes not only the correct species (such as *Festuca rubra* var. *commutata*) but also a modern cultivar of that species. For further details on lawn seed mixtures and single species grasses see *Sowing Rates*, p.394, and for the range of turf types see "Turfing", p.392.

The grass mixture should not contain agricultural cultivars; these are bred to produce vigorous, vertical leaf growth for grazing and need frequent mowing. They also tend to spread less, and so do not always produce a dense, uniform cover.

Non-grass lawns

Although lawns are usually established with grasses, other evergreen species are sometimes used. These

FLOWERS IN GRASS
The grass in this informal orchard is dotted with bright yellow buttercups (Ranunculus) *and the vivid red, white, and purple cups of naturalized tulips.*

include chamomile (*Chamaemelum nobile*), *Cotula*, *Dichondra micrantha*, and even various species of moss. Unlike grasses, these ground-cover plants do not stand up to heavy, continual wear, so they are rarely the best choice for a main lawn; they may, however, be used for primarily ornamental areas. Grow them in a patio or courtyard garden to provide a welcome patch of green; as a living surround at the base of a fountain, raised pond, pedestal urn, or statue; or next to a patio or path to creep over the edges and relieve the rigidity of the hard surface.

Chamomile leaves release a sweet, apple-like fragrance when crushed underfoot but they do not tolerate heavy wear; the non-flowering clone, 'Treneague', is naturally low-growing and especially suitable for lawns.

Cotula, which has fern-like leaves, is considerably more hard-wearing as it forms a thick carpet of creeping stems; it also flourishes in moist conditions. *Dichondra* grows most successfully in warm areas and does not survive temperatures lower than -4°C (25°F).

Another option is to create a "tapestry lawn" with a patchwork effect by growing a number of low, mat-forming plants together. It is best to use plants that grow at a similar rate, such as the various creeping thymes (such as *Thymus caespititius*, *T.* 'Coccineus', *T.* 'Doone Valley', and *Thymus polytrichus* subsp. *britannicus*), otherwise one species may gradually predominate and so upset the balance of the original design. As for other non-grass lawns, tapestry lawns should not be heavily used.

CHAMOMILE LAWN
The soft, spreading cushion of a chamomile lawn provides a central focal point in a herb garden or a patio, and softens the hard effect of the gravel edging and formal sundial.

THOROUGH site preparation is the key to establishing a successful new lawn. Although this may be time-consuming and expensive, in the long run it is easier and cheaper to prepare the site properly at the outset than to try to alleviate problems later. The general principles of preparation apply to all sites, but decisions on drainage, soil improvement, and irrigation should depend on the individual site and the climate.

Clearing the site

It is important to clear the site completely, removing any large stones and rubble, and all plant growth, including any tree stumps or roots. If the site is already partially turfed but in too poor a condition to be worth renovating, then remove all the turf (see also "Renovating a neglected lawn", p.399).

Eradicating weeds

Take particular care to eliminate any perennial weeds that have underground rhizomes or deep tap roots, such as couch grass or quackgrass (*Elymus repens*), dandelion (*Taraxacum officinale*), docks (*Rumex*), and the perennial stinging nettle (*Urtica dioica*), because they regenerate rapidly from small pieces of root or rhizome (see PLANT PROBLEMS, "Perennial Weeds", pp.670–673). Once the lawn grass is established, broadleaved weeds may still be controlled using selective weedkillers, but weed grasses will be more difficult to eliminate, so it is sensible to use a weedkiller to clear the ground initially.

Annual weeds, such as fat-hen (*Chenopodium album*) and shepherd's purse (*Capsella bursa-pastoris*), may be controlled by mowing after the grass has germinated. It is preferable, however, to remove annual weeds before sowing as part of the site preparation.

Preparing the soil

The ideal topsoil for a lawn is a well-drained, sandy loam at least 20cm (8in) and preferably 30cm (12in) in depth, overlying a well-structured and free-draining subsoil. In these conditions the grass becomes deep-rooted and obtains ample water and nutrients from the soil. If the soil depth varies, during dry weather brown patches will rapidly appear where the soil is shallow.

Other soils may also be suitable, but if the soil does not drain freely and the lawn is likely to be heavily used, especially in wet conditions, the drainage should be improved. If the topsoil is very shallow or poor, it may be necessary to add new topsoil; this may be moved from other parts of the garden or bought, although for large areas the latter is very expensive.

If the soil has a naturally high sand content, and is, therefore, too free-draining, incorporate some well-rotted organic matter to help retain nutrients and water (see "Soil structure and water content", p.620). Be careful, however, not to add too much because organic matter quickly rots down, and this may result in soil sinkage and an uneven surface.

After clearing the site, plough, cultivate, or dig over the whole area, removing any large stones that are brought to the surface, then rake the ground to produce a fine tilth. Breaking up the soil in this way makes subsequent levelling easier, as well as relieving compaction and improving the soil structure. On heavy, clay soils, however, rotavating or ploughing may create a compacted layer below the soil surface which could impede drainage; if necessary, break it up using a subsoiling machine or by double digging. For further information, see "Soil cultivation", pp.618–621.

Drainage

Lawns on free-draining soils, and those in regions with low rainfall, are unlikely to require draining. In heavy, clay soils, drainage may be improved by incorporating up to two parts of sand to every one part of soil by double digging, but this is expensive and laborious. In any soil that is not free-draining, it is preferable to install a drainage system during the preparation stage to avoid continual and expensive attempts to alleviate the problem after the lawn has been established.

The best type of drain for lawns consists of a row of pipes laid in a trench, which is backfilled with gravel. The ideal depth of the drain, and the distance between drains, will vary from site to site depending on the type of soil and the rainfall. For most loamy soils receiving moderate rainfall, one drain every 5–8m (15–25ft) is needed. Heavier, clay soils or sites in areas with a high rainfall will need drains laid at closer intervals (see also SOILS AND FERTILIZERS, "Improving drainage", p.623).

How to Level the Ground

1 Firm the site well, especially at the edges, by tamping with the back of a rake or by treading. Mark some pegs at the same distance from the top of each. Insert a row of pegs at the site edge. If next to paving, the marks should be level with its surface.

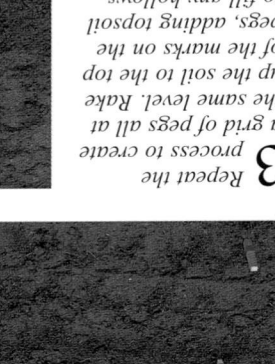

2 Add a second, parallel row of pegs about 1m (3ft) from the first row. Place a spirit level on top of these to check that they are level with the previous row. Adjust the pegs as necessary.

3 Repeat the process to create a grid of pegs all at the same level. Rake up the soil to the top of the marks on the pegs, adding topsoil to fill any hollows. Once the ground is level, the pegs may be removed.

Levelling the site

In gardens that have only minor undulations and deep topsoil, the site may be roughly levelled by raking soil from the high spots to fill the hollows, firming at intervals to consolidate the ground. Although it is not essential for the ground to be precisely level, awkward bumps and

Adjusting the soil pH

For new lawns, the pH is unlikely to need adjusting, unless previous use has left the site in extremely poor condition. Most grasses grow satisfactorily at pH levels of 5.5–7. Fine fescues and bents grow best at pH 5.5–6.5, while perennial ryegrass, the meadow grasses, and many warm-season grasses grow better at pH 6–7. Soil-testing kits for measuring pH are available from most garden centres.

If the soil is very acidic (below pH 5), dig or cultivate lime into the soil, the exact amount depending on the degree of acidity (see "Liming", p.625). Then leave the site for about a month before applying fertilizer. Lime may be added once the lawn is

established but, as large amounts spread on grass may encourage certain diseases, only use a small quantity and repeat the following year if necessary. If uncertain about what to do, seek advice from an agricultural or horticultural college, or an agricultural advisory service.

ACCURATE LEVELLING

To level the ground, first create a grid of pre-marked pegs and knock them into the soil at the same depth. Add or remove soil until it is level with the marks on the pegs.

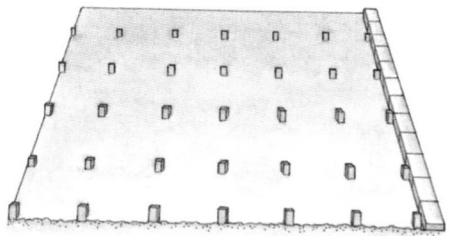

hollows may cause problems when mowing. In some instances – for example, for a paddock or an area of rough grass – levelling by eye is sufficient. But if a perfectly level surface is required, such as for a formal lawn, a more accurate method should be used.

Achieving an accurate level

After levelling the ground roughly, an exact level may be achieved by knocking pegs into the ground all at the same depth to form a grid.

Start from a straight edge such as a path or patio, or create a taut line with string. Then take a number of identical pegs and make a mark on each one at the same distance from the top. Starting from the straight edge, knock the pegs into the ground at equal intervals so that the marks are at the required level of the lawn or approximately 2cm (¾in) below this if turfing. Add a second row of pegs and then further rows until the site is covered by a grid of pegs.

Use a spirit level – placed on a straight plank of wood if necessary to span across the rows – to check

that the pegs within the rows are all at the same height. Then adjust the level of the soil so that it is aligned with the mark on each peg.

Substantial levelling

If the site needs more substantial levelling or the topsoil is very shallow, the subsoil must be levelled first. To do this, remove the topsoil, rotavate or dig over the subsoil, then rake, level, and firm it roughly before replacing the topsoil in an even layer at least 20–30cm (8–12in) deep. To prevent the filled areas from sinking later, firm them thoroughly at intervals, adding more topsoil if necessary, and allow the site to settle before preparing the surface.

Creating a slope

Making the lawn slope gently away from the house or patio improves drainage and ensures that water does not drain into the foundations. A method similar to levelling is used, but each successive row of pegs is marked farther up or down to form a sloping grid. For example, to create a gradient of 1:100, make the marks

on each row of pegs successively lower by 2cm (¾in) and space pegs 2m (6ft) apart. A lawn angled towards a house must have its drain or soakaway sloping in the opposite direction, that is away from the house, to prevent water from reaching the building.

Final site preparations

Once the soil has been drained and levelled, the final surface may be prepared so that the site is ready for establishing a lawn.

Firming and raking

Tread the soil evenly all over to firm it and to ensure there are no soft spots which might later sink, making the turf vulnerable to being scalped during mowing. It may be necessary to tread the area about three times before the soil is sufficiently consolidated, but take care not to compress the soil too much, and do not firm wet soil as it will become compacted. Even after firming, the soil may settle further over the course of a year or two, leaving small hollows. These should be levelled by applying a sieved, sandy top-dressing (see p.398).

After firming, thoroughly rake the surface to produce a fine tilth and a level surface. If sowing seed, remove any stones larger than about 1cm (½in) across during raking; if turfing, it is only necessary to remove stones over 2.5cm (1in).

Leave the prepared site for about three to four weeks to allow any weed seeds to germinate; any emerging weeds should then be either hoed off carefully or treated with a contact weedkiller and gently raked off two or three days later once they have died, taking care not to disrupt the levelled soil unduly.

Fertilizing

A few days before establishing the lawn, and once the surface has been prepared, apply fertilizer to the site. This should contain the three major nutrients to ensure good growth: nitrogen (N), phosphorus (P), and potassium (K). Sites that have not been fertilized for many years may be deficient in all three. Phosphorus is especially important during the early stages of growth. Use a balanced organic fertilizer, such as pelleted chicken manure, or a compound granular or micro-granular fertilizer that contains all three of the nutrients; apply it according to the manufacturer's instructions at a rate of 150–200g/sq m (4–6oz/sq yd).

1 *Firm the surface by treading it evenly, or by tamping it with the back of a rake. Repeat, if necessary, until the entire site is well firmed.*

2 *Rake the soil to a fine tilth and leave it to allow any weeds to germinate. When they appear, apply a contact weedkiller and, after about 2–3 days, rake off the weeds.*

3 *Apply a base dressing of a compound granular organic fertilizer and lightly rake it into the surface. Leave the site for a few days before turfing or seeding.*

CREATING A SLOPE

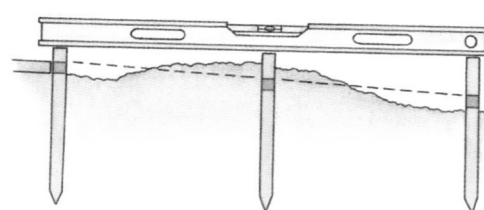

Decide how many rows of pegs will be used and mark the pegs for each row at different heights in order to achieve the desired gradient (see above). Using a spirit level, create a grid of pegs as for levelling, and rake soil up to the marks.

INSTALLING A DRAIN

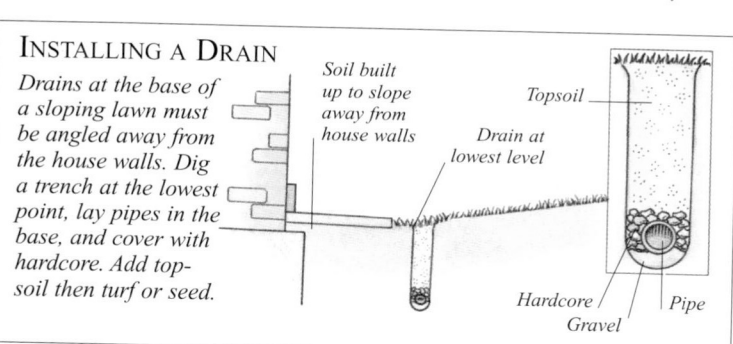

Drains at the base of a sloping lawn must be angled away from the house walls. Dig a trench at the lowest point, lay pipes in the base, and cover with hardcore. Add topsoil then turf or seed.

Soil built up to slope away from house walls

Topsoil

Drain at lowest level

Drain at lowest level

Hardcore

Pipe

Gravel

Establishing a lawn

THERE are various methods of establishing a lawn. For cool-season grasses in temperate areas, the gardener may choose between seeding or turfing; for warm-season grasses in subtropical and tropical regions, vegetative propagation methods may also be used.

Seeding a lawn is usually the cheapest method, but it takes up to a year before the lawn can be subjected to heavy wear. Establishing a lawn by vegetative means takes longer and is more costly than seeding. Turfing, although more expensive, gives an immediate visual effect, and the lawn may be used within two to three months; it is advisable to use turf if you have pets that may disturb grass seedlings before they are established.

Turfing

There is a wide range of turf types available, including purpose- and custom-grown turf, meadow and treated meadow turf, and sea-marsh turf; the type chosen largely depends on considerations of site and expense. Always buy turf from a reputable garden centre or turf farm.

If possible, inspect the turf before buying it to make sure that it is in good condition, of the right quality (see "Selecting the right grass", p.388), and that the soil is a free-draining loam rather than a heavy clay. Check that there are no weeds, pests, or diseases, nor an excessive amount of thatch (the organic matter consisting of decaying grass, stolons, and rhizomes that accumulates on the soil surface); there should, however, be enough organic matter to hold the turf together.

Purpose-grown turf
Purpose-grown turf is widely available and contains different grasses for various uses. It is raised from the newest grass cultivars and treated to make it free from weeds and disease. Turf that is guaranteed free of annual meadow grass (*Poa annua*) is also available from the top producers, although at a high price. If you need a very large quantity of special turf, and are prepared to wait 18 months for it to be grown and harvested, it may also be grown to order, but this is expensive.

Meadow turf
This is usually grown for agricultural purposes and therefore is less fine in texture; it may have been

1 *Lay the first row of turf alongside a straight edge such as a patio or path. Place each new piece or roll exactly flush with its neighbour.*

2 *Place a plank on the first row of turf. Use this to kneel on. Then lay the next row with the turf joints staggered, as in a brick wall. Proceed in exactly the same way for the rest of the lawn.*

3 *Tamp down each turf with the back of a rake to make sure that there are no air pockets. Alternatively, roll the lawn with a light roller.*

4 *Apply a light top-dressing of sieved, sandy loam and brush this in well, filling any gaps between the turves.*

5 *If no rain is forecast, water the turves well. Take care to keep them moist until they have rooted into the topsoil or they may shrink and gaps will appear.*

either sown recently or grown in a long-established field. It is usually the cheapest turf, as it may contain coarse, vigorous, agricultural grasses and broadleaved weeds such as daisies (*Bellis perennis*). The quality varies greatly, however, so it is especially important to buy meadow turf from a reputable supplier to ensure that it is of reasonable quality. If the weeds are eliminated by the use of selective weedkillers, the improved turf is described as treated meadow turf. Lawns established with meadow turf may have a coarse appearance and need more frequent mowing, but are perfectly adequate for utility or family use.

Sea-marsh turf
Once considered the finest turf available, sea-marsh turf contains fine fescues and bents. As it frequently grows in river estuaries where there are silt and clay deposits, however, it may contain a silty layer, which restricts drainage, thus reducing its wear-tolerance. Purpose-grown turf, containing new cultivars of fine

fescues and bents, is often preferred, since it is usually grown on better soil and is readily available.

Turf sizes
Turf is available in a range of sizes and shapes. High-quality turf is often sold in rolls 40cm (16in) wide and up to 2.2m (7ft) long, and lower quality turf in shorter lengths. Major producers also usually supply turf of all qualities in units of 1sq m (1sq yd).

STORING TURF

Lay the turves as soon as possible; if it is essential to store them, spread them out flat – grass side up – so that they receive enough light, and keep them watered.

Storing turf
Turf is best lifted and relaid in its new position within the same day. If there is an unavoidable, long delay, lay the turf flat on paving or plastic sheeting, preferably in a slightly shaded area, and keep it watered; in hot weather, it may dry out very quickly, so check it regularly. If turf is left rolled up, it will not receive enough light, so the grass will turn yellow and eventually die.

Laying turf

Turf may be laid at almost any time of the year except during prolonged spells of extreme temperatures. If possible, choose a time when rain is expected in the next day or two. Turf should be laid on moist, but not wet, soil to encourage rapid rooting. Provided the site is correctly prepared, turf is comparatively easy to lay. Expert contractors will, however, do the job for you, if required.

Starting at the edge of the site, lay the first row of turf in a straight line. Standing on planks placed on the turf, rake over the soil on which the next row is to be laid. Lay this next row so that the end of each turf piece or roll is staggered with adjacent pieces or rolls.

Do not finish a row with a small segment of turf beside the edge, as it will be vulnerable to damage and drying out. If necessary, lay the last complete piece of turf at the edge, and fill the gap behind with the trimmed segment. Lay further rows until the site is covered.

When all the turf has been laid, cut the edges to shape. For a curved edge,

TRIMMING THE LAWN EDGE

CURVED EDGE
Lay a hose or rope to the required shape and secure with wire hoops. Standing on a board, cut just inside the hose.

STRAIGHT EDGE
Stretch a taut string along the required line and align a plank with this. Then, standing on the plank, cut along its edge.

LIFTING TURF FOR RELAYING

1 *Cut the turf to be lifted into strips: insert 2 short canes a little way apart, 30cm (12in) in from the turf edge, and lay a plank flush against them. Stand on the plank and cut along its edge.*

2 *Cut each strip into turves about 45cm (18in) long, then undercut the turves to a depth of at least 2.5cm (1in). To stack them, lay grass to grass, soil to soil, on a path or piece of plastic sheeting.*

3 *Trim the lifted turves so that they are all the same depth: place each turf upside down in a prepared box and slice off any soil above the correct level. Relay the turves as required.*

lay a hose or rope along the curve required, and cut just inside it. For a straight edge, mark the proposed lawn edge with taut string. Align a plank with this guideline and cut along it using a half-moon or powered edger. Move the plank along the guideline and repeat the procedure until the entire edge has been cut.

Aftercare
Either tamp down the turves with the back of a rake or roll the lawn with a light roller to ensure that there are no air pockets. In wet conditions, however, do not roll until the turves have rooted and knitted together. Brush or lute a light top-dressing (see p.398) between the turves to encourage the roots to spread.

Do not allow the turf to dry out before the grass has rooted through. It is essential to water the turf thoroughly so that it reaches the soil below, otherwise the turves may shrink in dry or hot weather.

Moving turf

Sometimes it may be necessary to lift and relay an area of turf. It should be cut and lifted in uniformly sized pieces so that they fit together easily when they are relaid.

Cutting
First, divide the turf to be lifted into lengths 30cm (12in) wide by cutting along the edge of a plank with a half-moon edger. Move the plank 30cm (12in) in from the previous cut to form each new length. Then cut each length at right angles to form pieces about 45cm (18in) long. Alternatively, a mechanical turf lifter may be hired; this cuts the turf to the size and depth required and also lifts it.

Lifting
Once cut, lift the turves with a flat spade or turf float, carefully severing them from the underlying soil and roots. Remove a wedge of turf next to the first piece to be lifted, then insert the spade under the turf without damaging the edge. Undercut each turf to a depth of at least 2.5cm (1in). Stack the lifted turf grass to grass, soil to soil, on a hard surface such as paving.

Trimming
After the turves have been lifted, trim them all to the same depth using a specially constructed shallow box the same size as the cut turves. Leave one of the shorter sides open and, if possible, cover the remaining top edges with a smooth metal strip. Place each turf upside down in the box and, using a sharp blade, remove the excess soil by slicing along the top of the box.

Establishing a non-grass lawn

To create a new lawn from broad-leaved species, such as chamomile (*Chamaemelum nobile*), prepare the site as for a grass lawn, including a dressing of fertilizer on the base. Plant pot-grown specimens, rooted cuttings, divisions, or seedlings at 15–30cm (6–12in) intervals. They may be planted closer together or farther apart – the closer they are, the faster they will form a lawn and, of course, the greater the expense. Keep the site well watered during dry periods. Once the plants have covered the site, trim the lawn with a rotary mower, nylon-line trimmer, or hand shears when necessary. If growing chamomile, it is best to use the non-flowering cultivar 'Treneague' which is naturally very low-growing. Flowering forms may be grown from seed but they require more frequent trimming and the dead flowerheads may be unsightly.

1 *Plant rooted cuttings or divisions (here chamomile) 15–30cm (6–12in) apart in prepared ground. Keep the area well watered and free from weeds.*

2 *After several weeks, when the plants have grown together to form a lawn, lightly trim them with a nylon-line trimmer or garden shears.*

Seeding

Grass seed is best sown in warm, moist conditions so that it will germinate and establish quickly: early autumn is usually best. Spring-sown grass is also successful but the soil is colder than in autumn and there is more competition from weeds. Seed may be sown in summer if irrigation is available, but in hot conditions young grass seedlings suffer heat stress and may wilt or even die.

Sowing rates

Grass sowing rates vary, depending on the mixture or species (see chart, below). Although there is some leeway to allow for factors such as depletion caused by birds eating the seeds, it is important not to sow seed in much greater or smaller quantities than the recommended rate. Sowing too little seed may allow weed seedlings space to compete with the grass, and the lawn will take slightly longer to establish. Sowing too much seed may cause more problems by producing humid conditions among the seedlings. This encourages damping off (see p.664), which can damage the young lawn in a very short time, particularly in warm, humid weather (see also "Lawn problems", p.668).

Sowing seed

Seed may be sown either by hand or, faster and more evenly, by a machine. First calculate the amount of seed needed by multiplying the size of the area to be sown (in square metres or yards) by the recommended sowing rate (the amount of seed per square metre or yard). Before sowing the seed, shake the container to mix the seeds thoroughly and ensure that small seeds do not settle to the bottom and thus give an uneven distribution of grass types.

Sowing by machine

This is the best way to sow grass seed over a large area. Measure out the correct amount of seed for the lawn and divide it in half. For even coverage, sow half of the seed in one direction and half at right angles to this. A well-defined lawn edge may be achieved by laying plastic sheeting or hessian at the site edge and running the machine just over it; this also prevents the uneven distribution that may occur when stopping the machine at the end of a strip.

Sowing by hand

If sowing by hand, first divide the area into small, equal-sized sections, using string and canes or pegs; this makes it easier to sow the seed evenly. Then measure out the correct amount of seed for one section and accurately divide the batch of seed in half. Transfer one half-batch into a measure, such as a small cup, to make it easier and faster to measure out each subsequent amount. Work on one section at a time, scattering half the seed of a batch in one direction, then sowing the other half at right angles to this before moving on to the next section.

Aftercare

After sowing, lightly rake over the surface. Unless rain is forecast, water the site with a sprinkler. Germination will occur in one to two weeks, depending on grass species, soil and air temperature, and moisture. Protect the site from birds by covering it with netting or brushwood until the seedlings have established.

ESTABLISHING A LAWN BY SOWING SEED

1 *If using a machine, sow half the seed in one direction and half at right angles to this. For a defined edge, lay down plastic sheeting and push the machine just over it at the end of each row.*

ALTERNATIVE STEP
If sowing by hand, mark the site into equal areas. Weigh out enough seed for a single area, then scatter it evenly, half in one direction and half at right angles to this.

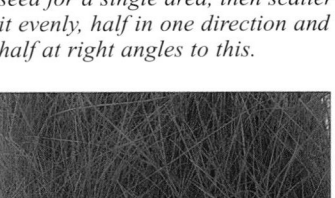

2 *After sowing, lightly rake over the surface. In dry conditions, water the site regularly to encourage the seeds to germinate.*

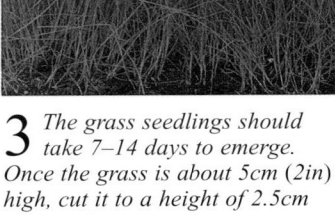

3 *The grass seedlings should take 7–14 days to emerge. Once the grass is about 5cm (2in) high, cut it to a height of 2.5cm (1in) with a rotary mower.*

Water the site regularly in dry weather since young grasses are very susceptible to drought. Once the seedlings have emerged, the surface may be gently firmed with a light-weight roller (100kg/220lb), although this is not essential.

Cutting

When the grass has reached approximately 5cm (2in), cut it to a height of 2.5cm (1in). For the first two or three cuts, use a rotary mower, because a cylinder mower with a roller may tear the vulnerable young leaves. Then carefully rake up and remove all excess clippings. If the lawn was sown in late summer or early autumn, continue to mow when necessary through late autumn in order to maintain it at about 2.5cm (1in) high. During the following spring, gradually lower the height of the cut until the desired height is reached, depending on the type of grass used (see also "Frequency and height of cut", p.395). Young grasses are particularly vulnerable to damage by wear, so try to use the lawn as little as possible during its first full growing season.

Vegetative propagation

Lawns grown from warm-season grasses, or the cool-season creeping bentgrass (*Agrostis stolonifera*), which produce vigorous stolons and rhizomes, may also be established by vegetative means such as stolonizing, sprigging, or plugging. The best time of year for creating a lawn by one of these methods is late spring or early summer, on a site prepared as for sowing grass seed. It will take about two months for the material to root and spread over the soil. As for grass seedlings, regular irrigation is essential.

To establish a lawn by stolonizing, spread stolons evenly over the soil at the supplier's recommended rate, top-dress with a light, sandy soil, roll, and water. Alternatively, for sprigging, stolons and rhizomes are planted in holes or furrows 2.5–5cm (1–2in) deep and 8–15cm (3–6in) apart, then firmed in and watered. For plugging, small pieces of turf, or plugs, are planted at intervals of 25–45cm (10–18in).

SOWING RATES

MIXTURES	g/sq m	oz/sq yd
Fescues and bents	25–30	³⁄₄–⁷⁄₈
Perennial ryegrass and other species	35–40	1–1¹⁄₈
Flower-rich mixtures (depending on mixture)	2.5–5	¹⁄₁₆–¹⁄₈
SINGLE SPECIES		
Bents (*Agrostis*)	8–10	¹⁄₄–⁵⁄₁₆
Carpet grass (*Axonopus*)	8–12	¹⁄₄–³⁄₈
Common Bermuda grass (*Cynodon dactylon*)	5–8	¹⁄₈–¹⁄₄
Centipede grass (*Eremochloa ophiuroides*)	1.5–2.5	¹⁄₂₄–¹⁄₁₆
Red fescue (*Festuca rubra* var. *rubra*)	15–25	¹⁄₂–³⁄₄
Perennial ryegrass (*Lolium perenne*)	20–40	⁵⁄₈–1¹⁄₈
Bahia grass (*Paspalum notatum*)	30–40	⁷⁄₈–1¹⁄₈
Smooth-stalked meadow grass/Kentucky blue grass (*Poa pratensis*)	10–15	⁵⁄₁₆–¹⁄₂

Routine care

Once the lawn is well established, regular maintenance is needed to ensure its health and attractive appearance. The attention required depends on the lawn's size and type as well as the site and climate. In general, the most frequent tasks are mowing and watering, but annual maintenance may include fertilizing, top-dressing, aerating, and, where necessary, controlling moss, weeds, pests, and diseases. For large lawns, using mechanical or powered tools, which may be hired, often makes maintenance tasks faster and easier (see "Lawncare tools", pp.558–559).

Mowing

In addition to making the lawn a pleasure to walk on, regularly cutting the grass helps to create a dense, healthy sward with an even, attractive finish. Mowing is needed most frequently in the warm, moist conditions of early and late summer; during drought conditions, however, it is best either not to mow at all or to set the mower to a higher cut. Delay mowing during very wet or frosty weather: wet grass can clog the mower or the mower may slip, and mowing in frost damages the grass. If mowing a fine lawn, brushing with a besom beforehand raises the grass and so achieves a better cut. Brushing the lawn in the morning also helps to remove dew and dries the grass surface, making it considerably easier to mow.

Mowers
For most lawns, a cylinder or reel mower, or a rotary (including the hover type) mower is suitable. A mower with a roller provides the finest finish for a lawn and creates

BRUSHING AWAY DEW

To remove excess moisture and raise the grass before mowing, brush away the dew with a besom; for large areas, drag a piece of hessian over the lawn.

stripes, but a mower with no roller gives a perfectly acceptable surface for a utility lawn. A mulching mower leaves clippings on the lawn to nourish the grass – ideal in an organically managed garden. The type of mower selected should depend on the size of the lawn and the finish required (see also "Lawnmowers", p.557).

Frequency and height of cut
The frequency of mowing and the height of cut depends on a number of factors, including the type of grasses grown, how the lawn is used, and the time of year, but little and often is a good general rule to follow. Try to remove no more than a third of the leaf growth at any one time. If the grass is cut sporadically and drastically, it will struggle to recover after each mowing and there will be a noticeable decline in the lawn's quality. Frequent mowing is necessary in summer when the grass grows quickly; during spring and autumn, the rate should be reduced and, in winter, occasional "topping" – removing just the grass tips – may be all that is needed.

High-quality lawns may be cut even as low as 0.5cm (¼in) but they should be mown frequently – every two or three days in summer – to maintain their appearance. Utility lawns should be left to grow longer than this, because the grasses do not tolerate such a low cut; this also helps to protect the surface against heavy wear and tear.

It is not necessary to mow all areas to the same height. Try two or three heights of cut for different grass areas to add texture and interest to the garden. For practical reasons, cut the main area to be used for walking or playing to a height of about 1–2.5cm (½–1in). Keeping the grass at this length protects the surface against wear. Mow the areas under trees less frequently – every one or two weeks in summer – to a height of 5–10cm (2–4in). Leave any areas of flower-rich grassland at 10cm

MOWING STRIPES

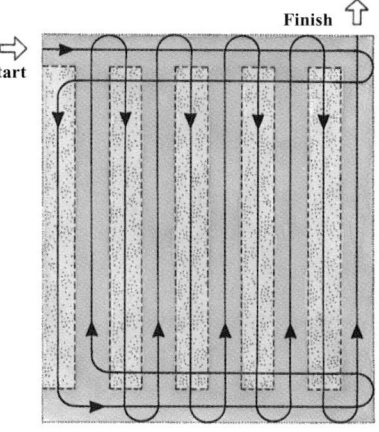

REGULAR SHAPE
First mow a wide strip at each end of the lawn for turning space, then mow up and down the lawn in slightly overlapping runs.

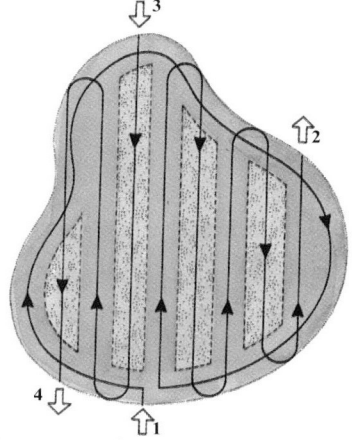

IRREGULAR SHAPE
Mow a strip around the lawn edge, then mow a straight strip up the centre. Mow up and down one half of the lawn, then the other half.

(4in) or more; they will need no more than three cuts per year and should not be cut until the flowering species have shed their seed in mid-summer (see MEADOW GARDENING, p.401). Since they are mown infrequently, these areas produce much more growth and debris which should be raked up and removed after mowing.

Mowing stripes
Use a mower fitted with a roller to achieve a classic, striped finish to the lawn. If the lawn is square or rectangular, first mow a wide strip at either end of the lawn. Then mow up and down in straight strips, slightly overlapping the previous run to make sure that all the grass is mown.

If the lawn is of an irregular shape first mow all around its edge. Then, starting at the centre of one end, mow a straight line down the middle by picking out an object or tree beyond the end of the lawn and then pointing the mower directly towards it. Mow straight strips up and down

one half of the lawn, then return to the centre and mow the other half in a similar fashion.

Mowing sports lawns
On areas to be used for ball games, such as croquet, bowls, or putting, vary the direction each time you mow to prevent a "grain" from developing. Grain is produced by grass growing in one direction and affects the run of the ball.

Grass clippings
On fine lawns where a high-quality finish is required, use a mower that collects grass clippings as it cuts or rake them up afterwards and add them in layers to the compost heap. Do not compost them, however, for the first few cuts after application of weedkiller. Removing grass clippings tends to discourage earthworms and lessens the spread of annual meadow grass and weeds such as speedwell. It may also help to prevent a build-up of thatch and thus maintain a finer finish to the lawn.

FREQUENCY AND HEIGHT OF CUT

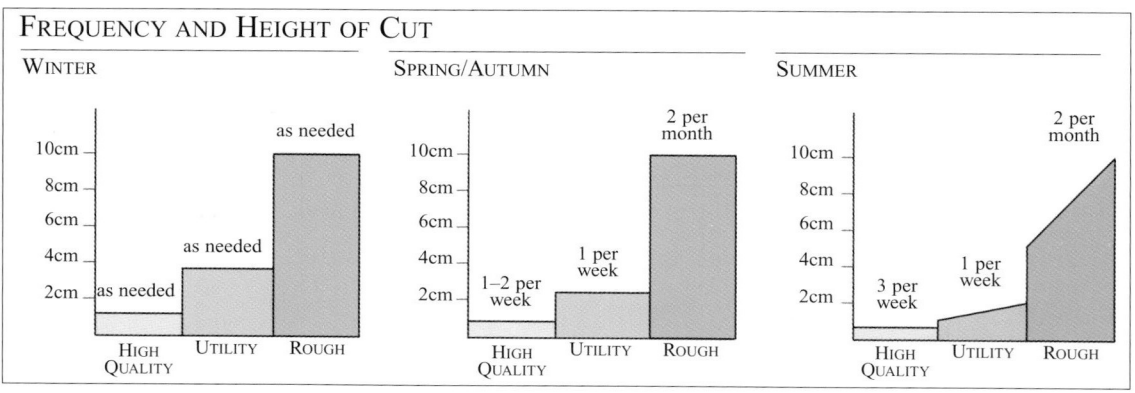

Utility lawns containing earthworms may benefit from a light layer of clippings left on the lawn as they will be recycled by the worms, thereby returning plant nutrients to the soil. The majority of the clippings should be raked up, however, as excessive amounts may cause damage to the turf beneath as they rot down. In general, it is better to remove grass clippings and replace the lost nutrients by feeding.

Removing fallen leaves

In autumn and winter, clear away any fallen leaves from the lawn by brushing or raking them up and removing them; a layer of leaves left on the lawn reduces evaporation, and the resulting humidity can encourage turf diseases.

Trimming edges

After mowing, create a neat finish by trimming the lawn edges with long-handled edging shears, a mechanical edging machine, or a nylon-line trimmer with an adjustable head for edging (see "Lawncare tools", pp.558–559). If the lawn edges become irregular, recut them once or twice a year with a half-moon edger, cutting against a plank for a straight line; for very large lawns, it is faster and less laborious to use a powered edging machine for this task.

CLEARING LEAVES

Remove any fallen leaves and debris by brushing the lawn briskly with a besom or a spring-tined rake. For large lawns, use a leaf-sweeper or blower to speed up the task.

Watering

Established grass generally resists and recovers from drought well without watering, although growth slows down and the turf turns brown in prolonged dry spells. It is, however, essential to water newly made and high-quality lawns thoroughly in dry periods to maintain growth and colour – provided that there are no hosepipe restrictions in force.

A seep hose or hosepipe is perfectly satisfactory for most lawns but areas of grass that need regular watering may be better served by a built-in, pop-up sprinkler system installed underground. For more information on irrigation tools, see "Watering aids", pp. 560–561.

Start to water as soon as you notice that the grass does not spring back up after the lawn has been walked on – a state known as "footprinting". The best time to water is either in the early morning or in the evening to minimize evaporation. It is vital to give the lawn enough water; after watering, the soil should be moistened to a depth of 10–15cm (4–6 in). Shallow watering encourages plant roots to remain near the surface, making the lawn more susceptible to drought. Dig a small hole to check that the soil is damp to the required depth; make a note of the time that it took to water the lawn sufficiently to guide you in future. Alternatively, a battery-powered moisture meter may be used to register the soil moisture level.

On heavy soils, where the drainage is restricted, it is important not to apply too much water as this inhibits oxygen and mineral intake by the grass roots. If pools of water remain on the lawn for some time after heavy rain or watering, the lawn may need additional drainage (see "Improving drainage", p.623).

Fertilizing

As with all plants, grasses require nutrients to grow, and regular applications of fertilizer help ensure a vigorous, healthy lawn. Most of the nutrients essential for growth are plentiful within the soil, but four – nitrogen (N), phosphorus (P), potassium (K), and iron (Fe) – are often applied as a supplement. Nitrogen is the nutrient most commonly added, especially when grass clippings have been removed: it is essential for producing further growth that is stimulated by mowing. Nitrogen-deficient grass is generally yellow-green in appearance and lacking in vigour.

Fertilizers are the easiest way to apply nutrients to a lawn; both organic and artificial products are available (see also "Soil nutrients and

fertilizers", pp.624–625). The exact amount of fertilizer that is required depends on how quickly water drains from the soil, how much rainfall or irrigation is received by the lawn, whether or not the grass clippings are removed, and on the type of grasses grown. On heavy, clay soils that are rich in nutrients, and where rainfall or irrigation rates are low, only light fertilizing is necessary. Light, sandy soils, however, that are well watered and that lose nutrients quickly by leaching need greater amounts.

Types and constituents of fertilizer

For most lawns, two applications of fertilizer a year are sufficient (see chart, opposite). Apply a spring/summer fertilizer at the beginning of summer, and an autumn/winter one after routine maintenance in early autumn. Both contain nitrogen, phosphorus, and potassium, but in differing proportions, because nitrogen, applied too late in the year, may stimulate soft, lush growth and encourage diseases such as snow mould/*Fusarium* patch (see p.667). Select a fertilizer that contains a mixture of both slow- and fast-release nitrogen; this helps the lawn to "green up" within two to three days and stay green for several weeks.

Soluble lawn tonics are high in fast-release nitrogen, and are applied to the grass by watering can or hose. Such summer feeds have a quick but short-lived, greening effect.

Iron (Fe), although not generally used on its own, is a constituent of lawn sand, which is used to control moss. Some complete fertilizers also contain iron. "Weed and feed" compounds are available to control moss and broadleaved weeds and to fertilize the lawn all in one operation. Iron darkens the grass, making it appear greener without stimulating growth. It is especially useful in autumn when the grass may lose some of its colour but excessive growth is undesirable.

How to apply fertilizer

It is essential to apply fertilizer evenly to avoid variations in growth and the risk of damaging or even

---

CUTTING THE EDGE OF THE LAWN

EDGING BY MACHINE
Periodically recut the lawn edge to retain the lawn's shape and create a well-defined finish. For large lawns, use a powered edger: align the cutting blade along the required new edge and guide the machine forward.

TRIMMING THE EDGE
After mowing, trim the grass overhanging the lawn edge with long-handled edging shears; or use a nylon-line trimmer adapted to work vertically.

EDGING BY HAND
If recutting the edge manually, use a sharp half-moon edger, cutting along the line of a plank for a straight edge.

WATER PENETRATION

Shallow watering may make the lawn vulnerable to drought (right); apply enough water to moisten the soil to a depth of about 10–15cm (4–6in) (far right).

HOW TO APPLY FERTILIZER

Weigh out the correct amount of fertilizer for the area and divide it in half. Apply the first half in one direction, working up and down the lawn in adjoining but not overlapping runs. Apply the second half at right angles to this. Close off the supply when you turn the machine at the end of each run.

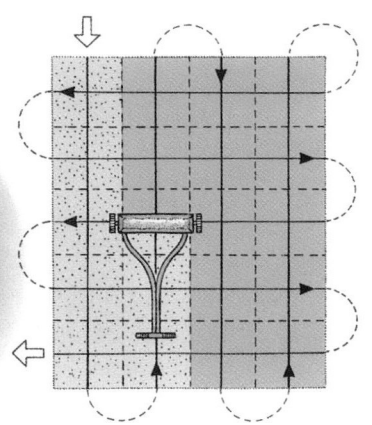

killing the grass. Any variation in the rate of application will generally be more than obvious within a week, and excessive doses may leave a bare patch behind. Although fertilizer may be spread manually, it is both easier and more accurate to apply it by machine.

Probably the simplest method is to use a continuous belt or drop spreader. This is pushed up and down the lawn, as if mowing, but so that each pass abuts the previous one, without overlapping it. To ensure even coverage, it is best to divide the fertilizer into two batches and apply half in one direction; the rest is distributed at right angles to it.

Alternatively, a spinning disc or broadcast spreader may be used to apply the fertilizer over a larger area; the spread may be uneven, however. To reduce the risk of fertilizer being distributed unevenly, set the machine to half the application rate and make adjacent runs at half the distance apart of the machine's spread. For example, if the extent of spread is 2m (6ft), make the runs 1m (3ft) apart. After using either type of machine, be certain to wash it out thoroughly because fertilizers are corrosive and may, therefore, damage any metal parts.

UNEVEN DISTRIBUTION

Take care to apply fertilizer evenly as uneven distribution may make the lawn patchy; it may damage or even kill areas of grass.

Before applying fertilizer, calibrate the spreader to obtain the correct distribution rate. To calibrate a spreader, first find a dry, flat area of concrete or asphalt, and chalk out a measured area of 4sq m (4sq yd), for example. Set the spreader to medium and fill it a quarter full. Using the machine, spread the fertilizer as evenly as possible over the marked area, as if over the lawn, then brush up all the fertilizer within the area and weigh it. Divide this weight by the area, in this case 4sq m (4sq yd), to give the application rate in grams per square metre (ounces per square yard). Adjust the machine setting accordingly, and then check the

application rate again over the same measured area. Continue this process until the rate is correct.

Annual maintenance

In addition to routine tasks such as mowing and watering, regular maintenance is required to keep a lawn healthy and to reduce the risk of serious pest or disease problems (see chart, below). A maintenance programme should involve aeration (including thatch removal, or scarifying), fertilizing, and the control of weeds, moss, pests, and diseases (see "Lawn weeds", p.400, and "Pests and diseases", p.400).

It is also important for the continued good health of the lawn to topdress the grass as well as to rake or brush it regularly to clear away leaves and other debris (see "Removing fallen leaves", p.396). Tasks that may be necessary at least once a year include recutting any edges that have become uneven or jagged and repairing any damaged or worn patches of grass by returfing or reseeding (see "Repairing lawn damage", p.399). Winter, when the lawn is no longer in need of quite such regular attention, is the most convenient time to check all equipment carefully. Sharpen all cutting edges,

oil tools where necessary, and send the mower for servicing, so that it will be in peak condition for the first cut of the new season.

Aerating the turf

Aeration is vital since it allows deep root growth and so helps the turf to become established as well as reducing soil compaction. It is also important to reduce excessive thatch, the organic matter consisting of decaying blades of grass, rhizomes, and stolons that accumulates on the soil surface. A certain amount of thatch – up to about 1cm (½in) deep – is beneficial as it reduces evaporation and helps to protect the lawn from wear. In excess, however, it prevents water from reaching the soil beneath and may itself become saturated, interfering with drainage. The removal of thatch also encourages new grass growth and so promotes a healthy, vigorous sward.

There are several ways of aerating the soil and removing thatch. These include scarifying, slitting, hollow tining (also known as coring), and spiking. It is preferable not to undertake these tasks in dry conditions, however, because they make the lawn more vulnerable to drought in the short term. Autumn is often the best time since the warm, moist conditions allow the grass to recover

ANNUAL MAINTENANCE PROGRAMME

MAINTENANCE PROCEDURE	EARLY/ MID SPRING	MID/LATE SPRING	EARLY/MID SUMMER	MID/LATE SUMMER	EARLY/MID AUTUMN	MID/LATE AUTUMN	WINTER
Mowing	Roll before mowing if turf is lifted by frost	Mow weekly. Adjust mower to summer cut height	Mow 1–3 times a week as required	Mow 1–3 times a week (set mower higher in dry periods)	Raise height of cut as growth rate slows	Set mower to winter cut height	Lightly mow if there is new growth
Watering		May be needed in dry regions	Water as necessary	Water well in dry periods	Occasionally water if dry		
Fertilizing		Apply spring fertilizer	Summer fertilizer		Apply autumn fertilizer		
Aerating and scarifying		Lightly scarify		Spike or slit areas subject to heavy wear	Scarify and aerate lawn, or hollow tine to remove thatch	Aerate lawn if not done in early autumn	
Weed and moss control		Apply lawn sand in place of spring feed if moss present	Apply weedkiller	Apply weedkiller if not applied in early summer	Apply weedkiller; treat moss with lawn sand		
Pest and disease control					Apply pesticide/ fungicide as necessary		
Other procedures	Recut edges if required. Carry out any restoration work	Brush away any worm casts on the lawn			Top-dress after autumn renovation	Remove fallen leaves	Remove leaves. Service tools

SCARIFYING

BY MACHINE
For large areas of lawn, use a mechanical or powered scarifier. Work the machine back and forth across the lawn as if mowing.

BY HAND
Pull a spring-tined rake vigorously across the lawn to remove thatch and dead moss. Ensure that the tines of the rake reach well down into the soil surface.

quickly from these renovation procedures. Whichever the aeration technique, first mow the lawn to its normal summer height. After maintenance work, apply a low nitrogen feed and avoid using the lawn for one to two weeks to encourage recovery.

Scarifying

This technique helps to remove thatch and permits air to enter the surface of the lawn. These processes are important because the soil organisms that naturally break down thatch require air to live. For small areas, scarifying may be done manually by vigorously raking the lawn with a wire or spring-tined rake. This is hard work, however, so it may be worth hiring a mechanical or powered scarifier instead. To remove the maximum amount of thatch, scarify the lawn in two directions, one at 90° to the other. Any moss should be killed prior to scarifying so that it will not spread to other parts of the lawn (see "Moss", p.400).

Slitting

For slitting, a special machine is used that penetrates the soil with flat, knife-like blades to a depth of 8–10cm (3–4in). The blades cut slits through the thatch which allow air into the soil thereby encouraging a dense, healthy sward.

Hollow tining or coring

This removes thatch, aerates the soil, and relieves soil compaction, all in one operation. A mechanical or hand tiner removes a core of grass, thatch, and soil, making a series of holes across the lawn, about 10cm (4in) apart. Remove the cores, then fill the holes with a sandy top-dressing (see below) to prevent them from closing and to allow air and water into the lawn. Hollow tining may take longer to do than spiking and slitting because soil is removed rather than simply pushed sideways.

Spiking

This allows air into the soil, thereby encouraging root growth; it can also relieve soil compaction. Use a mechanical or hand spiker, or, for small areas, a garden fork. Angle the spikes back slightly to raise the turf gently without breaking it up. This encourages deep root growth by creating fissures in the soil.

AERATING

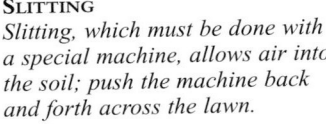

AERATING BY MACHINE
For large lawns, use a mechanical or powered aerator; work the machine in slightly overlapping runs.

SLITTING
Slitting, which must be done with a special machine, allows air into the soil; push the machine back and forth across the lawn.

HOLLOW TINING
Use a purpose-designed tool, working methodically across the lawn to lift out cores of grass and soil 0.5–2cm (¼–¾in) wide.

SPIKING
For small lawns, spiking using a garden fork is adequate; insert the fork straight, then lean it back slightly to let in more air.

Top-dressing

Immediately after autumn maintenance work, apply a top-dressing, on a dry day if possible. This helps reduce thatch by keeping the lawn open and aerated, fills core holes, and helps to level the surface. For most lawns, a sandy mixture of six parts medium-fine sand, three parts sieved soil, and one part peat substitute, peat, or leaf mould is suitable.

After scarifying, apply the mixture of top-dressing at a rate of 1kg/sq m (2lb/sq yd), but if the lawn has been both scarified and hollow tined, apply the dressing at the rate of 3kg/sq m (6½lb/sq yd).

Ensure that the top-dressing does not smother the grass by luting or brushing it into the surface and any core holes. Luting also helps level any slight surface irregularities.

TOP-DRESSING

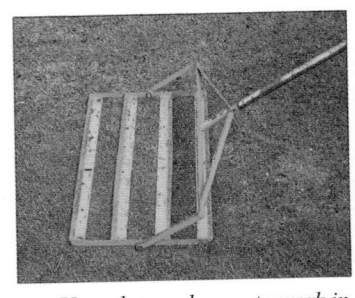

Medium-fine sand

Sieved soil

Peat substitute

1 *Prepare the top-dressing by mixing medium-fine sand with topsoil and peat substitute, peat, or leaf mould. Pass the mixture through a 5mm (¼in) mesh sieve.*

2 *Weigh out the correct amount of top-dressing for the lawn area and apply it on a dry day. For a large lawn, it is best to use a machine.*

ALTERNATIVE STEP
For small areas, the top-dressing may be applied by hand; spread it evenly over the lawn with a shovel or spade.

3 *Use a lute or besom to work in the dressing, keeping a steady pressure to distribute it evenly, and water thoroughly.*

Rolling

Rolling is not essential, but if done in spring it may help to resettle the surface after any maintenance work carried out the previous autumn and any possible upheaval caused by frost. A roller or, alternatively, a cylinder mower may be used; if using the latter, raise the blades to prevent damaging the lawn. The traditional practice of rolling lawns frequently is unnecessary and could cause problems of compaction, particularly on heavy soils.

Renovating a neglected lawn

In some cases, a neglected, patchy lawn may be improved by renovation; if, however, it is dominated by weeds and moss, it may be preferable to remove the old turf and establish a new lawn instead. The best time to start renovation work is in spring because the grass will grow well during spring and summer and should therefore be well established by the end of the season.

A renovation programme involves a series of procedures that restore the lawn to a good condition. First, in early spring, cut the grass to about 5cm (2in) using a rotary mower, and remove any clippings. After one week, mow again, preferably with a cylinder mower set at its highest cut. Over the next couple of weeks gradually reduce the height of cut until it reaches the correct level. At this stage, feed the lawn with a liquid or granular fertilizer and, two weeks later, apply a weedkiller. If there are any bare or uneven patches, they may be reseeded after one or two weeks. At the beginning of autumn, aerate the lawn, top-dress, and apply an autumn feed. A regular maintenance programme should then be followed so that the lawn is kept in tiptop condition (see *Annual maintenance programme*, p.397).

Repairing lawn damage

If an area of the lawn becomes damaged or patchy, perhaps because of uneven wear, it may usually be repaired by removing the affected part, then turfing or seeding. It is important to use turf or seed that is the same type as the rest of the lawn; if this is unknown, use a piece of turf from a less prominent part of the lawn to replace the damaged area. If the problem of lawn damage occurs repeatedly, it may be necessary to consider introducing a completely different and more hard-wearing surface, such as gravel or paving (see STRUCTURES AND SURFACES, pp.584–605).

Repairing a damaged edge
Edges that have been damaged in only one or two small areas may be repaired quite simply. Using a half-moon edger and a straight edge, such as a short plank of wood, mark out a small section of turf containing the damaged part. Slice under the section of turf with a turf float or spade and push it towards the lawn edge until the poor area is outside the lawn. Then trim off the damaged part to align the turf with the existing lawn edge. This leaves a gap within the lawn, which should be gently forked over and a granular or liquid fertilizer added. Then returf or add a little soil and reseed with an appropriate grass mixture. Ensure that the repair will be flush with the rest of the lawn.

Alternatively, lift the turf, then turn it around and replace it so that the damaged area is within the lawn. Repair the damage by turfing or seeding, taking care to ensure that any new turf is laid level with the surrounding lawn.

Repairing a damaged patch
If there is a damaged patch within the lawn, first cut out and lift a piece of turf containing the damaged area. Fork over the soil then fertilize it, if required, and lightly firm the soil.

HOW TO REPAIR A DAMAGED EDGE

1 *Using canes and string, mark out a small, straight-sided section of turf containing the damaged part; cut out the area with a half-moon edger.*

2 *Carefully undercut the turf with a spade, then slide it forward until the damaged part is beyond the lawn edge.*

3 *Align a plank with the lawn edge, then cut along it to trim off the damaged section so that the turf is level with the rest of the lawn edge.*

4 *Cut a new piece of turf to fit the resulting gap and ease it into the hole; if it is too large, trim it so that it forms an exact fit.*

5 *Adjust the soil level beneath the new turf, if necessary, by adding or removing soil until the new piece sits level with the rest of the lawn.*

6 *Once the level is correct, tamp the new piece firmly into place with the back of a rake or a medium-weight roller.*

7 *Sprinkle some sandy top-dressing over the repaired area, particularly into the joins, and water thoroughly.*

ALTERNATIVE METHOD

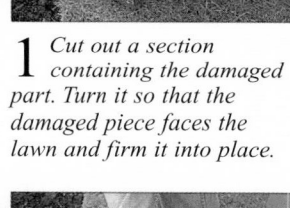
1 *Cut out a section containing the damaged part. Turn it so that the damaged piece faces the lawn and firm it into place.*

2 *Add a little sandy loam, if necessary, so that the damaged part is level with the rest of the lawn, then sow grass seed over the damaged section, and water well.*

HOW TO REPAIR A DAMAGED PATCH

1 *Using a half-moon edger and the edge of a plank, cut around the damaged area, then undercut the turf with a spade and remove it.*

2 *Lightly fork or rake over the area of exposed soil to loosen it, and then apply a liquid or granular fertilizer if required.*

3 *Carefully tread over the soil to consolidate it and firm the surface before returfing.*

Lay a new piece of turf to fit the exposed space, raising or lowering the soil level beneath, if necessary, so that the new turf is level with the rest of the lawn, and tamp it down in position with the back of a rake or your hands. Top-dress and water the repaired surface well.

Levelling a hump or hollow

Small humps or hollows within the lawn may be levelled easily. First cut a cross through the turf on the affected area and peel back the cut turf. To level a hollow, fork over the soil beneath and fill in with topsoil, then lightly firm the ground. For a hump, remove the excess soil until the ground is level, and firm. Fold back the cut turf and tamp it down with the back of a rake before top-dressing and watering.

On larger uneven areas, it may be necessary to remove complete sections of turf entirely, level the soil beneath (see "Levelling the site", pp.390–391), and then carefully relay the turf over the original area.

4 *Place a new piece of turf in the hole, cutting it to fit with a half-moon edger.*

5 *Check that the new turf is level with the rest of the lawn; if necessary adjust the soil level beneath the turf. Then firm in the turf and water well.*

Lawn weeds

Although some weeds, such as slender speedwell (*Veronica filiformis*) and daisies (*Bellis perennis*), may look attractive in utility lawns, they are generally considered undesirable in high-quality, closely mown lawns. Many broadleaved weeds can survive in grass that is mown, but excessive numbers may make the grass suffer so, even in a utility lawn, control may be needed. Unless the lawn clippings are collected, mowing may even spread weeds that can root from small pieces of stem. On small lawns, daisies and plantains (*Plantago*) may be cut out individually by hand, but for a large lawn, the simplest method is to use a "weed and feed" mixture.

This may be applied with a fertilizer spreader or by hand, according to the instructions given.

Moss

Almost always undesirable, moss may be found in lawns for many reasons, including soil compaction, poor drainage, low fertility, insufficient light, mowing too closely, and extremes of soil pH. If the lawn is occasionally affected by moss, treat it with a chemical moss killer or lawn sand, then remove it by scarification (see p.398). If the problem continually recurs, identify and correct the possible causes; this may involve improving soil aeration, drainage, and fertility and, on light soils, top-dressing to assist water retention. Adopting an annual maintenance programme should help to control the problem. For further details see PLANT PROBLEMS, "Lawn weeds", pp.672–673.

Pests and diseases

Several turf diseases, including brown patch (see "Drought", p.667), dollar spot, fairy rings, snow mould/*Fusarium* patch, and red thread attack lawns, particularly in hot, humid countries; *Fusarium* patch is a problem in cold regions too and may even occur under snow. Preventive sprays may be necessary, but in cooler temperate and maritime climates it is usual to spray only in serious cases. For treatment of pests and diseases, see "Lawn problems", pp.667–668.

Earthworm casts should be tolerated because of the good these creatures do in the garden environment. The casts, however, provide ideal sites for the germination of weed seeds so they should be regularly dispersed with a besom, particularly before mowing the lawn.

LEVELLING A HOLLOW OR HUMP

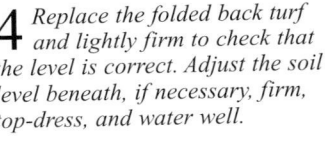

1 *Cut a cross right through the hump or hollow in the turf, using a half-moon edger; the cross should reach just beyond the affected area.*

2 *Fold back the cut sections of turf, taking care not to pull them too harshly or they may crack.*

3 *For a hollow, fill in the ground beneath with a good, sandy topsoil; for a hump, remove some of the soil until the entire surface is level.*

4 *Replace the folded back turf and lightly firm to check that the level is correct. Adjust the soil level beneath, if necessary, firm, top-dress, and water well.*

Meadow gardening

A WILD-FLOWER meadow is an attractive and colourful feature that brings a breath of the countryside into the city or suburbs. It can be the ideal way of using a part of the garden that is difficult to cultivate conventionally, perhaps because it is too dry, slopes steeply, or has poor soil, and can play a small part in the conservation of species that are threatened by the destruction of their natural habitats. A meadow also attracts seed-eating birds, small mammals, and insects into the garden – many butterflies and beneficial insects rely on long grasses as food for their larval stages.

Types of meadow

Grassland plants occur in habitats ranging from cornfields and dry downlands to wetlands and woodland margins. When planning a meadow, take into account soil type, moisture levels, and the degree of sun and shade – the growing conditions determine the plants that will both thrive and look natural. An open, sunny site with well-drained soil is ideal for ox-eye daisies (*Leucanthemum vulgare*), field scabious (*Knautia arvensis*), and lady's bedstraw (*Galium verum*). It also suits a cornfield area with annual poppies (*Papaver rhoeas*) and cornflowers (*Centaurea cyanus*), for which the soil must be well cultivated each spring if they are to persist. In damp ground, plants such as meadowsweet (*Filipendula ulmaria*), ragged robin (*Lychnis flos-cuculi*), and common spotted orchid (*Dactylorhiza fuchsii*) will flourish. Shady areas beneath trees are perfect for dog's-tooth violets (*Erythronium denscanis*) and snowdrops (*Galanthus nivalis*). A look at the local wild flora will indicate which species to grow, but never take plants or seeds from the wild. A huge range of wild flowers is now offered by specialist nurseries as plugs and young plants.

Extending the season

Meadows generally peak in summer, but can be given a longer span of interest. Try introducing spring bulbs, such as crocus (especially *C. tommasinianus, C. vernus*, and *C. chrysanthus* cultivars), wild daffodils (*Narcissus pseudonarcissus* and *N. poeticus*), snake's head fritillaries (*Fritillaria meleagris*), and tulips. Early summer bulbs include starry-flowered quamash (*Camassia quamash* and *C. leichtlinii*) and for autumn there are *Colchicum autumnale* and *Crocus speciosus* cultivars (see "Naturalizing bulbs", p.228).

Establishing meadows

Meadow flowers are perfectly adapted to soils of low fertility and thrive best among fine turf grasses, such as bents (*Agrostis*) and fescues (*Festuca*),

THE WILD-FLOWER MEADOW
Many wild species bloom more profusely in the garden than in the wild, providing a rich food source for bees, butterflies, and their larvae.

that will not swamp them. Many ordinary grass seed mixes contain vigorous, hard-wearing rye grass (*Lolium perenne*) that out-competes the wild flowers, so choose a mix that does not include it. Various meadow mixes are available that are appropriate for different sites and soils. The simplest way to reduce soil fertility is to avoid using fertilizers and to mow regularly and remove the clippings. Stripping existing turf helps, but it is not advisable to remove topsoil unless it is very deep and fertile, since this may damage soil structure.

Sowing and planting

Sow a meadow in early autumn, or in spring in cold areas or on wet soils. Eliminate all perennial weeds with weedkiller or a black plastic sheet mulch. Cultivate the soil to a fine tilth and water. Allow a flush of annual weeds to germinate and hoe them off, then firm the soil by treading or rolling. Sow seed at the recommended rate and rake in lightly.

If establishing a meadow in existing grassland, such as an orchard, reduce fertility over one or two years by mowing and removing the clippings weekly. Introduce pot- or plug-grown wild flowers in spring or autumn.

Maintenance

Spot treat vigorous perennial weeds with weedkiller or dig them out. Reduce the sward to 8cm (3in) with a scythe or nylon-line trimmer. For a spring-flowering meadow, do not mow the meadow between early spring and midsummer; and cut the sward from midsummer onwards. Leave the mowings to dry and shed their seed before raking up and removing. For later summer flowers, cut the sward from early autumn onwards and again as grass growth begins in spring. Gather the spring mowings immediately.

AIDING NATURAL DISTRIBUTION
After cutting, allow clippings to dry and then shake out the seeds. It is worth collecting some to grow on as pot or plug plants for next year.

FLOWERING PLANTS FOR MEADOW HABITATS

Leucanthemum vulgare
(ox-eye daisy)

Geranium pratense
(meadow cranesbill)

Primula veris
(Cowslip)

Campanula glomerata
(Clustered bellflower)

Galanthus nivalis
(snowdrop)

**Erythronium
dens-canis**
(dog's-tooth violet)

CHAPTER

15

GROWING HERBS

WHETHER GROWN ON their own as an ornamental feature, with other plants in a border, or among the ordered ranks of a vegetable plot, herbs are an invaluable addition to any garden. They have always been prized for their culinary, cosmetic, or curative uses, but they also make decorative garden plants. Although few have spectacular flowers, many are graced by attractive foliage and almost all are worth growing for their scent alone – ranging from the citrus tang of lemon balm to the aniseed aroma of fennel and the sweet apple perfume of chamomile. Their fragrance is hard to resist and their nectar-filled flowers tempt bees and butterflies, so adding the drowsy hum of insects to complete the restfulness of a herb garden.

Designing with herbs

HERB growing combines the delights of the flower garden with the productivity of the vegetable plot. The results are decorative, excellent in aroma and flavour, and inexpensive to produce. By definition, a herb is any plant that has culinary or curative uses, so the range is surprisingly wide. Herbs include annuals, perennials, shrubs, and trees, not just herbaceous plants.

Historically, herbs have been used for flavouring and preserving food, and, in addition, for making medicines and toiletries. Their aesthetic appeal has always been important, too, and their ornamental qualities, as well as their practical uses, are of equal value today.

STRUCTURED INFORMALITY
Growing a rich profusion of herbs brings a wealth of fine scents and contrasting textures to the garden. In this herb garden, clipped dwarf hedges add structure while bold blocks of herbs such as golden marjoram contrast with casual plantings of feathery fennel and low alpine strawberries.

Herbs in the home

Although fresh and dried herbs are widely available, they rarely have as fine an aroma or flavour as those harvested from your own garden. Enjoy their scents indoors as well as outside by using them fresh in flower arrangements or dried to make pot-pourri or to fill herb pillows. All over the world, herbs are considered invaluable in cooking to enhance and enliven other foods, elevating even the simplest meal to the level of *haute cuisine*. The curative and cosmetic properties of herbs are also renowned: for thousands of years, they have been used in many medicines and beauty products.

Culinary uses
Freshly harvested herbs are an important ingredient in many classic combinations, such as tomato and basil salad, potato mayonnaise with chives, and Pimm's with borage. In some cases, the flowers may be used as an edible decoration: borage, chives, elder, and marigold are all simple to grow and produce attractive flowers. Stalks, such as angelica for crystallizing, or branches of rosemary for barbecues, are also easily grown but are rarely available otherwise. Aromatic seeds, or spices, are easier to obtain but again are mostly cheap and easy to produce.

Certain herbs, such as lemon balm and peppermint, may be infused in boiling water to make herb teas, which are good alternatives to ordinary tea and coffee since they do not contain tannin or caffeine. Most are made from dried leaves, flowers, or seeds, although they may also be made from fresh herbs.

Medicinal herbs
In many parts of the world herbal medicine is commonplace and the herb garden is a source of home-grown treatments for all sorts of ailments; mint, for example, is a mild local anaesthetic, a powerful antiseptic, and a remedy for digestive problems. The essential oils of many herbs are also used by trained aromatherapists when massaging different parts of the human body. In general, it is inadvisable to use herbs for medicinal purposes without specialist knowledge or advice.

Cosmetic and scented preparations
A number of herbs have beneficial effects on the condition of skin or hair, and are included in beauty products: rosemary, chamomile, and mint are used in shampoos and conditioners, thyme as an antiseptic for mouthwashes, and marigold and elderflower in skin lotions.

Aromatic herbs may be enjoyed all year round if they are made into scented household articles such as pomanders and linen sachets.

Herbs in the garden

The majority of herbs grown today are still the wild species, but many cultivars are also now available, differing in habit or in the colour of their foliage or flowers. This diversity makes them more valuable as decorative garden plants, while their scent and other properties are usually similar to if not identical with that of the species.

The appeal of herbs lies largely in their fragrance which, in contrast to other plants, usually derives from the foliage rather than the flowers. Essential oils are released when the leaves are warmed or crushed: on a sunny day, the scent of a herb garden fills the air.

A few herbs have brightly coloured flowers which may be used to great effect: the orange of marigolds (*Calendula officinalis*) offset by bronze fennel (*Foeniculum vulgare* 'Purpureum'), or the brilliant blue of borage (*Borago officinalis*) with silver-grey wormwood (*Artemisia absinthium*), for example.

Certain herbs are reputed to benefit other plants: some pungent plants such as southernwood (*Artemisia abrotanum*) are considered to repel insects if crushed or infused, while growing chamomile (*Chamaemelum nobile*) in the garden reputedly increases the health and vigour of other plants nearby.

Where to grow herbs

As for other plants, herbs should be grown in conditions that are similar to their natural habitat to ensure that they are healthy and vigorous. Many herbs are Mediterranean in origin, and these usually prefer plenty of sunshine and a free-draining soil.

Some herbs tolerate a damp, partially shaded site, however, provided that they are not waterlogged or in dense or permanent shade. Most variegated and golden cultivars thrive in light shade. Pineapple mint (*Mentha suaveolens* 'Variegata') and golden forms of lemon balm

---

HERBS THAT TOLERATE MOIST SHADE

Angelica (*Angelica archangelica*)
Chervil (*Anthriscus cerefolium*)
Chives (*Allium schoenoprasum*)
Elder (*Sambucus nigra*, *S. nigra* 'Aurea', *S. nigra* 'Marginata')
Feverfew (*Tanacetum parthenium*, *T. parthenium* 'Aureum')
Lemon balm (*Melissa officinalis*, *M. officinalis* 'All Gold', *M. officinalis* 'Aurea', *M. officinalis* 'Variegata')
Lovage (*Levisticum officinale*)
Mint (*Mentha*)
Parsley (*Petroselinum crispum*)
Sorrel (*Rumex acetosa*)
Sweet cicely (*Myrrhis odorata*)
Tansy (*Tanacetum vulgare*)
Woodruff (*Galium odoratum*)

(*Melissa officinalis*) and feverfew (*Tanacetum parthenium*) retain their colour best in a position that is lit by morning or evening sun but shaded at midday.

Herbs may be grown in a variety of situations, the choice largely depending on personal preference and convenience. A separate herb garden in an attractive design provides an appealing feature and need not take up much space, but it may be preferable to have a culinary herb patch, or herbs in containers, within easy reach of the kitchen. Some herbs are decorative enough to be grown with other plants in a bed or border, while others may be better sited in the vegetable garden. Herbs intended for culinary or medicinal use should always be sited away from possible contamination by pets or roadside pollution.

Herb gardens

If there is space, it is worth creating a separate herb garden and growing many different herbs together for a strong impact and to reap the benefit of their combined scents in one place. Making a special feature of the plants allows plenty of opportunity to create an interesting pattern or design using blocks of complementary or contrasting colours. As well as being a highly ornamental way of displaying the herbs, it makes harvesting easier. Traditionally, herb gardens have been bordered by low, clipped hedges of box (*Buxus sempervirens*), but a less formal edging of hyssop (*Hyssopus officinalis*) or lavender (*Lavandula*) would also be suitable.

Beds and borders

Herbs may also be grown with other ornamental garden plants. This is useful where there is no space for a separate herb garden, or for herbs that are border plants in their own right, such as bergamot (*Monarda didyma*) and rue (*Ruta graveolens*). Grey-leaved species are especially fine in a silver border or as a contrast to plants with blue, purple, or pink colouring, such as purple sage (*Salvia officinalis* 'Purpurascens').

Stately, architectural plants are valuable as focal points on their own or at the back of a border. Fill any gaps in borders with colourful annuals, such as poppies (*Papaver*), blue borage, and dark opal basil (*Ocimum basilicum* var. *purpurascens*).

Planting aromatic herbs next to doorways, paths, and seats makes it easy to enjoy their scents to the full. Low, spreading herbs, such as wild thyme (*Thymus serpyllum*), lawn chamomile (*Chamaemelum nobile*

'Treneague'), and creeping savory (*Satureja spicigera*), are suitable for rock gardens or en masse to form a fragrant carpet. These and other, more upright, herbs such as chives (*Allium schoenoprasum*) make an unusual and attractive edging to a border or path.

Herbs in the vegetable garden

For culinary herbs that are used in large quantities, such as parsley (*Petroselinum crispum*), the vegetable plot may be the best site. This may also be the most convenient place for fast-growing herbs, such as chervil (*Anthriscus cerefolium*) and dill (*Anethum graveolens*), that are sown in succession and do not transplant successfully. The herbs may be grown in straight rows among the vegetables or as an ornamental border around the edge of the vegetable garden.

Growing herbs in containers

Many herbs grow well in containers. From a hanging basket to a chimney pot, almost any container is suitable, provided that it has drainage holes and that a layer of porous material is added before planting in it.

In small gardens or on balconies, the entire herb garden may consist of containers, imaginatively positioned on walls, steps, shelves, and windowsills, as well as at ground level. If space is at a premium, using a strawberry planter (a pot with planting pockets) offers an attractive and functional way of growing a number of different plants together. Even if you have a separate area for herbs or grow them with other ornamentals or vegetables, it is often convenient to have one or two pots of commonly used herbs near the door.

Some of the best herbs to grow in containers are chervil, parsley, chives, compact marjoram (*Origanum vulgare* 'Compactum'), rock hyssop

CONTAINER GARDENING
Even in the smallest garden, there is room to grow a variety of aromatic herbs in a group of pots.

(*Hyssopus officinalis* subsp. *aristatus*), and thymes (*Thymus*). Large plants, such as rosemary (*Rosmarinus officinalis*) and bay (*Laurus nobilis*), often look good grown as single specimens in pots or tubs. Growing slightly tender herbs, such as myrtle (*Myrtus communis*), lemon verbena (*Aloysia triphylla*), and rose-scented geranium (*Pelargonium graveolens*), in containers is convenient because they may be brought inside during winter; they also make good conservatory plants.

Paving and patios

Planting herbs in the gaps between paving stones is an attractive option for those herbs that prefer well-drained conditions, such as thymes and creeping savory; allow the plants to spread onto the paving so that an occasional light tread may release their fragrance.

Patios are often ideal for displaying a variety of tender or Mediterranean herbs that enjoy warmth and shelter, while an exotic touch may be added by including tender plants such as lemon trees (*Citrus limon*), cardamom (*Elettaria cardamomum*), or ginger (*Zingiber officinale*) grown in ornamental containers.

Raised beds

Growing herbs in raised beds makes it easier to enjoy their fragrance at close quarters as well as being practical for the disabled or elderly, providing easy access for planting, maintenance, and harvesting. Raised beds must have strong retaining walls and should be no more than approximately 75cm (30in) wide and at a comfortable height for working (see also STRUCTURES AND SURFACES, "Raised beds", p.599).

CARTWHEEL BED
A cartwheel design provides a decorative and practical way of growing a small range of herbs.

Raised beds are also a good option on paved areas against a wall (but not above the damp course in a house wall) and in any site where the soil is not free-draining. Choose small, compact herbs for raised beds, and control their spread by regular pruning and dividing.

Designing a herb garden

Whether informal or formal, a herb garden should be designed so that it is congruous with the style of the rest of the garden and the house. Take into account maintenance resources when planning: in general, informal herb gardens need less initial structural work than formal ones, and routine care may be less time-consuming, depending on the plants used and the size and complexity of the design. It is also possible to combine elements of both formal and informal designs; for example, a well-defined, symmetrical pattern of paths could form a framework for a free planting of herbs of different heights, habits, and colours.

Informal designs
An informal design largely depends for its success upon the complementary habits and colours of the herbs. Variegated and coloured-leaved forms, such as golden marjoram (*Origanum vulgare* 'Aureum') and purple sage, are especially effective in such a scheme. Try green- and gold-leaved plants together, for example, or those with purple and silver foliage.

There is greater freedom to use plants of different heights and habits than in a formal scheme: tall ones may be introduced to create a striking effect without upsetting the bal-

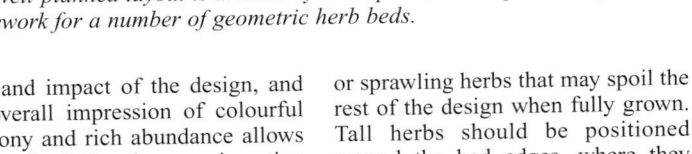

FORMAL HERB GARDEN
This well-planned layout is divided by brick paths, which provide a formal framework for a number of geometric herb beds.

ance and impact of the design, and the overall impression of colourful harmony and rich abundance allows greater flexibility for experimenting with bold combinations.

Formal designs
These designs are usually based on geometric patterns and framed by low hedges or paths. Each small bed created by the pattern is then planted with one kind of herb, giving bold blocks of colour and texture. At its simplest, the design may take the form of a cartwheel bedded into the soil with a different herb planted in each segment. These designs often look particularly impressive when viewed from above, so consider siting the herb garden where it may be overlooked from an upper window or a slope. When choosing plants, do not include tall, invasive,

or sprawling herbs that may spoil the rest of the design when fully grown. Tall herbs should be positioned around the bed edges, where they will not swamp neighbouring plants

A formal garden with paths is labour-intensive initially but soon looks mature and needs little structural maintenance. One that includes a framework of dwarf hedges that require regular clipping may be considerably more demanding. The

hedging may outline the design or take on the complex shapes of a knot garden (see also "Formal Gardens", p.18). Suitable plants for dwarf hedges include hyssop, lavenders, box, germander (*Teucrium* x *lucidrys*), and winter savory (*Satureja montana*) planted 22–30cm (9–12in) apart.

Making a plan
To draw up a plan, first measure the site and surrounding features accurately, taking account of any changes in level. Also note where shadows fall at different seasons as well as at different times of day.

Whether the garden is to be formal or informal in style, remember that herbs should be within arm's reach for convenient harvesting; for beds or borders in open ground, provide access by paths or stepping stones so that the soil is not walked on as this could lead to compaction.

Transfer the measurements to squared paper, working to scale; in order to compare a number of different designs, draw each scheme on a sheet of tracing paper laid over the master plan.

Finally, decide on which herbs to grow, taking into account their cultivation requirements, habit, colour, eventual height and spread, and the amounts that will be required for harvesting, then mark them on the plan. Herbs in containers may also be included in the design to provide focal points in the garden.

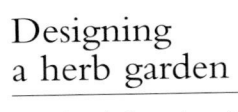

HERBS IN A PATIO GARDEN
Enliven a patio or courtyard, and soften the effect of the hard materials, by planting herbs directly into the gaps between paving or in gravel.

PLANNING A FORMAL HERB GARDEN

There are many possible formal designs, although imagination should be restrained by considerations of balance and proportion. Cartwheel and chessboard schemes are popular but unusual geometric patterns also provide plenty of opportunity to create an eye-catching feature.

Directory of common herbs

Chives
(Allium schoenoprasum)

Hardy, herbaceous, clump-forming perennial needing sun or semi-shade and moist but well-drained, rich soil. Good as a low edging for borders. May be forced for winter use (see p.411). Use the leaves, which have a mild onion flavour, as a garnish and flavouring in salads, dips, soft cheeses, and soups; the edible flowers make a decorative addition to salads.
Harvesting and storing Cut leaves and flowers as available to use fresh. For freezing and drying, cut leaves before flowering occurs and chop finely.
Propagation By seed sown in spring (see p.198) or by division in autumn or spring (p.200).
Related species and variants Variations in height, flower colour, and flavour are available; Chinese or garlic chives (*A. tuberosum*) have a mild garlic flavour and white flowers.

Lemon verbena
(Aloysia triphylla)

Half-hardy, upright, deciduous shrub requiring a sunny, well-drained soil. Plants may be cut back by frost but usually grow again. The leaves have a strong, clean, lemon scent and are used in herb teas, desserts, and, dried, in pot-pourri and teas.
Harvesting and storing Pick leaves during the growing season for using fresh or drying.
Propagation By softwood or greenwood cuttings (see p.111).

Dill *(Anethum graveolens)*

Hardy, upright annual with feathery, blue-green leaves. Grow in sunny, well-drained, rich soil but not near fennel, because cross-pollination may result in the loss of its distinctive flavour. Runs to seed quickly. Use the leaves or, for a stronger flavour, the aromatic seeds in soups, sauces, potato salad, pickles, and fish dishes.
Harvesting and storing Pick leaves in spring and summer before flowering occurs. Cut seedheads as they ripen in summer.
Propagation By seed sown in spring and early summer (see p.216); may not transplant well.

Angelica
(Angelica archangelica)

Hardy biennial with large, divided leaves and large flowerheads. Grow this bold, architectural plant in sun or shade and moist, rich soil. Unless seeds are required, remove seedheads before ripening to pre-

vent unwanted seedlings. The young stalks may be candied; the leaves are used in cooking, especially in fruit desserts and fish dishes.
Harvesting and storing Gather fresh leaves in spring and summer. Cut young stalks for crystallizing in spring or early summer. Cut seedheads as they ripen in summer.
Propagation By seed sown in autumn or spring (see p.216).

Chervil
(Anthriscus cerefolium)

Hardy annual needing semi-shade and moist, rich soil. Runs to seed quickly in hot, dry conditions. The leaves have a fine, subtle flavour, reminiscent of parsley and anise. Use the leaves in egg dishes, salads, soups, and sauces.
Harvesting and storing Gather leaves before flowering occurs. Freeze or dry them gently to preserve their delicate flavour.
Propagation By seed sown at monthly intervals from spring to early autumn (see p.216); do not transplant. May also be sown in trays under glass in early autumn for winter use.

Horseradish
(Armoracia rusticana)

Hardy perennial with persistent, stout, white-fleshed roots, which have a pungent flavour and are grated into coleslaw, dips, and sauces, especially in horseradish sauce. Young leaves are used in salads or sandwiches. Needs sun and moist but well-drained, rich soil.
Harvesting and storing Pick the young leaves in spring. Harvest the roots in autumn when the flavour is best, or as required.
Propagation By 15cm (6in) root cuttings in winter (see p.203) or by seed sown in spring (p.198).

Southernwood
(Artemisia abrotanum)

Hardy, semi-evergreen subshrub with finely divided, grey-green foliage. May be used to form a low hedge or in mixed borders. Grow in sunny, well-drained, rich, neutral to slightly alkaline soil. Use the aromatic leaves in pot-pourri and as an insect repellent.
Harvesting and storing In summer, pick leaves as required for using fresh or for drying.
Propagation By semi-ripe heel cuttings in late summer (see p.113).

Wormwood
(Artemisia absinthium)

Hardy, deciduous subshrub with deeply divided, greyish-green leaves. Good as a border plant or informal hedge. Requires sun and well-drained, neutral to alkaline, rich soil. Prune to within 15cm (6in) of the ground in spring. The aromatic leaves are intensely bitter; they were formerly used to flavour alcoholic drinks but are now regarded as toxic. The foliage is attractive in herbal decorations and posies.
Harvesting and storing Pick foliage in the summer for use fresh or dried in decorative arrangements.
Propagation By semi-ripe heel cuttings in late summer (see p.113).
Variants 'Lambrook Silver' is a cultivar with deeply divided, silver-grey foliage.

French tarragon
(Artemisia dracunculus)

Half-hardy, subshrubby perennial with upright stems and glossy, narrow leaves. Grow in sun and well-drained, neutral to alkaline, rich soil. In cold areas, may need winter protection, but may be forced for winter use. The leaves are commonly used in *sauce béarnaise*, *fines herbes*, tartare sauce, in egg and chicken dishes, and to flavour vinegar.
Harvesting and storing Cut sprigs of foliage throughout the growing season, leaving two thirds of the stem to regrow. The leaves are best frozen but may also be dried satisfactorily.
Propagation By division of rhizomes in autumn or spring (see p.201). Seed is not available: that sold as tarragon is the Russian subspecies.
Related species Russian tarragon (*A. dracunculus* subsp. *dracunculoides*) is hardier but it has an inferior flavour.

Borage
(Borago officinalis)

Hardy, upright annual needing sunny, reasonably drained soil. Add the cucumber-flavoured leaves, and the flowers, to cold drinks (such as Pimm's) and salads. Crystallize the flowers for use in cake decoration.
Harvesting and storing Pick young leaves and use fresh. Gather the flowers (without calyces) in summer to use fresh, freeze in ice cubes, or crystallize.
Propagation By seed sown in spring (see p.216). Self-sows in light soils.
Variants There is also a form with white flowers, *B. officinalis* 'Alba'.

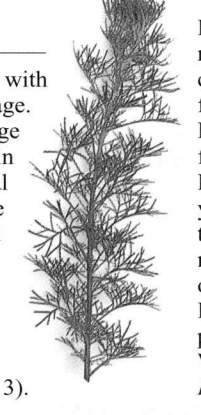

Marigold
(Calendula officinalis)

Bushy, hardy annual with bright orange flowers. Grows in sun and well-drained, even poor soil. Dead-head to prolong flowering. Use the petals to flavour and colour rice, soft cheese, and soups, and to garnish salads. Chop the young leaves into salads. Dried petals may be used to add colour to pot-pourri.
Harvesting and storing Pick open flowers in summer and remove petals for drying. Gather leaves when young.
Propagation By seed sown in autumn or spring (see p.216). Self-sows freely.
Variants Double-flowered forms in cream, yellow, orange, and bronze are widely available.

Caraway
(Carum carvi)

Hardy biennial needing sunny, well-drained, rich soil. Aromatic seeds are used in baking, confectionery, cheeses, and meat stews such as goulash. Add the leaves to soups and salads.
Harvesting and storing Gather leaves when young. Collect the ripe seedheads in summer.
Propagation By seed sown in spring, late summer, or early autumn (see p.216).

Chamomile
(Chamaemelum nobile)

Hardy, dense, creeping, evergreen perennial needing sunny, light, well-drained, sandy soil. Good at the edge of paths and borders, or between paving stones. May be planted as an ornamental lawn (see p.393). Use the apple-scented leaves in pot-pourri; the aromatic flowers are used in pot-pourri and herb teas.
Harvesting and storing Pick leaves at any time as required. Gather flowers when fully open in summer and dry whole.
Propagation By seed sown in spring or autumn (see p.198) or by division in spring (p.200).
Variants 'Treneague' is a dwarf, non-flowering form that is particularly suitable for lawns and gaps in paving. *C. nobile* 'Flore Pleno' has attractive double flowers.

Coriander
(Coriandrum sativum)

Hardy annual with divided foliage and small, white or pale mauve flowers. Grow in sun or semi-shade and well-drained, rich soil The plants have an unpleasant smell and should not be grown indoors. The lobed, lower leaves are used in curries, chutneys, sauces, and salads. The seeds,

which have a sweet, spicy flavour, are used in curry powder, baking, chutneys, and sausages.
Harvesting and storing Pick young leaves for using fresh or for freezing. Gather seedheads as they ripen and use whole or ground.
Propagation By seed sown in spring (see p.216).

Cumin
(Cuminum cyminum)

Tender annual with white or pale pink flowers. Needs sunny, well-drained, rich soil, and heat for the seeds to ripen. The aromatic seeds are used in curries, pickles, yoghurt, and Middle Eastern dishes.
Harvesting and storing Gather seedheads as they ripen.
Propagation By seed sown in early spring in a warm situation or under cover (see p.217).

Fennel
(Foeniculum vulgare)

Hardy perennial with fine, filigree leaves and clusters of yellow flowers. Grow in sun and well-drained, rich soil. Use the leaves and leaf sheaths for their aniseed flavour in salads, and meat and fish dishes. Seeds are used in baking, fish dishes, and herb teas.
Harvesting and storing Cut leaves and leaf sheaths when still young. Gather seedheads as they ripen.
Propagation By seed sown in autumn or spring (see p.198) or by division in spring (p.200).
Variants 'Purpureum' is an attractive bronze cultivar; Florence fennel (*F. vulgare* var. *dulce*) is grown as an annual for use as a vegetable (see p.540).

Woodruff
(Galium odoratum, syn. *Asperula odorata)*

Hardy, creeping perennial with star-shaped, white flowers that appear above the whorls of narrow leaves in spring and early summer. An excellent ground-cover plant in damp shade. The dried leaves are used in pot-pourri and herb tea.
Harvesting and storing Gather the leaves for drying just before the flowers open in spring.
Propagation By division in autumn or spring (see p.200) or by seed sown in early autumn (p.198).

Hyssop *(Hyssopus officinalis)*

Hardy, semi-evergreen subshrub with spikes of small, dark purple-blue flowers. Needs sunny, well-drained to dry, neutral to alkaline soil. The aromatic leaves are used in soups, bean dishes, stews, game, and pâté.
Harvesting and storing Gather leaves any time for fresh use; pick young leaves in early summer to dry.
Propagation By seed sown in autumn or spring (see p.114) or by softwood cuttings in summer (p.111).

Orris *(Iris* 'Florentina')

Hardy perennial with off-white flowers and sword-shaped leaves, needing sunny, well-drained soil. Plant so that the rhizomes are partially exposed. The thick rhizome develops a violet scent after drying and prolonged storage. It is ground for using as a perfume fixative in pot-pourri and linen sachets.
Harvesting and storing In autumn, dig up rhizomes at least three years old. Peel, split, and dry, leaving for up to two years before grinding.
Propagation By division or offsets in late summer (see p.201).

Bay *(Laurus nobilis)*

Hardy, evergreen tree or shrub needing sun or semi-shade and moist but well-drained soil. In cold areas, it may need protection from frost and wind. May be clipped for topiary or pruned hard to restrict size. Use the leaves in *bouquet garni*, and for flavouring stock, marinades, sauces, milk desserts, and meat and fish dishes.
Harvesting and storing Pick leaves any time for using fresh. Dry mature leaves in summer.
Propagation By seed in autumn (p.114) or by semi-ripe cuttings (p.79).
Variants 'Aurea' has yellow-flushed leaves.

Lavender
(Lavandula angustifolia)

Hardy, evergreen, bushy shrub with upright, mauve flower spikes. Grow in sunny, well-drained soil. Good for low hedging. The flowers are used in pot-pourri, linen sachets, herb pillows, and tea. They may also be crystallized or used to flavour oil or vinegar.
Harvesting and storing Gather flowering stems in summer, and air-dry.
Propagation By seed in spring (see p.114) or by semi-ripe cuttings in summer (p.112).
Related species There are several other species and many cultivars, varying in habit, foliage,

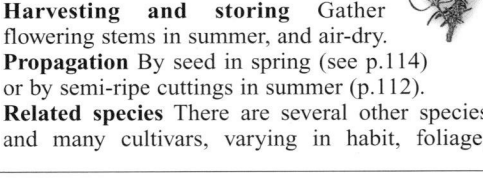
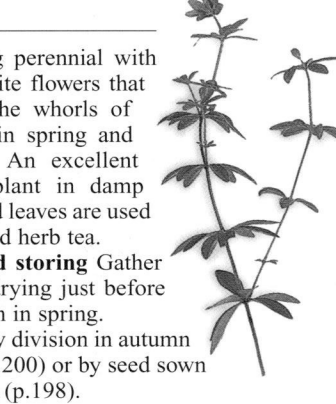

flowering time, and flower colour. They include dwarf cultivars, such as 'Hidcote', and white-flowered forms, for example 'Nana Alba'; French lavender (*L. stoechas*), which is borderline hardy, has purple flowers crowned by purple bracts.

Lovage
(*Levisticum officinale*, syn. *Ligusticum levisticum*)

Hardy perennial needing sun or semi-shade and deep, moist but well-drained soil. A tall plant, suitable for the back of a border. The leaves have a strong flavour, resembling celery and yeast, and are used in soups, stocks, and stews; add the fresh, young leaves to salads. The aromatic seeds are used in baking and vegetable dishes, and the young stalks may be crystallized. Blanch plants under pots in spring for use as a vegetable.

Harvesting and storing Pick young leaves in spring and freeze or dry. In spring, gather young stalks for crystallizing. Cut stalks after two to three weeks of blanching in spring, leaving central shoots to grow.

Propagation By seed sown as soon as ripe in late summer or autumn (see p.198) or by division in spring (p.200).

Lemon balm
(*Melissa officinalis*)

Hardy, clump-forming perennial needing sunny, moist but well-drained, poor soil. Add the lemon-scented leaves to cold drinks, sweet and savoury dishes, or infuse them.

Harvesting and storing Pick leaves before flowering for using fresh or for drying.

Propagation By seed sown in spring (see p.198) or division in spring or autumn (p.200). Self-seeds.

Variants Yellow-variegated cultivars, such as 'Aurea', are available; grow them in partial shade to avoid leaf scorch.

Mint
(*Mentha spicata*)

Hardy, herbaceous perennial that may be invasive (see p.411). Grow in sun and poor, moist soil. Use the leaves to make mint sauce, in salads, drinks, and with potatoes or peas.

Harvesting and storing Pick leaves before flowering and dry or freeze, or chop and infuse in vinegar.

Propagation By stem tip cuttings in spring or summer (see p.202), by division in spring or autumn (p.200), or by seed sown in spring (p.198).

Related species There are numerous species and cultivars with slightly differing foliage and scents. Some, such as pineapple mint (*M. suaveolens* 'Variegata'), have variegated leaves. Peppermint (*M.* x *piperita*) has purplish-green leaves used in

peppermint tea and in syrups and desserts, while eau-de-cologne mint (*M.* x *piperita* f. *citrata*) has a fine perfume. Bowles' mint (*M.* x *villosa* var. *alopecuroides*) has rounded leaves with a fresh, spearmint aroma and purplish-pink flowers.

Bergamot
(*Monarda didyma*)

Hardy, herbaceous perennial with heads of red, claw-shaped florets in summer. An excellent border plant for sunny, rich, moist soil. Infuse the aromatic leaves in tea for an "Earl Grey" flavour, and add them to summer drinks, salads, pork dishes, or pot-pourri. Use the attractive florets to add colour to salads and pot-pourri.

Harvesting and storing Pick leaves in spring or just before flowering occurs in summer for using fresh or drying. Gather flowers in summer, to dry.

Propagation By seed sown in autumn or spring (see p.198), by stem tip cuttings in spring (p.202), or by division in spring (p.200).

Related species and variants Hybrids with red, pink, white, or purple flowers are available. *M. fistulosa* has lavender flowers and tolerates drier soil.

Sweet cicely
(*Myrrhis odorata*)

Hardy, herbaceous perennial needing semi-shade and moist, rich soil. The fern-like leaves, which have an aniseed flavour, are used in fruit dishes or are added to salads. The thick tap root can be eaten raw or cooked as a vegetable. The large seeds are added to fruit dishes.

Harvesting and storing Pick leaves in spring and early summer for drying. Collect unripe seeds in summer and dry or pickle them. Dig up roots in autumn for using fresh.

Propagation By seed sown outdoors in autumn (see p.199) or by division in spring or autumn (p.200). Self-sows readily.

Basil
(*Ocimum basilicum*)

Half-hardy annual with toothed, pointed oval leaves. In cold regions, basil must be grown under cover or in a sheltered, sunny position in light, well-drained to dry, rich soil. Grows well in pots on a sunny windowsill. The highly aromatic leaves are used in salads, vinegars, pesto, and tomato pasta dishes.

Harvesting and storing Pick leaves when young in summer and freeze, dry, or use to flavour herb oil or vinegar; or pack leaves in jars of oil.

Propagation By seed sown in spring (see p.217).

Related species and variants Var. *purpurascens* is an attractive, purple-leaved variety with pink flowers. The compact bush basil (*O. minimum*) is hardier but has less flavour. *O. basilicum* 'Green Ruffles' has crinkled, toothed, pale green foliage.

Marjoram
(*Origanum vulgare*)

Hardy, herbaceous perennial with tiny, white, pink, or mauve flowers in summer. Needs full sun and well-drained, preferably alkaline soil. The aromatic leaves are used widely in cooking, especially in pizzas and pasta sauces.

Harvesting and storing Pick leaves for immediate use during the growing season. For drying or freezing, pick just before flowers open.

Propagation By seed sown in spring or autumn (see p.198), by division in spring or autumn (p.200), or by stem tip cuttings in spring (p.202).

Variants There are various species and hybrids, differing in hardiness, flavour, and flower and foliage colour, for example golden marjoram (*O. vulgare* 'Aureum'). The low-growing 'Compactum' is ideal for containers and edging.

Parsley
(*Petroselinum crispum*)

Hardy biennial with bright green, crinkled leaves. Grow in sun or semi-shade and well-drained, rich soil. Good for growing in pots. Use the leaves whole or chopped as a garnish and in *bouquet garni*, sauces, and egg and fish dishes.

Harvesting and storing Pick leaves from plants in their first year and use fresh or freeze.

Propagation By seed sown at intervals from early spring to autumn (see p.216).

Variants Italian parsley (*P. crispum* var. *neapolitanum*) is flat leaved, with a stronger flavour.

Aniseed
(*Pimpinella anisum*)

Half-hardy annual with deeply divided leaves and, in late summer, heads of tiny, white flowers. In cold regions, it must have a sunny, sheltered position in well-drained, sandy soil for the seed to ripen. Add the leaves to fruit salads. The aromatic seeds are used in baking, confectionery, and both sweet and savoury dishes.

Harvesting and storing Pick lower leaves in spring for immediate use. Collect seedheads as they ripen in autumn.

Propagation By seed sown in spring in its final position, because it is difficult to transplant successfully (see p.217).

Rosemary
(*Rosmarinus officinalis*)

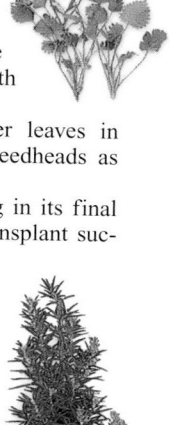

Hardy to frost hardy, evergreen shrub with dense, needle-like leaves and pale blue flowers in spring and summer or, in mild regions, all year round. Grow in sunny, well-drained, poor to moderately fertile soil. May be grown as an informal hedge. The leaves, which have a strong, resinous aroma, are used in meat dishes, especially with lamb, and to make pot-pourri and hair rinses. The flowers may be added to salads.

Harvesting and storing Pick leaves and flowers as required for immediate use. Gather sprigs for drying during the growing season.

Propagation By seed sown in spring (see p.114) or by semi-ripe cuttings in summer (p.112).

Variants Cultivars with flowers in various shades of blue, pink, and white are available. The vigorous, erect cultivar 'Miss Jessopp's Upright' is suitable for hedging; 'Severn Sea' has bright blue flowers and a dwarf, arching habit ideal for containers.

Sorrel
(*Rumex acetosa*)

Hardy, upright perennial needing sun or semi-shade and moist soil. Remove the flower spikes to prolong leaf production. Protect with cloches for a winter supply. The sour-tasting, young leaves are used in salads, soups, and sauces.

Harvesting and storing Pick young leaves before flowering occurs, for using fresh or freezing. May be frozen.

Propagation By division in either spring or autumn (see p.200), or by seed sown in spring (p.198).

Related species The low-growing species, French, shield, or buckler-leaf sorrel (*R. scutatus*), has small, fine-flavoured leaves.

Rue
(*Ruta graveolens*)

Hardy, evergreen subshrub with divided, grey-green foliage and greenish-yellow flowers in summer. Thrives in a hot dry position. An excellent plant for borders or low hedges. Handling rue on sunny days may cause a skin rash. Use the pungent leaves with discretion in salads, sauces, and to flavour cream cheese.

Harvesting and storing Pick leaves as required for immediate use, protecting hands with rubber gloves on sunny days.

Propagation By seed sown in spring (see p.114), or by semi-ripe cuttings in summer (p.112).

Variants There are cultivars that have cream-variegated and blue leaves, for example, 'Variegata' and the compact 'Jackman's Blue'.

Sage
(*Salvia officinalis*)

Hardy, evergreen subshrub with grey-green foliage. Grow in sunny, well-drained, rich soil. An excellent plant for shrub borders and rose gardens. The aromatic leaves are used in stuffings, meat dishes, to flavour cheese, and in herb teas.

Harvesting and storing Pick leaves as needed to use fresh. Gather leaves before the flowers open for drying.

Propagation By seed sown in spring (see p.114), softwood cuttings in spring and summer (p.111), or semi-ripe cuttings in early autumn (p.112).

Variants Cultivars include purple sage (*S. officinalis* 'Purpurascens') with strongly flavoured, purple leaves, and the less hardy 'Tricolor', with white-margined, pink-flushed leaves.

Cotton lavender
(*Santolina chamaecyparissus*)

Hardy, evergreen subshrub with silver-grey leaves and, in summer, masses of yellow, button flowerheads. Grow in sun and well-drained, poor to moderately fertile soil. Good as a low hedge, it also provides a contrasting colour in knot gardens (see "Formal garden styles", p.18). Add the scented leaves to pot-pourri, and dry the flowers for decorative purposes.

Harvesting and storing Pick leaves for drying in spring and summer. In summer, gather flowers as they open for drying.

Propagation By cuttings of semi-ripe sideshoots in late summer (see p.112).

Winter savory
(*Satureja montana*)

Hardy, evergreen subshrub with tiny, white to pink flowers in summer. Grow in sunny, well-drained soil. Use the aromatic leaves in bean and cheese dishes.

Harvesting and storing Pick any time for using fresh. Gather leaves to dry or freeze as flower buds form.

Propagation By seed sown in spring (see p.114), by division in spring or autumn (p.118), by softwood cuttings in summer (p.111), or by layering in spring (p.116).

Related species Creeping savory (*S. spicigera*) is a low species ideal for containers, edging, and rock gardens. The annual summer savory (*S. hortensis*) has lilac flowers and a fine flavour.

Alecost
(*Tanacetum balsamita*, syn. *Chrysanthemum balsamita*)

Hardy perennial needing semi-shade and well-drained soil. The leaves have a citrus-mint fragrance; use them sparingly in cooking and also in pot-pourri.

Harvesting and storing Gather fresh leaves in spring and summer for using fresh or for drying.

Propagation By division (see p.200), seed (p.198), or basal cuttings (p.202) in spring.

Variants Subsp. *balsametoides* is camphoraceous.

Feverfew
(*Tanacetum parthenium*, syn. *Chrysanthemum parthenium*)

Hardy, semi-evergreen perennial with long-lasting, daisy-like flowers in summer and autumn. Grow in a sunny, well-drained soil in borders and containers. Use the pungent leaves in sachets to deter clothes moths. The aromatic flowers are added to pot-pourri.

Harvesting and storing Pick leaves and flowers in summer for drying.

Propagation By seed sown in spring or autumn (see p.198), by division in spring or autumn (p.200), or by basal or stem tip cuttings in spring or early summer (p.202). Self-sows freely.

Variants There are cultivars varying in height and foliage, with single or double flowers. Highly recommended is the golden-leaved 'Aureum'.

Thyme
(*Thymus vulgaris*)

Hardy, evergreen, low-growing subshrub with tiny leaves and, in summer, pale lilac flowers. Grow in sunny, well-drained soil. May be grown as an edging for borders, between paving stones, and in containers. Add the aromatic leaves to *bouquet garni*, stuffings, sauces, soups, stocks, and meat dishes.

Harvesting and storing Pick leaves at any time to use fresh. Gather flowering tops for drying, stripping leaves and flowers from the stalks when quite dry. Fresh sprigs may also be infused in oil or vinegar.

Propagation By seed (see p.114) or division (p.118) in spring, by layering in spring or autumn (p.116), or by softwood or semi-ripe cuttings in summer (p.112).

Related species and variants There are many species and cultivars, varying in height, foliage, and flower colour. Wild thyme (*T. serpyllum*) is a low, mat-forming plant with mauve flowers; *T. serpyllum* 'Snowdrift' and *T.* 'Coccineus' have, respectively, white and magenta flowers; and *T.* 'Doone Valley' has scented foliage with gold markings. *T. × citriodorus* has lemon-scented leaves and lilac flowers; *T. vulgaris* 'Silver Posie' produces silver-margined leaves.

Ginger
(*Zingiber officinale*)

Tender, deciduous perennial needing sun or semi-shade and well-drained soil. The thick, tuberous rhizome is highly aromatic and is used in baking, preserves, confectionery, chutneys, sauces, and many Oriental dishes.

Harvesting and storing Dig up young rhizomes and peel them for using fresh or preserving in syrup. For drying, dig up the rhizomes as the leaves turn yellow.

Propagation By division of rhizomes as they start to sprout (see p.201).

Soil preparation and planting

THE ideal site for a herb garden is sunny, open but sheltered, with neutral to alkaline soil, and good drainage. These conditions suit the majority of common herbs such as lavender (*Lavandula angustifolia*), winter savory (*Satureja montana*), sage (*Salvia officinalis*), marjoram (*Origanum vulgare*), rosemary (*Rosmarinus officinalis*), and thyme (*Thymus vulgaris*), most of which are Mediterranean in origin.

Preparing the site

If possible, prepare the ground well in advance, preferably in autumn. First, remove all weeds, taking care to eliminate any persistent, perennial weeds such as couch grass (see PLANT PROBLEMS, "Perennial weeds", p.670). Then dig over the soil, leaving it in a rough state, to be broken down by frost.

In early spring, remove any weeds that have appeared subsequently, fork in well-rotted organic matter (such as garden or mushroom compost), and rake the soil to a fine, level tilth. The aim is to provide a free-draining and reasonably fertile soil. Feeding with manure or artificial fertilizers is not recommended, especially for Mediterranean herbs, since it produces soft growth with little aroma or resistance to frost.

On heavy, clay soil, it may be necessary to improve the drainage (see SOILS AND FERTILIZERS, "Improving drainage", p.623); alternatively, grow the herbs in raised beds or containers. Most herbs tolerate a slightly acid soil; if the pH is below 6.5, however, add a dressing of lime when preparing the soil (see SOILS AND FERTILIZERS, "Liming", p.625).

Planting invasive herbs

If planting invasive herbs, such as mint (*Mentha*), tansy (*Tanacetum vulgare*), or woodruff (*Galium odoratum*, syn. *Asperula odorata*), in open ground, restrict their spread by growing them in sunken containers. Old buckets, large pots, or even heavy-duty plastic bags are suitable, although you must make drainage holes at the base. For best results, lift and divide the plants each spring and replant young, vigorous pieces in the containers using fresh compost; if not replenished, nutrients are quickly depleted and the herbs may deteriorate and become more prone to disease, such as rusts (see p.648).

1 *Dig a hole large enough to accommodate a large pot or old bucket. Make drainage holes in the pot base, then place it in the hole and fill with a loam and compost mixture.*

2 *Plant the herb (here mint), firming in well; add enough compost to conceal the pot's rim, and water thoroughly. Each spring, replant and replace the compost in the pot.*

Herbs in winter

Although herbs are harvested mainly in spring and summer, the availability of many can be extended almost all year round.

Sown in late summer or early autumn, a number of herbs such as chervil (*Anthriscus cerefolium*), coriander (*Coriandrum sativum*), and parsley (*Petroselinum crispum*) continue to grow throughout the winter if they are protected from frost by a cold frame or cloches. They also grow well in pots placed on a sunny windowsill.

Herbaceous perennials that die down in winter, such as chives (*Allium schoenoprasum*), French tarragon (*Artemisia dracunculus*), and mint, may be forced for winter use. In early autumn, dig up mature plants, divide them, and replant in containers of loam-based potting compost. If kept in a light place that is free from frost and draughts, they produce fresh shoots throughout the winter that may be harvested regularly. Discard forced plants in spring or plant them out; if planted out, do not pick their leaves for at least a season to allow them time to recover vigour.

Evergreen herbs, such as winter savory, thyme, and rosemary, may be gathered throughout the year, but limit winter harvesting as there is no new growth at this time.

Planting container-grown herbs

Container-grown herbs may be planted throughout the year, but the best time is in spring when they establish rapidly. If they have been kept in a heated greenhouse during the winter, gradually harden them off (see p.220) in a cold frame before planting them out.

Soak well before planting, as dry root balls are difficult to wet once below ground. To avoid trampling and compacting the soil in a bed, it is best to stand on a plank in order to reach the planting positions. Set out the herbs, while still in their pots, according to your planting plan and check that each has sufficient room to develop, depending on its growth rate and spread.

Whatever the weather, water thoroughly after planting in order to settle the soil around the plants and provide even moisture for new root growth. After planting, pinch out the tips of clump-forming herbs and trim back shrubby herbs to encourage new sideshoots and to develop a bushy habit.

HOW TO GROW HERBS FOR FRESH WINTER USE

1 *Choose a dry day in early autumn to lift a clump of herbs (here chives) from the garden using a fork.*

2 *Divide the clump into smaller pieces with your hands or a hand fork. Shake loose as much of the soil from the roots as possible.*

3 *Plant up the divided pieces into pots or trays of potting compost; water well and cut back the top-growth.*

4 *Place the plants in a light, frost-free place. Once they are about 10cm (4in) high, harvest the leaves regularly to maintain a supply of new growth.*

Planting a herb garden to a design

Whether creating an intricate, formal design or a simple, informal one, careful planning, both on paper and on site, is essential for success. Make plans well in advance: start in the winter for planting in the spring, or as early as the preceding summer if you are raising the plants yourself.

As for all planting, thoroughly prepare the ground, clearing any weeds and raking the surface of the soil to a fine tilth (see "Preparing the site", p.411).

Once you have determined the design and the planting scheme on paper, mark the basic outline of the herb garden, including any paths, on the prepared site. Make any adjustments to the layout at this stage if required. It is most convenient to use container-grown herbs, since they can easily be set out according to the plan and the arrangement checked before actual planting begins.

If using turf or heavy materials such as paving, bricks, or stone, lay them before planting, while paths made of lighter, loose materials, such as grit, gravel, or bark chippings, may be laid before or after planting. When making paths of grit or gravel, provide retaining battens or edging tiles to prevent the material from spreading onto the plants in the beds.

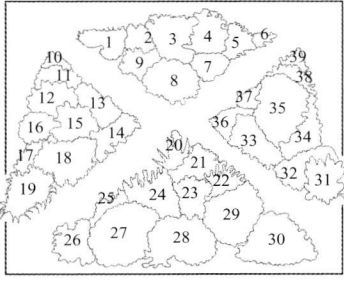

1 *First prepare the soil for planting. Then, using string and canes, or grit, mark out the planned design for the herb garden, including any paths or paved areas, on the site.*

2 *Lay out the plants, still in their pots, to check the overall effect and spacing. If using grit or gravel for the paths, sink battens at the edges to keep the material in place.*

3 *Once the design is finalized, plant the herbs and water them; you may prefer to plant them densely to achieve the desired effect quickly.*

4 *Lay the paths, adding grit or gravel evenly in between the battens; level the surface.*

5 *Keep the herb garden watered and weeded. Pinch out growing tips to promote bushy growth and prune as necessary.*

DESIGN FOR A HERB GARDEN

1 Chives (*Allium schoenoprasum*)
2 Compact marjoram (*Origanum vulgare* 'Compactum')
3 Bergamot (*Monarda didyma*)
4 Wormwood (*Artemisia absinthium*)
5 Hyssop (*Hyssopus officinalis*)
6 Wild thyme (*Thymus serpyllum*)
7 Silver-variegated thyme (*Thymus vulgaris* 'Silver Posie')
8 Marjoram (*Origanum vulgare*)
9 Pineapple mint (*Mentha suaveolens* 'Variegata')
10 Chamomile (*Chamaemelum nobile*)
11 Buckler-leaf sorrel (*Rumex scutatus*)
12 French tarragon (*Artemisia dracunculus*)
13 Variegated sage (*Salvia officinalis* 'Icterina')
14 Parsley (*Petroselinum crispum*)
15 Sweet cicely (*Myrrhis odorata*)
16 Cotton lavender (*Santolina chamaecyparissus*)
17 Creeping savory (*Satureja spicigera*)
18 Golden lemon balm (*Melissa officinalis* 'Aurea')
19 Chinese chives (*Allium tuberosum*)
20 Orris (*Iris* 'Florentina')
21 Borage (*Borago officinalis*)
22 Pink hyssop (*Hyssopus officinalis* 'Rosea')
23 Purple sage (*Salvia officinalis* 'Purpurascens')
24 Pink lavender (*Lavandula angustifolia* 'Loddon Pink')
25 Common thyme (*Thymus vulgaris*)
26 Purple basil (*Ocimum basilicum* var. *purpurascens*)
27 Rosemary (*Rosmarinus officinalis*)
28 Summer savory (*Satureja hortensis*)
29 Southernwood (*Artemisia abrotanum*)
30 Sweet marjoram (*Origanum majorana*)
31 Alecost (*Tanacetum balsamita*)
32 Golden feverfew (*Tanacetum parthenium* 'Aureum')
33 Chervil (*Anthriscus cerefolium*)
34 Marigold (*Calendula officinalis*)
35 Bronze fennel (*Foeniculum vulgare* 'Purpureum')
36 Woodruff (*Galium odoratum*)
37 Cotton lavender (*Santolina chamaecyparissus* 'Lemon Queen')
38 Sorrel (*Rumex acetosa*)
39 Lemon thyme (*Thymus* x *citriodorus*)

This small garden includes a wide range of aromatic and culinary herbs; they have been grouped in beds of restricted colour and divided by symmetrical paths for a traditional, formal effect, softened by the informal plant groupings within the beds.

Routine care

Most herbs flourish and require little attention once established. Maintenance largely consists of cutting back plants in spring and summer to encourage healthy growth, and tidying up dormant plants in winter. Herbs in containers usually need routine watering and feeding during the growing season, while periodic repotting or top-dressing is also necessary. Growing herbs in the right conditions should minimize any pest or disease problems; take action as necessary (see Plant Problems, pp.639–673) but you must wait one or two weeks after any chemical treatment before using the herbs.

Cutting back
Herbs that are valued for their fresh, young foliage may be cut back to produce a regular supply of leaves. Remove the flowering stems of sorrel (*Rumex acetosa*) as they appear; chives (*Allium schoenoprasum*) and marjoram (*Origanum vulgare*) may be left until after flowering as the flowers are useful as flavourings; variegated forms of marjoram, mint (*Mentha*), and lemon balm (*Melissa officinalis*) produce bright new foliage if the plant is cut back shortly before flowering as its colours fade.

The growth of invasive herbs should be checked regularly: even when planted in sunken containers, they produce surface runners which must be removed before they spread too far. Remove any reverted, plain shoots from variegated herbs as soon as they appear.

Dead-heading and pruning
Unless planning to save the seed, remove the dead flowerheads from most herbs so that energy is channelled into growth. Dead-heading annuals such as borage (*Borago officinalis*) lengthens the flowering season. Certain herbs such as angelica (*Angelica archangelica*) self-sow prolifically; these may become a nuisance if they are left to set seed.

Dead-head and prune shrubby herbs, such as lavender (*Lavandula*) and thyme (*Thymus*), by trimming lightly with shears after flowering. Hard pruning in spring encourages sideshoots and new growth from the base; thyme, however, is best pruned little and often during the growing season.

Mulching
Mulch only established herbs that thrive in moist soil, such as mint and bergamot (*Monarda didyma*). In summer, mulch after rain to retain moisture and to improve the soil as it breaks down. Use an inorganic mulch such as grit around Mediterranean or grey-leaved plants in heavy soil to reduce the risk of rotting.

Autumn clearance
The extent to which herbs are cut back in autumn partly depends on personal preference. In cold areas, leaving the dead foliage of herbaceous perennials until spring helps to protect them against frost and wind. Remove any dead leaves that have fallen on thyme and other low-growing, evergreen herbs as they may encourage fungal attack.

Winter protection
In cold weather, tender herbs should either be brought under cover or otherwise protected (see Frost and Wind Protection, pp.612–613). In spring, cut them back and plant them out again, or propagate new plants

Pruning Lavender

1 In late summer or early autumn, cut off all the dry flower stalks with secateurs and lightly clip the shrubs to maintain a neat finish.

2 Early the following spring, cut back shoots by 2.5cm (1in) or more of the previous year's growth, making sure that some green growth remains.

Replanting a Strawberry Planter

1 Each spring, replace or divide and replant the herbs in a strawberry planter if they have outgrown the pot or need rejuvenating.

2 First lift the plants from the top, then dig out the compost, carefully removing the plants from the pockets. Tip out any remaining compost. Replace the drainage material.

3 Add fresh compost up to the level of the lowest pockets. Divide or replace the old plants. Place each plant at the inside of a pocket, then gently pull the foliage through the hole.

4 Pack compost around the roots and up to the next level, firming well after each addition. Water the compost thoroughly.

from cuttings. The hardiness of a number of herbs, such as sage (*Salvia officinalis*) and lavender, depends on the variety; check this when buying.

Herbs in containers
Most herbs are easy to grow in containers and require little maintenance (see also Container Gardening, p.318). In hot weather, check soil moisture daily and water thoroughly when dry. During the growing season, feed the herbs every two weeks with a weak liquid fertilizer.

In cold periods, bring herbs in containers under cover in good light.

Frost-proof pots may be left outdoors, but insulate them with sacking to protect the herbs' roots.

Repotting
Inspect herbs periodically to check that they are not becoming pot-bound. Also look out for such signs as rapid drying out, pale foliage, and weak new growth. Repot during the growing season to encourage new root growth.

If repotting is impractical, renew the top 2.5–5cm (1–2in) of compost, incorporating well-rotted organic matter or a slow-release fertilizer. It will then be unnecessary to feed the herbs for about a month.

Propagation

HERBS may be propagated by a wide variety of methods, depending on the type of plant and the quantity of new plants required. Sowing seed is a simple, inexpensive way to raise a large number of plants and is necessary for annuals and biennials, although it may also be used for other plant groups. Cuttings are used to propagate various perennials as well as shrubs and trees, while division is suitable for a number of perennials and layering is a good method for some shrubby herbs. For further information on propagating individual species and cultivars, see "Directory of common herbs", pp.407–410.

Raising new plants from seed

It is easy to collect seed from most herbs and to grow them from your own seed (see PRINCIPLES OF PROPAGATION, "Seeds", p.629); they may be sown in containers or, where large quantities are required, in drills in the open ground. Seed may also be sown direct into the cracks between paving stones where it would be difficult to insert plants. Prepare a fine seedbed for any seedlings that you intend to transplant outside from containers. Spring is generally the best time for sowing seed, although some annual herbs may also be sown in early autumn.

Annuals and biennials

Hardy annuals such as borage (*Borago officinalis*) and marigolds (*Calendula officinalis*) may be sown in the spring or – to provide flowers late in the next spring – in autumn. Sow biennial herbs, such as caraway (*Carum carvi*) and angelica (*Angelica archangelica*), outdoors in late summer or early autumn for flowering the following summer. Thin out the seedlings twice: once after germination so that two or three remain at each position, and again after a few weeks so that only the strongest is left in place.

Short-lived, hardy herbs that are used regularly in large quantities, such as parsley (*Petroselinum crispum*), coriander (*Coriandrum sativum*), and chervil (*Anthriscus cerefolium*), may be sown at intervals of three to four weeks from early spring to early autumn. This provides a succession of foliage for harvesting throughout the year, although in some areas it may be necessary to provide protection from frost with cloches. Annual herbs of the Umbelliferae family – chervil and dill (*Anethum graveolens*) for example – are difficult to transplant successfully and are best sown directly in their ultimate positions.

Basil (*Ocimum basilicum*) is one of the more difficult herbs to grow from seed in cold areas. Sow basil seed very thinly in late spring, and keep it at a minimum temperature of 13°C (55°F). Prick out the seedlings once they are large enough to handle and keep them in a sunny, well-ventilated place. In cold, damp conditions, basil seedlings are prone to damping off (p.664) and grey mould (*Botrytis*) (p.653). Plant out the seedlings once all danger of frost is past or, in poor summers, grow them in containers under cover. In warm climates, basil may be sown directly into an outdoor seedbed (see ANNUALS AND BIENNIALS, "Sowing in open ground", p.217).

Perennials

If raising perennial herbs from seed, sow the seed in warmth in spring and grow on the seedlings in pots until they are large enough to be hardened off and planted out. Plant and care for them as for container-grown herbs (see p.411).

Most cultivars of perennial herbs do not come true from seed and must be propagated by cuttings or layering; an exception to this is variegated rue (*Ruta graveolens* 'Variegata'). Non-flowering forms, such as lawn chamomile (*Chamaemelum nobile* 'Treneague'), cannot be raised from seed; propagate by cuttings or division to obtain new plants.

Mound layering

This method is particularly suitable for propagating shrubs such as sage (*Salvia officinalis*), rosemary (*Rosmarinus officinalis*), lavender (*Lavandula*), and thyme (*Thymus*) that tend to become woody at the base or centre with little or no new growth. In spring, mound free-draining soil over the base of the plant, leaving just the top exposed. This stimulates new shoots to develop roots in a manner similar to stooling (see ORNAMENTAL SHRUBS, p.117). Leave the soil in place, replenishing it if it is washed away, until new roots have grown in late summer or autumn. Then cut the shoots off from the parent plant and treat them as rooted cuttings.

SOWING PARSLEY SEED IN CONTAINERS

1 *Soak the seed in warm water for several hours, then dry it. Tap seeds from a piece of paper onto firmed seed compost. Just cover with sieved compost.*

2 *Once the seedlings are large enough to handle, carefully lift them with a widger, holding them by the leaves not the stems.*

3 *Prick out the seedlings individually into prepared modules or pans of firmed compost. When they are approximately 5–6cm (2–2¹/₂in) high, transplant them outside into prepared ground.*

MOUND LAYERING SHRUBBY HERBS

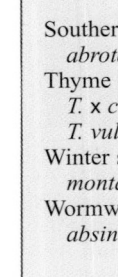

1 *To stimulate rooting, mound 7–12cm (3–5in) of sandy loam over the crown of the plant (here thyme) so that just the tips of the shoots are visible.*

2 *Once the layered stems have established new roots, remove them with a knife or secateurs. Pot up the rooted layers individually or plant them out.*

HERBS TO PROPAGATE BY MOUND LAYERING

Cotton lavender (*Santolina chamaecyparissus*, *S. pinnata*, *S. rosmarinifolia*)
Hyssop (*Hyssopus officinalis*)
Lavender (*Lavandula angustifolia*, *L. stoechas*)
Rosemary (*Rosmarinus officinalis* 'Prostratus')
Sage (*Salvia lavandulifolia*, *S. officinalis*)

Salvia officinalis

Southernwood (*Artemisia abrotanum*)
Thyme (*Thymus cilicicus*, *T.* x *citriodorus* and cvs, *T. vulgaris* and woody cvs)
Winter savory (*Satureja montana*)
Wormwood (*Artemisia absinthium*)

Harvesting and preserving

THE flavour of herbs may vary according to the growing conditions, the season, and the time of day. As the level of essential oils fluctuates with light and temperature, it is important to harvest herbs at the right time to ensure that the oil levels are at their peak. There are various methods of preserving herbs so that their scents and flavours may be enjoyed all year round. For advice on specific herbs, see the "Directory of common herbs", pp.407–410.

Harvesting

Herbs should be harvested on a fine, dry day after the dew has dried but before the plants are exposed to hot sunshine, which evaporates the essential oils. Always try to harvest herbs in a way that helps to maintain the plant's shape and vigour: choose straggly or invasive shoots, and with

1 *Pick healthy, unblemished shoots or leaves (here sage) on a dry morning, before the heat of the day releases the herb's essential oils.*

2 *Tie the shoots into bundles, then hang them upside-down in a warm place; once dry, strip the leaves from the stalks and store them in dark glass jars.*

PRESERVING HERBS BY AIR-DRYING

clump-forming herbs, such as chives (*Allium schoenoprasum*) and parsley (*Petroselinum crispum*), pick the outer leaves to encourage new growth in the centre. Only use foliage free from damage and insects.

Leaves and shoots may be picked at any time during the growing season but are at their best before the herb develops flowers. Evergreen herbs may be harvested lightly in winter. Handle aromatic leaves gently as bruising releases the essential oils. Use or preserve herbs as soon as possible after harvesting.

Collecting flowers, seed, and roots

When harvesting flowers, pick them on a warm, dry day, when they are fully opened. Collect seed by cutting off whole seedheads in summer or early autumn as they turn brown but before they are completely ripe and starting to shed. Roots may be lifted at any time of year, but the flavour is best in autumn.

Preserving

The main methods of preserving herbs are drying and freezing. In addition, a number are suitable for flavouring vinegars, oils, or jellies, while a few may be crystallized (candied) for decorating cakes and desserts. Store dried herbs in dark glass or ceramic containers, as exposure to light speeds the deterioration of their aromas.

Air-drying

Do not wash herbs as this may encourage moulds to develop. Dry herbs by hanging them upside-down in a warm, dry place such as an airing cupboard. Alternatively, place leaves, flowerheads, or petals in a single layer on a rack covered with muslin, netting, or kitchen paper. Leave them in a warm, dark, well-ventilated place until crisp.

Microwave drying

Wash the herbs and pat them dry, then place sprigs or leaves in a single layer on kitchen paper. Microwave them for two to three minutes, checking every 30 seconds and rearranging them if necessary to ensure even drying. Cool, then crumble and store as for air-dried herbs.

Drying seedheads

Cut seedheads in summer or early autumn as they turn brown, then place them in a paper bag or hang

FREEZING HERBS IN ICE CUBES

Freeze borage flowers and mint leaves singly in ice-cube trays for adding to drinks. Chop fresh herbs such as parsley or chives and place in ice cube trays, adding about 1tbsp of water to each 1tbsp of herb.

them upside-down and cover them with muslin to hold the seeds as they fall. Keep them in a warm, dry place to ripen; when dry, remove the seeds and store them. Seed for sowing should be kept in a cool, dry, frost-free place.

Drying roots

Most roots are best used fresh, but some may be dried and ground. First wash the roots thoroughly, then peel, chop, or slice them, before spreading them out on absorbent paper. Dry them in either a cool oven or a warm airing cupboard at 50–60°C (122–40°F) until brittle, then crush or grind them before storing.

Freeze-drying

Many soft-leaved herbs, such as parsley and basil, retain their colour and flavour better when frozen than when dried. Simply pack whole sprigs

DRYING SEEDHEADS

Cover the seedheads with muslin or a paper bag, secured in place with string or an elastic band, then hang them upside-down in a warm place until dry.

into labelled plastic bags, and freeze them; they crumble easily for use once frozen. For long-term storage, blanch them before freezing by dipping them first in boiling water, then in iced water. Pat dry and freeze.

Freezing in ice

Herbs may be frozen in water to form ice cubes; this is a good way of preserving borage flowers and mint leaves to use as a decorative addition to drinks, and the ice also protects the herbs from damage during storage. Herbs for cooking should be chopped before freezing since this is difficult to do once they have thawed. Place the ice cubes in a sieve and drain the water before use.

Making herb vinegars

Many herbs, such as French tarragon, thyme, oregano, and lavender, may have their flavours preserved by being steeped in vinegar.

To make flavoured herb vinegars, lightly crush some fresh herbs and then loosely fill a clear glass jar with the crushed herbs. (Do not use metal-lidded containers to make the herb vinegar, because the acid vinegar will corrode the lid and so taint the contents.) Warm either wine or cider vinegar and pour it over the herbs, and seal the jar. Leave the jar in a sunny spot for two weeks, shaking or stirring daily. Strain and bottle, adding a fresh sprig of the herb for identification. For a stronger flavour, replace the herbs and leave the herb vinegar for a further two weeks.

Basil leaves may be preserved by being packed in jars of oil; the leaves themselves may then be used in pasta sauces and other cooked dishes. Never be tempted to make your own herb-flavoured oils, because there is a risk of botulism.

CHAPTER

16

GROWING FRUIT

THE SATISFACTION OF growing, harvesting, and tasting your own fresh fruits is one of the great pleasures of gardening. A fruit garden may be highly decorative as well as productive: some plants have attractive, fragrant blossom or fine foliage while, in many cases, the fruits themselves are as ornamental as they are edible. In most areas, a wide range of fruits may be grown, while in cool regions growing under cover makes it possible to cultivate an even greater variety. In a large garden, there may be room to devote an area exclusively to fruit – whether in a formal layout with neat rows of trees, bushes, and canes, bordered by trained fans or cordons, or in an informal orchard. If space is limited, incorporate fruits into the rest of the garden, perhaps edging a bed with alpine strawberries or growing a grape vine over a pergola. Even in a small patio garden, there should be space for one or two citrus trees in pots or wall-trained apples or pears.

Planning the fruit garden

FRUITS have traditionally held a prominent place in the garden, and today, with a wide range of cultivars and many dwarf fruit trees available ideal for the average garden, fruit growing is increasing in popularity. There are always some fruits that will thrive in the given climatic and growing conditions, although the majority prefer a good loam and a sunny situation. In warm climates, a wide range of fruits may be cultivated outdoors although some fruits that require periods of cold dormancy before flowering will not usually be successful.

Where only a few fruit plants are required, the gardener may prefer to grow them within the ornamental garden rather than in a specialized fruit garden; many fruit trees are suitable for growing as specimens in a lawn. Alternatively, if space is very limited, most fruits may be cultivated in containers, either free-standing or trained against a support such as a garden fence, or grown on a "family" tree (see p.420).

If planning to grow plants in large numbers, however, it is best to create a separate fruit area within the garden; this makes it possible to grow fruits with similar require-ments together, and to protect them against birds and frost damage. This is possible even in a small garden, as long as suitable rootstocks are cho-sen and trees are carefully trained. If grown as espaliers, fans, or cordons around the borders of a garden, fruit trees may be both ornamental and a source of fresh crops.

Another consideration may well be the type of blossom you wish your trees to bear: some cultivars such as 'Arthur Turner', 'Ashmead's Kernel', and 'Bramley's Seedling' produce flowers in particularly impressive colours and/or sizes.

Thoughtful planning as well as careful selection of cultivars and methods of training make it possible to provide fresh fruit supplies over several months, and if there is some storage and freezing space available, the produce from a fruit garden may be enjoyed all year round.

In cool areas, the range of fruits that may be grown is even wider if some protection under cover is available. Reliable crops of peaches, nectarines, figs, grapes, or more tender fruits may be obtained by growing plants in a greenhouse, although ample room is needed for even a single tree. Protection and shelter is required by many of these fruits if they are grown outdoors.

The range of fruits

The different groups of fruit plants may be categorized according to their stature, their growth and fruit-ing habit, and their frost-hardiness.

WALL-TRAINED PEACH TREE
A sunny, south-facing garden wall is ideal for accommodating a fan-trained peach tree, providing warm and sheltered ripening conditions and a high yield of fruits from a limited space.

TREE FORMS

When selecting a tree form, there are three main factors to consider: growth habit, space, and maintenance. An espalier, for example, is ideal for growing against a wall, particularly for apples, which develop naturally on short spur shoots. Several cordons will occupy the same space as a fan, and so might be better in a small garden. Multiple cordons may be grafted with more than one cultivar, which provides an opportunity to have one "arm" as a pollinator for the main cultivar. Free-growing forms, such as bush or spindle, need pruning only once a year, while more elaborate shapes, such as cordons and espaliers, require training and pruning more often.

BUSH HALF-STANDARD STANDARD SPINDLEBUSH

PYRAMID DWARF PYRAMID CORDON MULTIPLE CORDON

ESPALIER FAN PALMETTE STEPOVER

Tree fruits (top fruits) include apples, peaches, and figs. The term embraces both pome fruits (those containing a core with pips, such as apples, pears, and medlars) and stone fruits (those containing stones, such as cherries, peaches, and plums), as well as a few other fruits, including mulberries and persimmons. The term "vine" may also be used to describe woody, fruiting climbers, such as kiwi and passion fruits, in addition to its more normal usage for *Vitis vinifera*, the grape vine.

The category soft fruits includes bush fruits, cane fruits, and strawberries, which are almost herbaceous. Bush fruits are naturally shrubby, forming a compact, bush shape, although they may also be trained into other forms. Blackcurrants, redcurrants, whitecurrants, and gooseberries are the most commonly grown bush fruits. Plants described as cane fruits produce cane-like shoots that bear the fruits; raspberries, blackberries, and hybrid berries, such as loganberries, are in this group. Most develop their canes in one season, and bear fruit on these the next, while producing new canes that will fruit in the following year.

Certain fruit-bearing plants cannot withstand frost and need warm, subtropical temperatures to develop and ripen fully; these may be categorized as tender fruits. Tender fruits include citrus, pomegranates, pineapples, tamarillos, and prickly pears. Some are also tree fruits, but have been grouped here with tender fruits because of their need for consistently warm temperatures.

Nuts include all plants that produce fruits with a hard outer shell around an edible kernel, for example cobnuts, almonds, and pecans.

Unrestricted and trained forms

Many fruits, particularly tree fruits, and to a lesser extent vines and some soft fruits, may be trained into a variety of forms. When deciding which forms to grow, bear in mind the space available, the relative ease of harvesting, and the degree of pruning and training needed to produce a plant that crops well. The choice of rootstock for fruit trees also determines their ultimate size (see "Rootstocks and tree size", p.423).

With the correct technique, trees and bush fruits may be trained almost as desired. The principle is to train young shoots into the required shape while they are still pliable; the branches then retain this form with regular, basic pruning.

Unrestricted tree forms

These forms develop, with limited pruning, in much the same way as a natural tree; they include the bush tree, standard, half-standard, and spindlebush. The bush and spindlebush are more compact than the standard and half-standard, and are suitable for small gardens.

A bush tree has a trunk up to 90cm (3ft) tall, with branches radiating out from the top third. It has an open centre, thus allowing the branches maximum light and space. Bush trees are small to medium sized, that is 1.5–4m (5–12ft).

The half-standard is similar to the bush but the trunk measures 1–1.5m (3–5ft) and the overall height is 4–5m (12–15ft). The standard is similar in form, but with a trunk measuring 1.5–2.2m (5–7ft) and an overall height of 5m (15ft) or more.

The spindlebush is a small tree growing up to 2.2m (7ft) tall with branches that are trained to radiate out from the central leader at a wide angle. It has fewer branches than other lightly pruned forms, but each branch is pruned to be as productive as possible. The lowest branch is usually about 45cm (18in) from ground level.

Trained forms

Some fruit trees and bushes are suitable for growing in trained (or restricted) forms. These include cordons, fans, and espaliers. They need careful training initially, and are then maintained by regular summer pruning, to restrict vegetative growth, with a minimum of winter pruning. Most require support wires, either secured to free-standing posts or against a wall or fence. Wall-trained forms are often favoured in temperate climates for fruits such as peaches because the fruits receive maximum sun and also benefit from the reflected heat of the wall. All the trained tree forms are ideal for small gardens as they make it possible to cultivate a variety of fruits in a restricted space. Maiden trees that have been grafted onto dwarfing rootstocks are usually used for training restricted forms.

A cordon is restricted to a single stem, 1.5–2m (5–6ft) long, clothed with fruiting spurs to produce a high yield in a small area. It is usually grown against a wall, or on posts and

FAMILY TREES
In a small garden, a convenient way to grow a variety of fruits is to plant a family tree, in which two or more cultivars are grafted onto the same rootstock so the tree bears different fruits on different branches.

FRUIT FOR FROST-FREE AREAS
Oranges grow well in warm, virtually frost-free regions such as Mediterranean countries, South Africa, and California. They often produce two crops a year and may bear flowers at the same time as an earlier orange crop is maturing.

wires, and is planted at an angle of about 45°. It may also be grown vertically or horizontally. Most commonly used for apples and pears, it is useful for red- and whitecurrants and gooseberries, too. Double (sometimes known as "U"), triple, or multiple cordons may be formed by pruning a maiden plant so that it forms two or more parallel stems. Cordons that have more than a single stem are usually trained vertically, while stepover cordons, with the main stem trained horizontally, are increasing in popularity. They are usually free-standing, supported on strong wires, and can be used to create an attractive, low edging to a bed.

A fan is trained with the main branches radiating in a fan shape from a short 24cm (10in) trunk and is suitable for tree fruits that are grown against walls and fences.

An espalier is trained with matching pairs of horizontal branches extending at regular intervals from a central stem. Each branch is clothed with short, fruiting spurs. The number of pairs of branches is variable

depending on space and tree vigour. This method is particularly suitable for apples and pears grown against walls or fences. It should not be used for stone fruits. A less rigid variation on the espalier is the palmette tree form, in which staggered tiers of branches are angled slightly upwards rather than horizontally.

Unlike the other trained forms, the pyramid is free-standing; its branches radiate from a central trunk, with an overall pyramidal form that is maintained by regular summer pruning to produce trees of small to medium size. Dwarf pyramids are similar but are grown on a more dwarfing rootstock.

Apple and pear trees can be trained into complicated forms such as arcure and goblet. These shapes, among others such as espalier, are of French origin. For the arcure, leading shoots are trained left then right in alternate years, curving downwards in a gentle arc. The goblet has shoots trained horizontally from a predetermined height on the trunk. From these, further shoots are trained

upwards, to form the goblet. For all such shapes, wires and bamboo canes are used to train the shoots and so achieve the desired form. All surplus shoots should be removed in summer, once those required are in place and established (see p.438).

"Family" trees

"Family" trees carry several cultivars – usually three – of the same fruit on a single tree. Such trees provide for a succession of fruit and are a very useful space-saving measure. Used originally by the Greeks and Romans, they were reintroduced during the 1950s and have become an increasingly popular way to grow apples and pears.

When young, a tree is grafted with two other cultivars suitable for cross-pollination and of similar vigour. Good apple combinations include: 'Egremont Russet' with 'James Grieve' and 'Sunset'; 'Bramley's Seedling' with 'Red Pippin (Fiesta)' and 'Falstaff'; and 'Charles Ross' with 'Discovery' and 'James Grieve'. Successful "family" pear trees include 'Beth' with 'Conference' and 'Concorde'; and 'Williams' Bon Chrétien' with 'Conference' and 'Doyenne du Comice'.

All such trees are available on a variety of rootstocks, and it is important to select one that will suit your soil and grow to the tree size required (see pp.435 and 444). 'MM106' is used for medium-sized apple trees, and 'Quince A' for pears. Apple 'M9' and pear 'Quince A' are for smaller "family" trees. Smallest of all is 'M27', which is best for pot-grown

"family" apple trees. 'Quince C' rootstsock is generally reserved for a few of the most vigorous cultivars such as 'Doyenné du Comice'.

Trees grown on 'M9', 'M27', and 'Quince A' must be permanently staked, because of their small, brittle root system.

Integrating fruits into the garden plan

Fruits may be grown either in a separate area on their own or intermingled with other, ornamental plants; the choice depends on space, personal preference, and the range of fruits

TRAINED CORDONS
Apple cordons provide good coverage of a fence, while alpine strawberries edge the border.

to be included. In either case, assess the impact that the fully grown fruit plants will have on the adjacent or surrounding plants. Planning and siting are particularly important because most fruits are long-term plants that require consistently good conditions to flourish and crop well over many years; in addition, with the exception of a few fruits such as strawberries, it is seldom practical or worthwhile transplanting them to other positions.

The planned fruit garden
Where a range of different fruits is required, it is well worth growing the plants together in a single area. When planning a fruit garden, take into account the preferred growing conditions of each type of plant and recommended planting distances; for example, site tall fruit trees where they will cast least shade on smaller bushes nearby. Also make sure that the space allocated for each plant is sufficient for it to develop naturally to its mature size.

Plants that have similar cultivation requirements may be grouped together to simplify practical operations such as applying fertilizer: for

example, redcurrants and gooseberries need more potassium than other fruits. Grouping plants also makes it easier to protect them from birds (with a fruit cage) or wind damage (with a windbreak).

For an eye-catching border, edge the fruit garden with a row of trained trees; cordons (especially stepover ones) or dwarf pyramids are particularly suitable because they need a minimum of support and occupy comparatively little space.

In planning the position of fruit trees (particularly apples, pears, sweet cherries, and some plums), remember that a self-sterile cultivar should be sited near a cultivar with which it will cross-pollinate (see "Pollination requirements", p.424), or it will produce few if any fruits.

For many fruits there is a wide choice of cultivars that ripen at different times; this makes it possible to plan for a succession of fruits that may be regularly harvested rather than a single glut. Some fruits, late-ripening apples and pears for example, may be stored for long periods, so if a steady supply is required, more space should be devoted to these than to earlier-ripening cultivars.

ORNAMENTAL DIVIDER
Trained apples form an attractive screen providing a fine display of spring blossom followed by handsome fruits in autumn.

Fruit in the small garden
There are various ways to make the most of a limited area for fruit growing so that it provides a high yield and is an attractive feature. Whenever possible, choose trees grafted on dwarfing rootstocks (see p.423) and

use training methods that make the best use of the available space. For example, plant "family" trees (see p.420) or Ballerina cultivars (see p.435). Train trees and soft fruits such as redcurrants and gooseberries as cordons against the house or

PLAN FOR A LARGE FRUIT GARDEN

A large plot, 11 x 17m (35 x 56ft), provides space for a range of fruit. Here, the chosen apple and pear cultivars will crop over a long period, and the soft fruit has been

grouped for easier maintenance. The more tender peaches and grapes thrive in a lean-to greenhouse.

1 Apple 'Discovery' (on 'M26'/'MM106')
2 Apple 'Epicure' (on 'M26'/'MM106')
3 Apple 'St Edmund's Pippin' (on 'M26'/'MM106')
4 Apple 'Sunset' (on 'M26'/'MM106')
5 Apple 'Cox's Orange Pippin' (on 'M26'/'MM106')
6 Apple 'Ashmead's Kernel' (on 'M26'/'MM106')
7 Plum 'Czar' (on 'Pixy')
8 Plum 'Victoria' (on 'Pixy')
9 Damson 'Prune' (on 'Pixy')
10 Pear 'Onward' (on 'Quince A')
11 Pear 'Concorde' (on 'Quince A')
12 Pear 'Doyenné du Comice' (on 'Quince C')
13 Pear 'Joséphine de Malines' (on 'Quince A')
14 Blackcurrant 'Boskoop Giant'
15 Blackcurrant 'Ben Lomond'
16 Blackcurrant 'Ben Sarek'
17 Redcurrant 'Red Lake'
18 Gooseberry 'Careless'
19 Gooseberry 'Leveller'
20 Raspberry 'Autumn Bliss'
21 Acid cherry 'Morello'
22 Raspberry 'Malling Jewel'
23 Loganberry (thornless)
24 Tayberry
25 Blackberry 'Merton Early'
26 Grape 'Black Hamburgh'
27 Peach 'Peregrine' (on 'St Julien A')
28 Strawberry 'Elsanta'
29 Sweet cherry 'Stella' (on 'Colt')
30 Fig 'Brown Turkey'

garden wall, rather than as bushes, since cordons require less room for a comparable fruit yield than fans or espaliers. Grow grape vines over a sturdy pergola or ornamental arch as part of the garden design. Cane fruits may also be trained in a variety of ways depending on space. Strawberries may be grown in vertical growing bags attached to a stake, fence, or other similar structure.

If there is room for only a single tree then it is essential to choose a self-fertile cultivar (see "Pollination compatibility", p.423). It is also worth selecting plants with a prolonged cropping season, unless there is ample storage and freezer space.

Mixed planting

In a garden that is largely ornamental or where there is insufficient space for a dedicated fruit garden, fruits may be planted among other plants. One or more fruit trees may make attractive specimens in the lawn, or grown in containers on a sunny terrace or patio. Fruit cordons or dwarf pyramids look effective when used as an ornamental divider, providing an unusual and productive screen, with attractive blossom in spring and ripening fruits from late summer to autumn. Trained forms of bushes or trees may be grown on almost any type of garden structure such as a pergola, fence, or shed, provided that the aspect is suitable.

When fruits are planted with ornamentals, make sure that all the plants' needs are compatible. If, for example, the fruits need protection from birds with netting, this may impede the growth of surrounding plants and look out of place. Particular care is also needed to ensure that fruit tree sprays do not adversely affect any nearby ornamental plants.

Strawberries are often grown among other plants either in the veg-

FRUIT IN A BORDER
The compact, rounded shape of a lemon tree laden with fruit punctuates an informal planting, providing a pleasant contrast to the colourful display of roses and double daisies.

SMALL FRUIT GARDEN

This small, fenced area supports no fewer than 17 fruit cultivars, providing abundant crops from early summer through to autumn. The plot measures only 4 x 9m (12 x 28ft) with a 2m (6ft) fence surrounding it; careful choice of cultivars and rootstocks coupled with correct training of the trees allows a wide range of fruits to be accommodated. The apple and pear cordons provide especially good yields from a limited space.

1 Sweet cherry 'Stella' (on 'Colt')
2 Pear 'Beth' (on 'Quince C')
3 Pear 'Concorde' (on 'Quince C')
4 Pear 'Doyenné du Comice' (on 'Quince C')
5 Raspberry 'Leo' (summer-fruiting)
6 Plum 'Victoria' (on 'Pixy')
7 Raspberry 'Autumn Bliss' (autumn-fruiting)
8 Peach 'Rochester' (on 'St Julien A')
9 Gooseberry 'Invicta'
10 Gooseberry 'Leveller'
11 Whitecurrant 'White Grape'
12 Redcurrant 'Red Lake'
13 Apple 'Epicure' (on 'M9')
14 Apple 'Lord Lambourne' (on 'M9')
15 Apple 'Sunset' (on 'M9')
16 Blackcurrant 'Ben Sarek'
17 Acid cherry 'Morello' (on 'Colt')

etable garden or – a popular use for alpine strawberries – along the edge of a border or raised bed.

Choosing a site

A sunny, sheltered position, where the plants will produce fruits of good quality and flavour, is ideal. Sites with some light shade are also acceptable but provide fewer ripening hours, so are best used for soft fruits or early-ripening cultivars of apples, pears, and plums. Plants on a south-facing slope may produce crops earlier than elsewhere but, as they also flower earlier, they are more likely to suffer frost damage.

Growing against supports

Walls, fences, pergolas, and arches all provide an ideal site for growing trained trees, especially if they are exposed to maximum sun. These structures make good use of space and allow the fruits to develop and ripen well; fruits trained on supports are also easier to protect from birds and frost than fruits in the open garden. The wall or fence must be high enough to accommodate the chosen fruits: 1.2m (4ft) would be enough for soft fruits, or apples or pears trained as cordons or espaliers, but a height and spread of 2m (6ft) or more are required for a fan-trained apple, pear, cherry, plum, or peach. Pergolas and arches are likely to provide sufficient height, but ensure that there is enough space for the plants to spread as they mature. The structure must be sufficiently sturdy to be able to support heavy crops, even in strong winds.

Frost and wind

Avoid planting in frost-prone sites because flowers, unopened buds, and fruitlets are all susceptible to frost damage. The coldest air collects where the ground is lowest, and a frost pocket will form in a valley floor or at the foot of a sloping garden, behind walls, hedges, or buildings.

Exposure to wind discourages pollinating insects and therefore greatly reduces the regularity of cropping. Strong winds also cause considerable crop damage. Draughty sites, such

as between two buildings, are not recommended, but a suitable, well-placed windbreak may be very effective in diverting or filtering wind to improve the conditions. Trees or large shrubs are preferable to solid barriers as they filter wind that would otherwise swirl over the barrier and damage plants on the other side (see also CLIMATE AND THE GARDEN, "How a windbreak works", p.611).

Growing fruits under cover

Crops native to warm climates, such as peaches, nectarines, and grapes, are ideal for greenhouse cultivation in cooler climates, but skill and attention to detail are required to maintain them in good condition and obtain satisfactory crops. Greenhouse or frame protection can also be a very satisfactory means of growing temperate fruits, such as strawberries, because, with careful selection of early-fruiting cultivars, the season can be lengthened by several weeks in early summer. In areas with a short growing season that experience early autumn frosts, it also improves cropping of perpetual or late-fruiting cultivars.

If fruits are to be grown with other plants in the same greenhouse, ensure that their temperature, humidity, and ventilation requirements are compatible. It is important that the

A CORDON ARCH
Fruit trees trained as vertical cordons over a series of arches provide an attractive, architectural feature as well as abundant crops of fruit. The structure must be sufficiently strong to support the weight of trees heavily laden with fruit in autumn.

greenhouse has the maximum possible number of bottom and top vents to provide a free flow of air. As for planting in open ground, the soil needs to be fertile and well-drained for the plants to thrive.

A number of tender fruits such as tamarillos (tree tomatoes) and pomegranates and even olives may be grown successfully under cover; in temperate climates, they are often grown as ornamentals since they seldom crop heavily, even under glass.

Trained fruits

Compatible tree and soft fruits that are suitable for training may also be grown in a greenhouse. Check that there is sufficient space for the chosen cultivar to develop and grow to its mature size, and ensure that suitable fittings for training the plant in the chosen form are in position before it is planted.

Fruits in pots

Strawberry plants that are grown in individual pots in a greenhouse or under a cloche will produce ripe fruits earlier than those in the open, thereby prolonging the fruiting season if both cultivation methods are used. Tender fruit trees such as citrus may be grown in pots that are placed outdoors during summer and returned under cover for winter.

Growing fruits in containers

Container-growing is useful for cultivating fruits where space is limited. The pots should be placed in sunny, sheltered sites and may be used on paved areas such as patios to provide ornamental features as well as crops of fruits. It is also a way of controlling the root growth, and therefore the vigour, of plants such as figs that (particularly in temperate climates) may make excessive vegetative growth at the expense of the crop. Container-grown fruit trees can also be moved in and out of cover to avoid frost or to give the plant a higher or lower temperature, according to its seasonal needs. Early-flowering trees such as peaches and nectarines in particular benefit from such flexible growing conditions.

Most fruits may be grown successfully in a large pot, half barrel, or similar container with a diameter of at least 30cm (12in). Strawberries may be grown either singly in 10cm (4in) pots or in strawberry planters (containers with side planting pockets). Fruits need more regular care in containers than when in the open ground, particularly with watering and feeding, because the root systems are confined and easily dry out.

Deciding which plants to grow

Whether planning an entire fruit garden or choosing just two or three trees, it is vital to select plants that will thrive in the given soil and climatic conditions without growing too large for their allotted space.

It also makes sense to choose well-flavoured, less commercial cultivars that are seldom readily available in the shops. More unusual fruits, such as red- or whitecurrants, are also worth considering, because they are often expensive to buy. If freezing soft fruits, such as strawberries or raspberries, is a priority, seek out cultivars that are suitable for the purpose.

Check the compatibility of different cultivars for pollination purposes before deciding which to grow (see "Pollination requirements", p.424). The final choice should also depend on the size of the crop required and the harvesting time.

Rootstocks and tree size

Tree size is determined largely by the rootstock onto which the tree has been grafted. Choose rootstocks that are of appropriate vigour for the planting area or training space available. Apple trees grown on dwarfing rootstocks such as 'M27' or 'M9', for example, are likely to suit most gardens; their relatively small size makes picking, pruning, and spraying easier. If a large tree is required, select one that is grown on a more vigorous rootstock. For further details, see pp.424 and 435.

Pollination compatibility

Most cultivars of apples, pears, sweet cherries, and some plums are not satisfactorily self-fertile, and therefore need to be planted close to one or more suitable cultivars of the same fruit that are in flower at about the

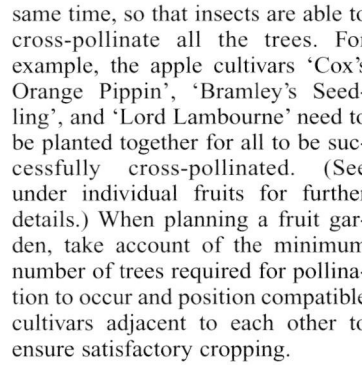

GRAPE CANOPY
A grape vine thrives in the warm but well-ventilated atmosphere of a conservatory or greenhouse. Care must be taken to prevent the ripening bunches from becoming scorched by the sun.

same time, so that insects are able to cross-pollinate all the trees. For example, the apple cultivars 'Cox's Orange Pippin', 'Bramley's Seedling', and 'Lord Lambourne' need to be planted together for all to be successfully cross-pollinated. (See under individual fruits for further details.) When planning a fruit garden, take account of the minimum number of trees required for pollination to occur and position compatible cultivars adjacent to each other to ensure satisfactory cropping.

Crop size and timing

Within the limits of space available, the amount of fruits that are required will determine the number of plants that should be obtained, bearing in mind that crop levels inevitably vary from year to year. The amount of storage or freezer space available may govern the size of crop that can be handled. Try to balance the numbers of early-, mid-, and late-ripening cultivars of each fruit grown in order to provide a consistent supply over a long period rather than a brief glut.

Early-ripening apples and pears do not keep well for more than a day or two, so do not grow more than can be consumed quickly: one or two cordons yielding 2–5kg (5–11lb) per tree should suffice. If you have plenty of storage space, plant a high proportion of late-ripening cultivars, the fruits of which can be stored for several months. Plums are also liable to produce gluts and the fruits must be used quickly unless they are frozen or otherwise preserved.

When deciding whether to plant early- or late-ripening cultivars, remember to take climatic factors into account: for example, late-ripening apples or pears are not a good choice for a region with a short summer or if the proposed site is shady, because there will not be enough time or sun for the fruit to ripen fully.

Site, soil preparation, and planting

ALL fruits require soil that is well-structured, adequately drained, and fertile to thrive. Before planting fruits, therefore, choose and prepare a suitable site so that it provides the necessary conditions.

Preparing the site

Prepare the site at least two months before planting. Remove all weeds, especially perennial ones, before any soil preparation takes place (see PLANT PROBLEMS, "Weeds", pp.669–673).

Soil types
A loam soil is ideal and produces high yields of good-quality fruits. Clay soils may produce very good crops if drainage is good but are slow to warm up in spring; growth and therefore cropping may be later. On sandy soils, plants come into growth earlier since the soil warms up quickly in spring. Heat is lost equally rapidly, however, which creates a greater risk from frost; sandy soil is also prone to drought. Sandy soils are usually less fertile than others, so the quality and flavour of fruits grown on these may be inferior to those produced on more fertile soil.

On chalk soils, lime-induced chlorosis caused by manganese and iron deficiencies (see p.651) may be severe, causing the leaves of plants to turn yellow and adversely affecting the quality and yield of fruit. In extreme cases, it will prove impossible to grow certain fruits satisfactorily; pears and raspberries, in particular, suffer badly. The use of sequestered iron alleviates the problem, but regular treatment may be necessary and is expensive. Annual mulches of farmyard manure and compost help by providing some of the trace elements required.

Improving the soil
For soft fruits, dig in generous amounts of well-rotted manure or garden compost and fertilizer to improve water retention and fertility. In preparation for planting tree fruits, fertilizers should not be used unless the soil is very poor and infertile, since it may produce excessive, soft growth rather than fruiting wood.

Drainage problems
Although poor drainage is more likely on heavy, clay soils, it may occur in many types of soil. Improve the soil structure where possible (see SOILS AND FERTILIZERS, "Soil structure

and water content", p.620), and install a drainage system if necessary (see "Installing drains", p.623). Where drains cannot be installed, plant fruits in raised beds (see STRUCTURES AND SURFACES, "Raised beds", p.599).

Adjusting the pH level
Soil with a pH level of 6–6.5 is ideal for all fruits except blueberries, which need an acid soil of pH4–5.5. Soils below about pH5.8 will need liming (see p.625). If planting in soil with a pH level over 7, top-dress regularly with sulphate of ammonia and mulch with acid compost to reduce the pH in the short term.

Preparing the support for a trained fruit tree or bush
If a fruit tree or bush is to be trained against a solid support such as a wall or fence, fix horizontal, parallel wires to the support with vine eyes and a tightener to keep the wires taut as the fruits develop. The vine eyes should hold the wires 10–15cm (4–6in) from the support to allow air to circulate around the branches and leaves of the plant. The spacing of the wires will vary, depending on the type of fruits grown. If using a free-standing post-and-wire support, secure the wires firmly to the posts. Just before planting, attach bamboo canes to the wires at the appropriate angles, and tie in the young plants to begin the training process.

Buying plants

Always choose fruits that will thrive in the conditions in your garden. Check that the ultimate size of the plant or tree will fit the available space and that there is room to train it into the desired form. Pollination needs also must be considered before deciding which cultivars to buy.

Specialist fruit nurseries are often the best and most reliable source of supply. They offer a wide range of old and new cultivars and will also advise about suitable rootstocks. Wherever possible, buy fruits that are certified free from disease.

It is best to buy young plants, since these become established quickly and may be shaped and trained to your own requirements. Plants are available bare-root or in containers. Container-grown plants are available all year round, but bare-root plants only in late autumn and winter when the plants are dormant and may safely be lifted. Reject plants

BUYING FRUIT TREES
BARE-ROOT TREE

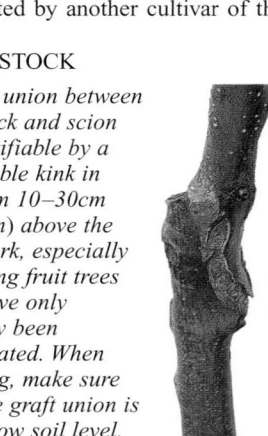

Well-spaced sideshoots (feathers)

Well-developed, healthy, balanced root system

CONTAINER-GROWN TREE

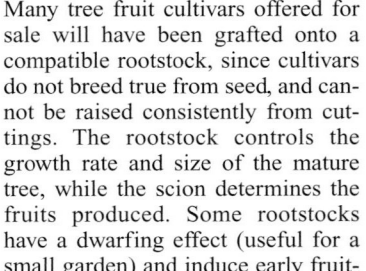

Vigorous, healthy roots that have not become congested and pot-bound

Moist, weed-free compost

with a pot-bound root system, since they seldom develop well. When buying bare-root plants, make sure the roots have not dried out and select plants with balanced main and fibrous roots.

Choose fruit trees that are healthy with sturdy growth and, if two or three years old, with well-spaced laterals. Inspect plants carefully and do not buy any with signs of pest infestation, damage, disease, or those that are lacking in vigour.

Pollination requirements
Most soft fruits and some tree fruits are self-fertile, that is they produce a crop without needing a pollinating cultivar nearby, and may therefore be grown singly. Apples, pears, nearly all sweet cherries, and some plums are not reliably self-fertile, however. To produce a successful crop, self-sterile cultivars need to be cross-pollinated by another cultivar of the

ROOTSTOCK

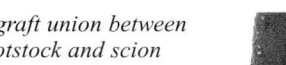

A graft union between rootstock and scion is identifiable by a noticeable kink in the stem 10–30cm (4–12in) above the soil mark, especially on young fruit trees that have only recently been propagated. When planting, make sure that the graft union is not below soil level.

same fruit. Usually, one pollinating cultivar is sufficient but some apples and pears must be grown close to two other cultivars for all trees to produce good crops.

For cross-pollination to occur, the flowering periods of the different cultivars must overlap. Cultivars are therefore divided into flowering groups, from early to late, which are indicated by numbers under the individual fruit entries. Cultivars for cross-pollination should be in the same, preceding, or following group. A cultivar in group 3, for example, is compatible with others in groups 2, 3, and 4.

Certain cultivars of some fruits, however, will not cross-pollinate, although they may flower at the same time. For sweet cherries and pears, these are classified in incompatiblity groups, which are indicated in the lists. Seek advice, if in doubt. A few sweet cherry cultivars will pollinate all other cultivars in flower at the same time; these are known as universal pollinators.

Selecting rootstocks
Many tree fruit cultivars offered for sale will have been grafted onto a compatible rootstock, since cultivars do not breed true from seed, and cannot be raised consistently from cuttings. The rootstock controls the growth rate and size of the mature tree, while the scion determines the fruits produced. Some rootstocks have a dwarfing effect (useful for a small garden) and induce early fruiting. A few rootstocks are resistant to certain pests and diseases.

Selecting fruit trees

Young fruit trees may be purchased at several stages of growth – choose the one most appropriate for the form that the tree is to take. Maiden whip trees (with no sideshoots) take at least one year longer than other forms to train and fruit. One-year-old feathered maidens are popular with experienced growers since their sideshoots enable the earliest possible training. Two-year-old trees fruit more quickly, and good specimens are easily trained. Three-year-old, trained trees are more expensive and can be harder to re-establish.

Planting in open ground

Container-grown plants may be planted at any time of year except when the ground is frozen or waterlogged, or during drought. Plant bare-root plants preferably from late autumn to early spring, while they are dormant; soak the roots well before planting. In frosty periods, heel them in temporarily in moist, frost-free soil until conditions are suitable for planting.

Planting fruit trees

If planting a number of trees, measure the site and mark out the planting positions with canes. Dig a hole for each tree at least one third wider than the tree's root system; firm the base of the hole and slightly mound it.

Insert a stake into the hole about 7cm (3in) away from the centre to allow for the tree's growth in girth as it matures. The height of the stake depends on the form into which the tree is to be trained (for details, see under individual fruits). Fruit trees on dwarfing rootstocks need permanent staking; remove the stake of those on other rootstocks after three years.

Place the tree in the hole, making sure that the soil mark on the stem is at ground level, and spread out the roots. Do not cover the union between rootstock and scion, since this encourages scion-rooting and the rootstock's influence will be lost.

Backfill in stages with soil, while another person holds the tree upright, shaking it gently from time to time so that the soil settles in between the roots. Firm the soil; when the hole is nearly full, break up the soil around the edges to obtain a uniform soil firmness over a greater area. Firm and level the area, and attach the tree to the stake using a soft, pliable, plastic tie with a firm cushion between tree and stake to prevent chafing. Protect the tree from rabbits and other animals with a wire netting surround.

Fruit trees to be planted against a wall or fence should be positioned 15–22cm (6–9in) away from the support, with the branches sloping gently inwards. This ensures that the roots are in good soil and allows for future expansion of the trunk.

Planting soft fruits and vines

Bush and cane fruits are planted as for fruit trees, but no staking is needed. Plant only up to the soil mark: planting too deeply inhibits the plants' growth. For vines, make the planting holes or trench wide enough for the roots to be fully extended, and train the vines against a support.

Planting in containers

Water the young plant thoroughly before planting. Use a moist, soil-based potting compost, leaving 2.5cm (1in) between the compost surface and the rim of the pot for watering. Water again after planting and keep the compost moist until growth begins, then water regularly.

PLANTING CORDONS

IN THE OPEN GROUND
Space trees 75cm (2¹/₂ft) apart (top). Attach a cane at an angle of 45° to horizontal wires (bottom left) stretched between sturdy posts. Tie each tree securely to a cane (bottom right).

AGAINST A FENCE
Fix wires 10–15cm (4–6in) away from the fence to allow for the growth of the trees and to promote good air circulation. Plant the trees 15–22cm (6–9in) from the fence.

PLANTING A FRUIT BUSH

1 *Dig a hole large enough to accommodate the roots of the bush when spread out. Place a cane across the hole to check that the level of the surrounding soil is the same as the soil mark on the main stem.*

2 *Backfill the hole with soil; tread in the soil gently to ensure that no air pockets remain between the roots. Rake over the soil lightly to level the surface.*

PLANTING A FRUIT TREE

1 *Dig a hole one third wider than the tree's root system. Drive in a stake to a depth of 45cm (18in) about 7cm (3in) from the centre of the hole.*

2 *Slightly mound the soil at the base of the hole and place the tree in the centre. Use a cane to check that the soil mark on the stem is level with the soil surface.*

3 *Spread out the tree's roots, then gradually fill the hole with soil. Firm to ensure that the tree is well anchored and that there are no air pockets between the roots.*

4 *Attach a buckle-and-spacer to the top of the stake and then to the tree so that the cushion is between the stem and the stake (see inset). Adjust as necessary.*

Routine care

Most fruit plants need regular maintenance to ensure that they are healthy and produce high-quality crops. Routine operations vary, depending on the type of fruit, growing conditions, and season.

Fruit thinning

Fruit thinning is necessary for a number of tree fruits, particularly apples, pears, and plums, to provide good-sized, high-quality fruits. It also prevents branch breakages by ensuring balanced crop distribution. In addition, thinning helps to prevent biennial bearing (to which some fruit cultivars are prone), that is, bearing heavy crops one year and little or none the next.

Thin by hand or with scissors, leaving the fruits room to develop fully and receive enough sun and air to ripen. Details of how and when to thin are given under each fruit.

Fertilizing, mulching, and watering

Apply manures and fertilizers when needed, observing crop performance and checking for any leaf discoloration that may denote nutrient deficiencies. In hot, dry summers, watering will usually be necessary; a seep hose (see p.561) uses water most efficiently, and a soil auger is invaluable for ascertaining visually the level of soil moisture at depth.

Care of tree fruits
In early spring, mulch newly planted trees and any that are not thriving with manure or compost. At the same

HOW TO THIN FRUIT

1 *Thinning of some fruits is required to obtain fruit of a good size and quality; if it is left unthinned, the fruit is usually small and of poor flavour.*

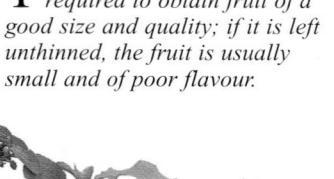
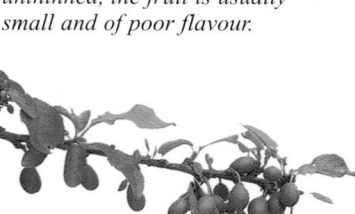

2 *Remove unhealthy or disfigured fruits first, then reduce the remainder to at least 5–8cm (2–3in) apart, depending on the type of fruit.*

time check that any problem is not caused by a pest or disease; if it is, treat as recommended in PLANT PROBLEMS, pp.639–673. Once the trees reach flowering size, a balanced fertilizer can be applied at a rate of 105–140g/sq m (3–4oz/sq yd) in early spring. Do not overfeed, particularly with nitrogen, as this may produce soft, disease-prone growth.

If a particular nutrient is needed, use specific fertilizers: potassium sulphate to correct potassium deficiency; ammonium nitrate to supply nitrogen; superphosphate to provide

phosphorus. Apply these in spring at a rate of 35g/sq m (1oz/sq yd), except superphosphate, which is normally applied at three times this rate every three or four years. Correct magnesium deficiency (p.651) by spraying the foliage, after flowering, with a solution of Epsom salts. In severe cases, repeat the treatment after three weeks. Other deficiencies, especially of manganese/iron (p.651), may also arise. If, more rarely, deficiencies of zinc, copper, or other elements are suspected, seek specialist advice.

Apply fertilizers evenly over an area just beyond the branch spread. Where trees are grown in grass, mow regularly and leave the mowings *in situ*; they rot down and return nutrients to the soil, helping particularly to avert potassium deficiency.

Care of soft fruits
Mulch soft fruits regularly in spring with well-rotted manure. Use fertilizers as indicated for tree fruits; nitrogen and potassium are the most essential nutrients. Apply fertilizer over the whole area; in the case of raspberries, spread the dressing at least 60cm (2ft) either side of the row, avoiding the foliage. With strawberries, dig in manure before planting.

Fruit in containers

Although soil-based potting composts contain nutrients, plants should be fed in the growing season in order to replace the nutrients as they are used; nitrogen and potassium in particular are often needed. Fruit plants in containers require watering

more frequently than those planted in open ground. Check the compost regularly – at least once a day in hot, dry weather – and keep it moist.

Each winter, fruit trees and bushes in pots should be top-dressed or re-potted. To top-dress, replace the top 2.5cm (1in) of compost with fresh compost. In alternate winters, where possible, repot the plant. Remove the plant from its container, and gently comb away some of the old compost from the root ball, using a hand fork or wooden stick. Cut out any coarse roots, taking care not to damage the fibrous roots, and repot into a larger, clean container (see also "Planting in containers", p.425).

Stakes and ties

The stakes and ties of both free-standing and trained fruits should be checked regularly. When the cushioning or ties are weak or worn out, the tree may rub against the stake, and *Nectria* canker (p.664) on apples, or bacterial canker (p.665) on stone fruits may develop. Check the base of the stake: this may rot and then topple with the tree in high winds, particularly just before a heavy crop is to be gathered. On trained trees, ensure that branches are not tied too tightly to canes or wires since this will restrict growth. Loosen any ties if necessary.

Supporting branches
Tree fruits grown in unrestricted forms may need to have their branches supported when the tree is heavily laden with fruit, even if the fruits have been correctly thinned. If

FERTILIZING FRUIT TREES

Using string and a peg, mark a circular area around the tree, slightly beyond the spread of the branches. This indicates where fertilizer should be applied – over the whole span of the tree's root system.

SUPPORTING LADEN BRANCHES

Tie several pieces of nylon string to a centrally placed pole attached to the main trunk. Use a nail to stop the string slipping down the pole. Tie at least one string to each heavily laden branch (away from the fruits) to support it.

only one or two branches are affected, support them on forked stakes or rope them to stronger branches. If several branches are overloaded, secure a sturdy stake either to the trunk or to the main stake and tie a rope to each branch and to the top of the stake; this technique is known as "maypoling".

Protecting plants

Fruit trees and bushes may need to be protected from bad weather or frost with windbreaks or fleece. Protection against birds and animals may also be required.

Wind protection
Maintain windbreaks (see p.611) properly so that they remain effective, and prune natural barriers such as trees or shrubs if they become thin to encourage bushier growth. Check that posts supporting windbreak netting or fences are secure and repair them as necessary.

Frost protection
Most frost damage is caused by spring frosts that kill or injure buds, flowers, or fruitlets overnight. Severe winter frosts may cause bark splitting and dieback, but in areas where low temperatures are common, select cultivars that are bred to withstand the conditions. In subtropical regions, there should be few problems; if necessary, cover small trees and bushes with polyester fabric or spun polypropylene sheets.

A very slight frost seldom causes any serious damage: -2°C (28°F) is frequently the danger point. The duration of the frost is usually more important than the temperature alone: -3°C (27°F) for a quarter of an hour would cause little or no damage whereas, sustained over three hours, it could cause substantial losses.

If frost is forecast, protect strawberries, bushes, and even small trees by using fleece, hessian, or layers of newspaper to cover the plant completely and trap warm air around it. Remove the covers each day once the temperature has risen above freezing point, and replace when frost is again forecast. For further information, see FROST AND WIND PROTECTION, pp.612–613.

Protection from birds
In winter, bullfinches and tits damage fruit buds by feeding on the nutritious centre of the buds and discarding the outer bud scales. This damage is much more serious than the loss of ripe fruit because it denudes whole branches permanently, making it necessary to prune them back to obtain new, young shoots, which will not fruit for two or more seasons. The best protection is to place nets over the trees or bushes. If snow is forecast, support the net or remove it temporarily because the weight of the snow on the net may damage branches underneath.

Ripening fruit should also be protected against birds; small areas may be temporarily covered with netting but for large areas it is preferable to erect a fruit cage instead. It is impractical to protect large fruit trees, although those trained against supporting supports may be enclosed by attaching netting to the support. The mesh of any net used must be small enough to exclude tiny birds. Protect strawberries in a patch with a low, temporary cage.

Pest, disease, and weed control

It is advisable to check plants once a week for signs of pest and disease problems; they may then be treated at an early stage before extensive damage has been caused (see PLANT PROBLEMS, pp.639–673). If virus diseases (pp.649 and 659) are suspected, seek professional advice to ensure that this is the problem; strawberries, raspberries, loganberries, blackberries, and blackcurrants are especially vulnerable. The only practical solution is to dig up infected specimens with their roots and burn them, otherwise the virus may spread to adjacent plants.

Weed control is also essential. Remove seedling weeds and mulch to inhibit germination of weed seeds. Perennial weeds should be dug out or spot-treated as soon as they are noticed. For further details, see "Weeds", pp.669–673.

Plants under cover

In cool-temperate climates, some fruits may need to be grown under cover. These include all the tender fruits, and a number of other fruits which either have flowers that are vulnerable to damage by spring frosts or require a long ripening period, for example peaches and many late-ripening grapes.

In subtropical climates, fruit trees are rarely grown under cover, since the only climatic problems encountered are exceptionally cool periods and heavy rainfall, which most are able to tolerate.

Plants that need to be under cover all year are best grown in greenhouses; walk-in polytunnels are of limited use because temperature levels and adequate ventilation are hard to maintain (see also GREENHOUSES AND FRAMES, "Choosing a greenhouse", pp.568–571).

Particular care is needed to maintain free air circulation around plants grown in greenhouses to discourage diseases that may be caused by the increased heat and humidity. Support wires for trained fruits should be secured at least 30cm (12in) away from the glass or plastic of the greenhouse. Control any pests and diseases and apply fertilizer as recommended under individual tree fruit entries. For details of pruning fruits grown in a greenhouse, see "Pruning under cover", p.430.

Growing tender fruits (for example citrus, guava, pomegranate, and olive) in containers makes it possible to bring them under cover when necessary. In cool areas, place tender plants grown in pots outside in a sunny position in spring and bring them under cover again in autumn. Overwinter the plants in the greenhouse at a temperature of at least 10–15°C (50–59°F).

PROTECTING AGAINST BIRD AND ANIMAL DAMAGE

BUD-STRIPPING
Birds stripping buds from branches over winter cause permanent damage, leading to unproductive, bare wood.

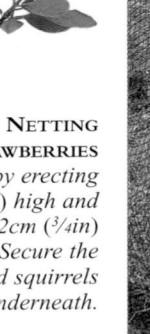

NETTING STRAWBERRIES
Protect fruit by erecting a frame 1.2m (4ft) high and draping and tying 2cm (³/4in) mesh netting over it. Secure the base so that birds and squirrels cannot get underneath.

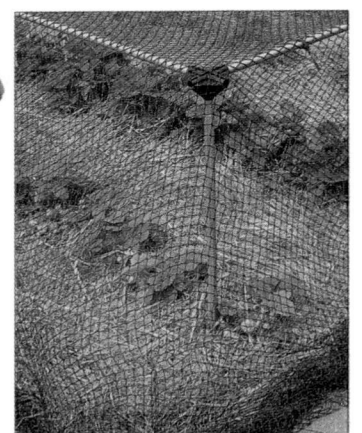

FRUIT CAGE
Fruit bushes or small fruit trees may be protected by a cage constructed from metal supports covered with wire or plastic netting.

PROTECTING TRAINED TREES
Fruit trees trained against supporting wires may be protected with a 2cm (³/4in) mesh net fixed at the top and secured firmly to the support.

Pruning and training

FRUIT trees and bushes need correct, regular pruning and, in many cases, training to yield a good crop. The degree and method required depend on the desired shape and the fruiting time and habit as well as on the individual type of fruit. Relatively limited pruning is needed to produce an open-centre bush tree, for example, while extensive, formative pruning and training are required for a fan or espalier to produce a symmetrical network of well-trained branches.

Aims of pruning and training

Initially, young trees and bushes should receive formative pruning and training to produce the desired shape (such as a bush) and to develop a strong, balanced framework. With established plants, the aim of subsequent pruning is to maintain the health and shape of the plant and ensure a good yield of fruit.

Pruning

This is the cutting out of unwanted shoots and branches, either because they spoil the plant's framework or because they are unproductive. Correct pruning maintains an open, uncrowded structure to allow the maximum amount of sun to reach the ripening fruits and to simplify spraying and harvesting. It also includes the removal of dead, diseased, damaged, or old, unfruitful wood.

On young plants, pruning may be combined with training to form a particular shape; unwanted shoots are removed completely, while those retained may be cut back to stimulate the growth of sideshoots. The established, cropping tree, bush, or plant is pruned to encourage optimum growth and fruit production.

Training

The selection and, in many cases, the tying in of shoots to create a specific shape is known as training. Forms close to the natural shape, such as the bush, require much less training than, for example, a fan, which is produced by precise selection, spacing, and tying in of individual shoots onto a supporting framework.

Over- and underpruning

Take care not to over- or underprune as this restricts fruitfulness and may encourage disease. Repeated, severe pruning results in increased, vigorous, vegetative growth, and little or no fruit, since few fruit buds are able to develop. This is especially damaging on a plant that is already vigorous. Underpruning leads to overcrowded branches that will receive less sun, which is essential to ripen the fruit; the branches may also rub together, exposing the tree to the risk of diseases such as *Nectria* canker (p.664). Pruning a young tree too lightly may also cause early overcropping that could stunt the tree and even break branches by overloading them.

When to prune

The time of pruning depends both on the specific treatment and on the kind of fruit. In the pruning procedures described here and under the individual fruits, "year one" refers to the first twelve months after planting, "year two" to the following twelve months, and so on.

Winter pruning is standard practice on all untrained apple, pear, quince, and medlar trees, on vines, and on black-, red-, and whitecurrants, gooseberries, and blueberries. Pruning of untrained trees of stone fruits (plum, cherry, peach, nectarine, and apricot) must be delayed until spring for young trees or summer for established ones, to minimize the risk of silver leaf infection (p.647). Summer pruning is essential on trained forms of tree fruits, grape vines, currants, and gooseberries. This reduces their vigour and contains them within the restricted space they occupy; it also concentrates the plants' energies on fruit production. Many tender fruits are pruned directly after fruiting.

How to prune

When deciding on the extent of pruning apple and pear trees, always take into account the vigour both of the individual shoot and of the whole tree. Vigorous growth should be pruned lightly; this usually involves thinning out a percentage of shoots completely and leaving the remainder unpruned. Prune weak growth more severely, but check first that no disease, such as canker, is causing the weakness.

Where to cut

It is important always to prune to just above a healthy bud and to make a clean cut; cutting midway between buds or leaving a ragged end may cause dieback and increase the shoot's vulnerability to disease. If removing a shoot or branch completely, cut it back to the point of origin but leave the bark ridge and branch collar intact rather than cutting flush with the parent stem.

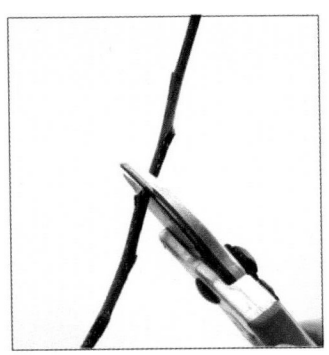

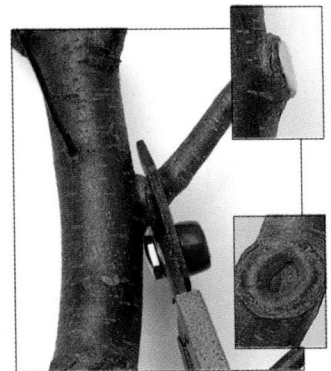

INCORRECT PRUNING

UNDERPRUNING
A tree that is pruned irregularly or very lightly will develop overcrowded shoots that will not receive sufficient light to ripen the fruits, which may be small. The branches may also rub together, increasing the risk of certain diseases.

OVERPRUNING
If a fruit tree is pruned excessively, this will stimulate a mass of vigorous, vegetative shoots. These shoots will produce few, if any, fruit buds, so the crop will be poor.

REMOVING A BRANCH

1 *Using a pruning saw, make the first cut approximately 30cm (12in) away from the trunk. Saw at right angles to the branch from underneath, to about one quarter of the way through.*

2 *Start the second cut at the top of the branch, slightly further out than the first cut. Saw right through the branch; if it breaks away, the bark will tear only as far as the first cut.*

3 *When making the final cut, take care not to damage the bark ridge at the top of the branch or the collar at the base. If necessary, start the cut from below and cut down from above to meet it.*

4 *Pare away rough edges with a sharp knife. The exposed area will seal itself more quickly with the bark ridge and collar left intact. This also reduces the risk of disease entering the wound. Do not apply wound paint, as it might seal in an existing infection.*

To prevent the branch or bark from tearing before cutting is completed, undercut first before finishing the cut from above. Cut back to the point of origin or to a well-placed, healthy branch as a suitable replacement. Do not leave a stub or the cut end will die instead of healing. Pare away any rough edges with a sharp knife.

Fruiting habits

How a plant is pruned depends on its fruiting habit. For example, sweet cherries form fruit mainly on spurs of two-year and older wood, so many of the older shoots must be retained. Acid cherries, however, fruit on one-year-old shoots; when pruning, leave most of the young shoots but remove some of the old, unproductive wood.

Training for shape

A young tree is usually bought as a "feathered maiden" (a one-year-old tree with sideshoots). Initial pruning consists of selecting shoots to be retained, shortening them as required, and removing unwanted shoots. If a young tree is bought as a maiden whip (a one-year-old tree without sideshoots), it should be cut down to a bud after planting, the height depending on how the tree is to be trained. This encourages the growth of sideshoots. When these develop, the tree, now two years old, is equivalent to a feathered maiden. Formative pruning continues for the first two or three years until the desired shape has been obtained.

Training for fruitfulness

The vigour and fruitfulness of shoots may be adjusted by raising or lowering selected laterals or, with oblique cordons, the whole tree. Horizontal growths are more fruitful than vertical ones, so tying a lateral closer to the horizontal makes it produce more fruit. If one lateral is less vigorous than another and more sideshoots are needed, raising it will stimulate vegetative growth. For an established, cropping tree or bush, pruning is more important than training; even on an untrained tree, less fruitful or unbalanced shoots may be tied down in summer to increase their yield.

PRUNING A MAIDEN WHIP TO FORM A FEATHERED TREE

WINTER, YEAR 1
To produce vigorous "feathers" (sideshoots) on a maiden whip tree, cut it back with an angled cut just above a bud at the required height.

WINTER, YEAR 2
By the following winter, a number of new sideshoots should have been produced below the pruning cut.

TRAINING ON CANES

1 *The vigour of laterals of trained trees may be altered by adjusting the angle at which they are trained. This technique corrects uneven growth on either side of the same tree.*

2 *Lower a young, strong-growing lateral, with its cane, at the start of or during the summer to reduce its vigour; raise a lateral to encourage it to grow more quickly. Retie the canes to the wires.*

3 *By the end of the summer, the branches may be returned to their original positions; they should be more even in length.*

Curbing excessive vigour

Extremely vigorous trees that produce rapid vegetative growth at the expense of cropping may benefit from root pruning. On apples and pears only, bark-ringing (see p.437) may also be used as a last resort to curb vigour; it should not be used on stone fruits as it may kill them. Both methods will induce the formation of fruit buds, so the beneficial effects will be seen in increased blossom and fruiting one or possibly two years later.

Root pruning

Trees may be root pruned at any age, but only when they are dormant. When pruning the roots of a young tree, first lift it by digging around it, then remove soil carefully from around the fibrous roots, taking care not to damage them. Cut back a few of the thick roots in the process. Then replant the tree firmly and stake it.

Larger trees need to be root pruned *in situ*, pruning one side of the root system one winter, and completing the other side a year or two later. To do this effectively, make a trench 45cm–1.2m (18in–4ft) wide, depending on the size of the tree, to expose the main roots. These should be severed and a section of each root removed. Then fill in the trench, firm, and mulch; in some cases, staking may be required to provide support until the tree is fully stable.

Pruning under cover

Prune back branches and shoots of plants grown in a greenhouse so that they do not touch the glass or plastic surfaces, as otherwise they may suffer sun scorch and growth will be constricted or damaged. Regular pruning also allows more light to reach the developing fruits and helps them to ripen.

Renovation

If a tree is too old to crop well, and has rotten or severely diseased branches or trunk, it should be grubbed out and burnt. If the trunk and the main branches are sound, however, and the tree is merely overcrowded, it can be rejuvenated by means of renovative pruning followed by correct, routine care.

Renovation work should be carried out in spring or summer on stone fruits and in winter on apples, pears, and other pome fruits. Cut out any branches that are dead, damaged, or diseased, or so low that they may trail on the ground when laden with fruit. Also remove crowded or crossing branches, because these will shade the developing fruits, and, if they rub together, may become prone to diseases such as canker. On a vigorous tree, it is advisable to stagger this pruning over more than one year; pruning too severely on a single occasion may only induce more vigorous, vegetative growth.

Once this initial thinning has been achieved, more precise pruning, such as spur thinning, may be carried out (as described for routine pruning under individual fruit entries). Chemical inhibitors are available to curb the regrowth of water shoots around the cuts, but wound paints are not recommended because they may seal in any infection.

ROOT PRUNING TO IMPROVE FRUITING

1 *Mark out the position for a trench around the tree using string and a peg. The trench should be at the same distance from the tree all the way round, just below the outermost spread of the branches.*

2 *Dig out a trench around the tree at the marked line; it should be at least 45cm (18in) wide and approximately 60cm (24in) deep.*

3 *At the base of the trench, use a fork to remove soil from around the thick roots without damaging the fibrous roots.*

4 *Sever each woody root on either side of the trench with a pruning saw, discarding the central section. Leave the fibrous roots unpruned.*

5 *Backfill the trench with soil, firm well, then cover the area with an organic mulch to retain moisture and help the tree re-establish. Stake if necessary.*

RENOVATING A NEGLECTED TREE

1 *Remove overcrowded, rubbing, or crossing branches to let in light and air by cutting them back to their point of origin, or to a vigorous sub-lateral facing the required direction.*

2 *Any branches that are damaged or affected by a disease such as canker (shown above) should be removed completely, or cut back to a healthy shoot.*

Harvesting and storing

MANY home-grown fruits may be enjoyed long after their normal harvesting time if correctly harvested and stored. While most are at their best eaten fresh, a number keep their flavour well even after prolonged storage. For details on harvesting and storing specific fruits, see the individual fruit entries.

Harvesting

Most fruits are best picked when fully ripe for using fresh. Fruits for storing are usually harvested slightly earlier, however, when they are mature but not yet completely ripe and still firm. Since not all the fruits on a single plant ripen at the same time, it is usually necessary to harvest over a period and this provides a succession of fresh supplies.

For tree fruits such as apples and pears, test for ripeness by holding a fruit in the palm of the hand, then gently lift and twist. If ripe, the fruit will come away easily complete with its stalk, otherwise it should be left for a day or two.

When harvesting, discard any damaged, diseased, or bruised fruits as they will quickly become infected with rot, which then spreads rapidly to adjacent fruits when in storage.

Soft fruits must be picked completely dry otherwise many may be affected by rot unless the fruits are used immediately. Regular picking, at least every other day, is advisable for strawberries, raspberries, blackberries, and hybrid berries.

Always take care not to damage the plant when harvesting – by pulling fruit off sharply, for example. Some types of fruit, such as cherries, grapes, and mangos, should be cut off the plant to avoid the risk of accidental damage.

Storing

There are various ways of keeping fruits for later use, including cool storage, freezing, and preserving; the most suitable method depends on the type of fruit. Some fruits, especially those such as apples, apricots, and figs that have a high acid and sugar content, may also be oven-dried at 120–140°F (49–60°C) but this is difficult to do successfully at home.

FREEZING SOFT FRUITS

Spread out soft fruits, such as raspberries, on trays so that they are not in contact with each other, then freeze them. Once they are frozen, they may be packed into suitable containers and kept in the freezer until they are required for use.

When preparing fruits for storage, handle them carefully to avoid bruising. Always store different cultivars in separate containers that are free from any residues or aromas that may taint the fruits.

Cool storage

Apples and pears in particular may be kept for several weeks, or even months in the right conditions – consistently cool, dark, and slightly damp. Various other tree fruits, such as lemons, may also be stored this way although they do not usually keep for such a long period, while most nuts keep well for up to a few months. Soft fruits cannot be stored in this way. The required temperature and degree of humidity vary for different fruits, but most should be stored in slatted trays and boxes to allow free air circulation. Some apple and pear cultivars, however, tend to shrivel and are better kept in clear plastic bags. Check unwrapped fruits regularly and remove any that show signs of disease or rotting.

Freezing

This is ideal for most soft fruits, except strawberries, and for a number of tree fruits. Small fruits such as raspberries are usually frozen whole, while large fruits such as apples are best chopped or sliced beforehand to ensure even and thorough freezing. Remove any stalks (and "strigs" of currants) then open-freeze whole fruits spread out on trays. Once they are frozen – after two to four hours – transfer the fruits to plastic boxes or bags, excluding as much air as possible, and keep them frozen until needed. Strawberries and some soft-fleshed tree fruits such as plums are often puréed before being frozen.

Preserving and bottling

All soft fruits and a number of tree fruits such as apricots and damsons may be made into preserves. In most cases, the entire fruit is used, while some such as grapes and blackberries are better strained and only the juice used to make a sweet jelly.

Citrus fruits, pineapples, and most stone fruits such as cherries may be bottled in sugar syrup with alcohol (such as rum, brandy, or *eau de vie*) if desired to preserve them. Citrus peel may also be candied or dried for use in baking.

STORING APPLES

1 *Wrap each fruit individually in greaseproof paper to prevent rot and keep it in good condition.*

2 *Carefully fold the greaseproof paper around the fruit, holding it lightly so that you do not bruise it.*

3 *Place each wrapped fruit on its folded end in a wooden slatted box, or other well-ventilated container, and store in a cool place.*

ALTERNATIVE METHOD

Store fruits of cultivars that tend to shrivel quickly in a plastic bag. Make several holes in the bag before filling it with no more than 3kg (6lb 8oz) of fruit. Seal the bag loosely.

FRUITS THAT FREEZE WELL

Apples **P**
Apricots **P**
Blackberries and all hybrid berries **Sk**
Blackcurrants **Sk**
Blueberries **Sk**
Cherries (acid) **Sk**
Cherries (sweet) **Sk**
Damsons **Sk** (with or without stones)
Gages **Sk**
Gooseberries **Sk**
Grapes **Sk**
Nectarines **P**
Peaches **P**
Plums **Sk**
Raspberries **Sk**
Redcurrants **Sk**
Whitecurrants **Sk**

KEY
P *Remove cores or stones and slice and peel if required*
Sk *Remove stalks (and stones where applicable)*

Propagation

TREE fruits (except figs) are usually propagated by grafting; figs, vines, and many soft fruits by cuttings, although if *Phylloxera* (see p.461) is a problem, grape vines should be grafted. Some fruits produce runners, layers, or suckers, all of which may be used to produce new plants. Several tender fruits and some nuts may be grown from seed but hardy fruits seldom come true.

Bud-grafting

Both chip-budding and T-budding are used to increase the stock of fruit trees. They are economical methods of propagation, since a new tree is produced from a single bud. Grafting should be carried out in midsummer, using as the rootstock an established plant with a stem that is at least 1cm (½in) thick. A bud from the scion plant is cut from a ripe shoot (the budstick) of the current season's growth, and grafted onto an incision in the rootstock.

Propagating by chip-budding
Select a healthy budstick and carefully remove a bud (the bud chip), taking care not to damage the cambium layer. Remove a sliver of rind from the rootstock and place the bud chip onto the exposed wood of the rootstock so that the cambium layers are in close contact. Bind the bud chip tightly onto the rootstock to hold it in place. When the bud and rootstock have united the bud will start to swell and the binding may be removed. The following winter, trim the rootstock just above the grafted bud to encourage a strong shoot to develop from the graft in spring.

CHIP-BUDDING

1 *Choose a vigorous shoot of the current season's ripened wood as the budstick. The shoot should be approximately pencil thick and have well-developed buds.*

2 *Hold the budstick firmly and, using a clean, sharp knife, slice off the soft tip and remove all the leaves to produce a clear length of stem.*

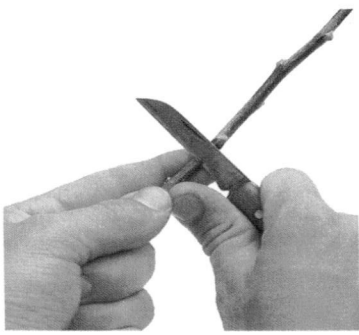

3 *To remove a bud chip, first slice into the budstick about 2cm (¾in) below a bud. Cut down to a depth of about 5mm (¼in), slanting the blade at an angle of 45°.*

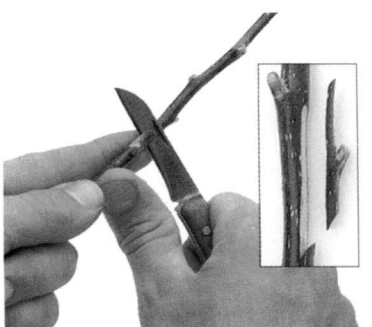

4 *Make another incision about 4cm (1½in) above the first. Slice downwards behind the bud towards the first incision, taking care not to damage the bud.*

5 *Remove the bud chip, holding it by the bud to keep the cambium layer clean. Place the bud chip in a plastic bag to stop it drying out.*

6 *To prepare the rootstock, stand astride the plant and, using a sharp knife, remove all the shoots and leaves from the bottom 30cm (12in) of stem.*

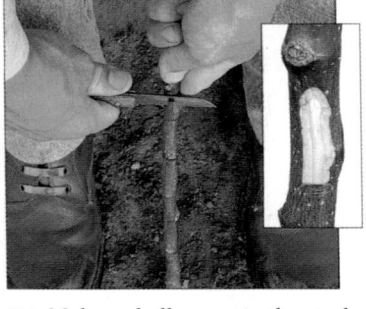

7 *Make a shallow cut in the stock. Remove a sliver of rind to reveal the cambium layer (see inset), leaving a "lip" at the base. Do not touch the exposed wood.*

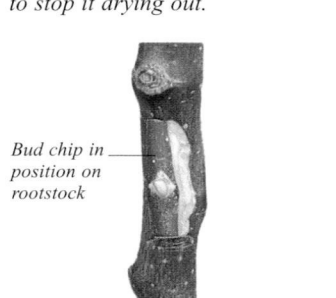

Bud chip in position on rootstock

8 *Place the bud chip onto the prepared lip of rind, offset if necessary, so that the exposed cambium layers of bud chip and rootstock match and touch.*

9 *Bind the bud chip to the rootstock with plastic tape. Carefully remove the tape after a few weeks when the bud chip has united with the rootstock.*

10 *The following late winter, remove the top of the rootstock. Cut cleanly with secateurs just above the grafted bud, using an angled cut.*

11 *During the summer, a shoot from the grafted bud will develop. The new tree is then at the maiden whip stage (see "Selecting fruit trees", p.425).*

Propagating by T-budding

In this technique the rootstock and scion bud are prepared in a similar way to chip-budding, except that two slits are made in the rootstock, to form the shape of a "T". This allows the bark of the rootstock to be lifted slightly so that the scion bud may be tucked behind it. Removing the scion bud with a leaf stalk attached makes it easier to handle; the stalk is removed before the bud is bound to the rootstock. The rootstock should be cut back the next winter.

For this technique to be successful, the bark of the rootstock must lift smoothly: in dry weather, rootstocks need to be watered for up to two weeks before T-budding takes place.

Whip-and-tongue grafting

This is a common method of grafting for tree fruits. It may be used as an alternative to budding but it is usually more successful with pome than with stone fruits. Use well-established rootstocks that have been planted either the previous winter or, preferably, two winters before grafting takes place.

The scion material should have at least three buds and should be taken in mid-winter from a healthy shoot of the previous season's growth. Heel it in until ready for grafting. In late winter or early spring, prepare the stock by cutting off the top of the stem and removing any sideshoots.

Using a sloping cut, slice off a small piece of bark from the top of the remaining stem; make a further shallow incision in the exposed cambium layer, to create a tongue.

Trim the scion to a length of three or four buds then, using a sloping cut, slice off a small piece of bark close to a bud but on the opposite side to it. Make a further, shallow incision, to match that in the stock, and hook the resulting tongue onto the one on the rootstock. Make sure that the two cambium layers are in

---

T-BUDDING

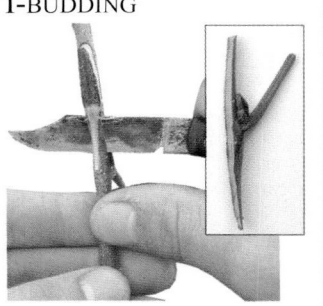

1 *Select a ripened shoot as the scion from the current season's growth and remove the leaves. Remove a bud by slicing underneath it (see inset).*

2 *Make a "T"-shaped cut in the stock about 22cm (9in) above ground level and prise open the flaps of bark.*

3 *Place the bud behind the flaps of bark, trimming the top level with the horizontal cut on the stock. Bind the bud as for chip-budding.*

WHIP-AND-TONGUE GRAFTING

1 *In mid-winter, remove healthy, vigorous hardwood shoots from the scion tree. Cut lengths of about 22cm (9in), cutting obliquely just above a bud.*

2 *Make bundles of 5 or 6 scions. Choose a well-drained, sheltered site and heel them in to keep them moist but dormant, leaving 5–8cm (2–3in) above the soil surface.*

3 *In late winter or early spring, prepare the rootstocks just before bud break. Cut off the top of each rootstock about 20–25cm (8–10in) from ground level.*

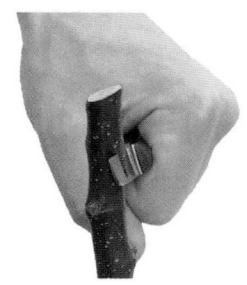

4 *Trim off any shoots from the rootstock with a sharp knife, then make a 3.5cm (1½in) upward-sloping cut on one side to receive the scion.*

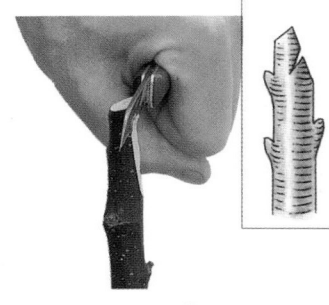

5 *Make a slit 1cm (½in) deep about one third of the way down the exposed cambium layer, to form a tongue into which the scion may be inserted (see inset).*

6 *Lift the scions, cut off any soft growth at the tips, and trim to 3 or 4 buds. For each, cut off a piece of bark behind a bud that is about 5cm (2in) from the base.*

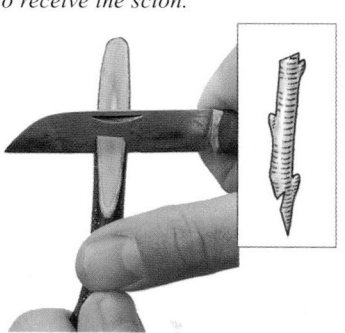

7 *Without touching the cut surface with your hand, cut the cambium layer (see inset) to match the tongue in the rootstock.*

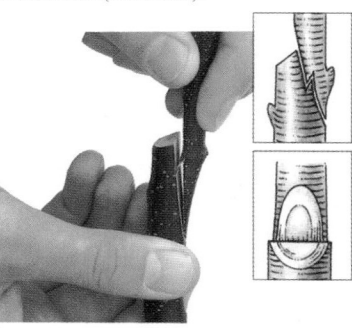

8 *Place the scion into the tongue on the stock (inset, top). Use the arches of the cambium layers as a guide (inset, bottom) to ensure the exposed surfaces fit together well.*

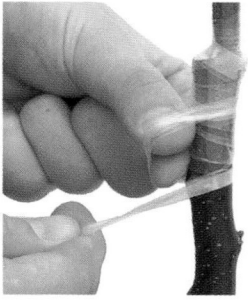

9 *Bind together stock and scion with clear plastic tape. When the cut surfaces start to callus, remove the tape by carefully scoring it downwards.*

close contact, then bind the graft firmly. Remove the binding carefully when a callus has formed around the graft union. By spring, buds on the scion will have started to grow. Select the best shoot that develops (keeping others pinched back) to form a maiden whip tree (see "Selecting fruit trees", p.425).

Cuttings

Hardwood, softwood, and leaf-bud cuttings may be used to propagate certain fruits. Cutting material should always be selected from a healthy parent plant that crops regularly.

Hardwood cuttings
Figs, vines, currants (white, red, and black), and gooseberries may be propagated from hardwood cuttings, usually taken in autumn.

Select a well-ripened shoot of the current season's growth and trim off the leaves and soft tip. Remove some or most of the buds, depending on the fruit being propagated, and trim off the top and base. The exact preparation and length of the cuttings vary slightly; details are given under individual fruit entries.

If the soil is well cultivated and not too heavy, the cuttings may be inserted into a narrow trench in the open ground. If the soil is heavy, however, place the cuttings in a pot of moist, sandy compost. The cuttings should be ready for transplanting one or two years later.

Softwood cuttings
Guavas, pomegranates, tree tomatoes, and blueberries are propagated from softwood cuttings (where the climate is warm enough for the wood to ripen sufficiently, blueberries may also be propagated from hardwood cuttings). Take the cuttings in midsummer and place them in pots of cutting compost (see p.478). Harden off the young plants before transplanting to their permanent positions.

Leaf-bud cuttings
Stocks of blackberries and hybrid berries may be increased quickly by leaf-bud cuttings (see p.472). Take the cuttings in late summer: remove short lengths of stem, each with a bud and leaf attached; insert them in compost with the buds just above the surface. Once rooted, the cuttings may be potted up or planted out.

Runners, layers, and suckers

Some fruits send out runners, layers, or suckers, which root naturally at stem nodes while still attached to the parent plant. This process may be exploited to increase fruit stocks.

Runners
Strawberries (but not all alpine strawberries) produce creeping horizontal stems, or runners, which root where they come into contact with the ground and may be used for propagation. As the runners are produced, spread them out evenly. Allow them to root, and then lift and sever them (see p.470).

Layers
Blackberries and hybrid berries may be propagated by layering, although some hybrids are slow to root. The tip of a shoot is induced to root by carefully pegging it down in the soil or in a pot of moist compost (see "Tip layering", p.471). A year later, when the tip has rooted and produced new growth, it may be severed from the parent plant and transplanted to its permanent position.

Suckers
Established cane fruits such as raspberries naturally produce suckers that are usually hoed off. If retained, rooted suckers may be lifted and severed in autumn, when the plants are dormant but the soil is still warm. Transplant the rooted suckers directly to their permanent positions (see *Propagating by Suckers*, p.474). Figs, cobnuts, and filberts also produce suckers: if the suckers have good root systems, sever them with a spade and replant in the same way.

Seed

Propagation from seed is the usual method of increasing stock of many tender fruits, including avocado (see p.486), guava, and papaya.

The alpine strawberry is one of the few hardy fruits that may be raised successfully from seed (see p.470). Cobnuts, filberts, walnuts, and sweet chestnuts may also be raised from seed with a reasonable chance of success, although cultivars selected for the quality of their fruit need to be propagated vegetatively. For details, see ORNAMENTAL TREES, "Raising trees from seed", p.80.

HARDWOOD CUTTINGS

1 Dig a narrow trench 15cm (6in) deep. If the soil has a high clay content, sprinkle a little sand into the base of the trench to improve drainage.

2 Choose a ripened stem from the current season's growth (here, from a fig tree). Remove lengths of at least 30cm (12in), cutting flush with the main stem.

3 Cut off all the leaves and the soft growth at the tip of each cutting, then trim to about 23cm (9in): make an angled cut above the top bud and a straight cut at the base.

4 Place the cuttings in the prepared trench, spacing them 10–15cm (4–6in) apart and burying two thirds of the stems. Firm the soil, and label.

5 The cuttings will take several months to root. Towards the end of the following growing season, they should have developed sturdy new growth.

6 After leaf-fall in autumn, carefully lift the rooted cuttings, wrapping the roots in plastic to stop them drying out. Transplant the cuttings to their permanent positions to grow on.

Tree fruits

THE fruits in this group, known also as "top fruits", are the largest-growing forms in the fruit garden. They may be divided into two main categories: "pome fruits", such as apples and pears, have a pip-containing core; "stone fruits", such as cherries and apricots, have a hard, central stone. There are also certain other fruits within this group that fit into neither of the above categories, such as figs, mulberries, and persimmons.

Cultivating tree fruits is a long-term undertaking that requires careful planning. The size and shape or form of the trees are important considerations. Left to grow naturally, many fruit trees would become impracticably large for the average-sized garden. Smaller forms grown on dwarfing rootstocks have been developed, however; fruit trees may also be trained and pruned as fans, espaliers, or cordons and grown flat against walls or fences, making it feasible to grow them successfully in even the smallest of spaces.

Another factor to consider is the number of trees required. Many fruit trees are self-sterile and, to produce crops, need at least one other suitable cultivar of the same fruit to act as a pollinator. Even self-fertile trees crop more heavily if pollinators are present.

Some tree fruits such as figs prefer a long, hot growing season and are difficult to cultivate in cooler climates; growing them under cover provides protection and improves fruit and crop size, as well as flavour.

Once a tree fruit has been selected and planted, it is important to follow the correct pruning methods. Good pruning not only builds a strong framework of branches, but also encourages and maintains maximum cropping for many years.

Pears
Apples
Apples
Quinces
Apples
Medlars

Apples (*Malus sylvestris* var. *domestica*)

Apples are one of the most widely grown, hardy fruits and both dessert and culinary cultivars offer a great variety of flavours and textures.

Tree size may also be varied – dwarfing rootstocks and "family" trees (see p.420) allowing a number of different apples to be grown in a small garden where only one large tree could have been accommodated before. Apple trees may readily be trained into almost any shape. Cordon-, espalier-, and fan-shaped forms are particularly useful for growing against walls and fences. Ballerina trees are dwarf, single-stemmed, compact apple trees with short fruiting spurs. Several cultivars are now available in this form.

The extensive choice of cultivars covers a period of ripening from mid-summer to late winter, and fruit may be stored until mid-spring, given suitable conditions. There are cultivars and rootstocks suitable for most climates, including those with severe winter temperatures. For flowering to occur, the trees must be subjected to at least 900 hours below 7°C (45°F): the chilling requirement. Apples are not grown successfully in tropical or subtropical regions.

Site and planting

When planting, make sure that each tree has sufficient space to develop to its full size. Select the most appropriate size of tree (largely determined by the rootstock) for your garden. In most cases, more than one apple tree will be required for pollination.

Site

A sunny, sheltered site is essential for consistently good crops. Walls for trained fruit should preferably be in full sun. For shaded areas or those in a region with short summers and cool temperatures, choose cultivars that ripen early. Where late frosts occur, select late-flowering cultivars so that the blossom will not be damaged.

Apples will grow in most well-drained soils, given adequate preparation (see p.424). The more dwarfing the rootstock, however, the more fertile the soil should be.

Rootstocks

Choice of rootstock depends on the tree size required and the soil type. Apple rootstocks are prefixed by M or MM, which stand for Malling and Malling Merton respectively, the research stations where the rootstocks were developed. A wide range of rootstocks is available, from 'M27', which is very dwarfing, to the extremely vigorous 'M25'. For normal garden purposes, 'M9' is recommended for dwarf trees, 'M26' for larger ones, and 'MM106' for medium-sized trees (see *Planting Distances*, p.436). Cultivars on 'M27' bear fruit within three years of being grafted but demand good growing conditions to maintain high yields. Where the soil is poor, use a more vigorous rootstock to compensate: for example, where a dwarf tree is required use 'MM106' instead of 'M9' or 'M26'. The vigour of the chosen cultivar also determines the size of the mature tree. Triploid cultivars grow larger than diploids (see below); use a more dwarfing rootstock for a triploid than for a diploid cultivar to attain a tree of similar size.

Pollination

No apples are reliably and consistently self-fertile: diploids must be planted near a second, compatible cultivar; triploid apples, which will not pollinate other cultivars, require two compatible cultivars nearby to pollinate them. Cultivars are divided into flowering groups according to their time of flowering; a cultivar from one group may be cross-pollinated by another from the same group or one in the group before or after it if flowering times overlap (see also *Recommended Dessert Apples*, p.436, and *Recommended Culinary Apples*, p.437). Some cultivars are incompatible: of those listed on pp.436 and 437, 'Cox's Orange Pippin' will not pollinate 'Kidd's Orange Red' or 'Suntan' and vice versa. If in doubt about compatibility, ask a fruit nursery for advice.

Planting

Bare-root trees are best planted when dormant, preferably in autumn when the soil is still warm; they may be planted until late winter (except when it is frosty) but keep them moist in spring so that they establish well. Container-grown trees may be planted at any time, unless the ground is frozen or very wet; water before planting so that the roots are moist. Using the soil mark as a guide, plant each tree at its original planting depth (see also *Planting a Fruit Tree*, p.425).

If the tree is to be trained, fit the supports and wires securely in place before planting (see under individual tree forms for details). For all untrained trees, staking when planting is essential and should be permanent for those on dwarfing rootstocks.

Planting distances (see p.436) depend upon how the trees are to be trained, as well as on the vigour of the chosen rootstocks and cultivars.

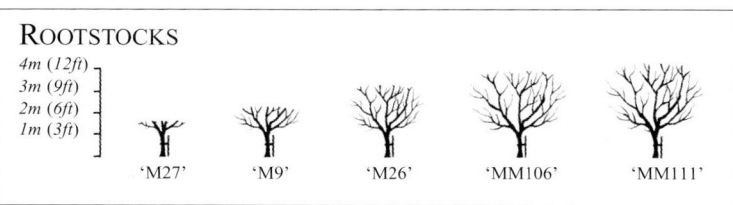

ROOTSTOCKS

4m (12ft)
3m (9ft)
2m (6ft)
1m (3ft)

'M27'   'M9'   'M26'   'MM106'   'MM111'

Routine care

Establish a regular maintenance programme to ensure that trees stay healthy and crop well. Feed and mulch periodically as required. Pruning and fruit thinning are annual tasks required to ensure satisfactory cropping. Check trees regularly for signs of pests and diseases and damage from rubbing stakes and ties.

Blossom thinning and biennial bearing

Certain cultivars, such as 'Laxton's Superb', tend to produce heavy crops in alternate years, with little or no blossom or fruit in intervening years. This is known as biennial bearing.

Blossom thinning can largely correct this; it involves removing nine of every ten blossom clusters by pinching them out, leaving the rosette of young leaves around each intact. The tree then produces a moderate, rather than heavy, crop and its resources are channelled into producing fruit buds for the following year, which would otherwise have been fruitless. On large trees, where it would be impractical to thin blossom over the entire tree, biennial bearing can be corrected by blossom-thinning a few branches.

If trees that normally crop regularly start to crop biennially, this may be due to the loss of blossom from frost and hence the crop; this may then induce a tree to overcrop the following year. The tree may not have sufficient resources to develop adequate fruit buds for the third year and a biennial tendency is set in motion. Disease or pest infestation causing a setback in one year may have a similar effect.

Fruit thinning

Thinning is essential where heavy crops have set, to improve fruit size, quality, and flavour, and to help prevent branches from breaking. On young trees, over-heavy cropping strains the tree's resources and slows the growth of new buds. Some thinning is useful on the young fruitlets, but it is simpler to carry out the main task in early summer, after the "June drop", when the tree naturally sheds imperfect and infertile fruits.

Use scissors to remove the centre (or "King") fruit of each cluster, which is sometimes abnormally shaped; then cut out any fruits that are damaged. In about mid-summer, thin the clusters again so that there is one good fruit per cluster. Fruit of dessert cultivars should be spaced 10–15cm (4–6in) apart, and that of culinary cultivars 15–22cm (6–9in) apart; these distances may vary according to the individual cultivar and the size of fruit required.

Fertilizing, watering, and mulching

Water trees in spells of hot, dry weather, apply fertilizer annually, and mulch as necessary (see "Care of tree fruits", p.426). If growth is poor, apply ammonium sulphate in spring at a rate of 35g/sq m (1oz/sq yd).

Stakes and ties

Inspect stakes and ties regularly to check that they are not rubbing against the bark of trees and that ties are effective; adjust them as necessary. Trees grown on dwarfing rootstocks such as 'M9' and 'M26' produce few tap roots and therefore need permanent staking to provide support and compensate for their lack of anchorage.

Pests and diseases

Common pests that may be troublesome include birds (p.657), wasps (p.659), codling moth (p.659), and aphids (p.646). The most common diseases that can affect apples include scab (p.658), powdery mildew (p.658), brown rot (p.658), bitter pit (see "Calcium deficiency", p.658), and *Nectria* canker (p.664).

PLANTING DISTANCES

TREE FORM	ROOTSTOCK	DISTANCE BETWEEN TREES	DISTANCE BETWEEN ROWS
Bush	'M27'	1.2–2m (4–6ft)	2m (6ft)
	'M9'	2.5–3m (8–10ft)	3m (10ft)
	'M26'	3–4.25m (10–14ft)	5m (15ft)
	'MM106'	3.5–5.5m (11–18ft)	5.5m (18ft)
Half-standard	'MM111'	7.5–9m (24–28ft)	7.5–9m (24–28ft)
Standard	'MM111', 'M25' (or seedling crab)	7.5–10.5m (24–32ft)	7.5–10.5m (24–32ft)
Spindlebush	'M9' or 'M26' (and triploids on 'M27')	2–2.2m (6–7ft)	2.5–3m (8–10ft)
	'MM106'	2–2.2m (6–7ft)	4m (12ft)
Cordon	as bush	75cm (30in)	2m (6ft)
Fan/espalier	'M9'	3m (10ft)	
	'MM106'	4.25m (14ft)	
	'MM111'	5.5m (18ft)	
Dwarf pyramid	'M27'	1.2m (4ft)	2m (6ft)
	'M9' or 'M26'	1.5m (5ft)	2–2.2m (6–7ft)
	'MM106'	2m (6ft)	2.2m (7ft)

APPLE THINNING

1 *Thinning is essential if the apple tree is carrying a heavy crop. After the "June drop", which is a normal occurrence, the remaining fruits will require further thinning if the crop is still heavy.*

2 *Remove sufficient small fruitlets (especially any that are malformed or very small) to leave about 10–15cm (4–6in) between each and only one fruitlet per cluster.*

Pruning and training techniques

Apple trees produce flowers and fruit mainly on two-year-old and older shoots and on short spurs produced on the older wood. Two-year-old shoots carry both large fruit buds and smaller, pointed growth buds. Fruit buds produce flower clusters and then fruit, while growth buds form into fruit buds for the following year or into sideshoots or fruiting spurs. One-year-old shoots may also carry fruit buds but these flower later than those on older wood. Tip-bearing cultivars produce markedly fewer spurs (see below).

Once their branch framework is established, trained trees need to be pruned (mainly in summer) to maintain shape, curb vegetative growth, and stimulate the production of fruit buds. Untrained trees require moderate pruning in winter to stimulate growth for the next season's fruit and to maintain an open, well-balanced structure so that they crop well and the fruit is of good quality.

FRUIT BUDS AND GROWTH BUDS

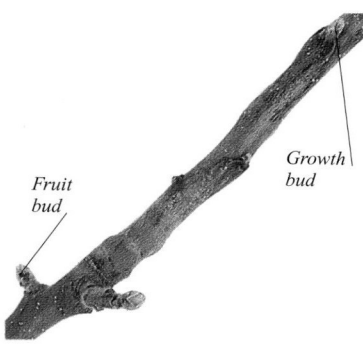

Fruit bud

Growth bud

Large fruit buds develop on 2-year-old and older wood. The smaller buds are growth buds, and are found mainly on one-year-old wood.

NICKING AND NOTCHING

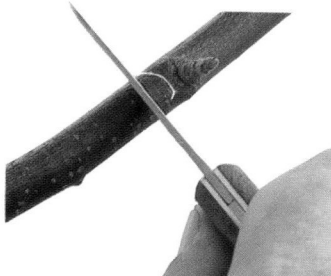

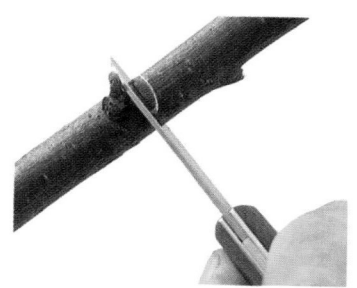

NICKING
To weaken bud growth, make a nick in the bark just below the bud and into the cambium layer.

NOTCHING
To stimulate bud growth, make a notch through the bark into the cambium layer just above the bud.

Tip bearers and spur bearers

Cultivars differ in the way they bear most of their fruit. Tip bearers carry much of the crop at, or near, the shoot tips, whereas spur bearers carry it along the whole shoot on short-jointed spurs from which further growth develops each year.

Tip bearers are not easily trained as cordons, espaliers, fans, or pyramids, because on each shoot there is bare, unproductive wood that limits the cropping capacity of the tree. They are best grown as standard, half-standard, or bush forms; once they are established, they need renewal pruning only (see p.438).

Nicking and notching

Sometimes it may be necessary to correct the balance of the branch framework of a trained tree; this may be achieved by nicking, which weakens the growth of a particular bud, or notching, which strengthens it. Notching may also be used to stimulate the production of sideshoots on bare lengths of stem.

Nicking and notching are most effective in spring when the sap is rising. Make a nick or a small incision with a sharp knife just below a bud to inhibit its growth; make a notch just above it to increase its vigour and stimulate new growth.

Bark-ringing

On excessively vigorous apple and pear trees (but not on stone fruits) that produce unsatisfactory crops, bark-ringing may be used as a last resort to curb vegetative growth and induce a greater fruit set. In late spring, remove a narrow band of bark from around the trunk through to the cambium layer at a height of about 1m (3ft). This reduces the flow of nutrients and hormones back to the roots, so that they are concentrated in the upper part of the tree.

Bark-ringing must be carried out carefully or the tree may die. First measure out the width of the band, which must be only 3mm (⅛in) on a small tree, graduating to no more than 1cm (½in) on a very large tree, then score the band with a knife. Cut through the bark and the cambium layer and remove the bark within the band down to the hardwood all the way round. Seal the wound at once with several layers of water-proof adhesive tape – it must cover the wound without touching the cambium layer.

BARK-RINGING

1 *Stick tape around the trunk as a guide for 2 parallel cuts. The ring may be 3mm–1cm (⅛–½in) wide, depending on the age and size of the tree.*

2 *The parallel cuts should be made through both the bark and the cambium layer. Carefully remove the ring of bark with the blunt side of the knife blade.*

3 *Wind water-proof tape around the ring so that it covers the wound without touching the cambium layer. Remove the tape when the wound has healed.*

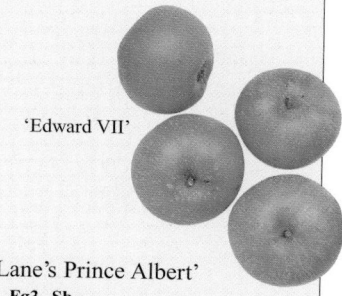

The wound should heal over by the autumn, when the waterproof tape may be removed. The following year, the tree should produce much more blossom and, consequently, a much heavier crop of fruit because the reaction of any wounded plant is to reproduce.

Winter pruning

There are three main techniques for winter pruning, all of which stimulate new growth. Spur pruning and thinning should be carried out only on cultivars that produce plenty of spurs, not on tip bearers. Renewal pruning is appropriate for spindlebushes and all tip bearers, as well as for vigorous cultivars that would be overstimulated by hard pruning. Regulated pruning is suited to cultivars that are naturally very vigorous, particularly triploids such as 'Bramley's Seedling', 'Blenheim Orange', and 'Jonagold'.

It may be necessary to vary the degree and type of pruning from year to year depending on the extent of growth, the quantity of fruit produced, and the age of the tree.

Spur pruning involves cutting back branch leaders and young laterals to stimulate the growth of sub-laterals and fruiting spurs. The extent of pruning required depends on the tree's vigour – the greater the vigour, the lighter the pruning, since pruning stimulates growth.

Shorten branch leaders on vigorous trees by no more than a few buds but on weaker ones by up to one third to stimulate new sub-laterals to form. Shorten young laterals to three or six buds where growth is good but to three or four buds on weaker trees so that spurs form. On a stronger tree, shoots up to 15cm (6in) long may be left unpruned.

Spur thinning is necessary as a tree ages to prevent fruits from becoming overcrowded. If left unthinned, the spurs become entangled and carry inferior fruit. When spur systems become congested, remove the older wood in favour of the younger. In time, it may be necessary to saw off whole spur systems.

Renewal pruning involves the annual cutting back of a proportion of older, fruited shoots to their base to stimulate the growth of new, young wood. Keep the centre of a bush tree open by pruning out any vigorous growth that is crossing or shading other laterals so that all the branches are well spaced. Remove a little, if any, of the tip from branch leaders and none at all on vigorous trees.

Regulated pruning consists of removing shoots and sometimes long sections of large branches that are crowded or crossing, particularly in the centre of the tree, to keep the branch framework open. Remove old wood to make room for young shoots. Do not tip prune the branch leaders.

Summer pruning

This is carried out to keep trained trees within their allotted space. It involves removing a large proportion of the new growth each summer to slow down vegetative growth.

The Modified Lorette System is the standard method of summer pruning in temperate climates with cool, unpredictable summers. It is carried out once the young shoots have become woody at the base. Maiden (new) laterals more than 22cm (9in) long that grow directly from the main stem or a main branch should be reduced to three leaves above the basal cluster. Prune back sideshoots arising from spurs and existing laterals to one leaf above the basal cluster. Continue to prune in this way as shoots mature. To help prevent sideshoots, or sec-

WINTER PRUNING
SPUR PRUNING

1 *Cut back young laterals to between 3 and 6 buds of the current growth, depending on the vigour of the shoot.*

2 *Prune back the current season's growth on branch leaders by one quarter to one third of their length.*

SPUR THINNING

On older trees, spur systems may become too dense. Thin these out by removing weak spurs and any on the undersides of the branches.

RENEWAL PRUNING

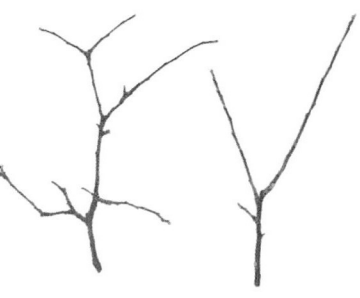

Prune out a good proportion of the older shoots that have already borne fruit (left). This will encourage new shoots to develop (right).

REGULATED PRUNING

On this tree there is congested growth; correct this by removing any branches that are crossing or touching each other, and thinning out any sub-laterals or laterals that are overcrowded.

SUMMER PRUNING (MODIFIED LORETTE SYSTEM)

Prune trees when the lowest third of all new growth has become woody.

Cut back laterals on the main stems to 3 leaves above the basal cluster.

Basal cluster

BEFORE PRUNING

Trim any sideshoots to 1 leaf.

AFTER PRUNING

ondary growths, from developing behind the pruning cut, leave a small number of the longer shoots unpruned; tie these shoots securely to other branches so that they are roughly horizontal and draw the sap down. Do not shorten any of them until after fruiting. Then, in mid-autumn, cut back any secondary growth shoots to one bud.

The Full Lorette System should be used in warmer climates. Prune back new laterals to about 5cm (2in), repeating at intervals through the summer. Shorten the laterals to 2cm (¾in) once they are woody at the base. Prune any secondary growths in late summer in the same way.

APPLE BUSH
YEAR 1, WINTER PRUNING

Prune back the leader to a selected lateral, leaving 2 or 3 strong laterals below it.

Cut back each of these laterals by two thirds to an upward-facing bud. Remove all other laterals.

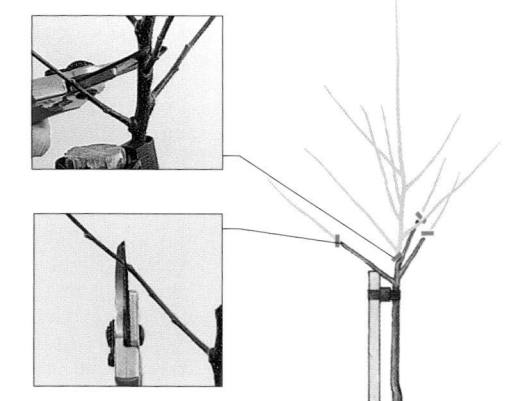

YEAR 2, WINTER PRUNING

Sub-laterals that are not needed for secondary branches should be pruned back to 4 or 5 buds.

Prune back branch leaders and well-placed sub-laterals by half to outward-facing buds.

Bush

The open-centre or goblet-shaped bush is comparatively simple to maintain; it is ideal for larger gardens where there is plenty of space.

Formative pruning
Start with a well-feathered maiden tree; the laterals will form the first branches. After planting, while the tree is dormant, cut back the leader to a strong lateral 60–75cm (24–30in) above ground level, leaving at least two or three well-spaced laterals below it radiating out like the spokes of a wheel. These form the basis of the branch system; shorten them by two thirds, cutting to an upward-pointing bud. Remove all other laterals.

If a maiden whip is used, or a feathered maiden tree that has few or no suitable laterals, cut back the leader in winter to a strong bud 60–75cm (24–30in) from the base, then make a small nick under the top two buds; this depresses their growth and encourages shoots from the lower buds to grow at wider angles. Remove any unwanted laterals completely.

By the end of the following summer, three or four strong, healthy laterals should have developed to produce a plant equivalent to a pruned, feathered maiden.

Strong growth should develop the following summer. If one lateral grows faster than the others, tie it down nearly horizontally to slow its growth. Remove weak, inward-, and downward-growing shoots.

In the second winter, select several well-spaced growths arising from the original laterals to build up the branch framework, and shorten them by half, cutting to outward-facing buds. If any are not needed for the framework, shorten them to four or five buds, and remove altogether any shoots crossing the open centre. As growth continues in the second

summer, remove any vigorous, upright shoots that unbalance the shape of the tree. By the third winter, the final branch formation should be established, with eight to ten main branches as well as several subsidiary ones.

Routine pruning
Only winter pruning (see p.438) is necessary for bushes once the framework is established; the pruning required will depend on the amount of growth made by the tree and on whether it is a tip or spur bearer. A tip bearer requires renewal pruning. Spur bearers require spur pruning and thinning.

ESTABLISHED BUSH, SPUR PRUNING IN WINTER

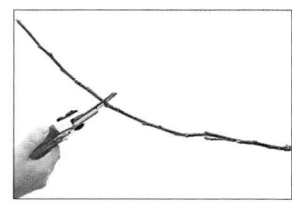

Prune weak branch leaders, leaving half the previous season's growth. Strong branch leaders should be cut back by one quarter or less. Leave very vigorous leaders completely unpruned.

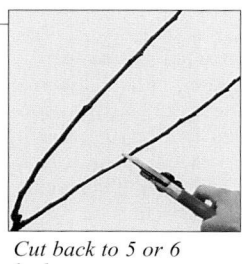

Cut back to 5 or 6 buds any young sideshoots growing from permanent branches to form spurs.

ESTABLISHED BUSH, RENEWAL PRUNING IN WINTER

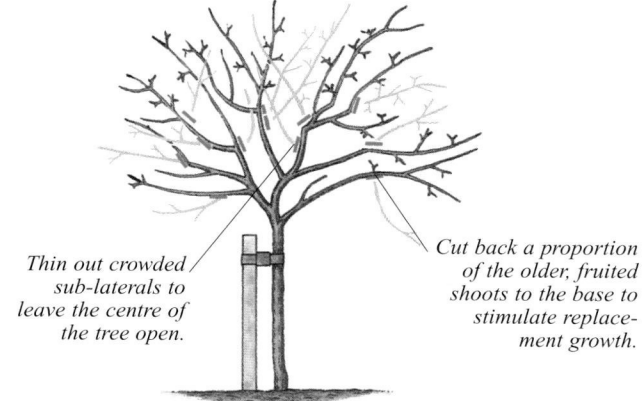

Thin out crowded sub-laterals to leave the centre of the tree open.

Cut back a proportion of the older, fruited shoots to the base to stimulate replacement growth.

Standard and half-standard

Few gardens are large enough to accommodate a standard or half-standard tree, but they make fine specimen trees where there is space.

Two or three years' training and pruning is needed to produce a clear stem of 1.2–1.3m (4–4½ft) for a half-standard, or 2–2.1m (6–6½ft)

for a standard. After planting a feathered maiden or maiden whip, tie in the leading shoot to a cane and cut any laterals hard back to 2.5cm (1in) in winter. In spring and summer, periodically pinch or cut back any feathers to a few leaves; this helps to thicken the main stem. Repeat this procedure in the second year.

In the following winter, remove most of the laterals and cut back the leader to the desired height, either

for a half-standard or standard; if the tree is not of the required height, grow it on for a third year. Several laterals should then develop below the cut; select and retain three or four well-spaced laterals to form the basic branch framework. Then train as for an open-centre bush (above).

Subsequent pruning of the tree is also as for a bush, but growth will be much stronger because the tree is grafted on a vigorous or extremely vigorous rootstock. Carry out regulated pruning on the established tree; it is only necessary to prune hard if the tree is not growing satisfactorily.

Spindlebush

A spindlebush is trained into the shape of a pyramid or cone, to a height of 2.2m (7ft); once it is established, only renewal pruning and pruning to keep the shape are required.

Numerous variations of the spindlebush have been developed but the basic aim is to keep the three or four lowest branches dominant by removing shoots that would otherwise develop in the centre of the tree. Any shoots that do develop higher in the tree are allowed to fruit and are then pruned hard back, to be replaced by fresh growth.

Formative pruning

Plant a strong feathered maiden of a spur-bearing cultivar (see *Recommended Dessert Apples*, p.436), supporting it with a 2m (6ft) stake. Cut back the leader in the winter to about 1m (3ft), or to just above the topmost lateral if this is higher. Select three or four vigorous and evenly spaced laterals that are about 60–90cm (2–3ft) from the base. Prune back each lateral by half to a downward-pointing, healthy bud and remove all other laterals.

If growth is strong, tie down any upright laterals towards the end of the first summer, in order to suppress growth and encourage the tree to fruit. If growth is weak, the upright laterals do not need to be tied down until the next summer.

Tie down the laterals with strong string secured to wooden or hooked metal pegs driven into the ground at an angle around the tree. If using wooden pegs, hammer a large "U" staple into the top of each one so that a string may be secured to it. Tie each string loosely so that it pulls down the branch to a 30° angle. Long branches may need to be tied in two places.

Remove any excessively vigorous shoots growing upwards from the main stem or laterals; do not attempt to tie them down since they may break. Train the central stem vertically by tying it to the stake.

The second winter after planting, shorten the central leader by one third of the new growth, cutting to a bud on the opposite side of the pruning cut made the previous winter. This helps to maintain a straight stem. Make sure that the strings are not constricting the tied-down shoots; once the growths have hardened and will remain in a more or

less horizontal position, remove the strings. The following summer, tie down some of the vertical shoots and remove completely any that are exceptionally vigorous or too close to the main stem, or that unbalance the branch framework.

By the third winter, laterals higher in the tree should have developed and been tied down to form further tiers of branches. They should be nearly horizontal, as this encourages early fruiting, and should not overshadow the lower framework branches if this can be avoided.

In the third summer, when the tree should produce fruit for the first time, tie down selected new sideshoots in late summer and remove any excessively strong shoots.

Routine pruning

From the fourth or fifth year onwards, renewal pruning (see p.438) is necessary in winter: shorten some of the old, fruited wood. Some of the shoots, particularly those that are higher in the tree, should be pruned hard back close to the trunk to encourage the development of replacement growths.

If the central leader is too vigorous, it may be cut back a little to a weaker lateral that will replace it. This concentrates vigour in the lower branches and helps to retain the pyramid shape, allowing maximum light to reach the fruits. In summer, continue cutting out completely any excessively vigorous and strongly upright-growing shoots.

Cordon

A spur-bearing feathered maiden may be trained as an oblique cordon on wires that are secured to posts or to a wall or fence. Tip bearers are not suitable as cordons (see "Tip bearers and spur bearers", p.437). Space three horizontal wires about 60cm (24in) apart; the lowest wire should be 75cm (30in) from the ground. Fix the wires about 10–15cm (4–6in) clear of the supporting wall or fence to allow free air circulation and so prevent the build-up of pests and diseases. Attach a cane to the wires at an angle of 45°, then plant a feathered maiden by it (see p.425) and tie in the main stem to the cane, using a figure-of-eight knot.

APPLE SPINDLEBUSH
YEAR 1, WINTER PRUNING

Prune the leader by making an angled cut just above a suitable bud about 1m (3ft) from the ground.

Cut back 3 or 4 strong laterals by half to downward-facing buds. Remove other laterals.

YEAR 1, SUMMER PRUNING

Tie down each of the 3 or 4 main laterals to pegs in the ground so that the branches are at a 30° angle.

Cut to the base any vigorous upward-pointing laterals or sub-laterals.

YEAR 2, SUMMER PRUNING

Repeat summer pruning as for Year 1, concentrating on removing any upright growths.

ESTABLISHED SPINDLEBUSH, WINTER PRUNING

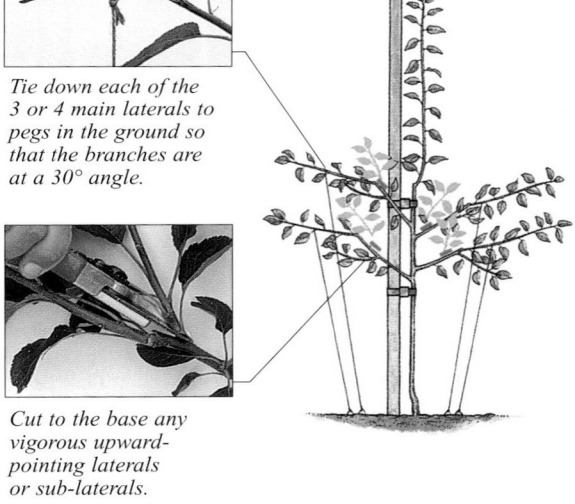

Cut back to 1 bud any large, old, upper branches with loppers or secateurs.

Cut out any weak, unproductive spurs completely.

Prune sub-laterals on the lower 4 permanent branches if they are unproductive, crossing, or inward-growing.

Formative pruning

In the winter immediately after planting, shorten to three or four buds all lateral shoots that are over 10cm (4in) in length. For tip-bearing cultivars, shorten the leader by about one third; do not attempt to prune the cordon further.

From the first summer onwards, prune the new shoots in mid- to late summer, once they have become woody at the base. Not all shoots ripen together, so pruning should continue over several weeks. Use the Modified or Full Lorette System (see "Summer pruning", pp.438–439).

Routine pruning

Winter pruning is essential to prevent congestion: reduce overgrown spur systems and remove completely those that are overcrowded. If the cordon is not producing enough well-spaced laterals, shorten the leader by about one quarter of its length to encourage strong growth.

Once a cordon has extended beyond the top wire, lower its angle of growth slightly to provide space for the leader to extend. When it reaches the top wire, trim it back to one leaf of new growth in late spring. Alternatively, if the leader is vigorous, cut it back in late spring to a sideshoot near the top wire.

Continue pruning on the Modified or Full Lorette System; on an established cordon, this largely involves cutting sideshoots to one leaf.

Double cordon

A double cordon is usually grown vertically. Feathered maidens and maiden whips may be trained as double cordons. The process is similar in each case, except that maiden whips must be pruned to stimulate low sideshoots before training can begin (see "Forming a double cordon", right). Alternatively, cut back a feathered maiden to two suitable and oppositely placed laterals. Tie them at about 30° to support canes and shorten by half. In summer, once a spacing of 45cm (18in) between the young leaders is attainable, turn and tie them to an upright position.

Fan

A wall or fence is an ideal support against which to grow a fan-trained apple tree; select a spur-bearing cultivar on a dwarfing rootstock so that it may be comfortably accommodated in the available space. Tip bearers are not suitable to grow as fans (see "Tip bearers and spur bearers", p.437). Fix horizontal support wires about 15cm (6in) apart, starting at

---

YEAR 1, WINTER PRUNING

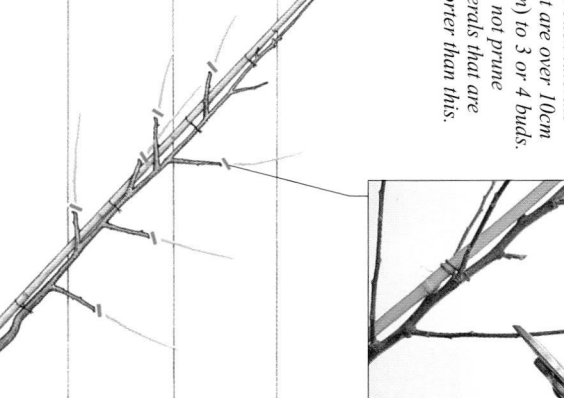

Cut back laterals that are over 10cm (4in) to 3 or 4 buds. Do not prune laterals that are shorter than this.

ESTABLISHED CORDON, WINTER PRUNING

Thin spurs as they become congested on older cordons.

YEAR 1, SUMMER PRUNING

Once the bases of the shoots have become woody, prune all new laterals to 3 leaves.

Trim back any sideshoots to 1 leaf.

ESTABLISHED CORDON, SUMMER PRUNING

Trim any maiden laterals to 3 leaves.

When the bases of the laterals have become woody, cut back the new growth to 1 leaf.

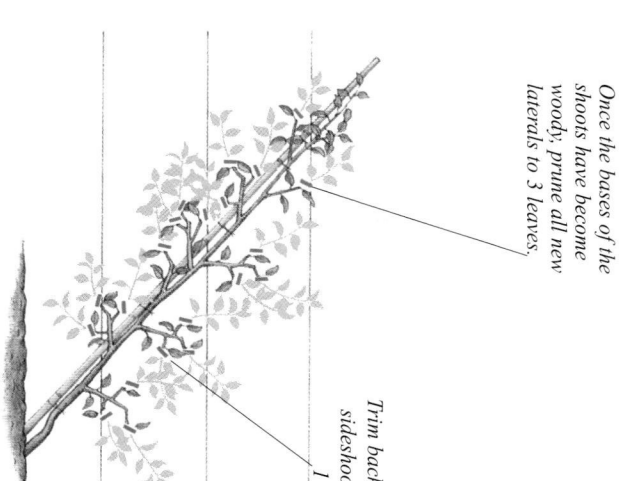

Forming a double cordon from a maiden whip

To train a maiden whip as a double cordon, cut back the newly planted tree to about 24cm (10in) from soil level during the first winter, leaving a strong bud on either side below the cut. The following summer, when new shoots have been produced, tie the two uppermost shoots to canes at an angle of 45°, lowering them to 30° later in the season. When the tips of these shoots are more than 45cm (18in) apart, train them upwards by tying them to vertical canes.

Once the basic "U"-shape of the double cordon has been formed, the two vertical arms should each be pruned in the same way as a single cordon.

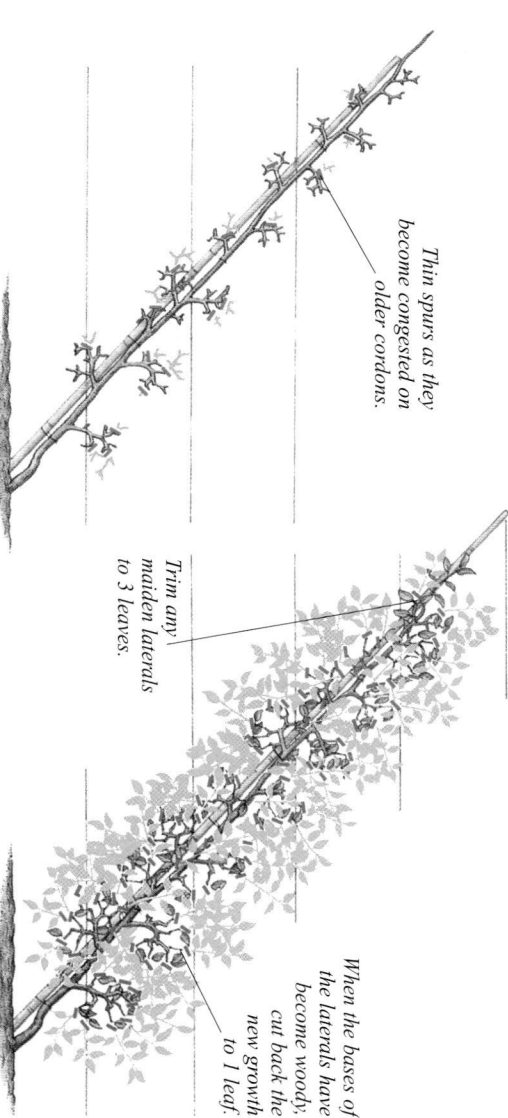

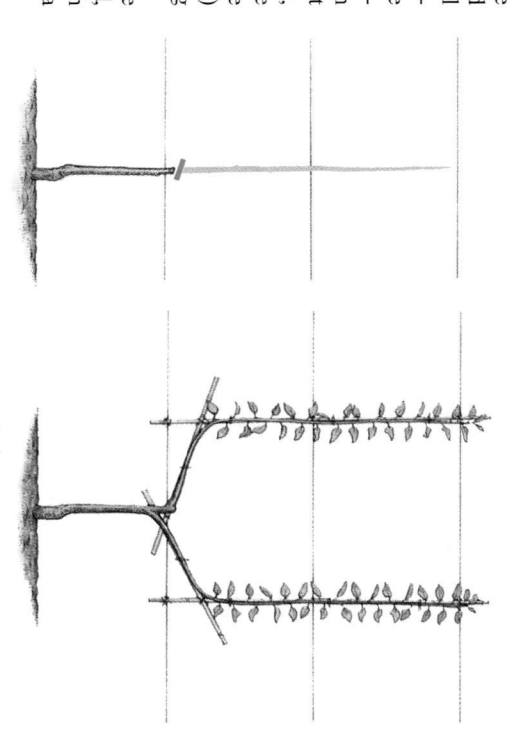

38cm (15in) from soil level. The initial development of the framework is as for peaches (see p.453); once established, it should be pruned on the Modified Lorette System (see p.438) with each rib being treated like a single cordon.

Espalier

For this tree form, one or more pairs of opposite shoots are trained at right angles to the main stem onto support wires 38cm (15in) apart. An espalier usually has two or three tiers but more are possible with trees of sufficient vigour. If a maiden whip is

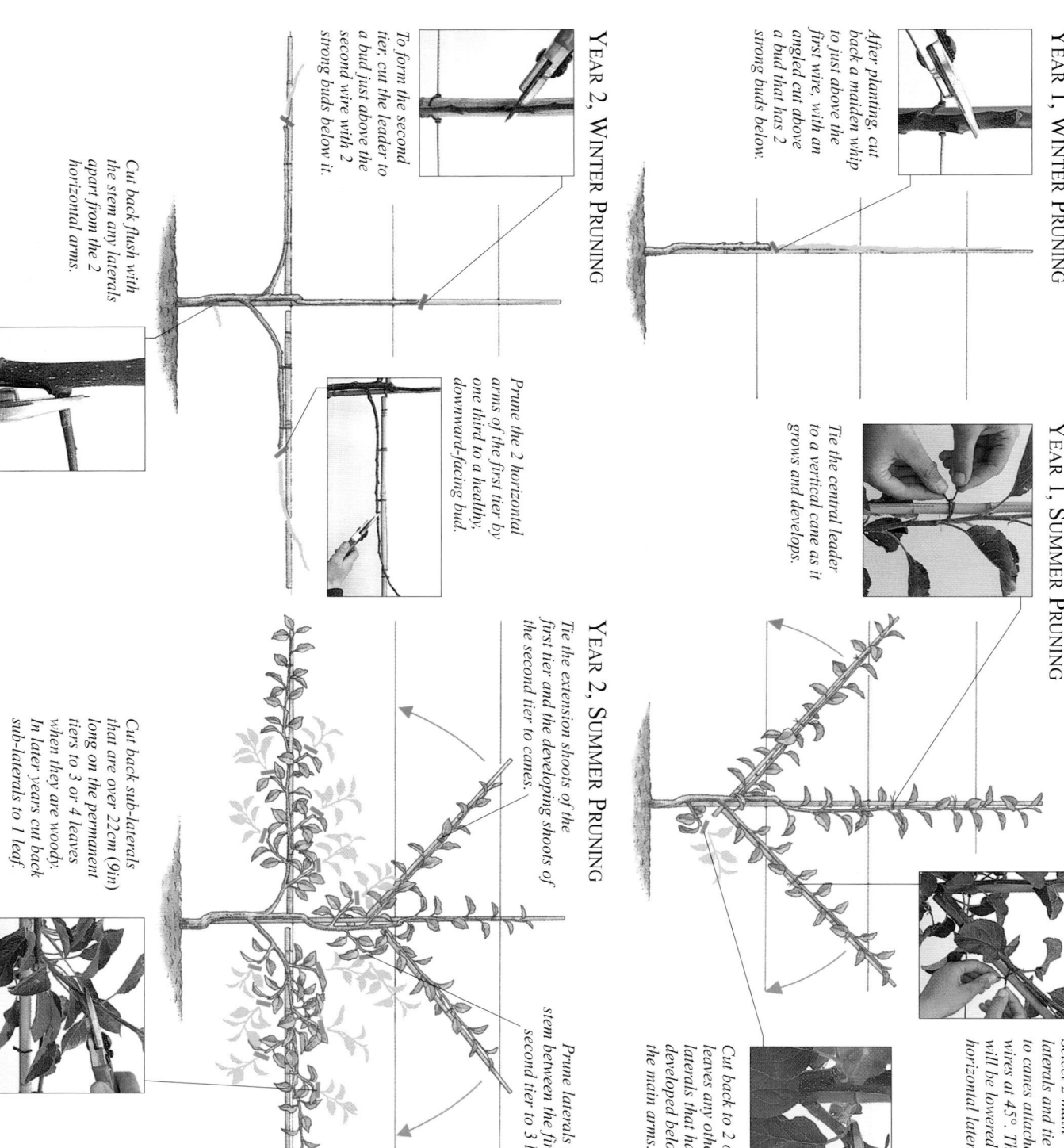

used, the first tier may then be trained more readily at the required height. Only spur bearers are suitable to grow as espaliers (see "Tip bearers and spur bearers", p.437).

Formative pruning

After planting a maiden whip, prune back the leader to a bud just above the lowest wire. The following summer, train the uppermost shoot vertically to form a new leader. The two strongest laterals below this develop, tie each to a cane at an angle of 45° to form the first branch tier. Cut or pinch back all other, lower shoots to two or three leaves. Tie down the laterals of the first tier into

their horizontal position towards the end of the first growing season. If the two main arms develop unevenly, lower the more vigorous shoot to check growth and raise the weaker shoot to induce vigour. Once the two are balanced, tie them into their horizontal positions (see also *Training on Canes*, p.429).

The following winter, remove completely any laterals that have developed other than the main arms. To create the second tier, first look for two strong buds about 38cm (15in) above the first tier, then cut back the central leader to the bud above these. Shorten each first tier arm by one-third to a downward-

facing bud; where growth is very vigorous, leave the arm unpruned.

The bud to which each arm is cut back will produce a shoot that should be trained horizontally during the second summer after planting. Cut back other sub-laterals according to the Modified Lorette System (see p.438). The second pair of arms will form and these should be trained in the same way as the first pair. Repeat this process as necessary to obtain the required number of tiers.

Routine pruning

Once the arms of the top-most tier are well established, prune back the central leader in winter to just above

APPLE ESPALIER
YEAR 1, WINTER PRUNING

After planting, cut back a maiden whip to just above the first wire, with an angled cut above a bud that has 2 strong buds below.

YEAR 1, SUMMER PRUNING

Tie the central leader to a vertical cane as it grows and develops.

Select 2 main laterals and tie them to canes attached to wires at 45°. These will be lowered to horizontal later.

YEAR 2, WINTER PRUNING

To form the second tier, cut the leader to a bud just above the second wire with 2 strong buds below it.

Prune the 2 horizontal arms of the first tier by one third to a healthy, downward-facing bud.

Cut back flush with the stem any laterals apart from the 2 horizontal arms.

YEAR 2, SUMMER PRUNING

Tie the extension shoots of the first tier and the developing shoots of the second tier to canes.

Cut back sub-laterals that are over 22cm (9in) long on the permanent tiers to 3 or 4 leaves when they are woody. In later years cut back sub-laterals to 1 leaf.

Prune laterals on the stem between the first and second tier to 3 leaves.

Cut back to 2 or 3 leaves any other laterals that have developed below the main arms.

PICKING

Support the apple in the palm of the hand and twist it slightly. If the apple comes away easily from the spur, it is ready for picking.

this tier. The espalier should thereafter be pruned in summer following the Full or Modified Lorette System (see pp.438–439).

Dwarf pyramid

The dwarf pyramid is a compact tree form suitable for a small garden or container. Such a shape is suitable for spur-bearing cultivars (see "Tip bearers and spur bearers", p.437). It needs permanent staking if grown on an 'M27' or 'M9' rootstock; cultivars on other rootstocks need staking for four or five years. For pruning, see "Pear: Dwarf pyramid", p.445.

Secondary growth often develops after summer pruning. These unwanted shoots inhibit the formation of fruit buds, so prune two or three weeks later than usual to help retard their growth if this is a problem. If secondary growth continues to appear, leave one or two shoots unpruned to act as sap-drawers (see "Summer pruning", p.438).

Harvesting and storing

Early-ripening apples should be gathered just before they are fully ripe or they soon become mealy. Late-maturing cultivars must not be picked too soon, however, or the fruits will shrivel in store.

Wrap fruits individually in grease-proof paper and store them in slatted boxes or crates in a cool place (see p.431). Fruits from young or over-vigorous trees store less well than those from more mature trees and should therefore be used first. For further information on harvesting and storing, see p.431.

Propagation

Apple trees may be propagated by chip-budding or T-budding in summer (see pp.432 and 433) or whip-and-tongue grafting in early spring (see p.433). If possible, use certified scions and rootstocks.

Grafting over

Grafting over is a technique used to graft scions of a selected cultivar onto an established apple or pear tree to replace the original cultivar or to create a "family" tree (see p.420). This is usually done to introduce a new pollinator for adjacent trees or to try a new cultivar; as the roots and main branch system are already established, the new cultivar should bear fruit quickly. There are two methods: top-working and frame-working.

Top-working
Initially, this entails heading (cutting) back most of the main branches to within 60–75cm (24–30in) of the main branch fork in spring. Leave one or two smaller branches unpruned to act as sap-drawers to reduce the number of new shoots that may form around the pruning cuts. Trim the cuts where branches have been sawn off. Two or three scions are used per branch but only the most vigorous one is grown on; the presence of the others may initially help to stop canker developing. These may be either rind- or cleft-grafted (the latter is rarely used by amateurs).

For rind grafting, take dormant scions from the previous season's growth of the desired cultivar and prepare them with angled top cuts and tapering basal cuts. Cut away a sliver of bark on the other side of the tapering cut to prevent the bark from being damaged when inserted into the branch. When rind grafting branches of about 2.5cm (1in) in diameter, place two scions opposite each other. Larger branches can accommodate three, evenly spaced scions. Make a vertical cut for each scion in the bark of the prepared branch. Carefully lift the bark and slide the scion into position underneath. Bind the graft firmly into position and seal the cut surfaces with grafting wax. Scion growth is rapid and ties must be released.

Retain the most vigorous scion and remove the others. Frequently, more than one shoot will develop from the selected scion; allow the best one to grow unchecked as the basis for the new branch. Shorten any others if they are less vigorous than the retained shoot but remove them completely if they are of equal vigour. After three or four years the new cultivar should start to crop regularly. Subsequently prune the new branch, according to the individual tree form.

Frame-working
In this method, most of the branch framework is retained and many scions are grafted onto different parts of the tree. Frame-working is preferred by commercial growers as trees crop more quickly than if top-worked.

HOW TO RIND GRAFT

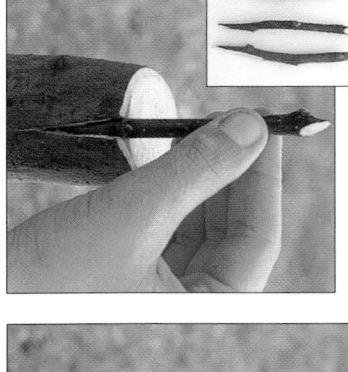

1 In early spring, cut off most of the main branches to within 60–75cm (24–30in) of the trunk. Leave 1 or 2 branches uncut to draw the sap.

2 Make a vertical cut 2.5cm (1in) long through the bark of one of the trimmed branches. If it is 2.5cm (1in) in diameter, make 2 evenly spaced cuts; if larger, make 3 cuts.

3 Use the blunt side of the knife blade to ease the bark away from the cambium layer.

4 Prepare scions 3 buds long, each with an angled cut at the top and a 2.5cm (1in) tapering cut at the base. Insert them with the tapering cut facing inwards.

5 When 2 or 3 scions have been inserted, bind the grafts tightly with strong string or grafting tape, winding it round the whole branch to hold the scions in place.

6 Apply grafting wax to the exposed areas. When the scions have united with the branch, retain the most vigorous and remove the others.

Pears (*Pyrus communis* var. *sativa*)

Pears need more consistently warm conditions than apples to crop reliably. Late-ripening cultivars require dry and warm conditions throughout late summer and early autumn. They have a winter chilling requirement of 600–900 hours below 7°C (45°F).

Pears may be trained in a similar way to apples; bush, dwarf pyramid, cordon, and espalier forms are the most suitable for small gardens. They are usually grown on quince, rather than pear, rootstocks. Some new rootstocks are under trial (see also "Family trees", p.420).

Site and planting

Pears flower earlier than apples, in mid- to late spring, and may be damaged by frosts. Pears are not fully self-fertile, cross-pollination is needed for a good crop.

Site

Pears require a warm, sheltered, and sunny site. The soil should retain moisture – particularly for trees on quince rootstocks (see below) – but must also be well drained; pears tolerate wetter conditions than apples.

Trees on poor or sandy soils produce fruits of inferior flavour, while those on shallow soils overlying chalk may suffer from lime-induced chlorosis, a nutritional problem caused by deficiencies of manganese/iron (see p.651). Such sites may be improved by regularly mulching with large amounts of organic matter and occasionally applying chelated iron and manganese.

before coming into growth, which may occur very early in a mild spring. Planting distances (see below) depend on the choice of rootstock and the form in which the trees are grown (see "Pruning and training", right).

Routine care

Regular maintenance including fruit thinning, feeding and watering, and checking for pest and disease problems, is similar to that required for apples (see p.436). For general information, see pp.426–427.

Fruit thinning

After the natural shedding of fruitlets at or soon after mid-summer, thin out to leave one fruit per cluster if the crop is heavy, but two if cropping is lighter.

Feeding, watering, and mulching

Water and fertilize trees as needed (see p.426). It is particularly important to give pears adequate nitrogen: in spring, apply light dressings of up to 35g/sq m (1oz/sq yd) of ammonium sulphate to maintain levels during the growing season. Mulch around newly planted trees in spring.

Pests and diseases

Pears may be affected by birds (p.657), rabbits and hares (p.666), wasps (p.659), aphids (p.646), winter moth caterpillars (p.645), firebright (p.649), pear midge (p.658), scab (p.649), and brown rot (p.657). Pear leaf blister mites produce pustules in the leaves, and gall mites (p.662) cause blackish-brown leaf blotches

and stunted leaves. Some pears, especially 'Conference', may develop parthenocarpic fruits. These have a cylindrical shape and may be produced when partial fertilization has occurred; the fruit grows but is misshapen. Treat by providing a suitable pollinator and giving shelter to encourage more pollinating insects.

Pruning and training

Pruning requirements and techniques are similar to those for apples, but pears tolerate harder pruning once they have started to crop. Fruiting occurs predominantly on two-year-old and older wood. On pears, spur production is usually more prolific than on apples, and spurs should be thinned regularly on established trees. Very few pear cultivars are tip bearers.

Training and pruning to develop a cordon or an espalier are as for apples. Both are pruned by the Modified Lorette System in temperate areas or, in warmer climates, by the Full Lorette System (see "Apples: Summer pruning", pp.438–439). A fan is formed in the same way as for peaches (see p.453) but, once established, prune as for an apple fan (see p.441). Pears should be pruned two or three weeks earlier than apples, once shoots mature at the base.

Where excessive vigour occurs at the expense of cropping, root pruning (see p.430) where practicable or, as a last resort, bark-ringing (see p.437) may be carried out.

Bush

Initial training and pruning of a bush are as for apples (see p.439). Several pear cultivars (for example 'Doyenné du Comice') have an upright growth habit; when pruning branch leaders of these cultivars, cut to an outward-pointing bud. Shoots that are upright should be tied down before they ripen fully at the base, as part of the initial training process, to encourage a wider angle of growth. Pruning on very vigorous trees should be much lighter after the second year. Where vigour is lacking, shorten new laterals to five or six buds or fewer.

The few tip bearers (for example, 'Jargonelle' and 'Josephine de Mallines') need to be renewal pruned as described for tip-bearing apples (see p.437). Established spur-bearing trees need considerable spur shortening and thinning, and occasional branch thinning, in winter.

Rootstocks

ROOTSTOCKS

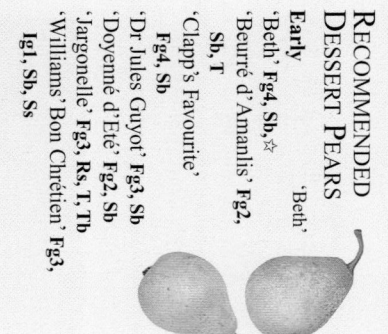

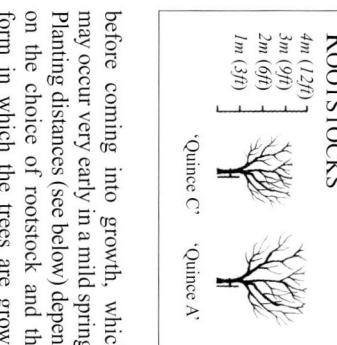

As well as producing relatively small trees, growing pears on quince rootstocks induces early fruiting. 'Quince A' is moderately dwarfing (similar to 'M26' in apple); 'Quince C' is more dwarfing (similar to 'M9' in apple). A few cultivars, however, do not make a good union with quince rootstocks and may need double-working (see p.446).

Pollination

Provision for cross-pollination should always be made by planting two compatible cultivars. Some cultivars are triploid, and a very few are male sterile: these require two pollinators nearby. Incompatible cultivars are indicated in the lists *Recommended Dessert Pears*, left and p.445, and *Recommended Culinary Pears*, p.445.

Planting

Plant pears in autumn when the soil is still warm or by mid-winter at the latest. This allows trees to establish

ROOTSTOCKS

4m (12ft)
3m (9ft)
2m (6ft)
1m (3ft)

'Quince C'   'Quince A'

RECOMMENDED DESSERT PEARS

Early
'Beth' **Fg4, Sb,** ☆
'Beurré d'Amanlis' **Fg2, Sb, T**
'Clapp's Favourite'
'Doyenné d'Eté' **Fg2, Sb**
'Dr Jules Guyot' **Fg3, Sb**
'Jargonelle **Fg3, Rs, T, Tb**
'Williams' Bon Chrétien **Fg3, Ig1, Sb, Ss**

Mid-season
'Abbé Fetel' **B, Fg3, Sb**
'Belle Guérandaise' **Fg2, Sb**
'Belle Julie' **Fg3, Sb**
'Bergamotte Esperen **Fg3, Sb**
'Beurré Hardy' **Fg3, Sb**
'Beurré Superfin' **Fg3, Sb,** ☆
'Bristol Cross' **Fg4, Sb**
'Calebasse Bosc' **Fg4, Sb**
'Comte de Lamy' **Fg4, Sb**
'Concorde' **Fg4, Sb**
'Conference' **Fg3, Sb**
'Cosica' **Fg3, Tb**

'Doyenné du Comice' **Fg4, Ig2, Sb, Ss,** ☆
'Fertility' **Fg3, Sb**
'Fondante d'Automne' **Fg3, Ig1, Sb,** ☆
'Louise Bonne of Jersey' **Fg2, Ig1, Sb**
'Marie Louise' **Fg4, Sb**
'Merton Pride' **Fg3, Sb, T**

'Beth'

'Conference'

KEY
B Biennial bearing
Fg Flowering group (numbers indicate period of flowering)
Ig Incompatibility group (pears within each period of flowering)
Rs Some resistance to scab
Sb Spur bearer
Ss Scab susceptible
T Triploid (unsuitable as pollinator)
Tb Tip bearer or partial tip bearer
☆ Excellent flavour

PLANTING DISTANCES

TREE FORM		ROOTSTOCK	DISTANCE BETWEEN TREES	DISTANCE BETWEEN ROWS
Bush		'Quince C'	3.5m (11ft)	5.5m (18ft)
		'Quince A'	4.75m (14ft)	5.5m (18ft)
Cordon		'Quince A' or 'C'	75cm (30in)	2m (6ft)
Espalier		'Quince C'	3.5m (11ft)	
		'Quince A'	4.75m (14ft)	
Fan		As espalier	As espalier	
		'Quince C'	1.2m (4ft)	2m (6ft)
Dwarf pyramid		'Quince A'	1.5m (5ft)	2m (6ft)

Dwarf pyramid

Prune back the leading shoot of a feathered maiden after planting to 50–75cm (20–30in) from the ground, and reduce any laterals to 15cm (6in); remove weak or low laterals. In the first summer, prune extension growth on the laterals, and any new laterals, to five or six leaves to downward-facing buds. This encourages horizontal growth and induces early fruiting. Cut back sub-laterals to three leaves. The following winter, prune the leading shoot to leave 25cm (10in) of the new growth, cutting to a bud on the opposite side to that of the previous year's pruning. In each subsequent year, prune the leader to buds on alternate sides. When the leader reaches the required height, prune back in late spring to leave one bud of the new growth.

Once the initial framework has been formed, nearly all pruning is carried out in mid- to late summer, depending on season and location. It is important that shoots have become

PEAR, DWARF PYRAMID

YEAR 1, WINTER PRUNING

Cut back the leader with an angled cut just above a bud, 50–75cm (20–30in) from the ground.

Prune back each lateral to a downward-facing bud about 15cm (6in) from the main stem.

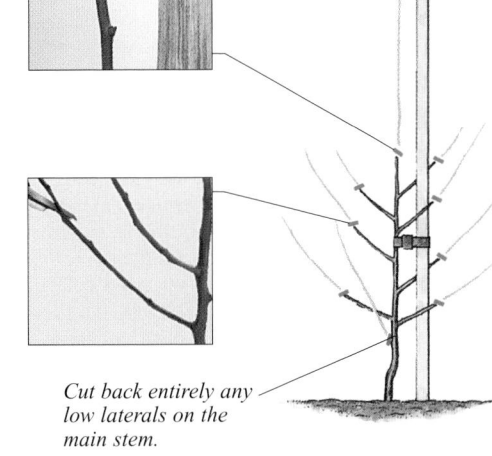

Cut back entirely any low laterals on the main stem.

YEAR 1, SUMMER PRUNING

Cut back new growth at the tips of the main laterals to 5 or 6 leaves on the extension growth.

Prune new laterals growing directly from the main stem to 5 or 6 leaves.

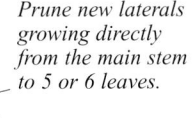

Cut back any sub-laterals growing from the main laterals to 3 leaves. These will start to form spurs for the following summer.

YEAR 2, WINTER PRUNING

Prune the previous season's growth on the leader to about 25cm (10in).

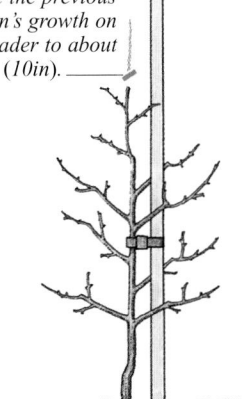

YEAR 2 AND ROUTINE SUMMER PRUNING

Trim sub-laterals from existing laterals or spurs to 1 leaf beyond the basal cluster.

Cut back new growth at the ends of the permanent branches to 5 or 6 leaves.

Cut back laterals growing from the main branches to 3 leaves.

ESTABLISHED DWARF PYRAMID, WINTER PRUNING

When the leader reaches the required height, prune it to 1 bud of the previous season's growth.

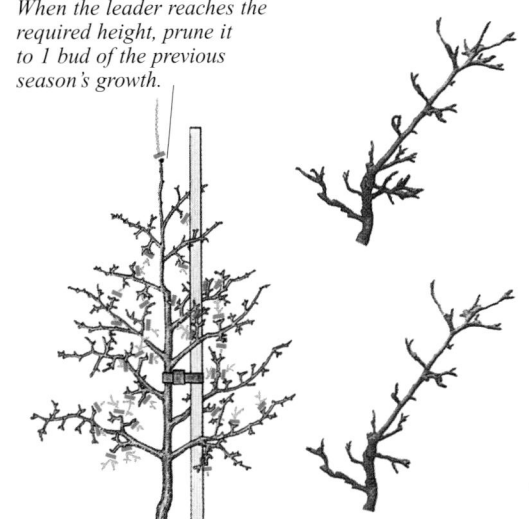

BEFORE
The spurs on the darker wood at the base of this shoot are congested and require thinning.

AFTER
Thin by removing any unproductive or overlapping spurs. Trim out excess fruit buds to leave 2 or 3 evenly spaced buds per spur.

woody at their base before they are pruned; the operation is therefore spread over three or four weeks and a few shoots may not be ready to prune until early autumn. Do not shorten shoots that are 15cm (6in) or less in length. Cut back branch leaders to six leaves of new growth and prune any sub-laterals to one leaf above the basal cluster. Any shoots arising directly from the main branches should be shortened to three leaves. If secondary growth develops, leave a few shoots unpruned as for apples (see "Summer pruning", p.438) to draw the sap.

The only major operation for winter pruning is the shortening of the central leader already described plus, in later years, some spur thinning and shortening. If the spur systems are allowed to become congested, the tree loses vigour and small, over-crowded fruits are produced.

Harvesting and storing

Time of picking is most important, especially for cultivars that ripen in late summer and early autumn. If left on the tree too long, the fruits will have turned "sleepy" and brown at the centre. Gather them at the first sign of a change of ground colour on the skin from dark to slightly lighter green. If in doubt, gently lift and twist

a fruit: if it comes away easily, it is almost ripe and will be at peak flavour in a few days. If the stalk breaks, wait for some days longer. Several harvests need to be made because all fruits do not ripen simultaneously. Fruits of late-ripening cultivars and those grown in cool climates must be left on the tree until mature to develop their full flavour.

Store pears in cool conditions, laying them in slatted boxes; do not wrap otherwise the flesh discolours. The fruits of later-ripening cultivars should be conditioned before eating: keep them at room temperature for a day or two and eat when the flesh gives under gentle pressure by the thumb near to the stalk. The flavour should then be at its fullest.

Propagation

For most pear cultivars, whip-and-tongue grafting or chip- or T-budding (see "Propagation", p.432) onto a 'Quince A' or 'Quince C' rootstock is usually successful. Grafting over may also be used to change the cultivar of an existing tree to another, preferable cultivar (see p.443).

Double-working pear cultivars

The few pear cultivars that are incompatible with quince rootstocks need to be double-worked: a cultivar that is compatible with both the quince rootstock and the selected scion cultivar is used as an "interstock" between the two. The cultivar 'Beurré Hardy' is the most widely used interstock; 'Vicar of Winkfield', 'Pitmaston Duchess', and 'Beurré d'Amalis' may also be used for all pear cultivars that require double-working. These include 'Dr Jules Guyot', 'Souvenir de Congrès', 'Marguerite Marillat', 'Williams' Bon Chrétien', 'Marie Louise', 'Packham's Triumph', and 'Thompson's'. Two methods of double-working may be used: double chip-budding and double grafting.

Double chip-budding entails carrying out chip-budding two years in succession: in the first

DOUBLE BUDDING
Insert the bud chip 5cm (2in) above the first graft and on the opposite side, so that the resulting stem will grow out straighter when the bud develops. Cut off the interstock above the new bud once the scion shoot has developed. Remove any shoots on the interstock.

year, a scion of the interstock is budded onto a quince rootstock; in the second year, a scion of the selected cultivar is budded onto the interstock on the opposite side. The method is as for chip-budding (see p.432).

For double grafting the same principle is followed. Graft the interstock onto the quince rootstock in early spring using the whip-and-tongue

DOUBLE GRAFTING
This follows the same principle as double budding: cut back the interstock a year after it is grafted, once the sap starts to rise, and graft on the required scion. Leave 5cm (2in) between grafts; position the scion graft on the opposite side from the previous one.

method (see p.433). In late winter or early spring, cut back the grafted interstock and graft the incompatible cultivar scion onto the interstock. Alternatively, it may be budded onto the interstock in summer, following the grafting of the interstock in spring. Remove shoots from the interstock but retain those from the cultivar scion.

Quinces (*Cydonia oblonga*)

Quinces are fruits grown mainly in temperate regions. As bushes, they reach 3.4–5m (10–15ft); they may also be trained as fans. The fruits are apple- or pear-shaped and are covered with greyish-white down. The most widely grown cultivars are 'Meech's Prolific' and 'Vranja'. Quince trees have a chilling requirement of 100–450 hours below 7°C (45°F) in order to flower.

Site and planting
Quinces require a reasonably sunny, sheltered site. The protection provided by a wall may be beneficial in cold areas. Moisture-retentive, slightly acidic soils are preferred; marked alkalinity usually causes lime-induced chlorosis.

'Quince A' is normally used as a rootstock. Where trees are grown on their own roots, suckering may be difficult to control. Quinces are generally self-fertile but the provision of pollinators is claimed to improve cropping levels. Plant quinces in

autumn or winter if bare-root, or throughout the year if container-grown, spacing them approximately 4–4.5m (12–15ft) apart.

Routine care
Cultivation requirements are as described under "Care of tree fruits", p.426. Once established, quinces need little attention. Occasional feeding at the standard rate may be necessary, particularly on poor soils, while watering and mulching may also be required. Quinces are comparatively easy to grow but fungal leaf spots (p.648) may be troublesome.

Pruning and training
Quinces fruit on spurs and on the tips of the previous summer's growth. Bushes may be left to grow into multi-stemmed trees or pruned in the early stages as for apple bushes (see p.439) with an open-centred, well-spaced branch framework.

Pruning of established trees is minimal, with occasional thinning in

winter of old, overcrowded growth. Not every lateral should be pruned, however, since this removes too many fruit buds.

Harvesting and storing
Pick the fruits when the skins have turned from green to gold, usually in late autumn. Store in boxes in a cool, well-ventilated, dark place. Do not wrap the fruits: quinces stored in plastic bags will discolour internally.

Because quinces have a strong aroma, they should be stored separately, so that they do not contaminate other fruits. They are often used in preserves.

Propagation
Quince trees may be propagated either by chip-budding onto 'Quince A' rootstocks in summer (see p.432) or by taking hardwood cuttings in autumn (see p.434).

QUINCE TREE
Leave a generous grass-free area around young quinces, so that all the nutrients are absorbed by the trees and not shared with the grass.

Medlars (*Mespilus germanica*)

Medlars are decorative, spreading trees with golden autumn colour and large, white or pinkish-white flowers in mid- to late spring. Medlar trees are most commonly grown as bushes, or as half-standards where larger specimens are required. They are self-fertile and have a chilling requirement of 100–450 hours below 7°C (45°F). The fruits are apple-shaped and somewhat flattened with prominent, horny calyces. Their flavour is an acquired taste; the fruits are used to make preserves.

RIPENING MEDLARS
The small, brown fruits ripen in autumn and measure 2.5–5cm (1–2in) across.

Site and planting

A sunny, sheltered site is preferable, although medlars tolerate partial shade. They may be grown in a wide range of soils, with the exception of those that are very chalky or badly drained. Adequate moisture is essential to obtain strong growth and a good crop of fruits.

Trees grown for the quality of their fruits are usually grafted on 'Quince A' rootstocks, although half-standards are sometimes available on seedling pear rootstocks.

Medlar trees are best planted in late autumn to winter. Half-standards should be spaced at a distance of 8m (25ft), and bushes at 4.25m (14ft).

Routine care

Cultivation requirements are generally as for apples (see p.436). Medlars may sometimes be affected by leaf-eating caterpillars (p.645) and fungal leaf spots (p.648).

Pruning and training

Train a bush tree as for apples (see p.439). For half-standards, pruning is initially as for apples. Once the main framework is established, occasionally thin branches in winter to maintain an open framework, removing overcrowded, diseased, or dead growth.

Harvesting and storing

Leave fruits on the tree for as long as possible so that they develop their full flavour. Pick them in late autumn

MEDLARS

when the stalk parts easily from the tree, preferably in dry weather. The fruits are unpalatable immediately after picking, and must be stored before use. Dip the stalks in a strong salt solution to prevent rotting, then store the fruits, calyces downwards, on slatted trays, so that the fruits do not touch. Use when the flesh has become soft and brown.

Propagation

Propagate by chip- or T-budding (see pp.432 and 433), or whip-and-tongue grafting (see p.433).

Plums, gages, damsons, and bullaces (*Prunus* x *domestica*)

Various kinds of plum are grown for their fine fruits. These include: European plums (selections of *Prunus* x *domestica*); gages (*P.* x *domestica* and *P. insititia*); damsons, Mirabelles, and bullaces (*P. insititia*); cherry plums (*P. cerasifera*); and the Japanese or Salicine plums (*P. salicina*, syn. *P. triflora*).

Regions with cool-temperate climates are ideal for European plums, damsons, and bullaces; in warmer areas with earlier springs, Japanese plums and Mirabelles are more widely grown. All types of plum prefer areas that have plenty of sun and relatively low rainfall. Cherry plums, or myrobalan, are rarely grown for their fruit, but are often used as vigorous rootstocks for a number of fruiting plums, and for some ornamental trees.

There is a wide range of cultivars adapted to different climates and, with more dwarfing rootstocks now available, plums are ideal for even small gardens; damsons usually make smaller trees than plums. The compact pyramid tree and dwarf bush forms are particularly suitable for small gardens; for the choicest fruit in cool climates, grow fan-trained trees on warm, sunny walls. European plums and damsons have a chilling requirement of 700–1,000 hours below 7°C (45°F), and the Japanese plum one of 500–900 hours.

Site and planting

Plums need a warm, sheltered site to ensure that the flowers are pollinated successfully. Their pollination requirements are complex – some cultivars are self-fertile while others require suitable pollinators planted nearby. Make sure that there is enough room on the proposed site for the required number of trees, allowing for their mature height.

Site

All plums flower early in spring, Japanese plums markedly so and cherry plums earlier still, so that spring frosts are always a hazard. They are, therefore, best planted in a relatively frost-free site. Plums need to be sheltered from wind to avoid damage to the trees and also to encourage pollinating insects.

Most soils are suitable, but avoid those that are very chalky and poorly drained. Plums on poor, sandy soils need extra feeding and watering to maintain good growth and cropping, and to improve flavour (see "Feeding, watering, and mulching", p.448).

Rootstocks

'Pixy' (dwarfing) and 'St Julien A' (moderately vigorous) are best for small to medium-sized plum trees, 2.2–4m (7–12ft). For trees up to

ROOTSTOCKS

4m (12ft)
3m (9ft)
2m (6ft)
1m (3ft)

'Pixy' 'St Julien A' 'Brompton' 'Myrobalan B'

4.25m (14ft), choose 'Myrobalan B' (incompatible with some cultivars) or 'Brompton' (universally compatible). 'Marianna' is excellent for Japanese plums, but is incompatible with some European plums. Plum trees tend to produce suckers, but this is less common with modern rootstocks.

Pollination

European plums and damsons may be self-fertile, partially self-fertile, or self-sterile. Fortunately, some very popular cultivars, such as 'Victoria', are self-fertile, but planting suitable pollinators nearby will ensure more consistent cropping. Cultivars that

are not self-fertile must always be planted with compatible pollinators nearby. Cherry plums are self-fertile. Some Japanese plums are self-fertile, but most give better results when planted near a suitable pollinator. Plum cultivars that will not pollinate certain others are indicated in the lists of recommended cultivars on pp.448 and 449, which also give details of flowering times. Seek advice about pollination of individual trees when buying.

Planting

This should be completed as early as possible in late autumn or early

PLANTING DISTANCES			
TREE FORM	ROOTSTOCK	DISTANCE BETWEEN TREES	DISTANCE BETWEEN ROWS
Bush	'St Julien A'	4–5m (12–15ft)	5.5m (18ft)
Half-standard	'Brompton' or 'Myrobalan B'	5.5–7m (18–22ft)	7m (22ft) minimum
Fan	'St Julien A'	5–5.5m (15–18ft)	
Pyramid	'St Julien A' or 'Pixy'	2.5–4m (8–12ft)	4–6m (12–20ft)

447

winter as growth starts early in spring. All trees are best staked for two years; stake those on 'Pixy' rootstocks permanently. Planting distances (see p.447) are determined by the chosen tree form and by the vigour of the rootstock.

Routine care

Feed and water trees regularly, and check for pests and diseases. Fruit thinning should be carried out as necessary. If spring frosts are likely, protect wall-trained trees in bloom with a cover (see FROST AND WIND PROTECTION, pp.612–613).

Fruit thinning

This is an important procedure both to give larger, better-flavoured fruits and to reduce the risk of branches breaking from the weight of too many fruits. Fruitlets may be thinned early if the set is heavy. After the stones have formed and natural fruit drop has occurred, thin the remaining fruit to about 5–8cm (2–3in) apart for small fruits and 8–10cm (3–4in) for larger cultivars (such as 'Victoria'). Scissors are best for this job since they are quicker to use than secateurs.

Feeding, watering, and mulching

Plums require plenty of nitrogen; apply a spring dressing at the rate recommended under "Care of tree fruits", p.426. Mulch annually with well-rotted manure or compost, and water as required, particularly in prolonged spells of hot weather. Plums planted against walls or fences will need more regular watering than those grown in the open.

Pests and diseases

Plums may be attacked by rabbits and hares (p.666), wasps (p.659), aphids (p.646), and winter moth caterpillars (p.645). Diseases that

may affect plums include silver leaf (p.647), bacterial canker (p.665), and brown rot (p.658). Any trees that are badly infected with silver leaf, bacterial canker, or (less commonly) with viruses (p.649) should be dug up and burnt without delay.

All stone fruit trees may be affected by the physiological disorder known as gumming. Trees that have this problem exude a translucent, amber-coloured, gum-like substance from the trunk and branches, while plums may also form gum around the stone within the fruit. The gum is produced by the trees as a result of stress caused by disease, adverse soil conditions, or physical damage caused by, for example, strong winds or a heavy crop. If gumming is noticed, try to identify the cause and alleviate the problem if possible.

Birds may also be troublesome; if they attack the fruit buds, it may be necessary to place fine mesh nets over the trees during the winter to prevent damage (see also p.657).

PLUM BUSH
YEAR 1, EARLY SPRING PRUNING

Prune back 3 or 4 laterals by about two thirds to a half, cutting to outward-facing buds.

Prune out the leader above the top-most selected lateral, using an angled cut.

Cut off any laterals below those selected flush with the main stem.

Pruning and training

Plum trees produce fruit at the base of one-year-old shoots, as well as on two-year-old wood and spurs. Once initially trained, they require less pruning on unrestricted forms than apples or pears. In cool-temperate climates it is essential to prune in summer (after training) to minimize the risk of silver leaf (p.647). Trained trees require routine summer pruning to maintain their restricted shape. Remove any damaged or diseased branches immediately, cutting back to healthy wood.

Bush

In early spring when the buds are breaking, start training a newly planted feathered maiden. Select three or four strong, evenly spaced laterals, the highest at about 90cm (3ft) from ground level, and prune them by about two thirds or a half, to healthy, outward-facing buds. These laterals will form the basic

YEAR 2, EARLY SPRING PRUNING

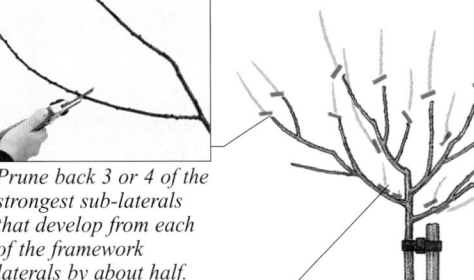

Prune back 3 or 4 of the strongest sub-laterals that develop from each of the framework laterals by about half.

Remove other weak, badly placed, or narrow-angled laterals completely.

FRUITING HABIT

Plum trees develop fruit at the base of one-year-old shoots and then along the stems on two-year-old wood and spurs.

framework of branches. Then prune out the leader, making an angled cut above the highest of the selected laterals. Cut back to the main stem unwanted laterals below those selected.

The following early spring, choose three or four of the strongest sub-laterals that have developed on each of the pruned laterals and shorten them by half. To achieve a balanced framework, trim off weak or badly placed laterals and pinch out any shoots growing from the main stem. Subsequently, restrict pruning of young trees to the removal in summer of excessively vigorous or awkwardly placed growths. With older trees, thin some branches in summer to avoid overcrowding, and seal wounds with bituminous paint.

If using a maiden whip, prune it to about 90cm (3ft). The following spring, laterals should have developed, and it may then be trained as a feathered maiden.

Half-standard

Choose three or four well-spaced laterals on a feathered maiden; cut back the leader just above the uppermost lateral at 1.3m (4½ft), then prune each of the chosen laterals by one third to a half. Remove any lower laterals. Subsequent pruning of the sub-laterals and training to form an open-centre head is the same as for a bush. Half-standard trees are less easy to manage than pyramid or bush plums when mature because of their greater size.

Spindlebush

Similar in shape to a plum pyramid (see p.450), the spindlebush requires a little more space but does not need the same annual summer pruning. Pruning and training are as for apple spindlebushes (see p.440) but prune in early spring when the buds break.

Tie down upright shoots and keep the top of the tree in check by removing the more vigorous shoots and retaining the less vigorous ones to produce fruit. In this way the conical shape is maintained.

Fan

Train a plum fan initially as for a peach fan (see p.453) to produce main branches or ribs to train against horizontal support wires. When

ESTABLISHED PLUM FAN
SPRING PRUNING

Thin new sideshoots to about 10cm (4in) apart.

Cut out any sideshoots that are growing towards the centre of the fan or are badly placed.

SUMMER PRUNING

Tie in any ribs needed to extend the framework or replace older wood.

Cut back sideshoots that are not needed for the permanent rib framework to 5 or 6 leaves.

Cut back wrong-pointing or awkward shoots to shoots facing in the required direction or flush with the rib.

AFTER FRUITING

In the autumn, after the fruit has been harvested, prune back to 3 leaves all the sideshoots that were shortened to 5 or 6 leaves earlier in the summer.

training the young fan, retain some sideshoots to fill in gaps and pinch back others to one bud. Remove any very vigorous sideshoots or those growing at an awkward angle.

On an established fan, in spring or as soon as they appear, remove sideshoots growing inwards towards the wall or fence, or the centre of the fan. Thin the remainder to 10cm (4in) apart and pinch or cut them back to six leaves during the summer unless they are required to fill spaces in the fan framework. After the crop has been picked, shorten these shoots to three leaves.

Pyramid

Plant a feathered maiden against a strong stake and, in early spring, cut back the central leader to a healthy bud at a height of about 1.5m (5ft). Remove any laterals growing below 45cm (18in) from the ground. Shorten the remaining laterals over 22cm (9in) long by half their length. When the bases of the young shoots are turning woody later in the summer, cut back extension growth on the main branches and new (maiden) laterals, to about 20cm (8in); at the same time, reduce sub-laterals to about 15cm (6in). To start forming the pyramid shape, cut main branches and sub-laterals back to downward-facing buds so that growth is more or less horizontal. Remove any laterals that are very vigorous or upward-pointing. Tie in the central leader to the stake, but do not prune it until the following spring, then shorten it by two-thirds of its new growth. Once the tree has reached a height of about 2m (6ft) on 'Pixy' or 2.5m (8ft) on 'St Julien A', cut back the central leader. This should be delayed until late spring, however, since this reduces its subsequent growth; cut it back to a bud about 2.5cm (1in) from the old wood. Continue annual summer pruning as previously described, cutting branch leaders to downward-pointing buds and removing any excessively vigorous, upright shoots, especially those growing in the upper parts of the tree, to maintain the pyramid shape.

On mature pyramids, overcrowding will develop; in summer, trim off any badly placed, old wood as necessary. Maintain the pyramid shape by keeping any vigorous or dominant upper branches in check.

Harvesting and storing

For the best flavour, allow fruits to ripen fully; for freezing or preserving, pick them when ripe but still firm. In wet weather, gather the ripening crop before brown rot or wasps spoil it. Split skins may occur with some cultivars in moist conditions. Keep the fresh fruits in a cool, dark place and use within a few days.

Propagation

Chip- or T-budding is most usual (see pp.432 and 433); whip-and-tongue grafting (see p.433) is less reliable for plums than for apples and pears.

PLUM PYRAMID

YEAR 1, EARLY SPRING PRUNING

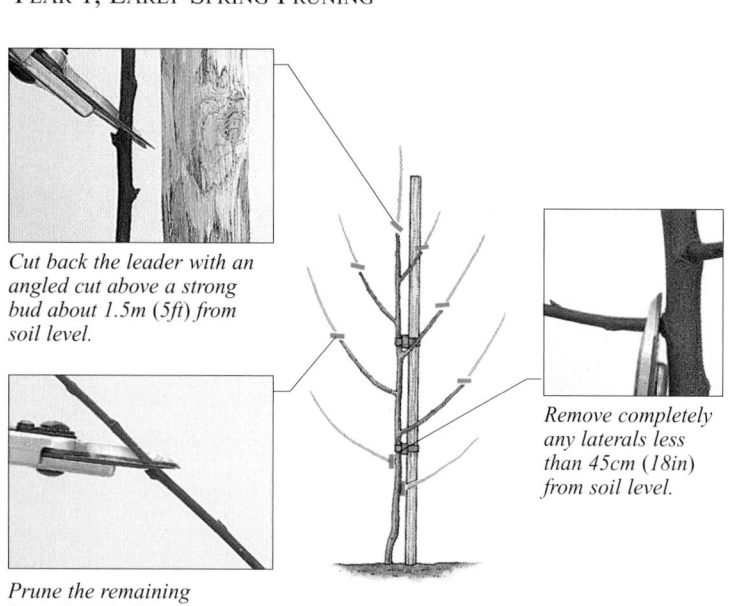

Cut back the leader with an angled cut above a strong bud about 1.5m (5ft) from soil level.

Prune the remaining laterals by half to downward-facing buds.

Remove completely any laterals less than 45cm (18in) from soil level.

YEAR 1, SUMMER PRUNING

Any new laterals forming too narrow an angle with the main stem should be removed. Do not prune the central leader.

Cut back any sub-laterals to 15cm (6in) with an angled cut just above a leaf.

Cut back new growth at the tips of the main branches to about 20cm (8in) and to a downward-pointing bud.

YEAR 2, EARLY SPRING PRUNING

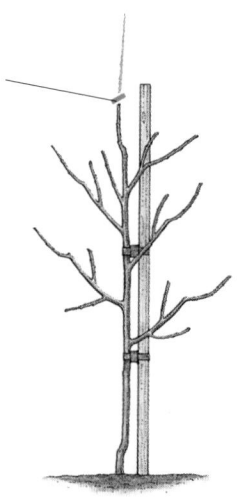

Just before bud burst, shorten the central leader by two thirds of its new growth.

ESTABLISHED PYRAMID, SUMMER PRUNING

Remove any sub-laterals that are crossing or overcrowded.

Repeat the routine summer pruning of main branches and sub-laterals.

Cut back any dead or unproductive wood to a healthy shoot or to the point of origin.

Peaches and nectarines (*Prunus persica* and *P. persica* var. *nectarina*)

Peaches and nectarines are grown in many temperate regions. They have a chilling requirement of 600–900 hours below 7°C (45°F). Sunny, reasonably dry summers are essential to produce good crops; in cooler climates, peaches may be grown under cover. A range of cultivars is available for different climates (see *Recommended Peaches*, right, and *Recommended Nectarines*, p.452); they are yellow-, pink-, or white-fleshed. On cling peaches the flesh tends to cling to the stone; other peaches are known as freestone. The nectarine is a smooth-skinned form of the peach and requires very similar treatment, although it prefers warmer growing conditions.

Peaches and nectarines are usually grown in bush form, but fans are popular in temperate climates since they allow the fruits to receive maximum sunlight for ripening. Some naturally compact (genetic dwarf) cultivars are ideal for growing in pots.

Site and planting

Peaches flower early in the year and so should be protected from frost; a south-facing wall is an ideal site.

Site
Maximum sun is necessary, in a sheltered site that is not susceptible to spring frosts. In cooler climates, a sunny wall or a greenhouse is needed. Peach trees in areas with high rainfall may be badly affected by peach leaf curl (p.651) unless given some protection (see "Routine care", right).

Deep, fertile, slightly acid soils (pH6.5–7) are ideal for growing peaches. If grown on sandy soils they need extra feeding and watering; shallow, chalky soils often give rise to lime-induced chlorosis.

Rootstocks
The plum rootstock 'St Julien A' is used to provide a moderately vigorous tree, while 'Brompton' is used if more vigour is required. In some areas, peach seedling rootstocks are preferred, using vigorous selections resistant to root-knot eelworms.

HAND-POLLINATION

Peaches may be hand-pollinated once the blossom is fully out. On a warm, dry day, use a small, soft brush to transfer the pollen from the anthers of one flower to the stigmas of another.

Pollination
All recommended cultivars are self-fertile, so a crop can be obtained from a single tree. In areas with wet or uncertain weather, pollination may be erratic but can be improved by hand-pollination using a soft brush or rabbit's tail.

Planting
Plant peach trees by midwinter if possible, as growth starts very early. Stake bush trees for the first two years. Planting distances vary depending on the tree form and choice of rootstock (see chart, below).

Routine care

For details of maintenance and cultivation requirements, see "Care of tree fruits", p.426. Lime-induced chlorosis may lead to manganese/iron deficiency (p.651), which must be treated as soon as possible. Protect the developing foliage of fan-trained

ROOTSTOCKS

4m (12ft)
3m (9ft)
2m (6ft)
1m (3ft)

'St Julien A' 'Brompton'

PROTECTING PEACH FANS

In the autumn, at leaf fall, cover the tree with a polythene shelter open at both ends for ventilation. This keeps the leaf buds dry and inhibits peach leaf curl spores from germinating.

peaches against peach leaf curl, and frost to some extent, with a polythene lean-to in winter and early spring.

Fruit thinning
To produce large fruits, thinning will be needed. When the fruitlets are the size of hazelnuts, thin them to one fruit per cluster. Later, when they are walnut-sized and some fruitlets have been shed naturally, thin to a spacing of 15–22cm (6–9in); in warm climates closer spacing may be used.

Feeding, watering, and mulching
In dry areas, watering is necessary to support growth and fruiting. Mulching in spring once the soil has warmed up helps the soil to retain its

RECOMMENDED PEACHES
Early
'Amsden June' **Wh**
'Duke of York' **Wh,☆**
'Earliglo' **Y**
'Hales Early' **Y**
'Saturn' **P**
'Waterloo' **Wh,☆**

'Earliglo'

Mid-season
'Bonanza' **Gd,Y**
'Garden Anny' **Gd,Y**
'Garden Lady' **Gd,Y**
'Peregrine' **Wh,☆**
'Redhaven' **Y**
'Rochester' **Y**

'Peregrine'

Late
'Barrington' **Y,☆**
'Bellegarde' **Y,☆**
'Dymond' **Y,☆**

KEY
Gd *Genetic dwarf (good for pot culture)*
P *Pink flesh*
Wh *White flesh*
Y *Yellow flesh*
☆ *Excellent flavour*

THINNING

1 *As they form, thin peaches to one fruit per cluster, removing first any fruits growing towards the wall or fence.*

2 *These remaining fruits will need thinning again later, in order to leave one fruit every 15–22cm (6–9in).*

PLANTING DISTANCES

TREE FORM	ROOTSTOCK	DISTANCE BETWEEN TREES	DISTANCE BETWEEN ROWS
Bush	'St Julien A'	5–5.5m (15–18ft)	5.5m (18ft)
	'Brompton' or seedling peach	5.5–7.5m (18–24ft)	7.5m (24ft)
Fan	'St Julien A'	3.5–5m (11–15ft)	

Early
'Early Rivers' ☆
'John Rivers' ☆

Mid-season
'Elruge' ☆
'Humboldt' ☆
'Lord Napier' ☆

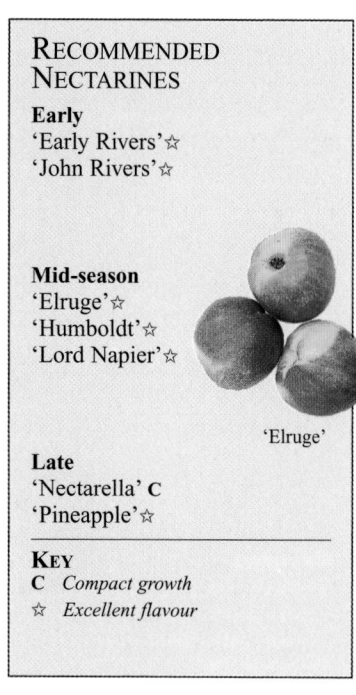

'Elruge'

Late
'Nectarella' **C**
'Pineapple' ☆

KEY
C *Compact growth*
☆ *Excellent flavour*

moisture. Adequate nitrogen is essential to promote new growth for cropping and potassium is needed to enhance hardiness and fruit quality.

Pests and diseases
Peaches may be attacked by aphids (p.646), birds (p.657), red spider mite (p.646), earwigs (p.644), and root-knot eelworms (p.660); common diseases include peach leaf curl (p.651), bacterial canker (p.665), grey mould (*Botrytis*) (p.646), and gumming (see "Plums: Pests and diseases", p.448).

Growing under cover

Peach trees under cover are best fan-trained so that the fruits receive maximum sun. The greenhouse must be able to accommodate a minimum span of 2.75m (9ft). Fertile, moisture-retentive soil is essential.

A trained tree should be grown against suitable support wires spaced at 15cm (6in) intervals, starting at 38cm (15in) from the ground. Secure the wires so that they are held about 22cm (9in) away from the glass. Full ventilation is essential in winter to allow adequate chilling.

In early spring, but not too early if no heat is available, reduce ventilation to start the tree into growth. Keep the temperature at 8–10°C (46–50°F) for up to two weeks and then raise it to 20°C (68°F).

Trees under cover grow rapidly; always feed and water them well. Occasional, copious watering is preferable to frequent, light applications. Syringe the foliage with a mist of tepid water and damp down the greenhouse floor on bright days.

Pollinate the trees by hand when in bloom (see *Hand-pollination*, p.451). Do not syringe or damp down during the flowering season as this

may prevent pollination, but start again once the flowers have dropped in order to help control red spider mites and mildew; stop syringing and damping down when the fruits begin to ripen.

Fruit thinning is essential to ensure that the fruits develop to their full size (see p.451).

Pruning and training

Peach and nectarine trees bear fruit only on shoots produced the previous year. The first fruits usually develop the third year after planting. Pruning is aimed at encouraging new growth and replacement shoots to maintain a well-balanced, open branch framework. There are three different kinds of bud: plump fruit buds; small, pointed growth buds; and triple buds that have a plump, central fruit bud with growth buds

PEACH BUSH

YEAR 1, EARLY SPRING PRUNING

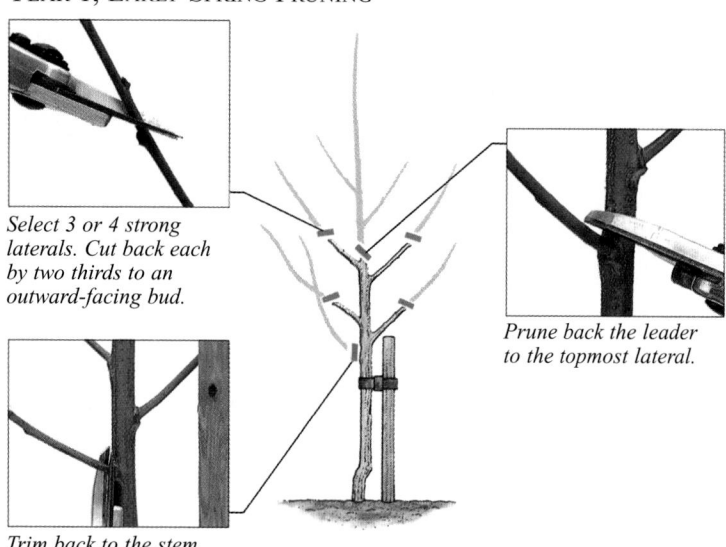

Select 3 or 4 strong laterals. Cut back each by two thirds to an outward-facing bud.

Trim back to the stem any unwanted laterals.

Prune back the leader to the topmost lateral.

YEAR 1, SUMMER PRUNING

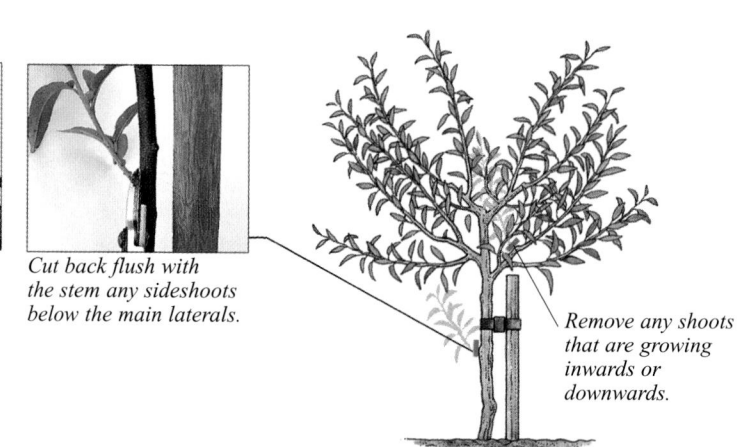

Cut back flush with the stem any sideshoots below the main laterals.

Remove any shoots that are growing inwards or downwards.

YEAR 2, EARLY SPRING PRUNING

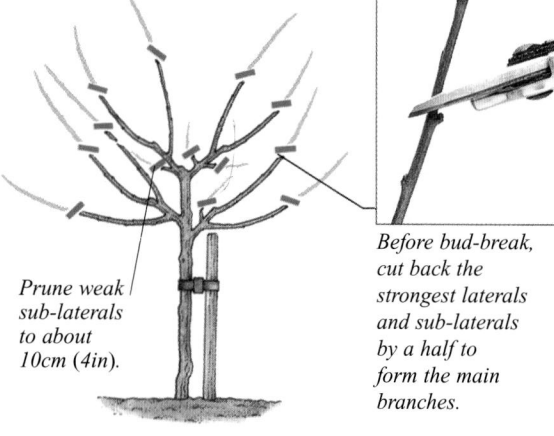

Prune weak sub-laterals to about 10cm (4in).

Before bud-break, cut back the strongest laterals and sub-laterals by a half to form the main branches.

ESTABLISHED BUSH, EARLY SUMMER PRUNING

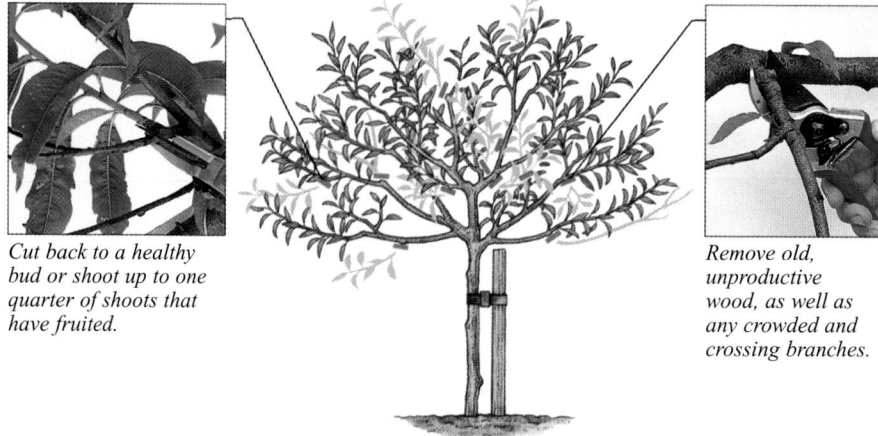

Cut back to a healthy bud or shoot up to one quarter of shoots that have fruited.

Remove old, unproductive wood, as well as any crowded and crossing branches.

on either side. On branches where extension growth is required, prune back to a growth bud, or, failing this, to a triple bud.

Bush

Plant a feathered maiden between late autumn and late winter. In early spring select three or four strong, well-spaced laterals with the topmost one about 75–90cm (2½–3ft) from the ground; prune back the leader to just above the top lateral. Prune back each of the selected laterals by two thirds and remove all other unwanted laterals. During summer, remove any badly placed or low shoots that have developed.

The following early spring, before bud-burst, select strong laterals and sub-laterals to form the basic framework. Cut these back by about half to a bud; prune any other sub-laterals to about 10cm (4in).

Once the tree is well established, keep the centre open by removing some of the older, fruited shoots each summer; occasionally, unproductive branches may need to be cut out.

Fan

Partially trained fans are sometimes available; if buying one of these, make sure that it has been correctly trained (as shown below). A fan should be developed from two laterals trained out approximately 30cm (12in) above the ground at 40°. The central leader immediately above them should have been removed to channel vigour equally to both sides of the tree. A fan that retains its long, central leader and has laterals radiating out at an angle along its length will produce excessive growth at the top of the fan, leaving the base bare.

Formative pruning

Set up support wires as for an apple fan (see p.441). After planting a feathered maiden, choose two laterals about 30cm (12in) above the ground and remove the leader above them. Prune the selected laterals to about 38cm (15in) to form the first two "arms" and tie them to canes at 40°. Prune back all other laterals to one bud as a reserve until the two arms have developed.

In summer, tie in the leader and arms to canes as they develop, to start forming the framework "ribs". Select and train in two equally spaced shoots on the upper side of each arm and one underneath. Pinch back any other shoots on the stem to one leaf, and remove any shoots on the ribs that are badly placed. Before bud-burst in the second spring, cut back the extension growth on the ribs by one third to a strong, healthy bud, in order to promote growth and the fan's development.

In early summer, continue tying in the selected developing ribs. Pinch back weak shoots and remove any that are very vigorous or pointing in the wrong direction.

The following early spring, shorten the ribs by one quarter of last year's growth. During the third summer, select further shoots to complete the main ribs of the fan. Any space in the centre of the tree will soon be filled in by sideshoots. Thin sideshoots produced from the ribs early in the season to 10–15cm (4–6in) apart; retain those that lie naturally along the plane of the fan but remove any that are awkwardly

placed and growing straight outwards or inwards towards the wall or fence. Tie in the retained shoots; they should produce fruit the following year. Pinch back any shoots that are overlapping, to four to six leaves.

Routine pruning

The aim of pruning in spring is to ensure a constant supply of well-placed, young shoots each year. At the base of each flowered shoot that will carry fruit in the forthcoming summer, there are usually two buds or young shoots; pinch out (disbud) one of these to prevent growth from becoming congested. The remaining one will carry fruit the following year. A second bud about halfway up the shoot may also be retained as a reserve in case the other one becomes damaged. After harvesting, remove the fruited wood, and tie in a replacement shoot at the base of each shoot that is cut out.

Continue this process annually; retain two replacement shoots if there is space in the framework. Without rigorous pruning, a peach tree soon becomes congested with old wood that bears no fruit.

PEACH FAN

YEAR 1, EARLY SPRING PRUNING

Choose 2 laterals, one on either side, 30cm (12in) from the ground to form the main arms. Cut out the leader just above the higher lateral.

Prune back each arm to about 38cm (15in) to a strong bud to encourage shoots, or "ribs", to form.

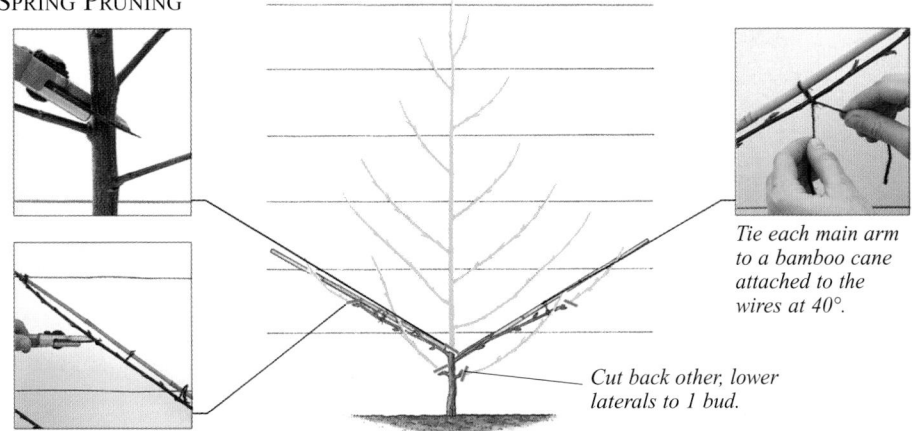

Tie each main arm to a bamboo cane attached to the wires at 40°.

— Cut back other, lower laterals to 1 bud.

YEAR 1, SUMMER PRUNING

Choose 2 ribs on the top of each arm and 1 underneath and tie them to well-spaced canes attached to the wires. Pinch back other shoots to 1 leaf.

YEAR 2, EARLY SPRING PRUNING

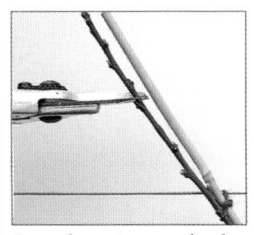

In early spring, cut back the extension growth on the ribs by one third to strong, healthy buds facing in the required direction.

YEAR 2, EARLY SUMMER PRUNING

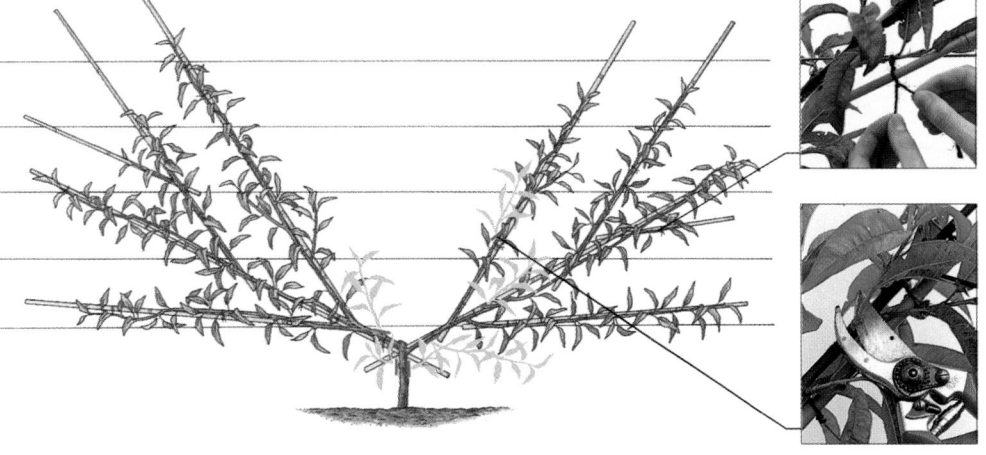

Train in developing ribs by tying them to canes to extend the permanent framework.

Cut back any wrong-pointing sideshoots to the point of origin, and remove any shoots emerging below the two main arms.

YEAR 3, EARLY SPRING PRUNING

Cut back each of the main ribs by one quarter to stimulate further growth and extend the framework.

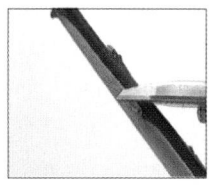

YEAR 3, SUMMER PRUNING

Pinch back any shoots that overlap the ribs to 4–6 leaves as they develop.

As the remaining sideshoots develop, tie them to canes to fill in the framework. These shoots should fruit the following year.

YEAR 3, EARLY SUMMER PRUNING

Thin young sideshoots to 10–15cm (4–6in) apart by pinching out unwanted shoots. Pinch out any shoots that are growing towards the wall or fence or in the wrong direction.

ESTABLISHED FAN, PRUNING AFTER FRUITING

Cut back each fruited shoot to a suitable replacement near its base.

Tie in the replacement shoot to fill the gap. These shoots should be evenly distributed over the whole fan.

Harvesting and storing

Harvest the fruits when they are fully ripe. Rest them in the palm of the hand and apply gentle pressure with your thumb on the part of the fruit nearest to the stalk. If the flesh "gives" slightly, the fruit is ready for picking. For the finest flavour, peaches and nectarines are best eaten as soon as possible after picking. If necessary, they can be stored for a few days by placing the fruits in a container lined with soft material and keeping it in a cool place.

Propagation

Peaches and nectarines are usually propagated by chip- or T-budding (see pp.432 and 433) in summer. Seedling peaches are variable in quality, but are often vigorous and may produce excellent crops.

Apricots (*Prunus armeniaca*)

Apricots are more difficult to grow than many other fruits. Not all cultivars thrive in certain areas, so always seek advice when selecting trees. The chilling requirement for apricots is 350–900 hours below 7°C (45°F), most cultivars being at the lower end of this range. They flower extremely early in the year.

Although dry, sunny summers are needed for successful cropping, drought conditions may cause serious bud drop late in the season. In cool climates, apricots may be grown under cover or fan-trained against a warm wall. In warm areas, the bush form is popular.

Site and planting

Apricot trees should be planted in a sunny, sheltered, and frost-free site in order to produce good crops of fruit. In cool areas, it is essential to grow them against a sunny wall or in a greenhouse to protect the flowers from frost and low temperatures in late winter and early spring.

A deep, slightly alkaline loam is the most suitable soil. Apricots are least likely to thrive on sandy and chalky soils. It is also best to avoid planting them on heavy soils, particularly in areas that have cool, wet winters, since this may make them prone to die-back.

For rootstocks, both seedling apricots and peaches are widely used. A seedling peach rootstock tolerates wetter conditions than a seedling apricot rootstock and produces a smaller tree. The plum rootstock 'St Julien A' is also often used; this is moderately vigorous.

Apricots are self-fertile; in cool areas, however, flowers should be pollinated by hand.

Plant in late autumn or very early winter (see *Planting Distances*, p.455) before bud-break. Stake bush trees securely for the first two years.

PLANTING DISTANCES

TREE FORM	ROOTSTOCK	DISTANCE BETWEEN TREES	DISTANCE BETWEEN ROWS
Bush	'St Julien A'	4.5–5.5m (15–18ft)	5.5m (18ft)
	Seedling peach or apricot	5.5–7m (18–22ft)	7m (22ft)
Fan	'St Julien A'	4.5–5.5m (15–18ft)	

Routine care

In general, maintenance and cultivation requirements are as for other tree fruits (see "Care of tree fruits", p.426).

In warm regions where heavy cropping is common, blossom may need thinning to counteract biennial bearing (see p.436). Remove badly placed fruitlets and carry out the main thinning after any fruits have dropped naturally and the stones have started forming. Thin so that there is a single fruit on each truss, to leave about 7cm (3in) between fruits.

In cool areas, branch die-back occurs quite frequently; cut back affected branches to clean wood as soon as possible. Birds (p.657), earwigs (p.644), bacterial canker (p.665), brown rot (p.658), and gumming (see "Plums: Pests and diseases", p.448) may be troublesome.

Pruning and training

Fruits are borne both on one-year-old shoots and on older spurs. Pruning is aimed at maintaining the shape of the tree and removing any old, unproductive wood. If young trees are too vigorous, they may be root-pruned (see p.430). Prune and train an apricot bush as for plums (see p.448).

The initial training of a fan is as for peaches (see p.453). On an established fan, thin young shoots to 10–15cm (4–6in) apart as they develop in the spring, and remove any shoots that are pointing downwards, towards the centre of the fan, or inwards to the wall. Retain growths that are needed to fill gaps in the framework. Pinch back sub-laterals to six leaves if they are not required to fill gaps and any sideshoots to one leaf later in the season. After fruiting, prune sub-laterals to three leaves.

Harvesting

Pick the fruit when it is fully ripe and comes away easily from its stalk. Use immediately because fresh apricots do not store well; alternatively they may be frozen, used in preserves, or dried (see p.431).

Propagation

Apricots may be propagated by chip- or T-budding (see pp.432 and 433), using seedling peach or 'St Julien A' rootstocks.

ESTABLISHED APRICOT FAN, EARLY SUMMER PRUNING

To fill gaps in the framework, tie in young sideshoots once they have hardened at the base.

Cut or pinch out altogether any shoots pointing downwards or towards the wall or fence.

Cut or pinch back to 5 or 6 leaves any sub-laterals not needed as replacement shoots.

THINNING

Thin out the young shoots to leave them 10–15cm (4–6in) apart. Tie them in to the wires as they develop.

AFTER FRUITING

Using secateurs, cut back to 3 leaves the shoots that were reduced to 6 leaves earlier in the summer.

Sweet cherries (*Prunus avium*)

Sweet cherry trees may grow to a height and spread of 7.5m (25ft) or more and, as most cultivars are self-sterile, two trees are often necessary to produce a crop. There are as yet no reliable dwarfing rootstocks (see p.456) so sweet cherries are best suited to an orchard or large garden. For an average garden, choose a self-fertile cultivar; ideally, this should be fan-trained on a wall or fence, since this restricts its growth and makes it easier to protect the tree from attack by birds and from rain just before picking, which may cause the fruits to split. Sweet cherries have a chilling requirement of 800–1,200 hours below 7°C (45°F).

Duke cherries are thought to be hybrids between the sweet cherry and the acid cherry. They are not very widely grown but where chosen require similar treatment and spacing to sweet cherries. Some Duke cherry cultivars are self-fertile and combinations of acid cherries and Duke cherries are compatible.

Site and planting

Sweet cherries need a warm, sheltered site to produce a good crop. It is important to choose cultivars carefully to make sure that they will pollinate each other; this should be checked before buying trees (see "Pollination requirements", p.424).

ROOTSTOCKS

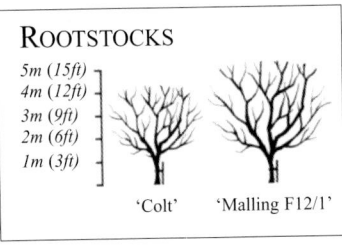

5m (15ft)
4m (12ft)
3m (9ft)
2m (6ft)
1m (3ft)

'Colt'   'Malling F12/1'

RECOMMENDED SWEET CHERRIES

Early
'Early Rivers' Fg1, Ig1, Ss,☆
'Waterloo' Fg2, Ig2,☆

Mid-season
'Merton Bigarreau' Fg3, Ig2,☆
'Merton Glory' Fg2, Ss, Up,☆
'Sunburst' Fg4, Sf

Late
'Bigarreau Gaucher' Fg5, Ss, Up
'Lapins' Fg4, Sf
'Merton Favourite' Fg2, Ig2
'Napoleon Bigarreau' Fg4, Ig3
'Noir de Guben' Fg1, Ss, Up,☆
'Stella' Fg4, Sf,☆

'Stella'

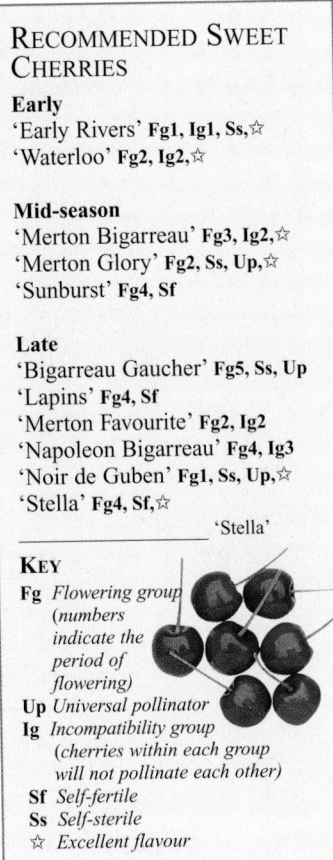

KEY
Fg *Flowering group (numbers indicate the period of flowering)*
Up *Universal pollinator*
Ig *Incompatibility group (cherries within each group will not pollinate each other)*
Sf *Self-fertile*
Ss *Self-sterile*
☆ *Excellent flavour*

Site

Choose an open, sunny, and sheltered site. If the cherry is to be grown as a fan, the support must be at least 2.5m (8ft) high and 5m (15ft) wide, with a reasonably sunny aspect; a tree grown on a cold wall will produce fruit of poor quality and flavour. A good, deep, well-drained soil is essential, as trees grown on shallow, poor soils produce small fruits and are less long-lived.

Rootstocks

'Colt', a semi-dwarfing rootstock, is suitable for bush or fan-trained trees in small gardens. 'Malling F12/1', which is very vigorous, is used where there is space. Two new dwarfing rootstocks, 'Inmil' and 'Camil', are under trial; their longevity and cropping potential are as yet unproven.

Pollination

The pollination requirements of sweet cherries are complex. The majority are self-sterile and they fall into distinct groups within which any combination is incompatible. Unless a self-fertile cultivar is obtained, it is important to choose a pair of trees that are from different groups and that flower at the same time. A few sweet cherries are universal pollinators, that is they will pollinate any cherries that flower at about the same time (see *Recommended Sweet Cherries*, left).

Planting

Sweet cherries should be planted in late autumn or winter if bare-root, or at any time if container-grown.

Construct the necessary supports and wires before planting fan-trained plants. Allow 5–5.5m (15–18ft) between trees that are to be fan-trained and between half-standards.

Routine care

Fruit thinning is unnecessary. Little or no feeding should be needed, apart from mulching as described under "Care of tree fruits", p.426. If growth is poor, apply ammonium sulphate at the standard rate of 35g/sq m (1oz/sq yd). Sweet cherries need thorough watering in dry conditions, but sudden watering on dry soils may cause the fruits to split.

As the fruits begin to colour, protect them from birds by draping netting over fan-trained trees. Bush and half-standard trees are difficult to net, however, so pick fruits as soon as they ripen.

The most likely pests and diseases to afflict sweet cherries are birds (p.657), cherry blackfly (see "Aphids", p.646), winter moth caterpillars (p.645), brown rot (p.658), silver leaf (p.647), and bacterial canker (p.665); cut out any branches with signs of silver leaf or bacterial canker as soon as they are noticed.

Pruning and training

Sweet cherries fruit on spurs on two-year-old and older wood. Mature trees should be pruned in summer to restrict vegetative growth and induce the formation of fruit buds. Train and

prune half-standards and bushes as for plums (see p.448).

Fan

Sweet cherry fans are established as for peaches (see p.453). If there are conveniently placed laterals on a feathered maiden, however, it may be possible to select four rather than two arms to speed up the development of the fan. Tie these arms to canes (attached to wires), which radiate out at 35–45° from the stem. In the spring following planting, prune back the arms to 45–60cm (18–24in) and remove all other laterals that have developed.

During the summer, select two or three well-placed shoots, or "ribs", from each arm and tie them in to fill the available space; remove the remainder. All ribs on the young tree may be tip pruned at bud-burst (but never earlier) to reduce the risk of silver leaf and bacterial canker.

On older fans, spurs may be thinned or shortened in spring (see "Winter pruning", p.438) and ribs pruned to shorter replacement shoots to reduce height. In summer, pinch back all shoots not needed for the framework to six leaves, then to three after fruiting. Upright or very vigorous growths should be removed or tied horizontally to prevent the fan from becoming unbalanced.

Harvesting and storing

Pick fruits when fully ripe, complete with stalks, and eat or cook them immediately. If the fruits are to be frozen (see p.431), pick when firm.

Propagation

Chip- or T-budding are the usual methods of propagation (see pp.432 and 433). 'Colt' rootstocks are compatible with all cultivars, as is the more vigorous 'Malling F12/1' rootstock.

ESTABLISHED SWEET CHERRY FAN, SUMMER PRUNING

Tie in shoots that are needed to replace old ribs or fill bare spaces.

Cut back to 5 or 6 leaves any new growth not needed to extend the fan framework.

AFTER FRUITING

After the crop has been harvested, cut back all the sideshoots that were pruned to 6 leaves in early summer to 3 leaves.

Acid cherries (*Prunus cerasus*)

Acid or sour cherry trees are much smaller than sweet cherries and most cultivars are self-fertile so they are more suitable for the average garden. The fruiting habit also differs in that the crop is mostly borne on one-year-old shoots produced the previous summer. The fruit is not usually eaten raw but is prized for preserves and other culinary uses. Acid cherries have a chilling requirement of 800–1,200 hours below 7°C (45°F).

Site and planting

Site and soil requirements are generally as for sweet cherries (see p.455) except that acid cherries may also be grown successfully against a north- or east-facing wall or fence.

The recommended rootstock, as for sweet and Duke cherries, is 'Colt'. It is best to obtain cultivars such as 'Morello' (the most popular) from a specialist fruit supplier since inferior, less fertile selections exist.

ROOTSTOCK

4m (12ft)
3m (9ft)
2m (6ft)
1m (3ft)

'Colt'

Plant trees to be trained as bushes and fans 4–5m (12–15ft) apart and for fans provide a minimum support height of 2.1m (6½ft).

Routine care

Acid cherries have the same cultivation requirements as sweet cherries (see p.455). Greater attention to feeding, particularly with nitrogen, may be necessary to encourage young, replacement shoots, but do not overfeed. Irrigation is important in dry areas. Netting is essential to protect the fruits from birds (see p.427); since acid cherries may be trained into small tree forms, such as the bush or dwarf pyramid, they may be grown in a fruit cage. Acid cherries are affected by the same pests and diseases as sweet cherries (see "Routine care", p.456).

Pruning and training

Acid cherries are pruned on a renewal system to produce a constant supply of one-year-old wood on which fruit is produced. A proportion of the older wood should be removed each year. Prune trees in spring and summer since this reduces the risk of silver leaf (p.647).

Fan

This is trained as for a peach fan (see p.453). Renewal pruning to encourage young growth once cropping starts is important because of the restricted space. In spring, on an established fan, pinch out badly placed or overcrowded new shoots

---

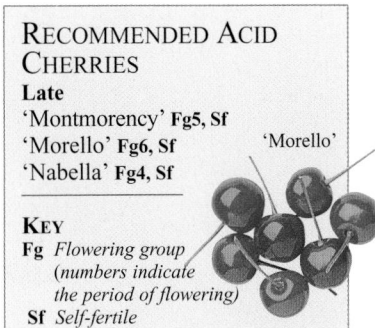

RECOMMENDED ACID CHERRIES

Late
'Montmorency' **Fg5, Sf**
'Morello' **Fg6, Sf**
'Nabella' **Fg4, Sf**

'Morello'

KEY
Fg *Flowering group (numbers indicate the period of flowering)*
Sf *Self-fertile*

---

and thin the rest to leave them 10cm (4in) apart. Tie these into support wires as they develop. Retain one or, where space permits, two developing shoots low down on each fruiting shoot. Tie in one of these to replace each fruiting shoot that is cut out after harvesting. The second shoot may be used as a reserve in case the first is damaged, or to fill a gap in the fan. To rejuvenate older fans, prune back to young shoots on older wood in spring and autumn.

ESTABLISHED ACID CHERRY FAN

SPRING PRUNING

Remove any wrong-pointing, young shoots, cutting them back flush with the stem.

Thin the young, developing shoots to about 10cm (4in) apart, if necessary.

SUMMER PRUNING, AFTER FRUITING

Cut back each fruited shoot to a suitable replacement near its base.

Tie in the replacement shoots to maintain even spacing. These should fruit the following year.

Remove any wrong-pointing shoots that have developed and were not removed in the spring, cutting them back flush with the stem.

ESTABLISHED ACID CHERRY BUSH, PRUNING AFTER FRUITING

Cut back one quarter of the fruited shoots to replacement shoots near the base of each.

Each year, cut back a few older, crossing, or unproductive laterals to replacement shoots.

Bush

The bush is built up as for peach (see p.453). After the third or fourth year, once the bush is established, renewal pruning is essential. In early autumn, after fruiting, cut out one quarter of the fruited shoots, preferably to replacement shoots, to maintain even spacing and leave room for the young growth that will carry the next year's crop. Remove old or unproductive wood at the same time. If pruning is neglected, fruiting will decrease and be restricted to the tree's outer edge.

Harvesting

Cut the stalks with scissors as hand picking may injure the shoots and encourage infection. Cook, freeze, or preserve soon after picking (see "Harvesting and storing", p.431).

Propagation

The most common methods are chip- or T-budding (see pp.372–373). All cultivars are compatible with 'Colt' and 'Malling F12/1' rootstocks.

HARVESTING ACID CHERRIES

Harvest by cutting each stalk close to the lateral, not by pulling as this may damage the bark and increase the risk of bacterial canker.

Persimmons (*Diospyros kaki*)

Persimmons are deciduous, slow-growing trees that will eventually reach a height of 10–15m (30–50ft) and a spread of about 10m (30ft). The fruits are usually globular, and they may be yellow, orange, or red when fully ripe; some cultivars produce seedless fruits.

Outdoor cultivation in subtropical areas with a minimum temperature of 10°C (50°F) is possible, but a range of 16–22°C (61–72°F) during autumn is preferable. Most cultivars have a low chilling requirement of 100–200 hours below 7°C (45°F); in addition, during the active growing season they need at least 1,400 hours of sunshine to fruit successfully.

Site and planting

A sheltered and sunny site is preferable; provide protection with windbreaks, if necessary. A well-drained and fertile soil is essential, with a pH of 6–7; mature trees are relatively drought-resistant, but they require irrigation if there is inadequate rain in the growing season.

PERSIMMON

Vigorous seedlings of *Diospyros kaki* are suitable as rootstocks, but *D. virginiana* is most frequently used for this purpose.

Although some persimmon cultivars have both male and female flowers on the same tree, a number have only one or the other. The most widely grown cultivars have only female flowers; these will produce fruit without pollination but the fruits are small and astringent. A pollinator cultivar, with male flowers, must therefore be grown nearby. A ratio of one pollinator plant to eight or ten female-flowering plants is usually adequate.

In well-manured ground, prepare planting holes; add organic material and general-purpose fertilizer. Trees should be spaced at about 5m (15ft).

Routine care

Apply fertilizer around the trees every three to four months, using a general-purpose mixture with medium nitrogen levels. Conserve moisture in the soil by mulching with organic matter, and water regularly in the dry season. Keep the ground around the trees weed-free.

The major pests that affect persimmons grown in the open are thrips (p.647), mealybugs (p.646), scale insects (p.648), and fruit flies (p.659). Common diseases that may cause problems include crown gall (p.655), anthracnose (p.666), and other fungal leaf spots (p.648).

If cultivating persimmons under cover, pests such as red spider mite (p.646) and whiteflies (p.646) may also be troublesome.

Growing under cover

If growing persimmons in a greenhouse, plant them in prepared beds or in large containers with a minimum diameter of 35cm (14in); use a very fertile compost incorporating a general-purpose fertilizer with medium nitrogen levels. Maintain a temperature of at least 16°C (61°F) and a humidity of 60–70 per cent. Water regularly during the growing season and apply a general-purpose fertilizer every three to four weeks.

It is necessary to pollinate the flowers by hand for a successful fruit set (see *Hand-pollination*, p.451). During the summer, move plants in containers into the open; leave them until the autumn until their chilling requirement has been met.

Pruning and training

Cultivars vary greatly in vigour. Dwarf and semi-dwarf cultivars are usually trained in a similar way to an apple spindlebush (see p.440). Prune trees for the first three years during the dormant season to form a framework. Subsequent pruning should be relatively light: restrict it to the removal of crowded, crossing, or unproductive branches, and to cutting back branch leaders annually by about one third of their new growth.

Harvesting and storing

Pick fruits when they are fully ripe. Cut fruits from the tree, leaving the calyx and a short fruit stalk attached. Seal the fruits in clear plastic bags and store them at 0°C (32°F); they should remain in good condition for up to two months.

RECOMMENDED PERSIMMONS

'Fuyu'
'Gailey' (pollinator)
'Hachiya'

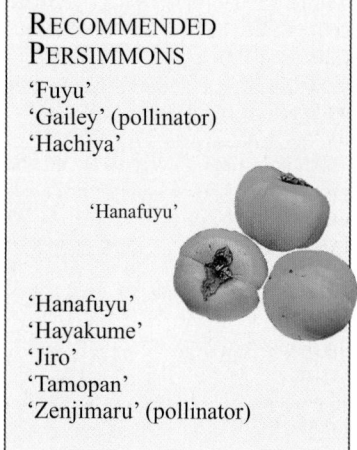

'Hanafuyu'

'Hanafuyu'
'Hayakume'
'Jiro'
'Tamopan'
'Zenjimaru' (pollinator)

Propagation

Persimmon trees may be propagated by seed, by grafting, from cuttings, or from rooted suckers.

Sow seed taken from mature fruits immediately in containers; kept at 28°C (82°F), it usually germinates in two to three weeks. In 12 months, the seedlings provide stocks suitable for grafting. Handle seedlings carefully when transplanting.

Cultivars may be propagated by chip- or T-budding (see pp.432 and 433), or by whip-and-tongue grafting (see p.433). Softwood cuttings (see p.79) taken in summer and treated with hormone rooting powder should root in a mist unit with basal heat.

Rooted suckers may be detached from the base of the parent tree (provided that it has not been budded or grafted). Establish them in containers before planting them out in their final positions.

Figs (*Ficus carica*)

Figs are among the oldest fruits in cultivation, and belong to the family Moraceae. They have a low chilling requirement of 100–300 hours below 7°C (45°F) and thrive in regions with a long, hot growing season.

Site and planting

Figs require a sunny position and in cool areas need a wall or fence for more warmth and protection from frost; this should be at least 3–3.5m (10–11ft) wide by 2.2m (7ft) high.

Figs prefer slightly alkaline, deep, rich, moisture-retentive soils, and a warm, dry climate. Cooler, wetter conditions induce too much growth, with poorer crops. When the pH is less than 6, lime the soil (see p.625).

Where space is limited, a concrete or brick "pit", or box, may be built below soil level to restrict the root system and produce a smaller tree. The pit should be 60cm (2ft) square and have a base that is not solid but filled with broken bricks or stones to a depth of 25–30cm (10–12in); this will provide drainage and restrict root growth downwards.

In cool climates, figs may also be grown in pots placed in a sunny, sheltered site and transferred to cold but frost-free conditions in winter. Use a container 30–38cm (12–15in) in diameter, with several large drainage holes, and filled with a loam-based potting compost.

No specific rootstocks have yet been introduced, and trees are grown on their own roots. Modern cultivars are self-fertile.

Select two-year-old, pot-grown specimens and plant these in winter, teasing the roots gently loose from the soil ball before planting. Unrestricted trees need to be spaced 6–8m (20–25ft) apart; those planted in a pit need only half this spacing.

Routine care

To protect branches carrying the embryo figs from frost, tie a dense layer of bracken or straw around

FRUIT PLACEMENT

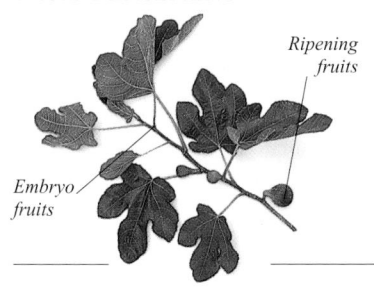

Ripening fruits

Embryo fruits

them (see also FROST AND WIND PROTECTION, *Hessian and Straw Cover*, p.612). At the same time, remove any unripe figs from the previous summer. It may be necessary to protect the ripening fruits against birds and wasps.

Feeding, watering, and mulching

A spring mulch of well-rotted manure is all that is normally required, but trees with restricted roots need extra nutrients. This may be in the form of a balanced fertilizer applied at a rate of 70g/sq m (2oz/sq yd), and supplemented during the summer with occasional liquid feeds. Avoid overfeeding fig trees.

Watering is essential in hot, dry weather, especially where the roots are restricted. Pot-grown figs need regular watering throughout the growing season. Repot and root-prune them every two years.

Pests and diseases

Figs in the open are usually problem-free, but wasps (p.659) and birds (p.657) may attack fruits. Under cover, red spider mite (p.646), mealybugs (p.646), whiteflies (p.646), wasps, (p.659), mice (p.662), and *Nectria* canker (p.664) may be troublesome.

Growing under cover

In cool areas, fan-trained figs may be grown under glass and will crop more regularly than in the open. The roots must be contained to restrict growth. Once growth starts, water regularly but reduce watering as the fruits ripen to prevent the skins splitting. Prune as for figs grown outdoors but leave a more open tree to allow as much light as possible to reach the leaves and fruit.

Pruning and training

In warm climates, figs need only light pruning and are usually grown in bush form. Two crops per season are normally produced, an early one from embryo figs (about the size of small peas) formed late in the previous season, followed by the main crop which is both formed and ripened during the same summer. Meanwhile, further embryo fruits develop to repeat the process.

In cool climates, figs are trained either as open bushes or fans. Only the first crop from embryo figs will have time to ripen. Remove those

ESTABLISHED FIG BUSH
SPRING PRUNING

Cut back frost-damaged shoots to healthy wood and thin out wrong-pointing shoots and any that are overcrowded.

Cut out a proportion of the remaining shoots or, on older trees, branches to 1 bud to promote new growth.

SUMMER PRUNING

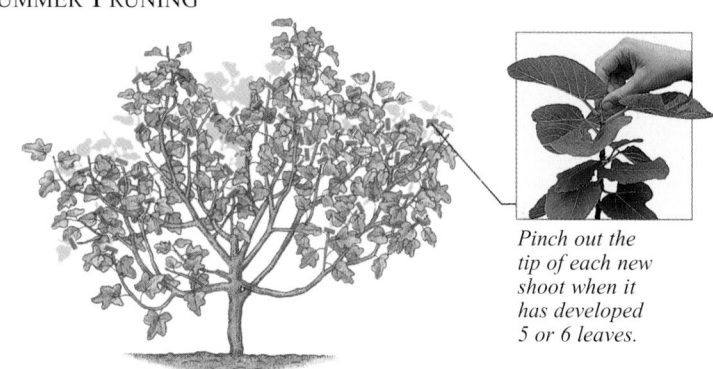

Pinch out the tip of each new shoot when it has developed 5 or 6 leaves.

that do not ripen to concentrate the tree's energies into producing new embryo fruits.

Bush

Purchase a tree with three or four branches arising about 60cm (2ft) above ground. Prune these back by half their length in the first winter to encourage further branches to form and establish a basic framework. Pot-grown trees should branch at 38cm (15in) from the base so that they are compact and not top-heavy.

Pruning of established trees differs with the climate. In warm climates in spring, shorten spreading branches to more vertical shoots and leave some growth in the tree's centre to protect the bark from sun scorch. In cooler climates, remove all crowded, crossing, or frost-damaged branches; keep the centre open by taking out all upright shoots and pruning to buds on the lower sides of branches.

Lengths of bare wood should be cut back to one bud to promote new growth. In the summer, pinch out new shoots or sideshoots to five or six leaves to encourage fruit to form.

Fan

Plant a two-year-old tree with two or three strong shoots. Tie down the two best-placed as for peach fans (see

RECOMMENDED FIGS

Early
'Black Ischia' ☆
'St Johns' ☆
'White Marseilles' ☆

Mid-season
'Brown Turkey'
'Brunswick'
'Negro Largo' ☆

'Brown Turkey'

Late
'Bourjasotte Grise'

KEY
☆ *Excellent flavour*

p.453) and tip prune lightly. Prune back trees without suitable sideshoots to about 40cm (16in) to encourage lateral growth. The fan is then developed as for peaches but with greater space between branches to allow for the fig's larger foliage.

Prune the established fan in early spring to remove old, fruited wood and any that is frost-damaged or badly placed, and leave the younger wood. Also prune back a proportion of younger shoots to one bud to induce fresh growths close to the main branches. Wherever possible, tie in the unpruned shoots to fill any

459

spaces and remove all others. Pinch out the tips of new growths to five leaves in midsummer. The resulting new shoots should then develop embryo fruits for overwintering.

Harvesting and storing

Pick the fruits when fully ripe. Ripe fruits tend to hang down, are very soft to the touch, and may have slight splits in the skin. Figs are best eaten fresh, but may also be dried.

Propagation

Seed-raised plants vary in fruit quality. Hardwood cuttings of one-year-old wood from selected cultivars should be used. Take cuttings (see p.434) 30cm (12in) long and insert them in well-prepared, well-drained ground. Protect them from frost with cloches. Figs may also be propagated by rooted suckers, severed from the parent tree and transplanted.

ESTABLISHED FIG FAN
SPRING PRUNING

Once all risk of frost has passed, cut all frost-damaged shoots back to their point of origin.

Cut back a proportion of young shoots to 1 bud to encourage replacement growth that will produce embryo fruits.

Tie in the shoots so that they are evenly spaced over the fan.

Cut off wrong-pointing shoots to the point of origin or to a well-placed sub-lateral.

Cut back a proportion of old, bare wood to 1 bud or node to promote new growth.

SUMMER PRUNING

Pinch back new shoots to 5 leaves to encourage embryo fruits to form in the leaf axils.

Mulberries (*Morus nigra*)

Mulberries belong to the Moraceae family. Black mulberries reach a height of 6–10m (20–30ft), and are grown for their fruit. White mulberries (*M. alba*) are not usually grown for their fruit. They grow up to 3m (10ft) tall. The chilling requirement is high and the trees begin growth late in the season.

Site and planting
Moist, slightly acid soils are preferable. Mulberries are usually grown on their own roots, and are self-fertile. Plant in late autumn to winter, 8–10m (25–30ft) apart; in cold areas, plant in spring.

Routine care
Cultivation is similar to that of apples (see p.436). Mulch and water in dry weather. Mulberries are mainly untroubled by pests and diseases.

Pruning and training
Mulberries are grown as either half-standards or standards. Prune only to establish a strong framework of four to five branches, and thereafter only remove branches if they are badly placed or crowded. The trees should be pruned when fully dormant in winter since shoots and roots bleed profusely if cut or damaged between early spring and autumn. If bleeding

does occur, cauterize the wounds as quickly as possible with a hot poker or other iron implement.

Harvesting and storing
Pick the fruit when fully ripe in late summer, or allow it to drop onto a suitable temporary surface (such as a sheet of plastic) to keep it clean. Eat mulberries fresh, or freeze them.

Propagation
Mulberries may be propagated by simple or air layering (see p.116) or by hardwood cuttings about 18cm (7in) long, taken with a heel (see p.113), known as "truncheons".

BLACK MULBERRY

Vines

VINES require warm, sheltered positions for successful fertilization, and to ripen their fruits. Grapes, kiwi fruits, and passion fruits all belong to this group. In cool areas, they should be given a sheltered environment or they may be grown under glass. Vines fruit on long, flexible stems of one-year-old wood and need to be pruned after fruiting each year to encourage them to produce a supply of new shoots; these grow rapidly and need to be carefully trained into their supports so that they receive the maximum amount of light and air.

Black dessert grapes

White dessert grapes

Kiwi fruits

Grapes (*Vitis vinifera*)

Through the ages grapes have traditionally been one of the choicest fruits for eating or for wine-making. The European grape (*Vitis vinifera*) and its cultivars are generally considered to be of the highest quality. The American grape (*V. labrusca*) tolerates colder climates and has been hybridized with *V. vinifera* to widen the choice in cooler climates of cultivars for dessert and wine grapes. Many cultivars are suitable for both dessert and wine use.

The fruits need a hot, dry summer to ripen. Warm-temperate regions suit a wide range of cultivars; many may be grown successfully in cooler climates, however, in protected sites or in greenhouses. Decorative pergolas, arches, or other suitable structures may support vines. Pruning methods vary: vines grown for dessert grapes are pruned to produce fewer, higher-quality fruits; vines grown for wine grapes are pruned to obtain the greatest quantity of fruits.

Dessert grapes

It is comparatively easy to produce high-quality dessert grapes in warm areas. In cooler climates, they may be grown against a sunny, warm wall or, preferably, in a greenhouse. Dessert grapes are usually divided into sweetwater, muscat, and vinous groups. Sweetwater are sweet grapes, ripening earliest; muscats have the finest flavour and are second to mature; vinous grapes tend to have less flavour, but are strong-growing and crop late. Vines are usually self-fertile and wind-pollinated, but hand-pollination is advised when growing them under glass (see right).

Site

A warm, sheltered, sunny site free from frosts at flowering time is ideal. Vines need a reasonably fertile, well-drained soil, with a pH of 6–7.5. Avoid planting them on very rich soil as this encourages excess growth at the expense of fruits. Sharp drainage is essential as grapes will not tolerate wet soils; improve the soil or install a drainage system if necessary (for details, see SOILS AND FERTILIZERS, "Improving drainage", p.623).

In cool climates, vines grown on a warm, sunny wall give reasonably good results but will not match the quality of vines grown under glass. Early-ripening cultivars should be used for wall cultivation to obtain dessert fruits by late summer. Support vines with horizontal wires, held in place by vine eyes, 2.5–5cm (1–2in) from the wall.

Vines are usually grown on their own roots, except in areas where *Phylloxera* is a hazard (see "Pests and diseases", right); in this case, seek local advice on which rootstock to use. The use of a rootstock may have other advantages, too, such as greater tolerance of a high pH or wet soil conditions, and control of overvigorous growth.

Planting

Cultivate the soil thoroughly before planting. In poor or sandy soils, incorporate upturned turves at the foot of the planting trench, adding ample, well-rotted manure or compost, then firm the area and water well. Plant bare-root vines in winter but containerized specimens may be planted at any season. Space single cordons at least 1.2m (4ft) apart, double or "U" cordons at twice that spacing; the arms of multiple cordons should be 60cm (24in) apart.

Routine care

Water thoroughly during the growing season whenever conditions are dry, reducing watering as the fruit ripens. Particular care is needed with grapes grown on a wall, since they may be in a rain shadow. Mulch to retain moisture. Once vigorous young shoots develop, feed with a high-potash fertilizer every two or three weeks; if growth is poor, give high nitrogen instead. Stop feeding as soon as the fruits start to ripen.

If using the cordon system, retain no more than one bunch per 30cm (12in) of vertical stem, or rod, for best-quality grapes; remove intermediate bunches at an early stage. Thin the fruits to obtain both well-shaped bunches and large, evenly sized grapes (and to discourage mildew). Do not touch the fruits themselves since this may spoil their bloom. Some cultivars need a second thinning as the fruits develop further.

Pests and diseases

Vines are affected by problems such as scale insects (p.648), vine weevil (p.645), wasps (p.659), downy mildew (p.646), and grey mould (*Botrytis*) (p.658). Under cover, red spider mite (p.646), whiteflies (p.646), mealybugs (p.646), and powdery mildew (p.658) may also be troublesome.

Vine *Phylloxera* is a serious pest in warmer climates, where this aphid-like insect attacks the roots of European vines; galls may also form on the leaves. The attack causes severe stunting and is often fatal. Little treatment is available, although the use of resistant rootstocks and resistant hybrids of American grape cultivars has greatly reduced its incidence. Net vines to protect them against birds (see "Protection from birds", p.427).

Growing under cover

In cool climates, grow vines in a greenhouse, preferably with heating. Other crops with compatible temperature and humidity requirements may also be grown in the greenhouse. In a lean-to greenhouse, the warmth from the back wall is particularly beneficial, especially if there is little or no direct heating. Greenhouses with both top- and side-ventilation give the best results.

The soil must be fairly fertile, weed-free, and well drained, with a pH of 6–7.5. Any drainage must be 75cm (2½ft) deep as vines are deep-rooted. Plant as for vines in the open.

Either train vines directly onto the back wall or plant them at the foot of the glass wall, training them on support wires that are 22cm (9in) or more from the glass. In freestanding houses, plant vines at one end, then train up and along the roof on wires. For details of cultivation, see "Routine care", above. A soil auger may be used to gauge levels of moisture in the soil; use tepid water for the first waterings of the season.

Control ventilation carefully; keep it at a maximum in winter to ensure adequate winter chilling of the vines.

THINNING GRAPES

1 *Once the bunches have been thinned to 30cm (12in) apart, the fruits will need thinning as they swell to increase the size of individual grapes and allow air circulation between them.*

2 *Use a forked cane and vine scissors to expose portions of the bunch and snip off unwanted grapes. The thinned bunch should be wide at the top and tapering towards the base.*

RECOMMENDED DESSERT GRAPES

Early
'Angers Frontignan' (black) **Vi**
'Ascot Citronelle' (white) **Mu**
'Auvergne Frontignan' (white) **Mu**
'Black Frontignan' (black) **Mu**
'Cardinal' (black) **Sw**
'Chasselas Rose' (white) **Sw**
'Chasselas Vibert' (white) **Sw**
'Ciotat' (white) **Sw**
'Foster's Seedling' (white) **Sw**

'Foster's Seedling'

'Gagarin Blue' (black) **Vi**
'Gamay Hatif' (black) **Sw**
'Himrod Seedless' (golden) **Sw**
'King's Ruby' (black) **Sw**
'Lady Hastings' (black) **Mu**
'Madeline Royale' (white) **Sw**
'Madresfield Court' (black) **Mu**
'Perle de Czaba' (white) **Mu**
'Primavis Frontignan' (white) **Mu**
'Roem van Boskoop' (black) **Sw**
'Royal Muscadine' (white) **Mu**
'St Laurent' (white) **Mu**
'Thompson's Seedless' (white) **Sw**

Mid-season
'Black Monukka' (black) **Mu**
'Canon Hall Muscat' (white) **Mu**
'Grizzley Frontignan' (white) **Mu**
'Madeira Frontignan' (black) **Mu**
'Muscat Bleu' (black) **Mu**
'Muscat Hamburgh' (black) **Mu**
'New York Muscat' (white) **Mu**
'Oliver Irsay' (white) **Mu**
'Reine Olga' (black) **Sw**

Late
Late-ripening cultivars ripen outside only in areas with reliably warm summers.
'Alicante' (black) **Vi**

'Alicante'

'Appley Towers' (black) **Vi**
'Mrs Pearson' (white) **Mu**
'Mrs Pince's Black Muscat' (black) **Mu**
'Muscat of Alexandria' (white) **Mu**
'Trebbiano' (white) **Vi**

'Muscat of Alexandria'

KEY
Mu *Muscat*
Sw *Sweetwater*
Vi *Vinous*

Reduce to a minimum in late winter to induce growth. Vary the amount according to the weather to maintain even temperatures. Slight ventilation is always advisable and adequate warmth is needed at flowering to aid pollination. Pollination requires extra attention under glass. With many cultivars, a shake of the rod around midday, or sharp tap with a stick, is usually sufficient to ensure pollination. Muscat grapes need more positive treatment. This entails running cupped hands down and over the blossom trusses to allow adequate pollen distribution. After fruit set, good air circulation is needed to control grey mould (*Botrytis*) and mildew.

Damping down and mist-spraying help control red spider mite. Do not damp down on dull days, or during flowering or ripening periods.

Fork over the bed carefully in late winter, avoiding the root area; remove 1cm (½in) of soil from the surface and replace it with loam-based compost. After the first watering, mulch with well-rotted manure or compost around the base of the vines.

Once the fruits ripen, they need a "finishing period" during which they remain on the vine to attain maximum colour and flavour: allow two to three weeks for early cultivars, and longer for late-ripening ones. Provide good ventilation, netting ventilators to exclude birds if these are a problem.

Pruning and training
The usual method for dessert grapes is to develop single or double ("U") cordons or rods on which permanent fruiting spurs are formed. These produce high-quality fruits.

Vines fruit on the current season's growth. Spring and summer pruning, therefore, is aimed at restricting new growth from the rods so that one bunch of grapes develops from each spur. It also restricts the growth of foliage sufficiently to expose the developing fruit to sun, particularly in cool climates. In hot climates, take particular care that sun scorch does not occur on the vine. Carry out winter pruning before midwinter to restrict sap-bleeding.

Single cordon After planting, while the vine is dormant, shorten the stem to a strong bud a few centimetres above the ground. In summer, train one leading shoot onto a vertical bamboo cane and pinch or cut back any laterals to five or six leaves. Shorten all the sub-laterals (shoots that are growing from the laterals)

GRAPE, SINGLE CORDON
YEAR 1, WINTER PRUNING

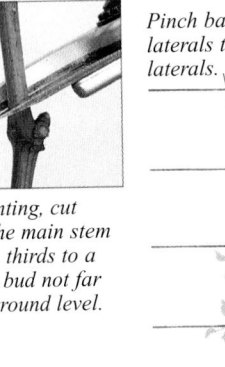

At planting, cut back the main stem by two thirds to a strong bud not far from ground level.

YEAR 1, SUMMER PRUNING

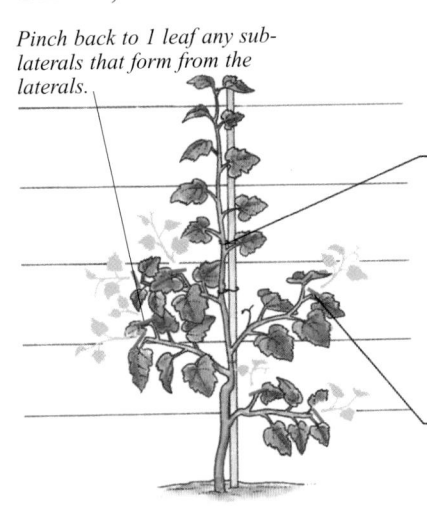

Pinch back to 1 leaf any sub-laterals that form from the laterals.

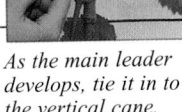

As the main leader develops, tie it in to the vertical cane.

Cut back each of the main laterals to 5 or 6 leaves.

YEAR 2, WINTER PRUNING

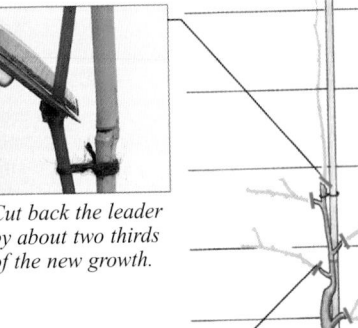

Cut back the leader by about two thirds of the new growth.

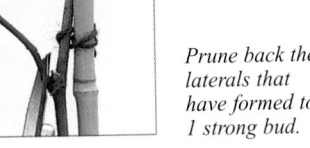

Prune back the laterals that have formed to 1 strong bud.

YEAR 2, SUMMER PRUNING

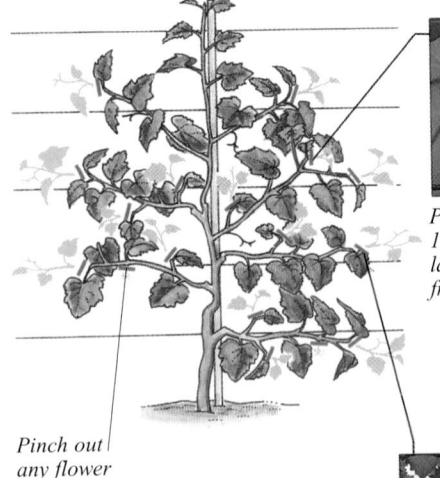

Pinch back to 1 leaf any sub-laterals that form from the laterals.

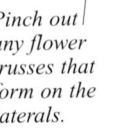

Pinch out any flower trusses that form on the laterals.

Cut back each lateral when it has reached 5 or 6 leaves.

back to one leaf. Remove any shoots that develop from the base.

During the second winter, reduce the leader by two thirds of the new growth to well-ripened wood and prune laterals back to one bud. In the second summer, tie in the leading shoot as it extends. Pinch or cut sideshoots back to five or six leaves and sub-laterals to one leaf, as for the first summer. Remove any flower trusses; do not allow the vine to fruit until the third year.

In the third winter, shorten the leading shoot by two thirds of its new growth and cut back all the laterals to one strong bud to create spurs that will bear fruiting shoots.

Routine pruning Carry out routine pruning from the third year onwards. In spring, let two shoots grow at each spur and pinch out others. Retain the

stronger of the two for fruiting, and pinch back the weaker to two leaves, keeping it as a replacement in case the fruiting shoot breaks. In summer, as flower trusses develop, retain the best, pruning out the others to leave one per lateral. Stop laterals at two leaves beyond the chosen flower trusses. Pinch out laterals not carrying flowers at about five leaves and any sub-laterals at one leaf.

Each winter continue to remove two thirds of the new growth from the leader, but when it has reached the top of its support cut it back annually to two buds. Cut laterals to one strong bud. If spur systems become congested in later years, either remove part of the system with a pruning saw or, if there are too many spurs on the rod, remove some of them completely. The spurs should

be 22–30cm (9–12in) apart. The rod should be untied from its wires to about halfway down its length and bent over until nearly horizontal for a few weeks during winter to encourage the even development of shoots the following spring; then retie the rod vertically.

Double cordon This may be formed by training in two shoots horizontally in the first summer. Prune each back to 60cm (2ft) the following winter. The next year, train the extension growths vertically. These form two vertical arms; prune each arm as a single cordon.

Multiple cordon Train in two shoots in the first summer and in winter prune each back to 60cm (2ft). Train the extension growths horizontally, and choose a strong shoot every 60cm (2ft) to train vertically in order

HARVESTING DESSERT GRAPES

Avoid touching the fruits and spoiling the bloom. Cut each bunch complete with a "handle" consisting of 5cm (2in) of woody stem from either side of the bunch.

YEAR 3, WINTER PRUNING

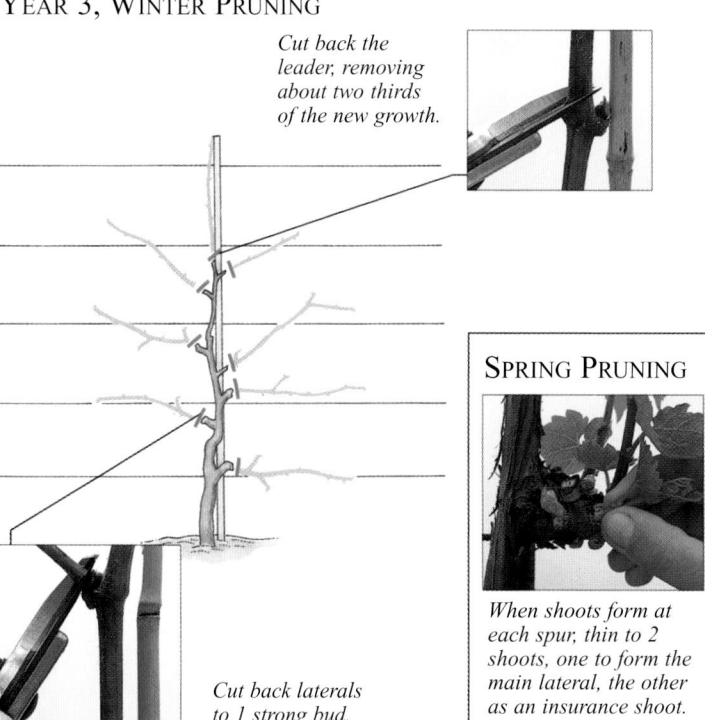

Cut back the leader, removing about two thirds of the new growth.

Cut back laterals to 1 strong bud.

SPRING PRUNING

When shoots form at each spur, thin to 2 shoots, one to form the main lateral, the other as an insurance shoot.

ESTABLISHED SINGLE CORDON, SUMMER PRUNING

If any lateral is not fruiting, cut back the tip to 5 or 6 leaves.

Cut all fruiting laterals back to 2 leaves beyond the flower truss.

Pinch back any sub-laterals that form on the laterals to 1 leaf.

Pinch out any weak flower trusses to leave no more than 1 per lateral.

ESTABLISHED SINGLE CORDON, WINTER PRUNING

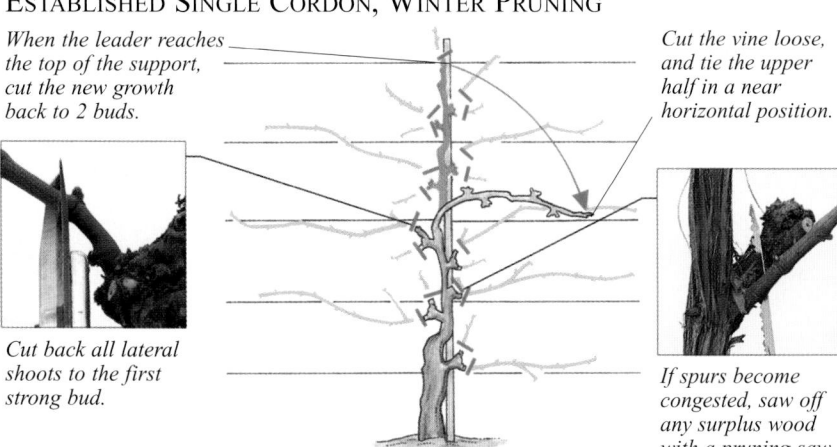

When the leader reaches the top of the support, cut the new growth back to 2 buds.

Cut the vine loose, and tie the upper half in a near horizontal position.

Cut back all lateral shoots to the first strong bud.

If spurs become congested, saw off any surplus wood with a pruning saw.

MULTIPLE CORDON

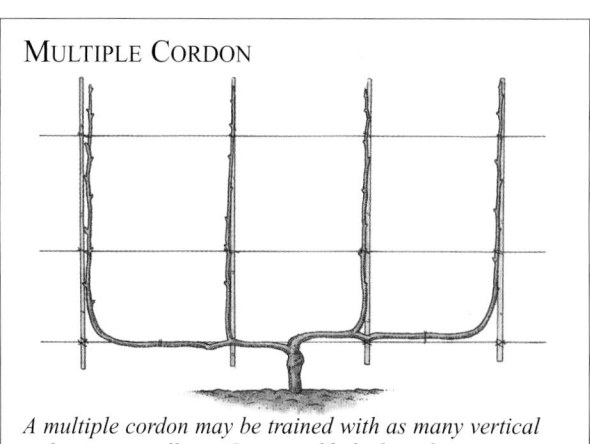

A multiple cordon may be trained with as many vertical rods as space allows. Once established, each arm is pruned in the same way as a single cordon.

'Siegerrebe'

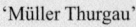

'Müller Thurgau'

'Black
Hamburgh'

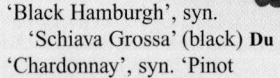

to form the number of arms required. Once established, prune each arm as a single cordon.

Alternative pruning methods Some cultivars will not produce adequate fruit-bearing shoots from the basal buds left by spur pruning. In such cases, longer lengths of ripened wood, or canes, are retained when winter pruning the buds from which fruit-bearing shoots will be produced. Other canes are cut back to three or four buds to produce strong new growths to replace the old fruiting canes the following winter. This process is repeated annually. Many other renewal systems may also be used to train dessert grapes (for details on the double Guyot system, see "Pruning and training: Guyot system", p.465).

Harvesting and storing
Tie back or remove some of the foliage to allow more sun to reach the ripening fruits. Cut ripe bunches from the vine with a short piece of woody stem – the "handle" – and place in a container with soft lining so that the fruits are not damaged and their bloom is not spoiled.

Bunches may be stored for a week or two at room temperature by cutting a longer handle and placing this in a narrow-necked container of water, with the fruit hanging down on the outside of the container.

Propagation
Vines may be propagated by hardwood cuttings or grafting (for details, see "Wine grapes: Propagation", p.466, and "Bud-grafting", p.432).

Wine grapes

Grapes may be grown for wine in areas with long, dry, sunny summers and adequate soil moisture. In cooler climates, early- and mid-season cultivars grown on warm walls or under cover give good results.

Site and planting
Most well-drained soils with a pH of 6–7.5 are suitable. Clear weeds before planting. Rootstocks are as for dessert grapes (see "Dessert grapes: Site", p.461). The flowers are usually self-fertile, and are wind-pollinated. Before planting, erect a row of support posts. Fix a single wire 38cm (15in) above the ground and double wires at 75cm and 1.2m (30in and 4ft). Each of the double

GRAPE, DOUBLE GUYOT
YEAR 1, WINTER PRUNING

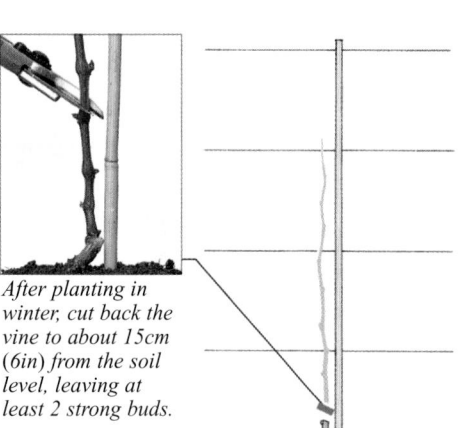

After planting in winter, cut back the vine to about 15cm (6in) from the soil level, leaving at least 2 strong buds.

YEAR 1, SUMMER PRUNING

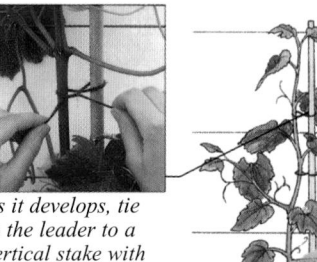

As it develops, tie in the leader to a vertical stake with a loose figure-of-eight knot.

Prune any laterals that develop back to 5 leaves.

Remove any competing shoots developing below the main leader.

YEAR 2, WINTER PRUNING

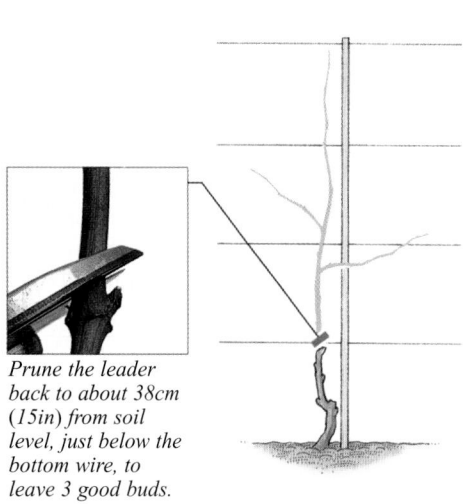

Prune the leader back to about 38cm (15in) from soil level, just below the bottom wire, to leave 3 good buds.

YEAR 2, SUMMER PRUNING

Cut back any other shoots flush with the stem.

Allow 3 main shoots to develop; tie them loosely to a central stake by looping string around all 3 shoots and the stake.

wires is looped round the posts to form a figure of eight. Plant one- or two-year-old vines in winter, 1.5–2m (5–6ft) apart, in rows 2m (6ft) apart.

Routine care

Remove any weeds, and water to establish young vines in dry conditions; water cropping vines only in drought conditions since too much water reduces grape quality. Give a light, annual, early spring application of a balanced fertilizer, and apply sulphate of potash in alternate years. Use a foliar spray of magnesium sulphate to correct deficiencies of magnesium (see p.651). Mulch every other year with plenty of well-rotted compost, or annually if the soil quality is poor. Fruit size is not important for wine quality so thinning is only necessary in cold areas, to improve sugar levels.

Pruning and training

Some cultivars need spur pruning (see "Dessert grapes: Pruning and training", p.462); many, however, require annual replacement of old canes to fruit regularly.

Guyot system This is widely used for wine grapes, since it produces a prolific crop in a limited space. It involves annual training of horizontal rods from which fruiting shoots are trained vertically. In the double

YEAR 3, WINTER PRUNING

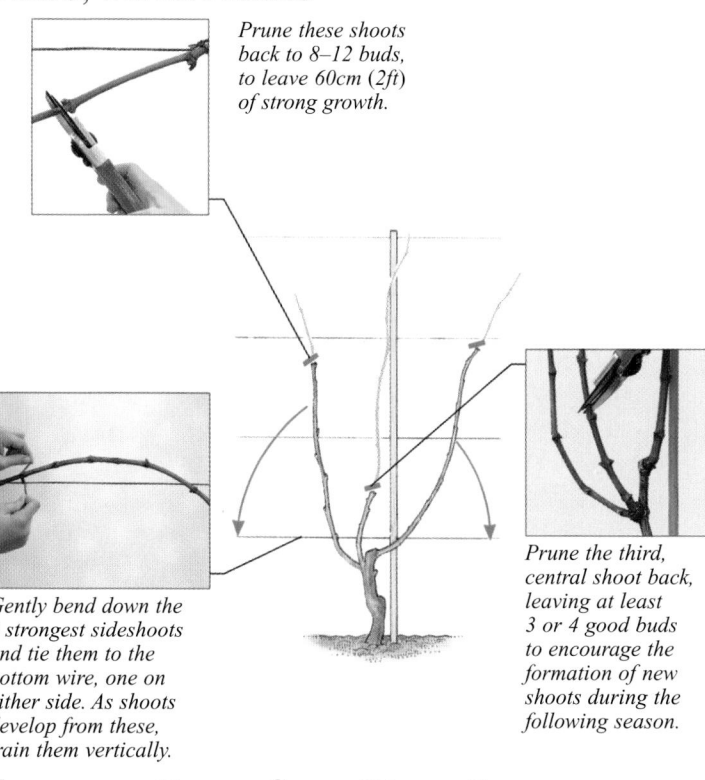

Prune these shoots back to 8–12 buds, to leave 60cm (2ft) of strong growth.

Gently bend down the 2 strongest sideshoots and tie them to the bottom wire, one on either side. As shoots develop from these, train them vertically.

Prune the third, central shoot back, leaving at least 3 or 4 good buds to encourage the formation of new shoots during the following season.

YEAR 3, SUMMER PRUNING

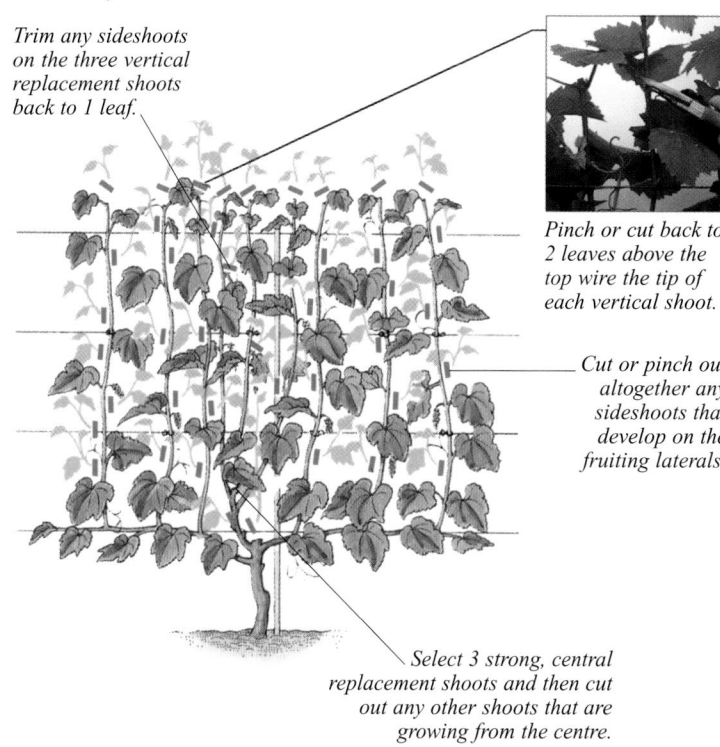

Trim any sideshoots on the three vertical replacement shoots back to 1 leaf.

Pinch or cut back to 2 leaves above the top wire the tip of each vertical shoot.

Cut or pinch out altogether any sideshoots that develop on the fruiting laterals.

Select 3 strong, central replacement shoots and then cut out any other shoots that are growing from the centre.

ESTABLISHED DOUBLE GUYOT, WINTER PRUNING

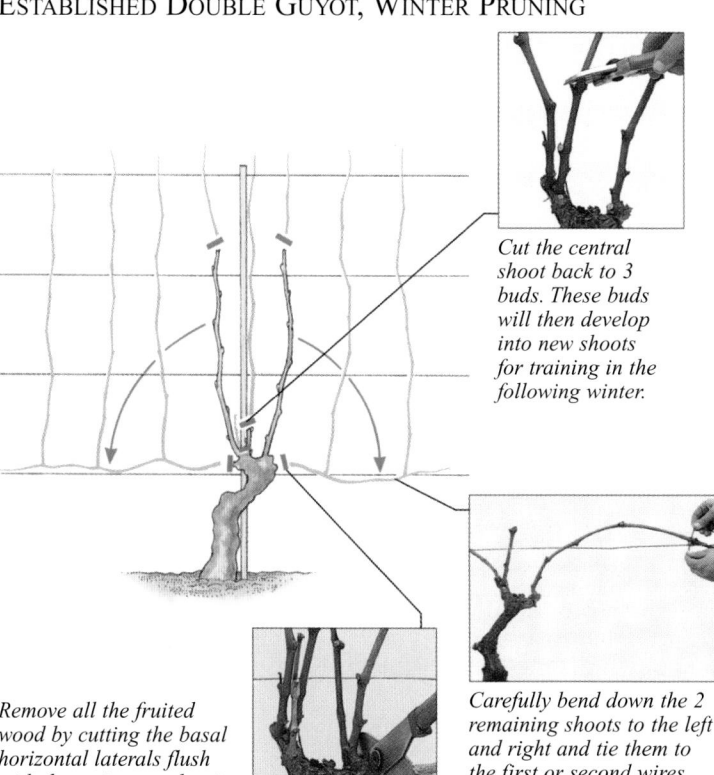

Cut the central shoot back to 3 buds. These buds will then develop into new shoots for training in the following winter.

Remove all the fruited wood by cutting the basal horizontal laterals flush with the main stem, leaving the 3 replacement shoots.

Carefully bend down the 2 remaining shoots to the left and right and tie them to the first or second wires. Tip prune to 8–12 buds.

ESTABLISHED DOUBLE GUYOT, SUMMER PRUNING

Pinch out the tips of the vertical fruiting shoots, 2 leaves above the top wire.

Pinch or cut back to 1 leaf any sideshoots that have been produced on the 3 vertical replacement shoots.

Cut out overcrowded shoots that are either likely to obscure the developing fruits or are surplus to requirements.

Pinch out completely any sideshoots on fruiting shoots.

Guyot two rods on each plant are trained in this way, in the single Guyot system only one.

To train a vine by the double Guyot system, cut it back during the first winter to two strong buds above ground level. In the first summer, let one shoot develop and tie it to a vertical cane or wires. Remove other

REMOVING FOLIAGE

When the grapes are developing, cut off any leaves that shade the ripening fruit directly. Do not remove too many as this may cause scorch from excess sunlight.

HARVESTING WINE GRAPES

Bunches of wine grapes may be harvested simply by cutting the stalk with secateurs.

low shoots and cut any laterals to five leaves. In the second winter, cut back to just under the lowest wire, making sure that there are at least three strong buds remaining.

The next summer, let three strong shoots develop and tie them in vertically. Remove low shoots. In the third winter, tie down two of the shoots to the bottom wire, one on either side. Tip prune these to eight to twelve buds; they will produce fruiting shoots the following summer. Cut the third shoot back to three or four buds to produce replacement shoots, so that the whole process may be repeated. (For the single Guyot system allow two shoots to develop; tie down one and cut back the other.)

During the third summer, select three of the best central shoots growing from the rod and tie loosely to a central post or cane; cut out other, weaker, central shoots. Pinch back to one leaf any sideshoots that form on the three replacements. Train the shoots from the two arms vertically through the parallel wires. If growth is strong, allow a few bunches of grapes to develop on them. Pinch or cut out shoot tips at two leaves above the top wire; remove any sideshoots on the fruiting shoots.

Routine pruning For winter pruning, cut out all old, fruited wood leaving only three replacement shoots. Tie two of these down, one on either side, and tip prune as for the third winter. Prune the third shoot to three strong buds. Routine summer pruning and training of replacement shoots is as for the third summer. Cut out any overcrowded shoots obscuring the fruits. Remove any leaves shading the grapes six weeks before they are expected to ripen.

Harvesting
Cut the bunches from the vines with secateurs; the grapes should be fully ripe and completely dry.

Propagation
Propagate from hardwood cuttings prepared in winter when pruning, using wood from the hardened base of one-year-old shoots. To plant in the open, take sections about 20cm (8in) long, trimming above and below a bud, and insert the cuttings 15cm (6in) deep in sandy soil.

Under cover it is possible to use shorter one- or two-bud cuttings. Grow these singly in 9cm (3½in) pots or insert five cuttings in a 21cm (8in) pot. Place the pots in a cold frame. Pot on each young rooted plant the following summer.

HARDWOOD CUTTINGS

Trim the stems into lengths of about 20cm (8in), making an angled cut above a bud at the top and a flat cut below a bud at the base. Insert the cuttings to two thirds their length into a trench in sandy soil.

TWO-BUD CUTTINGS

1 *While pruning at leaf fall, trim off a long section of ripened wood from the current season's growth. Then remove any leaves or tendrils remaining.*

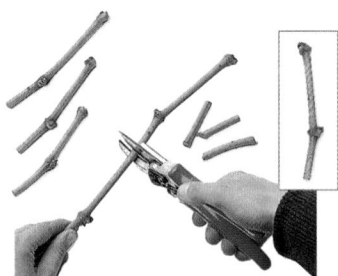

2 *Divide the stem into cuttings with 2 buds, with an angled cut above the top bud and a horizontal cut between 2 nodes below the lower bud. Remove a 1cm (½in) length of rind above the lower cut.*

3 *Insert cuttings in a compost of 2 parts peat, 1 part loam, and 1 part sand, the lower bud just below the surface. Label, water, and place in a greenhouse.*

4 *When the cuttings have rooted, they should be potted on individually into 10cm (4in) pots to grow on.*

Kiwi fruits (*Actinidia deliciosa*)

Deciduous trailing climbers, kiwi fruits were originally known as Chinese gooseberries. The vines will grow up to 9m (28ft) in length. The berries have a hairy, brown skin and green pulp, with small, black seeds.

Warm, moist conditions are preferable during the growing season, the optimum temperature range being 5–25°C (41–77°F). Dormant plants will, however, tolerate several degrees of frost and require chilling for a period of at least 400 hours below 7°C (45°F) to encourage good flower production.

Site and planting
Kiwi fruits can only be grown in the open in sunny, sheltered areas, since plants in growth are sensitive to adverse weather conditions. The soil should be well-aerated, deep, and rich in organic matter, with a pH of 6–7. Incorporate a general-purpose fertilizer into the site at a rate of 50–110g (2–4oz) per plant.

Kiwi fruits are dioecious, with plants bearing either male or female flowers. One male is needed for every eight or nine female plants to ensure adequate fertilization.

Erect a post and wire support, with wires at 30cm (12in) intervals. Plant either rooted cuttings or grafted plants 4–5m (12–15ft) apart in rows 4–6m (12–18ft) apart, staking the vines until they are tall enough to reach the supporting wires.

Routine care
Mulch the plants heavily and apply a general-purpose fertilizer rich in phosphate and potassium. Water regularly, particularly in prolonged dry periods. Keep rows weed-free. Fruit thinning is rarely necessary.

RECOMMENDED KIWI FRUITS

'Abbot' **F**
'Allison' **F**
'Bruno' **F**
'Hayward' **F**
'Montgomery' **F**
'Saanichton' **F**
'Tomuri' **M**
'Vincent' **F**

'Bruno'

KEY
F *Female*
M *Male*

HOW TO SUPPORT KIWI FRUIT

A common method is to train the plants as espaliers on horizontal wires with two main laterals per plant arising from the main stem, with fruiting laterals (see inset) at intervals of about 50cm (20in).

Plants grown in the open may be liable to root rot (see *Phytophthora* root rots, p.661). Under cover they may be infested with thrips (p.647), scale insects (p.648), and root-knot eelworms (p.660). Fruit rots may also occur as a result of infection of the petals. Infection spreads to the fruits, which then drop early. The spread of the disease is promoted by high humidity. Spraying flowers at petal fall with thiram or a similar fungicide gives reasonable control.

Growing under cover

This is rarely practicable due to the long, trailing growth of the plants; in exposed conditions, however, plants grown in the open may be protected from excessive wind and hail by a light plastic screening material.

Kiwi fruits may be grown in walk-in polytunnels if the appropriate environmental conditions can be provided. Soil preparation and cultivation details are the same as for plants grown in the open.

Pruning and training

Commercial crops are often grown on a "T" bar or overhead pergola structure. Another commonly used system is to train plants as espaliers on horizontal wires: each plant then has two main laterals arising from the main stem, and fruiting branches at intervals of 50cm (20in). For details, see "Apple: Espalier", p.442.

The fruits are produced on one-year-old wood only, so all fruited sideshoots should be cut back to two to four buds in the dormant season.

Harvesting and storing

Kiwi fruits start to bear fruit three to four years after planting. Harvest them as they soften. Snap or cut them from the branch, with the calyx attached; keep them cool. If wrapped in plastic film, fruits store for several months at 0°C (32°F).

Propagation

Both soft- and hardwood cuttings may be rooted successfully. Softwood cuttings should be taken in spring; trim to 10–15cm (4–6in) and insert in cutting compost (see p.434). Hardwood cuttings are taken in late summer; these should be 20–30cm (8–12in) long and inserted in sandy compost (see p.434).

Selected cultivars may also be grafted onto vigorous seedling stocks; the most common methods are T-budding and whip-and-tongue grafting (see p.433).

Passion fruits (*Passiflora* spp.)

Passion fruits are climbing plants, with individual stems reaching many metres in length. The globular fruits are either purple or yellow when ripe, and may be up to 7cm (3in) in diameter. The two species most commonly grown for their fruits are the yellow-fruited *P. edulis* f. *flavicarpa* and the purple *P. edulis*.

The optimum temperature range for the purple passion fruit is about 20–28°C (68–82°F). The yellow passion fruit prefers temperatures over 24°C (75°F) and does not tolerate frost; purple types may withstand frost for short periods. Moderate to high humidity is required for satisfactory growth.

Site and planting

Select a sunny site, protected by windbreaks, if necessary. Soils may vary in type but must be well drained, with a pH of about 6.

Cross-pollination by insects, normally bees, is usual, but hand-pollination may be necessary in wet weather; hand-pollination has been found to increase the yield of plants that are grown in the open.

Passion fruits require support, in the form of a wire trellis. Before planting, insert stout uprights, 3m (10ft) long, at intervals of 4m (12ft) each way. Link adjoining uprights in rows by tying with one or two strands of wire.

Take care to prepare the planting holes thoroughly, adding both organic material and a general-purpose fertilizer with medium to high levels of nitrogen. Establish the plants at about 3–4m (10–12ft) apart each way, or less if only a few plants are grown. The yellow form is usually planted 3m (10ft) apart each way.

Routine care

Apply a general-purpose fertilizer that has a medium to high nitrogen content at a rate of 0.5–1kg (1–2lb) per plant per year, preferably in equal dressings at intervals of three to four months. Apply an organic mulch in spring, and weed and water regularly during the dry season.

Pests affecting plants in the open as well as under cover include fruit flies (p.659), aphids (p.646), red spider mite (p.646), and various scale insects (p.648). Root-knot eelworms (p.660) and *Fusarium* wilt (p.654) may also be serious in some subtropical areas. "Woodiness" is caused by cucumber mosaic virus (see "Viruses", p.659), which is transmitted by aphids. As passion fruit vines are susceptible to eelworms and various wilt diseases, replace the plants every five or six years with healthy seedlings, rooted cuttings, or grafted plants.

Growing under cover

This is possible in temperate areas, but fruits may not be produced unless the optimum temperatures and conditions are provided; hand-pollination is generally necessary. Provide wire supports as for outdoor plants. Grow plants either in prepared beds or in large containers at least 35cm (14in) in diameter. Use a well-drained, fertile compost with

PASSION FRUITS

a high organic content and incorporate a general-purpose fertilizer into the compost before planting. Maintain a minimum temperature of 20°C (68°F) and humidity of 60–70 per cent. Apply a liquid feed or a general-purpose fertilizer at monthly intervals, and water regularly.

Pruning and training

Train two main growing stems along the wires to form a permanent framework. If these have not produced laterals by the time they are 60–90cm (2–3ft) long, pinch out their tips. Allow the lateral shoots, on which the fruits will be produced, to hang down as they develop each spring. Prune these laterals so that they are never less than 15cm (6in) from the soil. Once the plant is established, each winter cut back the current season's fruited shoots as these will not bear fruit again.

Harvesting and storing

Pick fruits when they begin to change colour, from green to either purple or yellow. The fruits should be ripe 8–12 weeks after fruit set depending on the cultivar. Fruits may be stored for up to 21 days if maintained at an even temperature of at least 6–7°C (43–45°F) and at a constant humidity level of 85–90 per cent.

Propagation

This is usually by sowing seed or raising cuttings; passion fruits may also be propagated by bud-grafting.

Seed may be extracted from the fully ripe fruits, and should be fermented for three to four days, then washed and dried. Sow the seed under cover in trays or 7–9cm (3–3½in) pots of seed compost, and keep at a temperature of at least 20°C (68°F). When the germinated seedlings are 20–35cm (8–14in) tall, transplant them to open ground, after hardening off, or grow them on under cover.

Cuttings 15–20cm (6–8in) long should be prepared and inserted into a tray or pot filled with cutting compost. Apply bottom heat and mist-spray to encourage rooting.

For details of bud-grafting, see p.432. Healthy bud-grafted plants should be transplanted into their permanent positions to grow on when approximately 15cm (6in) tall.

If eelworms or wilt diseases are a serious problem, the purple cultivars may be grafted onto resistant rootstocks. Vigorous seedlings of the yellow-fruited type are normally used for this purpose.

Soft fruits

Blackberries

Yellow raspberries

Blueberries

Strawberries

Boysenberries

Redcurrants

Raspberries

Aᴌᴌ the usually cultivated soft fruits are bush or cane fruits, except for strawberries, which are herbaceous perennials. Bush fruits include blueberries, gooseberries, and black-, red-, and whitecurrants. Cane fruits include blackberries, hybrid berries, and raspberries. All produce succulent fruits that are eaten fresh, or preserved, bottled, or frozen. Most soft fruits grow best in cool climates. They prefer a well-drained, moisture-retentive, and fertile soil. A sunny site is best and gives fine-quality fruit, but in most cases a little shade is tolerated. Almost all cultivars are self-fertile. Pruning methods depend on whether fruit is produced on one-year-old wood, on older wood and spurs, or on both.

Strawberries (*Fragaria* x *ananassa*)

Strawberries are low-growing, herbaceous plants that may be grown in most gardens, either in the open ground or in containers. There are three distinct types of strawberry plant: summer-fruiting, perpetual-fruiting, and alpine.

Summer-fruiting strawberries produce nearly all their fruit in an intensive two- to three-week period in midsummer. Some cultivars also give a smaller, autumn crop.

Perpetual-fruiting (ever-bearing) strawberries crop briefly in summer, cease for about two months, and then produce a succession of fruits in autumn. They grow best in regions that have mild, frost-free autumn weather.

Alpine strawberries, which are raised from seed, produce small, delicately flavoured fruits.

Variations in daylength (see GROWING VEGETABLES, p.495) affect the formation of flowers in some cultivars. It is therefore important to choose those appropriate for the latitude of the particular garden: nearer the tropics, for example, the cooler temperatures that are essential for growth and cropping may be found only at high altitudes.

Site and planting

Strawberries are best grown where new plantings may be made regularly on fresh ground, since cropping, fruit size, and plant health deteriorate if the same ground and plants are used after the third year. If you have room, grow one-, two-, and three-year-old plants in succession, discarding the oldest plants and planting new runners in fresh ground each year.

Site

Sunny, warm sites give the best-flavoured fruit. Sandy soils produce the earliest crops, loams and well-drained clays the heaviest and most finely flavoured; chalky soils do not produce good results. Slightly acid conditions with a pH of 6–6.5 are ideal. Good drainage is vital to avoid soil-borne diseases. Planting strawberries after potatoes can be risky, since the ground may be infected with *Verticillium* wilt (p.653).

To prolong the fruiting season, plantings may be split – choose a warm, sheltered position for the earliest crops, sunny, open ground for the main crop, and a less sunny site for late-ripening fruits.

Pollination

Most cultivars are self-fertile. The cultivar 'Pandora', however, fruits well only if several plants of a different cultivar that flowers at the same time are planted nearby.

Planting

The planting time for strawberries depends on geographical location. Seek expert advice if in doubt. In cool-temperate regions, late summer to early autumn planting is best and ensures the heaviest crops the following summer. For later plantings, remove flowers in spring to allow plants to become well established before they begin to bear fruit.

Use plants of certified stock, if possible, and plant in fresh ground, where strawberries have not been grown for at least three years. Replace plants every two or three years and grub out and burn any old plants nearby to prevent the spread of virus diseases. Clear all weeds and apply generous amounts of well-rotted farmyard manure, unless plenty remains in the soil from the preceding crop. On hungrier sandy or chalky soils, rake in a dressing of a balanced fertilizer as well, at a rate of

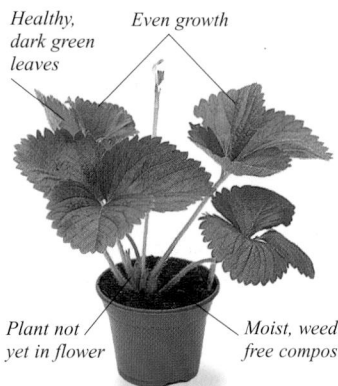

Healthy, dark green leaves

Even growth

Plant not yet in flower

Moist, weed-free compost

105g/sq m (3oz/sq yd), just before planting. Space strawberries at 45cm (18in) intervals in slightly raised rows, 75cm (2½ft) apart, so that rainwater runs off. Plant with the base of the central crown at soil level, firm in the plants, and water well. On wet sites, plant in raised beds (see STRUCTURES AND SURFACES, "Raised beds", p.599).

Strawberries may also be planted through sheets of black plastic, which smother weeds, retain soil moisture, and encourage early cropping by

PLANTING STRAWBERRIES UNDER A PLASTIC MULCH

1 *In moist soil, mark out a 90cm (3ft) wide bed with string. Mound the soil in the centre, and cover the bed with a length of black plastic 1.2m (4ft) wide.*

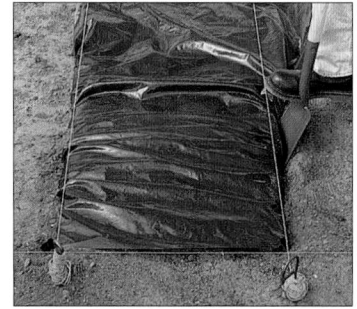

2 *Dig a narrow trench on either side of the bed and, using a spade, anchor the edges of the plastic sheet firmly in the trenches to stop it blowing away.*

3 *Make cross-shaped cuts in the plastic (see inset) at 45cm (18in) intervals. Plant the strawberries through the slits and firm the soil around their crowns.*

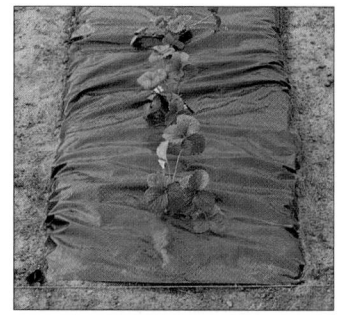

4 *Tuck in the cut plastic around the crowns of the plants. The finished row of strawberries should be slightly raised so that rain drains away from the plants.*

warming the soil. Anchor the plastic firmly, then make planting slits at the required intervals.

Routine care

Strawberries need regular watering. Ripening fruits should be netted against pests, and kept off the soil to keep them clean. Remove surplus runners, weed, and regularly check for pests and diseases. Flowers may need protection from frost in spring: fleece or double-thickness sheets of newspaper are very effective.

Protecting the fruits

Before the fruit trusses develop fully, lay clean, dry straw or proprietary mats beneath them to prevent soil splash on the fruits; this is unnecessary for plants grown through plastic. Protect the fruits from birds before they redden, using posts to support fruit nets (see p.427).

HOW TO KEEP STRAWBERRIES CLEAN

When the strawberries are in flower or the fruits are forming, put a thick layer of straw underneath and between the plants to prevent the ripening fruits from touching the soil.

ALTERNATIVE METHOD

Alternatively, strawberry mats may be laid carefully around the crowns to protect the developing fruits.

REMOVING RUNNERS

Remove excess runners as they develop. Pinch them out close to the parent plant, taking care not to damage any other foliage.

Controlling runners

Pinch out runners as they appear, unless they are needed to help form matted rows (see "Growing under cover", below).

Watering and weeding

Water strawberries when newly planted, then regularly during the growing season, especially after flowering to promote the development of quality fruits. Water plants under plastic only in very dry weather, watering through the planting slits. Keep beds free of weeds.

Pests and diseases

Strawberries may be eaten by birds (p.657), grey squirrel (p.659), and slugs (p.644), and are vulnerable to aphids (p.646), viruses (see p.659), grey mould (*Botrytis*) (p.658), fungal leaf spots (p.648), and red spider mite (p.646). Dig up and burn diseased or stunted plants. Red core and strawberry beetles are not widespread, but are serious where they occur. Red core is a soil-borne disease, more prevalent in heavy soils, causing the foliage to collapse and die. The only remedy is to change the site. Strawberry beetles take seeds from the outside of the fruits, encouraging rotting. They feed on weed seeds, so weed beds well.

Growing under cover

Strawberries grown in a heated greenhouse fruit up to one month earlier than those grown outdoors, but have less flavour. Establish runners in 6cm (2½in) pots of seed compost as early as possible (see p.470). Before the roots fill the pots, transplant into 15cm (6in) pots of potting compost; keep the plants outside until midwinter, protected from heavy rain, then place them in the greenhouse in a position of maximum

PICKING FRUITS

Pick dessert strawberries by the stalk to avoid bruising the fruit. Strawberries for jam may be picked without the stalk.

light. When new leaves form, maintain minimum temperatures of 7°C (45°F) at night and 10°C (50°F) during the day.

Adjust the ventilation to maintain these temperatures. Water and damp down frequently to keep a moist atmosphere and reduce the risk of red spider mite infestation. Increase the temperature by about 3°C (5°F) when flower trusses start to develop; during flowering, raise the temperature again by the same amount and stop damping down. Pollinate flowers by hand with a soft brush; do this around midday on a bright day. Remove late-forming flowers to improve the size of the ripening fruits. To enhance their flavour, lower the temperature as they begin to ripen.

For plants grown in the open, cloches placed over plants in late winter advance ripening by about three weeks, and polytunnels by one to two weeks (see p.582). Both should be well ventilated on warm days. Under cloches or plastic tunnels, strawberries may be grown in "matted rows", in which the planting distance is halved to give maximum yield. Runners may be retained to increase the density of the planting. Revert to the usual spacing after the first year by removing every other plant, otherwise fruit quality deteriorates and routine care becomes difficult.

Harvesting and storing

Harvest dessert strawberries when fully ripe, complete with stalks, and use them at once for the best flavour. Pick strawberries for jam when ripe but still firm. Pick the fruit every other day and remove and burn diseased or damaged fruit. Strawberries may also be bottled or preserved. If

469

frozen, the fruits, except those of the cultivar 'Totem', lose their firmness.

After harvesting, clear surplus runners, weeds, and straw from the site. Cut off the old foliage from plants, taking care not to damage the young leaves. Apply a balanced fertilizer and water it in if the soil is dry. Where plants are growing through a plastic mulch, make a fresh planting unless they are thriving.

Propagation

Each year plant one or two certified virus-free young plants well away from established fruiting beds. Control aphids and remove all flowers. The plants will produce a healthy supply of runners for up to two years; then start afresh with new, certified stock. Some perpetual-fruiting cultivars produce few runners.

CLEARING THE FOLIAGE AFTER HARVESTING

As soon as the crop has been picked, remove the old foliage to leave 10cm (4in) of stem above the young leaves and crown. Clear away and burn straw, foliage, and other debris from around the plants to minimize the risk of pests and diseases.

HOW TO PROPAGATE BY RUNNERS

1 *Plant certified virus-free plants especially to produce runners. As they form, spread them out evenly around the parent plant.*

2 *Once a runner has rooted and is making vigorous new growth, lift it carefully, using a hand fork, without damaging the roots.*

3 *Sever the rooted runner from the parent plant. Transplant it to well-prepared soil or pot it up singly for planting out later.*

Alpine strawberries

Alpine strawberries (*Fragaria vesca* 'Semperflorens') have small, fragrant, sweetly flavoured fruits and make a neat and attractive edging for flower borders or vegetable plots. They tolerate cooler conditions than most other strawberries and prefer partial shade in the summer in warm areas. Their fruiting season lasts from midsummer through to late autumn.

Plants deteriorate after about two years, so should be propagated regularly from either runners or seed. To separate seed from the fruits, leave the strawberries to dry and squash them between finger and thumb. Sow the seed in pots of standard seed compost and maintain them at 18–24°C (64–75°F). Prick out seedlings when they have two true leaves. Plant out young strawberries in early summer.

ALPINE STRAWBERRY

HOW TO PROPAGATE FROM SEED

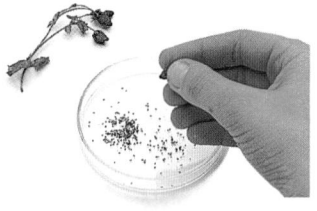

1 *Use dried fruits, squashing them gently between finger and thumb so that the seeds fall off. Hold the fruits over a clean container to collect the seeds.*

2 *Fill a 6cm (3in) pot with seed compost. Sprinkle the seeds thinly on the surface, then cover them with a thin layer of compost and a layer of fine grit.*

Blackberries and hybrid berries (*Rubus fruticosus* and *Rubus* hybrids)

The fruits of cultivated blackberries and hybrid berries such as loganberries and boysenberries are borne on canes in late summer. The hybrids have arisen from crosses between different *Rubus* species or cultivars.

Site

Before planting, the ground should be well prepared and fertilized, as for raspberries (see p.472). Buy blackberries and hybrid berries from specialist nurseries and, if possible, choose plants that are included in a certification scheme to ensure healthy, virus-free stock. Thornless cultivars are usually less vigorous than prickly ones. Blackberries and hybrid berries are all self-fertile and consequently may be grown singly.

Blackberries and hybrid berries need a sunny or partially shaded position. Do not plant them in exposed sites.

Provide support for the canes: walls and fences, with horizontal wires set up at 30cm (12in) intervals, are ideal.

A post 3m (10ft) long sunk 60cm (2ft) into the ground may also be used as a basic support, but for vigorous cultivars erect a post-and-wire fence. Position the posts at 4–5m (12–15ft) intervals with four horizontal wires running between them, the lowest at 90cm (3ft) from the ground, the highest at 2m (6ft). On light, sandy soils, you should provide extra support for the end posts by bracing them with diagonal wooden props. This will help to prevent the wires from sagging under the weight of the canes.

Planting

Plant during winter; if the weather is severe, delay until late winter or early spring. Some hybrids may be killed in very cold areas so seek local advice. Plant shallowly, spreading out the roots well and firming the soil at the base of the plants. Space more vigorous cultivars 4–5m (12–15ft) apart, less vigorous ones 2.5–3m (8–10ft) apart. After planting, shorten the canes to 22cm (9in).

BUYING HEALTHY BLACKBERRY PLANTS

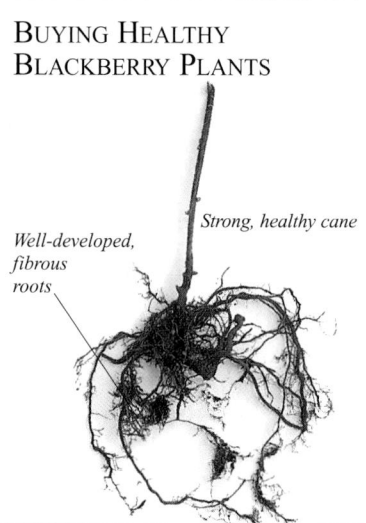

Strong, healthy cane

Well-developed, fibrous roots

METHODS OF TRAINING

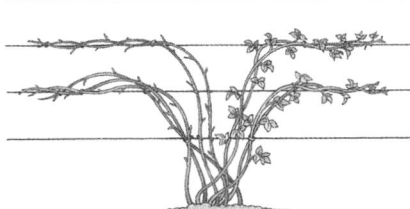

ALTERNATE BAY
Train new canes to one side of the plant, while the older ones fruit on the other side.

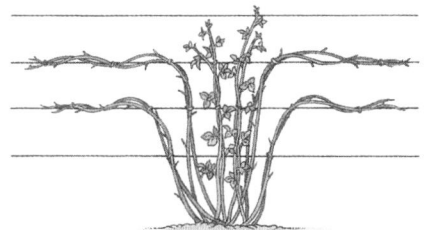

ROPE
Train fruiting canes in groups along wires, leaving new canes to grow centrally.

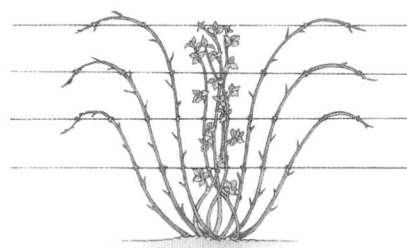

FAN
Fan-train fruiting canes individually to the left and right, and train new canes centrally.

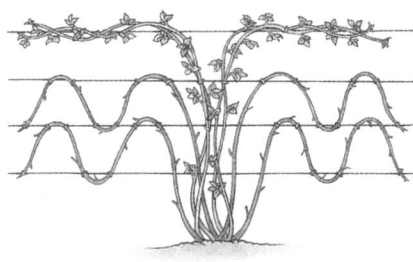

WEAVING
Weave fruiting canes through the lower wires. Train new canes centrally and along the top wire.

RECOMMENDED BLACKBERRIES

Early
'Bedford Giant' **Rg**
'Himalaya Giant' **Rg**
'Merton Thornless'
'Silvan'
Late
'Ashton Cross'
'Fantasia'
'John Innes'
'Loch Ness'
'Oregon Thornless'
'Thornfree'
'Waldo'

'Bedford Giant'

RECOMMENDED HYBRID BERRIES

Boysenberry
Loganberry
Tayberry
Tummelberry
Thornless
    Loganberry

Tayberry

KEY
Rg *Rampant growth*

ESTABLISHED BLACKBERRIES AND HYBRID BERRIES
PRUNING AFTER FRUITING

Cut down all the fruited canes to ground level near the base of the stem.

Tie the new canes securely to the horizontal wires according to the training system used.

TIP PRUNING FROST-DAMAGED STEMS

Inspect the canes for signs of frost damage in early spring and, if necessary, cut back the tips of affected canes to healthy wood.

Routine care
Maintenance requirements are as for raspberries (see p.472).

Pests and diseases
Problems may be caused by raspberry beetle (p.658), birds (p.657), grey mould (*Botrytis*) (p.658), and viruses (p.659), although resistance varies from one hybrid to another.

Pruning and training
The plants fruit on one-year-old wood, so training needs to separate fruiting canes from newly developing ones. For small gardens, the rope and fan methods (see above) are best. The alternate bay and weaving systems use much more space, but weaving is the best method for vigorous plants.

After cropping, cut out the fruited canes at ground level. Retain and tie in those canes that have grown during the current season but remove any that are weak or damaged. In early spring, cut back the tip of each cane if it shows any signs of die-back resulting from frost.

Harvesting and storing
Pick the fruits regularly; unlike raspberries, the central plug stays within the picked fruit. For exhibiting, pick fruits complete with their stalks. They may be stored by bottling, preserving, or freezing.

Propagation
To provide a few new plants, use tip layering (see below). In summer,

TIP LAYERING

1 *Bend over the tip of a healthy, vigorous shoot and place it in a hole 10cm (4in) deep. Fill the hole with soil and firm down well.*

2 *Once the tip has rooted in late autumn or winter, cut the old stem close to the young, rooted plant to sever it from the parent. Pot it up, if required, or transplant in spring.*

bend a shoot to ground level and place the tip in a hole dug in the soil. Cover it with earth and firm. Once the tip has rooted in late autumn or winter, sever it from the parent plant. Transfer the young plant to its final growing position in spring.

To produce a larger number of young plants, remove shoots, 30cm (12in) long, of the current season's growth in late summer; take leaf-bud cuttings from them, with a leaf and a piece of stem. Place several cuttings in one 14cm (5½in) pot in a moist atmosphere or cold frame; they should root in six to eight weeks. Harden them off and plant them out in late autumn or, where winters are harsh, in early spring. Transplant the young canes to their final positions a year later.

HOW TO PROPAGATE BY LEAF-BUD CUTTINGS

1 *Select a strong, healthy shoot from the current season's growth, taking at least 30cm (12in) of stem with plenty of well-developed leaf buds.*

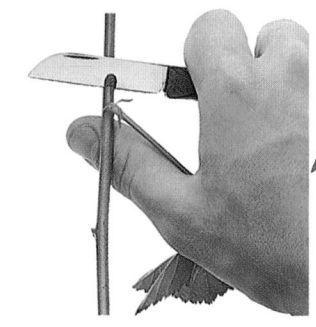

2 *Make a cut 1cm (½in) above a bud: slice downwards to remove the bud and a portion of stem about 2.5cm (1in) long, with a leaf attached.*

3 *Place 3 cuttings in a 14cm (5½in) pot, with the stem portions at an angle and growth buds just above the soil. Water, label, and place in a cold frame.*

Raspberries (*Rubus idaeus*)

A number of raspberry cultivars have been produced by crossing the European wild red raspberry (*Rubus idaeus*) with the American raspberry (*R. idaeus* var. *strigosus*) and the North American black raspberry (*R. occidentalis*).

Raspberries are a cool-season crop, growing best where there is plenty of moisture. Fruits vary in colour from dark red through to yellow. There are two main types of raspberry: summer-fruiting, which has a short season of heavy cropping in high summer, and autumn-fruiting, which has a protracted cropping period beginning in late summer and continuing until the start of winter frosts.

Site and planting

The site needs thorough preparation before planting, since raspberries do not crop well on poor soils, particularly if in competition with weeds. Raspberries are self-fertile.

Site

Raspberries should be planted in a sheltered, sunny position. They tolerate partial shade, and in hotter regions some shade may be a positive advantage.

The soil should be rich in humus and moisture-retentive but also well drained, as raspberries do not tolerate poor drainage. Sandy, chalky, and poor, stony soils need an annual, heavy dressing with humus-rich material, and regular watering. In addition, if raspberries are grown on lime-rich soil they may suffer from chlorosis (see "Manganese/iron deficiency", p.651).

Preparation

Clear all perennial weeds before planting as they are extremely difficult to deal with later. Prepare an area at least 90cm (3ft) wide and dig in plenty of well-rotted manure.

Construct permanent supports. For a post-and-wire support, set a single row of stout posts 3m (10ft) apart. Run three lengths of wire or nylon string between the posts setting them at heights of 75cm (30in), 1.1m (3½ft), and 1.5m (5ft). Keep the wires or strings taut and tie in the canes with twine by "continuous lacing" (weaving between the canes and wires) to prevent the canes from being blown along the row.

The parallel wires method requires two rows of posts, with posts at the above spacing and rows 75cm (30in) apart. Run two pairs of parallel wires along the posts, one pair at 75cm (30in), the other at 1.5m (5ft), then criss-cross between them with wire or strong string. The canes are supported by the cross-wires and do not need to be tied in.

For the Scandinavian system, erect two rows of posts, as above, but with 90cm (3ft) between rows, then run a single wire along each row at a height of 90cm (3ft). Twist fruiting canes along the wires, allowing new canes to grow in the open, central space.

Obtain certified virus-free canes; otherwise use suckers taken from established plants of known good health and cropping performance.

Planting

Plant dormant canes in well-manured ground at 38–45cm (15–18in) intervals, in rows 2m (6ft) apart. Plant in autumn or early winter, as this

SUPPORTING AND TRAINING METHODS

The post-and-wire method is useful if space is limited. The parallel wires method gives the canes more room, but is not suitable in windy conditions. The Scandinavian system bends young canes around each other and the wire; the canes are not tied in or tip pruned. This method needs more space than the others.

SCANDINAVIAN SYSTEM

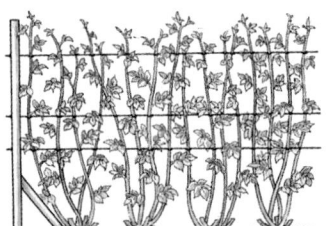

POST AND WIRES

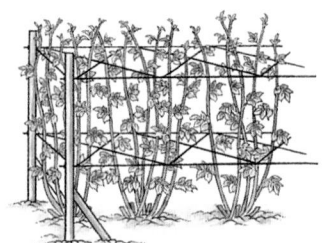

PARALLEL WIRES

HOW TO PLANT RASPBERRIES

1 *Prepare a trench 5–8cm (2–3in) deep in well-manured ground. Plant the canes 38–45cm (15–18in) apart. Spread out the roots carefully and backfill the trench with soil.*

2 *Firm the soil around the bases of the canes, ensuring that they remain vertical. Prune canes back to a bud, about 25cm (10in) from the ground. Rake over the soil lightly.*

encourages the canes to establish quickly. Spread out the roots evenly at a depth of 5–8cm (2–3in), and gently firm them in. Prune the canes to 25cm (10in) from the ground.

Routine care

In spring, mulch with well-rotted manure. Apply this on either side of the row, taking care not to bury the canes. If manure is unavailable, apply regular dressings of a balanced fertilizer (see "Care of soft fruits", p.426) and mulch with compost or leaf mould to conserve moisture.

Flowers usually appear too late to be damaged by frost so do not need protection. Remove weeds and water the plants regularly and thoroughly. Remove any suckers more than 22cm (9in) from the main row.

Pests and diseases

Raspberry beetle (p.658) and birds (p.657) are the main pests. Grey mould (*Botrytis*) (p.658), spur blight/cane blight (p.653), and viruses (p.659) may also be a problem.

Pruning and training

As soon as new canes are established, by about midsummer, cut out the canes that were shortened at planting time.

Summer-fruiting raspberries should have all fruited canes removed at ground level after cropping. Tie in the new canes (see *Supporting and Training Methods*, p.472), spacing them evenly 8–10cm (3–4in) apart. Cut out damaged and weak canes so that those remaining receive as much light and air as possible. Loop over and tie in tall canes to prevent wind damage.

The following spring, trim canes to 15cm (6in) above the topmost wire, cutting back any tips with frost damage. Remove dead, diseased, or crowded canes or any growing more than 22cm (9in) from the row.

Autumn-fruiting raspberries (see p.474) should have all canes cut to ground level in late winter. The new canes grow, then fruit in the autumn.

Harvesting and storing

Pick the fruit when it is firm to ripe for preserves and freezing, and when it is fully ripe for eating fresh, harvesting every other day, if possible.

HOW TO REMOVE UNWANTED SUCKERS

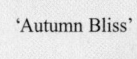

If suckers become overcrowded or are growing too far outside the row, as here, lift them and sever from the parent plant.

PRUNING AT THE END OF THE FIRST SEASON

1 *By about midsummer, cut down to ground level the old canes that were shortened when planting was carried out.*

2 *Tie the current season's strongest canes to the support wires (see inset) when they reach about 90cm (3ft). Remove weak shoots and those growing more than 22cm (9in) from the row.*

ESTABLISHED RASPBERRIES, PRUNING AFTER FRUITING

1 *When all the fruit has been picked, cut back all the fruited canes to ground level.*

2 *Tie the current season's strongest canes to the support wires when about 90cm (3ft) tall, spacing them 10cm (4in) apart: here the continuous lacing method is used.*

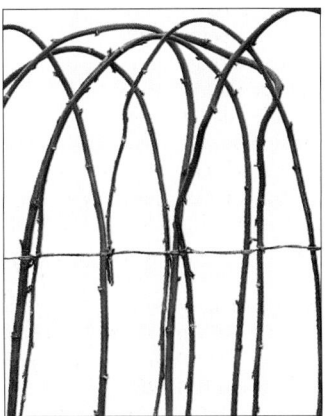

3 *At the end of the growing season, loop any tall canes over the top wire and tie them in.*

SPRING PRUNING

Before the growing season begins, tip prune all the canes to a healthy bud. Wherever possible, the cut should be made about 15cm (6in) above the top supporting wire.

Detach the fruit from the central plug and the stalk; fruits for exhibiting should be picked complete with stalk, however. Remove and burn diseased or damaged fruits promptly to prevent the spread of infection to healthy fruits.

Propagation

In late autumn, select strong suckers that are growing away from the main fruiting row, and lift and replant them while they are dormant. Ensure that they are from plants that are known to be healthy and free-cropping; where doubt exists, use certified virus-free canes from specialist nurseries instead.

PROPAGATING BY SUCKERS

Lift suckers carefully in autumn and sever them from the parent plant. Remove any remaining foliage. Ensure that the suckers are healthy and replant where new stock is required. Water in thoroughly.

Autumn–fruiting raspberries

These should be sited in a sunny, sheltered position where the plants will quickly become established and the fruits should ripen in as short a time as possible. The fruits are borne freely on the upper part of the current season's canes. Planting and cultivation requirements are as for summer-fruiting raspberries.

Pruning of autumn-fruiting raspberries is carried out in late winter before growth starts; the fruited canes are all cut down to the ground to stimulate new canes, which will fruit in the autumn.

LATE WINTER PRUNING
Before new growth starts, cut down all the canes to ground level. Fruit will be produced in autumn on the new season's canes.

Blackcurrants (*Ribes nigrum*)

Blackcurrants thrive only in cool-temperate regions. The bushes flower early, so are prone to frost damage on exposed sites. They fruit in midsummer. In parts of the USA their cultivation is prohibited because they are hosts for a rust disease on white pine. Jostaberries, a hybrid between blackcurrants and gooseberries, are cultivated in the same way.

Site and planting

The ground should be well prepared before planting to provide the best conditions for the continual production of new fruiting shoots. Remove all weeds from the site before planting and dig in plenty of manure.

Site

Choose a sunny, sheltered site; some shade is tolerated. Protect blackcurrants from spring frosts if necessary (see FROST AND WIND PROTECTION, pp.612–613). Blackcurrants grow in a range of soils but deep, moisture-retentive soil is most suitable; avoid wet, poorly drained ground. A pH of 6.5–7 is preferable; lime very acid soils (see p.625). Blackcurrants are self-fertile.

Planting

Plant disease-free bushes from certified stock. Bushes sold under certification schemes are normally two years old, but one-year-old plants from disease-free stock are also ideal. Planting in late autumn is preferable but blackcurrants may be planted throughout the winter. Handle the plants carefully to avoid damaging the basal buds. Space the bushes 1.2–1.5m (4–5ft) apart, with the same distance between the rows. After planting, cut down all the shoots to one bud to encourage strong, new growth.

Routine care

In winter, apply sulphate of potash at a rate of 35g/sq m (1oz/sq yd) and a nitrogenous fertilizer at the same rate in spring. Mulch well in spring all round the bushes, with well-rotted manure, compost, or leaf mould, to conserve soil moisture.

Water in dry weather, but not as the fruits ripen, since this may cause the skins to split. Net bushes to protect ripening fruits from birds.

Pests and diseases

Aphids (p.646), big bud mites (p.655), winter moth caterpillars (p.645), and birds (p.657) may affect blackcurrants. Grey mould (*Botrytis*) (p.658), powdery mildew (p.658), and fungal leaf spots (p.648) may also be troublesome.

Pruning and training

Blackcurrants are grown with as many young shoots as possible originating at or near ground level. Most of the fruits are borne on shoots produced the previous season, and regular pruning is essential to maintain high yields. Pruning, together with adequate feeding, encourages strong, new shoots to develop.

Cut all stems to one bud above ground level immediately after planting. The following year, remove any very weak, downward-pointing, or horizontal shoots. Thereafter, prune established bushes as buds begin to burst, before late winter, by cutting to the base one quarter to one third of two-year-old wood, and any older, weak wood. No tip pruning is required. New shoots are a pale tea colour, two-year-old wood is grey, and older wood black.

If a bush needs rejuvenating cut out a greater proportion of the old wood, retaining only those branches from which strong, young shoots have

NEW AND FRUITED SHOOTS

Pale, new shoot

Dark, fruited wood

developed. If few shoots develop yet the bush is healthy, cut down the whole plant to just above ground level in winter. Most bushes then rejuvenate well if fed and mulched, but one year's crop is sacrificed. The new shoots that develop may need thinning, retaining the strongest. After ten years or so it is better to replace a bush than to try to rejuvenate it.

BLACKCURRANT BUSH
YEAR 1, WINTER PRUNING

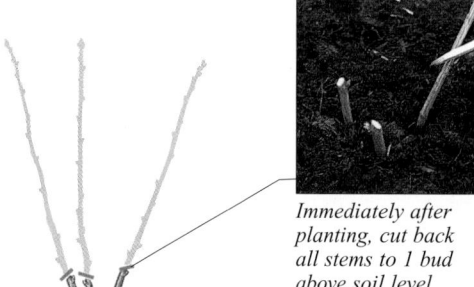

Immediately after planting, cut back all stems to 1 bud above soil level.

YEAR 2, WINTER PRUNING

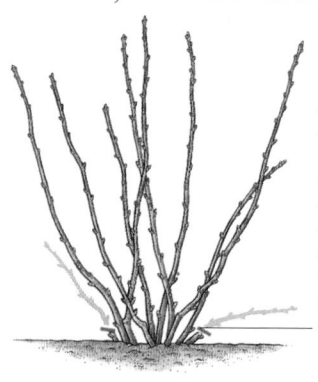

The bush should develop 7 or 8 strong, new shoots. Cut back any weak or low-growing shoots to about 2.5cm (1in) above soil level, to encourage new growth from the base.

ESTABLISHED BUSH, PRUNING AFTER FRUITING

Cut out the old wood and one quarter to one third of two-year-old stems to stimulate new growth.

Remove any weak, damaged, or low-growing shoots, cutting close to the main stem.

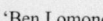
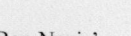

Harvesting and storing

Blackcurrants are borne on "strigs" in bunches. Harvest the fruits when dry and ripe but still firm. Remove the whole bunch, not the individual fruits, which may otherwise be damaged. Early-ripening cultivars soon shed their fruits but late-ripening cultivars retain their fruits much longer. Fruits may either be eaten fresh or stored by bottling, preserving, or freezing.

Propagation

Blackcurrants are propagated from hardwood cuttings (see p.434) taken from healthy bushes in autumn. Retain all buds on the cuttings to encourage basal shoots to grow.

HARDWOOD CUTTINGS

Insert 20–25cm (8–10in) cuttings in a trench, leaving two buds exposed.

Red- and whitecurrants (*Ribes sativum*)

Red- and whitecurrants require a cool climate. Whitecurrants are simply a colour variant of redcurrants; both fruit in midsummer and need the same growing conditions.

Site and planting

Red- and whitecurrants need a sunny site but tolerate some shade; in hot climates some shade may be necessary. Protect plants from winds to prevent stems breaking, and in high temperatures to prevent scorching.

Prepare the soil well before planting, as for blackcurrants (see p.474). Heavier, moisture-retentive, but well-drained soils are preferable. Potassium deficiency may occur on very sandy soil. All cultivars are self-fertile.

When buying young bushes, ensure that the plants are from healthy stock that crops well. There is no certification scheme, however. Plant in autumn or winter: space bushes 1.2–1.5m (4–5ft) apart, cordons at 30cm (12in), and fans at 1.8m (6ft).

Routine care

For details of maintenance, see blackcurrants (p.474). Maintain high potash levels by applying potassium sulphate if necessary (muriate of potash may scorch the foliage).

Pests and diseases

Keep the plants covered with netting throughout the winter to prevent birds from damaging the buds. If the buds are damaged, delay winter pruning until just before bud-burst and then prune to healthy buds. Aphids (p.646), sawfly larvae (p.645), grey mould (*Botrytis*) (p.658), and coral spot (p.665) may affect plants.

Pruning and training

Red- and whitecurrants are normally grown as open-centre bushes but may be trained on supporting wires as cordons, double cordons, or fans. Fruits develop on spurs produced by pruning back the sideshoots.

Bush

A one-year-old bush should have two or three strong, young shoots; shorten these by half in late winter. Remove any that are less than 10cm (4in) from the ground to produce a short leg.

The following winter, shorten new growth by half to form the main branches, pruning to an outward-pointing bud. Prune sideshoots

REDCURRANT BUSH
YEAR 1, WINTER PRUNING

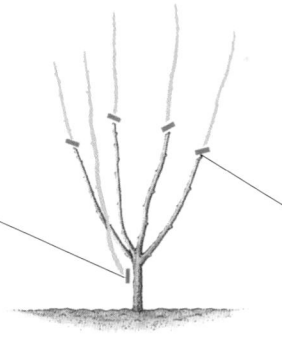

Remove any side-shoots growing within 10cm (4in) of soil level by cutting flush with the stem. This will form a short leg at the base.

Prune each stem to an outward-facing bud (or to an upright shoot) about half-way along its length.

YEAR 2, WINTER PRUNING

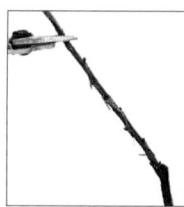

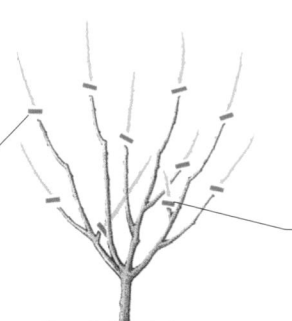

To form the permanent branches, shorten leaders and sideshoots by half of the new growth, cutting to outward-facing buds.

Cut back to 1 bud any sideshoots crowding the centre or growing downwards.

ESTABLISHED BUSH, WINTER PRUNING

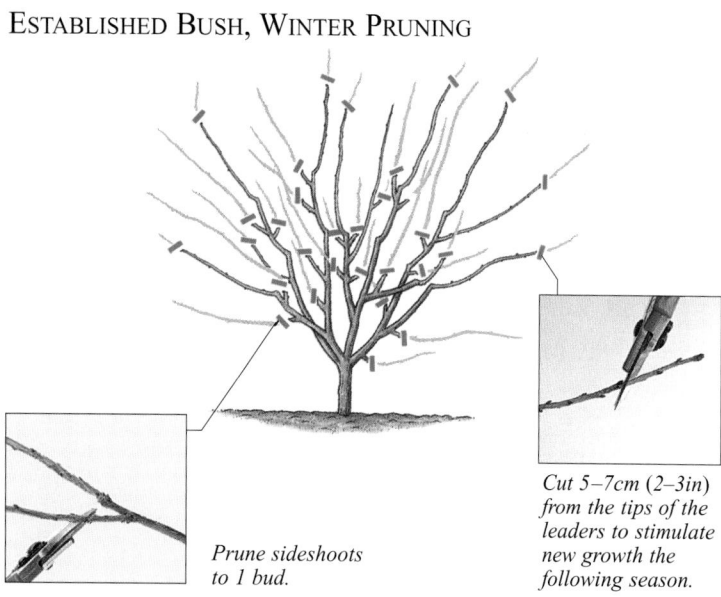

Prune sideshoots to 1 bud.

Cut 5–7cm (2–3in) from the tips of the leaders to stimulate new growth the following season.

growing in- or downwards to one bud. Prune established bushes by cutting back sideshoots to one bud and tip pruning main branches.

Cordon

Single cordons are usually trained vertically. Set up wires at 60cm (24in) and 1.2m (4ft) from the ground. Select a main shoot on a one-year-old plant and train it against a cane;

prune back the shoot by half, then cut back all other shoots to one bud.

In summer, prune sideshoots to five leaves of new growth. Shorten these sideshoots to one or two buds in winter, and prune the leader by one quarter of the new growth. When the leader reaches the top of its support, trim it to one bud. A double cordon is developed by training two shoots at about 30° to the ground as

for apples (see "Forming a double cordon", p.441); they are subsequently trained vertically when 30cm (12in) apart. Each branch is then pruned as for a single cordon.

Fan

Fan-trained red- and whitecurrants are established as for a peach fan (see p.453). Each branch should then be pruned as a cordon.

Harvesting and storing

Harvest red- and whitecurrants as for blackcurrants. The plants tend to retain their ripe fruits a little longer than most blackcurrants. They may be bottled, preserved, or frozen.

Propagation

Take hardwood cuttings in early autumn. Use young shoots 30–38cm (12–15in) long, and remove all but the top three or four buds, to produce a plant with a short stem.

Insert the cuttings in moist, fertile soil, burying them by about half their length, and firm well. Once rooted, transplant the young plants to their final positions.

HARDWOOD CUTTINGS

Cuttings should be 30cm (12in) long. Retain only the top few buds.

REDCURRANT CORDON
YEAR 1, WINTER PRUNING

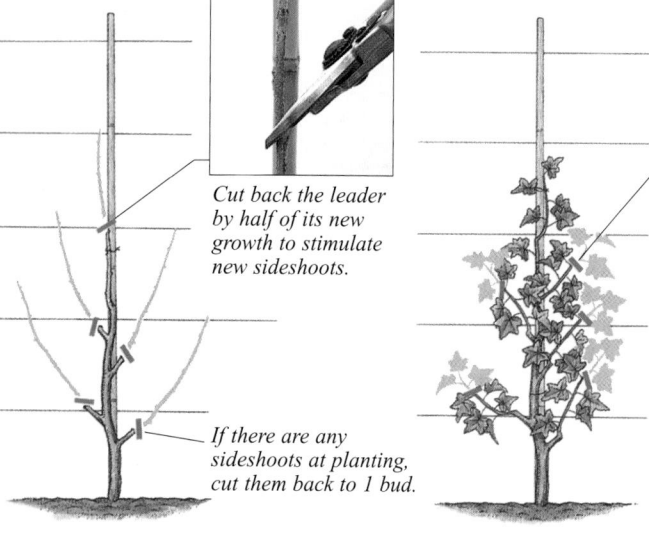

Cut back the leader by half of its new growth to stimulate new sideshoots.

If there are any sideshoots at planting, cut them back to 1 bud.

YEAR 1, SUMMER PRUNING

Prune back the current season's sideshoots to 5 leaves.

ESTABLISHED CORDON, WINTER PRUNING

If the leader has reached the top wire, prune to 1 bud, or prune it back by one quarter of the summer's growth.

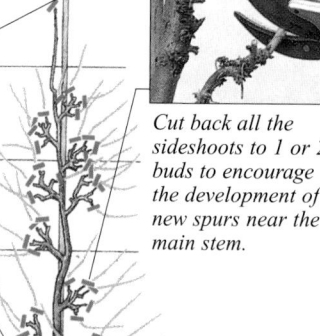

Trim back to the point of origin any shoots growing less than 10cm (4in) from the ground.

Cut back all the sideshoots to 1 or 2 buds to encourage the development of new spurs near the main stem.

Gooseberries (*Ribes uva-crispa*)

Gooseberry fruits ripen yellow, red, white, or green, depending on the cultivar. The Worcesterberry (*Ribes divaricatum*) resembles an over-vigorous, very thorny gooseberry bush, with small, red-purple fruits that make excellent jam, and has similar needs to a gooseberry bush.

Site and planting
Gooseberries are easy to grow. Like currants (*Ribes*), they need cool conditions and, if summer temperatures are high, adequate shade. Growing conditions and planting distances are as for redcurrants (see p.475). All cultivars are self-fertile.

Routine care
General maintenance is largely as for blackcurrants (see p.474). Gooseberries require high potassium levels and regular mulching, ideally with well-rotted manure. New shoots on young bushes are vulnerable to breakage and need protection from

strong winds. If the crop is heavy, thin the fruits in late spring.

Pests and diseases
Birds (p.657) may cause severe bud loss, so cover plants with netting. If the buds have been attacked, delay winter pruning until bud-burst, then

prune to live buds. Gooseberry plants may be affected by powdery mildew (p.658), sawfly larvae (p.645), and bacterial or fungal leaf spots (p.648).

Pruning and training
Young plants may be trained as bushes, cordons, or fans as for red-currants. A number of gooseberry cultivars, such as 'Leveller', have a natural drooping habit, however; to prevent stems from trailing to the ground, prune to upward-pointing buds, particularly when training young bushes.

Bush For initial pruning, see red-currants (p.475); aim to create an open-centre bush on a stem 10–15cm (4–6in) long. Established bushes may be pruned by regulated or spur pruning in winter, to give large fruits.

Regulated pruning is the simpler method: remove low, crowded, and crossing shoots to maintain well-spaced growth at the centre of the bush; also remove any old, unproductive branches and select new, young shoots to replace them.

Spur pruning is more labour-intensive: all the sideshoots are shortened to a suitable bud 8cm (3in)

GOOSEBERRY STANDARD

from the main branches. The branch leaders also need to be tip pruned.

Standard Cultivars to be trained as standards are grafted onto *Ribes odoratum* or *R. divaricatum* stock. Select one shoot of the rootstock and train it vertically, keeping any sideshoots short. It will take about three years to grow to a suitable height. When the stem has thickened and reached about 1.1–1.2m (3½–4ft), trim off the sideshoots and graft on the selected cultivar using whip-and-tongue grafting (see p.433). Use a strong stake to support the stem. The scion will develop and branch naturally the following summer. The next winter establish the framework as for a bush and then prune and train in the same way.

Cordon and fan These are trained as for redcurrants (see p.476). Once established, prune in summer, reducing new sideshoots to five leaves. In winter, shorten shoots to 8cm (3in) and tip prune leaders.

Harvesting and storing
Fruits should ripen by midsummer. Gooseberries for cooking should be picked while still green, but allow dessert-quality cultivars to ripen fully on the bush for the best flavour, ensuring that they are protected from

birds. Yellow-, white-, and red-berried cultivars should be left to ripen to their full colour before they are picked. Gooseberries freeze well.

Propagation
Take hardwood cuttings in early autumn. Gooseberry hardwood cuttings may be difficult to root; retaining all the buds often improves the success rate. Remove all low buds and sideshoots when the rooted cutting is lifted. If this is not done, troublesome suckers will develop.

GOOSEBERRY BUSH
YEAR 1, WINTER PRUNING

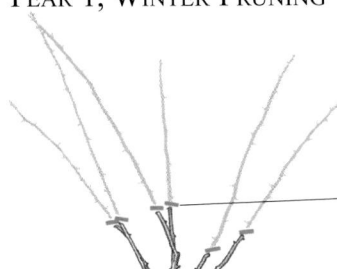

Prune back all the shoots by a half to three quarters to an outward-facing bud.

ESTABLISHED BUSH, REGULATED PRUNING, WINTER

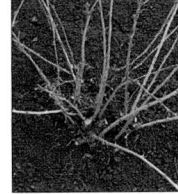

Cut out older branches to prevent overcrowding and to maintain an open centre.

The bush should have mainly young shoots, evenly spaced, pointing up- or outwards.

ESTABLISHED BUSH, SPUR PRUNING, WINTER

Prune all new sideshoots to a bud about 8cm (3in) from their base.

Tip prune the branch leaders to 3 or 4 buds of the new growth. This encourages the formation of spurs.

HARDWOOD CUTTINGS

1 *In early autumn, trim young shoots to 30–38cm (12–15in), with an angled cut above a bud at the top and a straight cut at the base. Dip in rooting hormone and insert in a trench to half their length.*

2 *The following autumn, carefully lift the rooted cuttings. Remove basal buds or shoots less than 10cm (4in) from the base (see inset), before transplanting the young plants.*

Blueberries (*Vaccinium corymbosum*)

Highbush blueberries are derived from the American wild blueberry. They produce clusters of fruits that are a dark, hazy purple-blue with a grey bloom; their flavour is enriched by cooking or preserving. They require a cool, moist climate, needing 700–1,200 hours below 7°C (45°F) and very acid soil (pH 4–5.5). Highbush blueberries grow to a height of 1.3–2m (4½–6ft) and are deciduous, with white flowers in spring, and striking gold and scarlet autumn colour.

Rabbit-eye blueberries (*Vaccinium ashei*) are grown in the same way as the highbush group, but tolerate less acid soils and drier conditions; they are cultivated mainly in Australia and the USA. The fruits are smaller and more gritty than highbush blueberries.

Cropping, in mid- to late summer, is light at first but after five or six years yields of 2.25kg (5lb) of fruit per bush may be obtained, and on older bushes considerably more. Blueberries are self-fertile, but crop better when two or more cultivars are planted close together.

Site and planting

Blueberries need a sunny location, although they tolerate some shade. The soil must be well drained. Clear all perennial weeds from the site before planting and, if the soil is alkaline, correct this by mixing a 15cm (6in) layer of acidic compost with the existing soil to a depth of at least 60cm (2ft). Alternatively, apply flowers of sulphur at a rate of 50–120g/sq m (2–4oz/sq yd).

Blueberries may also be grown in large pots or tubs with a diameter of 30–38cm (12–15in), filled with ericaceous compost.

HIGHBUSH BLUEBERRY BUSH

Plant from late autumn to late winter, spacing bushes 1.5m (5ft) apart. Cover the roots with 2.5–5cm (1–2in) of soil, and mulch with acid compost or leaf mould. Growing a mixture of cultivars results in better fertilization and heavier crops.

Routine care

To promote growth and cropping and to maintain acidity, apply a dressing each spring of sulphate of ammonia at 35g/sq m (1oz/sq yd), sulphate of potash at 35g/sq m (1oz/sq yd), and bone meal at 105g/sq m (3oz/sq yd). Keep plants mulched with acid compost, and water with rainwater. Avoid root disturbance when weeding.

Pests and diseases

The fruits may be eaten by birds, so provide protection by netting the bushes (see "Protection from birds", p.427). Other pests and diseases rarely cause any trouble.

ESTABLISHED BLUEBERRY BUSH, WINTER PRUNING

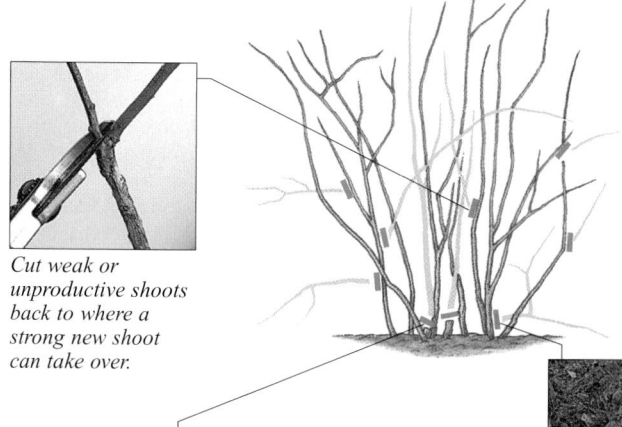

Cut weak or unproductive shoots back to where a strong new shoot can take over.

Cut to ground level older, non-fruiting branches to stimulate new basal shoots.

Cut back any low or downward-pointing branches to their point of origin or to a branch growing in the required direction.

Pruning and training

Blueberries fruit on two- or three-year-old wood. New bushes need little pruning for two or three years, but cut out weak shoots to provide a strong basic framework.

Thereafter, prune to ensure regular production of new shoots from the base, as for blackcurrants (see p.474), by cutting out some of the oldest wood each year.

Harvesting and storing

The fruits ripen over a period of several weeks. Pick over the bushes carefully, harvesting only the ripe fruits, which part easily from the cluster. Blueberries may be successfully stored for later use by preserving, bottling, or freezing.

Propagation

Take 10–15cm (4–6in) softwood cuttings in midsummer, dip them in hormone rooting powder, and then insert them in an acidic, peat/sand rooting medium. Place the cuttings in a propagator until rooted, then transplant to a larger pot. Harden off before planting out.

RECOMMENDED HIGHBUSH BLUEBERRIES

Early
'Bluecrop'
'Bluetta'   'Bluetta'
'Earliblue'
'Patriot'

Mid-season
'Berkeley'
'Herbert'
'Ivanhoe'
'Spartan'

Late
'Coville'
'Goldtraube 71'
'Jersey'

BLUEBERRY SOFTWOOD CUTTINGS

1 *Select suitable softwood material and take cuttings at least 10cm (4in) long. Cut just above a leaf joint.*

2 *Trim the base of each cutting just below a node with a sharp knife, and remove the leaves from the lower third of the cuttings. Dip the ends of the cuttings in hormone rooting powder.*

3 *Prepare a pot of acid cutting compost. Make holes with a dibber and insert each cutting so that the basal leaves are just above the compost. Water, label, and place the pot in a propagator.*

Tender fruits

Most tender fruits originate from tropical and subtropical regions, where they thrive in the warm, dry conditions. Apart from olives, many may be eaten straight from the tree, or stored for a short period of time in suitable conditions. Members of the citrus family that are too acid for eating, such as lemons and limes, are grown either for their juice or for use in preserves and marmalades. Since tender fruits are generally grown in hot climates, where the soil may be lacking in nutrients, it is important to prepare the site

adequately when planting: an extra 110–180g (4–6oz) of slow-release fertilizer forked into the base of the planting hole will help the plants to establish quickly.

In cool-temperate climates, some tender fruits may still be grown, in containers or under cover, as long as the correct temperature and humidity levels are provided (see CONTAINER GARDENING, "Subtropical container gardens", p.318). Although many do not consistently ripen their fruits under cover, they nevertheless make attractive ornamentals.

Pineapple · Sweet oranges · Avocado pear · Limes · Lemons · Mango

Pineapples (*Ananas comosus*)

Pineapples are tropical perennials that produce terminal fruits each composed of up to 200 seedless fruitlets. For best results they need full sun and temperatures of 18–30°C (64–86°F) with humidity of 70–80 per cent. Cultivar groups include the Cayenne Group, the Queen Group, and the Spanish Group, of which the Spanish has the sweetest flavour.

Site and planting
Select a sunny site that is sheltered from strong winds. Pineapples tolerate a wide range of soils, but prefer a sandy, medium loam with a pH of 4.5–5.5. Plant "slips" or suckers about 30cm (12in) apart, with 60cm (24in) between rows, or at a spacing of 50cm (20in) each way.

Routine care
Use a general-purpose fertilizer with medium potassium and high nitrogen levels at intervals of two to three months, at a rate of 50g (2oz) per

plant. Correct any iron and zinc deficiencies by spraying with a 2 per cent solution of ferrous or zinc sulphate. Water pineapples regularly in dry weather and apply an organic mulch to conserve soil moisture.

Pests and diseases
Pests that may affect pineapples include mealybugs (p.646), root-knot eelworms (p.660), scale insects (p.648), red spider mite (p.646), and thrips (p.647).

The most serious disease affecting pineapple plants in the open is heart rot, caused by *Phytophthora cinnamomi* and *P. parasitica*, fungi that often affect pineapples grown in wet conditions. Since this is difficult to treat, it is advisable to guard against infection by planting resistant cultivars where these are available; all suckers that are required for propagation should be dipped in a fungicide, since the fungus enters through wounds.

Growing under cover
Plant rooted pineapple "slips" or cuttings in well-prepared beds with good drainage, or use pots at least 30cm (12in) in diameter. Use compost with a high organic content and apply a liquid feed every three to four weeks. Maintain a temperature of at least 20°C (68°F) and humidity of about 70 per cent. Water regularly and thoroughly, particularly while young plants are establishing.

Harvesting and storing
Harvest the fruits when they begin to turn yellow by cutting the stem 2.5–5cm (1–2in) below each fruit. Pineapples may be stored for up to three weeks at 8°C (46°F) and at 90 per cent humidity.

Propagation
The terminal crown shoot may be used as a cutting; remove it with about 1cm (½in) of the fruit attached. Pineapples may also be propagated

PROPAGATING PINEAPPLES FROM SUCKERS

Sever basal slips or suckers and leave to dry before inserting in a sandy cutting compost (see inset).

by "slips" or suckers that develop from below the fruit or suckers produced in the leaf axils; these may be detached with a sharp knife. Dip the cut surfaces of slips or suckers in a fungicide, then leave them to dry for several days. Remove the lower leaves and insert the cuttings in pots of sandy compost. Pot them on into 15cm (6in) pots when rooted.

PINEAPPLE

PROPAGATING PINEAPPLES FROM THE CROWN SHOOT

1 *Scoop out the crown shoot of a ripe pineapple with a sharp knife, ensuring that you do not cut through the base of the shoot. Dip the wound in fungicide and leave for several days to dry.*

2 *Insert the prepared cutting into a pot of cuttings compost and maintain at a temperature of at least 18°C (64°F). The cutting should be rooted and ready to pot on within a few weeks.*

RECOMMENDED PINEAPPLES

Cayenne Group
'Baronne de Rothschild'
'Cayenne Lissa'
'Smooth Cayenne'

Queen Group
'Natal Queen'
'Ripley Queen'

Spanish Group
'Red Spanish'
'Singapore Spanish'

Papayas (*Carica papaya*)

Papayas (or paw-paws) are slender, generally single-stemmed, tropical trees, growing up to 4–5m (12–15ft) with a spread of 1–2m (3–6ft) at the crown. The fruits may be up to 20cm (8in) long when mature. A temperature range of 22–28°C (72–82°F) with humidity of 60–70 per cent is normally required; some cultivars will withstand temperatures as low as 15°C (59°F), although flowering and fruiting may then be poor.

Site and planting
Choose a warm, sunny site with protection from strong winds. Papayas require fertile, well-drained soil,

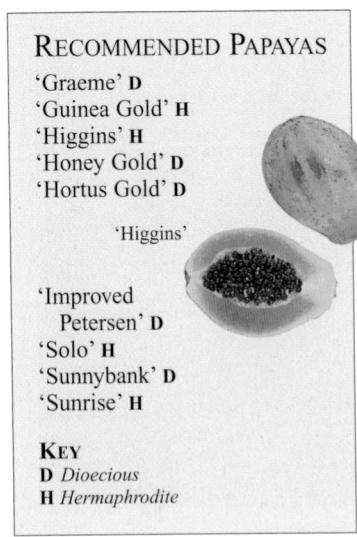

RECOMMENDED PAPAYAS

'Graeme' **D**
'Guinea Gold' **H**
'Higgins' **H**
'Honey Gold' **D**
'Hortus Gold' **D**

'Higgins'

'Improved Petersen' **D**
'Solo' **H**
'Sunnybank' **D**
'Sunrise' **H**

KEY
D *Dioecious*
H *Hermaphrodite*

with a pH of 6–7; good drainage is essential, since the trees are sensitive to waterlogging.

Many cultivars of papaya are dioecious, with male and female flowers produced on separate plants, but hermaphrodite cultivars are sometimes available. One male tree is usually sufficient to pollinate five or six female trees. Pollination is normally by insects and wind. Plant at a spacing of 2.5–3m (8–10ft).

Routine care
Apply a general-purpose, balanced fertilizer, 1–1.5kg (2–3½lb) per tree per year, in two or three separate dressings during the growing season. Water regularly in dry conditions and conserve moisture with an organic mulch (see SOILS AND FERTILIZERS, "Organic mulches", p.626). Papayas may be affected by viruses and eelworms after three or four years; if this happens, they should be replaced with either young plants of named cultivars or seedlings.

Pests and diseases
Common pests in the open are root-knot eelworms (p.660); papaya diseases include anthracnose (p.666), powdery mildew (p.646), and damping off of seedlings (p.664). Papaya trees grown under cover may also be attacked by aphids (p.646), thrips (p.647), whiteflies (p.646), and mealybugs (p.646).

Growing under cover
In temperate areas, papayas may be grown successfully under cover, if adequate light and temperature levels are provided. Raise seedlings or cuttings as described under "Propagation", below. Transplant them when they are 20–25cm (8–10in) tall into prepared beds, or pots with a minimum diameter of 35cm (14in). Use a fertile compost, to which a slow-release fertilizer has been added. Maintain a temperature of at least 22°C (72°F) and humidity of 60–70 per cent. Apply a liquid feed or light dressings of fertilizer with medium to high nitrogen content every three to four weeks. The plants should be watered regularly.

Pruning and training
Remove any lateral branches, since these are unproductive. After fruiting, prune to 30cm (12in) from the ground; of the new shoots that arise, select the strongest as the new leader and cut back the others.

Harvesting and storing
Harvest the fruits when they are orange to red. They may be stored at 10–13°C (50–55°F) with 70 per cent humidity for up to 14 days.

Propagation
Seed is the usual method of propagation. Sow the seed under cover in trays or, preferably, in bottomless

PAPAYA TREE

pots 6–9cm (2½–3½in) in diameter. Handle the seedlings carefully, since papayas are sensitive to root disturbance. Harden them off, then plant them out when they are 30–45cm (12–18in) tall. To obtain adequate numbers of female plants when dioecious cultivars are used, plant seedlings in clumps of three or four, thinning to one female plant after flowering begins. Hermaphrodite seedlings may be planted singly.

Cuttings are usually obtained by pruning mature trees to 30–40cm (12–16in) from the ground and using the new shoots as cuttings. Dip their bases in hormone rooting powder and grow them on under cover.

Citrus (*Citrus* spp.)

The genus *Citrus* includes oranges, lemons, and a number of other edible species (see p.481). Citrus form small, widely branching trees on trunks of 50–60cm (20–24in) in circumference. The trees will reach a height of 3–10m (10–30ft) and a spread of 5–8m (15–25ft). Limes are the most compact, grapefruits the largest and most vigorous. Lemon trees have a more upright habit than the other species. Also discussed here is the kumquat, which was formerly included within the genus *Citrus* but is now classified as *Fortunella*. Its cultivation requirements are similar to those of *Citrus*.

Citrus is a subtropical genus. All species and hybrids are evergreen and have aromatic leaves. For optimum growth, they require a temperature of 15–30°C (59–86°F), although most species will survive short periods at 0°C (32°F). They thrive at altitudes of 100m (320ft)

or above, with humidity levels of 60–70 per cent, unless otherwise stated. Flowering is not seasonal but occurs during warm periods with regular rainfall; flowers and fruits may coincide. Many species of citrus make excellent plants for growing in containers under cover in temperate areas.

Site and planting

Citrus prefer a sunny aspect and should be protected by windbreaks in exposed areas. They tolerate a wide range of soils but do best in fertile, well-drained, slightly acid soils (pH 6–6.5). Young citrus respond well to a high soil fertility.

Rootstocks
Sweet orange may be used, since it is compatible with all widely grown citrus species and cultivars. Rough

lemon rootstocks produce early-bearing, vigorous trees tolerant of tristeza (quick decline) viruses, but their fruits may have thick rinds and a low acid and sugar content. Sour orange is also a good universal rootstock, but it is susceptible to tristeza viruses.

Trifoliate orange is a dwarfing rootstock that is suitable for cooler areas. It has some resistance to eelworms but is not compatible with certain cultivars of lemon. Cleopatra mandarin and Troyer citrange are also used as rootstocks. Seedling rootstocks may also be raised – for details, see "Propagation", p.481.

Pollination
Most citrus, including sweet orange, are self-fertile, so a pollinator is not normally required; many, for instance the 'Washington' sweet orange, also produce seedless fruits.

Planting
Planting distances vary between 5m (15ft) and 10m (30ft) each way, depending on the vigour of the species or cultivar chosen. Citrus are sensitive to waterlogging, so on a site

SWEET ORANGE TREE

where the soil is not sufficiently well drained, plant each tree on a slight mound, 5–7cm (2–3in) high. For pot-grown citrus see CONTAINER GARDENING, "Planting large and long-term plants", p.324.

Routine care

During the first few years, feed citrus trees with a balanced fertilizer that has a high nitrogen and medium potassium level at a rate of 1kg (2lb 4oz) per tree per year. The fertilizer should be given in two or three doses, applied at regular intervals around the base of each tree, when the trees are in active growth. Double the quantity of fertilizer after five years. A mulch helps to retain moisture.

Remove all weeds around the bases of the trees, and water thoroughly in dry weather, particularly when the flowers or fruits are developing. The non-seasonal habit of fruiting makes fruit thinning unnecessary. Remove any suckers.

Pests and diseases

Various mealybugs (p.646), scale insects (p.648), thrips (p.647), red spider mite (p.646), aphids (p.646), root and crown rots (see "*Phytophthora* root rots", p.654), anthracnose (p.666), blue mould (p.658), and scab (p.649) may affect citrus grown in the open ground as well as under cover. Root-knot eelworms (p.660) may be serious pests on some soils. In the tropics and subtropics, fruit flies may be a problem (p.659).

Many citrus species and cultivars may be infected with tristeza virus, which is spread by aphids and causes stem pitting on grapefruits, limes, and citrons. Infected trees will lose vigour and produce small fruits. The virus is most likely to affect cultivars that are budded onto sour orange rootstocks. Spray against aphids, or use alternative rootstocks.

Growing under cover

In temperate areas, several cultivars of sweet orange, tangerine, lemon, and lime, as well as the Seville orange and kumquat, may be grown under cover, although they may not be relied on to bear fruit. Prepare the beds well, or use large containers, at least 60cm (2ft) in diameter, filled with a nutrient-rich compost. Maintain a minimum temperature of 20°C (68°F) with at least 75 per cent humidity, and water the plants regularly. Apply a liquid fertilizer each month once the young trees are well established.

Pruning and training

Shorten the main branches of newly planted trees by one third in the first year. This encourages lateral growth and produces a rounded shape. After fruiting, prune only to remove dead, diseased, or crossing branches and any that touch the soil. Citrus may also be trained as standards or half-standards (see p.439), particularly if grown as ornamentals.

Harvesting and storing

Citrus fruits may take from six to eight months, or even longer, from fruit set to ripen, depending on the climate (the lower the temperature, the longer the period required). In areas of low sunshine, mature citrus fruits may remain green.

Harvest the fruits when they have ripened by cutting them at the fruit stalk with secateurs or a sharp knife or by pulling the fruit stalk from the tree with a slight twist. Undamaged fruits may be stored for several weeks at 4–6°C (39–43°F).

Propagation

Some citrus may be raised from seed. Most citrus seeds are polyembryonic and therefore "clonal", reproducing characteristics of the parent tree. The quality of fruits from non-polyembryonic cultivars is variable. For named cultivars the usual means of propagation is by budding.

To raise citrus trees from seed, use fresh seed, sowing it in trays or pots of seed compost at a depth of 3–5cm (1¼–2in). Water the seeds frequently and maintain a temperature of 25–32°C (77–90°F). When the seedlings are large enough to handle, prick them out into 10 or 12cm (4 or 5in) pots. When they are 20–30cm (8–12in) high, transplant them into 21–30cm (8–12in) pots, or plant them out, after hardening them off. Alternatively, repot them into 25–38cm (10–15in) pots and plant in the open when they are 60–90cm (2–3ft) tall.

T-budding (see p.433) is the usual method of propagating citrus vegetatively. Use seedling citrus stocks with stems 1cm (½in) in diameter. After three to four weeks, remove the budding tape and cut the stock growth above the budded area halfway across. When the bud shoot is 2.5cm (1in) long, the stock growth above the budded shoot may be removed entirely.

RIPE SWEET ORANGES

Species of citrus

Limes (*Citrus aurantiifolia*)
There are two main groups of lime. One has an acidic taste, the other is fairly sweet and is often used as a rootstock. One of the acidic cultivars grown most commonly is 'West Indian'. Its fruits are round, small, and thin-skinned, with few seeds; the skin and pulp are green.

Most limes are grown as seedlings but may also be reproduced by budgrafting onto rough lemon rootstock.

Sour, Seville, or bitter oranges (*Citrus aurantium*)
The sour, or bitter, orange is an upright-growing tree, which is relatively cold-hardy. The fruits, which are used for making marmalade, are about 7cm (3in) in diameter, rounded, with thick peel. They are fairly acidic, but some forms bear fruits that have a lower citric acid content.

Lemons (*Citrus limon*)
Most lemon cultivars produce seeded fruits that may remain green, rather than turning yellow, even when fully mature. To grow successfully in the open, they prefer an altitude of 300–500m (1,000–1,600ft), with little variation in temperature, and need a minimum temperature of 20°C (68°F). As with other citrus, fruits may take 9–11 months to mature, and they often appear on a tree at the same time as its flowers.

Citrons (*Citrus medica*)
The fruits of the citron are ovoid and yellow, with a thick rind and a rough surface, and may be up to 15cm (6in) long; the pulp contains little juice.

Two main groups of citron cultivars have been recorded: acid cultivars such as 'Diamante' and 'Etrog', and non-acid cultivars such as 'Corsican'. Citrons are grown mainly for their peel, which is usually

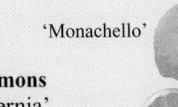
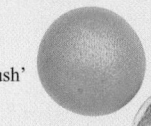

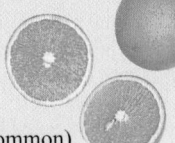

candied for use in the confectionery trade. Citrons make very attractive ornamentals, however; in temperate areas they may be grown under cover (see p.481).

Grapefruits (*Citrus* x *paradisi*)
The fruits of the grapefruit are large, rounded, up to 10–15cm (4–6in) in diameter, and yellow. Most cultivars are well adapted to growing at or just above sea level, provided the temperature exceeds 25°C (77°F). There are two principal groups of grapefruit in cultivation, one with white pulp, the other with pink; seeded and seedless cultivars are available in both groups.

Mandarins or tangerines (*Citrus reticulata*)
Mandarins, or tangerines, generally require temperatures above 18°C (64°F), but very high temperatures may result in loss of fruit quality.

Cross-pollination between trees frequently occurs; this gives rise to fruits with many seeds.

The Satsuma Group is the one most frequently cultivated; the fruits of cultivars in this group are mainly slightly flattened and seedless, with a well-developed orange colour and sweet flavour. Some cultivars have a "navel", a miniature fruit that develops at the end of the fruit. The other three groups are the Cleopatra Group, which is widely used as a rootstock but has unpalatable fruits itself, the King Group, and the Common Mandarin Group (which includes the cultivar 'Clementine').

Tangelos or ugli fruits (*Citrus* x *tangelo*)
This hybrid between the grapefruit and the mandarin inherits some characteristics from each of its parents; the orange fruits are larger than those of the mandarin but have a relatively

thin, easily peeled skin. They may be grown under cover in temperate areas, where they may occasionally bear fruit.

Sweet oranges (*Citrus sinensis*)
Sweet orange cultivars are usually classified into three groups: Valencia, navel, and blood oranges. Most sweet oranges, including the widely grown 'Jaffa' orange, belong to the Valencia (or Common) Group. The fruits are medium to large and spherical to ovoid, with few or no seeds. Oranges in this group may have a slightly acid taste but have an excellent flavour.

Navel oranges have a small secondary fruit at the main fruit apex and are usually seedless. They grow well in slightly cooler climates, peel and separate easily, and have excellent flavour. Blood oranges are similar but their pulp, juice, and rind are red (except when they are grown at high temperatures).

Sweet oranges are usually grown from seed, but a few specific cultivars are propagated vegetatively by bud-grafting (see p.432). Seedlings are also widely used as rootstocks for grafting with other species. Two sweet orange crops at different stages of development may be borne on a tree at the same time.

Kumquats (*Fortunella japonica, F. margarita*)
Originating in China, kumquats are hardier than the citrus fruits described above: they can withstand temperatures down to -5°C (23°F) for short periods. The fruits, which may be eaten unpeeled, are small and yellow. Those of *Fortunella japonica* are rounded in shape, while those of *F. margarita* are ovoid.

The calamondin (x *Citrofortunella microcarpa*) is a mandarin-kumquat hybrid; it is grown as an ornamental in temperate regions.

Tamarillos (*Cyphomandra betacea*, syn. *Solanum betaceum*)

Also known as tree tomatoes, tamarillos are subtropical trees growing to 3–5m (10–15ft), with a spread of 1.5–2.5m (5–8ft). They are most productive at 20–28°C (68–82°F) with 70 per cent humidity. The red, orange, or yellow fruits are ovoid and may be 7.5cm (3in) long.

RIPE TAMARILLOS

Site and planting
Tamarillos require a sunny position and protection from the wind in exposed sites, since the stems are quite brittle. Fertile, loam soils produce the best results. Allow a planting distance of about 3m (10ft) each way.

Routine care
A general-purpose fertilizer with medium to high nitrogen should be applied every two to three months at a rate of 110g (4oz) for each tree. Water well during dry periods, and use an organic mulch around the base of the plants to prevent loss of moisture from the soil.

Pests and diseases
Tamarillos in the open may be affected by aphids (p.646). They are susceptible to cucumber mosaic virus and potato virus "Y" (see "Viruses", pp.649 and 659); *Phytophthora palmivora* and *P. infestans* (see "Tomato/potato blight", p.649) may also cause problems. Under cover,

plants may be attacked by thrips, (p.647), whiteflies (p.646), red spider mite (p.646), and powdery mildew (p.658).

Growing under cover
Tamarillos may be grown in containers with a diameter of at least 35cm (14in) or in well-prepared beds. Use compost mixed with a general-purpose fertilizer. Maintain the correct temperatures and humidity, water regularly, and apply a liquid feed every three to four weeks.

Pruning and training
When plants reach a height of 1m (3ft), remove the growing point to encourage branching. Little pruning is needed apart from removing crowded and crossing branches, and diseased or dead wood.

Harvesting and storing
Tamarillos usually fruit one to two years after planting. Detach the fruits using a sharp knife when they start to

TAMARILLOS

change colour. They may be stored for up to two weeks at a temperature of 4–6°C (39–43°F).

Propagation
Sow seed under cover; pot the seedlings individually into 10cm (4in) pots when they are 3–5cm (1¼–2in) tall. When they reach 15–25cm (6–10in), harden them off and plant them out in the open. Propagation is also easy from virus-free softwood cuttings: select shoots 10–15cm (4–6in) long and use a sandy (but not acid) compost. Follow the procedure as for blueberries (see p.478).

Loquats (*Eriobotrya japonica*)

A member of the family Rosaceae, the loquat is an attractive, evergreen tree growing to 7m (22ft) or more tall, with a spread of about 5m (15ft). Loquats are best suited to a subtropical environment and need a minimum temperature of 15°C (59°F) to flower and fruit regularly. They are widely grown in the Mediterranean

region. In cooler climates loquats may be successfully grown under cover, since they are able to withstand relatively low temperatures for short periods. Some cultivars have a low chilling requirement.

Loquats bear clusters of fragrant, cream-coloured flowers, followed by bunches of round, yellow fruits

3–8cm (1¼–3in) long with tough skins. The pulp is soft and sweet.

Suitable rootstocks for loquats include quince (*Cydonia oblonga*), medlar (*Mespilus* spp.), and vigorous loquat seedlings. Most loquat cultivars are self-pollinated, but cross-pollination by insects may also occur.

Site and planting
Select a warm, sunny situation. Windbreaks should be erected to reduce wind damage and moisture evaporation. Loquats tolerate a wide range of soils, but prefer a well-drained, fertile, slightly acid loam. The trees should be planted at a distance of 4–5m (12–15ft) each way.

Routine care

Apply a top-dressing of general-purpose fertilizer at a rate of about 450g (16oz) per tree every three to four months. Loquats must be regularly watered to keep the roots moist during dry periods; regular applications of organic mulch help to reduce water loss. Keep the surrounding area free of weeds.

To ensure the production of large fruits, thin the bunches at an early stage of their development. Remove any that are weak or damaged, leaving healthy, evenly spaced fruitlets.

Pests and diseases

Plants in the open have few problems. Under cover, however, loquats may be attacked by thrips (p.647), mealybugs (p.646), red spider mite (p.646), whiteflies (p.646), and powdery mildew (p.658).

Growing under cover

Young, seed-raised plants may be grown in containers or planted out in well-prepared beds when they are about 45cm (18in) tall. Use a loam-based compost, with a slow-release fertilizer incorporated, and maintain a temperature of at least 18°C (64°F) during the summer. Water them regularly, and apply a liquid feed every month.

Pruning and training

Minimal pruning is required for loquats other than tip pruning all over-vigorous shoots and removing wayward branches; any crossing, damaged, dead, or diseased branches should also be removed.

Harvesting and storing

Harvest when the fruits soften and begin to turn rich yellow or orange. Short-term storage is possible at temperatures of 5–10°C (41–50°F).

Propagation

Loquats may be propagated by seed, sown 2–3cm (¾–1¼in) deep in pots of sandy seed compost, and main-

RIPE LOQUATS

LOQUAT TREE

tained at not less than 18°C (64°F). Transplant the seedlings to their final positions when they are 7–10cm (3–4in) high. Other techniques that may be used for propagating loquat cultivars include T-budding (see p.433), spliced side grafting (see *Propagating Trees by Spliced Side Grafting*, p.82), and air layering (see INDOOR GARDENING, p.383).

Mangos (*Mangifera indica*)

Mangos are tropical, evergreen trees that often reach 30m (100ft) when grown from vigorous seedlings. If dwarfing rootstocks and compact-growing clones are used, the trees' height may be restricted to 7–10m (22–30ft). The spread is about 8m (25ft) for dwarf types.

Mango fruits vary from 5 to 30cm (2 to 12in) in length and may weigh from 100g (3½oz) up to about 2kg (4lb 6oz). They have a leathery skin and may be orange, yellow, green, or red, depending on the cultivar. The single seed may comprise 25 per cent of the total volume of the fruit. Cultivars are available that are adapted to growing in subtropical areas with a temperature range of

MANGO TREE

21–25°C (70–77°F) with humidity above 60 per cent; the higher temperature is regarded as the optimum for most cultivars. For successful flowering and fruit set, mangos require a high light intensity and a dry period.

Site and planting

Select a warm, sunny aspect. If necessary, provide protection from strong winds, since high moisture loss may seriously affect the growth of the trees; very low humidity may worsen the situation, and lead to leaf scorch, seed abortion, and fruit drop.

Soil type is less important for mangos than it is for most other tree crops, and both sandy loams and medium clays are suitable, provided they are well drained. Mangos need a pH of between 5.5 and 7.5.

Dwarfing rootstocks are rapidly becoming available; these are often more suitable, particularly for small gardens, than non-selected local cultivars. If dwarfing rootstocks are not available, polyembryonic seedlings produced from parent trees selected for their high quality of fruit and yield are to be preferred.

Pollination is only successful in relatively dry weather, since high humidity and heavy rainfall limit fertilization (flowering usually begins after a period of cool or dry weather). A solution of potassium nitrate, applied as a spray, may promote flowering. Pollination is mainly by insects, although some mango cultivars are self-fertile.

Space compact and dwarf cultivars 8m (25ft) apart each way; more vigorous cultivars require a spacing of 10–12m (30–40ft).

Routine care

Feed with a general-purpose fertilizer with medium potassium and high nitrogen levels, at a rate of 1–1.5kg (2–3½lb) per tree, per year. This should be applied in three or four doses during the growing season; after the fourth year of growth, double the amount.

Water mangos well during dry periods, particularly in the first three years of growth, since plenty of moisture is essential for root development. An organic mulch retains moisture and suppresses weed (see "Organic mulches", p.626). Fruit thinning is rarely necessary.

Pests and diseases

In the tropics, mangos are liable to attack by fruit flies (p.659) and mealybugs (p.646); various types of scale insect (p.648) may also be a problem. Diseases that may affect trees in the open include anthracnose (p.666) and powdery mildew (p.646).

Mangos grown under cover may also be subject to damage by aphids (p.646), whiteflies (p.646), thrips (p.647), red spider mite (p.646), and certain forms of powdery and downy mildew (p.646).

MANGOS

Growing under cover

Mangos grown from seed are likely to be too vigorous for growing under cover unless they have been grafted onto a dwarfing rootstock, when they will form attractive, ornamental trees. They may be grown in large containers or well-prepared beds. In temperate regions, flowering will generally occur under cover only towards the end of the growing season, and only if the optimum growing conditions have been provided. Fruiting cannot be guaranteed, however, and is dependent on successful pollination.

Transplant young plants when they are about 1m (3ft) tall. They will require a compost containing a slow-release fertilizer with a medium potassium and high nitrogen content. Ensure that a minimum temperature of 21–25°C (70–77°F) and humidity of about 75 per cent are maintained. Mangos grown under cover should

be watered regularly and given a liquid feed every month. Supplement this with sprays of a nitrogenous fertilizer if the leaves turn yellow due to lack of nitrogen.

Pruning and training

Restrict pruning to tip pruning the leading shoot when it is about 1m (3ft) long to encourage lateral branching. Remove overcrowded or very vigorous growth during the early years to ensure an evenly spaced, rounded tree canopy. Once the tree is established, pruning is limited to the removal of diseased, dead, or crossing branches, or those that are congested.

Harvesting and storing

Mangos fruit three to four years after planting. The fruits should be picked when they begin to change colour. Handle them carefully to avoid any damage by bruising.

Any mangos that are slightly immature may be stored at 10°C (50°F) for two to four weeks, maintaining humidity of 90–95 per cent; they should ripen during this time.

Propagation

Propagation from seed is possible for polyembryonic cultivars, or various methods of grafting may be used instead. For seed propagation, remove the pulp of ripe fruits; to hasten germination, soak the seed in water for 48 hours and carefully remove the seed coat. Sow immediately in beds or containers, using well-prepared compost, and with the convex side of the seeds uppermost, lightly covering them with compost, and water.

The resulting seedlings may be polyembryonic and similar to the parent tree, but they are also likely to be very vigorous and take five to eight years to bear fruits that may prove variable in quality. A mango seed usually produces at least one such vigorous seedling resulting from self- or cross-pollination; any such seedlings should be discarded. The remaining seedlings are ready for transplanting to containers at least 15cm (6in) in diameter within six to eight weeks and may be used for rootstocks. Alternatively, they may be grown on as fruiting trees.

Mangos may also be propagated vegetatively, although stem cuttings often fail to root successfully. "Approach" grafting is a recommended alternative. Take a container-grown rootstock that is about one year old. Place the container near the scion branch still growing on the parent tree. Using a sharp knife, take a shallow, vertical slice 5–6cm (2–2½in) long from the side of the rootstock and scion, thus exposing the cambium layers. Place the matching cut surfaces together and bind them firmly. After two or three months the two should have united; cut the top off the rootstock, and sever the scion from the parent plant.

Other successful methods of propagating mangos are by T-budding (see p.433) and air layering (see INDOOR GARDENING, p.383).

Olives (*Olea europaea*)

Olives are evergreen trees, growing 9–12m (28–40ft) tall, with a spread of 7–9m (22–28ft). The fruits may be gathered while they are still green, or when they are fully ripe and have turned black. They may measure up to 4cm (1½in) long.

Olives grow well in subtropical areas with an optimum temperature range of 5–25°C (41–77°F). They need long, hot summers for the fruits to ripen fully, followed by winter temperatures that are low enough to meet the chilling requirement of the specific cultivar, so seek specialist advice on which cultivars grow best in your area. Very low winter temperatures may result in frost damage. Hot, dry winds and cool, wet weather in the flowering period reduce fruit set. In temperate areas olives are occasionally grown as ornamental trees (but seldom flower or fruit) or else in containers (see "Subtropical container gardening", p.318). Given suitable growing conditions, an olive tree may attain a great age.

Site and planting

A wide range of soils is suitable, although low to medium fertility is preferable, since soils that are very fertile are likely to result in excessive vegetative growth. The site must be well drained. Olives grow well on alkaline soils, including those with a high level of salts, provided that the pH level does not exceed 8.5. In exposed areas, grow by a wall or use a windbreak for protection.

Most cultivars are self-fertile but pollinators may be necessary to increase fruit yield in cooler climates. Olives are mainly pollinated by wind but also by insects; high humidity levels inhibit pollination.

The usual planting distance varies from 5m (15ft) to 7m (22ft) each way, depending on the habit of the cultivar; all olives should be staked to avoid wind damage. Closely planted trees may be thinned by removing alternate trees when the canopies begin to overlap.

Routine care

Top-dress with a general-purpose fertilizer with medium to high levels of nitrogen at a yearly rate of about 0.5–1kg (1–2lb) per tree, applied in two or three doses when the trees are in active growth. Applications of potassium and, possibly, boron supplements may be necessary on some soils. Water olives regularly during dry periods, particularly for the first two to three years after planting. Mulching with organic material is also beneficial. Keep the planting area free of weeds.

OLIVE TREE

Fruit thinning may be necessary, if the trees show signs of biennial bearing (see "Apples: Blossom thinning and biennial bearing", p.436). Thinning is generally done by hand, although professionals use a spray containing α-naphthalene acetic acid after flowering.

Pests and diseases

Olives grown in the open may be affected by various types of scale insect (p.648) and root-knot eelworms (p.660). Olive diseases include *Verticillium* wilt (p.653). Trees grown under cover may be affected by whiteflies (p.646), thrips (p.647), and red spider mite (p.646).

Growing under cover

Rooted cuttings or budded plants should be grown either in prepared beds, or in containers no smaller than 30–35cm (12–14in) in diameter; use a fertile compost that incorporates a slow-release fertilizer with medium levels of potassium

OLIVES

and nitrogen. Apply a liquid feed every three to four weeks and water the trees regularly.

Maintain a high temperature – above 21°C (70°F) – in summer and as low a temperature as possible in winter. Olives grown in containers may be placed in the open during the summer months.

Pruning and training

Prune newly planted olives by removing the leading shoot when it is about 1.5m (5ft) tall; select three to four strong laterals to provide the basic branch framework of the tree. Subsequent pruning consists of removing older branches to encourage the growth of new shoots, because fruits are produced on one-year-old wood mostly at the edges of the tree canopy.

Harvesting and storing

Olive trees grown in the open are likely to flower and fruit in three to four years from planting; yields generally increase until the tree is 15 years old, after which they remain fairly constant.

Olives are processed to remove their bitterness by immersion in a brine (5–6 per cent sodium chloride) solution. Fruits used for this treatment should be harvested when they are fully ripe but still green. Olives for eating may be harvested when black and firm, then packed in dry salt. When thoroughly dehydrated, the olives are stored in oil. Fruits for oil production should be left on the tree until they are fully ripe. They are harvested by shaking the tree so that the olives fall onto a cloth or fine netting placed on the ground below the tree canopy.

Propagation

Olives are usually propagated by stem cuttings, but selected cultivars may also be increased by bud-grafting. Cuttings may be hardwood (from one- or two-year-old wood), leafy, semi-ripe cuttings from the current season's growth, or softwood ones.

Hardwood cuttings, which are taken during winter, should be about 30cm (12in) in length. Remove the leaves from the lower half of each cutting, and soak its base for 24 hours in hormone rooting solution. Insert the cuttings to half their length in cutting compost, leaving them for about 30 days to root while maintaining a temperature of 13–21°C (55–70°F). Transplant the rooted cuttings singly into pots, and raise them in greenhouse conditions.

Alternatively, take softwood or semi-ripe cuttings 10–15cm (4–6in) long (see ORNAMENTAL TREES, p.79). Named olive cultivars may be propagated by T-budding (see p.433), always budding onto vigorous, olive seedling rootstocks.

Prickly pears (*Opuntia ficus-indica*)

This member of the cactus family is grown mainly in the subtropics. Although many of its forms are relatively low-growing and spreading in habit, some may eventually attain a height of 2m (6ft).

Most prickly pears will tolerate semi-arid conditions, with an optimum temperature range of 18–25°C (64–77°F); they will survive at lower temperatures, with a minimum of 10°C (50°F). Full sunlight is essential for satisfactory growth.

The stems of prickly pears consist of flattened, elliptic sections, 30–50cm (12–20in) long, which

PRICKLY PEAR

are almost spineless in many of the cultivated forms but very spiny on wild and naturalized plants.

Prickly pear fruits, which are produced from the upper part of the sections, are purple or red when ripe, and about 5–10cm (2–4in) long. They contain a soft, juicy pulp with many seeds. Prickly pears are pollinated by insects.

Site and planting

Prickly pears thrive in subtropical regions, where they are able to tolerate lengthy periods of drought. They are sensitive to poor drainage and saline conditions, however, and prefer sandy, well-aerated soils, with an ideal pH of 5.5–7.

Rooted sections are usually established 2–2.4m (6–7½ft) apart, with a spacing of 2–3m (6–10ft) between each row.

Routine care

Fertilizers are not normally required, unless the soil is particularly poor. Keep the planting site weed-free. Pests are rarely serious. Some forms of *Pythium* spp. (see "Damping off" p.660), however, may affect prickly pears in humid conditions.

Growing under cover

Use a sandy compost to which a slow-release fertilizer has been added. Maintain the temperature at

PROPAGATING PRICKLY PEARS FROM STEM SECTIONS

1 Using a sharp knife, cut a whole section away from the parent plant. It is advisable to wear gloves, since the spines irritate the skin.

2 After allowing the section to dry out for a few days, place it in a sandy compost, and firm it in. The section should have rooted in 2–3 months.

18–25°C (64–77°F) with humidity of 60 per cent or below. Little watering is required once the plants have become established.

Harvesting and storing

Prickly pears produce fruits three to four years after planting. Detach them carefully from the stem sections using a sharp knife. They are best eaten within a few days after they have been harvested, but may be stored for short periods in cool conditions, if necessary.

Propagation

Detach whole stem sections from the parent plant; if these are very large, cut them horizontally into two or three pieces. Allow them to callus in a sunny, sheltered place for several days before inserting them into a sandy compost. The sections should take two to three months to root; they may then be potted on into 15–20cm (6–8in) pots, or transplanted to their final positions. Water the new plants regularly until they are established.

Avocado pears (*Persea americana*)

The avocado pear is a subtropical, evergreen tree that may grow to a height of 10–15m (30–45ft), with a similar spread. Its fruits are pear-shaped, with a large, central, rounded seed. Fruit size and skin texture vary with the cultivar and colours range from green to russet. The three main types of avocado are Guatemalan, Mexican, and West Indian.

The optimum temperature range for growth and fruit development is 20–28°C (68–82°F) with humidity of over 60 per cent; some Mexican and Guatemalan cultivars and hybrid forms are able to withstand temperatures as low as 10–15°C (50–59°F), but they do not usually produce flowers at such low temperatures.

Site and planting

Avocado trees may be grown in the open in subtropical areas, provided the temperature is within the range given above. Their branches are brittle, so it is necessary to provide windbreaks in exposed areas to prevent them from being seriously damaged by the wind.

Select a site with maximum exposure to sun if possible. Avocados need a well-drained soil, since their roots are extremely sensitive to waterlogging. Medium loam soils with a pH of 5.5–6.5 are preferable, but sandy or clay loams may

RECOMMENDED AVOCADO PEARS

'Ettinger' (Mexican x Guat.)
'Fuerte' (Mexican x Guat.)
'Hass' (Guatemalan)
'Lula' (Guatemalan)
'Nabal' (Guat.)
'Pollock' (West Indian)
'Zutano' (Mexican x Guat.)

'Lula'

AVOCADO TREE

It is not normally necessary to thin the fruits on avocado trees.

Pests and diseases
Avocados may be affected by avocado root rot (see "*Phytophthora* root rots" p.654), anthracnose (p.666), and *Cercospora* spot or blotch (see "Fungal leaf spots", p.648); also by such pests as whiteflies (p.646), thrips (p.647), red spider mite (p.646), and mealybugs (p.646).

Growing under cover
Establish young plants either in well-prepared beds or in containers with a minimum diameter of 21cm (8in). Maintain temperatures of 20–28°C (68–82°F) and humidity of 70 per cent. For container-grown plants, pot on into containers at least 30cm (12in) in diameter, taking care not to disturb the plants' root systems.

Water containerized avocados regularly, and apply either a general-purpose fertilizer with a medium level of both potassium and nitrogen at intervals of two to three weeks, or a liquid feed. In temperate climates, flowering and fruiting are rare under cover, due to the trees' daylength and light intensity demands.

Pruning and training
Avocado trees need little pruning beyond shaping the tree during its early growth to ensure that an evenly spaced, rounded canopy develops. Once the tree is established, remove any diseased, damaged, or crossing branches after fruiting.

Harvesting and storing
Seed-raised trees start to bear fruit when they are between five and seven years old; budded or grafted plants are productive at three to five years after planting. The fruits may remain on the tree for up to 18 months without maturing, but they usually ripen rapidly after harvesting.

Cut the fruits from the tree using secateurs. Handle them carefully to avoid bruising. Store them at temperatures above 10°C (50°F) and at 60 per cent humidity. Any damaged fruits should be discarded.

Propagation
Avocado trees are easily grown from seed and reproduce virtually true to type. Select healthy, undamaged seeds and soak them in hot water for 30 minutes at 40–52°C (104–125°F) to inhibit infection from avocado root

RIPE AVOCADOS

rot. Cut a thin slice from the pointed end, then dip the wound in a fungicide. Sow the seed in sandy compost with the cut end slightly above the soil surface; germination usually takes about four weeks. The seedlings may be grown on in containers until they are about 30–40cm (12–16in) tall. They should then be ready for transferring to their final positions.

To propagate named cultivars onto disease-resistant rootstocks, side-wedge grafting (see PRINCIPLES OF PROPAGATION, p.636) or saddle grafting (see ORNAMENTAL SHRUBS, p.118) may be used.

also be suitable, if the drainage is good, or has been improved (see also "Preparing the site", p.424).

If grafted plants are to be used, those on rootstocks that are known to be both vigorous and resistant to avocado root rot (*Phytophthora cinnamomi*) are preferable. Avocados may be self-pollinated, but the best crops are produced if at least two cultivars are planted near to each other. Choose cultivars whose flowering periods coincide or overlap. When planting, allow 6m (20ft) each way between the trees.

Routine care
Apply a general-purpose fertilizer with a medium potassium and nitrogen content, when the trees are in active growth. The recommended rate is 1.5–2kg (3½–4½lb) per tree every year, preferably in two or three doses. Use an organic mulch around the base of each tree, leaving 25cm (10in) clear around the stems.

Water avocado trees during dry periods, particularly during the first three years when they are becoming established. Keep the area around the base of the trees free from all weeds.

GROWING AVOCADOS FROM SEED

1 Soak the seed in hot water and then prepare it by cutting about 1cm (½in) off the pointed end with a sharp knife. Dip the wound in fungicide.

2 Place the seed in a 15cm (6in) pot of moist seed compost so that the cut top of the seed is just above the soil surface.

3 Several weeks later the seed will have germinated to produce a shoot and roots.

Guavas (*Psidium guajava*)

Guava trees grow to a height of up to about 8m (25ft) and have a spread of 7m (22ft). They are widely grown in both tropical and subtropical regions and thrive in temperatures ranging from 22–28°C (72–82°F). The preferred humidity level is 70 per cent or less: a higher level may affect the quality of the fruits produced.

Guava fruits are 2.5–10cm (1–4in) in diameter, with either white or pink flesh. The flowers are normally pollinated by insects, particularly bees.

Site and planting
A sheltered site is preferable, protected by windbreaks if necessary. Guavas will tolerate a wide range of soils, but a well-drained loam is ideal. The pH may range from 5 to 7, but a pH of approximately 6 is most desirable.

When planting, allow a spacing of 5m (15ft) in each direction between the trees. The young trees should be securely staked in areas that are exposed to strong winds.

Routine care
Guavas respond well to applications of a general-purpose fertilizer with a medium potassium and nitrogen content. Use this at a rate of 1–2kg (2–4½lb) of fertilizer for each tree per year, divided into two or three top-dressings during the growing season. Weed the area around the bases of the trees, keep them well watered, and apply a mulch of organic matter, which will help to retain soil moisture.

GUAVAS

GUAVA TREE

Pests and diseases

Pests are rarely a serious problem, but in the open, aphids (p.646), fruit flies (see p.659), and root-knot eelworms (p.660) may require control. Anthracnose (p.666) occurs in many areas. Plants under cover may also be infested by whiteflies (p.646), and thrips (p.647). Guava seedlings are sensitive to damping off (p.660).

Growing under cover

Guavas may be grown in well-prepared beds or containers at least 30–35cm (12–14in) in diameter, using a fairly rich potting compost mixed with a slow-release fertilizer. Maintain a minimum temperature of 22°C (72°F) with humidity of 70 per cent. Water plants regularly, and apply a liquid feed every three to four weeks. To improve the chances of fruiting, cross-pollination by hand may be necessary. A relatively dry atmosphere should be maintained during the flowering period.

Pruning and training

When the young trees are about 1m (3ft) tall, cut back the leading shoot by about two thirds, to encourage branching. Subsequent pruning can be limited to the removal of any dead, crossing, or diseased branches, and any low branches that droop down and touch the soil.

Harvesting and storing

Guavas cultivated in the open generally fruit after one to three years, depending on cultivar and environmental conditions. The fruits ripen about five months after fertilization and may be picked when they begin to turn yellow. Handle them carefully, since they bruise easily.

They may be stored for up to three or four weeks at a temperature of 7–10°C (45–50°F), with relative humidity of 75 per cent.

Propagation

Guavas are usually propagated from seed; for the increase of specific cultivars, air layering, cuttings, or grafting may be used.

Sow seed in a fertile, sterile compost in trays or 7cm (3in) containers; germination normally occurs in two to three weeks. The seedlings may vary in quality: pot the strongest ones on into 15cm (6in) pots when they are 20cm (8in) tall. Harden the young plants off and transplant them when they are 30cm (12in) tall.

Selected guava cultivars may be side-wedge grafted (see p.636) onto vigorous seedling guava rootstocks, the stems of which should have a diameter of at least 5mm (¼in). No specific rootstocks are recommended; select only strong, healthy plants, preferably self-pollinated, as parents for rootstock seeds.

Guavas may also be increased by softwood cuttings 12–16cm (5–6in) long (see p.632). Plants produced by

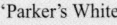
these graftings or cuttings may be planted out when they are about 30cm (12in) tall. In the open, guavas may be increased by simple layering (see ORNAMENTAL TREES, p.81) or by air layering (see INDOOR GARDENING, p.383). With the latter, hormone rooting powder applied to the girdled sections increases the success rate.

Pomegranates (*Punica granatum*)

Pomegranates form small, ornamental trees or bushes 2–3m (6–10ft) tall with a spread of 1–1.5m (3–5ft). They are evergreen in the subtropics but deciduous in cooler climates. The globular fruits are up to 10cm (4in) in diameter with leathery, yellow or red skins. The optimum temperature range is 18–25°C (64–77°F), but temperatures just below freezing are tolerated for short periods. Dry weather and a high temperature, ideally 35°C (96°F), are required for fruiting. In temperate climates, therefore, pomegranates are usually grown for their orange-red summer flowers and autumn colour; a dwarf variant of the species, *Punica granatum* var. *nana*, fruits freely under cover in temperate areas.

POMEGRANATE FLOWER AND FRUIT

Site and planting

Select a sunny aspect, sheltered by windbreaks in exposed conditions. Heavy loam soils with a pH level of about 7 are generally suitable, if they are well drained. Most cultivars are self-fertile. Plant seedlings, rooted cuttings, or suckers 4–6m (12–20ft) apart each way.

Routine care

Once plants are established, apply a general-purpose fertilizer every two to three months at a rate of 110g (4oz) for each tree per year. Mulch the site and keep it free of weeds; water the trees regularly during dry weather. Cut out all suckers.

Pests and diseases

Pomegranates grown in the open are generally trouble-free; under cover, they may be affected by whiteflies (p.646), aphids (p.646), red spider mite (p.646), and thrips (p.647).

Growing under cover

Plant pomegranates in well-prepared beds or containers with a minimum diameter of 35cm (14in), using potting compost with slow-release fertilizer added. Maintain a temperature range of 18–25°C (64–77°F) and humidity of 60–70 per cent. Apply a liquid fertilizer every three to four weeks, and water the plants regularly. Plants in containers may be moved into the open in summer.

Pruning and training

Select three or four main branches to form a framework and remove any crowded, crossing, or diseased branches. Cut out any suckers not required for propagation.

Harvesting and storing

Fruiting should start about two to three years after planting. Harvest the pomegranates when they turn yellow or red; they may then be stored for several weeks at 4–6°C (39–43°F).

Propagation

Pomegranates are usually propagated from cuttings or root suckers. Insert hardwood cuttings (see p.434) in sandy compost, and give bottom heat until they have rooted. Softwood cuttings (see *Blueberry Softwood Cuttings*, p.478) require bottom heat and mist (use compost with neutral pH). Pot on both types into 10–15cm (4–6in) pots when they have rooted. Root suckers may be carefully separated from the parent plant and replanted. Alternatively, dry off the seed; sow it in pots or trays of seed compost, maintaining a temperature of 22°C (72°F).

POMEGRANATE TREE

Nuts

Pecan nuts — Walnuts — Cobnuts — Sweet chestnuts — Almonds

SEVERAL nut-bearing trees and bushes are suitable for gardens; they prefer a sunny, open situation. Some, such as sweet chestnuts, walnuts, and pecans, eventually form large trees and make handsome specimens. In small gardens, an almond tree may make a fine feature, although it may produce nuts only in warm climates. Cobnuts and filberts may be pruned as compact bushes in a fruit garden or planted in informal groups in a wild garden. Most nuts (but not almonds) are monoecious, having separate male and female flowers on the same plant.

Pecan nuts (*Carya illinoinensis*)

Pecans are deciduous trees that may grow to 30m (100ft) high with a spread of 15–20m (50–70ft), so they are suitable only for large gardens. They grow best in warm-temperate climates: temperatures over 38°C (100°F) may lead to bark damage and the production of low-quality nuts; flowers may be damaged if the temperature drops below 1°C (34°F). Pecans have a chilling requirement of 150–250 hours below 7°C (45°F) in order for flowering to occur.

Pecans are monoecious but the male flowers are often open before the females on the same tree, so it is best to grow two or more cultivars near to each other to ensure that fertilization takes place. Since pecans are wind-pollinated, heavy rainfall when the trees are flowering may adversely affect pollination; after such conditions, crops may be poor. The nuts are ovoid, 2–2.5cm (¾–1in) long, and have a relatively thin shell.

Site and planting

Choose selected cultivars that have been grafted onto pecan seedling stock as trees raised from seed may not produce fruit of good quality. Pecans quickly develop a long tap root, so plant young trees: older, pot-grown plants with congested roots are seldom successful. Pecans need a site that is sheltered from strong winds and thrive on deep, fertile soils with a pH of 6–6.5.

Plant the trees when they are dormant (see *Planting a Fruit Tree*, p.425), spacing them 8m (25ft) apart.

PECANS

Routine care

Apply a top-dressing of a balanced fertilizer at a rate of 70–140g/sq m (2–4oz/sq yd) annually. Keep the planting site weed-free, and water the trees during dry periods until they are established. Pecans are moderately resistant to drought but require plenty of water during the summer months.

Pecan trees are seldom affected by pests and diseases; *Phytophthora* root rots (p.661) and aphids (p.646) may sometimes be a problem.

Pruning and training

Train pecans with a central leader initially (see "Central-leader standard trees", p.72). Once the trees are established, pruning is restricted to removing crossing and congested branches and any dead wood.

Harvesting and storing

The first crop may be produced after five years; full production is reached after 15–20 years. The nuts are usually harvested by hand. They may be stored, in cool, dry, airy conditions, for several months.

Propagation

Whip-and-tongue grafting of selected cultivars onto vigorous pecan seedling rootstocks is the most usual method of propagation (see p.433). The seedlings to be used as stock plants should be raised in deep pots or plastic sleeves, since their long tap roots are sensitive to damage during transplanting.

RECOMMENDED PECANS

'Desirable'
'Elisabeth'
'Elliot'
'Mohawk'
'Moore'
'Moreland'

Sweet chestnuts (*Castanea sativa*)

Sweet or Spanish chestnuts are deciduous, summer-flowering trees up to 30m (100ft) tall with a spread of 15m (50ft). They are monoecious and wind-pollinated. Some cultivars may need a pollinator. The shiny, rich brown nuts are borne most consistently in areas with cold winters and warm summers. Two or three kernels are usual, but in some cultivars, such as 'Marron de Lyon' and 'Paragon', a single kernel is formed.

Site, planting, and routine care

A fertile, moisture-retentive soil with a pH of 6 is preferred; allow 10–12m (30–40ft) between trees (see *Planting a Fruit Tree*, p.425). Water young trees and keep the site weed-free. On well-prepared sites, applications of fertilizer are unnecessary. Trees may be affected by honey fungus (p.665).

Pruning and training

Train as central-leader standards (see p.72). On established trees, remove congested, crossing, or dead branches.

SWEET CHESTNUTS

Harvesting and storing

Nuts are borne after about four years. Harvest them in the autumn. Hull the nuts, soak them for 48 hours, discarding any that darken, then dry and store them in a cool, airy place.

Propagation

Propagate from selected cultivars by bud-grafting or whip-and-tongue grafting onto seedling stock of sweet chestnut (see pp.432 and 433).

Cobnuts and filberts (*Corylus avellana* and *C. maxima*)

Cobnuts (or hazels) and filberts are valued for their winter catkins and their nuts. Unpruned, they reach a height and spread of 4–5m (12–15ft). They are deciduous and monoecious, and crop best in cool, moist summers. The chilling requirement is 800–1,200 hours below 7°C (45°F). Winter temperatures below -10°C (14°F) may damage the male flowers (catkins), although the female flowers are usually less vulnerable. The outer husk or calyx of the cobnut does not completely envelop the nut. The filbert has a husk that is longer than the nut and often completely encloses it; a sub-group of filberts has frilled husks and is known as frizzled filberts. Cobnuts and filberts are wind-pollinated; many are self-fertile. For cobnuts, recommended self-fertile cultivars include

COBNUTS

FILBERTS

'Cosford' and 'Nottingham' (syn. 'Pearson's Prolific'); a recommended self-fertile filbert is 'Kentish Cob'. The nuts of cobnuts and filberts are brown and egg-shaped.

Site and planting
A partially shaded, sheltered position is preferable. A soil pH of 6 is best; very rich soil may cause excessive soft growth at the expense of cropping. Adequate moisture with good drainage is important. Plant in autumn or early winter, 5m (15ft) apart (see *Planting a Fruit Tree*, p.425).

Routine care
Weed and mulch regularly; water in dry spells. On poor soils apply a balanced fertilizer in spring at a rate of 100g/sq m (3oz/sq yd). Trees are usually trouble-free, but the fruits may be attacked by hazelnut weevil, for which there is no chemical control for amateur gardeners.

Pruning and training
Cobnuts and filberts are usually grown as open-centre bushes, each with a 45cm (18in) stem and eight to twelve main branches. On young plants, prune the leaders in winter to 55cm (22in); good laterals should then develop. Remove any shoots growing low down on the main stem and all but the best-placed, strongest shoots needed to develop the framework. Shorten these by one third in winter. The following winter remove any excessively strong, upright growth and, if necessary, tip prune sideshoots to form a well-balanced framework.

Established bushes bear heavier crops if pruned in late summer using

BRUTTING COBNUTS

In the late summer, strong shoots of the current season's growth that are about 30cm (12in) long are broken and left hanging. This helps the formation of flower buds.

a technique known as "brutting". Break the longer sideshoots halfway along their length, and let them hang. This opens up the bush and encourages more female flowers to form. In winter, when the catkins release pollen, shorten the brutted shoots to three or four buds; remove old or overcrowded shoots.

Harvesting and storing
Nuts are borne after three or four years. Gather them when the husks begin to yellow. Dry, then store.

Propagation
Suckers produced from tree roots may be used for propagation. In winter, remove them, each with a root ball, and grow on in a nursery bed or plant directly in their final positions. Trees may also be propagated by simple layering (see p.116) in autumn.

Walnuts (*Juglans regia*)

English walnuts (strictly speaking Persian) are deciduous trees that may reach a height of 18m (60ft) with a similar spread; they are suitable only for large gardens. Named cultivars should always be planted for fruit, since seedlings may produce poor-quality nuts. Walnuts are monoecious and wind-pollinated. Most are self-fertile but some cultivars produce male catkins and pollen before the female flowers are receptive. To overcome this problem, plant nearby a reliable pollinator such as the old French cultivar 'Franquette'. Walnuts have a chilling requirement of 500–1,000 hours below 7°C (45°F). The gnarled nuts develop within a pitted shell.

Site, planting, and routine care
A well-drained, moisture-retentive soil is best. Walnuts prefer a pH of

Walnuts may be slow to establish, but after two or three years, once the root system is well developed, stronger growth occurs. Bacterial leaf blotch and blight may be a problem (see "Bacterial leaf spots and blotches", p.648).

Pruning and training
Walnuts should be trained as central-leader standards (see p.72). Prune in midwinter since the trees do not bleed when they are dormant. Remove any strong shoots that make a narrow angle with the stem, to leave a well-balanced framework of evenly spaced branches. Thereafter, little pruning is required apart from cutting out overcrowded, crossing, or congested branches in winter and removing dead wood as required.

Harvesting and storing
Walnut trees may need many years before they start bearing. Walnuts for pickling should be picked in summer before the hulls and shells harden. In early autumn, the hull or casing cracks to release the nut, still in its shell.

WALNUTS

Gather the crop before the shells become discoloured. Clean, then gently dry the nuts. Store them in cool, airy, slightly humid conditions.

Propagation
The usual methods are whip-and-tongue grafting (see p.433) or chip-budding (see p.432) cultivars onto seedlings of the American black walnut (*Juglans nigra*). In cool climates keep a grafted tree under glass until the graft has taken, then move the container to a protected site in the open. Plant young trees in their final positions in autumn or winter.

Almonds (*Prunus dulcis*)

Unpruned, sweet almonds grow about 5–6m (15–20ft) tall, with a similar spread. They crop regularly only in areas with warm, dry summers and frost-free winters. The chilling requirement is 300–500 hours below 7°C (45°F). In cool areas they are often grown as ornamentals. Almonds are insect-pollinated. Most cultivars are partly self-fertile, but crops will be better if a pollinator is planted nearby. The nuts are flattened and pointed, with a pitted shell.

Site, planting, and routine care
Almonds require a sheltered, frost-free site and a well-drained soil, preferably with a pH of 6.5. Plant them 6–7m (20–22ft) apart (see *Planting a Fruit Tree*, p.425).

Cultivation of almonds is as for peaches (see p.451). Peach leaf curl (p.651) and bacterial canker (p.665) may affect almond trees.

Pruning and training
Almonds are usually pruned and trained as bushes, as for peaches (see p.452). Nuts are borne on one-year-old wood. In summer, on established trees, remove one quarter of the old shoots that have cropped in previous seasons to encourage fresh growth.

Harvesting and storing
The nuts are borne after three to four years. Gather them as their hulls start

RECOMMENDED WALNUTS

All cultivars listed are self-fertile.
'Broadview'
'Buccaneer'
'Franquette'
'Lara'
'Mayette'
'Parisienne'

6.5–7 but tolerate some alkalinity. Since flowers and young shoots are susceptible to frost damage, avoid cold sites. Walnuts have a long tap root, so select young plants rather than older, pot-grown ones whose roots may be congested. Plant in late autumn or winter (see *Planting a Fruit Tree*, p.425), with 12–18m (40–60ft) between trees.

ALMONDS

to crack. Clean and dry the almonds before storing them.

Propagation
Almonds are usually propagated by chip-budding (see p.432). Root stocks vary according to soil type: almond seedlings are often used in dry regions while peach seedlings are more suitable for heavier soils.

RECOMMENDED ALMONDS
'Balatoni'
'Macrocarpa'
'Titan'

CHAPTER

17

GROWING VEGETABLES

MORE AND MORE gardeners are discovering the deep satisfaction of growing their own vegetables. They do so for many reasons: for the majority it is the joy of savouring a freshness and flavour that is so often missing from shop-bought produce, while some relish the chance to grow unusual cultivars. Organic gardeners want to harvest crops that are untainted by chemical residues. Then again, there are those who find a well-tended vegetable patch every bit as beautiful as a herbaceous border. Modern science and methods of cultivation, coupled with the outstanding vigour and disease-resistance of many of today's vegetable cultivars, enable even newcomers to vegetable growing to experience the satisfaction of bringing to the table fine vegetables that they have sown, tended, and harvested in their own gardens.

Designing a vegetable garden

A HEALTHY, productive area for growing vegetables may be created in a garden of any size, from a large, sunny area to a few containers on a patio. The vegetables may be grown in a separate vegetable plot or integrated with flower beds.

Good growing conditions are essential if vegetables of quality are to be produced. Virtually any site can, however, be made suitable, perhaps by erecting windbreaks if it is exposed, or taking the necessary steps to improve soil fertility and drainage. This cannot be done overnight, but within a year or two very satisfactory results may be obtained.

Choosing the site

Most vegetables lead short but pampered lives so the ideal situation for a vegetable garden provides warmth, sunlight, shelter, and fertile, well-drained, loamy soil with an adequate water supply. The chosen site should be open but not exposed, and not overshadowed: trees shade and drip on plants and remove nutrients and moisture from the soil, while buildings may create shade and funnel damaging winds across the plot.

Shelter from wind
Providing shelter from wind is one of the most important factors in vegetable growing. Wherever possible,

A WELL-DESIGNED GARDEN
This thriving vegetable garden is both well designed and effectively maintained, with an open, but not exposed, *aspect. The beds all contain different crops, and a network of paths allows easy access to each bed.*

avoid windy sites: even light winds may decrease vegetable yields by 20–30 per cent, while strong winds are often devastating. Vegetables in coastal gardens may be damaged by desiccating wind-borne, salt spray.

Windbreaks

In gardens exposed to wind, windbreaks should be erected; they should be about 50 per cent permeable, allowing the wind to filter through, rather than solid structures which force the wind over them, creating an area of turbulence on the other side (see also FROST AND WIND PROTECTION, pp.612–613, and CLIMATE AND THE GARDEN, "Wind", p.610).

An effective windbreak may be either a living barrier, such as a hedge, or a structure such as a slatted fence or a screen of windbreak netting. Hedges are attractive but take time to become established, require maintenance, take up considerable space, and compete for soil, water, and plant nutrients; they are therefore only appropriate in quite large gardens. For further information, see HEDGES AND SCREENS, pp.84–85. A windbreak of trees could be considered at the boundaries of a very large garden. In smaller sites, fences, hurdles, or windbreak netting battened to posts or stakes are more practical.

A windbreak gives maximum shelter over a distance roughly five times its height. A very exposed garden may need a windbreak at least 2m (6ft) high. In this case, nets and posts must be strong, as they will be subjected to great strain in high winds. Alternatively, erect lower, short-term windbreaks between rows of plants or beds; netting windbreaks

no more than 45cm (18in) high and 3–4m (10–12ft) apart, attached to canes, are very effective for this.

If gaps in buildings or trees create a wind funnel across the garden, erect a barrier extending 1m (3ft) across the gap in each direction. Deciduous shrubs or a hedge may be planted in the gap, with an artificial windbreak to shelter the plants until they are established.

Slopes

A sloping site is less easy to work than a flat one and soil erosion after heavy rain may be a problem on steep slopes; setting the beds across the slope may help. A site on a south-facing slope is an advantage in cool-temperate climates because it warms up rapidly in spring. In hot climates, site beds on a north-facing slope because here they will have relief from intense sun.

Positioning

The orientation of vegetable beds often makes little difference to open-ground crops, but greenhouses and frames should be oriented so that their sloping surfaces face the sun to maximize efficiency. Position tall crops, such as climbing beans, carefully: in temperate climates, place them where they will not shade dwarf-sized plants from the sun, but in hotter climates use them to provide such shade.

Sites below garden walls

In temperate and northern climates, the ground at the foot of a south-facing garden wall is a warm, sheltered place that is useful for growing early spring and late autumn crops

ALLOCATING SPACE
Each element in this garden has been sited to produce optimum growing conditions for the crops. The greenhouse and frame are positioned to receive maximum light, the hedge filters the prevailing wind, and tall plants, such as the runner beans, do not overshadow the smaller vegetables.

and, in summer, tender, sun-loving crops such as tomatoes and aubergines. Keep these beds well watered so that the soil does not dry out. North-facing walls can provide some shade for plants such as lettuces and peas that suffer in high temperatures.

Maintaining soil fertility

A friable loam is ideal for growing vegetables: it is rich in plant nutrients, and supports a population of earthworms and micro-organisms to break down organic matter. It has a good structure, and remains workable even in adverse conditions: it

does not become sticky during wet weather or dusty in dry periods, but always retains a crumbly texture, so that the soil is well aerated; this is important for both the living organisms in the soil and the roots of the vegetables themselves. An ideal soil is both well drained and moisture-retentive, and should be slightly acid (pH6–6.5). In such a soil, most vegetables grow well, and need little extra feeding.

Soil types

Vegetables may be grown successfully on a range of different soil types. At one extreme are porous, sandy soils, which warm up quickly in spring and are ideal for early crops. They are easy to cultivate year-round, but lose nutrients rapidly to leaching, so that crop feeding and irrigation are especially important. At the other extreme are heavy clays, which hold nutrients well, but are relatively slow to warm, sticky, and prone to waterlogging; they are best cultivated in autumn and winter.

In practice, many soils are a mixture of types. The key to success is timely cultivation and, above all, the incorporation of well-rotted organic matter to improve nutrient and water-holding capacity. Adequate lime content is critical in soil fertility and sites should be tested for pH levels frequently. For further information, see "Soil and its Structure", pp.616–617.

Using organic matter

Crops continuously remove nutrients from the soil and from naturally decomposing organic matter. In almost all soils, fertility must be maintained by replenishing organic

ALTERNATING ROWS
Provided that the fertility of the soil is maintained, rows of vegetables may be arranged to maximize yields by alternating rows of fast- and slow-growing crops (here different types of lettuce and a range of brassicas). The fast-growing lettuces will have been harvested by the time the brassicas have reached maturity.

matter regularly. The main forms available to gardeners are animal manures (preferably with a high straw content but little sawdust or woodshavings), spent mushroom compost, seaweed, or homemade garden compost.

A layer of organic matter 8–10cm (3–4in) deep, applied over most of the ground each year, will maintain structure and fertility. It may be spread on the surface or dug into the soil. If organic matter is spread on the soil surface in the autumn, earthworms will work it in. This is particularly beneficial on light soils where heavy winter rainfall can cause leaching of nutrients. Any organic matter remaining on the surface in spring should be forked in. Dig organic matter into heavy soils in autumn, or into light soils in spring, spreading it evenly throughout the soil as deeply as possible Well-rotted organic matter is a useful mulch and can be used at any point in the growing season (see also "Mulching", p.502).

Green manuring

This is the practice of growing crops specifically to dig into the soil to improve its fertility. In the vegetable garden green manures may be grown and dug in between crops, or grown over winter to augment soil nutrients and avoid leaving the soil bare (see SOILS AND FERTILIZERS, "Green manures", p.625).

INTERCROPPING
Lettuces and sweet corn planted together mature at varying rates. The fast-growing lettuces are ready to harvest before the sweet corn is fully grown.

Drainage

Good drainage is absolutely essential; where there is a serious problem, it may be necessary to lay land drains (see SOILS AND FERTILIZERS, "Improving drainage", p.623).

In most cases, working in copious quantities of organic matter improves drainage markedly, since this will encourage earthworm activity, which improves the soil structure by creating an extensive network of small drainage channels.

Preserving soil structure

Good soil structure is easily destroyed by physically damaging it, for example, by walking on it or cultivating it when it is either very wet or very dry, or from heavy rain beating down on the surface. Laying out the garden in narrow beds (see THE BED SYSTEM, p.496) to minimize the need to tread on the soil, and keeping the surface mulched (see "Mulching", p.502) will help to preserve the structure.

Planning the vegetable garden

The layout of a vegetable garden is determined by the size, shape, and nature of the garden and the demands of the household. It is important to plan for crop rotation (see CROP ROTATION, p.498) so that the four main vegetable groups – legumes, brassicas, roots, and crops of the onion family – can be grown on different sites in successive years to minimize the build-up of pests and diseases. Gardeners with space for a kitchen garden usually opt either for traditional, allotment-style rows, or for permanent beds in which different crops are grown each year (see THE BED SYSTEM, pp.495–496), but there are alternatives for those with limited space. It is also important to plan for perennial vegetables and herbs.

A place for perennials

Most vegetables are grown as annuals on a different piece of ground each year. The few perennial vegetables, such as rhubarb, asparagus, and globe artichokes, should be grouped in a permanent bed at one side or end of the garden, separated from the annual vegetables. If there is space, they may be intercropped with other, fast-growing vegetables (see "Maximizing space", below).

Vegetables in containers

Gardeners who are limited to terraces, concreted yards, patios, roofs, or balconies often grow vegetables in containers to provide a productive display that can also, especially with imaginative cultivar choices, be very attractive (see CONTAINER GARDENING, p.318). Although vegetables are more difficult than flowers to grow successfully in containers, they are still worth the effort involved. Place containers on paths and low walls to make the best use of the space available, and plant them up with dwarf and the more decorative cultivars. Suitable containers range from terracotta pots and tubs to proprietary growing bags filled with compost.

Maximizing space

To maximize yields in a given area, crops may be combined in a single bed. Seeds of a fast-growing crop, such as radishes, can be intersown simultaneously and in the same row as slower growing parsnips. Garlic, shallots, onion sets, and bunching onions are also suitable for intercropping. Likewise, a rapidly maturing "catch crop" such as lettuce, can be grown among slow-maturing brassicas. A chequerboard pattern gives maximum efficiency, but alternate rows also work well. Alternatively, catch crops can be sown before or between rows of slower crops, for example, spinach with tomatoes or winter brassicas. The fast-growers make immediate use of the available space, but mature before the slower-growing crops need the room. Ensure that the short-term crop is not shaded by the slower-growing one.

Vegetables in flower beds

As many gardens are too small to allow a complete area to be devoted to vegetables, there has been a move in recent years towards integrating them into flower beds, or planting them in groups of beds to create an attractive pattern. Wherever possible, vegetable cultivars are selected for their decorative qualities, and then grouped to display them to maximum effect. This approach is known as "potager gardening" in Europe and "edible landscaping" in the USA. There is enormous scope to develop individual ideas. The only requirement for growing vegetables in flower beds is to ensure that soil fertility is maintained at the level necessary for the chosen vegetables.

A PATCHWORK OF CROPS
Square beds with soil paths between them provide a neat framework for manageable rows of vegetables. A plot laid out like this allows a variety of crops to be grown, and is designed for a simple method of crop rotation.

Climatic factors

Most vegetables grow only when the average daytime temperature rises above about 6°C (43°F) between spring and autumn. The number of "growing days" with suitable daytime temperatures that occur between these seasons is governed by factors such as latitude, altitude, and degree of exposure, and largely determines sowing dates and the type of crops that may be grown outdoors in any given locality.

Temperature requirements

Vegetables are sometimes classified as warm- or cool-season crops, depending on their physiological needs, particularly those relating to temperature. Most brassicas and several bulb and stem vegetables cannot withstand intense heat, whereas more tender vegetables, such as tomatoes, are damaged or killed by freezing temperatures. Cultivars of some vegetables have been bred to resist cold, and the growing season of many vegetables may be extended at either end of the season by growing them under cover (see p.505). See individual vegetables for specific temperature requirements (pp.507–548).

Daylength

The number of daylight hours, or daylength, differs according to the latitude and season, and vegetable cultivars have a varying response to daylength at different stages of their growth. Short-day plants grow and seed only if the daylength is less than 12 hours; long-day plants only if it is more than 12 hours.

This affects the sowing time, particularly of crops that are grown for their seeds, such as beans; others must be harvested before flowering. Onions, for example, are naturally long-day plants: when the daylength is 16 hours or more, onions stop making leafy growth and start to develop a bulb. The more leafy growth that has been made up to this point, the larger the bulb that forms; onion seeds should therefore be sown early in the year so that the plant will develop as much leafy growth as possible before the daylength increases.

Cultivars are available that have been specially bred and adapted to long or short days, or that are daylength neutral. Examples are mentioned under individual vegetables later in the chapter; the safest course is to choose cultivars recommended for your area.

Rainfall

The average annual rainfall of a district has a significant influence on the growth of vegetables. In areas of low precipitation, there is a risk of drought at the important stages of crop development, such as the swelling of peas and beans, or leaf growth in lettuces. In low-rainfall areas, watering and surface mulching to conserve moisture become critical considerations.

In high-rainfall areas, it is essential to maintain or create free soil drainage and more vigilance is called for to recognize and deal with the effects of slugs, snails, and fungal leaf diseases, all of which proliferate in damp conditions. With high rainfall, nutrients are also more likely to be leached from the soil and supplementary feeding may be necessary.

Aspect

Although the climatic factors of a locality cannot be altered, their worst effects can be alleviated by good soil management and by taking steps to improve the microclimate (the environmental conditions within a garden). It is important to develop and take advantage of physical aspects. Providing wind shelter with fences, screens, or hedges reduces water loss from vegetables and the soil and promotes higher average soil temperatures, which aids growth. Walls or fences facing the sun form warm niches that are particularly beneficial to crops such as tomatoes, peppers, and sweet corn, which do best at higher temperatures. Ground that slopes towards the sun warms soonest in spring and is ideal for early vegetables. Conversely, be alert to the disadvantages of tall walls in producing shade from sun and rain.

A PRODUCTIVE DISPLAY
This example of potager planting groups marrows climbing a supporting arch with a profusion of yellow and red nasturtiums beneath. All thrive in warm, sunny conditions.

COMBINING VEGETABLES AND HERBS
This informal garden has vegetables intermingled with herbs. Runner beans climb up an arch, parsley and chives ring red and green "Salad Bowl" lettuces at the edge of the centre bed, and sweet corn develops among feathery dill.

VEGETABLES IN A WINDOWBOX
Vegetables can thrive in small containers, such as this windowbox. Here shallow-rooted lettuces, young cabbages, tomatoes, and strawberries have been chosen not only for their culinary uses, but also for their decorative qualities.

The bed system

FRUIT and vegetables are best grown in open ground, either on the flat or in raised beds. In these situations the soil benefits from rainfall and weathering, and the plants have a free root run. In the traditional garden, it is usual to set aside a particular garden area specifically for fruit and vegetables. This area can be a wide, open plot, but an excellent, more modern alternative is to set out the vegetable garden as a series of narrow beds divided by pathways.

The traditional vegetable patch

In the traditional kitchen garden, long rows of vegetables usually run across the plot. This is a perfectly good way to grow produce; it allows large areas of ground to be cultivated and used with maximum flexibility.

Growing crops, however, requires constant access for sowing, thinning, planting out, watering, top-dressing, pest and disease control, weeding, harvesting, and clearing. Each task involves treading on the ground, which compresses the soil. This reduces the air in the soil, impedes drainage, and results in poor growth. Compaction can be reduced by taking care not to tread on wet soil and by walking on planks to spread the weight, but narrow beds totally avoid the need to walk on cropped areas.

Using beds

In a bed system, the cropping area is divided into semi-permanent or fixed beds. The beds should be narrow enough to bring their central areas within arm's reach, so that all cultivation tasks can be carried out from

CLOSE CROPPING
The high soil fertility in this raised bed permits close and equidistant plant spacing in staggered rows. Narrow beds like these are also particularly convenient when using a standard width of horticultural fleece to protect crops.

the dividing pathways, without stepping onto the soil. This avoids soil compaction and has the additional advantage that harvesting and other tasks can be done soon after rain without the usual risk of damaging soil structure. There is also less need to dig beds once they are established and fertile, and what cultivation is necessary is greatly reduced because of the smaller cropped area. Since the regular addition of bulky organic manures is concentrated on a smaller area, it is easier to build up high

levels of fertility, and to improve soil aeration and drainage, which in turn leads to stronger root growth.

The concentration of cropping areas into relatively confined spaces makes the bed system an ideal solution for worthwhile vegetable production in small gardens. The increase in soil fertility and lack of need for access along crop rows allows plants to be grown at closer spacings. Lettuces, for example, may be grown 20cm (8in) apart each way in staggered rows, as opposed to

rows 30cm (12in) apart in more traditional layouts. Each plant gains the maximum root space in the smallest possible area, making the best use of the soil available and increasing the total yield.

The close spacing of plants has further indirect benefits. Irrigation using low-level distribution systems such as seep hoses (see p.561) becomes more manageable, since smaller areas are served; water can also be used less wastefully using more conventional watering techniques.

MAKING A RAISED BED

1 *Measure and mark out beds. Edge with 15 x 2.5cm (6 x 1in) boards, sunk into a 5cm (2in) slit trench and supported by timber pegs driven into the ground every 1–1.2m (3–4ft).*

2 *Fill the bed with good-quality topsoil that has been enriched with organic matter such as well-rotted manure or garden compost. Take care to avoid creating air pockets at the edges and corners.*

3 *Spread out the soil evenly using a rake. Break up any lumps, aiming to achieve an even, firm texture. Make the finished soil surface roughly level with the top of the boards, topping up as necessary.*

4 *Level the soil with the back of the rake to leave a smooth finish. Top up with more soil as necessary in later weeks when the filled bed settles and the level of the soil falls.*

PLANTING IN A BED

The bed should be no more than 1.5m (5ft) wide, so that the centre is within easy arm's reach from either side. All work can then be carried out from the surrounding paths without any need to tread on the soil, thus avoiding damage to the soil structure.

Close spacing results in more effective smothering of annual weed growth, so weeding is also reduced.

Using a bed system can make crop rotation (see p.498) much easier, as each crop group can be allocated to a bed and moved on to a different one the following year according to the rotation requirements.

Planning bed layouts

Beds may be rectangular, square, or even curved; the prime consideration is that they must allow the whole bed to be cultivated from the paths.

The ideal width is 1.2m (4ft); this can be increased to 1.5m (5ft) if this makes better use of available space, or reduced to 1m (3ft) for areas that are to be protected with glass or plastic cloches. Narrow strips are particularly suitable for strawberries, for ease of mulching and harvesting.

The bed length can be adjusted to suit the site and, while their orientation is not of vital importance, running them from north to south generally ensures the most even distribution of sunlight.

The width of the paths between beds needs to be at least 45cm (18in) wide to allow for easy access, both on foot and with wheelbarrows.

Types of beds

Many terms are used to describe beds: they include flat or semi-flat beds, deep beds, and raised beds. A flat or semi-flat bed is simply marked out from the surrounding garden and cultivated. With repeated annual addition of bulky organic dressings, soil depth is increased as the bed surface is gradually raised above path level.

Deep beds

Organic growers often aim to minimize soil cultivation to preserve its natural structure and fertility and reduce the growth of weeds. Deep beds are an ideal way of achieving this. In deep beds, soil is improved to the required depth with one thorough cultivation that incorporates large amounts of organic matter (see *Double digging*, p.620). After this, further digging is avoided so that a natural soil structure develops, encouraged by the organic matter and a high worm population. Further organic matter is added only as mulches and top-dressings. The only disturbance to the soil surface occurs when planting, so weed seeds below germination level remain dormant and only weed seedlings from wind-blown seeds need to be removed.

Raised beds

Raised beds are constructed by marking out beds and building the sides up to 30cm (12in) high, using timber, such as railway sleepers, bricks, or cement blocks. Walls can be dispensed with, but in that case, the base of the bed should be about 30cm (12in) wider than the finished top to ensure stability.

Raised beds bring all the advantages of flat beds, but have improved drainage and warm up faster in spring. Making a raised bed higher along one side than the other, so that the sloping surface faces the sun, warms the bed even more effectively and promotes early plant growth.

Raised beds provide a means of gardening successfully on the most unpromising ground, such as where a site is naturally very badly drained or perhaps even concreted over.

Higher beds can also extend the pleasure of gardening to people of limited mobility. Walls can be built up to 60–90cm (24–36in) and the base filled with rubble (for good drainage). The bed is then topped with 30–45cm (12–18in) of fertile soil.

Making paths

Paths between beds can be maintained as soil areas from which weed growth is regularly skimmed off. A mulched path requires more initial effort, but reduces longer-term maintenance, especially if it is laid over a weed-suppressing landscape fabric. When topped with bark or gravel, this creates a firm, hard-wearing surface.

Grass pathways are most successful when a durable edging, for example rigid plastic or concrete blocks, is laid around the beds; the grass surface must stand proud of the edging to allow for unobstructed mowing.

The "no-dig" system

Cultivating the soil paradoxically creates conditions in which weeds flourish; it exposes weed seeds to the light needed for germination. It may also cause a natural soil structure to deteriorate as air incorporated by digging causes more rapid breakdown of organic matter. The "no-dig" system is a method of cultivation used by organic gardeners to preserve soil structure and reduce loss of nutrients. It exploits minimal soil disturbance and regular surface applications of organic matter (applied well in advance of cropping so earthworms can incorporate it) to help suppress weeds, conserve moisture, and maintain soil fertility and structure. The success of the technique demands thorough initial weed clearance, especially of perennial weeds, by means of sheet mulches (or chemicals for non-organic gardeners). The no-dig technique is well suited to bed systems, and can be very useful in reducing the labour of trenching and earthing up potatoes.

NO-DIG POTATOES

1 *To grow potatoes, lay the tubers on the soil surface, then cover with a 15–20cm (6–8in) layer of mulch.*

2 *Cover the mounded mulch with black plastic, fixing it down securely. Make slits for potato shoots to grow through.*

MAKING A PATH BETWEEN BEDS

1 *Mark out, level, and firm the path. Cut a 2.5cm (1in) slit along each edge. Cut landscape fabric to length, and 20cm (8in) wider than the path.*

2 *Fold the fabric edge into the slit on one side. Secure with 10 x 2.5cm (4 x 1in) wood edging and hammer level. Pull fabric taut and repeat on opposite side.*

3 *Cut crosses in opposite pairs in the fabric close to each plank, 2m (6ft) apart. Knock a wooden peg through each cross, to 2.5cm (1in) below the plank top.*

4 *Apply the mulch (here of bark chips). Rake and tamp down, so that the mulch is level with the plank tops and the support pegs are concealed.*

Crop rotation

Crop rotation is a system by which vegetable crops are grown on different areas of the plot in succession in consecutive years.

Advantages of rotation

The principal reason for rotating crops is to prevent a build-up of soil-borne pests and diseases specific to one group of crops. If the same type of "host" crop is grown every year in the same soil, its pests and diseases increase rapidly in number and often become a serious problem, whereas in the absence of their host they gradually die out. Various types of potato and tomato eelworm (nematodes), clubroot which attacks almost all brassicas (crucifers), and onion white rot are some of the common garden problems that may be alleviated by rotation.

Other benefits stem from rotating vegetables. Some crops, for example potatoes, blanket the soil so well that they smother most weeds, so it is useful to follow them with crops that are difficult to weed, such as onions. In addition, most root vegetables, and especially potatoes, help break up the ground and keep the soil structure open and well aerated.

Most vegetables in the legume family, including peas and beans, fix nitrogen in the soil by means of nodules on their roots and make it available for the next crop. Therefore nitrogen-hungry crops, such as leafy brassicas, potatoes, or spinach, should follow legumes. Conversely, root crops, which have a relatively low nitrogen requirement, can follow on from brassicas.

Several vegetables, including perennial types and many salad plants, do not fall into a principal rotation group. Salad plants stay in the ground for a short time and are therefore useful for intercropping or to fill temporary gaps in vegetable beds. As with the other vegetables, they should not be grown in the same patch of ground year after year. Perennial vegetables are best grown in a permanent bed of their own and so are not rotated. For the most important vegetable groups, see *Rotation of Vegetable Crops*, above right.

Drawbacks of rotation

A weak point in the rotation theory is that to be completely effective rotation should take place over a much longer timescale than the usual three or four years: clubroot and white rot infections can stay in the soil for up to 20 years. Rotations on that scale are out of the question in small gardens. Another shortcoming is that,

in practice, the distance between beds is often so small that soil-borne pests and diseases can easily spread from one to the next.

Crops in the general groups are likely to be required in different quantities, so plot size will vary. Some crops, such as parsnips and brassicas, will be very long-season crops that stand in the ground for progressive harvest. Each of these considerations make strict rotation difficult in the garden. Some gardeners maintain that, in very small areas, there is merit in not following a rotation, preferring to crop repeatedly on the same ground, then avoiding it selectively when a pest or disease infestation builds up.

It is, however, better to regard rotation as an aid to the suppression of pests and diseases, rather than as a means of total prevention or cure. On balance, the best advice is to move crops around the vegetable garden, endeavouring to have a break between growing crops in the rotation groups outlined.

Planning for rotation

Despite the disadvantages, rotation is a sensible practice, and gardeners should try to build it into their garden plans. The most crucial aspect is to have at least one but preferably two complete cropping seasons without repeating a vegetable group in a given site if at all possible.

Draw up a list of the main vegetables that you want to grow, with a rough indication of the quantities required. Growing vegetables that are climatically unsuited to the area is usually unsatisfactory, particularly in small gardens. Neither is it sensible to grow crops that are likely to be cheap to buy when your own crop is ready.

List the various beds in the vegetable garden. Group the selected vegetables in their rotation groups (for example all legumes and pod crops, or all brassicas), with a miscellaneous category for vegetables not in the main groups (see *Rotation of Vegetable Crops*, above right). Members of the miscellaneous group may be placed in one main group or another, depending on available space and quantities required.

Month–by–month planning

Make a chart with a column for each month of the year, and for every vegetable on your list fill in the months during which it will be in the ground. Remember that this period may be shortened by raising plants in containers (see "Sowing indoors", p.501) for transplanting later, and lengthened by the use of some form

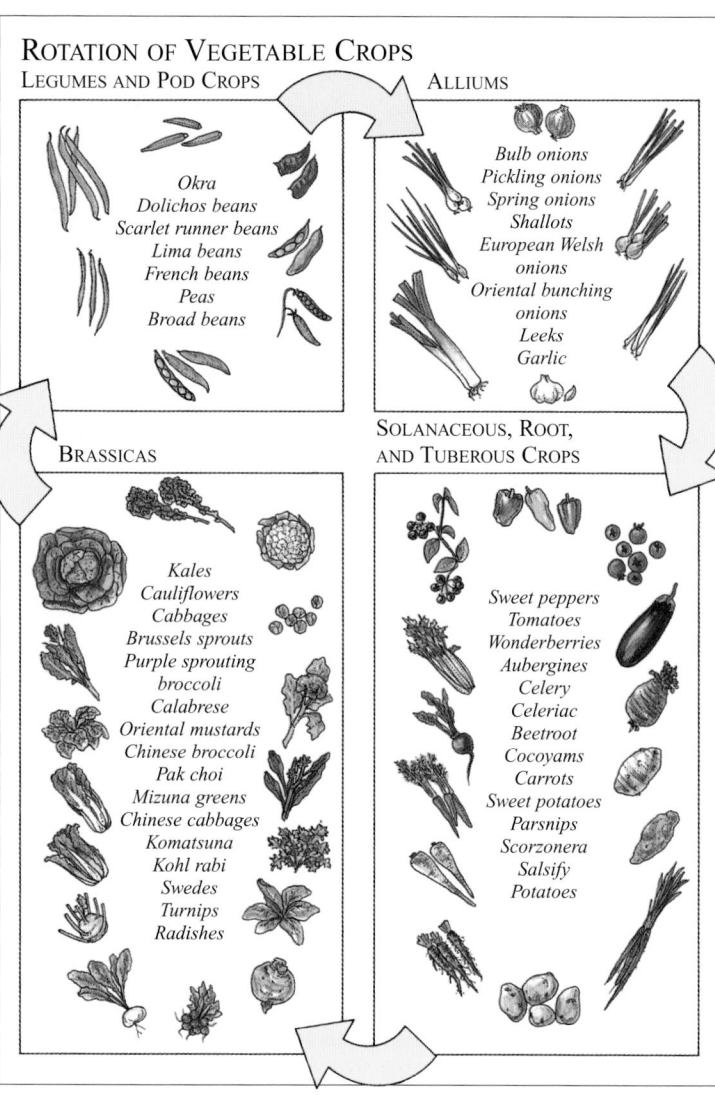

ROTATION OF VEGETABLE CROPS

LEGUMES AND POD CROPS

Okra
Dolichos beans
Scarlet runner beans
Lima beans
French beans
Peas
Broad beans

ALLIUMS

Bulb onions
Pickling onions
Spring onions
Shallots
European Welsh
onions
Oriental bunching
onions
Leeks
Garlic

BRASSICAS

Kales
Cauliflowers
Cabbages
Brussels sprouts
Purple sprouting
broccoli
Calabrese
Oriental mustards
Chinese broccoli
Pak choi
Mizuna greens
Chinese cabbages
Komatsuna
Kohl rabi
Swedes
Turnips
Radishes

SOLANACEOUS, ROOT, AND TUBEROUS CROPS

Sweet peppers
Tomatoes
Wonderberries
Aubergines
Celery
Celeriac
Beetroot
Cocoyams
Carrots
Sweet potatoes
Parsnips
Scorzonera
Salsify
Potatoes

of cover early and late in the season (see "Growing under cover", p.505). Some crops are sown once a year (parsnips and winter cabbages, for example), but with others, such as lettuces and radishes, repeat sowings may be made to provide a continuous supply throughout the year.

Planning a layout

Allocate each bed (or several beds if needed) to a different rotation group of vegetables, and write in the most important crop that each bed will grow. Refer to your month-by-month chart, and indicate a suitable crop to precede or follow it. For example, if Brussels sprouts are cleared from the ground in mid-spring, they may be followed by carrots, lettuces, or peas. Assume that most pieces of ground will bear only two crops a year. Use this basic plan in subsequent years and move the crops to different beds.

It is best to look on the overall plan as a rough guide only. Many factors – not least the unpredictability of the weather and seasons – have a bearing

on the success and failure of crops. The real key to success lies as much in the flexibility of the plan as in strict adherence to it.

Keeping records

Keeping a record of operations in the vegetable garden is always time well spent and a diary of each year's planting is especially valuable in planning rotations. It is also helpful to make notes on weather conditions, most importantly the dates of the first and last frosts in the locality. Such records can provide an invaluable guide to improving performance in future seasons.

Detailed records of cultivars grown, sowing and planting dates, quantities harvested – and those particularly enjoyed – form a valuable reference for subsequent years. They can help identify gluts and shortcomings, so as to avoid them in following years. It is also useful to record problems encountered and treatment given, whether they be pests and diseases or cultural disorders: to be forewarned is to be forearmed.

Sowing and planting

THE most common method of raising vegetables is from seed. There are several methods for sowing outdoors or under cover; use the most suitable for the chosen cultivar and the space available. Care in the early stages ensures healthier, more productive crops. Thin or transplant seedlings to their final position in a bed, greenhouse, or container before they become overcrowded.

Choosing seed

In the past, seed was sold only as ordinary, "naked" seed, but it is now also available prepared in a variety of ways to make sowing and germination easier. Seed can also be purchased pre-germinated.

Purchasing seed
Always buy good-quality seed, preferably vacuum-packed to preserve viability. Many of the best cultivars are F1 hybrids, bred by crossing two selected parents. Although expensive, they are very vigorous and productive. Vegetable seeds differ widely in their viability: to be safe, use seed under three years old, or test a sample before sowing.

Prepared seed
Pelleted seeds are individually coated with clay to form tiny balls and are easier to sow evenly than naked seed. This is particularly useful for handling small seeds such as those of carrots. Pelleted seeds should be carefully placed in a drill one by one, which saves transplanting later. They are sown in the normal way, but it is important that the clay coating is kept moist until after germination.

Seed is also available embedded, evenly spaced, in paper sheets or tapes, which disintegrate in the soil after sowing. The tapes are laid in a drill and covered with soil, as for ordinary seed. The backing gives protection in the early stages of germination and reduces thinning later.

Sometimes seeds are marketed in a gel in small tubs. They grow to the seedling stage in the tub, and may then be pricked out into a pot or directly into the ground. This saves an initial thinning after sowing.

Pre-germinated seed
Chitted or pre-germinated seed is purchased and sown just after germination, when the first root is emerging. Chitted seed is dispatched in small plastic containers; each seed is then sown carefully into a pot or seed tray. This is a good method for seed that needs temperatures that are difficult to maintain without an electric propagator or for those in which germination is unreliable.

To start ordinary seed early, it may be pre-germinated at home. This is useful for seed that germinates slowly in cold soil and may rot before germination. Space seeds on damp, paper towelling and put them in a warm place. Keep them moist until germination, then sow them carefully in containers or in open ground. This method may also be used to test a sample of old seed for viability before sowing.

Sowing outdoors

Vegetables are either sown *in situ*, where they grow to maturity, or in a seedbed from where they are transplanted to their permanent position. *In situ* sowing is used for crops that are harvested young, such as spring onions and radishes, or vegetables that do not transplant well, such as carrots and parsnips. Most other vegetables may be sown in a seedbed, in rows up to 15cm (6in) apart.

Successful sowing outdoors requires warm and well-prepared soil. Germination occurs for most vegetables once temperatures are over 7°C (45°F), so do not sow seed in cold soil. In several cases, lettuces for example, germination is poor at high temperatures. Particular temperature requirements for germination are given under individual vegetables. Soil temperature may be measured with a soil thermometer but most gardeners use their own knowledge of the soil to assess if it is warm enough for germination to occur.

Preparing the ground
Before sowing, dig the soil, then rake the surface until it has a fine texture or tilth, removing stones and large clods of earth. Rake when it is neither very wet and heavy nor very dry. If soil sticks to your shoes, delay until it has dried out a little, but not so much that it is dusty.

If sowing in wet soil, standing on a board prevents damaging the structure of adjacent soil. This is not necessary with the bed system (see p.496) since the seed may be sown from the surrounding path.

Guidelines for sowing
Seeds are sown at different depths according to their size. Unless otherwise directed, sow small seed, such as onions, about 1cm (½in) deep, brassicas 2cm (¾in) deep, peas and sweet corn about 2.5cm (1in) deep, and beans up to 5cm (2in) deep. The most important requirement is to sow thinly so that seedlings are not crowded in the early stages. Various methods of sowing are described below; whichever is used, it is vital to conserve surface moisture. In dry weather, cover the soil after sowing with plastic sheeting or newspaper. Remove any covering when the first seedlings appear.

Sowing in a drill
This is the most common method of sowing vegetables. Mark a row with a string line and make a small, even channel (a "drill") in the soil to the required depth. There are several methods of sowing: sprinkle a pinch of seed from between thumb and fingers, or gently tap seed out from the palm of the hand or from the packet. Small hand-held devices are available designed to release differently sized seeds gradually. Alternatively, station sow at intervals in groups of three or four seeds to be thinned later to one seedling per station. If the seed is sown *in situ*, space the stations at half the required distance between the mature plants to allow for losses; stations may be closer if seedlings are to be transplanted. After sowing, cover the seed with soil, drawing it back lightly with a hoe or rake, firm the area gently, and water with a can fitted with a fine rose.

If sowing in unavoidably wet conditions, line the drill before sowing with dry, sharp sand or vermiculite. If conditions are very dry, water the drill before sowing, lightly press each seed into the soil and then cover

SOWING IN A DRILL

1 *Mark out the drill using pegs and string. Use the corner of a hoe or a trowel to make the drill, ensuring that it is the depth required for the seed.*

2 *Sprinkle the seeds thinly and evenly along the drill. Stand on a plank placed parallel to the drill to prevent compaction of adjacent soil. Cover the seeds without dislodging them.*

ALTERNATIVE METHODS

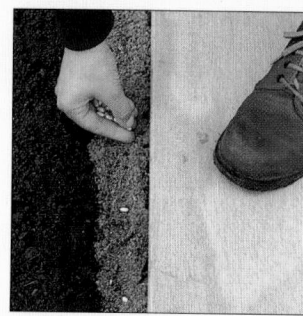
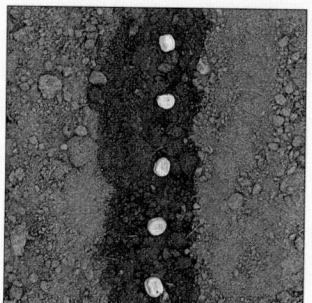

WET CONDITIONS
If the soil drains slowly or is very heavy, sprinkle a layer of sand at the base of the drill, sow the seed, then cover it.

DRY CONDITIONS
When the soil is very dry, water the base of the drill, then sow the seeds and lightly press them in before covering with dry soil.

SOWING IN A WIDE DRILL

1 Use a draw hoe to mark out parallel drills 15–23cm (6–9in) wide and flat at the base.

2 Sow seeds the required distance apart in the drill.

3 Cover the seeds with soil using the hoe. Take care not to dislodge them.

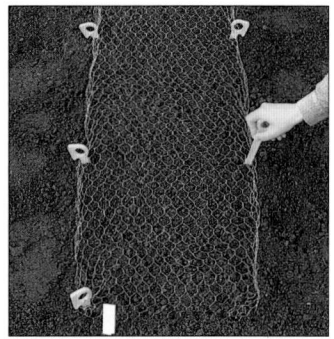

4 Protect them from birds or animals by pegging wire netting over the drill.

them with dry soil. This slows down the evaporation rate and helps keep seeds moist until germination.

Wide drills

Use wide, flat drills for plants that are grown closely together, such as peas, early carrots, and crops grown for harvesting at the seedling stage (see "Successional crops", right). Make each drill up to 23cm (9in) wide and to the required depth. Space the seeds evenly in the drill, and cover carefully with soil.

Large seed

The seed of beans or pumpkins may be sown individually. Place a seed in a hole made by a dibber or a finger, ensuring that each seed is at the base of the hole and in contact with the soil. Cover sowings of tender plants, such as marrows, with glass jars or cut-off plastic bottles and remove them once the seedlings emerge.

Broadcasting seed

In this method, the soil is first raked to produce a fine tilth; the seed is then scattered as evenly as possible either by hand or from a packet. Rake the soil lightly again afterwards to cover the seed.

Successional crops

Vegetables that grow fast, but rapidly pass their prime or run to seed, for example lettuces, should be sown little and often. To avoid gluts or gaps in cropping, wait until one sowing emerges before making the next.

Many leafy or salad vegetables may be sown for harvesting at the seedling stage and, once cut, often re-sprout to produce successional flushes of cut-and-come-again vegetables.

This is a very productive way to make use of a small area, and such crops are ideal for sowing under or between other, slower-maturing vegetables. To obtain seedling crops, sow seed in wide drills and cover with fleece. Seedlings do not need thinning and will be ready for the first cut in a few weeks.

Using fleece for protection

Fleece tucked into the soil or held down at the edges with bricks, helps to warm the soil before sowing. After sowing, it encourages early establishment and keeps off birds and some insect pests. Remove it before the seedlings' growth is restricted.

Thinning

Young seedlings must be thinned to prevent overcrowding. Thin to the final spacing in stages, to allow for losses from pests and diseases; at each stage, aim to leave a seedling just clear of its neighbours. If the seeds have been sown in situ, continue to thin until they are at the spacing required for mature plants. Very small seedlings should be thinned by nipping them off just above ground level so as not to disturb the roots of adjacent plants. Clear thinnings away as their scent may attract pests. Seedlings of plants such as lettuces, cabbages, and onions may be lifted for transplanting, and the soil refirmed around the remaining seedlings.

Planting

Plant or transplant vegetables into their final position when they are as young as possible so that they can grow without further check. Exceptions to this are plants that have been raised in containers or modules (see

BROADCASTING

1 Prepare the area to be sown by raking carefully in one direction to produce a fine tilth. Sprinkle the seed thinly and evenly over the surface.

2 Rake lightly at right angles to the original direction to cover the seed, then water thoroughly with a can fitted with a fine rose.

THINNING SEEDLINGS

To thin small seedlings, nip them out at ground level so that the roots of the remaining seedlings are not disturbed.

p.501). Do not transplant root vegetables once the tap root has started to form as this may distort its shape. Before taking plants from a seedbed, water around their roots; if the ground into which they are being planted is dry, water it lightly. Pick up a plant by a leaf rather than the stem or roots, which are easily damaged. Make a hole slightly bigger than the roots and position the plant in the hole, replacing the soil so that the

TRANSPLANTING SEEDLINGS

Lift seedlings gently, keeping as much soil around the roots as possible. Before replanting, place the seedlings in a clear plastic bag to retain moisture.

PLANTING DEPTH

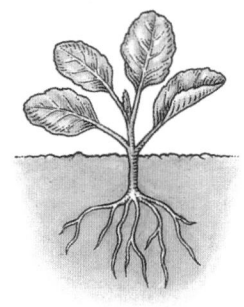

Plant vegetable seedlings so that their lowest leaves are just above soil level. Planting too high exposes the stalk, which may not support the weight of the mature vegetable.

lower leaves are just above soil level. Firm around the stem to anchor the plant. In hot weather, water seedlings, and then shade them with fine-mesh netting or newspaper cones until they are established. Keep the soil moist for a few days after planting (see "Critical watering periods", p.502).

Spacing

Different vegetables have individual spacing requirements, which sometimes determine their final size. Traditionally, vegetables are grown in rows with a recommended spacing between the plants, and between the rows. They may alternatively be grown with equidistant spacing between the plants – the average of the recommended spacing between plants and rows; so plants 15cm (6in) apart, in rows 30cm (12in) apart, may alternatively be grown 23cm (9in) apart each way. This method gives good results: plants have an equal share of light, air, moisture, and nutrients, and as they mature they form a canopy over the soil that suppresses weeds (see also THE BED SYSTEM, p.496). Vegetables may also be grown close together within widely spaced rows.

Sowing indoors

Vegetable seed may be sown indoors, in a cool greenhouse, or on a windowsill. This is helpful in climates with cool or short summers for tender vegetables, and for those needing a long growing season. It also helps to produce healthy seedlings and overcomes problems with germination, since temperature is more easily controlled. After germination, keep most seedlings at a lower temperature in a spacious, light, protected environment until they are planted out. Where this is impossible, it may be practical to buy more mature plants.

Seed trays

Sow seed in a small pan or seed tray, in standard seed compost (for details see ANNUALS AND BIENNIALS, "Sowing in pots or trays", p.218). When the seedlings have two or three small leaves, prick them out into a seed tray of potting compost, spaced 2.5–5cm (1–2in) apart. Seedlings usually need to be kept slightly warm. Put them in a well-lit, draught-free place to grow fast and evenly. Transfer larger plants to individual pots before planting them out.

Modules and small containers

Modules are individual units or small cells in which seeds are sown and plants grown on for planting out

---

SOWING AND TRANSPLANTING

1 *Fill the module with seed compost and make a hole 5mm (¼in) deep in each section. Sow one or two seeds per section. Cover with compost, then water.*

2 *Remove each plant from the module. Make a hole to take its root ball. Place the plant in the hole with its lower leaves just above the surface; firm and water.*

---

directly. This produces high-quality plants that grow on well: seedlings have no competition and develop a healthy root ball that is hardly disturbed when planted out in their final position. They do, however, need more space and compost in the early stages than those planted in trays.

Many types of module are available, the cheapest being plastic or polystyrene cellular trays. Small containers include clay or plastic pots, degradable pots, and soil blocks made of compressed compost. The compost may be enclosed in netting, which roots can penetrate.

Sow two or three seeds per unit; then thin the seedlings to leave the strongest. In some cases, such as onions and leeks, several seeds are sown and grown together, planted out as a unit at a wider spacing than usual, and grown on to maturity.

Hardening off

Plants raised indoors must be acclimatized to lower temperatures and wind before being planted in the open. Harden them off in cloches or cold frames over 10–14 days. Increase ventilation gradually during the day and then at night, until the seedlings can be left out all the time.

Vegetative propagation

A few vegetables are usually raised vegetatively, from offsets, tubers, corms, bulbs, or cuttings. This may be because they rarely set seed or, if raised from seed, are variable, or because vegetative propagation is faster. Details are given under individual vegetables (pp.507–548).

Growing vegetables in containers

Containers are useful for growing vegetables where space is limited, or to extend the vegetable garden into a paved area. They are also used in the greenhouse, especially if the soil is infected with soil-borne diseases and it is impractical to sterilize or replace it. Vegetables need a richer growing medium and more consistent and thorough watering than flowers and so are hard to grow well in containers unless carefully maintained (see also CONTAINER GARDENING, p.328).

Choosing the vegetables

The best vegetables for containers are compact, quick-maturing plants, such as lettuces, radishes, and beetroot, or robust, undemanding, leafy vegetables, such as spinach beet; fruiting vegetables, such as peppers, aubergines, and tomatoes, also flourish. Fast-maturing, seedling crops also grow well. Dwarf cultivars are excellent since they do not need support. Do not use vegetables that are deep-rooting, slow to mature, very tall or large, or gross feeders, such as brassicas, parsnips, or celery. Raise plants for containers in modules; sow cut-and-come-again seedling crops directly in the container.

Preparing the container

The larger the container, and the greater its volume of compost or

soil, the better. Large vegetables and gross feeders, such as potatoes and tomatoes, generally need a container that measures at least 25cm (10in) deep and wide. It should also be strong and stable.

Good drainage is essential. If there are no drainage holes, make several of at least 1cm (½in) diameter in the base; cover them with crocks to prevent blockage. For growing bags, follow the maker's instructions; drainage holes are not usually made since they would allow infection to enter when laid on diseased soil.

The soil or compost must be light and well aerated, since frequent watering will compact it. Lighten garden soil with well-rotted compost mixed with coarse sand and peat substitute or peat.

In hot and windy weather containers dry out rapidly by evaporation through the top and, if not made of plastic, the sides. To minimize this do not put them in exposed sites or at the foot of a hot wall. Line non-plastic containers with plastic sheeting perforated with drainage holes.

Fast-maturing, compact lettuces

Dwarf broad beans

Stable plastic container to retain moisture

Peas supported by peasticks

Routine cultivation

THE best vegetables are produced when the plants are maintained in the optimum conditions for growth. Keep them free from weeds and water them thoroughly as required. Mulches may be used to retain moisture and to suppress weeds. The level of nutrients needs to be maintained as the crop grows.

Watering

Most vegetables need reasonably moist soil; they vary, however, in the amount of water they require as well as when they most need it (see "Critical watering periods", below). Overwatering may lead to loss of flavour in tomatoes and carrots, and, in root crops, to the development of leaves at the expense of root.

How to water
It is more effective to water heavily and occasionally rather than frequently and lightly; very young plants, however, should be watered lightly and frequently so that they never dry out. Light watering evaporates rapidly without reaching the plants' roots, and encourages shallow surface rooting rather than the deep rooting that enables plants to withstand drought. Direct the water at the base of each plant. Water in the evening when less moisture will evaporate, and allow time for the plants to dry before nightfall.

Watering equipment
Use a can fitted with a fine rose to water young plants. For general watering in small gardens, a can may be adequate; in larger gardens, use a hand-held hose, regulating the flow with a fixture attached to the end.

A practical choice in vegetable gardens is either a seep hose or a porous hose laid among the plants (see also TOOLS AND EQUIPMENT, "Seep hoses", p.561). Water seeps through the holes or pores, usually watering a strip about 30cm (12in) wide. The tubing can be easily moved from crop to crop, and some types of porous hose may be buried shallowly in the soil.

Critical watering periods
There are periods in the growing cycle of vegetables when water is particularly beneficial; these vary according to the individual vegetable. In prolonged, dry weather confine watering to these periods.

Germinating seeds, seedlings, and newly transplanted plants should never be allowed to dry out, so water frequently and lightly.

Leafy and salad vegetables, such as spinach, chard, most brassicas, and lettuces, require frequent watering to help them crop heavily. The most critical period is between ten days and three weeks before maturity; during this period, but only in very dry conditions, apply a single, heavy watering of 22 litres/sq m (5 gallons/sq yd). Outside this period, give half this amount weekly during dry weather.

The critical point for fruiting crops such as tomatoes, peppers, beans, courgettes, cucumbers, and peas is when the flowers are forming and fruits or pods are developing. If conditions are dry during this time, water weekly at the rate for leafy crops (above). Do not water heavily before the critical period since this produces leafy growth at the expense of fruit.

Root crops such as carrots, radishes, and beetroot need moderate watering during the growing period. In the early stages, water at a rate of 5 litres/sq m (1 gallon/sq yd) if the soil is dry. Increase this rate four-fold when the roots start to swell, watering every two weeks if dry conditions persist.

Minimizing the need to water
To conserve soil moisture, particularly in dry areas, dig the soil deeply, working in plenty of organic matter to improve soil structure and moisture retention and to encourage deep rooting. Keep the soil surface mulched (see "Mulching", right), and keep down weeds, which compete for moisture. Do not hoe in dry weather since this encourages moisture to evaporate from the soil. Erect windbreaks to protect from desiccating winds (see "Shelter from wind", p.492). In areas prone to drought, adopt slightly wider spacing so that the roots can spread further to take moisture from a larger area.

Controlling weeds

A vegetable garden should be free of weeds. They compete for water, nutrients, and light, may physically suffocate plants, and may harbour pests and diseases (see PLANT PROBLEMS, "Weeds", pp.669–671).

Perennial weeds
Wherever possible, clear a vegetable garden of perennial weeds before starting to grow crops. Dig out

A seep hose laid between rows of vegetables ensures that the water reaches the roots of the plants and penetrates deeply into the soil.

deeply rooted and spreading perennials, taking care not to leave in the soil small pieces of root that will sprout again. Where a weed problem is very serious, either use appropriate weedkillers or smother the weeds with a light-proof mulch, such as old carpet or heavy, black, plastic sheeting. Most (except very persistent weeds) will die if covered for six to twelve months. While crops are growing, take care to prevent or control perennial weeds.

Annual weeds
These germinate and grow very rapidly and become a nuisance if they are allowed to seed freely in the vegetable garden. Pay particular attention to weeding in the first three weeks after crops germinate, when they are most affected by competition. Pull up weeds by hand or hoe shallowly to avoid bringing deeper weed seeds to the surface. Remove the weeds to prevent re-rooting.

Minimizing weed growth
During the growing season weed growth may be greatly reduced by mulching crops (see below) and also by growing vegetables at equidistant spacing (see "Spacing", p.501). Once they have reached a reasonable size, most form a canopy over the ground, which suppresses weeds.

Stale seedbeds
Spring sowings or plantings are the most vulnerable to annual weeds. Where the soil has not been cultivated recently and may be full of weed seeds, prepare the soil in advance; allow the first flush of weeds to germinate, and hoe them off before sowing or planting (see also SOILS AND FERTILIZERS, "The stale seedbed technique", p.620).

Mulching

A mulch is a layer of organic or inorganic material laid on the soil around plants. Where the surface is kept mulched, the need to cultivate is lessened or even eliminated.

Organic mulches
Bulky organic mulches add nutrients to the soil and improve the soil structure. They may be in the form of well-rotted, straw-rich, animal manures, garden compost, spent mushroom compost, dried lawn clippings, or seaweed. Do not use any materials derived from wood, such

Vegetables such as runner beans drop their flowers if the soil around their roots dries out. Water the crops well, then apply a mulch by forking it onto the border. A mulch prevents soil-moisture evaporation, and also insulates the soil, suppresses weeds, protects the surface from heavy rain and erosion, and reduces damage to soil when it is trodden on.

as sawdust and pulverized or shredded bark, unless they are at least two years old because their decomposition uses up soil nitrogen.

Organic mulches are best applied to growing crops in spring and early summer when the soil is moist. They maintain the temperature and moisture levels of the soil once they are applied so, if possible, mulch after the soil has warmed up in spring but before it starts to dry out. Never mulch cold, wet, or very dry soil. In areas with high rainfall and on heavy soil, however, an organic mulch is best spread on the ground in autumn to allow the worms to work it in.

In practice, it is often easiest to apply organic mulches when planting, watering plants first if necessary. Alternatively, mulch young seedlings that are already planted and growing strongly and are at least 5cm (2in) high. A mulch may be 2.5–7cm (1–3in) deep or more; aim for a deep mulch if the purpose is to keep down weeds.

Plastic film mulches

These are sheets of plastic that may be black, white, or transparent. Depending on which kind is used, they raise soil temperatures to bring on crops early, suppress weeds, reflect heat up to ripening fruit, and keep fruiting vegetables clean and free from soil splash. Shiny film mulches help deter flying pests.

Black films are mainly used to suppress weeds, although they also raise the soil temperature. Early potatoes may be grown under black films instead of being earthed up (see "Potatoes", p.547).

White films are mainly used to reflect light and warmth onto ripening fruit such as tomatoes and melons. Some films are made with the lower side black to suppress weeds, and the upper side white to reflect light. These films raise soil temperatures about 7°C (12°F) more than black films. Transparent films are used mainly to warm up the soil in spring, or to prevent soil splash.

It is simpler to lay films before planting or sowing crops. If desired, lay seep or porous hoses in position first, then lay the film on the ground or over the bed to be covered. Make slits 7–10cm (3–4in) deep in the soil around the bed, and anchor the mulch by tucking the edges into the soil, using a spade (see *Anchoring Plastic Sheeting*, p.626). This is simpler on slightly mounded beds. To plant, cut cross-shaped slits in the film with a knife, make a hole in the soil beneath, then carefully ease the plants through into the soil, and firm. Sow large seeds such as sweet corn

PLANTING THROUGH A BLACK-AND-WHITE PLASTIC MULCH

1 *Dig a trench around the area to be planted, lay down the mulch with the white side upwards, and secure its edges firmly into the earth.*

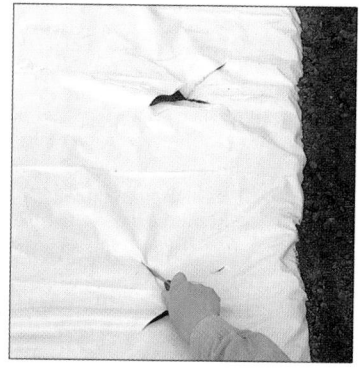

2 *Make cross-shaped slits in the plastic the required distance apart and dig a hole in the soil large enough to take the plant's root ball.*

3 *Remove the plant (here a tomato) from its pot, and place it in the hole. Firm the soil around the root ball and water. Stake if necessary.*

by making holes in the plastic and pushing the seeds through. When seedlings appear, guide them through the holes so that they are not trapped.

When necessary, water carefully through the planting holes. Slugs may be attracted to films: lift the film edges carefully and remove them or use a proprietary slug killer.

Feeding

In fertile garden soils, into which plenty of organic matter is regularly worked, most vegetables will grow satisfactorily without the use of additional fertilizers. As it takes a few years to build up soil fertility, however, supplementary feeding will be necessary on poor soils or to correct deficiencies and, in some cases, to obtain higher yields.

Soil nutrients

Plants need a range of nutrients; the three most important for vegetables, and those most often in short supply, are phosphorus (P), nitrogen (N), and potassium or potash (K). For further information, see "Soil nutrients and fertilizers", pp.624–625.

Maintain adequate levels of phosphorus and potassium with an annual application of garden compost at 2–5kg/sq m (5–11lb/sq yd) or manure at 5.5kg/sq m (12lb/sq yd). Alternatively, use artificial fertilizers such as superphosphate or triple superphosphate (for P) and potassium sulphate (for K) at levels recommended by the manufacturer, or apply them in compound fertilizers containing N, P, and K.

Potassium is washed out of the soil only slowly, so reserves last into the following season. Phosphorus is not

lost through leaching, but may be "locked up" in insoluble forms and not available to plants; reserves may need replenishing if soil analysis indicates that they are low. Nitrogen is constantly leached out and reserves need to be replenished continually, by adding either organic matter (which releases nitrogen as it breaks down) or artificial fertilizers.

Vegetables vary in their need for nitrogen. For further information, see *Nitrogen Requirements*, p.504. This indicates the broad requirements of different groups using a fertilizer with 21 per cent N content. Rates therefore vary according to the fertilizer used; nitrogenous fertilizers include ammonium sulphate, ammonium nitrate, and nitrate of potash.

Applying fertilizers

Fertilizers are sold in dry forms (dusts, granules, and pellets) and as concentrated liquids (see "Types of fertilizer", p.624). They can be applied either as a base-dressing before sowing or planting, or as a top-dressing to give a boost during growth (see "Applying fertilizers", p.625).

Apply nitrogenous fertilizers in spring, a month before sowing or planting; additional applications may be made later in the growing season. Never apply nitrogen in the autumn or it will be washed out of the soil before most vegetables are planted. Phosphate and potassium fertilizers are applied at any time, often in the autumn, or, where compound fertilizers are used, at the same time as nitrogen, in spring.

Feeding in organic systems

If extra feeding is necessary, use slower-acting organic fertilizers. These include fish, blood, and bone

meal, a general fertilizer applied as a base- or top-dressing, and dried blood (relatively fast-acting) and hoof and horn (slower-acting), both of which provide a source of nitrogen.

Various proprietary and general-purpose liquid feeds are available, some based on animal manures and others on seaweed extracts. The latter appear to be particularly beneficial to growth, even though their nutrient levels are not very high. They are either watered in or applied as a foliar feed.

Container-grown vegetables

The compost in containers can dry out very rapidly in hot weather. To conserve moisture, keep the upper surface mulched with up to 5cm (2in) of organic material, stones, or a sheet mulch. Be prepared to water thoroughly twice a day.

Occasional feeding may be necessary; use an organic or artificial fertilizer at diluted strengths, according to the manufacturer's instructions. Top-dress the compost in the container in spring, and change the compost completely every two or three years when it becomes compacted and less productive.

Pests and diseases

Healthy plants can resist most pest and disease attacks. Therefore good basic care of plants will keep problems caused by pests and diseases to a minimum. Learn to recognize the most common pests and diseases in your garden, and take the appropriate preventive measures wherever feasible. Avoid using chemicals in the vegetable garden as far as possible. Apart from their inherent danger and the risk of residues in the soil as well as on the plants, they may kill the natural enemies of many pests and diseases. If using chemical controls seems unavoidable, try to use organically approved products at least. In a few cases, biological control – the introduction of a pest's natural enemy – may be used. For general information and details about specific pests and diseases, see PLANT PROBLEMS, pp.639–673.

Healthy practices

To reduce problems with pests and diseases, keep the soil fertile and well drained, work in plenty of organic matter, and rotate crops regularly (see p.498). Grow suitable crops for the climate, choosing, wherever possible, cultivars with pest and disease resistance or tolerance (see the lists of recommended vegetable cultivars, pp.507–548). Raise plants in modules wherever feasible and harden off plants raised indoors. If you must purchase plants, ensure they are disease free. If growing plants under cover, always use clean seed trays and pots and sterilized potting compost.

Common pests

Animals and birds that may attack vegetables include deer, rabbits, mice, moles, and pigeon. In cases of persistent attack, erect wire fences or nets around the garden or over crops, use humane animal traps, and deter large birds with humming wire and small ones with strands of black cotton. In damp climates slugs and snails may be the most serious of all pests. They are mainly night-feeders – collect them after dark by torchlight and discard them. Where chemical controls are used, they must be handled carefully.

Soil pests, such as slugs and cutworms, commonly attack young plants, sometimes biting through the stems of plants at ground level. They tend to be worse in newly cultivated ground. Thorough digging exposes them to the birds. Many soil pests are night-feeders and may be easily caught by torchlight.

Microscopic soil pests known as eelworms or nematodes attack certain groups of plants, including potatoes. Rotate crops to prevent the pests from becoming established, and grow resistant cultivars where they are available.

Sucking insects, including many species of aphid, as well as carrot fly, cabbage root fly, and thrips or thunderflies, damage a range of plants by sucking the sap; they may spread virus diseases in the process. Knowledge of the pests' habits may help to prevent attacks – by earlier or later sowings, for example. Use sticky, yellow traps to catch aphids, collars (see *Collaring Seedlings*, p.507) to deter cabbage root fly, and film barriers against carrot fly (see p.544). Chemical or organic sprays may control outbreaks.

Various caterpillars attack a wide range of plants. Pick them off by hand or use the biological control *Bacillus thuringiensis*, or organic or chemical sprays. Fine nets placed over vegetables prevent the adult butterflies or moths from laying eggs on the plants. Small beetles, such as flea beetles, nibble seedling leaves of brassicas. They may be controlled with sprays, and plants may be protected with fine nets. Large beetles such as the Colorado beetle pose serious problems in some countries.

Pests may multiply very rapidly in the high temperatures under glass. The most serious are glasshouse whitefly and red spider mite, both of which attack a wide range of crops. They have become very resistant to most standard chemical sprays. Discourage them with maximum ventilation and by damping down to increase humidity. As soon as these pests are noticed, introduce some form of biological control to restrict their numbers (see "Biological control", p.642).

Keep vegetable beds (here of ornamental cabbages and carrots) and paths free of weeds and debris; remove and burn diseased plant material. Water and feed carefully – excess can be as damaging as insufficiency. Thin seedlings early to avoid overcrowding, and remove the thinnings. Encourage rapid germination of home-grown plants by sowing indoors if conditions are adverse outside.

Common diseases

Diseases are caused mainly by fungi, bacteria, and viruses. Infected plants develop a range of symptoms which in some cases merely disfigure plants, but in others will kill them. Damping off diseases, for example, infect and usually kill young seedlings; dig up and burn affected plants.

Diseases spread very rapidly in conditions that are favourable to their development and once established are difficult to control. Preventive measures and good garden hygiene are vitally important to prevent diseases from spreading and becoming established. A few sprays may be used in anticipation of an attack. Choose disease-resistant cultivars.

Clubroot, a soil infection, is one of the most serious problems affecting members of the cabbage family. Raising the soil pH by applying lime (see "Liming", p.625), and raising plants in sterile soil in modules so that they are vigorous, may help to control this infection.

Physiological disorders

Some problems experienced with growing vegetables are due to incorrect cultural conditions. Most common among these problems is premature bolting (flowering and setting seed), which may be caused by sudden low or high temperatures, drought, or sowing at the wrong time. Fruits failing to set may be due to lack of pollination, erratic watering, or drought. If there are mineral deficiencies in the soil, cauliflower curds may fail to grow. Further details are given under individual vegetables (see pp.507–548), with advice on how to create healthy growing conditions.

NITROGEN REQUIREMENTS (using fertilizer with 21 per cent N content)				
VERY LOW 12g/sq m (½oz/sq yd)	**LOW** 25–35g/sq m (1–1⅓oz/sq yd)	**MEDIUM** 45–55g/sq m (1½–2oz/sq yd)	**HIGH** 70–100g/sq m (2½–3½oz/sq yd)	**VERY HIGH** 110g/sq m (4oz/sq yd)
Carrots Garlic Radishes	Asparagus Beans (all) Celeriac Chicory (all) Courgettes Cucumbers Endive Florence fennel Gherkins Globe artichokes Kohl rabi Marrows New Zealand spinach Okra Onions (all) Parsnips Peanuts Salsify Scorzonera	Amaranths Aubergines Broccoli raab Cabbages (for storage) Calabrese Cauliflowers Cocoyams Hot peppers Jerusalem artichokes Kales Lettuces Potatoes (early) Pumpkins Rhubarb (young) Spinach Sprouting broccoli Sweet corn Sweet/chilli peppers Sweet potatoes	Beetroot Brussels sprouts Celery Ceylon spinach Leeks Potatoes (maincrop) Spinach beet Sweet melons Swiss chard	Cabbages (spring, summer, winter) Chinese broccoli Chinese cabbages Komatsuna Oriental mustards Mizuna greens Pak choi Rhubarb (cutting years)
(Peas do not require any extra nitrogen)	Swedes Tomatoes Turnips (and turnip tops)	Watermelons Wonderberries		

Growing under cover

THE productivity of a vegetable garden may be increased greatly in climates with a short growing season by growing plants under cover in a protected environment for some or all of their life cycle. The shorter the growing season, the more effective the cover will be.

Under cover, air and soil temperatures are increased, and crops are sheltered from chill winds. This lengthens the growing season by up to two months. The quality and yields of many crops are improved by higher temperatures and shelter.

Cover may be used to start crops early in spring for planting outside when temperatures rise. Half-hardy summer vegetables that would not mature outdoors during the growing season may ripen under cover; in cool climates, okra and aubergines, for example, only ripen fully under cover. The winter cropping period of many vegetables may be extended; for example lettuces, peas, Oriental brassicas (see p.513), and spinach all stop growing in the open but continue under cover.

Make the most of cover by ensuring that the soil underneath is fertile and weed-free. Vegetables require extra watering under cover – mulch them where practical to cut down watering. Plants started under cover may be set back if abruptly exposed to the elements. Harden them off gradually where appropriate.

Greenhouses and frames

Cover may be provided by anything from a greenhouse to a cold frame or a plastic tunnel cloche. For full details, see GREENHOUSES AND FRAMES, pp.566–583.

Greenhouses

A permanent, glazed greenhouse provides an excellent growing environment. It is easily ventilated and retains heat at night better than plastic film. Diseases may build up in soil if crops such as tomatoes are grown for several consecutive years, and the soil must then be changed or sterilized, or crops grown in containers. Supports may be required for tender, climbing vegetables.

Walk-in polytunnels

These are made of heavy-duty, clear plastic sheeting on metal supports. They are cheaper and easier to erect than greenhouses, and may be moved

Use wire hoops pushed into the ground 90cm (3ft) apart to support plastic film, which is tied at each end to a stake. Tie strings over the plastic and secure them at the base of each hoop.

to a different site if required. Ventilation is hard to control, however, increasing the risk of pests and diseases if temperatures rise rapidly; holes may be cut in the film in summer and taped over in winter. The film needs to be renewed every two or three years.

Tunnel cloches

These are cheap, mobile, and flexible; the lightweight plastic film may be rolled back for ventilation and watering. They provide shelter from wind and are useful in most gardens, especially for the final stages of hardening off seedlings and protecting vegetables in unsettled spring and autumn weather. Low polytunnels are limited by their height and flimsiness, however, and give little protection from low temperatures. They also need to be well anchored in windy situations.

Garden frames

Being relatively small, frames are most beneficial in gardens lacking space for a greenhouse or polytunnel. Some types are portable. They are easily ventilated, and may be heated by electric soil-warming cables. They are useful for raising and hardening off seedlings; their low height limits the range of crops grown, although the lids may be removed to allow semi-hardy crops to mature. Garden frames may be blacked out for forcing crops such as Witloof chicory and endive.

Cloches

Although individual cloches only cover a small area, when placed end to end they can be used to cover an entire row. To make maximum use of cloches, move them from one crop to another during a season; for example protect overwintering salads, start tender early potatoes or dwarf beans in spring, then ripen melons in midsummer.

Floating mulches

These are various types of film, including perforated plastic film, fine netting film, and non-woven fleecy film. All may be laid over low tunnel cloche hoops or directly over crops after sowing or planting, and anchored shallowly in the soil or weighted down. The mulches are lifted by the crops as they grow.

Floating mulches promote earlier crops and higher yields by raising temperatures and protecting plants from wind as well as, in some cases, insect pests. All give better ventilation than unperforated plastic films.

Weed beds carefully before laying floating mulches, since they are awkward to lift for weeding later.

Perforated plastic films

These are perforated with tiny slits or holes. They are generally used in the early stages of growth. Disadvantages include overheating in hot weather, minimal frost protection, and the risk of plants being chafed. To "wean" plants, slit plastic films down the centre a few days before removing them completely.

Netting films

Fine netting films are strong and last for several seasons. They are well ventilated so may usually be kept on until plants mature. They have little effect on temperature, but protect against wind. Provided that they are well anchored at the edges, they protect against many insect pests.

Fleecy or fibrous films

These light, soft, non-woven films usually last one season. Depending on the film's weight, it may protect against frost and flying insect pests; the films are more permeable to light and air than plastics. Many vegetables may be grown under fleecy film until they are nearly mature.

PERFORATED PLASTIC FILM
Floating mulches are spread over a bed of seedlings and earthed in at the edges so that they are loose enough to allow for growth. Perforated plastic film protects the seedlings but allows ventilation.

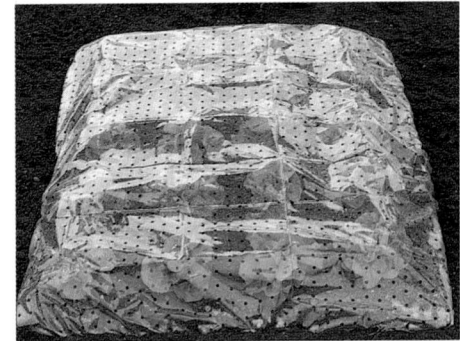

NETTING FILM
This protects plants against insect pests and wind damage.

FLEECY FILM
This is effective against frost as well as deterring insect pests.

Harvesting and storing

How and when vegetables are harvested, and whether they are used fresh, stored, or both, depends on the nature of the vegetable and the climate. The shorter the growing season and the more severe the winter, the greater the incentive to store vegetables, either naturally or by freezing. For details, see individual vegetables (pp.507–548) and *Vegetables that Freeze Well*, below.

Harvesting

Follow the guidelines under individual vegetables for how to harvest. Most vegetables are harvested at maturity, but some, notably leafy plants and brassicas, may be cut at various stages, and will often resprout for a second and third crop.

Cut-and-come-again harvesting

This method of harvesting is suited to vegetables that resprout after an initial cut has been made, enabling them to be used fresh over a fairly long period. Crops may be harvested at the seedling stage, or later when they are semi-mature or mature.

Harvest seedling crops when they are 5–10cm (2–4in) high, cutting about 2cm (³⁄₄in) above soil level. Some, for example salad rocket, salad rape, and cress, may be cut and left to resprout several times in succession. See also "Successional crops", p.500.

Some semi-mature or mature crops, if harvested by cutting 2.5–5cm (1–2in) above soil level, will resprout and after a few weeks produce more leaves and, in some cases, edible flowering shoots (see "Cultivating Oriental brassicas", p.513).

The technique is suited to certain types of lettuce, endive, sugar loaf chicory, Oriental greens, and Swiss chard. It is useful in cool climates in autumn and early winter as plants treated this way survive lower temperatures than they would otherwise and may be very productive, especially under cover.

Storing

The length of time that vegetables may be stored depends on the storage conditions and on the vegetable or cultivar. For details, see individual vegetables. The main cause of deterioration after harvesting is water loss, so aim to keep this to a minimum. Do not store damaged or diseased specimens since they may rot.

Vegetables often freeze well; almost all need to be blanched either in steam or boiling water and cooled quickly before freezing. The only exception to this is sweet peppers, which may be frozen without any initial preparation.

Leafy vegetables and brassicas

Leafy vegetables and various types of brassica, such as calabrese and cauliflower, have such a high water content that few of them store well. An exception is the winter storing cabbage, which may be stored either hanging in nets or on a bed of straw, in a frost-free shed or cold frame.

Several brassicas freeze well: some cultivars are bred for the purpose. Freeze only top-quality produce.

Fruiting vegetables

Vegetables such as tomatoes, aubergines, and cucumbers usually have an optimum time for harvesting, although fruits may also be harvested immature. If they are to be stored for winter use, they are best made into preserves or deep frozen.

Sweet peppers keep in good condition for many months if whole plants are pulled up and hung in a dry, frost-free place. Some cultivars of marrow and squash may be stored for several months. Leave the fruit on the plant until mature, then pick and "cure" it in the sun to harden the skin so that it forms an effective barrier to water loss, and store it in a dry, frost-free environment (see also "Pumpkins and winter squashes", p.525).

Bulbs

Certain cultivars of onion, shallot, and garlic will keep for many months. Lift the crop when mature or nearing maturity, and dry it in the sun (or under cover in wet climates), until the outer skins are papery. Handle the bulbs carefully to avoid bruising. Hang them as plaited strings, in nets, or spaced out on trays, in well-ventilated, frost-free conditions (see also *Storing Onions in a Box*, p.535).

Root vegetables

Some root vegetables, such as carrots and potatoes, may be either harvested young and eaten immature or left to mature and lifted and stored at the end of the season. A few, such as parsnips, are extremely hardy and, except in severe winters, may be left in the ground until required.

Prepare vegetables carefully for storing, removing any foliage since this will rot. Store only healthy, unbruised specimens. Potatoes are susceptible to frost; store them packed in light-proof sacks in a frost-free place.

Root vegetables such as beetroot and carrots easily lose moisture, so store them in layers in boxes of moist sand, peat substitute, or peat in a cool shed or cellar (see *Storing Carrots*, p.544). They may also be stored in outdoor clamps: pile them on straw and cover with more straw, and, in cold areas, a layer of soil to give protection against frost (see *Making a Swede Clamp*, p.543).

STORING STRINGS OF ONIONS
Plait together the dried onion leaves to form strings of bulbs. These may be hung outside in warm weather to dry further, and then brought indoors to be stored in frost-free conditions.

STORING RED CABBAGES

Lay the cabbages on slats covered with straw in a cool, well-ventilated, frost-free place. Leave gaps between them to allow free air circulation and discourage rotting.

VEGETABLES THAT FREEZE WELL

Asparagus 1
Aubergines 1 2
Beetroot 1 3
Broad beans 1
Broccoli raab 1
Brussels sprouts 1
Cabbages 1 2
Calabrese 1
Carrots 1 3
Cauliflowers 1 2
Celery 2
Chinese broccoli 1
Chinese cabbages 1 2
Courgettes 1
Dolichos beans 1
French beans 1
Hot peppers 1 2
Kales 1
Kohl rabi 1 2
Lima beans 1
Marrows 1 2
New Zealand spinach 1
Okra 1
Parsnips 1 3
Peas 1
Potatoes (small and new potatoes only) 1
Pumpkins 2
Rhubarb 2
Scarlet runner beans 1
Spinach 1
Spinach beet 1
Spring onions 2
Sprouting broccoli 1
Swedes 1 2
Sweet corn 1
Sweet peppers
Swiss chard 1
Tomatoes 1
Turnips 1 2 3
Wonderberries 1

KEY
1 Blanch
2 Dice, slice, purée, or shred
3 Freeze only when young

Western brassicas

WESTERN brassicas include kales, cauliflowers, cabbages, Brussels sprouts, sprouting broccoli, calabrese, turnip tops, broccoli raab, kohl rabi, swedes, and turnips. For kohl rabi, swedes, and turnips, see pp.540, 542, and 543 respectively.

Western brassicas are naturally biennial but are cultivated as annuals for their leaves and roots, and as biennials for flowerheads and shoots. Each type displays considerable variation, and there is often a range of cultivars for different seasons. They are usually cooked, but some are used raw. Western brassicas are

COLLARING SEEDLINGS

Where cabbage root fly are a problem, place a collar around the stem of each seedling. Make sure that it is flat on the ground to prevent the adult fly from laying its eggs at the base of the stem.

cool-season crops with varying degrees of frost tolerance; most perform poorly at high temperatures, so in warm climates grow them in winter. In temperate climates, they may provide crops for much of the year.

Siting Western brassicas
An open situation with fertile, well-drained, moisture-retentive soil is required. Rotate brassicas (see p.498) to avoid a build-up of clubroot. If this is a problem, lime the soil (see p.625) to bring the pH to 6.5–7 and discourage the disease. Most Western brassicas need high levels of nitrogen (see p.504), but they should not be planted on freshly manured ground since this causes overlush, leafy growth that is prone to pests and is more tender. A base-dressing may be applied to the area before planting (see "Applying fertilizers", p.503).

Sowing and planting Western brassicas
Western brassicas prefer firm soil; they may be planted after a previous vegetable crop without forking the soil. Sow *in situ*, or in a seedbed, or indoors in trays or modules for transplanting. If the soil is infected with clubroot, sow in modules, transferring to pots before planting out, so that the plants have a healthy

start and are more likely to mature without infection. Tall, top-heavy brassicas, such as Brussels sprouts or sprouting broccoli, should be planted 10cm (4in) deep. Earth up the stem as it grows by building a small mound of soil around it to a depth of about 10cm (4in); in windy sites, support the stem with a stake 1m (3ft) high. Plant brassicas firmly, with the lower leaves just above soil level. In some cases, spacing may be varied to determine the size of the brassica. If plants are widely spaced, they may be intercropped with salad seedlings or radishes.

Cultivating Western brassicas
Mulch after planting to suppress weeds. In dry weather, water as for leafy vegetables (see "Critical watering periods", p.502). Apply a nitrogenous fertilizer during growth.

Flea beetles (p.644), slugs and snails (p.644), damping off (p.660), cabbage root fly (p.660), white blister (p.646), whiptail (p.652), and cutworms (p.660) all affect young plants. Caterpillars (p.645), cabbage whitefly (p.646), mealy aphids (see "Aphids", p.646), clubroot (p.649), and birds (p.657) attack plants at all stages of growth.

Image labels: Winter cabbage; Calabrese; Cauliflower; Curly kale; Savoy cabbage; Brussels sprouts

Kales (*Brassica oleracea* Acephala Group)

Grown as annuals or biennials depending on the type, dwarf kales are 30–40cm (12–16in) tall, with a 30cm (12in) spread; tall types grow to 90cm (36in) and spread up to 60cm (24in). Some American kales are known as collards. Most kales produce leaves from a central stem; the leaves may be plain or curly (see below) or curly-broad hybrids. Good

CURLY KALE

cultivars include 'Afro', 'Black Tuscany', 'Redbor', 'Red Russian', and 'Reflex'. The leaves of all kales, and the spring-flowering shoots and young leaves of broadleaved types, are used cooked or raw. Kales are the hardiest brassicas, some surviving at -15°C (5°F); many also tolerate high temperatures. All prefer fertile, well-drained soils and need medium nitrogen levels (see p.504).

Sowing, planting, and routine cultivation
Sow seed in early spring for summer crops, and in late spring for autumn and winter crops. Sow *in situ* or in seedbeds or seed trays for transplanting; dwarf forms should be spaced 30–45cm (12–18in) apart, tall forms 75cm (30in) apart.

Give overwintering types a nitrogenous top-dressing in spring to encourage growth. In severe winters, grow dwarf cultivars under cloches or low polytunnels. Kales are usually unaffected by pests and diseases.

Growing under cover
For very early, tender kales, sow seed in early spring in rows 15cm (6in) apart, or in wide drills. Either harvest them as large seedlings, or thin the seedlings to 7cm (3in) apart and cut when they form plants 15cm (6in) tall, leaving the stumps to resprout for a second harvest.

Harvesting and storing
Some cultivars mature seven weeks after sowing, but plants can stand a long time in the ground. Snap off the leaves as required in autumn and winter to encourage new growth. Pick the shoots in spring when they are about 10cm (4in) long, before the flowers open. Kales freeze well.

ORNAMENTAL KALES

Ornamental kales are grown mainly for winter decoration in the garden or for garnishing salads. Leaves are variegated green, red, white, or purple.

Cauliflowers (*Brassica oleracea* Botrytis Group)

Grown as annuals or biennials, cauliflowers form an average head (or curd) of about 20cm (8in) in diameter; the plants are 45–60cm (18–24in) tall, with a spread of up to 90cm (36in). They are classified by the main season of use, usually winter (with a distinction between those for frosty and frost-free areas), summer, and autumn, although these groups overlap (see *Cauliflower Types*, below). Most types of cauliflower have creamy or white curds, but there are attractive, distinctively flavoured types with green or purple curds. The curds, and in some cases the young green leaves surrounding them, are cooked or used raw in salads. Smaller curds, or mini-cauliflowers, about 5cm (2in) in diameter, may be specially grown from early summer cultivars.

Cauliflowers are a cool-season crop and do not usually grow well in areas with high summer temperatures. Several cultivars are frost hardy, but cauliflowers may only be harvested all year round in areas with frost-free winters. For soil and site see "Siting Western brassicas", p.507; overwintering cauliflowers need a sheltered situation outside,

and are not usually grown to maturity under cover. All cauliflowers need a moisture-retentive soil, with medium nitrogen levels (see p.504), and a pH of 6.5–7.5.

Sowing and planting
Success with cauliflowers depends on sowing the correct cultivar at the appropriate time, and allowing plants to develop with as few checks to growth (from transplanting or dry soil, for example) as possible. Where drought is likely in summer, grow spring-heading types, which will benefit from autumn rainfall, or fast-maturing mini-cauliflowers.

The main sowing times and spacings are given in the chart below. Cauliflowers are usually sown in seed trays, modules, or a seedbed for transplanting, but may be sown *in situ* and thinned to the correct spacing. Generally, the later the planting, the larger the cauliflower will grow and the wider the spacing required. Seed germinates best at a temperature of about 21°C (70°F).

For a very early summer supply, sow seed in autumn, in modules or seed trays, then pot up seedlings in small pots. Put the pots into a well-ventilated frame or under cloches for the winter. Alternatively, sow *in situ* in frames or under cloches, thinning to 5cm (2in) apart. Harden off seedlings before planting them out in spring. For a later crop, sow indoors in gentle heat in early spring, and prick out into small pots.

PROTECTING CAULIFLOWER CURDS

1 *In winter and early spring, mature curds of overwintering types may need protection from severe frost.*

2 *Wrap the leaves up around the central curd, securing them with soft string.*

For summer/autumn and winter groups, sow the first batch indoors in seed trays or modules, or *in situ* in frames or under cloches. Successive sowings may be made in a seedbed outdoors, or in modules for transplanting later on.

To obtain mini-cauliflowers, select an early summer cultivar to be sown in spring or early summer; sow several seeds per station, 15cm (6in) apart, thinning to one seedling after germination. Alternatively, raise plants in modules and plant them out 15cm (6in) apart. For a continuous supply, make successive sowings.

Routine cultivation
Cauliflowers need regular water throughout the growing period. In dry conditions, water at a rate of 22 litres/sq m (5 gallons/sq yd) every two weeks. Overwintering cauliflowers require low nitrogen levels when planted or they will be too soft to survive the colder conditions. A nitrogenous fertilizer or organic liquid feed may be applied in spring.

To prevent white curds from discolouring in sunny weather, tie the leaves over the curds. This may also be done in winter and spring to protect curds of overwintering types from the elements; most modern cultivars, however, have leaves that naturally tend to cover the curds.

Pests and diseases
For cauliflower pests and diseases, see "Cultivating Western brassicas", p.507. Cauliflowers are also attacked by pollen beetles (p.657).

Harvesting and storing
The time from sowing to maturity varies from approximately 16 weeks for summer/autumn cauliflowers to about 40 weeks for winter ones. Cut the curds while they are still firm and tight. Mini-cauliflowers mature about 15 weeks after sowing and should be picked immediately since they deteriorate quickly. All cauliflowers, and in particular the mini-cauliflowers, freeze well.

RECOMMENDED CAULIFLOWERS

Winter
'Astra'
'Penduick'
'Vilna'
'Walcheren Winter 3-Armado'
'Walcheren Winter Armado May'

Summer
'Beauty' F1
'Fargro' F1
'Idol'
'Perfection'

Autumn
'Autumn Glory'
'Barrier Reef'
'Kestrel'
'Plana' F1
'Wallaby'
'White Rock'

Green cultivars
'Alverda'
'Minaret'
'Romanesco'

Purple cultivars
'Graffiti'
'Purple Cape'
'Violet Queen'

MINI-CAULIFLOWERS

PURPLE-HEADED CAULIFLOWER

CAULIFLOWER TYPES

GROUP	WHEN TO SOW	WHEN TO PLANT	SPACING	WHEN TO HARVEST
Winter (frost-free areas)	Late spring	Summer	70cm (28in)	Winter/very early spring
Winter	Late spring	Summer	63cm (25in)	Early spring
Summer	Autumn/early spring (sow under glass)	Spring	52cm (21in)	Early to midsummer
Autumn	Mid- to late spring	Early summer	55–63cm (22–25in)	Late summer to late autumn

Cabbages (*Brassica oleracea* Capitata Group)

Most cabbages are grown as annuals. Plants are generally 20–25cm (8–10in) tall, with a spread of up to 70cm (28in). The average head is about 15cm (6in) in diameter.

They are grouped according to their season of maturity, although there is some overlap between the groups. Leaves are dark or light green, blue-green, white, or red, and smooth or crinkled (savoy). Cabbage heads are pointed or round, and vary in their density. Spring greens are either loose-leaved cultivars or standard spring cabbages harvested before the head forms. Cabbage leaves are eaten either cooked or raw and sliced in salads. They may also be pickled. If they are tender enough, stems and stalks may be sliced finely and cooked. Some types of winter cabbage may be stored.

Cabbages grow best at 15–20°C (59–68°F). Do not plant in temperatures over 25°C (77°F). The hardiest cultivars may survive temperatures as low as -10°C (14°F) for short periods. Cabbages are not usually grown under cover.

To grow well, cabbages need soil that is fertile, moisture-retentive, and humus-rich with a pH level above 6. Spring, summer, and fresh winter cabbages require very high nitrogen levels, and winter storage cabbages medium nitrogen (see p.504). Do not

MATURE SPRING CABBAGES

give spring cabbages a nitrogenous base-dressing at planting, since the nitrogen will probably be washed from the soil over the winter; top-dress in spring instead.

Sowing and planting

Sow the chosen cultivars at the correct time for their group (see *Cabbage Types*, below). Sow seeds in seedbeds or modules and transplant seedlings to their final position on average five weeks later. Appropriate spacing varies according to type (see chart below) and it may be modified

to vary the size of the head; adopt closer spacing for smaller heads, and wide spacing to produce larger heads. A collar may be placed around each seedling stem when transplanting to protect against cabbage root fly (see *Collaring Seedlings*, p.507). Ensure that young seedlings have sufficient moisture until they are well established.

For spring greens either grow a greens cultivar, spacing the plants about 25cm (10in) apart, or use a heading spring cultivar and space plants 10–15cm (4–6in) apart. Cut

AUTUMN CABBAGE

RED SUMMER CABBAGE

SAVOY CABBAGE

CABBAGE TYPES

GROUP (TIME OF MATURITY)	DESCRIPTION	MAIN SOWING PERIOD	AVERAGE SPACING
Spring	Small, pointed or round heads	End of summer	30cm (12in)
	Loose-leaf greens	End of summer	25cm (10in)
Early summer	Large, mainly round heads	Very early spring (sow under glass)	35cm (14in)
Summer	Large, round heads	Early spring	35cm (14in)
Autumn	Large, round heads	Late spring	50cm (20in)
Winter (for storage)	Smooth, white-leaved, winter white types	Spring	50cm (20in)
Winter (to use fresh)	Blue, green, and savoy leaf types	Late spring	50cm (20in)

RECOMMENDED CABBAGES

Spring
'Dorado'
'Duncan' F1
'Durham Elf'
'Greensleeves' (greens only)
'Myatt's Offenham Compacta'
'Pixie'

'Prospera' F1
'Pyramid' F1

Early summer
'Charmant' F1
'Golden Cross'
'Hispi' F1
'Wivoy' F1 (savoy)

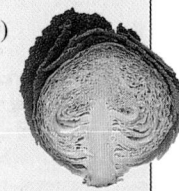

Summer
'Castello'
'Derby Day'
'Minicole' F1
'Spitfire'

Autumn
'Autoro' F1
'Quickstep'
'Rapier' F1
'Winnigstadt'

Winter (for storage)
'Hidena'
'Holland Winter White'

Winter (to use fresh)
'Celtic' F1
'Holly' F1
'January King Hardy
    Late Stock 3'
'Marabel' F1
'Protovoy' F1
'Tarvoy' F1

Red cabbage
'Rodeo'
'Ruby Ball'

HARVESTING SPRING GREENS

Plant spring cabbages 15cm (6in) apart. When they have grown on, but before they start to form a compact heart, harvest alternate plants, cutting them at the base. Use these as spring greens.

HOW TO OBTAIN A SECOND CROP

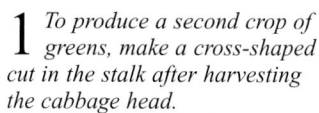

1 *To produce a second crop of greens, make a cross-shaped cut in the stalk after harvesting the cabbage head.*

2 *A few weeks later, several miniature heads should have sprouted, ready for a second harvest.*

them young as loose greens; every second or third plant may be left to heart up if a heading cultivar is used.

Routine cultivation

To increase their stability, earth up winter cabbages as they grow. Protect spring cabbages under cloches or floating mulches, and apply a liquid feed or a nitrogenous top-dressing in spring; feed others in the growing season. Keep cabbages moist throughout growth (see "Critical watering periods", p.502).

Pests and diseases

For pests and diseases that may affect cabbages, see "Cultivating Western brassicas", p.507. Seedling blight (p.654) may also occur.

Harvesting and storing

Spring and summer cultivars vary in their ability to stand in good condition once the head has matured; modern cultivars often stand longer than traditional ones. Normally the plant is dug up once the head has been cut, but spring and early summer cultivars may produce a second crop if the head is cut to leave a 10cm (4in) stalk in the ground. Using a sharp knife, make a shallow cross in the top of the stem to encourage new growth. Provided that the soil is fertile and moist, three or four more heads may develop together on the stalk.

Storage cabbages (winter white cultivars and appropriate red cabbages) should be lifted before heavy

PREPARING CABBAGES FOR STORING

Before storing cabbages, carefully remove any loose or discoloured, outer leaves without damaging the head (see inset). Inspect the cabbages regularly while they are in store and remove leaves that are rotting.

frost. Dig them up and carefully remove any loose, outer leaves. Place them on slatted supports or straw on the floor of a shed, or suspend them in nets. Store the heads at just above freezing point, with relatively high

humidity. They may also be stored in a cold frame, provided that it is ventilated on warm days to discourage rotting (see also *Storing Red Cabbages*, p.506). Cabbages may keep for four or five months.

Brussels sprouts (*Brassica oleracea* Gemmifera Group)

These are biennials grown as annuals, and vary in height from about 35cm (14in) for the dwarf forms to 75cm (30in) for the tall forms, with a spread of up to 50cm (20in) in both cases. Brussels sprouts are loosely divided by their time of maturity into early, mid-season, and late groups. The earlier types tend to be dwarfer and less hardy. The modern F1 cultivars are an improvement over older, open-pollinated ones; they perform better on fertile soils, are less prone to lean (as they have a stronger root system), and have more compact, even sprouts. The tight sprouts that develop on the stem are cooked but may also be shredded raw into salads. The mature leaves at the top of the plants may also be eaten. There is a well-flavoured, but less productive, red cultivar, 'Rubine'.

Brussels sprouts are typical cool-season brassicas; the hardiest cultivars survive temperatures of -10°C (14°F). If sown in succession, Brussels sprouts provide a constant crop from early autumn to late spring. A general base-dressing may be applied shortly before planting; high nitrogen levels are needed (see p.504). Avoid using freshly manured ground as this encourages blown and loose, rather than firm, sprouts. For soil and site requirements, see "Siting Western brassicas", p.507.

DWARF BRUSSELS SPROUT PLANT

EARTHING UP BRUSSELS SPROUTS

About a month after planting out, earth up Brussels sprouts by drawing the soil around the base of the stem to increase stability. At this stage they may also be staked if they are in an exposed site.

Sowing and planting

Sow in succession from early to mid-spring as the soil begins to warm up, starting with the early-maturing cultivars. For a very early crop, sow in gentle heat under cover in early spring. Sow either in seed trays or in

a seedbed for transplanting, or *in situ* in firm ground; most Brussels sprouts do not grow well in modules.

Thin out or transplant to the required spacing in early summer, generally four to five weeks after sowing. Plant dwarf cultivars about

45cm (18in) apart, and tall cultivars about 60cm (24in) apart. Use closer spacing to produce smaller sprouts of a more uniform size, and wider spacing for large sprouts that mature in succession and so may be picked over a longer period. Wide spacing also encourages good air circulation, which keeps plants healthy and disease-free. Plant tall cultivars deeply and earth up the stems as they grow to provide extra stability. Keep young plants moist until they are well established.

REMOVING LEAVES

Snap off any yellowing or diseased leaves that develop as these may carry fungal diseases that could spread to the whole crop. This also improves air circulation.

Brussels sprouts, with their slow rate of growth, may be intercropped in the first few months with fast-maturing vegetables.

Routine cultivation
Keep beds weed-free. Since plants are widely spaced, extra watering is required only in very dry conditions, when they should be watered at the rate for leafy crops (see "Critical watering periods", p.502). A top-dressing of a nitrogenous fertilizer or an organic liquid feed may be applied in late summer if the plants are not growing vigorously. Remove any withered or diseased leaves from the stems as they appear.

If sprouts are wanted for freezing, grow an early cultivar that matures in autumn, and nip off the sprout top or growing point in late summer, when the lower sprouts are roughly 1cm (½in) in diameter. All the sprouts will then mature for picking together, rather than in succession.

Pests and diseases
Mealy aphid can colonize individual sprouts; to control, treat with insecticidal soap, pyrethrum, rotenone, or bifenthrin. Downy mildew is also a common problem (p.646). For other diseases likely to affect Brussels sprouts, see "Cultivating Western brassicas", p.507.

Harvesting and storing
Brussels sprouts are ready to harvest about 20 weeks after sowing. Their

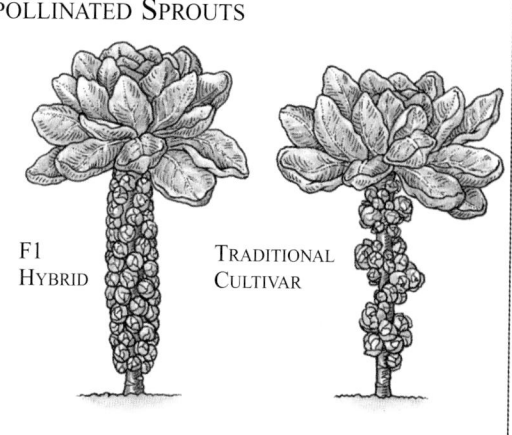

F1 AND OPEN-POLLINATED SPROUTS

Modern F1 hybrids produce sprouts that are compact, evenly spaced, and of uniform size. Traditional, open-pollinated cultivars are more likely to produce blown sprouts widely varying in size.

F1 HYBRID

TRADITIONAL CULTIVAR

flavour is improved after exposure to frost. Pick the lowest sprouts first by snapping them off at the base; the upper sprouts will continue to develop. If the sprouts are intended for freezing, pick them before the outer leaves are damaged by winter weather; freeze only top-quality sprouts. Sprout tops may be harvested by cutting them off at the end of the season.

After harvesting, dig up the plants and break up the stems with a hammer. This deters the build-up and spread of brassica diseases, and enables the stems to rot down more quickly when composted.

Where winters are very severe, uproot the whole plants before the ground freezes and hang them in a cool, frost-free place; the sprouts will remain fresh for several weeks.

RECOMMENDED BRUSSELS SPROUTS

Early
'Braveheart' F1
'Diablo' F1
'Oliver' F1
'Peer Gynt' F1

Mid-season
'Evesham Special'
'Roger' F1
'Romulus' F1

Late
'Cascade' F1
'Wellington' F1

Sprouting broccoli (*Brassica oleracea* Italica Group)

These large, biennial plants may reach a height of 60–90cm (2–3ft) and a spread of 60cm (2ft). There are purple and white forms; the purple is more prolific and hardier. The flowering shoots that develop in spring are eaten cooked. Sprouting

PURPLE SPROUTING BROCCOLI

broccoli is grown mainly in the British Isles, where it is considered one of the hardiest winter vegetables, surviving temperatures of about -12°C (10°F). Because it is a slow-maturing vegetable that occupies the ground for up to a year, broccoli

requires a fertile soil and medium nitrogen levels (see p.504). Avoid shallow and sandy soils and sites exposed to strong, winter winds.

Sowing, planting, and routine cultivation
Sow from spring to midsummer, either in a seedbed or in modules. Transplant from early to midsummer, spacing plants at least 60cm (2ft) apart, and planting them deeply for stability.

Plants may need staking in the autumn. If wood pigeon (p.645) eat leaves, cover the plants with netting for the winter. For further cultivation requirements, see "Cultivating Western brassicas", p.507.

Pests and diseases
Sprouting broccoli is prone to the common brassica pests (see "Cultivating Western brassicas", p.507); in mild years it may be host to whiteflies. Pigeons can be attracted in winter.

RECOMMENDED SPROUTING BROCCOLI

'Claret' F1
'Nine Star Perennial'
'Purple Sprouting'

'White Sprouting'

Harvesting and storing
Depending on the cultivar, pick shoots from early spring to late summer, when they are about 15cm (6in) long, while the flowers are in bud. Pick regularly to encourage more shoots; plants may crop for up to two months. Sprouting broccoli freezes well.

Calabrese (*Brassica oleracea* Italica Group)

Also known as American or Italian broccoli, calabrese is grown as an annual or biennial, and produces compact plants about 45cm (18in) tall, with a spread rarely over 38cm (15in). Cultivars are classified as early, mid-season, and late, with the earliest maturing the fastest. F1 hybrids are more productive than the original cultivars. The compact, terminal head and the young sideshoots are eaten lightly cooked.

Calabrese is a cool-season crop and should not be grown in areas where the average mean temperature is above 15°C (59°F). Young plants tolerate some frost, but it may damage embryonic and young heads once they start to develop. Calabrese needs an open site in moisture-retentive, fairly fertile soil with medium nitrogen levels (see p.504).

HARVESTING CALABRESE

1 *Just before the flower buds open, harvest the first central head by cutting through the stalk.*

2 *This encourages sideshoots to develop; these can also be harvested and more sideshoots will be produced.*

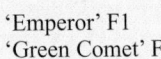
Sowing and planting
Sow in succession from spring to early summer for a crop during summer and autumn. Calabrese seedlings do not transplant well, so either sow two or three seeds per station *in situ*, or sow in modules and transplant seedlings to moist ground, disturbing the roots as little as possible. For an early crop, make the first sowings indoors; these are, however, especially prone to bolting when transplanted.

Calabrese plants grow well at various spacings. For the highest overall yield, space plants 22cm (9in) apart each way, or 30cm (12in) apart in rows spaced at 45cm (18in). Closer spacing produces smaller terminal shoots, which mature together and are suitable for freezing.

Routine cultivation
Keep the bed weed-free. Calabrese plants need plenty of water to crop well – 11 litres/sq m (2 gallons/sq yd) every two weeks. In very dry conditions, water as for leafy crops (see "Critical watering periods", p.502). A nitrogenous top-dressing or an organic liquid feed may be applied once the terminal heads have been cut in order to encourage additional sideshoots to develop.

Pests and diseases
For pests and diseases that may affect calabrese, see "Cultivating Western brassicas", p.507. Problems may also be caused by pollen beetles (p.657) and downy mildew (p.646).

Harvesting and storing
Calabrese is a fast-maturing brassica, ready 11–14 weeks after sowing. The main head should be cut when it is 7–10cm (3–4in) in diameter, while still firm and before the flower buds open. Sideshoots will subsequently develop; cut these when they are about 10cm (4in) long. Calabrese freezes well.

Turnip tops and broccoli raab (*Brassica rapa*)

Over the centuries different brassicas have been grown for cutting in the immature stages for use as quick-maturing greens. The two types commonly used for this purpose today are turnip tops (*Brassica rapa* Rapifera Group) and broccoli raab (*Brassica rapa* Utilis Group), which is also known as turnip rape and by a number of Italian names such as *cime di rapa*, *rapini*, and *broccoletti*.

They are grown as annuals or biennials, generally with single stems that reach a maximum height of about 30cm (12in). The leaves, young stems, and sweetly flavoured young flowerheads are eaten cooked as spring greens, or raw in salads.

Turnip tops and broccoli raab are cool-season brassicas. Grow them in spring and autumn in hot climates, or all year where summers are cool. All turnip cultivars are suitable; broccoli raab has no named cultivars. Both grow best in fertile, moisture-retentive soil and require low to medium nitrogen levels (see p.504).

Sowing, planting, and routine cultivation
Sow thinly broadcast or in rows about 10cm (4in) apart. For larger plants only, thin to 15cm (6in). For an early crop in cold areas, make the first sowing indoors in early spring. Plants need little attention subsequently.

Harvesting and storing
Harvest plants within seven to eight weeks of sowing. Make the first cut when they are leafy and 10cm (4in) tall, or wait until the immature flowering shoots appear and the plant is

TURNIP TOPS

20–25cm (8–10in) tall. Cut about 2.5cm (1in) above ground level. In cool weather, the plants resprout to give two or three further cuttings over a period of four or five weeks. Cut as long as the stems are tender. Use turnip tops and broccoli raab fresh as they do not store well.

BROCCOLI RAAB

Oriental brassicas

SEVERAL Oriental brassicas are now being introduced to the West. They have many features in common with Western brassicas but tend to be faster growing and have a wider range of uses than Western brassicas. If they are given the right conditions they are highly productive. They are grown as annuals or biennials.

Oriental brassicas are cultivated mainly for the leaves and leafy stems, but also for the young, sweetly flavoured flowering shoots. Leaf shape and colour vary from the glossy, white-ribbed leaves of some pak choi cultivars, and the feathery green leaves of mizuna greens, to the purplish-green of Oriental mustards. Oriental brassicas are nutritious, succulent, and crisp, and are mild to peppery in flavour. Cook them, preferably by stir-frying or steaming, or use young leaves and shoots raw in salads.

Oriental brassicas are best suited to climates with cool summers and mild winters, although many cultivars are available that are adapted for hotter climates. Most will withstand light frost, especially if harvested when they are semi-mature as a cut-and-come-again crop (see p.506). A few Oriental brassicas, such as komatsuna and some of the mustards, are extremely hardy.

In temperate climates, Oriental brassicas grow best in late summer and autumn. Where winter temperatures fall several degrees below freezing, they may be grown as a winter crop under cover in unheated structures; if planted late in the summer, they may crop from autumn to spring, although they will stop growing at low temperatures.

Oriental brassicas require similar conditions to Western brassicas (see "Siting Western brassicas", p.507) but, being fast-growing, hungry, and thirsty plants, the soil must be rich in organic matter, moisture-retentive, and fertile. They never develop well in poor, dry soil. Most of them have very high nitrogen requirements (see p.504).

Sowing and planting Oriental brassicas

All standard methods of sowing may be used; where there is a risk of plants going to seed prematurely (bolting), sow seed in modules or *in situ*. Many have a tendency to bolt when days are lengthening, particularly when this is combined with low spring temperatures. In these cases, in northern latitudes, delay sowing until midsummer, unless plants are started off in heat or cultivars with bolting resistance are used. If bolting continues to be a problem, grow Oriental brassicas as seedling crops, and harvest the leaves before the plants start to bolt.

Their rapid rate of growth makes Oriental brassicas ideal for intercropping among slower-maturing vegetables, especially for cutting as a cut-and-come-again seedling crop, when their flavour is superb.

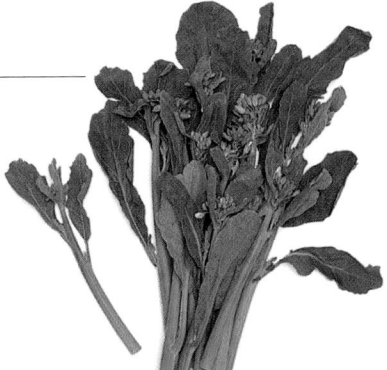

Loose-leaved Chinese cabbage

Tight-headed Chinese cabbage

Pak choi

Pak choi

Cultivating Oriental brassicas

Oriental brassicas are generally shallow-rooting and so need regular watering. In very dry conditions, water at the rate for leafy crops (see "Critical watering periods", p.502). They should also be kept mulched.

Oriental brassicas are susceptible to the same pests and diseases as Western brassicas (see "Cultivating Western brassicas", p.507). Those with tender leaves are very prone to slugs and snails (p.644), caterpillars (p.645), and flea beetles (p.644). They may be grown under fine nets to provide some protection.

Harvesting and storing Oriental brassicas

Most Oriental brassicas mature within two to three months after being sown. They may be harvested at four different stages from seedling to mature plant.

At the seedling stage they may be harvested using cut-and-come-again techniques (see "Cut-and-come-again harvesting", p.506), or left a few weeks longer and cut as semi-mature plants. When the plants are fully mature they may be either harvested all at once or alternatively cut about 2.5cm (1in) above ground level so that they sprout again for a second crop. The flowering shoots that develop naturally from mature plants may also be harvested before the flowers open.

In the West, Oriental brassicas are mainly used fresh, although most will keep for a few days if refrigerated. In the Orient, leaves are pickled or dried, and Chinese cabbages are stored for off-season supplies.

Oriental mustards (*Brassica juncea*)

The mustards are a varied group of annuals and biennials, forming large, often coarse-leaved plants. Leaf texture may be smooth, blistered, or deeply curled (for example 'Art Green'). Some cultivars are purple-leaved. The mustards are naturally very robust and less prone to pests and diseases than most Oriental brassicas. Several, including the purplish-green 'Miike Giant', 'Osaka Purple', and 'Xue Li Hong' survive at least -10°C (14°F). The distinctive flavour may be piquant in some cultivars, becoming stronger as they run to seed. The leaves are used cooked but may also be eaten raw in salads when young or if sliced.

Sow from mid- to late summer in temperate climates, and until early autumn in warm climates, for harvesting from autumn to spring. The seed is small and is sown in shallow soil *in situ* or in modules. Thin or plant out seedlings 15cm (6in) apart for harvesting young, and 35cm (14in) apart for larger plants. If they are planted under cover in autumn, plants are more tender, but will run to seed earlier the following spring.

Oriental mustards mature in 6–13 weeks, depending on the cultivar. Cut single leaves as required.

PURPLE-LEAVED ORIENTAL MUSTARD

Chinese broccoli
(*Brassica rapa* var. *alboglabra*)

These annuals, also known as Chinese kale, form stout plants with thick, blue-green leaves, growing up to 45cm (18in) tall. The succulent, fine-flavoured, chunky flower stems, which may be 2cm (¾in) thick, are generally cooked.

Chinese broccoli tolerates higher summer temperatures than many other brassicas, and withstands light frost. In warm and temperate climates, sow from late spring to late summer. For a very early crop, make the first sowings under cover in spring to transplant outside. For a protected early winter crop, plant under cover in autumn. In cool climates, delay sowing until midsummer since sowings earlier than this may bolt.

Sow seed *in situ* or in modules. For small plants, to be harvested whole as soon as the flowering shoots appear, grow plants 12cm (5in) apart

CHINESE BROCCOLI

with 10cm (4in) between rows. For large plants, to be cropped over a longer period, space plants 30cm (12in) apart each way. Cut the main shoot first, as for calabrese (see p.512); further sideshoots will continue to develop for harvesting later. Large plants take nine to ten weeks to mature.

Pak choi
(Brassica rapa var. chinensis)

Pak choi is a biennial usually grown as an annual, forming a loose head of fairly stiff leaves with wide midribs that broaden out markedly and overlap at the base. There are many types, the most common being white-ribbed or green-ribbed, available as F1 cultivars 'Joi Choi' (white) and 'Shanghai' (green). They vary in size from squat forms about 10cm (4in) tall to large plants about 45cm (18in) tall. Pak choi is succulent and mild in flavour, and may be eaten either cooked or raw.

Pak choi grows best at cool temperatures of 15–20°C (59–68°F). Most cultivars will tolerate some frost in the open but survive lower temperatures under cover grown as winter cut-and-come-again crops. A few are suited to hotter climates.

In temperate climates, sow seed throughout the growing season. There is some risk of premature bolting with spring sowings, so confine these to cut-and-come-again seedling crops. Sow seed *in situ* or in modules. Spacing depends on the cultivar and size of plant required, ranging from 10cm (4in) apart for small cultivars to about 45cm (18in) apart for the largest cultivars. In late summer, transplant pak choi under cover for an autumn crop.

Pak choi may be harvested at any stage from seedlings to the young flower shoots of mature plants.

PAK CHOI

HARVESTING SEEDLINGS

Pak choi may be harvested at the seedling stage. If they are cut about 2.5cm (1in) from the ground, new leaves will sprout.

Seedling leaves will be ready for harvesting in three weeks. They may be cut 2.5cm (1in) above ground level and will resprout. Mature plants may be cut higher and will also resprout for a second harvest.

Mizuna greens *(Brassica rapa var. nipposinica)*

Annuals or biennials, depending on climatic conditions, mizuna greens have dark green, glossy, deeply serrated, almost feathery leaves and slender, white, juicy stems forming a rosette up to 45cm (18in) in diameter and about 23cm (9in) tall. They are highly decorative, especially when grown as an edging or in blocks. Mizuna greens are eaten cooked, or raw when leaves are harvested young and tender.

They are very adaptable, capable of tolerating both high summer temperatures (provided that they are in moisture-retentive soil) and winter temperatures down to -10°C (14°F).

They may be sown throughout the growing season. Bolting resistance is good and seed may therefore be sown in seed trays or modules, in a seedbed for transplanting, or *in situ*. For an extra, tender, winter crop, sow in late summer to transplant under cover. Space plants 10cm (4in) apart for small plants harvested young, up to 45cm (18in) apart to obtain large plants. Mizuna greens are useful for intercropping if cut at the seedling stage.

Mizuna greens mature eight to ten weeks after sowing and may be harvested at all stages; seedling leaves may be ready within two or three weeks (see "Harvesting and storing Oriental brassicas", p.513). The plants are vigorous, and are capable of resprouting several times after they have been cut initially.

MIZUNA GREENS

Chinese cabbages *(Brassica rapa var. pekinensis)*

These are annuals or biennials usually grown as annuals. Chinese cabbages have dense, upright heads. The leaves are marked by prominent white veins, the broadened midribs overlapping at the base rather like pak choi. The barrel type forms a stout head about 25cm (10in) high, the cylindrical type a longer, less compact head up to 45cm (18in) high. Leaf colour ranges from dark green to almost creamy white, especially in the centre. There are also some very attractive, loose-headed types. Mild-flavoured with a crisp texture, Chinese cabbages are excellent in salads and lightly cooked.

For preferred climatic conditions, see "Pak choi" (left). Most headed types are likely to bolt if they are sown in spring, unless a temperature of 20–25°C (68–77°F) is maintained during the first three weeks of growth. It is safer to delay sowing until early summer. Some loose-headed types may be sown in spring. If they start to bolt, treat them as cut-and-come-again crops, although the leaves of some cultivars may be rough-textured and hairy when young. Sow seed in modules or *in situ*; thin or transplant seedlings to 30cm (12in) apart. Plenty of moisture throughout growth is vital. Chinese cabbages have soft leaves which are susceptible to pests (see "Cultivating Oriental brassicas", p.513).

Chinese cabbages mature eight to ten weeks after sowing, and can be harvested at any stage since they respond well to cut-and-come-again treatment both after the main heads have been cut, and during growth, as semi-mature plants.

HARVESTING CHINESE CABBAGES

1 *Harvest Chinese cabbage (here a loose-leaved cultivar) by cutting about 2.5cm (1in) above soil level.*

2 *After a few weeks, new leaves will have formed and may be cut. Stumps may resprout several times.*

Komatsuna *(Brassica rapa var. perviridis)*

The komatsuna group, also known as spinach mustard, is extremely diverse; its members form large, productive, robust, healthy plants, often with glossy leaves that may be up to 30cm (12in) long and 18cm (7in) wide. The flavour of the leaves resembles cabbage, with a touch of spinach, and they are eaten cooked, or raw, finely sliced in salads.

Komatsuna plants tolerate a wide range of temperatures and will survive -12°C (10°F). Some cultivars are suitable for tropical climates.

Plants are less likely to bolt from early spring sowings than most Oriental brassicas and are more drought-tolerant. For sowing and spacing, see "Mizuna greens" (left). Komatsuna makes a useful and successful winter crop under cover.

KOMATSUNA

Leaves may be harvested at all stages (see "Harvesting and storing Oriental brassicas", p.513). Mature plants are usually ready to be harvested eight weeks after sowing.

Leafy and salad vegetables

THIS group of vegetables is grown for the great variety of leaves that it produces, which may be eaten raw in salads, or cooked. The freshly picked leaves are delicious and highly nutritious. The range of leaf colour also gives them decorative value. Careful choice of cultivar and the right growing conditions ensure a year-round supply. If seeds are sown in succession, gluts of crops maturing together may be avoided. Due to the high moisture content of the leaves, many store for only two or three days; a few are suitable for freezing, however.

Butterhead lettuce
Loose-leaf lettuce
Spinach
Cos lettuce
Witloof chicons

Amaranths (*Amaranthus* spp.)

These rapidly growing annuals reach a height of about 60cm (24in) and a spread of 30–38cm (12–15in). *Amaranthus cruentus*, the most commonly grown as an edible crop, has oval, light green leaves; amaranth cultivars are mostly local – they include 'Fotete', 'Green Spinach', and 'Stubby'. *A. tricolor*, or Chinese spinach, has red, yellow, or green leaves and greenish-white flowers; cultivars include 'Lal Sag Rouge', 'Tampala', 'Banerjee's Giant', and 'Crystal'. *A. caudatus* has pale green leaves and is often grown as an ornamental plant for its vivid red, tassel-like flowers. Amaranth species are also known as African or Indian spinach. The leaves of the plants and immature flower buds are cooked and eaten in the same way as spinach.

Amaranths are tropical and subtropical plants that require temperatures of 22–30°C (72–86°F) with a humidity of above 70 per cent to crop well. They may also be grown in temperate climates in greenhouses or outdoors in a sunny, sheltered site. Moderately deep, well-drained, fertile soil with a pH of 5.5–7 and medium to high nitrogen levels are required (see p.504).

AMARANTHUS CRUENTUS

Sowing and planting
Sow outdoors in spring, once the temperature is high enough, in rows 20–30cm (8–12in) apart. Thin seedlings to l0–l5cm (4–6in) apart when they are about 5–7cm (2–3in) high. Protect with plastic covers or under cloches until the young plants have become established.

In cool areas, or for an earlier crop, seed may be sown in trays in a greenhouse; prick out seedlings into 6 or 9cm (3 or 3½in) pots when they are large enough to handle. Transplant them outdoors when they are 7–9cm (3–3½in) tall, spacing them 10–15cm (4–6in) apart.

Routine cultivation
Keep amaranth beds weed-free, and water regularly. Apply a balanced fertilizer or organic liquid feed every two to three weeks. Give additional dressings of nitrogen and potassium every three weeks on less fertile soils. Apply an organic mulch around the base of the plants to retain moisture and warmth. When the plants are 20cm (8in) tall, pinch out the growing point to encourage lateral shoots and to produce a heavier crop.

Pests and diseases
Downy mildew (p.646), powdery mildew (p.646), caterpillars (p.645), and aphids (p.646) may affect amaranths outside, and thrips (p.647) and damping off (p.664) under cover.

Growing under cover
When seedlings are 7–9cm (3–3½in) tall, transplant them to 21cm (8in) pots, growing bags, or beds, spacing them 38–50cm (15–20in) apart each way. Keep them at a minimum temperature of 22°C (72°F). Water, and maintain 70 per cent humidity by damping down in hot weather.

Harvesting and storing
Amaranths are ready to harvest eight to ten weeks after sowing. Using a sharp knife, cut young shoots up to 10cm (4in) long when the plants are about 25cm (10in) tall; they will produce further shoots over several months. Continue picking them as required. Amaranths are best eaten fresh; alternatively, they may be stored for up to one week at 0°C (32°F) and 95 per cent humidity.

AMARANTHUS TRICOLOR

Ceylon spinach (*Basella alba*)

Also known as Indian or vine spinach, these short-lived, twining perennials may grow to 4m (12ft) tall if supported. Var. *alba* has dark green leaves; var. *rubra* has red leaves and stems. The oval or round leaves are eaten cooked; the purple berries are not normally eaten.

Ceylon spinach is a tropical and subtropical plant that requires a temperature of 25–30°C (77–86°F). Lower temperatures reduce the growth rate, resulting in smaller leaves. Larger leaves are, however, produced in light shade. Well-drained and highly fertile soil with a pH of 6–7.5 and high nitrogen levels (see p.504) is required for good growth.

Sowing and planting
Sow in seed trays or 6 or 9cm (3 or 3½in) pots, maintaining the required temperature range. When the seedlings are 10–15cm (4–6in) tall, transplant them to well-prepared beds, spacing the plants 40–50cm (16–20in) apart each way.

Routine cultivation
Support plants by staking or by tying in the stems to a vertical or horizontal trellis. Keep plants weed-free and water as necessary. Mulch with organic material. Apply a balanced fertilizer or liquid feed every two to three weeks during the growing period. When the seedlings reach a

SUPPORTING CEYLON SPINACH

Ceylon spinach may be supported on a trellis parallel to the ground, raised about 30cm (12in) above soil level. The stems should be evenly spaced on the trellis so that they do not become overcrowded.

height of about 45cm (18in), remove the growing point to encourage branching. Remove flowering shoots to encourage leaf production.

Propagate plants by taking cuttings 10–15cm (4–6in) long; insert these in small pots until rooted and then transplant as described for seedlings.

Pests and diseases
Ceylon spinach is generally free of pests and diseases. Root-knot eelworms (p.660) may, however, affect plants, and, under cover, aphids (p.646), whiteflies (p.646), and glasshouse red spider mite (p.646) may also be troublesome.

Growing under cover
Transplant seedlings to growing bags or to 20–25cm (8–10in) pots. Remove the growing tips when the seedlings are about 30cm (12in) tall to encourage branching, and damp down regularly to maintain high humidity. Tie in developing shoots.

Harvesting and storing
Harvest 10–12 weeks after transplanting by cutting young terminal shoots that are 15–20cm (6–8in) long; this encourages further shoots to develop over several months. Eat leaves within two days of picking, or refrigerate them for a few days.

Swiss chard and spinach beet (*Beta vulgaris* subsp. *cicla* var. *flavescens*)

These spinach-like biennials belong to the beet family. Swiss chard, also known as seakale beet, forms large, glossy-leaved plants. Individual leaves may be up to 45cm (18in) long and 15cm (6in) wide. The mid-ribs widen into broad leaf stalks up to 5cm (2in) in diameter that may be white, red, creamy-yellow, or pink. Leaf colour varies with the cultivar, from deep green ('Fordhook Giant') to greenish-yellow ('Lucullus') and reddish-green ('Rhubarb Chard'). 'Bright Lights' is a very colourful cultivar. The leaves and mid-ribs are normally cooked; the latter require

WHITE-STEMMED SWISS CHARD

longer cooking and are often treated separately. Spinach beet, or perpetual spinach, forms smaller-leaved plants, with narrow, green leaf stalks. It is eaten lightly cooked or raw.

Although chard and spinach beet are essentially cool-season crops, growing best at 16–18°C (61–64°F), they tolerate higher summer temperatures than spinach (see p.519) without bolting, and survive winter temperatures of -14°C (7°F). They may be grown in a wide range of soils other than acid ones, provided that the soil is moisture-retentive and fertile, containing plenty of organic matter. Plants may remain in the ground for up to 12 months, and so need high nitrogen levels (see p.504).

Sowing and planting
For a continuous supply, sow seed in spring (plants may crop until late spring the following year), and again in mid- to late summer (for plants cropping until the following summer). Sow *in situ* in rows 38cm (15in) apart for spinach beet or, for Swiss chard, 45cm (18in) apart; thin seedlings early to 30cm (12in) apart. Plants may be grown closer together

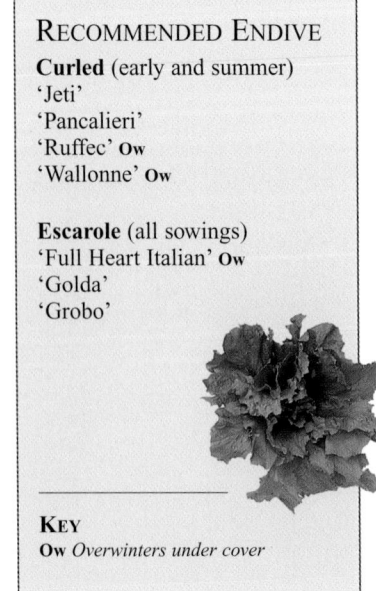

RED-STEMMED SWISS CHARD

in more widely spaced rows, but avoid overcrowding.

Alternatively, seed may be sown in seed trays or modules for transplanting. Germination is usually rapid. Spinach beet may be sown closely for use as a cut-and-come-again seedling crop (see "Successional crops", p.500).

Routine cultivation
The chards and spinach beet are naturally healthy and vigorous and usually require little attention. Give an organic mulch to keep down weeds and preserve moisture; apply

a nitrogenous fertilizer or organic liquid feed during the growing season if plants are not developing well.

Pests and diseases
Birds (p.657) may attack seedlings. Fungal leaf spots (p.648) and downy mildew (p.646) may also be problems.

Growing under cover
In cool climates, the chards and spinach beet are excellent winter crops under cover. Sow seed in modules in late summer and transplant under cover in early autumn, or broadcast spinach beet for cut-and-come-again seedling crops. They often crop throughout winter and early spring.

Harvesting and storing
Leaves are ready to be harvested 8–12 weeks after sowing. Cut the outer leaves first and continue picking as required; alternatively, harvest the whole plant by cutting the leaves about 2.5cm (1in) above ground level. Further leaves are then produced from the base over many months. Both Swiss chard and spinach beet may be frozen.

Endive (*Cichorium endivia*)

Endive is an annual or biennial plant that forms a flat or semi-upright rosette of leaves 20–38cm (8–15in) in diameter. The two most distinct types of endive are the serrated- or curled-leaved endive, and the broad-leaved escarole, but there are also intermediate types. Outer leaves are dark to light green and the more tender, inner leaves creamy-yellow. Endive is slightly bitter and is blanched to make it sweeter. Used mainly in salads, it is shredded to reduce bitterness, or may be cooked.

Endive is a cool-season crop that grows best at 10–20°C (50–68°F), but withstands light frost in the open; the hardier cultivars survive -9°C (16°F). Bitterness generally increases at high temperatures. Some curled types are quite heat-tolerant, while escarole types tend to with-

stand greater cold. There is a risk of premature bolting from spring sowings if temperatures fall below 5°C (41°F) for an extended period. Endive performs much better than lettuce in the low light levels of northern winters and therefore makes a useful winter greenhouse crop.

For soil and site requirements, see "Lettuces", p.518. Summer crops may be grown in light shade; always grow autumn crops on well-drained soil to avoid the risk of rotting. Endive has a low nitrogen requirement (see p.504).

Sowing and planting
Choose appropriate cultivars for each season. Sow in late spring for a summer crop or in summer for an autumn crop, either *in situ* or in modules or seed trays. Thin or plant out the

seedlings 25–38cm (10–15in) apart, using the wider spacing for spreading cultivars. Curled types may be sown as cut-and-come-again crops (see "Successional crops", p.500), most usefully in late spring and late summer.

Routine cultivation
To blanch leaves, choose nearly mature plants with dry leaves and blanch a few at a time since they deteriorate rapidly after blanching.

For complete blanching *in situ*, cover each plant with a bucket. For partial blanching, lay a large plate or piece of cardboard over the centre. With escarole types bunch up the leaves and tie them together. Protect the plants against slugs until they are ready for harvesting, which is after about ten days. In autumn, plants for blanching should be lifted before

BLANCHING ENDIVE

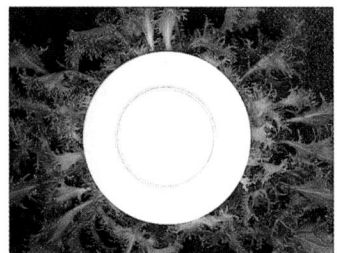

1 *Ensure that the endive is dry, then lay a plate over the centre to blanch the leaves partially.*

2 *The centre should have turned white and be ready for harvesting after about 10 days.*

severe weather disfigures them; transplant them into a darkened frame or dark area under greenhouse staging, then blanch as for Witloof chicory (see below).

Pests and diseases

Slugs (p.644) and aphids (p.646) are the most common problems. For other pests and diseases that affect endive, see "Lettuces", p.518.

Growing under cover

Protecting plants under cover provides a year-round supply. For use in winter and early spring, transplant seedlings in early autumn from seed trays or modules under cover. Sow as a cut-and-come-again seedling crop under cover in spring for harvesting early, and in early autumn for a late crop.

Harvesting and storing

Harvest endive between 7 and 13 weeks after sowing, depending on the cultivar and season. Pick individual leaves as needed, or cut across the crown, leaving the plant to resprout. Mature plants respond well to cut-and-come-again treatment (see "Cut-and-come-again harvesting", p.506). Endive leaves do not store well, so should be eaten fresh.

Chicory (*Cichorium intybus*)

There are many types of chicory, all with a distinctive, slightly bitter taste. Nearly all are hardy and are useful crops in the winter months. Their diverse colours make them attractive in salads, and some types may also be cooked. All types have low nitrogen requirements (see p.504).

Witloof or Belgian chicory

Similar in appearance to dandelions, these biennials have pointed leaves about 20cm (8in) long, with a spread of about 15cm (6in). Their "chicons" (the whitened, compact, leafy shoots obtained from lifting the roots and forcing and blanching them to make them sweeter) are eaten raw or cooked. The green leaves may also be used, but taste more bitter.

RECOMMENDED CHICORY

Witloof
'Videna'
'Witloof Zoom' F1

Red chicory
'Cesare' (early)
'Jupiter'
'Medusa' (early)
'Palla Rossa Verona'

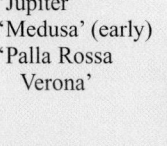

Sugar loaf
'Bianca di Milano'
'Biondissima di Trieste'
'Poncho'
'Snowflake'

Witloof chicory grows best at 15–19°C (59–66°F). It is generally forced for winter use. Grow the plants in an open site in reasonably fertile – but not freshly manured – soil.

The plants require a fairly long growing season. Sow seed outdoors *in situ* in spring or early summer, in rows 30cm (12in) apart. Thin the seedlings to about 20cm (8in) apart. Keep plants weed-free. Water the plants as necessary, to prevent the soil from drying out.

Witloof chicory may be forced *in situ* in light soils and areas with mild winters. In early winter, cut the green leaves about 2.5cm (1in) above ground level. Cover the stumps with soil, making a ridge about 15cm (6in) high; the chicons will grow and force their way through.

Force indoors if the garden soil is heavy or winters are severe, or if an earlier crop is required. Dig up the plants in late autumn or early winter. Cut the leaves to 2.5cm (1in) and trim the roots to about 20cm (8in); reject any that are very thin. The roots may be forced immediately or stored for forcing a few at a time in succession during the winter and early spring. To store the roots, lay them flat in boxes with moist sand between each of the layers and keep them in a frost-free shed or cellar until they are required.

To force indoors, plant several of the prepared roots in a large pot or box filled with compost or garden soil, and cover with an inverted pot or box of the same size. Block any drainage holes to keep out light. Keep the soil moist, and maintain a temperature of 10–18°C (50–64°F). Roots may also be planted under greenhouse staging, or in a garden frame. Make a light-proof area by stretching black plastic sheeting over wire hoops or attaching it to a wooden support. Do not use plastic sheeting in spring if temperatures soar, since aphid damage and rotting may occur. Witloof chicory is normally free of pests and diseases.

Harvest chicons forced outside after 8–12 weeks when about 10cm (4in) high by moving the soil and cutting the heads 2.5cm (1in) above the neck. Plants forced indoors should be ready after three to four weeks. Stumps may resprout to give a second crop of smaller chicons. Keep chicons wrapped or refrigerated after cutting since they become green and bitter on exposure to light.

FORCING AND BLANCHING CHICORY

1 *In late autumn or early winter, lift the mature plant carefully. The central leaves may be tender enough to eat.*

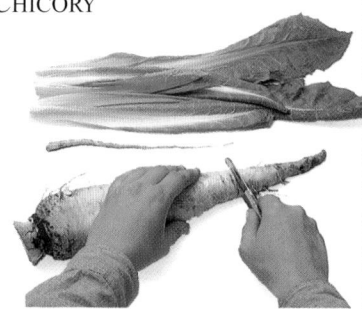

2 *Using a sharp knife, trim the leaves to 2.5cm (1in) from the crown and slice off the base of the root and any side roots, leaving a 20cm (8in) length.*

3 *Put a layer of moist potting compost or garden soil into a 24cm (9in) pot. Place three trimmed roots in the mixture and firm so that they stand upright, then fill the pot to within 2.5cm (1in) of the rim and firm, leaving the crowns exposed.*

4 *Line another pot with cooking foil or black plastic to cover the drainage holes and place it over the roots to block the light. Keep at 10–18°C (50–64°F). Harvest the chicons 3–4 weeks later by cutting just above soil level.*

Red chicory

This is a varied group of perennials usually grown as annuals. The typical red chicory, also known as radicchio, is a low-growing plant with bitter, reddish-green outer leaves and a compact heart. It is eaten raw in salads, shredded to reduce bitterness, or may be cooked.

Red chicory tolerates a wide range of temperatures and soil conditions, but is mainly grown for use in the cooler months. Cultivars vary in their frost tolerance. 'Treviso' is exceptionally hardy; it may be forced in the same way as Witloof chicory (see p.517). The new F1 hybrids produce more solid heads than traditional cultivars. Sow in early and midsummer,

in situ or in seed trays for transplanting. Plant 24–35cm (10–14in) apart depending on the cultivar. Transplant summer-sown crops under cover in autumn.

Eight to ten weeks after sowing, pick single leaves or harvest the whole head. Chicory stands a long time after maturing; in cold climates, protect with low tunnels in late autumn so that the plants develop more solid heads.

Sugar loaf chicory

Sugar loaf chicory is green-leaved, forming a conical head not unlike cos lettuce in both shape and size. Its inner leaves are naturally blanched

and slightly sweetened. For use, and for climate, soil, and cultivation requirements, see "Red chicory" (left).

Sugar loaf chicory may be sown in spring as a cut-and-come-again seedling crop (see p.500); harvest the seedlings before temperatures rise, causing leaves to coarsen. For mature plants, thin seedlings to 25cm (10in) apart, and harvest in late summer to autumn. The plants tolerate light frost, and provide winter crops if grown under cover.

Harvest leaves as needed, or cut the heads when mature. The heads keep for a few weeks in cool, dry, frost-free conditions. They may also be piled up, turned inwards and covered with straw to form clamps (see *Making a Swede Clamp*, p.543).

SUGAR LOAF CHICORY

Lettuces (*Lactuca sativa*)

Lettuces are annual, low-growing plants; they usually have green leaves, although some cultivars have red or reddish-green leaves.

There are several distinct types. Cos (romaine) lettuces have long, substantial, well-flavoured leaves with fairly loose hearts; semi-cos are shorter with very sweet, crunchy leaves. Butterhead lettuces have smooth, soft leaves, forming a rounded, compact heart; crispheads (known as icebergs when marketed with the outer leaves removed) have crispy leaves forming a heart. Loose-leaf lettuces, typified by the "Salad Bowl" types, do not form hearts so are slow to bolt and may be cut over a long period; their leaves are often indented and are very decorative. They are the most nutritious form of lettuce and may also be used for cut-and-come-again seedling crops (see p.500).

Lettuces vary from 10cm (4in) to over 30cm (12in) in spread. The cos types are about 25cm (10in) tall, others about 15cm (6in) high. Lettuces are primarily used as salad vegetables, but outer and older leaves may also be cooked or used in soups.

Lettuces are cool-season crops, growing best at 10–20°C (50–68°F). Cool nights are essential for good results. Some cultivars are tolerant of heat or frost. Germination is poor above 25°C (77°F); at these temperatures, plants tend to bolt rapidly and may become bitter, although loose-leaf lettuces are slower to bolt than other types.

Grow in an open site, or in light shade in very hot weather. Lettuces need fertile, moisture-retentive soil and, although they fall into none of the rotation groups, should not be

LOOSE-LEAF LETTUCES ('LOLLO ROSSA')

grown in the same patch of soil for two years in a row to prevent the build-up of fungus disease. They require medium nitrogen (see p.504).

Sowing and planting

Cultivars appropriate for the season must be sown. For a year-round supply in cool climates, sow from early spring to late summer at two- to three-week intervals. At the end of summer or in early autumn, sow hardy cultivars that overwinter outdoors or under cover for a spring crop. In warm climates, only heat-tolerant cultivars should be sown during the summer.

In cool climates, sow seed *in situ*, in a seedbed, or in trays or modules for transplanting. Sowings in summer are best made *in situ*, since seedlings wilt when transplanted unless they have been raised in modules. Seed may become dormant in high temperatures; this is most likely to occur several hours after

sowing and may be overcome by watering after sowing to cool the soil, by putting seed trays or modules in a cool place to germinate, or by sowing seed in the afternoon so that the critical period occurs at night when temperatures are lower.

HARVESTING LOOSE-LEAF LETTUCES

Loose-leaf lettuces may be harvested by cutting across the leaves 2.5cm (1in) above ground level. Leave the stump to resprout.

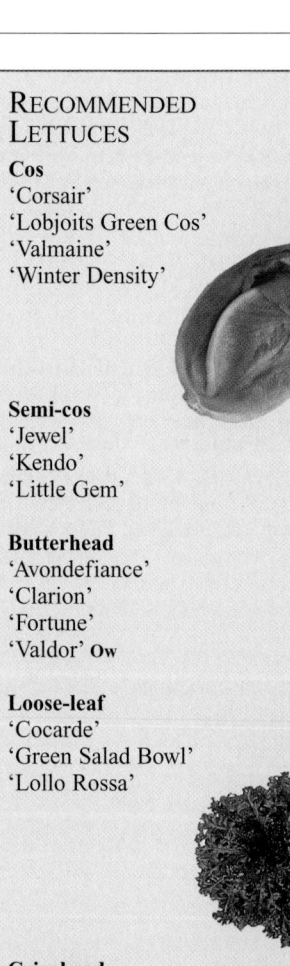

RECOMMENDED LETTUCES

Cos
'Corsair'
'Lobjoits Green Cos'
'Valmaine'
'Winter Density'

Semi-cos
'Jewel'
'Kendo'
'Little Gem'

Butterhead
'Avondefiance'
'Clarion'
'Fortune'
'Valdor' **Ow**

Loose-leaf
'Cocarde'
'Green Salad Bowl'
'Lollo Rossa'

Crisphead
'Beatrice'
'Lakeland'
'Saladin'
'Warpath'
'Webb's Wonderful'

KEY
Ow *Overwinters under cover*

Transplant lettuces in moist conditions when they have five or six leaves, with the base of the leaves positioned just above soil level. In hot weather, shade young plants until they are established. Space small cultivars 15cm (6in) apart, and larger ones about 30cm (12in) apart.

Sow hardy cultivars for over-wintering outdoors *in situ* or under cloches or in frames; thin to about 7cm (3in) apart in autumn and to the full distance apart in spring. Floating mulches or cloches put over the plants in spring improve their quality, and help them to mature earlier.

Most types of lettuce may be grown as cut-and-come-again seedling crops, especially the loose-leaf lettuces, including the traditional European "cutting" cultivars, and some cos varieties (see "Successional crops", p.500).

Routine cultivation
Keep lettuce beds weed-free. Apply a nitrogenous fertilizer or organic liquid feed if growth is slow. In dry conditions, water the plants at a rate of 22 litres/sq m (5 gallons/sq yd) per week. The most critical watering period is about seven to ten days before maturity (see also p.502). In late autumn or early winter, protect lettuces with cloches to improve the quality of the crop.

Pests and diseases
Problems include greenfly and root aphid (see "Aphids", p.646), cutworms (p.655), leatherjackets (p.660), slugs (p.644), mosaic virus (see "Viruses", p.649), downy mildew (p.646), boron deficiency (p.654), and grey mould (*Botrytis*) (p.653); birds may attack seedlings (p.657). Some cultivars show aphid resistance

PROTECTING SEEDLINGS

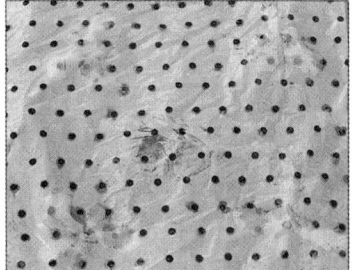

Protecting seedlings with perforated film or fleece helps them mature more quickly early in the season.

and others show some tolerance to mosaic virus and downy mildew.

Growing under cover
In cool climates, earlier lettuce crops may be obtained by sowing

or planting in early spring in an unheated greenhouse, beneath cloches or perforated fleecy films, or in cold frames. Some cultivars may also be grown under cover in winter for early spring cropping; for midwinter crops, gentle heat is usually required.

Harvesting and storing
Loose-leaf lettuces should be ready about seven weeks after sowing, butterheads after 10 or 11 weeks, and cos and crispheads after 11 or 12 weeks. Cut cos, butterhead, and crisphead types soon after maturing to prevent bolting. They may be stored for a few days in a refrigerator. Pick the leaves of loose-leaf types a few at a time, as required, since they do not store well, or cut across the plants 2.5cm (1in) above soil level, leaving the stumps to resprout within a few weeks.

Spinach (*Spinacia oleracea*)

Spinach is a fast-growing annual that reaches a height of 15–20cm (6–8in), with a spread of about 15cm (6in). The highly nutritious leaves are smooth or crinkled, and round or pointed, depending on the cultivar. They are eaten lightly cooked or, when young, raw in salads.

A cool-season plant, spinach grows best at 16–18°C (61–64°F), although it will grow well at lower temperatures. Small plants and seedlings may survive -9°C (16°F). Grow cultivars recommended for the area; for example, many are prone to bolt in long days (see "Daylength", p.495), especially after a cold period or in hot, dry conditions. Recommended spinach cultivars include 'Atlanta', 'Monnopa', 'Palco', and 'Spokane'. Spinach plants tolerate light shade

during summer, and need a soil with medium nitrogen levels (see *Nitrogen Requirements*, p.504). For other soil requirements, see "Swiss chard and spinach beet", p.516.

Sowing and planting
Sow in cool seasons as spinach will not germinate in temperatures above 30°C (86°F). Sow *in situ*, placing individual seeds about 2.5cm (1in) apart in rows spaced about 30cm (12in) apart. For a continuous crop, sow in succession, after seedlings of the previous sowings have appeared. Thin early as for Swiss chard (see p.516), to about 7cm (3in) for young plants, or to 15cm (6in) apart for large plants.

Spinach may also be grown as a cut-and-come-again seedling crop

for use in salads (see p.500). For this, sow in early spring and early autumn under cover, and also in late summer for an overwintering crop in the open. For routine cultivation, pests and diseases, and growing under cover, see "Swiss chard and spinach beet", p.516.

Harvesting and storing
Cut leaves between five and ten weeks after sowing at any stage once the plants are about 5cm (2in) tall. Either cut individual leaves, or cut the heads about 2.5cm (1in) above the ground and leave them to resprout; alternatively, pull up whole plants. In warm areas, harvest plants young, before they start to run to seed. Use the leaves fresh soon after picking, or store by freezing.

SPINACH

New Zealand spinach (*Tetragonia tetragonioides*, syn. *T. expansa*)

A half-hardy, creeping perennial, New Zealand spinach is also grown as an annual. The plants have thick, triangular leaves about 5cm (2in) long with a spread of 90–120cm (3–4ft). The leaves are used in the same way as spinach (see above).

New Zealand spinach tolerates high, even tropical, temperatures, and drought, but cannot withstand frost. It grows best in an open site on reasonably fertile and moisture-retentive soil, and needs low nitrogen (see p.504). It is generally less prone to bolting than spinach.

Seeds may be slow to germinate, so to aid germination soak them in

water for 24 hours before sowing. In cool climates, sow seed indoors and plant out at 45cm (18in) each way after all risk of frost has passed. Otherwise sow seed *in situ* outdoors after the last frost, thinning in stages to the final spacing. Keep seedlings weed-free (mature plants cover the soil, suppressing weeds). Pest or disease problems are rare.

Start picking the young leaves and the tips of the stems six or seven weeks after sowing. Pick frequently to encourage further young growth for three or four months. New Zealand spinach should be used fresh immediately after cutting, or frozen.

PICKING NEW ZEALAND SPINACH

Pick the young leaves and tips of stems of New Zealand spinach before seedheads start to form. Plants will continue to make new growth that may be harvested until the first frosts.

Minor salad vegetables

THERE are many lesser-known vegetables worth cultivating to use raw in salads, either on their own or mixed with other vegetables. They are suitable for growing in small gardens and containers. The leaves are distinctly flavoured and nutritious, especially if used young. Apart from summer purslane and iceplants, all tolerate a few degrees of frost, or even lower temperatures on well-drained soil with wind protection. In cool climates, most may be grown under cover in winter for higher yields. Most salad plants are fast-maturing but make lusher growth in nitrogen-rich soil. Many are best sown as cut-and-come-again crops (see p.500). They are usually free of pests and diseases.

Land cress (*Barbarea verna*)

This biennial, low-growing plant has a spread of 15–20cm (6–8in); land cress is also known as upland cress. The glossy, deep green leaves have a strong flavour similar to watercress, and are used as a watercress substitute, either raw or cooked. Land cress is very hardy, remaining green in winter. It grows best in the shade; in heat it runs to seed rapidly, becoming coarse and very hot-tasting. It may be intercropped between taller vegetables or used to make a neat edging for beds.

Grow land cress in fertile and moisture-retentive soils. Sow seed in spring for an early summer crop, or in late summer for an autumn and overwintering crop. It may be grown in unheated greenhouses in winter. Sow *in situ*, thinning to 15cm (6in) apart, or in seed trays to transplant. Pick leaves seven weeks after sowing when they are 7–10cm (3–4in) long.

LAND CRESS

If a few plants are left to run to seed in spring they seed freely, and the seedlings may be transplanted where they are needed. Flea beetles (p.644) may affect young plants.

Mustard (*Sinapis alba*)

Mustard is similar to cress in its habit and is often partnered with it. It is grown for the sharply flavoured seedling leaves which may be used raw in salads. It is a cool-season crop that runs to seed very rapidly in hot weather; its leaves tend to become coarse if it is grown in areas with heavy rainfall.

In temperate climates, outdoor sowings are most successful in spring and autumn *in situ*, using any of the methods suggested for cut-and-come-again seedlings (see p.500).

Mustard, like cress, is a useful crop for growing under cover from autumn to spring. It may be sown without soil either on moist paper towelling in a saucer placed on a windowsill, or in a sprouter; alternatively it may be sown in a seed tray of potting compost or soil. These methods may be used all year round. Mustard germinates faster than cress, so if the two are required together, sow the mustard two or

MUSTARD

three days later than the cress. A sowing every seven to ten days ensures a continuous supply.

Harvest mustard by cutting as required when the seedlings are about 3.5–5cm (1½–2in) tall. It runs to seed much more rapidly than cress, and will normally provide no more than two or three cuts.

Salad rape (*Brassica napus*)

This annual plant has light green, mild-flavoured leaves and is often used as a substitute for mustard in mustard and cress packs. It is fast-growing but slower to run to seed than mustard or cress. The leaves are used raw as seedlings, while larger leaves may be cooked as greens.

Salad rape survives temperatures of -10°C (14°F), and tolerates moderate heat. The plants grow in a wide range of soils. In temperate climates, sow under cover in early spring and late autumn; sow in succession outdoors until early autumn. Indoors, grow on a windowsill as for mustard (below, left). Outdoors, sow broadcast, or in rows or wide drills. Make the first cut after ten days; when plants reach 60cm (24in), harvest small leaves over several months.

HARVESTING SALAD RAPE

Cut leaves of salad rape at any stage from seedling to 7cm (3in) long. In good conditions, three cuts of seedling leaves may be possible.

Salad rocket (*Eruca vesicaria*)

This hardy, spicy-leaved Mediterranean plant is used in salads; older plants may be cooked. Salad rocket is also known as rucola, erugala, Mediterranean rocket, or roquette. It grows best in cool weather in moisture-retentive soil; in cool climates, it is excellent under cover in winter, and as a cut-and-come-again crop. Sow broadcast or in rows to cut as seedlings, or thin to 15cm (6in) to cut when larger. Seedlings are ready in three weeks. Flea beetles (p.644) may attack salad rocket.

SALAD ROCKET

Cress (*Lepidium sativum*)

This fast-growing plant is grown for its seedling leaves, which are used raw. Cress is also known as garden cress, curly cress, or peppercress. There is a fine-leaved and a broad-leaved form. It is a moderately hardy, cool-season crop, running to seed rapidly in hot weather, unless sown in light shade. In cool climates, cress grows well under cover in the winter months. It may stop growing at very low temperatures, but starts again when temperatures rise. It is useful for inter- and undercropping.

Except in very cool areas, cress is best sown in spring and late summer or early autumn; avoid sowing in hot weather. Either sow on moist paper in a saucer and place on a windowsill or sow in a sprouter; this will give one cut. To obtain several consecutive cuts, sow in a seed tray of light soil, or in the ground, broadcast, in

BROAD-LEAVED CRESS

single rows, or in wide drills. Cut ten days after sowing when seedlings are up to 5cm (2in) high. If sown in the ground, up to four successive cuts may be made.

Iceplants (*Mesembryanthemum crystallinum*)

Grown as perennials in warm climates and as tender annuals elsewhere, iceplants have a sprawling habit, succulent stems, and thick, fleshy leaves, covered with sparkling bladders. The leaves and young stems taste refreshing and slightly salty. They are used raw in salads or cooked like spinach.

Iceplants need a sunny position in light, well-drained soil. In warm climates, sow *in situ* outdoors; in cool climates, sow indoors in the spring, transplanting to 30cm (12in) apart after all risk of frost has passed. Slugs (p.644) may attack seedlings. Plants may be propagated by means of cuttings (see PERENNIALS, "Stem tip cuttings", p.202). The first picking of the young leaves and tender pieces of stem may be made about

ICEPLANTS

four weeks after planting. Harvest plants regularly to encourage further growth, and remove any flowers that appear. Leaves and stems keep fresh for several days.

Winter purslane (*Montia perfoliata*)

This is a hardy annual with heart-shaped leaves and dainty flowering shoots. The mildly flavoured, slightly succulent leaves, stems, and flowering shoots are used raw in salads. Also known as miner's lettuce or claytonia, it thrives in cool weather. It prefers well-drained conditions but grows well even in poor, light soil. Once established, it self-seeds rapidly; invasive seedlings are shallow-rooted and easily pulled up.

Make the main sowing in late summer for an autumn to early winter crop outdoors. Sow in spring for a summer crop. Grow either broadcast as a cut-and-come-again seedling crop, or in rows, or 10cm (4in) wide drills; seed may be sown *in situ*

WINTER PURSLANE

or in seed trays. Transplant or thin seedlings to 15–23cm (6–9in) apart. Start cutting 12 weeks after sowing, leaving the plants to resprout.

Summer purslane (*Portulaca oleracea*)

This half-hardy, low-growing plant has slightly succulent leaves and stems that are used raw or cooked. There are green- and yellow-leaved forms; the green type has thinner leaves, is more vigorous, and possibly better flavoured, but the yellow or golden form is attractive in salads. The plants need a warm, sheltered site with light, well-drained soil.

Grow summer purslane either as a cut-and-come-again seedling crop or as single plants. In cool climates, sow in a seed tray in late spring, planting out 15cm (6in) apart, after all risk of frost. Make earlier and late summer sowings under cover as a cut-and-come-again seedling crop. In warm climates, sow *in situ* outside throughout the summer. Cut the seedlings, or young shoots of single

GOLDEN SUMMER PURSLANE

plants, from about four to eight weeks after sowing. Cut regularly, always leaving two basal leaves, and remove any flowers that develop. Slugs (p.644) may attack plants.

Watercress (*Rorippa nasturtium-aquaticum*)

A hardy aquatic perennial, watercress (also known as *Nasturtium officinale*) has nutritious, sharply flavoured leaves that are used in salads and soups. Its natural habitat is fresh running streams, with slightly alkaline water at about 10°C (50°F).

Root cuttings by placing stems in fresh water; they will soon root and may be planted at the edge of a stream in spring, spaced 15cm (6in) apart. Watercress may be grown in moist garden soil, but it is easier to grow in 15–21cm (6–8in) pots. Put a layer of gravel or moss in each pot, fill with rich soil, and stand it in a dish of cool, clean water. Plant three or four rooted cuttings per pot, and

WATERCRESS GROWN IN A POT

stand it in a sheltered position in good light. Change the water at least daily in hot weather. Cut leaves as needed.

Dandelions (*Taraxacum officinale*)

Hardy, perennial weeds, dandelions spread up to 30cm (12in). Wild and cultivated forms are grown for the young leaves, which are used raw. The cultivated forms are larger and slower to run to seed. Dandelion leaves are slightly bitter but blanching sweetens them. The flowers and roots are also edible. Dandelions tolerate a range of well-drained soils.

Sow in spring, in seed trays for transplanting, or *in situ*, spacing 35cm (14in) apart. Blanch in succession from late summer, covering dry plants with a large, light-proof bucket. Harvest the leaves when they are elongated and creamy-yellow. Dandelions die back in winter, but reappear in spring; the plants will continue to grow for several years.

BLANCHING DANDELION

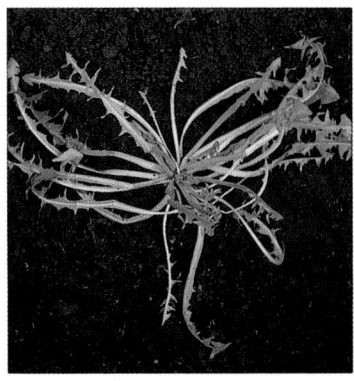

When the plant has several leaves, cover it with a bucket 30cm (12in) tall. Harvest the creamy-yellow, elongated leaves after several weeks.

Corn salad (*Valerianella locusta*)

Grown for autumn and winter salads in cool climates, these hardy annuals form small, mild-flavoured plants. Corn salad is also known as lamb's lettuce or mache. There are two types: the floppy, large-leaved type, and the smaller, upright type with darker green leaves, which is reputedly the hardier. They tolerate a wide range of soils. In cold climates, grow them under cover in winter to obtain more prolific and tender-leaved plants. Corn salad is a useful crop for inter- or undercropping vegetables such as winter brassicas.

Corn salad may be grown as a cut-and-come-again seedling crop, or as individual plants. Sow from midsummer onwards *in situ*, broadcast, in rows, or in wide drills. Keep the seeds moist until they have germinated. Thin seedlings to 10cm (4in) apart. Corn salad is slow-growing

LARGE-LEAVED CORN SALAD

and may take 12 weeks to mature. Harvest leaves individually or cut across the plants, leaving them to resprout for a second cut.

Fruiting and flowering vegetables

Honeydew melon

Aubergines

Marrow

Sweet peppers

Courgettes

Cherry tomatoes

Musk melon

Plum tomatoes

Greenhouse cucumber

Sweet peppers

Sweet corn

SOME of the most exotic and succulent vegetables fall into the fruiting and flowering group of vegetables. Many – tomatoes, peppers, aubergines, and melons, for example – are tropical or subtropical in origin; in cooler areas these may need to be grown under cover or in a warm situation. In temperate climates, others such as marrows, sweet corn, and pumpkins need to be germinated indoors but may be planted outdoors to grow to maturity. All need a warm, sheltered situation to ripen their fruits and for pollination to be successful.

Sweet peppers (*Capsicum annuum* Grossum Group)

Also called capsicums, or bell peppers, these annuals have a bushy habit and may grow up to 75cm (30in) tall with a spread of 45–60cm (18–24in). The fruits are usually oblong, ranging in size from 3–15cm (1¼–6in) long and 3–7cm (1¼–3in) in diameter, and may be green, cream, yellow, orange, red, or dark purple. The mature fruits are eaten cooked or raw, whole or sliced.

Sweet peppers are tropical and subtropical plants needing a minimum temperature of 21°C (70°F) with a humidity of 70–75 per cent. Temperatures over 30°C (86°F) may reduce fruit set and cause buds and flowers to drop. In temperate climates, plants may be grown under cover or outside in a sunny, sheltered site. Moderately deep, fertile, well-drained soil with medium nitrogen levels (see p.504) is required.

Sowing and planting
Sow seed in spring in the greenhouse in trays of compost with a pH of 5.5–7. Prick out the seedlings into

SWEET PEPPERS

6–9cm (3–3½in) pots and plant out 10–12 weeks after sowing in well-prepared beds, spacing the plants 45–50cm (18–20in) apart each way. In temperate climates, pot on seedlings and do not plant out until all risk of frost has passed.

Routine cultivation
Pinch out the terminal growing point of established plants to encourage a bushy habit and stake cultivars over 60cm (24in) tall. Water regularly to prevent leaf and bud drop, and mulch with organic material. Apply a balanced fertilizer or liquid feed every two weeks during the growing season. Protect plants outdoors with plastic covers, if necessary.

Pests and diseases
Plants may be attacked by aphids (p.646); under cover they may also be affected by glasshouse red spider mite (p.646), whiteflies (p.646), thrips (p.647), and blossom end rot (see "Calcium deficiency", p.658).

Growing under cover
Sow as above in early spring. When the seedlings are 8–10cm (3–4in) tall, pot them into 21cm (8in) pots or transplant into growing bags or well-prepared greenhouse beds. Space plants at least 50cm (20in) apart and

stake taller cultivars. Maintain the recommended temperature and a humidity of 70–75 per cent by regularly damping down.

Harvesting and storing
Harvest the peppers 12–14 weeks after transplanting and before the first frost if the plants are growing outside. Some cultivars are best used when the fruits are green, but others may be left on the plants for two to three weeks until they change colour to red or creamy-yellow. Cut off individual peppers; they may be stored in cool, humid conditions for up to 14 days at 12–15°C (54–59°F). Entire plants may also be stored (see "Fruiting vegetables", p.506).

RIPENING SWEET PEPPERS
As they ripen, the fruits change colour from green to red, yellow, or dark purple, and the flavour becomes sweeter.

HARVESTING SWEET PEPPERS

Some peppers are best harvested when green; others may be left to turn red or yellow. Cut the stalk about 2.5cm (1in) from the fruit.

RECOMMENDED SWEET PEPPERS
'Ace' F1
'Ariane' F1
'Bell Boy' F1
'Bendigo' F1

'Canape' F1
'Gypsy' F1
'Luteus'
'Mavras' F1

'Purple Beauty'
'Redskin'
'Unicorn' F1

Chilli peppers (*Capsicum annuum* Longum Group)

This form of *Capsicum annuum* has pointed fruits up to 9cm (3½in) long. Popular chilli pepper cultivars include 'Jalapeno', 'Thai Hot Dragon', and 'Apache'.

The plants are cultivated in the same way as sweet peppers (see above); chilli peppers are slightly more tolerant of high temperature levels, however. They may be picked for use at any stage when the colour is green to red. If they are growing outside, they should be harvested before the first frost is expected.

The hot flavour increases with the maturity of the chilli fruit and comes from the white pith and seeds inside. If the flavour is too hot, the pith and seeds may be removed and discarded.

RIPENING CHILLI PEPPERS

RED CHILLI PEPPERS

Hot peppers (*Capsicum frutescens*)

These plants, also known as cayenne peppers, are branching perennials that grow to 1.5m (5ft) tall and bear small, narrow, orange, yellow, or red fruits which may hang from the branches or be carried upright, depending on the cultivar. They are highly pungent and are used in sauces and as a general flavouring.

Hot peppers are tropical and subtropical plants and therefore cannot tolerate frost. Plants should be spaced 60cm (24in) apart in each direction, and cultivated in the same way as sweet peppers (see p.522), although they generally require more water. Staking is not normally necessary.

Hot peppers need a long growing period, and the first fruits are usually produced about 15–18 weeks after planting. They should be allowed to ripen fully before being picked. They may be frozen or dried and stored for several months.

HOT PEPPERS

Watermelons (*Citrullus lanatus*)

Watermelons are annual, tropical or subtropical plants with spreading stems that grow to 3–4m (10–12ft). Their fruits are rounded or oblong, green or cream, striped or mottled, and may grow to 60cm (24in) in length; they are eaten raw. Plants need a temperature of 25–30°C (77–86°F) and may be grown outdoors only in sunny, sheltered areas, but may also be grown under cover. Well-drained, sandy loam soils with medium levels of nitrogen (see p.504) and a pH of 5.5–7 are needed. Incorporate well-rotted manure and a general-purpose fertilizer into the soil before planting.

WATERMELON

Sowing and planting
Sow in early spring under cover, in trays or 6–9cm (3–3½in) pots, at a temperature of at least 22–25°C (72–77°F). When the seedlings are 10–15cm (4–6in) tall, harden them off. Plant them out after all risk of frost has passed, spaced at least 1m (3ft) apart. Protect from wind and cold weather with plastic screens.

Routine cultivation
Mulch to retain moisture and apply a balanced fertilizer or liquid feed every two weeks until the fruits begin to develop. Pinch out the growing points of the main shoots when they are 2m (6ft) long and train sideshoots between other plants in the row. To assist formation of fruits, hand-pollinate the flowers (see "Marrows and courgettes", p.526). Reduce sub-lateral growths from the sideshoots to two or three leaves after fruits start to develop, and place a pad of dried grass or a block of wood beneath each fruit to protect it from soil-borne pests and diseases.

Pests and diseases
Humidity levels over 75 per cent encourage leaf diseases, particularly powdery mildew (p.646) and mosaic virus (see "Viruses", p.649). Other common pests include aphids (p.646), root-knot eelworms (p.660), and fruit flies (p.659).

Growing under cover
Watermelons are extremely vigorous and are not normally grown in a greenhouse. They may be grown under plastic covers, spaced 1m (3ft) apart; remove covers at flowering time to reduce humidity and encourage insect-pollination.

Harvesting and storing
Harvest 11–14 weeks after sowing; mature fruits give a hollow sound when tapped. They may be stored for 14–20 days at 10–12°C (50–54°F).

Sweet melons (*Cucumis melo*)

These climbing annuals, normally trained as cordons, reach a height of about 2m (6ft) with laterals extending to 60cm (24in). The three major types are cantaloupe, winter or casaba, and musk (including honeydew) melons. Cantaloupe melons have grey-green, thick, rough skins with deep grooves; individual fruits weigh up to 750g (1lb 11oz). Winter melons have smooth, yellow, or yellow and green striped skin, and weigh up to 1kg (2lb 2oz). Musk melons vary in size but are usually smaller than cantaloupe and winter melons and often have fine reticulated markings on smooth skins. Winter melons and some cultivars of cantaloupe melons are suitable for growing in a greenhouse.

Sweet melons are tropical plants requiring a minimum temperature of 18°C (64°F) for germination, rising to 25°C (77°F) during the growing period. In very sunny, sheltered sites, growing in the open is possible but in temperate climates plants are grown in cold frames or in a greenhouse. They need a well-drained, fertile soil with a pH of 6.5–7, a high humus content, and high nitrogen levels (see p.504). Add a general-purpose fertilizer and well-rotted compost or manure.

Sowing and planting
Sow seed under cover in early spring in trays or in 6–9cm (3–3½in) pots (two seeds per pot), removing the weaker one if both germinate. After about six weeks, and when risk of frost is passed, harden off and plant out the seedlings, spaced 1m (3ft) apart with 1–1.5m (3–5ft) between rows. Plant each seedling on a slight mound and protect young plants until they are established from wind and cold weather with plastic tunnels.

MUSK MELON

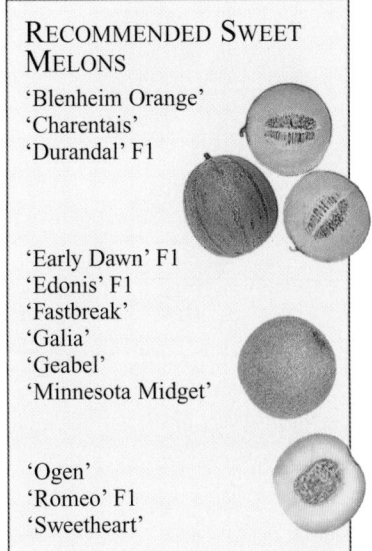

STOPPING SWEET MELONS

Allow 1 flower per lateral to set, and then pinch or cut out the growing tip of each lateral at 2–3 leaves beyond the developing fruit.

Routine cultivation

After five leaves have developed, pinch out each growing point to encourage further shoots. When these are well developed, reduce them to about four of the most vigorous shoots. Train two shoots on either side, between adjacent plants in the row. Remove any protective covering when the plants begin to flower to encourage insect-pollination. Hand-pollinate if required (see "Marrows and courgettes", p.526).

Thin to one fruit per shoot when the fruits are 2.5cm (1in) in diameter, and stop all sub-laterals at two to three leaves beyond the developing fruits. Pinch out the main shoots when they are 1–1.2m (3–4ft) long and remove any further sub-laterals that form. Place a pad of dried grass, a tile, or a piece of wood beneath each developing fruit to protect it from soil-borne diseases.

Water regularly and feed every 10–14 days with a liquid feed as the fruits begin to develop; reduce watering and feeding as the fruits ripen.

Pests and diseases

Aphids (p.646) and powdery mildew (p.646) may be troublesome. Under cover, the plants may be affected by glasshouse red spider mite (p.646), the fungal disease powdery mildew (p.646), whiteflies (p.646), and *Verticillium* wilt (p.653).

Growing under cover

To raise sweet melons in a cold frame, plant seedlings singly in the centre of the frame. Train the four laterals to grow towards the corners. As the plants develop, increase ventilation and gradually reduce humidity. Once the fruits start forming, remove the lights, replacing them at night only in cold weather. In hot weather, shade lightly.

Sweet melons may be grown in a greenhouse if the distance from the base of the side walls to the ridge is at least 2m (6ft). Plant seedlings onto well-prepared mounds (see "Cucumbers and gherkins", below). Grow as single or double cordons, training on canes tied to horizontal wires up to the ridge. Space plants 38cm (15in) apart for single cordons, 60cm (24in) for double cordons.

They may also be grown in growing bags or 24–25cm (9–10in) pots placed on greenhouse staging.

For a single cordon, pinch out the growing point when the main shoot is 2m (6ft) long to encourage lateral growth. Stop laterals at five leaves and sub-laterals at two leaves beyond the flowers. For a double cordon, pinch out the main shoot and let two shoots develop vertically; train as above. Support developing fruits in 5cm (2in) mesh slings or nets fixed to the ridge. To aid pollination do not damp down during flowering. Maintain a temperature of 24°C (75°F) at night and 30°C (86°F) in the day.

Harvesting and storing

Harvest 12–20 weeks after sowing. Cantaloupe and musk melons are sweet-smelling when mature, and the fruit stalks crack. Separate the fruits gently from the stalks. Store for 14–50 days at 10–15°C (50–59°F), depending on the cultivar.

Cucumbers and gherkins (*Cucumis sativus*)

Most are annual, trailing vines that grow to 1–3m (3–10ft); there are a few compact bush cultivars. The immature fruits are eaten raw, pickled, or cooked in soup.

Outdoor or ridge cucumbers are characteristically rough-skinned, spiny, and 10–15cm (4–6in) long. Modern, improved cultivars, many of Japanese origin, are smoother and up to 30cm (12in) long, with improved cold tolerance and disease resistance. They are mainly grown outdoors or in frames and are insect-pollinated. Gherkins are ridge cucumbers with short, often stumpy fruits up to 7cm (3in) long, harvested young, and used mainly for pickling. Apple and lemon cucumbers are round, yellow-skinned, ridge cucumbers that grow up to 6cm (2½in) in diameter. European or greenhouse fruits are smooth and over 30cm (12in) long. They do not require pollination to set fruit and, if pollinated, may produce bitter, swollen fruits; use the modern all-female cultivars to remove the risk of accidental pollination.

Cucumbers are warm-season vegetables, growing best at a mean temperature of 18–30°C (64–86°F).

They have no frost tolerance and most are damaged at temperatures below 10°C (50°F). In northern latitudes, ridge types may produce male flowers alone early in the season; female flowers, then fruits, occur later. Grow cucumbers in a sheltered site in fertile, humus-rich soil that is well drained but moisture-retentive: the roots must not be allowed to dry out. Lime very acid soils. The plants need low nitrogen levels (see p.504). Rotate indoor crops.

Greenhouse types must be grown with minimum night temperatures of 20°C (68°F) and in high humidity. Never grow ridge types in the same greenhouse as all-female cultivars since cross-pollination will occur.

Sowing and planting

Cucumbers transplant badly, so seed for outdoor varieties should be sown *in situ* after all risk of frost has passed or alternatively in small pots or modules. If sowing outside, prepare holes at least 30cm (12in) wide and deep, working in plenty of well-rotted compost or manure as you backfill. Cover with about 15cm (6in) of manured soil made into a small mound to ensure sharp drainage. Place seeds on their side about 2cm (¾in) deep, sowing two to three per pot or site.

Seed germinates at a minimum soil temperature of 20°C (68°F). Thin to one seedling after germination. Seed sown in pots needs a minimum temperature at night of 16°C (61°F)

GHERKIN

until the seedlings are planted out, about four weeks after sowing. Space climbing types 45cm (18in) apart; bush types, and climbing types if trailing over the ground, should be spaced about 75cm (30in) apart. In cool climates, protect plants with cloches or fleecy film after planting.

Routine cultivation

Grow trailing types up supporting fences, nets, or canes, or allow them to twine up strings. Nip out the growing point after five or six leaves have appeared, and train the resulting stronger growths up the support, tying them in if necessary. When these shoots reach the top of the support, nip them out two leaves beyond a flower; laterals will develop on which more fruits will form. As fruiting continues, feed plants every two

SOWING AND PLANTING OUT

1 *Fill a 5cm (2in) pot with seed compost to within 2.5cm (1in) of the rim. Place 2 or 3 seeds on their sides in the compost, then cover them to a depth of about 2cm (¾in). Water well and label.*

2 *Prepare a hole 30cm (12in) wide and 30cm (12in) deep, and fill with well-rotted compost. Pile the soil on top to make a mound about 15cm (6in) high. Plant the cucumber on top of this mound. Firm in and water.*

BUSH CUCUMBERS

Pests and diseases
Cucumbers may be affected by snails (p.644), aphids (p.646), powdery mildew (p.646), cutworms (p.655), glasshouse red spider mite (p.646), whiteflies (p.646), cucumber mosaic virus (see "Viruses", p.649), and foot and root rots (p.654).

Growing under cover
Grow as in the open using appropriate cultivars – the all-female selections are recommended. Stop the main shoot of each plant at the top of the supports and nip off sideshoots beyond the first leaf. Damp down greenhouses to control pests.

Harvesting and storing
Harvest cucumbers regularly from about 12 weeks after sowing when the sides of the fruits are parallel and they are about 15–20cm (6–8in) long. Harvest gherkins when they are 2.5–7cm (1–3in) long or when they have reached pickling size.

weeks with a high-potash fertilizer or equivalent organic liquid feed. Regular watering is essential during the growing period, particularly after transplanting so that plants establish quickly, and during flowering and fruiting (see "Critical watering periods", p.502).

CLIMBING CUCUMBERS

Pumpkins and winter squashes (*Cucurbita maxima, C. moschata, C. pepo*)

This is a very diverse group of annuals, also known as winter squashes, with fruits ranging from 450g (1lb) to over 30kg (66lb). The skin may be smooth, warted, or ridged, and green, cream, blue-green, yellow, orange, red, or striped – the colour often changing with maturity. Their shapes vary considerably and may be round, long, squat, onion-shaped, or a two-layered, "turban" shape. Most form very large trailing plants with huge leaves; some are compact and bushy. Both young and mature fruits may be eaten cooked, either fresh or after storage. Shoots and young leaves may be cooked and flowers may be eaten raw or cooked. Some cultivars have edible seeds.

PUMPKINS ON A TRIPOD

For climate, site, and soil preparation requirements, see "Cucumbers and gherkins", p.524. Pumpkins require medium to high nitrogen levels (see p.504).

Sowing and planting
Seed may be soaked overnight before sowing to hasten germination. Sow as for cucumbers (see p.524). Space plants 2–3m (6–10ft) apart, depending on the cultivar. For large cultivars, prepare holes up to 45cm (18in) deep and 60cm (24in) wide. Insert a marker cane when planting so that the centre of the plant can be found if watering is necessary. Protect and mulch after planting.

Routine cultivation
A top-dressing of a general fertilizer may be applied soon after planting. Shoots may be trained in circles on the ground using bent wire to hold down the stems, or grown on supports, such as tripods, which for vigorous cultivars must be very strong. Where only a few large fruits are needed, remove all but two or three of the other fruits while still young.

Hand-pollinate as for marrows (see p.526), if necessary. Pumpkins are deep-rooting so watering should only be needed in very dry weather.

Pests and diseases
The most serious pests and diseases are slugs (p.644) in the early stages and cucumber mosaic virus (see "Viruses", p.649).

Harvesting and storing
Cut away any foliage shading the fruits to encourage them to ripen. Harvest pumpkins 12–20 weeks after planting. Leave fruits for storing on the plant to mature as long as possible: the stem starts to crack and the skin hardens when the fruit is ripe. Pick before the first frosts, cutting each fruit with a long stalk.

After harvesting, most storage types must be exposed to the sun for ten days to "cure" or further harden the skin so that it forms a barrier, slowing the rate of water loss. Cover the fruits at night if frost threatens, or cure indoors at 27–32°C (81–90°F) for four days. 'Acorn' may be stored without curing. Store pumpkins in a well-ventilated place at about 10°C (50°F) with a humidity of 95 per cent. They may be kept from four to six months, and, in some cases, even longer, depending on the conditions and the cultivar grown.

CURING PUMPKINS

When it is ripe, cut the pumpkin off the plant with as long a stalk as possible. Leave the pumpkins in the sun for about 10 days so that the skin hardens.

Marrows and courgettes (*Cucurbita pepo*)

Also known as vegetable marrows or summer squashes, marrows are annuals that trail for several metres or form compact plants of 90cm (3ft) spread. They commonly have cylindrical fruits about 30cm (12in) long and 13cm (5in) in diameter. Courgettes are marrows harvested young; only tender-skinned cultivars are suitable. Marrows are usually trailing, while courgettes are bushy. The skin of marrows may be green, yellow, white, or striped. Custard marrows have flattish, fluted-edged fruits; crookneck squashes have swollen fruits with a bent neck. There are also round-fruited cultivars. Spaghetti marrows are marrow-like in shape, but with hard skins; their flesh resembles spaghetti when cooked. All the fruits are generally cooked. Young leaves and shoot tips may also be cooked, and flowers eaten raw or cooked.

Marrows and courgettes are warm-season crops, needing temperatures of 18–27°C (64–81°F). Frost tolerance, soil, and soil preparation are as for cucumbers (see p.524). They need low nitrogen levels (see p.504).

Sowing and planting
Sow as for cucumbers (see p.524) when the soil temperature is at least

BUSH MARROW

Hand-pollinating

Marrows and courgettes are generally insect-pollinated but in cold seasons, if fruits are not setting, it may be necessary to hand-pollinate. The female flower has a tiny bump (the embryonic fruit) behind the petals which the male flower lacks (see below); this makes it easy to distinguish between them.

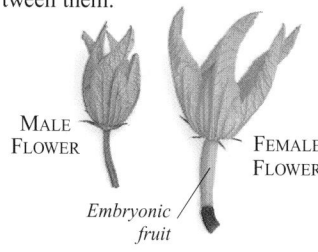

MALE FLOWER   FEMALE FLOWER

Embryonic fruit

To hand-pollinate, take a male flower, remove all the petals and press it against the female flower. Alternatively, use a fine paint-brush to transfer the pollen from the stamens of the male flower to the stigma of the female.

15°C (59°F). Place each seed about 2.5cm (1in) deep or a little deeper in light soils. Sow seed *in situ* after all risk of frost has passed, or germinate in pots indoors. Space bush types 90cm (3ft) apart, and trailing types 1.2–2m (4–6ft) apart. In cool areas, protect young plants with cloches or floating mulches. In hot areas, floating mulches will protect young plants against insects. Mulch after planting.

Routine cultivation
Trailing types may be grown up strong supports. The shoots may also be trained in circles, using bent wire to peg down the stems. Towards the end of the season, nip off the ends of the shoots. Feed and water as for cucumbers (see pp.524–525).

Pests and diseases
Slugs (p.644) may attack in the early stages of growth; cucumber mosaic virus (see "Viruses", p.649) may also be a problem.

Growing under cover
This is only appropriate in cool climates when a very early crop is required. Use bush cultivars.

Harvesting and storing
Harvest marrows seven to eight weeks after planting. Some types may be stored for a few weeks if they are kept well ventilated at about 10°C (50°F) with a humidity of 95 per cent. Spaghetti marrows may be stored for several months. Pick courgettes when they are about 10cm (4in) long, preferably with the flower attached as this indicates freshness. Harvest shoots from the top 15cm (6in) of stem; new growth is soon made. If harvesting flowers, pick male ones after the females have set.

HARVESTING COURGETTES

Cut courgettes when they are 10cm (4in) long, with a short stalk. Handle the fruits carefully to avoid bruising them. Regular harvesting will encourage more fruits.

RECOMMENDED MARROWS AND COURGETTES

Marrows
'Badger Cross' F1
'Clarita' F1
'Custard White'
'Emerald Cross'

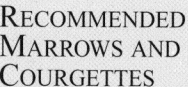

'Long Green Trailing'
'Minipak'
'Patty Pan'
'Sunburst'

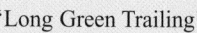

'Tender and True'
'Tiger Cross' F1

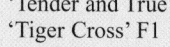

Spaghetti marrows
'Tivoli'
'Vegetable Spaghetti'

Courgettes
'Ambassador' F1
'Bambino' F1
'Defender' F1
'Early Gem' F1
'Elite' F1
'Rondo di Nice'

Globe artichokes (*Cynara scolymus*)

These perennial plants have blue-grey leaves and thistle-like flowers. Globe artichokes may grow up to 1.2–1.5m (4–5ft) tall with a 90cm (3ft) spread. They are grown for the green and purple flower buds, which have edible, fleshy pads (the "hearts") at the base of the outer

scales and the top of the flower stem; the hearts are cooked or pickled. A reliable cultivar is 'Vert de Laon'.

Globe artichokes grow best in cool climates at 13–18°C (55–64°F) and tolerate light to medium frosts. They need an open but not exposed site, with fertile, well-drained soil into

which plenty of compost or well-rotted manure has been dug, and low levels of nitrogen (see p.504).

Sowing and planting
Globe artichokes are normally increased by division. Using a sharp knife, two hand forks, or a spade,

divide healthy, established plants in the spring; each division should have at least two shoots with a tuft of leaves and a good root system. Plant these divisions 60–75cm (24–30in) apart and trim the tips of the leaves to 13cm (5in). Globe artichokes may be raised from seed either indoors or

DIVIDING GLOBE ARTICHOKES

In spring, lift an established plant and divide it using two hand forks, a spade, or a knife. Each division should have at least two shoots, and strong roots.

outdoors in spring, but the results are variable; thin or plant out seedlings at the correct spacing. In future years, divide the most productive plants to build up a good stock. Named cultivars can only be raised from divided offsets. Plants should be replaced every three years to maintain vigour and cropping levels.

Routine cultivation

Keep the planting area free of weeds and well mulched to conserve soil moisture. Do not allow the roots of globe artichokes to dry out in summer or become waterlogged in winter. If heavy frosts are expected, earth up the base of each plant, covering with a thick layer of straw; remove the covering in spring.

Pests and diseases

Root aphids (see "Aphids", p.646) may cause problems.

Harvesting and storing

In favourable conditions, some heads may be cut in the late summer of the first season. More flowering stems will be produced in the second season. Pick before the scales open, when the buds feel plump. Remove the hairy choke and stalk before freezing; the hearts may be pickled.

GLOBE ARTICHOKE

Tomatoes *(Lycopersicon esculentum)*

These are annual plants in temperate areas and short-lived perennials in the tropics. The main trailing stem of the indeterminate (mid-size, non-bushy) types grows to over 2.5m (8ft) long in warm climates, with vigorous sideshoots. The shorter (semi-determinate) types and the bush (determinate) types stop growing earlier than the indeterminates, with the stems ending in a fruit truss. Compact dwarf types may grow up to 23cm (9in) across and as tall.

Ripe tomato fruits are red, yellow, orange, pink, or white, and round, flat, plum- or pear-shaped. The tiny currant tomatoes (*Lycopersicon pimpinellifolium*) are 1cm (½in) in diameter, cherry types 2.5cm (1in), the ribbed Marmande and giant beefsteak types up to 10cm (4in). All are eaten raw or cooked.

Tomatoes grow best at 21–24°C (70–75°F), but do not grow well below 16°C (61°F) or above 27°C (81°F) and do not tolerate frost. They need high light intensity. In cool climates, grow them in a sheltered site outdoors or under cover; they are often grown in containers. Tomatoes tolerate a wide range of fertile and well-drained soils, with a pH of 5.5–7; lime very acid soils (see "Liming", p.625). Crops need to be rotated (see p.498).

Prepare the ground by working in plenty of well-rotted manure or compost at least 30cm (12in) deep, since tomatoes are deep-rooted and gross feeders. Apply a basic fertilizer before planting: tomatoes need high levels of phosphorus (see "Soil nutrients", p.503) but low levels of nitrogen (see p.504).

Sowing and planting

In warm climates, sow seed *in situ* in spring and thin seedlings to the correct spacing. In cool climates, six to

BUSH TOMATOES

eight weeks before the last frost, sow seed 2cm (¾in) deep, at about 15°C (59°F), in seed trays or modules. Transplant into 5–6cm (2–3in) pots at the two- or three-leaf stage; give the seedlings ample ventilation, space, and light. They can stand short periods of low temperatures if day temperatures rise to compensate. Harden off before planting out when night temperatures are over 7°C (45°F) or soil temperatures at least 10°C (50°F) and the risk of frost is over. Plant when the flowers on the lower truss are visible.

Cordons Train indeterminate and semi-determinate types as cordons with 38–45cm (15–18in) between plants in single rows 45cm (18in) apart, or in double rows with 90cm (3ft) between the pairs of rows.

Bush and dwarf types Bush types sprawl on the ground; space them 30–90cm (12–36in) apart, depending on the cultivar. Dwarf types may be more closely spaced than this. Cover with cloches or floating mulches in the early stages. Bush types grow well when mulched with plastic film (see "Mulching", p.502).

Routine cultivation

All types of tomato should be watered and mulched heavily once the soil is warm. In dry conditions, water tomatoes weekly at a rate of 11 litres (2 gallons) per plant. Plants in containers need more frequent watering and supplementary feeding with a tomato fertilizer. Take care not to overwater or overfeed as this may reduce flavour.

Cordons Tie in cordons to the support canes or wires as they grow, and remove all sideshoots when they are about 2.5cm (1in) long. In late summer, remove the terminal shoot two leaves above a truss to allow the remaining fruits to develop and ripen before the first frost. In cool climates, remove supports at the end of the season, bend over the plants *in situ* on straw, and cover with cloches to encourage ripening (see p.528).

TRAINING CORDON TOMATOES

1 *On cordon tomatoes, regularly pinch out sideshoots as they develop to concentrate the plant's energies into swelling the fruits.*

2 *When the cordon has reached the required height in late summer, nip out the tip of the main shoot 2 leaves above the top flower truss.*

RECOMMENDED TOMATOES

Cordon
'Dombito' F1 (beefsteak)
'Gardener's Delight' (cherry)
'Golden Sunrise' (yellow)
'Mirabelle'

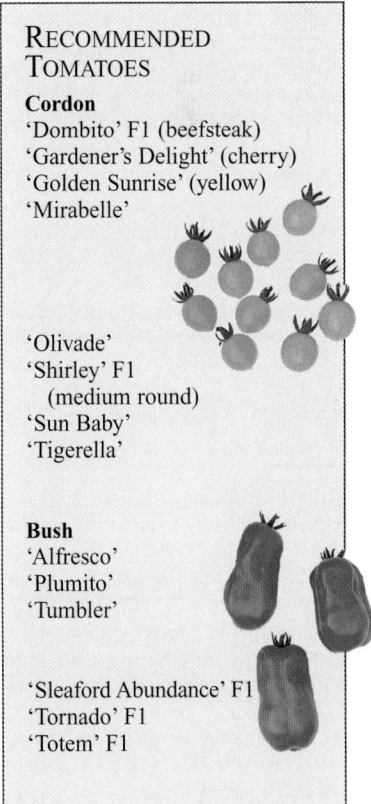

'Olivade'
'Shirley' F1
    (medium round)
'Sun Baby'
'Tigerella'

Bush
'Alfresco'
'Plumito'
'Tumbler'

'Sleaford Abundance' F1
'Tornado' F1
'Totem' F1

TOMATOES RIPENING UNDER A CLOCHE

In cool climates, tomatoes will continue to ripen at the end of the season if they are cut down from their supports, leaned over horizontally on a bed of clean, dry straw, and covered with cloches. The roots stay in the ground.

Pests and diseases

Outdoor tomato plants are affected by damping off in seedlings (p.660), leafhoppers (p.647), potato cyst eelworms (p.666), and tomato blight (p.658). Tomatoes under cover are affected by whiteflies (p.646), potato mosaic virus (see "Viruses", p.649), tomato leaf mould (p.648), grey mould (*Botrytis*) (p.658), magnesium deficiency (p.651), boron deficiency (p.654), seedling blight (p.654), foot and root rots (p.661), and blossom end rot (see "Calcium deficiency", p.658). Use disease-resistant cultivars where possible. Interplanting with French marigolds may deter whiteflies.

Growing under cover

In cool climates, tomatoes may be grown in greenhouses or poly-tunnels. Polytunnels, which can be moved to a fresh site, are better than greenhouses, where soil-borne diseases may develop unless the soil is replaced every three years. Alternatively crops may be grown in containers or by ring culture (plants are grown in "rings" or bottomless pots filled with compost, resting on shingle or gravel). Cultivars may also be grafted onto disease-resistant rootstocks. After the first truss has set feed weekly with a high-potash fertilizer or an organic liquid feed.

Harvesting and storing

Pick fruits as they ripen. Harvest the earliest bush types seven to eight weeks after planting; before the first frosts, these may be pulled up by the roots and hung upside-down indoors to ripen. Harvest cordon types after 10–12 weeks. Tomatoes freeze well.

GROWING BAGS

Tomatoes may be planted in growing bags outdoors or in greenhouses. Growing in bags prevents the plants from being infected by soil-borne diseases.

Wonderberries *(Solanum x burbankii)*

These annual plants grow to about 75cm–1m (30in–3ft) tall with a spread of 60cm (24in). Several cultivated forms of the wonderberry, or sunberry, are grown; all have oval, light green leaves as well as round, purple berries up to 1cm (½in) in diameter. The leaves and young shoots are used like spinach. The unripe fruits contain a poisonous alkaloid, so pick only ripe berries and cook them thoroughly.

Wonderberries are tropical and subtropical plants requiring temperatures of 18–25°C (64–77°F) with a humidity of at least 70 per cent. They may be grown in the open in sunny, sheltered sites, but in temperate areas, greenhouse cultivation is recommended. A fertile, well-drained soil with a pH of 5.5–7 is preferable; medium nitrogen levels are required (see p.504).

Sowing and planting

Sow seed in spring in trays in the greenhouse. Prick out the seedlings when they are large enough to handle, into 6–9cm (3–3½in) pots. When they are 8–10cm (3–4in) tall, harden them off and transplant them; space plants 40–50cm (16–20in) apart, with about 60cm (24in) between rows.

Routine cultivation

Wonderberries need high levels of soil moisture; mulch well and water regularly. Apply a general-purpose fertilizer or an organic liquid feed every 10–14 days during the growing period. Pinch out the growing point when plants are 30cm (12in) tall to encourage lateral branching, and stake plants that grow higher than 60cm (24in). Keep the ground around plants free from weeds.

Pests and diseases

Aphids (p.646) are the major pest. Under cover, glasshouse red spider mite (p.646) and thrips (p.647) may also attack plants.

Growing under cover

When seedlings are about 10–15cm (4–6in) tall, transplant into 21cm (8in) pots or growing bags, leaving at least 50cm (20in) between plants, or transplant into well-prepared greenhouse beds, spacing plants 50–60cm (20–24in) apart each way. Reduce the level of humidity during flowering to promote pollination.

Harvesting and storing

Harvest shoots 9–11 weeks after transplanting; continue removing shoots 10–15cm (4–6in) long to encourage lateral growths. To produce berries, do not remove shoots

WONDERBERRIES

but allow the plants to become bushy and to flower. Harvest the fruit about 14–17 weeks after sowing, removing bunches with a sharp knife. Ripe berries may be stored for 10–14 days at 10–15°C (50–59°F).

Aubergines *(Solanum melongena)*

Short-lived perennials normally cultivated as annuals, aubergines form small bushes about 60–70cm (24–28in) tall with a spread of about 60cm (24in). Also known as eggplants or garden eggs, cultivars differ mainly in the shape, size, and colour of the fruits, which may be oval, pear-shaped, or round, dark purple, yellowish-green, or white, and weigh 200–500g (7–18oz). The fruits are generally sliced and cooked.

Aubergines are tropical and subtropical plants requiring temperatures of 25–30°C (77–86°F), with a minimum humidity of 75 per cent. Below 20°C (68°F) growth may be checked, although many cultivars may be grown in temperate areas in greenhouses or outdoors in a sunny, sheltered site, with protection.

Aubergines require a deep, fertile, well-drained soil and medium nitrogen levels (see p.504).

Sowing and planting

In spring, sow seed under cover in trays using a light, slightly acid (pH 6–6.5) compost: soak the seed in warm water for 24 hours first to aid germination. Prick out into 6–9cm (3–3½in) pots. In warm climates, plant out the seedlings into well-prepared beds when they are 8–10cm (3–4in) tall, spacing them about 60–75cm (24–30in) apart each way. Pinch out their terminal growing

points to promote a bushy habit. In temperate climates, pot up singly into 15cm (6in) pots; plant out after risk of frost has passed. Protect from heavy rain, wind, and low temperatures.

Routine cultivation

Stake cultivars over 60cm (24in) tall. Keep plants well watered, otherwise leaves and buds are liable to drop, and mulch to preserve moisture. Apply a balanced fertilizer or liquid feed every two weeks during the growing season. Prune back mature plants to stimulate growth. To produce large fruits, restrict the number per plant to five or six.

Pests and diseases

Aubergines may be attacked by aphids (p.646). Under cover, red spider mite (p.646), mealybugs (p.646),

caterpillars (p.645), thrips (p.647), and powdery and downy mildew (p.646) may be troublesome.

Growing under cover

Sow seed in early spring at 20–30°C (68–86°F). When the seedlings are 8–10cm (3–4in) tall, transfer them to 20cm (8in) pots or growing bags, and pinch out the tips. Maintain the temperature above the minimum required during the growing period. Damp down greenhouses to help discourage red spider mite.

Harvesting and storing

Harvest 16–24 weeks after sowing, when fruits reach full colour and are unwrinkled. Cut the fruit stalks close to the stem. Aubergines may be stored for up to two weeks in humid conditions at 12–15°C (54–59°F).

AUBERGINES

HARVESTING AUBERGINES

Cut aubergines while their skin is still purple and shiny; once it loses its shine, the flesh will taste bitter. Cut the stalk at least 2.5cm (1in) from the fruit.

Sweet corn (*Zea mays*)

Sweet corn is an annual that grows to at least 75cm–1.7m (2½–5½ft) and has an average spread of 45cm (18in). Male tassels and female ears (cobs) are borne on the same plant. The cobs are golden, white, or bicoloured white and yellow, and cooked or eaten raw when young. New, "supersweet" (sugar-enhanced) cultivars are available.

Sweet corn needs a long growing season of 70–110 frost-free days after planting. It requires temperatures of 16–35°C (61–95°F), but pollination is poor in hot, dry conditions; in warm climates, grow in an open site. In cool climates, grow early-maturing cultivars in a frost-free, sheltered site. Sweet corn is shallow-rooting and grows on a wide range of fertile, well-drained soils with medium nitrogen (see p.504).

Sowing and planting

Seed does not germinate at soil temperatures below 10°C (50°F). In warm climates, sow seed in spring *in situ*, 2.5cm (1in) deep and 7cm (3in) apart, thinning to the correct spacing after germination. Seed may be sown through plastic mulches. In cool climates, sow indoors in modules and plant out seedlings when the soil temperature reaches 13°C (55°F), or sow *in situ* after all risk of frost has passed. In wet soils, use treated seed that will not rot.

To ensure good pollination and full cobs, plant corn in blocks of at least four plants each way. The average spacing is 30cm (12in) apart; short cultivars may be closer, tall ones further apart. In cool climates, cover with floating mulches or

SWEET CORN PLANTED IN A BLOCK

Male and female flowers are carried on the same plant. The male flowers (inset, top), which release pollen, are produced in tassels up to 40cm (16in) in length at the tip of the plant. The female flowers (inset, bottom) are silky strands under which each cob forms. The strands are sticky to collect pollen. The female flowers are wind-pollinated so plant in a block rather than a row to ensure good pollination.

cloches after sowing or planting, removing them at the five-leaf stage. Fine-net floating mulches will protect the plants against frit flies. Supersweet types need higher temperatures to germinate and grow and should not be planted with other types as the sweetness will be lost if they are cross-pollinated. Mini-corn is obtained by planting early cultivars about 15cm (6in) apart and harvesting them when the cobs are about 7cm (3in) long.

Routine cultivation

Hoe shallowly when weeding to avoid damaging the roots. In exposed areas, earth up the stems to 13cm (5in) to increase stability. Watering is not necessary, except

in very dry conditions, until flowering starts and again later when the grains are swelling. Water at a rate of 22 litres/sq m (5 gallons/sq yd).

Pests and diseases

Mice (p.662), slugs (p.644), and birds are the most serious pests. The maggots of frit flies may attack the bases of seedlings, causing the growing points to wilt and die. Raise seedlings in pots, or under fine nets, until past the five- or six-leaf stage.

Harvesting and storing

Plants normally produce one or two cobs. Pick just before required, as the sweetness soon deteriorates; supersweet types retain their flavour for about a week. Sweet corn freezes well.

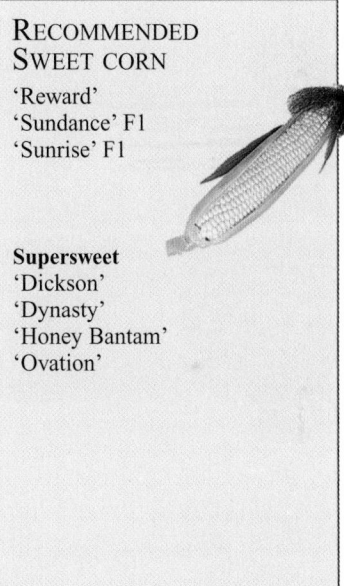

TESTING SWEET CORN FOR RIPENESS

Once the silks have turned brown, peel back the sheath and press into a kernel with a fingernail. If the liquid that appears is milky, the cob is ripe; if watery, it is underripe, and if doughy, overripe.

Podded vegetables

French beans

Scarlet runner beans

Dried French beans

Peas

Mangetout peas

Haricots

Broad beans

French beans

Sugar peas

Peanuts

Shelled peanuts

VEGETABLES in this group all produce seed pods. Some are grown for these pods, which may be cooked and eaten whole, while others are grown for the seeds, which are extracted and cooked or eaten raw. The seeds of some may be dried; most may be frozen. Several of the plants are decorative as well as functional and may be used for screening, or trained over arches. Podded vegetables often need sheltered conditions at specific temperatures for pollination; they generally require a rich soil to which organic matter has been added before planting.

Okra (*Abelmoschus esculentus*)

OKRA

These tender, annual plants are also known as ladies' fingers. The fast-maturing cultivars may grow to 1m (3ft) with a spread of 30–40cm (12–16in); the slow-maturing ones (mainly grown in tropical areas) are up to 2m (6ft) tall. The pods are 10–25cm (4–10in) long and white, green, or red. Recommended cultivars include 'Clemson Spineless', 'Pure Luck', and 'Penta Green'. Immature pods are eaten as a cooked vegetable; mature pods may also be dried and powdered for use as a flavouring.

In warm-temperate and subtropical areas, plants may be grown in the open only in very favourable, sunny conditions. Seeds germinate only at soil temperatures of at least 16°C (61°F); after germination a stable temperature in the range 20–30°C (68–86°F) is needed for optimum growth. Most modern cultivars are daylength-neutral (see "Daylength", p.495). Plant in well-drained soil, adding plenty of organic material. Okra plants need low to medium nitrogen levels (see p.504).

Sowing and planting
Soak seed for 24 hours before sowing to aid germination. When soil temperatures reach 16–18°C (61–64°F), sow seed *in situ* in rows 60–70cm (24–28in) apart, leaving 20–30cm (8–12in) between plants. In warm-temperate areas, sow in spring under cover at 20°C (68°F) or above, in trays or 6–9cm (3–3½in) pots. When seedlings are 10–15cm (4–6in) tall, harden off and transplant to well-prepared beds, spacing as above.

Routine cultivation
Stake tall plants and protect from strong winds with plastic covers or screens, if necessary. Remove all weeds, water regularly, and apply an organic mulch to retain soil moisture. Pinch out the growing points when seedlings are about 60cm (24in) tall to promote branching. Apply a general-purpose fertilizer or liquid feed at two-week intervals to encourage rapid growth. Do not overfeed with nitrogen since this delays flowering.

Pests and diseases
Plants are likely to be damaged by aphids (p.646), caterpillars (p.645), and powdery mildew (p.646); white-flies (p.646), glasshouse red spider mite (p.646), thrips (p.647), and fungal leaf spots (p.648) may also be troublesome under cover.

Growing under cover
Seedlings may be transplanted into well-prepared beds in the greenhouse or in growing bags, spacing the young plants at least 40cm (16in) apart. Maintain a temperature above 20°C (68°F) and a humidity of over 70 per cent. Spray the plants as necessary to control pests and diseases, and apply an organic liquid feed or a general-purpose fertilizer.

Harvesting and storing
Four to six pods per plant are produced. They may be harvested approximately 8–11 weeks after sowing, depending on the cultivar. Sever the pods from the plant with a sharp knife when they are bright green; overmature pods may become fibrous. Pods may be stored in perforated bags at 7–10°C (45–50°F) for up to ten days.

Peanuts (*Arachis hypogaea*)

These tender, annual plants, also known as groundnuts and monkeynuts, originate from South America. Plants grow to a height of 60cm (24in) with a spread of 30cm (12in) for the more upright Spanish-Valencia types, or up to 1m (3ft) for the less common, prostrate, Virginia types. The Spanish-Valencia types are often divided into Spanish, with two seeds per pod and light brown seed coats, and Valencia, with up to four seeds per pod and dark red seed coats. The stems of the Valencia types are usually thicker than those of the Spanish. The Virginia forms have two seeds per pod, with dark brown seed coats.

The fertilized flowers produce shoot-like structures that penetrate the soil where the immature fruits develop into peanuts. Removed from their pods, the nuts are eaten fresh or roasted, or used in cooking.

Peanuts are tropical plants that need average temperatures of about 20–30°C (68–86°F) and a relative humidity of 80 per cent, although some forms grow well in the warmer subtropics. A frost-free site is essential. Rainfall at flowering time may adversely affect pollination.

Peanut cultivars are generally daylength-neutral (see "Daylength", p.495). Sandy, well-drained loams with a pH of 5.5–6.5 containing calcium, potassium, and phosphorus are preferable. The plants also need low nitrogen levels (see p.504).

Sowing and planting
Sow seeds *in situ*, removed from their shells, in spring or when soil temperatures exceed 16°C (61°F). In temperate climates, sow under cover in trays or 9cm (3½in) pots, keeping temperatures over 20°C (68°F).

When the seedlings are 10–15cm (4–6in) tall, harden them off and transplant them to well-prepared beds. Whether directly sown or transplanted, the plants should be spaced 15–30cm (6–12in) apart with about 60–70cm (24–28in) between the rows. Protect them with cloches or polytunnels where necessary.

Routine cultivation
Earth up around the roots when the plants are 15cm (6in) tall, and hoe regularly to encourage the fertilized flowers to penetrate the soil. Remove all weeds, and water well in dry periods. Do not water plants during the flowering period, however, as this may lead to poor pollination.

SPANISH-VALENCIA PEANUT PLANT

Pests and diseases
Plants may be affected by aphids (p.646), thrips (p.647), and caterpillars (p.645); under cover, glasshouse red spider mite (p.646) and whiteflies (p.646) may be a problem. Fungal leaf

spots (p.648), root and stem rots (see "Seedling blight", p.654), and rosette virus (see "Viruses", p.649) may also be troublesome.

Growing under cover
Sow seed as described above. Transplant the seedlings when they are 10–15cm (4–6in) tall into growing bags, or well-prepared greenhouse beds. Maintain a temperature over 20°C (68°F), reducing humidity at flowering time to aid pollination.

Harvesting and storing
Harvest the pods 16–20 weeks after sowing for the upright types, and three to four weeks after this for the prostrate types. Virginia types, which produce two seeds per pod, may require up to 25 weeks from sowing to harvesting. Assess the stage of maturity by uprooting one or two pods; they keep for several months. Dry the pods in the sun, then remove the peanuts for storing in cool, dry conditions.

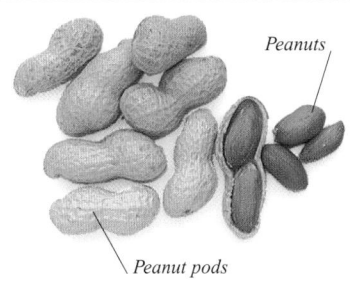

Peanuts

Peanut pods

Dolichos beans (*Lablab purpureus*)

These dwarf or climbing, short-lived, tender perennials are also known as hyacinth beans and lablab beans. Both long- and short-podded cultivars occur. Climbing forms may grow to 4–6m (12–20ft), while dwarf forms reach 1m (3ft) with a spread of about 60cm (2ft). The pods range in colour from green to purple. Young pods and mature seeds are eaten cooked; the latter should be cooked thoroughly. Young seedlings, raised in the dark, may be used as bean sprouts.

Dolichos beans may be grown in subtropical and warm-temperate regions in very favoured, sunny sites with protection. The plants require a temperature of 18–30°C (64–86°F) with a minimum humidity of 70 per cent; cool weather may adversely affect pollination since it discourages pollinating insects. Daylength-neutral cultivars are available (see "Daylength", p.495).

Most soils are suitable for dolichos beans, particularly those containing plenty of organic matter; good drainage is essential. Some cultivars respond well to applications of superphosphate. Dolichos beans need low nitrogen levels (see p.504).

DOLICHOS BEANS

Sowing and planting
Sow *in situ*, in spring or at other times of the year if temperatures are high enough. In temperate areas, sow seeds under cover, in trays, or in 6–9cm (3–3½in) pots at a depth of 2.5cm (1in). When the seedlings are 10–15cm (4–6in) tall, harden them off and transplant into well-prepared beds. Space climbing cultivars 30–45cm (12–18in) apart, allowing 75–100cm (30–36in) between rows; space dwarf cultivars 30–40cm (12–16in) apart with a distance of 45–60cm (18–24in) between rows.

Routine cultivation
Climbing cultivars should be supported by stakes, at least 2m (6ft) high. Water the plants regularly, and mulch to conserve moisture. Protect as necessary with plastic screens or covers and remove all weeds. Apply a general-purpose fertilizer or liquid feed every 10–14 days until flowering. Pinch out the growing points of dwarf cultivars to encourage them to develop a bushy habit; the shoots of climbing cultivars should be trained or tied in to the stakes.

Pests and diseases
Aphids (p.646), thrips (p.647), caterpillars (p.645), root-knot eelworms (p.660), powdery mildew (p.646), fungal leaf spots (p.648), and some viruses (p.649) may be troublesome; under cover, whiteflies (p.646) and glasshouse red spider mite (p.646) may also affect plants.

Growing under cover
Transplant seedlings to growing bags or well-prepared beds in the greenhouse, spacing the plants at least 50–60cm (20–24in) apart. Alternatively, seedlings may be grown on in 21–25cm (8–10in) pots (two plants may be grown in the larger pots). Maintain a temperature of at least 20°C (68°F) and reduce humidity by providing adequate ventilation at flowering time to improve pollination. Dolichos beans may also be propagated from softwood cuttings (see PRINCIPLES OF PROPAGATION, "Stem cuttings", p.632), taken early in the growing season, which root readily in high humidity.

Harvesting and storing
Harvest the young pods six to nine weeks after sowing, when they are fully grown but before the seeds develop; the mature pods containing seeds may be harvested after 10–14 weeks before they become fibrous. If the plants remain healthy after the first crop, cut back the main stems to about half their length to encourage a second crop. Dolichos beans freeze well.

Scarlet runner beans (*Phaseolus coccineus*)

SCARLET RUNNER BEANS

These perennial climbers are grown as annuals in temperate and cool climates. Plants grow to over 3m (10ft) tall, with a spread of about 30cm (12in); some naturally dwarf cultivars form bushes about 38cm (15in) tall. They have pink, red, white, or bicoloured flowers.

The flat pods, over 25cm (10in) long and up to 2cm (¾in) wide, are eaten cooked; immature seeds and mature, dried seeds may also be cooked. With some cultivars, it may be necessary to remove the "strings" along the pods.

Scarlet runner beans are a temperate or cool-season crop that does not withstand frost. Plants need a growing season of about 100 frost-free days and they grow best at 14–29°C (57–84°F). At higher temperatures, especially if combined with high humidity, the pods may not set unless the plants are in light shade. In cool climates, choose a sheltered situation to encourage pollinating insects. Plants are deep-rooting and need fertile, moisture-retentive soil. Prepare the soil by digging a trench one spade deep and 60cm (24in) wide, working in well-rotted straw or compost. Runner bean crops should be rotated (see p.498), and need low nitrogen levels (see p.504).

Sowing and planting
Before planting climbing types, erect a strong support system of poles or canes over 2.5m (8ft) long, tied to a horizontal pole or to each other to form a "wigwam". Commercial supports or towers are available. Plants

RECOMMENDED SCARLET RUNNER BEANS

Standard
'Enorma'
'Kelvedon Marvel'
'Liberty'
'White Emergo'

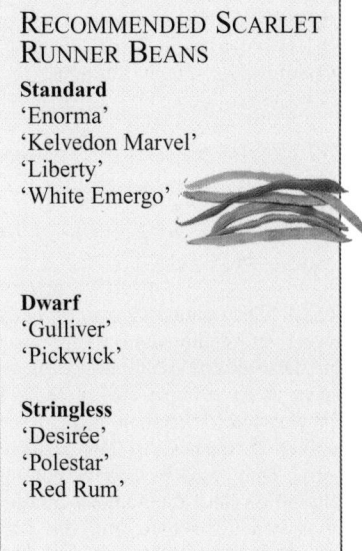

Dwarf
'Gulliver'
'Pickwick'

Stringless
'Desirée'
'Polestar'
'Red Rum'

may also be twisted up nylon netting, strings, or wires pegged to the ground; do not use plastic-coated netting since the plants do not cling onto it. Sow seed *in situ* 5cm (2in) deep, after all risk of frost has passed bearing in mind that a minimum soil temperature of 12°C (54°F) is needed for germination. In cool areas, sow seed indoors in seed trays and harden off seedlings before transplanting outside. Grow climbers in double rows 60cm (2ft) apart or in circular "wigwams", spacing the plants 15cm (6in) apart. Bush forms may be grown in groups at the same spacing. Mulch well to retain moisture after germination or planting out.

BEAN SUPPORTS

There are various ways to support climbing beans, depending on the space available. Mature plants will obscure the support structure beneath.

CROSSED CANE ROW

Two rows of 2.5m (8ft) canes, crossed and secured to a horizontal bar

WIGWAM

2.5m (8ft) canes tied near the top

NETTING SUPPORT

10cm (4in) square nylon net fixed to a pole frame

RUNNER BEANS ON A WIGWAM

Routine cultivation

Protect seedlings with cloches or floating mulches. To convert climbing forms into bushes, nip out the growing shoots when plants are 23cm (9in) high. Such plants crop earlier but have lower yields.

Watering is especially important when the flower buds appear and pods are setting (see "Critical watering periods", p.502). At these times water at a rate of 5–11 litres/sq m (1–2 gallons/sq yd) twice a week.

Pests and diseases

Slugs (p.644) in the early stages, pollen beetles (p.657), bean seed fly (p.666), anthracnose (p.666), foot and root rots (p.654), halo blight (see "Bacterial leaf spots and blotches", p.648), seedling blight (p.654), and viruses (p.649) may be troublesome.

Harvesting and storing

Harvest after 13–17 weeks. Pick pods when they are at least 17cm (7in) long and tender; continue picking at frequent intervals to prolong the cropping period. Runner beans freeze well.

Lima beans (*Phaseolus lunatus*)

DWARF LIMA BEANS

Also known as butter beans, lima beans are tender annuals and short-lived perennials. Some forms of lima bean climb while others are dwarf and branching. Climbing cultivars may grow to a height of 3–4m (9–12ft), dwarf cultivars to 90cm (3ft), spreading to 40–45cm (16–18in). The young pods and mature seeds are eaten cooked; the seeds may also be dried or germinated in the dark for use as bean sprouts.

The lima bean is a tropical plant that requires a minimum temperature of 18°C (64°F) for germination. Temperatures above 30°C (86°F) may adversely affect pollen formation. In subtropical and warm-temperate areas, growing in the open is possible only in full sun, using plastic screens or covers for protection until the plants are fully established.

Small-seeded cultivars flower only in short daylengths of about 12 hours but the large-seeded cultivars are normally daylength-neutral (see "Daylength", p.495). Most cultivars thrive in a wide range of soil types, but a sandy, well-drained loam with a pH of 6–7 is preferable. Lima beans require low to medium nitrogen levels (see p.504). The procedures for sowing, planting, routine cultivation, and growing under cover are as described for dolichos beans (p.531).

Pests and diseases

Aphids (p.646), thrips (p.647), caterpillars (p.645), whiteflies (p.646), and glasshouse red spider mite (p.646) may be troublesome. Diseases include powdery mildew (p.646), fungal leaf spots (p.648), and some viruses (p.649).

RECOMMENDED LIMA BEANS

Climbing
'Challenge'
'Florida Butter'
'Wilber'

Dwarf
'Fordhook 242'
'Henderson'

Harvesting and storing

Harvest whole pods young, mature seeds about 12–16 weeks after sowing. Store both above 4°C (39°F) at 90 per cent humidity for up to two weeks. Lima beans may be frozen.

French beans (*Phaseolus vulgaris*)

These tender annuals have climbing, dwarf, and intermediate forms. They are also known as kidney, snap, or string beans. Height and spread are as for scarlet runner beans (see p.531). The pods are 7–20cm (3–8in) long. They may be round, flat, or curved in shape; diameter ranges from pencil-thickness (for the filet types) to about 2cm (¾in); they may be green, yellow, purple, red, or green flecked with purple. The yellow, waxpod types have a waxy texture and excellent flavour. Types vary in the stringiness of the pods; stringless cultivars are available. Never eat the pods raw as the seeds inside contain toxins that must first be destroyed by cooking. Use the immature pods, the half-ripe, shelled bean seeds (flageolets), or the dried, mature bean seeds (haricots). Special cultivars are grown for drying.

French beans grow in similar conditions to scarlet runner beans (see p.531) but the seeds need a minimum temperature of 12°C (54°F) to germinate. The optimum growing temperature is 16–30°C (61–86°F); seedlings do not tolerate temperatures below 10°C (50°F). The plants are self-pollinated, and grow best in rich, light soil. Good drainage is essential to prevent root rot. Work plenty of well-rotted compost or manure into the soil before planting, and always rotate crops (see p.498). Seed may be dressed with the appropriate rhizome inoculant, or rhizobium granules may be applied to the soil at planting; this treatment increases current and subsequent yields by encouraging the formation of nitrogen-fixing root nodules. French beans usually need low nitrogen levels (see p.504).

PRE-GERMINATING FRENCH BEANS

1 *Spread the beans out on moist tissue paper in a tray without drainage holes. Keep damp, at a minimum of 12°C (54°F).*

2 *When the delicate shoots begin to appear and before they turn green, carefully pot up the beans or sow them directly in their final position outside.*

Sowing and planting
Seed may be pre-germinated before sowing. Sow seed or pre-germinated seeds 4cm (1½in) deep *in situ* or indoors as for scarlet runner beans (see p.531), and make successive sowings throughout the summer. If necessary, warm the soil beforehand with cloches or an inorganic sheet mulch. Space climbing forms as for scarlet runner beans. Dwarf types may be grown at an equidistant spacing of 22cm (9in) in staggered rows for the highest yields. In cold climates, protect after planting with cloches or floating mulches.

Routine cultivation
Support climbing types as for scarlet runner beans; use twigs to support intermediate types. Stems may also be earthed up to keep plants upright. Mulch and do not allow plants to dry out completely; extra watering at a rate of 22 litres/sq m (5 gallons/sq yd) may be necessary in dry conditions at flowering time.

Pests and diseases
Slugs (p.644), bean seed fly (p.666), root aphids and black bean aphid (see "Aphids", p.646), anthracnose (p.666), foot and root rots (p.654), halo blight (see "Bacterial leaf spots and blotches", p.648), and viruses (p.649) may affect French beans.

Growing under cover
In cold climates, dwarf French beans may be grown to maturity in a greenhouse or polytunnel, or under cloches. Space plants as in the open.

EARTHING UP
Plant out the beans 15cm (6in) apart, and once they have formed several pairs of leaves earth them up to support them.

Harvesting and storing
Harvest after 7–13 weeks. Pick young beans regularly to use fresh or freeze. For shelled beans, see below; store in an airtight jar.

DRYING FRENCH BEANS

In damp climates, pull up plants and hang them by the roots in a dry, frost-free place. Once dried, remove the pods and extract the beans.

RECOMMENDED FRENCH BEANS
Dwarf
'Aramis' (filet; anthracnose resistant)
'Chevrier Vert' (for flageolets and drying)
'Cropper Teepee' (green roundpod)
'Delinel' (filet)
'Dutch Brown' (for drying)
'Masai' (stringless)
'The Prince' (green flatpod)
'Purple Queen' (purple podded)
'Purple Teepee' (purple podded)
'Tendergreen' (stringless)
Climbing
'Borlotti'
'Kingston Gold'
'Kwintus'

Peas (*Pisum sativum*)

Peas are annuals that grow from 45cm (18in) to over 2m (6ft) tall, with an average spread of 23cm (9in). Plants cling to supports with tendrils; modern semi-leafless types are almost self-supporting. Peas are grouped according to the time taken to mature. The early groups are shorter and lower yielding than later types. Pods are usually green but there are purple-podded cultivars.

Shelling-pea types are grown for the fresh peas in the pods; some may be dried. Petit pois are small, fine-flavoured peas. Wrinkle-seeded cultivars are usually sweeter but less hardy than the smooth-seeded types. Edible-podded types (mangetout, sugar peas) are eaten before the peas mature. Mangetout types are flat-podded and eaten young; the round-podded sugar types are used when semi-mature. Peas and pods are usually cooked, but may be eaten raw.

SEMI-LEAFLESS PEAS

Peas are a cool-season crop, growing best at 13–18°C (55–64°F). The flowers and pods cannot withstand frost. Grow peas in an open site, in reasonably fertile, moisture-retentive, well-drained soil; they will not tolerate cold, wet soil, or drought. Work

plenty of well-rotted compost or manure into the soil before planting. Peas should be rotated (see p.498). The plants have nitrogen-fixing nodules on their roots, and do not require any extra nitrogen during growth.

Sowing and planting
Make the first outdoor sowings as soon as the soil is about 10°C (50°F). Germination is much slower at lower temperatures. The first sowings may be made under cloches or floating mulches using dwarf cultivars. For successive crops, either sow seeds at 14-day intervals or sow cultivars from different groups at the same time so that they mature in succession. Avoid midsummer sowings in warm areas, as high temperatures also affect germination. If sowing an early type late, allow about ten weeks before frost is expected for the pods to ripen. Where winters are mild, sow

hardy, early-maturing cultivars in late autumn to overwinter. There is a high risk of loss to mice, but surviving plants crop very early.

Sow the seed 3cm (1¼in) deep in patches so that plants can support each other, spacing individual seeds 5–7cm (2–3in) apart. Alternatively, make a flat-bottomed drill up to 23cm (9in) wide, spacing seeds 5cm (2in) apart each way (see "Wide drills", p.500). The drills should be 60–90cm (24–36in) apart, using wider spacing for tall cultivars. Seed may also be sown in double rows 23cm (9in) apart, spacing seeds 1cm (½in) apart.

Routine cultivation
Protect seedlings against birds with horizontal netting as pea guards. Once the tendrils have developed, remove the pea guards and erect supports: use wire netting, pea nets, or brushwood on either side of a drill. Semi-leafless

and dwarf types need less support. When the peas have several leaves, mulch them to keep the roots cool.

Once plants are flowering and forming pods, water every week (unless rainfall is high) at a rate of 22 litres/sq m (5 gallons/sq yd).

Pests and diseases
Jays (p.659), wood pigeon (p.645), pea moth (p.659), and pea thrips (p.659) are the most common pests; mice (p.662) may also be troublesome since they eat seeds. Damping off (p.660), foot and root rots (p.654), seedling blight (p.654), and *Fusarium* wilt (p.654) are occasional problems.

Growing under cover
Early spring and late autumn sowings may be made under cover; grow dwarf peas to maturity under cloches for early or overwintering crops.

Harvesting and storing
Harvest early types 11–12 weeks after sowing, and maincrop peas after 13–14 weeks. Pick edible-podded

SUPPORTING PEAS

When seedlings have developed tendrils, push peasticks into the ground, as upright as possible, all around the outside of the patch (above). As the peas grow, the tendrils wrap around the peasticks and the peas grow up them (right).

types when the immature peas are just forming inside the pods, shelling peas and sugar snap types when the pods have swollen. Edible-podded

types may be left to mature and shelled normally. All may be frozen. For storing pods on plants, see *Drying French Beans*, p.533.

Broad beans (*Vicia faba*)

These annual plants are also known as fava beans. They range in height from 30cm (12in) for dwarf cultivars to about 1.5m (5ft), with an average spread of 45cm (18in). Broad beans are grouped according to the time they take to mature. The broad pods are up to 2.5cm (1in) wide and 7–15cm (3–6in) long, with green, white, or pinkish-red seeds 2–2.5cm (¾–1in) long. The immature bean seeds, as well as the young pods and leafy shoot tips, may be cooked. The shelled beans freeze well.

Broad beans are a cool-season crop, growing satisfactorily only at temperatures below about 15°C (59°F). Some cultivars are very hardy, the immature plants surviving -10°C (14°F) on well-drained soil. Some that are adapted to higher temperatures have recently been bred. Grow spring and early summer sowings in an open site, and autumn sowings for overwintering in a sheltered site, in reasonably fertile, well-manured soil. Rotate broad bean crops (see p.498). The plants need low nitrogen levels (see p.504) because their root nodules fix atmospheric nitrogen.

Sowing and planting
Sow seed *in situ* in spring and early summer as soon as the ground is workable. Seed germinates at fairly low temperatures. For an early crop, sow seed in late autumn to early

DWARF BROAD BEANS

winter of the previous year – the plants need only be 2.5cm (1in) high before winter. In very cold areas seed may be sown indoors in winter and transplanted outside in spring after the risk of frost has passed.

Sow seed about 4cm (1½in) deep, spaced about 23cm (9in) apart each way. Grow either in double rows, with 90cm (3ft) between the pairs of rows, or evenly spaced in blocks across a bed. The taller cultivars may be supported with strands of wire attached to strong canes or poles placed around the rows or blocks of plants. If necessary, dwarf cultivars may be supported with twigs to keep their pods clear of the ground. Overwintering crops and those sown in

early spring may be protected with cloches or floating mulches in the early stages of growth.

Routine cultivation
Do not allow the plants to dry out; water as for French beans (see pp.532–533). Once flowering starts, pinch out the growing tips to encourage pods to form and to combat blackfly. Earth up overwintering plants to protect them.

Pests and diseases
Mice (p.662), jays (p.659), wood pigeon (p.645), tropical root rots

PINCHING OUT

When the beans are in full flower, pinch out the growing tip of each plant. This will remove any blackfly and concentrate the plant's energy into producing beans.

(p.661), blackfly (see "Aphids", p.646), chocolate spot (p.649), and foot and root rots (p.654) may affect broad beans.

Harvesting and storing
Harvest broad beans that were sown in spring after 12–16 weeks, and those sown in autumn after 28–35 weeks. Pick them while the pods are plump with the swelling beans and before they become leathery. The beans may be frozen, or dried at the end of the season for use during the winter months as for French beans (see pp.532–533).

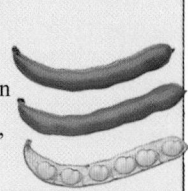

Bulb and stem vegetables

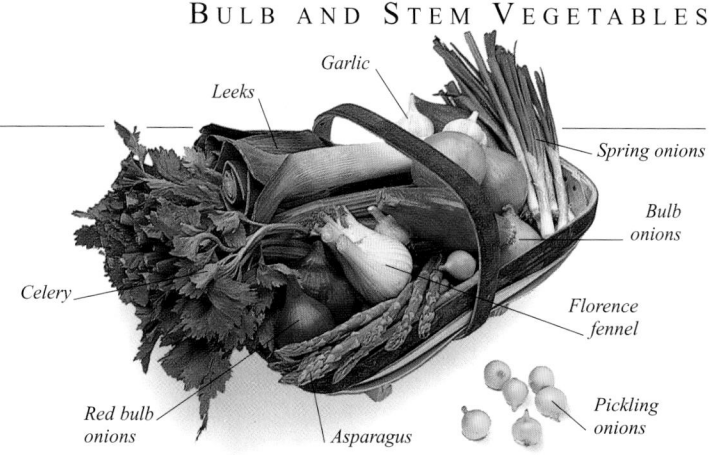

Garlic

Leeks

Spring onions

Bulb onions

Celery

Florence fennel

Red bulb onions

Asparagus

Pickling onions

Vᴇɢᴇᴛᴀʙʟᴇѕ grown for their bulbs or stems include members of the onion family as well as a varied group of other plants that, with the exception of Florence fennel, are mostly hardy and slow-maturing. Celeriac, kohl rabi, and Florence fennel form swollen stems just above ground level, rather than true bulbs. The onion family should be rotated as one group; for rotation groups for the other vegetables, see p.498. Both asparagus and rhubarb are perennial vegetables that should be planted in permanent beds that have been specially prepared for them.

Bulb onions (*Allium cepa*)

These are grown as annuals. The bulbs may be rounded, flattened, or have a long, torpedo shape. They normally have brown or yellow skins with white flesh, although some have red skin and pinkish-white flesh; the leaves grow 15–45cm (6–18in) long. Immature and mature bulbs are eaten either raw or cooked. Some cultivars are suitable for storage. The green-leaved thinnings may be used as spring onions (see p.536).

Bulb onions are a cool-season, frost-tolerant crop, growing best at 13–24°C (55–75°F). Cool temperatures are required in the early stages of growth. Cultivars need different daylengths in order for the bulbs to swell; long-day types should be chosen for northerly latitudes, and short-day types for southerly latitudes (see also "Daylength", p.495).

Grow them in an open site, on fertile, medium to light soil that is well drained. Prepare the soil by digging in a good deal of well-rotted manure, preferably the autumn before planting. Do not plant on newly manured ground. A general feed may be worked into the seedbed before sowing. They have low nitrogen requirements (see p.504).

Sowing and planting

Onions may be raised from seed or sets (small bulbs specially grown and harvested immature the previous year). Seed is cheaper but slower to develop; sets are easier to grow but usually only available for certain cultivars. Bulb onions require a long growing season, particularly if large bulbs are required or if they are to be stored.

Sow in spring when the soil is workable, on a firm seedbed, sowing seed very thinly 1cm (½in) deep, in rows 23–30cm (9–12in) apart. Thin out the seedlings in stages. For the highest yield of medium-sized onions, space 4cm (1½in) apart; for larger onions, thin seedlings to 5–10cm (2–4in) apart.

To extend the growing season in northern latitudes, start under cover in seed trays or modules at temperatures of 10–15°C (50–59°F) from late winter to early spring. Harden off seedlings at the two-leaf stage and plant out at the appropriate spacing. Modules may also be multi-sown with five seeds per section and each section planted out as a unit, with 25cm (10in) between units (see also *Transplanting Leeks*, p.537).

Certain cultivars may be sown in summer or autumn to overwinter for earlier crops the following year. This is inadvisable where winters are very severe or very wet since seeds may rot before germination. Traditional, summer-sown cultivars are reasonably hardy and may be sown *in situ* in late summer, thinning to 2.5cm (1in) apart in autumn and in stages to the final spacing in spring. Japanese overwintering onions are also suitable for sowing at this time; they are hardier than other bulb onions, but are unsuitable for storage. The precise sowing date for these is critical. Sow during the summer at the recommended date for the area, spacing and thinning as above.

Most sets are planted in the early spring. If using heat-treated sets, consult the suppliers for planting times. Plant at the above spacing in shallow furrows so that the tips protrude just above the soil. Recently introduced sets for planting during autumn may be available.

Routine cultivation

Keep the site weed-free, especially when the onions are young and susceptible to competition from weeds. Onions are fairly shallow-rooted and need little water once established, except in very dry conditions. Overwintering onions may be given a nitrogenous fertilizer or organic liquid feed if necessary in spring.

Pests and diseases

Onion fly (p.663), bean seed fly (p.666), onion white rot (p.663), downy mildew (p.646), and, in storage, onion neck rot (p.663) are common problems that affect onions.

Harvesting and storing

Spring-sown bulb onions will take 12–18 weeks to mature; summer-sown onions up to 42 weeks. Pull or lift them as needed to use fresh.

For storage, wait until the leaves have died back naturally (do not bend them over by hand), and then carefully uproot all the onions. In sunny conditions, leave them in the sun to dry for about ten days, either hung in nets or supported off the ground on an upturned seed tray to allow maximum ventilation. In wet conditions, hang them in a greenhouse. The outer skins and leaves must all be thoroughly dry before the bulbs are put into storage.

Handle the bulbs gently since any bruises may encourage storage rots. Do not store onions that are bull-necked; these should always be used first. Store onions either hanging in nets or plaits (see *Storing Strings of Onions*, p.506) or packed carefully in layers in boxes. They must be kept at 0–7°C (32–45°F) and in low humidity (ie below 40 per cent). Average storage life is three to six months, depending on the cultivar.

RECOMMENDED BULB ONIONS

Onions for autumn harvesting
'Buffalo' F1
'Giant Fen Globe'
'Rijnsburger Balstora'
'Rijnsburger Robusta'

Red onions (use fresh or store)
'Long Red Florence'
'Mammoth Red Onion'
'Red Baron'

Traditional and Japanese overwintering onions
'Express Yellow'
'Imai Early Yellow'
'Reliance'
'Senshyu'
'Sonic'
'Southport Red Globe'

Sets for autumn planting
'Centurion' F1
'Sturon'

STORING ONIONS IN A BOX

Prepare onions carefully for storing. Bull-necked onions (those with thick necks above the bulbs, see far right) should be rejected. Be careful not to damage any onions for storing as this encourages rot. Place them in layers in a box and store them in a place that is well ventilated and frost-free.

Spring onions

Traditional European spring onions, or bunching onions, are cultivars of bulb onions suitable for using young when the green leaves are 15cm (6in) tall, with a whitened shank and tiny bulb. A widely grown cultivar is 'White Lisbon'. For climate, soil requirements, and pests and diseases see "Bulb onions", p.535. Lime acid soil (see p.625).

In spring, sow thinly *in situ*, in rows 10cm (4in) apart, or bands 7cm (3in) wide and 15cm (6in) apart. For continuous crops, sow every three weeks in summer. Overwintering cultivars (eg 'White Lisbon Winter Hardy') may be sown in late summer for an early spring crop; protect them in winter with cloches. Water the onions in dry conditions. Spring onions are ready for pulling after two months.

THINNING SPRING ONIONS

If densely sown, harvest seedling spring onions to leave the others spaced 2.5cm (1in) apart. Those remaining will continue to grow and may be harvested when required.

Pickling onions

These bulb onion cultivars produce small, white bulbs (also known as mini-onions) in northerly latitudes, and larger bulbs in southerly latitudes. They may be used when they reach about thumb-nail size, either fresh or for pickling. Cultivars include 'Barletta' and 'Paris Silver Skin'. They prefer fertile soil, but tolerate fairly poor soil. For climate, cultivation, and pests and diseases, see "Bulb onions", p.535.

In spring sow seed *in situ*, either broadcast or in bands about 10cm (4in) wide, spacing seeds 1cm (½in) apart. Thin them only if larger onions are required. Harvest them after about eight weeks when the foliage has died back; use them fresh, or dry and store as for bulb onions (see p.535) until required for pickling.

PICKLING ONIONS

Shallots (*Allium cepa* Aggregatum Group)

These distinctly flavoured, onion-shaped bulbs form clumps of about a dozen bulbs. There are yellow- and red-skinned forms; all may be eaten raw or cooked, and used fresh or after storing. The leaves of young shallots may be used as spring onions. Suitable cultivars are 'Pikant' and 'Atlantic'.

Climate and soil requirements, routine cultivation, and pests and diseases are as for bulb onions (see p.535). Shallots are very hardy. Buy virus-free sets that are ideally about 2cm (¾in) in diameter. Plant in early spring or during winter in mild areas.

Plant as for bulb onion sets (see p.535), spacing the sets about 18cm (7in) apart each way. Each set will develop into a clump, maturing in early summer. For an early crop of green leaves, plant small sets in autumn, spacing them in the ground, or in seed trays under cover about 2.5cm (1in) apart.

Harvest green leaves as needed. For good-sized bulbs, do not pick the leaves; lift the bulbs once the foliage has died down. To store them, dry as for bulb onions (see p.535); good stocks store for up to a year.

PLANTING SHALLOTS

Make a drill 1cm (½in) deep. Push the sets into the drill about 18cm (7in) apart so that the tips show above the soil.

SHALLOTS

European Welsh onions (*Allium fistulosum*)

These onions are very hardy perennials. They have hollow leaves up to 45cm (18in) tall and 1cm (½in) in diameter, growing in clumps of 23cm (9in) diameter on average; the bases of the leaves are thickened at and below ground level. The leaves remain green all year, even at temperatures as low as -10°C (14°F), so they are a useful winter vegetable. The leaves and tiny bulbs may be eaten either raw or cooked.

Climate and soil requirements, cultivation, and pests and diseases are as for bulb onions (see p.535). Sow seed *in situ* in spring or summer in rows about 30cm (12in) apart. Thin the seedlings in stages until they are about 23cm (9in) apart, or propagate by dividing established clumps and carefully replanting the younger, outer sections of the clumps to the above spacing. Leaves may be

WELSH ONIONS

harvested from 24 weeks after sowing; cut individual leaves as required, or pull up part or all of the clump. Established clumps can become very thick and should be divided every two or three years. Welsh onions do not store well.

Oriental bunching onions

These have been developed from European Welsh onions. They are perennials usually grown as annuals or biennials for harvesting at any stage from seedlings to large plants. Mature plants have thickened, white shafts 2.5cm (1in) in diameter and 15cm (6in) high. All parts are edible. There are cultivars for planting and harvesting year-round, and for a wide range of climatic conditions.

For soil requirements, see "Bulb onions" (p.535). Sow seed *in situ* in spring and summer, in rows 30cm (12in) apart. Thin out in stages up to 15cm (6in) apart, depending on the size required. Seed may also be sown in trays and planted out. Sow the hardiest cultivars, such as 'White

Evergreen' or 'Ishikura', in autumn and overwinter to use in early spring. Some cultivars, such as 'Ishikura', may be earthed up several times during growth to obtain long, white shafts. Young leaves may be picked four weeks after sowing.

ORIENTAL BUNCHING ONIONS

Leeks (*Allium porrum*)

These are biennials grown as annuals, reaching 45cm (18in) tall and 15cm (6in) across. The edible part is the sweetly flavoured, thick, white shank that forms below long, blue-green leaves. This may be blanched by earthing it up or by deep planting. Leeks with short, thick shanks are called pot leeks. All types are used cooked, as a vegetable or in soups.

Leeks are a cool-season crop, and grow best below 24°C (75°F), but will tolerate higher temperatures if kept moist. Cultivars range from early and moderately hardy to late and very hardy. Grow in open sites on fertile, moisture-retentive soil, working in plenty of manure or compost and a nitrogenous fertilizer if the soil is low in nitrogen (high levels are needed; see p.504). Do not plant on compacted soils. Leeks must be rotated (see p.498).

Sowing and planting

Leeks need a long growing season; start them as early in the year as possible, sowing in succession. Sow 1cm (½in) deep in an outdoor seedbed for transplanting when 20cm (8in) tall. Alternatively sow *in situ* in rows 30cm (12in) apart. Thin or transplant

LEEK PLANTS

SOWING IN A MODULE

Fill a module with seed compost to within 1cm (½in) of the top. Sow 4 leek seeds in each module on the surface of the compost. Cover with a thin layer of compost, and water.

the seedlings at the three-leaf stage to 15cm (6in) apart. Use closer spacing if smaller leeks are preferred. For well-blanched stems, make holes 15–20cm (6–8in) deep with a dibber and drop a seedling in each, making sure that the roots reach the soil at the base. Water gently, then allow soil to fall in around the plants as they grow. Leeks may also be planted on the flat and blanched by hoeing up soil around the stems, 5cm (2in) at a time, as they grow.

To extend the growing season, sow under cover as for bulb onions (see p.535). Leeks respond well to being multi-sown in modules with up to four seeds per cell. Plant out the groups of seedlings at an even spacing of 23cm (9in).

Routine cultivation

Water thoroughly until the leeks are well established, and thereafter only in exceptionally dry conditions. Keep beds weed-free. Mulch to retain soil moisture if necessary.

Pests and diseases

Stem and bulb eelworms (see "Eelworms", p.652), onion fly (p.663), rusts (p.648), and onion white rot (p.663) may be troublesome.

TRANSPLANTING LEEKS

Each section of a module may be planted out as a whole; plant the clumps 23cm (9in) apart.

SINGLE SEEDLINGS

Leeks sown outdoors may be transplanted to their final position in holes 15–20cm (6–8in) deep and 10–15cm (4–6in) apart.

Harvesting and storing

Leeks may be harvested 16–20 weeks after sowing but can stand for many months. Lift them as required from summer onwards; the hardy cultivars may be lifted throughout

HEELING IN LEEKS

To store outdoors, lift the leeks and lean them against one side of a "V"-shaped trench. Cover the roots and white stems with soil and firm lightly. Lift and use as required.

winter into spring, except in very severe climates. Leeks do not store well out of the ground. If the site they occupy is required, prolong the season by digging them up and heeling them in elsewhere.

RECOMMENDED LEEKS

'Autumn Mammoth – Argenta' l
'Autumn Mammoth – Goliath' e, m, l
'Cortina' m
'Jolant' e
'Kayak' l
'King Richard' e
'Longbow' m, l
'Mammoth Blanch' e, m
'Swiss Giant – Pancho' e
'Toledo' m
'Upton' F1 m
'Wintra' l

KEY
e *early*
m *mid-season*
l *late*

Garlic (*Allium sativum*)

Biennials grown as annuals, garlic plants grow up to 60cm (2ft) tall with a spread of about 15cm (6in). Each produces an underground bulb up to 5cm (2in) in diameter. There are pink- and white-skinned forms and many selections are available that are adapted to different climatic zones. Suitable garlic cultivars include 'Germidour', 'Novatop', 'Sultop', and 'White Pearl'. The strongly flavoured cloves, used for seasoning, may be eaten both cooked and raw, and are either used fresh or may be stored for a year-round supply.

Garlic tolerates a wide range of climates, but needs a period of one to two months at about 0–10°C (32–50°F) in winter. Some variants are extremely hardy; use those recommended for your area. Garlic grows best in an open, sunny position on light soil that does not have to be very fertile, so do not grow it on freshly manured ground. Good drainage is vital. Garlic needs very low levels of nitrogen (see p.504).

Sowing and planting

For planting, split off individual cloves at least 1cm (½in) in diameter from a mature bulb. Always use healthy, virus-free stock. To produce large bulbs, garlic needs a long growing season, so wherever possible plant cloves in the autumn. In very cold areas and on heavy soils, delay planting until the early spring, or plant the cloves in modules in winter, one per section. Then place the modules in a sheltered position outdoors to provide them with the necessary cold period. Plant them out in the ground after they have started to sprout in spring.

Plant the cloves upright with the flat base-plates downwards, at about twice their own depth. Space them

PLANTING GARLIC CLOVES IN MODULES

Plant one clove 2.5cm (1in) deep in each section of a module. Cover the cloves with more compost.

about 18cm (7in) apart each way or 10cm (4in) apart in rows 30cm (12in) apart. The bulbs tend to push themselves upwards as they grow.

Routine cultivation

Little attention is required during growth other than keeping the beds free of weeds. For pests and diseases that may affect garlic, see "Bulb onions", p.535.

Harvesting and storing

Garlic takes between 16 and 36 weeks to mature, depending on the variant and when it has been planted.

Uproot the plants as soon as the leaves have started to fade so that the bulbs do not resprout; if they are allowed to resprout they are much more likely to rot when stored.

Dry them thoroughly after lifting as for bulb onions (see p.535). Handle the bulbs very carefully when preparing them for storage to avoid bruising. Store the bulbs hanging in bunches or plaits made with the dried leaves or place them loose on trays kept in dry conditions at 5–10°C (41–50°F). Garlic may be stored for up to ten months, depending on the variant and storage conditions.

STORING GARLIC

After harvesting the garlic, tie the leaves loosely together with raffia or plait them. Then hang each bunch in a cool, dry place.

Celery (*Apium graveolens*)

A biennial plant, celery grows to 30–60cm (12–24in) tall, with a spread of 30cm (12in). Traditional trench celery has large, white, pink, or red stems that are blanched before use. Self-blanching types have creamy-yellow stems that may be partially blanched. There are green-stemmed types, and intermediates are also available. Celery stalks are eaten raw or cooked and the leaves used as a seasoning or garnish.

As a temperate-climate crop, celery grows best at 15–21°C (59–70°F). Depending on the cultivar and conditions, it tolerates light or moderate frost; trench cultivars with red stems are hardiest. Some have improved resistance to bolting. Grow celery in an open site in fertile, moisture-retentive, but well-drained soil; lime acid soil (see p.625). Rotate celery (see p.498), but do not plant it near parsnips since both are susceptible to celery fly. Dig plenty of well-rotted organic matter into the soil before planting. For trench celery,

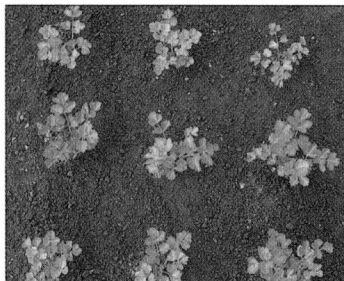

CELERY SEEDLINGS IN A BLOCK

prepare a trench 38cm (15in) wide and 30cm (12in) deep in autumn before planting; work in manure or compost, and replace the soil to ground level. Celery needs high nitrogen levels (see p.504).

Sowing and planting

Sow in spring *in situ* after all risk of frost is past, or indoors in seed trays or modules at 15°C (59°F) no more than ten weeks before the last expected frost. Use seed treated with a

fungicide to avoid celery leaf spot. Sprinkle it onto the compost or cover it shallowly as light is needed for germination. Do not sow too early; plants may bolt if the temperature falls below 10°C (50°F).

Thin out seedlings with four to six true leaves; plant out indoor-sown seedlings after all risk of frost is past. Reject any with blistered leaves. Plant self-blanching types 23cm (9in) apart in blocks to increase natural blanching. Young plants may be covered with cloches or floating films which should be removed after a month. Plant trench celery seedlings 38cm (15in) apart in single rows. They may be planted in trenches, or on the flat.

Routine cultivation

Celery requires steady growth, with no checks from water shortage or sudden drops in temperature. Apply a nitrogenous fertilizer or organic liquid feed about a month after planting. Once the plants are established, water them weekly at a rate of 22 litres/sq m (5 gallons/sq yd).

To sweeten self-blanching types, tuck a thick layer of loose straw around the plants when they are 20cm (8in) tall. To blanch celery in a trench, tie the stems loosely together with soft string and fill in the trench gradually, earthing up the stems as they grow. If planted on the flat, wrap purpose-made collars or 23cm (9in) strips of heavy, light-proof paper around the stems when the plants are 30cm (12in) tall. To extend the blanched area, add a second collar three weeks later. In winter, cover trench celery with straw or bracken to protect against frost.

Pests and diseases

Slugs (p.644), celery fly (see "Leaf miners", p.647), carrot fly (p.660), boron deficiency (p.654), fungal leaf

RECOMMENDED CELERY

Self-blanching
'Celebrity'
'Lathom Self Blanching'
'Victoria' F1

Trench
'Giant Pink'
'Giant White'
'Ideal'

Green
'Hopkins Fenlander'
'Tango'

LIFTING CELERY

Lift self-blanching celery plants before the first frosts. Clear the straw from around the stem and use a fork to uproot the whole plant.

spots (p.648), and violet root rot (p.661) are the most common pests and diseases.

Harvesting and storing

Harvest self-blanching and green celery 11–16 weeks after planting and trench celery in late autumn. Cut the stalks before they become pithy. Before frost threatens, lift and store the remaining plants in high humidity in a cool, frost-free place. They will keep for several weeks.

BLANCHING CELERY

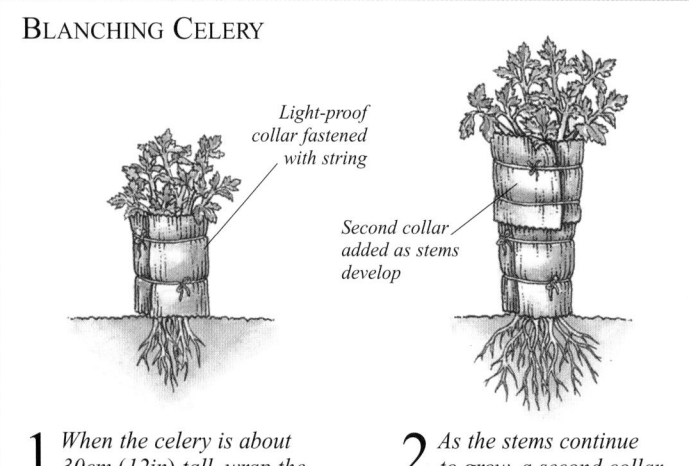

Light-proof collar fastened with string

Second collar added as stems develop

1 *When the celery is about 30cm (12in) tall, wrap the stems loosely with light-proof paper so that the leaves are still exposed to the light.*

2 *As the stems continue to grow, a second collar may be added to blanch the new growth.*

Celeriac (*Apium graveolens* var. *rapaceum*)

This is a biennial plant that grows about 30cm (12in) high with a spread of 38cm (15in). The swollen "bulb" at the stem base is cooked and also grated raw in salads. The leaves are used for seasoning and garnishing.

Celeriac is a cool-temperate crop, withstanding temperatures of -10°C (14°F) if the crowns are protected with straw. Plants tolerate light shade.

PLANTING OUT CELERIAC FROM A MODULE

Plant out celeriac from a module when it is 8–10cm (3–4in) high with 6 or 7 leaves. Space the young plants 30–38cm (12–15in) apart; take care not to bury the crowns.

if the soil is moist. For soil requirements, see "Celery", p.538; celeriac needs low nitrogen levels (see p.504).

Sowing and planting

Celeriac needs a six-month growing season for the bulb to develop. Germination may be erratic. Sow seed indoors in early spring, preferably in modules. If using trays, prick out the seedlings to 5–7cm (2–3in) apart or pot them singly into small pots or modules. Harden off the young plants before planting out when they are about 7cm (3in) tall. Space them 30–38cm (12–15in) apart with their crowns at soil level, not buried.

Routine cultivation

Mulch after planting, and water well, especially in dry conditions. Plants may be fed during the growing season (see "Celery", p.538). Towards the end of the summer, remove some of the coarse, outer leaves to expose the crowns; this encourages the bulbs to develop. To protect from frost, tuck a loose layer of straw 10–15cm (4–6in) thick around the crowns.

Pests and diseases

Celeriac may be affected by the same pests and diseases as celery (see p.538), but is normally healthy.

Harvesting and storing

Celeriac may be harvested from late summer until the following spring. The bulbs are ready for use when they are 7–13cm (3–5in) in diameter.

The flavour is best and the bulbs will keep longer if the roots are left in the ground over winter. Where winters are very severe, dig up the plants in early winter without damaging the bulbs; trim off the outer leaves, leaving a central tuft, and store the plants in boxes of damp soil in a cool, frost-free place.

RECOMMENDED CELERIAC

'Alabaster'
'Balder'
'Ibis'
'Monarch'
'Prinz'
'Snow White'

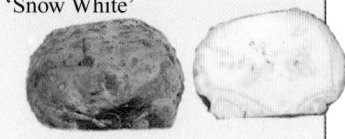

Asparagus (*Asparagus officinalis*)

Asparagus is perennial and may be productive for up to 20 years. Its light, fern-like foliage grows over 90cm (3ft) tall, with a spread of about 45cm (18in). It is cultivated for the delicious young shoots or spears that push through the ground in spring. Male and female plants are available; the females produce berries. Male plants are higher yielding; very productive, all-male, F1

PLANTING ASPARAGUS CROWNS

Dig a trench about 30cm (12in) wide and 20cm (8in) deep with a central, mounded ridge that is 10cm (4in) high. Place the asparagus crowns on the ridge about 38cm (15in) apart. Spread the roots out evenly and cover them with about 5cm (2in) of soil to the level of the crowns.

hybrid cultivars are now also readily available. Asparagus is normally eaten cooked.

Asparagus is a cool-season crop, growing best at 16–24°C (61–75°F) in regions with cool winters that provide the necessary dormant period. Choose an open site, avoiding exposed situations and frost pockets. Asparagus tolerates a very wide range of moderately fertile soils

although acid soils should be limed (see p.625). Good drainage is essential. Do not make a new asparagus bed where asparagus has been grown before, since soil-borne diseases may persist. Remove all perennial weeds from the site and prepare the ground by digging it over and working in manure or compost. Asparagus may also be grown in raised beds to improve drainage. It has low nitrogen requirements (see p.504).

Sowing and planting

Asparagus is traditionally grown by planting one-year-old purchased plants or "crowns" in spring. The crowns are fleshy and must never be allowed to dry out before planting.

Grow them about 38cm (15in) apart, either in single or double rows, with the rows spaced 30cm (12in) apart. Plant the crowns about 10cm (4in) deep by first making a small trench with a central, mounded ridge along the flat base. Spread out the roots evenly over the ridge and cover them with soil to the level of the crowns. Fill in the rest of the trench

RECOMMENDED ASPARAGUS

Traditional
'Connover's Colossal'
'Giant Mammoth'
'Martha Washington'

All-male cultivars
'Backlim'
'Cito'
'Franklin'
'Gijnlim'
'Grolim'
'Lucullus'

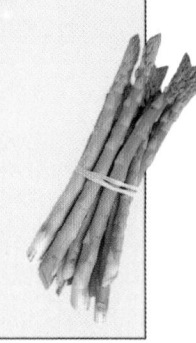

with soil gradually as the stems grow, always leaving 8–10cm (3–4in) of the stems exposed.

Raising asparagus from seed is cheaper, but the results are more variable. Sow seed 2.5cm (1in) deep *in situ* in spring, and thin out to about 7cm (3in) apart. Plant out the

CUTTING BACK ASPARAGUS STEMS

Using secateurs, cut back the stems in autumn to within about 2.5cm (1in) of ground level.

largest the following spring. Alternatively, sow seed indoors in modules in early spring at 13–16°C (55–61°F). The seedlings grow rapidly, and may be planted out in permanent positions in early summer.

Routine cultivation

Asparagus requires little attention other than keeping the beds weed-free. Hoe shallowly to avoid damaging the roots. When the foliage turns yellow in autumn, cut the stems back to about 2.5cm (1in) above the soil.

Pests and diseases

Slugs (p.644) at an early stage and asparagus beetle (p.644) on more mature plants are the most serious

pests. The soil-borne fungal disease violet root rot (p.661) may destroy plants in long-established beds.

Harvesting and storing

Asparagus must be allowed to build into a strong plant before it is harvested in mid-spring. Good, modern cultivars may be cut lightly in the second season. The following year, limit cutting to a six-week period; subsequently, cutting may continue over eight weeks if the plants are growing well. Harvest the spears when they are about 15cm (6in) high and fairly thick. Cut at an angle, taking care not to damage other nearby spears. Remaining spears will continue to grow. Asparagus freezes well.

HARVESTING ASPARAGUS

When the spears are 12–15cm (5–6in) high, cut each stalk 2.5–5cm (1–2in) below soil level.

Kohl rabi (*Brassica oleracea* Gongylodes Group)

These annual plants from the brassica family are grown for the white-fleshed, turnip-like, swollen stem or "bulb" that forms just above the ground. Kohl rabi reaches 30cm (12in) high and has an average spread of 30cm (12in). The outer skin is green (sometimes described as "white") or purple. The bulbs are nutritious, well flavoured, and used cooked or raw.

Kohl rabi is a cool-season crop, growing best at 18–25°C (64–77°F). Young plants tend to bolt prematurely in temperatures below about 10°C (50°F). For soil requirements, see "Siting Western brassicas", p.507. Kohl rabi grows well in light soils and withstands drought better than most brassicas. It has low nitrogen requirements (see p.504).

Sowing and planting

In mild climates, sow seed outdoors in succession from spring through to late summer, using the hardier purple

forms for late sowings. In hot climates, sow in spring and autumn. Sow *in situ* either in rows about 30cm (12in) apart, thinning seedlings to about 18cm (7in) apart, or space the seeds about 25cm (10in)

GREEN KOHL RABI

apart in each direction. Under cover, sow earlier in gentle heat in trays or modules. Plant out seedlings when they are no more than 5cm (2in) high. Protect early outdoor crops with cloches or floating mulches.

Routine cultivation

Kohl rabi is fast-maturing; little attention is required during growth other than keeping beds weed-free.

Pests and diseases

Flea beetles (p.644), cabbage root fly (p.660), and clubroot (p.660) may affect kohl rabi. See also "Cultivating Western brassicas", p.507.

Harvesting and storing

Depending on the cultivar and season, kohl rabi may be ready for cutting between five and nine weeks after sowing. Traditional cultivars should be eaten when they are no larger than tennis balls or they will

RECOMMENDED KOHL RABI

'Adriana'
'Green Vienna'
'Kongo' F1

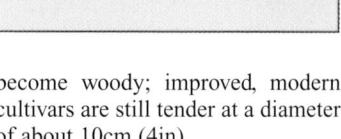

'Purple Danube'
'Quickstar' F1

become woody; improved, modern cultivars are still tender at a diameter of about 10cm (4in).

Leave later crops in the earth until heavy frost threatens, since the flavour deteriorates once lifted. In cold areas, lift in autumn. Leave a central tuft of leaves on each bulb to help keep them fresh; store them for up to two months in boxes of moist sand.

Florence fennel (*Foeniculum vulgare* var. *dulce*)

Grown as an annual, Florence, or sweet, fennel is distinct from the perennial herb fennel. The plants grow up to about 60cm (2ft) high and have a spread of about 45cm (18in). The anise-flavoured, flattened "bulb" of overlapping scales that develops at the base of the leaf stalks is eaten cooked or raw. The highly decorative fern-like foliage may be used as a flavouring or garnish.

Florence fennel tolerates a wide range of climates, from temperate to subtropical. It thrives at a warm, even temperature, but mature plants can withstand a light frost. Grow it in an open situation, in very fertile,

moisture-retentive, but well-drained soil into which plenty of humus has been worked. Florence fennel grows well in light soils but must not be allowed to dry out. It has low nitrogen requirements (see p.504).

Sowing and planting

In cool, northern latitudes, sow seed from early to midsummer; traditional cultivars are likely to bolt if sown in spring, so use modern, bolt-resistant cultivars for earlier sowings. In warmer climates, sow in spring for a summer crop and again in late summer for an autumn crop. Florence fennel does not transplant

well and may bolt prematurely if checked, so either sow seed *in situ* or in modules for transplanting when the seedlings have no more than four leaves. Space the young seedlings about 30cm (12in) apart each way. Early and late crops may be protected from the frost by covering with cloches or floating mulches.

Routine cultivation

Little attention is required; keep beds weed-free. Florence fennel needs to be kept moist, so water thoroughly and mulch. When bulbs start to swell, earth them up to half their height to make them whiter and sweeter.

FLORENCE FENNEL

HARVESTING FLORENCE FENNEL

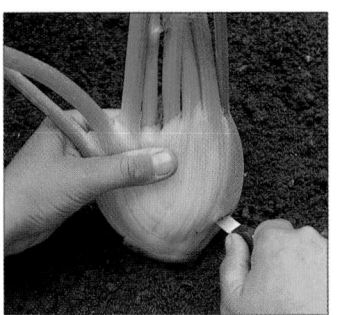

1 *Cut the fennel bulb about 2.5cm (1in) above soil level. Leave the base in position.*

2 *Feathery leaves will usually sprout from the base of the stem within a few weeks.*

Pests and diseases

Florence fennel rarely suffers from any pests or diseases. Most problems stem from lack of water, fluctuating temperatures, or from transplanting, all of which may cause bolting.

Harvesting and storing

Harvest the bulbs when they are well rounded, about 15 weeks after sowing or two to three weeks after earthing up. Pull them up whole, or cut across the bulbs about 2.5cm (1in) above ground level. The stump will normally resprout to produce small sprigs of ferny foliage that may be used for flavouring or as a garnish. Florence fennel does not store well; eat it as fresh as possible.

RECOMMENDED FLORENCE FENNEL

'Cantino' **Br**
'Carmo' F1
'Perfection'
'Romanesco' **Br**
'Rudy'
'Selma'
'Zefa Fino' **Br**

KEY
Br *Bolt-resistant*

Rhubarb (*Rheum* x *cultorum*)

This perennial lasts over 20 years in good conditions. Rhubarb grows about 60cm (24in) or more high and up to 2m (6ft) across. The leaves may be 45cm (18in) wide. The pale-green or pinkish-red leaf stalks, which may be 60cm (2ft) long, are harvested young and used cooked.

Rhubarb is a temperate-climate crop and does not thrive at high temperatures; the roots survive at least -15°C (5°F). Recommended cultivars include 'Champagne', 'Timperley Early', and 'Victoria'. It grows on a wide range of soils, as long as they are rich and well drained. Before planting, dig in plenty of manure or compost. Rhubarb needs medium nitrogen levels when young and very high nitrogen once it is mature (see p.504).

Sowing and planting

Rhubarb is normally propagated by planting "sets", each consisting of a fleshy rootstock with at least one bud. Sets are about 10cm (4in) in diameter. Plant them in the dormant season from autumn to spring, preferably autumn. Either buy virus-free sets, or separate a set from a healthy, two- or three-year-old plant, once its leaves have died back, by lifting the plant and slicing through the crown; replant the parent. On light soils, plant the set so that 2.5cm (1in) of soil covers the buds; on heavy or wet soils, plant with the buds just above ground level. Space the plants 90cm (3ft) apart.

Rhubarb may also be raised from seed, although the results are variable. Sow seed in spring, 2.5cm (1in) deep in rows 30cm (12in) apart, in a seedbed outdoors. Thin the seedlings to 15cm (6in) apart, and plant out the strongest-looking ones in their permanent positions in autumn, or in spring the following year.

Routine cultivation

Mulch the plants heavily, and water them in dry weather. Apply a heavy dressing of manure or compost every

DIVIDING RHUBARB

1 *Lift or expose the crown. Cut through it carefully using a spade, ensuring there is at least 1 main bud on each section. Prepare the soil by digging in manure.*

2 *Replant the sections (sets) 75–90cm (2½–3ft) apart. Fill in around each root so that the bud is just above the surface. Firm, and rake around the bud.*

autumn or spring and a nitrogenous dressing or organic liquid feed in spring. Remove any flowering stems.

Rhubarb may be forced in the dark to obtain very tender sticks. Cover the dormant crowns in late winter with a 10cm (4in) layer of straw or leaves, then a forcing pot, or a large bucket, at least 45cm (18in) high; leave this on for about four weeks until stems are large enough.

Pests and diseases

Honey fungus (p.661), crown rot (p.665), and viruses (p.649) may attack established plants.

Harvesting and storing

Harvest in spring and early summer. With set-raised plants, start pulling lightly the first year after planting; with seed-raised plants, wait until the second year. In subsequent years, pull heavily until the quality starts to deteriorate in summer. Forced stems are ready to harvest about three weeks earlier than unforced ones.

HARVESTING RHUBARB

When the rhubarb stems are ready, they may be harvested by gripping each stem at the base and twisting it while pulling it upwards and outwards.

FORCING RHUBARB

For an earlier, tender crop, cover the dormant buds (see upper inset) in winter with straw or leaves inside a forcing pot or any large container that excludes the light. The plant will produce tender, pink stems a few weeks later (see lower inset).

Root and tuberous vegetables

Sweet potato — *Carrots*
Swede — *Sweet potato*
Turnips — *Potatoes*
Jerusalem artichokes — *Parsnips*

Root vegetables are the mainstay of the kitchen garden. As the name suggests, most are grown for their swollen roots or tubers. A few, such as turnips, beetroot, and cocoyams, are also used for their young, leafy growth; some radish cultivars also produce edible seed pods. A variety of root vegetables may be grown and harvested in succession for a steady supply; many store quite easily, sometimes still in the ground, for use throughout the winter. Salsify and scorzonera may both be overwintered for their flowering shoots, produced in the spring.

Beetroot (*Beta vulgaris* subsp. *vulgaris*)

Beetroot is a biennial plant grown as an annual. It grows to about 15cm (6in) tall and about 12cm (5in) across. The swollen root forms at ground level and may be round, flat, or cylindrical. It is on average 5cm (2in) in diameter, and about 10cm (4in) or more deep in the long forms. The flesh is normally red but may be yellow, white, or even have concentric pink and white rings. The skin is similarly red, yellow, or off-white. The sweetly flavoured roots are mainly used cooked, either fresh or stored, but may also be pickled. The fresh, young leaves (tops) may be used as greens.

Beetroot grows best and develops the deepest colours in cool, even temperatures, ideally of 16°C (61°F). Grow it in an open site on rich, light soil with high nitrogen levels (see p.504). Apply half the nitrogen before sowing. Lime very acid soils.

THINNING SEEDLINGS

When the beetroot seedlings have produced 3 or 4 leaves, thin clumps growing close together to the required spacing by nipping off the top green leaves at soil level without disturbing the remaining seedlings.

Sowing and planting

Beetroot "seeds" each contain a cluster of two or three seeds, the seedlings of which must be thinned out early. Some cultivars, such as 'Cheltenham Mono' and 'Monopoly', have been bred to produce single, or monogerm, seed, which needs little or no thinning.

To overcome slow germination, soak seed in warm water for 30 minutes before sowing. Some cultivars may bolt if sown early or in unfavourable conditions so choose bolt-resistant cultivars for early sowings.

In spring, sow seed *in situ* outdoors when the soil is workable and has warmed up to at least 7°C (45°F). Sow seed 1–2cm (½–¾in) deep, with the spacing determined by the type of beetroot and the size required. Grow maincrop beetroot in rows 30cm (12in) apart, thinning to 7–10cm (3–4in) apart. For pickling beetroot about 2.5cm (1in) in diameter, space rows 7cm (3in) apart, thinning seedlings to 6cm (2½in).

For earlier crops, sow in early spring under cloches, in frames, or indoors in seed trays or modules, transplanting outside when the seedlings are 5cm (2in) tall. Sow three monogerm or ordinary seeds per module (see "Modules and small containers", p.501), thinning as necessary. Early beetroot needs plenty of space, so plant indoor-sown seedlings in rows 23cm (9in) apart, then thin them to 9cm (3½in) apart. For continuous supplies of young beetroot, sow seed at intervals of two to three weeks throughout summer. Sow cultivars intended for

HARVESTING BEETROOT

Grip the stems and pull the beetroot from the soil; it should lift easily since it is shallow-rooted. Avoid damaging the roots, which will bleed if they are cut.

storage in late summer, at least ten weeks before the first heavy frost is expected.

Routine cultivation

Water only to prevent the soil from drying out, at a rate of 11 litres/sq m (2 gallons/sq yd) every two weeks. Apply the remaining nitrogenous fertilizer during active growth.

Pests and diseases

Beetroot may be affected by sparrows (see "Birds", p.657), cutworms (p.655), aphids (p.646), damping off (p.660), fungal leaf spots (p.648), and boron deficiency (p.662).

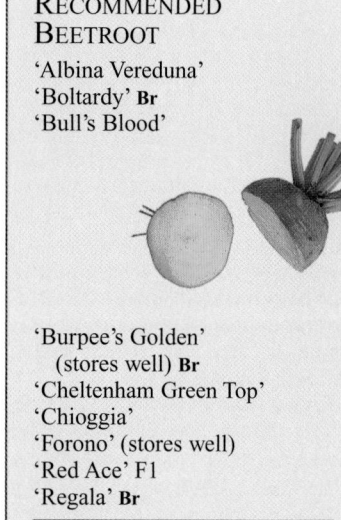

Harvesting and storing

Harvest beetroot at any stage from small, immature roots 2.5cm (1in) in diameter to fully mature roots; this will be from 7 to 13 weeks after sowing, depending on the cultivar, the season, and the size required. In mild areas, beetroot may be left in well-drained soil in winter, protected with a layer of straw up to 15cm (6in) deep, but they eventually become rather woody. Otherwise lift them before severe frost. Twist off the leaves (cutting causes "bleeding") and store the roots in moist sand in a frost-free place. Beetroot normally keeps until mid-spring.

Swedes (*Brassica napus* Napobrassica Group)

Biennials from the brassica family, swedes are grown as annuals and reach a height of 25cm (10in) with a spread of 38cm (15in). The root flesh is usually yellow, but sometimes white, and the skin generally purple, buff, or a combination of both. The large, often irregularly shaped, underground roots, which may be 10cm (4in) in diameter and as long, are sweetly flavoured and used cooked. This hardy, cool-season crop grows best on light, fertile soil with low nitrogen levels (see p.504). For climate and soil requirements, see "Siting Western brassicas", p.507.

Sowing and planting

Swedes need a growing season of up to 26 weeks to mature fully. Sow seed from early to late spring *in situ*, 2cm (¾in) deep in rows 38cm (15in) apart, thinning early and in stages until the seedlings are about 23cm (9in) apart.

Routine cultivation
Keep beds weed-free and if conditions are very dry, water at a rate of 11 litres/sq m (2 gallons/sq yd).

Pests and diseases
Downy mildew (p.646), powdery mildew (p.646), boron deficiency (p.662), and violet root rot (p.661) may affect swedes. Some cultivars are resistant to mildew. For other pests and diseases, see "Cultivating Western brassicas", p.507.

Harvesting and storing
Swedes generally mature in autumn and, being hardy, may be left in the soil until the end of the year, when they should be lifted carefully to prevent them from becoming woody; except in very cold climates, covering with a thick layer of straw provides sufficient protection until the swedes are lifted. Store swedes in clamps outdoors or in wooden boxes under cover (see *Storing Carrots*, p.544) for up to four months.

MAKING A SWEDE CLAMP
Choose a sheltered, well-drained site and stack the roots on a 20cm (8in) layer of straw in a pyramid, with their necks facing outwards. Cover with a layer of longer straw. In very cold climates, protect further with a 10cm (4in) layer of soil.

Turnips (*Brassica rapa* Rapifera Group)

These are biennials from the brassica family grown as annuals. The plants are about 23cm (9in) high with a spread of about 25cm (10in). The underground roots swell to 2.5–7cm (1–3in) in diameter and are round, fairly flat, or long. The flesh may be either white or yellow and the skin white, pink, red, or yellow. The young leaves, known as turnip tops, may be eaten as greens (see "Turnip tops and broccoli raab", p.512). Turnip roots are used either fresh or stored and are normally cooked.

Turnips are a temperate-climate crop, growing best at about 20°C (68°F). They are reasonably hardy, tolerating light frost. For general climate and soil requirements, see "Siting Western brassicas", p.507. Grow turnips in moist soil as they bolt prematurely in dry conditions. Early types, many of which are small and white, are fast-growing and excellent for early spring and summer crops; the hardier types are used fresh during summer and winter and for storage. They require low to medium nitrogen levels (see p.504).

Sowing and planting
Start sowing seed of early turnips in spring as soon as the ground is workable, or sow under cover. Make

HARVESTING TURNIPS

Harvest turnips by pulling them from the soil by their leaves. Do not leave them in the ground too long or they may become woody.

successive sowings at three-week intervals until early summer. Sow maincrop types from mid- to late summer *in situ*, 2cm (¾in) deep. Space early types in rows that are 23cm (9in) apart, thinning seedlings to 10cm (4in); space maincrop types in rows 30cm (12in) apart, thinning to 15cm (6in).

Routine cultivation
Keep beds weed-free. In dry conditions water at a rate of 11 litres/sq m (2 gallons/sq yd).

Pests and diseases
Flea beetles (p.644) may affect seedlings; other problems include violet root rot (p.661) and boron deficiency (p.662). Turnip gall weevil causes hollow swellings on the roots that may be mistaken for clubroot but are rarely serious; discard all affected plants. For other pests and diseases, see "Cultivating Western brassicas", p.507.

Harvesting and storing
Harvest early turnips after about five weeks, maincrop types after six to ten weeks. Pull them before they become woody. Lift turnips for storage before the first frost, then store them for up to three or four months in outdoor clamps covered with straw.

RECOMMENDED TURNIPS
'Golden Ball'
'Green Top Stone'
'Ivory'
'Market Express' F1
'Purple Top Milan'
'Snowball'
'Tokyo Cross' F1

Cocoyams (*Colocasia esculenta*)

These herbaceous, frost-tender perennials grow to about 1m (3ft) tall, with a spread of 60–70cm (24–28in). The plants have large, long-stalked leaves, which may be green or greenish-purple. Cocoyams, sometimes known as taro, are grown for their large, swollen tubers, which are

COCOYAM PLANT

eaten cooked. The young leaves and shoots are also edible, and may be cooked and used as greens.

Cocoyams are tropical and subtropical plants that require temperatures of 21–27°C (70–81°F), with humidity levels over 75 per cent. In temperate areas they need a very sheltered, sunny site, or they may be grown under cover. Cocoyams are adapted to short daylengths of about 12 hours (see "Daylength", p.495); they rarely produce flowers. Some forms are tolerant of light shade. Moisture-retentive soil is essential because many forms of cocoyam are sensitive to dry soil conditions.

Fertile soil that has a high organic content and a slightly acid pH level of 5.5–6.5 is recommended. Cocoyams require medium to high levels of nitrogen (see p.504).

Sowing and planting
Seeds are rarely available, so propagation is usually from existing tubers. Plant mature tubers or portions of tubers with dormant buds *in situ* in well-prepared beds. Space the tubers about 45cm (18in) apart with 90cm (3ft) between rows.

Cocoyams may also be propagated by cuttings. Sever the tops of tubers with a horizontal cut; each cutting should consist of several leaves 10–12cm (4–5in) long, a central growing point, and a small portion of the tuber. Plant the cuttings in their final positions at the above spacing; if the temperature is below the optimum 21°C (70°F), plant them in 21–25cm (8–10in) pots of standard compost to grow on under cover until the temperature is high enough for transplanting outside.

Routine cultivation
Cocoyams need a constant supply of water for the highest yields, so water regularly. Apply an organic mulch to conserve moisture, and feed with a general-purpose fertilizer at two- to three-week intervals. Keep beds free of weeds. The plants should be earthed up around the stems once they are established to encourage the tubers to develop.

Pests and diseases
These are rarely serious for cocoyams that are grown in the open, but aphids (p.646), thrips (p.647), red spider mite (p.646), and fungal leaf spots (p.648) may reduce tuber yields. Under cover, cocoyams are liable to the same pests and diseases as those grown outside; whiteflies (p.646) may also be troublesome.

Growing under cover

Propagate from tubers (see p.543). When these have rooted, transfer them to well-prepared greenhouse beds, 21–30cm (8–12in) pots, or growing bags, ensuring that the roots are disturbed as little as possible.

Water and feed the plants regularly, maintaining a temperature of 21–27°C (70–81°F) and humidity of more than 75 per cent by damping down. Tubers that are cultivated under cover tend to be smaller than those grown outdoors.

Harvesting and storing

Cocoyams are slow to develop and reach maturity. Harvest the tubers 16–24 weeks after planting when the leaves start to turn yellow and plants die down. Lift cocoyams grown in the open carefully using a fork; plants under cover may be lifted gently out of their pots or growing bags. Try not to damage the tubers since this encourages rotting.

Healthy tubers may be stored for about eight to twelve weeks at a temperature of 11–13°C (52–55°F), with humidity of 85–90 per cent.

COCOYAM TUBER

Carrots (*Daucus carota*)

These are biennials grown as annuals. Their swollen, orange tap roots may be up to 5cm (2in) in diameter at the neck and up to about 20cm (8in) in length. The feathery, green foliage grows to about 23cm (9in), with a 15cm (6in) spread. Carrots are normally long and tapered but may be rounded. There are many types: early ones are usually small and slender and used young; maincrop types are larger and used fresh or stored. All are eaten either cooked or raw.

Carrots are a cool-season crop, and tolerate the same temperatures as beetroot (see p.542). Grow in an open site on light, fertile soil. Deep-rooted types require reasonably deep, stone-free soil. Work in plenty of organic matter, preferably in the autumn before sowing. The fertile, loose soil of established raised beds is particularly suitable for growing carrots. Rake the soil into a fine tilth before sowing. Carrots should be rotated (see p.498). They need very low nitrogen levels (see p.504).

Sowing and planting

Sow early types in spring *in situ* as soon as the soil is workable and has warmed up to 7°C (45°F). Earlier sowings may be made under cloches, in frames, or under floating mulches; remove these after a few weeks. Sow maincrop types from late spring until early summer. A second sowing of early types may be made in late summer and protected with cloches.

Sow seed sparingly about 1–2cm (½–¾in) deep, either broadcast or in rows 15cm (6in) apart. Thin early carrots to 7cm (3in) apart; maincrop carrots should be thinned to 4cm (1½in) to obtain medium-sized carrots or farther apart if large carrots are needed. Carrots do not transplant well unless sown in modules: sow seed of deep-rooted cultivars singly, those of round-rooted ones, several together. Round-rooted carrots sown in modules do not need thinning and should be planted out as a group at slightly wider spacing than for maincrop carrots.

Routine cultivation

Remove weeds regularly once the carrots have germinated and until the foliage hinders further weed growth. Water at a rate of 16–22 litres/sq m (3–5 gallons/sq yd) every two or three weeks.

Pests and diseases

Carrot fly (p.660) may be a serious problem; surround with a low barrier where possible. The egg-laying, adult fly is attracted by the smell of carrot foliage; thin in the evening, nipping off the seedlings at ground level and removing the tops from the site. Root and leaf aphids (see "Aphids", p.646), carrot motley dwarf virus (see "Viruses", p.649), violet root rot (p.661), and boron deficiency (p.662) may be troublesome.

Harvesting and storing

Harvest early cultivars about seven to nine weeks after sowing, maincrop cultivars after 10–11 weeks. Pull them by hand or fork them out. On well-drained soils in areas with mild winters, carrots may be left in the soil in winter (see *Protecting Parsnips*, p.546). Otherwise lift them before heavy frost, cut or twist off the foliage, and store healthy roots in boxes in a cool, dry place for up to five months.

PROTECTION AGAINST CARROT FLY

Surround the patch of young carrots with a protective barrier 60–90cm (2–3ft) high. The barrier may be made either of fine mesh netting or stiff, clear plastic, both of which also help to warm the soil inside.

THIN SOWING

Sow carrot seeds about 2.5cm (1in) apart so that the seedlings will need little thinning later. The seed should be 1–2cm (½–¾in) deep.

HARVESTING YOUNG

Early cultivars may be harvested when they are very young. Pull them up in a bunch when they are 8–10cm (3–4in) long.

STORING CARROTS

Twist the foliage off the carrots; place them on a layer of sand in a box. Cover them with more sand and continue in layers.

Jerusalem artichokes (*Helianthus tuberosus*)

These are perennial plants, also known as sunchokes or girasoles. The distinctively flavoured tubers are 5–10cm (2–4in) long, about 4cm (1½in) in diameter and, in most cultivars, very knobbly. 'Fuseau', however, produces smooth tubers. The plants may grow up to 3m (10ft) tall. The tubers are normally cooked but may be eaten raw. Jerusalem artichokes grow best in temperate climates and are very hardy. They tolerate a wide range of soils and require medium nitrogen levels (see p.504). They may be planted as a windbreak screen.

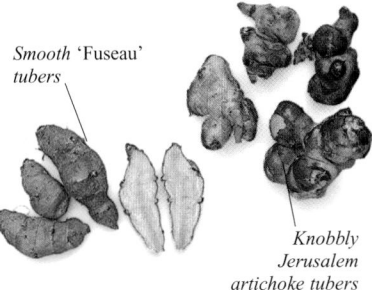

Smooth 'Fuseau' tubers

Knobbly Jerusalem artichoke tubers

Sowing and planting

Plant tubers as soon as the ground is workable in spring. Those the size of a hen's egg may be planted whole; cut large ones into pieces, each with several buds. Make a drill, planting about 12.5cm (5in) deep and 30cm (12in) apart. Cover with soil.

Routine cultivation

When the plants are about 30cm (12in) tall, earth up the stems to half their height for stability. In late summer, cut the stems back to 1.5m (5ft), removing any flowerheads at the same time. In very exposed sites, stake or support the stems. Water in very dry conditions. When the leaves start to yellow, cut the stems back to just above ground level.

PLANTING

Make a drill 10–15cm (4–6in) deep. Place the tubers in the drill 30cm (12in) apart with the main bud facing upwards. Cover carefully so the tubers are not dislodged.

Harvesting and storing

Harvest the tubers 16–20 weeks after planting. Lift them only when required, since they keep best in the ground, and take care not to damage the roots. Save a few tubers to replant or leave some in the soil for the

CUTTING DOWN

Towards the end of the summer, cut down the stems to about 1.5m (5ft), so that the plants will not suffer wind damage. The tubers will continue to develop unchecked.

following year. Otherwise, remove even small tubers since they rapidly become invasive. In severe climates or on heavy ground, lift in early winter and store in a cellar or in clamps outdoors (see *Making a Swede Clamp*, p.543) for up to five months.

Sweet potatoes (*Ipomoea batatas*)

These tender perennials are grown as annuals. They have trailing stems that grow to 3m (10ft) or more if unpruned. Cultivars vary considerably in leaf shape and tuber size, shape, and colour. Tubers are eaten cooked; the leaves may be used in the same way as spinach (see p.519).

Sweet potatoes are tropical and subtropical plants, requiring a temperature of 24–26°C (75–79°F). In warm climates, they need a sunny aspect; in temperate climates, they should be grown under cover, but tuber yields are smaller. Most cultivars are short-day plants (see "Daylength", p.495).

Highly fertile, well-drained, sandy loams with a pH of 5.5–6.5 and medium to high nitrogen levels (see p.504) are required.

Sowing and planting

In the tropics and subtropics, plant sweet potatoes at the start of the rainy season. In warm and temperate climates, plant in spring. Make raised ridges about 75cm (30in) apart, then plant the tubers 5–7cm (2–3in) deep in the ridge, spacing them 25–30cm (10–12in) apart. Alternatively, take 20–25cm (8–10in) long stem cuttings from mature plants and insert them to half their length just below the apex of the ridge.

Cultivars raised from seed will provide reasonable crops. Sow indoors in trays or 21–25cm (8–10in) pots at a temperature of at least 24°C (75°F). When seedlings are 10–15cm (4–6in) high, harden them off and transplant outside.

Routine cultivation

Water and weed regularly, and mulch to conserve moisture. Train shoots to spread around the plant. Apply a general-purpose fertilizer at two- to three-week intervals until the tubers have formed. Protect from winds.

Pests and diseases

Aphids (p.646), caterpillars (p.645), root-knot eelworms (p.660), fungal leaf spots (p.648), *Fusarium* wilt (p.661), seedling blight (p.654), and various viruses (p.649) affect sweet potatoes growing outdoors. Under cover, whiteflies (p.646), thrips (p.647), and glasshouse red spider mite (p.646) may be troublesome.

Growing under cover

Sow seed, as described below left, transplanting seedlings to growing bags or prepared beds. Alternatively, take cuttings and insert three or four into 15cm (6in) pots. Maintain a minimum temperature of 25°C (77°F) and a humidity of over 70 per cent by damping down regularly. When roots develop, transfer plants to greenhouse beds or growing bags. Water regularly and remove the growing points of shoots longer than 60cm (2ft) to encourage lateral shoots. Keep the temperature below 28°C (82°F), and the growing area well ventilated.

Harvesting and storing

Harvest 12–16 weeks after planting, when the stems and leaves turn yellow. Crops from seed are ready three

SWEET POTATO PLANT

or four weeks later. Lift the tubers, using a fork, without damaging them. In order to store sweet potatoes they must first be cured for four to seven days at temperatures of 28–30°C (82–86°F) and humidity of 85–90 per cent (see "Pumpkins and winter squashes", p.525). They may be stored in shallow trays at 10–15°C (50–59°F) for several months.

STEM CUTTINGS FOR GROWING UNDER COVER

1 *Select healthy, vigorous shoots and cut them off the parent plant with secateurs.*

2 *Remove the lower leaves and trim each shoot below a node to 20–25cm (8–10in). Insert in pots and grow on under cover.*

RECOMMENDED SWEET POTATOES

'Centennial' (orange-fleshed)
'Eland' ✱ (orange-fleshed)
'Gem' (white-fleshed)
'Gold-rush' (orange-fleshed)
'Jewel' (white-fleshed)
'Nemagold' ✱
  (orange-fleshed)

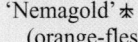

KEY
✱ *Resistant to root-knot eelworms*

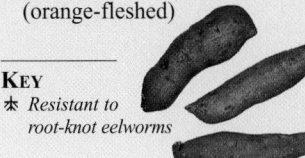

Parsnips (*Pastinaca sativa*)

Parsnips are biennials grown as annuals. The tap root grows to 5cm (2in) across at the neck and about 10cm (4in) long in short forms and up to 23cm (9in) in long types. The leaves are about 38cm (15in) long and 30cm (12in) wide. The roots are eaten cooked.

Parsnips are a hardy, cool-season crop, and prefer light, deeply cultivated, stone-free soils. On shallow soils, grow the shorter forms. Lime very acid soils and rotate crops (see p.498). Parsnips have low nitrogen requirements (see p.504).

RECOMMENDED PARSNIPS

'Avonresister' (short)
'Cobham Improved Marrow' (medium)
'Gladiator' F1 (long)
'Javelin' (long)
'Tender and True' (long)
'White Spear' (long)

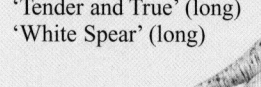

Sowing and planting

Always sow fresh seed. Parsnips need a long growing season and so should be sown as soon as the soil is workable in spring, but not in cold or wet soil. Sow seed *in situ* 2cm (¾in) deep in rows 30cm (12in) apart. Thin the seedlings to 10cm (4in) apart to produce large roots, or 7cm (3in) for smaller roots. A faster-germinating crop such as radishes may be intersown; to allow for this, station sow several parsnip seeds at intervals of 10cm (4in), and thin to one seedling per station. To start parsnips earlier, sow seed in modules with gentle heat under cover and transplant seedlings before the tap roots develop.

Routine cultivation

Always keep beds free of weeds. In very dry conditions water the plants as for carrots (see p.544).

Pests and diseases

Parsnips may be attacked by celery fly (see "Leaf miners", p.647), root aphids (see "Aphids", p.646), and carrot fly (p.660). Use cultivars resistant to parsnip canker (p.661) where possible; of those recommended, all but 'Tender and True' are resistant. Boron deficiency (p.662) and violet root rot (p.661) may occasionally be troublesome.

Harvesting and storing

Parsnips mature in about 16 weeks. Their flavour is improved by frost and, except in very severe climates, they may be left in the soil during winter and lifted as required. The leaves die back in winter, so mark the ends of the rows with canes so that the plants are easily found to harvest. Where winters are very severe, cover the rows with 15cm (6in) of straw to keep the soil from freezing and to make lifting easier. Young parsnips may be lifted and frozen.

INTERSOWING

In a prepared drill, sow 3 parsnip seeds every 10cm (4in) and then sow radish seeds between them, about 2.5cm (1in) apart.

PROTECTING PARSNIPS

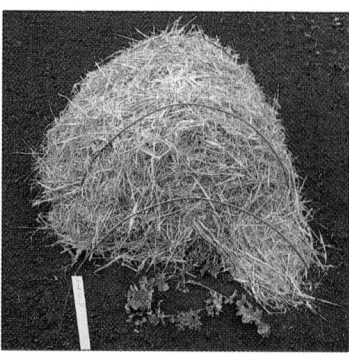

In severe climates, cover the plants with layers of straw or bracken, to a depth of 15cm (6in). Hold in place with wire hoops and mark each row.

Radishes (*Raphanus sativus* and *Raphanus sativus* Longipinnatus Group)

There are several types of radish, some biennial and others annual; all are grown for the swollen roots. Small, round types have roots up to 2.5cm (1in) in diameter; small, long types up to 7cm (3in) long. The leaves of both may grow to about 13cm (5in) high. Large forms include oriental radishes (Longipinnatus Group), known as mooli or daikon, and the large, overwintering, winter radishes. Roots of large, round cultivars may be over 23cm (9in) in diameter, those of large, long cultivars up to 60cm (24in) long, while the plants grow 60cm (24in) tall with a spread of 45cm (18in).

Radish skin colour is red, pink, white, purple, black, yellow, or green; the flesh is normally white. Small roots are used raw when fresh, and large roots are used raw or cooked, fresh or stored. Immature seed pods from cultivars such as 'Münchner Bier' and young seedling leaves from most cultivars are edible raw.

Radishes are mainly a cool-season crop, but there are cultivars suited to a wide range of growing conditions. Some mooli and all overwintering types are frost-tolerant. Grow radishes in an open site, although midsummer crops tolerate light shade.

Radishes prefer light, rich, well-drained soil, preferably manured for the previous crop, and very low nitrogen levels (see p.504). Radishes should be rotated (see p.498).

Sowing and planting

Sow standard, small types outdoors throughout the growing season, starting when the soil is workable. Sow at 15-day intervals for a continuous crop. Very early and late sowings may be made under cover, using small-leaved cultivars bred for growing under cover. Delay sowing most oriental mooli until summer to prevent bolting. Some bolt-resistant cultivars may be sown earlier. Sow overwintering radishes in summer.

Radishes are normally sown *in situ*. Small types grow very fast and may be used for intercropping (see "Parsnips", above). Broadcast seed very thinly, or sow 1cm (½in) deep in drills 15cm (6in) apart. Thin the seedlings to at least 2.5cm (1in) apart, never allowing them to become overcrowded. Alternatively, seeds may be spaced 2.5cm (1in) apart so that no thinning is needed. Sow large types about 2cm (¾in) deep, in rows about 23cm (9in) apart, thinning to 15–23cm (6–9in), depending on the cultivar. Small types may be used for cut-and-come-again seedling radish leaves (see "Successional crops", p.500).

Routine cultivation

Radishes should never be allowed to dry out. In periods of dry weather, water the crop every week at a rate

HARVESTING

Radishes are ready to harvest 3–4 weeks after sowing. If the radishes are being used for intercropping, pull them up carefully without disturbing the roots of the other seedlings in the row.

RECOMMENDED RADISHES

Small
'Cherry Belle'
'Crystal Ball'

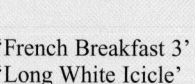

'French Breakfast 3'
'Long White Icicle'
'Pink Beauty'
'Scarlet Globe'
'Sparkler'

For sowing under cover
'Helro'
'Robino'
'Saxa'

Mooli
'April Cross' F1 (slow bolting)
'Minowase Summer Cross' F1

Overwintering
'Black Spanish Round'
'Cherokee' F1

of 11 litres/sq m (2 gallons/sq yd). Overwatering, however, encourages leaf rather than root development.

Pests and diseases
Radishes may be attacked by flea beetles (p.644), cabbage root fly (p.660), and slugs (p.644).

Harvesting and storing
Small radishes mature three to four weeks after sowing, most large types after eight to ten weeks. Pull small types soon after they mature, since most will become woody if they remain in the ground for long. Large types, however, may be left in the ground for several weeks with no risk of deterioration. Overwintering radishes may be left in the soil for lifting when required, except in severe winter weather or if they have been grown in heavy soil. In these cases, lift the roots and store them in boxes of moist sand in a frost-free place, or outside in clamps for three or four months (see *Making a Swede Clamp*, p.543). Where radish seed is required for propagation, leave a few plants to produce seed. Harvest the pods while they are still young and green, then dry them, and collect the seeds.

Scorzonera (*Scorzonera hispanica*)

This hardy perennial is normally grown as an annual. Plants grow to about 90cm (3ft) tall and have yellow flowerheads. The black-skinned, white-fleshed roots are 20cm (8in) or more long, and about 4cm (1½in) across at the neck. They have an unusual flavour and are eaten cooked. The young leaves and shoots (chards) of overwintered plants are edible, and the young flower buds and their flower stalks are also delicious cooked. For soil, climate,

SCORZONERA PLANTS

and manuring requirements, see "Carrots", p.544. A fertile, deep, light soil is essential for good roots to develop. Scorzonera has low nitrogen requirements (see p.504).

Sowing and planting
Sow fresh seed *in situ* in spring about 1cm (½in) deep, in rows about 20cm (8in) apart, thinning out seedlings to 10cm (4in) apart. Water at a rate of 16–22 litres/sq m (3–5 gallons/sq yd) in dry spells. For routine cultivation, see "Carrots", p.544. Pests and diseases rarely affect scorzonera.

Harvesting and storing
The roots need at least four months to develop. They may be left in the soil throughout the winter (see *Protecting Parsnips*, p.546), or lifted and stored in boxes in cool conditions. Start lifting the roots for use in the autumn and continue into spring. If they are only pencil-thin, leave the remaining plant roots to thicken for harvesting the following autumn.

For chards, cover the plants with about 13cm (5in) of straw or leaves in early spring. The young, blanched leaves will push through this layer. Cut them when about 10cm (4in) tall.

For flower buds, leave a few roots in the soil during winter with no covering; these will flower the following spring or early summer. Pick the unopened buds with about 8cm (3in) of stem.

SCORZONERA ROOTS

Salsify (*Tragopogon porrifolius*)

A hardy biennial with purple flowers, salsify is known as vegetable oyster or oyster plant, due to its taste. It is similar to scorzonera in appearance and use, and has the same climate, soil, cultivation, harvesting, and storage requirements. Salsify roots need to be eaten in their first winter.

SALSIFY ROOTS

If the roots are overwintered, the flower buds may be eaten the following spring. Pick the buds with short stalks, preferably in the morning before they open.

Potatoes (*Solanum tuberosum*)

Potatoes are tender perennials that grow to an average height of 60cm (2ft), with a similar spread. There are numerous potato cultivars, displaying enormous variation in their underground tubers.

A typical mature tuber is about 7cm (3in) long and 4cm (1½in) wide with white or pinkish-red skin and white flesh, but there are yellow- and blue-fleshed cultivars, often used in salads. Potatoes are eaten cooked, fresh or after storing.

Potatoes are a cool-season crop, growing best at 16–18°C (61–64°F). Neither plants nor tubers tolerate frost. Depending on the cultivar, they require a growing season of 90–140 frost-free days. They are divided into early, second early, and maincrop groups, depending on the number of

days required to mature. The earlies grow fastest but are generally lower-yielding. Potatoes need at least 500mm (20in) of rainfall or irrigation during the season.

Grow potatoes in an open, frost-free site; they need well-drained, fertile soil at least 60cm (2ft) deep that is rich in organic matter. Although tolerant of a wide range of soils, acid soils (pH5–6) are preferred.

Potatoes are subject to several soil-borne pests and diseases, and so crops must always be rotated (see p.498). Prepare the ground well by digging in plenty of organic matter. A general fertilizer may be worked in just before planting. Early potatoes need medium nitrogen; high nitrogen is required for maincrop potatoes (see p.504).

Planting
Grow cultivars recommended for the area. Plant small tubers (known as "seed potatoes") that have been specially raised and are certified disease-free. In northern latitudes with a short growing season, potatoes (especially the earlies) are sprouted, or chitted, indoors to start them into growth about six weeks before planting. Place the tubers in a shallow tray, with the eyes or buds uppermost, in even light in a cool but frost-free room. Planting is easiest when the sprouts are about 2cm (¾in) long, but they may be planted with sprouts of any length. For large, early potatoes, leave only three sprouts per plant, rubbing off the others. Otherwise, the more sprouts per tuber, the higher the yield.

SPROUTING SEED POTATOES FOR PLANTING

To sprout seed potatoes, place them in a box or tray in a single layer with the end of the potato containing the most "eyes" uppermost. Store in a light, frost-free, but well-ventilated place until the sprouts have grown to about 2cm (¾in) in length.

Plant outside when there is no longer risk of heavy frost and once the soil temperature has reached 7°C (45°F). Make drills 7–15cm (3–6in) deep or make individual holes, and place tubers upright with the eyes or sprouts at the top, covering them with at least a 2.5cm (1in) layer of soil. Plant early potatoes 35cm (14in) apart in rows 43cm (17in) apart, second early and maincrop potatoes 38cm (15in) apart in rows 68cm (27in) and 75cm (30in) apart respectively.

In cool areas, cover early potatoes with cloches, clear plastic sheeting, or floating film mulches (see p.505). When shoots emerge, cut holes in the film and ease the foliage through. Remove floating films about a month later, cutting them down the centre first to acclimatize the potatoes to cooler conditions for a few days.

RECOMMENDED POTATOES

Early
'Accent'
'Arran Pilot'
'Concorde'
'Foremost'
'Maris Bard'
'Pentland Javelin'
'Winston'

Second early
'Estima'
'Charlotte'
'Kondor'
'Picasso'
'Roseval'
'Wilja'

Maincrop
'Cara'
'Desirée'
'Maris Piper'
'Maxine'
'Navan'
'Nicola'
'Pentland Squire'
'Romano'
'Sante'

For salads
'Pink Fir Apple'
'Ratte'

Early potatoes may also be planted under black plastic sheeting, which excludes light and makes earthing up unnecessary; this is not recommended for maincrop potatoes since watering is difficult. Lay the plastic on the ground, anchor the edges in the soil, and plant the potatoes through cross-shaped slits in the plastic. Alternatively, plant the potatoes, cover them with plastic, make slits, and pull the stems through when the plants start to push up the plastic.

Potatoes are sometimes grown from seedlings, plantlets, or eyes. These are planted in seed trays and transferred outside, after hardening off, once all risk of frost has passed.

Routine cultivation
If frost threatens after the leaves have appeared, cover them at night with a light layer of straw or newspaper. Plants normally recover from light frost damage. Unless grown under black plastic, potatoes need to be earthed up to prevent tubers near the surface from becoming green and unpalatable and sometimes toxic. When the plants are about 23cm (9in) tall, hoe up soil around the stems to a depth of about 13cm (5in). This may be done in stages.

In dry conditions, water early potatoes every 12 days at a rate of 16 litres/sq m (3 gallons/sq yd). Delay watering maincrop potatoes until the young potatoes are the size of marbles – check the size of the tubers by scraping back the soil beneath one plant – then give one watering of at least 22 litres/sq m (5 gallons/sq yd). Potatoes may be given an organic liquid feed or a nitrogenous top-dressing during growth.

Pests and diseases
Cutworms (p.660), slugs (p.644), potato cyst eelworms (p.666), millipedes (p.644), blackleg on potatoes (p.664), and violet root rot (p.661) may be troublesome. For full details of potato blight (including resistant cultivars) and other pests and diseases affecting potatoes, see "Potato tuber problems", p.662.

Harvesting and storing
Harvest early potatoes when, or just before, the flowers open. Potatoes under black plastic may be harvested by lifting the sheeting – they should be on the surface. Leave healthy maincrop potatoes in the soil for as long as possible; in autumn, cut the haulm (the stems) of each plant to about 5cm (2in) above ground level, and leave the potatoes for another

two weeks, to harden the skins, before lifting. In areas with warm, wet summers where potato blight is prevalent, cut the haulm in late summer and burn the foliage; lift the potatoes two weeks later.

Lift potatoes for storage on a dry, sunny day and leave them in the sun for two hours, then store them in the dark in paper sacks in a cool, frost-proof place. Give extra protection if frost threatens. Potatoes may also be stored for up to six months outdoors in well-insulated clamps (see p.543) or in a cellar. Young or new potatoes may be frozen. For new potatoes to be eaten during winter, plant a few tubers in the middle of summer and cover with cloches in autumn.

PLANTING POTATOES

1 *Make a drill 7–15cm (3–6in) deep, using a draw hoe. If planting maincrop potatoes, place them in the drill 38cm (15in) apart with the sprouts upwards. Cover carefully once planted.*

2 *Draw up the soil around the stems when the foliage is about 23cm (9in) high. Earthing up prevents tubers that form near the surface from turning green and being unfit to eat.*

ALTERNATIVE METHOD

1 *To plant under black plastic, unroll the plastic and anchor it by burying the edges. Make a cross-shaped cut where each potato is to be planted. Place each potato 10–12cm (4–5in) deep in the soil under each cut.*

2 *Once the haulm has been cut, the plastic can be pulled back and the crop of potatoes will be lying on the soil surface, ready to harvest.*

HARVESTING POTATOES

In autumn, cut the haulm (stems) cleanly with a knife just above ground level. Leave the potatoes in the ground for another 2 weeks before lifting.

Salsify (*Tragopogon porrifolius*), see Scorzonera, p.547

PART TWO

MAINTAINING THE GARDEN

PRACTICAL ADVICE ON TOOLS AND EQUIPMENT, GREENHOUSES, AND BUILDING MATERIALS AND TECHNIQUES; UNDERSTANDING SOIL TYPE AND CLIMATE, HOW PLANTS GROW AND REPRODUCE, AND HOW BEST TO DEAL WITH PROBLEMS

1
TOOLS AND EQUIPMENT

KEEPING A GARDEN looking its best throughout the year involves a certain amount of maintenance, from routine tasks such as mowing the lawn to occasional procedures such as deep-soil cultivation. While it is unnecessary and expensive to invest in an entire catalogue's worth of garden equipment, having the correct tool for the job makes the work easier and produces a more professional result. Besides basic tools that will be in almost constant use, for example a spade, fork, or pair of secateurs, there will be other items that you cannot do without – perhaps a wheelbarrow for moving garden refuse, or a sprinkler system for watering. Assessing the type of work you do in the garden makes it easier to decide which tools you need; choosing them with care ensures that they will be comfortable to use as well as durable and functional.

Buying and using tools

Most modern gardening tools are based on traditional designs, although some may be improvements or variations on old concepts. A few completely new tools, however, have been successfully introduced. For example, until the 1980s, shredders and nylon-line trimmers were hardly known; yet they are now firmly established because they fulfil a demand not met by traditional tools.

Before buying a tool, the most important point to bear in mind is its function – it must perform correctly the task it is meant to do. Consider exactly what you need a particular tool for and how frequently you will use it. A simple, inexpensive pair of secateurs, for example, will be adequate if wanted only for pruning a few rose bushes once a year; if required for intensive use, however, it is much better to invest in a high-quality pair. Before purchasing a tool, wherever possible always try to check that it is:
• the best type of tool for the task;
• the right size and model to suit your needs;
• comfortable to use.
In large gardens, or for laborious or time-consuming tasks, consider using powered tools; however, since they are expensive and require careful handling and safety precautions, be sure that they are really needed.

To ensure that tools perform well and last a long time, it is important that they are properly maintained. Immediately after use, always clean off any soil, grass clippings, or other plant material and wipe metal parts with an oily rag; all pruning and cutting tools will also need regular sharpening. Tools that are not needed over the winter months should be cleaned and well oiled and then stored in a dry place.

In addition, factors such as expense and storage space must be taken into account: if a tool is needed only infrequently, hiring may be a more sensible option, especially for relatively expensive, bulky tools.

Hiring tools

If you decide to hire, book equipment in advance, especially tools likely to be in seasonal demand, such as powered lawn rakes and cultivators, and check whether the hire firm will deliver and collect the tools.

The condition of hired tools varies considerably. Some, especially powered tools, may even be potentially dangerous to operate. For this reason, you should always:
• Check for missing or loose parts. These may not be obvious, but if in doubt do not accept the tool.
• Look for loose bolts and fittings on tools such as powered cultivators that are subject to vibration.
• Ask for powered tools to be started, and check carefully for excessive vibration and noise.
• On electrical tools, check that the voltage is correct or that a suitable transformer is supplied if relevant. Look for frayed, cut, or exposed wires. Do not assume that the wiring is satisfactory just because the tool works adequately.
• On four-stroke engines, check the oil in the engine and transmission.
• Ask for a demonstration or instructions if you have never operated the tool before. This is particularly important with tools such as chainsaws, which can be dangerous to use.
• Buy or hire any recommended protective clothing (for example goggles, gloves, and ear protectors).
• Before signing the delivery note, comment on the contract or delivery note if you have noticed any faults.

Safe use of tools

If you are not sure how to use a tool, ask for advice when buying or hiring, or contact the manufacturer. Correct use gives good results and helps prevent accidents. Make sure that the weight and length of the tool are suitable: a tool that is too heavy will be difficult to handle; one that is too short may cause back strain. Keep all powered tools in good repair and follow any safety recommendations. To minimize risks, make sure that a mains electric tool is fitted with a residual current device – sometimes called an earth leakage circuit breaker – which severs the supply in microseconds if the circuit leaks power (see also "Electrical safety", p.556).

DIGGING CORRECTLY
Keeping your back straight, not curved, when digging, hoeing, or raking helps to prevent backache.

USING POWERED TOOLS
Take particular care when using powered tools, and always wear appropriate protective clothing.

Cultivation tools

The type of cultivation tools required depends on the nature of your garden. If you grow mainly vegetables or are cultivating a new garden, tools for digging will be a priority. If, however, the garden is well established, with lawns and perennial borders, surface cultivation tools such as hoes will be more important.

Spades

A spade is an essential tool, excellent for general cultivation, lifting soil, and digging holes for planting. There are two major types: standard digging spades, and the smaller and lighter border (also called ladies') spades. Some manufacturers also produce an intermediate-sized or medium spade that is suitable for general digging but lighter than a standard spade.

Some spades have a tread, which makes it easier to push the blade into the soil and less likely to damage footwear; these spades are, however, heavier and more expensive. For extensive digging, a larger spade (known as a "heavy"), which has a 30 x 20cm (12 x 8in) blade, may prove quicker to use.

If you find digging difficult or have a large area to dig, it may be worth buying an automatic spade to make the task less of a strain.

Forks

Garden forks are used for general cultivation, lifting rootcrops (which are more likely to be damaged with a spade), and shifting bulky material such as manure and garden compost. They are also ideal for relieving soil compaction, and for lightly forking in top-dressings of organic matter. Two forks back-to-back can be used to divide congested clumps of perennials with little effort.

Most garden forks have four square metal prongs, and are generally available in two sizes: standard and border (or ladies'). Less common are medium, or youth, forks, an intermediate size between standard and border forks. Other variations are also sometimes found. For example, a potato fork has broad, flat prongs and, generally, a larger head than a standard fork; it may be easier to use than a spade when digging heavy ground.

The head and neck of a fork should be forged in a single piece, the shaft fitting into a long socket in the neck.

STANDARD DIGGING SPADE
This is useful for shifting large amounts of soil, but it is heavy and therefore may be unsuitable or uncomfortable for some gardeners. It has a rectangular blade of about 28 x 19cm (11 x 7in).

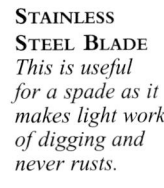
"D"-type moulded hilt gives a good grip

Plastic hilt is comfortable even in cold weather

Tread makes digging easier

Coated blade may be easily cleaned

STAINLESS STEEL BLADE
This is useful for a spade as it makes light work of digging and never rusts.

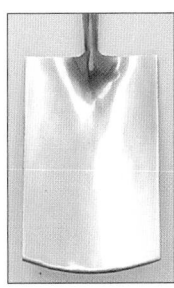

AUTOMATIC SPADE
Operating on a spring-and-lever system, the spade throws the soil forward without the need to bend. It may be worthwhile for the disabled or for those with back trouble or with a large area to dig.

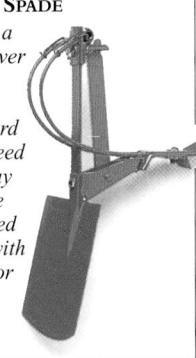

BORDER SPADE
With a blade only 23 x 13cm (9 x 5in), this is designed for digging in confined spaces, for example a planting hole in a border, but it is also good for any general light work.

STANDARD FORK
This fork is useful for cultivating heavy soil, lifting vegetables, and shifting large loads, but some people may find it heavy to manoeuvre. Its head is about 30 x 20cm (12 x 8in).

Wooden shaft fitting into long socket in neck

Neck and head formed from one piece of metal for strength

Head

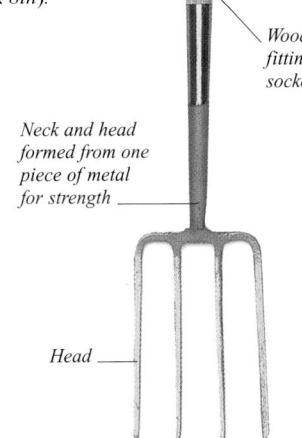

POTATO FORK
Primarily for lifting potatoes, this flat-tined fork may also be used for digging, and moving compost or garden refuse.

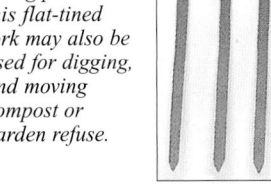

BORDER FORK
This is best for light work in borders and similar restricted areas. The size of the head – 23 x 14cm (9 x 5½in) – makes it suitable for anyone needing a small, lightweight fork.

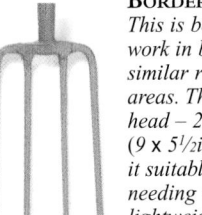

Which metal?

Carbon steel is used for most garden tools. If cleaned and oiled after use, it should not rust, and it can be sharpened. Although stainless steel is more expensive and cannot be sharpened, it does make digging easier since the soil falls away from the blade more readily. Tools that have a "non-stick" coating may make working the soil and cleaning easier but the coating may wear off after long use.

Handles and hilts

A spade or fork shaft should be the correct length for the user's height to minimize back strain. The standard shaft length is 70–73cm (28–29in); a longer shaft, available up to 98cm (39in) long, will almost certainly be more comfortable for people over 1.7m (5ft 6in) tall.

Shafts are made from wood or metal, the latter sometimes covered with plastic or nylon. Both are generally strong, but even metal shafts may break if put under too much stress, and, unlike wooden ones, they cannot be replaced. Metal shafts, even plastic-coated, are colder than wood to hold in winter. Handle the tool, as if using it, to assess which type feels best.

"D"-TYPE HILTS
These are the most common type, but they may be uncomfortable for those with large hands, particularly when wearing gloves.

"Y"-TYPE HILTS
Similar to "D"-type hilts, but they may be weaker as they are formed by splitting the shaft wood.

"T"-TYPE HILTS
These have a cross-piece joined to the shaft end. Some gardeners find them comfortable, but they are not commonly available and may have to be ordered.

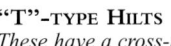
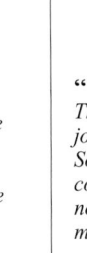

Hoes

Hoes are used for weeding and aerating soil; some types may be used to form seed drills. The Dutch hoe is probably the most versatile and is ideal for weeding between rows of plants and for creating drills. Apart from draw, digging, and onion hoes, there are proprietary hoes available for specific uses.

USING A DUTCH HOE
Hold the hoe so that the blade is parallel to the soil surface.

DUTCH HOE
This traditional hoe is excellent for weeding around plants. It cuts through surface weeds without damaging the plant roots.

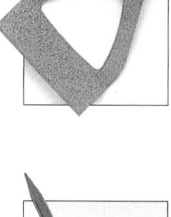

COMBINATION HOE
This is suitable for chopping off weeds, drawing drills, and earthing up. Use the prongs to break up soil and draw seed drills.

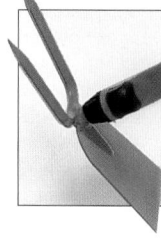

TRIANGULAR HOE
Use the point for drawing a "V"-shaped drill; the flat side is for weeding narrow spaces in between plants.

DIGGING HOE
This has one or two chisel-like blades. It is used with a swinging motion to break up small areas of hard ground.

Short-handled hoe for use in confined areas

ONION HOE
This small hoe (above), also called a hand, or rock garden, hoe, is for weeding between onions and other closely grown plants where a normal hoe might cause damage. It is like a short-handled version of a draw hoe, and is used while squatting or kneeling.

DRAW HOE
This hoe (right) is good for chopping weeds, drawing up earth around plants, making flat-bottomed seed drills, and, with the blade corner, making "V"-shaped drills.

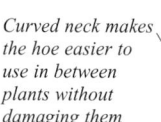

Moulded handle ensures a secure grip

Curved neck makes the hoe easier to use in between plants without damaging them

Rakes

Rakes are excellent for levelling and breaking up the soil surface before planting and for gathering garden debris. There are two main types: general garden rakes and lawn rakes (see "Rakes and aerators", p.559).

A one-piece rake head is stronger than a bolstered (riveted) one, and the wider the head, the faster an area is covered; 12 teeth are adequate, 16 or more are preferable for large areas. A 1m (3ft) wide wooden rake is useful in a large garden.

Heads and shafts

Most rake and hoe heads are made from solid carbon steel; stainless steel ones are more expensive and do not work any better, although they are easier to clean and do not rust. Some rakes have a "non-stick" coating.

Shafts may be made from wood, aluminium, or plastic-covered metal. Shaft length is important: you should be able to stand upright while hoeing or raking to reduce strain on the back. Most people find a 1.5m (5ft) shaft comfortable, but a longer handle may be preferred.

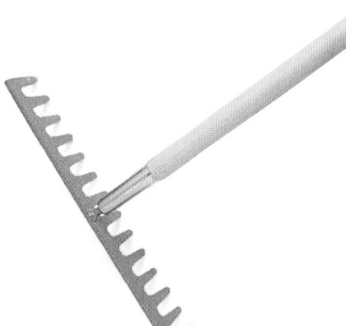

GARDEN RAKE
This has short, wide, rounded teeth and is valuable for levelling soil, clearing the ground, and general garden tidying.

BOLSTERED RAKE
This cheaper garden rake has nail-like, riveted teeth.

Trowels and hand forks

A trowel is useful for digging holes for small plants and bulbs, and for working in containers and raised beds. A hand, or weed, fork may be used for weeding, lifting small plants, and for planting.

Most trowel blades and hand fork prongs are made from stainless steel, coated steel (eg chrome-plated), or ordinary carbon steel. Unlike carbon steel, stainless steel does not rust and is easy to keep clean but it is expensive. Coatings gradually tend to wear off in time. Some trowels have extra-long handles – up to 30cm (12in) – for more leverage. Hand forks with handles 1.2m (4ft) long reduce the need to bend when weeding the back of a border. Wooden, plastic, and plastic-coated handles are all generally comfortable to hold; metal ones tend to be cold.

HAND FORK
Often used for lifting small plants or loosening the soil when weeding. Unlike a trowel, it does not compact the soil, so it may be preferable to use when planting in heavy soil.

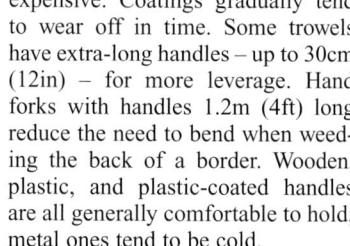

NARROW-BLADED TROWEL
Sometimes known as a rock garden or transplanting trowel, this is ideal for working in very confined areas such as rock gardens as well as for general transplanting tasks.

WIDE-BLADED TROWEL
This is useful for planting bulbs and bedding or other small plants, especially in confined areas such as containers and windowboxes.

Hand-weeding tools

For weeding between paving, bricks, or rocks, a patio weeder, which has a narrow, hooked blade, is ideal. A daisy grubber has a pronged blade suitable for levering up lawn weeds.

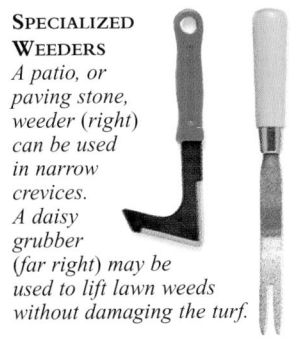

SPECIALIZED WEEDERS
A patio, or paving stone, weeder (right) can be used in narrow crevices. A daisy grubber (far right) may be used to lift lawn weeds without damaging the turf.

Manual cultivators

A hand, or pronged, cultivator is used to break up the surface of compacted soil or to loosen weeds. It has a three- or five-pronged, metal head on a long shaft and is pulled through the soil, generally from a standing position. Some adjustable models have removable, central prongs.

Specialized hand cultivators may be useful for certain regular tasks. A star-wheeled cultivator, or miller, for example, forms a fine tilth when pushed to and fro through the soil, so is good when preparing a seedbed.

ADJUSTABLE MODELS
Cultivators with removable central prongs are suitable for tasks such as cultivating each side of a row of seedlings. Some models have a detachable handle which may be fitted to other types of compatible tool head, for example a rake or hoe.

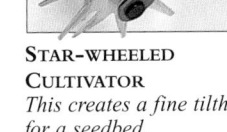

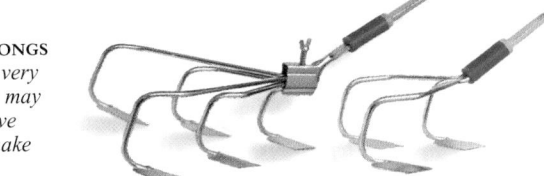

A single detachable handle may be combined with a variety of tool heads

STAR-WHEELED CULTIVATOR
This creates a fine tilth for a seedbed.

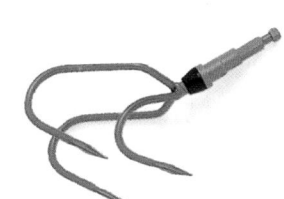

REMOVABLE PRONGS
When working in very confined areas, it may be useful to remove some prongs to make the head smaller.

Powered cultivators

A powered cultivator is used for tackling laborious tasks like turning over the soil in neglected ground. It breaks up compacted soil and reduces it to a tilth fine enough for planting. It is impractical for use in heavily planted areas, however, and does not eliminate the need for hand digging. Petrol-powered cultivators are powerful and generally have a wide range of attachments but need more maintenance than electric ones. Electric cultivators are excellent for small jobs. They are easier to manoeuvre, less noisy, and cheaper than petrol-engined types but trailing cables may be a problem.

On most cultivators the handle height is adjustable. Some also have handles that pivot and lock sideways, allowing you to walk alongside the machine without trampling the ground already cultivated.

Cultivators come in three main types: front-, mid-, and rear-engined. **Front-engined cultivators** have rotors behind the driving wheels. They are easy to steer, but, because of the way the weight is distributed, are best for shallow cultivation. **Mid-engined cultivators** are propelled by rotors rather than wheels. This may make control difficult, but the engine weight over the rotors makes deep cultivation easier than with a front-engined type. **Rear-engined cultivators** are best for manoeuvring in difficult places and for forming deep holes. The rotors, on a boom at the front, are swept from side to side as the cultivator is propelled along. The machines may be tiring to control.

POTATO LIFTER
This attachment lifts potatoes out onto the soil surface for easy collection.

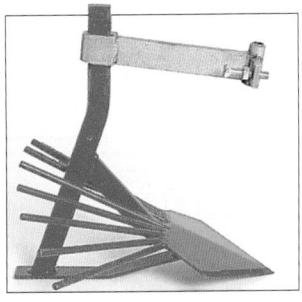

FIVE-TINE CULTIVATOR ATTACHMENT
This is used to weed between rows and for general cultivation. The tines can be adjusted for depth and width.

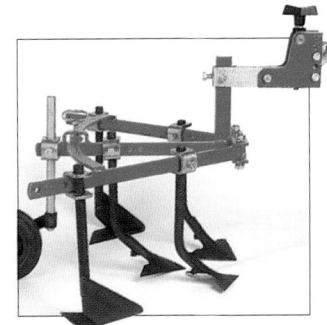

POWERED CULTIVATOR
This front-engined petrol model is stable and easy to control. It is expensive, but makes an excellent job of straightforward cultivation over a large area.

Deadman's handle (cuts power if grip relaxed)

Blade engagement

Accelerator

Clutch

Horizontal handle adjuster

Vertical hand height adjuster

Choke

Lever adjusts depth of cultivation

Fold-away stand ensures stability when machine is not in use

Transporter wheel aids steering

Rotors should be well away from operator's feet

Rear rotors produce a fine finish for a seedbed

Pruning and cutting tools

When pruning, it is important to use the appropriate tool for the task and to make sure that it is sharp so that it cuts cleanly, easily, and safely. Using a blunt blade can leave a plant with a ragged wound that is prone to infection or that can cause die-back. Take particular care when working with powered tools, such as hedge-trimmers or brushwood cutters (see "Electrical safety", p.556).

Secateurs

Secateurs are used for pruning woody stems up to about 1cm (½in) thick and soft shoots of any thickness; they may also be used for taking cuttings for propagation. They can be used single-handed and are more controllable and easier to handle safely than a knife, particularly by inexperienced gardeners.

There are three main types of secateur: by-pass, parrot-beak, and anvil. By-pass and parrot-beak secateurs have a scissor-like action; anvil secateurs have a sharp, straight-edged upper blade that cuts against a square-edged lower anvil. In some designs (swing anvils), the blade is pivoted in such a way that it remains parallel to the anvil as it cuts, slicing rather than crushing the stem.

For cutting soft-stemmed plants, a light, comparatively cheap pair is perfectly adequate. For pruning fruit trees and shrubs with woody shoots up to 1cm (½in) thick, a pair of heavy-duty secateurs is well worth the additional expense as the mechanism will not become strained.

If possible, try out the secateurs to check that they are comfortable and easy to operate; the handle material and shape, how wide they open, and the pressure of the spring keeping

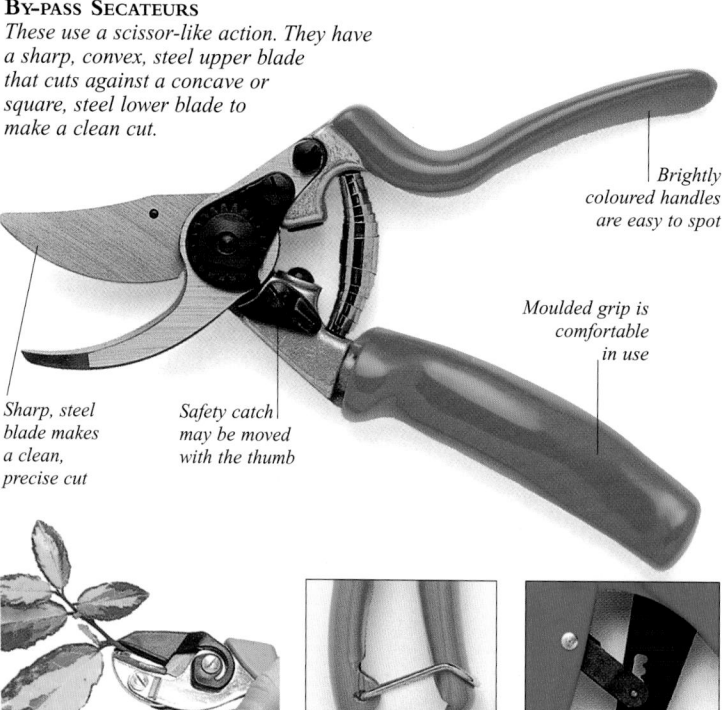

BY-PASS SECATEURS
These use a scissor-like action. They have a sharp, convex, steel upper blade that cuts against a concave or square, steel lower blade to make a clean cut.

Brightly coloured handles are easy to spot

Moulded grip is comfortable in use

Sharp, steel blade makes a clean, precise cut

Safety catch may be moved with the thumb

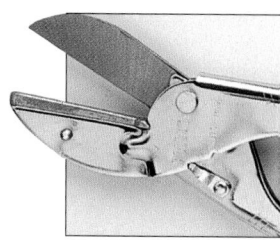

ANVIL SECATEURS
These must be kept sharp, otherwise the blade crushes the stem against the anvil instead of cutting it.

PARROT-BEAK SECATEURS
These give a clean cut, but may be damaged if used to cut wood more than 1cm (½in) thick.

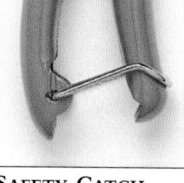

FLOWER GATHERERS
These are designed to grip the flower stem after cutting.

SAFETY CATCH
This catch clips the handles together.

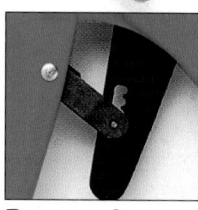

RATCHET SYSTEM
This makes cutting tough stems easier.

them open all vary considerably. Metal handles may be very cold to hold, but most handles are now plastic or plastic-covered metal. All secateurs are fitted with a safety catch that locks the blades in the shut position. Check that it is easy to operate with one hand and that it cannot be flicked off accidentally.

Secateur blades may be made from stainless steel, carbon steel, or coated steel. Coated blades are easy to wipe clean, but are unlikely to last as long as high-quality stainless or carbon steel blades, which keep their sharp-

ness and cut cleanly and easily. When buying high-quality secateurs, ensure that they can be dismantled for sharpening without special tools and that new blades are available.

Some models have a ratchet system for cutting through a stem in stages. These require less effort and so are suitable for those who find conventional models a strain.

Flower gatherers, or flower pickers, hold the flower stem after cutting. They are invaluable if cutting flowers often, otherwise secateurs or scissors will suffice.

Maintenance

Clean the blades of cutting tools after each use with an oily rag or wire wool to remove any sap that has dried on; then lightly oil them. Periodically tighten the blade tension of garden shears; this makes them cut more efficiently and produces a better finish.

Most pruning tools are easy to sharpen. Remove blades that are badly blunted or damaged, and regrind or replace them.

Long-handled pruners or loppers

A pair of long-handled pruners, or loppers, is useful for removing woody stems or branches 1–2.5cm (½–1in) thick, where secateurs might be damaged, and for thinner branches that are difficult to reach.

The long handles give additional leverage, making it easier to cut through thick stems. They are usually wood or plastic-covered tubular steel or aluminium. Blades are made of stainless steel, carbon steel, or coated steel, as for secateurs.

The weight and balance of long-handled pruners are important as you may have to hold them at full

stretch or above your head. Make sure that you will be able to operate them easily and without strain.

Most long-handled pruners have a by-pass blade motion, others an anvil action. Both are satisfactory designs, and the choice is a matter of personal preference. Designs with a ratchet are sometimes available and are particularly useful for cutting through thick or tough branches and to reduce the strength needed for cutting.

All long-handled pruners require regular maintenance to keep them in peak working condition.

LONG-HANDLED BY-PASS PRUNERS
Using long-handled pruners makes it possible to prune stems that are high up or that are too tough or thick for secateurs.

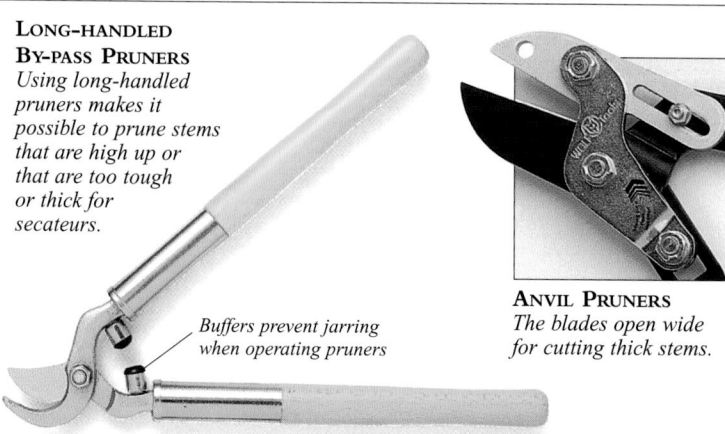

Buffers prevent jarring when operating pruners

ANVIL PRUNERS
The blades open wide for cutting thick stems.

Tree pruners

A tree pruner is suitable for cutting branches up to 2.5cm (1in) thick that would otherwise be out of reach. The cutting device is positioned at the end of a pole that is usually 2–3m (6–10ft) long, although some extend to 5m (15ft). The carbon steel blade is operated by a lever system or a cord; both are efficient, although the lever system is more popular. Some cord models have telescopic poles so that the length may be adjusted; they are also more convenient to store. Tree pruners may have saw or fruit-picker attachments.

TREE PRUNER

Hooked end is lowered over the branch to be cut

Pruning saws

Use a pruning saw for severing branches more than about 2.5cm (1in) thick. Because sawing in a confined space between other branches, and often at an awkward angle, may be difficult, various types of pruning saw have been developed. Those most commonly available are: general-purpose pruning, Grecian or rigid-handle curved, double-edged or two-edged, folding, and bow saws. If pruning is a major task in the garden, it may be necessary to have more than one saw for different types of work. A Grecian saw is one of the most useful pruning saws for an amateur gardener.

All pruning saws should have hardpoint, heat-treated teeth, which are harder and stay sharper for longer than ordinary saw teeth. They must be professionally sharpened. Saw handles are plastic or wood; choose whichever feels more comfortable and has a secure grip. Score a groove in the branch in which to insert the saw blade in order to reduce the risk of its slipping during use.

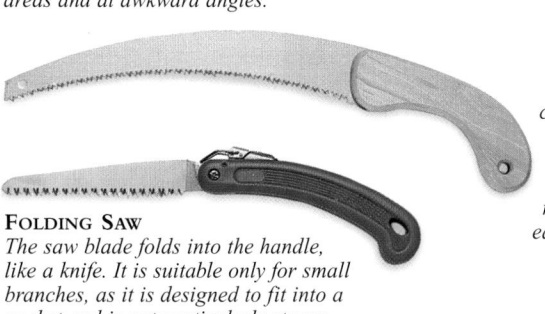

GENERAL-PURPOSE PRUNING SAW
Invaluable for most pruning jobs, this saw has a small blade, generally not more than 45cm (18in) long, so that it can be easily used in confined areas and at awkward angles.

FOLDING SAW
The saw blade folds into the handle, like a knife. It is suitable only for small branches, as it is designed to fit into a pocket and is not particularly strong.

GRECIAN SAW
This is excellent for confined spaces as it has a curved blade and cuts only on the pull stroke. In restricted areas, it is easier to use pressure on a pull, rather than a push, stroke.

DOUBLE-EDGED PRUNING SAW
This is very flexible as it has both coarse and fine teeth but may be difficult to operate in confined spaces without the top teeth damaging a nearby branch.

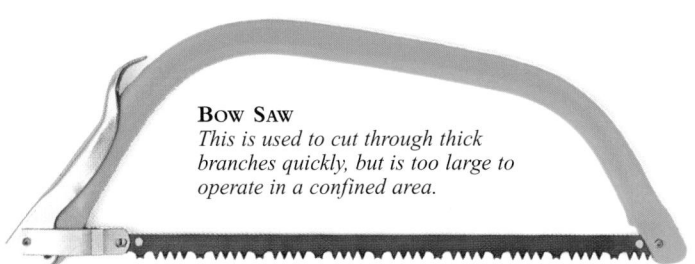

BOW SAW
This is used to cut through thick branches quickly, but is too large to operate in a confined area.

Garden knives

A garden knife may be used for light pruning tasks instead of secateurs, and is more versatile. It is also convenient for taking cuttings, preparing material for grafting, harvesting certain vegetables, and cutting string.

There are various types of garden knife available, including general-purpose, grafting, budding, and pruning or peach pruners. Most knives have a carbon steel blade which is either fixed or folds into the handle. If choosing the folding type, check that it is easy to open, and that the spring holding the blade in position is neither too strong nor too slack. Always dry knife blades after use, and wipe them over with an oily rag. Sharpen knives regularly, to the same angle as when new.

A Stanley-type knife with disposable blades is a good alternative to a garden knife, or use disposable craft knives and scalpels for taking cuttings.

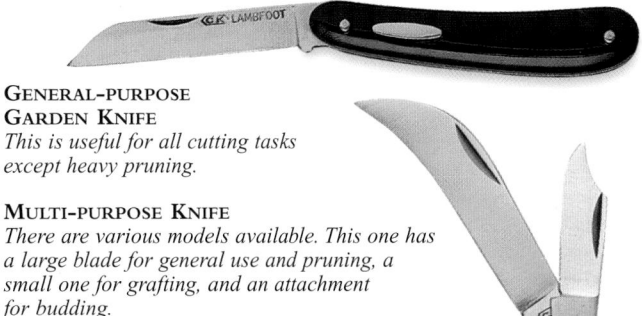

GENERAL-PURPOSE GARDEN KNIFE
This is useful for all cutting tasks except heavy pruning.

MULTI-PURPOSE KNIFE
There are various models available. This one has a large blade for general use and pruning, a small one for grafting, and an attachment for budding.

GRAFTING
This straight-bladed knife is suitable for general tasks, and for making accurate cuts when grafting.

BUDDING
The blade projection is used for prising open the rootstock incision when propagating by bud-grafting.

PRUNING
The large blade curves downwards for a controlled cut when pruning.

Garden shears

Shears are used mainly for trimming hedges, but are also invaluable for cutting small or awkward areas of long grass (see also "Lawncare tools", pp.558–559), clipping topiary, and cutting back herbaceous plants.

For soft-stemmed hedges, a light pair is adequate but for large hedges with tough, woody stems a heavy-duty pair will be needed.

Weight and balance are important; before buying, check that the shears are centrally balanced and the blades are not too heavy, or they will then be tiring to operate.

Most shears have straight blades although a few have wavy edged blades: these cut through mature wood easily and help to trap the shoots so that they are not pushed out with the scissor-action of the blades. They are difficult to sharpen (see also "Maintenance", p.554).

STANDARD SHEARS
Shears usually have one notched blade to hold a thick shoot during cutting.

SINGLE-HANDED SHEARS
These have a spring mechanism similar to secateurs that allows them to be operated with one hand. Some types have blades that swivel – useful for cutting at an angle or vertically (as for edging a lawn). They are only suitable for cutting grass or very soft stems.

Hedgetrimmers

For gardeners with large hedges to cut, a powered hedgetrimmer may be worthwhile as it takes much less time and effort to use than ordinary manually operated shears.

The longer the blade, the faster the hedge can be cut and the easier it is to reach a tall hedge or across the top of a wide one. Hedgetrimmers with very long blades are heavy and often poorly balanced, however. A 40cm (16in) blade is adequate for normal garden use, but if cutting extensive hedges a 60cm (24in) blade saves considerable time. Blades may be either single- or double-sided; the latter speed up the cutting time but are not as easy to control as single-sided blades, so hedge-shaping may be more difficult.

The ease of handling is also affected by the blade action. Models with reciprocating- or double-action blades, which move against each other, are generally preferable for the majority of gardeners. Single-action models, in which one moving blade cuts against a second, stationary blade, cause vibration and can therefore be tiring to operate.

The finish of the cut is largely controlled by the spacing of the teeth along the blade. Teeth that are narrowly spaced produce a smooth, even

PROTECTIVE CLOTHING
When operating powered tools, wear protective clothing such as goggles, ear protectors, and thick gardening gloves (see also p.563).

POWERED HEDGETRIMMER
This makes hedgetrimming faster and easier than it is when using garden shears. Electric models are light and easy to manoeuvre, while petrol versions are powerful and unhampered by trailing cables.

finish on a hedge that is regularly trimmed, while more widely spaced teeth usually cope better with thicker twigs but leave a rougher cut.

Petrol or electricity?
Hedgetrimmers may be powered by petrol or electricity, either from the mains or batteries. Petrol hedgetrimmers may be operated anywhere and are generally powerful and relatively free from vibration. They are, however, noisier, heavier, and more expensive than electric ones and usually require more maintenance.

Electric hedgetrimmers are more commonly used by amateurs and are better for small jobs. Being lighter, they are easier to handle than petrol trimmers; they are also cleaner to use and cheaper to buy.

Mains electric hedgetrimmers are the most convenient for hedges within 30m (100ft) of a power supply. As with other electric tools, the trailing cable can be inconvenient and even hazardous, and the machine must not be used in wet conditions. Safety features are very important when handling such a potentially

dangerous tool: for example, they should always be operated with a residual current device, or earth leakage circuit breaker (see also "Electrical safety", below).

Battery-powered hedgetrimmers are good for hedges in a distant part of a large garden or where there is no convenient power supply. They are usually run from a spare car battery. When fully charged, they are reasonably powerful but maintaining a charged battery and moving it around the garden can be time-consuming and laborious. They are more expensive than mains electric models.

Rechargeable hedgetrimmers

Hedgetrimmers powered by a rechargeable battery are cordless, easy to manoeuvre, and comparatively cheap. They are excellent for small, regularly trimmed hedges, but they lack the power to cut thick shoots and long hedges satisfactorily. As there are no trailing cables, rechargeable machines present fewer safety hazards than other types of electric trimmer. They can be recharged from a special mains unit.

Brushwood cutters

A brushwood cutter is excellent for slashing through tough weeds, undergrowth, and very long grass. The rotating head has a metal slasher or fine-toothed blade. This makes it suitable for far heavier tasks than those that can be tackled with a nylon-line trimmer (see "Lawncare tools", pp.558–559), but it is more tiring to operate. Some models take

plastic blades, but these are not as tough or durable. In addition to their cutting blade, some may be fitted with a nylon line for trimming grass.

As they need powerful engines to work effectively, most brushwood cutters are petrol-driven. Electric models are usually lighter, less noisy, and require less maintenance, but are less efficient for heavy work.

Electrical safety

• Keep leads only just as long as is necessary. Trailing cables are inconvenient and potentially hazardous, as they may be cut by moving blades.
• Have outside sockets installed by a qualified electrician at suitable points in the garden to keep leads short and safe.
• If extension leads are needed, ensure that they have the same number of wires as the tool: if the tool is earthed, the extension cable should be too.
• If the circuit is not already protected, attach a plug fitted with a residual current device (RCD) to the tool, or buy an adaptor RCD to insert between the plug and socket.
• Do not use an electric tool during or just after rain as this may cause electrical faults.
• Always disconnect the power supply before adjusting, inspecting, or cleaning a tool.
• Never touch a severed or damaged cable before disconnecting it from the mains.

Chainsaws

Chainsaws are suitable for sawing logs or large branches and for extensive tree surgery and felling. As they cut with a powered, toothed chain revolving at high speed, they can be extremely dangerous; it is essential to be trained in their use and never to work alone, in case of accidents. As with all electrical equipment, you must always wear appropriate safety equipment and follow strict rules for the safe use of electricity (see right).

Electric chainsaws are useful for small jobs and are cheaper than petrol types, which are more powerful, noisy, heavy, often difficult to start, and create fumes.

ELECTRIC CHAINSAW
An electric chainsaw is suitable for most sawing tasks; it is lighter and easier to handle than a petrol-powered version and generally requires less maintenance.

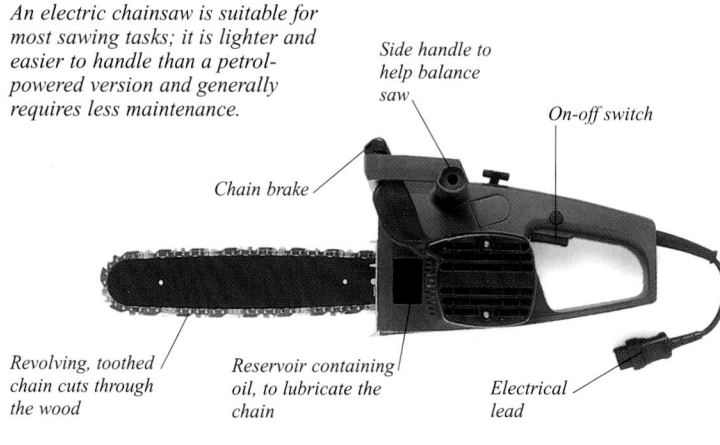

Side handle to help balance saw

On-off switch

Chain brake

Revolving, toothed chain cuts through the wood

Reservoir containing oil, to lubricate the chain

Electrical lead

Lawnmowers

When choosing a lawnmower, take into account the size of your lawn and the type of cut required. If only a small area needs mowing, a manual lawnmower may suffice, but for a larger lawn, buy a powered one. There are cylinder, rotary, and hover mowers available: cylinder models usually provide the finest cut, while rotary types are better for long, overgrown grass; hover mowers are best for irregular lawns.

Grass should be mown more closely in summer than in winter, so check that the height of cut is easily adjustable (see also THE LAWN, "Frequency and height of cut", p.395). A mulching mower chops grass finely and discharges the clippings close to the soil surface, for rapid decomposition and soil nourishment. If you need a fine finish without loose grass, choose a lawnmower with a grass collector. Such models are more usually cylinder mowers than hover ones (see also "Grass clippings", p.395).

Manual lawnmowers

Manual mowers are relatively cheap, quiet, have no awkward cables, and need very little maintenance. There are two types: those driven by wheels at the side and those operated by a chain drive from a heavy rear roller. A side-wheel mower is easy to push but awkward at the edge of a lawn.

Powered lawnmowers

There are two basic types of powered lawnmower: cylinder, and rotary or hover (hover mowers work on the same principle as rotary ones). Most run on petrol, mains electricity, or rechargeable battery. Powered mowers are potentially dangerous on steep slopes as they are designed for flat surfaces. Ride-on or tractor-hauled models are convenient for large areas.
Cylinder mowers are self-propelled or have a powered blade; the latter type may be heavy and tiring to operate. Most have a rear roller, which is essential if you want a lawn with a striped pattern; the heavier the roller, the more pronounced the stripe.

Petrol-driven cylinder mowers often have broader cutting widths than electric ones. This reduces the cutting time but makes them more difficult to manoeuvre.
Rotary and hover mowers have replaceable metal or plastic blades that cut the grass with a scissor-like

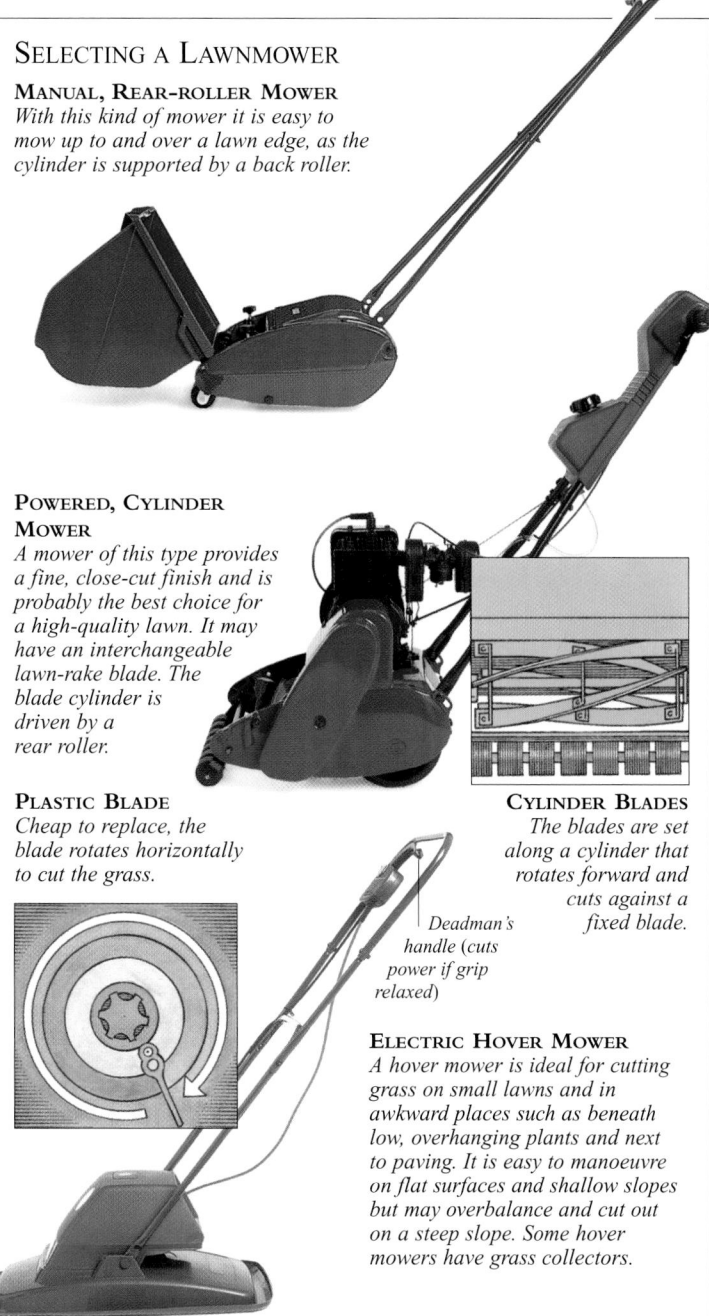

SELECTING A LAWNMOWER

MANUAL, REAR-ROLLER MOWER
With this kind of mower it is easy to mow up to and over a lawn edge, as the cylinder is supported by a back roller.

POWERED, CYLINDER MOWER
A mower of this type provides a fine, close-cut finish and is probably the best choice for a high-quality lawn. It may have an interchangeable lawn-rake blade. The blade cylinder is driven by a rear roller.

PLASTIC BLADE
Cheap to replace, the blade rotates horizontally to cut the grass.

CYLINDER BLADES
The blades are set along a cylinder that rotates forward and cuts against a fixed blade.

Deadman's handle (cuts power if grip relaxed)

ELECTRIC HOVER MOWER
A hover mower is ideal for cutting grass on small lawns and in awkward places such as beneath low, overhanging plants and next to paving. It is easy to manoeuvre on flat surfaces and shallow slopes but may overbalance and cut out on a steep slope. Some hover mowers have grass collectors.

PETROL-DRIVEN ROTARY MOWER
A ride-on mower is useful for extensive grassed areas, including rough and long grass, as it has a powerful engine. The replaceable metal blade cuts horizontally.

motion, as they rotate horizontally. Rotary mowers have wheels while hover mowers ride on a cushion of air. Some rotary mowers are fitted with rollers, and these are best for fine lawns. Both types work better than cylinder mowers for sites that are slightly uneven or have long grass, but most models cannot cut the grass very low. Rotary blades can become unbalanced so regular service checks are advisable.

Which power source?
Batteries and electricity are more convenient and cleaner than petrol, but not suitable for powerful engines. For cordless mowers, a handy power outlet is needed for recharging – batteries cannot always be removed from the mower. For an electric mower, access to a power supply is also essential, but the trailing flex may be a hazard. Electric mowers should not be used on wet grass.

Petrol lawnmowers are also not hampered by cables but are more expensive to buy and maintain. They may not start readily unless they are fitted with an electric ignition.

Safety
• Blades must be well protected so that they do not come into contact with the operator's feet, especially when using on slopes. The operator should always wear strong shoes.
• The blade brake must stop the blades rotating within five seconds of being turned off.
• The mower should have a lock-off switch, which requires two operations to turn on an engine. This reduces the risk of a child accidentally switching it on.
• A deadman's handle should be fitted. Held when mowing, this turns off the engine when released.

Maintenance

A few simple precautions keep a mower working efficiently.
• After use, disconnect power, then clean engine and blades.
• Check that the blades are sharp and replace blunt ones.
• Oil and lubricate regularly.
• Service the mower yearly.
• Periodically check that spark plugs are clean and adjusted.
• Clean filters and air intakes of petrol mowers regularly.
• Periodically check the oil level on four-stroke engines.
• Before you store a petrol-powered model, drain the tank.

Lawncare tools

As well as a lawnmower, a number of other tools are useful for maintaining a healthy and attractive lawn. Manual tools are usually adequate for most lawns but, for large areas, powered tools are faster and less tiring to use.

Edging tools

A neat, well-defined edge provides the perfect finishing touch to a well-mown lawn and emphasizes the lawn's shape and outline (see also *Cutting the Edge of the Lawn*, p.396). There are two main lawn edging tools: half-moon edgers and long-handled shears, although powered edging machines and certain nylon-line trimmers may be used.

Shafts for long-handled shears are wooden, steel, or plastic-coated steel; all are strong and the choice is really a matter of personal preference.

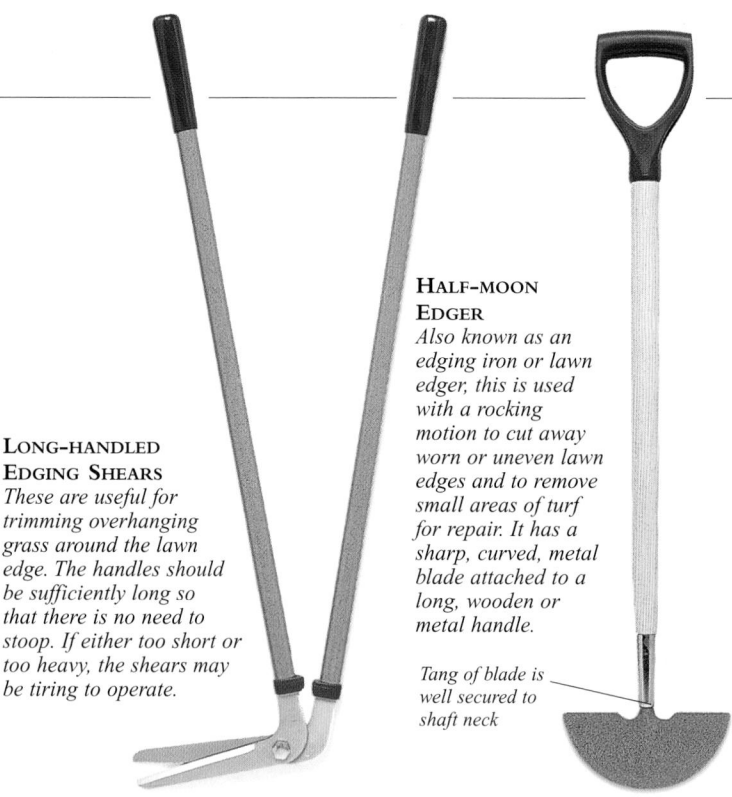

LONG-HANDLED EDGING SHEARS
These are useful for trimming overhanging grass around the lawn edge. The handles should be sufficiently long so that there is no need to stoop. If either too short or too heavy, the shears may be tiring to operate.

HALF-MOON EDGER
Also known as an edging iron or lawn edger, this is used with a rocking motion to cut away worn or uneven lawn edges and to remove small areas of turf for repair. It has a sharp, curved, metal blade attached to a long, wooden or metal handle.

Tang of blade is well secured to shaft neck

Lawn edging materials

To prevent a lawn from gradually decreasing in size when turf is removed with tools such as a half-moon edger, outline the lawn with bricks, paving slabs, terracotta edging tiles, or metal or plastic edging strips. This helps to ensure an even edge to the lawn and inhibits grass from spreading onto paths and borders. A brick or paving-slab edge also enables hover and side-wheel mowers to be driven right to the lawn edge. Plastic strips, which are usually coloured green, are less likely than metal edging strips to damage mower blades, and are also cheaper.

Nylon-line trimmers

A nylon-line trimmer is useful for trimming grass in awkward areas that cannot easily be reached by a mower. It may also be used for slashing ground-cover plants or soft-stemmed weeds, although a more powerful brushwood cutter may be needed for tough undergrowth (see p.556). As the nylon cutting line is flexible and easily replaced, it is possible to work right up to a wall or paving without damaging the tool. It is also safer than a fixed blade if there is an accident. Always wear goggles, as flying stones may be hazardous.

Nylon-line trimmers may be driven by mains-powered electricity, rechargeable battery, or petrol, and similar considerations of safety, convenience, and weight apply. Mains-powered electric models are light and easy to operate, but their area of use is restricted by the cable length. For safety, they should have a deadman's handle and be connected to a residual current device. Cordless nylon-line trimmers with rechargeable batteries are suitable for small to medium areas, especially where there is no external power supply. They too are lightweight, quiet, and easy to use. Under no circumstances must electric-powered trimmers be used while grass is wet (see also "Electrical safety", p.556).

Petrol-driven trimmers are ideal for larger gardens, but they are heavier, more expensive, and need more maintenance than other trimmers. For safety, they should have a quick, easy way to stop the engine.

Garden rollers

A garden roller, which may be made of metal or water-filled, hollow plastic, is used to level the surface during initial ground preparation before sowing grass seed or laying turf. It also settles the soil around young grass seedlings. Rolling established lawns regularly is no longer recommended, however; on heavy soils particularly, it tends to compact the turf and therefore impede drainage, which may cause problems such as moss and poor grass growth.

TRIMMER
This has a flexible, nylon, cutting line which rotates at high speed to cut through grass and other soft-stemmed plants or weeds. Some models have an adjustable head that may be tilted vertically for trimming lawn edges.

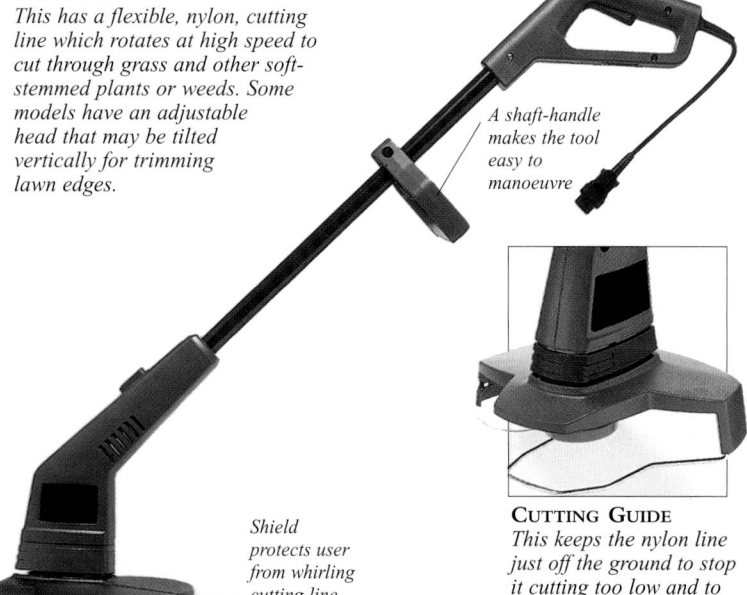

A shaft-handle makes the tool easy to manoeuvre

Shield protects user from whirling cutting line

CUTTING GUIDE
This keeps the nylon line just off the ground to stop it cutting too low and to produce an even trim.

Long-handled lawn shears

Long-handled lawn shears are helpful for trimming grass in awkward places, such as beneath overhanging plants or around trees, paving, or walls, and for tidying any stalks missed during mowing. The blades, set at right angles to the handles, are positioned parallel to the ground, not vertically as in edging shears.

While lawn shears are useful for very small areas, they have now largely been superseded by powered, nylon-line trimmers, which are faster and more versatile. Trimmers are heavier to hold and manoeuvre than shears, however, and less energy-efficient than hand tools.

LONG-HANDLED LAWN SHEARS
These may be useful for cutting grass in small areas that would be difficult to cut with a mower.

Rakes and aerators

Tools for clearing up fallen leaves and garden debris and for reducing thatch (a layer of decaying organic matter) and soil compaction help to keep a lawn in good condition.

Lawn rakes are primarily used to gather up fallen leaves. Some types may be helpful in removing thatch and dead moss. There are three types of lawn rake: spring-tined, flat-tined, and scarifying, or aerator, rakes (see also "Rakes", p.552). In addition, powered lawn rakes are available, which are suitable for large lawns.

Aerators help to reduce thatch and let air into the soil, encouraging good root growth. On very small areas, aerating may be done with a garden fork, but for most lawns a purpose-built machine such as a hollow-tined aerator or a slitter is better.

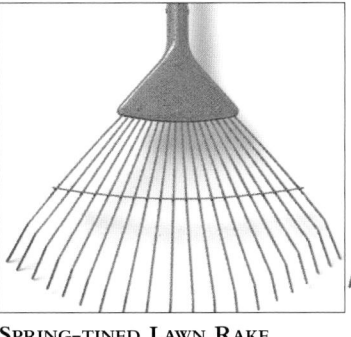

SPRING-TINED LAWN RAKE
This is used for clearing out dead grass and moss, removing small stones and debris, and lightly aerating a lawn. Its light head has long, flexible, rounded wire tines.

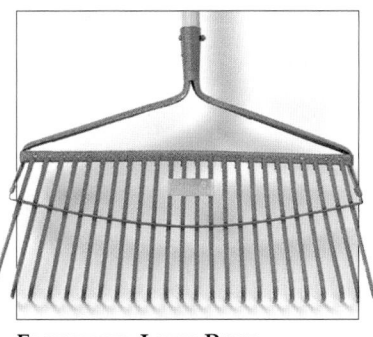

FLAT-TINED LAWN RAKE
Excellent for gathering up leaves and loose material, this has long, flexible, flat tines of plastic or metal, and a light head to minimize damage to new growth.

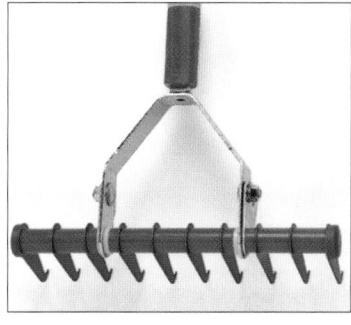

SCARIFYING RAKE
This cuts deeply into thatch and even into the turf itself. Its rigid, metal tines are usually flat, with sharp points. As it may be heavy and tiring to use, a model with wheels either side of the rake head may be preferable.

POWERED LAWN RAKE
Easier to use than an ordinary rake, its plastic or metal tines effectively scarify turf, while its collecting box removes debris.

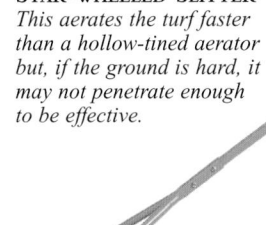

STAR-WHEELED SLITTER
This aerates the turf faster than a hollow-tined aerator but, if the ground is hard, it may not penetrate enough to be effective.

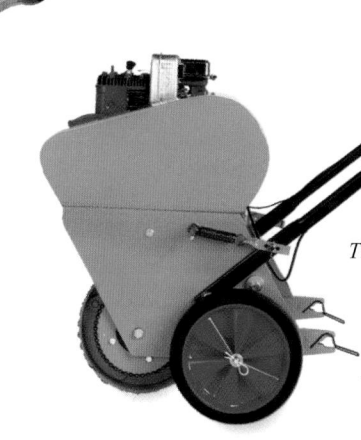

HOLLOW-TINED AERATOR
This powered, hollow-tined aerator penetrates deeply through the turf into the soil. The tines remove cores of soil, opening up compacted turf.

Sweepers and blowers

At its simplest, a leaf sweeper may be an ordinary besom brush or stiff broom used to sweep away small debris; this kind of basic sweeper is ideal for clearing pathways and small areas of the garden.

For large-sized lawns, however, using a purpose-designed leaf sweeper saves both labour and time. The leaves are lifted from the surface of the grass by rotating brushes and they are then thrown into a large collecting bag, from which they can be readily emptied and composted.

Electric- or petrol-powered vacuum leaf collectors and blowers may prove worthwhile in very large gardens, but they are expensive to buy and they may be noisy to operate.

Some powered models have flexible attachments designed for use among flower beds and other areas of the garden that are particularly hard to reach.

BESOM
This is an inexpensive brush suitable for sweeping up leaves and light debris.

LEAF SWEEPER
This gathers up garden leaves, using rotating brushes, and collects them in a large bag. It is light, easy to push, and quiet in operation.

BACKPACK LEAF BLOWER
This blower is carried on the operator's back while it blows, rather than sweeps, garden leaves into a pile for collection. It is useful for small, tight, or irregularly shaped areas, but is bulky to store and noisy, so always wear ear protection when operating such a machine.

Control handle and starter

Fertilizer spreaders

A fertilizer spreader is suitable for the accurate distribution of fertilizer, grass seed, and granular weedkillers. It comprises a hopper on wheels with a long handle. Check that the application rate is adjustable and that the flow may be switched off when turning at the lawn edge. After setting the application rate always check that it is correct by fertilizing a test area first (see "Applying fertilizers", p.625). A hose attachment for applying a fertilizer with water is useful for feeding a lawn (see "Sprayers", p.560).

FERTILIZER SPREADER
A spreader applies fertilizer evenly, so avoiding scorching the grass.

Watering aids

Irrigation makes it possible to grow plants that require more water than is provided by rainfall, and to grow plants both indoors and in the greenhouse. Equipment such as hoses and sprinklers help make routine watering easier and faster.

Watering cans

A watering can is practical in the house, greenhouse, or for small areas outside. Choose a lightweight can that will not be too heavy to carry when full. The opening of the watering can should be wide enough to make filling easy, and the can itself should feel comfortable and well balanced. A can that has a strainer at the base of the spout helps to prevent the rose from becoming clogged by debris in the water.

Water butts

A water butt collects rainwater from the house or greenhouse roof, which is invaluable during dry periods and for acid-loving plants. The butt should have a tap, and a lid to keep out debris, which pollutes the water and might block the tap. If necessary, raise the butt on blocks so a watering can will fit under the tap. Some butts divert water back to the drain when they are full. See WATER CONSERVATION AND RECYCLING, pp.614–615.

GARDEN WATERING CANS
These should have a generous capacity to reduce the need for repeated refilling. For general-purpose use, a 9 litre (2 gallon) can, which holds 8kg (18lb) of water, is a convenient size.

INDOOR WATERING CAN
This should have a long spout to reach into plant pots and windowboxes, and to help control the flow.

PLASTIC OR METAL?
Most watering cans are now made from plastic, but traditional galvanized metal ones, which are heavier and more expensive, are still available; both types are sturdy and durable.

GREENHOUSE WATERING CAN
This has a long spout, so that it is easy to reach plants at the back of a bench, and a reversible rose for both fine and coarse sprays for watering seedlings and mature plants.

Caution with weedkiller

Do not use the same watering can or sprayer for watering the garden and for dispensing liquid weedkillers. Keep a dedicated one, clearly marked, for applying chemicals.

Which rose?

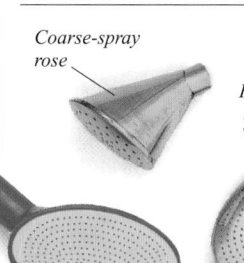

Coarse-spray rose

Fine-spray brass rose

Fine-spray, brass-faced, plastic rose

A fine rose is best for seeds and seedlings because the resulting spray does not damage them or wash the compost or soil away from them. For more established plants, a coarse-spray rose, which delivers the water faster, is preferable.

Roses are manufactured in a choice of materials: brass, brass-faced plastic, and all-plastic. Plastic is less durable and cheaper than brass but is still satisfactory for most uses. In general, metal roses give a finer spray.

Using a dribble bar, which is attached to a watering can, makes it more accurate than a rose for applying weedkiller. It also reduces spray drift which can be a problem with a rose.

Hosepipes

A hosepipe is invaluable for irrigating distant parts of the garden and for areas that require copious watering. Most hosepipes are made from PVC; they vary in the way they are finished or reinforced, which affects their durability, flexibility, and resistance to kinking. Any kinks interrupt water flow and eventually weaken the hose wall. Double-walled and reinforced hoses are resistant to kinking but relatively expensive. Some hosepipes are available on a wall-mounted, retractable reel, for tidy storage, while others are on wheels or retract into a plastic box with a carrying handle. These allow waterflow through the hose even when partially wound, so the hose can always be tidy yet ready for immediate use.

All types of hose are made in various fixed lengths with connectors and nozzles pre-fitted or as accessories. Some hoses can be lengthened with one or more extensions.

Wherever an external, cold-water supply is connected to a garden hose, it is advisable to fit the tap or outlet with a double-check, or non-return, valve, to prevent back siphonage of potentially contaminated water into other parts of the system. Check with your local water authority if this is a legal requirement in your area.

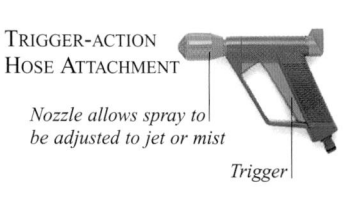

HOSE REEL
A reel with a handle or wheels is easy to move around the garden. Some reels allow waterflow through the hose even when partially wound.

Sprayers

Use sprayers to apply pesticides, herbicides, and fertilizers, and to water or mist-spray plants. Compression types, pumped up before use, are most suitable for general use; small trigger-pump sprayers are for misting house plants or applying pesticides to a few plants. In countries where regulations permit, hose attachments that incorporate reservoirs are available for dispensing fertilizers and weedkillers.

TRIGGER-ACTION HOSE ATTACHMENT

Nozzle allows spray to be adjusted to jet or mist

Trigger

FERTILIZER PULSE HOSE ATTACHMENT

Central chamber for fertilizer

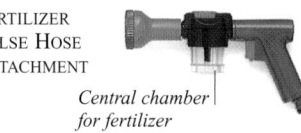

COMPRESSION SPRAYER
This sprayer is pumped up with the handle and is suitable for treating large areas.

HOSE-END ATTACHMENTS
Most attachments simply allow the intensity and range of the water spray to be adjusted. Some have a trigger-action nozzle.

Seep hoses

Seep hoses are useful for irrigating lawns or rows of plants. They are plastic or rubber hoses with small perforations along their entire length. With the holes facing upwards, a seep hose produces a fine spray over a rectangular area such as a lawn. With the holes placed towards or under the soil, water is directed to the base of plants – an excellent way to irrigate vegetables and other plants grown in rows.

Porous hoses are variations on seep hoses, and are particularly suitable for newly planted beds and borders and vegetable gardens. These hoses enable water to seep slowly into the soil and can be attached to a hose timer. They can be buried at a depth of up to 30cm (12in) below the surface as a permanent irrigation system, although a shallow covering is suitable for most situations. Porous hoses can also be laid on the soil surface, around established plants for example, but they must be covered with a mulch. Because water is released directly into the area of the plant's roots, it is distributed very economically and there is no run-off and little evaporation. The low humidity levels reduce the incidence of fungal diseases as well as the spread of pests and diseases, often triggered by water splash. Weed germination is also discouraged by the dry soil surface.

Porous hoses can be simply and easily cut into flexible lengths and laid in any shape or pattern provided there is no kink. They also work effectively on a slope, particularly if laid along rather than down the incline. The pipes can remain outside throughout the year, even if installed on the soil surface. However, the connections can be varied, and the system moved around as required.

TYPES OF SPRINKLER

   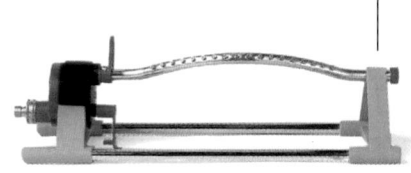

STATIC SPRINKLER
Static sprinklers are intended primarily for use on lawns, most being mounted on a spike to push into the ground. They usually deliver water in a circle, but a few water in a semi-circular, rectangular, or fan shape. They are liable to form puddles, so must be moved around to achieve an even distribution of water.

ROTATING SPRINKLER
Good for lawns, beds, and borders, this type of sprinkler covers a large circular area and applies the water evenly. The spray is delivered through nozzles on the arms, which are attached to a spinning pivot, driven by the force of the water. Those that are fitted with long stems are the best type for watering beds and borders.

PULSE-JET SPRINKLER
This type of sprinkler is invaluable for covering large, circular areas of lawn, beds, or borders. It has a single jet on a central pivot, which rotates in a series of pulses, ejecting spurts of water. Except on lawns, the delivery head is generally set on a tall stem for increased coverage.

OSCILLATING SPRINKLER
This is best used at ground level; it is not suitable for positions where surrounding foliage will interfere with the range of the spray. Water is sprayed through a series of brass jets in the oscillating arm. This sprinkler delivers water fairly evenly over a rectangular area, the size of which may be easily adjusted.

Garden sprinklers

A garden sprinkler automatically delivers a fine spray of water over a specific area. Because it works while unattended, it saves time and effort. However, if water is applied in hot, sunny weather, much is lost by evaporation, and so sprinklers are not as efficient as seep and porous hoses.

A sprinkler is generally attached to a garden hose or a static water-pipe. There are various types to suit a range of needs: some are best for a lawn, for example, while others are preferable for irrigating a flower bed or vegetable patch. The simplest form is a static sprinkler. Other types of sprinkler, such as the rotating, pulse-jet, and oscillating ones, use water pressure to rotate the sprinkler heads and this provides better and more even coverage.

A travelling sprinkler (also called a walking sprinkler) is useful for large, level areas such as a big lawn; it is convenient but expensive. The sprinkler delivers spray over a rectangular area while it is propelled along a track (usually a hosepipe) by the force of the water.

Underground sprinkler systems
These are permanent systems, ideal for irrigating lawns and rock gardens. They are unobtrusive and simple to operate, and are best installed when the area needing irrigation is first constructed, preferably by a professional. PVC pipes and connecting joints are laid in the form of a grid so that they supply various watering heads, to which hoses or sprinklers are attached. The sprinkler from each head delivers an even supply of water to a circular area. Always continue watering until the ground is thoroughly wet, because this helps to even out the distribution to any overlapping areas. This type of watering system requires non-return valves to meet water authority standards, and possibly a water meter.

Hose timers

Hose timers may be used with ordinary garden sprinklers or more elaborate watering systems. They fit between a tap and the hose or irrigation pipe. Most such timers turn off the water after a predetermined time. The more sophisticated ones will turn on and off several times a day and can be pre-programmed as well as linked to a moisture detector that prevents watering if the ground is sufficiently wet.

COMPUTERIZED TIMER
This allows you to programme watering times and duration in advance, to irrigate plants while you are busy or on holiday.

WATER TIMER
This can be set to turn off the water after a pre-set period, from about 5 minutes to 2 hours.

Trickle, or drip feed, systems

These are used for plants that benefit from individual watering; plants, for example, that need more water than others growing around them. The water drips or is sprayed gently beside the plant – a variety of nozzles being available. A trickle system works well in a shrub border, along a hedge, or for rows of vegetables. On a smaller scale, it is ideal for plants in containers, growing bags, and windowboxes. Unless fitted with a hose timer, trickle systems tend to waste water, and they need regular cleaning to prevent the tubes and drip heads from becoming blocked with algae and debris.

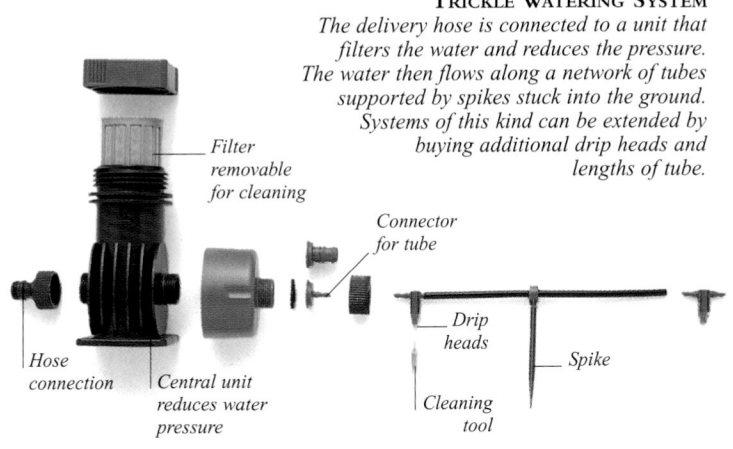

TRICKLE WATERING SYSTEM
The delivery hose is connected to a unit that filters the water and reduces the pressure. The water then flows along a network of tubes supported by spikes stuck into the ground. Systems of this kind can be extended by buying additional drip heads and lengths of tube.

Filter removable for cleaning

Connector for tube

Drip heads

Spike

Hose connection

Central unit reduces water pressure

Cleaning tool

General garden equipment

As well as tools for cultivating and maintaining the garden, a wide range of other accessories, such as carrying equipment and planting aids, may be useful, depending on your own individual requirements.

Wheelbarrows

Wheelbarrows are useful for transporting plants, soil, and materials such as compost and garden debris. They may be made of metal or plastic, the former being more durable. Painted metal soon rusts if the paint is chipped; even galvanized metal bins rust eventually. Plastic bins, although lighter, may split.

A ball-wheeled wheelbarrow is more stable than a standard model, making it easier to use over recently dug ground. Most suitable for very heavy work is a builder's barrow, which has an inflatable tyre to cushion the load. Barrows with two wheels and a pram-type handle (sometimes called garden carts) are stable and easy to load and unload, but are less manoeuvrable than standard barrows on uneven ground.

Sheets and bags

A carrying sheet or bag is suitable for transporting light but bulky garden waste such as hedge clippings; when not in use, it takes up very little space. It should be lightweight,

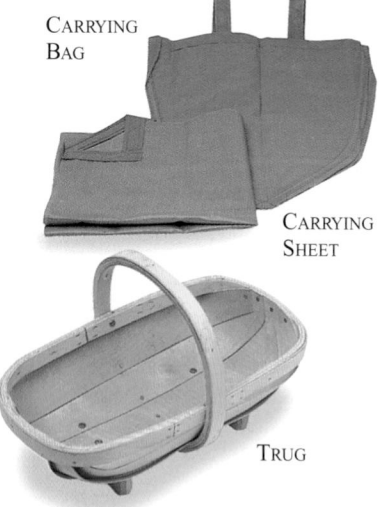

CARRYING BAG

CARRYING SHEET

TRUG

with strong handles, and made of a tough, tear-proof material, such as woven plastic. Carrying bags have a larger capacity than sheets. Trugs and baskets are good for light tasks such as carrying flowers or fruit.

TYPES OF WHEELBARROW

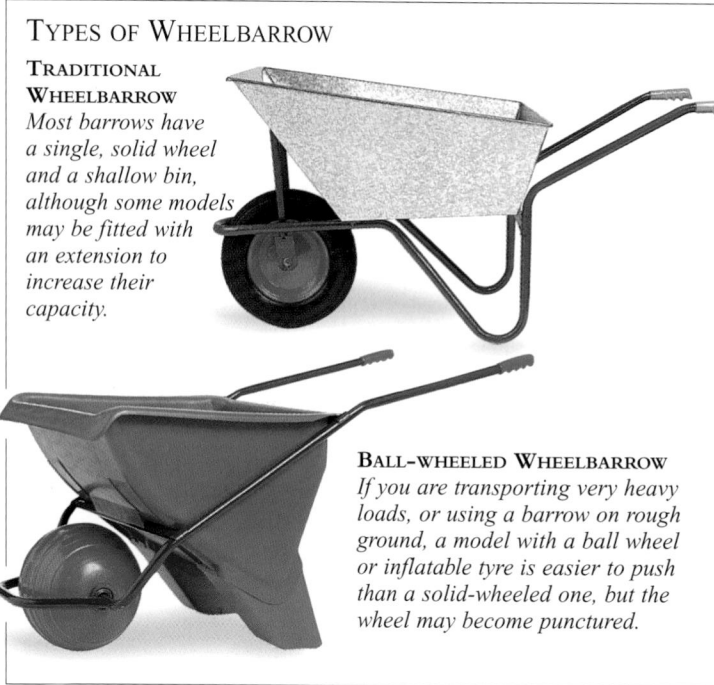

TRADITIONAL WHEELBARROW
Most barrows have a single, solid wheel and a shallow bin, although some models may be fitted with an extension to increase their capacity.

BALL-WHEELED WHEELBARROW
If you are transporting very heavy loads, or using a barrow on rough ground, a model with a ball wheel or inflatable tyre is easier to push than a solid-wheeled one, but the wheel may become punctured.

Plastic bags

Clear plastic bags are excellent for a number of purposes: preventing cuttings material from drying out after collecting it, for example, and for covering cuttings in pots to raise humidity around them. Most food and freezer bags are suitable provided that they are made of polythene and are not too thin – other materials being less effective at retaining moisture.

Kneelers and knee pads

A cushioned-pad kneeler, covered with a waterproof material, is simply knelt on for extra comfort, when weeding, for example, whereas knee pads are strapped to the knees and often sold in only one size, so check

that they fit before buying. Kneeling stools support the knees on a slightly raised platform and have hand rests to give support when kneeling and standing. They may also be turned upside-down for use as a small stool for working at raised beds or greenhouse benches.

KNEELERS
A kneeling stool (top) can be inverted for use as a stool and is light to carry. A cushioned pad (bottom) keeps knees clear of damp, hard ground.

Compost bins

A compost bin should have a lid to keep warmth in, easy access to the compost by slats or panels, and a capacity of at least 1 cu m (1 cu yd) to generate sufficient heat to accelerate the rotting process. Avoid wire mesh bins or those with large gaps between the slats, because they allow the heat generated to escape.

Traditional, wooden compost bins are available pre-cut for easy

self-assembly. Plastic compost bins are generally more effective than metal or wooden ones because they conserve moisture and reduce the need to water. There are plastic bins available that may be rotated to turn the compost, but this does not necessarily make good compost more quickly than a well-designed, traditional bin. See also SOILS AND FERTILIZERS, *Making a Compost Bin*, p.627.

Incinerators

Incinerators burn rubbish more quickly and cleanly than bonfires, but many gardeners now prefer to recycle garden waste by shredding and composting it. Open-mesh incinerators, some of which may be folded up after use, are good for burning dry material such as twigs and leaves, while galvanized steel, dustbin-type incinerators are suitable for slowly burning damp, woody material. Both types must be well ventilated.

Shredders

A compost shredder chops woody or tough garden waste, such as old Brussels sprout stems and prunings, until it is fine enough to break down quickly on a compost heap. Shredders are usually electrically powered and should not be left outdoors when not in use. Most machines operate by a fast-spinning blade but some have a crushing–cutting action and these are much quieter and easier to use.

Small shredders accept only thin, woody stems and need constant, time-consuming feeding. It may therefore be better occasionally to hire a bigger machine that will chew up relatively large branches, too.

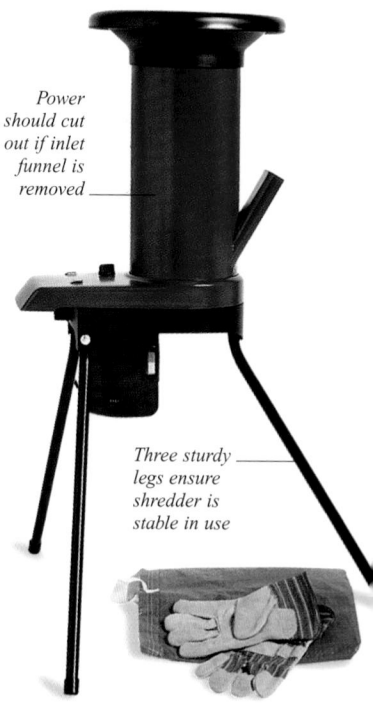

Power should cut out if inlet funnel is removed

Three sturdy legs ensure shredder is stable in use

USING A SHREDDER
The inlet funnel should not allow direct access to the blades. Wear goggles and gloves to protect against flying debris and thorny stems.

Planting and sowing aids

General garden tools or household items are often used for planting and sowing; for example a stick or pencil, instead of a dibber, will make a planting hole. Specialized tools, however, do make some tedious and repetitive jobs simpler and quicker.

Seed sowers and planters

These facilitate accurate and even sowing of seed. There are four main types: shakers, plungers, wheeled sowers, and seed-tray sowers.

Shakers are hand-held devices that may be used for sowing seed in prepared drills. Skill is required to ensure even seed distribution.

Plungers insert each seed individually to a predetermined depth.

Wheeled seed sowers are good for distributing seeds evenly. With a long handle, they can be worked from a standing position.

Seed-tray sowers are thin, plastic or wooden boards with moulded protrusions on one side. When pressed onto the seed compost they firm the surface and make evenly spaced holes for sowing seed.

Bulb planters

A bulb planter is useful if planting a number of bulbs individually; for planting groups of small bulbs, a trowel or hand fork is better. A bulb planter is usually pushed into the soil with your foot. It removes a plug of soil or turf, which is then replaced on top of the bulb after planting; those with a claw-like action release the plug by pressure on the handle.

Gardening gloves

There is a range of gardening gloves for various purposes: some keep hands clean when working with soil or compost, while others also provide protection against thorns.

Leather and fabric gloves are useful for tasks such as pruning roses to guard against thorns. When buying leather ones, check that the leather extends far enough to protect all of the palm. All-leather or suede gloves give very good protection, but may be uncomfortably hot in warm weather. Gauntlet types cover the wrists and lower forearms.

Many gloves are made of fabric and vinyl. Some are impregnated with vinyl, others just have a vinyl grip on the palms. They are good for most jobs and keep hands cleaner than fabric alone. Vinyl-coated gloves are useful for messy jobs, such as mixing concrete, but are too thick for jobs needing a sensitive touch.

FABRIC WITH VINYL GRIP

SUEDE GAUNTLETS

SUEDE AND FABRIC

COTTON FABRIC

Dibbers and widgers

A dibber is a pencil-shaped tool used for making planting holes. Use a small dibber to transplant seedlings or insert cuttings, a large one for transplanting vegetables such as leeks that require a wide hole to allow space for growth, and for planting through a plastic mulch. A widger, which is like a narrow spatula, is good for lifting seedlings and rooted cuttings with the minimum of root disturbance.

Garden lines

A garden line is mainly used in vegetable plots as a guide for forming straight rows, but is also invaluable

for other tasks, such as marking out areas when planning or designing, or forming a straight edge when planting up a hedge or constructing a wall or patio.

GARDEN LINE
Most garden lines have a pointed stake at either end for inserting into the ground. Grooves allow you to stretch a level line between the stakes.

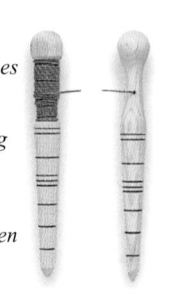

Sieves

Garden sieves generally have a mesh of 3–12mm (⅛–½in) and are used to separate out coarse material from soil or potting compost. Choose a sieve with a large mesh to remove twigs and stones from soil before sowing or planting; use one with a smaller mesh when covering fine seeds after sowing. Those with a wire-mesh tend to be more effective and durable than plastic ones.

WIRE-MESH SIEVE

SIEVE WITH FINE, PLASTIC MESH

Thermometers

The best type of thermometer for garden and greenhouse use is a minimum-maximum thermometer, because this records both the lowest and highest temperatures reached. A greenhouse thermometer together with a hygrometer, which measures air humidity, are useful to monitor conditions under glass. A soil thermometer outdoors is helpful in deciding when to sow seed.

MINIMUM-MAXIMUM THERMOMETER

GREENHOUSE THERMOMETER

Rain gauges

A rain gauge is used for measuring amounts of rainfall or irrigation; it is helpful for identifying areas of the garden that are affected by rain shadow. It should have clear markings and a smooth inside surface for easy cleaning. Many gauges have a short spike for inserting into the ground.

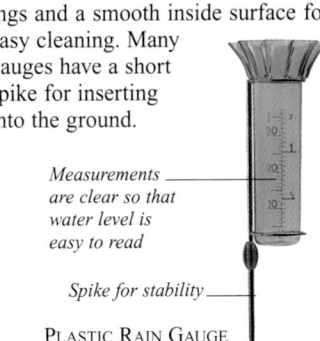

Measurements are clear so that water level is easy to read

Spike for stability

PLASTIC RAIN GAUGE

PLANTING AND SOWING TOOLS

SMALL DIBBER

WOODEN GARDEN DIBBER FOR OUTDOOR USE

BULB PLANTER

WIDGER

WHEELED SEED SOWER

METAL GARDEN DIBBER

Ties and supports

Ties are used for various purposes in the garden but in particular to secure a climbing, scrambling, or fragile plant; supports are needed to protect some plants from wind or rain. Ties must be secure without constricting the stem, and must be checked annually; use a light material such as twine or raffia on soft-stemmed plants.

General ties

Garden string or twine in 3-ply is adequate for most tying jobs. Raffia, which is good for binding joins after grafting and as a lightweight tie, and soft strings, such as jute fillis, may disintegrate after a year or so. Clear plastic tape is excellent for use in grafting; special rubber ties are also available. Tar-impregnated string or polypropylene twine is a reliable, weather-resistant tie.

Plastic-coated tying wire is strong and lasts for several years. It is good for fixing labels to training wires or trellis and for joining canes. It may come on a reel with a built-in cutter, which is convenient to use.

Plant rings

These are split rings of wire; plastic-covered rings are also available. Plant rings are designed to be opened and closed easily around a plant stem and its support. They are suitable for light jobs, such as attaching a house plant to a cane.

Labels and markers

Labels for garden use should be durable, weather-resistant, and large enough to contain all the information you want to note. Plastic labels are cheap and may be reused; if written on with pencil, they should remain legible for a season. Most plastic labels discolour gradually with age and become brittle, but they are ideal for labelling trays of seeds and cuttings. Looped labels and those with ties may be secured around the stem of a plant and are useful if labels at eye level are required.

For more permanent, water-resistant markers, use those coated with a black material; these are written on by scratching through to the white plastic beneath, but they cannot be marked with a new name. Aluminium labels, which are more expensive, will last almost indefinitely, but the lettering may have to be renewed every few years.

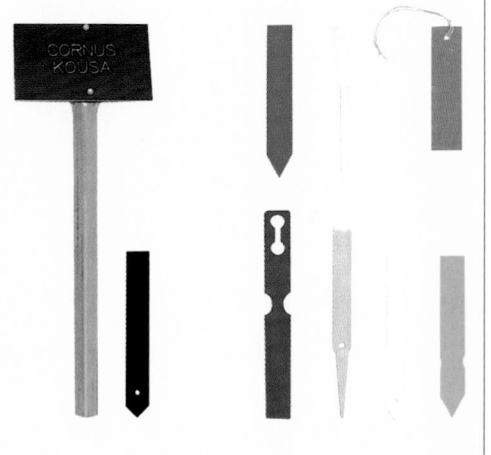

Tree ties

Rubber tree ties are strong, durable, and good for securing a young tree to a stake. They should be easily adjustable so that an expanding stem is not constricted. Select one with a buffer so that the stake does not chafe the stem, or use a padded tie in a figure-of-eight form (see also "Tree ties", p.65). Nail ties to the stakes.

Wall fixings

Purpose-designed plant stickers may be used for tasks such as securing the stem of a climber direct to a wall or other support. Lead-headed nails are stronger; they have a soft spur that may be bent over to fix stems and small branches to a wall.

Vine eyes hold stretched wires to which wall plants are then secured. On wall masonry, use flat vine eyes; for timber and wall plugs, screw in eyelet vine eyes.

Canes and stakes

Bamboo canes are excellent for supporting single-stemmed plants, but they eventually split and rot. More permanent and expensive are PVC stakes and plastic-covered steel rods. Support clumps of border plants with metal link or ring stakes (see PERENNIALS, "Staking", p.192). Trees and standard roses should be supported with sturdy, wooden stakes.

Netting

Netting is available in various materials and mesh sizes for a range of uses, such as supporting plants, protecting fruit from birds, and shading greenhouse plants (see "Shading", p.576). For plant support, choose a mesh of 5cm (2in) or more; it may be hard to disentangle plants from a smaller mesh. For plants such as sweet peas, thin, flexible plastic netting is adequate; heavier plants need semi-rigid plastic nets.

For fruit protection, use purpose-designed, plastic netting with a mesh of 1–2cm (½–¾in). Protect seedlings and winter vegetables from birds with 2.5cm (1in) mesh netting, or, if you are worried about bird safety, with cellulose-thread webbing, which repels not traps birds, and is biodegradable. Wire netting may be

placed around plants to provide protection from animals such as rabbits. It is also useful for reinforcing concrete when constructing a pond or trough. For general pest and weather protection. cover plants with a finely woven mesh sheet that is reusable.

Use windbreak netting to protect vulnerable plants in exposed sites (see *Windbreaks*, p.611). Knitted plastic netting may deteriorate in about four years, whereas moulded plastic should last at least twice as long. Windbreak webbing is even more long-lasting but very obtrusive.

NETTING

PLASTIC
NETTING
*Shade
netting*

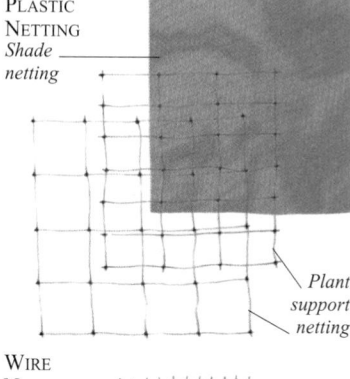

*Plant
support
netting*

WIRE
NETTING

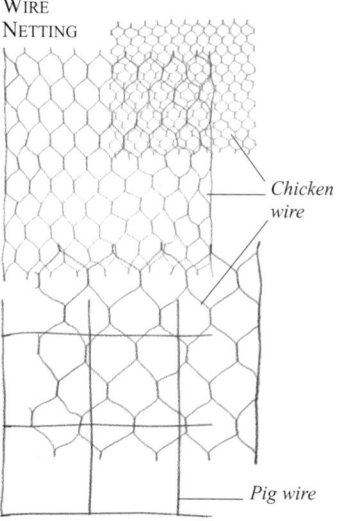

*Chicken
wire*

Pig wire

PLANT SUPPORTS AND TIES

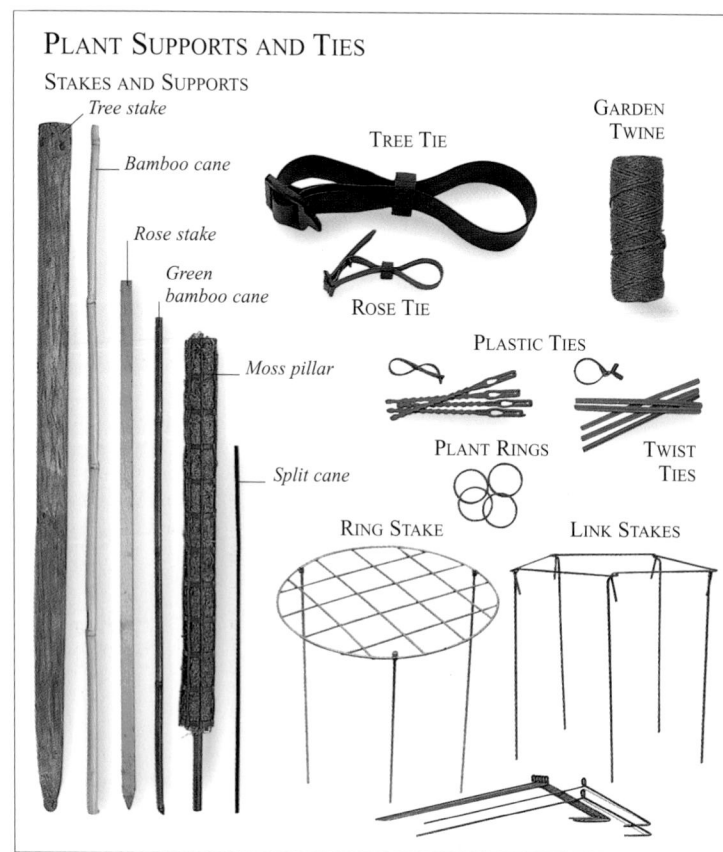

STAKES AND SUPPORTS
Tree stake
Bamboo cane
Rose stake
*Green
bamboo cane*
Moss pillar
Split cane

TREE TIE
ROSE TIE

GARDEN
TWINE

PLASTIC TIES
PLANT RINGS
TWIST
TIES

RING STAKE
LINK STAKES

WALL FIXINGS

FLAT VINE EYE

EYELET VINE EYE

LEAD-HEADED NAIL
WITH SPUR

Pots, trays, and growing media

Pots are available in a wide range of sizes but there are two basic shapes: round and square. Although round pots are traditional, square pots hold more compost for the same diameter; to save space use square pots, which pack neatly together. Round pots are classified by the inside diameter at the rim; square ones by the length of the rim along one side. Most pots have slightly sloping sides so that a plant and its root ball may be easily removed intact for repotting or planting out.

Pots are usually made of clay (terracotta) or plastic. Clay is traditional; plastic, however, is more common. Most plastic pots are manufactured from polypropylene, which deteriorates in cold weather. Pots made of a polypropylene and polythene mix do not become brittle in cold weather.

Standard pots are as deep as they are broad; they are the most common type of pot. Pans or seed pans are one third the depth of a standard pot of the same diameter. They are useful for germinating seeds. Half-pots are half to two thirds the depth of a standard pot of the same diameter. They are often used commercially for plants with relatively small root balls, such as evergreen azaleas. For very deep-rooted seedlings, sweet pea tubes or – for plants that will remain in the pot for some time – long Toms are used. Whalehide ring pots are designed to be used for the ring culture of tomatoes (see

SINGLE AND MULTI-CELLED SEED TRAYS
These are used for sowing seeds, inserting cuttings, or growing on young plants. Use a rigid, outer tray to hold flimsy, single-use modules containing plastic cells. Cells are useful for pricking out seedlings and sowing seeds singly.

POTS AND PANS
Pots and pans are used for cultivating plants both indoors and outside. The smaller pots, pans, and half-pots are suitable for propagating and growing on young plants.

Ornamental terracotta pots

Standard pots

Half-pot

Large standard pot

Seed pan

Pans

Seed, seedling, and cutting pots

p.528) in greenhouses. Other containers designed for specific uses include lattice pots with mesh sides, which can be used for aquatic plants.

Degradable pots and pellets
These are good for plants that resent root disturbance, because they can be planted out into the bed. The plants' roots grow through the sides and base of the pots into the surrounding ground. They are generally made from compressed peat and various other fibres (often sphagnum moss and wood fibre, sometimes impregnated with plant food).

Peat pellets are good for seeds and for rooting cuttings and must be expanded with water before being

used. Many gardeners create their own degradable pots from cones made from double-thickness newspaper.

Seed trays
Traditional, wooden seed trays have largely been replaced by plastic ones, which are easier to clean but often more fragile. Very thin plastic trays are cheap and flexible but are unlikely to last more than a season. Strong plastics are more rigid and expensive; they may become brittle and split with age but, if stored out of sunlight when not in use, they should last for several years.

Module trays
Multi-celled, or module, seed trays are particularly good for seedlings such as peas and broad beans that hate being pricked out. The tapered sides to each cell allow young plants to be transplanted with only minimal damage to their fragile roots, so they establish quickly in their new surroundings. Module trays are available in plastic, polystyrene, and biodegradable paper, and in a wide range of cell sizes and numbers, from four to several hundred.

Growing media
When sowing seed and rooting cuttings, a higher success rate is achieved using propagation composts.

Standard seed compost
Fine seed needs good contact with the compost to germinate and should be sown in purpose-made seed compost, which is fine-textured, moisture-retentive, and low in nutrients, as salts may damage seedlings.

Standard seed compost (based on the John Innes formula) is made using 2 parts (by volume) sterilized loam, 1 part peat substitute (or peat), and 1 part sand. To each cubic metre is added 1.2kg superphosphate of lime and 600g ground limestone (2lb and 1lb respectively for a cubic yard).

Standard cuttings compost
Compost mixes for rooting cuttings are free-draining and intended for use in high-humidity environments. They may be based on bark, perlite, or mixes containing a high percentage of coarse sand. Cuttings composts are low in nutrients, so cuttings need feeding once rooted.

A standard cuttings compost typically contains 50:50 sand and peat substitute (or peat). To each cubic metre (yard) is added 4.4kg (7½lb) dolomitic lime; 1.5kg (2½lb) each of hoof and horn or dried blood, superphosphate of lime, and calcium carbonate; and 150g (4oz) each of potassium nitrate and potassium sulphate. A specialist micro-nutrient fertilizer should also be added.

Inert growing media
Sterile inert growing materials do not harbour the potential pest and disease problems associated with soil-based or loamless potting composts. Some of the most popular are rockwool, perlite, vermiculite, and clay granules (see also "Hydroculture", p.375).

LONG TOM
This pot suits deep-rooted plants that would be restricted by a standard pot.

WHALEHIDE RING POT
This bottomless pot for ring culture holds the potting compost over the aggregate.

SWEET PEA TUBES
These are excellent for seedlings that quickly develop long root systems.

BULB BASKET
Such a basket protects bulbs from animals and is also easy to lift after flowering.

BIODEGRADABLE POTS
Use for propagating plants that resent root disturbance when transplanted.

LATTICE POT
This pot for aquatics lets in water, but should be lined with hessian to retain soil.

2
GREENHOUSES
AND FRAMES

MANY PEOPLE RESIST the idea of installing a greenhouse in the mistaken belief that it is expensive or requires detailed gardening knowledge to maintain and use properly. This is not the case. The rewards of gardening under cover more than compensate for the initial cost and effort and open up a whole new world of gardening pleasures. As well as being an all-weather space for tasks that crop up throughout the year, a greenhouse can be a cost-effective investment, allowing you to propagate plants for the garden at little cost. Even if you have a small plot you will be able to find a compact model to suit; or you could consider installing a cold frame – smaller in scale but a great boon to practical gardening.

Gardening under cover

Greenhouses, cold frames, and cloches are useful additions to any garden and are available in an extensive range of sizes to fit whatever space is available. Each type of structure has a distinctive function but they are usually used in conjunction with each other. The most productive gardens use all three.

Unheated structures

Unheated greenhouses are used primarily to advance or extend the growing season of hardy and half-hardy plants. Cold frames fulfil a similar function, although they are also often used for hardening off plants that have been propagated in a greenhouse and for storing "resting plants". Cloches are used *in situ* over plants in the garden itself.

Heated structures

A heated greenhouse is far more versatile than either an unheated greenhouse or a cold frame, and allows a much greater range of plants to be grown. These include many frost-tender species that do not grow satisfactorily in temperate or cold climates without protection. In addition, a heated greenhouse provides a suitable environment in which to propagate plants.

GREENHOUSE STYLE
This traditional-style greenhouse is an integral part of the garden, which extends right up to the sides of the greenhouse. The hedges and trees provide shelter but are not close enough to reduce light penetration significantly. The timber framework will need to be treated every year or so with wood preservative to give weather resistance but otherwise only minimal maintenance is required.

ELEGANT DESIGN
Greenhouses with plastic-covered frames can be extremely attractive, as well as functional. This one is a decorative garden feature in its own right.

Siting the greenhouse

An amateur greenhouse is best positioned so that it blends in with the overall garden design. It should also be positioned in a sheltered site but where enough light is available for the plants to grow and thrive: too much shade will limit the range of plants that may be grown easily, whereas an exposed site will make the greenhouse expensive to heat or may mean that the plants are not adequately protected on cold nights.

Early planning
It is always worth spending the time to make sure that you have chosen the right spot before buying a greenhouse. If possible, make detailed notes in winter or spring of where shadows are cast in the garden by

POSITIONING THE GREENHOUSE

If the greenhouse is used mostly in the summer, its longer axis should run north to south. If good light in spring is a priority, however – when the sun is lower in the sky – orient the greenhouse east to west to make the best use of available light.

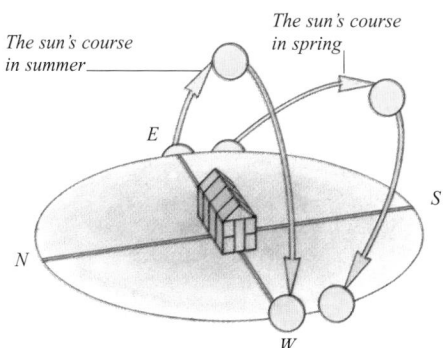

The sun's course in summer
The sun's course in spring
E
N
S
W

houses and any neighbouring garages, trees, or other large, nearby features, so that you do not site a greenhouse where it will be in shade for more than a few hours each day. Orienting the greenhouse north–south by its longer axis makes the best use of light in summer. For raising plants in spring, or overwintering tender specimens, an east–west orientation provides good light for much of the day.

If there is a possibility that you will want to extend the greenhouse later, or build a second, smaller one, allow enough space on the site.

Free-standing greenhouse
The best place to site a free-standing greenhouse is in a sheltered, light area away from buildings and large trees. If the site is high or exposed, choose a position that is sheltered by a hedge that acts as a windbreak, or build a fence or other screen. Windbreaks should not cast too much shade onto the greenhouse itself, however; they need not be tall – a 2.5m (8ft) hedge provides shelter for a distance of 12m (40ft) or more.

Do not position a free-standing greenhouse near or between buildings, since this could create a wind funnel effect that may damage the greenhouse and the plants inside. Positions at the bottom of a slope or near walls, hedges, or fences on the side of a slope should not be used to site a greenhouse because cold air may become trapped there (see CLIMATE AND THE GARDEN, "Frost pockets and frost damage", p.607).

Lean-to greenhouse
Place a lean-to greenhouse against a wall that receives a mixture of sun and shade. Do not site it where there is sun for most of the day, otherwise the greenhouse may overheat in summer, even with shading and a good ventilation system.

Access
Bear in mind the need for easy access. A site that is reasonably close to the house is preferable to one at a distance. Also make sure that there is a clear area in front of the greenhouse door for loading and unloading. Any paths leading to the greenhouse should be level. They should preferably have a hard, resilient surface and be wide enough to accommodate a wheelbarrow.

Mains services
Choose a site that will be convenient for mains water and electricity connection, if these services are needed. Although electricity is not essential for heating, it is useful for lighting as well as for some thermostatic controls and timing switches. A mains water connection makes watering plants more convenient, especially if an automatic system is used, and reduces the need to trail lengths of hose around the garden.

CHOOSING THE SITE

An open but sheltered site is best for a greenhouse – it should not be positioned in the path of a wind funnel. If there is no natural protection from the wind, construct a windbreak.

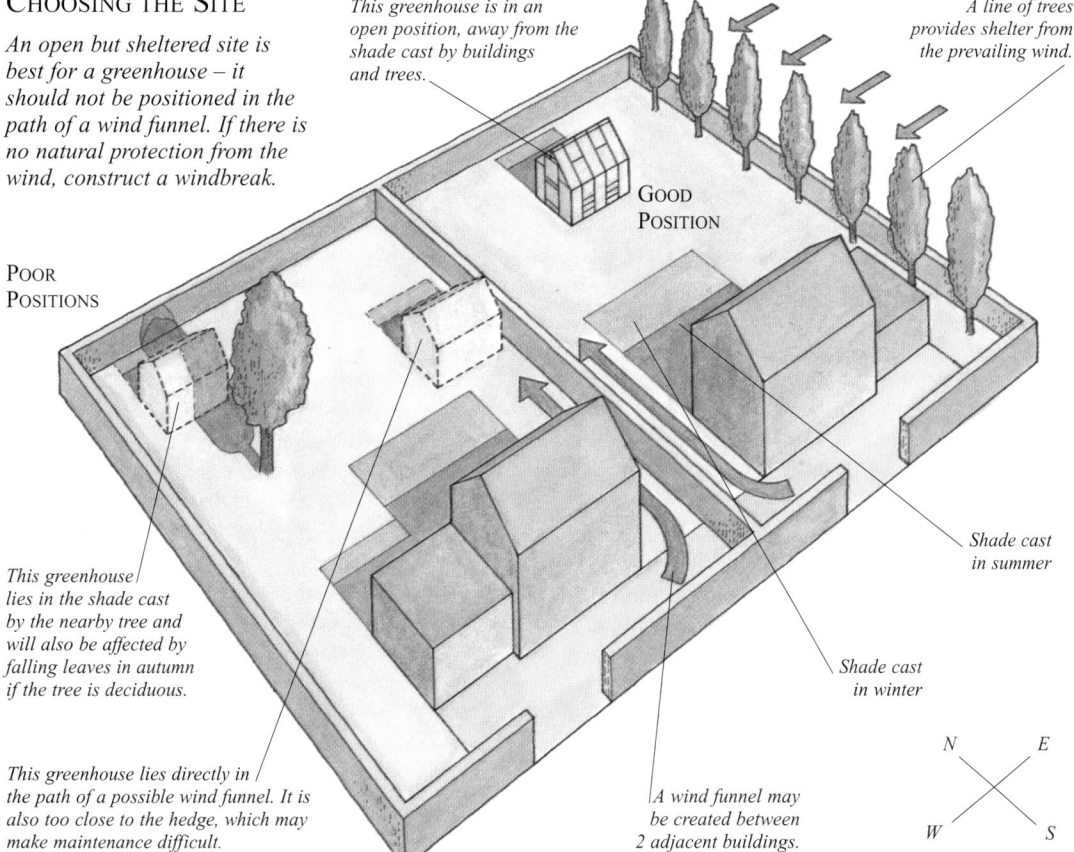

This greenhouse is in an open position, away from the shade cast by buildings and trees.

A line of trees provides shelter from the prevailing wind.

GOOD POSITION

POOR POSITIONS

This greenhouse lies in the shade cast by the nearby tree and will also be affected by falling leaves in autumn if the tree is deciduous.

This greenhouse lies directly in the path of a possible wind funnel. It is also too close to the hedge, which may make maintenance difficult.

A wind funnel may be created between 2 adjacent buildings.

Shade cast in summer

Shade cast in winter

N E
W S

Choosing a greenhouse

Before buying a greenhouse, consider carefully how it will be used in order to select the most suitable style, size, and materials – a greenhouse that is used as a garden room, for example, will differ significantly from one that is purely functional. If growing tropical and subtropical plants, an attractively shaped greenhouse, perhaps with room for central staging, might enhance the floral display.

Many different styles of greenhouse are available. Some make best use of space or provide optimum ventilation; others conserve heat well or allow better light penetration. When priorities have been decided, the final choice of style will depend on personal preference.

Conventional greenhouses

The more conventional types of greenhouse are suitable for a wide range of plants and include traditional span, Dutch light, three-quarter span, lean-to, and Mansard (or curvilinear) greenhouses. All of

TRADITIONAL SPAN

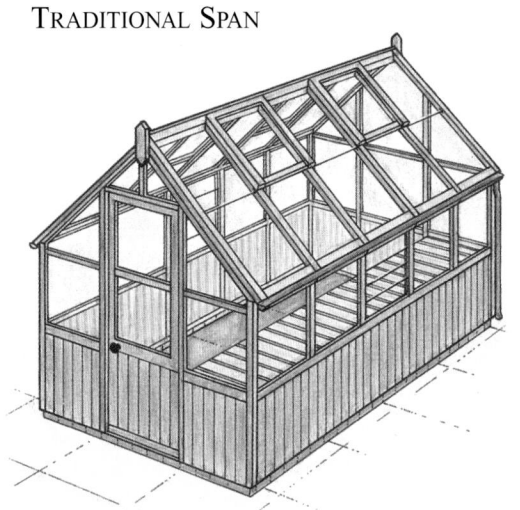

DUTCH LIGHT

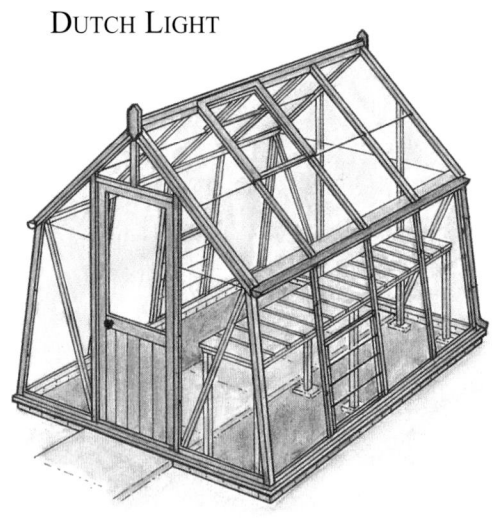

these may have an aluminium or timber framework, and either all-glass or part-solid walls (except Dutch light greenhouses). Conventional greenhouses also have a wide range of compatible accessories, including staging and shelves.

Traditional span
The vertical sides and even span roof of a traditional span greenhouse are extremely practical in terms of

growing space and headroom. For raising seedlings and growing border crops, a traditional span greenhouse is likely to provide the best use of space for the least cost.

Dutch light
The sloping sides of Dutch light greenhouses are designed to allow in maximum light, so these greenhouses are suitable for border crops, especially low-growing ones such

as lettuces. The large sheets of glass are expensive to replace because of the size – the traditional dimensions are 145 x 77cm (59 x 30¾in). The glass panes slide into the frame and are secured using cleats fixed with galvanized nails.

The panes of glass on the roof overlap slightly to keep out rain and increase rigidity. This may cause loss of heat, however, if the panes overlap too loosely.

THREE-QUARTER SPAN

LEAN-TO

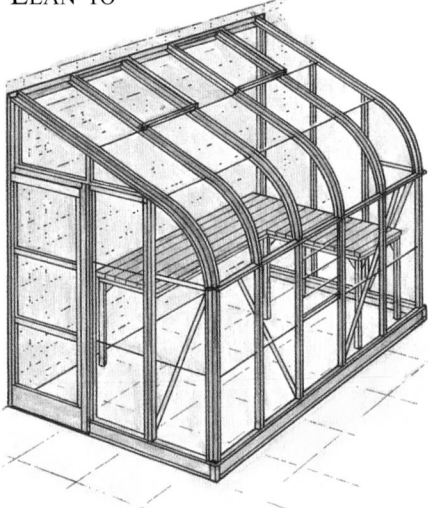

MANSARD

Three-quarter span
A three-quarter span greenhouse is positioned with one of its sides against a wall. Light is a little more restricted than in a free-standing model, so this type of greenhouse is best positioned beside a sunny wall, although this may mean that extra shading is required in summer. The wall provides extra warmth and insulation in the greenhouse, especially if it is a house wall (see also "Lean-to", right).

Lean-to
Where there is insufficient space for a free-standing structure, a lean-to greenhouse is an invaluable choice, particularly if a mainly decorative show-house is favoured.

Many are similar in appearance to conservatories, and may be used as garden rooms. Installing electricity, mains gas, or a water supply in a lean-to that is adjacent to a house wall is cheaper and generally involves less work than laying cables

or pipes to a greenhouse that is some distance from the house. In addition, the warmth of the house wall may reduce the level of heating required; brick walls store heat, from both the sun (especially if the wall is south-facing) and the domestic heating system, which is then released into the greenhouse.

The brick wall also provides good insulation, so that less heat escapes from a lean-to than from many other types of greenhouse.

Mansard
The Mansard (curvilinear) greenhouse has slanting sides and roof panels that are designed to allow maximum entry of available light. The full benefit is gained only in an open position with no shade from surrounding buildings or trees. A Mansard greenhouse is suitable for plants that need maximum light during the winter, when daylight hours are short and light levels are also frequently low.

DOME-SHAPED

POLYGONAL

ALPINE HOUSE

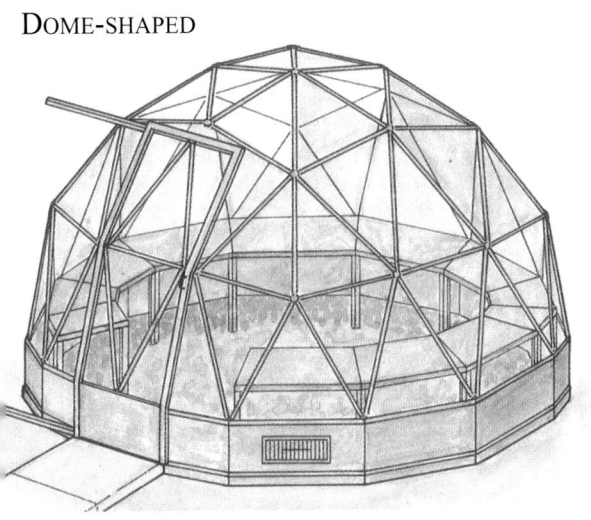

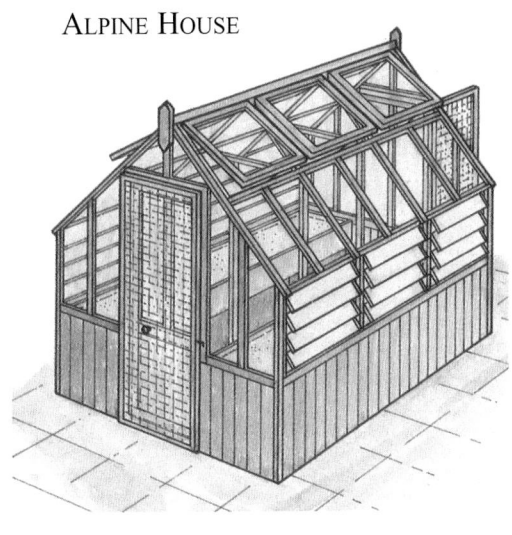

Specialist greenhouses

There are many specialist types of greenhouse, including dome-shaped, polygonal, alpine house, conservation, mini, and "polytunnel", all of which differ markedly in appearance from the more conventional types. Some are designed as highly decorative garden features in their own right, while others may offer particularly good value for money or be for specific types of plant.

Dome-shaped
This is an elegant design that is particularly useful in exposed positions as it is stable and offers less wind resistance than traditional greenhouses. Light transmission is excellent because the multi-angled glass panes and aluminium frame allow maximum light transmission. Dome-shaped structures may have limited headroom around the edge, and plants may also be difficult to reach. Extensions are not generally available and fittings may be limited to those produced by the manufacturer.

Polygonal
Octagonal and other polygonal greenhouses are frequently chosen where appearance is important, and may provide a focal point within the garden. They are generally more expensive than traditional greenhouses of similar size and, because they are not very common, there may be a limited choice of accessories. The irregular shape may also restrict growing space. Fitting replacement panes of glass in a polygonal greenhouse is more difficult than in a conventional structure.

Alpine house
This type of greenhouse is traditionally timber-framed with louvre vents extending all along the sides for the most effective ventilation. Usually, alpine houses are not heated and are closed only in the coldest winter weather, so insulation is not required. Unsuitable for tender plants, they are used for plants that thrive in bright, well-ventilated conditions, yet which require some overhead protection from dampness and rain. Their shape is similar to that of a traditional span greenhouse.

CONSERVATION

MINI

POLYTUNNEL

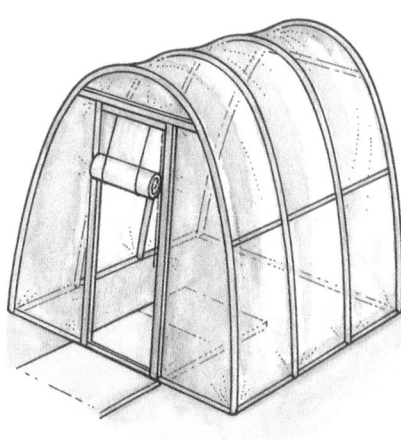

Conservation greenhouse
This type of greenhouse has many special features that are designed to save as much energy as possible. It is therefore usually more expensive than other types of greenhouse of similar size. The roof panels are angled to allow optimum light penetration, and mirrored surfaces are also used to reflect light within the greenhouse itself. Plastic double glazing and purpose-made insulation are fitted as standard.

Mini-greenhouse
These useful, low-cost greenhouses are good for a limited space, as they are available in various heights, widths, and depths. There are also free-standing and wheeled versions. A mini-greenhouse is the best choice if only a small number of plants is to be grown. It is covered with glass or plastic and is usually aluminium framed. It should preferably face south–east or south–west so that maximum light penetrates. The staging is available in a range of depths and movable heights. Access may be a problem – all work has to be done from the outside. Rapid temperature changes often occur, so fit a louvre vent if available. Shading in summer is also essential if plants are not to scorch.

Plastic "polytunnel" greenhouse
Where visual appearance is not important and low-cost protection is required – such as in the vegetable plot – a "polytunnel" greenhouse has many benefits. It comprises a large, tunnel-shaped frame covered with heavy-duty transparent plastic sheets and is widely used for crops that require some protection but not the warm conditions of a traditional greenhouse. Polytunnels keep out the worst of the winter cold and provide useful wind protection throughout the year. Since they are light and relatively easy to move, they are often used in plots where crop rotation is carried out.

For a very large growing area, commercial polytunnels are a cost-effective investment, but for a small garden a more traditional shape may be a better choice. A few polytunnels include some staging, although most are intended primarily for growing crops at ground level, planted either directly into the soil, in pots, or in growing bags.

Ventilation may be a problem: the door offers a reasonably efficient method of ventilation – especially in large tunnels with openings at each end – and some have sides that roll up. The plastic sheeting may need to be replaced every few years – it will gradually become opaque, restricting light penetration.

Choosing the size

A greenhouse will almost inevitably seem too small once it is filled with plants so, if possible, buy one that may be extended. Although a large greenhouse costs more to heat than a small one, it is possible to partition off a section in winter, and leave the remainder unheated (see "Thermal screens", p.574).

Space considerations

A greenhouse that is used primarily for ornamentals should have plenty of room inside for staging, which may be tiered, and possibly a central or end display. To provide space for propagation and growing on, it may be necessary to divide up the space with a partition. Alternatively, use a cold frame for propagation.

Length, width, and height

A length of 2.5m (8ft) and a width of 2m (6ft) are the minimum, practical dimensions for a general-purpose, traditional greenhouse. A smaller greenhouse than this limits the range of plants that may be grown, and may make it difficult to control the environment – draughts and rapid heat build-up in summer tend to be more of a problem in small greenhouses, and may lead to sudden fluctuations in temperature. In greenhouses that are more than 2m (6ft) wide, it may also be difficult to reach pots and ventilation towards the back of the staging. Staging to a width of 60cm (2ft) on either side allows a path of the same width down the middle.

If border crops are to be grown, choose a greenhouse that is 2.5m (8ft) wide with borders to a width of 1m (3ft). A width of 2.5m (8ft) is also suitable if a wider path is required for a wheelchair or to enable a wheelbarrow to be used easily.

Many small greenhouses have low eaves and comparatively low ridges, which make it tiring to work over the border or staging for long periods. To gain more height, build the greenhouse on a brick base or dig out a sunken path.

Choosing the materials

Greenhouses are made in a range of materials. The most important considerations when choosing both the framework and glazing for the greenhouse are practicality, expense, and the amount of maintenance required. The appearance of the materials may also be important.

BUYING A GREENHOUSE

Before buying a greenhouse, use the following as a checklist; it may save disappointment later.

Ridge height should be at least 2.1m (6½ft); remember to allow for roof ventilator openings protruding.

Roof ventilators are usually inadequate as supplied – the total ventilation area should equal one sixth of the floor area. Extra ventilators may be needed.

Glass should be easy to replace; use panes of a standard size – 60cm (24in) square or 60 x 45cm (24 x 18in). The large panes of Dutch light greenhouses are expensive to replace. Consider double-glazing if high temperatures are to be maintained, although this adds considerably to the cost.

Cross bracing on aluminium alloy greenhouses must be strong enough to make the structure rigid.

Doors may be hinged or sliding. They must be wide enough: 60cm (24in) is the minimum practical width. For wheelchair or wheelbarrow access they should be wider and without a "lip". Sliding doors are easily adjusted for ventilation and are less likely to slam in wind than hinged doors. Check that doors are a good fit when closed, otherwise they may let in draughts.

Eaves height affects the headroom – it should be at least 1.3m (4½ft) for ease of working.

Use ground anchors if the structure is not secured to a brick base.

A kick panel at the foot of the door minimizes the risk of breaking the glass panel.

Gutters and downpipes reduce the risk of water cascading from the roof and damaging the plants nearby.

A base may be an optional extra – bear this in mind when comparing prices since most timber-framed greenhouses need one. Some have a step that makes wheelchair access and use of a wheelbarrow difficult.

Use base cladding to reduce heat loss in the winter, unless border crops are to be grown.

Side ventilators allow free circulation of air. Louvre windows must close tightly to minimize heat loss in cold weather.

The framework

Timber frameworks have been the traditional choice and are generally considered to be the most attractive. They tend to be expensive, however, and are also heavy to construct. If possible, choose a durable wood. Always look for a manufacturer that offers hardwood frames made from renewable sources. A quality greenhouse will be rot-resistant, will not warp easily, and, if treated every year or two with special wood preparation, will retain its colour well.

Greenhouses constructed with redwood and deal are cheaper than those described as "cedar". Before being assembled, they should be pressure-treated with preservative; they also require regular painting to prevent rotting (see also "Timber framework", p.583).

Greenhouses with aluminium alloy frames are almost completely

CONSTRUCTION MATERIALS

TIMBER
A timber frame is the traditional choice for garden greenhouses. Hardwoods are low maintenance.

ALUMINIUM
Aluminium alloy frames are light but extremely sturdy and need only minimum maintenance.

STEEL
Plastic-coated, steel frames are very strong but must be treated regularly to prevent rust.

maintenance-free. They do not retain heat quite as well as timber frames but the difference is minimal.

Galvanized steel is also often used for greenhouse frames. Steel frames are light and easy to construct but extremely strong. They are cheaper than timber or aluminium frames but must be painted regularly (see "Metal framework", p.583).

Aluminium and steel frames are narrower than timber ones and allow larger panes of glass to be used, resulting in better light penetration.

Glass panes

Horticultural glass is the most satisfactory glazing material for a greenhouse: it allows excellent light penetration but is thinner and less expensive than ordinary glass. It is easy to clean, does not discolour, and retains considerably more heat than plastic glazing materials. Glass is not as robust as plastic glazing, however, so breakages and cracks may be a problem, since the panes must be replaced quickly.

Plastic glazing

Plastics are generally more expensive and less durable than glass; they discolour more readily and also tend to become scratched over time, which is both unsightly and, more importantly, may cut down on the amount of light that is transmitted if the discoloring is severe.

Acrylic sheets are used to glaze the curved eaves of many greenhouses because the acrylic may be shaped easily to give an elegant outline to the structure. Condensation occurs more readily on its surface than on a conventional glass pane. Rigid polycarbonate sheets are also often used to glaze greenhouses. They are easy to handle, lightweight, virtually unbreakable, and have good insulating properties. They are relatively easily scratched, however, and tend to discolour.

Twin-walled polycarbonate has particularly good insulating qualities, but its opacity may be a major problem in a greenhouse.

Sizing

Most local glass merchants will cut glass panes to size for little cost. It is important to make sure that any measurements you give are accurate; calculate them carefully, ensuring that there will be sufficient clearance for the glass to engage with the mounting system that is to be used.

GLAZING MATERIAL

Rigid plastic glazing material is light and easy to fit. This is twin-walled polycarbonate, which provides good insulation.

If plastic glazing material is used it will be supplied in sheets and is not usually difficult to cut to size at home using a sharp craft knife and straight edge.

Erecting the greenhouse

A greenhouse requires far less maintenance and lasts much longer if it is properly erected in the first place. The information listed below is necessarily of a general nature, because it applies to many different greenhouse types and designs: always follow the manufacturer's instructions for particular advice. If in doubt on any point, check the details with either the supplier or the greenhouse manufacturer.

Some manufacturers that supply by mail order also erect greenhouses, if required, but usually expect the ground to be levelled beforehand and any brick base (see below) to be prepared in advance.

Preparing the site

Always erect a greenhouse on firm, level ground, otherwise the frame may warp and become twisted and cause the glass to crack. The chosen site must first be cleared of weeds, since persistent weeds are very difficult to eradicate when the greenhouse is erected and in position. If the site selected for the greenhouse has been recently dug over, allow the soil to settle for a few weeks, and then consolidate it with a heavy roller.

Foundations

Aluminium greenhouses that are smaller than 2m wide and 2.5m long (6 x 8ft) do not usually require a thick concrete base. Simply dig a hole at each corner approximately 25–45cm (10–18in) deep, then wedge in the ground anchors (see p.572) with rubble and pour in a concrete mix to fix them securely.

If a more substantial foundation is required, dig a trench approximately 25cm (10in) deep, filling it with 15cm (6in) of consolidated hardcore. Fix the anchoring bolts in place and finish off with poured concrete or paving slabs, making sure that the ground is level.

Brick bases

A brick base must be constructed to the precise measurements provided by the greenhouse manufacturer, on solid concrete footings approximately 13cm (5in) deep (see *How to Make a Concrete Footing*, p.596). The finished level of the footings should be at or below soil level.

Wooden greenhouses

The sections of a wooden greenhouse are usually supplied complete and only need to be bolted together and then fixed to the base.

Base

Interlocking concrete blocks may be used for the base, otherwise a solid concrete foundation or brick base should be built (see "Foundations" and "Brick bases", above).

Sides, gable ends, and roof

Before the greenhouse is delivered, check what kind of bolts or fixings are required and whether they will be supplied. First bolt the sides and gable ends together to form the main framework. Follow the manufacturer's advice for the exact method of fixing this to the base or foundations, as designs vary. The foot of the frame may contain integral anchorage points for securely bolting it down. Bolt any internal partitions to the frame, then add the roof sections and bolt them in place.

Some wooden greenhouses are supplied as sections with unglazed frames, with the glass or plastic glazing supplied separately. Others have pre-glazed frames but these are heavy to move – two or more people may be required to support them.

If the timber has not been treated and is not rot-resistant, it is important to paint all the woodwork with a preservative at this stage, before the greenhouse is glazed.

BUILDING A BRICK BASE

If using a brick base for the greenhouse, build it in advance, and lay proper foundations first. Check with the greenhouse manufacturer before building the base to make sure that the dimensions are correct.

Glazing

If putty is to be used for glazing it is usually supplied with the greenhouse. Apply it to the glazing bars, and bed-in the glass carefully. The glass panes are usually secured in place with galvanized steel or brass sprigs; if these are not supplied, they may be purchased from any hardware shop.

If a dry glazing system (that is, one that does not require putty) is to be used, simply follow the supplier's instructions.

Whichever method is used, glaze the sides and gable ends first, overlapping the panes by 1cm (½in). Use soft metal overlap clips to hold the glass panes firmly together.

CONCRETE FOUNDATIONS

For solid greenhouse foundations, dig a trench to match the dimensions of the greenhouse, filling it with hardcore and a layer of concrete.

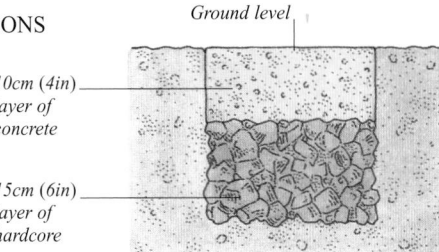

Ground level

10cm (4in) layer of concrete

15cm (6in) layer of hardcore

GLAZING BARS AND CLIPS FOR METAL GREENHOUSES

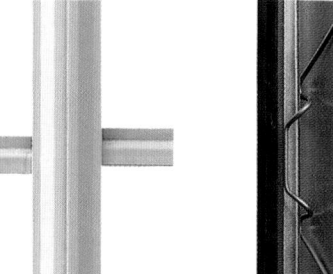
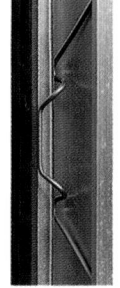

GLAZING BARS
These form the framework of the greenhouse.

"W"-SHAPED WIRE CLIP
Use this type of clip to hold glass and plastic panes firmly in place.

SPRUNG BAND CLIPS
An alternative clip, these fix onto the frame.

Ventilators and door

Ventilators are supplied as an integral part of the pre-assembled sections, so the number you ordered should be in place. Screw on hinged doors and simply insert sliding doors into the runners.

Metal greenhouses

Greenhouses with metal frames are delivered in home-assembly kit form, and the frame is supplied in sections – the base, sides, gable ends, and roof. The sections are in turn divided into separate component pieces that need to be bolted together.

Base

Assemble the base first, ensuring that it is perfectly level and square to prevent any warping and twisting of the frame; measure from each corner to the one diagonally opposite – the measurements must be the same. The base must be securely anchored; this is particularly important in windy or exposed areas.

If fixing ground anchors to a concrete foundation, use the anchoring

A GROUND ANCHOR

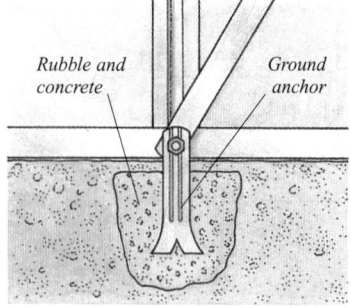

Rubble and concrete

Ground anchor

Small greenhouses may be secured using ground anchors. Wedge them in place with rubble first before pouring in a concrete mix.

bolts provided, otherwise simply set the ground anchors in rubble and concrete at each corner of the base.

Sides, gable ends, and roof

Assemble the sides, gable ends, and roof sections in the sequence recommended by the manufacturer in the instruction sheet. The sides are usually put together first.

First make sure that everything has been included, as listed by the kit contents list, then before assembly lay out on the ground all the pieces for each section, in their correct relative positions. Bolt the pieces for each section (sides and gable ends) together. Decide at this point where the vents are to be positioned and leave suitable gaps for them, as necessary. Do not fully tighten the nuts until all the sections are assembled and have been loosely put together.

Bolt the sections together one to another, and then to the base, then bolt on the roof bars and ridge bar.

Ventilators

Ventilator frames are assembled separately, then bolted onto the roof and sides as required, before glazing. This gives greater flexibility than with wooden greenhouses when choosing both the number and position of ventilators. The hinges of roof ventilators usually slide in a groove in the moulding.

Glazing

Glazing strips are usually used for metal greenhouses. Cut the strips to the appropriate length and then press them into the grooves in the glazing bars – shaped pieces of metal that form the framework to hold the glass securely in position.

Glaze the sides of the greenhouse first, placing the glass squarely between the glazing bars, leaving about 3mm (⅛in) clearance on each

Installing electricity, gas, and water

Installing an outdoor power supply is not a job for the amateur. The installation of electricity in a greenhouse must be properly carried out by a qualified electrician, although considerable savings may be made by excavating the trench for the cable yourself and then refilling it later when the job is completed. Alternatively, the cable may be run overhead if your greenhouse is close to the house and it will not be unsightly; your electrician will be able to advise you on whether or not this is a practical option. Armoured cable and water-proof fittings should always be used for safety.

Electricity has many practical uses in the greenhouse: it provides power for heating, lighting, propagators, timers, soil-warming cables, and electrically powered garden tools of various types.

Mains gas is useful for heating the greenhouse, although mains gas heaters are less widely available than bottled gas heaters. Consult an approved fitter to discuss the feasibility and cost of laying on mains gas. Again, you can save money by offering to do the spadework yourself.

If you already have an outdoor water tap, you may be able to take a spur from this and run it to the greenhouse. The pipe must be buried below frost level – at least 30cm (12in) deep – and the above-ground parts should be very well lagged. In the UK, it is essential that an anti-siphoning device is incorporated in order to meet legal requirements.

side of the glass panes for the glazing clips to be attached. The upper panes of glass should overlap the lower ones by about 1cm (½in). Secure them with overlap glazing clips – pieces of metal bent into "S" shapes that hook over the lower pane and hold the upper one firmly in position.

Once each pane is in position, use glazing clips, pressing them into place between the glazing bars and panes to hold the glass. A little pressure will be required to overcome the natural spring in the metal.

Glaze the gable ends of the greenhouse and then the roof, using the same technique.

Fitting the door

Metal greenhouses usually have sliding doors. These should be bolted together and slid into the runners provided in the end frame. A stop is supplied for bolting on afterwards to prevent the door from coming off the runners if it is opened too quickly. The door should be glazed when it has been fixed in position.

Fitting the staging

The staging supplied by the manufacturer is designed to be bolted or screwed to the framework. This is best done at the same time as the greenhouse is erected, if possible, especially for octagonal and dome-shaped greenhouses, which have staging specially designed to fit. If solid staging is used, leave a gap several inches wide between the inside of the greenhouse and the staging, to allow free air circulation.

FITTING A PANE IN A METAL GREENHOUSE

Attach overlap glazing clips to the base pane. Wearing gloves, lift the pane into place, gently pressing the top edge into position before hooking the bottom edge onto the lower pane. Secure the pane with glazing clips (see inset), pressing them gently until they slot into position.

Creating the right environment

Creating the right balance of conditions in a greenhouse to suit the plants grown there is the essence of successful greenhouse gardening.

For tender plants, the temperature maintained is vital. In a heated greenhouse, choose an efficient, reliable, and economic heater. In any greenhouse, good insulation to retain heat and keep out draughts must be balanced with the need for thorough ventilation. Shading is essential in most greenhouses during the summer to help prevent the plants from overheating; see PRINCIPLES OF PROPAGATION, *Shading Greenhouses* (*Temperate climates*), p.636.

Atmospheric humidity should be kept at a level that suits the plants being grown. Automatic methods of watering tend to increase humidity so, for most plants, special humidifiers may not be essential. Special lighting is often useful to increase the growth potential of plants.

Greenhouse temperature

The choice of plants to be grown in a greenhouse is determined largely by the temperature at which it is maintained (see "The greenhouse environment", p.359). There are four categories of greenhouse: cold, cool, temperate, and warm. The environment is controlled slightly differently in each type.

Cold

A cold greenhouse is not heated at all. Insulation (see p.574) is needed to keep out the worst of the winter cold and some form of shading (see p.576) is needed in summer. Thorough ventilation (see p.575) is important all year round.

A cold greenhouse may be used to grow summer crops, to overwinter slightly tender plants, or to propagate cuttings (although a propagator will increase the success rate, see p.580). An unheated greenhouse may also permit an early display of hardy plants and many types of spring bulb.

An unheated greenhouse is suitable for alpines – some are specifically designed to provide maximum ventilation for this type of plant (see "Alpine house", p.589), although any greenhouse with louvre ventilators along the sides is adequate.

Cool/frost-free

A cool greenhouse is one that is heated just enough to keep out frost. This means that a minimum daytime temperature range between 5°C (41°F) and 10°C (50°F), and a night-time temperature of no less than 2°C (36°F), is needed.

To ensure that these temperatures are maintained, a heater capable of a large temperature lift is a necessity in winter, in case the outside temperature falls many degrees below freezing. An electric heater with a thermostat (see p.574) is most likely to do this efficiently.

Insulation, thorough ventilation, and shading control are necessary, as with cold greenhouses.

A frost-free greenhouse may be used to grow all the types of plant mentioned for cold greenhouses. In addition, frost-tender plants may be overwintered, and summer crops or flowering pot plants grown. A propagator will be needed for germinating seeds. Young seedlings will benefit from the extra light provided by a growing lamp (see p.577).

Temperate

A slightly warmer greenhouse with a minimum daytime temperature range between 10°C (50°F) and 13°C (55°F), and with a minimum night-time temperature of 7°C (45°F), is suitable for growing a good selection of hardy, half-hardy, and tender pot plants, as well as vegetables.

Additional warmth is necessary in spring for propagation, supplied by a propagator or by boosting the ordinary heating for the required period. Supplementary lighting provided by a growing lamp is useful. Shading and good ventilation are required, especially in summer.

Warm

A warm greenhouse has a daytime temperature range between 13°C (55°C) and 18°C (64°F), with a minimum night-time temperature of 13°C (55°F). Such high temperatures enable an amateur gardener to grow a large range of plants, including

tropical and subtropical ornamentals, fruits, and vegetables. A warm greenhouse may also be used for propagating plants and raising seedlings without the aid of propagation equipment, although a growing lamp will be useful.

In hot weather very good ventilation, preferably automatic, an efficient method of shading, and high humidity (see p.576) are essential.

THE "GREENHOUSE EFFECT"

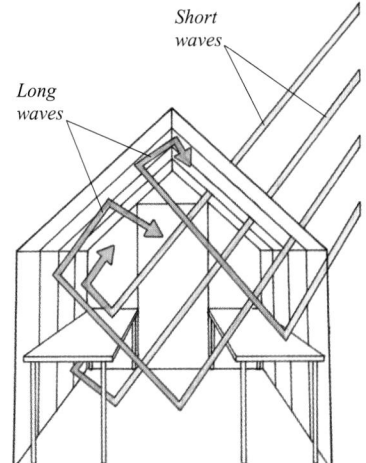

Short waves

Long waves

Light passes through glass as short-wave radiation, warming everything inside, including floor, staging, soil, and plants. Heat then re-radiates from these as long waves, which cannot pass through the glass, leading to a build-up of heat inside the greenhouse.

HOW TO BALANCE THE ENVIRONMENT OF A GREENHOUSE

	HEATING (see p.574)	INSULATION (see p.574)	VENTILATION (see p.575)	SHADING (see p.576)	HUMIDITY (see p.576)	WATERING (see p.577)	LIGHTING (see p.577)
COLD No minimum temperature	None.	Insulate against severely cold draughts and damp, foggy weather in winter.	Through ventilation is essential to prevent damp, stagnant conditions in winter.	Shade vulnerable plants in summer with a shading wash, blinds, meshes or fabric, or rigid sheets.	Unlikely to be a problem in summer. Maintain a "dry" atmosphere in winter by ventilating.	Water by hand in winter. Use a capillary system, seep hose, or trickle system in summer.	Growing lamps are unlikely to be needed for the type of plants grown.
COOL Minimum temperature 2°C (36°F)	A thermostatically controlled electric heater is preferable but gas or paraffin heaters may also be used. A frost alarm is useful if tender plants are grown.	In winter, as for a cold greenhouse. In spring, good insulation is extremely important if frost-tender plants are grown.	Ventilate freely, especially if a gas or paraffin heater is used, to disperse water vapour and toxic fumes.	Shade to control the temperature in summer – shading washes or blinds do this most efficiently. Fit automatic blinds, if possible.	"Damping down" is beneficial to increase humidity in summer.	As for a cold greenhouse, except that an overhead system may also be used in summer.	Growing lamps may be useful, especially in spring when natural light is poor, for plants at an early stage of development.
TEMPERATE Minimum temperature 7°C (45°F)	A heater (preferably electric) fitted with a thermostat is required. A frost alarm is also essential.	As for cold and cool greenhouses. Thermal screens are useful in spring for propagation.	As for a cool greenhouse. Automatic vent openers are extremely useful in summer.	As for a cool greenhouse.	Maintain high humidity in spring and summer, especially around cuttings and seedlings.	An automatic watering system is useful throughout the year.	Growing lamps are useful in winter and spring for extending daylength.
WARM Minimum temperature 13°C (55°F)	As for a temperate greenhouse.	Good insulation is essential throughout the year to minimize heating costs.	Automatic vent openers fitted to several vents simplify temperature control enormously.	Automatic blinds are desirable in summer.	High humidity is required throughout the year.	As for a temperate greenhouse.	As for a temperate greenhouse.

Heating

It is important to maintain the correct temperature in the greenhouse for the range of plants you have chosen to grow. Select a heater that is powerful enough to maintain the required minimum temperature efficiently. Other factors to consider when choosing a greenhouse heater include convenience, the cost of installation, and running costs.

Electric heaters

These are the most reliable, efficient, and convenient to use in the greenhouse, although an electricity supply will be needed to run them (see "Installing electricity, gas, and water", p.572). They are usually thermostatically controlled, which means that no heat is wasted, and they do not require regular refuelling or maintenance. In addition, electric heaters do not produce fumes or water vapour.

A number of different types of electric heater is available. These include fan heaters and water-proof tubular heaters, both of which heat the greenhouse effectively. Convector heaters are also used but these do not distribute heat as efficiently. Tubular heaters need to be fitted to the sides of the greenhouse, just above floor level. Other heaters may be moved around as desired.

Electric fan heaters are particularly useful because they promote good air circulation, which helps to maintain an even temperature and minimizes the spread of disease. They may also be used to cool the greenhouse in warm weather if the heating element is switched off.

Gas heaters

Gas heating systems may be run off the mains supplies (see "Installing electricity, gas, and water", p.572) or from bottled gas. They are not as convenient to use as electric heaters: although they may have thermostats, these are not usually calibrated in degrees so you will need to experiment to find the correct setting.

If bottled gas is used, the cylinders need to be regularly replaced: always have two bottles connected by an automatic switch-over valve in case one runs out. Propane gas releases fumes and water vapour as it burns, so ventilation is important. Keep gas cylinders in a safe place and have them checked regularly by an authorized dealer.

Paraffin heaters

These are not as efficient as electric or gas heaters in their use of fuel because they are not controlled by a thermostat. Paraffin heaters may therefore be expensive to run if a high temperature needs to be maintained, since some energy may be wasted, although they are inexpensive to buy in the first place and there is no installation cost.

When using paraffin heaters, thorough ventilation is required because some plant-toxic fumes and water vapour are produced as a byproduct of combustion – a humid, stagnant atmosphere may encourage disease if ventilation is poor. Other drawbacks include the need to transport and store fuel, and to check the fuel level and wick every day to ensure that it is burning cleanly.

Circulated hot water

Solid fuel hot water systems are now rarely used in greenhouses. Oil- and gas-fired circulated hot water systems are still sometimes used, but seldom on the small scale of the amateur greenhouse.

Although the distribution of heat through hot water pipes provides good heat transfer, often only about 50 per cent of the energy released is used – the rest is lost through the glass walls. The need for regular stoking and clearing out of the fire also makes solid fuel inconvenient.

Thermometer and frost alarm

If the heater in a greenhouse is not thermostatically controlled, use a maximum/minimum thermometer to check that the correct overnight temperatures are being maintained for the plants grown.

In regions that suffer extremely low temperatures, a frost alarm is a useful safeguard if the greenhouse contains tender plants. If the air temperature unexpectedly drops to near freezing, for example through a power failure or heater breakdown, an alarm bell will sound remotely (this will usually be somewhere in the home), allowing you time to protect the plants.

A FROST ALARM

Install a frost alarm if growing tender plants that may be damaged or killed if the temperature falls.

INSULATION MATERIAL

Bubble plastic is useful for insulating a greenhouse and reduces heat loss considerably. Cut it to size and attach it securely to the framework.

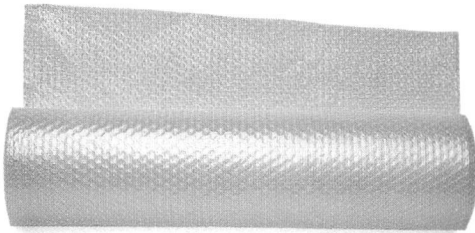

Insulation

Insulation in the greenhouse may reduce heating costs considerably; if a minimum temperature of 7°C (45°F) is required, for example, the cost of insulation may be recovered within just a few seasons – and even in a single winter period in particularly cold areas. The higher the temperature to be maintained, and the colder the region, the more cost-effective insulation is likely to be. Care in choosing the right material is required, however, since some insulation materials may reduce the amount of light reaching the plants.

Double-glazing

The most efficient method of insulating the entire greenhouse is to fit double-glazing. This is best done at the time of construction, if possible. Double-glazing is expensive, of course, but the benefits could be enormous.

Flexible plastic insulation

Bubble plastic, which consists of double or triple skins of transparent plastic with air cells in between, is a very efficient method of insulation. A single layer of plastic sheeting is not as efficient as bubble plastic at reducing heat loss but is less expensive and does not cut out so much light. Plastic sheets may be used in winter as a form of double-glazing. To attach the insulation material, use suction-pad fasteners or clips that fit into the greenhouse frame.

Thermal screens

These consist of sheets of clear plastic or translucent material, such as a cross-laminated fabric, that are attached to wires between the eaves and drawn horizontally across the width of the greenhouse in the evening. They are useful for conserving heat at night because they restrict the amount of heat that rises above the eaves, trapping the warmth lower down around the plants.

Vertical screens may also be used to partition off a heated section at one end of the greenhouse with plastic sheeting, leaving the remainder of the area unheated. Plants may be overwintered and early seedlings raised in the heated section.

Special kits for making thermal screens are available, or plastic sheeting and the necessary fixings may be obtained separately.

Base cladding

Base cladding on the floor of glass-to-ground greenhouses reduces heat loss significantly. In winter, place polystyrene panels along the foot of the glass panes to provide extra insulation, removing them before summer border crops are planted.

THERMAL SCREENS

Horizontal screen between the eaves

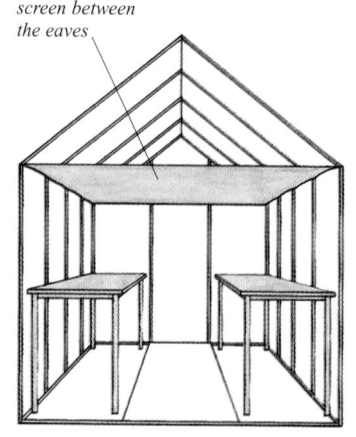

Vertical screen that acts as a partition

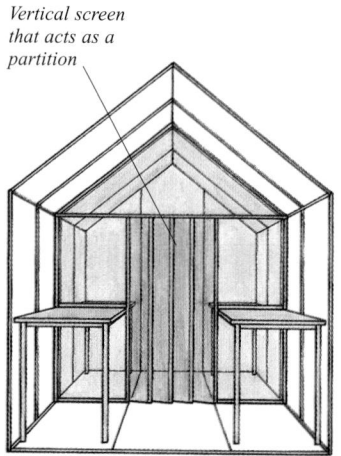

Thermal screens may be drawn horizontally between the eaves. They may also be drawn vertically to partition off a section of the greenhouse that needs to be heated to a high temperature.

Ventilation

Good ventilation is essential in a greenhouse, even in winter, to avoid a build-up of stuffy or damp, stale air, and to control temperature. It is important that the area covered by ventilators should be equal to at least one sixth of the floor area.

Extra ventilation

Few greenhouses are supplied with enough ventilators as standard, so order additional air vents, hinged and louvre windows, or extractor fans when buying a greenhouse. This is an especially important consideration with timber greenhouses, since it is usually difficult to add them later.

Extra ventilation is particularly important if paraffin or bottled gas heating systems are used, to prevent water vapour and fumes from building up to an unacceptable level.

Wind ventilation system

Air exchange in a greenhouse occurs when external movements of air, caused by gusts of wind, replace interior warm, humid air with fresh air. If ventilators are placed on the sides and roof of the greenhouse, and are also staggered, this will ensure that air circulates throughout the entire area – if vents are placed directly opposite one another, air will simply blow straight through the greenhouse.

Doors may also be kept open in summer to increase ventilation; it is worth fixing a sheet of netting across the doorway, however, to keep out birds and pets.

Chimney ventilation system

Chimney effect ventilation depends on warm, humid air rising out of roof vents and being replaced by fresh air that is drawn in as a result through lower ventilators, which are usually positioned along the sides of the greenhouse either above or below the staging.

Fan ventilation system

Fan ventilation is a mechanically driven system that works by extracting air from the greenhouse at head height, or slightly higher, and drawing in fresh air through vents lower down and usually at the opposite end of the greenhouse.

Hinged ventilators

These may be fitted to the sides or roof of the greenhouse and should open wide, to an angle of about 45°. This will allow maximum airflow while at the same time preventing direct gusts of wind from entering

THE PRINCIPLES OF GREENHOUSE VENTILATION

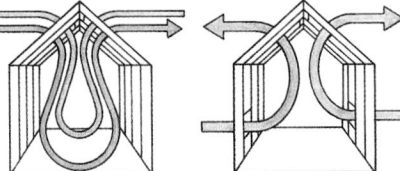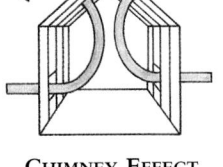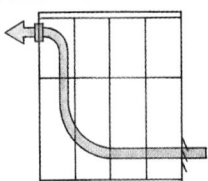

WIND EFFECT
Fresh air blows into the greenhouse, circulates, and then escapes through an open vent on the opposite side.

CHIMNEY EFFECT
Warm air rises and escapes through open vents in the roof, drawing fresh, cooler air in lower down.

FAN VENTILATION
Air is drawn out by a fan at the top of the greenhouse and drawn in through open vents lower down.

the greenhouse and possibly causing damage to the plants or even to the structure itself.

Louvre ventilators

Usually positioned below the height of the staging, louvre window ventilators are particularly useful for controlling the flow of air throughout the greenhouse in winter, when roof ventilators may allow too much heat to escape. The louvre vents must close tightly, however, so that they exclude all draughts.

Automatic vent openers

Autovent openers simplify temperature control significantly in the greenhouse, since they are designed to open automatically whenever the temperature inside rises above a predetermined level. These devices are essential if a heating system that has no thermostat has been installed in the greenhouse.

With any type of greenhouse, automatic vent openers should be fitted to at least some of the hinged or louvre ventilators; this is easily done by closely following the manufacturer's instructions.

They may be set to open at a range of temperatures, but make sure that you choose an automatic system that will function within the temperature range required in your greenhouse. It is best to set this to operate at a temperature that is just below the

optimum for the plants. In this way, the vents will open and the greenhouse will be well ventilated before the temperature inside rises to an unsuitable level for the plants.

Many different designs of autovent are available. Some models work by the expansion and contraction of a plug of wax that is contained in a metal or plastic cylinder; the movement of the wax works a piston that opens and closes the ventilator. Other models make use of metal rods that alter their shape as the temperature rises and falls, activating the ventilation mechanism.

Extractor fans

The type of extractor fan that is designed primarily for use in kitchens and bathrooms is also ideally suited for use in the greenhouse. An additional bonus with using these extractor fans is that most of them are fitted with a thermostatic control, which is an essential requirement for the greenhouse.

Choose a fan that is powerful enough for the particular size of your greenhouse – the extraction rate is usually quoted in cubic metres or cubic feet per hour. As a general guide, a 2 x 2.5m (6 x 8ft) greenhouse requires a fan with a capacity of 300cu m (10,000cu ft) per hour, but a smaller one may be perfectly adequate if other types of ventilation are also used.

A louvre window – positioned at the opposite end of the greenhouse to the extractor fan and set lower down – is essential to provide a flow of fresh air to replace the stale air that is drawn out by the fan.

Buy a fan that is fitted with louvre flaps that close when the fan is not actually working so that draughts are excluded. To extend the working life of the fan, the motor should not be set to run at maximum capacity; it is much better to choose a model that is slightly more powerful than is strictly necessary for the greenhouse.

LOUVRE VENTS

These are fitted on the side of the greenhouse above ground level to improve the flow of air through the interior. The opening mechanism has a lever and is simple to operate (see insets).

HINGED VENTS

Vents that open by a hinge mechanism are normally fitted to the roof of the greenhouse. Make sure that they open wide and that they are securely fixed when open.

AUTOVENT OPENER

This autovent works by the expansion and contraction of wax in a cylinder as the greenhouse temperature rises and falls.

Shading

This will help to control the temperature of the greenhouse if the ventilation system is insufficient. It also protects vulnerable plants from too much direct sunlight, reducing the risk of leaf scorch, and preventing flower colours from fading in strong sunlight. Shading applied primarily to control heat should be on the outside of the greenhouse; internal shading is unlikely to reduce the temperature significantly.

The amount of shade required in a greenhouse depends on the season and the plants being grown. In the months of strongest sunlight, shading that reduces the light by 40–50 per cent is suitable for a typical mixed greenhouse. Ferns generally prefer approximately 75 per cent filtering of light, while most cacti and other succulents require very little or no shading at all.

Shading washes

These are often the most effective and cheapest method of reducing heat from the sun, while still allowing enough light to penetrate for good plant growth. Paint or spray the wash onto the outside of the glass at the beginning of the sunny season and remove it in late summer by rubbing or washing it off, using a cleaning solution if necessary.

Shading washes are inexpensive but they may be messy to apply and remove, and their appearance is sometimes unattractive in a small garden where the greenhouse is a major feature. Some washes become more transparent when wet, so that on rainy days or when the weather is dull they allow more light penetration.

Blinds

These are used mainly on the outside of the greenhouse and control temperature effectively. They are more versatile than shading washes, since

they may be rolled up or down, depending on the intensity of light required. They may be used where only a section of the greenhouse needs to be shaded. Manually operated blinds need constant attention, however. Automatic blinds, which come into operation as soon as the temperature rises to a predetermined level, are more convenient to use, but they are expensive.

Meshes and fabrics

Flexible mesh shading materials are suitable for either interior or exterior use. They are less adaptable than blinds because they are generally fixed in position for the entire season, and they are less satisfactory than shading washes in helping to control plant growth.

Woven and knitted fabrics are also suitable for both interior and exterior greenhouse use. The amount of light reduction varies considerably, depending on the type of fabric fitted, but the quality of light allowed through to the plants is usually perfectly adequate for good growth, although the temperature is not significantly reduced.

FLEXIBLE MESH

Plastic mesh netting may be cut to length and used either internally or externally for shading plants in a greenhouse.

SHADING THE GREENHOUSE

Shading washes are applied to the outside of a greenhouse to prevent the temperature inside from rising too high, without greatly reducing light. The washes may be left on throughout the season.

ROLLER BLINDS

Blinds are a versatile method of shading the greenhouse. They should be hard wearing, since they will be in place for long periods.

Cross-laminated fabric and some plastic meshes are recommended for internal shading only.

Tinted bubble plastic may also be used for shading. It cuts down the light by almost 50 per cent, but it reduces temperature only slightly.

Rigid sheets

Rigid polycarbonate sheets (usually tinted) are sometimes used for shading in greenhouses. The sheets may be fixed either inside or outside, as recommended by the greenhouse manufacturer. They cut down the light effectively, but unless they are white in colour the quality of light transmitted may not be sufficient for good plant growth.

Humidity

Humidity is a measure of the quantity of water vapour in the air. The humidity of the air affects the rate at which plants transpire; this is their mechanism for drawing water (along with nutrients) from roots to leaves, where the water then evaporates from leaf pores into the air. As water evaporates, the plant is cooled down.

Establish the preferred humidity levels of the plants in your greenhouse, then control the amount of moisture in the atmosphere to suit them. Humidity may be increased using various techniques (see "Humidifiers", below) and reduced by ventilation (see p.575).

Plant requirements

A very humid atmosphere reduces the rate of transpiration and evaporation to a level that may be harmful to some plants and they may suffer

damage from overheating unless cooler, drier air is brought in by ventilation. Many tropical plants from humid climates, however, require high levels of humidity for healthy growth, and will not survive in a dry atmosphere.

If the air is dry and the humidity level low, plants transpire more rapidly, often losing a great deal of moisture. Plants that are not adapted to cope with low humidity will wilt as a result, unless additional water is supplied at the roots. Dry-climate plants often have specific anatomical features that reduce the transpiration rate in drought conditions (see WATER CONSERVATION AND RECYCLING, pp.614-615).

Measuring humidity

The level of humidity in a greenhouse depends to an extent on the temperature of the air – warm air is capable of holding more moisture than cold air before it becomes saturated. Relative humidity is a measure of the amount of water vapour in the air expressed as a percentage of saturation point at the same temperature. A "humid" atmosphere is defined as having a relative humidity of about 75 per cent; a "dry" atmosphere has a relative humidity of about 35 per cent.

Wet and dry bulb thermometers, used in conjunction with hygrometric tables, may be used to measure the relative humidity of the atmosphere. Hygrometers, which have a dial that gives readings for both the temperature and the humidity, are also available. As a general guide, a relative humidity below 75 per cent, but above 40 per cent, is beneficial for most greenhouse plants during the growing season – at levels above 80 per cent, diseases such as grey mould (*Botrytis*) and mildew may become a problem.

In winter, humidity should be maintained at a lower level, but the exact level required will depend on the types of plant grown and the temperature of the greenhouse.

Humidifiers

Greenhouses may be "damped down" during the summer by splashing water – predominantly on the floor and on any staging – from a watering can or hose. This has the effect of increasing the level of atmospheric humidity. An automatic spray system simplifies humidity control, especially for plants that require very high humidity. In a small greenhouse, mist-spraying by hand or providing a tray filled with water that slowly evaporates into the air is usually adequate.

Watering

A traditional watering can is still the best, if perhaps time-consuming, method of watering a mixed collection of plants in a small greenhouse. Because you can readily monitor the flow, it ensures that all the plants are watered according to their individual requirements.

An automatic watering system is a useful addition to a greenhouse in summer, however; if the greenhouse is left unattended on a regular basis, an automatic system becomes essential, since some pot plants may need to be watered several times a day in very hot weather.

Capillary systems

Watering systems that rely on capillary action to draw up water are often used in a greenhouse.

Plant pots may be placed on a 2–5cm (¾–2in) layer of clean sand (which retains moisture well) that is placed on the greenhouse staging and kept permanently wet. Moist sand adds considerable weight to the staging, however, so make sure that it is sturdy enough to take the extra load. In addition, protect wooden staging from the wet sand by lining it with sheets of heavy-duty plastic, otherwise it will rot. Alternatively, the sand may be placed in aluminium or plastic trays.

Add a length of plastic gutter to the edge of the bench and keep it filled with water. This may be done by hand or automatically from an overhead tank connected to the mains, in which case the system should be controlled by a ballcock.

Capillary matting, which is widely available in rolls and is simply cut to the required size, is far lighter, easier to keep clean, and just as effective as sand. To keep the capillary matting continuously moist, trail the edge into a water trough or other reservoir of water. The water may be topped up by hand or supplied automatically from the mains, as above.

For a capillary system to be effective, there must be sufficient contact between the compost in the pots and the source of moisture so that water is continuously supplied to the plants' root systems. Plastic plant pots usually allow good contact between the compost and the moist sand or matting. Clay pots, however, may each require a wick. This is cut out of a piece of spare capillary matting and placed in the drainage hole of the pot to bridge any gaps between the compost and the mat.

During the winter months, do not use capillary watering systems in the greenhouse, since most plants are dormant, or growing only slowly, and therefore require a reduced intake of water. The perpetually damp mat or sand may also increase humidity in the greenhouse to unsatisfactory levels for the plants (see "Humidity", p.576).

Overhead systems

A system of overhead pipes, with nozzles from which water is sprayed onto the plants below, is widely used in commercial greenhouses. This is an ideal system for watering a large number of plants that are all at a similar stage of growth. It is not suitable for the small, amateur greenhouse, however, that contains a wide variety of plants. Overhead watering systems are also expensive to install and create too humid an atmosphere if used in the winter.

Seep hoses

These are widely used in the garden, and inside the greenhouse to water border crops or to keep capillary matting moist. In very hot weather, however, seep hoses may not supply a sufficient flow of water to the plants (see also p.561).

Trickle irrigation systems

This type of irrigation system consists of a series of small-bore tubes, each with an adjustable nozzle. The tubes are placed in the individual pots or growing bags, or near plants growing in the greenhouse border.

Most trickle irrigation systems are fed with water from a reservoir that is filled in turn from a hose connected to the mains water supply. It is possible, however, to use water supplied direct from the mains.

The rate of water delivery must be monitored very carefully and adjusted according to the needs of the plants; these needs vary depending on time of year and the vagaries of the weather (see also p.561).

Lighting

If an electric power supply is already installed in the greenhouse (see "Installing electricity, gas, and water", p.572), lighting units are not expensive to add at any time, and running costs are also low. In addition, the lights produce a little extra heat for the plants. Ordinary fluorescent lamps provide enough illumination to work by comfortably.

Growing lamps

The special quality of lighting produced by growing lamps is required to increase light intensity and daylength (see THE VEGETABLE

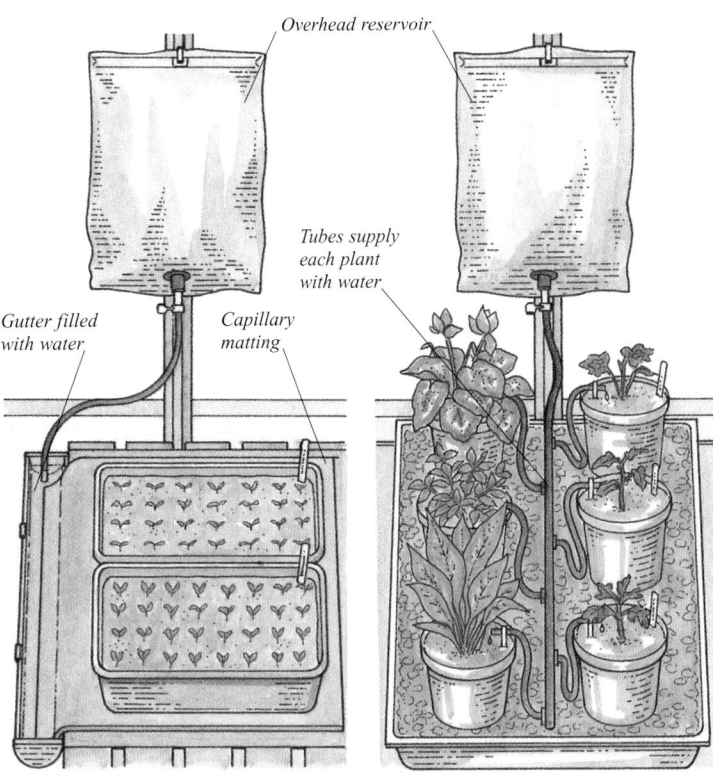

WATERING SYSTEMS

Overhead reservoir

Tubes supply each plant with water

Gutter filled with water

Capillary matting

CAPILLARY WATERING
An overhead reservoir feeds water to a gutter fixed to the staging. The matting soaks up water, which is absorbed by compost in the trays.

TRICKLE IRRIGATION
Trickle systems supply water directly to each pot by means of tubes, which are fed from an overhead reservoir.

GARDEN, "Daylength", p.495) for specific purposes during spring and winter when light levels are low.

Fluorescent tubes that produce good light to improve plant growth may be obtained from specialist aquarium suppliers and garden centres. They do not produce much heat, and so may be placed close to the plants. The lights are fitted with reflectors that cast the light downwards, where it will do the most good. For greatest effectiveness, the tubes should be mounted 25–30cm (10–12in) above the foliage. Mercury fluorescent lamps and mercury vapour lamps also provide a suitable quality of light to encourage good plant growth.

Metal halide lamps are the best, if most expensive, form of growing lamp, emitting light that is close to the spectrum of natural light. They illuminate a large area but cast their light in a circular pattern, which may be inconvenient in a small greenhouse, since the corners may not be strongly lit.

Most growing lamps that are suitable for use in the greenhouse need special fittings because of the moist, humid atmosphere. If in any doubt, always ask the advice of a qualified electrician.

Light meters

Where lighting is a very important factor, special plant light meters may be useful in the greenhouse, because they measure light levels much more accurately than can be judged by eye.

Light meters are usually supplied with information about the light levels that are preferred by a wide range of commonly cultivated plants, so follow the instructions for the particular plants grown.

A GROWING LAMP

This provides additional light to improve plant growth. Secure it directly above the plants, if possible.

Using the space

To make best use of the limited space in a greenhouse, plan the layout carefully. Cultivation in raised beds, borders, growing bags, or containers placed on the ground, staging, or shelves are all suitable methods; often, a combination is best.

Raised beds

These are used mainly in alpine houses, where sharp drainage is required. Raised beds may be expensive to construct using new bricks, but old bricks are satisfactory. Leave a large gap between a raised bed and the wall of a greenhouse so that air can circulate and moisture from the compost does not penetrate the wall. For details see STRUCTURES AND SURFACES, "Raised beds", p.599.

Beds that are raised to normal bench height are suitable only for lean-to greenhouses or for those with a tall brick base. For small plants that do not require a great depth of soil, a stone trough placed on brick pillars or "legs" may be used. Alternatively, construct a raised container by fixing rigid metal sheets or paving slabs on top of brick pillars, making the walls by laying several brick courses around the top, and lining with a sheet of butyl rubber. The butyl sheet should have several holes pierced in it to ensure that the bed will be adequately drained.

Raised beds for taller plants need not be so high and so do not need to stand on brick pillars. They are usually built up from ground level with basal seep holes for drainage and simply filled with compost.

Borders and growing bags

A glass-to-ground greenhouse is required to grow plants directly in the border, to ensure that plants receive enough light. Borders with a width of 1m (3ft) are acceptable in a greenhouse that is 2.5m (8ft) wide but make the beds wider if staging is placed over the borders, so that the staging does not prevent you from reaching the far side easily. Plants in containers may also be placed on top of the border rather than on staging, if required.

The soil in greenhouse borders may become infected with disease if the same plants are grown repeatedly over many years. If this is the case, or if the greenhouse floor is concreted over, growing bags may be used. Growing bags provide a convenient method of cultivation, since they retain moisture well and

INSIDE THE GREENHOUSE

Organize the elements within the greenhouse sensibly to make the best possible use of the limited space. Here is a well-planned layout for a lean-to greenhouse.

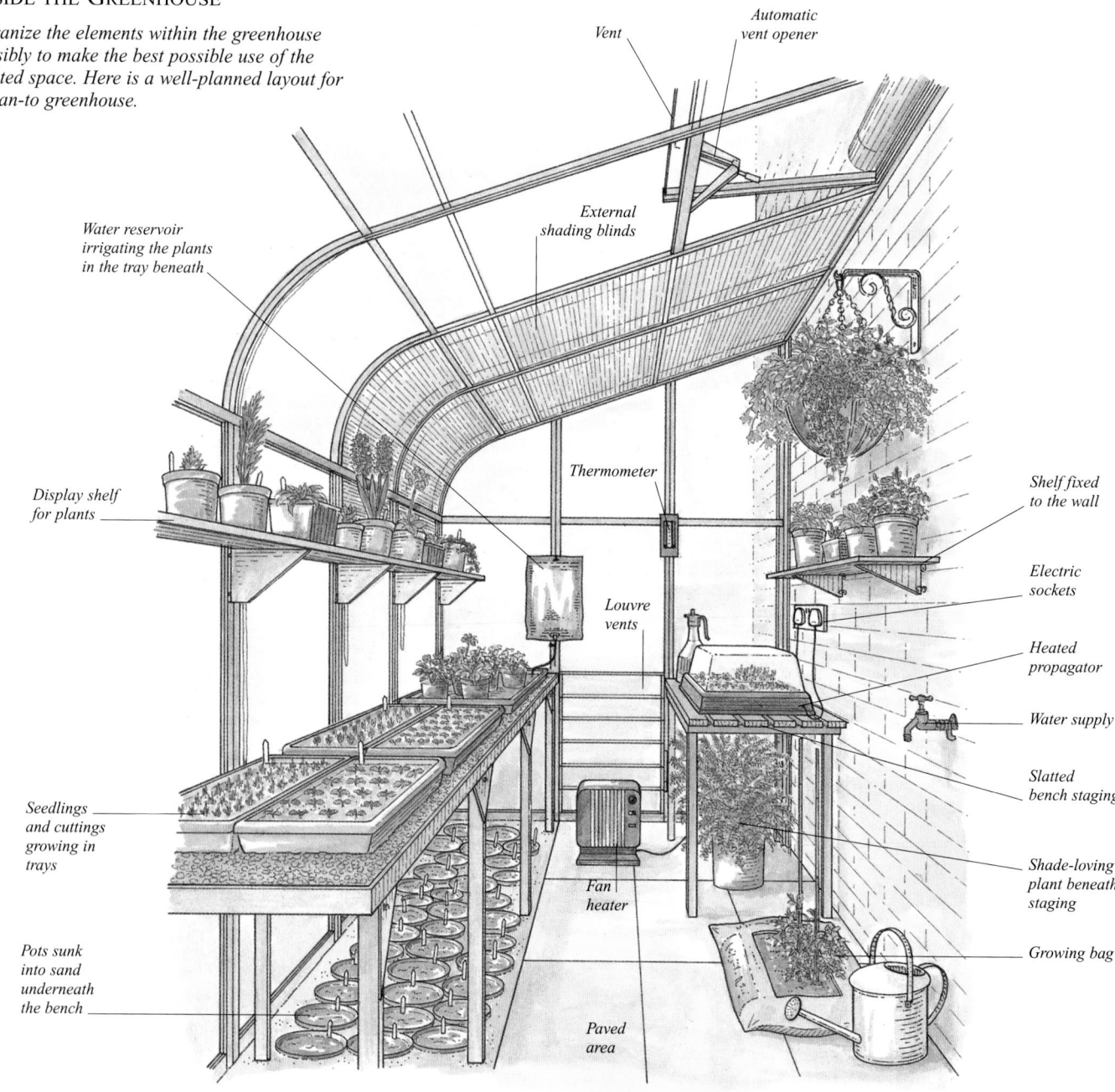

DISPLAYING THE PLANTS

Shelving and staging enable attractive tiered displays of plants of varying heights to be made. If the greenhouse is heated, a wide variety of plants may be grown throughout the year to maintain the display of flowers and foliage. Place dormant or "resting" plants beneath the staging to make more room for other plants in season.

remove the need to dig and fertilize the soil before planting. All the nutrients in the compost contained in the growing bags are used up during the season, so fresh growing bags should be used each year.

Staging

Staging is important for any ornamental or mixed greenhouse – by bringing plants to waist height, watering and care are made easier. Even if removed for summer crops, staging is necessary for propagating and growing on young plants.

Positioning the staging

The most satisfactory arrangement for a small or mixed greenhouse is to have a central path with staging along the sides, and possibly across one end, removing half of it for border crops when necessary and retaining the permanent staging to display ornamentals. The permanent staging should be positioned on the side where it will cast the least shade on the border crops.

Central staging

Larger ornamental greenhouses that are designed primarily as show houses may have staging placed in the centre, with a path around the edge. Two staging benches may be placed back-to-back, preferably with tiered staging in the centre to enhance the display of plants.

The right size and height

Most staging benches are 45–60cm (18–24in) wide. Wider benches are useful in a large greenhouse but they may be difficult to reach across. All staging needs to be of sturdy construction to support the considerable weight of plants, containers, and compost. Always leave a generous gap between the back of any staging and the sides of the greenhouse to allow air to circulate.

Most amateur greenhouses also have to serve as a potting shed. A convenient height for staging that is also used as a work surface is approximately 75–90cm (30–36in); it should be lower if a sitting working position is required.

Free-standing staging

It is sometimes useful to have staging that can be dismantled and stored away, bringing it into the greenhouse for short periods, for instance when raising seedlings in spring. Free-standing staging may not fit the

FREE-STANDING STAGING

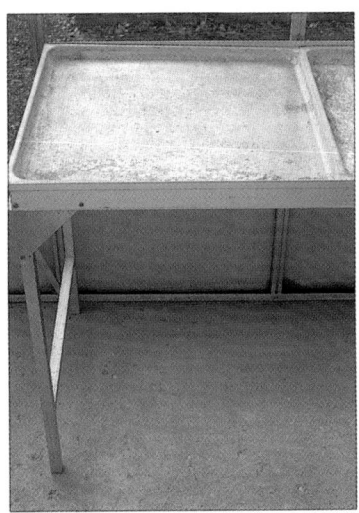

Movable benches allow great flexibility, since they may be moved around to accommodate the plants, or removed altogether.

FIXED STAGING

Most greenhouse manufacturers supply permanent, purpose-built staging that is made from the same materials as the greenhouse. It is best fitted at the same time as the greenhouse is constructed.

greenhouse quite so well as staging that is built-in and may not look as attractive but is more flexible in use. It must be easy to assemble and sturdy since it will be in use for many years. If border crops are grown for most of the year, open-mesh staging which folds back neatly against the side of the greenhouse is convenient for short periods.

Free-standing modular staging systems can be built up in tiers and provide an attractive way of displaying plants. Slatted, mesh, or solid modular systems are available.

Permanent staging

Built-in staging and shelves may put a strain on the framework of a greenhouse, especially light, aluminium alloy structures. Gravel or sand, if used, adds extra weight to the staging, particularly when it is wet. Buy staging that is purpose-built, if possible; if in doubt, check with the greenhouse manufacturer before fitting any permanent staging.

Slatted and mesh staging

If you are growing alpines or cacti and succulents in pots, it is preferable to use slatted or mesh benches, which allow a freer flow of air than solid staging. However, slatted and mesh staging are not suitable for capillary watering systems.

SLATTED STAGING

Wooden-slatted staging is an attractive choice. The slats allow better air circulation around the plants than solid-surface staging does, but slats are not suitable for a capillary watering system, unless pots are placed in trays on the bench.

For a timber greenhouse, use wooden slatted benches; for an aluminium alloy or galvanized steel greenhouse, metal or plastic-mesh benches are more appropriate.

Solid surface staging

Solid staging allows more pots to be accommodated than slatted staging (it is difficult to keep pots upright between the slats), but may require more ventilation.

If using a capillary watering system, choose solid aluminium staging that has a level surface for the matting or sand. Some types of staging have reversible sections that produce raised flat surfaces for mats if placed one way, and dish-like sections for sand or gravel if reversed.

Shelves

Shelves in the greenhouse may be used for both storage and display. Permanent shelves often cast shade on the plants below so it is preferable to install fold-away shelves, which may be used in spring when space is short and then put away for the rest of the year.

In a small greenhouse, shelves can be used to display trailing plants where there is not enough head-room for hanging baskets.

Propagation aids

The propagation of many plants requires higher temperatures than may realistically be maintained in the greenhouse. To save on fuel bills, therefore, propagation aids are often used to provide the extra heat required. They may also increase the success rate when sowing seed or rooting leafy cuttings. Choose a propagator for the greenhouse that is large enough to hold at least three standard seed trays.

An electric power supply in the greenhouse is essential if heated propagators, mist units, or soil-warming cables are to be used. Mist units require a mains water supply as well as a power supply.

Unheated propagators are of limited use in the greenhouse but usually provide sufficient humidity for rooting tip, softwood, or semi-ripe cuttings in summer. On a small scale, a similar effect is created by enclosing a pot of cuttings in a clear plastic bag.

Heated propagators

A heated propagator should have a heating element that is capable of providing a minimum compost temperature of 15°C (59°F) in winter and early spring, when temperatures outside may fall below freezing.

If tropical plants are to be propagated, the unit must have a more powerful heating element that can maintain a temperature of 24°C (75°F). The propagator should preferably be fitted with an adjustable thermostat, which allows greater flexibility of temperature.

Use rigid plastic lids, since these are more likely to retain the heat than thin plastic covers. Adjustable ventilators are useful because they allow moisture to escape and prevent the atmosphere inside the propagator from becoming too humid.

Domestic propagators

Some small heated propagators are designed for windowsill use. Usually holding just two seed trays, they are generally too small to be of practical use in the greenhouse and often do not have a thermostat. They may not generate enough heat in a cold or cool greenhouse, since the heating element is intended to operate in a room indoors.

Heated bases

These are designed to be used with unheated propagators or ordinary seed trays, either of which may be placed on the heated base. A plastic hood must be placed over seed trays to maintain warmth and humidity. Heated bases do not raise the temperature as efficiently as heated tray propagators (see below).

Heated tray propagators

These have a self-contained heating element in the base, and are best when fitted with an adjustable thermostat.

Mist units

Cuttings may often be rooted more rapidly and in greater numbers in a mist unit than by using other more conventional means. Mist units, which are normally used mainly by specialist horticulturists, automatically maintain a high humidity around cuttings and are useful for difficult plants.

The easiest and most convenient mist units to use are self-contained, enclosed ones that include a heating element, thermostat, sensor, transparent cover, and a misting head. The constantly humid atmosphere created by the misting head provides a suitable environment in which to root cuttings quickly – by maintaining a constant film of water on the propagating material. Heat loss by evaporation is also reduced, and there is also less risk of the cuttings being affected by fungal diseases because, when the misting head is in operation, most disease spores are washed out of the air and from the leaves before they can infect plant tissues.

For large numbers of plants, a mist propagation unit is more practical. Some units are designed for use without a cover on an open greenhouse propagating bench; they are used in conjunction with soil-warming cables and also require a specially constructed greenhouse bench. If sited in a greenhouse where a mixed collection of plants is grown, however, the high humidity created by an open mist unit may prove unsuitable for some types of plant. In this situation, it would be preferable to install a closed mist unit.

Soil-warming devices

An electric horticultural blanket or a heated tray filled with moisture-retentive matting or sand will also create the basal heat and high humidity needed for successful propagation. More expensive still are soil-warming cables intended primarily for heating the substrate in a conventional propagator or on a mist bench in the greenhouse. Such soil-warming cables may also be used to heat the air in an enclosed space, such as a cold frame or home-made propagator. The safest system to use is a cable with a wired-in thermostat that is connected to an insulated, fused socket. Buy a screened cable, as it is much less dangerous if the cable is accidentally cut.

Soil-warming cables are sold in lengths that are designed to heat a given area. A 75-watt cable, for example, measures 6m (20ft) and provides enough heat for a bench area of 0.7sq m (7sq ft) in a greenhouse that has some form of heating. A cable with a higher wattage would of course be needed for use in a similar area in an unheated greenhouse or in a cold frame that is outside the greenhouse.

The cable should be laid at a depth of 5–8cm (2–3in) in a series of "S" bends (ensuring that the loops do not touch) in a bed of moist sand.

PROPAGATING BLANKET

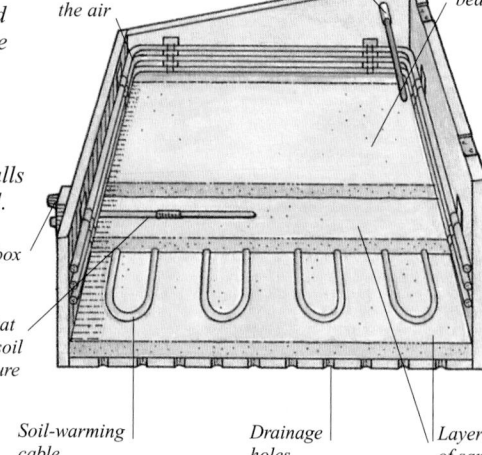

This specialized horticultural blanket is made of electric wires encased in aluminum foil to provide an even spread of heat. When not in use, it can be rolled up and stored.

Thermostat can be set to required temperature

Propagator

Probe monitors temperature at surface

Capillary matting

Plastic sheet protects blanket

Electric blanket

Polystyrene insulation pad

Greenhouse bench

USING SOIL-WARMING CABLES

In this propagating case, cables are used to heat the sand base and the air. Each set of cables has a thermostat, which ensures that the temperature never falls below a pre-set level.

Thermostat regulates air temperature

Cables also heat the air

Sand bed

Control box

Thermostat controls soil temperature

Soil-warming cable

Drainage holes

Layers of sand

A WINDOWSILL PROPAGATOR

Portable propagators should be used indoors, where they will retain the high humidity needed to germinate seeds or root cuttings.

Cold frames and cloches

Cold frames and cloches relieve pressure on greenhouse space, but they are also extremely useful in their own right. They are likely to be used most intensively in spring to harden off plants raised in a greenhouse, but they may also be used throughout the year to grow a wide range of crops. In the colder months, they are useful for protecting winter flowers, overwintering the seeds of hardy annuals sown in autumn, and sheltering vulnerable alpines from the worst of the wet weather.

Cold frames

The most popular type of cold frame has glass (or clear plastic) sides as well as glass "lights" (frame tops which contain the panes of glass), although sometimes timber and brick are used for the construction. Glass-to-ground models usually have a metal framework.

Frame lights

Choose a frame that has removable or sliding "lights" for easy access; some also have sliding front panels, which may be useful for extra ventilation. Hinged "lights" that are wedged open still provide protection from heavy rain but sliding "lights"

are often removed entirely during the day, leaving the plants very vulnerable to heavy rain. Lightweight aluminium frames with their "lights" wedged open may be at risk in strong winds, however, so choose a model which has a hinged top and adjustable casement stays to secure the "lights" safely.

Wooden frames

Traditional timber frames are now difficult to obtain and are usually expensive, but may be made cheaply at home from second-hand timber. The wooden sides retain heat well. It is not very difficult to fix soil-warming cables (see p.580) to the inside of the frame to provide extra warmth. Paint or stain the wood to preserve it.

Aluminium alloy frames

These are widely available and relatively inexpensive. They vary considerably in design but are usually sold packed flat for easy transportation, and assembled on site. Aluminium alloy frames let in more light than either wooden or brick frames, but they do not have such good insulating qualities and may not be as strong or robust. It may be necessary to use ground anchors for light-weight frames.

HOW TO USE COLD FRAMES

PLANTING IN THE FRAME
Plants may be grown directly in the cold frame, if required. Always prepare the base with a thick layer of drainage material, such as broken crocks or coarse gravel, before adding a 15cm (6in) layer of good garden soil or compost.

PROTECTING CROPS
Here, the cold frame has been placed directly onto the soil in the vegetable plot. Vegetables are growing through slits in a plastic mulch (see "Plastic film mulches", p.502) laid on the surface of the soil.

VENTILATION METHODS OF COLD FRAMES

HINGED LIGHTS
Hinged tops may be wedged open on warm days to prevent the plants from overheating.

SLIDING LIGHTS
Sliding tops are less vulnerable to gusts of wind but plants are not protected from heavy rain.

Brick frames

These are rarely used nowadays but they may still be built at home if a cheap supply of old bricks is available and if the "lights" can be made. Brick frames are generally warm and draught-proof.

Suitable sizes

The minimum practical size for a cold frame is 1.2m x 60cm (4 x 2ft). Often, however, the frame has to fit into whatever space is available (as near the greenhouse as possible), so choose the largest affordable frame that fits the space.

Height is important if the frame is to be used for plants in pots or for tall vegetable crops. In order to increase the height of a frame temporarily, raise it on loose bricks.

Insulation

The range of plants that may be successfully overwintered in a frame is increased if the frame is well insulated. The frame needs to be draught-proof; there should be no gaps around the glass or framework, and the top and any sliding front panels must fit well.

Glass-to-ground and plastic-sided frames may need insulating in cold weather with sheets of expanded polystyrene or bubble plastic (see "Flexible plastic insulation", p.574). Cut the sheets to size, and place them against the inside of the frame.

On cold nights, particularly when a sharp frost is predicted, frames may require additional outer protection: use layers of hessian or old carpet to cover the tops, tied down firmly or held in position with pieces of heavy timber. This protective covering should always be removed during the day, otherwise plants may suffer from lack of light. Alternatively, use

several layers of thick, clear plastic sheeting or bubble plastic for extra protection – this may be left in place during the day since it does not reduce the light to the same degree.

Ventilation

Good ventilation is essential in warm weather. Most frames have "lights" that may be wedged open to allow fresh air inside; often, the "lights" also slide along to allow more ventilation, and are eventually removed completely when young plants need to be hardened off.

Light

Aluminium frames (but not brick or wooden frames) may be moved around the garden to take advantage of the best light at various times of the year. If a frame is permanently sited, it should be positioned where it will receive the maximum amount of light in winter and spring, provided that the site is not too exposed.

Frames need shading in summer but, for year-round use, one that lets in as much light as possible is best.

Glazing materials

Horticultural glass is the best glazing material for cold frames; it transmits light well, allows the frame to warm up quickly, and retains heat better than most plastic materials. Broken or cracked panes should be replaced at once, so a frame that allows the individual panes to be replaced should be chosen. Some are glazed using glazing clips or glass panels that slide into the framework; this makes glass replacement fairly simple.

Where glass may be a potential danger for children or animals, or where the cost of the frame is the main consideration, use plastic glazing material.

Cloches

A range of cloche designs and materials is available – choose a cloche that suits the types of plant to be grown. Cloches tend to be used mainly in the vegetable garden but they are equally useful for protecting ornamental plants and seedlings that need a little extra warmth during winter or early in the season (see also "Frost protection", p.613).

Materials

Glass is the best choice of material if cloches are to be used extensively and moved from crop to crop. It has good light transmission and allows the frame to warm up quickly in sunlight. For safety, select toughened, 4mm (1/8in) float glass, which breaks into little pieces rather than large shards. Clear plastic material (of various thicknesses) is an alternative; plastic cloches are generally less expensive than those made of glass but do not allow such good light penetration, nor do they retain as much heat or last as long.

Single thickness plastic is the least satisfactory material for retaining heat, but is cheap and useful where high temperatures are not necessary. Plastic cloches last longer if they have been treated with an ultraviolet inhibitor and are stored out of direct sunlight when not in use.

The minimum thickness that is suitable for cloches is 150 gauge, but 300, 600, or 800 gauge provides much greater protection. PVC is thicker and more rigid, and has similar qualities to polypropylene (see below). Moulded PVC and PVC sheeting should last for five years or more if treated with an ultraviolet inhibitor.

Cloches made from twin-walled polycarbonate offer good insulation and should last for ten years or more. Polypropylene is used in some injection-moulded cloches and in corrugated sheets; it retains heat better than plastic, but not as well as

TENT CLOCHE

BARN CLOCHE

glass or twin-walled polycarbonate. It lasts for five years or more if treated with an ultraviolet inhibitor.

End pieces

These are an important part of most cloches – without them a cloche may become a wind tunnel, damaging the plants inside. The end pieces should fit well to preclude draughts but they should be easy to remove to provide ventilation when required.

Tent cloche

A tent cloche is inexpensive and simple to construct: two sheets of glass are held together by wire or plastic clips, to form a tent shape. It is suitable for germinating seeds, for protecting young seedlings in spring, and for low-growing plants.

Tunnel cloche

A tunnel cloche may be made from either rigid or flexible plastic. Generally, flexible plastic, continuous tunnel cloches are used for crops such as strawberries and early carrots. The plastic must be supported by wire hoops (positioned over the row of vegetables) and tensioned with wires. Use heavy-duty plastic that has been treated with an ultraviolet inhibitor.

Rigid models are generally more attractive but more expensive than tunnel cloches that are made of flexible plastic. They are also easier to

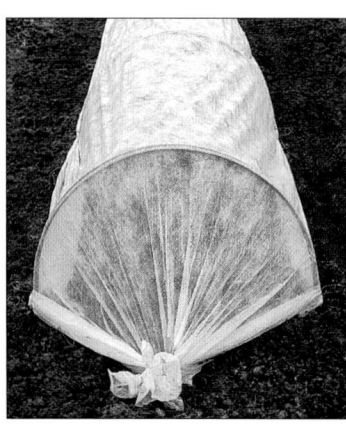

TUNNEL CLOCHE

move around, since they do not need to be dismantled first. Some tunnel cloches have self-watering features.

Barn cloche

This has almost vertical sides supporting a sloping, tent-shaped top. Its extra height makes it useful for relatively tall plants but extra materials and complicated fittings make it more expensive than a tent cloche.

Some glass and rigid plastic barn cloches have lifting or removable tops to provide ventilation in warm weather, while still offering wind protection. This makes weeding, watering, and harvesting easier.

Flexible PVC is sometimes used for barn cloches, but these tend to be lower and therefore less versatile than those using other types of material, unless the top is removable or can be wedged open.

Wall-of-water cloche

This unusual design of cloche is useful for single plants and consists of a circle of clear plastic tubes, into which water is poured. The tubes form the wall of the cloche, which alters in shape depending on the water level. The water protects the plant from several degrees of frost.

Self-watering cloche

Watering plants beneath cloches is difficult and time-consuming if the cloches have to be lifted or moved.

SELF-WATERING CLOCHE

A self-watering cloche is designed to allow rainwater to trickle through gradually to the plants below. Alternatively, it may have a tubular system that is connected to a hosepipe.

Floating cloche

A "floating" cloche (also known as a floating mulch) consists of a sheet of perforated plastic sheeting or polypropylene fibre fleece, which is placed over the ground where crops have been sown.

Floating cloches are permeable, allowing rainwater to penetrate to the soil below. This is a great advantage, since it reduces the need to water. The perforations in plastic floating

cloches enable the sheet to stretch a little as the crop grows beneath it. Fibre fleece is sufficiently lightweight to rise with the growing crop. Both perforated plastic and fibre floating cloches allow air to pass freely through the material and also have useful insulating properties; fibre fleece also protects plants from one or two degrees of frost. For further information, see GROWING VEGETABLES, p.505.

The sheets or fleeces should be anchored firmly into the soil at the edges of the beds with soil, stones, or pegs. Whole beds may be covered with a floating cloche, if desired, or pieces may be cut to fit smaller areas or even individual plants.

Individual cloche

These are usually used to protect individual plants in the early stages of growth but they may also be placed over any vulnerable, small plants during severe winter weather, such as frost, deep snow, heavy rain, and high winds.

INDIVIDUAL CLOCHE

Home-made individual cloches, such as waxed-paper protectors and cut-off plastic bottles, are easy to make and are much less expensive than purpose-made models but may not be so attractive as ready-made, rigid plastic or glass, bell or dome-shaped cloches. These have curved walls, from which condensation trickles to the ground rather than falling on the plants, and so possibly causing disease or scorching.

INDIVIDUAL BELL CLOCHE

Routine maintenance

Regular maintenance is necessary to preserve greenhouses, and to keep frames and cloches clean. Autumn is usually a convenient time to attend to the maintenance work: cleaning and disinfecting the greenhouse structure and equipment at this time of year minimizes problems from overwintering pests and diseases.

It is important to do this work on a mild day before the very cold weather begins. Tender plants may then be put outside while the preparations for winter are carried out.

CLEANING BETWEEN PANES

To remove dirt from between overlapping panes in the greenhouse, use a thin, rigid strip of plastic to loosen any deposits before spraying or hosing down with water.

MAINTAINING THE GREENHOUSE

Exterior maintenance

Choose a dry, still day for routine work on the outside of the greenhouse. Before making a start, gather together all necessary materials for cleaning, repairing, and repainting.

Cleaning glass and plastic glazing

Glass may be cleaned with water only, using a hose and long-handled brush, but if it has become very dirty, better results are achieved by brushing with a solution of kettle descaler. Protect skin and eyes by wearing gloves and goggles, and rinse off the solution thoroughly with running water.

A proprietary window cleaning solution may also be used but it will not remove ingrained dirt. Dirt also tends to become trapped between overlapping panes. Push a thin, plastic label between panes to loosen dirt and algae, then remove using a water jet from a hose. Shading washes are best removed by rubbing them off with a cloth.

Repairing glass

Panes of glass and plastic panes that are slightly cracked may be temporarily repaired with transparent glazing tape. Broken and badly cracked panes, however, should be replaced completely, as soon as possible after the damage is noticed, to prevent harm to plants.

To replace a pane in an aluminium alloy greenhouse, remove the spring glazing clips and the adjoining pane, if necessary, and reglaze using the old clips (see p.572).

If the panes are bedded on linseed putty (as in many older wooden greenhouses), remove the glazing tacks and the panes of glass carefully. Chip away the putty with a chisel to leave a smooth surface. Clean the glazing bars with abrasive paper before reglazing.

Apply a priming paint to any unpainted or untreated wood on the glazing bars. Pay particular attention to knots in the wood which may be potential entry points for moisture. When the paint is fully dry, replace the panes by setting them on a bed of putty or glazing mastic, using glazing tacks to hold them.

Gutters and downpipes

Check that gutters and downpipes are in good repair. Use a hosepipe to clear any blockages. Small leaks in gutters may be sealed with mastic or other sealant, but badly leaking sections of gutter will need to be replaced completely.

Metal framework

Aluminium greenhouses require only minimal structural attention. Although they lose their bright colour, the greyish patina that forms protects the metal from the weather.

Steel frames and fittings should be checked for rust and, if necessary, treated with rust remover. Repaint every few years.

Timber framework

Cut out any rotting wood and replace it, applying woodworm killer, and renewing rusty hinges, as necessary. Softwood greenhouses need regular painting: strip off flaking paint, wash down, then apply primer and good-quality exterior paint. Hardwood greenhouses are more rot-resistant, only requiring a coat of wood preservative every year or two, which also restores the colour.

Ventilators

Windows and ventilator fans should be checked for ease of operation, working parts oiled if necessary, and glass or plastic cleaned.

Inside the greenhouse

Before cleaning and disinfecting the inside of a greenhouse or frame, turn off any electric power supply at the mains, cover electric sockets and fittings with plastic, and remove all plants to a safe place.

Cleaning and disinfecting

Glass and plastic glazing materials should be cleaned as described under "Exterior maintenance", above. Clean the glazing bars by scrubbing with a disinfectant solution – fine wire wool may be used (but not on anodized "coloured" aluminium).

Scrub brickwork and paths with a garden disinfectant and rinse with clean water. The disinfectant may be used, diluted according to the manufacturer's instructions, to sterilize the staging and other surfaces. Paint it on with a paintbrush or spray on as a coarse spray, wearing protective gloves and a face mask and goggles while spraying.

Fumigation

Return the plants to the greenhouse and, if necessary, use a fungicidal and insecticidal smoke to fumigate inside, following the instructions supplied. Make sure that all vents are closed before lighting the fumigant. Do not inhale the smoke, and lock the door until it is safe to re-enter.

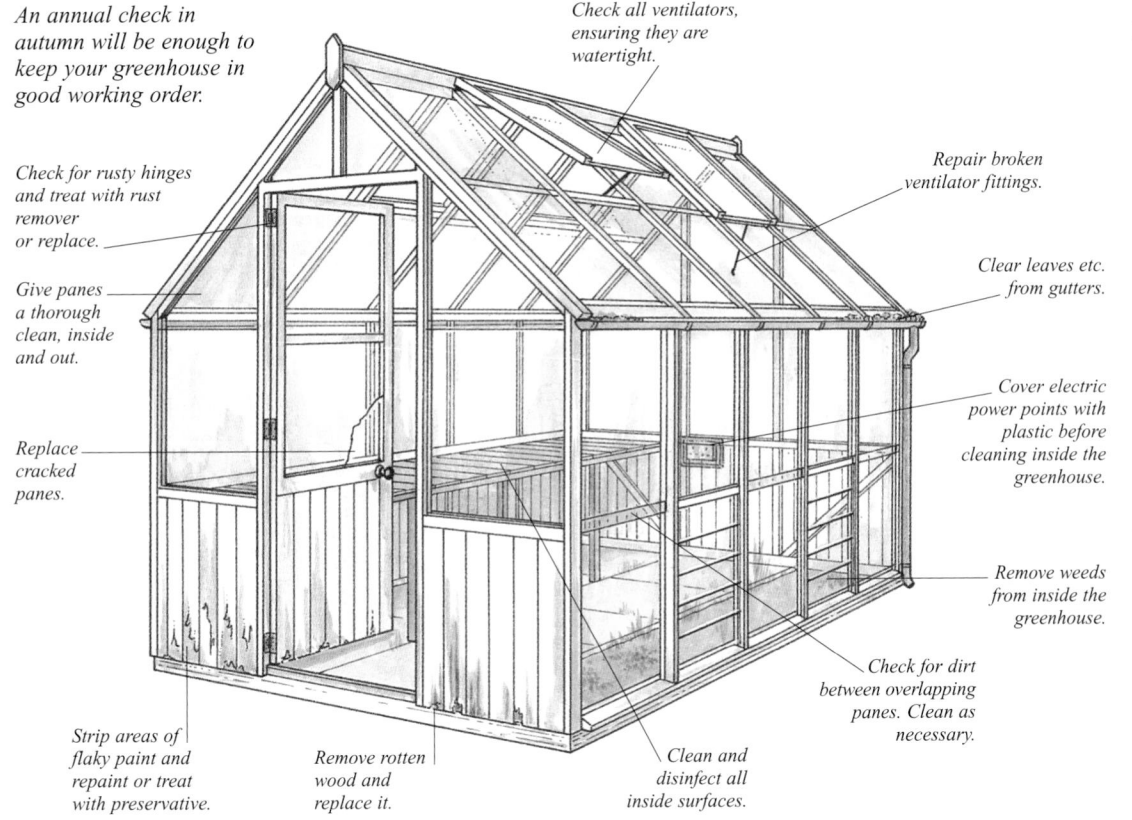

An annual check in autumn will be enough to keep your greenhouse in good working order.

Check for rusty hinges and treat with rust remover or replace.

Give panes a thorough clean, inside and out.

Replace cracked panes.

Strip areas of flaky paint and repaint or treat with preservative.

Remove rotten wood and replace it.

Clean and disinfect all inside surfaces.

Check for dirt between overlapping panes. Clean as necessary.

Remove weeds from inside the greenhouse.

Cover electric power points with plastic before cleaning inside the greenhouse.

Clear leaves etc. from gutters.

Repair broken ventilator fittings.

Check all ventilators, ensuring they are watertight.

3
STRUCTURES AND SURFACES

THE STRUCTURES AND hard surfaces of a garden act as the framework around which plants can grow and mature. Pergolas, fences, or trellis add vital height, as well as offering privacy and shelter, while paths lead visitors on a tour around the garden's splendours. A terrace adjoining the house can, depending on aspect, make the perfect setting for breakfast, or an ideal spot to relax in the evening sun. As well as being functional, structures and surfaces can be attractive design features, providing year-round architectural interest. They can also be used as foils for planting: a circular patio makes a striking contrast with spreading plants, while a large rustic arch will form a complementary support for rambling roses.

Designing with structures and surfaces

Hard landscape elements are vital in helping to form the framework of a garden design and may be as ornamental as they are functional. In a new garden, features such as a terrace or a pergola are valuable for providing interest while the plants are growing and becoming established. In a more mature garden, sympathetically designed structures complement softer elements such as a lawn or the planting in a border and give the garden solidity and substance all year round.

When planning and designing structures, consider them in the context of their setting and in relation to each other. Materials, style, size, and shape should all be congruous both with the house and the overall design of the garden. A terrace or wall adjacent to the house often looks most effective if built of the same materials, forming a cohesive link between house and garden. Local materials are often preferable because they tend to look appropriate in the setting. The degree of formality is another important consideration to be made; in a formal garden, for example, a mellow brick wall boundary would be ideal, while in an informal, cottage garden a picket fence or woven wattle hurdles would be more suitable.

Structures may be used to link, define, or separate different elements or parts of the garden. A gently

DESIGNING WITH HARD LANDSCAPE
Here, hard materials have been used to form the main framework of the design, creating interest while the planting is becoming established and providing a foil for the softer shapes of the plants. The curving path adds a sense of movement, while the innovative use of mixed materials provides satisfying textural contrasts.

curving path leads the eye along the garden, providing a unifying line, while a wide, straight path separates the features on either side. Steps create an interesting change of level and demarcate separate areas as well as joining them visually and providing access from one part to another. If the steps adjoin a patio, they may look best if constructed from the same materials and in a similar style – curved steps would look attractive linked to a circular patio, for example.

The order in which you undertake construction work largely depends on your individual priorities and the requirements of the site. It might be, for example, necessary to erect a flanking wall first because it will help to retain the soil of a raised bed; in another garden, laying a path might be the first priority to allow easy access with wheelbarrows to the rear of a site where work is in progress.

This chapter covers most straightforward structural projects that may be undertaken by an amateur, from hard surfaces such as patios, terraces, and paths, to boundaries and divisions, for example walls and fences, as well as other structures such as raised beds and pergolas. Certain hard landscape elements are covered in full in other chapters: see WATER GARDENING, pp.280–303, for details on constructing ponds and watercourses, and ROCK, SCREE, AND GRAVEL GARDENING, pp.252–280, for rock gardens and alpine troughs.

Patios and terraces

A patio is an ornamental feature as well as a functional one, providing an area for meals and relaxation, with plants in beds or containers, and perhaps a raised pool. An open paved area, with a balustrade or low wall, is more accurately described as a terrace. Patios and terraces are usually paved, although timber decking (see pp.591–592) has become increasingly popular as an alternative.

Choosing a site

Patios and terraces are usually sited close to the house, often with French windows allowing direct access. This is convenient for providing power sources for lights and other equipment, but if the site is not warm and sheltered, it may be better to choose an alternative position. Designing the patio at an angle of 45° to the house, perhaps at a corner, may ensure that it receives sun for most of the day. A patio may also be built away from the house to make use of a fine view across the garden.

Two or more small patios may be more useful than one large one. One may be sited in an open, sunny spot, the other in a cooler position to provide a welcome, shady retreat on a summer's day.

Shelter and privacy
A warm, sheltered patio can be enjoyed both earlier and later in the season than one that is subject to strong winds. If the site is overlooked, or exposed to winds, provide both shelter and seclusion with screens, such as trellis, covered with climbing plants. A pergola (see pp.603–604) roofed with trellis will screen the patio from above and provide shade. Avoid siting a patio near large trees, however: these will cast too much shade and drip long after rain has stopped, their roots may dislodge the paving, insects could be troublesome, and falling leaves and bird droppings may be a nuisance.

Mark a number of pegs at the same distance from the top of each, then knock them in, in rows 2m (6ft) apart – the first at the top of the slope. Put a 2.5cm (1in) offcut on a peg in the second row. Make the two rows of pegs level, remove the offcut, and repeat.

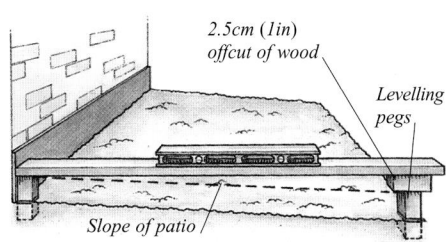

2.5cm (1in) offcut of wood

Levelling pegs

Slope of patio

A suitable size
Size is less important for a terrace that is simply a link between house and garden than for a patio that is to serve as an "outdoor room". It should be in proportion to the garden: if too small it may look trivial, if too large it may overpower a small garden. As a guide, allow about 3.3sq m (4sq yd) for each person likely to use it. For a family of four, a patio about 13sq m (16sq yd) is a practical size.

Choosing a surface

Simplicity is the key to good design. If the patio is to accommodate furniture, climbers, and container plants, paving should be unobtrusive. Bear in mind that coloured paving may look fussy and often weathers to dreary shades. Variety is best achieved by mixing textures: small areas of brick or gravel among paving slabs, railway sleepers intersecting bricks or clay pavers, or cobbles with stone slabs.

Also decide if, for example, a hard-wearing surface is needed, or one that is not slippery when wet: choose from such materials as concrete (p.586), paving slabs (p.587), natural stone (p.588), tiles (p.588), bricks and pavers (p.589), or granite setts and cobbles (p.591).

Foundations

Patios, paths, and drives (see p.593) need firm foundations to ensure that the paved surface remains stable once in use. The load-bearing requirements must also be taken into account: few patios will be required to support very heavy loads, but drives need more substantial foundations because they may be used by heavy vehicles as well as cars. Climate is another factor: in areas with prolonged dry periods, for example, concrete foundations may crack if not sufficiently deep; seek local advice if necessary.

Before undertaking any excavation work, check the location of all the service pipes and cables on your property with the local authority or supplier to avoid damaging them.

Water run-off
To drain off water, the surface of a patio should slope slightly; a fall of 2.5cm for every 2m (1in for every 6ft) is usually sufficient. Calculate the combined depth of the sub-base and surface material and mark this as a line at the same distance from the top of each of a number of levelling pegs. Insert one row at the top of the slope so that the mark is at soil level, the top of the peg indicating the desired level of the finished paving. Insert a second row of pegs 2m (6ft) down the slope. On each peg in this row in turn, place a small, 2.5cm (1in) thick offcut of wood, a "shim", and lay a spirit level on a plank between this peg and one in the first row. Adjust the height of the lower peg until the top of the shim and the upper peg are level. Remove the shim and repeat the process down the slope. Then rake the soil so that it is level with the mark on each peg. The base and surface of the finished construction should be parallel.

Basic procedure
Remove any plant growth from the area, including tree roots, then dig out loose topsoil until firm subsoil is reached. Consolidate this using a plate compactor. For most patios and paths, but not those that might bear heavy loads (see p.586), firm subsoil or a 10cm (4in) layer of hardcore, covered with 5cm (2in) sand, is an adequate foundation. Use more hardcore if necessary to bring the surface of the sub-base up to the required level.

On unstable soils, such as peat or heavy clay (which may shrink in dry weather and cause damage to the paving), lay 15cm (6in) of compacted hardcore as a sub-base. Top this up with sand or ballast to produce a level surface for laying.

PREPARING THE SUB-BASE FOR PATIOS AND PATHS

1 *Mark out the area with pegs and string, setting the string at the ultimate level of the path or patio. Use a builder's square to check that the corners are set at right angles.*

2 *Dig down to firm subsoil and tamp down with a plate compactor. Allow for a 10cm (4in) depth of hardcore, a 5cm (2in) layer of sand, if required, plus the thickness of the surface layer.*

3 *Drive in a grid of levelling pegs every 2m (6ft). For a patio, incorporate a slight slope so surface water drains away. Use a spirit level and plank to ensure that pegs are level with strings.*

4 *Spread a 10cm (4in) layer of hardcore over the entire site, and then compact it so that it is level, using the pegs as a guide. Add sand, if necessary, and compact the area again.*

HOW TO LAY CONCRETE

1 *After marking out the site, dig it out to a depth of 20cm (8in). Drive levelling pegs into the ground 1m (3ft) apart along the string lines. Set them horizontal using a plank and a spirit level.*

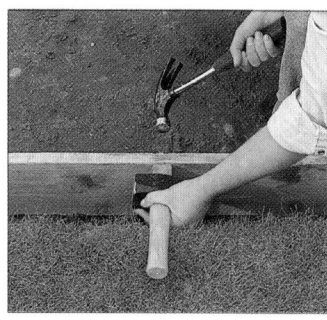

2 *Remove the string lines and nail wooden planks to the inner faces of the pegs, butted end-to-face at the corners. This formwork holds the concrete in place until it sets hard.*

3 *Divide large sites into sections no more than 4m (12ft) long using formwork. Spread hardcore 10cm (4in) deep and tamp it down with a roller or stout timber.*

4 *Starting with the first section, tip in the concrete and spread it level so that it is just proud of the formwork. Work the concrete well into the edges.*

5 *Using a wooden beam that spans the width of the formwork, compact the concrete with a downward chopping motion. Then slide the beam from side to side to level the surface.*

6 *Fill any hollows that appear after levelling using fresh concrete, and level it again.*

7 *Lay a protective, water-proof covering such as plastic sheeting over the concrete until it dries. Remove the formwork when the concrete has set hard.*

Load-bearing surfaces

For areas such as drives that need to support heavy weight (such as cars), lay a sub-base of at least 10cm (4in) of compacted hardcore or rubble, with a further 10cm (4in) of concrete on top. This concrete may be used as the top surface or as a base for another material such as asphalt or pavers bedded in mortar. On clay or unstable soils, or if the surface is to be used by heavy vehicles, lay 15cm (6in) of concrete on top of the hardcore. If mixing your own concrete for the foundations, see below. When laying large areas of concrete, it is essential to leave expansion gaps (see "Expansion joints", p.594).

Concrete

Concrete is relatively quick and easy to lay and makes a hard-wearing and durable surface. It may be made more attractive by adding a textured finish (see p.594).

Ordering concrete

If you intend to lay a large area of concrete and there is access for large vehicles, having ready-mixed concrete delivered will make the job easier and quicker. Give the supplier the site measurements and information about the intended use of the surface to ensure that the correct amount and mix is delivered or use a supplier who will mix it for you on site. This saves time and effort, but requires advance preparation and usually some helpers, since you have to tackle the job straightaway.

Concrete and mortar mixes

The following proportions for concrete and mortar mixes are suitable for most projects. For an explanation of terms, see p.591.

Wall footings, drive foundations, and bases for pre-cast paving
1 part cement
2½ parts sharp sand
3½ parts 20mm (¾in) aggregate
(or 5 parts combined aggregate to 1 part cement, omitting the sand)

***In situ* (poured) concrete paving**
1 part cement
1½ parts sharp sand
2½ parts 20mm (¾in) aggregate
(or 3½ parts combined aggregate to 1 part cement, omitting the sand)

Bedding mortar (for bedding paving, and jointing paving bricks)
1 part cement
5 parts sharp sand

Masonry mortar (for garden brickwork)
1 part masonry cement
3 parts soft sand

All these proportions are measured by volume and not by weight. The consistency of the mix required for different jobs varies considerably. When mixing either concrete or mortar, start by adding only about half a part of water to one part of cement. This will provide a very stiff mix. Continue to add water gradually until you reach the consistency you need.

In hot climates, setting retardants may sometimes be necessary in mortar and concrete mixes, while in cold climates, antifreeze products may have to be incorporated. Seek local advice, if necessary. It is best to avoid laying concrete and mortar when the weather is close to freezing or above 32°C (90°F).

Laying concrete

First mark out the area to be concreted with string and dig down about 20cm (8in) until firm subsoil is reached. Drive a number of wooden levelling pegs into the ground at intervals of 1m (3ft) around the edge, using the string as a guide. Nail planks to the inside faces of the levelling pegs to make a formwork at least 20cm (8in) deep, which confines the concrete until it sets.

Divide large sites up into small sections no more than 4m (12ft) long using more planks. On top of the subsoil, spread a 10cm (4in) layer of compacted hardcore. Taking one section at a time, pour the freshly mixed concrete inside the formwork to a depth of 10cm (4in) and work it well into the edges. Use a wooden beam spanning the width of the formwork to compact the mix, then level the concrete by drawing the beam back and forth across the top of the formwork.

Inspection covers

Inspection covers that allow access to mains services must always be unobstructed, so should never be paved over. Proprietary metal trays are available in which to bed paving slabs, clay pavers, or other materials. These minimize the unsightly impact of an inspection cover sited in an area of paving and may simply be lifted out when necessary. When it is important to maintain the same pattern of laying as the surrounding area, it may be necessary to cut the slabs or pavers that fit within the tray. The trays may also be filled with turf, or used for planting.

Paving slabs

Concrete paving slabs are popular for patios, paths, and drives. They are available in a range of sizes, textures, and colours, and are easy to lay once the base has been prepared. Many garden centres and builders' merchants stock a range of pre-cast concrete slabs. Some designs may be available only in one area. Large suppliers usually produce catalogues and deliver direct.

Sizes and shapes

Most slabs are either 450 x 450mm (18 x 18in) or 450 x 600mm (18 x 24in), with smaller slabs designed to integrate with them. Not all slabs have a shaped edge designed to butt join; a half slab may be slightly less than half the size of a full one, to allow for mortar between the joints.

Circular slabs are suitable only for stepping stones and small areas of paving with an infill of a loose material, such as gravel. Hexagonal slabs are useful if you prefer a pattern without regular, parallel lines; half slabs are available for a straight edge. Some slabs are made with a "bite" out of one corner, so that four slabs together form a planting hole.

Quantities

If laying a pattern with slabs of different sizes or colours, draw a plan on graph paper to calculate the number of each required, and allow up to five per cent extra for breakages (especially if many have to be cut, see p.588). Try to work to dimensions that minimize the need to cut slabs.

Laying paving slabs

If laying a patio, establish a line that you can use as a straight edge and ensure that there is a slight slope for drainage; always slope the patio away from a building. A house wall is a practical base line to work from, but you may want to leave a small gap between the wall and paving for planting. The top of the paving must be a minimum of 15cm (6in) below the damp-proof course. Mark out the area to be paved with pegs and string. Make it a size that requires as few slabs as possible to be cut. If the slabs are not to be butted, allow about 0.5–1cm (¼–½in) for mortar joints; metric slabs are usually designed to be laid with narrower joints than imperial slabs; if in doubt, seek advice from the supplier.

Preparing the site

Clear the site and prepare a sub-base of hardcore (see p.585). You will need wooden spacers about 1cm (½in) thick to place between the paving slabs to allow for mortar.

Positioning the slabs

Work from one corner, placing a row of slabs in each direction with spacers between to make sure that the dimensions are correct. Adjustments are easy to make at this stage. Using a bricklayer's trowel, lay a strip of bedding mortar along each edge where the slab is to be laid, to form an area slightly smaller than the slab. If the slab is 45cm (18in) or more across, lay a cross of mortar within the box. The mortar ridges should be about 3–5cm (1¼–2in) high. This "box and cross" method combines strength with easy adjustment. Lay the slab in position and tamp it down with the handle of a club hammer or mallet. Use a spirit level to check that it is firm and straight. Repeat with successive slabs, using spacers between each one. Check the levels in each direction after every three or four slabs. Remove the spacers while you can

PAVING SLAB STYLES

TEXTURE
Surface textures range from smooth to stippled, scored, or roughly pebbled.

HEXAGONAL PAVERS
These are an attractive alternative to rectangles or squares. Half blocks are used for straight edges.

WEATHERED PAVERS
If a more natural look is desired, a range of "weathered" stone pavers is available.

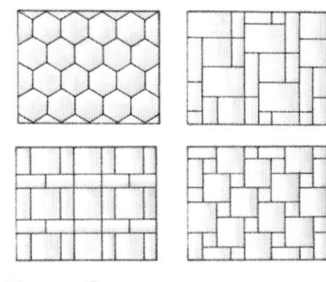

PAVING PATTERNS
A variety of pleasing patterns may be created with different shapes and sizes of paver.

POINTED SLABS
Some slabs are pointed to give special patterns or effects. Those with a "bite" taken out may be fitted together for a planting gap.

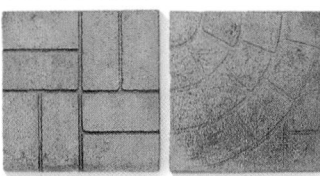

CAST AND PRESSED SLABS
Cast slabs (sloping edges) are for light/medium use. Pressed slabs (straight) are lighter but stronger.

HOW TO LAY PAVING SLABS

1 *Mark out the area and prepare the sub-base (see p.585). Lay strips of mortar to form a square just smaller than the slab. Include a cross strip for large slabs.*

2 *Position the slab and tamp down. Use a spirit level to check it is level. Repeat, using spacers for 1cm (½in) mortar gaps between the slabs.*

3 *Remove the spacers before the mortar sets. After two days, fill the joints with a stiff mortar. Scrape away so they are recessed about 2mm (¹⁄₁₆in). Brush slabs clean.*

USING A JIGGER
This device has a central slit. After aligning the slit and joint, the gap can be filled without spilling mortar on the slabs.

still reach them without walking on the paving, and before the mortar sets. If you have to walk on the paving before the mortar has dried, stand on planks to spread your weight.

Finishing off
After a couple of days, fill the joints with a very stiff mortar mix (it should almost be "crumbly" to avoid staining the surface of the paving). Rub a

dowel or a rounded piece of wood over the pointing for a crisp finish, leaving it about 2mm (¹⁄₁₆in) below the paving surface. Alternatively, brush a dry mortar of 1 part cement to 3 parts sand into the joints. Brush any surplus off the surface. Spray the joints with a fine mist from a compression sprayer or a watering can fitted with a fine rose. Sponge excess mortar from the surface immediately, before it stains the slabs.

Cutting paving slabs

If you have many slabs to cut, it is best to hire a block splitter or angle grinder. For only a few, use a bolster (a broad-edged cold chisel) and club hammer. Always wear goggles when cutting paving blocks. Score the line where you need to cut with a corner of the bolster all around the slab, then chisel a groove about 3mm (¹⁄₈in) deep along this line; you may have to work around the slab several times, using the bolster to define and deepen the groove. If the slab has to fit into a tight space, cut it about 6mm (¹⁄₄in) smaller than needed to allow room for any rough edges that may be left when the slab splits.

Place the slab on a firm surface and raise the smaller part of the slab to be cut on a length of timber. Tap it sharply with the handle of a club hammer until a split forms along the line of the groove. Trim any rough pieces carefully with the bolster.

Crazy paving

Crazy paving has an informal appearance. It can be laid on sand, which will allow plants to be grown

between the joints, or on mortar for a firmer finish; if using the latter, fill in the joints with bedding mortar.

Defining the edges
Use string lines to mark out the area to be paved and prepare a sub-base for the paving (see p.585). Allow a slight slope for drainage (see "Water run-off", p.585) if necessary. Define the edges by laying a few metres (yards) of edging material first, working from one corner if laying a patio, the two edges if laying a path. This may simply be large pieces of crazy paving, with at least one straight edge, which can be laid to form the sides of the patio or path, or it could be wood, brick, or concrete. If using paving slabs, mortar these into position, even if bedding the remaining slabs on sand.

Laying the crazy paving
Loose lay an area about 1m (3ft) square without mortar, fitting the pieces together like a jigsaw. Keep the gaps small. It may be necessary to trim some pieces to size. Introduce a large piece occasionally, and infill with smaller ones.

Bed the pieces on sand or mortar, using a spirit level on a straight edge to ensure that they are level. Use a mallet or a block of wood and a hammer to bed each piece firmly in position. Lift pieces and add or remove sand or mortar as necessary until they are level.

Filling the joints
If bedding crazy paving on sand, finish off by brushing dry sand into the joints. If using mortar, mix a stiff, crumbly, almost dry mortar and use a pointing trowel to fill the joints (see "Finishing off", above). If using a dark-coloured stone, such

as slate, use a concrete dye (a powder you mix with the sand and cement) to make the joints less conspicuous. The colour will look different when dry, so test the dye on a small area and leave it to dry before deciding on the amount of colour to add.

Natural stone

Natural stone looks good, but is expensive and difficult to lay. Some types, such as sandstone, may be available cut into regular sizes and with an even edge. "Dressed" stone looks more natural; it is trimmed to a regular shape and has an attractive, uneven finish.

Lay sawn or dressed stone in the same way as paving slabs, adding or removing mortar to produce a level surface. Random stone is irregular in outline and thickness, and has no straight edges. This stone is suitable for laying as crazy paving, and it looks much more appealing than broken concrete paving slabs.

Tile surfaces

Quarry tiles, which are made of clay fired to a very high temperature, are useful for linking outdoor and indoor areas – perhaps where the paving inside a conservatory links with that outside. Glazed ceramic tiles may be more ornamental, giving an enclosed patio the impression of a Mediterranean courtyard for example, but many are not frost-proof. When selecting tiles, always check that they are suitable for using outdoors in your area before buying them. Tiles are difficult to cut,

---

HOW TO CUT SLABS

1 *Place the slab on a firm, flat surface and, using the corner of a bolster and a straight edge, score a groove on both faces and edges to mark the cutting line.*

2 *Using a bolster and club hammer, carefully work along the scored line to deepen the groove on the faces and edges of the paving slab.*

3 *Raise the slab onto a length of timber. Align the groove with the edge of the timber and tap the slab sharply with a hammer handle until it splits.*

HOW TO LAY CRAZY PAVING

1 *Using string lines and pegs to mark the height of the edges, prepare a sub-base (see p.585). Lay the edging pieces first, placing their straight edges outermost.*

2 *Fill in the centre with large slabs, infilled with smaller ones. Check that central slabs are level with the edging pieces and bed them on sand or mortar. Use a block of timber and a club hammer.*

3 *Fill the joints with almost dry mortar, or brush in sand. With a mortar finish, use a trowel to bevel the mortar so that any surface water drains away from the slabs.*

especially if they are not rectangular, so where possible design the area to make use of full tiles.

Laying tiles
Since tiles are thin and sometimes brittle, they need to be laid on a concrete sub-base (see "Load-bearing surfaces", p.586). Quarry tiles may be laid on bedding mortar (see p.591). Soak the tiles for a couple of hours before use so that they do not absorb too much moisture from the mortar.

Glazed ceramic tiles are best glued to a level concrete base using outdoor tile adhesive (obtainable from a builders' merchant). Spread this on the back of the tiles, following the manufacturer's instructions, then press the tiles into position on the prepared concrete base.

Finish off an area of glazed tiles with a grout (available from builders' merchants) to fill the gaps, perhaps coloured to match or contrast with the tiles.

Bricks and pavers

Bricks and clay or concrete pavers are most effective when laid in small areas; a large expanse is best broken up with other materials, such as gravel or railway sleepers, otherwise the effect may well prove to be overwhelming.

For a patio situated next to a house built of brick, using bricks or pavers is an excellent way of linking the house and garden visually. Bricks and pavers also offer greater design flexibility than large, stone or concrete slabs, as they can be laid in a variety of patterns.

Choosing bricks
The range of bricks available is sufficiently extensive for it to be possible to find a type that suits a patio or terrace designed and constructed in any style.

For a large volume of bricks, contact a brick company to see if they will deliver. Builders' merchants supply bricks in any quantities. Be sure to choose bricks that are appropriate for outdoor paving and resistant to wetting and freezing.

Choosing pavers
Clay pavers are as attractive as bricks and are usually produced in shades of red. They have a thinner profile than concrete pavers or bricks. Concrete pavers may lack the warm colours of bricks but they will make a practical surface. They are generally found in grey, blue-grey, or buff shades and are produced in a range of shapes.

Laying bricks

First make a suitable sub-base (see p.585). Bricks should ideally be bedded on mortar. First lay edging strips (or edging bricks), bedded on a concrete footing and then fixed with mortar between the joints. Prepare the bedding mortar (see p.586) and lay it to a depth of 2.5cm (1in). Bed the bricks onto this, spacing them evenly to leave joints for mortar; use thin strips of hardboard or wood as spacers between bricks if desired. Once an area is complete, brush a dry mortar over the bricks. To remove air pockets, press this into the gaps with a narrow piece of wood. In damp weather, moisture from the ground and air will set the pointing; in dry weather, speed up setting by spraying with water.

HOW TO LAY BRICK PAVING

1 *First, prepare the sub-base (see p.585), allowing space for the edging bricks. Use string lines and pegs to set the edging bricks at the desired height.*

2 *Mortar in the edging bricks, and bed the others in the required pattern, tamping them level. At intervals, check levels in all directions.*

3 *Spread a thin layer of dry mortar over the surface and brush it between the joints. Sprinkle with water to set the mortar, and clean the surface.*

Patterns in brick

Bricks may be laid in several different ways to create attractive patterns; three examples are shown below.

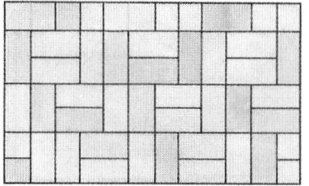

BASKET-WEAVE

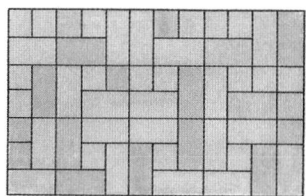

INTERLOCKING BOXES

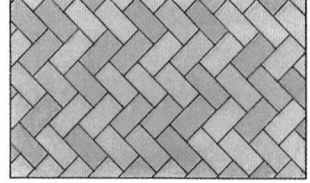

HERRINGBONE

Types of brick

Bricks are available in a wide range of styles, textures, and colours, providing an attractive and practical building material; take care to choose the most appropriate type so that they are suitable for the proposed purpose and that they coordinate well with the house, patio, or other hard landscape features.

ENGINEERING BRICKS
Engineering bricks are very hard-wearing. If used for paving, make sure they have good wet-weather grip. They may cost more than ordinary bricks.

CORED BRICKS
Cored bricks have holes. They may be used on edge for paving with a narrower profile, but are not economical for large areas.

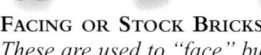

FACING OR STOCK BRICKS
These are used to "face" buildings, providing an attractive finish. They are available in a variety of colours, and may be rough or smooth in texture. They may be unsuitable for paving as they may not be able to withstand severe weather conditions.

BRICKS WITH "FROGS"
A frog is an indentation in one side of a brick. Frogged bricks may be used for paving, if they are laid on edge or the frogs face downwards.

Cutting bricks and pavers

Bricks and thick pavers may be difficult to cut. If cutting is necessary, the easiest option is to use a hydraulic block splitter. These are often available from hire shops and are operated by applying pressure on a lever. Using this method, the bricks and pavers are cut quickly and neatly.

Alternatively, bricks and pavers may be cut to the desired shape with a bolster and club hammer (see "Cutting paving slabs", p.588).

Laying pavers

Pavers are bedded onto sand using a plate compactor; they nest together with small gaps between. Since the pavers can be lifted and relaid, this type of paving is sometimes called "flexible paving". Blocks 60–65mm (2½–2¾in) thick are adequate for garden projects.

Preparing the site and laying edge restraints

First, prepare a sub-base of 8cm (3in) compacted hardcore on firm soil (see p.585). Where there are no existing firm edges (such as walls), lay permanent edging strips. The simplest way to do this is to use specially made edge restraints or edging pieces, which are available from paving manufacturers. These must be concreted into position. Alternatively, use 100 x 35mm (4 x 1½in) treated or creosoted timber held in place with strong pegs at least 50mm (2in) square.

Large areas should be broken up into manageable sizes, such as 1m (3ft) squares, using temporary timber rails. Spread a layer of sharp

Pavers, tiles, setts, and cobbles

Pavers (also called paviors) vary greatly in size, colour, and thickness. They are also finished in many different ways, so that their texture and final shape, either formal and geometric or more informal and natural, contribute greatly to the style of the garden. More distinctive effects may be possible using terracotta tiles, granite setts, Belgian blocks, or rounded cobbles.

CLAY PAVERS
These red pavers may be laid either as "stretchers", that is longitudinally, or as "headers", placed end on.

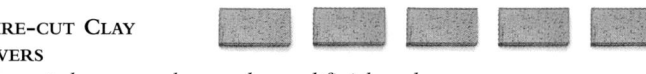

WIRE-CUT CLAY PAVERS
Wire-cut clay pavers have a dragged finish and a roughened surface on all sides, which serves to provide extra grip in the finished paving.

INTERLOCKING PAVERS
These clay or concrete pavers can be used to create unusual patterns. Pressed pavers in blocks (far right) are produced in a range of colours.

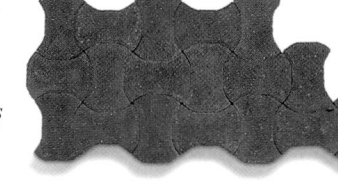

TERRACOTTA TILES
Like bricks, terracotta tiles are made of clay but allowed to dry in the sun. They are porous and may crack if used in areas prone to frost.

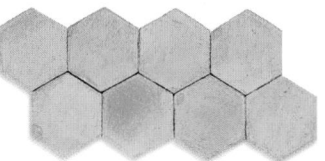

GRANITE SETTS
Cut from hard granite, this form of paving is extremely durable. Like cobbles, the roughened surface of the setts creates a natural effect.

"BELGIAN" BLOCKS

COBBLES
Cobbles (below) are large, rounded stones formed by the action of the sea or glaciers. To protect the environment, buy glacially formed cobbles that have been quarried commercially rather than coastal ones that may have been taken from a beach. Cobbles may be embedded separately in the ground or be edged and set in bedding mortar to form an interestingly textured finish.

IMITATION GRANITE SETTS
These reconstituted stone pavers are lighter and cheaper than granite. "Belgian" blocks have a more weathered look.

HOW TO LAY FLEXIBLE PAVING

1 *After preparing the sub-base (see p.585), set edging strips of concrete or timber in position around the edges of the site. Use a spirit level and a club hammer to tap the edges level.*

2 *Divide large areas into bays 1m (3ft) square with battens. Add 5cm (2in) of sand. Level the sand to the tops of the battens with a length of wood. Remove the battens and fill the vacated spaces with sand.*

3 *Lay the pavers to the required pattern, working from one corner of the site. Lay only whole blocks at this stage, leaving until last any cut ones required to fill the gaps in the design.*

4 *Vibrate the pavers into the sand or tamp down with a club hammer and length of timber. Brush dry sand over the surface and make 2 or 3 passes with a plate compactor.*

sand evenly to a depth of about 5cm (2in). The top surface of the sand should be about 4.5cm (1¾in) below the desired level of the finished paving when using 60mm (2⅜in) pavers, or about 5cm (2in) below when using 65mm (2½in) blocks.

Positioning and bedding the pavers

Do not walk on the sand while laying the pavers, and keep it dry. Working from one corner of the site, lay the pavers. When some are laid, place a kneeling board over the pavers to continue working. Lay as many whole blocks as possible, then fill in with cut pavers around obstacles such as inspection covers as necessary (see p.586).

When about 5sq m (6sq yd) of paving has been laid, bed the pavers into the sand. The easiest way to do this is with a plate compactor, but do not go too near the incompleted edge. If only laying a small area of paving, the blocks may be tamped down with a heavy club hammer over a block of wood that is large enough to span several pavers at once. Continue to lay pavers and bed or tamp them down.

When the whole area is finished, brush dry sand into the joints and settle in position with the plate compactor. Use a mowing edge of bricks, pavers, or concrete slabs where it is difficult to mow right to the lawn edge. Bed the paving material on mortar, with the top just below the grass level, so that the mower is not damaged.

A COMBINATION OF PAVING EFFECTS
A mixture of different paving materials, including square stone slabs, crazy paving, and brick edging, blends well with informal planting.

Setts and cobbles

Bed granite or imitation setts on 5cm (2in) of bedding mortar (see p.586) and brush stiff mortar into the joints (see "Finishing off", p.588). Spray the surface with water to clean it and set the mortar mix.

Cobbles may also be set in mortar. They are uncomfortable to walk on, so use them for small areas or with other materials. When laying, form firm edges with bricks or lengths of concrete edging. Lay 3.5cm (1½in) of bedding mortar over 8cm (3in) of compacted hardcore.

Terms explained

Aggregate is crushed stone or gravel used in making concrete. Graded 20mm (¾in) aggregate is suitable for most concreting jobs. Combined aggregate contains sand as well as stone.
Ballast is combined aggregate.
Bedding mortar is used for laying paving stones. It is made with sharp sand.
Cement is a grey powder containing limestone, the setting agent of concrete and mortar.
Concrete is a hard-setting building material made of a mixture of cement, aggregate, sand, and water.
Dry mortar is a stiff mix of sand and cement often used to fill the joints in paving.
Hardcore is rubble such as broken bricks used as a sub-base under concrete foundations.
Masonry cement has additives that make it unsuitable for concrete. Use only for mortars.
Mortar is a mixture of cement, sand, and water used principally for bricklaying.
Portland cement is not a brand name, but a type of cement. Use ordinary Portland cement for most concreting jobs. It can also be used for mortars.
Sand is graded by particle size. Sharp (concreting) sand is coarse; soft (builders') sand is more evenly graded for masonry mortar.

Decks

Timber decking is popular as a hard surface in warm, dry climates. Decks may be used anywhere, however, provided that timber pressure-treated with preservative is used.

It is best to build the deck on a level or gently sloping site. For a raised deck on a steep, sloping site and for decking that extends over water (see WATERSIDE DECKING, p.296), it is advisable to seek specialist assistance, since it would need to be well designed and constructed.

In some countries, building regulations state that all exterior areas of decking must be able to support a stipulated minimum weight. It may also be necessary to obtain a building permit and have the work inspected. If in doubt, check with your local authority building department. Simple parquet decking (see p.592) laid on gravel and sand should not require permission.

TIMBER DECKING
A wooden patio or verandah overlooking the garden makes a very imposing feature, especially when crowned with a pergola to provide summer shade. Timber decking, however, needs to be very well constructed, and it is usually best to have the job done by experts. Features such as rails, steps, and timber supports require regular maintenance (see p.592).

Timber for decking

Western red cedar is a good choice because of its natural rot resistance, although regularly treating it with a preservative ensures a longer life. Other timbers are suitable but must be pressure-treated with a preservative. Timber merchants will advise on the most suitable timber and grade to use. Short lengths of timber can be made up into decking panels to produce a variety of attractive patterns.

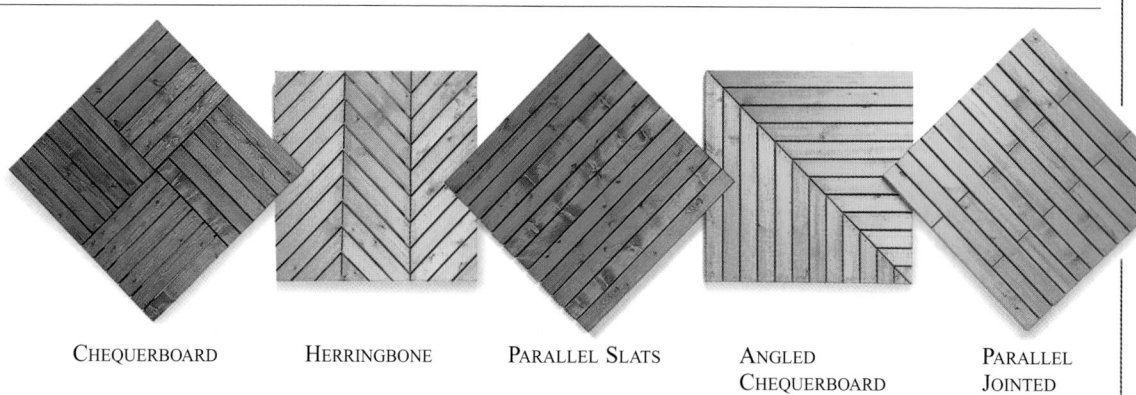

CHEQUERBOARD   HERRINGBONE   PARALLEL SLATS   ANGLED CHEQUERBOARD   PARALLEL JOINTED

Slatted decking

This type of decking is suitable for level or gently sloping ground. It is simple to construct.

For an area beside a house, construct a concrete foundation (see *How to Lay Concrete*, p.586) with a gentle fall away from the house for water drainage. Onto the concrete base, mortar a row of bricks spaced about one brick apart at right angles to the intended direction of the decking. Add further rows of bricks at intervals of 40cm (16in). Check constantly that all the bricks are level, because they will support the joists.

Lay joists 75 x 50mm (3 x 2in) over the bricks, inserting a sheet of plastic or other damp-proof material between the bricks and the joists. If joining lengths of timber, make sure there is a brick beneath the point where the joists abut and screw a plain bracket across the join. Check levels between joists accurately with a spirit level and a straight edge. Lay 250 x 25mm (10 x 1in) planks at right angles to the joists. Allow 10mm (½in) gaps for free drainage and a little movement in the timber. Ensure that joints in the decking are staggered from row to row and that the planks are butt-joined over a supporting joist. Secure the planks with brass or other rust-proof screws, countersunk beneath the surface. Fill the holes with wood filler that matches the colour of the wood.

Finish the deck neatly with a low brick or block edging, cutting the decking so that it overlaps the edging by 5cm (2in). Alternatively, a length of facing timber can be screwed or nailed along the cut edges.

Parquet decking

It is possible to buy small, parquet-type, timber squares intended primarily for paths, which can also be used for decking. Alternatively they can be easily made. About 1m (3ft) square is a practical size. Buy 100 x 50mm (4 x 2in) treated timber, cut into 1m (3ft) lengths, and sand the ends smooth. Two lengths form the supports at opposite sides of the square, while the others are laid across them as slats. Use spacers to ensure that the slats fill the area evenly and fix the slats with two nails at either end. Prepare a base on firmed ground or subsoil with 8cm (3in) of compacted gravel topped with 8cm (3in) of sand. Level and tamp before laying the squares in alternate directions. Nail them together if necessary to stop them moving, driving the nails in at an angle.

Applying stains

Western red cedar turns a very obvious red colour when wet. It may, however, be stained any colour to suit the surroundings. It is best to use microporous stains, which allow any moisture in the wood to escape; if trapped beneath an impermeable layer, it would eventually cause the surface colour to lift. All wooden surfaces for staining should be dry and free from dirt. Follow instructions regarding stirring or thinning and apply the stain with a good-quality paint brush, brushing in the direction of the grain. Do not overload the brush, since this will lead to uneven coverage, but work the stain well into the wood. Several applications will be needed, but wait until each coat is completely dry before applying more. See also "Wood preservatives", p.602.

Maintenance

All wooden surfaces need regular maintenance. Once a year, check all surface areas for splits or cracks. Damaged timbers will need to be replaced. Check, too, that no bolts, screws, brackets, or nails have rusted. If galvanized fittings are abraded, their protective coating may be damaged and rust will appear. Brass fittings, which do not rust, are preferable in timber decking. If the stain wears thin in areas of heavy foot traffic, clean the surface and re-apply the stain (see above). Fungus growths are likely to appear at some stage. Fungicides are available, but it is better to remove growths by brushing with a stiff broom or use a scrubbing brush and a mild solution of bleach.

DECKING STEPPING STONES
Decking can be used to create an unusual "stepping-stone" path across a pond. When positioned and angled for aesthetic effect, the squares add a stylish, geometric element to informal planting and the soft play of light on the pond surface. Here, parallel slats are laid in alternate directions to add a dynamic sense of movement to the overall design.

SUPPORT FOR TIMBER DECKING

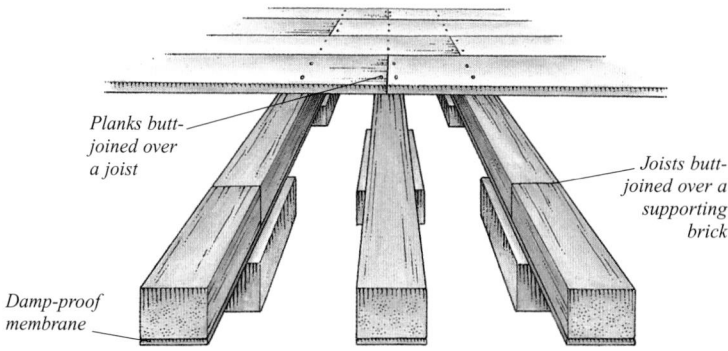

Planks butt-joined over a joist

Joists butt-joined over a supporting brick

Damp-proof membrane

When joining two lengths of timber to form a joist, make sure that the join lies over one of the supporting bricks. Lay the planks at right angles to the joists, positioning all butt-joints directly over a supporting joist.

Paths and steps

Paths and steps play a valuable part in good garden design. They help form the framework of the garden, link its various elements, and may lead the eye to a focal point. Consider setting a path at an angle, off-centre, or following an indirect route. Steps provide interesting changes of level and create very different effects, depending on whether they are straight or curved, wide or narrow, and shallow or steep.

Practical considerations
Paths to the garden shed or the greenhouse need to be wide enough to take a wheelbarrow and should also provide a dry and solid surface. Those to the front door or for strolling through the garden should be sufficiently wide for two to walk abreast: about 1–1.2m (3–4ft).

Materials and design
The choice of materials and the laying pattern may be used to set or enhance the garden style. Combining materials, for example paving stones with cobbles, bricks with gravel, or concrete paving slabs with bricks or clay pavers, often makes a very effective design for a path.

"Stepping-stone" paths may be laid in many parts of the garden. They are a good choice, for example, when you do not want to spoil the line of a lawn, but they can become muddy in wet weather. Place the paving stones on the surface first to check the spacing; they should be spaced at a natural pace. On lawns, set them into the grass so that their surface is safely below mowing level.

Where winters are relatively dry, paths may be made of timber, either in the form of log sections used as stepping stones or to make a series of square, slatted units as described in "Parquet decking", opposite.

On sloping sites, steps may be an essential part of a path. They may also be valuable as a design feature even on a relatively flat site. Steps should harmonize with their setting: for example, in a woodland garden, shallow log risers and gravel treads would be suitable while, in a modern setting, brick risers and concrete slab treads would be more appropriate.

Drives
A drive can have a considerable impact on a design, especially in a small garden. There may be little choice where to position a drive, unless a new garage is to be built at the same time; it is possible to make a drive look attractive, however, by choosing a suitable surface and positioning ornamental plants nearby.

Asphalt

Asphalt is best used for drives and paths that need not be attractive – the path to the shed, for example. It can also be used to cover a damaged concrete path. As well as black, asphalt is available in red and green. Stone chippings may be rolled into the surface to add texture. Asphalt is best laid in warm weather. Unless well laid, asphalt may break up after a few years; for heavily used areas such as a main drive it is worth having it laid by a qualified contractor.

Preparations
Asphalt can be laid on any firm surface, such as concrete or gravel. Never lay it on bare earth or hardcore

BRICK PATHWAYS
A brick path can become a design feature in its own right, adding texture and colour to a garden entrance. Here, the soft pink of the brick harmonizes with the surrounding plants and leads the eye to the rose-covered arch and the informal grass area beyond.

since it will be difficult to obtain a firm and level surface that will last. If necessary, make a stable base by spreading a mixture of gravel and sand 5–8cm (2–3in) thick over firm ground or compacted hardcore. If an old path or drive is the base, first paint inside any holes or cracks with bitumen emulsion (tar paint) and leave for about 20 minutes before filling them with macadam. To ensure good water drainage, lay a drive on a slight slope.

The edges of an asphalt path often weaken and crumble, so use concrete edging blocks (from builders' yards), bricks, or lengths of creosoted timber to provide a firm edging.

Application
Apply a layer of bitumen emulsion to bind the surface. Stir it first, then pour it from the container and spread it with a stiff brush. (Wash the brush in hot, soapy water afterwards.) When the emulsion has turned black, apply the macadam and rake it to an even depth of about 2cm (¾in).

Firm the surface by tamping it with the back of a rake to remove large air pockets, then make several passes with a heavy garden roller. Keep the surface of the roller damp to prevent the macadam sticking to it. Top up any visible depressions, and roll the surface again. If using stone chippings, sprinkle evenly and roll again to bed them in.

Bricks and pavers

The sympathetic colouring of bricks and clay pavers makes them excellent materials for paths within the garden. Because the individual units are small, it is relatively easy to

adjust to changes of level and even to lay a path to a curve. A variety of effects can be created depending on the laying pattern used (see "Patterns in brick", p.589).

Construction
Mark out the proposed line of the path with pegs and string, calculating where cut bricks or pavers may be needed to create a sharp curve. If the path will be subjected to heavy wear, prepare a concrete foundation (see "Load-bearing surfaces", p.586). For one that will receive lighter use, an 8cm (3in) sub-base of firmed hardcore levelled with ballast should be sufficient.

First lay a suitable edging (see p.594) along one side of the path, then lay the path itself in sections about 1m (3ft) long. Pavers should be bedded in a 5cm (2in) layer of dry sand (see "Laying pavers", p.590), while bricks will require a 2.5cm (1in) bed of mortar (see "Laying bricks", p.589). As you complete each section, tamp the bricks or pavers into place, checking that they are level with a straight edge and spirit level. Then lay the edging on the other side of the path to complete this section. Repeat the process until the path has been laid.

To finish off a path made of pavers, brush dry sand into the joints. For a brick path, brush a dry mortar mix in between the joints (see "Finishing off", p.588), making sure that there are no large air pockets. If necessary, compact the mortar using a piece of wood slightly thinner than the joints. Finally, sprinkle with water from a watering can fitted with a fine rose, or use a compression sprayer to moisten the mortar and clean the bricks if necessary.

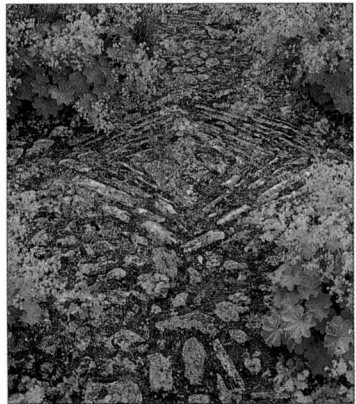

SUBTLETY WITH STONE
Here, the mottled texture of the embedded stones is complemented by Alchemilla mollis *and defined by seams of moss.*

LOG SECTIONS
Logs sawn into sections make a harmonious series of stepping stones through an area of woodland, blending perfectly with the setting.

Concrete

Concrete cast *in situ* is an economical and hard-wearing surface material that is especially suitable for wide paths and drives. Its appearance can be made more attractive by adding texture (see below). Concrete can also be coloured using special dyes added to the mix. Since the colour often looks different once the concrete has dried, use dyes with caution. Colour a small, test piece first and let it dry rather than judge the effect by the wet mix.

Break up a wide concrete path with rows of bricks or lengths of broad timber that will become part of the finished design. These will avoid the need for laying expansion joints during construction.

Preparing a base

Prepare a suitable foundation (see "Basic procedure", p.585). Next, make the formwork to hold the concrete in place until it sets. Use lengths of timber 2.5cm (1in) thick, and at least the depth of the concrete. Use 5 x 5cm (2 x 2in) pegs, not more than 1m (3ft) apart to hold the formwork in place. Lengths of timber may be satisfactorily joined by nailing a block of wood to the outside of the two pieces to bridge them together.

Making curves

To make gentle curves, mark out the shape that you want to create, and hammer pegs into the ground set closely together. Soak lengths of softwood in water to make them pliable and then bend and nail them to the pegs. Sharp curves can be made in a similar way, with the addition of a series of saw cuts on the inside of the curve. The saw cuts should reach about half-way through the timber to increase its flexibility. Alternatively, use several thicknesses of thin hardboard, which is easy to bend and shape.

Expansion joints

Concrete will crack if not laid with breaks to allow for expansion and a degree of movement. Divide the area into sections no more than 4m (12ft) long, using fixed pieces of timber as temporary divisions. If using ready-mixed concrete, where the load has to be used all at once, use hardboard cut into sections and leave these in position until the concrete has set.

Adding texture

An *in situ* concrete path can be made more attractive by adding texture. Use these techniques on a few sections only, or alternate patterns between sections, to create an interesting overall effect.

Exposed aggregate gives a pleasant, non-slip finish. Spread gravel or crushed stone evenly over the concrete before it sets, then tamp it gently into the surface. When the concrete is nearly hard, brush the surface to expose more of the aggregate, then spray it with water to wash away fine particles.

Brushed finishes are extremely easy to create. After tamping the concrete gently, push the bristles of a soft broom all over the surface to produce a fairly smooth finish; for a ridged effect, use a stiff broom once the concrete has begun to set. You can also brush in a series of swirls, or straight or wavy lines, as desired.

Stamped patterns can be made with special tools, but ordinary objects found in the home or garden may also be used imaginatively, for example pastry cutters and sea shells. This technique is best kept to very small areas. To create attractive leaf impressions, use large leaves, such as sycamore or horse chestnut. Press the leaves into the surface with a trowel and then brush them out once the concrete has hardened.

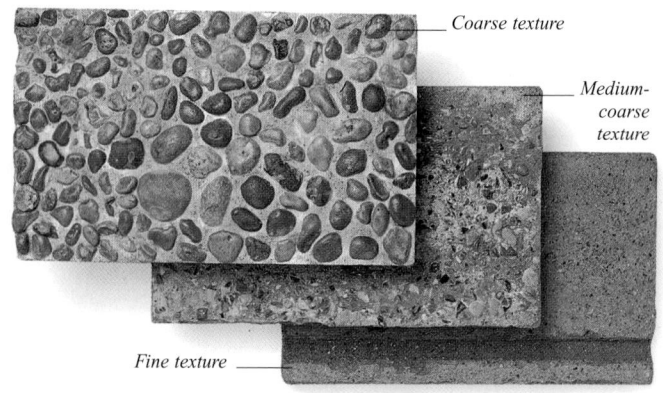

Coarse texture

Medium-coarse texture

Fine texture

1 *Dig out the base of the path to a depth of 18cm (7in) and set the edges. Compact the base. Drive in pegs at 1m (3ft) intervals to anchor the edge restraints.*

2 *If the path borders a lawn, excavate an extra 2.5cm (1in) so that the path is below turf level (inset). Put down successive layers of hardcore, sand and coarse gravel, and pea gravel. Rake level.*

Laying concrete

Make up the concrete (see p.586) and pour it into the formwork. If mixing in small batches, fill alternate "bays", then remove the dividers once the concrete has set and pour concrete into the remaining bays. Use a length of wood to tamp the concrete level, working from the centre towards the joints. If the path or drive is wide, a tamping board used with a helper will make the job easier. Tamping leaves a slightly ridged surface. If you require a smooth finish, use a wood float in gentle, sweeping motions. A steel float will produce an even smoother surface.

Concrete paving slabs

Paving slabs are available in a wide range of colours, shapes, and finishes. They are easier to lay than *in situ* concrete, but are more difficult to lay to a curve than bricks or pavers. They combine well with other materials, for instance with cobbles set along the edge, or with small strips of gravel between each slab. This is a useful technique for creating curved paths since it makes the uneven joints less obtrusive. For details on laying paving slabs, see p.587.

Grass

Grass paths are useful for linking a series of lawns, or for broad walks between beds. They should be as wide as possible or they will not stand up to concentrated wear. Put down turf for a grass path in the same way as for a lawn – for full instructions, see THE LAWN, "Laying turf", p.393.

Gravel

Gravel is easy to lay, presents no problems when creating curves, and is not expensive. However, unless well bedded and used with retaining edges, loose gravel can get onto adjoining surfaces, it can be uncomfortable and noisy to walk on, and it is not an easy surface on which to push a wheelbarrow or a pushchair. See also ROCK, SCREE, AND GRAVEL GARDENING, "Gravel beds and paving", p.256.

Construct a firm base by excavating the ground to take about 10cm (4in) of compacted hardcore, 5cm (2in) of a sand and coarse gravel mix, and 2.5cm (1in) of gravel. For a fine finish choose pea gravel. Gravel can also be laid over geotextile fabric (see p.265).

Apply the gravel in several stages, raking and rolling it to produce a slight camber for drainage and watering it to help compaction.

In a formal setting with mainly straight edges, concrete edging strips can be used; in other settings bricks or treated timber may be more appropriate. If using timber, anchor it with pegs about 1m (3ft) apart.

Edging paths

Plastic edge restraints, easily cut to size, are available to hold a path of bricks or pavers in place invisibly. Lengths of treated timber may also be used, held in place with wooden pegs. It is also possible to use timbers temporarily while building the path, then remove them and fill in the gaps with concrete. For a brick edging, lay the bricks on edge or angled at 45°, and secure with a little mortar.

Building steps

To calculate the number of steps you need to build, divide the height of the slope by the height of one riser (including the depth of the paving slab and mortar). It may be necessary to adjust the height of the steps to fit the slope. Mark the position of the risers with wooden pegs and then excavate the soil to form a series of earth steps.

Make a concrete footing (see p.596) for the base riser and leave it to set. Then construct the riser using bricks or blocks set in masonry mortar (see p.586). Check that they are level using a straight edge and spirit level, and backfill behind the riser with compacted hardcore or sand and gravel.

Prepare a bed of mortar on top of the riser and lay the first tread; it should slope forward slightly to shed water, and overlap the riser at the front by 2.5–5cm (1–2in). Mark the position of the next riser on the tread and mortar it into position.

Tread to riser ratio

For ease of use, it is important that the width of the tread and the height of the riser are in the correct proportion to each other. As a general rule, the width of the tread and double the height of the riser should total about 65cm (26in). First, choose the height of the riser, double it and deduct it from 65cm (26in) to give the width of the tread. You may wish to add 2.5–5cm (1–2in) for an overhang.

For the steps to be safe, the treads should measure at least 30cm (12in) from front to back. The height of the risers is normally between 10cm (4in) and 18cm (7in).

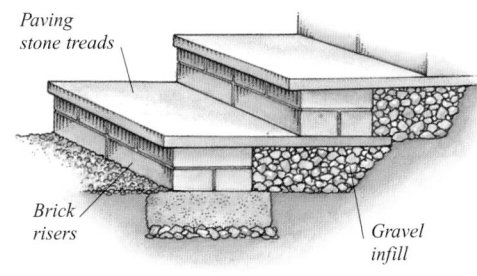

Paving stone treads

Brick risers

Gravel infill

TIMBER AND GRAVEL STEPS
Here railway sleepers are infilled with gravel to create a curving flight of gently rising steps, with flanking plants softening the edges.

HOW TO BUILD STEPS INTO A BANK

1 *Measure the height of the bank to work out how many steps are needed (see left). To do this, drive a peg into the top of the slope and a post at the bottom. Tie string horizontally between the two, then measure the distance between ground level and the string.*

2 *Use string and pegs to mark the sides, then run strings to mark the fronts of the treads. Dig out the steps and compact the earth at each tread position.*

3 *Construct a footing for the riser, 15cm (6in) deep and twice the width of the bricks. Fill with concrete over a 7cm (3in) hardcore base.*

4 *When the concrete has set, lay the first riser on the footing. Use a string line stretched between pegs to ensure bricks are straight and level.*

5 *Backfill with hardcore to the height of the bricks and tamp down. Set the paving slabs on 1cm (½in) of mortar, with a small gap between them.*

6 *The slabs should have an overhang of 2.5–5cm (1–2in) at the front and a slight, forward slope for drainage. Mark the position of the second riser on the slabs and mortar the bricks in place. Fill in and set the treads as before. Continue for the remaining steps. Lastly, mortar the joints between the slabs.*

Walls

Boundary walls have been a feature of gardens since the early days of enclosures. In the nineteenth century, walled gardens were a common feature on large estates, as they provided security, privacy, and ornament. Nowadays, however, large boundary walls are uncommon, having given way to cheaper fences or hedges.

Garden walls are often decorative as well as practical. Low walls are very suitable for dividing off parts of the garden. Because they require less substantial foundations and few or no supporting piers, low walls are also easy and cheap to construct (see opposite). If they have a planting cavity, low walls can look particularly attractive in the garden.

Materials

Boundary walls may be constructed from various materials including brick, and, for low walls, concrete walling blocks that are purpose-made for outdoor use. When buying bricks, always check with the supplier that they are suitable for garden walls: they should be frost-proof and able to withstand moisture penetration from both sides.

Walls may also be constructed from a combination of materials, for example brick with facing panels of local stone such as flint. Large, plain walls may be painted with a masonry paint (in pale or bright colours) on the garden side. This reflects the light and contrasts well with wall shrubs or other plants.

How high to build?

There may be restrictions placed on the height of walls in the deeds of the property, or in local authority or highway regulations. Check this before building. A low, decorative wall is a straightforward DIY job, but brick and concrete block walls higher than about 1m (3ft) require advice from a builder or structural engineer. Any wall higher than 1m (3ft) should have a strengthening pier every 2.5m (8ft).

COMBINED MATERIALS
Brick and flint are juxtaposed here to create a striking garden divider. The mixture of straight and curved lines reinforces the blend of styles. When combined in this way, diverse materials can effectively enhance each other.

Concrete footings for walls

The width of the footing for all walls should be two to three times the width of the wall. For walls lower than 1m (3ft), deep and substantial foundations are not necessary.

For a half-brick wall (i.e. the width of a single brick), dig a trench the length of the wall and 38cm (15in) deep. Place 13cm (5in) of hardcore in the bottom and tamp it down. Then pour in 10cm (4in) of concrete. Allow this to harden completely for a few days before laying the bricks or concrete blocks.

Walling materials

Bricks are the most popular choice of walling material, although concrete blocks manufactured to imitate natural clay bricks may also be used. If you want to build a wall to match the brickwork of existing buildings, used bricks are available in many colours and styles.

SMOOTH-TEXTURED BRICKS
These are most suitable for facing the front of a wall. They come in a range of colours.

MOTTLED ENGINEERING BRICKS
These contribute a rough-hewn appearance; they are also the hardest of all the bricks.

PRE-CAST CONCRETE BLOCKS
These contain medium-textured aggregate.

ROCK-FACED CONCRETE BLOCKS
The brick-red colour imitates the look of clay bricks. They are also available coloured to look like sandstone.

SMOOTH BLOCKS
Concrete blocks are suitable for a modern design.

HOW TO MAKE A CONCRETE FOOTING

1 *Mark out the site of the foundations with string lines stretched between wooden pegs.*

2 *Dig a trench of the required depth. Check that the base is level and the sides vertical. Drive in pegs to the level for the concrete. Align with a spirit level and a length of wood spanning the pegs.*

3 *Soak the trench with water and allow it to drain. Then add 13cm (5in) of hardcore and tamp it down. Pour in concrete, slicing into the mix with a spade to work it in and dispel air bubbles.*

4 *Compact the concrete by tamping it down firmly with a length of timber. Level it to the tops of the pegs. Leave the surface rough as a key for the mortar for the first course of bricks.*

HOW TO BUILD A SIMPLE LOW WALL

1 *Once the concrete footing has dried fully – at least 2 days – set out the position of the wall with 2 string guides, 2 bricks' width plus 10mm (½in) apart. Dry-position the lowest course, 10mm (½in) between bricks.*

2 *Chalk the brick positions on the footing. Throw a mortar bed 10mm (½in) thick along all the first course. As you set each brick on it, check that it is level both from end to end and front to back.*

3 *Before laying, butter an end face of each brick with 10mm (½in) of mortar. Fill the central gap.*

4 *Throw a mortar bed on top of the first course of lengthways bricks (the stretcher) and lay the next course (the header) at right angles to the first. Check constantly and adjust all levels.*

5 *Raise up both ends of the wall by 4 courses, alternating stretchers and headers. Scrape off excess mortar as you bed each brick. Neaten joints with a pointing tool. Then complete each course.*

6 *On the fourth row, insert a half brick after the first header, to maintain staggered joints and avoid having a weak joint running down the wall. As you build, regularly check the levels, as before.*

7 *Complete the wall with a header course, laying the bricks on edge. To help deflect rainwater, point the mortar joints by running a pointing tool against the vertical, then horizontal joints.*

For a full-brick wall, which is two bricks wide, or for a double wall with a space for planting cavities, dig the trench 5cm (2in) deeper and add 5cm (2in) extra concrete. For a brick or concrete block wall, the top of the footing need only be 15cm (6in) below ground level.

For screen block walling, the top of the footing may be just below ground level, provided reinforcing rods are used. On heavy clay or in cold areas, increase the depth of the footing so that it is below the frost line. For higher walls, specialist advice should be sought.

holes (un-mortared gaps between bricks) for drainage in the first course that is completely above ground level.

Before the mortar dries, use a pointing trowel to give the joints a neat, bevelled finish. Vertical joints should all be bevelled in the same direction, horizontal ones should slope slightly downwards to aid water run-off.

Combination bricks

"Combination blocks" that give the appearance of being several individual bricks may look crude close up, but once in a garden setting, and especially when weathered, they are far less noticeable, and make simple garden wall construction very much quicker and easier. Some are regularly shaped while others interlock, like a jigsaw, for greater stability.

COMBINATION COPING BLOCK

Bricklaying

To ensure that the first course is straight, stretch two parallel strings along the footing, the space between them equal to the width of the wall plus 10mm (½in). Lay a 10mm (½in) bed of masonry mortar (p.586) along the footing. The first brick of a course is laid un-mortared, then the second is "buttered" on one end and laid up against it. As you lay, check frequently with a spirit level that the bricks are level and horizontal. If too high, tap them down gently with the trowel handle. Insert more mortar under any that are too low. Check also that the mortar joints are all 10mm (½in) thick.

Repeat the process for each subsequent courses and reset the builder's line for a position guide. For walls with planting cavities, leave "weep"

Brick bonding

There are many brick bonding patterns. If you are a beginner at bricklaying, keep to one that is easy to lay and does not require many cut bricks. The simplest of all is a running, or stretcher, bond, in which all the bricks are laid lengthways.

Screen block walling

In parts of the garden where a brick wall would form too solid a barrier, a screen wall of purpose-made, pierced concrete blocks may be more appropriate. Such walls are supported by hollow pilaster blocks, normally reinforced with iron rods set in the footing and filled with mortar or concrete, yet they are not strong.

Some popular bonds

Running bond is used for walls one brick thick; Flemish and English bonds combine stretchers and headers (bricks laid respectively lengthwise and widthwise) in a full-brick wall.

RUNNING BOND

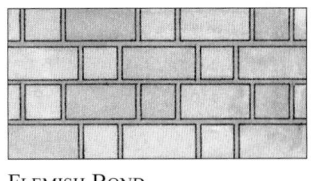

FLEMISH BOND

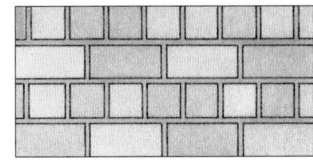

ENGLISH BOND

TYPES OF COPING

A DECORATIVE FINISH
Upright stones have been set in mortar as a coping for a dry limestone wall.

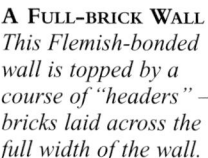

A FULL-BRICK WALL
This Flemish-bonded wall is topped by a course of "headers" – bricks laid across the full width of the wall.

STONE COPING
Large, stone slabs form a solid coping that complements a wall of flints mortared in courses.

SOFTENING THE WALL
The hard line of the wall's edge is softened by a colourful display of trailing flowering plants to create a curtain effect. The crevices between the dry stones provide ideal spaces for shallow-rooting rock garden plants.

Coping

Coping, which forms the top course of a wall, prevents frost damage by shedding rainwater so that it does not seep into the joints. It also gives the wall a "finished" appearance.

Specially made, curved coping bricks are available, but these are often only the width of the wall and are strictly cappings, as they do not throw the drips clear of the wall. Wider concrete slabs are used for copings on brick as well as concrete block walls. If an ordinary brick finish is required, lay a double course of flat roof tiles before the final row. Coping is especially important for pierced screen block walls, because it helps to bond the blocks.

Dry-stone walls

Dry-stone walls may be laid on a concrete footing (see p.596) or a foundation of rubble. They may be planted with alpines (see p.268), and look particularly attractive if a cavity is left in the top for trailing plants.

Dig a trench and make a firm base of compacted hardcore or rubble. The base of the wall should be one or two courses below ground level. Use a taut line to maintain a level construction, and build up the wall with broad tie-stones and smaller random stones to bond the wall together. The wall should be wider at the bottom than at the top. To achieve a consistent slope or "batter", make a batter board, a wooden frame in the shape of the desired cross-section of the wall. An inward slope of about 2.5cm for every 60cm (1in for every 24in) is usually sufficient. Use a spirit level to keep the batter board perpendicular. Finish off with large, flat stones or a row of vertical stones laid on edge (and mortared if desired) as a decorative coping.

Retaining walls

Retaining walls may be used to terrace a garden or contain the soil in a raised bed (see facing page). Dry stones, concrete walling blocks, or bricks may be used. Seek professional advice for any retaining wall more than 75cm (30in) high or one on a steep slope, because it may be necessary to reinforce it to withstand the pressure of soil and water. Rather than building one large retaining wall, terracing the garden in a series of shallow steps may be easier. In some countries, permission is required to build a high retaining wall, and regulations may demand that contractors be hired to construct it from poured concrete.

Insert a drain (see "Installing drains", p.623) running horizontally along the back of the wall, and backfill the lower half of the wall with gravel or rubble. If using bricks or concrete blocks, build the wall on a concrete footing (see p.596) set below the lower soil level, and leave "weep" holes for drainage between every second or third brick in the lower courses of the wall.

Dry-stone walling is a good choice for a low retaining wall, since alpines can be grown in the exposed face. Place large stones on a firm foundation of concrete or compacted hardcore, and lay subsequent courses of stone with an inward slope (a batter) of 2.5–5cm for every 30cm (1–2in for every 12in) of height. The wall should be perpendicular on the retaining side (see *How to Build a Dry-stone Retaining Wall*, p.268). If it is not to be planted with crevice plants, the wall may be mortared to make it stronger (see "Bricklaying", p.597); otherwise pack garden soil between the stones for additional stability.

Constructing retaining walls

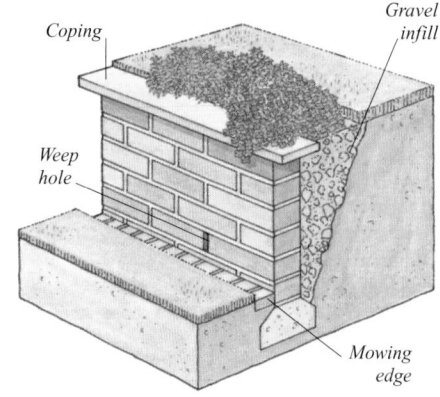

Coping
Gravel infill
Weep hole
Mowing edge

CONSTRUCTION
On the left is a section of a brick wall with a vertical, unmortared joint acting as a weep hole. On the right is a wall built of hollow concrete blocks (see below). Hollows may be filled with wet concrete, or with soil for plants.

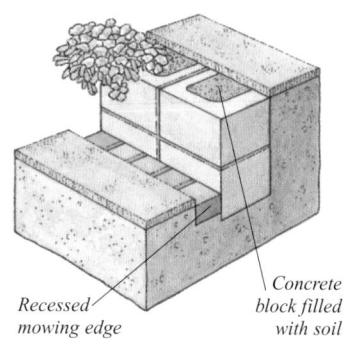

Recessed mowing edge
Concrete block filled with soil

Any retaining wall used to hold back soil on a slope must be extremely strong. Bear in mind that the higher the wall, the stronger it will need to be. Remember, too, that wet earth is heavier than dry earth, and water must be allowed to drain out through weep holes left at the base of the wall. If the units of construction are large, the retaining wall will be even stronger than if small bricks or blocks are used.

REINFORCING RODS
The strength of a wall built with hollow concrete blocks will be greatly increased if hooked rods are set in the concrete foundation. Further reinforcing rods may be added passing up through the blocks.

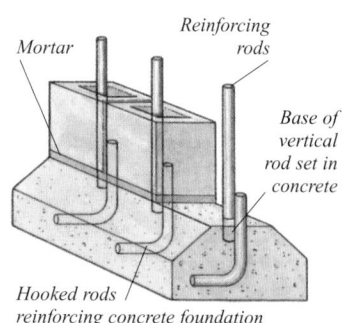

Mortar
Reinforcing rods
Base of vertical rod set in concrete
Hooked rods reinforcing concrete foundation

Raised beds

Raised beds provide a strong design element in a garden, perhaps surrounding a sunken garden or providing changes of level. Small groups of raised beds, or a series of linked beds, are ideal for an area that is mainly paved, while a single, distinctive raised bed makes a good home for an attractive specimen plant.

Where the soil in a garden is poor, or unsuitable for growing certain plants, raised beds can be extremely useful: they enable acid conditions to be created in a garden with alkaline soil, for instance. Moreover, plants in raised beds have more room to develop and require less attention than those in tubs and other containers, in which the soil dries out quickly.

Raised beds have the great advantage that they can be reached without stooping. Recessed or "kneehole" beds, also known as tabletop beds, make access particularly convenient for wheelchair users. A well-planned series of raised beds makes gardening a practicable possibility for elderly, disabled, or infirm gardeners. The height of the beds will need to be tailored to the requirements of the individual gardener and narrow enough for the whole bed to be within easy reach. The beds should be linked by easily negotiated, wide garden paths (see pp.593–594).

Materials

Raised beds may be built from a wide range of materials: mortared bricks (see "Types of brick", p.589), concrete walling blocks (see "Walling materials", p.596), unmortared natural stone (see "Dry-stone walls", p.598), railway sleepers, or sawn logs. If using bricks or concrete blocks, you may wish to finish off the bed with a coping (see p.598) wide enough to sit on.

Brick beds

A large, rectangular, brick bed is easy to construct, but may appear rather unimaginative. A number of smaller, linked beds at different heights will create a more visually stimulating feature, as will a circular raised bed. Always choose frost-proof bricks. A half-brick wall is usually strong enough.

Rectangular beds

Prepare a footing (see *How to Make a Concrete Footing*, p.596) at a depth that allows the first course of bricks to lie below ground level. When the footing has set, use a masonry mor-

tar mix (see p.586) to lay the courses of bricks (see "Bricklaying", p.597). Lay whole bricks at right angles to form the corners.

Circular beds

For a circular bed, the bricks should ideally be cut to give a smooth curve but it is possible to use full bricks. First lay the bricks loosely with a circumference large enough to ensure that there are no wide gaps at the edge. Prepare the footing, and, when this has set, lay the bricks so that they almost touch on the inside edge of the wall. Use wedges of mortar to fill the gaps on the outer face. Stagger the courses as with a conventional bond and use half bricks for the final course to give a better curve.

Ericaceous plants

If plants that require acid soil are to be grown in a raised bed, line the inside of the walls, when completed, with a butyl rubber liner or several coats of a waterproof, bitumen-based paint. This stops lime in the mortar from leaching into the bed.

Concrete block beds

Concrete walling blocks are a good choice for raised beds if matching materials have been used for other garden structures and surfaces. The blocks may be too large for circular beds, but are ideal for rectangular ones. The beds are constructed in a similar way to brick beds.

Natural stone

Raised beds may be built using natural stone laid dry. Use the technique for dry-stone retaining walls (see "Dry-stone walls" and "Retaining walls", p.598), but keep the beds low and small.

For a bed higher than about 60cm (24in), it is best to mortar the stones securely in place. Even with a low bed, it may be necessary to mortar the corners for stability.

Sleepers

Railway sleepers, which blend unobtrusively with most plants and garden surfaces, are ideal for large, low, raised beds, but they are heavy and difficult to handle: do not make the walls more than three sleepers high. Use a chainsaw to cut the sleepers to length, but build the walls

MATERIALS FOR RAISED BEDS

Half-brick wall using a running bond

Soil level

Hardcore base

2.5cm (1in) concrete footing

BRICK BED
Ideally, brick beds should be built with frost-proof bricks. After preparing the concrete footing (see p.596), lay the first course of bricks below soil level. Stagger the courses to strengthen the walls.

Sleepers laid like bricks in a running bond

Rammed gravel base

SLEEPERS
Railway sleepers are particularly good for low raised beds, but beds must be lined if the sleepers have been treated with toxic preservative. No footing is needed because the sleepers are themselves very stable.

in multiples of full or half sleeper lengths. This will reduce the amount of sawing involved.

It is not necessary to provide a footing, since the length and weight of the sleepers make them extremely stable. Create a level surface to lay them on, using rammed gravel, then bond the sleepers like bricks, and, if more than two courses high, use metal rods driven into the ground to secure them in place: either drill holes for the rods in the sleepers, or position the rods on the outside of the raised bed as a brace.

Sleepers may already be impregnated with bitumen or a wood preservative that is toxic to plants, in which case the bed sides must be lined with a geotextile fabric, PVC, or butyl.

Sawn logs

Logs make attractive edgings for woodland-style beds, and for very low, informal beds in a natural setting. For higher raised beds, logs of a

uniform size and thickness should be used. These may not be readily available, however, and the corner joints are difficult to construct. If this type of raised bed is to be built, it may be better to buy it in easily assembled kit form.

Watering

The growing medium in a raised bed will drain more rapidly than the soil in ordinary garden borders, so it is important to water plants more frequently. In particular, the soil in immediate contact with the retaining walls tends to dry out and shrink. In extreme conditions, this could expose the fibrous feeding roots of plants growing around the edges of the bed, making them vulnerable to frost, heat, or drought. Depending on the plants to be grown, it may also be necessary to add more humus to the soil to help retain moisture (see SOILS AND FERTILIZERS, "Using soil additives", p.621).

Fences

Fences are commonly used as property boundary markers, but they may also act as windbreaks or as a decorative feature within the garden. They may be erected more quickly and cheaply than brick- or block-built walls, and they have the additional advantage of providing almost instant privacy. In general they do, however, require more maintenance than a wall. To make a fence into a decorative element, it may be clothed with climbers or have trellis panelling fixed to the top or sides.

The first step before erecting any fence is to mark out the line of fencing with a string line. If it is to be on a boundary between two properties, all the fencing and fence posts must be on your side of the boundary. For other legal requirements regarding fences, see "Laws on fences", p.602.

Panel fences

One of the simplest forms of fencing is a panel fence. It may be constructed using wooden or concrete posts. With concrete posts, the panels are simply slotted into grooves on either side of the post. For details, see *How to Erect a Panel Fence*, facing page. Another advantage of concrete is that it does not rot.

If you prefer timber posts, the panels have to be screwed or nailed into position. Protect the bases of timber fence posts by using either metal post supports or concrete spurs (see facing page). The latter are short posts that are embedded in a firm concrete foundation. They are bought ready made with two holes through which the timber posts are bolted to the spur just above ground level.

To build a fence with timber posts dig a hole for the first post, then stretch a string line along the run of the fence to ensure that it is straight. For a panel 2m (6ft) high, you will need 2.75m (9ft) lengths of timber for the posts and the post holes should be 75cm (30in) deep. Fill the bottom with a 15cm (6in) base of hardcore, then stand the post in the hole and pack it round with more hardcore to

HOLE BORER

If a number of holes is needed for fence posts, hire a "corkscrew" hole borer. This device is reasonably easy to operate – simply turn the handle and apply a little pressure to make clean, deep holes. Powered versions are also available but they are heavy to support and can be difficult to use at first.

Fence types

Basket-weave fencing is usually sold as prefabricated panels, generally in a range of heights. Thin, interwoven slats of pine or larch are fixed in a light, softwood frame. It provides good privacy, but is not very strong.

Closeboard fencing consists of overlapping, vertical, feather-edged boards, usually of softwood, nailed to a pair of horizontal arris rails. The thick edges of the boards are nailed over the thin edges. It may be constructed *in situ*, but is also available (as shown here) in the form of panels. Closeboard is one of the strongest forms of fencing, offering good security and privacy.

Waney-edged fencing, made of overlapping, horizontal planks, is one of the most commonly used forms of panel fencing (see also p.605). It provides adequate levels of security.

Shingle fences consist of overlapping cedar shingles (wooden "tiles") that are nailed to a timber framework to produce a strong, solid fence. They offer good security and privacy, depending on their height.

Wattle hurdles are panels of interwoven woody stems and give a rustic effect. Two examples are shown here. They may be made *in situ* or bought as ready-made panels. They are held in place by stout stakes and are particularly useful when a new hedge is becoming established in a garden, offering interim privacy as well as good protection against both small and large animals. Within a relatively short period of time, however, they can begin to look ragged and unattractive, and they are also troublesome to maintain and repair.

Lattice fences are made from sawn timber or rustic wood. They resemble large partitions of diamond-shaped trellis. They are useful for an informal boundary marker, but offer little privacy.

Picket fences have vertical wooden "pales" spaced about 5cm (2in) apart, fixed to horizontal rails, and are more decorative than functional. Plastic picket fences are available that require far less maintenance than traditional wooden ones. Neither kind offers much security or privacy.

Ranch-style fencing uses thin, planed planks attached horizontally to stout posts. The timber is either painted or simply treated with preservative. There are plastic versions of this style of fencing available, which need less maintenance, but neither is secure.

Cleft chestnut paling consists of split vertical stakes about 8cm (3in) apart, linked by strands of galvanized wire. It is suitable only as a temporary fence.

Post-and-rail fences have two or more horizontal poles or rough sawn timber rails fixed between adjacent posts. They form an inexpensive boundary marker.

Interference fencing has horizontal boards fixed on both sides of the posts, the planks on one side facing the gaps on the other. It makes a better windbreak than a solid fence, and it provides acceptable if not total privacy.

Chain link consists of a wire mesh, which is usually attached to concrete, timber, or iron posts. Galvanized wire mesh lasts for ten years, plastic-coated wire mesh longer. It is a good choice where an animal-proof boundary is required.

Welded wire consists of an open, wire mesh stapled to wooden posts and rails. It is used primarily as a barrier to fence off larger animals where appearance is unimportant.

Post-and-chain fences may have chains made of metal or plastic which are attached to wooden, concrete, or plastic posts. They are used to mark boundaries where more substantial fences are not allowed.

Concrete fences are made of concrete panels, usually pierced, slotted into concrete posts. They offer the security and permanence of a masonry wall and require much less maintenance than a timber fence.

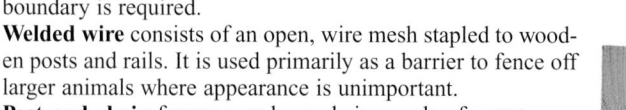

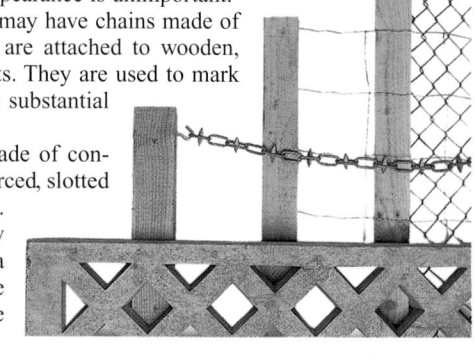

hold it in position. Check that it is upright with a spirit level. Using the panel as a width guide, dig a hole for the second post, making sure that it is aligned with the string line. Level the ground between the post and the hole and lay a gravel board – a length of wood (or concrete) fixed between fence posts at ground level to prevent panels from coming into contact with the soil and rotting. A wooden gravel board should be secured to the first post with galvanized nails. Attach a fence panel to the post using 75mm (3in) galvanized nails driven through pre-drilled holes, or screw them together with metal fixing brackets. Place the second post into its hole, ensuring that it is vertical and fits closely against the fence panel; fix the gravel board and panel as before. Repeat with the remaining posts, gravel boards, and panels.

Lodge the posts firmly in position with wedges of scrap timber and hardcore, checking that they are vertical with a spirit level. Pack a stiff concrete mix (see p.586) around the base of each post, and use a trowel to create a slope away from each side as a run-off for water.

Saw the tops of the posts to an equal height above the panels if necessary. Treat any sawn surfaces with wood preservative and finish each post with an overhanging wooden cap that deflects rainwater.

Metal post supports

Instead of digging holes for fence posts, metal post supports may be sunk into the ground instead, and wooden posts inserted into them. This reduces the length of the timbers needed for fence posts and keeps them out of contact with soil, thus prolonging the life of the wood. Use 60cm (24in) supports for fences that are up to 1.2m (4ft) high and 75cm (30in) supports for fences up to 2m (6ft).

Before driving the support into the ground, fit an offcut of wood from a post into the socket. This protects the support from damage. Most manufacturers also provide a special attachment that fits over the offcut of wood while the support is hammered into place.

Check continually that the spike is entering the ground vertically. Hold a spirit level against each of the four sides of the socket in turn. To secure the post, tighten the clamping bolts in the socket, or if these are not provided, fix it with screws or nails through the slatted holes. For added strength, metal post supports may also be set in a foundation of hardcore and concrete.

HOW TO ERECT A PANEL FENCE

1 Dig a hole 75cm (30in) deep and pack a 15cm (6in) layer of hardcore in the base. Insert the first concrete post and check the height of the post against the fence panel.

2 Pack hardcore round the post and pour in concrete. Tamp it down. Add more concrete and tamp again. Keep checking that the post is vertical.

3 Lay a fence panel on the ground to position the next hole accurately. Use a string line as a guide, then dig the next hole.

4 Fit a gravel board between the post holes. Level the ground until the board lies horizontally. Check with a spirit level.

CONCRETE SPURS

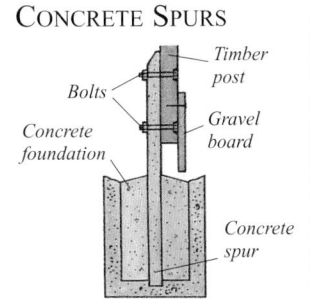

Bolts · Timber post · Concrete foundation · Gravel board · Concrete spur

To avoid damage through contact with damp soil, bolt timber fence posts to a concrete spur set in a concrete foundation.

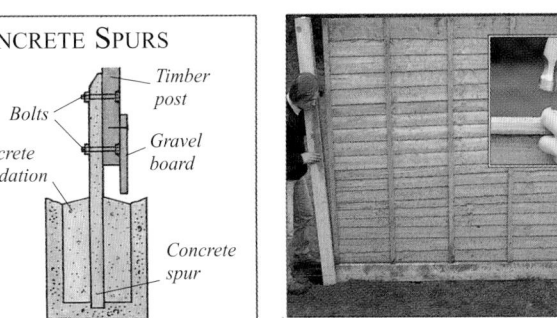

5 Slot the panel into the groove in the first post. Insert the next post and pack into position with hardcore. Secure moulded wooden coping to the top of the panel.

ERECTING A FENCE USING METAL POST SUPPORTS

1 Place an offcut of wood and the fixing accessory in the socket of the post support. Use a sledgehammer to drive the support directly into the ground.

2 Keep checking that the support is being driven in vertically. Hold the spirit level against all four sides in turn.

3 Insert the fence post into the socket at the top of the support and secure it by nailing through the slatted holes. Some sockets are fitted with clamping bolts.

4 Using a string guide, hammer in further post supports. Nail fencing (here a panel of picket fence supported on bricks to keep the rails horizontal) to the posts.

USING ARRIS RAILS

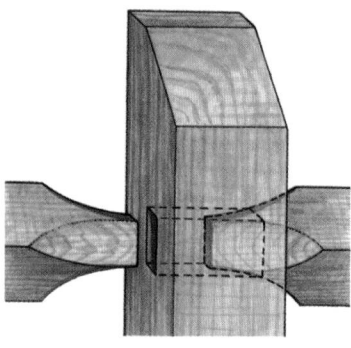

The ends of the rails are chiselled to fit into mortise slots cut in the support posts. Vertical, feather-edged boards are nailed to the back of the rails.

Closeboard fencing

The overlapping vertical boards of a traditional closeboard fence are nailed to two horizontal rails, triangular in section, which are known as arris rails. Fence posts are available with mortise slots cut into the sides to hold the rails, but it is possible to chisel out the slots yourself. The usual heights for the rails are 30cm (12in) below the top of the fence and 30cm (12in) above the ground. Shape the ends of the arris rails so that they fit into the mortise slots and treat the cut ends with preservative.

Set up the fence posts as for panel fences (see p.600). Insert the arris rails into the mortise slots as you go. Wedge the first post firmly in place with hardcore, then prop the next post loosely in position. Insert the first pair of arris rails in the slots, pulling the second post into position. Attach the arris rails so that the flat backs face the correct side for the panels. Check with a spirit level that the second post is vertical and that the rails are horizontal. You may need to raise or lower the post a little. When satisfied, ram hardcore around the base to secure it.

Assemble the remaining posts and rails in the same way and nail them together for added strength. Cement round the bases of the posts to make permanent foundations. As a base support, lay gravel boards along the bottom of the fence (see "Panel fences", p.600). Nail small blocks of wood to the bottom of the fence posts as brackets for the boards, or nail the boards to pegs driven into the ground.

To fix the first feather-edged board, rest it on the gravel board and attach it to the back of the arris rails by nailing through the thicker edge. Then lay the thicker edge of the next board over the thin edge of the first, overlapping it by about 1cm (½in) and hammer nails through the boards

into the rails. Cut a spacer from a piece of scrap wood to ensure that the overlap for all the boards is uniform.

Sloping ground

There are two ways to erect a fence on sloping ground: the fence may be constructed as a series of stepped horizontal sections or may slope with the ground. The method you should employ is largely dictated by the type of fencing you want to use.

A stepped fence

Panel fences, which cannot be satisfactorily cut, should be stepped. The upright posts need to be longer than they would be on level ground, the extra height depending on the width of the fence panels and the gradient. The triangular gap beneath each panel may be filled by building a low brick wall, stepped so that the panels sit on it. Alternatively, cut angled gravel boards and fix them in the gaps.

SLOPING GROUND

STEPPED FENCE
The panel fence is erected as it would be on level ground, except that the posts must be longer by the height of the supporting brick wall.

SLOPED FENCE
The line of the fence runs parallel to the slope, while the posts and the fencing boards are the same height they would be on level ground.

A sloped fence

To build a fence that slopes with the ground, set a temporary post at the top of the slope and stretch a string line between this and the bottom post. Use a fencing system that consists of individual planks nailed to rails (such as a closeboard or a picket fence). Instead of running horizontally between the posts, the rails run parallel to the slope. Cut the base of each plank at an angle to match the slope. Fix the planks to the rails vertically, resting them on a gravel board.

Wood preservatives

If possible, buy timber that has been factory-impregnated with preservative in a special vacuum press, since home treatments, usually applied only with a brush, are much less effective in penetrating the wood. When constructing a fence with pre-treated timber, any cut ends should be soaked in preservative for 24 hours before use. Keep all preservatives away from plants, and always wear gloves and old clothes.

Unless fences are made of a natural rot-resisting timber, such as oak or cedar, treat them regularly with a wood preservative. Preservative should be applied only to dry timber.

Creosote is a widely used and effective treatment for preserving fencing. It has a very powerful smell, however, which many people find unpleasant. Wear protective clothing when applying this substance, since it is poisonous if swallowed, inhaled, or absorbed through the skin. Creosote is not recommended for fences used to support plants. It is also harmful to wildlife. Alternatives favoured by organic gardeners are based on natural plant oils and resins.

Water-based preservatives are less unpleasant to use, and less toxic to plants. They improve the appearance of the timber and prevent the growth of surface moulds. They are, however, generally less effective at controlling rot. Many now come in a range of colours, either as stains or

paints. Wood stains darken and/or colour the timber and are translucent, allowing the natural beauty of the wood to show through, whereas paint is opaque and several layers – of primer, undercoat, and top coat – may be required to provide full protection to the wood.

Maintenance

Broken timber support posts are one of the most common problems. If the damage is at soil level, the most effective method of repair is to use a concrete spur (see p.601). This is a short post sunk into the ground alongside the existing one and bolted to it to give support.

Dig a hole 45–60cm (18–24in) deep around the damaged post and saw off the rotten part. Paint the cut end of the timber post with a wood preservative. Place the concrete spur in the hole, resting it against the post, and pack hardcore around the base to support it. Push bolts through the holes in the spur and hammer hard enough to leave an impression on the wooden post. Remove the bolts and spur, then drill holes through the post for the bolts. Bolt the concrete spur onto the post, tightening the nuts from the spur side so that the wooden post is not damaged.

Make sure that the post and spur are vertical, if necessary bracing them in position temporarily with stakes driven into the ground. Then fill the hole with a fairly stiff concrete mix (see "Concrete and mortar mixes", p.586), ramming it down firmly to remove any air pockets. After about a week, once the concrete has set, remove the supporting stakes and saw off any surplus length from the protruding bolts.

Broken arris rails are easily repaired with specially angled metal brackets. Some of these brackets are designed to brace a broken rail in the middle, others to support a rail that has rotted where the end fits into the post. Both types are simply screwed into place.

Trellises

Trellises, which are usually made of wood, are both a practical and a decorative feature in a garden. They may be secured to the tops of fences or walls or fixed against them. Alternatively they may be used on their own as partitions or screens. Curved and more intricately designed trellis panels are available for creating garden arbours. Panels are available in a range of shapes and patterns, most consisting of standard diamonds or squares; herringbone trellis is particularly effective for screening.

Trellises are most frequently used to support climbing plants. For a free-standing screen, heavy duty trellis is essential, particularly if it is to support vigorous climbers; the timber frame should be at least 2.5cm (1in) in section. If the trellis is to be used to extend the height of a wall or a fence, a lighter weight may be acceptable. When buying trellis, make sure it has been pressure-treated, and treat any sawn ends with a wood preservative (see p.602).

Trellis primarily intended for supporting climbers is also available in wire and plastic.

Erecting trellis

For a free-standing trellis, panels may be fixed to fence posts in the same way as ordinary fence panels (see "Panel fences", p.600). To attach panels to a fence with timber posts, use metal post extenders. Remove the post cap and slide the metal extender over the top of the post. Insert the required length of extension post and replace the original cap on top of the extension. To fix a lightweight trellis above a masonry wall, attach long battens of 5 x 2cm (2 x ³⁄₄in) timber to the sides of the trellis and screw them to the wall. If the trellis is to be fixed against a wall, allow at least 2.5cm (1in) between the wall and the trellis for good air circulation. Hinged fixings allow access for maintenance (see CLIMBING PLANTS, "Fixing a trellis panel to a wall", p.130).

Pergolas and rustic work

The term pergola originally meant a covered walkway formed by plants grown up trellis. Today the term describes any structure consisting of uprights supporting horizontal beams, over which plants are grown.

Traditionally pergolas were made of rustic poles, but sawn timber is often a better choice, especially where the pergola is combined with timber decking, or where the house forms one of the supports. Sawn timber may be used in combination with brick columns or with painted scaffold poles serving as uprights. Hardwoods such as oak are often used for sawn timber pergolas, but softwoods are perfectly adequate, provided they have been pressure-treated with a preservative.

Pergola construction

Draw your design on graph paper to work out the quantities of materials required, but buy a little more than you think you will need, as you may wish to modify the design slightly during construction. The height of the pergola should be at least 2.5m (8ft) if plants are to be grown over it so as to allow room to walk beneath. If the pergola spans a path, the uprights should be positioned far enough apart to allow for the growth of plants on either side.

Supports

Set wooden support posts in hardcore and concrete in holes at least 60cm (2ft) deep (see "Panel fences", p.600), or use metal post supports (see p.601). If you are building a pergola over a patio, special metal shoes designed to be fixed in a concrete base are available. To avoid breaking up an existing concrete or

TIMBER PERGOLA ON A BRICK PATIO
The materials used to construct this pergola are few and simple, yet the design is most effective. A large square trellis has been fixed behind the square brick pillars that support the cross-beams.

paved surface, build a brick shoe and fit the post into it (see *Joints and Supports*, p.604).

Sawn timber support posts should be 100 x 100mm (4 x 4in) in section. Scaffold poles may be used instead of timber uprights but must be set in concrete because of their greater weight. Alternatively, if the weight that is to be carried is substantial, build brick or concrete block columns on substantial footings (see "Bricklaying", p.597).

Cross-beams

For cross-beams (roof beams), use either the same timber as for the uprights or planks 50 x 150mm (2 x 6in) in section. These are sometimes sold ready-shaped and notched to fit

JOINTS AND SUPPORTS

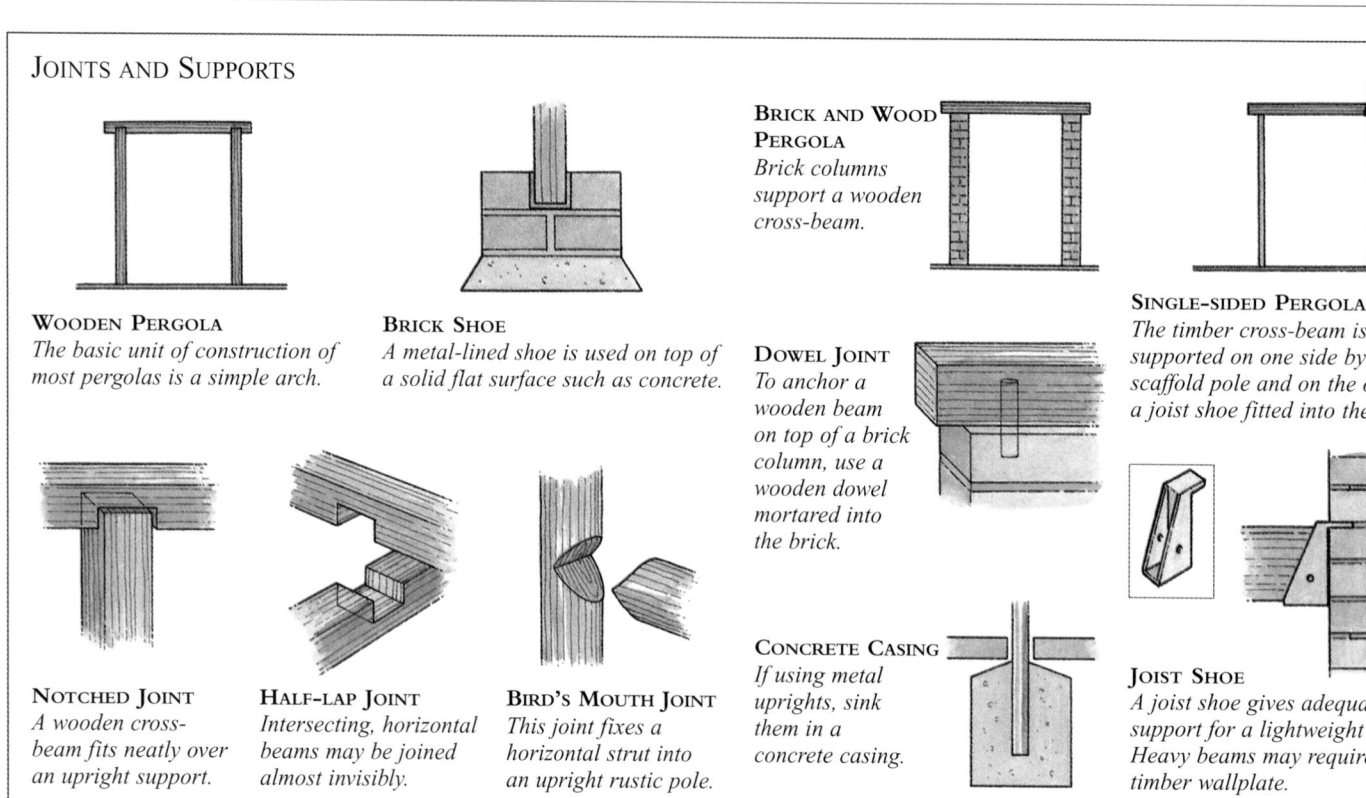

WOODEN PERGOLA
The basic unit of construction of most pergolas is a simple arch.

BRICK SHOE
A metal-lined shoe is used on top of a solid flat surface such as concrete.

BRICK AND WOOD PERGOLA
Brick columns support a wooden cross-beam.

DOWEL JOINT
To anchor a wooden beam on top of a brick column, use a wooden dowel mortared into the brick.

SINGLE-SIDED PERGOLA
The timber cross-beam is supported on one side by a scaffold pole and on the other by a joist shoe fitted into the wall.

NOTCHED JOINT
A wooden cross-beam fits neatly over an upright support.

HALF-LAP JOINT
Intersecting, horizontal beams may be joined almost invisibly.

BIRD'S MOUTH JOINT
This joint fixes a horizontal strut into an upright rustic pole.

CONCRETE CASING
If using metal uprights, sink them in a concrete casing.

JOIST SHOE
A joist shoe gives adequate support for a lightweight beam. Heavy beams may require a timber wallplate.

over the tops of the uprights. Lighter timber may be used for decorative rafters laid between the cross-beams.

Joints for beams and uprights
It is possible to assemble all the overhead timberwork by means of galvanized brackets and screws, but the structure will be stronger, and more attractive, if you use carpentry joints (see above). To fix an overhead beam to an upright, use a simple notched joint. This kind of joint is especially useful if the cross-beams are to project beyond the uprights – to serve as supports for hanging containers, for example.

Treat the cut surfaces of the joint with wood preservative (see p.602) before nailing them together. Avoid driving the nails in at right angles; skew-nailed joints hold together better when the structure flexes in the wind. If extra strength is needed, screw a "T"-bracket where the upright meets the horizontal.

If you are using scaffold poles to support timber cross-beams, effective joints may be created by drilling circular holes of the same diameter as the scaffold into the beams. The depth of the holes should be half the thickness of the timber.

Timber pergolas are often supported by a wall of the house. To attach a wooden cross-beam to the wall you will need to use a metal joist shoe mortared into the brickwork. When the supports are brick columns, the wooden horizontals are

fixed with dowels, which are mortared into the brick (see above).

You may wish to roof over the pergola with a network of intersecting rafters. Where two beams of equal thickness meet, a half-lap joint gives a strong, neat finish.

Many designs also incorporate corner braces between the uprights and the cross-beams to give the pergola greater rigidity. The timber for the braces should measure about 50 x 50mm (2 x 2in) and should fit as closely as possible into notches cut in the beams.

Cut the braces to the required length, then hold them up to the framework to mark the position and shape of the notches. Use a drill and chisel to cut the notches. When all the necessary adjustments have been made, treat all the cut surfaces with preservative before nailing the braces into the notches.

Rustic work

Rustic work comprises all kinds of garden structures made from poles (usually of larch or fir), rather than sawn timber. A popular material for arches and screens as well as pergolas, the poles may either be dressed, that is with the bark stripped off, or be left with the bark on as an attractive finish. If you use poles with bark, bear in mind that the bark is likely to become a refuge for wildlife including garden pests.

The vertical poles that support the structure should be about 10cm (4in) in diameter. They may be bedded in concrete (see "Panel fences", p.600) or set in the open ground. In the latter case, sink them to 45–60cm (18–24in) of their length to ensure stability. If the bark is to be left on, strip it from the bases of the poles up to a point that extends 2.5cm (1in) above soil level when they are in position. Whether the bark is left on the poles or stripped off, soak the ends in wood preservative overnight. Set the uprights in their positions. The cross-beams and corner braces needed to complete the structure may be fixed later, once the concrete around the supports (if this is used) has set.

The poles used for the main cross-beams and corner braces should have a diameter of about 8cm (3in), but thinner poles may be used for the decorative latticework.

It is possible to pre-assemble some sections of the structure by laying them out on the ground according to the design, then cutting some of the poles to length and making the necessary joints. Saw all the cross-pieces only as you need them to ensure that they fit exactly.

There are many joints that may be used in the construction of a rustic pergola or arch. Half-lap joints (see above), similar to those used for sawn timber, are useful where the poles intersect. To attach a horizontal cross-beam to an upright, use a bird's mouth joint (see above). All cut ends

should be painted with preservative before you assemble the structure.

As with sawn timber, it is always best to nail the joints together at an angle to give them extra rigidity.

Other plant supports

It is possible to provide support for climbers without erecting a trellis or pergola. Striking effects can be achieved with interwoven willow wands and other relatively simple structures (see also WILLOW WALLS, p.87, and CLIMBING PLANTS, "Climbing methods and supports", p.124).

Tripods
Rustic tripods are an excellent way of integrating climbers into a mixed or herbaceous border. Dressed rustic poles are better than those with bark for this purpose, as they are less likely to attract pests. For large plants, use poles of about 15cm (6in) diameter. If the tripod is in a bed, sink the poles in holes filled with gravel.

Pillars
For a more formal effect along the back of a border or to flank a path, erect a row of single pillars made of brick or reconstituted stone. The bases of the pillars should be set firmly in concrete. To help climbers grow up the pillars, use plastic-covered large-mesh netting. Secure the net around the pillars by tying together with plastic-covered wire.

Garden sheds

Sheds are valuable outbuildings for storing garden tools and equipment. They may house a miscellany of domestic items from bric-à-brac to bicycles, and sometimes double as a workshop, too. A simple tool store will keep hand tools dry and clean, but a larger shed with space to set up a workbench along one of the walls is a better investment.

Designs

Different designs of shed are available. Some have an apex roof (like an inverted "V"), while others have a pent roof (sloping in one direction only) or a flat roof.

An apex-roof shed has more headroom in the centre than a pent-roof shed, an advantage if a workbench is to be placed along one side.

A pent-roof shed usually has its door and window on the higher side.

A sensible arrangement is to place a workbench beneath the window and to store tools on the lower side.

As a rule, flat roofs are found only on sheds made of concrete.

Materials

Garden sheds may be constructed from a variety of materials – wood, concrete, steel, aluminium, or glass-fibre. The choice of material depends on the intended life and uses of the shed as well as on expense and maintenance requirements.

Wood

The most widely used material for a garden shed is wood; it blends in sympathetically with plants, especially after the new timber has weathered with age. Durable woods such as cedar are preferable, since they are naturally resistant to rot.

Most sheds, however, are made of softwood, which is much cheaper than cedar. Try to find a shed made of pressure-treated timber rather than of wood that has simply been dipped or painted. Treat with a preservative when new, and maintain regularly. Wooden sheds should be lined with water-proof building paper (from a builder's merchant) to reduce the risk of moisture penetration and to protect tools from rusting.

Concrete

Sheds made from concrete are robust and long-lasting but not particularly attractive, so are best sited alongside the house rather than in a conspicuous part of the garden. Generally constructed of pre-cast concrete sections, the roof is usually flat; many have plastic sections in the roof to admit light. A concrete shed must be erected on a firm, concrete base (see p.586).

The concrete walls may have a finish of exposed aggregate or imitation brick. When painted, these may make an excellent background for climbers and wall shrubs.

Metal

Steel sheds are very durable if they have been treated during manufacture to resist rust. They are usually green, but may be painted and usually do not include windows.

Sheds made of interlocking sheets of aluminium are also available. Most have a sliding door, and some an acrylic sheet window. Often small, these sheds are intended primarily as tool stores and are virtually maintenance-free.

Glass-fibre

Small glass-fibre sheds are available that are easy to assemble, and require no maintenance. They are just large enough to store tools.

CHOOSING A TIMBER SHED

The life of a wooden shed depends on the quality of the construction and of the timber. Whenever possible, compare erected sheds – most major suppliers will have a good selection to choose from. Pay close attention to the features indicated below.

ROOFING FELT
Choose a thick felt with a stone-chip finish. Poor felt will let in moisture that will damage the wood after three or four years.

ROOF
It must be strong, and should not sag or flex if you push the centre of one of the roof panels.

GUTTERS
They can help to extend the life of the shed by keeping the cladding dry. Although not a standard fitting, they are easy to fix yourself.

WINDOWS
These must fit well and should have rust-proof fittings. If hinged from the top, water is less likely to enter if they are left open in the rain. Check that there is a sloping sill and a drip groove underneath to prevent water from damaging the cladding.

EAVES
These should overhang the sides and ends by at least 5cm (2in).

HEADROOM
Make sure that you can stand comfortably; bear in mind that cross-braces are found in some designs.

DOOR
This should be solid with good cross-bracing. Check for strong hinges and a good lock. Metal fittings should be rust-resistant – galvanized metal or aluminium.

FLOOR
It should be firm – test it by jumping up and down on it.

CLADDING
Inspect the shed from the inside to make sure that no daylight is visible through the boards. See right for different types of cladding.

BEARERS
If the shed is not erected on a concrete base, pressure-impregnated bearers help to keep the shed timber dry. If not using bearers, lay the shed on a damp-proof material.

TYPES OF CLADDING

TONGUE-AND-GROOVE
This cladding usually offers good weather protection.

FEATHER-EDGED, OVERLAPPING WEATHERBOARD
This may warp or buckle unless it is thick.

REBATED WEATHERBOARD
This gives a closer fit than feather-edged weatherboard.

REBATE SHIP-LAP
This is durable, and has an attractive finish.

WANEY-EDGED WEATHERBOARD
This rough-edged board (also called rustic cladding) may be less weather-proof.

4
CLIMATE AND THE GARDEN

CLIMATE HAS A major influence on plant growth, and much of the satisfaction in gardening lies in meeting the challenges of the weather, often by exploiting its effects to the gardener's advantage. Choosing plants that thrive in the prevailing climate is fundamental to success, although many will adapt to weather conditions alien to their natural habitat. The effects of climate on plants are complex, and responses to the weather are shaped by many factors, including a plant's location within the garden, stage of maturity, and the length and intensity of exposure to inclement conditions. Through an understanding of the effects of climate, a gardener will be better able to grow healthy, productive, and attractive plants.

Climate zones

World climate may be divided into four broad but clearly defined zones; these are tropical, desert, temperate, and polar.

Tropical climates are characterized by high temperatures and heavy, sometimes seasonal, rainfall, and support luxuriant, evergreen vegetation. Deserts have average daytime temperatures in excess of 38°C (100°F) but often very cold nights, with annual rainfall of less than 25cm (10in); only adapted plants, such as cacti, survive in these conditions. Temperate regions have changeable daily patterns but rainfall is generally evenly spread throughout the year and temperatures are less extreme than in the tropics or deserts; deciduous plants are more common than evergreens, as they are better adapted to these conditions. Polar regions experience extreme cold, strong winds, and low rainfall, so little plant growth is possible.

In addition to these four broad zones, intermediate zones, including subtropical and Mediterranean, are also recognized.

Regional climate

Conditions within climate zones are determined by geographical factors such as latitude, altitude, and proximity to the sea, which increases rainfall and moderates temperature.

The European continent
The great extremes of summer and winter temperature in north-eastern and central parts of Europe are influenced by latitude and the continental land mass. The Atlantic ocean and Mediterranean sea are too far away to have any moderating influence on temperatures in winter, when the cold land mass of Asia is more influential.

Further south, however, the combined influences of the sea and relative proximity to the equator mean that the Mediterranean climate consists of mild winters with limited rainfall and hot, dry summers.

The British Isles
The maritime climate of the British Isles is influenced by warm air currents and rain from the surrounding oceans. Westerly parts, in particular, benefit from the tempering influence of warm air currents from the Gulf Stream, so winters there are milder and prolonged frosts rare.

The North American continent
North America has much regional variation. For example, the average minimum temperature in the region from Saskatchewan to Labrador in the north of the continent is between -50°C (-58°F) and -35°C (-31°F), whereas that in the area between Arizona and Virginia in the south is between 5°C (41°F) and 10°C (50°F).

SPRING FROST
The play of light on the frost-tinged foliage and flowers of hardy plants brings an ethereal quality to the garden. Selecting plants to fit your local weather patterns should help produce satisfying results throughout the year.

Elements of climate

The elements of climate that directly affect plants and the techniques used to grow them are temperature, frost, snow, rain, humidity, sun, and wind. Of these, temperature is usually regarded by gardeners as the most important: it determines the choice of plants to be grown as well as the length of the growing season.

Temperature

Vital plant processes such as photosynthesis, transpiration, respiration, and growth are significantly affected by temperature. Each plant species has a minimum and a maximum temperature beyond which these processes fail to take place. The maximum temperature is around 35°C (96°F) for most plants, while the minimum is highly variable. Where extremely low temperatures occur, plant tissue may be physically destroyed (see "Freezing and thawing", below).

Air and soil temperatures are the most important climatic factors influencing the onset and breaking of dormancy in plants, which, in turn, largely determine the length of the growing season.

Air temperature

Sunshine produces radiant energy that raises the ambient or air temperature significantly. In temperate and cooler climates, a sheltered site that benefits from the warming effect of full sun may be used to grow plants from warmer regions that might not otherwise thrive.

Altitude has an important effect on air temperature: given the same latitude, highland sites are cooler than lowland ones – for every 300m (1,000ft) increase in altitude, the temperature drops by 0.5°C (1°F). High-altitude sites thus have a shorter growing season, which together with the cooler temperatures affects the range of plants that may be grown.

Soil temperature

The temperature of the soil is important for good, healthy, root growth and affects the rate at which plants are able to absorb water and nutrients from the soil. The successful germination of seeds and development of shoots also depend on suitable soil temperatures (see PRINCIPLES OF PROPAGATION, "Requirements for germination", p.630).

The speed at which soil warms up and the temperature maintained during the year depend on soil type

and the aspect of the site. Sandy soils warm up more quickly than clay, and well-drained, fertile soils stay warm longer than those that are compacted or infertile (see also SOILS AND FERTILIZERS, "Soil types", p.616).

Sites with a natural, gentle incline towards the south warm up quickly in spring because they gain more benefit from the sun than level or north-facing ground. They are therefore ideal for early vegetable crops. North-facing slopes, on the other hand, stay relatively cool and may be used to grow plants that thrive in cooler conditions.

Dormancy

Plants become dormant to limit their exposure to winter weather; most having at least a short period of full dormancy. Many woody plants shed their leaves in autumn to avoid excessive transpiration, while most herbaceous and bulbous plants die down completely in winter and remain dormant below the ground.

The temperature of the soil and air are the most important factors involved in the onset and breaking of dormancy. It is possible to exploit this knowledge by, for example, keeping plants in a dormant state through cold storage – dormant scions for grafting may be stored until sap begins to rise in the rootstock, and shrubs may be stored in the same way, if necessary, until the soil is warm enough for planting.

On the other hand, bulbs grown in pots and winter-flowering azaleas, for example, may be awakened from dormancy and brought into early flowering if they are placed in a warm greenhouse.

Frost

Frost is a great hazard in gardening and considered to be more crucial than the average minimum temperature for the area. An unexpected severe frost has serious implications; even hardy plants may be vulnerable to unusually low temperatures, particularly after they have produced new growth in spring.

Frost occurs when the temperature is consistently below freezing, and takes several forms: in a hoar frost, crystals of ice are formed from water that has condensed from a humid atmosphere; black frost is more likely in a dry atmosphere, and blackens the leaves and stems of plants. Ground frost results whenever the temperature of the soil falls

FROST POCKETS

As relatively warm air rises, cold air sinks to the lowest point it can reach, and a "frost pocket" may occur. Valleys and ground hollows are ideal for frost pockets, and any plants in the vicinity will suffer as a result. Frost also collects behind closely planted hedges and other solid obstructions such as walls and fences, with the same effect.

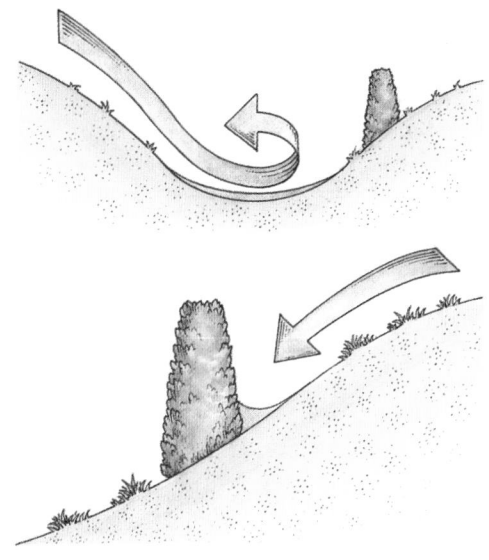

below freezing point; the depth of penetration of ground frost depends on its intensity and duration. Still, clear nights when the cold air collects at a level just above the ground are particularly dangerous. Most at risk are those trees, shrubs, and climbers whose woody tissue has not ripened (hardened) well, usually due to a lack of sun and warmth during autumn.

The risk of spring frost in any area determines the date after which it is safe to sow or plant out tender plants, such as chrysanthemums, runner beans, tomatoes, dahlias, and half-hardy bedding plants, and the onset of the autumn frost determines the end of their growing season. If to be kept from year to year, tender plants should be taken indoors or given adequate protection (see FROST AND WIND PROTECTION, pp.612–613).

Frost pockets and frost damage

Where dense, cold air flows downwards, pools of frost may collect; any valley or hollow is therefore a potential frost pocket. Cold air accumulates in the depression, increasing the area of potential damage as it backs up the sloping sides of the valley.

Thick barriers formed by established trees or hedges along hillsides may obstruct the passage of cold air down a slope, but frost pockets will form in front of them. The problem may be avoided by thinning or removing the trees or hedges to allow cold air to flow through.

When the ground is frozen, water is no longer available to the roots of plants. Deep-rooted trees are not affected by heavy frosts, as their roots penetrate well below the frost-line, but plants with shallow roots,

such as small evergreen shrubs, may not be able to replace the moisture lost by continuing transpiration. Severe ground frost also often causes newly planted, young, or shallow-rooted plants to rise or "lift" out of the soil; these should be carefully refirmed as soon as the thaw begins.

The risk of frost damage to plants kept permanently outside in the garden may be reduced by various means. For details, see FROST AND WIND PROTECTION, pp.612–613.

Freezing and thawing

Frost itself does not always cause great damage to plants, and alternate freezing and thawing may be more devastating. Cell sap expands on freezing and can destroy plant cell walls, frequently killing tender plants. The flowers, shoots, buds, and leaves of hardier plants may also show damage when the thaw begins, and sometimes even the roots are harmed as well. In instances of severe frost, the bark of some woody plants may split open.

Repeated hard freezes followed by rapid thaws and subsequent waterlogging of the soil causes the greatest damage to roots. Late frosts in spring are particularly damaging to new top-growth, causing blackening of the leaves and injury to new buds and flowers.

Duration of frosts

The duration of the frost is also relevant to the amount of damage caused: for example, a temperature of -3°C (27°F) for a quarter of an hour might cause no damage, whereas the same temperature sustained over three hours could result in substantial losses.

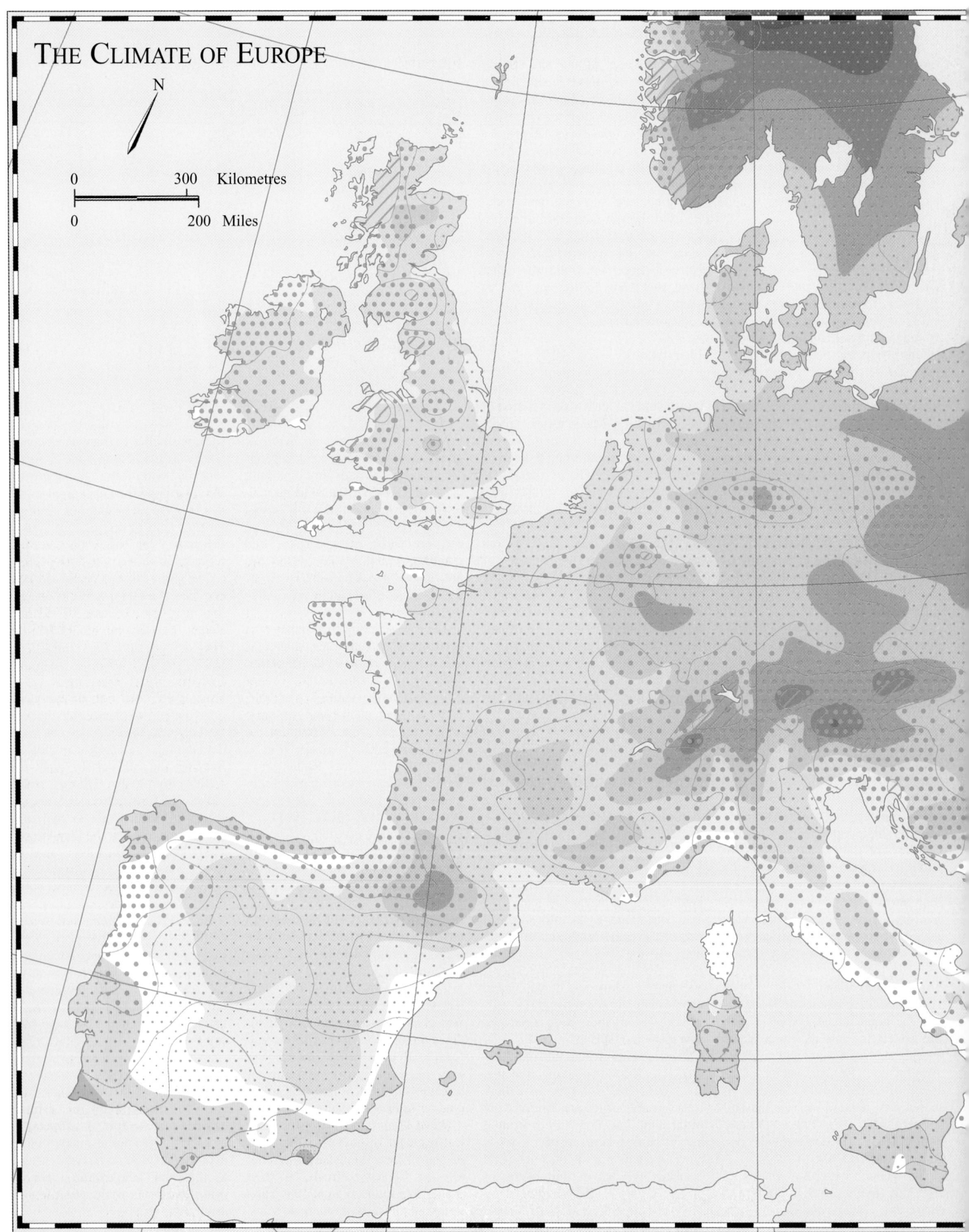

THE CLIMATE OF EUROPE

N

0   300   Kilometres

0   200   Miles

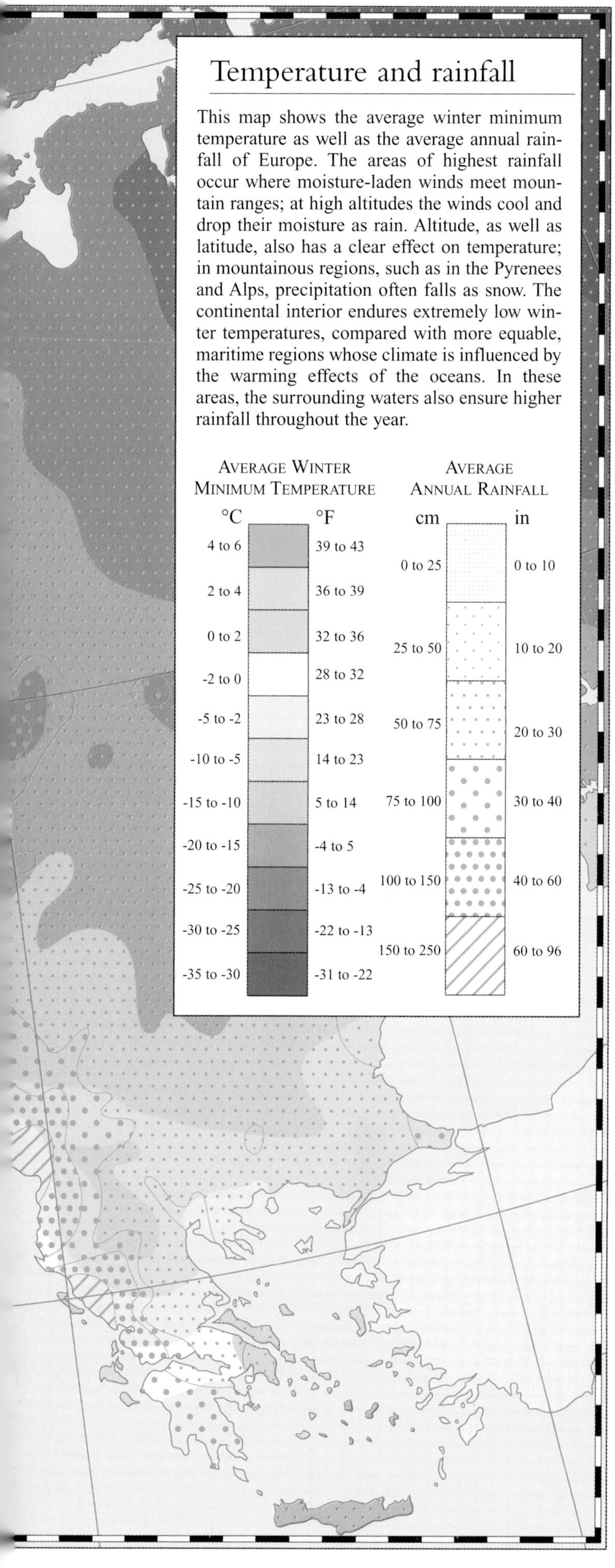

Temperature and rainfall

This map shows the average winter minimum temperature as well as the average annual rainfall of Europe. The areas of highest rainfall occur where moisture-laden winds meet mountain ranges; at high altitudes the winds cool and drop their moisture as rain. Altitude, as well as latitude, also has a clear effect on temperature; in mountainous regions, such as in the Pyrenees and Alps, precipitation often falls as snow. The continental interior endures extremely low winter temperatures, compared with more equable, maritime regions whose climate is influenced by the warming effects of the oceans. In these areas, the surrounding waters also ensure higher rainfall throughout the year.

AVERAGE WINTER MINIMUM TEMPERATURE			AVERAGE ANNUAL RAINFALL	
°C	°F		cm	in
4 to 6	39 to 43			
2 to 4	36 to 39		0 to 25	0 to 10
0 to 2	32 to 36			
-2 to 0	28 to 32		25 to 50	10 to 20
-5 to -2	23 to 28		50 to 75	
-10 to -5	14 to 23			20 to 30
-15 to -10	5 to 14		75 to 100	30 to 40
-20 to -15	-4 to 5			
-25 to -20	-13 to -4		100 to 150	40 to 60
-30 to -25	-22 to -13			
-35 to -30	-31 to -22		150 to 250	60 to 96

THE EFFECTS OF SNOW

SNOW DAMAGE
The considerable weight of thick snow may force apart hedges or evergreen shrubs and trees if it is allowed to settle for too long. Always clear snow from such plants as soon as possible.

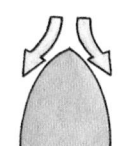

ARCHED HEDGE
Shape a hedge to prevent snow collecting on it.

Frost as an aid to cultivation
Despite the danger to plants, frost may sometimes be helpful in cultivation. For example, soil water expands when it freezes, shattering clods into much smaller soil particles; this is particularly useful on clay soils, in aiding the development of tilth. Low soil temperatures also reduce the numbers of some soil-inhabiting pests.

Snow

When atmospheric temperature falls close to (but not below) freezing, water droplets freeze in clouds or rain and may fall as snow.

Snowfall provides a useful supply of water on thawing and often provides valuable insulation for plants; a blanket of snow prevents the soil beneath from falling below 0°C (32°F) even though the temperature of the air may drop below this point. Heavy snow followed by severe frost, however, may damage shoots and branches. Wherever possible, remove thick layers of snow from vulnerable plants.

Rainfall

Water is the main constituent of cell sap and is vital for photosynthesis, the complex means by which carbon dioxide and water are converted into living plant tissue. Photosynthesis is also fundamental to the process of transpiration, whereby a plant is kept turgid and nutrients are transported through it. Respiration, germination of seeds, and the subsequent development of roots, shoots, leaves, flowers, and fruit are also dependent upon good water supplies.

Rainfall is the principal source of water for plants grown in the open. Much rainfall is lost through evaporation and run-off but any moisture that soaks into the soil is absorbed by soil particles or held as a thin film around them. Water and essential nutrients, which are absorbed in solution, are then extracted from the soil by plant root hairs.

SNOW PROTECTION
A snow blanket protects high-altitude plants from freezing temperatures.

For optimum growth, plants need a steady supply of water. In practice, rainfall is variable, however, in both regularity and quantity.

Waterlogging
In badly drained soil, a build-up of water leads to waterlogging. Most plants are able to survive an occasional heavy downpour, but where waterlogging is prolonged, roots may die through asphyxiation, except in the case of specially adapted plants, such as marginal aquatics, swamp cypress (*Taxodium distichum*), and willows (*Salix*). On permanently waterlogged sites, most plants fail to establish unless drainage is improved (see SOILS AND FERTILIZERS, p.623).

Drought
Plant development is more often restricted by too little available water rather than by too much. Drought during the summer, when temperature and sunlight are at maximum levels, is a common problem. Wilting is the first outward sign of drought; plant functions slow down until more water is available, and water loss by transpiration is reduced by partial closure of stomata in the leaves. See BASIC BOTANY, "Leaves", p.675.

Plants that originate in regions of low rainfall often have special adaptations, such as hairy, sticky, glossy, spiny, narrow, or fleshy leaves, that help to reduce water loss through transpiration. Cacti and other succulents, which have water-storing tissue in their leaves, stems, or roots, can survive long periods of drought.

The soil
In areas of low rainfall, various techniques may be used to increase the amount of water available to

RAIN SHADOW

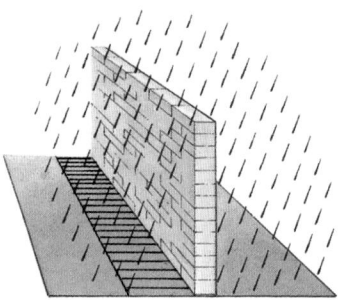

Ground in the lee of a wall or solid fence (see shaded area above) receives less rainfall than ground on the windward side, since the wall or fence creates an area of rain shadow.

plants from the soil, such as removing weeds (see pp.669–673), mulching, and increasing humus content by digging in organic matter (see SOILS AND FERTILIZERS, "Mulches", p.626, and "Using soil additives", p.621). In addition, plants derive more benefit from rainfall if grown in an open position away from buildings, fences, and trees, which often produce areas of rain shadow.

Torrential rain may damage soil structure but the worst effects can be avoided by gardening on well-drained sites. Where this is not possible, drainage may be improved by deep digging or by installing artificial drainage aids (see SOILS AND FERTILIZERS, "Double digging", p.620, and "Installing drains", p.623).

Humidity

Humidity levels are determined by the quantity or proportion of water vapour in the atmosphere and the moisture content of the soil.

The point at which the air becomes saturated varies according to sunlight, temperature, and wind. Atmospheric humidity is usually referred to as "relative" humidity, which is

the amount of water vapour present in the air expressed as a percentage of saturation point.

The effects of humidity

In areas of heavy rainfall, atmospheric humidity is high. Certain plants thrive in conditions of exceptional humidity – ferns and mosses, for example. If necessary, humidity may be increased by damping down around plants (see GREENHOUSES AND FRAMES, "Humidifiers", p.576). This is also of great value when propagating plants to reduce loss of water by transpiration.

High relative humidity may have unfavourable effects, however: fungal diseases, for example grey mould, flourish in the moist conditions created by high humidity.

Sunlight

Sunlight provides radiant energy to raise the temperature and humidity of soil and air, and plays a major role in stimulating plant growth.

For most plants, sunshine and the consequent high temperatures encourage maximum new growth, flowering, and fruiting. A sunny summer also results in greatly enhanced food storage in plants and helps to firm protective tissue, which means that better propagating material is produced.

Daylength

The duration of daylight in a given 24-hour period (daylength) is determined by latitude and season, and affects flowering and fruiting in some plants, such as strawberries, *Kalanchoe*, and chrysanthemums. "Short" days have less than 12 hours of daylight, while "long" days have more than 12 hours. By using artificial lighting or blacking out the natural light, the flowering times of plants that are daylength-sensitive may, if required, be manipulated to

SUNSHINE AND SHADE

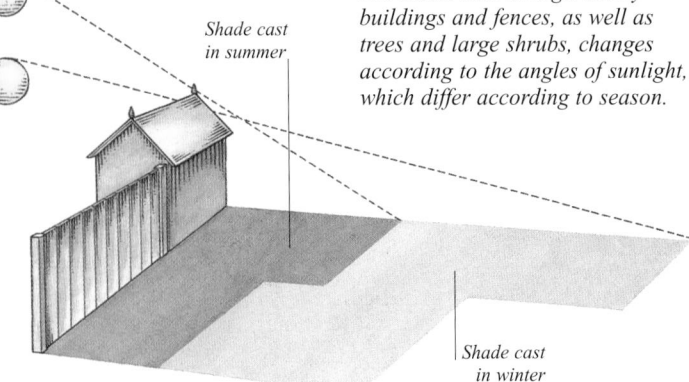

Shade cast in summer

Shade cast in winter

The shade cast on a garden by buildings and fences, as well as trees and large shrubs, changes according to the angles of sunlight, which differ according to season.

WIND TURBULENCE

Exposed areas on rising ground may suffer severe wind damage. Gusts of air meeting resistance from the land are diverted around the sides and over the top of hills, gathering in intensity at the same time.

WIND FUNNELLING

A wind funnel created between buildings and trees may cause a great deal of damage to plants in its path, since air is forced through the narrow channel at great speed. If gardening in such an area is unavoidable, construct a windbreak to protect your plants.

advantage. Germination of seeds and seedling development may be advanced by the same method (see GREENHOUSES AND FRAMES, "Growing lamps", p.577).

How plants respond to sunlight

Plants always grow towards the direction of sunlight: a shrub that is positioned close to a wall, for example, will develop more shoots and foliage on the side farthest from the wall. In the same way, plants that are subjected to a poor or localized light source become drawn or etiolated as they try to reach more light. The intensity of sunlight dictates flower opening in some plants: for example *Ornithogalum umbellatum* only opens its flowers in good light conditions.

Sun or shade

Most leafy plants require the maximum amount of light to achieve optimum growth. Some garden plants thrive in direct, strong sunshine, while others will not tolerate it. Half-hardy plants, most fruits and vegetables, roses, and plants of Mediterranean origin all thrive best in full sun. On the other hand, many rhododendrons prefer to have some shade, whereas ivies (*Hedera*) and periwinkles (*Vinca*) tend to do best in heavily shaded areas.

Excessive sunshine

Strong sunlight may scorch the flowers and leaves of plants, especially if they have been recently watered. It occasionally causes split-

ting of fruits or bark. To prevent such problems, always choose an appropriate site when planting, and for vulnerable plants provide artificial shade in summer, most especially in greenhouses and frames (see GREENHOUSES AND FRAMES, "Shading", p.576).

Wind

Wind often damages plants and adversely affects their environment but it also has some benefits: it plays an important part in pollen and seed dispersal and may also be useful in cooling plants down, provided that they have enough water to prevent desiccation. In addition, gentle winds prevent the development of a stagnant atmosphere, and deter plant diseases that might otherwise thrive

On the other hand, wind may discourage beneficial insects and make it difficult to control pests, diseases, and weeds: spraying is likely to be less effective in windy conditions or damaging to non-target plants due to spray drift. Many more serious problems are caused by the wind, however, although there are various ways of protecting plants.

Wind damage

If woody plants are exposed to strong winds continuously, their top-growth becomes unbalanced, giving the plants a one-sided appearance. The exposed shoot tips are also likely to be damaged or "scorched". Trees that grow on hill tops and on exposed, coastal sites are examples.

Strong winds and gales

The greater the velocity of wind, the more damage it causes. In high winds, shoots and stems of plants may be broken and, in gale force conditions, trees may be uprooted or their root systems seriously weakened. Strong winds may also cause damage to fences, greenhouses, and other structures in the garden. On sandy or peat soil, the wind may cause soil erosion.

Wind scorch

Strong winds in high temperature increases the rate at which water is lost from plants, leading to desiccation of leaves and shoots. Even moderate winds have a detrimental effect, and may prevent plants from reaching their full growth potential. Similar wind damage occurs if temperatures are very low; plants cannot replace lost moisture if soil water is frozen (see p.607).

Effects of topography

The severity of the wind depends to a large extent on topography. Coastal sites often have no natural protection from salt-laden wind coming in from the sea. Hill-top sites may be equally exposed, because the wind gusts around and over the hill.

Wind funnels are created by the channelling of air between hillsides and along valleys, through corridors of established trees, or between adjacent buildings. This has the effect of intensifying wind speed and strength, so avoid planting in these areas if possible. Windbreaks are an effective means of providing shelter from wind. They may be either artificial, such as fences or screens, or natural, for example tree or shrub hedges (see HEDGES AND SCREENS, pp.84–86).

How a windbreak works

Whichever type of windbreak is used, it should be about 50 per cent permeable. Solid barriers deflect the wind upwards, producing an area of low pressure directly behind them, which draws air downwards to fill the vacuum, causing further turbulence.

Fences or screens need to be up to 4m (12ft) high for maximum protection as a garden boundary, but may be as low as 50cm (20in) for low-growing plants such as vegetables and strawberries. To achieve the greatest benefit across a large area, windbreaks should be placed at regular intervals roughly equal to ten times their height.

WINDBREAKS

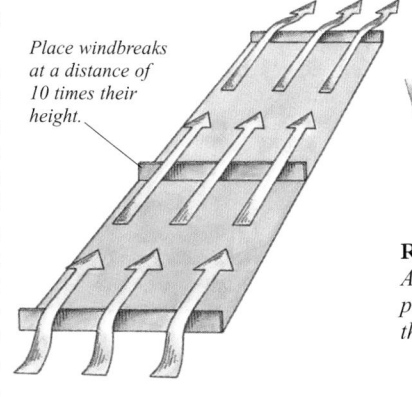

Place windbreaks at a distance of 10 times their height.

A SERIES OF WINDBREAKS
Across a large area of flat ground, construct several, semi-permeable fences or screens to break the force of the wind.

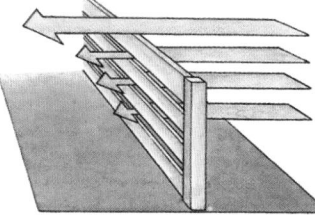

REDUCING WIND SPEED
A windbreak should be semi-permeable. Gusts of air still pass through, but at reduced speed.

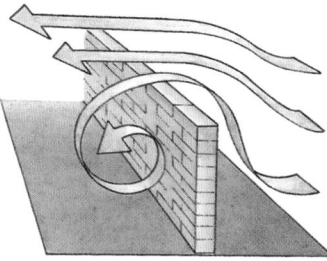

NON-PERMEABLE WINDBREAK
A solid windbreak is ineffective. Air is forced upwards, then pulled down to create a downdraught.

Microclimate

Differences in topography frequently mean that local microclimates show variations from the more generalized pattern within a specific climatic region. A site in a natural dip or hollow may be relatively warm if it is protected from the wind; on the other hand, if the hollow is shaded from sunshine it will be quite cool and may form a frost pocket in winter (see p.607). Rainfall may be significantly less in gardens in the lee of high ground than in others in the same locality but on the windward side.

The garden and its plants further modify local climate and introduce features that give rise to a microclimate specific to the garden; this may differ markedly from that of the surrounding area. To alter the microclimate of a garden, a gardener can readily adapt certain features to provide specific conditions.

Orientation

The soil in raised or sloping beds that face the sun will warm up quickly in spring, producing ideal conditions for early crops or flowers. If the soil is free-draining, the same area may be used for plants that prefer dry conditions.

South-facing fences and walls are excellent places to grow tender climbers, wall shrubs, and trained fruit trees, since they are in sun for much of the day, which improves flowering and fruiting. Walls also absorb a great deal of heat that is then released overnight; this can confer a few degrees extra frost protection during winter.

Wind shelter

A row of trees or a fence provides a sheltered area for plants that might otherwise suffer wind damage. The growing conditions on each side of such a windbreak will be different: the ground close to a hedge or fence on the leeward side will rarely receive rain and may also be sheltered from the warming effect of the sun.

Shaded areas

Areas of shade in the garden beneath tree canopies, hedges, or large shrubs receive the same sort of light as in natural woodland and may be suitable for plants that enjoy such an environment. If a greater degree of shade is required, plants may be grown against north-facing walls, although these sites will be colder.

A bog garden

The edges of a pond or stream, or a low-lying part of the garden, may be used to create the bog-like conditions in which moisture-loving plants thrive.

Greenhouses and frames

Using greenhouses, frames, and cloches gives complete control over the elements, enabling a gardener to provide a variety of microclimates in a small space (see GREENHOUSES AND FRAMES, pp.566–583).

THE MICROCLIMATE OF A GARDEN

The potential for several different growing environments exists in even the smallest gardens. Naturally occurring features create their own areas of microclimate and garden features may be either exploited or manipulated, as necessary, to provide the conditions that plants from many different regions enjoy.

Avoid planting in areas of wind turbulence.

Raised beds provide well-drained conditions.

Trees provide a natural windbreak.

A sunny terrace is suitable for tender and sun-loving plants.

The edges of a pool may be planted with bog plants.

Water plants thrive in a pool.

A greenhouse provides a suitable environment for tender plants.

Frost and wind protection

Select plants that will thrive in a given climate zone before attempting to alter the growing conditions. Trying to grow very tender plants in a cold climate will almost certainly end in disappointment. For species that normally do well in a site but may suffer in harsh winters, providing protection against frost and wind is a sensible precaution. Efficient wind protection enables gardeners to grow a wide range of plants and is particularly useful for large plants, for those in open ground that cannot easily be brought under cover, and for early-flowering plants and trees that are more susceptible to frost than later-flowering species. Protection is also needed from strong winds, which can cause broken stems and browning of foliage. In regions that regularly experience extremes of low temperatures, plants such as roses may need to be trenched before winter.

Preventive measures

Gardeners can take precautions to avoid the worst effects of frost: do not plant in frost pockets and choose sheltered sites (such as in front of a warm wall or on a sunny bank) for susceptible plants. Tender climbers,

---

PROTECTING SMALL TREES AND SHRUBS

BRACKEN OR STRAW INSULATION
Tie in the branches, then surround the tree with wire netting secured to 3 canes in a partial circle 30cm (12in) from the tree. Pack bracken into the gap, then secure the netting to a fourth stake. Cover the top with more straw. Attach a sheet of plastic to the netting.

STRAW BARRIER
Pack a thick layer of straw between 2 layers of wire netting. Surround the plant, filling any gaps with extra straw, and tie in place.

HESSIAN STRIPS
Tie in the branches or leaves of the crown, then wrap the tree in strips of hessian, winding it round and tying it in place at intervals with string or twine. Protect the base of the trunk with straw or bracken.

HESSIAN AND STRAW COVER
Pack straw around the shrub's branches, working from the bottom up. Loosely wrap hessian around, and tie with string.

NETTING OVER A FRAMEWORK
When wall-trained fruit trees blossom, protect them from frost at night with woven nylon netting, rolled down to cover the tree but held away from the blossom by canes.

STRAW AND NETTING FOR WALL-TRAINED PLANTS
Protect a tree or shrub against a fence or wall by packing straw or bracken behind the branches. Fix netting at the top and bottom of the fence. Pack more straw between netting and plant, until it is covered.

TRENCHING ROSES (EXTREME WINTER-COLD REGIONS ONLY)

MOUNDING UP EARTH
Protect the graft union of bush roses from extreme cold by mounding up earth around the crown, to a depth of 12cm (5in).

1 *Loosen the root ball then dig a trench long enough to take the height of the bush when laid on its side and about 30cm (12in) deeper than the width of the bush.*

2 *Line the trench with a 10cm (4in) layer of straw and lay the bush down. Pack straw around and above the shoots.*

3 *Insert stakes and tie strings between them to hold the bush down. Infill with soil, mounding it up to cover the bush to a depth of 30cm (12in).*

for example, may be grown against a house wall (which will be warmer than a garden wall) or in containers that can easily be moved to a sheltered position. Seedlings, summer bulbs, and tubers should only be planted out when all danger of spring frost has passed, and roses and other shrubs should not be fed late in the season, since this encourages new, soft growth that may then be damaged by autumn frost. Allowing herbaceous plants to die down naturally means that the foliage and stems will protect the crowns in winter, while a deep mulch of slowly decomposing organic matter provides useful protection for the roots of all plants. Check plants regularly in winter, firming any that have been lifted out of the ground by frost.

Frost protection

The aim of frost protection is to insulate the plants from the extremes of freeze and thaw conditions by maintaining a constant temperature.

Insulation

Wrapping plants in hessian, carpet, or double thicknesses of newspaper is effective in protecting the topgrowth from damage. Any warm air escaping from the soil is trapped beneath the cover and acts as an insulating layer. Hessian helps to slow the warming process caused by a thaw and keeps the plant dormant through any mid-winter mild spells. Bracken or straw packed around the plant beneath the hessian provides additional insulation and is suitable for wall-trained trees and shrubs, climbers, potatoes, strawberries, and small fruit trees and bushes. Once

temperatures rise above freezing this cover can be removed. Wall-trained plants need to be detached from their support if possible and the stems gathered together before wrapping.

Small shrubs and trees growing in areas below their usual winter hardiness level can be protected by building a loose wire-netting cage around them and then packing this with dry leaves or straw. Plastic sheeting tied or stapled over the top of the cage will keep the insulating layer dry. Alternatively, pack the straw in between and behind the stems before covering over.

Mounding with mulches or soil

For perennial plants that die down to a resting crown, place a mulch or a few forkfuls of leaves over the crown and keep it in place with bracken or prunings from evergreens. Roses and other woody plants can be protected by mounding earth around the base or laying them in a trench. In very cold regions, the earth mound should be covered with a layer of straw. Root vegetables can be protected from frost damage in the same way and can then be harvested even during frosty spells.

Cloches

If only a few individual plants need protection, the best solution is to use a cloche, which acts like a miniature greenhouse, warming the soil and maintaining an even temperature. Emerging shoots of frost-sensitive plants, such as asparagus, can be protected with almost any household container: an old bucket, a large plant pot, or a tough cardboard box will all do the job quite adequately. Specially designed, clear plastic cloches are commercially available. More permanent cloche protection

can be provided by glass cloches, polythene panels, polytunnels, or cold frames (see GREENHOUSES AND FRAMES, pp.566–583).

Wind protection

Wind protection aims to reduce the wind speed before it reaches any plants, thereby reducing physical damage to branches and stems and preventing further water loss. Many tender plants have greatly improved chances of survival if they are planted in the lee of a good hedge. A 1.5m (5ft) hedge will reduce the wind speed by 50 per cent for plants within 7.5m (23ft) of the hedge (see HEDGES AND SCREENS, pp.84–86).

Tree and shrub species vary widely in their ability to withstand wind. The most tolerant are those with small, thick, spiny, or waxy leaves, such as *Thuja plicata*, *Escallonia*, and hollies (*Ilex*). Of deciduous trees, alders (*Alnus*), rowan (*Sorbus aucuparia*), willows (*Salix*), common elder (*Sambucus nigra*), and hawthorn (*Crataegus monogyna*) are particularly wind hardy. Windbreaks made from canes and netting, or proprietary products, will aid a hedge while it is becoming established.

WINDBREAKS

DOUBLE NETTING
Protect plants with fragile stems from wind by using flexible double netting supported by canes pushed into the soil.

PROPRIETARY WINDBREAKS
Protect plants with proprietary windbreaks fixed to stout stakes.

WOVEN HURDLES
Place woven hurdles at intervals between the plants, setting them at an angle into the prevailing wind, to deflect any strong gusts.

COVERS FOR FROST AND SNOW PROTECTION

CLOCHE
Use a cloche to protect seedlings, tender herbaceous plants, or young shrubs. Cover the open ends with glass or plastic to stop wind blowing straight through.

TUNNEL CLOCHE
Protect low-growing plants such as strawberries with a tunnel cloche stretched over wire hoops. The polythene may be raised at either side for ventilation during the day.

NEWSPAPER
Protect the new growth of potatoes and other tender crops against frost at night by covering them with sheets of newspaper, earthed in on either side to keep them in place.

HORTICULTURAL FLEECE
This lightweight woven fabric warms the soil and gives frost protection while at the same time allowing light and water to pass through to the plants below.

Water conservation and recycling

WATER conservation in the garden begins with choosing the right plants for the soil and climatic conditions. In dry areas, where the need for water conservation is at its greatest, select species that have fleshy or waxy-surfaced leaves and grasses, which are well adapted to withstand drought, as are a great many plants native to Mediterranean climates. The appropriate plants must then be planted in well-prepared soil (see SOILS AND FERTILIZERS, "Soil cultivation", p.618). Improving the soil by incorporating organic matter (see "Soil structure and water content". p.620) and the use of mulches (see "Top-dressings and mulches". p.626) can largely eliminate the need for supplementary watering. It will, however, be necessary to water plants in containers, which are unable to develop extensive root systems and receive little benefit from natural rainfall. They are also much more susceptible to drying out in windy situations. Where extra watering is needed (see "Reducing high water dependency", right), apply it as efficiently as possible, using the following guidelines.

To reduce transpiration, water plants early in the morning or in the evening. Always avoid watering in direct sunlight. Water thoroughly when required, ensuring the moisture reaches the plant roots. Refrain from simply wetting the soil surface by indiscriminate hosing or by giving a little water at frequent intervals (see SOILS AND FERTILIZERS, "Watering techniques", p.622). Inadequate amounts of water simply encourage surface rooting, which in the long term makes the plant more vulnerable.

ENHANCING WATER RETENTION IN SOIL
Water absorption can be a problem on poorly structured light or neglected soil (left). Such soils should be improved by the addition of bulky organic matter such as well-rotted farmyard manure or garden compost (right).

When symptoms of water stress first occur, apply no more than 24 litres of water per sq m (4.5 gallons per sq yd); give this every 7–10 days to maintain plant growth if necessary. Avoid the use of a sprinkler, which indiscriminately and wastefully discharges high volumes of water over a wide area.

Collecting water

In many temperate areas, the water collected from rain falling on the roof of an average house could and should be used to supplement water from the mains supply, which should be used as efficiently as possible. As a rough guide to the amount of water that could be saved from a roof, multiply its surface area by the annual rainfall in the vicinity (all in metres). To convert to litres, multiply the resulting figure by 1,000. For example, with an annual rainfall of 0.6m (2ft), runoff from a garden shed roof measuring 2.5 x 3.5m (8 x 11ft) would be more than 5,000 litres (1,100 gallons). A house roof measuring 17 x 7m (56 x 22ft) would shed nearly 72,000 litres (16,000 gallons).

Rainwater is readily stored by connecting a water butt or tank to a downpipe. If the butt or tank has a lid and is free from algae, the water will remain oxygenated for about 6 months. (Anaerobic water should not be used on plants.) Such water reservoirs should stand on a firm base and, to facilitate filling a watering can from the bottom tap, they should be raised on a plinth of bricks or walling blocks.

As rainfall occurs at irregular intervals, often in heavy bursts, a rainwater butt will frequently overflow. The amount stored can easily be increased by using several butts joined to one another by short pipes inserted into the overflow sockets.

PLANTING THROUGH SHEET MULCH
Cut a slit in a sheet mulch such as geotextile fabric and plant through the hole. The mulch will reduce evaporation and suppress weeds.

Reducing high water dependency

Although some garden features and crops do require supplementary watering, their needs can be reduced in the following ways.

New plantings
• Create a saucer-shaped dip around each plant stem to hold water and avoid runoff.
• Lay trickle, or drip feed, irrigation, which targets water to the roots of each plant (see p.561).
• Ensure that the growing mix of container-grown plants is saturated by immersing the plants in a bucket before planting; this ensures that the air is completely expelled. Water again thoroughly immediately after planting.
• Destroy competitive weeds by hoeing the soil shallowly.

Containers and hanging baskets
• Incorporate water-retaining granules in the growing mix.
• Level the growing mix to within 2.5–5cm (1–2in) of the container rim so there is space for sufficient water to soak the growing mix thoroughly at each watering.

• Place plants in a sheltered spot that is shaded for part of the day. Keep away from drying winds.
• Group containers together rather than placing them individually.

Food crops
• Select crops carefully, especially in dry areas. Several vegetables will fail to develop adequately if short of water at critical periods in their development. Examples are potatoes, which need plenty of water as their tubers are ripening, and tomatoes, courgettes, and runner beans when flowering and fruit is swelling.
• Irrigate with seep or trickle hoses so that supplementary watering is targeted where it is most needed.

Lawns
• Reduce the size of the lawn and create gravel beds or surfaces.
• Select a mixture of lawn grass species that are relatively resistant to drought conditions.
• Raise the mower blade height at which the grass is cut, from eg 1cm (½in) to 2.5cm (1in).
• Feed the lawn with an appropriate fertilizer during autumn to encourage drought resistance in the sward.

Patios
• Create partial shade with timber structures, to reduce the considerable glare from the sun on some patio surfaces. The reflection may affect adjacent plants, increasing their moisture loss. Although trees will provide shade, dry zones occur around the roots, and these can nullify the advantage of shade.
• Angle any slope on a patio so water runs off onto the garden and is not lost in adjacent drains.
• Use decking, which allows water to percolate through the gaps, rather than concrete or stone slabs.

Water features
• Convert moving water to still water features. The former inevitably has a higher evaporation rate, particularly when placed in a sunny, exposed position.
• Plant water lilies to minimize evaporation from ponds and similar uncovered surfaces.
• Top up any water loss with stored rainwater rather than mains water.

SEEP HOSES
Hoses with small perforations along their entire length are an excellent way to irrigate strawberries (here) and other plants grown in a row.

TARGETED WATER OUTLETS
Trickle, or drip feed, systems deliver water through individual drippers that are placed permanently near the roots of each plant.

RECYCLING GREY WATER
Water from showers or baths can be diverted from dedicated downpipes to an adjacent water butt, for immediate distribution and reuse around garden plants. The water butt must be covered with a lid not only for safety but also to prevent the accumulation of debris and algae.

Larger water tanks are also available. and any recycled ones must be thoroughly cleaned of residues from previously stored fluids.

By adjusting the downpipes from rainwater gutters, water butts can be placed against a wall, which should not be in full sun. If the butt or a series of butts are obtrusive, the rainwater downpipe can be fitted with a small device that diverts the rainwater through a pipe to a more distant receptacle – for example, one sited behind a garden shed or trellis.

Where there is an insufficient slope for the water to run naturally into these storage tanks, a sump pump should be installed in a small butt or receptacle at the base of the downpipe. Very large storage tanks,

RAINWATER BUTT
Collect rainwater off greenhouse, shed, and house roofs by attaching pipes between each gutter and water butt. Always buy as large a butt as you can afford and position it sufficiently high for a watering can to fit conveniently under its tap.

even if they are placed low enough to be gravity fed from the house, will need a pump to redistribute the water around the garden. Sump pumps that have an on/off, cut-out float on the intake are ideal because they prevent damage to the pump if the tank runs dry and the pump has been left on accidentally. The system can be constructed so the pump drives water through a series of small diameter pipes to the areas of the garden requiring irrigation.

Rainwater diverters fitted on the downpipe or the overflow socket on a rainwater butt can also channel the excess water to a garden pond. Ponds used for this purpose should be free of blanketweed and should preferably contain oxygenating plants. In a

large informal garden, a saucer-shaped, heavily planted pond can be created with a pebbled edging, for a beach-like effect (see WATER GARDENING, "Styles of pond edging", p.291). This will conceal any large variance in water level from summer to winter. As with other water reservoirs, any pond is likely to require an electric submersible pump to redistribute the water to the rest of the garden.

Grey water

Grey water is the term used for domestic waste water other than sewage (which is referred to as black water). As large volumes of water are available from this source – the average bath using 120 litres (26 gallons) – in extreme drought conditions it can be a valuable source of water provided it is not too heavily contaminated with soaps, detergents, fats, or grease. Buckets of grey water can be taken direct from a bath (or sink) to the garden, or the water could be siphoned from the bath to the garden using a garden hose. Siphoning aids are available from good hardware merchants. Pipe diverters used in the same way as rainwater diverters can be fitted to the waste-water drain from the bathroom and fed into a dedicated grey-water butt or reservoir, for use soon after it has cooled.

Some types of domestic waste water are better than others. In order of preference they are shower, bath, bathroom sink, and utility sink, provided bleaches or strong detergents have not been used. Water from dishwashers and washing machines is generally unsuitable for garden use, as it contains too much detergent.

Grey water should never be used on newly propagated or container-grown plants or those grown in a conservatory or greenhouse.

How to use grey water

• Store in a dedicated container and don't mix with other water.
• Use grey water as soon as it has cooled and never keep longer than a few hours. Storing it on summer days can quickly produce a bacterial soup, which can smell unpleasant and breed disease pathogens.
• Apply grey water on soil or compost adjacent to a plant; never water directly on foliage.
• Never use grey water on fruit, vegetables, or herbs or on acid-loving plants as the detergents in the water will be alkaline.
• Never apply grey water with a sprinkler to the lawn or to any area where the water might form puddles, as such water is unhygienic. Insects (such as mosquitos) may breed in the water; children may be attracted to play in the puddles, and animals may drink from them.
• Avoid using grey water with "dripper" or fine nozzle irrigation systems, because these will quickly clog up.
• Try to rotate the types of water applied to the garden and avoid the persistent use of grey water in one particular area. Harmful sodium levels may build up if grey water is overused. This can be detected by a soil test. If the pH level is over 7.5, plant growth may be adversely affected. Over-high levels can be remedied with gypsum; apply at a rate of 1kg per 10 sq m (1lb per 50 sq ft). until the pH level reaches 7 or below.

5
SOILS AND FERTILIZERS

SOILS ARE HIGHLY complex and dynamic materials that are made up of minute particles of weathered rock and organic matter, known as humus, as well as plant and animal life. Healthy soil is essential to successful plant growth: it physically supports plants and supplies them with water, air, and mineral nutrients. If the soil in your garden does not at first appear to be ideal, there are many solutions and most soils can be improved with a little time and effort. For example, waterlogged soil can be drained and its structure improved, and the water-holding capacity of light soils can be increased by digging in organic matter, such as compost or well-rotted manure. Fertilizers increase nutrients, and lime can be applied to make acidic soils more alkaline, while mulches prevent weed seeds from germinating and reduce water loss from the soil. Finally, nutrients from organic waste can be returned to the soil by making garden compost.

Soil and its structure

Most soil is classified according to its clay, silt, and sand content. The size and proportion of these mineral particles affects the chemical and physical behaviour of the soil. Particles of clay are less than 0.002mm ($\frac{1}{16,000}$in) in diameter; silt particles are up to 25 times larger than the largest clay particles; and sand particles may be 1,000 times larger – up to 2mm ($\frac{1}{16}$in) in diameter.

Soil types

Loam soils have the ideal balance of mineral particle sizes, with between 8 and 25 per cent clay, which results in good drainage and water retention, combined with high fertility.

Clay soils are heavy, slow draining, and slow to warm up in spring, but are often highly fertile. They are easily compacted, however, and may bake hard in summer.

Both sandy and silt soils have a low proportion of clay particles, making them much less water-retentive than clay. Sandy soils are particularly light and free-draining and need frequent irrigation and feeding; however, they warm up quickly in spring and are easily improved with organic matter. Silts are more retentive and fertile than sandy soils but tend to compact more easily.

Soil characteristics

Clay soils have more than 25 per cent clay particles and are characteristically wet and sticky. Soils containing less than 8 per cent clay are classified as either silt or sandy soil, depending on whether silt or sand particles predominate. Peat is formed where wet, acid conditions prevent full decomposition of organic matter, which therefore remains on or near the soil surface. Chalky soil, however, is alkaline and free-draining, and allows organic matter to decompose rapidly.

SANDY SOIL
A dry, light, free-draining soil, easy to work but relatively infertile.

PEAT
Rich in organic matter, peat is dark and moisture-retentive.

CLAY
A heavy, slow-draining soil, usually with a high nutrient value.

CHALK
Pale, shallow, and stony, chalk is free-draining and moderately fertile.

SILT
Silt is reasonably moisture-retentive and fertile but compacts easily.

Organic or peat soils are wet and acidic; they support excellent plant growth, however, if drained, fertilized, and limed.

Chalk or limestone soils are shallow, free-draining, and alkaline, and have moderate fertility.

The profile of the soil

Soils may be divided into three layers, or horizons: topsoil, subsoil, and a layer derived from the parent rock. Topsoil contains most soil organisms and many of the nutrients. It is generally dark, because it contains organic matter that is added artificially or naturally by leaf fall. Subsoil is usually lighter in colour; if it is white, the parent rock is probably chalk or limestone. If there is little or no colour change between topsoil and subsoil, the topsoil may be deficient in organic matter.

Weeds and wild plants help to indicate the type of soil in a garden and any characteristics that it may have, although their presence is only a guide. Birch (*Betula*), heathers (*Calluna, Daboecia, Erica*), foxgloves (*Digitalis*), and gorse (*Ulex europaeus*) are all signs of acid soil, as are many garden plants such as rhododendrons. Beech (*Fagus*) and

SOIL PROFILES

Topsoil contains organic matter and is usually dark

Subsoil is lighter and less fertile than the topsoil

Soil is usually made up of layers of topsoil and subsoil, and a lower layer derived from underlying rock. The depth of each layer can vary.

Identifying your soil

Rub a small amount of moist soil between your fingers. A sandy soil feels quite gritty and will not stick together or form a ball, although a sandy loam is slightly more cohesive. A silt soil feels silky or soapy to the touch. A silty loam may show imprints when pressed with a finger. A loamy clay soil holds together well and may be rolled into a cylindrical shape. Heavy clay soil may be rolled even more thinly, and develops a shiny streak when smoothed. All clay soils feel sticky and slightly heavy.

SANDY SOIL
Sandy soil feels gritty when rubbed between finger and thumb. The grains do not stick together.

CLAY SOIL
Clay soil feels sticky when wet and may be rolled into a ball that changes shape when pressed.

---

ash (*Fraxinus*) indicate that the soil is likely to be alkaline. Wild plants may also reveal the chemical profile of the soil: nettle and dock, for example, suggest a rich, fertile soil that is high in phosphorus, while clover indicates a soil that is low in nitrogen.

Acidity and alkalinity

Soil pH is a measurement of acidity or alkalinity – the scale ranges from 1–14. A pH below 7 indicates an acid soil, while a pH higher than 7 indicates an alkaline soil. Neutral soil has a pH of 7.

The pH of soil is usually controlled by its calcium level. Calcium is an alkaline element that almost all soils tend to lose through leaching (meaning that it is washed through the soil by water). Soils over chalk or limestone, which are rich in calcium, are more or less unaffected; other soils, especially sands, gradually turn more acidic.

Alkalinity may be increased, if necessary, by liming (see p.625), or introducing lime-rich material such as mushroom compost.

TESTING pH LEVEL

Soil test kits use a chemical solution that changes colour when mixed with soil in a small test tube. The colour is then matched against a chart that indicates the pH level of the soil sample.

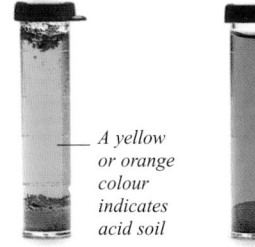

A yellow or orange colour indicates acid soil

Bright green indicates neutral soil

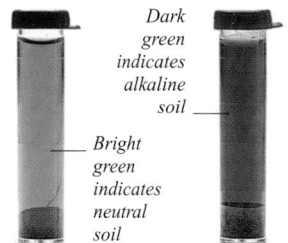

Dark green indicates alkaline soil

Electronic pH meters and soil test kits may be used to measure soil pH. Make several tests in different parts of the garden, as the pH often varies, even within a small area; readings are particularly unreliable after the soil has been limed.

The effect of pH

Above all, pH affects the solubility of soil minerals and hence their availability to plants. Acid soils tend to be deficient in phosphorus. Alkaline soils tend to lack manganese, boron, and phosphorus.

Soil pH also affects the number and type of beneficial soil organisms, as well as pests and diseases. For example, worms dislike acid soils, but clubroot, leatherjackets, and wireworms are common in acid conditions. On alkaline soils, potato scab occurs more frequently.

Optimum pH

The pH range for good plant growth is between 5.5 and 7.5. A pH of 6.5 is usually optimum, depending on the plants to be grown. Peaty soils have an optimum pH of 5.8, however. The highest vegetable yields are

---

generally obtained from neutral soils but most ornamentals tolerate a wide pH range. Some are more sensitive; calcicoles (lime lovers) and calcifuges (lime haters) are adapted to extreme pH ranges and their growth suffers if they are planted in soil with the wrong pH level.

Soil organisms

Certain soil organisms are essential to maintain soil fertility. Beneficial bacteria and fungi prefer well-aerated soil and generally tolerate a wide pH, although most fungi prefer acidic soil conditions. Some fungi (mycorrhizae) live in association with plant roots, and improve the take-up of nutrients from the soil.

Small soil animals, such as mites, play a vital part in the breakdown of organic matter. Microscopic worms and nematodes (eelworms) help to control pests – although some are themselves pests.

Larger soil animals, particularly earthworms, improve soil structure when feeding and burrowing; the passage of soil through an earthworm's body binds soil particles into crumbs, increasing aeration and improving drainage.

BENEFICIAL ORGANISMS

DEVIL'S COACH-HORSE BEETLE

GROUND BEETLES

EARTHWORM

CENTIPEDES

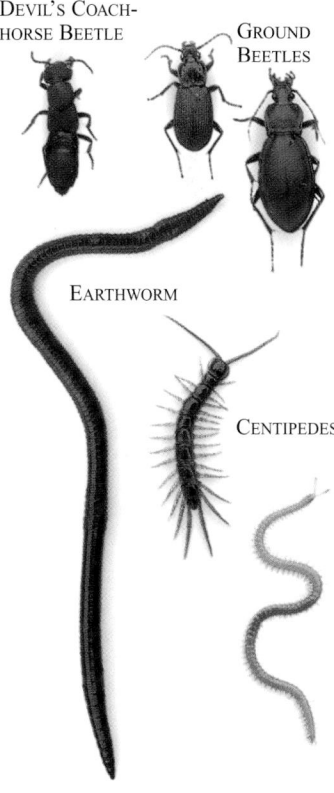

Healthy soil contains a teeming community of earthworms and other organisms, which help to aerate the soil and break down organic matter.

Soil cultivation

Correct methods of soil cultivation, including weeding, digging, and adding soil improvers, are vital to successful long-term plant growth.

Weeds compete with cultivated plants for space, light, nutrients, and water – in fact, all the essentials. They may also harbour diseases of many types, which makes their eradication or control vital.

Several digging techniques are used to cultivate the soil in different ways, depending on the condition of the soil and the plants that are to be grown. If the condition of the soil is poor, it may be improved by the addition of organic material, usually at the same time as digging.

Clearing an overgrown garden

Badly neglected, overgrown plots may be cleared using either tools or chemicals: use whichever method is convenient (see also PLANT PROBLEMS, "Controlling weeds", p.669).

Mechanical clearance

Slash as much top-growth as possible using a nylon-line trimmer, brushwood cutter, or scythe, and clear it away from the area. Then, with a rotary mower, cut any remaining growth as low as possible before digging out and removing all the vegetation that is left on the site.

Alternatively, use a rotavator to churn up the soil and chop up the weeds. Make several passes with the rotavator to break up the matted vegetation, then rake it up and remove it from the surface. The chopping action of the tines, however, will cut the roots or rhizomes of

perennial weeds into pieces that regenerate rapidly. After rotavating, therefore, it is essential to rake over the plot and remove by hand all remaining weed fragments. Repeat treatments will be necessary.

Chemical clearance

Following the manufacturer's instructions carefully, spray with a translocated weedkiller, leave it to take effect, and then cut down the top-growth. If necessary, respray any vegetation that escaped the first application of weedkiller.

Remove the dead vegetation or incorporate it into the soil. Most gardeners prefer to prepare the whole site for planting, but trees, shrubs, and other vigorous ornamentals may be planted directly into holes prepared in the dead vegetation.

On sandy soil, many weedkillers are rapidly leached out, so use only weedkillers that break down when in contact with soil. In organic gardens, where it is not desirable to use chemicals, or if the layout of a garden makes it difficult to apply weedkiller evenly, use mechanical or other methods of weed control, such as mulching (see p.626) and organic practices, including the deep-bed system (see p.496).

Weed control

In practically all gardens the soil is full of weed seeds and fragments of perennial weed roots. Weed seeds are brought into the garden from neighbouring land by the wind and in the soil or compost around bought plants. Cultivation, by its very nature, disturbs the soil, and often brings weed seeds to the surface,

where they are able to germinate (see "The stale seedbed technique", p.620). Soil cultivation also allows small pieces of perennial weed roots to regenerate and start a new growth cycle over again.

It is virtually impossible to clean a soil completely of weeds, but regular weeding, rather than sporadic attempts that are then followed by periods of neglect, is the best method of control. Although tedious, hand-weeding, using a hand fork, is one of the most effective methods of controlling weeds, since you can ensure that the whole plant is removed from the bed. It also causes the least disturbance to existing plants.

Hoeing

Hoes are used to remove annual weeds and also help to aerate the soil (see also p.552). Unless used carefully, however, they may damage

the surface roots and top-growth of nearby cultivated plants. Hoeing mainly affects the surface soil and seldom goes deep enough to destroy the roots of perennial weeds; dig these out or destroy them with a translocated weedkiller (see PLANT PROBLEMS, "Foliage-acting weedkillers", p.671).

Sterilizing the soil

Some soil pests and diseases, such as honey fungus (*Armillaria*) and nematodes, are so aggressive and persistent that soil sterilization may be the only effective treatment to eliminate them.

Soil sterilants should only be used as a last resort, since they are indiscriminate and kill all organisms, beneficial as well as harmful. This may lead to long-term problems in the garden, because harmful pests

CLEARING A SITE OF WEEDS

USING WEEDKILLER
A neglected or weed-infested site must be thoroughly cleared before planting takes place. Treat coarse weeds with a chemical weedkiller.

FORKING OUT WEEDS
Fork up the roots of large weeds and pull them out, holding the main stem close to the soil so that the whole root system is removed.

ROTAVATING THE SOIL

1 *For cultivating large areas of soil, it is worth hiring a motorized rotavator. Adjust the handlebars to a comfortable position and press down on the handlebars so that the tiller blades penetrate the soil to their full depth.*

2 *After rotavating, rake up and remove any pieces of perennial weeds from the surface of the soil, otherwise they will re-establish and grow again.*

SOIL STERILIZATION

Soil sterilization may be the only method of eradicating some pests or diseases. Cover the sterilized soil with plastic weighted down (any soil used for this should be discarded).

are likely to re-invade and thrive unhindered, since there will be no natural predators to control them.

Chemical soil sterilants are highly poisonous and should be applied only by a trained operator. The sterilant is applied as a drench that percolates and vaporizes through the pores of the soil. The soil surface is then covered with plastic to prevent the gases from escaping. After a soil sterilant has been applied, it will be several weeks before it is safe to plant in the treated soil.

Digging and forking

Cultivating the soil by digging and forking helps to provide suitable conditions for good plant growth by aerating the soil and breaking up any surface crust (cap). Organic matter and fertilizers may be added at the same time, if required. On heavily compacted ground, digging helps to improve soil structure and drainage.

The most common method of cultivation is digging with a spade; single and double digging are in general the most effective and labour-efficient digging methods. Some garden beds, however, may not be suited to such a methodical approach to soil cultivation, especially where there are already many established plants. In these circumstances, forking and simple digging may be useful alternatives.

Disadvantages of digging
Digging increases the rate of breakdown of organic matter, particularly in sandy soils, which in the long term reduces soil fertility. Also, digging heavy, wet soils can cause compaction and make conditions worse. If these soils have a good existing structure, digging can be avoided, particularly for tree and shrub beds.

FORKING

Fork over the soil when it is moist but not waterlogged. Work methodically, inserting the fork then turning it over (see inset) to break up the soil and aerate it.

The "no-dig" and deep-bed techniques, popular with organic gardeners in particular, are cultivation methods that minimize soil disturbance, even in the vegetable garden (see THE BED SYSTEM, p.496). In most cases, initial deep cultivation of the soil, incorporating organic matter to improve its structure, is necessary before these methods can be successfully adopted.

When to dig
It is preferable to dig in autumn, if possible. The soil is then exposed to winter frosts and snow, which help to break down large clods of soil and improve soil structure, especially on heavy ground.

From mid-winter until early spring, the ground is often wet or frozen and impossible to work. Heavy soil must never be dug when it is wet.

Using a fork
Much digging work involves lifting and turning the soil. Forks, which are shaped to penetrate the soil easily, are excellent for opening up and loosening soil – but not for lifting it. Forking is less harmful to the soil structure than using a spade, because it tends to break the clods along existing, natural, fracture lines rather than along artificially sliced ones.

Forking is suitable for rough digging and for turning the soil but not for creating fine tilths (see "Forming a tilth", p.620). It is also useful for clearing weeds from the soil, particularly perennial weeds such as couch grass (*Elymus repens*), without leaving behind small pieces that will regenerate.

Simple digging
When digging, some gardeners prefer simply to lift out a spadeful of soil, invert it, drop it back in its original position, and chop it up. This method is known as simple digging. It is a quick and relatively easy form of cultivation and is suitable for cleaning the soil surface of any debris and non-persistent weeds, incorporating small amounts of manure and fertilizers, or creating a surface tilth. Simple digging is often the best option when working in irregularly shaped beds or around existing plants.

Single digging
Single digging is the term applied to a methodical and labour-efficient approach to cultivation that ensures an area has been completely dug, to a uniform standard, and to the depth of a spade (known as a "spit").

Mark out with lines the area to be cultivated; then, beginning at one end

SIMPLE DIGGING

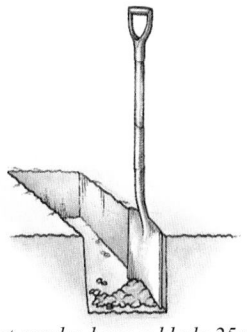

Most spades have a blade 25cm (10in) long. This is the depth of trench required when digging 1 "spit" deep.

1 *Drive the spade into the soil to its full depth, keeping the blade upright. Press down firmly on the blade with the ball of your foot.*

2 *Pull back on the handle and lever soil onto the blade. Bend knees and elbows to lift the spade; do not try to lift too much, especially where the soil is heavy.*

3 *Twist the spade to turn the soil over. This introduces air into the soil and encourages the breakdown of organic matter.*

SINGLE DIGGING

Mark out the bed, then dig a series of trenches, working backwards so that you do not compact the soil. Turn the soil from each trench into the one in front, using soil from the first trench to fill the last.

1 *Dig out a trench 1 spit deep and about 30cm (12in) wide. Insert the spade vertically and lift the soil onto the ground in front.*

2 *Dig a second trench, turning the soil into the trench in front. Invert the soil to bury annual weeds and weed seeds.*

of the plot, dig out trenches to a spade's depth and about 30cm (12in) wide. Place the soil from the first trench in a pile on the ground in front. Work backwards along the plot, turning the soil from each subsequent trench into the one in front.

Adopt this method on regularly shaped plots and in situations where soil uniformity is important – in vegetable gardens and allotments, for example. Single digging is also useful where large quantities of organic matter need to be dug in.

Take the opportunity to incorporate lime (if needed) and fertilizers, such as bonemeal, into the bottom of each trench before replacing the soil. Weeds, especially deep-rooting perennial ones, should be removed as a matter of course.

Double digging

Double or trench digging, in which the soil is worked to a depth of two spits rather than one, should be carried out if the ground has not been previously cultivated or if drainage needs to be improved. Lime and fertilizers should be incorporated, if required, and perennial weeds removed, as in single digging.

On sites where the topsoil is less than two spits deep, standard double digging should be used, since this method ensures that the soil from the upper and lower spits are kept separate. The lower spit containing subsoil should not be brought to the surface – it may be forked or dug over *in situ*, although if more thorough cultivation is required it is also turned.

First mark out the area with lines, as for single digging, then remove the soil from the upper and lower spits of the first trench and from the upper spit of the second, laying it aside on the ground in three separate, clearly marked, piles. Soil may then

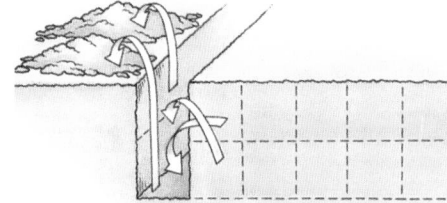

DOUBLE DIGGING FOR DEEP TOPSOILS
Where the topsoil is at least 2 spits deep, soil from the upper and lower spits may be mixed or transferred. Dig out 2 spits from the first trench, setting the soil aside to fill the final trench, then transfer soil from the upper spit of the second trench to the bottom of the first. Soil from the lower spit of the second trench should be transferred to the top of the first, and so on.

be transferred from the lower spit of the second trench to the base of the first trench, and from the upper spit of the third trench to the top of the first. In this way, topsoil and subsoil remain completely separate. Continue digging further trenches in the same way and, at the end of the bed, use soil saved from the first two trenches to fill the appropriate spits of the final two.

If the topsoil is more than two spits deep, there is no need to keep soil from the upper and lower spits separate, and all the soil from one trench may simply be transferred to the trench in front (see above).

Forming a tilth

A "tilth" is a fine surface soil that is suitable for seed germination. It consists largely of small, even soil particles, and is moisture retentive and level. A surface tilth ensures good contact between seed and soil, so that moisture is absorbed easily.

IMPROVING STRUCTURE

To improve soil structure, dig in organic material such as well-rotted manure or compost, according to the needs of the soil.

Prepare seedbeds about one month before sowing by digging the soil and then leaving it to weather. Just before sowing, break up any remaining clods of soil with a rake, level the ground by treading gently, and then rake the surface to provide the fine tilth required for seeds.

Soil structure and water content

For plants to grow and flourish over a period of many years, the soil needs to have a good, inherent structure. On medium and heavy soils, in particular, plant growth depends on good soil structure.

In a well-structured soil, the particles form crumbs that exist as part of an interconnecting network of pores, through which water, nutrients, and air circulate. The structure of the soil therefore affects its ability to hold water, the rate at which it drains, and soil fertility. A poorly structured soil may become too freely drained or waterlogged, and nutrients will be lost by leaching.

SURFACE TILTH

A crumbly, even-textured soil with fine particles makes a good tilth for seed germination. It retains water and nutrients, while providing free drainage needed for good growth.

The stale seedbed technique

This method of cultivation involves disturbing the soil by shallow digging to bring weed seeds to the surface. Any existing weeds are removed at the same time. The weed seeds are then allowed to germinate and grow, and the seedlings killed with a contact weedkiller or by shallow hoeing – this time disturbing the soil as little as possible. Seed may then be safely sown in the weed-free ground, as required. Further weed seeds inevitably germinate during the season, but since the main weed flush has been destroyed, subsequent weed control will be relatively simple.

1 *As an experiment, the soil on the right of this plot has been dug over, while the soil on the left has been left undisturbed.*

2 *After a few weeks, weed seeds have germinated on the cultivated ground. The undisturbed soil has relatively few weeds.*

Poorly structured soil

A poorly structured soil tends to be too wet in winter and too dry in summer. Water frequently runs off the surface rather than percolating deep down, yet once the soil is wet it drains slowly. A soil such as this is difficult to work, and in summer it may become hard and concrete-like. As a result, plant roots have great difficulty penetrating the soil and plant growth is adversely affected.

Cultivating heavy soil during wet weather may make it compacted. When soil particles are compressed, the amount of air in the soil is reduced and so drainage is hindered.

Walking on the soil in wet conditions damages the structure of the surface layer – the soil crumbs break down and fine particles at the surface form a crust, which then effectively prevents air and oxygen from reaching the plants' roots and also prevents seeds from germinating. This is known as "capping" and may occur on some soils, particularly silts, following heavy rain or if the soil is watered too heavily.

Improving soil structure

To improve poor structure, cultivate the soil to as great a depth as possible by double digging (without mixing subsoil with topsoil), incorporating organic or inorganic additives to help bind the soil particles into crumbs. This will do much to improve both aeration and water retention. On severely waterlogged sites, a suitable drainage system may need to be installed (see p.623).

Using soil additives

The choice of additives to use is dependent on the type of soil. Most may either be applied to the surface or incorporated into the soil. Organic material such as animal manure and garden compost improves the structure of any type of soil and also provides valuable nutrients. In addition, animal manure encourages earthworms, which will further benefit soil structure (see "Soil organisms", p.617).

A light, sandy soil may be improved with small amounts of clay (a process known as marling), but enormous quantities of grit or sand would be needed to lighten a very heavy soil.

On compacted soil and clay soil, add manure, compost, and/or lime (but not for acid-loving plants) to improve its structure by encouraging crumb formation.

On silt, add small amounts of clay to improve soil structure, and use manure and compost to encourage crumb formation.

The amount of additive required depends on the soil condition, but a good rule of thumb is to apply about a 5–10cm (2–4in) layer of bulky additives. Some materials, particularly inorganic compounds and water-retaining gels, should be added in much smaller quantities, so it is important to follow the manufacturer's instructions.

Subsidiary benefits of soil additives

Additives also maintain a good balance of air and water in soil. Sand, gravel, and coarse organic matter may be used to improve drainage in silty, compacted, and heavy clay soils. Sand or gravel should be used along channels in the soil, keeping a path open for water, rather than being worked in. Some additives, such as peat substitute, peat, well-rotted manure, and water-holding gels (which hold many times their weight in water) act as "sponges" and may be used to improve water retention in free-draining, sandy soil. On compacted soil, water-holding gels are useful for improving water retention without reducing aeration.

Additions of clay will improve the fertility of impoverished soil. Clay, peat substitutes (or peat), and, to some extent, bark help to retain nutrients that might otherwise be lost by leaching.

Problems with additives

Some additives should not be used in certain soil conditions. Fine sand, for example, added in small amounts to heavy soil may make poor drainage worse by blocking the soil pores. Use a more open material, such as gravel or coarse sand, instead.

SOIL ADDITIVES

Adding composts, well-rotted manure, or peat substitutes such as coconut fibre improves the soil structure and helps to hold moisture in the soil. Mushroom compost is alkaline in nature and therefore should not be used with plants requiring acid conditions. Lime binds clay soil particles together into crumbs by a process known as flocculation.

MUSHROOM COMPOST MANURE

LIME COCONUT FIBRE

Fresh manure gives off ammonia and sometimes other substances that may be toxic to plants. If it is not possible to compost the manure or mature it until it is well rotted, apply it to the soil surface in the autumn and leave the soil uncultivated over winter. The manure will gradually rot down and be incorporated into the soil by earthworms.

Fresh straw, leaves, and bark use up nitrogen during their decomposition process, contributing to a possible nitrogen deficiency in the soil unless additional nitrogen fertilizer is applied to the soil at the same time.

For garden compost (see p.627), never use plant remains that are infected with viruses or any material that contains perennial weeds – both are difficult to control or eradicate. This material should be burned.

COMPARING SOILS

GOOD SOIL
A well-structured soil has a crumbly, moist texture, with a network of pores that holds both air and water. The soil crumbs bind together but do not form a hard "cap".

POOR SOIL
This topsoil is hard and compacted, making it almost impossible to cultivate. Drainage will be poor. Cracks appear where the soil has dried out.

SOIL PROBLEMS

COMPACTION
In compacted soil, the pores between the soil particles have been badly compressed. This results in slow drainage and poor aeration.

BLUE MOTTLING
Blue mottling on the soil surface indicates stagnant, waterlogged soil that needs to be drained. The soil may also have an unpleasant smell.

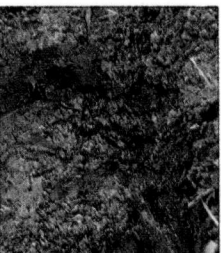

HARDPAN
This is an almost impermeable layer of severely compacted soil. Water will not drain through until the hardpan is broken up and drains are installed.

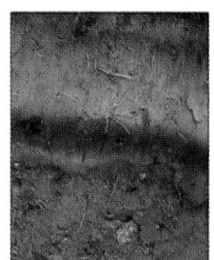

CAPPING
A crust or "cap" forms on the soil when soil crumbs on the surface are damaged by heavy rain or watering, or by walking on the soil when it is wet.

Water

Adequate water is crucial for good plant growth; the amount available depends to some extent on the plant itself but also on soil type and structure, and the method of watering. Water is often in short supply and should not be wasted, so it is important to use good watering and water-conserving techniques. It is also useful to know which plants are susceptible to drought (and when) and which are drought resistant.

An excess of water in the soil (waterlogging) can be as damaging to plants as a lack of soil water. Cultivating the soil and adding organic matter and grit will do much to improve drainage in saturated soil but on severely waterlogged sites an effective drainage system should be installed.

Soil water

In a well-structured soil, water is held in fine capillary pores, which are usually less than 0.1mm ($\frac{1}{160}$in) in diameter, with air in the larger pores; it is therefore possible for soil to be described as "both moist and well drained".

Water is most readily available to plants from pores of the largest diameter. As the pores become smaller, it becomes increasingly difficult for the plants to extract moisture, which means that some soil water always remains unavailable.

Clay soils

Clay soils hold the greatest amount of water but they have a high percentage of fine capillary pores, so plants are not always able to extract enough water for their needs.

HOW NOT TO WATER

Do not water plants at a rate that causes puddling on the soil surface, since this leads to run-off and erodes the soil.

METHODS OF WATERING

BASIN WATERING
Scoop out soil from around the base of the plant, and fill the resulting basin with water.

POT WATERING
Bury a large pot that has a drainage hole close to the plant and fill the pot slowly with water.

Sandy soils

Sandy soils contain coarse pores; the water held within them is more readily available than in clay. Sandy soils, however, drain quickly, and there is relatively little capillary movement of water sideways and upwards.

Loams

Loams usually contain a balanced mix of coarse and relatively fine pores – the coarse pores allow rapid drainage while the finer ones retain water, much of which may be extracted by plants in dry conditions.

The water table

Moisture rises towards the soil surface by capillary action from the water table below. Heavy clay soils may be saturated to 2m (6ft) above the water table, with some moisture available to plant roots as much as 3.5m (11ft) above it. Silt and most clay soils are saturated to 1.5m (5ft), with moisture available to roots 2.5m (8ft) above the water table. The figures for fine sand are 1.5m (5ft) and 2.4m (7½ft) respectively, and for coarser sand 30cm (1ft) and 1m (3ft). On gravel, there is no water rise at all. In many gardens the water table is too low to have any influence.

Watering techniques

The aim of watering is to recharge the soil so that reserves will be sufficient to last until the next watering or rainfall. Always water thoroughly so that water is available deep in the soil. Frequently applying a little water is of limited value, because much of it simply evaporates off the soil surface before it has a chance to penetrate down to the roots of plants.

Moisture take-up

The water supply to a plant is limited by the size of its root system. When planted in soil where the drainage has been improved (see p.623) and any compaction rectified by double digging (see p.620), plants are able to develop deeper root systems, with a comparative increase in growth.

The main limitation when watering, however, is the rate at which the soil takes up the moisture. On average, soil absorbs about 8mm ($\frac{3}{8}$in) depth of water per hour. Water applied to the soil faster than it is absorbed (for example, by a hand-held hose or watering can with a rose) collects in a pool on the surface until the area covered is sufficient to take it all in. After watering in dry conditions, it is worth testing the soil with an auger – it may be surprising just how little the water has penetrated. If the soil around the plant roots is still dry, give the area several further applications once the water from the first application has soaked in.

To reduce run-off, the ground may be modified by terracing or "dishing" to create a hollow trough around each plant (see above), which ensures that water reaches the roots. Pot watering (see above), sprinklers (see p.561), and trickle or drip feed systems (see p.561) are efficient methods of watering, since water is supplied to the roots over several hours.

Water-conserving techniques

Mulching the surface of the soil (see p.626) improves rain penetration and minimizes evaporation. By controlling weeds effectively (see p.618), you will ensure that no soil water is wasted on unwanted plants. See also WATER CONSERVATION AND RECYCLING, p.614.

Water deficiency

Once a plant begins to wilt, its growth rate has already begun to slow down. In many areas, water use will exceed water supply during summer, so the soil suffers a net loss of moisture. Digging additives such as manure into the soil improves structure (see p.621) and water retention, which helps to prevent a water deficit from occurring, but unless an existing deficit is made up by irrigation, the soil becomes progressively drier. Regular watering is therefore essential.

The local meteorological office will have figures for the typical monthly water loss from the soil and through leaves by transpiration (known as potential evapotranspiration), and also for the average monthly rainfall. These figures are useful when calculating how often to water but, for greater accuracy, it is better to take your own rainfall measurements each month rather than using the average figures.

Seasonal and establishment needs

The point at which a water deficit begins to affect plant growth depends on the plants themselves. High-yield plants usually need plenty of water, so the soil should be kept moist. Some plants have critical periods of growth, during which time water supplies are vital: the first half of summer, for example, is much more important than the second for young ornamental trees. Fruit trees need ample water as the fruits swell, as do potato tubers.

Watering is especially important for newly planted or transplanted plants, and those in shallow soils and in containers. Seedlings, too, have low drought resistance, and a reliable water supply is essential. Standard trees are likely to require watering throughout their first season, since their top-growth is frequently out of proportion to their roots.

Drought conditions

Even well-established garden plants suffer during prolonged drought, although no perceptible damage may be seen for some time. Moderate drought may, however, improve the flavour of some fruits and vegetables, especially tomatoes.

In areas of low rainfall, there is increasing interest in using plants that are adapted to droughts (xerophytes): *Pieris*, lavenders (*Lavandula*), and *Phlomis*, as well as many grey- and silver-leaved plants, are good examples.

Grass tolerates prolonged, dry weather well; although lawns may become brown, they quickly recover once rain falls. Regular watering in summer is not essential, therefore, unless you want to keep your lawn looking green.

Waterlogged soil

Waterlogging occurs when the amount of water entering the soil exceeds the amount draining out. Particularly vulnerable are areas where the water table is high (see p.622) or where the soil is compacted and thus poorly structured.

Roots (except those of bog plants) are unable to function effectively in waterlogged soil and may eventually die if drainage is not improved. Wet soil is often low in certain nutrients (notably nitrogen) and, as a result, mineral deficiencies may prove a problem. Since wet soil tends to be cold, plant growth may be slow in spring. Diseases such as clubroot

(see p.649) also flourish in water-logged soil. Rushes, sedges, and mosses growing on the ground suggest that the soil may be water-logged, and a sharp division between peaty topsoil and subsoil also indicates poor drainage. On waterlogged clay, the soil may have a stagnant smell and a yellow or blue-grey colour, which is known as gleying.

Poor drainage may be confirmed by pouring water into a hole 30–60cm (12–24in) deep. If the water remains for hours or even days, then the soil needs draining. If digging deeper or trying to push a metal rod into the soil meets with resistance, this indicates that there is a layer of hardpan (see *Soil Problems*, p.621).

Improving drainage

Where waterlogging is not severe and there is excess surface water only, this may be diverted from the site by shaping garden surfaces so that the water flows into drainage

ditches. To improve drainage where there is a high water table, install an underground drainage system, preferably using a specialist contractor to carry out the work. If drains already exist, check for blockages in the drainage ditches, or for damaged pipes. Underground drains will not help if there are drainage barriers, such as a hard pan, above them.

Ditches and French drains
A system of open ditches is the best method of carrying away any excess water from the surface. These should be 1–1.2m (3–4ft) deep, with sloping sides. Just as effective but less obtrusive are French drains, which are gravel-filled drainage ditches topped with upturned turf and topsoil.

Drainage systems and soakaways
A soakaway is a rubble-filled pit into which excess water runs via underground drains or drainage ditches (see below). This method of drainage is effective on sites where there is surface compaction, since it breaks

through any layer of hardpan. To construct a soakaway, dig a hole approximately 1m (3ft) wide and at least 2m (6ft) deep. Fill it with broken bricks or stones completely surrounded by geotextile fabric. Install perforated plastic pipes or tile drains at least 60cm (24in) below ground level (see below) to lead from the surrounding land to the soakaway.

Water storage areas
Alternatively, create a water storage area where water collects in a pond or large container, or gradually soaks away. A pond is beneficial to wildlife, but its success depends on the degree of sediment in the drainage water – too much will make the pond rich in nutrients, therefore becoming prone to silting up and excessive algal growth.

Water collected in containers may be recycled for use in the garden. Collecting water that is allowed gradually to soak away helps to replenish groundwater reserves and reduces silt pollution of rivers.

How to Build a Soakaway

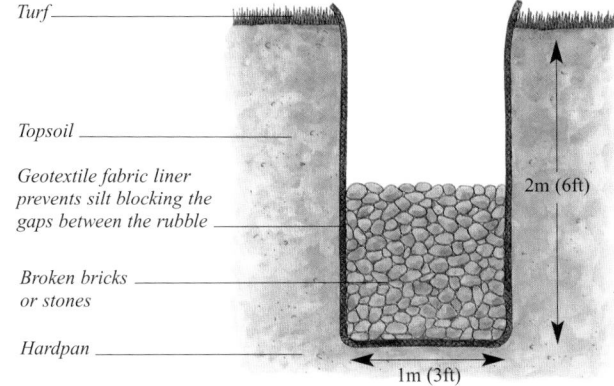

Turf

Topsoil

Geotextile fabric liner prevents silt blocking the gaps between the rubble

Broken bricks or stones

Hardpan

2m (6ft)

1m (3ft)

1 *In a waterlogged part of the garden, dig a hole 2m (6ft) deep with 1 x 1m (3 x 3ft) sides. Line the sides and bottom with a geotextile fabric. Then fill the lined soakaway hole with rubble, such as broken bricks or stones, to a depth of 1m (3ft).*

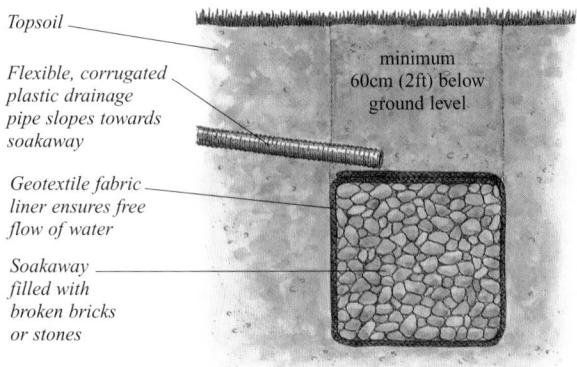

Topsoil

Flexible, corrugated plastic drainage pipe slopes towards soakaway

Geotextile fabric liner ensures free flow of water

Soakaway filled with broken bricks or stones

minimum 60cm (2ft) below ground level

2 *Fold the liner over the rubble. Then place the end of a perforated plastic pipe on top of the liner, so that it is ideally 60cm (2ft) below ground level. Fill in the hole with topsoil, and turf the top.*

Installing drains

A system of perforated corrugated plastic pipes laid in a herringbone pattern underground provides an effective method of drainage into a rubble-filled ditch or soakaway. Lay the pipes well below ground level, so they do not interfere with future cultivations. Water from the surrounding site can seep into the pipes, which must be angled so they carry

the water to the soakaway. Compared with tile drains (see below), plastic pipes are flexible, easily cut, and absorb the natural movements within the soil. To join two pipes, cut a hole in one pipe to match the diameter of the other pipe; then push it in. Install drains before plants are in place, if possible, as the work causes great upheaval.

A Tile Drainage System

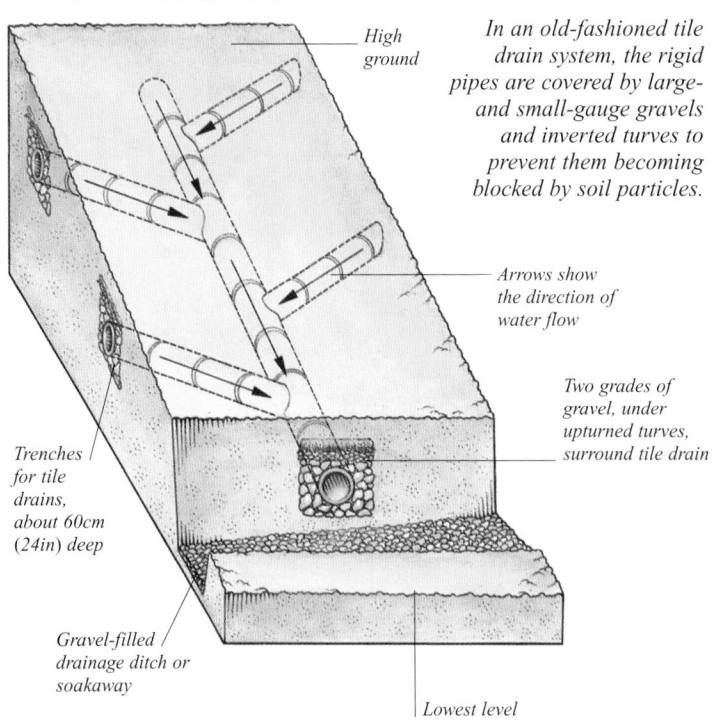

High ground

In an old-fashioned tile drain system, the rigid pipes are covered by large- and small-gauge gravels and inverted turves to prevent them becoming blocked by soil particles.

Arrows show the direction of water flow

Two grades of gravel, under upturned turves, surround tile drain

Trenches for tile drains, about 60cm (24in) deep

Gravel-filled drainage ditch or soakaway

Lowest level

623

Soil nutrients and fertilizers

The nutrients utilized by plants are composed of mineral ions, absorbed in solution from the soil through the roots and used with carbon dioxide and water to make food. Macronutrients, required in relatively large amounts, include nitrogen (N), phosphorus (P), potassium (K), magnesium (Mg), calcium (Ca), and sulphur (S). Micronutrients, or trace elements, are equally important but required only in small amounts; they include iron (Fe), manganese (Mn), copper (Cu), zinc (Zn), boron (Bo), molybdenum (Mb), and chlorine (Cl).

To ensure healthy plant growth, fertilizers containing nutrients may be added to the soil but this is only necessary when the soil is unable to provide adequate amounts of the nutrients required. On the majority of soils, only nitrogen, which promotes vigorous growth, phosphorus (phosphates), for assisting strong root growth, and potassium (potash), which improves flowering and fruiting, need to be added regularly. Nitrogen deficiency (see p.650) causes reduced growth, and potassium deficiency (see p.650) causes leaf discolouration. Phosphate deficiency (see p.650) is less common but is most likely to occur in young plants with poor root systems. Manganese/iron deficiency (see p.651) causes browning of leaves, and may be a problem if acid-loving plants are grown in alkaline soil or watered with hard water.

Types of fertilizer

Deciding the amount and which type of fertilizer to apply can be complex. Understanding how each type works will make gardening more productive and even perhaps more environmentally friendly. It should be noted that in this context, the term "organic" may simply be used to mean "of living origin", while "inorganic" refers to artificial, chemical formulations. Gardeners practising organic growing, in the environmentally conscious sense, should carefully check the labelling and provenance of any fertilizer to ensure that it meets their concerns.

Bulky organic fertilizers

Weight for weight, bulky organic fertilizers supply fewer nutrients than inorganic fertilizers. For example, 1 tonne/ton of manure typically contains 6kg (13.2lb) of nitrogen, 1kg (2.2lb) of phosphorus and 4kg (8.8lb) of potassium; the equivalent amount of nutrients in a chemical form is provided by only 30kg (66lb) of inorganic fertilizer.

Manures are, however, integral to organic growing because the organic "waste" matter that makes them so bulky provides greater benefits than a simple nutrient analysis would suggest. Manures, although they may vary in quality, normally contain high levels of micronutrients, and are a long-term source of nitrogen. They also provide conditions in which worms thrive. Additions of manure improve the structure and water content of most soils (see p.620); and since this encourages root growth, it increases plant uptake of nutrients.

Concentrated organic fertilizers

Traditional examples of concentrated organic fertilizers include dried blood, fish and bone meals, and hoof and horn. Seaweed meal and pelleted chicken manure are popular alternatives with gardeners practising organic methods. Compared with bulky organic materials, they are easy to handle and contain fairly consistent proportions of nutrients but are relatively expensive for each unit of nutrient. Their characteristic slow release of nutrients is partly dependent on breakdown by soil organisms, so they may not be effective when these organisms are inactive, as in cold weather.

Despite some gardeners' concerns, there are no documented health risks from processed animal-protein fertilizers, such as bone meal, manufactured for domestic gardens; indeed some argue that they are an environmentally sound way of utilizing waste. However, wearing gloves and a dust mask when applying such products, and hand-washing produce (or indeed substituting garden compost where edible crops are being grown) will provide added peace of mind. If you prefer not to use animal-derived products at all, seaweed meal is normally a perfectly adequate source of plant nutrition.

Soluble inorganic fertilizers

Concentrated inorganic fertilizers contain high percentages of a given nutrient, weight for weight, and most are easy to transport, handle, and apply, although a few are unpleasant to handle; wearing gloves and a dust-excluding mask is always advisable. They are usually the cheapest source per unit of nutrient. They give a quick-acting boost to plants deficient in nutrients, and permit precise control over the timing of nutrient release. However, a large proportion of soluble fertilizer may be wasted on sandy soils because of leaching.

When using soluble inorganic fertilizers, be selective about which mineral ions are applied to the soil, since some may damage particular plants. Redcurrants, for example, are

NUTRIENT CONTENT OF FERTILIZERS

	% Nitrogen (N)	% Phosphate (P_2O_5)	% Potash (K_2O)
ORGANIC			
Animal manure	0.6	0.1	0.5
Blood, fish, and bone	3.5	8	–
Bone meal	3.5	20	–
Cocoa shells	3	1	3.2
Garden compost	0.5	0.3	0.8
Hoof and horn	13	–	–
Mushroom compost	0.7	0.3	0.3
Pelleted chicken manure	4	2	1
Rock phosphate	–	26	12
Seaweed meal	2.8	0.2	2.5
Wood ash	0.1	0.3	1
INORGANIC			
Ammonium sulphate	21	–	–
Growmore	7	7	7
Potassium sulphate	–	–	49
Single superphosphate	–	18	–
Slow-release fertilizer	14	13	13

COMPARING FERTILIZERS

GARDEN COMPOST

MUSHROOM COMPOST

COCOA SHELLS

BLOOD, FISH, AND BONE

SOLUBLE INORGANIC FERTILIZER

These comparisons show the relative amounts of different types of fertilizer required to supply roughly the same quantity of nutrients.

SLOW-RELEASE FERTILIZERS

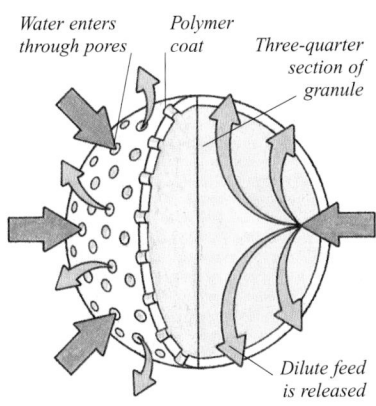

Water enters through pores | *Polymer coat* | *Three-quarter section of granule*

Dilute feed is released

Water enters the fertilizer granules through pores in the polymer coat, which builds up pressure inside, splitting the granules open.

sensitive to chloride salts, such as potassium chloride; sulphates should be used instead. Large applications of some inorganic salts make the soil more saline and may harm beneficial soil organisms. Apply soluble inorganic fertilizers in split applications, sparingly but fairly frequently, rather than in a single, large dose.

Slow-release fertilizers
These are complex fertilizer formulations that are designed to release nutrients gradually, over many months or even years in some cases. Some slowly degrade in the soil, while others absorb water until they swell and burst open. Many have membranes of varying thickness that gradually release nutrients from an internal store. These fertilizers are expensive and not generally economical to use in the wider garden, but they are especially valuable in the care of container plants (see p.323).

Green manures
These are plants that are grown purely to be dug back into the soil to improve fertility and add to the

organic content. They are used on land that would otherwise be left fallow and can help to prevent nutrients from being washed away, since fallow land is more prone to leaching. Do not use invasive plants as green manures, however.

Borage (*Borago officinalis*), ryegrass (*Lolium perenne*), and comfrey (*Symphytum officinale*) are excellent perennial green manures. Mixtures of fast-germinating annuals are also used. Legumes such as annual lupins have nitrogen-fixing bacteria in root nodules which enable them to obtain nitrogen from air in the soil. The organic matter these plants provide may contribute as much nitrogen as would be added in a standard fertilizing regime; it has a low carbon:nitrogen ratio and so breaks down rapidly, providing easily available nitrogen.

Applying fertilizers

Concentrated fertilizers may be scattered over the surface of the soil or placed around individual plants. Some fertilizers are also available in liquid form for application to the soil surface or as foliar feeds directly onto leaves. All products, organic or inorganic, should be handled with care. Always wear protective clothing where advised. Do not apply on windy days and spread granular or powdered products carefully on the soil – never touching plant stems. Use only the recommended quantities; too much can damage plants.

Broadcast fertilization
Scattering fertilizer over the whole soil surface benefits the greatest area of soil and minimizes the risk of plant injury from overfeeding. In dry weather, however, the uptake of some nutrients may be poor, particularly of immobile nutrients such as phosphates so, whenever possible, dig phosphates into the soil.

Fertilizer placement
Fertilizing around the base of a plant is an economical and efficient feeding method, as plant roots quickly spread through the fertilized area.

Liquid fertilizers
Dissolving fertilizer in water before application is an efficient method of applying nutrients, especially if the soil is dry. Do not use liquid feeds when rain is forecast, since the liquid may be washed away. Liquid fertilizers sprayed onto leaf surfaces, known as foliar feeds, may be used to correct mineral deficiencies caused by certain soil conditions, such as high pH. For deep-rooted plants, such as fruit trees, foliar feeds may also be used to correct deficiencies in nutrients that are relatively insoluble.

Liming

Liming or adding lime-rich material such as mushroom compost increases the alkalinity of the soil. This is sometimes desirable to improve yields on the vegetable plot but is seldom worthwhile for ornamental plants – it is better to choose plants adapted to the existing conditions.

Types of lime
Ordinary lime (calcium carbonate) is bulky but easy to handle and relatively safe to use. Quicklime (calcium oxide) is more efficient at raising pH but is caustic and may scorch plants; there is also a risk of over-liming with quicklime. Slaked or hydrated lime (calcium hydroxide), made by treating quicklime with water; is slightly less efficient than quicklime but less caustic.

Applying lime
Lime may be spread on the soil at any time of year, but it should be applied as far in advance of planting as possible and preferably be well

LIMING

Using a spade, spread the lime over the surface of the soil, then distribute it evenly with a rake (see inset). Do not plant or sow for about a month.

dug in. Choose a windless day and always wear goggles. Do not lime every year, as overliming may contribute to nutrient deficiencies, and always take pH readings in several different parts of the plot first, since any uneven rates of breakdown may cause temporary, localized problems. The table below indicates the average amount of lime required for particular soils of a given pH to achieve a

STARTING pH	SAND (g/sq m)	LOAM (g/sq m)	CLAY (g/sq m)
4.5	190g	285g	400g
5.0	155g	235g	330g
5.5	130g	190g	260g
6.0	118g	155g	215g

level of pH 6.5 (see also "Optimum pH", p.617). To raise soil pH quickly, add lime during digging. If required for established plantings, lime may be applied as a top-dressing and watered in. Do not apply lime at the same time as manure: lime reacts with manure to release nitrogen in the form of ammonia. This may damage plants and wastes nitrogen. If required, apply lime and manure in alternate years.

GREEN MANURING

Sow seed for green manures on fallow ground. Cut the plants to the ground when about 20cm (8in) tall, digging them in after a day or two.

HOW TO APPLY FERTILIZER

BROADCASTING
To apply fertilizer in accurate amounts over large areas, mark out the plot into square metres or yards, using string or canes. Fill a pot or bowl with the recommended quantity of fertilizer and sprinkle it evenly over each section of the plot.

PLACEMENT
Sprinkle the fertilizer around the base of the plant, making sure that none touches the leaves or stem.

Top-dressings and mulches

Top-dressings and mulches are materials that are applied to the surface of the soil. They are used to improve plant growth in some way, either by adding nutrients to the soil, by increasing the organic content, or by reducing water loss from the soil. Alternatively they may be used in a decorative manner.

Top-dressings

The term "top-dressing" is used in two ways. First, it describes surface applications of soluble fertilizers around plants. Second, it refers to additives that are applied to the soil surface or to lawns. For example, a lawn may be top-dressed with sand or fine organic material, which will eventually be washed in by rain.

Gravel or grit is sometimes used as a top-dressing for plants in beds and containers to provide quick drainage away from the "collars" of plants that are sensitive to excess moisture. They also act as a mulch and discourage growth of mosses or lichens on the soil surface.

Plants may also be top-dressed with gravel or stone chippings simply to achieve a decorative effect.

Mulches

Mulches are available in organic and inorganic forms and improve plant growth in several ways: they regulate soil temperature, keeping plant roots

MATERIALS USED AS TOP-DRESSINGS

TOP-DRESSINGS AS ADDITIVES
Some top-dressings, such as well-rotted manures and compost, are added to the soil around plants to provide humus and a steady supply of nutrients. Sand, mixed with loam and peat or coir, is used as a top-dressing on lawns to improve aeration.

SAND

DECORATIVE TOP-DRESSINGS
Materials such as gravel and grit are added to the compost surface in containers or to the soil surface in a border or bed, particularly around low-growing plants such as alpines. These materials improve surface drainage as well as setting off the plants.

GRAVEL

COMPOST

LEAF MOULD

COARSE GRIT

CORNISH GRIT

warm in winter and cool in summer; they reduce water loss from the soil surface; and they help to stop weed seeds germinating by preventing light from reaching them.

Always remove all perennial weeds before mulching, otherwise they benefit from the effects of the mulch, to the detriment of your plants. A mulch should not be applied when the soil is cold or frozen, since the insulation effect will be counter-productive, and the soil remain cold – instead, wait until the soil has warmed up in spring.

Organic mulches
To be effective, an organic mulch should be long-lasting and not easily dislodged by rain. It should also have a loose structure that allows water to pass through it quickly.

Coarse bark is one of the most useful organic mulches because it inhibits weed seeds in the soil from germinating, and weeds that do appear are easily removed. Garden compost, leaf mould, and peat substitutes such as coir are not quite as effective because they provide an ideal medium for the germination of weed seeds and are quickly mixed into the soil, although they do improve the soil's texture as a result.

Inorganic mulches
Inorganic mulches made of biodegradable horticultural paper or thin sheets of woven or bonded, water-permeable fabrics (known variously as sheet mulches, landscape fabric, or geotextile) are widely available and simple to lay and

secure with metal pegs. They are easy to plant through, and provide good weed suppression while allowing water to penetrate to plant roots.

A disadvantage of sheet mulches is that, once they are in place, organic matter cannot be incorporated into the soil. However, because they form such a barrier, they are useful laid beneath a layer of loose mulch to extend its life.

Mulches made from impermeable plastic sheet are particularly useful when laid temporarily to warm soil before sowing early crops, or longer-term for perennial weed suppression. However, once in place, almost no water evaporates from the soil; do not, therefore, lay plastic sheet mulches over waterlogged soil.

"Floating" mulches are sheets of light perforated plastic or fibre fleece used like cloches – as the crop grows, the floating mulch is raised by the plants. Their main purpose is to increase temperature; they may also act as a barrier against pests.

LOOSE MULCHES

APPLYING THE MULCH
A loose mulch regulates soil temperature, retains moisture, and discourages weeds. It should preferably be about 10–15cm (4–6in) deep.

AREA TO MULCH
For small to medium-sized plants, spread a mulch to the full extent of the foliage canopy.

ANCHORING PLASTIC SHEETING

A plastic sheet mulch controls weeds effectively over a large area and raises soil temperature slightly. Using a spade, anchor the sheet by sinking the edges into 5cm (2in) slits dug into the soil.

Composts and leaf mould

There are two distinct forms of compost: garden compost is decayed organic matter and is a soil additive; potting and propagation composts are made from precise combinations of (mainly) organic materials, and are used for growing plants in containers (see CONTAINER GARDENING, "Composts for containers", p.322) and for propagation (see PRINCIPLES OF PROPAGATION, "Requirements for germination", p.630).

Garden compost

The contribution of garden compost to the productivity of the garden can be enormous. As well as supplying nutrients directly, the high levels of humus it contains increase the soil's nutrient-holding capacity and help improve soil drainage and aeration. It also contributes a healthy population of beneficial soil micro-organisms. It should be added to the soil when the rate of breakdown of the organic matter has levelled off; by this stage, it should be dark, crumbly, and smell sweet and earthy.

Making garden compost
To make a compost heap, build up a mixture of nitrogen-rich material (such as grass clippings) and carbon-rich material (such as bark and shredded newspaper), preferably in a ratio of 1:2. Almost any vegetable matter, including seaweed, may be composted, but protein and cooked vegetable waste should not be used, as these attract vermin.

Do not put grass clippings on the heap for the first few mowings after the application of a weedkiller, and never add thick layers of grass clippings, as they inhibit air movement. In fact no vegetation that has been treated with herbicide should be used, as the chemicals may persist, making the compost unsuitable for food crops; it may also damage plants mulched with contaminated compost. There is a health risk, too, especially to children, if cat or dog waste is included, which may contain eggs of the *Toxocara* parasite.

Pruning clippings may be added to a compost heap, although any woody stems must be shredded first. Avoid any material that is diseased or infested with pests. Use only young weeds; those with seed, or about to set seed, should be put in a dustbin, as should all pernicious, perennial weeds. It is especially important to avoid those with creeping root systems, such as couch grass (*Elymus repens*) and ground elder (*Aegopodium podagraria*).

Compost additives
Many materials compost satisfactorily, but additional nitrogen will speed up the process. The nitrogen may be provided as artificial fertilizer, proprietary, high-quality, nutrient-rich, starter compost, or as manure, which has the advantage of containing high levels of beneficial micro-organisms. Add this, as needed, to the compost heap, so that there are alternate layers of organic material and manure.

If the material in the compost heap is too acidic, micro-organisms will not work efficiently – adding lime will make it more alkaline.

The composting process
The process by which organic matter is broken down in a compost heap relies on the activity of beneficial, aerobic bacteria and micro-fungi. To proliferate and work efficiently, these micro-organisms need air, nitrogen, moisture, and some warmth.

To ensure adequate airflow, first make the base of the compost heap from a thick, open layer of twiggy material. To maintain good aeration, it is essential that the compost materials are never allowed to become compacted or too wet. Mix fine- and coarse-textured matter when building the heap, if necessary putting fine materials to one side until there is an opportunity to mix it with coarser grades. Turn the compost regularly to avoid compaction and speed up the composting process.

TWIN COMPOST BIN SYSTEM
Fill the first bin (left) with alternating layers of organic matter. When it is full, turn the contents into the second bin (right) to continue rotting, and start refilling the first bin. Keep both bins well covered at all times.

MAKING A COMPOST BIN

1 *To make the first side, lay 2 timber battens (to act as the uprights) on the ground at least 1m (3ft) apart. Nail planks across them, butting the joints together. Leave an 8cm (3in) gap at top and bottom.*

2 *Make the second side; nail scraps of wood across the top to hold the sides in place temporarily. Nail on the back planks.*

3 *Nail 2 battens inside each upright (inset) for the front planks to slide between. Fix a piece of wood at the base as a "stop".*

4 *Nail planks across the top and bottom of the front panel, to stabilize the bin when the front planks are removed.*

5 *Check that the front planks slide easily between the battens. If necessary, saw a little off the ends.*

USING THE BIN
Place a thick layer of twiggy material at the base; build up the heap in 15cm (6in) layers, sprinkling each layer with a little manure.

Manure

Garden and kitchen waste

During composting the heap should be damp, but not wet, so water it in dry weather, if necessary. Cover with sacking, plastic sheeting, or carpet.

The process of bacterial decomposition itself generates a high temperature, which speeds the natural breakdown of organic matter and also helps to kill weed seeds and some pests and diseases. To heat up sufficiently, a compost heap should be at least 1 cubic metre (1 cubic yard) in size but 2 cubic metres (2 cubic yards) is preferable. Compost reaches its maximum temperature in two or three weeks and matures in about three months.

An ammonia odour indicates that the compost is too rich in nitrogen; add in more carbon-rich material, such as cardboard egg boxes or kitchen paper rolls. A smell of rotten eggs means that the heap lacks air; turn the heap and incorporate coarse, bulky materials.

Slow composting

Composting may be undertaken in a non-intensive way. Heaps of pruning clippings, for example, eventually rot down, even if they are not in a bin. No starter material is added, and the heap is not turned. There will, however, be some material that does not break down fully – this will need to be composted again.

Municipal composting

An increasing number of local authorities operate community recycling centres that produce garden compost from "green" waste. This is derived from municipal parks and gardens and from separated domestic collection by their waste-management divisions. The product is often offered for resale to the home gardener and makes a good mulch material.

Worm compost

Worm-worked compost is highly fertile and is formed when worms consume and digest organic matter, expelling the end-product as fine-textured wormcasts. The most productive are small, red brandling worms and striped tiger worms. Wormeries are ideal for recycling kitchen waste, and can be purchased in kit form, or as a worm "culture" for making a homemade worm bin.

To give the culture a good start, introduce the worms into a 5cm (2in) layer of garden compost or manure over a layer of damp straw or shredded newspaper. Add layers of kitchen waste – to a depth of no more than 15cm (6in) at a time – and allow the worms to work most of it before adding more.

The worms work only at temperatures above 15°C (59°F), so store the wormery under cover during winter. Do not allow excess liquid to build up in the bin. When the bin is full, remove the worms from the compost by sieving and use them to start the next culture.

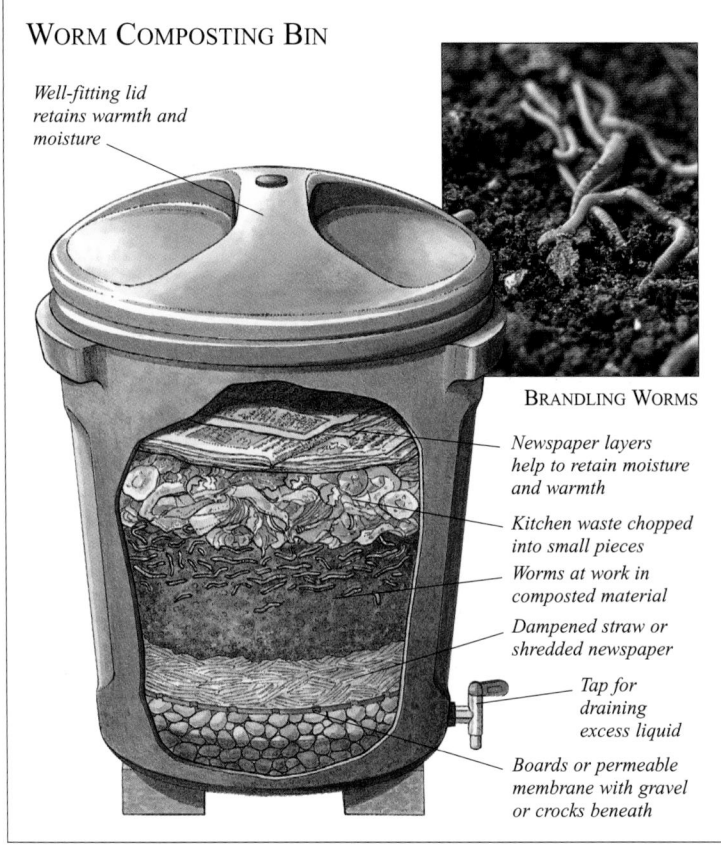

WORM COMPOSTING BIN

Well-fitting lid retains warmth and moisture

BRANDLING WORMS

Newspaper layers help to retain moisture and warmth

Kitchen waste chopped into small pieces

Worms at work in composted material

Dampened straw or shredded newspaper

Tap for draining excess liquid

Boards or permeable membrane with gravel or crocks beneath

Leaf mould

Although leaves can be included on the compost heap, they are best composted separately as they are slow to break down. They rely more heavily on micro-fungi than on bacteria, and need less air and warmth. Stack leaves, as they are collected in autumn, in a wire netting cage or bin, treading them down firmly each time the bin is filled. Except for watering in dry weather, they need little further attention while they decompose.

MAKING A LEAF MOULD BIN

1 *Staple chicken wire to 2 wooden stakes of equal length. Then hammer the stakes 30cm (12in) into the ground.*

2 *Insert 2 more stakes into the ground, and staple the wire to them, securing the 2 cut ends of wire to one of these stakes.*

THE FINISHED BIN
A leaf mould bin should be broad and reasonably low, to allow for easy access to the middle. You will need to compact the leaves after putting them in by treading on them, or firming with a rake.

USING THE BIN
Leaf mould is an excellent soil conditioner and mulching material. It can also be used as a compost additive in homemade potting. It should not be removed from the bin until it has decomposed completely, which is likely to take a year or more. Use one bin while the other is rotting down.

6
PRINCIPLES
OF PROPAGATION

PLANT PROPAGATION is not difficult once the basic principles are understood, and it is the best and cheapest way to increase plant stocks. In addition, it provides many opportunities for gardeners to exchange plants, thereby increasing the varieties available in cultivation. Techniques range from the simple division of overcrowded perennials to more advanced methods, such as hybridizing in order to create plants with new characteristics, such as novel flower colours. For many people, the transition from a seed into a healthy plant, or the development of a cutting into a new tree or shrub, is fascinating. Successful propagation is well within the reach of any gardener once they grasp the techniques in this chapter.

Seeds

Seed is much the commonest way by which flowering plants reproduce in nature. It is normally a sexual method and, as such, always presents the possibility of a variety of genetic combinations, so that the resulting seedlings are variable. Such variation provides the basis by which plants adapt to their environment, and enables the breeding and selection of cultivars with new combinations of desirable characteristics. Seeds may more or less breed true but often vary greatly within a species. In horticulture, variation is disadvantageous if the plants raised are to retain particular characteristics, but advantageous when new, improved characteristics are being sought.

REPRODUCTIVE PARTS OF A ROSE FLOWER

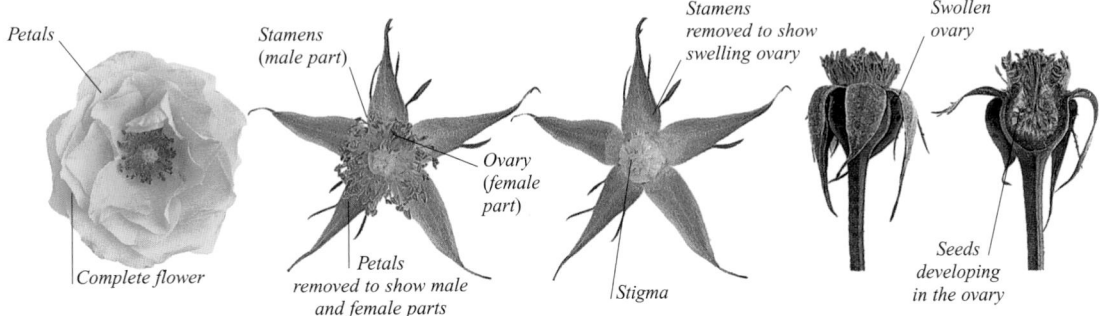

Petals

Stamens (male part)

Ovary (female part)

Complete flower

Petals removed to show male and female parts

Stamens removed to show swelling ovary

Stigma

Swollen ovary

Seeds developing in the ovary

The parts of a flower needed for reproduction are the stamens – the male part, which bears the pollen – and the pistils – the female part, which comprises one or more stigmas, style, and ovary. The petals attract pollinators.

How the seed develops

Most plants are hermaphrodite – that is, each flower bears male and female parts. As the flower matures, pollen is transferred onto one or more stigmas of the same flower (self-pollination) or of a flower on another plant of the same species (cross-pollination) by insects, birds, water, or wind. The pollen grains then produce pollen tubes, which grow down the style towards the ovules in the ovary, and fertilization occurs when the male and female nuclei fuse. From these develop the embryos, which, nourished by adjacent storage tissue in a seed, are capable of forming complete new plants.

Collecting and storing seed

In general, seed should be collected as soon as it is ripe and then stored in a cool, dry, dark, airy place such as a domestic refrigerator until it is used. Certain seeds, however, have special needs. Some are viable for only short periods and should be sown as soon as possible. Others may be stored for very long periods at low temperatures without losing viability. Fleshy fruits should be soaked and softened in water, the seeds removed from the flesh, and then air-dried at 10–20°C (50–68°F). Before they are sown, however, seeds of most stone fruits (eg cherry) and that of some berried shrubs (eg *Berberis* and *Cotoneaster*) need stratifying (see p.630).

As soon as a seed capsule splits, harvest it together with other capsules that are nearing maturity. Dry them in clean paper bags before separating out the seeds. When mature, wind-distributed seed will start dispersing, so quickly cover the seed-bearing branches with fine muslin or paper bags; or cut one or two seed-bearing branches and place them in water indoors to mature.

How to overcome dormancy

The seeds of some plants have inbuilt mechanisms to assist in controlling the time of germination; for example, many seeds do not germinate in late autumn, when conditions are unfavourable for seedling growth, but remain dormant until the temperature and other factors are more suitable. This dormancy is achieved by a variety of means including the presence of chemical inhibitors in the seed, by hardened seed coats that must rot or be breached before the seed can germinate, or by the need for the seed to experience alternating cold and warm periods. Several methods have been developed horticulturally to overcome this natural dormancy so the seeds will germinate more quickly and are therefore less likely to fail.

Scarification
The aim is to break down the hardened seed coat and allow water to enter, thereby speeding up germination. Large, hard-coated seeds, such as those of the legume family, may be nicked

SCARIFICATION

Before planting, carefully nick the hard coat on seeds such as Paeonia lutea *with a clean, sharp knife so that the seed can absorb moisture.*

with a knife. Smaller seeds may be shaken in a jar lined with abrasive paper or one containing sharp gravel.

Warm stratification

This is used for hard-coated seeds of many woody species (see *Tree Seed Requiring Stratification*, p.81). Place the seeds in a plastic bag in moist (but not wet) standard seed compost, and store for 4–12 weeks at 20–30°C (68–86°F). This is usually followed by a period of cold stratification before sowing. See also "Breaking seed dormancy", p.115.

Cold stratification

Soak the seeds for a period of up to 24 hours, then add them to moist (but not wet) vermiculite in a plastic bag or place them in an open dish on moist filter paper. Refrigerate the seeds at 1–5°C (34–41°F) for 4–12 weeks. If germination has occurred, sow the seeds immediately.

Alternatively for large seeds, place the seeds in a pot containing 1 part seed to 3 parts moist sand. Cover with mesh and leave in a cold frame for one or two winters until they germinate; then sow the seed at once.

Requirements for germination

In order to germinate, a seed needs water, air, warmth, and, for a few

POST-SCARIFICATION SOAK

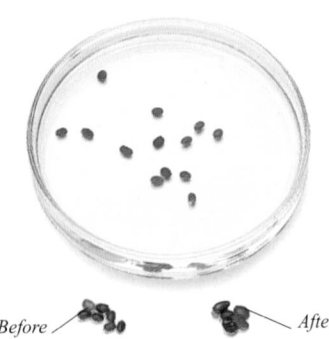

Before / *After*

After scarification, soak seeds such as lupin in water for 24 hours, so they swell slightly, then sow them.

species, light. The growing medium needs to be a fine compost capable of drawing water up to seeds placed near its surface. To aid this capillary rise, the compost is firmed lightly. Without this firming, air pockets occur, and the water columns essential for capillary rise are broken. The compost, however, must not be compacted or so damp that air cannot penetrate; seeds will almost certainly fail in such anaerobic compost as they cannot obtain the oxygen vital for growth. For most successful results, the temperature for germination of most seeds should be 15–25°C (59–77°F); heated propagators are useful for maintaining a steady temperature (see "Heated propagators", p.637). Some large seeds such as those of *Hippeastrum* germinate easily if floated on water rather than laid on soil (see BULBOUS PLANTS, "Tender bulbs", p.247).

Light requirements vary during germination: a few seeds need light (eg *Alyssum, Begonia, Calceolaria,* and *Genista*), but others are inhibited by it (eg *Allium, Delphinium, Nigella,* and *Phlox*). There is no way of distinguishing seeds requiring dark conditions from those needing light by physical examination: if the dark/light requirement is unknown, initially sow the seed in the dark; if it fails to germinate after a period of some weeks, place it in the light.

Sowing and aftercare

After sowing the seed in containers or in open ground, do not allow the compost to dry out or become too waterlogged. Cover the containers with 5mm (¼in) of coarse sand or fine (5mm) grit for autumn-sown seeds; for spring sowings, replace the grit with a 1cm (½in) layer of vermiculite: fine grade for small or medium-sized seeds, and medium grade for large seeds. Place the containers in a suitable environment (see "The propagation environment", p.636). The first sign of germination

HOW A SEED GERMINATES

In hypogeal germination (right), the cotyledons, or seed leaves, stay below soil level, whereas in epigeal germination (far right), they appear above ground.

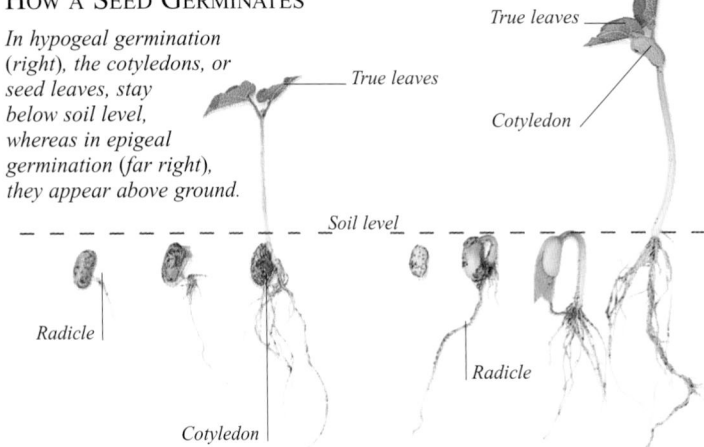

Radicle

True leaves

Soil level

Cotyledon

True leaves

Cotyledon

Radicle

Evenly coloured, rich green foliage

Long, thin stems

HEALTHY SEEDLINGS

Sturdy, well-spaced nasturtium (Tropaeolum) *seedlings flourishing under glass and ready to be pricked out.*

UNHEALTHY SEEDLINGS

If not pricked out early enough, the seedlings will become pale, crowded, and etiolated – and may die.

is the emergence of the radicle, or primary root, followed, in epigeal germination, by the cotyledons, or seed leaves, which provide the initial food reserves. The true foliage leaves appear later and generally differ from the cotyledons.

When the seedlings are large enough to handle, they should be "pricked out" (see ANNUALS AND BIENNIALS, "Pricking out", p.219). Failure to do so results in weak growth, because the crowded seedlings compete for light and nutrients and readily succumb to fungal infection. Once transplanted, return the seedlings to the warm ger-

TRUE LEAVES

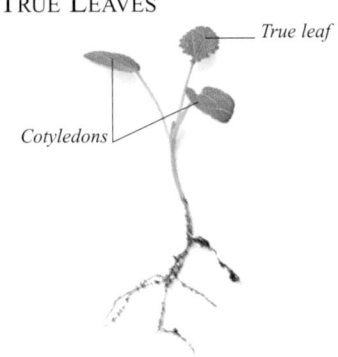

True leaf

Cotyledons

As the cotyledons, or seed leaves, wither, the true leaves gradually take over the process of photosynthesis.

mination environment to re-establish; then gradually harden them off by placing the containers in cooler conditions (see "Hardening off", p.637). A cold frame, closed at first, then opened in stages, provides a suitable environment for hardening off seedlings.

Producing hybrids

When hybridizing plants, it is important to prevent self-pollination. For controlled cross-pollination, petals, sepals, and stamens are removed from the flowers on the proposed female parent and the denuded flowers protected from insects by paper or plastic bags until the stigmas on the female plant are sticky and receptive. Pollen, previously collected from air-dried stamens, is then transferred to the stigmas and the flowers are protected from insects once again until fertilization has occurred. Hybrid seed will develop in the ovaries and should be collected when ripe and according to its requirements (see also ROSES "Hybridizing", p.168).

F1 and F2 hybrids

For the gardener seeking uniformity and near-perfection, F1 and F2 hybrid seed is available for a limited range of plants, mostly annuals. Such seed needs a complex plant breeding technique and is therefore more expensive.

The first generation derived from crossing two carefully maintained, genetically inbred plants of the same species is termed "first filial generation", or F1, hybrid. F1 hybrids are usually more vigorous than their parents and give uniformity in flower characteristics such as colour and form that seldom occurs with open-pollinated seed. Sometimes two controlled crosses from four selected lines are used to produce a "second filial generation", or F2, hybrid – retaining some of the vigour and uniformity of the F1 parents but often with other favoured characteristics less evident in the F1s.

Layering

Layering is a natural form of propagation: roots are induced to develop by covering a stem with soil while it is still attached to the parent plant. The rooted portion of stem is then separated from the parent plant and grown on.

The stem to be layered is often cut, ring-barked, or twisted. This partially interrupts the flow of hormones and carbohydrates, which, as they accumulate there, help to promote root growth. The tissues beyond the constriction are slightly water-stressed, and this, too, favours root formation. Another important root stimulus is the exclusion of light from the stem: light-starved cells then become thin-walled and roots form more readily. In order to stimulate rooting further, use a rooting hormone at the point of layering.

Methods of layering

Layering methods are classified in three groups: those in which a stem is brought down to the soil (simple, serpentine, natural, and tip layering); those in which soil is mounded over a stem (stooling, trench layering, and French layering); and air layering, where the "soil" is brought up to the plant stem. The word "soil" is used loosely here to mean any growing medium such as peat, sand, sawdust, or sphagnum moss.

Simple layering

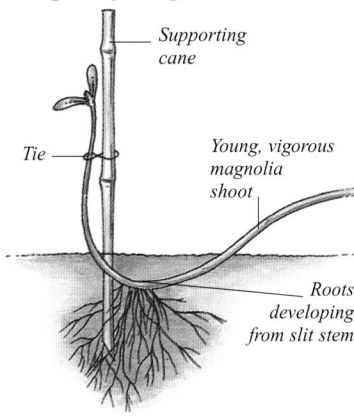

Supporting cane

Tie

Young, vigorous magnolia shoot

Roots developing from slit stem

This method is best carried out between autumn and spring. The parent plant should be young and pruned the previous season to produce vigorous, flexible stems, which can be brought down to soil level and will root readily. A slanting cut is made on the underside of the stem to be layered, which is firmly secured at this point into the soil. The shoot tip is tied to a cane, inserted in the soil. The following autumn, if the layer is well rooted, it can be cut from the parent plant (see also ORNAMENTAL SHRUBS, "Simple layering", p.116, and CLIMBING PLANTS, "Simple layering", p.145).

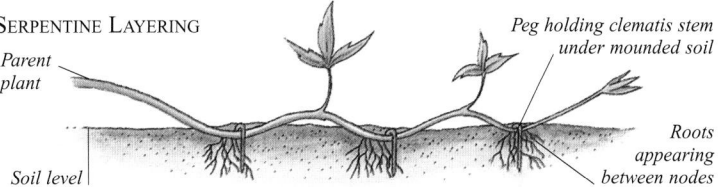

SERPENTINE LAYERING

Parent plant

Soil level

Peg holding clematis stem under mounded soil

Roots appearing between nodes

Serpentine layering

This modified form of simple layering is used for plants with pliable stems, such as clematis. Long, young stems are mounded with soil, leaving buds exposed to produce aerial shoots (see also CLIMBING PLANTS, "Propagation by serpentine layering", p.145).

Natural layering

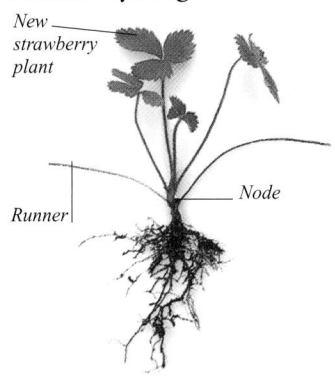

New strawberry plant

Runner

Node

Some plants, such as strawberries, reproduce naturally by sending out a series of runners. These then root at a node, forming a new plant. Once the new plant is fully established, sever it from the parent and grow on (see also "Strawberries: Propagation", p.470).

Tip layering

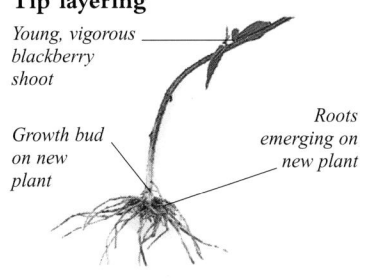

Young, vigorous blackberry shoot

Growth bud on new plant

Roots emerging on new plant

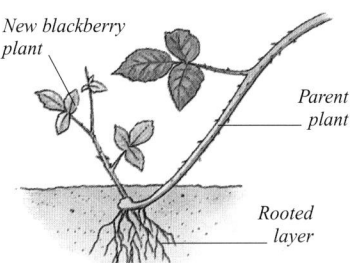

New blackberry plant

Parent plant

Rooted layer

This method is for shrubs and climbers that produce roots from their shoot tips; one of the commonest examples in nature is the blackberry. In summer, a young, vigorous shoot tip is buried in soil in a hole 7–10cm (3–4in) deep. A new shoot, which has developed from the tip, appears a few weeks later; the young plant may then be separated from its parent. Grow on the rooted layer *in situ*; transplant it the following spring, if required (see also *Tip Layering*, p.471).

Stooling

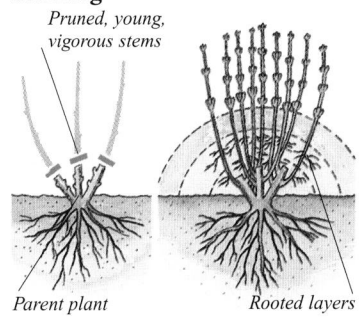

Pruned, young, vigorous stems

Parent plant

Rooted layers

Although important for the commercial production of rootstocks, stooling, or mound layering, is used by amateurs only for a few woody plants. The stems of a young parent plant are cut back in late winter or early spring to within 8cm (3in) of the ground. When the new shoots are about 15–20cm (6–8in) long, mound soil up over their bases, and again twice more until summer. With plants that root easily, such as thyme and sage, there is no need to cut the stems back before mounding. By autumn, the stems will have rooted; they are then separated from the parent plant and transplanted (see also GROWING HERBS, "Mound layering", p.414).

Trench layering

Trench, or etiolation, layering is primarily for fruit rootstocks, especially those that are hard to root. The parent plant is planted at an angle, so that its shoots can readily be pegged down in shallow trenches and covered with soil. The rooted shoots can be detached from the parent to form new plants.

TRENCH LAYERING

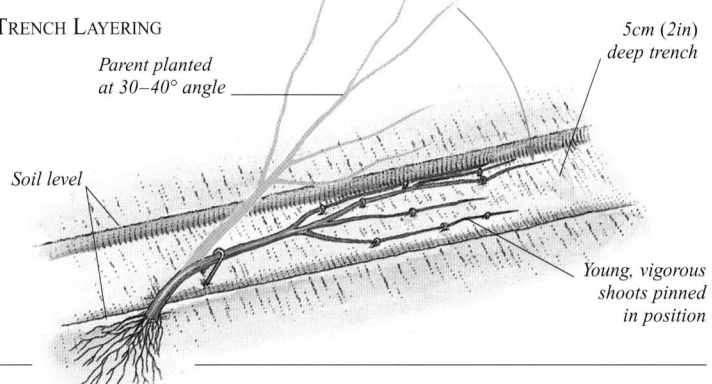

Parent planted at 30–40° angle

Soil level

5cm (2in) deep trench

Young, vigorous shoots pinned in position

French layering

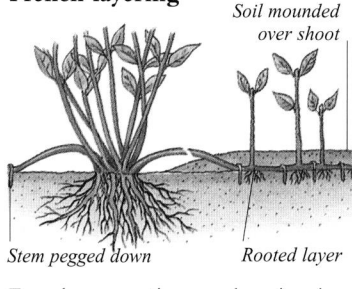

Soil mounded over shoot

Stem pegged down

Rooted layer

French, or continuous, layering is a modified form of stooling. In late winter, peg young shoots from the parent stem to the ground. Any new growths are gradually earthed up to a depth of 15cm (6in). These new shoots should have rooted by autumn and after leaf fall may be separated and grown on (see also ORNAMENTAL SHRUBS, "French layering", p.117).

Air layering

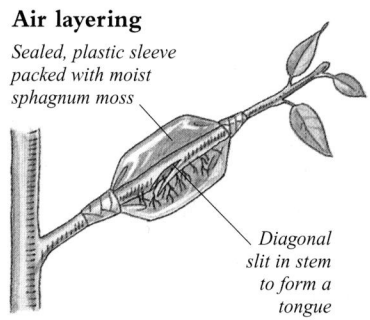

Sealed, plastic sleeve packed with moist sphagnum moss

Diagonal slit in stem to form a tongue

Use air, or Chinese, layering – also known as marcottage – on some trees, shrubs, climbers, and house plants, such as rhododendrons, magnolias, and rubber plants (*Ficus elastica*). In spring or summer, choose a strong-growing, healthy shoot of one- to two-years old, as these root most readily. Trim off sideshoots and leaves for 30cm (12in) back from the tip. Make a slit in the stem and apply hormone rooting compound to it. Keep the wound open by packing it with moist sphagnum moss. Then cover the wounded area with more sphagnum moss and seal with plastic, preferably black, until roots develop (see *Air Layering a Shrub*, p.117, and INDOOR GARDENING, "Air layering", p.383). Rooting may take up to two years.

Cuttings

Propagation from cuttings is the commonest vegetative method. There are three main types: stem, leaf, and root. Stem cuttings produce roots directly from the stem itself or from the mass of thin-walled, wound-healing tissue (callus) that develops at its base. These roots are called adventitious, which means added, or artificial. Some large leaves can be used as cutting material and will develop adventitious roots from near their veins. Vigorous, young roots may also be used for cuttings – propagation by root cuttings is a simple and economical method neglected by most gardeners. Suitable species will produce both adventitious stem buds and roots on the root cutting.

How roots form

Adventitious roots most often develop from young cells produced by the cambium – a layer of cells that generates tissues involved in the thickening of stems. They are usually located close to food- and water-conducting tissues, which provide nourishment as they develop.

Adventitious root growth is also helped by natural hormones called auxins, which accumulate in the base of a cutting. Natural auxins can be supplemented by synthetic auxins, which are available as talc-based powders or as solutions. These aid rooting when applied to the bases of cuttings and are recommended for all plants except those that root very easily. Use only a little hormone, however, as too much could harm immature tissue.

Rooting hormones can be bought with low concentrations of active ingredients for soft cuttings and higher concentrations for hardwood material; some contain a fungicide, which helps to prevent infections entering the cuttings through the wounded tissues.

CALLUS PADS

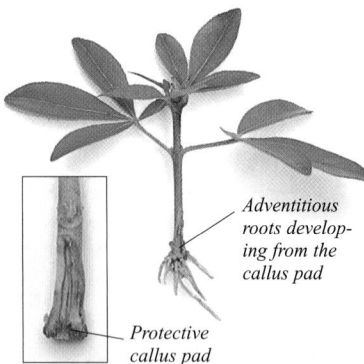

Adventitious roots developing from the callus pad

Protective callus pad

Some plants (here Choisya ternata) form a protective callus pad of wound-healing tissue at the base of a stem cutting, where they have been severed from the parent plant.

SOFTWOOD CUTTINGS

Prepared cutting trimmed below the node

Rooted cutting

The soft, green stem on a softwood cutting (here Hydrangea macrophylla) usually turns brown as it matures and develops its root system.

Stem cuttings

Stem cuttings are often classified by the maturity of the stem tissue into softwood, greenwood, semi-ripe, and hardwood (or ripewood). The distinction is useful, though imprecise, because tissues develop continuously throughout the growing season.

Softwood cuttings
These are taken in spring and are generally made from the tips of shoots (tip cuttings) on the parent plant, but the new, young basal shoots (basal cuttings) of herbaceous perennials are also used (see PERENNIALS, "Basal stem cuttings", p.282). Since young material roots most readily, softwood cuttings often provide the best chance of rooting species that are difficult to propagate. Retain the soft tip where possible, as this is where the rooting auxins are produced. Softwood cuttings need a supportive environment, because they lose water and wilt quickly (see "The propagation environment", p.636).

Greenwood cuttings
These are taken from early to midsummer, from slightly more mature wood, when growth begins to slow. They root slightly less readily but survive better than softwood cuttings, although they still require a supportive environment in which to develop.

Semi-ripe cuttings
Taken in late summer, semi-ripe cuttings are less prone to wilting since the stem tissues are firmer and woody (see ORNAMENTAL SHRUBS, "Semi-ripe cuttings", p.112). Some species with large leaves, for example Ficus and camellia, may be propagated more economically by taking a short section from a semi-ripe stem just above and below a leaf bud, retaining a single leaf (see ORNAMENTAL SHRUBS, "Leaf-bud cuttings", p.113).

Hardwood cuttings
Fully mature, hardwood (or ripewood) cuttings are taken at the end of the growing season from autumn through to spring, when the tissues are fully ripened. They are the easiest to maintain in a healthy condition but are often slow to root. Hardwood cuttings fall into two categories: leafless deciduous cuttings and broadleaved evergreen cuttings. Growth of many glossy-leaved evergreens, such as holly (*Ilex*) and rhododendron, wilts readily when young early in the season since their protective leaf waxes develop slowly; they are therefore best propagated by semi-ripe or hardwood cuttings (see also ORNAMENTAL TREES, "Hardwood cuttings", p.78; CLIMBING PLANTS, "Propagation from hardwood cuttings", p.143; and ROSES, "Hardwood cuttings", p.165).

SEMI-RIPE CUTTINGS

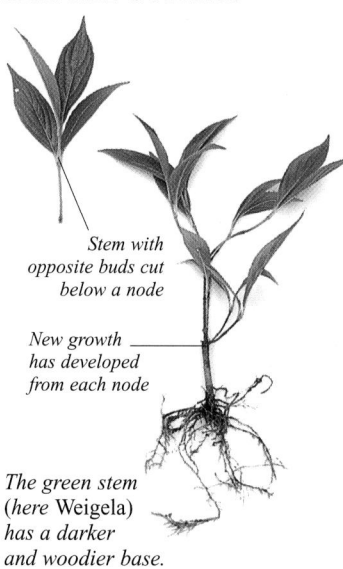

Stem with opposite buds cut below a node

New growth has developed from each node

The green stem (here Weigela) has a darker and woodier base.

LEAF-BUD CUTTINGS

Healthy, green leaf

Leaf bud from which new shoot will develop

A short piece of semi-ripe stem (here camellia) provides sufficient food reserves for a leaf-bud cutting, since it produces some food through its leaf.

HARDWOOD CUTTINGS

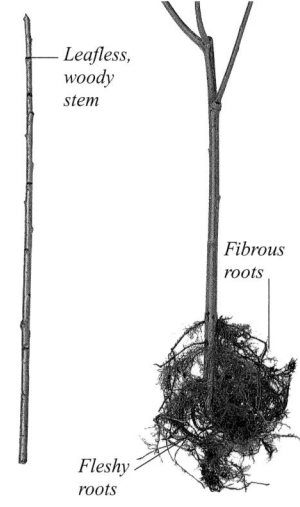

Leafless, woody stem

Fibrous roots

Fleshy roots

Hardwood cuttings (here Salix alba) are the longest type of stem cutting since they need large food reserves while their roots slowly develop.

When to take stem cuttings

There are no hard and fast rules about when to take stem cuttings of a particular species, so if cuttings taken in spring fail to root, further cuttings can be taken later in the season and treated according to the relative maturity of the shoots.

Plants that are difficult to root are best propagated early so that the new plants have time to mature before winter. As the action of root-producing hormones is suppressed by flower-initiating ones, use cuttings without flower buds wherever possible; if cuttings with flower buds have to be used, remove the flower buds.

Preparing stem cuttings
Stem cuttings are normally prepared by trimming just beneath a node, or leaf joint, where the cambium (the layer of cells involved in stem thickening) is most active. Many easy-rooting

NODAL CUTTING

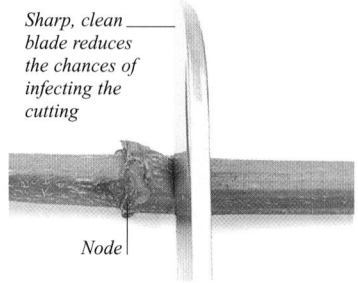

Sharp, clean blade reduces the chances of infecting the cutting

Node

Most cuttings (here Hydrangea paniculata) root most satisfactorily at their nodes and so should be trimmed just below a node.

INTERNODAL CUTTINGS

Internodal cuttings (here Clematis montana) *maximize propagating material in an economical way.*

cuttings, for example willows (*Salix*), have pre-formed roots at the nodes, and these start to develop when the stem is cut from the parent plant. For these and for cuttings with densely crowded leaves on each stem, cut between nodes (internodal cutting).

The length of the cutting will depend on the species but is commonly 5–12cm (2–5in) or about five or six nodes in length. The lower leaves are stripped to give a clean stem for insertion. To assist the cuttings in rooting, semi-ripe and hardwood cuttings are often "wounded" by removing a sliver of bark from the lowest 2.5cm (1in) of the cutting. This exposes a greater area of cambium and thereby stimulates roots to form. Some cuttings, especially semi-ripe ones, may be taken by pulling a sideshoot away from the main shoot with a small "heel" of bark still attached (see ORNAMENTAL SHRUBS, "Heel cuttings", p.113). A heel may provide a cutting with added protection until it has produced roots, although there is no satisfactory scientific explanation for this response.

With the exception of leafless, hardwood stem cuttings, which contain food reserves from the previous

WOUNDING

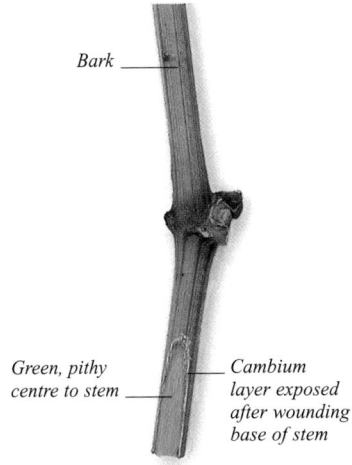

Use a very sharp, clean knife to make a shallow, angled, downward cut at the base of semi-ripe and hardwood cuttings such as vine (Vitis).

PREPARING CUTTINGS

To reduce stress from water loss on leafy cuttings (here rhododendron), remove some leaves, halve others.

growing season, few cuttings are able to produce roots and shoots without supplementing their food reserves through photosynthesis. However, active leaves lose water through their pores, which is not easily replaced, and excessive water loss will cause failure. To achieve a balance between retaining photosynthetic tissue and reducing water loss, trim away all but four full-sized leaves, leaving any immature leaves. If the remaining leaves are large, as on many broad-leaved trees and large shrubs, reduce each by half to minimize water loss.

Leaf cuttings

For some plants, whole leaves (with or without leaf stalks) or sections of leaves may be taken as cuttings and inserted or secured onto the compost. With whole leaves laid flat, the veins should be nicked at intervals as new plantlets form at the cut surfaces of large leaf veins. Propagate plants such as *Sinningia* and *Streptocarpus* from cut sections of fully expanded, undamaged leaves. African violets

LARGE LEAVES

Large leaves of plants such as begonia may be divided into small pieces, each of which will form callus at a nicked vein and then adventitious roots.

(*Saintpaulia*) and *Peperomia* may be propagated from entire leaves with their stalks (see INDOOR GARDENING, "Propagating from leaves", p.381).

Root cuttings

Root cuttings are taken in the dormant season from young, vigorous roots of about pencil thickness for most trees and shrubs, but the roots may be somewhat thinner for some herbaceous plants such as phlox.

The length of the cutting
This is dependent on the environment in which the root cutting is to develop: the warmer the environment (within reason), the faster new shoots will appear and, therefore, shorter cuttings with smaller food reserves may be used successfully although these should not be less than 2.5cm (1in) in length. Root cuttings are preferably grown on in a greenhouse. A cold frame is also suitable, but the cuttings may be slower to develop shoots. For *Ailanthus* and lilac (*Syringa*), which can be propagated in open ground, 10–15cm (4–6in) long root cuttings should be used.

Inserting root cuttings
It is important to insert root cuttings the correct way up since the new roots always form at the distal end (that is, the end that was farthest from the crown of the parent plant). Cuttings should be inserted vertically so that their other (proximal) ends are flush with the soil surface; herbaceous root cuttings, however, are frequently inserted horizontally (see also PERENNIALS, "Root cuttings", p.203).

The rooting medium

Cuttings need air (to obtain oxygen) and water in their rooting medium, but if the medium is too wet, the cuttings rot. Standard cutting compost must, therefore, have a more open structure than loam-based potting compost. The rooting medium should

SMALL LEAVES

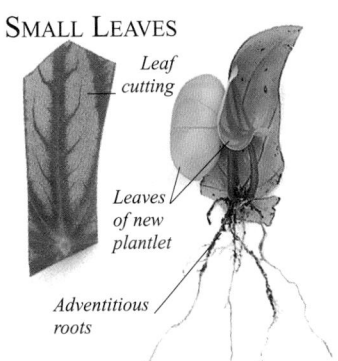

To encourage callus to form, and rooting to occur, small leaves such as Peperomia *may be trimmed at the edges.*

ROOT CUTTINGS

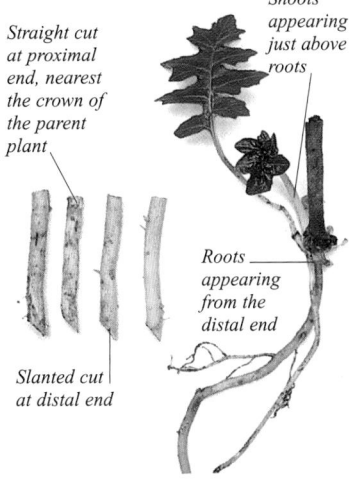

To help distinguish the two ends when taking root cuttings (here Acanthus mollis), *make differently angled cuts.*

PROTECTIVE ENVIRONMENT

Leafy cuttings grow best in a humid environment, such as within a plastic bag secured over a container; keep the plastic away from the leaf surfaces.

also be warm in order to speed up development of the roots: 18–25°C (64–77°F) is ideal for cool temperate species, and up to 32°C (90°F) for those from warm climates. If necessary, use bottom heat (see p.636).

Caring for the cuttings

After insertion, keep leafy cuttings turgid in the humid atmosphere of a closed case, mist unit, propagator, or other similar environment. Leafless cuttings that have been planted outdoors, either direct in the soil or in a container, should be protected by a clear plastic tunnel or a cold frame.

Every ten days or so, water the rooting medium lightly if required, and spray with a fungicide to help prevent disease; at the same time, lift the lights or remove the plastic over enclosed cuttings, to enable air to circulate, for a 5–10-minute period.

Once rooted, cuttings should be potted up individually and those growing under cover gradually hardened off (see p.637).

Storage organs

Storage organs have diverse structures, and include bulbs, corms, rhizomes, root and stem tubers, and turions. Most plants with storage organs will increase naturally by producing offsets, which should be lifted and divided to prevent overcrowding. Offsets will flower more quickly than seed-raised plants and will be identical with the parent, whereas seed-raised plants may be variable in character.

The main propagation methods apart from division are to cut the storage organs into sections and to stimulate them to produce offsets by wounding; these sections or offsets will soon form complete plants if provided with a warm, dark place in which to develop. The cut surfaces should always be dusted with a fungicide as they easily succumb to fungal attack.

Bulbs

NON-SCALY, OR TUNICATE, BULB

Wide, fleshy, inner scale leaves

New shoot arising from leaf axil

Membranous, dry, outer scale leaves on Narcissus bulb

Root

SCALY BULB

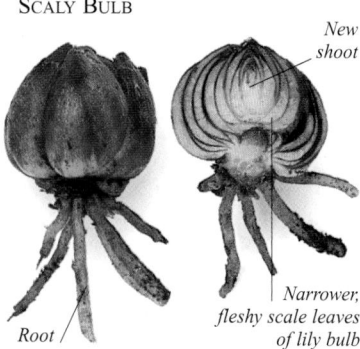

New shoot

Narrower, fleshy scale leaves of lily bulb

Root

Bulbs may be propagated by chipping; division of offsets, bulbils, or bulblets; scaling or twin-scaling; and scooping or scoring. The gardener can tell only from experience which is best for which bulb, but for lists of plants appropriate to each method, see BULBOUS PLANTS, "Propagation", pp.245–250.

Chipping

Non-scaly, or tunicate, bulbs such as snowdrops (*Galanthus*) that do not naturally increase quickly may be multiplied rapidly by chipping. This method involves cutting each bulb into up to 20 pieces, depending on its size. Each piece, which generally comprises three or more scale leaves and

CHIPPING

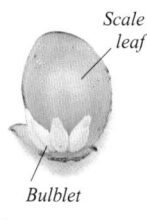

Scale leaf

Bulbil develop between the scale leaves on a chipped bulb such as snowdrop (Galanthus) *in air temperatures that do not exceed 25°C (77°F).*

Bulblet

a section of basal plate, is then soaked in or dusted with a fungicide. The chips may be incubated (see "Chipping", p.249) or placed in vermiculite in a container in a frost-free greenhouse and left undisturbed. New bulbs form usually within 12 weeks, but a few may take almost two years. Separate the bulblets and repot or replant.

Division of offsets

Bulbs have wide, fleshy scale leaves, which act as food storage organs. At their base are axillary buds, which may enlarge naturally to form offsets. When the bulbs are lifted at the end of the growing season, these may be separated and planted out individually (see "Dividing bulbs", p.245).

DIVISION OF OFFSETS

Carefully remove each offset from a bulb (here Narcissus) *by cutting or pulling.*

Offset

Parent bulb

Bulbils or bulblets

Bulbils are produced on flowerheads or stems; bulblets develop on the bulb itself or on stem roots. Both may be detached and planted up to develop into new bulbs (see also LILIES, "Bulbils and bulblets", p.251).

Scaling

Scaling involves the removal of bulb scales, which are then induced to form bulblets. It is used for bulbs such as fritillaries (*Fritillaria*) and lilies

BULBLETS AND BULBILS

Some lilies (Lilium), *for example* L. lancifolium, *produce small, bulb-like structures known as "bulbils" on their stems above the ground. Others, for example* L. longiflorum, *may develop similar bulblets on bulbs or stem roots in the soil.*

Lily bulblets

Lily bulbils

Old stem, which has developed roots

SCALING

Bulblets appear at the base of individual scale leaves of loose-scaled bulbs, here lily (Lilium).

Scale leaf

New top-growth

Rooted bulblet

TWIN-SCALING

Two leaf scales and a section of basal plate are used for non-scaly bulbs (here Narcissus).

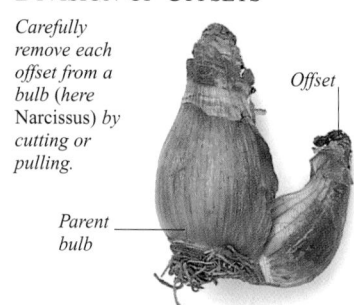

Fleshy scale leaves

Bulblet

Basal plate

(*Lilium*) that are made up of fairly loose scales. Individual scale leaves are pulled away from the basal plate of a mature bulb and then left in a plastic bag containing moist vermiculite or a peat:grit mix, in a warm, dark place. Bulblets appear at the scale bases, usually after two months. Grow on the scales in a container until the bulblets are large enough to be separated (see also "Scaling", p.248).

Twin-scaling

Non-scaly, or tunicate, bulbs such as daffodils and snowdrops may be twin-scaled. In this, the bulb is cut vertically into eight to ten sections and each of these is divided into pairs of bud scales with a small section of basal plate. These are then incubated and grown on in the same way as in scaling above. (See also "Twin-scaling", p.249.)

Scooping and scoring

Some bulbs, such as hyacinths, can be propagated by either scooping or scoring the bulb. This causes callus tissue to develop, which encourages bulblets to form. For scooping, the basal plate of a mature bulb is scooped out at the centre, leaving just the outer

SCORING

Callus tissue

Bulblets developing inside cut

Basal plate

Shallowly cutting the basal plate of some bulbs (here hyacinth) stimulates the growth of bulblets.

edge of the basal plate intact; for scoring, two shallow cuts at right angles are made into the basal plate. The bulb is then stored basal plate uppermost, in a warm, dark place, until bulblets have formed; these are then detached and grown on (see also "Simple cutting", p.250; "Scooping hyacinths", p.250; and "Scooping and scoring trilliums", p.250).

Corms

GLADIOLUS CORM

Food storage tissue

Thickened stem base

Corms are reduced, compact, underground stems with a solid internal structure. Most corms produce several buds near the apex; each bud naturally forms a new corm. Miniature corms, or cormels, are produced as offsets

RAISING CORMELS

New corm

Separate the new corm and cormels from the old corm when dormant, and grow on.

Cormels

Old corm

DEVELOPMENT OF A CORMEL

Cormels may take up to three years to reach flowering size. The sequence below shows their development in the first year.

between the old and new corms in the growing season (see also BULBOUS PLANTS, "Gladiolus cormels", p.245). Larger corms may be increased artificially just before the growing season, by cutting them into pieces, each with a growing bud, and dusting with fungicide. Place in a pot or the open ground and lightly cover with soil, while new corms develop.

Rhizomes

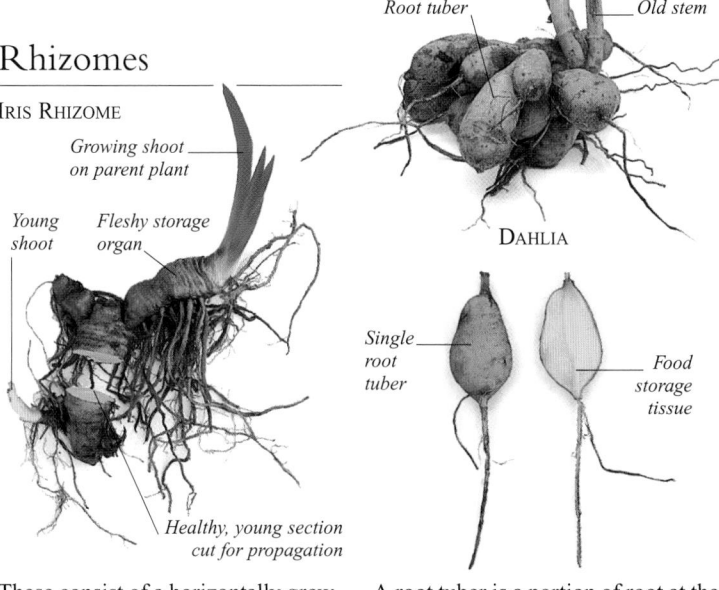

IRIS RHIZOME

Growing shoot on parent plant

Young shoot

Fleshy storage organ

Healthy, young section cut for propagation

These consist of a horizontally growing shoot, usually beneath but sometimes on the soil surface. They are propagated by cutting the rhizome into young, healthy sections, each with one

or more growth buds, which are planted up individually (see also PERENNIALS, "Division of rhizomatous plants", p.201; BULBOUS PLANTS, "Scooping and scoring trilliums", p.250; and ORCHIDS, "Division", p.371).

Root tubers

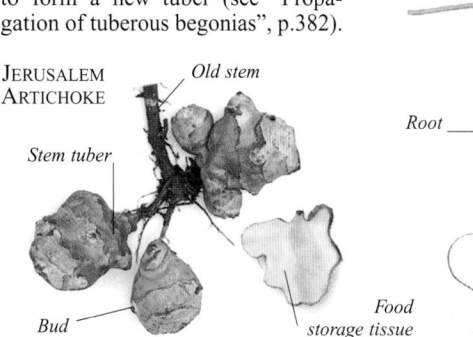

Root tuber   Old stem

DAHLIA

Single root tuber

Food storage tissue

A root tuber is a portion of root at the stem base that swells during summer and is modified into a storage organ, or tuber, as in dahlias. Such plants may be propagated in spring by

dividing a cluster of tubers into healthy pieces, each with a developing shoot (see also Cutting up Bulbs for Propagation, p.249). Root tubers may also be propagated by basal cuttings of the young, emerging shoots in spring (see DAHLIAS, How to Propagate by Basal Cuttings, p.235).

Stem tubers

The stems of some plants (eg potatoes) are modified to produce tubers, which act as storage organs. Tuberous begonias, for example, form perennial tubers at the bases of their stems. In spring, these can be cut into pieces, each with a growth bud and then dusted with fungicide. Each piece will produce basal shoots, which can be used as basal cuttings (see DAHLIAS, How to Propagate by Basal Cuttings, p.235) or grown on to form a new tuber (see "Propagation of tuberous begonias", p.382).

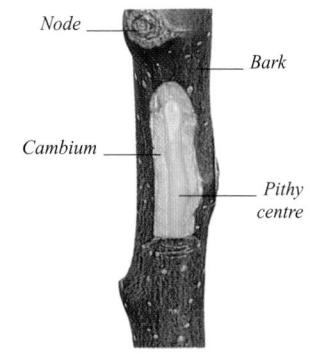

JERUSALEM ARTICHOKE   Old stem

Stem tuber

Bud   Food storage tissue

Other types of storage organ

Plants such as Saxifraga granulata and some Kalanchoe and Asparagus species develop round, bulb-like buds in their shoot axils. These buds can be separated and grown on individually in the same way as bulblets or cormels (see p.634).

In some water plants, such as Hydrocharis and Myriophyllum, these relatively large bud structures are known as "turions". When mature, they drop off the parent plant naturally, sink to the bottom of the water, and develop into new plants.

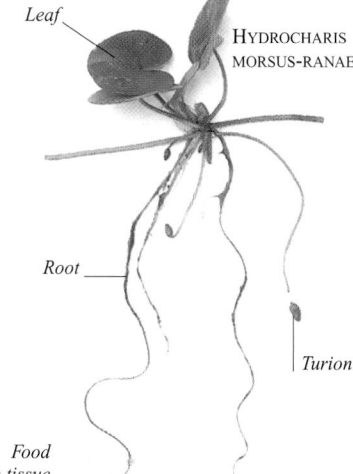

Leaf

HYDROCHARIS MORSUS-RANAE

Root

Turion

Grafting and budding

In a wide range of woody plants and a few herbaceous ones, a budded stem, or scion, is grafted onto a rootstock, or stock, of another species or cultivar, to achieve a composite plant with more desirable characteristics. Most apple, pear, and stone fruit trees are propagated in this way. The stock may be more resistant than the scion to root disease or more suited to a particular environment. Often (especially with fruit trees), the stock is selected because it controls the growth of the scion to produce a dwarfed or a particularly vigorous plant. Sometimes, a scion cultivar that is difficult to increase from cuttings is grafted onto easily rooted stock. The rootstock also influences the age at which the tree bears fruit and its size and skin quality – dwarfing rootstocks generally conferring earlier fruit-bearing. Conversely, the rootstock's growing cycle may be affected by the scion cultivar, which in its turn influences cold hardiness. Reactions to soil acidity can also be affected by interactions between rootstock and scion cultivars.

The scion may take the form of a single bud on a short portion of stem (usually known as budding) or it may be a multi-budded length of stem.

When to graft

Field (outdoor) grafting is normally undertaken from late winter to early spring, when the cambium is particularly active, and mild conditions also favour the growth of callus cells. Hot weather later in the season may dry out the thin-walled, cambial cells. Bench grafting, generally done in the greenhouse or potting shed, is undertaken in winter and summer.

T-budding, on the other hand, is most often done in mid- to late summer, when well-developed scion buds are available and young stock material is of suitable diameter. For success, the stock plant needs to be growing actively, so that the bark can be lifted from the wood to allow the bud to be inserted. Chip-budding, however, may be undertaken over an extended season because the chip is positioned beside the stock rather than slipped under its bark.

How to graft

Because grafting cuts inevitably damage plant cells, and the thin-walled cells at the graft union are

vulnerable to fungi and bacteria, it is essential that knives are sterile and sharp, so that a single cut is sufficient. The propagation environment, prepared plant material, and ties must also be scrupulously clean.

Once stock and scion material have been selected and cut to shape, according to the type of graft, position the two pieces carefully so that there is maximum cambial contact. If the grafting materials are of different widths,

CAMBIUM LAYER

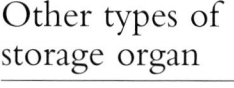

Node

Bark

Cambium

Pithy centre

For successful grafting, the scion cambium must be matched as closely as possible to that of the stock.

ensure the cambium on at least one side of the graft is in contact. Central to the grafting process is the activity of the cambium – a continuous, narrow band of thin-walled cells between the bark and the wood – which produces new cells that allow stem thickening. Within days of grafting, the region between the stock and scion should fill with thin-walled callus cells. The cambial cells on the stock and scion next to the young callus then link to neighbouring cells, so that a complete cambial bridge forms between the two parts. Further divisions of this new cambium produce water- and food-conducting tissue, which functionally joins the scion and stock.

Grafts should be bound with clear plastic tape, which seals the join well. Waxing is not necessary, except in hot-pipe callusing (see p.637). Pot-grown stocks once grafted should be kept in a suitable protective environment (see "Greenhouses", p.636, and "Cold frames", p.637).

Regularly examine the graft, and remove the tape once the graft appears to have taken. The following growing season, cut back the stock plant just above the new shoot that has developed from the grafted scion.

Chip-budding

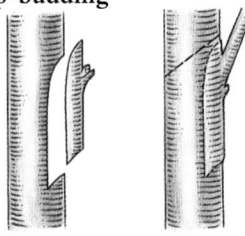

A "chip" of ripe wood is removed from the rootstock and replaced with a matching "chip" of similar size from the scion, or budstick, containing a bud (see "Propagating by chip-budding", p.432).

T-budding

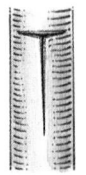

In this technique, just the scion bud is grafted onto the rootstock by cutting a "T" in the stock bark and inserting the bud beneath (see ROSES, "Bud-grafting", p.166).

Spliced side grafting

A short, downward cut through the cambium layer of the stock is followed by a sloping cut down towards the base of the first cut. The chip is removed and replaced by the scion, shaped to match the stock (see ORNAMENTAL TREES, "Spliced side grafting", p.82, and ORNAMENTAL SHRUBS, "Spliced side-veneer grafting", p.118).

Side-wedge (or inlay) grafting

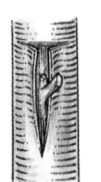  

A downward, slightly inward cut is made into the side of the stock. The scion is then prepared by making two oblique cuts at the base. The scion's wedge-shaped base is inserted into the rootstock cut so that the cambium aligns and is bound in position.

Apical-wedge grafting

A 2–3cm (³⁄₄–1¹⁄₄in) vertical cut is made centrally into the stock, into which the wedge-shaped scion is inserted (see ORNAMENTAL SHRUBS, "Apical-wedge grafting", p.119).

Saddle grafting

The top of the stock is saddle-shaped, with upward-sloping sides. The scion is then shaped so that it fits closely over the top of the root-stock (see ORNAMENTAL SHRUBS, "Saddle grafting", p.118).

Whip grafting

Cut back the stock at an oblique angle to 5–8cm (2–3in). Then prepare the scion to match. If the scion is thinner than the stock, first cut the stock horizontally, then obliquely to match.

Flat grafting

Both the stock top and scion base are cut horizontally (see CACTI AND OTHER SUCCULENTS, "Flat grafting", p.357).

Whip-and-tongue grafting

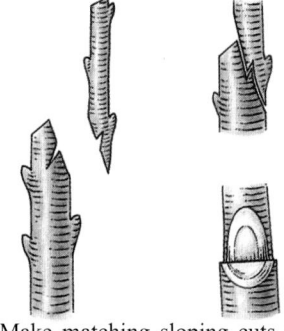

Make matching sloping cuts on the rootstock and scion, then cut shallow tongues along the sloping cuts, so that the scion interlocks securely with the stock (see GROWING FRUIT, "Whip-and-tongue grafting", p.433).

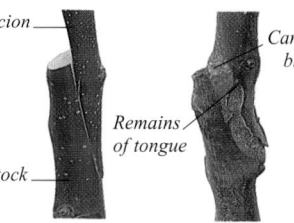

WHIP-AND-TONGUE GRAFT
The rootstock and scion gradually unite to function as one plant.

The propagation environment

During propagation, plants are at their most vulnerable and their environment is, therefore, vitally important. The choice of environment depends on which propagation method is chosen and on the relative maturity of the plant material itself. Propagation from leafy cuttings, for example, requires a more closely regulated environment than for leafless cuttings.

Greenhouses

It is essential that a greenhouse has adequate ventilation and, in the growing season, appropriate shading (see "Creating the right environment", p.573). From spring to early autumn, apply a shading wash to the outside of the glass so that plants are not stressed unnecessarily by extreme weather conditions (see "Shading washes", p.576). Additional protective shading can be provided by

mounting shade cloth on wire runners across or along the length of the bench or greenhouse. The curtain can be withdrawn during dull weather.

Protecting leafy cuttings

Because leafy cuttings, initially, have no roots and cannot easily take up water to replace that lost from the leaves, they must have further protection within the greenhouse.

Clear plastic sheeting or a plastic bag placed over a tray of cuttings and tucked under is perfectly satisfactory if appropriate shading is provided. Water vapour condensing on the inside of the plastic helps to protect the cuttings against desiccation. Soft cuttings may succumb to disease if the plastic touches them; insert a framework of split canes or wire in the compost to keep the plastic off the cuttings. In such closed systems, however, excessive air temperatures may build up in very hot conditions and the containers

RIGID-TOPPED PROPAGATOR

When the vents are closed, moisture is retained within the unit. Cuttings therefore remain turgid, and so are more likely to root quickly and healthily.

of cuttings should be kept in a shaded but light place out of the sun.

Rigid plastic propagators need similar shading to plastic sheeting. Initially the vents should be kept closed, to maintain a moist atmosphere. Once rooting has taken place and the cuttings are ready to be hardened off, the vents should be opened.

A mist unit provides the best system for summer propagation, but for winter and early- and late-season propagation it should be combined with bottom heat. Ideally, the mist unit should maintain a constant water film on the leaf surfaces; some water will still be lost from the leaves by transpiration but this is amply replaced by "applied" water from the misting process. Since the mist is applied in bursts, the greenhouse humidity fluctuates and so, inevitably, the water film on each leaf is imperfect, and some water loss occurs. Complete mist systems comprise supply pipes, water filter, nozzles, and a solenoid

and sensor to regulate the misting frequency (see "Mist units", p.580).

For softwood cuttings, which wilt readily, the best system is to arrange a low, clear plastic tent just above the misting nozzles. This ensures a higher ambient humidity between mist bursts than does open mist. It is important to shade such a closed mist system in bright weather.

Bottom heat

Most biological processes are speeded up when temperatures are higher, and so raising compost temperature usually increases the rapidity with which seeds germinate and cuttings root.

Cables or heating mats are most convenient for small greenhouses (see "Propagation aids", p.580). The temperature is controlled by a rod thermostat or electronic controller. If they are used in closed mist systems, excessive air temperatures may build up in bright conditions, during which the heating must be switched off.

To prevent the greenhouse from overheating when propagating, add one or more layers of shading, depending on the weather conditions and season. Greenhouses in open, sunny sites are particularly vulnerable to overheating.

		SPRING	SUMMER	AUTUMN	WINTER
DULL DAYS	Whitewash		███████		
BRIGHT DAYS	Layer of shade cloth	██████████████			
	Additional shade cloth		███████		
	Whitewash	█████████████████			

HOT-PIPE CALLUSING OF GRAFTS

1 *Cut 2.5cm (1in) wide slots in the pipe. Place each plant with its sealed and bound grafted area vertically inside a slot.*

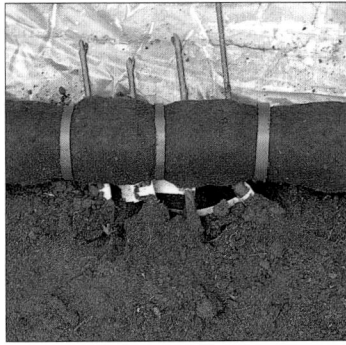

2 *Cover any roots with moist soil. Lay some capillary matting over the slots and secure with cut-out pieces of pipe or insulating tape.*

Hot-air grafts

Hot-pipe callusing applies thermostatically controlled hot air to a grafted plant to speed the formation of callus tissue, which is the first sign of a successful graft union. A soil-warming cable is threaded twice through a length of plastic drainpipe, 8cm (3in) across, in which slots have been cut – 2.5cm (1in) wide for bare-rooted stock; 8cm (3in) wide for container-grown ones. The pipe is then positioned just above ground level. Each scion and graft is sealed with melted wax, so it is less likely to dry out, and then taped and placed in a slot within the plastic pipe. Any bare roots are covered with soil, to keep them cool but moist, and then the whole pipe is wrapped with insulating material. If the temperature within the pipe is set to 20–25°C (68–77°F), callusing should occur within a few weeks.

Heated propagators

These self-contained units are very useful for extending the propagation season (see "Heated propagators", p.580). Since the units have heat loadings well in excess of the 160 watts/sq m (15 watts/sq ft) recommended for mist systems, they must be fitted with effective thermostats, otherwise high temperatures may damage cuttings in sunny weather.

Cold frames

Cold frames provide a valuable gain in soil and air temperatures while maintaining high humidity and providing adequate light for young plants. They can be used to raise seedlings early in the season, protect grafts, and propagate leafless and leafy cuttings. They may also, if required, be fitted with bottom heat (see p.636).

Because such low structures have no great volume, they easily overheat in sunny conditions unless ventilated and shaded well (see "Cold frames", p.581). Conversely, when temperatures fall below -5°C (23°F), frames must be insulated with thick layers of hessian, coconut matting, polystyrene tiles, or bubble plastic.

Cloches and polytunnels

Glass and clear plastic cloches and tunnels are most often used to give seedlings an early start in the season in the vegetable garden. A wide range of easily rooted cuttings also do well in such an environment (see "Cloches", p.582). Additional shading, such as shade netting, is required in bright, sunny weather.

Growing the propagated plant

To propagate plants effectively, a gardener needs not only to prepare the material properly but also to care for and grow on the young plants in a suitable environment until they have developed sufficiently to thrive in the garden. At key stages in propagation, practical inexperience or carelessness may kill well-rooted plants.

Caring for the plants

Since most forms of propagation involve cutting various parts of the plants being increased, plant tissues are exposed to possible disease infection; it is therefore important to maintain hygienic conditions in the propagating area. Tools and benches should be regularly and thoroughly cleaned (using a mild disinfectant if necessary), and dead and damaged plant material removed. Potting composts must always be fresh and sterile. Fungicidal solutions may also be applied to protect seedlings (eg Cheshunt compound) and leafy cuttings (eg captan), following the manufacturer's instructions.

When preparing pots or trays of compost for sowing seed, lightly firm the compost using a presser board, especially around the edges of the container. Water is drawn up through the compost by capillary action and, without this firming, air pockets occur and the water columns essential for capillary rise are broken. However, do not firm loam-based composts: a

FIRMING THE COMPOST

Ensure that seeds are germinated in evenly pressed, level compost so that capillary action and therefore seedling growth are not hindered by air pockets in the compost.

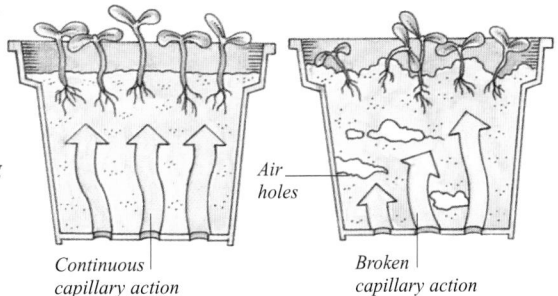

Continuous capillary action

Air holes

Broken capillary action

medium filled with roots must be well aerated and have an open structure for optimum plant growth.

The composts in which propagated plants are growing should be moist, but not wet, at all times. Too wet a medium will reduce the oxygen available and the roots may die or succumb to disease. It is also important to maintain the correct environment until the young plants are sturdy enough to be hardened off (see "The propagation environment", p.636). Prick out seedlings to avoid their becoming overcrowded, as unless air is allowed to circulate freely around the young plants stagnant conditions may arise and cause damping off (p.660). Remove fallen leaves and dead matter immediately.

Most organic potting mixes are acid, that is, with a pH value of less than 7, and the ideal range for an organic mix is pH 5–5.5. Simple test kits are available to measure the pH. A very alkaline soil or compost reduces the amount of phosphorus, iron, manganese, and boron available to the plant, whereas too acidic a soil means that calcium and magnesium may be in short supply. For feeding the plants, apply a proprietary liquid fertilizer strictly in accordance with the manufacturer's instructions.

DAMPING OFF

Seedlings are more likely to damp off if they are overcrowded, especially if grown in damp, poorly ventilated conditions, or if they are allowed to suffer frost damage.

Hardening off

Hardening off the propagated plants, by which process the young plants are acclimatized to the outside air temperature, must not be rushed, because, over a period of days, the natural waxes coating the leaves need to undergo changes in form and thickness to reduce water loss. The stomatal pores on the leaf also need to adapt to less supportive conditions.

First, turn off the heat, if appropriate, in the propagator or mist unit. Then, during the daytime, raise the covers for increasingly long periods. Finally, the covers may be removed for both day and night. If the plant has been in the protective environment of a greenhouse and eventually needs to be planted outdoors, move it next into a cold frame. This, too, should be closed at first, then opened in stages. Alternatively place in the shelter of a wall, fence, or hedge and cover with horticultural fleece, gradually lifting it first during the day, and then at night. The hardening off process may take two to three weeks.

Outdoor nursery beds

Large numbers of new plants and seedlings in containers can be grown on in an outdoor nursery bed, once they have been hardened off. At its simplest, this can be an area of cleared and levelled ground covered with water-permeable woven fabric, black polypropylene, or weed matting,

NURSERY BED WITH RAISED EDGES

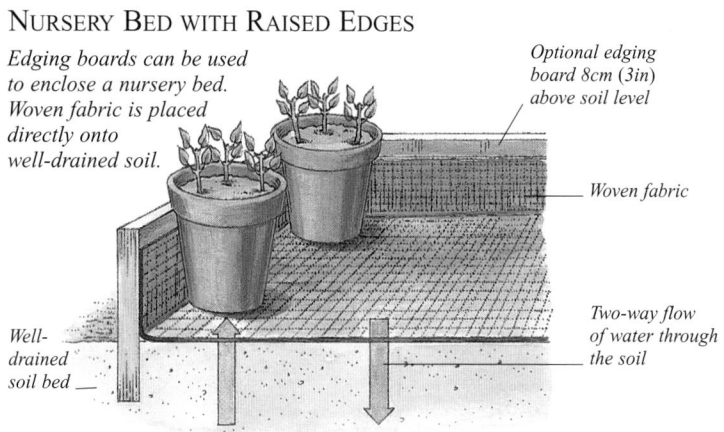

Edging boards can be used to enclose a nursery bed. Woven fabric is placed directly onto well-drained soil.

Optional edging board 8cm (3in) above soil level

Woven fabric

Well-drained soil bed

Two-way flow of water through the soil

SAND BED

With this type of nursery bed, woven fabric can be placed over an enclosed bed of coarse sand.

Plastic sheeting cut 2.5cm (1in) below the top of the edging boards

Edging board 8cm (3in) above soil level

Sand bed

Two-way flow of water through the sand

Soil bed

which will suppress weeds, provide a clean growing environment, and help to isolate plants placed on its surface from soil-borne diseases. The plants are placed on the fabric and gain access to soil water through capillary action. Edging boards can be added (as above) to "corral" the plants neatly and reduce the effect of drying winds, making watering more

effective. The fabric should be sterilized regularly to maintain a clean growing environment.

The nursery bed may be of any size, but it is essential that it is on free-draining soil. If your soil is a heavy clay, it is worth raising the nursery bed by first laying down plastic sheeting, and then adding a layer of coarse, lime-free sand, 8cm

(3in) deep. The entire sand bed will need to be enclosed by edging boards (see above right). The edging boards and plastic sheeting will retain moisture and ensure that watering is effective, while the drainage afforded by the sand will prevent a waterlogged environment. A covering layer of water-permeable woven fabric can be added to prevent erosion of

the sand by wind, and also disturbance by domestic animals, keeping the sand cleaner and more hygienic.

A sand bed has the advantage over a basic nursery bed of reducing the amount of watering necessary, minimizing the risk of potting composts drying out. More complex sand-bed designs incorporate drainage pipes and automatic watering systems.

Advanced techniques

Since the mid-20th century, many new propagation methods have been introduced commercially. Some are generally confined to "laboratory nurseries" using advanced technologies, but the following developments affect several branches of horticulture and have direct or indirect relevance to gardening. (See also INDOOR GARDENING, "Hydroculture", p.375.)

Micropropagation

Micropropagation uses explants, or tiny pieces of young plant material. Each explant is grown on in a glass or plastic container in a medium containing organic nutrients, mineral salts, hormones, and other elements needed for growth, and is placed in a closely controlled, sterile environment. The explant multiplies to form numerous shoots or complete plantlets, which

are then rooted as "microcuttings" or, if they have already rooted, weaned to greenhouse conditions. Sterile conditions are vital throughout, and transfer of the plant material from the culture to a greenhouse is especially difficult.

Micropropagation is used mainly for high-value plants, for example for the rapid introduction of new cultivars, for plants difficult to propagate by other means, and to produce disease-free stock.

Genetic modification

Also known as GM or genetic engineering, genetic modification uses modern DNA technology to identify and extract particular genes from a plant's cells and introduce them into another cell, not necessarily of the same species. The technique makes it possible to recombine genes of

fundamentally changed parents in the process of plant breeding and results in completely new plants. Using GM methods, resistance to certain pests and diseases can be engendered: for example, cucumber mosaic virus in susceptible lettuces, tomatoes, and peppers; and herbicide resistance in tobacco plants. Other potential benefits of GM include: extending colour and scent ranges in flowers; enhanced fruit flavours; greater tolerance of low temperatures and water shortages; and the production of medicinal compounds.

Fundamental interference with the natural order by the manipulation of genes raises public concern. Questions are asked about potential risks to the environment. Is it possible that progeny arising through GM may deliver genes into natural populations of plants, through normal cross-pollination, with deleterious consequences? Might GM plants themselves show undesirable traits such as invasiveness to produce "superweeds"? Are there potential hazards to human health through consumption of GM food crops? In addition, ethical issues arise including freedom of choice, dominance of commercial influence, and the non-reversibility of the basic procedures.

As the opportunity and challenges presented by genetic modification unfold, gardeners should be aware of facts in the case. Statutory regulations govern development of the technique and there are mechanisms in place to evaluate the benefits and potential risks.

Advances in seed propagation

New methods have been developed to improve the speed and uniformity of seed germination for the gardener. Seeds are soaked in solutions of salts, such as sodium chloride or potassium nitrate, or in polyethylene glycol solutions. They are thus primed for germination but are dried before the radicle emerges and are then packaged ready for sale. The seeds can be sown conventionally as required.

Fluid drilling and pelleted seed have been developed to make uniform seed sowing easier. In fluid drilling, seed primed for germination is contained within a gel base, for example in a fungicide-free wallpaper paste, which can then be squeezed along the seed drill. In pelleted seed, primed seed is coated in an inert material that may contain fungicides, nutrients, and/or a fluorescent dye. Such readily handled seeds can be sown very evenly.

Artificially produced seeds

Some flower tissues, when introduced into a special liquid culture medium, develop numerous embryos – each similar to the embryo within a seed. If these are given a synthetic coating (in a process known as somatic embryogenesis), vast numbers of genetically uniform, artificial "seeds" may eventually be produced.

MICROPROPAGATION

A microscopic portion of plant tissue is extracted from a plant under sterile conditions. This portion, or explant, is then divided (right) and grown on in test-tube conditions (far right). Once sufficiently large, these embryo plants may be further divided or grown on to form plantlets.

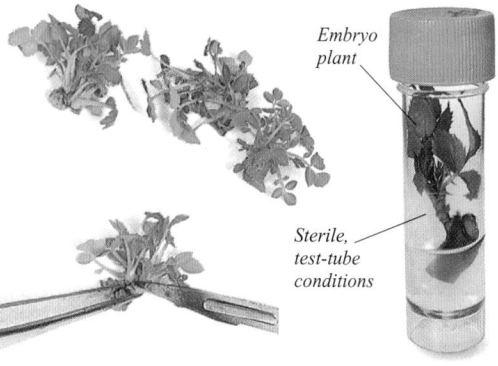

Embryo plant

Sterile, test-tube conditions

7
PLANT PROBLEMS

EVEN THE MOST experienced gardener may suffer problems caused by plant diseases and disorders, the ravages of pests, and the choking of plants by weeds. By following the principles of good cultivation and garden management, however, it should be possible to keep these problems to a minimum.

When problems do occur, it is important first to diagnose them correctly, before deciding upon the appropriate course of action required to remedy the situation. The choice of treatments now includes a wide and effective variety of organic and biological methods, as well as the use of chemicals.

Pests, diseases, and physiological disorders

Most plant problem symptoms are easy to see. A tree, shrub, or plant may wilt or become discoloured, or it may fail to come into leaf or to bloom at all. Insects, which may be the cause of the plant's poor health, may be seen on part or all of the plant. Sometimes an infestation or disease in the roots may be noticed first through symptoms in the leaves. This chapter gives detailed information on how to prevent and control the pests, diseases, and physiological disorders that can cause such problems.

What is a pest?

Pests are animals that cause damage to cultivated plants. Some, such as slugs, snails, and rabbits, are well known; most, however, are small invertebrates such as mites, eelworms, woodlice, and millipedes, which are less evidently plant pests. The largest group by far in this category are the insects. Pests may damage or destroy any part of a plant or, in some cases, even the whole plant. They feed in various ways – by sap sucking, leaf mining, defoliating, or tunnelling through stems, roots, or fruits. Sometimes they cause abnormal growths known as galls. Some pests also indirectly damage plants by spreading viral or fungal diseases, while others coat plants with a sugary excrement that encourages the growth of sooty moulds.

What is a disease?

A plant disease is any pathological condition caused by other organisms, such as bacteria, fungi, or viruses. Fungal diseases are commonest; bacterial diseases relatively rare. The symptoms that these organisms produce vary considerably in appearance and severity, but the growth or health of the plant is almost always affected and, in severe attacks, the plant may even be killed. The rate of infection is affected by factors such as weather and growing conditions. In some cases, the disease-causing organism (pathogen) is spread by a carrier, such as an aphid. The pathogen is sometimes visible as a discoloration on the plant, as with rusts. Symptoms such as discoloration, distortion, or wilting are typical signs of disease infection.

HOW TO DIAGNOSE PLANT SYMPTOMS

In a case where it is obvious that the leaves have been eaten away by some kind of pest, turn to the section on "Eaten leaves" to identify the cause.

When a plant shows several symptoms, look either in the section on the whole plant or in the part that deals with the worst aspect, here discoloured leaves.

What is a disorder?

Plant disorders usually result from nutritional deficiencies or from unsuitable growing or storage conditions. An inappropriate temperature range, inadequate or erratic water or food supply, poor light, or unsatisfactory atmospheric conditions may all lead to physiological disorders. Problems may also be caused by deficiencies of the mineral salts that are essential for healthy plant growth.

Weather, cultural, or soil conditions may lead to a range of plants being affected. The problems become apparent through symptoms such as discoloured leaves or stem wilt. A plant that lacks water, food, or the appropriate environmental conditions will not only appear unhealthy but will also be far less able to resist attack from either insect pests or diseases caused by fungi, viruses, or bacteria. Unless problems are correctly diagnosed and appropriately treated, in extreme circumstances affected plants may die.

How to use this chapter

This chapter is organized according to the site of symptoms (such as distorted flowers or discoloured leaves), in sections covering leaves, stems, flowers, fruit, roots and tubers, bulbs, whole plant, and lawns. Within these, symptoms are grouped by type; for example, all yellow leaf spots will be found together.

To identify a problem, look in the appropriate section. If you cannot find it there, turn to the cross-references at the end of that section. Each entry lists the plants affected, the symptoms, the cause of the problem, and how to control it. Some notes on the controls currently approved appear on p.668; however these are subject to change. Always check labelling for specific uses, as not all brands of any one chemical are recommended for the same problems or the same plants.

*A combination of
defences protects these
strawberry plants.
Netting prevents
depredations by birds,
while a layer of straw
maintains a clean,
dry environment
around the fruits,
discouraging moulds
and rots.*

same ground for a number of years may also lead to problems (see, for example, "Rose-sick soil", p.156). If a disease such as pansy sickness becomes evident, remove all the plants and grow other botanically unrelated plants that are not susceptible on the site.

Resistant plants
Some plants are resistant to attack by pests or diseases. Plant breeders have been able to profit from this and have produced cultivars with a higher-than-average resistance to some pests or diseases. Cultivated plants resistant to pests include some butterhead lettuces, which are seldom affected by the lettuce root aphid. Plants resistant to disease include some tomato cultivars, which resist tomato leaf mould, and the climbing rose 'Maigold', which shows some resistance to diseases such as powdery mildew, rusts, and black spot.

In some cases, the resistance appears to be total, but even a resistant plant may succumb to a given disease if its growing conditions are poor, for example, or if other factors, such as the weather, weaken the plant. Before buying plants, check if there are disease- or pest-resistant cultivars readily available. The range of resistant plants varies from year to year, so check catalogues annually for this type of information.

Integrated control

The phrase "integrated control" is used to describe what is widely agreed to be best practice in the limitation and management of pest and disease problems. It aims firstly to do everything possible to prevent problems occurring, but then, should this be inadequate, to consider all the options for dealing with a problem – for example, using organic or biological controls – before resorting to chemicals. Gardeners practising integrated control combine the best aspects of organic and inorganic methods, always opting for the organic one first. They choose resistant plants and maintain high standards of garden hygiene, ensuring plants are healthy and thus have the best chance of resisting attack; they practise crop rotation. They seek to prevent pests from landing on plants, by the use of traps, barriers, and repellents. Plants are inspected regularly to spot problems early, and care is taken to ensure an accurate diagnosis. Chemicals are used sensibly and correctly, and only when warranted by serious pest or disease attack.

PREVENTING BUILD-UP OF DISEASE

Practising crop rotation stops specific soil-borne problems building up in the same plot of ground, for example clubroot of brassicas – here, plants are being removed after cropping.

Prevention of problems

Always buy strong, vigorous plants that look healthy. Do not purchase plants that are showing dieback or discoloured stems, that have leaves that are an abnormal colour for the time of year, or that are wilted or distorted. Do not buy plants showing significant pest infestations or disease. Check the root ball of container-grown trees and shrubs: do not buy them if they are either pot-bound or showing poor root development.

Check that the plant is suitable for its intended position, taking into account the type, texture, and pH of the soil, the aspect of the site, and whether the plant is prone to frost damage. Plant carefully, making sure that the ground is well prepared and that the roots are properly spread out. Follow the individual plant's requirements for watering, feeding, and, where appropriate, pruning.

Garden hygiene
Maintaining a tidy and well-managed garden is one of the most important ways to reduce the risk of pest and disease attack. Examine plants regularly to identify any new problem as soon as possible, since a well-established infection or infestation is always far more difficult to deal with than one that is identified and treated early.

The regular removal and disposal of diseased parts of plants, and some pests such as cabbage white caterpillars, may be laborious but certainly helps to control problems. Debris from infested or diseased plants should in many cases be burned; otherwise the pest or pathogen may survive, overwinter, and re-infect plants in spring.

If a plant is badly diseased or infested by pests, it may be impossible to revive it; such plants should be removed, especially if there is a risk that the trouble might spread to healthy plants nearby.

Crop rotation and replant problems
Rotating vegetable crops, usually on a three- or four-year basis, helps prevent soil-borne pests and diseases from building up to a damaging level. For further details on planning a crop rotation system, see GROWING VEGETABLES, "Crop rotation", p.498. Although a strict rotation plan is generally used for vegetables, it is also worth rotating annuals and bulbs where feasible, as this reduces the build-up of diseases like pansy sickness and tulip fire. Growing a particular kind of plant in the

Correcting cultural disorders and deficiencies

Unsatisfactory growing conditions may result not only in poor general growth, but also in some very specific symptoms that closely resemble those caused by pests and diseases. When problems manifest themselves and an obvious cause – such as pest infestation – is not immediately apparent, it is worth considering the plant's growing environment as a whole – recent weather conditions, for example, or the health of your soil, or indeed whether some aspect of plant care was not provided. At best, the plant may be restored to complete health by some simple measure – the addition of a mineral supplement, for example, or less frequent watering. At worst, you may have to accept plant losses caused by freak extremes of weather – or learn that certain plants simply are not suited to the conditions you are able to provide.

SYMPTOMS OF CULTURAL DISORDER

Bitter pit in apples, caused by a lack of calcium, may be triggered by dry conditions in soils that in fact do contain sufficient calcium levels.

FRIENDS AND FOES

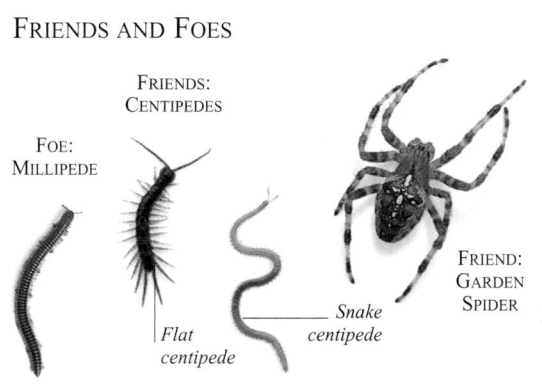

FOE:
MILLIPEDE

FRIENDS:
CENTIPEDES

Flat centipede

Snake centipede

FRIEND:
GARDEN SPIDER

FRIEND:
HEDGEHOG

COMPANION PLANTING
French marigolds (Tagetes patula) *attract hoverflies, which feed on aphids that may attack nearby plants.*

It is also worth remembering that the risk of certain pest and disease problems can be minimized by altering growing conditions. Liming in the vegetable garden (see p.625) is a classic example; by increasing the alkalinity of the soil, it reduces the risk of clubroot affecting brassica crops.

Organic controls

Organic control uses natural methods to help plants both resist and recover from attack by pests and diseases. Such methods have long played their part in gardening, but in recent years they have attracted an increasing level of interest, especially as some harmful organisms have become immune to chemicals that once controlled them. Gardeners have become increasingly aware of the damage that irresponsible use of chemicals can do to the environment, and especially to creatures that are the gardener's natural allies – those that are predatory on plant pests.

Attracting pest predators
Insects and other creatures found in gardens are by no means all destructive. Many are not only useful to the plant but actually essential for its survival; for example, a large number of fruits, vegetables, and flowers rely on pollinating insects, such as honey bees, to carry pollen from one flower to another to enable fertilization to take place. In other cases, some species of natural predator can help to control certain types of pest and should therefore be encouraged to visit the garden. A natural balance between pests and predators may take a few years to accomplish but, once established, such a garden will be much healthier than one that relies on chemical remedies alone.

Areas of undisturbed land will attract beneficial animals, especially if planted with a wide range of native species. Flat stones placed in the bed or border will be used by thrushes as anvils on which to smash snail shells. Predators such as hoverflies and ladybirds can also be encouraged by the introduction of colourful flowers, especially if flat or open-centred in form, and so they, too, will help keep pests to a minimum.

Recognizing beneficial garden animals
Hedgehogs, shrews, frogs, and toads feed on many ground-dwelling plant pests such as slugs and snails. Birds may be the cause of some damage in the garden, but this disadvantage is usually far outweighed by the enormous quantities of insect pests that many devour. Some invertebrates, for example centipedes, prey on soil-dwelling pests. It is possible to distinguish centipedes from the somewhat similar millipedes (which are often harmful) by the number of legs that are carried on each segment of their bodies: centipedes have only one pair

per body segment, whereas millipedes have two pairs (see also *Friends and Foes*, above).

Spiders are also useful allies as their webs trap countless insects. Certain insects, however, may be invaluable in the garden. Ladybird beetles are a familiar example in many countries, and both the larvae and the adult beetles feed on destructive pests such as aphids. Lacewing larvae, too, have a voracious appetite for aphids, and they can be encouraged by planting flowers, such as pot marigolds (*Calendula*), and the provision of a nesting box in which they can overwinter. Ants and wasps, whose activities might damage some plants, may still help the gardener by preying on other insect pests. Ground beetles are voracious consumers of numerous pest species.

Companion planting
Certain companion plants grown in association with a crop may help to reduce pest attack. For example, some strong-smelling herbs such as mint and garlic may repel pests that are attracted to plants by smell, thereby keeping them away from nearby plants. Deliberate planting of host plants may deflect pests away from other plants or attract predators to feed on the pests: nasturtiums (*Tropaeolum*), for example, are susceptible to aphids, so plant French marigolds (*Tagetes patula*) nearby as these attract hoverflies, which have larvae that feed on the aphids.

Traps, barriers, and repellents
These work by stopping pests getting near plants. Many are easily constructed from everyday items. Earwigs may be trapped in inverted flower pots,

and wireworms in old potatoes or carrots spitted on a stick and buried. In the greenhouse, saucers of water under bench legs will foil ants and woodlice – not in themselves pests of established plants, but extremely destructive to delicate seedlings. Glasshouse whiteflies, which are attracted to the colour yellow, may be caught on a piece of yellow card smeared with grease. Place these near the top of the plants and move them up as the plants grow. Inspect these traps regularly and dispose of the pests. Consider introducing biological controls (see p.642) if the infestation is increasing.

Pheromone traps can be purchased from most garden centres and by mail order. They synthesize the chemicals used by specific insects, such as the codling moth, to attract a mate. The trap eliminates the males by luring them onto a sticky sheet, thereby also reducing the mating success of the remaining females. Such a trap also allows the gardener to monitor infestation levels, and determine whether further control methods are needed.

Traps and barriers can be used to great effect against slugs and snails (see also "Controlling slugs and snails", p.642). Larger barriers, from horticultural fleece to fruit cages, can be erected around and over plants to deter winged insects such as carrot fly and cabbage whitefly, as well as

ORGANIC EARWIG TRAP

An inverted flower pot filled with dried grass and placed over a cane attracts earwigs (see p.644). Examine the pot and remove any earwigs daily.

CODLING MOTH TRAP

Hang a pheromone trap head high in apple and pear trees in spring. It will catch male codling moths and so reduce mating opportunities.

Controlling slugs and snails

There are many effective alternatives to slug pellets, which some gardeners prefer not to use. The value of hand-picking should not be underestimated, especially when several pairs of hands are available to help. Slugs and snails are most active at night, and can be readily spotted by torchlight, especially on a damp evening. Gather up the pests and kill them by dropping in a strong salt solution.

There are a number of environmentally friendly traps and barriers, both proprietary products and home-made. Some stop the slugs reaching the plants while others attract them to more tempting fare nearby.
• Lure slugs and snails into a hollowed-out grapefruit or orange half that has been set, open side downwards, on stones just above the ground. Slugs and snails, attracted by the citrus scent, will move under the fruit skin and are likely to remain there, until morning at least. The slugs can then be drowned in a strong salt solution.
• Part-fill a jar with beer or milk and almost sink it in the ground. The rim should be about 1cm (½in) above the surface so that useful predators such as ground beetles are prevented from toppling in. The smell of the beer or milk will attract slugs and snails, which should fall in and drown. Specially designed slug "traps" are available by mail order.
• Create a wide, physical barrier of a coarse material such as sand, grit, wood ash, soot, pine needles, or broken eggshells around special plants. These should be either too dry or too scratchy for slugs and snails to be attracted to cross.
• Surround vulnerable seedlings and very small plants with individual tubes, made from a plastic bottle with the top and bottom cut off. Press the plastic tube into the soil so it encircles a plant.
• Place a proprietary porous mineral product as a barrier around plants that need protection. Such a barrier, however, is less effective under wet conditions, which is when slugs and snails are most active.

birds, rabbits, and deer. Grease bands bar the way to pests climbing up trees and pots, and proprietary brassica collars, or ones cut from carpet or underlay, will prevent female cabbage root fly from laying their eggs around young brassica plants (see p.660).

Repellents, such as ultrasonic devices or humming tapes, are sometimes used to protect plants against moles, cats, and birds, which may be encouraged to move elsewhere in the vicinity. However, while bird-scaring devices and pet repellents may work initially, they often require changing frequently as the creatures become familiar with them.

Acceptable organic treatments

A few chemical preparations originate from natural sources; pyrethrum, for example, is derived from the pyrethrum daisy. Other organic treatments are derris dust, soft soap, vegetable oils, and sulphur dust. These may be obtained as ready-made powders or liquid sprays; copper-based ones are safe to use and spray damage is not a problem. They have short persistence, however, and act only on contact with the pest or disease, which necessitates regular and thorough applications. One disadvantage of organically "acceptable" insecticides is that most are non-specific in action, harming all insect life, whereas some "unacceptable" chemical controls have been carefully formulated to target only the harmful pest and not other beneficial creatures such as pest predators. Such non-organic treatments are arguably less environmentally damaging than organic alternatives.

Biological control

Some of the most troublesome pests, especially red spider mite, whiteflies, and vine weevil grubs, can be dealt with very effectively using the relatively recently developed technology of biological control. The term biological control describes the limiting of pest damage by the deliberate introduction of natural enemies, such as predators, parasites, or diseases. Biological controls are living organisms, usually nematodes or small predator insects or mites, which have no detrimental effects on non-target species. They are bred and supplied under controlled conditions, and as they are alive, they must be introduced onto your plants or into

INDIVIDUAL CLOCHE
Cut-down plastic bottles protect tender stems from voracious pests at ground level.

the soil as soon as they have been obtained. These tiny creatures may prey on their host or target pest during a specific stage of its development, or they may spread disease among them. For example, the microscopic pathogenic nematode *Heterorhabditis megidis* is watered into potting compost or soil containing vine weevil grubs, which it infects with a fatal disease, while the predatory mite *Phytoseiulus persimilis* feeds on the eggs, nymphs, and mature forms of red spider mite. Not all pests and diseases, however, can be countered by appropriate biological controls; other controls may be introduced as more research is carried out on insect and disease ecology.

Most of these organisms require daytime temperatures of at least 21°C (70°F) and good light intensity in order to breed faster than the pests. They can therefore be introduced into a heated greenhouse earlier than an unheated one or the

PEST	BIOLOGICAL CONTROL
Aphids	Fly larva predators (*Aphidoletes aphidimyza*)
Caterpillars	Bacterial disease (*Bacillus thuringiensis*)
Chafer grubs, leatherjackets	Pathogenic nematodes (*Heterorhabditis* and *Steinernema* spp.)
Fungus gnats larvae	Predatory mites (*Hypoaspis miles*)
Mealybugs	Ladybirds (*Cryptolaemus montrouzieri*)
Red spider mites	Predatory mites (*Phytoseiulus persimilis*)
Soft scale insects	Parasitic wasp *Metaphycus helvolus*
Thrips	Predatory mites (*Amblyseius* spp.)
Underground slugs	Pathogenic nematode (*Phasmarhabditis hermaphrodita*)
Vine weevil grubs	Pathogenic nematode (*Heterorhabditis megidis*)
Whitefly	Parasitic wasp *Encarsia formosa*

USING BIOLOGICAL CONTROLS

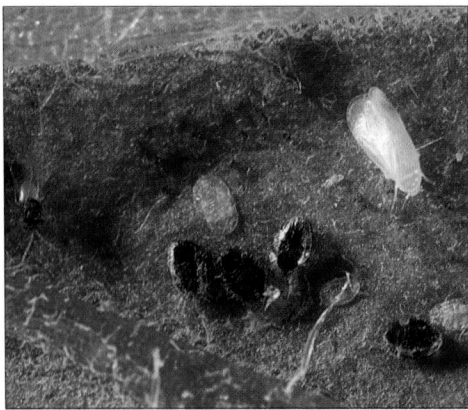

BIOLOGICAL CONTROL AT WORK
Minute Encarsia formosa *wasps attack and parasitize whitefly larvae, causing them to blacken and eventually die.*

YELLOW STICKY TRAP
A useful adjunct to biological controls, these can catch small numbers of pests and will alert the gardener if populations start to increase.

open ground. Another key to successful use is to ensure that the pest has been correctly identified and therefore the appropriate specific control measures adopted. If you are not sure what pests you have, lure them onto a sticky yellow trap, for easier identification.

Biological controls may be obtained from mail-order specialist suppliers. These generally advertise in the gardening press and on the internet. Good garden centres will also be able to provide advice on suitable controls and where to buy them.

Greenhouse controls
Some biological controls are suitable for use only in the greenhouse or conservatory. Introduce the control before plants are heavily infested, as it may be a number of weeks before it becomes effective. Restrict the use of pesticides, since most are harmful to biological controls; the exceptions are pirimicarb against aphids, and insecticidal soaps or vegetable oils, which control a range of small insects and mites.

Open-garden biological controls
Use of biological controls is less practicable in the relatively uncontrolled conditions of the open garden, especially where pesticides are used, since they may kill the controls as well as the pests. Of the controls listed in the table (facing page), only those for caterpillars, chafer grubs, leatherjackets, vine weevil, and underground slugs are suitable for use in the open garden, provided the soil temperature is suitably high.

Chemical control

Chemical control is the term used to describe the action of destroying plant pests and diseases by applying synthetic compounds to plants or soil. Although the emphasis on organic control is presently becoming stronger, the responsible and sparing use of chemicals still has a valuable role to play in pest and disease control. A sensible combination of the most suitable aspects of both methods may provide the best solution to these difficult and often recurrent problems.

Pesticides and fungicides
Most pesticides (which are used to kill insects, mites, and other pests) and fungicides (which are used to control diseases caused by fungi) either work by being brought into contact with the pest or disease organisms, or are systemic.

Contact pesticides kill pests when they crawl over a treated surface or when they are directly hit by the chemical (when sprayed, for example). Contact fungicides may kill germinating fungal spores and prevent further infection, but they have little effect on established fungal growths.

Systemic chemicals are absorbed into the plant tissues and are sometimes transported by the sap stream throughout the entire plant. Fungicides of this type, for example carbendazim, kill fungi in the plant tissues. Systemic pesticides, such as imidacloprid and pirimicarb, are predominantly used against certain sap-sucking pests and may be less useful against foliage pests that have chewing mouthparts, such as caterpillars, beetles, and earwigs. Thorough spraying of affected plants, especially on the undersides of leaves, is essential if these pesticides are to work.

Pesticide-resistant strains may sometimes occur, particularly with persistent greenhouse pests such as whitefly and red spider mite. Fungi that are

APPLYING CHEMICALS WITH CARE

THOROUGH APPLICATION
To avoid a wasted application, spray well into the centre of plants and beneath foliage, especially with products that have a contact action.

SEPARATE EQUIPMENT
Keep watering cans, sprayers and nozzles specifically for use with herbicides; residues in equipment can harm non-targeted garden plants.

frequently treated with systemic fungicides may also develop resistant strains. This problem can sometimes be overcome by using a different type of compound, but with greenhouse pests the use of biological control (where possible) is often a better alternative (see p.642).

Formulation of chemical preparations
The active ingredient of a chemical preparation kills the organism, and the way in which a preparation has been formulated determines its efficacy and use. Pesticides and fungicides are available as concentrated liquids, dusts, powders (with which a wetter may be incorporated to ensure thorough penetration of the active ingredient), smokes, baits, and ready-to-use dilute liquids. These are now formulated for maximum effectiveness and safety, for gardeners and for the environment, although in the past some environmentally harmful chemicals were available.

Phytotoxicity
Some plants are liable to suffer adverse reactions to fungicides and insecticides. This is known as phytotoxicity. The manufacturer's instructions often list those species that should not be treated. Such lists cannot, however, be complete, since the reaction of many ornamental plants to certain chemicals is as yet unknown. If in doubt about whether a certain chemical may be suitable, first test the fungicide or pesticide on a small area of the plant before undertaking treatment of the whole plant. Alternatively, where several plants of the same type are grown together, test the chemical on only one of them.

Various other factors, including the stage of growth and the environmental conditions surrounding the plant, can also increase the likelihood of a plant being damaged by chemical treatments. For example, young seedlings, cuttings, and flower petals are much more sensitive than is mature foliage to variations in the growing conditions, and may therefore be adversely affected by the application of some chemical treatments. Similarly, plants that are suffering any stress should never be treated with chemicals.

In order to avoid problems with side-effects on mature plants, never spray them when they are in bright sunlight, or when they are either dry around the roots or have been exposed to unusually high or low temperatures.

Using chemicals safely

If the instructions are followed precisely – that is, only in the way and for the purpose that the manufacturer describes – chemicals should prove effective with little risk to the user or to the environment. It is now illegal in some countries for gardeners to use chemicals other than in accordance with the instructions provided. Always take the following precautions:

• think before you spray: is it really necessary, or could you use organic remedies or biological controls instead?
• choose the chemical carefully – make sure it is the right one for the job;
• apply the preparation at the rate and frequency stated on the label;
• never use any type of chemical on plants in ponds;
• never mix chemicals unless the manufacturer recommends this;
• always observe any suggested precautions;
• always spray when the wind is still, or almost still, to avoid damaging adjacent plants;
• always spray in the evening, when there are few bees and hoverflies around;
• do not spray on hot, sunny days, as such weather increases the risk of scorching plants;
• avoid contact with the skin and eyes by wearing goggles, rubber gloves, and long-sleeved clothing;
• do not inhale dusts, smokes, or sprays;
• make sure that the chemical does not drift into other people's gardens;
• keep pets and children away during treatment;
• never eat, drink, or smoke when applying a chemical;
• dispose of any excess carefully and wash out any apparatus thoroughly;
• do not use apparatus for anything other than chemicals;
• store chemicals out of reach of children and animals;
• store chemicals in their original containers, with their original labels, and keep any explanatory leaflets with them.

Leaf problems

Eaten leaves

Slugs and snails

Plants affected Non-woody plants, especially young ones (see also "Slugs", p.662).
Symptoms Holes appear in the foliage and stems may be left on the leaves or the soil surface. Small holes on the outside of potato tubers lead to large cavities inside.
Cause Slugs (eg *Milax*, *Arion*, and *Deroceras* spp.) and snails (eg *Helix aspersa*), slimy-bodied

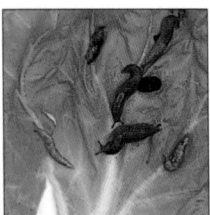
Slugs under leaves

Holes in leaves

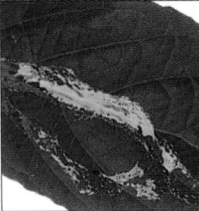
Silvery slime trails

Stems stripped

molluscs that feed mainly at night or after rain.
Control Cultivate regularly to expose eggs. Use traps or barriers (see p.641), or handpick. 'Kestrel' potatoes are slug-resistant. Biologically control underground slugs with the pathogenic nematode *Phasmorhabditis hermaphrodita*. Scatter organic granules or metaldehyde slug pellets, spray plants and the soil surface with liquid metaldehyde, or use an aluminium sulphate-based product.

Earwigs

Plants affected Shrubs, perennials, and annuals, commonly dahlias, chrysanthemums, and clematis. Also apricots and peaches.
Symptoms Young leaves are eaten in summer. See p.657 for other symptoms.
Cause Earwigs (*Forficula auricularia*), which are yellowish-brown insects 2cm (¾in) long with a pair of curved pincers. Earwigs hide during the day and feed at night.
Control Place inverted pots, that have been loosely stuffed with hay or straw, on canes among susceptible plants; earwigs use these as daytime shelters from which they can be removed and destroyed. Alternatively, spray at dusk with bifenthrin or dust with permethrin.

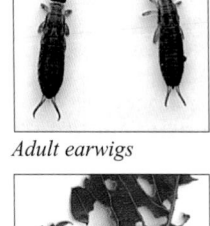
Adult earwigs

Leaves eaten away

Woodlice

Plants affected Seedlings and other soft growth, including strawberry fruits.
Symptoms Holes may appear in seedlings and in leaves near shoot tips but woodlice are not generally pests; they mainly eat decaying plant material and are often found on plants that have already been damaged by other pests and diseases.
Cause Woodlice (eg *Oniscus*, *Porcellio*, and *Armadillidium* spp.), also known as slaters or pill bugs. They are grey or brownish-grey, sometimes with white or yellow markings, and up to 1cm (½in) long with hard, segmented bodies. They feed at night and hide away out of sight in dark shelters during the day.
Control Always clear away plant debris and keep greenhouses tidy to reduce shelter. Protect seedlings with bendiocarb dust if damage is occurring.

Millipedes

Plants affected Seedlings and other soft growth, strawberry fruits, and potato tubers.
Symptoms Seedlings and soft growth are eaten; slug damage on bulbs and potato tubers is enlarged. Damage is rarely serious.
Cause Millipedes (eg *Blaniulus*, *Brachydesmus*, and *Cylindroiulus* spp.), black, grey, brown, or creamy-white animals that feed below or at soil level. They have hard, segmented bodies with two pairs of legs per segment (centipedes, which are beneficial predators, have only one pair per segment). The spotted snake millipede (*Blaniulus guttulatus*) is the most damaging species. Its slender, creamy-white body is up to 2cm (¾in) long with a row of red dots along each side. Millipedes are encouraged by soils that have a high organic content.
Control Cultivate the soil thoroughly and maintain good hygiene. Use inorganic rather than organic fertilizers in areas where millipedes are a problem, especially where potatoes are being grown. Millipedes are difficult to control but are rarely a problem in their own right; slug control helps to avoid millipede problems.

Common millipedes

Flea beetles

Plants affected The seedlings of brassicas, turnips, swedes, radishes, wallflowers (*Erysimum*), and stocks (*Matthiola*).
Symptoms Small holes and pits are scalloped from the upper surface of the leaves; plants may die.

Cause Small, black or metallic-blue beetles (eg *Phyllotreta* spp.), sometimes with a yellow stripe running down each wing case. They are usually 2mm (¹⁄₁₆in) long, with enlarged hind legs that enable them to leap off plant surfaces when disturbed. They overwinter in plant debris.
Control Clear away plant debris, particularly in autumn. Sow seed in warm soil and water seedlings regularly to help rapid growth through the vulnerable stages. Dust emerged seedlings with derris or pyrethrum if damage occurs.

Asparagus beetle

Plants affected Asparagus.
Symptoms Leaves are eaten; the epidermis is removed from stems, causing the upper growth to dry and turn brown. Damage occurs between late spring and early autumn.
Cause Both the adult and larval asparagus beetle (*Crioceris asparagi*). The adult beetles are 7mm (¼in) long, with yellow

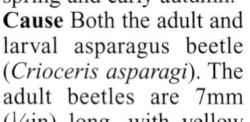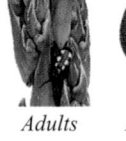
Adults   *Larvae*

and black wing cases and a reddish thorax. The larvae are greyish-yellow.
Control Pick off light infestations by hand. If serious, spray with pyrethrum or derris; if plants are in flower, spray at dusk to protect bees.

Viburnum beetle

Plants affected *Viburnum*.
Symptoms Holes are eaten in the leaves; this occurs initially during early summer, when the foliage may be reduced to just veins, and then reappears once again in late summer.
Cause The viburnum

beetle (*Pyrrhalta viburni*). The first period of damage in early summer is caused by the creamy-white larvae of the viburnum beetle, which are up to 7mm (¼in) in length and have black markings. The second phase of damage, occurring in late summer, is caused by the adult beetles, which are greyish-brown in colour.
Control Spray with bifenthrin or pyrethrum when the larvae first appear.

Red lily beetle

Plants affected Bulbous lilies (*Lilium*), fritillaries (*Fritillaria*), and occasionally Solomon's seal (*Polygonatum*).
Symptoms Leaves and flowers are eaten from early spring to mid-autumn.
Cause The adult and

larval red lily beetle (*Lilioceris lilii*). Adults are 8mm (⅜in) long and bright red. Larvae are reddish-brown with black heads, and covered in black excrement.
Control A long egg-laying and emergence period (mid-spring to midsummer) makes control difficult. Pick off by hand; otherwise spray with bifenthrin or imidacloprid + methiocarb.

Vine weevil

Adult vine weevil

Plants affected Shrubs, mainly rhododendrons, hydrangeas, *Euonymus*, and camellias; also grape vines (*Vitis vinifera*), strawberries, and many herbaceous plants.
Symptoms Notches appear in leaf margins, often near the ground, from mid-spring to mid-autumn.
Cause The adult vine weevil (*Otiorhynchus sulcatus*), a greyish-black beetle 9mm (⅜in) long, with a short snout and a pair of elbowed antennae. It feeds at night and hides by day.

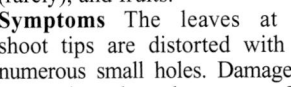
Irregular holes in leaf margins

Control Damage occurs over an extended period, and control is difficult, although good hygiene and the removal of plant debris reduce the number of hiding places. Use a biological treatment to control the grub stage, watering the nematode *Heterorhabditis megidis* onto the compost in late summer. Once established, plants can tolerate damage to their leaves.
See also "Vine weevil grubs", p.666.

Capsid bugs

Plants affected Shrubs and perennials (especially chrysanthemums, fuchsias, hydrangeas, *Caryopteris*, and dahlias), annuals, some vegetables (rarely), and fruits.
Symptoms The leaves at shoot tips are distorted with numerous small holes. Damage occurs throughout the summer. See p.657 for other symptoms.
Cause Capsid bugs (eg *Lygus rugulipennis* and *Lygocoris pabulinus*), green or brown insects 6mm (¼in) long that suck sap from shoot tips. Their toxic saliva kills plant tissues, causing leaves to tear.
Control In winter, clear up plant debris. Spray at first sign of damage using bifenthrin.

Leaf-cutting bees

Plants affected Roses mainly but also trees and other shrubs.
Symptoms Lozenge-shaped or circular pieces of uniform size are removed from the margins of the leaf.
Cause Leaf-cutting bees (*Megachile* spp.), which use the leaf pieces to build their nests. They are up to

1cm (½in) long, and have ginger hairs on the underside of their abdomen.
Control Leaf-cutting bees are of some benefit as pollinating insects and, unless plants are heavily damaged, control is not necessary. If they are a persistent nuisance, swat them as they return to the leaf.

Sawfly larvae

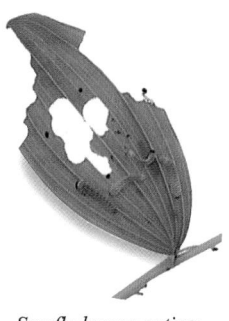
Sawfly larvae eating

Plants affected Trees, shrubs, herbaceous perennials, and fruits. Particularly affected are conifers, willows (*Salix*), *Aruncus dioicus, Geum, Aquilegia*, Solomon's seal (*Polygonatum*), roses, gooseberries, and currants.
Symptoms Plants are defoliated.
Cause The larvae of various sawfly species (eg *Nematus, Pristiphora*, and *Diprion* spp.); caterpillar-like larvae that are up to 3cm (1¼in) long and generally green, sometimes with black spots. The larvae of the Solomon's seal sawfly (*Phymatocera aterrima*) are greyish-white in colour. Most larvae grip the leaf edge and wave their bodies in an

Leaves eaten away

"S" shape when they are disturbed, but this does not occur with those on *Geum* or Solomon's seal.
Control Where possible, remove by hand. Spray serious infestations with pyrethrum, bifenthrin, or derris.

Winter moth caterpillars

Plants affected Many deciduous trees, fruit trees, and roses.
Symptoms Leaves are eaten between bud burst and late spring. Blossom and fruitlets may also be severely damaged.
Cause Pale green caterpillars, 2.5cm (1in) long, of the winter moth (*Operophtera brumata*).
Control Place sticky grease bands at least 15cm (6in) wide around tree trunks in mid-autumn, in order to prevent the wingless female moths from climbing up to lay eggs on the branches. Use the bacterial control *Bacillus thuringiensis*, or spray after bud burst with derris, pyrethrum, or bifenthrin.

Cabbage caterpillars

Plants affected Mainly brassicas, including cabbages, cauliflowers, and Brussels sprouts. Some perennial and annual ornamentals, eg nasturtiums (*Tropaeolum*).
Symptoms Holes appear in the foliage between

late spring and early autumn, and caterpillars may be found in the hearts of brassicas and on leaves.
Cause Caterpillars of the large cabbage white butterfly (*Pieris brassicae*), which are yellow and black with distinct hairs; those of the small cabbage white (*P. rapae*), pale green with velvety hairs; and those of the cabbage moth (*Mamestra brassicae*), yellowish-green or brown, with few hairs.
Control Pick off the young caterpillars by hand. For serious infestations, spray the foliage with the bacterial control *Bacillus thuringiensis*, or apply derris, pyrethrum, or bifenthrin.

Wood pigeon

Plants affected Brassicas and bush fruits, especially blackcurrants, and the seeds of peas, beans, and other vegetable crops.
Symptoms Leaves of brassicas are eaten, especially in cold weather, and young plants are uprooted; blackcurrants are stripped of buds, leaves, and fruits; seeds are eaten.
Cause The wood pigeon (*Columba palumbus*).
Control Netting is the only effective way to prevent damage to crops. Scaring devices, such as humming tapes, scarecrows, or aluminium foil strips, work only initially; they soon lose their deterrent effect as birds become used to the devices. Repellent sprays, based on aluminium ammonium sulphate, must be used very frequently to remain fully effective.

Caterpillars

Plants affected Many garden plants.
Symptoms Leaves, and possibly flowers, are eaten.
Cause Caterpillars of various species of butterfly and moth, which feed on plant material. The most common in gardens are winter moth and cabbage caterpillars (see left), webber moth caterpillars (see p.647), and tortrix moth caterpillars (see p.648).
Control Pick off caterpillars by hand, if practicable, and cover crops with horticultural fleece. For serious infestations, spray the foliage with the bacterial control *Bacillus thuringiensis*, or apply derris, pyrethrum, or bifenthrin.

Rabbits and hares

Plants affected Low-growing plants, young trees.
Symptoms Low-growing leaves are eaten, and the bark of young trees is gnawed away, especially during spells of cold weather.
Cause and control See p.666 for details.

Deer

Plants affected Most garden plants, especially trees, shrubs (including roses), and herbaceous plants.
Symptoms Shoots and leaves are eaten; tree bark is rubbed and frayed, and stripped in winter.
Cause and control See p.666 for details.

See also "Webber moth caterpillars", p.647; "Tortrix moth caterpillars", p.648; "Bacterial leaf spots and blotches", p.648; "Shothole", p.648; "Cutworms", p.655; and "Birds", p.657.

Discoloured and wilted leaves

Aphids

Plants affected Most plants.

Symptoms Leaves are often sticky with honeydew (aphid excrement), blistered, or blackened by sooty moulds; stems and buds may also be covered. See also p.651.

Blackfly on stem

Cause Aphids (including those known as greenfly, blackfly, or plant lice) that cluster on stems and the undersides of leaves, sucking the sap; some attack roots. They are up to 5mm (¼in) long, and green, yellow, brown, pink, grey, or black; some, eg the woolly beech aphid, are covered in a fluffy, white

Blistered leaf

wax. Aphids may transmit viruses (see p.649).

Control Apply a tar oil wash in winter against aphid eggs on deciduous fruit trees and bushes. Encourage ladybirds and lacewings. In greenhouses, hang yellow sticky cards or introduce biological-control *Aphidoletes aphidomyza* and *Aphidius* spp. Spray outdoor plants, before heavy infestations develop, with bifenthrin, vegetable oils, insecticidal soaps, pyrethrum, or derris, or use a systemic insecticide, such as imidacloprid or pirimicarb. Pirimicarb is selective, leaving most other pests and beneficial insects unharmed.

Whiteflies

Plants affected Indoor and greenhouse plants, some vegetables and fruits.

Symptoms Leaves are covered with sticky honeydew (whitefly excrement) and a form of sooty mould. Small, white insects fly off the plants when they are disturbed.

Adult whiteflies

Cause Whiteflies, active, white-winged insects 2mm (¹⁄₁₆in) long; the immature, scale-like nymphs, which are immobile, whitish-green (or black if parasitized), flat, and oval are also found here. Several species occur, the most widespread of which is the glasshouse whitefly

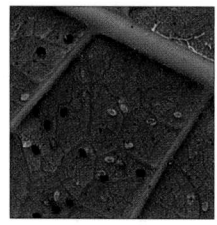

Whitefly nymphs

(*Trialeurodes vaporariorum*). In the open, brassicas are attacked by the cabbage whitefly (*Aleyrodes proletella*).

Control The parasitic wasp *Encarsia formosa* provides effective biological control in greenhouses from mid-spring to mid-autumn, if introduced early. Both greenhouse and garden whiteflies may be sprayed with bifenthrin, pyrethrum, insecticidal soaps, or vegetable oils on three or four occasions at five-day intervals; pesticide-resistant strains of greenhouse whitefly do, however, occur.

Mealybugs

Plants affected Indoor and greenhouse plants, cacti and other succulents, vines (*Vitis*), some tender fruits, *Citrus*.

Symptoms A fluffy, white substance appears in leaf and stem axils. Plants may be sticky with honeydew (excrement) and black-

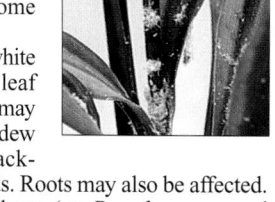

ened with sooty moulds. Roots may also be affected.

Cause Various mealybugs (eg *Pseudococcus* and *Planococcus* spp.); soft-bodied, greyish-white, wingless insects up to 5mm (¼in) long, often with white, waxy filaments trailing from their bodies. Root damage is caused by root mealybugs.

Control During the warmer months introduce the ladybird *Cryptolaemus montrouzieri* for biological control. If this fails, spray with imidacloprid + methiocarb, vegetable oils, or an insecticidal soap on several occasions at intervals of two weeks.

White blister

Plants affected The Cruciferae family, commonly brassicas, honesty (*Lunaria*), *Arabis*, and *Alyssum*.

Symptoms White, glistening, fungal spore clusters, often grouped in concentric circles, develop on lower leaf surfaces. Severely affected foliage, and the heads

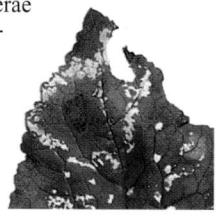

of brassicas, may also be distorted by this condition.

Cause The fungus *Albugo candida*, which is most troublesome on closely spaced plants.

Control Remove and burn affected leaves. Rotate plantings, and increase spacing. Cultivars such as Brussels sprout 'Saxon' resist white blister well.

Powdery mildew

Plants affected Most outdoor and many indoor plants.

Symptoms A fungal growth, usually white and powdery, appears on the leaves; on rhododendrons it is buff-coloured and felty. Usually found on the upper surface, it may

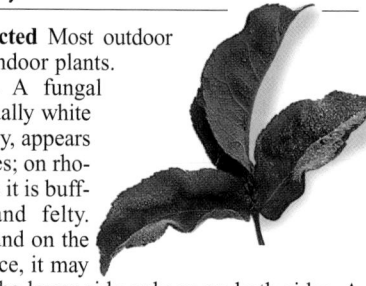

appear on the lower side only or on both sides. A purple or yellow discolouration may develop. Leaves yellow and fall early. Flowers and fruits (see p.658) are also affected.

Cause Various fungi, including species of *Sphaerotheca*, *Oidium*, and *Uncinula*, which thrive on plants growing in dry soil. Some have restricted host ranges; others attack widely. Spores are spread by wind and rain splash, and the fungus may overwinter on host-plant surfaces.

Control Avoid growing susceptible plants on dry sites, and water and mulch as necessary. Remove affected areas immediately. If the problem persists, spray with sulphur, myclobutanil, or bupirimate + triforine; avoid wetting foliage.

Downy mildew

Plants affected Perennials, annuals, bulbous plants, vegetables, some fruits, including brassicas, stocks (*Matthiola*), lettuces, and seedlings.

Symptoms A fluffy or mealy, white fungal growth develops on the lower surface of the foli-

age, while the upper surface is blotched either yellow or brown; the older leaves are usually the most seriously affected. Growth is stunted and the plant is prone to secondary infections such as grey mould (*Botrytis*) (see below).

Cause Species of *Peronospora* and *Bremia* fungi, which are encouraged by humid conditions.

Control Sow seeds thinly and do not overcrowd plants. Improve ventilation, air circulation, and drainage; avoid overhead watering. Remove affected leaves.

Grey mould (*Botrytis*)

Plants affected Trees, shrubs, perennials, annuals, bulbous plants, vegetables, fruits, and most indoor plants. Soft-leaved plants are particularly vulnerable to this condition.

Symptoms A fuzzy, grey fungal growth appears on the foliage, causing it to discolour and rapidly deteriorate; the infection may then spread into the main body of the plant. See pp.653, 656, and 658 for other symptoms.

Cause and control See p.653 for details.

Red spider mite

Plants affected Trees, shrubs, perennials, annuals, bulbous plants, cacti and other succulents, vegetables, and fruits. Beans, cucumbers, melons, apples, and plums are particularly susceptible.

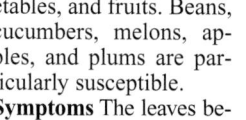
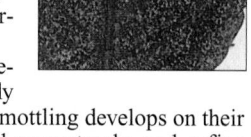

Symptoms The leaves become dull and increasingly yellowed as a fine, pale mottling develops on their upper surface. They fall prematurely, and a fine silk webbing may cover the plant.

Cause Red spider mites, eight-legged animals less than 1mm (¹⁄₁₆in) long. They are yellowish-green with black markings, but may be orange-red in autumn. There are several species, the most common of which is the two-spotted, or glasshouse, red spider mite (*Tetranychus urticae*); this affects both garden and indoor plants in summer.

Control The rapid reproduction of the mites and the existence of pesticide-resistant strains makes control difficult. Discourage those in greenhouses by spraying water underneath leaves and maintaining high humidity; the predatory mite *Phytoseiulus persimilis* provides an effective biological control of *T. urticae* if introduced before heavy infestations develop. Non-resistant red spider mites may be controlled with sprays of bifenthrin, vegetable oils, or insecticidal soaps on three or four occasions at five-day intervals.

Thrips

Plants affected Shrubs, perennials, annuals, bulbous plants, vegetables, fruits, and indoor and greenhouse plants.
Symptoms A silver-white discolouration with tiny black dots appears on the upper leaf surface. See p.656 for other symptoms.
Cause Various species of thrips or thunderfly (eg *Thrips simplex*, *T. tabaci*, *Frankliniella occidentalis*, and *Kakothrips pisivorus*), which are brownish-black insects with narrow bodies up to 2mm (1/16in) long, sometimes crossed with pale bands. The immature nymphs are a pale yellow-orange but otherwise resemble the adults. Both adults and nymphs feed on the upper surface of the leaf. They thrive in hot, dry conditions.
Control Water plants regularly and reduce the temperature in greenhouses with shading and ventilation. Before heavy infestations arise, use biological-control *Amblyseius degenerans* against western flower thrips (*Frankliniella occidentalis*). Spray all thrips with pyrethrum or bifenthrin as soon as damage is seen.

Silver leaf

Plants affected Broadleaved trees and shrubs, especially those in the Rosaceae family; plums and cherries are most commonly attacked.
Symptoms A silver-grey discolouration appears on the foliage, often starting on a single branch and then gradually spreading throughout the crown. The branches subsequently die back and infected limbs have a central dark stain.
Cause The fungus *Chondrostereum purpureum*, which is also commonly found on felled logs and dead branches. The spores are produced from small, leathery brackets attached to the bark. The upper surface of the bracket is pale grey and slightly hairy, the lower surface purple and smooth. Spores may infect fresh wounds (less than a month old). There is no risk of infection from the silvered foliage.
Control Avoid injury to plants. Prune susceptible trees in summer, when infection is less likely to occur. Remove affected limbs to 15cm (6in) past the stained wood.

Leafhoppers

Spots on leaves

Plants affected Trees, shrubs, perennials, annuals, vegetables, and fruits. Rhododendrons, roses, pelargoniums, primulas, and tomatoes are usually the most vulnerable.
Symptoms A coarse, pale spotting appears on the upper leaf surface, except on rhododendrons where damage is restricted to the spreading of rhododendron bud blast (see p.656).
Cause Leafhoppers, such as the rose leafhopper (*Edwardsiana rosae*) and the glasshouse leafhopper

Adult leafhoppers

(*Hauptidia maroccana*), green or yellow insects 2–3mm (1/16–1/8in) long that leap from the plant when disturbed. Their bodies are widest just behind the head and taper back. The rhododendron leafhopper (*Graphocephala fennahi*) is turquoise-green and orange, and 6mm (1/4in) in length. The creamy-white, immature nymphs are less active.
Control Spray beneath the leaves with bifenthrin or pyrethrum when leafhopper activity is seen – adults readily jumping off leaves when disturbed.

Pear and cherry slugworm

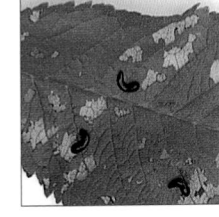

Plants affected Pear and plum trees; also fruiting and ornamental cherries (*Prunus*), *Chaenomeles*, hawthorns (*Crataegus*).
Symptoms The leaves develop whitish-brown patches where the larvae graze away the surface.
Cause The pear and cherry slugworm (*Caliroa cerasi*), which is the larval stage of a small black-bodied sawfly. The larvae are up to 10mm (1/2in) long and are broadest at the head end. They are covered by a black slimy substance and consequently resemble slugs. They feed mainly on the upper leaf surface. Two or three generations occur between early summer and early autumn.
Control Spray thoroughly with pyrethrum, derris or bifenthrin as soon as the larvae are first seen.

Suckers (psyllids)

Plants affected Bay (*Laurus nobilis*), box (*Buxus*), and pears.
Symptoms The leaf margins of bay are yellowed, thickened, and curled; box leaves are stunted; pear leaves are sticky with honeydew (excrement) and blackened with sooty mould. Damage occurs throughout the summer. See p.651 for other symptoms.
Cause Suckers (eg the bay sucker, *Trioza alacris*, the box sucker, *Psylla buxi*, and the pear sucker, *Psylla pyricola*), the flattened and immature nymphs of small, aphid-like, winged insects. The nymphs are 2mm (1/16in) long, and generally grey or green in colouring.
Control Prune out and burn affected shoots immediately. Spray the plant thoroughly with pyrethrum or bifenthrin, either in spring or when the damage is first seen.

Leaf and bud eelworms

Dark patches

Plants affected Annuals and many herbaceous perennials. Most commonly attacked are penstemons, chrysanthemums, and *Anemone* x *hybrida*.
Symptoms Brownish-black patches appear on leaves as islands or wedges between the larger veins.

Cause Microscopic nematodes (*Aphelenchoides* spp.) that feed in large numbers inside infested leaves.
Control Burn all affected leaves or destroy the whole plant as soon as the infestation is noticed. For chrysanthemums, dip the dormant stools in clean water held at 46°C (115°F) for five minutes to obtain clean cuttings. There is no effective pesticide available to amateur gardeners.

Wedges between veins

Leaf miners

Linear blotching

Plants affected Trees, shrubs, perennials, and vegetables, especially lilacs (*Syringa*), hollies (*Ilex*), apples, cherries, chrysanthemums, and celery.
Symptoms White or brown areas appear within the leaf, often of characteristic shape for the particular leaf miner, eg linear, circular, or irregular.
Cause Larvae of various flies, eg the celery leaf miner (*Euleia heraclei*) and the chrysanthemum leaf miner (*Chromatomyia syngenesiae*); moths, for example the apple leaf mining moth (*Lyonetia clerkella*); beetles, such as the beech leaf mining weevil (*Rhynchaenus fagi*); and sawflies, eg the birch leaf mining sawfly (*Fenusa pusilla*).

Irregular discolouration

Control Remove and destroy affected leaves if the plant is lightly infested. None of the pesticides currently available to amateur gardeners is likely to control leaf miners.

Webber moth caterpillars

Plants affected Many trees, shrubs, perennials, and annuals, but most particularly fruit trees, willows (*Salix*), *Euonymus*, junipers (*Juniperus*), hawthorns (*Crataegus*), and cotoneasters.
Symptoms Shoots of the affected plant are defoliated, and the feeding area is completely covered with a dense, greyish-white, silk webbing.
Cause The caterpillars of various moths, such as the brown tail moth (*Euproctis chrysorrhoea*), the lackey moth (*Malacosoma neustria*), small ermine moths (*Yponomeuta* spp.), the hawthorn webber moth (*Scythropia crataegella*), and the juniper webber moth (*Dichomeris marginella*). The caterpillars of the last two species are no more than 2cm (3/4in) long; the other caterpillars are up to 5cm (2in) long and often have hairy bodies.
Control Remove small infestations by careful pruning. If the problem is very serious, spray the plants with biological-control *Bacillus thuringiensis*, pyrethrum, or bifenthrin.

Tortrix moth caterpillars

Plants affected Trees (ornamental and fruit), shrubs, perennials, annuals, and bulbous plants.

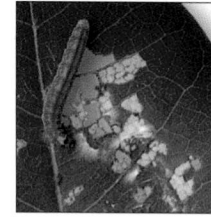

Symptoms Two leaves may be bound together with fine, silky threads, or one leaf may be either similarly attached to a fruit or folded over on itself. Brown, dry, skeletal patches appear on the leaves.

Cause The caterpillars of tortrix moths, such as *Cacoecimorpha pronubana*, which graze away the inner surfaces of leaves. They are up to 2cm (¾in) long, and are generally dark green with brown heads. The caterpillars wriggle backwards rapidly when they are disturbed.

Control Squeeze bound-up leaves to crush the caterpillars or pupae. Pheromone traps are available for use against *C. pronubana*; these trap the males and reduce the likelihood of the females mating successfully. If the problem is serious, spray the affected plants very thoroughly with *Bacillus thuringiensis*, bifenthrin, or pyrethrum.

Scale insects

Plants affected Trees, shrubs, cacti and other succulents, fruits, and indoor and greenhouse plants.

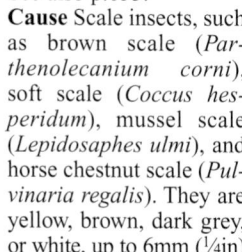
Soft scale

Symptoms Foliage may be sticky with honeydew (excrement) and blackened with sooty moulds. Plant growth may be slow. White, egg-containing deposits may also appear. See also p.653.

Cause Scale insects, such as brown scale (*Parthenolecanium corni*), soft scale (*Coccus hesperidum*), mussel scale (*Lepidosaphes ulmi*), and horse chestnut scale (*Pulvinaria regalis*). They are yellow, brown, dark grey, or white, up to 6mm (¼in)

Egg deposits

long, flat or raised, and circular, pear-shaped, or oval. They are found on lower leaf surfaces and stems.

Control Spray deciduous fruit trees with a tar oil wash in winter. Use biological-control *Metaphycus helvolus* on soft scale insects in greenhouses. Other plants may be sprayed with vegetable oils or fatty acids when the newly hatched scale nymphs are present – throughout the year on greenhouse plants, early to midsummer outside.

Bacterial leaf spots and blotches

Plants affected Trees, shrubs, roses, perennials, annuals, bulbous plants, vegetables, fruits, and indoor plants.

Symptoms Various spots or patches develop. They may appear water-soaked, and are often angular with a yellow edge or halo ("halo blight"). Black spots appear on delphinium leaves. See also "Fungal leaf spots", right.

Cause *Pseudomonas* bacteria, spread by insects, rain splash, or wind-borne seeds.

Control Avoid wetting the foliage. Remove any leaves affected by black spot. Spray plums and cherries with copper oxychloride or Bordeaux mixture.

Black spot on delphinium

Rusts

Plants affected Trees, shrubs, perennials, annuals, bulbous plants, vegetables, fruits, and indoor plants.

Symptoms Small, bright orange or brown patches of spores develop on the lower leaf surface, each corresponding to a yellow discoloration on the upper surface. Spores may appear in concentric rings or pustules, sometimes pale beige, eg those of chrysanthemum white rust. Winter spores, dark brown or black, are sometimes also produced. The leaves may also fall early. See p.653 for other symptoms.

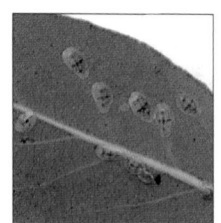
Small, brown spores

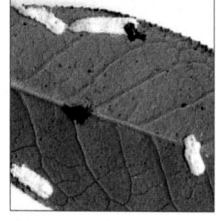
Pale discolouration

Cause Fungi, most often species of *Puccinia* and *Melampsora*, which are encouraged by high humidity. The spores are spread by rain splash and air currents. A few rusts are systemic.

Control Remove all affected areas. Improve air circulation by increasing ventilation and plant spacing wherever possible, and try to discourage the development of lush growth. Affected plants should be thoroughly sprayed with a fungicide containing penconazole or myclobutanil.

Rust on bluebell leaf

Corky scab

Plants affected Cacti and other succulents, especially *Opuntia* and *Epiphyllum*.

Symptoms Corky or brown, irregularly shaped spots appear. These areas later become sunken.

Cause Either extremely high humidity or excessively high light levels.

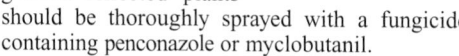

Control Take measures to improve the growing conditions of the plant. In extreme cases, however, the plant must be discarded, after having been used for propagation purposes, if desired.

Shothole

Plants affected Edible and ornamental cherries (*Prunus*), peaches, nectarines, plums, gages, and *Prunus laurocerasus*; also other trees, shrubs, and woody perennials.

Symptoms Discoloured (usually brown) spots develop on the foliage; the dead leaf tissue then falls away, leaving holes. In severe cases large areas of leaf are lost.

Cause The fungus *Clasterosporium carpophilum* is usually responsible for this condition, but occasionally other fungi or bacteria are involved. Plants that are lacking in vigour are most likely to show symptoms of shothole. The bacterium *Pseudomonas syringae* pvar. *morsprunorum* also causes shothole.

Control Try to improve the general growing conditions and the overall health of the affected plant. In *Prunus*, spray with a copper-based fungicide.

Fungal leaf spots

Plants affected Trees, shrubs, perennials, annuals, bulbous plants, vegetables, fruits, and many indoor plants.

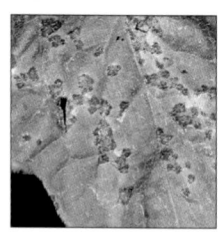

Symptoms Discrete, concentrically zoned spots appear on the leaves; close inspection may reveal pinprick-sized, fungal, fruiting bodies. Spots are often brown or slate grey. In severe cases they coalesce. Early leaf fall may occur, but in some instances there is little damage or effect on overall plant vigour.

Cause A wide range of fungi.

Control Remove all affected parts of the plant, and rake up and burn any leaves that have already fallen. Spray roses with myclobutanil, penconazole, bupirimate + triforine, flutriafol, or mancozeb. There is no effective fungicide available to amateur gardeners for most other leaf spots.

Tomato leaf mould

Plants affected Almost exclusively greenhouse tomatoes.

Symptoms Purplish-grey, fuzzy, fungal patches develop on the lower leaf surface, each corresponding to a yellow discolouration on the upper surface. Leaves turn brown, wither, and die but do not fall. The lower leaves are affected first.

Cause The fungus *Fulvia fulva* (syn. *Cladosporium fulvum*), which thrives in warm, humid environments. The spores are spread by insects, tools, and handling, or on air currents. They overwinter on plant debris and on greenhouse structures.

Control Remove affected leaves, and improve ventilation and air circulation. Consider growing cultivars bred for resistance to the disease, eg 'Shirley', 'Grenadier', and 'M.M. Super'. Spray with carbendazim; it is not worth spraying if the disease occurs towards the end of the season.

Chocolate spot

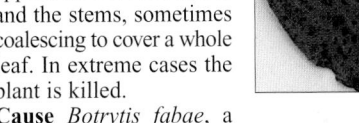

Plants affected Broad beans.
Symptoms Chocolate-coloured spots or streaks appear on both the leaves and the stems, sometimes coalescing to cover a whole leaf. In extreme cases the plant is killed.
Cause *Botrytis fabae*, a fungus that thrives in wet spring weather. Plants growing in very acid soils are susceptible, as are those with soft, lush growth. Winter-sown crops are most severely affected by this condition.
Control Sow seed thinly, first dressing the soil with sulphate of potash, and avoid excessive use of nitrogen fertilizers. Remove and burn affected plants at the end of the harvest. Spray with carbendazim.

Scab

Plants affected Pears, *Citrus*, loquats, pyracanthas, and *Malus*, including both ornamental and fruiting species.

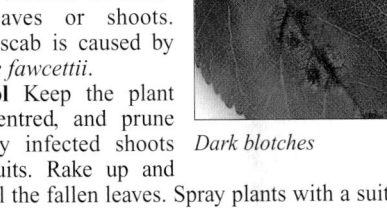

Brown patches

Symptoms Dark and greenish-brown patches, scabby and sometimes blistered, develop on the foliage; any affected leaves may fall early. See p.658 for other symptoms.
Cause The fungi *Venturia inaequalis*, *V. pirina*, *Spilocaea pyracanthae*, and *S. eriobotryae*, which thrive in damp weather. They may overwinter on infected leaves or shoots. Citrus scab is caused by *Elsinoe fawcettii*.
Control Keep the plant open-centred, and prune out any infected shoots and fruits. Rake up and

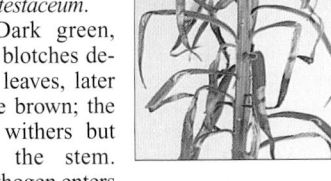

Dark blotches

burn all the fallen leaves. Spray plants with a suitable fungicide, such as mancozeb, myclobutanil, or carbendazim. Do not store any affected fruits.

Lily disease

Plants affected Lilies (*Lilium*), especially *L. candidum* and *L. x testaceum*.
Symptoms Dark green, water-soaked blotches develop on the leaves, later turning a pale brown; the foliage then withers but remains on the stem. Where the pathogen enters a leaf axil the stem may rot. Black sclerotia (fungal resting bodies) may form on dead tissues.
Cause The fungus *Botrytis elliptica*, which is encouraged by wet weather. Spores produced on the leaf lesions (or, in spring, from the sclerotia) are spread by rain splash and wind.
Control Grow on a well-drained site; clear away affected debris. There is no chemical treatment available for lily disease.

Viruses

Plants affected All plants.
Symptoms Leaves are undersized, distorted, or grouped in rosettes. Patterns of yellow discolouration (mosaics, ringspots, mottles) are common. See pp.656 and 659 for other symptoms.

Yellowish streaks

Ringspots

Cause A large number of viruses, some with very wide host ranges. Submicroscopic virus particles in the sap of infected plants may be transmitted to healthy tissues by sap-feeding pests such as aphids (p.646), by nematodes or other soil-borne pests, through handling, or on pruning or propagating tools; some are seed-borne.
Control Buy certified (virus-free) plants where possible. Keep potential carriers, eg aphids (see p.646), under control, and make sure that the site is free of weeds as these may harbour viruses. Remove and burn affected plants as soon as possible; always handle suspect plants after those which appear healthy, and do not propagate from them. Always use a new site for any replacement plants.

Tulip fire

Plants affected Tulips.
Symptoms The leaves are covered with pale brown, spore-producing blotches. Both leaves and shoots are deformed and stunted, and later become covered in dense, grey, spore-bearing, fungal growths, and black sclerotia (fun-

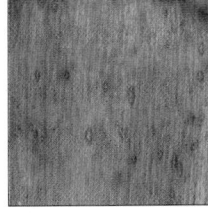

gal resting bodies). The bulbs develop sunken, brown lesions and small, black sclerotia. Plants may fail to mature or flower buds fail to open. See p.656 for other symptoms.
Cause The fungus *Botrytis tulipae*, which flourishes particularly in wet seasons; the spores are spread by wind and rain. The sclerotia persist on infected bulbs or in the soil, later germinating when tulips are planted again in the same area.
Control Remove and burn affected leaves and shoots (or preferably the whole plant) immediately. Plant from early winter onwards. Lift and dry bulbs at the end of the season, discarding any with sclerotia, and dust the remaining bulbs with sulphur. Wait at least two years before replanting the site with tulips; alternatively, change the soil.

Clubroot

Plants affected The family Cruciferae, especially brassicas (eg cabbages, Brussels sprouts, swedes), and radishes. Also some ornamentals, such as stocks (*Matthiola*), candytufts (*Iberis*), and wallflowers (*Erysimum*).

Symptoms Plants are stunted and discoloured; foliage wilts in hot weather. See also p.660.
Cause The slime mould *Plasmodiophora brassicae*, which thrives in poorly drained, acid soils, and on manure and plant debris. It is easily spread on boots and tools, and the spores remain viable for 20 years or more. Susceptible weeds (eg charlock and shepherd's purse) may be a source of infection.
Control Remove and burn affected plants. Keep the area free of weeds, where feasible improve drainage, and lime the soil. Choose resistant cultivars where available, such as calabrese 'Trixie', kale 'Tall Green Curled', swede 'Marian', and Chinese cabbage 'Harmony'. Raise new plants in pots of soil-based compost so that their roots are well developed when planted out. Proprietary chemical dips may be used at the planting stage.

Tomato/potato blight

Plants affected Tomatoes (in the open and occasionally under cover), potatoes.

Symptoms Brown discolouration develops on the leaf tips and edges; in damp conditions these may often be ringed with a white, fungal growth.
The leaf tissue is killed, and where the patches coalesce the whole of the affected leaflet may eventually die. See pp.658 and 662 for other symptoms.
Cause The fungus *Phytophthora infestans*, which thrives in warm, moist conditions. Spores produced on tomato and potato foliage, and on potato haulms, are carried by wind and rain; they may be washed into the soil to infect potato tubers.
Control Avoid overhead watering. Grow tomatoes under glass rather than in the open. Earth up potatoes deeply to provide a barrier for the tubers against falling spores, and choose resistant cultivars, for example 'Kondor', 'Romano', 'Cara', and 'Wilja'. Protect both tomatoes and potatoes by spraying thoroughly with mancozeb, Bordeaux mixture, or a suitable copper-based fungicide. In wet seasons spray plants before the blight appears; spray tomatoes as soon as they have been stopped.

Fireblight

Plants affected Members of the family Rosaceae that bear pome fruits, mainly pears, apples, some *Sorbus*, cotoneasters, and hawthorns (*Crataegus*).

Symptoms The leaves generally turn blackish-brown, shrivel and die, and they remain clinging to the stem; those of some *Sorbus* and hawthorns may turn yellow and fall. Oozing cankers appear on the branches, and the whole tree may eventually die. See p.665 for other symptoms.
Cause The bacterium *Erwinia amylovora*, which is produced from the cankers, attacks via the blossom. It is carried from plant to plant by wind, rain splash, insects, and pollen.
Control Remove the affected plants or prune out affected areas to at least 60cm (24in) past the damaged area; remember to dip the saw in disinfectant before using it on another tree. Fireblight is no longer a notifiable disease.

Pansy sickness

Plants affected Violets (*Viola*) and pansies (*Viola* x *wittrockiana*).
Symptoms The petals and leaves discolour and wilt as the stem rots at ground level. Roots are also susceptible to attack, and may eventually become quite loose in the ground.
Cause Microscopic fungi (primarily *Pythium violae* and *Aphanomyces euteiches*), which are soil-borne and build up in soils where pansies and violets have been grown for several years. Resting spores are produced and the soil may remain infected for several years.
Control Dig up and burn any affected plants as soon as the problem is noticed. Grow susceptible plants on a new site each year.

Primula brown core

Plants affected Primulas.
Symptoms Leaves yellow, wilt, and die, and the plant becomes loose in the ground as the roots rot back from the tips.
Cause and control See p.661.

Insecticide/fungicide damage

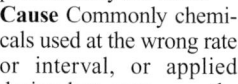
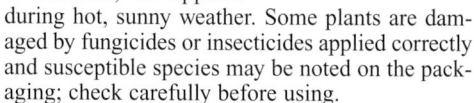

Plants affected Some indoor and garden plants.
Symptoms Discrete spots or patches, often bleached or scorched, appear on leaves, which may fall; the plant usually survives.
Cause Commonly chemicals used at the wrong rate or interval, or applied during hot, sunny weather. Some plants are damaged by fungicides or insecticides applied correctly and susceptible species may be noted on the packaging; check carefully before using.
Control Use proprietary chemicals for the specific uses and plants indicated on the product label and always follow the manufacturers' instructions.

Contact weedkiller damage

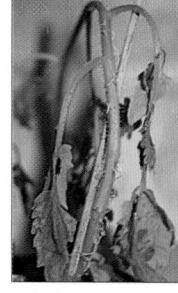

Plants affected All plants.
Symptoms Pale, bleached spots appear on the foliage, sometimes turning brown, and small bumps on stems. Bulbs exposed to contact weedkillers before their foliage has died down show a very pale, almost white, leaf colour the following season. In severe cases, vigour may be reduced and the plant may even die. Usually plants grow out of the symptoms.
Cause Spray drift due to windy conditions, or to careless application. Poorly cleaned sprayers and watering cans may also lead to contamination.
Control Follow the manufacturers' instructions. Use a dribble bar applicator or watering can in preference to a sprayer, and keep separate equipment for use with weedkillers only.

Drought

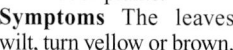

Plants affected All plants, especially those that are young and container-grown, or in light, sandy soils.
Symptoms Autumn colour develops early and defoliation may occur, sometimes followed by die-back. Plants wilt and growth is stunted. See pp.657 and 664 for other symptoms.
Cause Prolonged or repeated water shortage caused by dry soil, excessive water loss from leaves of plants on exposed sites, injured or restricted roots, or soil compaction. Plants in small containers are vulnerable in hot weather, since peat-based composts allowed to dehydrate are hard to re-wet.
Control Water plants regularly, especially those in hot positions. Mulch when soil is thoroughly moist, to improve moisture retention. It is easier to prevent drought than to treat it; plants, however, are less likely to be damaged by short, sudden droughts than prolonged ones.

High temperatures and scorch

Plants affected In particular plants with fleshy leaves or flowers, those near glass, and seedlings; also trees, shrubs, perennials, annuals, bulbous plants, vegetables, fruits, and indoor plants.
Symptoms The leaves wilt, turn yellow or brown, become dry and crisp, and may die; the tips and margins are often affected first. In extreme cases the stems die back. Scorching produces brown patches on the upper or exposed parts of the plant; foliage close to glass is very susceptible. Affected leaves may shrivel completely. Scorched petals turn brown and become dry and crisp. Roses may show "balling" (as the outer petals dry up they enclose the bud). Fruits are also affected (see p.658).
Cause Very high or fluctuating temperatures in a closed environment (eg a greenhouse); scorching is caused by bright, but not necessarily hot, sunlight. Scorch problems are increased by moisture on the leaves and fruit, and by faults in the glass near plants, both of which magnify the sun's rays. Apple fruits may discolour if picked too early or stored with insufficient ventilation.
Control Where possible shade greenhouses, provide adequate ventilation to keep temperatures down, and move plants away from any faults there may be in the glass. Avoid overhead watering and spraying in sunny weather. Harvest only ripe apples and store them under suitable conditions.

Low temperatures

Plants affected Trees, shrubs, perennials, annuals, bulbous plants, vegetables, fruits, indoor plants; seedlings and young plants are most vulnerable.
Symptoms Leaves, especially those of seedlings, are sometimes bleached, and brown, dry patches develop; evergreen foliage may turn completely brown. Frost injury results in puckered, withered, or discoloured (often blackened) leaves, and a lifting of the lower leaf surface, which gives the foliage a silvered appearance. Rotten patches, brown and dry or dark and soft, develop on the petals, especially on exposed flowerheads. Frost injury may leave petals withered or discoloured and the whole flower may be killed. See p.653 for other symptoms.
Cause Low temperatures or occasionally great fluctuations in temperature. Plants in exposed positions or frost pockets are likely to be affected.
Control Check the plant's suitability for the site. Provide winter protection for young or tender plants, and those grown in exposed positions.

Nitrogen deficiency

Plants affected Most outdoor and indoor plants.
Symptoms Pale green leaves are borne, and these sometimes develop either yellow or pink tints. Overall growth is reduced and the whole plant may eventually become slightly spindly.
Cause Growing plants either in poor, light soils or in restricted surroundings such as hanging baskets, windowboxes, or other types of container.
Control Use green manures on affected areas, or apply a high-nitrogen fertilizer, eg sulphate of ammonia, nitrochalk, or manure.

Potassium deficiency

Plants affected Edible and ornamental fruiting plants, mainly currants, apples, and pears.
Symptoms The foliage turns blue, yellow, or purple, with a brown discolouration either in blotches or on the leaf tips or margins. Some leaves may roll inwards; they are fairly soft and therefore prone to attack by pathogens. Flowering, fruiting, and general growth of the whole plant may be reduced.
Cause Growing plants in soils either with a light texture or with a high chalk or peat content.
Control Improve the soil texture. Dress with sulphate of potash or a high-potash fertilizer.

Phosphate deficiency

Plants affected Potentially all plants may suffer; but this particular deficiency is unlikely to occur in most gardens.
Symptoms Plant growth is slow and the young foliage may appear dull or yellowed.
Cause The leaching out of phosphates in acid soils and areas of high rainfall. Plants growing in either heavy clay soils or deep peat soils, as well as those overlying iron pans, are the most likely to be at risk from this condition.
Control Apply bone meal or superphosphate.

Manganese/iron deficiency

Plants affected Trees, shrubs, perennials, annuals, bulbous plants, vegetables, fruits, and indoor plants. Acid-loving plants growing in alkaline soils are often affected.
Symptoms A yellowing or browning starts at the leaf margins and extends between the veins. The overall leaf colour may also be rather yellow.
Cause The cultivation of plants in unsuitable soils or composts; acid-loving plants, in particular, are unable to absorb adequate trace elements from alkaline soils. Regular watering with very hard water, buried debris (e.g builders' rubble), and rain run-off from mortar in walls are all possible causes of a locally raised soil pH.
Control Choose plants that are compatible with the soil type and clear the area of any builders' debris. Use rainwater, not tap water, for susceptible plants. Acidify the soil before or after planting, and apply acid mulches. Apply a chelated or fritted form of trace elements and sequestered iron.

Magnesium deficiency

Plants affected Trees, shrubs, perennials, annuals, bulbous plants, vegetables, and fruits; also many indoor plants. Tomatoes, roses, and chrysanthemums are most often affected.
Symptoms Distinct areas of discolouration, usually yellow but occasionally red or brown, develop between the leaf veins (interveinal chlorosis), and the affected leaves may fall early.
Cause Acid soils; heavy watering or rainfall, both of which leach out magnesium; or high potash levels, which make it unavailable. Plants fed on high-potash fertilizers to encourage flowering or fruiting (eg tomatoes) are susceptible.
Control Treat plants and/or soil with Epsom salts in autumn; either add them neat to the soil at a rate of 25g/sq m (1oz/10sq ft), or apply a foliar spray of 210g Epsom salts in 10 litres of water (7½oz in 2¼ gallons), adding a wetting agent such as soft soap.

Waterlogging

Plants affected Potentially all plants.
Symptoms Leaves turn yellow and the plants wilt.
Cause Too much water in the growing medium, owing to poor structure or drainage, or overwatering.
Control Improve soil structure and drainage.
See also pp.660 and 664.

See also "Irregular water supply", "Oedema", "Peach leaf curl", "Hormone weedkiller damage", "Phytoplasmas", all below; "Azalea gall", p.652; "Smuts", p.652; "*Verticillium* wilt", p.653; "*Fusarium* wilt", p.654; "*Phytophthora* root rots", p.654; "Foot and root rots", p.654; "Etiolation", p.655; "Blossom wilt", p.656; "Carrot fly", p.660; "Narcissus eelworm", p.663; "Iris rhizome rot", p.663; "Onion fly", p.663; "Blackleg on potatoes", p.664; "*Seiridium* canker", p.664; "Clematis wilt", p.665; and "Anthracnose", p.666.

Distorted leaves

Irregular water supply

Plants affected Potentially all garden plants, especially those grown in containers.
Symptoms Leaves and flowers become puckered and distorted or are undersized. See pp.653 and 659 for other symptoms.
Cause An irregular supply of water, leading to irregular patterns of growth and consequent distortion in the upper parts of the plant.
Control Provide a regular and adequate supply of water for plants, especially in hot or windy weather, and pay particular attention to any plants that are growing in containers. Apply a regular mulch around the plants, where appropriate, since this will do most to conserve the moisture in the soil and prevent problems from occurring.

Oedema

Plants affected Potentially all plants, but particularly pelargoniums, camellias, *Eucalyptus*, and succulents.
Symptoms Raised, warty patches appear on the foliage. These are initially of a similar colour to that of the rest of the leaf but later turn brown.
Cause Excessively high moisture levels in either the air or the growing medium, which give the plant cells an unusually high water content. As a result of this, small groups of cells swell, forming the outgrowths, and later burst, leaving brown patches on the leaves.
Control Improve air circulation around the plants by increasing ventilation, and by attending carefully to plant spacing. Decrease the amount of watering and wherever possible try to improve drainage. Leaves affected with this condition should not be picked off at any time.

Peach leaf curl

Plants affected Peaches, nectarines, almonds, and closely related ornamental species (*Prunus*).
Symptoms Leaves become distorted, blistered, and sometimes swollen, later turning a deep red; a white, fungal growth then develops on the leaf surfaces. The foliage falls, but a second flush of healthy leaves will be produced afterwards.
Cause The fungus *Taphrina deformans*, which is encouraged by cool, wet conditions. Spores are carried by wind or rain to shoots, bud scales, and cracks in the bark, where they overwinter.
Control Pick off affected leaves. Shelter plants so that spores cannot land; an open-sided, wooden frame covered with heavy-duty plastic is ideal. To prevent infection, spray leaves with Bordeaux mixture or a suitable copper-based fungicide in mid- to late winter, repeating the application 14 days later.

Hormone weedkiller damage

Plants affected Broadleaved plants, mainly roses, tomatoes, grapes, and conifers.
Symptoms Leaves are small, narrow, often thickened, and with prominent veins. They may be cup-shaped and extremely distorted. The petioles become twisted. Small bumps may appear on stems. See p.659 for other symptoms.
Cause Contamination by a growth regulator or hormone-type weedkiller, often from a considerable distance; minute quantities may cause extensive damage. Common sources of trouble are spray drift, the use of contaminated sprayers or watering cans, and water from polluted butts.

Distorted leaves

Stunted leaf buds

Control Always apply weedkillers according to manufacturers' instructions, placing protective barriers around adjacent garden plants to prevent spray drift. Keep one sprayer or watering can for use with weedkillers only. Store weedkillers away from compost, fertilizers, and plants. Affected plants usually grow out of the symptoms.
See also "Selective weedkillers". p.671.

Aphids

Plants affected Trees, shrubs, climbing plants, perennials, annuals, bulbous plants, vegetables, and fruits.
Symptoms Leaves are stunted and distorted.
Cause and control See p.646 for details.

Suckers (psyllids)

Plants affected Bay (*Laurus nobilis*), box (*Buxus*), and pears.
Symptoms The leaf margins of bay are yellowed, thickened, and curled; box has stunted stems and cupped, slightly distorted leaves. Damage occurs to box in spring, and to bay throughout the summer. See p.647 for symptoms on pears.
Cause and control See p.647 for details.

Phytoplasmas

Plants affected Trees, shrubs, perennials, annuals, bulbous plants, vegetables, fruits (especially strawberries), and indoor plants.
Symptoms Leaves may be undersized, distorted, and covered with patterns of discolouration. This condition on strawberry plants causes green petals on the flowers and produces young leaves that are small, irregularly shaped, and yellowed; in addition, the older foliage turns a distinctly red colour when flowering has ceased. See p.656 for other symptoms of phytoplasmas.

Cause Phytoplasmas, which are believed to be related to bacteria. Phytoplasmas are spread from plant to plant by leafhoppers (see p.647), which commonly pick up the infection from clover plants that are suffering from a condition known as phyllody disease.
Control Discard all affected plants, buy only certified fruit stock, and control pests that are potential carriers (leafhoppers), and weeds, which may harbour the disease.

Gall mites

Plants affected Trees and shrubs, including plums, pears, walnuts, vines (*Vitis*), maples (*Acer*), limes (*Tilia*), elms (*Ulmus*), hawthorns (*Crataegus*), rowan (*Sorbus aucuparia*), broom (*Cytisus*), beeches (*Fagus*), and blackcurrants.

Pale leaf blotches

Symptoms These vary according to the species of mite, and include: whitish-green or red pimples or spikes on foliage (maples, elms, limes, and plums); creamy-white or pink hairs on lower leaf surfaces (maples, limes, and beeches); raised, blistered areas on upper leaf surfaces, with pale hairs underneath (walnuts and vines); thick, curling leaf margins (beeches and hawthorns); pale leaf blotches, later turning brownish-black (rowans and pears); and stunted leaves (broom). Plant vigour is not affected.

Stunted leaves

Cause Microscopic gall mites, or eriophyid mites, secreting chemicals that induce abnormal growth.
Control Remove affected leaves and shoots if desired. There is no effective chemical control.

Gall midges

Plants affected Many garden plants especially violets (*Viola*), *Gleditsia*, and blackcurrants.
Symptoms Violet leaves thicken and fail to unfurl. *Gleditsia* leaflets swell and fold over to form pod-like galls. Blackcurrant shoot-tip leaves fail to expand normally and the shoot tips may eventually be killed.
Cause Whitish-orange maggots up to 2mm (¹⁄₁₆in) long that feed within the galled tissues; three or four generations may occur in a summer. These are the larvae of three species of midge: the violet gall midge (*Dasineura affinis*), the gleditsia gall midge (*D. gleditchiae*), and the blackcurrant gall midge (*D. tetensi*). The adults are tiny, greyish-brown flies with tubular bodies and two pairs of legs.
Control Remove and destroy affected leaves. The larvae are well protected inside the galls, so there is little prospect of being able to control them with the use of pesticides.

Gall wasps/cynipid wasps

Plants affected Oaks (*Quercus*) and roses.

Symptoms Symptoms on oaks include: flat discs on the lower surface of leaves in autumn; benign, spherical, woody growths (marble galls) or pithy oak apples on shoots in spring; yellowish-green or red bunches of currant galls on the catkins; and yellowish-green, sticky "knopper" galls on acorns. Species rose stems and hybrid rose suckers develop swellings covered in yellowish-pink, moss-like leaves ("bedeguar" galls or "Robin's pincushions") in late summer. Damage to these plants is minimal.
Cause The larvae of gall wasps, or cynipid wasps; they secrete chemicals as they feed.
Control No treatment is necessary.

Azalea gall

Plants affected Rhododendrons and azaleas, especially Indian azalea (*Rhododendron simsii*) grown as an indoor plant.
Symptoms Fleshy, pale green swellings (galls) develop on the foliage or flowers, later turning white.

Cause The fungus *Exobasidium vaccinii* var. *japonicum*, which is encouraged by high humidity. The spores are insect- or air-borne.
Control Remove and destroy the galls as soon as they are seen, before the fungus produces spores.

Whiptail (molybdenum deficiency)

Plants affected All brassicas, most particularly cauliflowers and sprouting broccoli.
Symptoms The leaves develop abnormally and appear narrow and ribbon-like; the heads of cauliflowers and sprouting broccoli are extremely small or, more commonly, do not develop at all.

Cause A deficiency of the trace element molybdenum, most often occurring in acid soils.
Control Increase the alkalinity of the soil by liming. Treat the soil with molybdenum before sowing or planting out susceptible crops.

Bulb scale mite

Plants affected *Hippeastrum* and daffodils, especially those grown indoors.
Symptoms Growth is stunted, the leaves become curved, and saw-toothed scarring appears along the leaf margins and flower stems.

Cause The microscopic, white bulb scale mite (*Steneotarsonemus laticeps*), which feeds in the neck region of the bulb.
Control Discard infested bulbs. Buy only those of good quality from reputable suppliers. There is no chemical control available to amateur gardeners.

Rose leaf-rolling sawfly

Plants affected Roses.

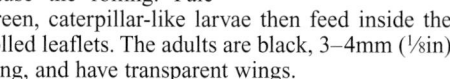

Symptoms Rose leaflets roll downwards at the edges to form tight tubes during late spring and early summer.
Cause Rose leaf-rolling sawfly (*Blennocampa phyllocolpa*). Females lay their eggs in the leaflets, secreting chemicals that cause the rolling. Pale green, caterpillar-like larvae then feed inside the rolled leaflets. The adults are black, 3–4mm (¹⁄₈in) long, and have transparent wings.
Control Pick off and burn rolled leaves. Alternatively, spray with bifenthrin against adult sawflies.

Smuts

Plants affected *Anemone*, *Trollius*, violets (*Viola*), and also winter aconites (*Eranthis hyemalis*).

Symptoms Round or elliptical swellings, often pale green or dirty white, develop on the leaves. They rupture, releasing powdery, black masses of spores; severely affected leaves then wither and die. Leaf stalks may show similar symptoms.
Cause Various fungi, eg *Urocystis* and *Ustilago*; the spores are spread by rain splash and air currents.
Control Burn affected plants; infection may recur even if the problem appears to have been controlled.

Eelworms

Plants affected Phlox and onion.
Symptoms Phlox are stunted, with narrow shoot-tip leaves and swollen stems; onion leaves and stems are swollen and soft. Plants may be killed by a heavy attack.
Cause Microscopic eelworms or nematodes (*Ditylenchus dipsaci*) feeding in the plant tissues.
Control Burn affected plants. Where infested onions have been growing, plant non-susceptible vegetables (lettuce and brassicas) for the next two years. Eelworm-free phlox can be obtained from root cuttings. There is no chemical control available for garden use.

See also "Powdery mildew", p.646; "Leaf and bud eelworms", p.647; "Scab", p.649; "Viruses", p.649; "Leafy gall", p.655; "Ink spot", p.663; "Narcissus eelworm", p.663; "Anthracnose", p.666.

Stem, branch, and leaf-bud problems
Stems discoloured or with pests visible

Low temperatures

Plants affected Trees, shrubs, perennials, annuals, bulbous plants, vegetables, fruits, and indoor plants. Soft-stemmed and young plants are most vulnerable.
Symptoms Brown, dry patches develop on the stems – especially those of *Acer*. Stems may blacken, wither, and crack or split, giving access to various organisms that cause die-back. The cracks become enlarged if moisture accumulates within them and then freezes, and this may lead to the death of the whole plant. See p.650 for other symptoms.
Cause Low temperatures or occasionally great fluctuations in temperature. Plants that are growing in exposed positions are the most likely to be affected by this problem.
Control Provide winter protection from frost and wind for young or tender plants, as well as for those growing in exposed positions.

Verticillium wilt

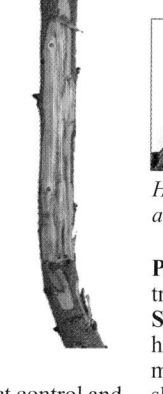

Plants affected Many garden and greenhouse plants.
Symptoms Staining of the vascular system of stems and roots, creating longitudinal brown stripes (revealed by removal of bark or outer stem). Woody plants deteriorate over several years, and may die.
Cause Several species of the fungus *Verticillium*, which may be present in the soil or in plant remains, or are introduced in new stock.
Control Remove any affected plants and soil in the immediate vicinity of the roots. Clean pruning tools thoroughly after use on diseased or suspect plants. Keep weeds under strict control and do not grow susceptible plants on the affected area.

Slime flux/wet wood

Plants affected Trees, shrubs, and woody perennials; clematis is particularly affected.
Symptoms The stem dies back and a pink, yellow, or off-white slime oozes from its base. This is often thick and may have an unpleasant smell.
Cause Injury to the stem (often through frost or wounding) when sap pressure is high, just before the leaves break. The sap released from the wound has a high sugar content and is colonized by various micro-organisms (in particular yeasts, bacteria, and fungi), which cause the thickening and discolouration.
Control Avoid injury to stems, particularly those of susceptible plants. Remove the affected stems immediately, cutting well back into healthy growth, below ground level if necessary. Given adequate food and moisture, the plant should subsequently produce more shoots.

Spur blight/cane blight

Plants affected Raspberries. Spur blight may also attack loganberries.
Symptoms With spur blight (shown here), purple areas develop around the nodes in late summer; these increase in size and turn a silvery-grey. Numerous tiny, black, spore-producing structures develop in the centre of each blotch. Buds may die, or may produce shoots that die. With cane blight, deterioration starts just above soil level as the fungus enters through points of injury and causes the base of the cane to develop dark discolouration and to become brittle. The foliage withers. Weakened plants are much more likely to be affected by this problem than well-maintained, strong specimens.
Cause The fungi *Didymella applanata* (spur blight) and *Leptosphaeria coniothyrium* (cane blight).
Control Maintain plants well. At the first sign of disease, cut out affected canes, going to below soil level for cane blight.

Scale insects

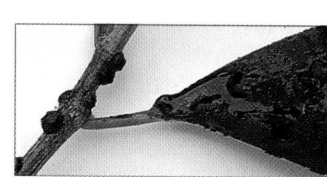

Hemispherical scale (above) and mussel scale (right)

Plants affected Indoor and greenhouse plants, trees, shrubs, fruits, and cacti and other succulents.
Symptoms The stems are sometimes sticky with honeydew (excrement) and blackened with sooty moulds. Heavily infested plants may also show slow growth. White, waxy deposits containing eggs also occasionally appear on the stems.
Cause and control See p.648 for details.

Rusts

Plants affected Trees, shrubs, perennials, annuals, bulbous plants, vegetables, fruits, and indoor plants; mints (*Mentha*), roses, raspberries, and blackberries are commonly affected.
Symptoms Pustules containing bright orange or dark brown spores develop either on, or apparently bursting from within, the stem. Some plants, eg junipers, develop gelatinous growths. In severe cases stems become extensively distorted and ruptured. Die-back may follow. See also p.648.
Cause A range of fungi encouraged by high humidity. Spores are spread by rain splash and air currents, and may overwinter on plant debris.
Control Remove affected areas and improve air circulation, increasing ventilation and plant spacing. Spray with a suitable fungicide, eg myclobutanil or bupirimate + triforine.

Grey mould (*Botrytis*)

Plants affected Trees, shrubs, perennials, annuals, bulbous plants, vegetables, fruits, and indoor plants. Soft-leaved plants are vulnerable.
Symptoms Dead and discoloured patches develop on the stems and leaves. Rapid deterioration may occur, causing the upper parts of the stem to die. Fungal spores develop on decaying plant material. See pp.656 and 658 for other symptoms.
Cause The fungi *Botrytis cinerea* and, on snowdrops (*Galanthus*), *B. galanthina*, which thrive in damp conditions and where air circulation is poor. Fungal spores are spread on air currents or by rain splash; infection is most likely where plants are damaged. Fruits may also become infected by contact with those already diseased. Hard, black, resilient sclerotia (fungal resting bodies), produced on plant remains, fall to the ground and may cause later infections.
Control Avoid injury to plants, clear up dead and dying plant material, and provide good air circulation, ensuring at all times that plants are adequately spaced and those under cover are well ventilated. Remove and burn any affected areas (and in the case of snowdrops the entire clump) immediately. Spray with a suitable fungicide that contains carbendazim.

Irregular water supply

Plants affected Potentially all plants, especially those in containers.
Symptoms The outer stem layer or bark of the stem or trunk may split or crack. See pp.651 and 659 for other symptoms.
Cause An irregular supply of water, leading to irregular growth. Sudden availability of water after a drought caused by climatic conditions or a prolonged dry period due to erratic watering brings rapid swelling, which causes the stem to rupture and crack.
Control Provide a regular and adequate supply of water, especially during hot or windy weather. Do not suddenly overwater plants after drought conditions in an attempt to make up for a severe lack of moisture. Mulch, where appropriate, to conserve as much moisture in the soil as possible.

Dutch elm disease

Plants affected Elms (*Ulmus*) and *Zelkova*.
Symptoms Notching appears in twig crotches, and young twigs may be crook-shaped. Longitudinal, dark brown streaks develop under the bark. Leaves in the crown wilt, yellow, and die. The tree

Crook-shaped twigs

may die within two years.
Cause *Ophiostoma novo-ulmi*, a fungus spread by elm bark beetles as they tunnel under the bark. Infected trees may pass the disease to healthy ones via common root systems.
Control Fell and remove affected trees.

Longitudinal streaks

Woolly aphid

Plants affected Apples, cotoneasters, pyracanthas.
Symptoms A fluffy, white, mould-like substance appears on the bark in spring. Starting on the larger branches around old pruning cuts and in bark cracks, it later spreads to the new shoots where soft swellings may develop. Aphids may be visible.

Cause The woolly aphid (*Eriosoma lanigerum*), which is a small, greyish-black insect that sucks sap from the bark and secretes white, waxy threads.
Control Spray plants with bifenthrin or pirimicarb when the pest is seen.

Froghoppers (cuckoo spit)

Plants affected Trees, shrubs, perennials, annuals.
Symptoms Globules of white froth containing a small insect appear on stems and leaves in early summer. Where the pest feeds on shoot tips growth may be distorted but damage is minimal.

Cause Froghopper nymphs, or spittlebugs (eg *Philaenus spumarius*), cream-coloured sap-suckers that secrete a protective froth over themselves. The adults are darker in colour, up to 4mm (⅛in) long, and live openly on the plant.
Control If treatment is necessary, remove nymphs by hand or spray with pyrethrum or bifenthrin.

Adelgids

Plants affected Conifers, particularly *Abies*, pines (*Pinus*), spruces (*Picea*), *Pseudotsuga menziesii*, and larches (*Larix*).
Symptoms A fluffy, white, mould-like substance appears on the leaves and stems. Knobbly swellings develop on *Abies*, and swollen stem tips (known as pineapple galls) appear on the young shoots of spruce.

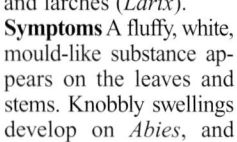

Cause Adelgids, or conifer woolly aphids (for example *Adelges* spp.), which are small, greyish-black, aphid-like insects that suck sap from the bark or the leaves. The bark- and leaf-feeders secrete white, waxy threads.
Control Established trees can tolerate the damage, but spray small trees with bifenthrin on a mild, dry day in mid- to late winter or early summer.

Fusarium wilt

Plants affected Perennials, annuals, vegetables, and fruits; most commonly affected are China asters (*Callistephus*), carnations (*Dianthus*), sweet peas (*Lathyrus odoratus*), beans, and peas.
Symptoms Black patches develop on stems and foliage; these patches are sometimes covered with a white or pale pink fungal growth. Roots turn black and die. Plants wilt, often suddenly.
Cause Various forms of the microscopic fungus *Fusarium oxysporum*, which are present in the soil or on plant debris, or are sometimes seed-borne; they may also be introduced on new stock. They will build up in the soil when the same type of plant is grown in the same site year after year.
Control There is no cure for affected plants. Remove them and the soil in their vicinity, and destroy the plants. Avoid growing susceptible plants in the area. Propagate only from healthy stock; if possible, grow resistant cultivars.

Phytophthora root rots

Plants affected Trees, shrubs, and woody perennials; maples (*Acer*), Lawson cypress (*Chamaecyparis lawsoniana*), apples, yew (*Taxus baccata*), rhododendrons, raspberries, and heathers are most commonly attacked.

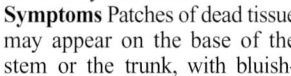

Symptoms Patches of dead tissue may appear on the base of the stem or the trunk, with bluish-black stains in the tissue beneath; the foliage is sparse and chlorotic. Die-back may follow, and plants may even be killed. See p.661 for other symptoms.
Cause Various species of the fungus *Phytophthora*, which is frequently found in wet or waterlogged soil. Roots are attacked by swimming spores that build up in the soil and in infected plant remains.
Control Always avoid heavy watering, and wherever possible improve soil drainage in the area. Dig up and burn all affected plants. Buy only good-quality plants from reputable sources, and choose those that are tolerant or resistant to *Phytophthora*, such as *Tsuga heterophylla* and x *Cupressocyparis leylandii*. There is no effective chemical control available to amateur gardeners.

Foot and root rots

Plants affected A wide range, especially petunias and other bedding plants, tomatoes, cucumbers, peas, beans, and young, container-grown plants.
Symptoms The stem bases discolour, and rot or shrink inwards. This causes the upper parts of the plant to wilt and collapse; the lower leaves will usually show the symptoms first. The roots turn black and break or rot.

Cause A range of soil- and water-borne fungi that flourish where growing conditions are not adequately hygienic. They are often introduced through the use of unsterilized compost and non-mains water, and build up in the soil, especially if susceptible plants are repeatedly grown on the same site.
Control Rotate susceptible plants. Maintain strict hygiene and only use fresh, sterilized compost, and mains water. Remove affected plants and the soil in the vicinity of their roots.

Seedling blight

Plants affected Many vegetable crops grown in warm climates, including beans, peas, peanuts, cabbages, sweet potatoes, and tomatoes.
Symptoms Seedlings show symptoms of damping off (see p.660). The collar or stem of older plants rots at soil level, and shoots yellow, wilt, and die.
Cause Invasion via the base of the plant by the fungus *Corticium rolfsii* (syn. *Sclerotium rolfsii*); nematode and insect wounds promote infection. Plants in light, sandy soils, well supplied with moisture, are most at risk.
Control Maintain crops well, remove diseased plants and debris, and avoid growing plants in contaminated areas; burn infected residues or bury them deeply.

Boron deficiency

Plants affected Carnations (*Dianthus*), lettuces, celery, and tomatoes; also all fruits (most commonly pears, plums, and strawberries). The condition is fairly rare.
Symptoms The growing tips die, causing the plants to become stunted and bushy. Celery stems

start to develop transverse cracks and the exposed tissues turn brown; lettuces fail to heart up. Pears become distorted and dimpled with brown, flecked flesh (very similar symptoms to those of the virus disease called stoney pit). Plums are misshapen and may show gumming (see "Pests and diseases", p.448). Strawberries are small and poorly coloured. See p.662 for other symptoms.
Cause and control See p.662 for details.

Clematis wilt

Plants affected Some large-flowered *Clematis* hybrids, eg 'Jackmanii'. *Clematis* species are generally resistant.
Symptoms The terminal shoots wilt, starting with the youngest stems, and the petioles darken where they join the leaf blade. Whole sections of the plant may be affected and start to die back. See also p.665.
Cause The fungus *Phoma clematidina*, which produces spore-releasing fruiting bodies on the older stems. Other, non-pathogenic causes of wilt (eg drought, poor drainage, slug damage, and graft failure) may be mistaken for this disease.
Control Cut back any affected stems to healthy tissue, below ground level if necessary. *C. montana* is regarded as resistant to clematis wilt, for which there is no effective treatment.

See also "Mealybugs", p.646; "Powdery mildew", p.646; "Chocolate spot", p.649; "Lily disease", p.649; "Contact weedkiller damage", p.650; "Smuts", p.652; "Etiolation", p.655; "Fungal brackets", p.655; "Lightning", p.655; "Chafer grubs", p.660; "Leatherjackets", p.660; "Damping off", p.664; "Blackleg on cuttings", p.664; "Blackleg on potatoes", p.664; "Coral spot", p.665; "Honey fungus", p.665; "Crown rot", p.665; "Replant disease/soil sickness", p.665; "Rose die-back", p.665; "Fireblight", p.665; "Peony wilt", p.665; and "Vine weevil grubs", p.666.

Stem distortion and abnormal growth

Etiolation

Plants affected Seedlings of all garden plants, and soft-stemmed plants.
Symptoms Stems are elongated and often pale, and the plant may grow towards the available light source, developing a lop-sided habit. The leaves are chlorotic and flowering is often reduced.
Cause Insufficient light, often due to poor siting of the plant or shading from adjacent plants, buildings, and similar structures. Overcrowded plants are susceptible to the condition.
Control Choose and site plants carefully. Ensure that adequate light is provided for seedlings as soon as germination has occurred. Plants only slightly affected should recover if conditions are improved.

Cutworms

Plants affected Low-growing perennials, annuals, root vegetables, and lettuces.
Symptoms Stem bases and leaves of low-growing plants are visibly gnawed and roots may also be affected. Plants grow slowly, wilt, and may ultimately die.
Cause Caterpillars of various moths (eg *Noctua* and *Agrotis* spp.), usually creamy-brown in colour and 4.5cm (1¾in) long. At night they feed above soil level.
Control Where damage is seen, search for and destroy the cutworms. Spray any vulnerable plants at dusk with bifenthrin, where leaf damage is occurring.

Hormone weedkiller damage

Plants affected Broadleaved plants (mainly roses, tomatoes, and grapes) and conifers.
Symptoms Small bumps may appear on stems. Leaves are distorted and petioles twisted or spiralled. See also pp.651 and 659.
Cause Contamination by a growth regulator or hormone-type weedkiller, often from a considerable distance; even minute quantities may cause extensive damage. Sources of trouble are spray drift and the use of contaminated sprayers or watering cans. Plants that have been affected usually grow out of the symptoms.
Control Apply weedkillers according to the manufacturers' instructions, placing protective barriers around adjacent plants. Keep one sprayer or watering can for use with weedkillers only, or preferably use dribble bars. Store weedkillers away from compost, fertilizers, and plants.

Leafy gall

Plants affected Shrubs, perennials, and annuals, especially dahlias, chrysanthemums, and pelargoniums.
Symptoms Tiny, distorted shoots and leaves develop on the stem at or near ground level.
Cause *Rhodococcus fascians*, a soil-borne bacterium that enters host plants through small wounds. It is easily spread on tools or through propagating from infected plants.

Control Destroy affected plants and remove the soil in their immediate vicinity, and wash after handling them. Maintain strict hygiene, sterilizing tools, containers, and the greenhouse regularly. Do not propagate from infected plants.

Crown gall

Plants affected Trees, shrubs (most commonly cane fruits and roses), and woody perennials.
Symptoms Irregular, rounded, often woody swellings occur on or burst from the stem, but plant vigour is not seriously affected. See p.661 for other symptoms.
Cause *Agrobacterium tumefaciens* bacteria, prevalent in wet soils, which enter through surface wounds.
Control Avoid plant damage and improve soil drainage. Cut out and destroy all the affected stems.

Forsythia gall

Plants affected Forsythias.
Symptoms Rough, woody rounded galls form on the stems of this shrub. They persist from year to year but rarely have adverse effects.
Cause Unknown; possibly bacterial infection.
Control No action is strictly necessary but the unsightly galled stems may be removed.

Fungal brackets

Plants affected Trees, shrubs, woody perennials.
Symptoms Fungal fruiting bodies, often bracket-shaped, appear commonly on the lower trunk, but also on the upper section or on the crown, sometimes near branch stubs or other wounds. Either short-lived or perennial, they vary in appearance, often according to weather conditions. General growth is slow, and the tree may develop an excess of dead wood and a thin crown.
Cause and control See p.661 for details.

Witches' brooms

Plants affected Trees, mainly birches (*Betula*) and hornbeams (*Carpinus*); shrubs; woody perennials.
Symptoms Dense clusters of small shoots appear on otherwise normal branches. Leaves discolour early and remain small but vigour is unaffected.

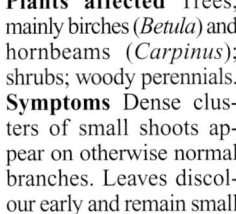

Cause Fungi (especially *Taphrina*) and mites (for example *Eriophyes*), which cause the mutations.
Control Cut branches back below the affected area.

Big bud mites

Plants affected Commonly hazels (*Corylus*), yew (*Taxus baccata*), brooms (*Cytisus*), and blackcurrants.
Symptoms The buds are abnormally enlarged and fail to break.
Cause Microscopic gall mites feeding inside the buds. Hazels are attacked by *Phytoptus avellanae*, brooms by *Eriophyes genistae*, yew by *Cecidophyopsis psilaspis*, and blackcurrants by *C. ribis*. Blackcurrant big bud mites can spread the virus-like disease known as reversion (see also "Viruses", p.659).
Control Remove and burn affected buds during the winter. Yew and hazels are fairly tolerant but heavily infested blackcurrants and brooms should be dug up and destroyed as soon as symptoms are noticed. The blackcurrant cultivars 'Farleigh' and 'Foxendown' are resistant to big bud mite.

Lightning

Plants affected Tall trees.
Symptoms Bark may be stripped, and a deep furrow may appear on one side, often following the spiral grain. The heartwood may be shattered, leaving the tree susceptible to disease. Dead wood increases in the crown and the upper crown dies.
Cause Lightning.
Control Lightning conductors may be fitted to valuable tall trees but this is unlikely to be feasible.

Mechanical wounding

Plants affected Potentially all plants.
Symptoms A neat-edged wound is visible on the stem or bark. Sap from the injured area may ferment into a slime flux (see "Slime flux/wet wood", p.653), and pathogens entering the wound cause die-back or even death. A healed wound may leave a raised area.
Cause Careless use of garden machinery and tools.
Control Remove severely damaged shoots or stems. Wounds on woody plants should be left alone.

Voles

Plants affected Shrubs and young trees.
Symptoms Bark is gnawed from stems and roots.
Cause Voles.
Control Mouse traps are the most effective solution, but poisoned bait may also be used. See also "Mice, rats, and voles", p.662.

> **See also** "Asparagus beetle", p.644; "Vine weevil", p.645; "Eelworms", p.652; "Rusts", p.653; "Irregular water supply", p.653; "Fasciation", p.657; "Grey squirrel", p.659; "Nectria canker", p.664; "*Seiridium* canker", p.664; "Honey fungus", p.665; "Replant disease/soil sickness", p.665; "Anthracnose", p.666; "Rabbits and hares", p.666; and "Deer", p.666.

Flower problems

Discoloured flowers

Grey mould (*Botrytis*)

Plants affected Trees, shrubs, perennials, annuals, bulbous plants, vegetables, fruits, and indoor plants.
Symptoms A fuzzy, grey, fungal growth appears on the flowers in patches, leading to total deterioration. This may later spread to the stems and body of the plant. See also pp.653 and 658.

Fungal patches

Cause The fungi *Botrytis cinerea* or *B. galanthina*.
Control Avoid injury to plants, clear up dead material, and provide good ventilation. Remove affected areas as soon as noticed. Spray with a suitable fungicide containing carbendazim.

Total deterioration

Viruses

Plants affected Most flowering plants, mainly bulbous plants and sweet peas (*Lathyrus odoratus*).
Symptoms Flowers are small and distorted, patterned with streaking or colour-breaking. See also pp.649 and 659.
Cause A large number of viruses. Submicroscopic virus particles in the sap of infected plants may be transmitted to healthy tissues by aphids, nematodes, and certain other pests, through handling, or on garden tools; some are seed-borne.
Control Buy certified (virus-free) plants. Control potential carriers, for example aphids, and keep down weeds. Remove and burn affected plants; handle suspect plants after healthy ones, and do not propagate from them. Use a new site for any replacement plants. There is no chemical control.

Thrips

Plants affected Perennials, often *Achimenes*, *Primula obconica*, *Sinningia*, *Streptocarpus*, African violets (*Saintpaulia*), chrysanthemums, cyclamen, roses, gladioli, pelargoniums.
Symptoms White flecks appear on the petals, and loss of pigmentation can

be severe. Heavy attacks prevent the buds opening. Leaves develop a silver-white discolouration.
Cause Various species of thrips, eg gladiolus thrips (*Thrips simplex*) and rose thrips (*T. fuscipennis*) in gardens, and western flower thrips (*Frankliniella occidentalis*) in greenhouses. They are sap-suckers that may enter and damage unopened flower buds. The adults are narrow-bodied, up to 2mm ($\frac{1}{16}$in) long, and brown or black; the immature nymphs are creamy yellow. They thrive in hot, dry conditions.

Control Water plants regularly and, in greenhouses, maintain a cool, humid atmosphere. Use biological control with the predatory mite *Amblyseius*, or spray with pyrethrum, derris, or bifenthrin.

Blossom wilt

Plants affected Apples, pears, cherries (*Prunus*), and quinces.
Symptoms The flowers turn brown and wither, but remain tightly clinging to the stem. The adjacent leaves then turn brown and die, and in severe cases

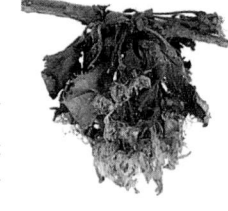

the spur may be extensively damaged. Many tiny, buff-coloured spore masses appear on the affected areas, and in winter pustules form on the bark.
Cause *Monilinia* spp., which flourish in damp conditions and also cause brown rot in fruits (see p.658). The spores are carried on air currents and infect the plant via the flowers.
Control Remove and burn all infected parts.

Tulip fire

Plants affected Tulips.
Symptoms Bleached, and often elongated, spots appear on the petals; severely affected flowers may wither. Some of the buds remain tightly closed and become covered in a dense, grey, fungal growth. See p.649 for symptoms affecting the leaves.

Cause The fungus *Botrytis tulipae*, which flourishes in wet seasons, because the spores are spread by wind and rain. The sclerotia (fungal resting bodies) persist in the soil, and will later germinate when tulips are planted in the area again.
Control Remove and burn affected leaves and shoots immediately. Lift and dry off bulbs at the end of the season, discarding any with sclerotia, and dust with sulphur. Wait two years before replanting the site with tulips, or change the soil. Plant from early winter onwards.

Phytoplasmas

Plants affected Trees, shrubs, perennials, annuals, bulbous plants, vegetables, fruits (especially strawberries), and indoor plants.
Symptoms Flowers are green, undersized, and sometimes distorted. They

do not revert to their usual colour and subsequent flushes are also green. Symptoms on clematis are similar to those caused by frost injury, but "frost-damaged" flowers will be replaced by normal-coloured blooms later in the season. On strawberries,

the condition causes green petals on the flowers and produces discoloured, misshapen leaves. See also p.651.
Cause Phytoplasmas, which are believed to be related to bacteria. They are spread by leafhoppers (see p.647), which commonly pick up the infection from clover plants suffering from phyllody disease.
Control Discard affected plants, buy certified fruit stock, and control both pests (potential vectors) and weeds (which may harbour the disease).

Rhododendron bud blast

Plants affected Rhododendrons and azaleas.
Symptoms The buds form but do not open. They turn brown and dry, sometimes developing a silver-grey sheen, and during spring become covered in black, fungal bristles. The affected buds are not shed.

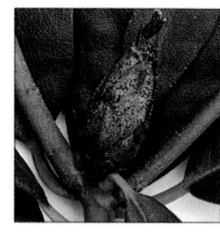

Cause The fungus *Pycnostysanus azaleae*, which infects through wounds made by the rhododendron leafhopper (*Graphocephala fennahi*).
Control If practical, remove and destroy all affected buds before midsummer, when the leafhoppers become prevalent; also spray against them in late summer and early autumn (see p.647).

Potassium deficiency

Plants affected Both edible and ornamental fruiting plants, but mainly currants, apples, and pears.
Symptoms Flowering, subsequent fruiting, and general growth may be reduced. See p.650 for details of other symptoms.
Cause Growing plants in soils with either a light texture or with a high chalk or peat content.
Control Improve the soil texture. Dress with sulphate of potash or a high potash fertilizer.

Apple sucker

Plants affected Apples.
Symptoms The blossom browns as though it is frost-damaged; small, green insects appear on the flower stalks.
Cause Apple sucker (*Psylla mali*) nymphs, which are flattened, pale green insects up to 2mm ($\frac{1}{16}$in) in length that suck sap. Heavy attacks will kill the blossom and prevent fruit set.
Control Apply a tar oil wash in winter. Alternatively, spray with pyrethrum or bifenthrin at the green cluster stage of bud development, before the petals show colour.

> **See also** "Powdery mildew", p.646; "High temperatures and scorch", p.650; "Low temperatures", p.650; "Azalea gall", p.652; "Chrysanthemum petal blight", p.657; "Michaelmas daisy mite", p.657; and "Fireblight", p.665.

Distorted and eaten flowers

Drought

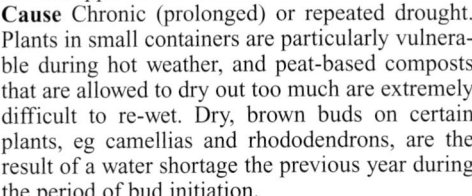

Plants affected All plants, especially those in light, sandy soils or containers.
Symptoms The buds fail to develop fully, and the flowers are small and sparse. See also pp.650 and 664.
Cause Chronic (prolonged) or repeated drought. Plants in small containers are particularly vulnerable during hot weather, and peat-based composts that are allowed to dry out too much are extremely difficult to re-wet. Dry, brown buds on certain plants, eg camellias and rhododendrons, are the result of a water shortage the previous year during the period of bud initiation.
Control Water plants regularly, and frequently check those in hot or sunny positions. Mulch, where appropriate, to improve moisture retention. Try to prevent drought rather than treat it: plants exposed to a chronic water shortage are far less likely to recover than those suffering a sudden shortage.

Capsid bugs

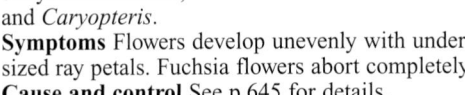

Plants affected Shrubs, perennials, and annuals, mainly dahlias, fuchsias, hydrangeas, chrysanthemums, and *Caryopteris*.
Symptoms Flowers develop unevenly with undersized ray petals. Fuchsia flowers abort completely.
Cause and control See p.645 for details.

Earwigs

Plants affected Shrubs, perennials, and annuals, commonly chrysanthemums, dahlias, and clematis. Also apricot and peach trees.
Symptoms Petals are eaten in summer. See p.644 for other symptoms.
Cause The earwig (*Forficula auricularia*), which is a yellowish-brown insect 2cm (¾in) long.
Control Place inverted pots, stuffed with hay or straw, on canes among plants; earwigs hide in these, and can be destroyed. Alternatively, spray at dusk with bifenthrin.

Fasciation

Plants affected All plants, most commonly delphiniums, forsythias, *Daphne*, and *Prunus subhirtella* 'Autumnalis'.
Symptoms Peculiar, broad, flattened flower stems develop. The main stems are also broad and flattened.
Cause In many cases, early damage to the growing point caused by insect, slug or frost attack, or handling; it may also be due to bacterial infection or genetic malfunction.
Control Fasciation does no harm; affected areas may either be left on the plant or pruned out.

Proliferation

Plants affected Mainly roses, especially the older varieties, but occasionally other ornamentals and fruiting plants.
Symptoms The flower stem grows through the centre of the existing flower, and a new flower may form above the first. In some cases several flower buds form together, surrounded by one set of petals.
Cause Early damage to the growing point of the bud, often through frost or insect attack. Where the problem recurs, a virus (see p.656) may be the cause.
Control Severely and repeatedly affected plants, which may be virus-infected, should be destroyed. In all other cases treatment is unnecessary.

Chrysanthemum petal blight

Plants affected Chrysanthemums and other members of the Compositae family and *Anemone*. The disease is rare.
Symptoms The outer florets develop brown or water-soaked oval spots; if the whole flowerhead becomes affected, it withers and dies. *Botrytis cinerea* may colonize the affected bloom (see "Grey mould/ *Botrytis*", p.656), masking the original symptoms.
Cause The fungus *Itersonilia perplexans*, which attacks susceptible plants, usually those under glass.
Control Remove and destroy affected blooms.

Michaelmas daisy mite

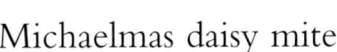

Plants affected Michaelmas daisies (*Aster*), especially *A. novi-belgii*.
Symptoms Plants flower poorly; some flowers may be converted into rosettes of small leaves. Greyish-brown scars appear on stunted stems.
Cause The Michaelmas daisy mite (*Phytonemus pallidus*), a microscopic mite that feeds in flower buds and shoot tips.

Distorted and healthy (inset) flowers

Control Discard infested plants, replacing them with less susceptible perennial asters, eg *Aster novae-angliae* or *A. amellus*. There is no effective chemical control available to amateur gardeners.

Hemerocallis gall midge

Plants affected Daylily (*Hemerocallis*).
Symptoms Flower buds become abnormally swollen and fail to open. The problem occurs between late spring and midsummer.
Cause The Hemerocallis gall midge (*Contarinia quinque-*

notata), a tiny fly that lays its eggs in the developing buds. Affected buds contain white maggots, up to 2mm (¹⁄₁₆in) long, feeding between the petals.
Control Pick off and burn galled buds. The late-flowering cultivars escape damage.

Pollen beetles

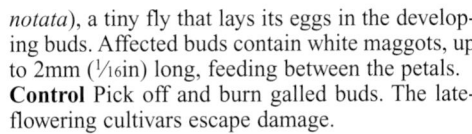

Plants affected Roses, sweet peas (*Lathyrus odoratus*), daffodils, marrows, runner beans, and other garden flowers.
Symptoms Small, black beetles are found in the flowers in spring and mid- to late summer.
Cause Pollen beetles (*Meligethes* spp.), which are 2mm (¹⁄₁₆in) long and black. They eat some pollen but otherwise cause little direct damage to the blooms.
Control Pollen beetles cannot be controlled, because vast numbers fly into gardens from oil seed rape fields, where they breed. It is not advisable to use insecticides: they can cause damage to the petals and harm useful pollinators, eg bees. Cut flowers can be freed of the beetles by placing them during the day in a shed or garage with one light source (eg an open door) towards which the beetles fly.

Birds

Plants affected Trees (ornamental and fruit), most fruits, and shrubs, especially forsythias, cherries (*Prunus*), pears, gooseberries, almonds, and *Amelanchier*, crocuses, primrose (*Primula vulgaris*), and polyanthus (*Primula*).

Bullfinch damage

House sparrow damage

Symptoms Flower buds are pecked from trees and shrubs; outer bud scales are left scattered on the ground. Crocus and primrose flowers are shredded. Vegetables, especially peas and beans, fruits, seeds, and seedlings are pecked or eaten.
Cause Birds, including bullfinches (trees, shrubs, and fruits) and house sparrows (crocuses and primroses). Vegetables, fruits, and seedlings may be pecked or eaten by many birds including wood pigeons (p.645), blackbirds and starlings (p.659), and jays (p.659).
Control Netting or very fine mesh is the only certain way of preventing damage. Scaring devices, eg humming tapes, scarecrows, or aluminium foil strips, are effective only initially; birds soon lose their fear. Repellent sprays, usually based on aluminium ammonium sulphate, must be used frequently to maintain their effectiveness.

See also "Caterpillars", p.645; "Low temperatures", p.650; "Irregular water supply", p.651; "Azalea gall", p.652; "Etiolation", p.655; "Viruses", p.656; "Thrips", p.656; and "Phytoplasmas", p.656.

Fruit, berry, and seed problems

High temperatures and scorch

Plants affected Soft fruits, tree fruits, tomatoes, and apples, especially green-skinned cultivars.
Symptoms Discoloured patches develop on the skin, particularly on the upper-most surfaces of fruits, or on the ones that are more highly exposed.
Cause and control See p.650 for details.

Grey mould (*Botrytis*)

Plants affected Fruiting trees, shrubs, perennials, annuals, and indoor plants. Soft, thin-skinned fruits, eg strawberries, raspberries, grapes, and tomatoes, are vulnerable.
Symptoms Normally, a grey, fuzzy, fungal growth develops on a soft, brown rot. The damage spreads rapidly and the whole fruit may collapse. Unripe tomatoes may develop "ghost spot", where a pale green ring appears on the skin but the rest of the fruit colours normally and does not rot (the unaffected parts may be eaten). See also pp.653 and 656.
Cause and control See p.653 for details.

Powdery mildew

Plants affected Most fruits, commonly grapes, peaches, and gooseberries.
Symptoms Whitish-grey, fungal patches appear on the skin, often turning brown as they mature. The berries of grapes become hard and extensively cracked, and may fail to swell fully; secondary fungi may then invade. Cracking of gooseberries is uncommon and fungal growth can be rubbed off.
Cause and control See p.646. Grow gooseberries showing some resistance, for example 'Invicta' and 'Greenfinch'.

Brown rot

Plants affected Culti-vated fruits, especially apples, plums, peaches, nectarines, and pears.
Symptoms Soft, brown areas develop on the skin, and penetrate throughout the flesh. Concentric rings of creamy-white pustules then start to appear on the surface. Affected fruits either fall or may become dry and wizened and remain on the tree.
Cause The fungus *Monilinia* (*M. fructigena* and *M. laxa*). The pustules produce spores, and these are then carried by wind or insects to other fruits;

infection occurs through wounds or blemishes on the surface of the fruit.
Control Prevent injury to fruits (eg that caused by pests), and pick off and burn those affected.

Tomato blight

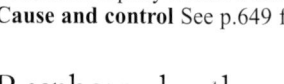

Plants affected Tomatoes, mainly in the open but also in greenhouses.
Symptoms The fruits first develop a brown discoloura-tion and then start to shrink and rot. Even fruits that may have appeared to be healthy when picked may begin to deteriorate rapidly within a few days.
Cause and control See p.649 for details.

Raspberry beetle

Plants affected Mainly rasp-berries, but also blackberries and hybrid cane fruits.
Symptoms Ripe fruits are dried up and brown at the stalk end; an insect larva may be found inside the fruit.
Cause The raspberry beetle (*Byturus tomentosus*). The females lay eggs on the flowers in early to midsummer. Brownish-white larvae up to 6mm (¼in) long hatch two weeks later. They feed initially at the stalk end of the fruit but then move to the inner plug.
Control Only chemical sprays provide an effective control. Apply bifenthrin or derris to raspberries when the first pink fruit appears; to loganberries when 80 per cent of the petals have fallen; to blackberries when the first flower opens. A second application may be required for raspberries and loganberries two weeks after the first. Spray at dusk to avoid harming bees.

Scab

Plants affected Pears, pyracanthas, *Citrus*, *Malus*, and loquats.
Symptoms Blackish-brown, scabby patches develop on the skin, and a severe attack will leave fruits small and distorted. In some cases cracks may develop, which will make the fruit vulnerable to secondary infections.
Cause and control See p.649 for details.

Calcium deficiency

Plants affected Apple (the condition is known as bitter pit), container-grown tomatoes, and sweet pep-pers (blossom end rot).
Symptoms The flesh of apples is brown-flecked and tastes bitter; the skin

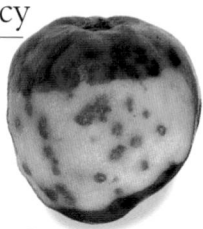

Bitter pit

is sometimes pitted. Bitter pit may affect fruits on the tree or in store. Tomato and pepper fruits develop a sunken, blackish-brown discolouration at the flower end.
Cause A lack of

Blossom end rot

calcium, possibly combined with other nutritional imbalances, resulting from an irregular or poor supply of moisture to the roots, preventing ade-quate calcium uptake. Groups of cells deprived of calcium collapse and discolour.
Control Avoid very acid growing media. Water regularly and, where feasible, mulch plants. Apples may be sprayed with calcium nitrate every ten days from early summer until harvesting.

Pear midge

Plants affected Pears.
Symptoms The fruitlets turn black, starting at the eye end, and fall from the tree. Small maggots are found inside fruitlets.
Cause The pear midge (*Contarinia pyrivora*). The adults lay eggs on the unopened flower buds; these hatch into orange-white maggots 2mm (¹⁄₁₆in) long that feed in the fruitlets, leaving them black and rotten.
Control Collect and burn damaged fruitlets before the maggots fall into the soil to pupate. Pear midge is difficult to control on large trees.

Shanking of vines

Plants affected Grape vines (*Vitis vinifera*).
Symptoms Berry stalks wither. Berries have a watery or sour taste; black varieties turn red, and white ones remain translucent. They may remain on the bunch but shrivel up and are vulnerable to disease, eg grey mould (*Botrytis*) (see above).
Cause Heavy cropping, either over- or under-watering, or stagnant soil conditions.
Control Cut out withered berries and regularly apply a foliar feed. Decrease the crop for a few years and try to improve general soil conditions.

Blue mould on citrus

Plants affected All *Citrus*, especially oranges.
Symptoms Circular patches of mould, usually with a central depression, appear on the rind. They extend rapidly and develop a distinct, blue coloration.
Cause The fungus *Penicillium italicum*, which enters fruits through bruised, wounded, or insect-damaged areas. It typically occurs on stored fruits.
Control Pick and handle fruits with great care, to minimize injury. Store only undamaged fruits, ensuring that they do not touch each other.

Irregular water supply

Plants affected Potentially all fruiting plants.
Symptoms Fruits are misshapen and undersized, and a sudden availability of water may cause their skin and flesh to crack, leaving them vulnerable to the diseases that cause rotting. See pp.651 and 653 for other symptoms.
Cause and control See p.651 for details.

Viruses

Plants affected Pears, cucumbers, melons, pumpkins, tomatoes, strawberries, and raspberries.
Symptoms Fruits may be undersized, distorted, discoloured, and grouped in rosettes. Cucumber mosaic virus produces warty, distorted cucumber, melon, and pumpkin fruits, blotched dark green and yellow; pear stony pit virus produces distorted and pitted pear fruits with patches of dead, stony cells. See also pp.649 and 656.
Cause and control See p.649 for details.

Hormone weedkiller damage

Plants affected All fruits, but commonly only tomatoes.
Symptoms Plum-shaped tomatoes form. Although they ripen normally and are safe to eat, they may taste unpleasant and be hollow. Fruits that have formed before contamination occurs are not usually affected. See p.651 for other symptoms.
Cause and control See p.651 for details.
See also "Selective weedkillers". p.671.

Fruit flies

Plants affected Tropical and subtropical fruits.
Symptoms Holes are bored in fruits. Secondary fungal and bacterial infection may occur.
Cause Larvae of fruit flies (*Dacus* and *Ceratitis* spp.), including the Mediterranean fruit fly (*C. capitata*).
Control Lay a bait of malathion and sugar solution.

Wasps

Plants affected Tree fruits, such as plums, pears, apples, and figs, as well as grapes.
Symptoms Large cavities are eaten in ripe fruits in late summer; wasps may be seen feeding.
Cause Wasps (*Vespula* spp.), which are attracted to fruits initially damaged by birds.
Control Protect fruits by placing bags made of muslin or nylon tights over the trusses before damage begins. Make a wasp trap using beer in a jar; cover it with a paper lid in which a wasp-sized hole has been pierced. Locate and destroy wasp nests, placing bendiocarb dust in the entrance at dusk when the wasps have stopped flying.

Blackbirds and starlings

Plants affected Tree and soft fruits.
Symptoms Peck marks appear on ripe tree fruits, leaving them susceptible to brown rot (see p.658); soft fruits are eaten whole.
Cause Blackbirds, starlings, and other birds (see p.657).
Control Either net the plants at fruiting time or grow them in a permanent bird-proof cage.

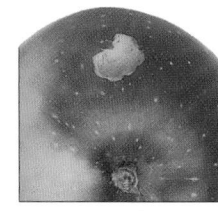

Codling moth

Plants affected Apples and pears.
Symptoms Holes are tunnelled in ripe fruits.
Cause The caterpillars of the codling moth (*Cydia pomonella*), which feed in the core of the fruit; when they are mature, each caterpillar makes a frass-filled tunnel to the outside of the fruit.
Control Hang pheromone traps in the trees from late spring to mid-summer to catch the male moths, thus reducing egg fertilization. Use of traps will also indicate when the males are flying, so sprays can be timed more accurately to control the caterpillars as they hatch. If needed, spray with bifenthrin in early summer and again three weeks later.

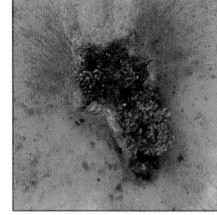

Plum moth

Plants affected Plums.
Symptoms The fruits ripen prematurely and then drop. A pink caterpillar and its excrement may be found inside the fruit.
Cause The plum moth (*Cydia funebrana*), which lays its eggs on the fruitlets during early summer. These hatch into caterpillars known as red plum maggots, which grow up to 1cm (½in) long.
Control Pheromone traps may reduce the mating success of the females, and consequently result in fewer maggoty fruits, if they are hung in the tree in late spring to catch the male plum moths. There are no effective insecticides available for garden use against the plum moth.

Apple sawfly

Plants affected Apples.
Symptoms Fruitlets are tunnelled and drop off during early to mid-summer. The damaged fruits will sometimes remain on the tree and become mature, but they are misshapen and have a long, ribbon-like scar on the skin.
Cause The larvae of the apple sawfly (*Hoplocampa testudinea*), white caterpillar-like insects up to

1cm (½in) long with brown heads. They are less widespread than codling moth (see above).
Control Spray with bifenthrin within seven days of petal fall, if sawfly have been a problem in previous years; spray at dusk to avoid harming bees.

Pea thrips

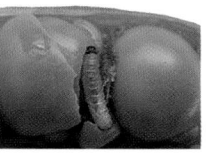

Plants affected Peas.
Symptoms The pods turn silver-brown and they may remain flat apart from a few seeds at the stalk end.
Cause The pea thrips (*Kakothrips pisivorus*), which is a narrow-bodied, blackish-brown, sap-feeding insect up to 2mm (¹⁄₁₆in) long. The immature nymphs have a similar appearance but are orange-yellow. Both the adults and the nymphs feed on the plants; they thrive in hot, dry conditions.
Control Water plants regularly where the damage occurs, and spray the plants with pyrethrum or bifenthrin.

Pea moth

Plants affected Peas.
Symptoms Peas in pods are eaten by caterpillars.
Cause The pea moth (*Cydia nigricana*), which lays eggs on pea plants in flower in early to mid-summer. The caterpillars are creamy-white with brown heads, and are up to 1cm (½in) long.
Control Use pheromone traps to catch the males, reducing the chances of the females mating successfully; or spray plants with bifenthrin, 7–10 days after flowering begins. Early- or late-sown peas should not need spraying.

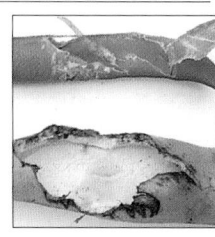

Jays and pigeons

Plants affected Peas and broad beans.
Symptoms Developing pods are pecked and the seeds are eaten.
Cause Jays and pigeons.
Control Netting is the only effective protection. Scaring devices are only effective initially as birds soon lose their fear. Repellent sprays must be used frequently if their effectiveness is to be maintained.

Grey squirrel

Plants affected Young trees, flower buds, fruits, and nuts.
Symptoms Bark is gnawed away. Flower buds, ripening fruits, and nuts are eaten.
Cause Grey squirrel.
Control Traps work only if used over a wide area.

See also "Woodlice", p.644; "Millipedes", p.644; "Winter moth caterpillars", p.645; "Wood pigeon", p.645; "Potassium deficiency", p.656; "Birds",p.657; "Boron deficiency", p.662; and "Drought", p.664.

Root and tuber problems

Waterlogging

Plants affected Potentially all plants.
Symptoms Some roots may rot off completely. Those remaining are frequently blackened with a peeling outer surface. The first visible symptom is usually wilting leaves.
Cause Excessive water

levels in the growing medium, owing to factors such as poor soil structure, compaction, impeded drainage, or overwatering.
Control Where feasible, improve the structure and drainage of the soil and, if necessary, choose plants that are likely to survive in wet conditions. Check that drainage holes for container-grown plants are adequate, and that flow through them is not impeded. Regular application of a foliar feed during the growing season may help to stimulate growth, allowing waterlogged roots to be replaced.

Damping off

Plants affected The seedlings of all plants.
Symptoms Affected roots darken and rot off, causing the seedling to collapse and die. The disease often starts at one end of the seed tray, spreading rapidly to the other. A fluffy, fungal growth may

appear on the compost as well as on dead seedlings.
Cause Various fungi – in particular *Pythium ultimum* and some *Phytophthora* – which are soil- or water-borne and attack seedlings via either the roots or the base of the stem. They flourish in moist and unhygienic conditions.
Control There is no effective control once the disease is established. To prevent it, sow seed thinly, improve ventilation, maintain strict hygiene, and avoid overwatering. Use only sterilized compost, mains water, and clean trays and pots. Water occasionally with a suitable copper-based fungicide.

Root-knot eelworms

Plants affected Many garden plants, including fruit trees, vegetables, and ornamentals in warm climates. Plants in greenhouses are also susceptible.
Symptoms Galls or swellings appear on the roots or tubers. Overall growth is stunted, and the plant may wilt, yellow, and sometimes even be killed.
Cause Root-knot nematodes (*Meloidogyne* spp.), which are thin, transparent, and only 0.5mm (1/32in) long. The larvae penetrate the roots.
Control Burn all affected plants. Rotate vegetable crops; choose resistant plants. There is no chemical control available to amateur gardeners.

Vine weevil grubs

Plants affected Many shrubs, perennials, bulbous plants, and those that are grown indoors; most commonly affected are begonias, cyclamen, fuchsias,

Impatiens, primulas (including the Polyanthus Group), *Sedum*, and strawberries. Container-grown plants are particularly vulnerable.
Symptoms The outer tissues of woody seedlings and cuttings are gnawed from the stem bases and roots below ground level. Plants grow slowly, have a tendency to wilt, and finally collapse and die.
Cause and control See p.666 for details.
See also p.666; and p.645 for information on damage caused to leaves by adult vine weevils.

Chafer grubs

Plants affected Young annuals, bulbous plants, lawns, and vegetables.
Symptoms Large cavities appear in root vegetables. Stem bases are eaten, and small plants wilt and may eventually die.
Cause The root-feeding, creamy-white larvae of beetles such as cock chafers (*Melolontha melolontha*) and garden chafers (*Phyllopertha horticola*). They are plump, "C"-shaped, and up to 5cm (2in) long, with brown heads and three pairs of legs.
Control Search for and destroy the larvae, or water in biological-control pathogenic nematodes (*Heterorhabditis megidis*) when the soil is moist and warm (at least 14°C/57°F) from midsummer.
See also p.667 for problems caused on lawns.

Cutworms

Plants affected Low-growing perennials, annuals, root vegetables, and lettuces.
Symptoms Cavities appear in root crops, and tap roots may be severed, causing plants to wilt and die. See p.655 for other symptoms.
Cause The caterpillars of various moths (eg *Noctua* and *Agrotis* spp.), usually creamy-brown in colour and up to 4.5cm (1¾in) in length. They eat roots and the outer tissues of stem bases.
Control Search for and destroy the cutworms near plants showing signs of damage.

Leatherjackets

Plants affected Young annuals, bulbous plants, lawns, and vegetables.
Symptoms The roots are eaten, the stems are severed at ground level, and plants turn yellow, wilt, and may eventually die.
Cause The larvae of crane flies, also known as daddy-long-legs (eg *Tipula* spp.), which feed on roots and stems. Leatherjackets are up to 3.5cm (1½in) long; they have tubular, greyish-brown bodies with no legs.
Control Where damage is seen on the plants, search for and destroy the leatherjackets, or in late summer apply biological-control pathogenic nematodes (*Steinernema carpocapsae*) to moist, warm (14–20°C/57–68°F) soil. Leatherjacket damage most commonly occurs on land that has recently been brought into cultivation, and so the problem should diminish within a few years.
See also p.667 for problems caused on lawns.

Carrot fly

Plants affected Mainly carrots, parsnips, parsley (*Petroselinum crispum*), and celery.
Symptoms Rusty brown tunnels are bored under the outer skin of mature roots. Small plants develop discoloured foliage and may eventually die.
Cause Creamy-yellow maggots, larvae of the carrot fly (*Psila rosae*), which feed in the surface tissues of the larger roots; in autumn they may bore deeper. They are slender, legless, and up to 1cm (½in) long.
Control Enclose susceptible plants within a clear polythene fence at least 60cm (24in) high, or grow under horticultural fleece, to exclude the low-flying female flies. Some cultivars, eg 'Sytan' and 'Flyaway', are less vulnerable to attack. Lift carrots for storage in autumn to limit damage.

Cabbage root fly

Plants affected Brassicas (including cabbages, cauliflowers, Brussels sprouts, turnips, swedes), radishes.
Symptoms Plants grow slowly and wilt; seedlings and transplants die; tunnels appear in root crops.
Cause Root-feeding larvae of the fly *Delia radicum*, white, legless maggots up to 9mm (3/8in) long. Several generations occur between mid-spring and mid-autumn, causing damage mainly to young plants.
Control Place collars of carpet underlay, roofing felt, or cardboard, about 12cm (5in) in diameter, around the base of transplanted brassicas to prevent the female flies from laying eggs in the soil, or lay landscape fabric over the whole planting area and insert the young brassicas through planting holes in the fabric. Alternatively, grow under horticultural fleece. There are no pesticides approved for garden use.

Clubroot

Plants affected The family Cruciferae, especially certain brassicas (for example cabbages, Brussels sprouts, and swedes) and radishes, and some ornamentals, including candytufts (*Iberis*), wallflowers (*Erysimum*), and stocks (*Matthiola*).
Symptoms Swollen and distorted roots; stunted and often discoloured plants; wilting in hot weather. See p.649 for other symptoms.
Cause The slime mould *Plasmodiophora brassicae*, which thrives in poorly drained, acid soils, and may also be found on manure and plant debris. It is easily spread on boots and tools, and the spores remain viable for 20 years or more, even in the absence of a host plant. Weeds susceptible to this disease (eg shepherd's purse and charlock) may be a source of infection.
Control Remove and burn affected plants as soon as any sign of disease appears. Keep the area free of weeds, improve drainage, and lime the soil. Raise new plants in soil-based compost to encourage the development of a strong and healthy root system.

Violet root rot

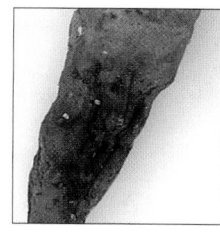

Plants affected Vegetables, mainly carrots, parsnips, asparagus, swedes, turnips, potatoes, celery.
Symptoms Roots, tubers, and any other parts below ground level are covered in a dense, matted, purple fungal growth to which soil particles become attached. The upper parts of the plant become stunted and discoloured. There may be secondary rotting.
Cause The fungus *Helicobasidium brebissonii*, which is harboured by some weeds. It thrives in both acid and waterlogged soils.
Control Burn infected plants immediately. Avoid growing susceptible plants on the affected site for at least four years; keep the area free of weeds.

Root aphids

Plants affected Lettuce, beans, carrots, parsnips, Jerusalem artichokes, auriculas, roses, *Dianthus*.
Symptoms Slow growth and tendency to wilt in sunny weather in mid- and late summer. A white waxy powder may appear on roots and nearby soil.
Cause Aphids, to 3mm (⅛in) long and generally creamy-brown, which feed on roots and stem bases. Different species of root aphid attack specific plants, for example *Pemphigus bursarius* on lettuce and *Thecabius auriculae* on auriculas.
Control Rotate vegetable crops and grow root-aphid-resistant lettuce cultivars. Root aphids are difficult to treat with insecticides, but lettuce and beans can be watered with diluted bifenthrin; treat pot-grown ornamental plants with imidacloprid.

Foot and root rots

Plants affected A wide range, especially petunias and other bedding plants, tomatoes, cucumbers, peas, beans, and young, container-grown plants.
Symptoms The roots turn black and break or rot. See p.654 for details of other symptoms.
Cause and control See p.654 for details.

Phytophthora root rots

Plants affected Trees, shrubs, and woody perennials; commonly maples (*Acer*), yew (*Taxus baccata*), Lawson cypress (*Chamaecyparis lawsoniana*), apples, rhododendrons, raspberries, and heathers.
Symptoms The larger roots die back from the stem or trunk, although the fine roots may appear perfectly healthy; affected roots usually turn black. See p.654 for other symptoms.
Cause and control See p.654 for details.

Tropical root rots

Plants affected Annual and perennial crops, temperate and tropical, including broad beans, French beans, cucumbers, melons, pumpkins, peanuts.
Symptoms Annual plants show a mid-season wilting, with rotting of the base of the stem and upper portion of the root; the infected tissues develop lesions and often turn red before decaying. The leaves become chlorotic as their water supply is restricted, and young seedlings may show signs of damping off (see p.660). Groundnut shells become blackened and rapidly decay. The infected tissues of perennial crops turn purple and the plants wilt.
Cause Various forms of the soil-borne fungi *Fusarium solani*, *Thielaviopsis basicola*, *Thanatephorus cucumis*, *Phytophthora* spp., and *Pythium* spp. among others. The disease is carried in the soil and infected debris; crops grown in poorly drained, acid soils are particularly at risk. High soil temperatures will encourage the development of pea root rot (*Aphanomyces entiches*).
Control Rotate crops on a long cycle. Use heat- or fungicide-treated seed, if feasible. Where possible, improve soil drainage.

Crown gall

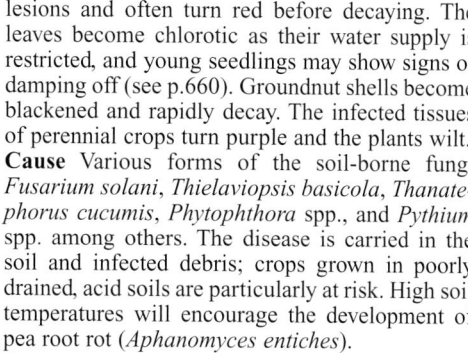

Plants affected Trees, shrubs (most commonly cane fruits and roses), and woody perennials.
Symptoms Irregular, rounded swellings develop on the roots, and occasionally the whole root system is distorted into a single, large swelling. See p.655 for symptoms.
Cause The bacterium *Agrobacterium tumefaciens*, prevalent in wet soils. The bacteria enter the plant through wounds made on the surface and cause cells to proliferate.
Control Avoid damaging plants and improve soil drainage. Cut out and destroy any affected stems in order to prevent secondary infection.

Honey fungus

Plants affected Trees, shrubs, climbers, and some woody perennials; most commonly affected are privets (*Ligustrum*), rhododendrons, and *Wisteria*.
Symptoms In autumn, fruiting bodies sometimes develop in clusters on underground roots, at the base of the trunk, and occasionally at some height from the ground; they die back after the first frost. The plant deteriorates and eventually dies. See p.665 for other symptoms.
Cause The fungus *Armillaria* (principally *A. mellea*) spread either by rhizomorph movement from an infected plant or stump, or through root contact.
Control Dig out and burn affected plants, stumps, and as much of the root system as possible; if necessary, have the stump chipped or ground out by a contractor. Avoid the more susceptible plants, choosing those showing some resistance, eg yew (*Taxus baccata*), *Cornus*, beech (*Fagus*), and *Hebe*.

Fungal brackets

Plants affected Mainly trees, and especially mature or overmature specimens, but also shrubs and woody perennials.
Symptoms Fungal fruiting bodies, often bracket-shaped, may appear above ground, following the line of the roots; they are attached to the roots by tiny fungal threads. They vary in appearance, often according to weather conditions. The roots may become hollow and eventually die, making the tree extremely unstable in the ground. Stems are also affected (see p.655).
Cause Various fungi, eg *Meripilus* or *Ganoderma*.
Control Seek professional advice, particularly if the tree poses a potential hazard. Removal of fruiting bodies will not prevent further internal decay, but does reduce the chances of spread to other trees.

Parsnip canker

Plants affected Parsnips.
Symptoms The shoulders of affected parsnips discolour and rot; the crown, shank, and roots of the plant may also rot, and the foliage may show some spotting. This condition occurs mainly in autumn and winter.
Cause Various species of fungus, primarily *Itersonilia pastinaceae*. Some are soil-inhabiting and others produce spores that are washed into the soil from leaf lesions.
Control Rotate crops. Prevent injury to parsnip roots, particularly the type of injury caused by carrot fly larvae (see p.660). Sow late and closely in order to produce parsnips with small roots, which are less prone to disease, and earth up the rows to provide a barrier against spores washed down from the leaf lesions. Remove all affected plants immediately. Grow parsnips in a deep loam soil with a high pH, and choose a resistant cultivar, eg 'Avonresister' or 'Gladiator'.

Verticillium wilt

Plants affected A large number of garden and greenhouse plants.
Symptoms The roots deteriorate and die, and if cut longitudinally in the early stages of degeneration they may show a central, vascular column of brown discolouration.
Cause and control See p.653 for details.

Fusarium wilt

Plants affected Perennials, annuals, vegetables, and fruits; most commonly affected are China asters (*Callistephus*), carnations (*Dianthus*), sweet peas (*Lathyrus odoratus*), beans, and peas.
Symptoms The roots of affected plants turn black and eventually die.
Cause and control See p.654 for details.

Primula brown core

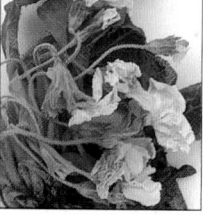

Plants affected Primulas.
Symptoms The roots rot and, if split longitudinally, show a distinct brown core; many are killed and plants become loose in the ground. Leaves yellow, wilt, and die. Flowers wilt.
Cause The fungus species *Phytophthora primulae*, which can remain viable in the soil for many years.
Control Dig up and burn all the affected plants. Grow any new primulas on an entirely fresh site.

Mice, rats, and voles

Plants affected Shrubs, young trees, crocus corms, seedlings of peas and beans, seeds, vegetables, and fruits kept in storage.
Symptoms The outer layer of stems and roots is gnawed. Seeds, seedlings, corms, vegetables, and fruits are eaten.
Cause Mice, rats, and voles.
Control Mouse or rat traps provide the best solution; difenacoum, brodifacoum, or coumatetralyl poisoned baits may also be used.

Boron deficiency

Plants affected Roots of carrots, parsnips, swedes, turnips, and beetroots. The condition is fairly rare.
Symptoms The roots are of a poor shape and texture, and are rather grey. They may split longitudinally and sometimes contain cavities. A brown discolouration – known as brown heart – may occur in the lowermost sections, often in concentric rings; it is found mainly in turnips and swedes, and leaves them poor tasting and fibrous. Beetroot shows internal discolouration and may develop cankers. See p.654 for other symptoms.
Cause A lack of boron in the soil, or an inability of the plant to take up the trace element owing to unsuitable growing conditions. Most common on very chalky or heavily limed soils, those that have been very dry, and those where the boron has been leached out. It rarely affects greenhouse plants.
Control Maintain correct soil moisture levels and avoid excessive liming. Before introducing a susceptible plant to a problem site, apply borax at 35g/20sq m (1oz/20sq yd), mixing with horticultural sand for easy and accurate application. Use fritted trace elements.

> **See also** "Aphids", p.646; "Mealybugs", p.646; "Pansy sickness", p.650; "Slugs", "Wireworms", below; "Onion fly", p.663; "Fungus gnats or sciarid flies", p.666; and "Bean seed fly", p.666.

Potato tuber problems

Slugs

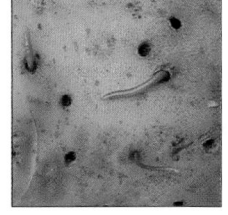

Plants affected Potatoes.
Symptoms Circular holes are bored in the outside of potato tubers, and extensive cavities appear in the interior during late summer.
Cause Slugs.
Control Use biological control with pathogenic nematode *Phasmarhabditis hermaphrodita*, or scatter metaldehyde pellets. Grow less susceptible cultivars; harvest tubers as soon as mature.
See also "Slugs and snails", p.644, for leaf problems.

Wireworms

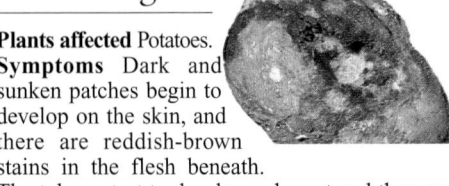

Plants affected Potatoes and other root crops, seedlings, perennials, annuals, and bulbous plants.
Symptoms Tunnels up to 3mm (⅛in) in diameter, superficially similar to those made by slugs, are bored through root crops.
Underground parts of other plants are damaged. Small plants wilt and die.
Cause The slender, stiff-bodied, yellowish-orange larvae of click beetles (eg *Agriotes* spp.), which feed on roots and stem bases. They are up to 2.5cm (1in) long, with three pairs of short legs at the head end and a peg-like protuberance beneath the rear end. The problem mainly occurs when grassland is brought into cultivation.
Control Where damage is seen, search for and destroy the wireworms. Lift root crops as soon as they are mature. The pest usually disappears once the ground has been cultivated for at least five years.

Potato blight

Plants affected Potatoes.
Symptoms Dark and sunken patches begin to develop on the skin, and there are reddish-brown stains in the flesh beneath.
The tubers start to develop a dry rot and they may also be affected by secondary, soft-rotting bacteria.

See p.649 for symptoms that affect the foliage.
Cause The fungus *Phytophthora infestans*, which thrives in warm, moist conditions. Spores produced on the foliage and on potato haulms are carried from plant to plant by wind and rain, and may be washed down into the soil to infect potato tubers. The same fungus may also attack tomatoes.
Control Avoid overhead watering. Earth up potatoes deeply to provide a barrier against falling spores, and choose resistant cultivars, eg 'Cara', 'Kondor', 'Romano', or 'Wilja'. Spray with mancozeb or a copper-based fungicide; in wet seasons spray before the blight appears.

Common potato scab

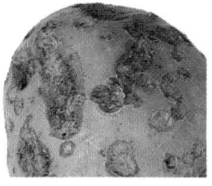

Plants affected Potatoes.
Symptoms Raised, scabby patches develop on the skin, and these sometimes rupture. Damage may be superficial, but in some cases the tuber becomes extensively cracked and disfigured. The flesh is not generally damaged.
Cause *Streptomyces scabies*, a bacterium-like but mycelium-producing organism, common in soils that are sandy and light with a high lime content, and those only recently cultivated. Disease development is most common during hot, dry summers, and when soil moisture levels are low.
Control Improve soil texture and avoid liming; water regularly. Do not plant potatoes on soil that has recently been used for brassicas. Grow resistant cultivars, for example 'King Edward'; very susceptible cultivars include 'Maris Piper' and 'Desiree'.

Bacterial rotting

Plants affected Potatoes.
Symptoms. The tuber is rapidly reduced to a slimy mass that has a strong smell, while growing or in storage.
Cause Bacteria enter the tuber either through wounds or through damage caused by infections.
Control Maintain good growing conditions, and harvest potatoes carefully in order to avoid injury. Remove all affected tubers immediately.

Internal rust spot

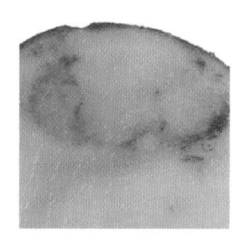

Plants affected Potatoes.
Symptoms Rust-brown flecks develop throughout the flesh of the tubers.
Cause Cultivation either in sandy, acid soils that are low in organic matter, or in soils that are generally low in nutrients – in particular potash and phosphorus.
Control Incorporate humus into the soil before planting and apply a general fertilizer in spring. Water regularly. Grow only potatoes showing some resistance to this condition, for example 'King Edward'.

Potato spraing

Plants affected Potatoes.
Symptoms A brown, arc-shaped discolouration, sometimes with a corky texture, develops inside the often misshapen tuber. Potatoes alone show these symptoms, but the viruses (p.649) can infect *Nicotiana*, China asters (*Callistephus*), gladioli, tulips, hyacinths, and *Capsicum*.
Cause A number of viruses, including tobacco rattle virus, and, less often, potato mop-top virus; these are transmitted by free-living nematodes in the soil.
Control Avoid growing other host plants on the affected site, and grow all potatoes on a fresh site.

Ring rot

Plants affected Potatoes in store.
Symptoms The vascular tissues of tubers become soft and decay. The disease may eventually reach the tuber surface, producing cracks near the eyes, and secondary rots may develop. Symptoms usually develop late in the growing season.
Cause *Corynebacterium sepedonicum*, a bacterium transmitted by infected tubers used as seed potatoes.
Control Inspect tubers on lifting, do not store any that are suspect, and ensure that all storage containers are clean. Plant only disease-free tubers.

> **See also** "Millipedes", p.644; "Blackleg on potatoes", p.664; and "Potato cyst eelworms", p.666.

Bulb, corm, and rhizome problems

Storage rot

Plants affected Bulbs and corms, especially if damaged or poorly stored.
Symptoms Discoloured, sometimes sunken patches develop on the surface of the bulb, or beneath the outer scales or skin. A fungal growth may appear on the patches, spreading

through bulb tissues, which become light and dry.
Cause A range of fungi. Infection is often restricted to a very few, closely related bulbs or corms, and may affect both those in the ground and those in store. Temperatures that are too low or too high and over-damp conditions encourage the disease.
Control Store and plant only healthy bulbs, and avoid injury to them. Store in suitable conditions, and immediately remove any that show signs of deterioration. Dusting them with sulphur may prevent attack.

Bulb flies

Plants affected Daffodils, *Hippeastrum*, snowdrops (*Galanthus*), bluebells (*Hyacinthoides nonscripta*), *Cyrtanthus purpureus*, and *Sprekelia*.
Symptoms Bulbs fail to grow or produce only a few grass-like leaves. Maggots may be found in the bulbs.
Cause The large narcissus bulb fly (*Merodon equestris*), which attacks sound bulbs, and small narcissus bulb flies (*Eumerus* spp.), which attack damaged bulbs. Large bulb flies lay eggs singly on bulbs in early summer. Adults resemble small bumblebees; larvae are brownish-white, up to 2cm (¾in) long, and fill the centre of the bulb with muddy excrement. Small bulb fly larvae are similar but never more than 8mm (⅜in) long; there are usually several in a bulb.
Control Avoid planting in warm, sheltered places, which attract adult flies. Discourage egg-laying by firming the soil around the necks of bulbs as they die down, or cover with fine-meshed screens or horticultural fleece in early summer.

Ink spot

Plants affected Bulbous irises, *Crocosmia*, *Lachenalia*.
Symptoms Inky stains appear on bulbs, and yellow dots or black craters on fleshy scales. Bulbs may rot away. Black patches or blotches appear on leaves.
Cause The fungus *Mystrosporium adustum*, which spreads through the soil to nearby bulbs.
Control Destroy diseased bulbs. Lift bulbs every year, and plant in a new area.

Narcissus basal rot

Plants affected Daffodils.
Symptoms After about one month in store, the basal plate of the bulb becomes soft and brown, and rots. The deterioration spreads to the inner scales, which turn dark brown, and a pale pink, fluffy, fungal growth may then appear

between the scales and on the basal plate. The bulb gradually dries out and becomes mummified. Bulbs which become infected in the ground may, if not lifted, rot away in the soil. In some cases, foliage symptoms of yellowing and wilting occur first.
Cause The soil-borne fungus *Fusarium oxysporum* f. *narcissi*, which infects bulbs through the basal plate; the fungus is encouraged by high soil temperatures. If the infected bulb is not lifted, it may infect adjacent bulbs. Stored bulbs that are infected but do not show symptoms also act as a source of infection when planted.
Control Lift bulbs early in the season, before soil temperatures rise, and dip them in a solution of carbendazim. Check bulbs thoroughly for signs of disease before storing.

Narcissus eelworm

Plants affected Daffodils, bluebells (*Hyacinthoides non-scripta*), and snowdrops (*Galanthus*).
Symptoms Bulbs cut transversely reveal brown concentric rings. Plant growth is stunted and distorted, and infested bulbs invariably rot.
Cause The narcissus eelworm (*Ditylenchus dipsaci*), which is a microscopic nematode that feeds within bulbs and foliage. Where bulbs have been naturalized, the area of infestation will increase each year as the pest spreads through the soil. Weeds may also harbour narcissus eelworm.
Control Dig up and burn both the infested plants and any others within 1m (1yd) of them. Immersing dormant daffodil bulbs in water at 44°C (112°F) for three hours kills the eelworms without causing bulb damage, but the constant temperature is difficult to maintain without special equipment. Avoid replanting affected areas with susceptible plants for at least two years, and keep weeds under control. No chemical treatment is available.

Iris rhizome rot

Plants affected Irises.
Symptoms The base of outer leaves decays and the rot then spreads into the rhizome, attacking the youngest parts first. The infected area is reduced to a foul-smelling mass.
Cause The bacterium *Erwinia carotovora* pvar. *carotovora*, which thrives in waterlogged soil. The bacteria enter the rhizomes through wounds or other damaged areas.
Control Check all rhizomes for any kind of damage before planting, and be extra careful to avoid injuring them. Plant the rhizomes shallowly, and always in good, well-drained soil. Take steps to ensure that slugs (see p.662), which may be the cause of injury to rhizomes, are kept under control. The prompt removal of any rotting tissue may help to check the problem temporarily, but in the long term the whole rhizome is best discarded.

Onion white rot

Plants affected Onions, shallots, leeks, garlic.
Symptoms The base of the bulb and the roots are covered in a fluffy, white, fungal growth in which hard, black sclerotia (fungal resting bodies) become embedded.

Cause The fungus *Sclerotium cepivorum*. Sclerotia in the soil will remain viable for at least seven years and, when stimulated by the presence of new host plant roots, they will germinate, causing infection again.
Control Dig up and burn affected plants as soon as possible. Do not grow susceptible crops on the affected site for at least eight years.

Onion neck rot

Plants affected Onions and shallots.
Symptoms The scales at the neck become soft and discoloured; a dense, fuzzy, grey, fungal growth develops on the affected area; and hard, black sclerotia (fungal resting bodies) may form. In some

severe cases the bulb eventually becomes mummified. The symptoms frequently do not appear until the bulbs are being kept in storage.
Cause The fungus *Botrytis allii*, spread mainly by seed-borne fungal spores and the sclerotia present on plant debris.
Control Obtain sets and seed from a reputable source. Encourage the growth of hard, well-ripened onions; do not feed after midsummer, avoid high nitrogen fertilizers, and water regularly. After harvesting, allow the tops of onions to dry off as rapidly as possible. Store under cool, dry conditions with good air circulation, discarding damaged bulbs. Avoid the more susceptible white-bulbed onions.

Onion fly

Plants affected Mainly onions, sometimes shallots, less often garlic and leeks.
Symptoms Growth is poor, the outer leaves turn yellow, and maggots may be found in the bulb.
Cause The root- and bulb-feeding larvae of the onion fly (*Delia antiqua*), white maggots up to 9mm (⅜in) long.

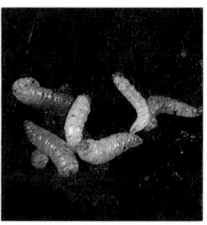

Control Carefully lift and burn infested plants. Egg-laying females can be excluded by growing onions under horticultural fleece. There are currently no pesticides available to amateur gardeners.

See also "Slugs and snails", p.644; "Millipedes", p.644; "Red lily beetle", p.644; "Tulip fire", p.649; "Bulb scale mite", p.652; "Grey squirrel", p.659; and "Mice, rats, and voles", p.662.

Whole–plant problems

Drought

Plants affected All plants, especially those that are young, container-grown, or in light, sandy soils.
Symptoms Autumn coloration develops early and defoliation, followed by die-back, may occur. Plants wilt and growth is stunted. Flowering and fruit set may decrease markedly. Fruits may be small, sometimes distorted, and of a poor texture. See pp.650 and 657 for other symptoms.
Cause Chronic (prolonged) or repeated drought due to inadequate or unavailable soil moisture; excessive water loss from the leaves of plants on exposed sites; injured or restricted roots; or soil compaction. Plants in small containers are vulnerable during hot weather, and peat-based composts that dry out too much are extremely difficult to re-wet. Dry, brown buds on certain plants, such as camellias and rhododendrons, are the result of a water shortage the previous year during the period of bud initiation.
Control Water plants regularly, and frequently check those in hot or sunny positions. Mulch, where appropriate, to improve moisture retention. Drought is more easily prevented than treated; plants exposed to chronic water shortage are less likely to recover once adequate water is supplied or temperatures fall than those suffering acute (sudden) shortage.

Low temperatures

Plants affected Trees, shrubs, perennials, annuals, bulbous plants, vegetables, fruits, indoor plants; seedlings and young plants are especially vulnerable.
Symptoms The leaves are sometimes bleached, and brown, dry patches develop; evergreen foliage may turn brown. Rotted patches develop on petals, especially on exposed flowerheads. Frost injury causes leaves to pucker and petals to wither or discolour. In some cases, whole flowers may be killed. See also pp.650 and 653.
Cause and control See p.650 for details.

Waterlogging

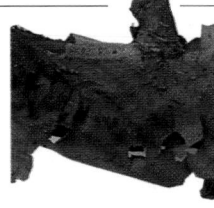

Plants affected Potentially all plants.
Symptoms Leaves may turn yellow, and plants tend to wilt. Bark peels off branches. Roots may rot off completely. Those remaining often begin to blacken and their outer surface peels away very easily.
Cause Excessive water levels in the growing medium, owing to poor soil structure, compaction, impeded drainage, or overwatering.
Control Where feasible, improve the structure and drainage of the soil and, if necessary, choose plants that are most likely to survive in wet conditions. Check that drainage holes for container-grown plants are adequate, and that flow through them is not impeded. The regular application of a foliar feed during the growing season may help to stimulate growth, allowing waterlogged roots to be replaced.

Damping off

Plants affected The seedlings of all plants.
Symptoms The seedlings collapse and die as their roots darken and rot off; the disease often attacks seedlings at one end of a seed tray, rapidly spreading to the other. A fluffy, fungal growth may appear both on the compost and on any dead seedlings.
Cause Various fungi (most particularly *Pythium ultimum* and some *Phytophthora*), which are soil- or water-borne and attack the seedlings via the roots or stem bases. These fungi flourish in moist and unhygienic conditions.
Control There is no control once the disease is established, so it must be prevented. Sow seed thinly, improve ventilation around seedlings, maintain strict hygiene, and avoid overwatering. Always use sterilized compost, mains water, and clean trays and pots. Water seedlings occasionally with a suitable copper-based fungicide.

Blackleg on cuttings

Plants affected Cuttings, most particularly those of pelargoniums.
Symptoms The stems become blackened, shrunken, soft, and rotten, usually at the base; the plant discolours and eventually dies.
Cause A variety of microorganisms, eg *Pythium* and *Rhizoctonia*, which are often spread by propagating in unhygienic conditions. Unsterilized compost, dirty pots, trays, and tools, and the use of non-mains water are commonly to blame. The disease is also transmitted by soil moisture.
Control Use clean equipment, sterilized compost, and mains water. Dip cuttings in rooting powder containing a fungicide before potting up. Remove affected cuttings immediately.

Blackleg on potatoes

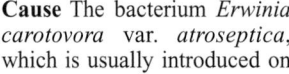

Plants affected Potatoes.
Symptoms The stems collapse, blacken and rot at the base, and the foliage discolours. The disease usually occurs at the start of the season, but any tubers that have formed may also rot. Most of the crop remains healthy; only a few plants show symptoms.
Cause The bacterium *Erwinia carotovora* var. *atroseptica*, which is usually introduced on slightly infected seed tubers that do not show any symptoms at all when they are being planted.
Control Remove affected plants immediately. Inspect tubers on lifting and do not store any that are suspect. The bacteria are unlikely to build up to dangerous levels in the soil, and potatoes can be planted on the site again under a rotation scheme.

Bad pruning

Plants affected Woody perennials, shrubs, and trees.
Symptoms The plant has a poor, unnatural, or uneven shape. Vigour may be reduced and flowering is limited. Snags or whole limbs may die back.
Cause The removal of limbs too close to, or far from, the main limb or trunk. A flush cut, where no snag is left, leaves a large wound and, more importantly, no branch collar – the area that most rapidly produces callusing wood to heal the wound. Conversely, too long a snag encourages die-back. Carelessly removed branches may damage adjacent bark.
Control When pruning a tree or shrub always be careful to follow the correct method at the appropriate time of year, checking the extent of pruning necessary. Use sharp pruning tools and do not leave any snags or flush cuts. If necessary, employ a reputable tree surgeon.

Nectria canker

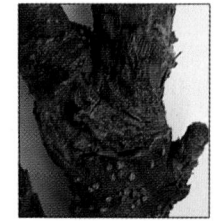

Plants affected Woody perennials, shrubs, trees, especially apples, flowering crab apples (*Malus*), beeches (*Fagus*), poplars (*Populus*), *Sorbus*, mulberries (*Morus*), and hawthorns (*Crataegus*).
Symptoms Small areas of bark, often close to a bud or wound, darken and sink inwards; the bark cracks, forming loose, flaky, concentric rings. Enlarged cankers restrict nutrient and water flow, and lead to stem and leaf deterioration. In extreme cases the whole shoot becomes ringed and dies back. White pustules appear in summer, red pustules in winter.
Cause Spores of the fungus *Nectria galligena* infect wounds caused by pruning, leaf fall, irregular growth, frost, and woolly aphids (see p.654).
Control Prune affected branches or, on larger limbs, remove the entire cankered area. Spray the affected tree with an appropriate fungicide, on a still day. Avoid susceptible cultivars, eg the apples 'Cox's Orange Pippin', 'Worcester Pearmain', and 'James Grieve'.

Seiridium canker

Plants affected Conifers, mainly cypresses (*Cupressus*) especially *C. macrocarpa* and *C. sempervirens*, and x *Cupressocyparis leylandii*.
Symptoms Some scattered branches develop dull foliage, which later yellows, dies, turns brown, and is eventually shed. Affected branches develop cankers, which produce copious amounts of resin and are covered with pinhead-sized, black, blister-like, fruiting bodies. When cankers girdle a branch or main stem it dies.

Cause Air-borne spores released from the fruiting bodies of the fungus *Seiridium cardinale* invade trees through the ends of cut branches, fine cracks in the bark, leaf scales, and twig crotches. Infection occurs most readily during the dormant season.
Control Cut out all affected branches or, if severely damaged, remove the whole tree. There is no available chemical control.

Bacterial canker

Plants affected *Prunus*, in particular cherries and plums.
Symptoms Flat or sunken, elongated cankers develop on the stems; droplets of golden or amber-coloured gum ooze from the affected area. The stem starts to deteriorate, and the foliage and flowers may wither and die, or the buds do not break. Foliage may show symptoms of shothole (see p.648).
Cause The bacteria *Pseudomonas syringae* pvar. *syringae* and *P. syringae* pvar. *morsprunorum*.
Control Remove cankered branches back to healthy wood. Spray the foliage with Bordeaux mixture or other suitable copper fungicide in late summer and early autumn.

Coral spot

Plants affected Broadleaved trees and shrubs, especially *Elaeagnus*, elms (*Ulmus*), beeches (*Fagus*), maples (*Acer*), magnolias, and currants.
Symptoms Affected shoots die back, and the dead bark becomes covered in orange-pink pustules about 1mm (¹⁄₁₆in) in diameter. Until recent years, the

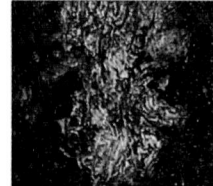

disease was most commonly found on dead branches and woody debris, but it has become more aggressive and now affects living shoots as well as dead.
Cause The fungus *Nectria cinnabarina*. Spores that have been released from the orange pustules are spread by rain splash and on pruning tools. They enter the wood through damaged or dying areas and wounds and infect the plant.
Control Clear away all woody debris. Cut back affected branches to a point well below the obviously infected area.

Honey fungus

Plants affected Trees, shrubs, climbers, and some woody perennials; especially *Wisteria*, rhododendrons, and privets (*Ligustrum*).
Symptoms A creamy-white mycelium develops under the bark at the base of the trunk or the stem, sometimes it also extends upwards; tough, black rhizomorphs (ie fungal strands) appear. In autumn fruiting bodies grow in clusters and die back after the first frost. Gum or resin exudes from cracks in the bark of conifers. Plants deteriorate and finally

Mycelium under bark

Fruiting bodies

die; prolific flowering or fruiting may occur shortly before death. Roots are also affected (see p.661).
Cause The fungus *Armillaria* (principally *A. mellea*) spread either by rhizomorph movement from an infected plant or stump, or through root contact.
Control Dig out and burn affected plants, stumps, and root systems; if necessary, have stumps chipped or ground out by a contractor. Avoid susceptible plants; choose those with some resistance, eg yew (*Taxus baccata*), *Cornus*, beech (*Fagus*), and *Hebe*.

Crown rot

Plants affected Mainly perennials and indoor plants; also trees, shrubs, annuals, bulbous plants, vegetables, and fruits.
Symptoms The base of the plant rots and may smell unpleasant. Plants may wilt, wither, and die.
Cause Bacterial and fun-

gal organisms entering the stem through surface wounds; over-deep planting also leads to infection.
Control Avoid injury to the stem base and keep the crown free of debris; do not mulch right up to the plant. Ensure that planting depths are correct. Complete removal of the affected area may prevent disease spread, but frequently the whole plant is killed and should be dug up and destroyed.

Replant disease/soil sickness

Plants affected Mainly roses, commonly those on *R. canina* rootstocks, and fruit trees.
Symptoms Vigour is reduced; growth and roots are stunted.
Cause Several factors may be involved, including soil-dwelling nematodes and the viruses they transmit, soil-borne fungi, and nutrient depletion.
Control Do not grow replacement plants in a site previously occupied by the same or a closely related species. Change the soil to a depth of at least 45cm (18in) and a width several centimetres greater than the spread of the roots. There is no suitable

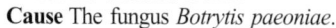

chemical sterilant available for amateurs, but the ground can be treated by a contractor.

Rose die-back

Plants affected Roses.
Symptoms The plants die back, and may discolour. A fungal growth may develop. Deterioration is extensive in some cases.
Cause Poor planting, poor maintenance, or a poor environment. Severe or repeated attacks of

frost, leaf disease, or fungi may also be responsible.
Control Plant roses correctly. Feed and water them regularly. Prune them, and keep diseases and pests under control. Remove all dead or diseased tissue back to healthy wood.

Fireblight

Plants affected Members of the family Rosaceae that bear pome fruits, mainly pears, apples, cotoneasters, hawthorns (*Crataegus*), and some *Sorbus*.
Symptoms Blossoms wilt and adjacent stem areas discolour. The foliage turns blackish-brown, shrivels,

and dies, but remains on the stem. Dark greenish-brown cankers then form on the branches, producing a bacterial ooze varying in colour between yellowish-brown and white, depending on the host. The inner surface of the bark and the wood beneath it may be stained brown. Affected limbs die and the tree is killed. See p.649 for other symptoms.
Cause The bacterium *Erwinia amylovora*, which is produced from the cankers and attacks via the blossom. It is carried by wind, rain splash, insects, and pollen grains.
Control Remove affected plants or prune out affected areas 60cm (24in) past the damage; dip the saw in disinfectant before using it on another tree. Fireblight is no longer a notifiable disease.

Clematis wilt

Plants affected Clematis, mainly large-flowered cultivars, eg 'Jackmanii'.
Symptoms The terminal shoots wilt, starting with the youngest foliage, and the petioles begin to darken where they join the leaf blade. A small spot of discolouration

may develop under the lowest pair of wilting leaves. Whole sections of the plant may start to die back.
Cause The fungus *Phoma clematidina*, which produces spore-releasing, fruiting bodies on the older stems. Other, non-pathogenic causes of wilt (eg drought, poor drainage, and graft failure) may be mistaken for this disease.
Control Cut back any affected stems to healthy tissue, below ground level if necessary. *Clematis* spp. are regarded as resistant to clematis wilt, for which there is no effective treatment.

Peony wilt

Plants affected Peonies (*Paeonia*).
Symptoms Affected shoots wilt, wither, and turn brown at the stem base. The infection generally starts at the stem base, which may become covered in a grey, fuzzy, fungal growth resembling grey mould. Small, hard, black, sclerotia (fungal resting bodies) form both on and within the affected stems.
Cause The fungus *Botrytis paeoniae*. The sclerotia drop into the soil and remain until conditions are favourable (wet years in particular); they then cause new infections.
Control Cut out the affected shoots of herbaceous peonies to below ground level, as soon as any signs of disease appear; thin out dense plants.

Anthracnose

Plants affected Willows (*Salix*) (mainly *S. x sepulcralis* var. *chrysocoma*); dogwood (*Cornus florida, C. kousa, C. nuttallii*); *Antirrhinum*.

Symptoms Dark, elliptical, rough cankers, about 6mm (¼in) long, on the stems; small, dark brown leaf spots turn yellow, curl, and fall early. The disease is rarely fatal.
Cause The fungus *Marssonina salicicola* on willow, *Discula destructiva* on dogwood, and one or more species of *Colletotrichum* on *Antirrhinum*. They are usually encouraged by mild, damp weather. Spores produced from the cankers and foliage lesions are spread by rain splash.
Control Prune out and burn the cankered shoots, where possible. Rake up and burn affected leaves.

Potato cyst eelworms

Plants affected Potatoes and tomatoes.
Symptoms Plants yellow and die, starting with the lower leaves, and potato tubers remain small. Roots of lifted plants show numerous white, yellow, or brown cysts up to 1mm (¹⁄₁₆in) in diameter.
Cause Root-dwelling eelworms, or nematodes, that disrupt water and nutrient uptake. Mature females swell and their bodies (known as cysts) burst through the root walls. Cysts contain up to 600 eggs; these remain viable for many years. Cysts of the golden cyst eelworm (*Globodera rostochiensis*)

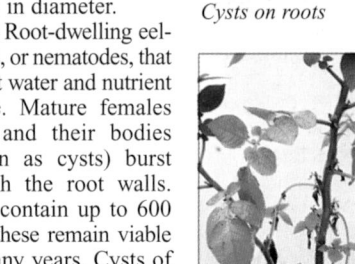

Cysts on roots

Yellowed leaves

change from white through yellow to brown as they mature; those of the white cyst eelworm (*G. pallida*) change directly from white to brown.
Control Crop rotation discourages the build-up of infestation. Some potatoes are resistant to the golden cyst eelworm, eg 'Accent', 'Pentland Javelin', 'Rocket', and 'Swift' (earlies), and 'Cara', 'Maris Piper', 'Sante', and 'Stemster' (maincrop); others, eg 'Maxine', are also tolerant of the white cyst eelworm. There is no chemical control available for amateur use.

Vine weevil grubs

Plants affected Shrubs, perennials, bulbous plants, and indoor plants; fuchsias, begonias, cyclamen, *Impatiens, Sedum*, primulas (including the Polyanthus Group), and strawberries are commonly affected. Container-grown plants are particularly vulnerable.

Symptoms Plants grow slowly, wilt, collapse, and die. Roots are eaten and the outer tissues of woody plants are gnawed from the stems below ground.
Cause The plump, white larvae of the beetle *Otiorhynchus sulcatus*, which are up to 1cm (½in) long and slightly curved, with brown heads and no legs. The adults lay eggs in spring and summer, and damage occurs from autumn to spring.
Control Maintain good hygiene to avoid providing shelters for the adults. Biological-control treatments using nematodes (*Heterorhabditis megidis*) are available; watered onto the potting compost in late summer, these treatments kill the larvae; a moist, well-drained compost with a temperature of 14–21°C (57–70°F) is required. Alternatively, treat susceptible plants with a drench of imidacloprid in late summer, or grow ornamental seedlings and cuttings in a compost premixed with imidacloprid, to kill small larvae.
See also "Vine weevil", p.645.

Fungus gnats or sciarid flies

Plants affected Plants grown under cover. Seedlings and cuttings are more susceptible than established plants.
Symptoms Both seedlings and cuttings fail to grow; greyish-brown flies run over the compost surface or fly among the plants. Larvae may be visible.
Cause The larvae of fungus gnats or sciarid flies (for example *Bradysia* spp.), which feed mainly on dead roots and leaves but may also attack young roots. They are slender, white-bodied maggots up to 6mm (¼in) long with black heads. The adult flies are of a similar length. They do not cause any problems on healthy, established plants.
Control Keep greenhouses tidy, and remove dead leaves and flowers from the soil surface to avoid providing shelters. Use sticky yellow traps suspended above plants to trap the adult flies. Introduce predatory mite *Hypoaspis miles* to feed on the flies' larvae. If necessary, use compost premixed with imidacloprid to control the larvae.

Bean seed fly

Plants affected French and runner beans.
Symptoms Seeds either fail to germinate or emerge blind. Seedlings are eaten.
Cause The larvae of the fly *Delia platura*, which are white, legless maggots up to 9mm (³⁄₈in) long that eat the germinating seeds and seedlings.
Control Avoid sowing when the soil is cold and wet (to encourage rapid germination), or pre-germinate seeds before sowing. If the problem is recurrent, sow seeds in pots or trays in a greenhouse and transplant once the seedlings have emerged.

Ants

Plants affected Many annuals and low-growing perennials.
Symptoms Plants grow slowly and have a tendency to wilt. Heaps of soil may also appear, sometimes burying some low-growing plants.
Cause Various species of black, yellow, or reddish-brown ants (eg *Lasius* and *Formica* spp.), which disturb the roots as they construct their nests. They do not usually feed on the plants, however, and cause relatively little damage.
Control Ants are often abundant and impossible to eliminate; as far as possible their presence should be tolerated. If the problem is severe, dust the soil with bendiocarb or permethrin.
See also p.668 for problems caused on lawns.

Rabbits and hares

Plants affected Young trees; low-growing plants.
Symptoms Tree bark is gnawed away, especially during cold weather. Low-growing plants are eaten, sometimes grazed down to ground level.

Cause Rabbits and hares.
Control Exclude the animals from gardens with wire netting at least 1m (3ft) high and sunk another 30cm (12in) below ground level. Alternatively, place less elaborate fencing around individual susceptible plants. Protect the base of trees with wire netting or spiral tree-guard collars. Repellent substances, based on aluminium ammonium sulphate or pepper dust, give only limited protection and need frequent application, especially during wet weather or periods of rapid plant growth.

Deer

Plants affected Most plants, especially trees, shrubs (including roses), and herbaceous plants.
Symptoms Shoots and leaves are eaten; tree bark is rubbed and frayed. In winter, bark may be eaten.
Cause Mainly roe and muntjac deer, which feed on shoots, leaves, and bark. Bark is frayed when males mark trees with their scent glands or rub the velvet from their new antlers.

Eaten rose shoots

Control Protect gardens with wire mesh fences at least 2m (6ft) high, or place wire netting around stems and trunks. Repellent sprays or scaring devices, such as hanging tin cans, provide only short-term protection from deer.

Branch damage

See also "Clubroot", p.649; "Pansy sickness", p.650; "Irregular water supply", p.651; "*Verticillium* wilt", p.653; "Slime flux/wet wood", p.653; "Spur blight/cane blight", p.653; "Grey mould (*Botrytis*)", p.653; "Dutch elm disease", p.653; "*Fusarium* wilt", p.654; "*Phytophthora* root rots", p.654; "Foot and root rots", p.654; "Cutworms", p.655; "Crown gall", p.655; "Fungal brackets", p.655; "Lightning", p.655; "Mechanical wounding", p.655; "Blossom wilt", p.656; "Root-knot eelworms", p.660; "Chafer grubs", p.660; "Leatherjackets", p.660; "Carrot fly", p.660; "Cabbage root fly", p.660; and "Wireworms", p.662.

Lawn problems

Drought

Plants affected Lawns and other grassed areas.
Symptoms Yellowish-brown, straw-like patches of variable size develop on the lawn; in extreme cases the whole area may become discoloured. Damage usually occurs in late spring or summer.
Cause Dry weather and inadequate watering. Free-draining, sandy soils are most at risk.
Control Water regularly in the early evening, providing enough water for deep penetration. To improve drought resistance, feed regularly, leave cut grass on the lawn if drought conditions are forecast, and spike and top-dress in the autumn. Allow the grass to grow fairly long before cutting, and avoid mowing too closely.
See also pp.650, 657, and 664 for problems caused to other plants.

Cats and dogs

Plants affected Lawns, seedlings, garden plants.
Symptoms Gardens, especially lawns and other grassed areas, are fouled with droppings; grass and foliage are scorched with urine; and newly sown areas are scratched up.
Cause Cats and dogs. Cats prefer dry soil and newly cultivated areas.
Control When cats and dogs are seen urinating on plants, wash it off immediately with water, to avoid scorching. Repellent substances based on pepper dust, naphthalene, or aluminium ammonium sulphate are available, but these often give only temporary protection. Ultrasonic devices may encourage cats and dogs to go elsewhere.

Dollar spot

Plants affected Lawns and other grassed areas, particularly those containing fine-leaved bents and creeping fescues.
Symptoms Small, pale, straw-coloured patches develop in early autumn. At first they are 2.5–7cm (1–3in) in diameter, but coalesce to form larger areas. They become darker as they age.
Cause The fungus *Sclerotinia homeocarpa*, encouraged by heavy or compacted soils and by a high pH; alkaline soils or those treated with lime are likely to produce symptoms. The disease appears mainly in mild, damp weather.
Control Improve soil aeration and remove thatch in the lawn, using a spring-tined lawn rake. Treat the affected area with a suitable fungicide.

Starvation

Plants affected Lawns and other grassed areas.
Symptoms The grass is thin, patchy, and often rather pale; it may be invaded by moss and weeds or attacked by pathogens. Growth is likely to be slow.

Cause Inadequate feeding or unsuitable fertilizers.
Control Feed the lawn in spring and preferably also in summer and autumn, choosing feeds appropriate to the time of year.

Snow mould/*Fusarium* patch

Plants affected Lawns, particularly those that contain a high proportion of annual meadow grass (*Poa annua*).
Symptoms Patches of grass become yellow and die, often coalescing to form large areas. In damp weather a white, fungal growth appears, causing the grass blades to stick together. It is most prevalent in late autumn and winter, especially on areas of grass that have been walked on while snow-covered.
Cause Principally the fungus *Monographella nivalis* (syn. *Fusarium nivale*), which is encouraged by poor aeration and excessive nitrogen fertilizers.
Control Improve maintenance in susceptible areas, regularly aerating and scarifying the turf. Avoid using high-nitrogen fertilizers in late summer to early autumn. Treat affected turf with a suitable fungicide.

Slime moulds

Plants affected Common grasses, and occasionally some other plants.
Symptoms Clusters of beige, orange, or white fruiting bodies smother individual blades of grass, and spores are then released, giving the slime mould a grey appearance; the grass looks unsightly but is not harmed. The condition is particularly common in late spring and again in early autumn.
Cause Slime moulds. They tend to thrive during periods of heavy rain.
Control Hose down the affected area.

Red thread

Plants affected Lawns, especially of finer grasses such as the fescues.
Symptoms Tiny, pale pink to red, gelatinous, branching threads of a fungus develop on small patches, about 8cm (3in) in diameter, of grass, which later become bleached. The lawn is very rarely killed completely but it is weakened and its general appearance is somewhat spoiled.
Cause The fungus *Laetisaria fuciformis*, which is common after heavy rain. It is also troublesome when the soil is nitrogen deficient or poorly aerated.
Control Improve turf maintenance and drainage, aerating, scarifying, and feeding as necessary.

Dog lichens

Plants affected Lawns and other grassed areas, particularly those that are in poor condition.
Symptoms Groups of greenish-black, curled, or leafy growths with a pale creamy-white lower surface appear in the lawn.
Cause *Peltigera canina*, which is most troublesome on grassed areas that are badly drained, poorly aerated, compacted, or shaded.
Control Rake out the lichens and treat with a suitable chemical. Improve aeration of the lawn and, if possible, the drainage. Remember to feed and top-dress the grass regularly.

Algae and gelatinous lichens

Gelatinous patch

Plants affected Lawns and other grassed areas.
Symptoms Slippery patches of green or greenish-black form on the surface.
Cause Gelatinous lichens and algae, which are particularly commonly found on any poorly drained, poorly aerated, or compacted sites.
Control Try to improve the drainage, and also aerate the lawn. Prune back any trees or shrubs that noticeably overhang the area, creating densely shaded, damp sections. Apply any proprietary lawncare products that contain dichlorophen.

Green, algal slime

Leatherjackets

Plants affected Lawns and other grassed areas.
Symptoms Brown patches appear in the lawn in midsummer, and maggots are sometimes visible.
Cause Leatherjackets, the larvae of crane flies, or daddy-long-legs (eg *Tipula* spp.), which feed on the roots. They are greyish-brown, tubular, legless maggots up to 3.5cm (1½in) long (see p.660).
Control Soak affected areas of the lawn with water, and cover with sacking or black plastic sheeting for a day to bring the leatherjackets to the surface; they can then be removed and killed. Alternatively apply biological-control pathogenic nematodes (*Steinernema carpocapsae*). Problems are worse following wet autumns.
See also p.660 for problems caused to other plants.

Chafer grubs

Plants affected Lawns and other grassed areas.
Symptoms Patches of the lawn are ripped up by birds, foxes, or badgers as they feed on chafer larvae. Damage occurs in autumn, sometimes continuing through a mild winter, and is found mainly on sandy soils where grass growth is already poor.

Cause The root feeding grubs of certain beetles, in particular the garden chafer (*Phyllopertha horticola*), and the Welsh chafer (*Hoplia philanthus*). The grubs are plump, "C"-shaped, and can be up to 2cm (¾in) long. They have white bodies, brown heads, and three pairs of legs.
Control Feed and water the lawn as necessary, to encourage good growth. If damage is severe, repair lawns by sowing or turfing in the spring. Water in biological-control pathogenic nematodes (*Steinernema carpocapsae*) from midsummer.
See also p.660 for problems caused to other plants by chafer grubs.

Toadstools

Plants affected Lawns and other grassed areas.
Symptoms Fungal, fruiting bodies develop, sometimes in distinct circles ("fairy rings"), and often on buried, woody material. Most cause little damage, but fairy rings are both harmful and disfiguring. Two circles of very lush, green grass form, one within the other, sometimes several metres in diameter, and the grass in between them dies off;

toadstools then emerge on the outer part of this middle zone. A white, fungal growth permeates the soil in the area of the ring.
Cause Various fungi, including *Coprinus*, *Mycena*, and the fairy-ring-producing *Marasmius oreades*. They all have underground mycelia and are spread to new sites by wind-borne spores.
Control Brush off *Coprinus* and *Mycena* when they first appear, before their spores are produced. If the fungi are on buried wood, remove them. There is no chemical control available to control fairy rings.

Ants

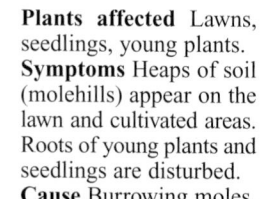
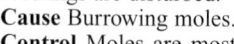
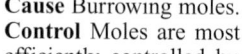

Plants affected Lawns and other grassed areas.
Symptoms Small heaps of fine soil are deposited on the surface of the lawn, mainly in summer.
Cause Ants (eg *Lasius flavus*), usually yellow-brown, which carry soil up to the surface as they remove it to extend their underground nests.
Control When the soil dries, remove the heaps with a brush. Dust the nest site with bendiocarb, permethrin, or pyrethrum.
See also p.666 for problems caused to other plants.

Earthworms

Plants affected Lawns.
Symptoms Small, muddy deposits or worm casts are left on the lawn surface in spring and autumn.
Cause Earthworms, mainly surface-casting types, especially *Allolobophora* spp.
Control Disperse dry casts by brushing. There are no effective organic or chemical treatments currently available to amateur gardeners.

Moles

Plants affected Lawns, seedlings, young plants.
Symptoms Heaps of soil (molehills) appear on the lawn and cultivated areas. Roots of young plants and seedlings are disturbed.
Cause Burrowing moles.
Control Moles are most efficiently controlled by trapping, although they may sometimes be driven away, at least temporarily, by ultrasonic devices.

Controls currently approved

Organic insecticides

Fatty acids/insecticidal soaps A modern version of the traditional soft soap spray for use against small insects, including aphids, whiteflies, red spider mite, thrips, scale insects, and mealybugs.

Pyrethrum Extracted from the flowers of *Pyrethrum cinerariifolium*. Available as sprays and dusts for controlling aphids, whiteflies, thrips, leafhoppers, ants, small caterpillars, and other small insects.

Rotenone or **Derris** Extracted from the roots of *Derris* and *Lonchocarpus* species. Available as sprays and dusts for controlling aphids, thrips, red spider mite, raspberry beetle, flea beetles, sawfly larvae, and other small caterpillars.

Vegetable oils Extracted from plants, including oil seed rape. Available as sprays for use against a similar range of pests as fatty acids.

Synthetic (non-organic) insecticides

Aluminium sulphate Applied to soil as crystals for the control of slugs and snails.

Bendiocarb A dust for controlling ants, woodlice, and wasp nests.

Bifenthrin A synthetic compound related to pyrethrum. Available as sprays for controlling aphids, white-

flies, thrips, leafhoppers, small caterpillars, beetles, and red spider mite.

Imidacloprid A systemic insecticide that is absorbed into the plant by the roots. Controls vine weevil grubs, fungus gnat larvae, whiteflies, and aphids. An aerosol that also contains methiocarb additionally controls red lily beetle, scale insects, and mealybugs.

Metaldehyde Pelleted baits or a liquid drench for controlling slugs and snails.

Permethrin Another synthetic pyrethroid. Available as a dust for controlling ants, earwigs, woodlice, and other crawling pests.

Pirimicarb Only available in the UK in combination with two fungicides for application as a spray. A selective insecticide that controls greenfly, blackfly, and other aphids only. It is absorbed into the foliage and so can reach aphids concealed under curled leaves.

Tar oil winter wash Spray for dormant fruit trees and bushes to control overwintering eggs of aphids, apple sucker, mussel scale, and other pests.

Organic fungicides

Bordeaux mixture A mixture of copper sulphate and calcium hydroxide approved under some organic regimes. Labelled in UK for control of potato and tomato blight, celery leaf spot, apple and pear canker, bacterial canker of *Prunus*, peach leaf curl, and some soft fruit rusts.

Sulphur Available in UK as dust, or as a liquid suspension with fatty acids. The dust may be used for control of a wide range of powdery mildews, and storage rots of bulbs, corms, etc. The liquid formulation is used for powdery mildew and pest control on roses and other ornamentals.

Synthetic fungicides

Bupirimate + triforine In UK, these two fungicides are only available as a mixture with the insecticide pirimicarb, for the control of rose black spot and rusts and powdery mildew on ornamentals.

Captan Only available in mixture with the rooting hormone ∝-naphthylacetic acid, to suppress infection in cuttings.

Carbendazim A systemic fungicide labelled for control of a wide range of scabs and powdery mildews, also some fruit and vegetable diseases and grey mould on many plants. Does not control rust diseases.

Cheshunt compound A copper-ammonium complex for control of damping-off problems in seedlings.

Copper oxychloride Protects against similar diseases to Bordeaux mixture.

Dichlorophen Available only in a mixture with 1-naphthylacetic acid rooting hormone for control of infection in cuttings, or as the sodium salt for control of mosses, algae, and lichens on hard surfaces (not for plant treatment).

Flutriafol Available in UK only mixed with the insecticide bifenthrin as a ready-to-use formulation for control of rose diseases and pests.

Mancozeb A protectant fungicide labelled in UK for control of lettuce downy mildew, potato and tomato blight, apple and pear scab, peach leaf curl, blackcurrant leaf spot, and some rusts.

Myclobutanil A systemic fungicide available in UK in several formulations for control of rose black spot, rusts, and powdery mildew on ornamentals, apple and pear scab, and some soft fruit powdery mildews.

Penconazole A systemic fungicide for control of powdery mildew on ornamentals and rose black spot; also provides some control of rusts on ornamentals. Some plants, for example fuchsias, may be sensitive to this product.

Phenolic formulations These form the basis of some wound paints, to protect exposed woody surfaces from fungal infections.

Tar acids and oils These are the basis of general disinfectants that also have labelling in UK for soil sterilization and control of honey fungus and clubroot. Also a component of some wound paints.

Thiophanate methyl A fungicide closely related to carbendazim, only available in UK as a seedling dip to control clubroot in brassicas.

Weeds

WEEDS are, quite simply, plants that grow where they are not wanted. They have important features in common: they are usually fast-growing and invasive, competing with cultivated plants for food and water; they are able to grow in almost any soil or site; and they often show a marked resistance to control. Weeds may occur in almost any part of the garden.

Cultivated plants may be placed in the weed category in certain circumstances, depending on their habit. If they prove too invasive for their site and overwhelm their neighbours, or if they self-seed freely throughout the garden, they may properly be classified as "weeds".

Categorizing weeds

Annual weeds complete their entire lifecycle within one year. They set seed which germinates freely; occasionally, as in the case of groundsel (*Senecio vulgaris*), they may even produce several generations in one season. It is important, therefore, to remove annuals at the seedling stage, before they are able to produce seed.

Perennial weeds, by contrast, survive from year to year. Some grow readily from seed, like annuals, but more usually persist by means of various storage organs, such as rhizomes, bulbs, bulbils, tubers, and thick tap roots. Many perennials are able to proliferate because of poor cultivation techniques that leave small pieces of rhizome or root in the soil when digging over or rotavating.

Controlling weeds

Weeds may be controlled in two main ways: they may either be discouraged from growing by the use of good, basic gardening techniques; or they may be removed by manual, mechanical, or chemical means.

The choice of how to remove different weeds depends on various factors: the habit of the plants themselves, the preference of the gardener, and the location of the weeds – whether in borders, lawns, paths, or neglected sites.

CULTIVATED PLANTS AS WEEDS

SNOW-IN-SUMMER
Any plant may become a weed if it dominates other garden plants. The dense growth and rapid spread of Cerastium tomentosum *may cause problems in a rock garden.*

RUSSIAN VINE
Although often planted to cover unsightly features rapidly, the Russian vine (Fallopia baldschuanica) *is an invasive climber that can soon swamp more delicate plants in the vicinity.*

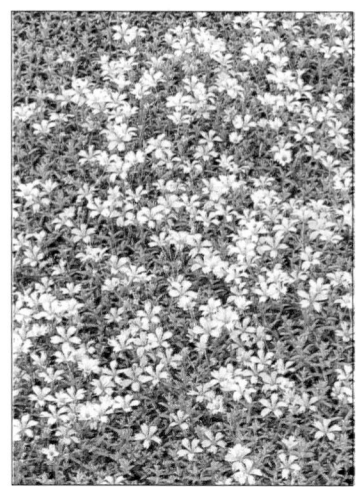

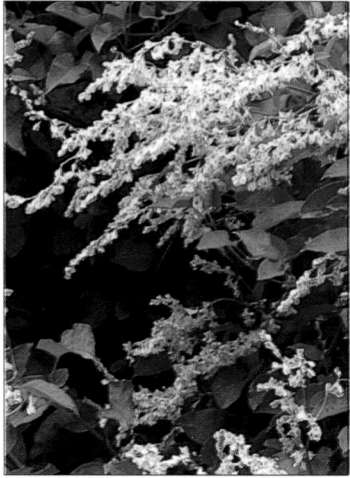

Annual weeds

In common with other annual plants, annual weeds grow, flower, set seed, and die within one year. They occur most frequently in regularly cultivated areas, such as vegetable plots or annual borders, where frequent digging deters perennial kinds. Their rapid growth makes them troublesome among crops raised from seed *in situ* as they smother slower-growing plants and reduce yields of others by competing for moisture, nutrients, and light.

The need for control

It is most important to destroy annual weeds before they produce seeds, since many seeds are small, light, readily wind-borne, and quick to germinate. Quick-maturing species such as shepherd's purse (*Capsella bursa-pastoris*) may produce several generations in a single season. Common chickweed (*Stellaria media*) smothers nearby plants and is another weed that should be controlled at the seedling stage. Its seeds start to germinate in the autumn and continue growing in a mild winter to form dense mats.

Many seeds may be buried once they are shed, and lie dormant for many years until they are brought to the surface during site or crop cultivation. The weeds then germinate and grow rapidly. If a site is heavily infested, it should be cultivated regularly when it is crop-free in order to kill germinating seedlings.

Annual weeds may be controlled by hand, mechanical, or chemical means (see "Preventing weeds", p.670).

COMMON ANNUAL WEEDS

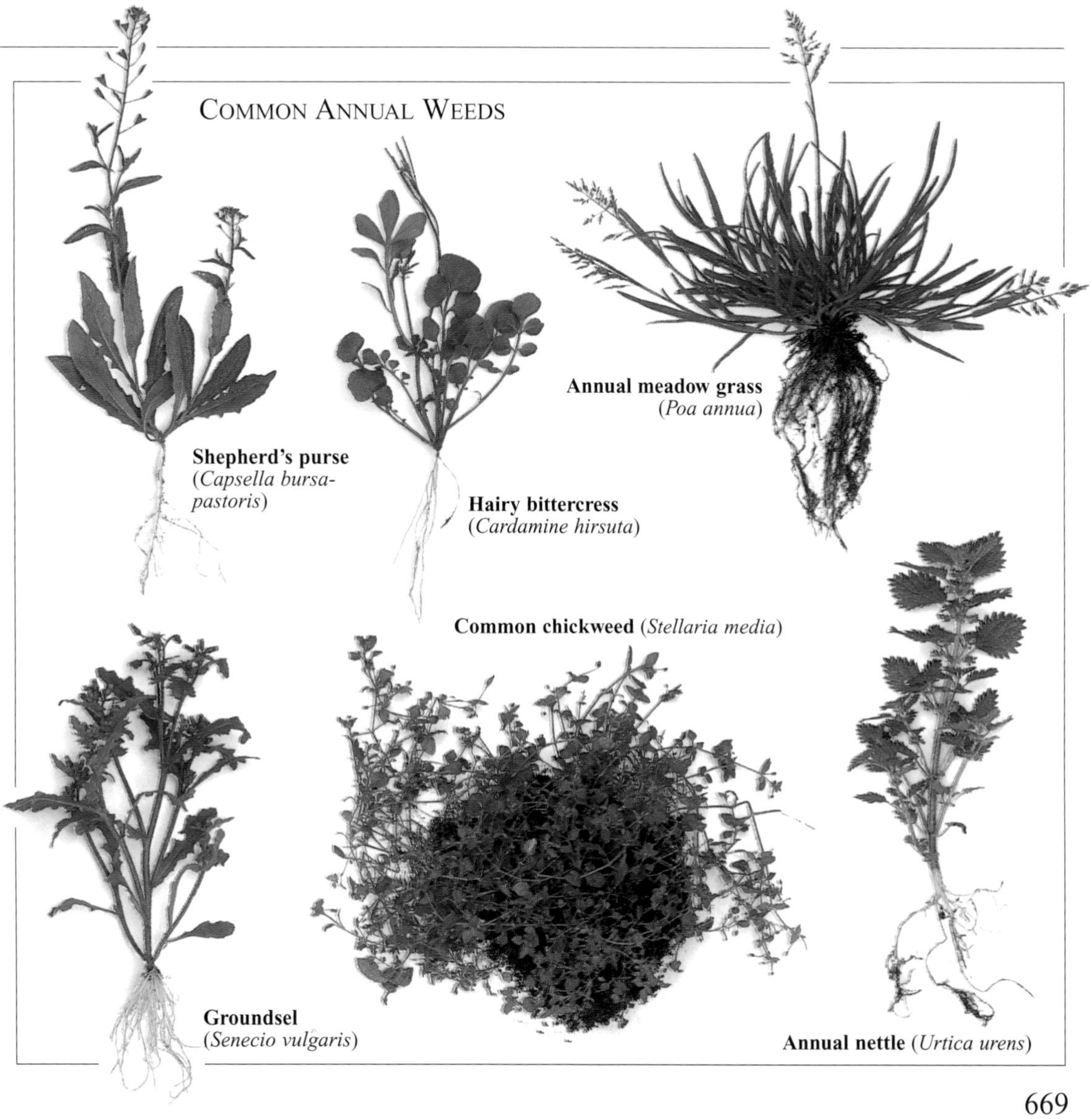

Shepherd's purse (*Capsella bursa-pastoris*)

Hairy bittercress (*Cardamine hirsuta*)

Annual meadow grass (*Poa annua*)

Groundsel (*Senecio vulgaris*)

Common chickweed (*Stellaria media*)

Annual nettle (*Urtica urens*)

Perennial weeds

Perennial weeds persist from year to year, surviving and resting through winter cold and summer heat by storing food reserves in fleshy roots, bulbs, rhizomes, or tubers.

They may be divided into two groups: herbaceous kinds and woody-stemmed kinds. Herbaceous perennials die back to ground level in the autumn. They survive the winter by storing food in their roots and then reappear in spring. Examples are the perennial stinging nettle (*Urtica dioica*), broadleaved dock (*Rumex obtusifolius*), and field bindweed (*Convolvulus arvensis*). Also included in this group are the stemless herbaceous perennials that have leaves arising directly from their roots or rhizomes, for example, dandelion (*Taraxacum officinale*) and ground elder (*Aegopodium podagraria*).

Woody-stemmed perennials, such as common elder (*Sambucus nigra*) and bramble (*Rubus fruticosus*), survive the winter by storing food in stems and branches. The woody-stemmed, evergreen, common ivy (*Hedera helix*) can also be an invasive weed.

The need for control
Perennial weeds have underground fleshy roots, rhizomes, and other storage organs that are not easily controlled. Hoeing and digging, along with machine cultivation, tend to break the roots and rhizomes into sections without killing them; many survive to grow and increase the infestation. With most perennial weeds, use of weedkillers is the most practical and effective approach.

Preventing weeds

Both annual and perennial weeds may be prevented from establishing in various ways. These will do much to avoid the need for tedious weeding later on, especially if you adopt methods that rely on the principle of depriving light from the soil surface. Without light, plants are unable to grow.

Working the soil
Before planting, it is extremely important to clear the site completely of all weeds, either manually or with chemicals. Weeds are often difficult to eradicate from among established plants, which may need to be lifted and the weeds extracted from the washed root system.

Conditioning very acid soils with lime will deter some lawn weeds, such as field woodrush (*Luzula campestris*), that thrive where the soil is acid.

Cultivating healthy plants
Vigorous, healthy plants are able to compete more effectively with weeds than are poor, weak specimens. Plants with spreading foliage provide a dark cover over the soil that discourages weed germination under the canopy.

Some vegetable crops, for example potatoes, compete well with annual weeds and may be grown to help maintain clean ground for a subsequent crop (see GROWING VEGETABLES, "Crop rotation", p.498).

Plastic mulch materials
Covering the soil with plastic mulch sheeting after planting prevents annual weeds from establishing. Such materials can also be effective in suppressing most perennial weeds if undisturbed for at least two years. Plastic mulch sheeting is generally permeable, allowing water and nutrients to pass through to the roots. Cover the sheeting with a bark mulch to improve its appearance. Black plastic sheeting is particularly useful in fruit and vegetable gardens; make slits in it through which the crops can grow.

Organic mulching
In early spring, apply a mulch 5–8cm (2–3in) thick of weed-free, organic material such as leaf mould, peat substitute, or processed bark to help prevent weed seeds germinating and smother weed seedlings. Do not use garden compost or insufficiently rotted manure as they often contain weed seeds.

Established perennial weeds may grow through the mulch but, as they tend to root into the loose material, they are easy to remove.

Ground-cover plants
Some plants grow in dense carpets that suppress the germination of weed seeds. They are useful for parts of the garden where, because of shade, or very wet or dry soil, weeds thrive. Choose ground-cover plants carefully as some are invasive (see PERENNIALS FOR GROUND COVER, p.180).

Grassing down borders
Some persistent perennial weeds, such as horsetail (*Equisetum arvense*) and oxalis (*Oxalis corymbosa* and *O. latifolia*), may resist repeated attempts to eradicate them with weedkiller or to dig them out. An alternative approach is to grass down any badly infested borders and maintain them as close-mown turf for several years. Given time, this treatment will generally eliminate most of the infestation of persistent perennial weeds.

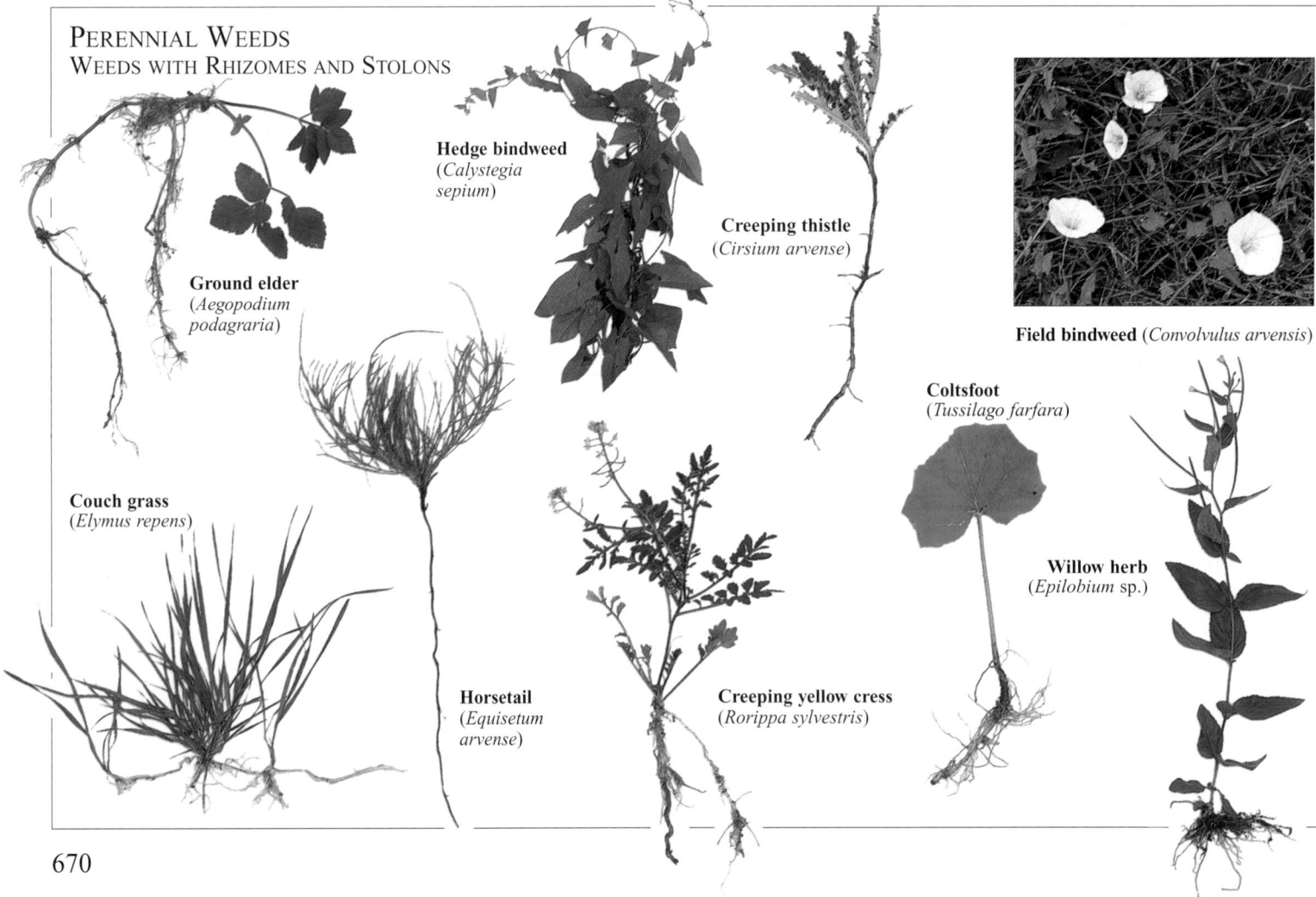

PERENNIAL WEEDS
WEEDS WITH RHIZOMES AND STOLONS

Ground elder
(*Aegopodium podagraria*)

Hedge bindweed
(*Calystegia sepium*)

Creeping thistle
(*Cirsium arvense*)

Field bindweed (*Convolvulus arvensis*)

Couch grass
(*Elymus repens*)

Coltsfoot
(*Tussilago farfara*)

Willow herb
(*Epilobium* sp.)

Horsetail
(*Equisetum arvense*)

Creeping yellow cress
(*Rorippa sylvestris*)

Controlling weeds

Once weeds are present, they may be eradicated in one of three ways: hand-weeding, mechanical control, and chemical control. There are three different types of weedkiller: those that act on the leaves, those that act on the soil, and those that act on specific types of plant.

Hand-weeding and hoeing

Hand-weeding, hoeing, and forking are often the only practical ways of removing weeds in flower beds, the vegetable garden, and small patches of ground, where weedkillers cannot be used safely without risk of harming nearby garden or crop plants.

Hand-weed or hoe in dry weather, if possible, so that the weeds shrivel and die rapidly. In wet weather, remove uprooted weeds from the site to prevent them from rooting back into the soil. Hoe only lightly around cultivated plants to prevent their surface roots from being damaged.

Removing weeds mechanically

Market gardeners often use rotary cultivators (rotavators) with hoeing or cultivating attachments for annual weed control between rows of vegetables, but they may be unsuitable for perennials. They simply cut the rhizomes of weeds such as couch grass and ground elder into many pieces that will continue to grow as new plants. Wherever possible, use weed-killers to kill persistent perennial weeds before digging or cultivating.

Foliage-acting weedkillers

Leaf-acting products enter the weeds through leaves or green stems and are applied with a sprayer or watering can and fine rose or dribble-bar. There are two different types: systemic and contact. The first acts by translocation, moving from the leaves to the roots, and so destroys both annual and perennial weeds. For maximum effect the weeds should be in vigorous growth. The second type works by killing only by direct touch. They destroy annual weeds and the green leaves and stems of perennial weeds, although not the roots of perennials, which will usually regrow strongly. Some weedkillers act through both leaves and roots.

Soil-acting weedkillers

These are applied to the soil and are absorbed into the roots of growing weeds. From there they move to the parts above ground, killing the weeds by interfering with their metabolism. They remain active in the soil, sometimes for months, killing weeds as the seeds germinate. They kill established annual weeds and may also kill or suppress many established perennial weeds. When planning to use areas that have been treated with soil-acting weedkillers, check the manufacturer's literature for details of residual activity and do not sow or plant until the recommended period has elapsed.

Selective weedkillers

These weedkillers kill broadleaved weeds but not narrow-leaved grasses.

Range of chemicals

From time to time the range of weedkillers available to gardeners changes – a new product is introduced or an existing one withdrawn. When buying weedkillers, always check within the range currently available that the products can be used safely and effectively in the situations where weeds are troublesome. A weedkiller may include one of these chemicals.

Glufosinate ammonium (contact action) and **paraquat with diquat** (contact action) are both quick-acting and will kill annual weeds but only check the growth of perennial weeds. They are useful for killing overwintering annual weeds before spring sowing or planting and are inactivated in soil.

Glyphosate (translocated, foliage-acting) is one of the most useful weedkillers for controlling perennial weeds. It is a foliage-acting weedkiller that moves down to the roots, killing or strongly checking even the most difficult weeds. It is not selective and should be kept well away from all garden plants, but especially raspberries, roses, and other suckering woody plants. With most weeds, it is most effective when growth is well advanced, usually from midsummer onwards, but check the manufacturer's recommendations. As it does not remain active in the soil it is safe to cultivate as soon as weeds are dead.

Ammonium sulphamate (foliage- and soil-acting) controls woody-stemmed perennial weeds such as bramble and various tree seedlings. Where they cannot be dug out easily, cut them back with secateurs or a pruning saw to leave a short stump. Then wet the newly cut surface and the whole stump down to ground level with a solution of ammonium sulphamate. Avoid run-off into the soil where there may be underlying roots of nearby garden plants.

Dichlobenil (soil-acting, granular) is a weedkiller that may be applied, before growth begins, to the soil around some well-established ornamental shrubs, including roses, to control or suppress some perennial weeds, such as ground elder, and to control germinating weed seeds. It is residual and continues to act for several months.

Amitrole (foliage-acting, translocated) is usually combined with contact and soil-acting herbicides to control weeds that have become established in cracks and crevices in paved areas, paths, and drives.

WEEDS WITH TUBERS AND FLESHY ROOTS

Bryony (*Bryonia dioica*)

Oxalis (*Oxalis corymbosa* and *O. latifolia*)

Lesser celandine (*Ranunculus ficaria*)

WEEDS WITH DEEP ROOTS

Japanese knotweed (*Fallopia japonica*)

Dock (*Rumex* sp.)

Bramble (*Rubus fruticosus*)

Perennial stinging nettle (*Urtica dioica*)

Using weedkillers safely

Care must always be taken when applying weedkillers:
• wear protective clothing, for example rubber gloves and old clothes, when mixing and applying weedkillers;
• do not apply weedkillers in windy conditions when there is a risk of spray being blown across to nearby plants, which may suffer serious damage;
• use only for appropriate purposes as recommended on the product label, for example do not use a path weedkiller to keep down weeds in a rose bed;
• always dilute soluble weedkillers according to the manufacturer's instructions;
• always apply weedkillers at the recommended rates on the labels;
• always keep in original containers and make sure that the labels are well secured to the containers so that contents are known and no errors in usage occur;
• never store diluted weedkillers for future use;
• store away out of reach of children and animals, preferably in a securely locked cupboard in a workshop or shed.

Lawn weeds

Various perennial weeds can be troublesome in lawns. Their common survival factor is their ability to grow and thrive in the adverse conditions of short, regularly mown grass. They usually originate from seeds carried by the wind or by birds. Once lawn weeds have germinated, most are then rapidly spread by the action of mowing and early treatment is necessary if they are to be eradicated.

Among the most troublesome lawn weeds are: slender speedwell (*Veronica filiformis*), field woodrush (*Luzula campestris*), annual meadow grass (*Poa annua*), and mind-your-own-business (*Soleirolia soleirolii*, syn. *Helxine soleirolii*). These persistent weeds do not respond to treatment by lawn weedkillers, and need other forms of treatment.

In lawns where the grass is too sparse to offer adequate competition, moss may also become a problem.

Preventing weeds and moss

Good lawn care is an effective preventive measure. The presence of numerous weeds in a lawn usually indicates that the grass is not growing sufficiently vigorously to prevent weeds from establishing. Lack of regular feeding and drought are among the most common reasons for poor growth. Soil compaction and mowing the grass too closely and too regularly may also lead to the spread of moss. For further details on lawn care, see THE LAWN, "Routine care", pp.395–400. Coarser weed grasses (for example, *Holcus lanatus*) may remain a problem, and clumps or affected areas of turf may need to be removed and the cleared patch returfed or re-seeded.

Raking before mowing and lifting creeping stems may help to check the spread of creeping weeds, such as trefoils (*Trifolium* spp.), slender speedwell (*Veronica filiformis*), and sorrels (*Rumex* spp.) if the grass is mown straight afterwards and the clippings picked up by the mower.

Removing weeds

There are two main ways of treating lawn weeds, depending on the severity of the problem. They may be removed by hand or treated with an appropriate weedkiller.

Weeding by hand
Hand-weeding is an effective method of removing a few, scattered rosetted weeds such as daisy (*Bellis perennis*), dandelion (*Taraxacum officinale*), and plantains (*Plantago* spp.). Use a daisy grubber or hand fork to lift the weeds, then firm back displaced turf.

Dealing with moss
Moss may be killed with moss preparations or lawn sand. This is only a short-term solution, however: unless the original conditions that encouraged moss are identified and corrected, the problem usually recurs.

Removing weeds with chemicals
Weedkillers intended specifically for use on lawns work by translocation – moving within the plant from the leaves to the roots – and the weeds begin to distort and shrivel within a few days of application. The chemicals are selective and do not harm lawn grasses at normal dilution rates, but do not use them on seedling grasses within six months of germination.

You should also avoid using lawn weedkillers on newly laid turf, until one growing season has passed after laying or planting.

LAWN WEEDS

Yarrow (*Achillea millefolium*)

Common mouse-ear chickweed (*Cerastium fontanum*, syn. *C. vulgatum*)

Mouse-ear hawkweed (*Hieracium pilosella*)

Field woodrush (*Luzula campestris*)

Broadleaved plantain (*Plantago major*)

Self-heal (*Prunella vulgaris*)

Creeping buttercup (*Ranunculus repens*)

Sheep's sorrel (*Rumex acetosella*)

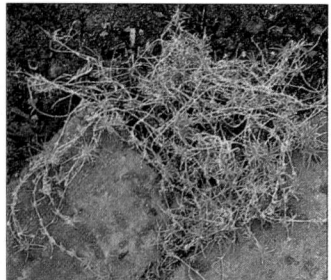
Pearlwort (*Sagina procumbens*)

Lesser yellow trefoil (*Trifolium dubium*)

Common white clover (*Trifolium repens*)

Slender speedwell (*Veronica filiformis*)

The range of chemicals

Proprietary lawn weedkillers normally combine two or more active ingredients in order to control a wider range of weeds. These include:
2,4–D a selective weedkiller that is particularly effective against broad-leaved, rosetted weeds, such as plantains and daisies. This chemical is usually combined with mecopropp.
Mecopropp which kills various difficult, small-leaved, and creeping weeds, such as trefoils (*Trifolium* spp. and *Lotus corniculatus*). It is usually combined with 2,4–D.
Dichlorophen which kills moss in lawns. It is quick-acting.
Ferrous sulphate the active ingredient in lawn sands; it is used to eradicate moss.
MCPA a selective herbicide used in both problem-weed mixtures and lawn weedkillers to control weeds that have resistance to other chemicals.
Dicamba usually combined with 2,4–D or MCPA to control a wider range of weeds.
Lime which may be applied on very acid soils in winter in the form of ground chalk or limestone at 50g/sq m (2oz/sq yd) to deter sorrels and field woodrush. Sorrels can be partially controlled by repeat treatment with 2,4–D preparations; field woodrush is resistant to lawn weedkillers.

Buying weedkillers

Lawn weedkillers are usually sold as a concentrated liquid and therefore need to be suitably diluted. They may also be obtained in the form of soluble powder, ready-to-use spray, aerosol, wax bar, or in combination with liquid or granular lawn fertilizers.

Applying weedkillers

Feed the lawn at the start of the growing season, applying weedkiller two to three weeks later when grass and weeds are growing strongly. In the spring, creeping lawn grasses soon colonize any bare patches left as weeds shrivel and die. Great care should be taken when applying weedkillers (see the recommendations on p.671).

Wheeled sprayers can be used for large areas; a watering can with a fine rose or dribble-bar attachment is better for small lawns. Divide the lawn into strips using two garden lines to ensure that the grass has been given complete and uniform coverage.

If possible, wait for two or three days after mowing before applying the weedkiller so that the weeds have time to develop new leaf surfaces to absorb the chemicals. Do not mow the grass for two or three days after spraying to allow time for the weedkiller to work its way down towards the roots. Also do not put the grass clippings on the compost heap for first few cuts after the application of weedkiller.

How often to apply

Some lawn weeds, such as daisies and plantains, are killed by one or two applications of weedkiller; others, for example the trefoils, may need two or three applications, at four- to six-week intervals.

Where a weed shows no response to repeated applications of various weedkillers, the only solution is to remove it by hand. This will either mean removing and replacing infested areas of turf or, alternatively, feeding, scarifying, and aerating the turf to strengthen it and weaken the weed.

Neglected sites

Different treatments need to be adopted according to how long the area has been neglected and how great a hold the weeds have obtained. Sites that have been neglected for some time may take a season, or even longer, to clear for vegetable growing.

Short-term neglect

On sites that have been neglected for up to a year, most of the weeds are likely to be annuals. Kill these with one or two applications of the contact weedkillers paraquat with diquat or glufosine ammonium in the spring or summer. This has the added advantage of defoliating and weakening any young perennials that may have appeared; it does not kill them, however. Dig these up two or three weeks after the treatment, when they have resprouted and can be identified.

If any weed seedlings appear in the meantime, either dig them in or destroy them with a further application of contact weedkiller.

Winter clearance

If the site is being cleared during the winter, remove any overwintering top-growth of annual weeds with a rotary mower. Then dig out any perennial weeds by hand, if possible, before cultivating the area. Clear neglected vegetable plots and allotments progressively, beginning at the warmer, sunnier end, where the earliest sowings of crops are to be made and the seedbeds are to be sited.

Longer-term neglect

After a second year of neglect, perennial weeds will become well established, competing vigorously with annual weeds. If the site remains neglected for a further year, by the end of the third growing season the weed population will usually be largely, or entirely, strong-growing perennial weeds. Badly infested sites are difficult to clear by hand or by use of a rotavator (the latter may do no more than turn the weeds back into the soil again). It is more practical to use translocated and soil-acting weedkillers, allowing a full growing season for treatment to take effect.

Cutting down weeds

If beginning clearance in spring, cut down weeds with woody stems, for example brambles or elder, to within 30–45cm (12–18in) from the ground, then spray the whole weed-infested area with ammonium sulphamate.

Using this weedkiller has a dual purpose: it not only kills woody weeds but is also effective against coarse grasses and broadleaved perennial weeds. It persists in the soil for about three months, which is a disadvantage; being highly soluble, it spreads easily through the soil and, for this reason, should not be used where there are underlying tree or shrub roots, or where it may leach into cultivated areas and affect plant growth there.

Any weeds that survive treatment with ammonium sulphamate and produce regrowth in late summer can then be treated with glyphosate.

Summer spraying

Another method is to cut the weeds back in spring and then allow them to grow unchecked until midsummer; then spray the site with glyphosate, which acts more effectively on the vigorous young growth stimulated by the spring cut. It is a translocated weedkiller and it usually takes three to four weeks to show any effect; it leaves no active residues in the soil and as soon as weeds are dead the site can be cultivated and planted. Very persistent weeds, such as horsetail and bindweed, may need subsequent spot-treatment, again with glyphosate, possibly for a further two or three growing seasons, to control them fully.

Uncultivated ground

Where previously cultivated land is to be left uncultivated, and is free from perennial weeds, it can be kept clear by regular light cultivations, at intervals throughout the year, with a hoe or with a mechanical tool, such as a rotary cultivator. Alternatively, at intervals, developing weed seedlings can be killed by application of the contact weedkillers, paraquat with diquat, or glufosinate ammonium.

If there are perennial weeds infesting the site, let them grow until midsummer, then spray with glyphosate.

Weeds in cracks and crevices

Weeds in the cracks in paths and brickwork are hard to remove by hand, so chemical control is usually required.

Path weedkillers

In early spring, apply a proprietary path weedkiller. Such weedkillers are mixtures of contact and soil-acting chemicals, the latter usually remaining active in the soil for several months. They may also include a foliage-acting, translocated herbicide, such as MCPA or amitrole, to deal with any established perennial weeds not usually controlled by the low-strength, soil-acting chemicals in these mixtures.

Spot treatment

Perennial weeds in paths may be spot-treated or sprayed with glyphosate when regrowth is vigorous. Dichlobenil granules carefully sprinkled or brushed into the spaces between paving stones will control weeds but should not be applied if crevice plants are being cultivated.

WEED-INFESTED PONDS

Filamentous algae (blanketweeds), which are often troublesome in too shallow or under-stocked ponds, can be kept under control with suitable pool algicides. However, there are no weedkillers approved for the control of invasive pool weeds such as the floating azollas and duckweeds. These are best controlled by periodically sweeping the pool's surface using a floating boom or net.

8
BASIC BOTANY

FAMILIARITY WITH THE BASICS of botany (the study of plants) helps the gardener to understand how to keep plants healthy as well as many horticultural techniques, such as propagation. The study of the internal arrangement of plant structures (anatomy) and their external construction (morphology), for example, provides an explanation of how to graft or make pruning cuts that heal quickly. Physiology – the study of a plant's metabolism – offers insight into a plant's need for water and light, the processes of photosynthesis, transpiration, and respiration, and the role of nutrients. The identification and classification of plants (taxonomy) shows close relationships between genera or species that have similar cultivation needs.

Plant diversity

There are more than 250,000 species of seed-bearing plant. They include annuals, which flower, seed, and die in a year or less; biennials, which grow from seed in their first year and then flower, seed, and die in the second season; and perennials, which live for several to many years, and include woody plants. Commonly, the term perennials is applied to herbaceous or border plants, while trees and shrubs are referred to as woody plants. The roots, stems, leaves, and flowers of plants may become modified for particular purposes and environments.

Roots

These anchor the plant in the soil and absorb water and mineral salts from which the plant manufactures its food. Fleshy tap roots penetrate vertically downwards, forming sparse lateral roots that are, in turn, finely branched. Fibrous roots comprise a network of fine, thread-like roots that emerge from the base of the stem or from tap roots in some plants. The root tips bear fragile root hairs, which are in intimate contact with soil particles from which water and mineral salts are absorbed. Roots are sometimes modified to form storage organs, as is the case in many terrestrial orchids or swollen tap roots such as carrots, or in some tubers such as dahlias.

Stems

Plant stems provide the above-ground framework of the plant, supporting the leaves, flowers, and fruits. Some stem cells are specialized to provide a strong framework; some conduct water and mineral salts (the xylem), or

BASIC PARTS OF A PLANT

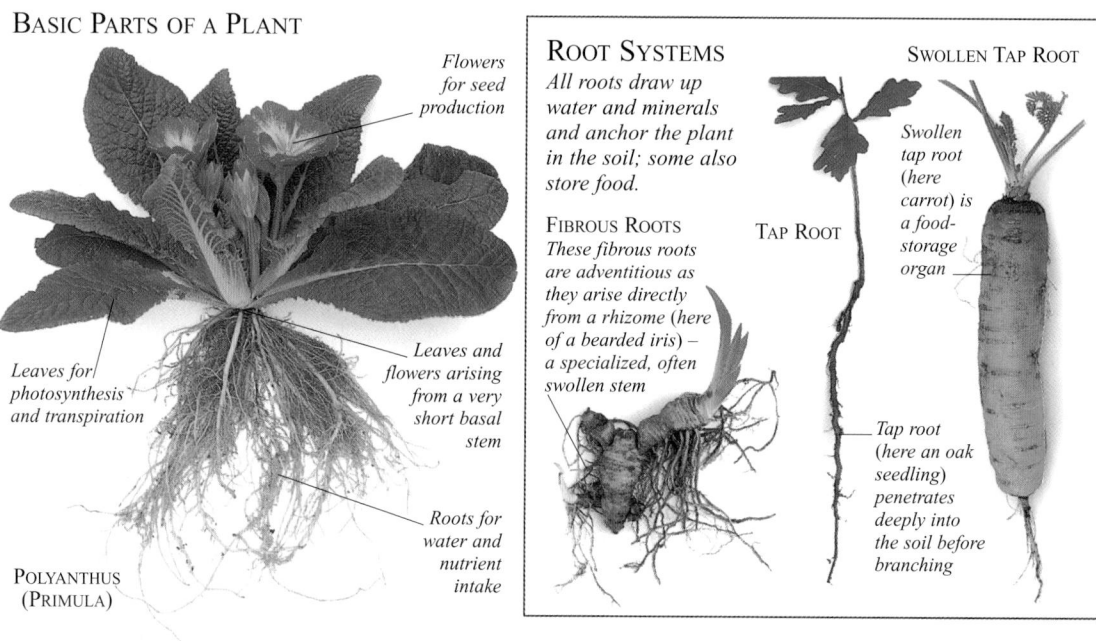

Flowers for seed production

Leaves for photosynthesis and transpiration

Leaves and flowers arising from a very short basal stem

Roots for water and nutrient intake

POLYANTHUS (PRIMULA)

ROOT SYSTEMS
All roots draw up water and minerals and anchor the plant in the soil; some also store food.

SWOLLEN TAP ROOT

FIBROUS ROOTS
These fibrous roots are adventitious as they arise directly from a rhizome (here of a bearded iris) – a specialized, often swollen stem

TAP ROOT

Swollen tap root (here carrot) is a food-storage organ

Tap root (here an oak seedling) penetrates deeply into the soil before branching

TYPES OF STEM

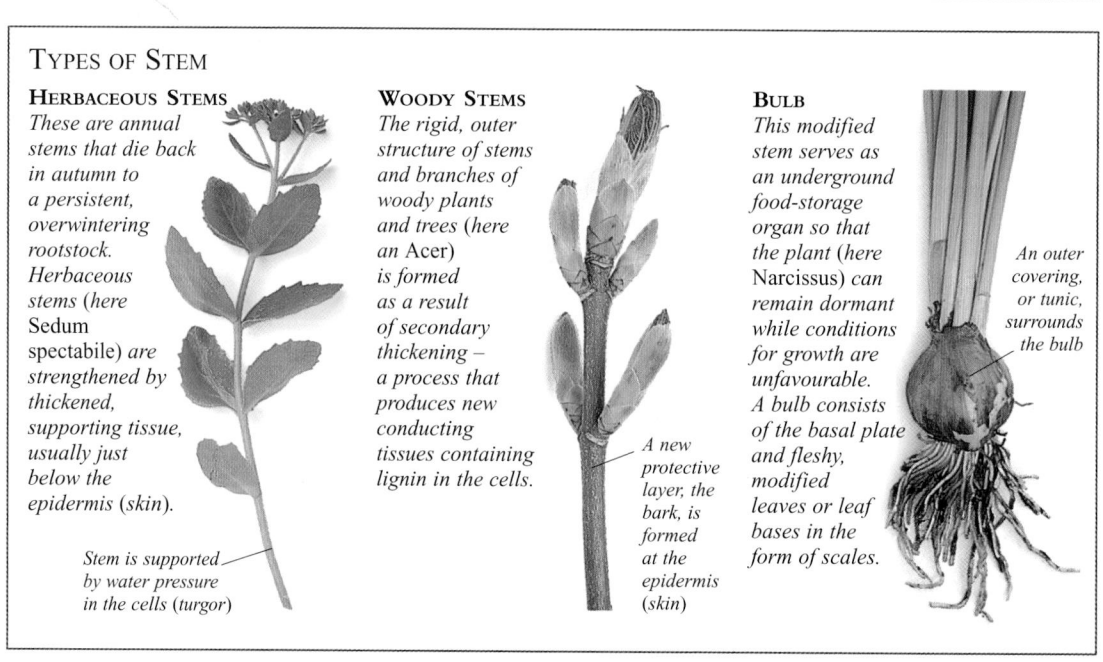

HERBACEOUS STEMS
These are annual stems that die back in autumn to a persistent, overwintering rootstock. Herbaceous stems (here Sedum spectabile) *are strengthened by thickened, supporting tissue, usually just below the epidermis (skin).*

Stem is supported by water pressure in the cells (turgor)

WOODY STEMS
The rigid, outer structure of stems and branches of woody plants and trees (here an Acer) *is formed as a result of secondary thickening – a process that produces new conducting tissues containing lignin in the cells.*

A new protective layer, the bark, is formed at the epidermis (skin)

BULB
This modified stem serves as an underground food-storage organ so that the plant (here Narcissus) *can remain dormant while conditions for growth are unfavourable. A bulb consists of the basal plate and fleshy, modified leaves or leaf bases in the form of scales.*

An outer covering, or tunic, surrounds the bulb

LEAF FORMS

SCALE-LIKE LEAF (*Chamaecyparis obtusa* 'Nana Aurea')

PINNATE LEAF (*Robinia pseudoacacia*)

BROADLY OVATE LEAF (*Camellia japonica*)

PINNATIFID LEAF (Swiss-cheese plant, *Monstera deliciosa*)

COMPOUND PINNATE FROND (*Dryopteris filix-mas*)

DIGITATE LEAF (Horse chestnut, *Aesculus hippocastanum*)

LINEAR LEAVES (Annual meadow grass, *Poa annua*)

manufactured food (the phloem) from the leaves to all parts of the plant. Stems are often modified for other functions. Corms, rhizomes, and many tubers are swollen, underground stems that are modified for food storage; in cacti, the frequently swollen stems contain water-storage tissue.

Leaves

Leaf form is extremely diverse and may be modified as spines, as in some cacti, or as tendrils, as in the garden pea. Whatever their form, leaves are

the manufacturing centres of a plant. They contain the green pigment chlorophyll, which absorbs the energy of sunlight in order to convert carbon dioxide from the air and water from the soil into carbohydrates by the process known as photosynthesis. The by-product, oxygen, is essential to all life. The energy required to drive the plant's metabolism is produced through respiration, which breaks down carbohydrates to release energy, carbon dioxide, and water.

Leaves present a relatively large surface so that they maximize absorption of light; they are thin enough

PHOTOSYNTHESIS

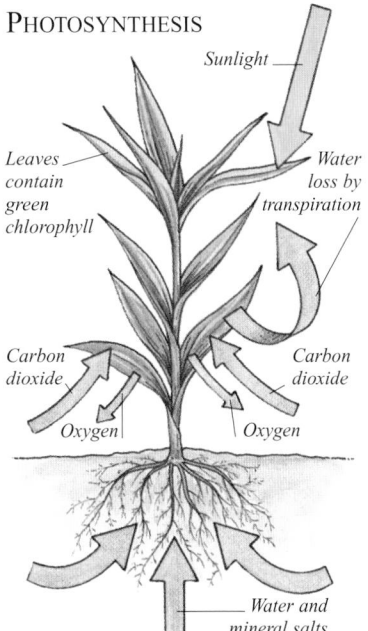

Sunlight

Leaves contain green chlorophyll

Water loss by transpiration

Carbon dioxide

Carbon dioxide

Oxygen

Oxygen

Water and mineral salts

Water and carbon dioxide are converted into carbohydrates and oxygen using the energy of sunlight, which is trapped by the chlorophyll in a plant's leaves.

for light to penetrate to the cells that contain chlorophyll, and to allow rapid movement of gases to all cells. Their surfaces contain numerous pores (stomata) through which oxygen and carbon dioxide pass in and out of the leaf. The stomata also control water losses through transpiration. A high evaporation of water vapour from the leaves and a lack of water entering through the plant roots is the cause of plants wilting in dry conditions.

Although only 1 per cent of the fresh weight of a plant consists of minerals, they are essential. In solution they

are directly concerned with the water balance of the cells, and help regulate the passage of substances between cells. They maintain the correct pH for biochemical reactions and are essential components of chlorophyll and enzymes, the biological catalysts of the plant's internal chemistry.

Fruits and seeds

Seeds are a flowering plant's means of reproduction. Each seed develops from a single, fertilized egg and one or more seeds is contained in a fruit. There are many types of fruit that disperse their seeds in various ways. Some seeds germinate rapidly with no special treatment; other seeds may need to undergo specific treatment in cultivation for them to germinate fairly rapidly. (See also PRINCIPLES OF PROPAGATION, "How to overcome dormancy", p.629.)

Pods and capsules are dehiscent fruits, splitting along a regular line or lines to release the seed, as in *Aquilegia*. Indehiscent fruits such as hazel (*Corylus*) do not split; they have a single seed (kernel) enclosed in a tough shell. These large seeds have a high moisture and fat content, and deteriorate quickly unless sown fresh or stored in cool, moist conditions. In roses, many small, indehiscent fruits, each containing one seed, are enclosed in a hollow receptacle – the hip. The individual seeds (strictly fruits) need to be extracted before sowing.

Succulent fruits, where the seed is enclosed in flesh, include berries (eg bananas, tomatoes, grapes), which have many seeds; drupes (eg plums, cherries, peaches), which typically have one seed in the form of a stone or pip; and pomes (eg apples, pears),

TRANSPIRATION

Stoma (pore) on lily leaf

Plant fluids

Guard cells controlling closing and opening of stomata

Water lost through open stomata (pores)

Water and minerals drawn up from roots

Evaporation of water from the leaf surfaces creates a constant flow of water and nutrients from the roots to the foliage; this is known as the "transpiration stream".

FRUIT TYPES

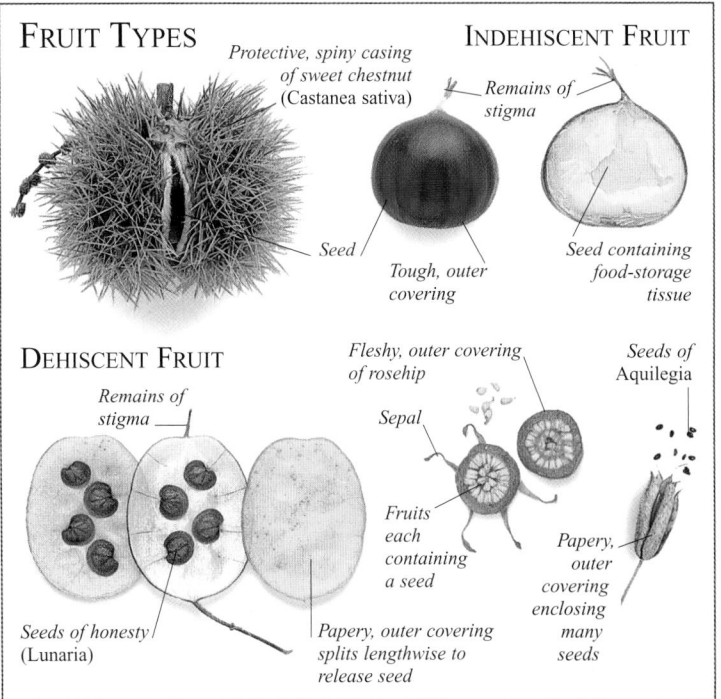

Protective, spiny casing of sweet chestnut (Castanea sativa)

INDEHISCENT FRUIT

Remains of stigma

Seed

Tough, outer covering

Seed containing food-storage tissue

DEHISCENT FRUIT

Remains of stigma

Fleshy, outer covering of rosehip

Seeds of Aquilegia

Sepal

Fruits each containing a seed

Seeds of honesty (Lunaria)

Papery, outer covering splits lengthwise to release seed

Papery, outer covering enclosing many seeds

which develop from parts of the flower as well as the ovaries. In all these types of fruit, the seed should be removed from the pulped flesh and cleaned before being sown.

Flowers

Flowers are the fourth basic part of a plant and they show extraordinary diversity in colour, scent, and form, with a wide range of adaptations to ensure that they fulfil their reproductive function. They may be borne as showy, individual flowers (*Hibiscus*, tulips) or in many-flowered spikes (*Kniphofia*), racemes (hyacinth), panicles (*Gypsophila*), umbels (*Agapanthus*), or in heads consisting of numerous small florets such as dahlias in the family Compositae.

A flower has four main parts: petals or tepals, sepals, stamens, and one or more carpels (which are collectively known as the pistil). Most conspicuous are the petals, carried above a whorl of (usually) green sepals. The male reproductive nuclei are carried in pollen grains, enclosed in an anther attached to a stem, the filament – the whole male part being a stamen; these vary greatly in number from three in crocuses to 30 or more in buttercups.

PARTS OF A FLOWER

Stigma
Anther
Filament] *Stamen*
Stylar column
Sepal
Petal
Pedicel (flower stalk)

SEXUALITY IN FLOWERS

Dioecious plants – being either male or female – need a plant of each sex growing close to one another to set seed. Monoecious plants bear separate male and female flowers on the same plant. Bisexual (hermaphrodite) flowers contain both male (stamens) and female (carpels) parts in the same flower.

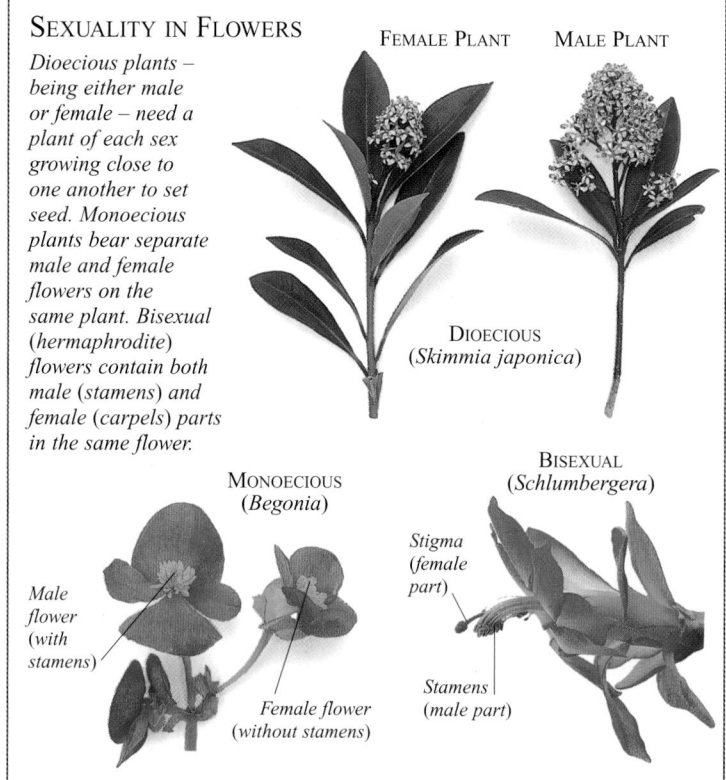

FEMALE PLANT   MALE PLANT

DIOECIOUS
(*Skimmia japonica*)

MONOECIOUS
(*Begonia*)

Male flower (with stamens)

Female flower (without stamens)

BISEXUAL
(*Schlumbergera*)

Stigma (female part)

Stamens (male part)

The carpels enclose the female egg nuclei and have a projecting style, or stylar column, with a stigma at its tip to receive pollen grains. Pollen grains germinate on the stigma and a pollen tube containing the male nuclei grows through the tissue of the style to fuse with the female nuclei (the process of fertilization) eventually forming seeds.

Many plants bear separate female and male (unisexual) flowers on the same plant, for example birch (*Betula*) and hazel (*Corylus*). They are known as monoecious plants. Bisexual, or hermaphrodite, plants have the male and female parts in each flower. A few species bear unisexual and bisexual flowers and are known as polygamous plants. In dioecious plants all the flowers produced are of one sex only; examples are many holly species

(*Ilex*), *Garrya*, and some *Skimmia* variants. Male and female plants must be grown together if they are to set seed; this is especially important in cases where plants are grown for their ornamental berries, as with many hollies and *Gaultheria* species and cultivars.

Different but related species do not normally interbreed because they often occur in dissimilar habitats, flower at varying times, or possess minor variations in flower characters that prevent successful interbreeding. In cultivation, such barriers can sometimes be overcome, and hybrids are often created by design (see "Producing hybrid plants", p.630).

Angiosperms and gymnosperms

Flowering plants of the division Angiospermae produce seeds that are enclosed in an ovary. The Gymnospermae (literally "naked seeds"), comprise non-flowering plants that produce seed that is only partly enclosed by tissues of the parent plant. Conifers (Coniferae) form the largest gymnosperm family and include many evergreen genera, such as pine (*Pinus*) and cedar (*Cedrus*), as well as some deciduous ones, such as larch (*Larix*), maidenhair tree (*Ginkgo*), and dawn redwood (*Metasequoia*). Also included in the gymnosperms are the cycads – ancient, slow-growing plants with handsome, evergreen, palm-like foliage – such as the genus *Encephalartos*.

CLASSES OF FLOWER

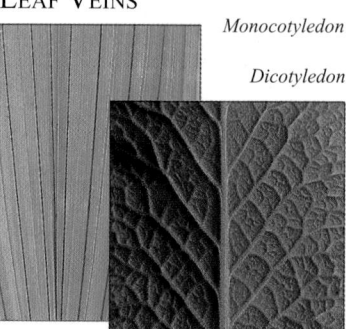

Flowering plants are grouped into two classes: monocotyledons and dicotyledons

Petals in multiples of two, four, or five

DICOTYLEDON
(*Ranunculus repens*)

Tepals in threes or multiples of three

Stamens in threes or multiples of three

Three-lobed stigma

MONOCOTYLEDON
(*Lilium*)

LEAF VEINS

Monocotyledon

Dicotyledon

Leaf vein patterns in monocotyledons (here Curculigo recurvata*) are usually parallel; those in dicotyledons (here* primula*) generally form a network.*

Angiosperms are divided into monocotyledons and dicotyledons, based on the number of "seed leaves" (cotyledons) within the seed itself. Monocotyledons have a single seed leaf, and mature leaves with (usually) parallel veins; also usually relatively slender, non-woody stems. Their flower parts are in threes or multiples thereof, and the sepals and petals are often very similar in shape. Irises, daffodils, all grasses including bamboos, and palms are all monocotyledons. Dicotyledons have leaves with a broad network of veins; the flower parts are in multiples of two, four, or five (occasionally, seven or more) and normally the sepals and petals differ markedly in size and colour from each other. Dicotyledons are very diverse in habit, varying from broadleaved trees, such as oak (*Quercus*), to herbaceous plants such as peonies (*Paeonia*).

Mutation

A mutation, also known as a sport, is a genetic change in a plant, either natural or induced, that may be exploited horticulturally by propagating the mutated material in order to introduce a new cultivar. Mutations may occur in all parts of the plant but those of horticultural interest are mainly colour mutants or doubled flowers and variegated shoots that occur on a normally green-leaved plant.

Chrysanthemum cultivars often produce mutations, for example one flowerhead in a spray having a different colour from the parent plant.

White cultivar with yellow sport

Plant names

In general plants are referred to by their botanical names throughout the *RHS Encyclopedia of Gardening*. However, for some plants, including vegetables, fruits, and herbs, the common names have been used in preference to their botanical one. To find out the botanical names of these plants, consult the index, which includes both common and botanical names for all plants mentioned in the book. The botanical name of a plant is based on a hierarchical system of classification and Linnaeus's binomial approach (genus followed by a specific epithet).

Classification and nomenclature

Plants are referred to scientifically by two names, generally written in italics. The first name, which always has its initial letter capitalized, is the genus, the second is the species name, or specific epithet: for example, *Rosa canina*. In nature, species often show minor variations in character; they are then given a third name, prefixed by "subsp." (subspecies), "var." (varietas), or "f." (forma): thus *Rhododendron rex* subsp. *fictolacteum* and *Daboecia cantabrica* f. *alba*. Sexual crosses between botanically distinct species or genera are known as hybrids and are indicated by a multiplication sign: thus *Epimedium* x *rubrum*. Non-sexual crosses – created through grafting plant tissues so they merge together – are known as graft-hybrids and are indicated by a cross sign: thus + *Laburnocytisus* 'Adamii'. Here, *Laburnum* and *Chamaecytisus* species have been combined to form the graft hybrid.

A cultivar (cultivated variety) is one that has been selected or artificially raised either from the wild or from gardens and grown in cultivation, and whose characteristics are preserved by some means of controlled propagation. The name of such a plant is written in Roman script with an initial capital letter and in single quotation marks: thus *Calluna vulgaris* 'Firefly'.

When plant breeders raise a new cultivar, it is given a code-name to ensure its formal identification: this may be different from the name under which the plant is sold. For example, the rose selling under the trade designation Queen Mother also has the code-name of 'Korquemu'; in this *Encyclopedia*, both names are cited in all but captions, and are styled thus: *Rosa* Queen Mother ('Korquemu'). To safeguard ownership of a cultivar, plant breeders may apply for Plant Breeder's Rights (PBR), which are granted using the code-name.

GLOSSARY

The glossary explains horticultural terms that are used in this book. Words in italic in a definition have a separate entry. Fuller explanations and illustrations may be found elsewhere by looking up the term in the index.

Acid (of soil). With a *pH* value of less than 7. (Cf *Alkaline* and *Neutral*.)
Adventitious. Arising from places where growths do not normally occur; for example, adventitious roots may arise from stems.
Adventitious bud. See *Bud*.
Aerate (of soil). Loosen by mechanical means in order to allow air (oxygen and carbon dioxide) to enter; for example, using a spiked roller to aerate a lawn.
Aerial root. A plant root growing above ground to provide anchorage and, on an *epiphyte*, to absorb atmospheric moisture.
Air layering. See *Layering*.
Alkaline (of soil). With a *pH* value of more than 7. (Cf *Acid* and *Neutral*.)
Alpine. A plant that grows above the tree line in mountainous areas; loosely applied to rock garden plants that may be grown at relatively low altitudes.
Alpine house. An unheated, well-ventilated greenhouse used for cultivating *alpine* and bulbous plants.
Alternate (of leaves). Occurring successively at different levels on opposite sides of a stem. (Cf *Opposite*.)
Anemone-centred (of flowers). Flowers or flowerheads in which the central petals or flowers (modified *stamens*) form a cushion-like mound and the outer rim of petals or ray florets are flat and spreading, as in some chrysanthemums.
Annual. A plant that completes its life cycle (*germination*–flowering–seeding–dying) in one growing season.
Anther. The part of a *stamen* that produces *pollen*; usually borne on a *filament*.

Apical. See *Terminal*. **Apical bud**: see *Bud*.
Apical-wedge grafting. See *Grafting*.
Aquatic. Any plant that grows in water; it may be free-floating, totally submerged, or rooted on the pond bottom with leaves and flowers above the water surface.
Asexual reproduction. A form of reproduction not involving *fertilization* and in propagation often involving mechanical methods (see *Vegetative propagation*).
Auxins. Naturally occurring or artificially synthesized plant growth substances controlling shoot growth, root formation, and other physiological processes in plants.
Awn. A sharp point or bristle, commonly found on a glume of a grass *inflorescence*.
Axil. The upper angle between a leaf and a stem, between a main stem and a lateral branch, or between a stem and a bract. (See also *Bud: Axillary bud*.)
Axillary bud. See *Bud*.
Back-bulb (of orchids). A dormant, old *pseudobulb* without leaves.
Ball. See *Root ball*.
Balled. 1) Of trees and shrubs that have been lifted and had their *root ball* wrapped in hessian or other material to keep it intact during *transplanting*. 2) Of a flower that does not open properly and rots when still in bud.
Bare-root. Of plants sold with their roots bare of soil.
Bark-ringing. The removal of a ring of bark from the trunk or branches of certain fruit trees, to reduce vigorous growth and to encourage fruit cropping. Also known as "girdling".
Basal plate. A compressed *stem*, part of a *bulb*.
Basal stem cutting. See *Cutting*.
Base dressing. An application of fertilizer or humus (manure, compost, etc.) applied to or dug into the soil prior to sowing or planting.
Bastard trenching. See *Double digging*.
Bed system. A method of planting vegetable crops in closely spaced rows, often in blocks or narrow beds for easy access.
Bedding plants. Annuals and biennials (or plants grown as such) raised almost to maturity and then planted out, "bedded out", often in large blocks for temporary display.
Biennial. A plant that flowers and dies in the second growing season after *germination*.
Blanch. To exclude light from developing leaves or stems in order to keep the plant tissue soft and palatable.
Bleed. To lose *sap* through a cut or wound.
Blind. Of a plant that fails to produce flowers, or a stem in which the growing point has been damaged.
Bloom. 1) A flower or blossom. 2) A waxy, white or bluish-white coating on a stem, leaf, or fruit.
Blown. Of flowers or hearted vegetables that are past full maturity and are fading.
Bog plant. A plant whose natural habitat is soil that is permanently damp, or one that thrives in such conditions.
Bole. The *trunk* of a tree from ground level to the first major branch.
Bolt. To produce flowers and seed prematurely.
Bract. A modified, often protective, leaf at the base of a flower or flower cluster. Bracts may resemble normal leaves, or be small and scale-like, or large and brightly coloured.
Branch. A shoot arising from the main stem or trunk of a woody plant.
Brassica. A member of the cabbage *family*.
Break. A *shoot* growing from an *axillary bud*.

Broadcasting. Scattering seed or fertilizer evenly over the ground, rather than in furrows or *drills*.
Broadleaved. Of trees or shrubs that bear broad, flat leaves rather than needle-like foliage.
Bromeliad. A member of the *family* Bromeliaceae.
Bud. A rudimentary or condensed shoot containing an embryonic leaf, leaf cluster, or flower. **Adventitious bud**: one produced abnormally, for example from the stem instead of from a leaf *axil*. **Apical** (or **terminal**) **bud**: the topmost bud on a stem. **Axillary bud**: one that occurs in an *axil*. **Crown bud**: a flower bud at the shoot tip, surrounded by other, usually smaller, flower buds. **Fruit bud**: one from which leaves and flowers (followed by fruits) develop. **Growth bud**: one from which only leaves or a shoot develop.
Bud union. The point at which the *scion* bud unites with the *rootstock*.
Budding. Bud-grafting, a form of *grafting*.
Budding tape. See *Grafting tape*.
Bud-grafting. See *Grafting*.
Budwood. A shoot cut from a tree to provide a *scion* for *bud-grafting*.
Bulb. A modified *stem* acting as a storage organ and consisting mainly of fleshy, more or less separate or tightly packed, scale leaves (a modified *bud*) on a much reduced stem (basal plate).
Bulb fibre. A mixture of *peat*, oystershell, and charcoal, in which *bulbs* are grown in containers, often without drainage holes.
Bulbil. A small *bulb*-like organ, often borne in a leaf *axil*, occasionally on a stem or in a *flowerhead*. (Cf *Bulblet*.)
Bulblet. A small developing *bulb* produced from the *basal plate* of a mature bulb outside the *tunic*. (Cf *Bulbil* and *Offset*.)

Bush. 1) A small shrub. 2) An open-centre fruit tree with a *trunk* of 90cm (36in) or less. **Bush fruit**: used of soft fruit bushes such as blackcurrants and gooseberries.

Cactus. A member of the *family* Cactaceae, characterized by fleshy, water-storing tissue in the stems and areoles (specialized groups of cells) from which spines, flowers, and shoots develop.

Calcicole. *Lime*-loving; a plant that thrives in *alkaline* soil.

Calcifuge. *Lime*-hating; a plant that will not grow in *alkaline* soil.

Callus. Protective tissue formed by plants over a wounded surface, particularly in *woody* plants but also at the base of cuttings.

Calyx (pl. **calyces**). The collective name for the *sepals*, the outer *whorl* of, usually green, segments that enclose the flower in bud.

Cambium. A layer of meristematic tissue capable of producing new cells to increase the girth of stems and roots. (See also *Meristem*.)

Capillary matting. Matting made of synthetic fibre that is used to draw water upwards by capillary action to irrigate pot plants on capillary beds or benches.

Capping. A crust that forms on the surface of soil damaged by compaction, heavy rain, or watering. (Cf *Pan*.)

Carpel. The female part of the flower of flowering plants that contains the *ovules*; several carpels in a flower are collectively known as the *pistil*.

Carpet bedding. The use of groups of closely planted, low-growing, colourful *bedding plants* in various designs.

Catkin. A racemose (see *Raceme*) flower spike, or a spike-like *inflorescence*, with conspicuous *bracts* and small, often unisexual flowers lacking petals.

Central leader. The central, usually upright stem of a *tree*.

Certified stock. Plants certified by the Department of Environment, Food & Rural Affairs (USDA in the USA) as free from certain pests and diseases.

Chilling requirement. The requirement of plants for a specific period of dormancy below a particular temperature in order for them to initiate flowering.

Chinese layering. An alternative name for air layering; see *Layering*.

Chip-budding. See *Grafting*.

Chlorophyll. The green plant pigment that is mainly responsible for light absorption and hence *photosynthesis* in plants.

Clamp. A method for storing root crops outdoors. The crops are heaped up and protected against frost by layers of straw and soil; a "chimney" hole filled with straw provides ventilation.

Climber. A plant that climbs using other plants or objects as support: **self-clinging climbers** by means of supporting, *adventitious*, *aerial* roots or adhesive tendril tips; **tendril climbers** by coiling their leaf stalks, leaf *tendrils*, or modified *terminal* shoots; **twining climbers** by coiling their *stems*. **Scandent**, **scrambling**, and

trailing climbers produce long, usually flexuous, stems that grow over or through plants or other supports; they attach themselves only loosely, if at all, to the support.

Cloche. A small, usually portable, structure made of clear plastic or glass, normally in a metal framework; used to protect early crops on open ground and to warm the soil before planting. (See also *Floating cloche*.)

Clone. 1) A group of genetically identical plants produced by *vegetative propagation* or *asexual reproduction*. 2) An individual plant in such a group.

Cold frame. A glazed, box-like, unheated structure, made from brick, wood, or glass, with a hinged or removable glass or clear plastic *light*, used to protect plants from excessive cold.

Collar. 1) The part of a plant where the roots meet the stem; also known as the "neck". 2) The part of a tree where a main branch meets the *trunk* (or a side branch meets a main branch).

Companion planting. Positioning plants together that are reputed to have a beneficial effect on neighbouring plants by discouraging pests and diseases or improving growth.

Compositae. The daisy *family*.

Compost. 1) A potting medium comprising a mixture of *loam*, sand, *peat*, *leaf mould*, or other ingredients. 2) An organic material, rich in *humus*, formed by decomposed plant remains, and other *organic* matter, used as a soil improver or *mulch*.

Compound. Divided into two or more subsidiary parts, for example a leaf divided into two or more *leaflets*. (Cf *Simple*.)

Cone. The densely clustered *bracts* and flowers of *conifers* and some flowering plants, often developing into a woody, seed-bearing structure as in the familiar pine cone.

Conifer. Gymnosperms, usually evergreen trees and shrubs that are distinguished from flowering plants (Angiosperms) by the naked *ovules* that are not enclosed in an *ovary* but are often borne in *cones*.

Contact action. The action of a *pesticide* or weedkiller that kills or damages the pest or weed by direct contact.

Coppicing. The annual pruning back of trees or shrubs close to ground level to produce vigorous, usually decorative, *shoots*.

Cordon. A trained plant (usually a fruit tree) generally restricted to one main stem by rigorous pruning. A **single cordon** has one main stem, a **double**, or **"U"**, **cordon** has two, and a **multiple cordon**, three or more stems.

Corm. A *bulb*-like, underground, swollen *stem* or stem base, often surrounded by a papery *tunic*. A corm is replaced by a new corm that develops from a *terminal*, or *lateral*, *bud*.

Cormel. A small *corm* developing around a mature corm, usually outside the main corm *tunic*, as in *Gladiolus*.

Cormlet. A small *corm* arising at the base (and usually within the old *tunic*) of a mature one. (See also *Offset*.)

Corolla. The interior *whorl* of the *perianth* of a flower, comprising several free or fused *petals*.

Cotyledon. A seed leaf; the first leaf or leaves to emerge from the seed after *germination*, often markedly different from mature leaves. Flowering plants (Angiosperms) are classified into *monocotyledons* (one) and *dicotyledons* (two) depending on how many cotyledons are contained in the mature seed. In Gymnosperms (*conifers*) they are often produced in *whorls*.

Crocks. Broken pieces of clay pot, used to cover the drainage holes of pots in order to provide free drainage and air circulation to the root system and to prevent the growing medium from escaping from or blocking the drainage holes.

Crop rotation. A system in which vegetable crops are grown on different sections of a plot on a three- or four-year cycle to minimize the build-up of soil-borne pests and diseases in one section.

Cross-fertilization. The *fertilization* of the *ovules* of a flower as a result of *cross-pollination*.

Cross-pollination. The transfer of pollen from the *anther* of a flower on one plant to the *stigma* of a flower on another plant; the term is often loosely applied to *cross-fertilization*. (Cf *Self-pollination*.)

Crown. 1) The basal part at soil level of a *herbaceous* plant where roots and stems join and from where new shoots are produced. 2) The upper, branched part of a tree above the *bole*.

Crown bud. See *Bud*.

Culm. The usually hollow stem of a grass or bamboo.

Cultivar. A contraction of "cultivated variety" (abbreviated to cv.); a group (or one among such a group) of cultivated plants clearly distinguished by one or more characteristics and which retains these characteristics when propagated either asexually or sexually. (Cf *Variety*.)

Cutting. A portion of a plant (a leaf, shoot, root, or bud) that is cut off to be used for *propagation*. **Basal stem cutting**: one taken from the base of a (usually *herbaceous*) plant as it begins to produce growth in spring. **Greenwood cutting**: one taken from the soft tips of young growth after the spring growth flush has slowed down; slightly harder and woodier stems than are used for softwood cuttings. **Hardwood cutting**: one taken from mature wood of both deciduous and evergreen plants at the end of the growing season. **Heel cutting**: one taken with a portion of the bark or mature wood at the base. **Internodal cutting**: one in which the basal cut is made between two *nodes* or growth buds. **Leaf cutting**: one taken from a detached leaf or part of a leaf. **Leaf-bud cutting**: one consisting of a short section of stem and a single or double pair of buds or leaves. **Nodal cutting**: one trimmed at the base just below a growth bud or *node*. **Ripewood cutting**: one taken from ripened wood,

usually of evergreens, during the growing season. **Root cutting**: one taken from part of a semi-mature or mature root. **Semi-ripe cutting**: one taken from half-ripened wood during the growing season. **Softwood cutting**: one taken from young, immature growth during the growing season. **Stem cutting**: one taken from any portion of a plant stem. **Stem tip cutting**: any cutting taken from the tip of a shoot; sometimes applied to softwood and greenwood cuttings.

Cyme. A usually flat-topped, *determinate inflorescence* in which the central or *terminal* flower opens first.

Damping down. Wetting greenhouse floors and staging with water to increase humidity, particularly in very hot weather.

Dead-heading. The removal of *spent* flowers or *flowerheads*.

Deciduous. Of plants that shed leaves at the end of the growing season and renew them at the beginning of the next; **semi-deciduous** plants lose only some of their leaves at the end of the growing season.

Degradable pot. A pot made from degradable material such as compressed peat or paper.

Dehiscence. Term used of *fruits* (usually capsules) and *anthers* to describe the process of opening at maturity to release their contents.

Dehiscent. Of a *fruit*, usually a capsule, or an *anther* that splits along definite lines to release seeds or pollen.

Determinate. 1) Used of *inflorescences* where the central or terminal flower opens first so that the main axis cannot extend further. (Cf *Cyme*.) 2) Used of bushy or dwarf tomatoes. (Cf *Indeterminate*; *Semi-determinate*.)

Dibber. A tool used for making holes in soil or potting compost into which seedlings or cuttings are inserted.

Dicotyledon. A flowering plant that usually has two *cotyledons* or seed leaves in the seed; it is also characterized by the (usually) net-veined leaves, the *petals* and *sepals* in multiples of two, four, or five, and by the presence of a *cambium*. (Cf *Monocotyledon*.)

Die-back. The death of tips of shoots as a result of damage or disease.

Dioecious. Bearing male and female reproductive organs on separate plants.

Disbudding. The removal of surplus *buds* to promote the production of high-quality flowers or fruits.

Distal end (of *cuttings*). The end that was originally farthest from the *crown* of the parent plant. (Cf *Proximal end*.)

Division. A method of increasing plants by dividing them into pieces, each with a root system and one or more shoots (or dormant buds).

Dormancy. The state of temporary cessation of growth and slowing down of other activities in whole plants, usually during the winter; **seed dormancy**: non-*germination* of seed when placed in conditions suitable for germination due to physical, chemical, or other factors inherent in the seed; **double (seed) dormancy**: non-germination of seeds due to two dormancy factors in the seed.

Double (of a flower). See *Flower*.

Double cordon. See *Cordon*.

Double digging. A cultivation technique in which the soil is worked to a depth of two *spits*. Also known as "trench digging" or "bastard trenching".

Drainage. The passage of excess water through soil; the term is also applied to systems of drainage used to remove excess water.

Drill. A narrow, straight furrow in the soil in which seeds are sown or seedlings planted.

Drupes. See *Stone fruits*.

Earthing up. Drawing up soil around the base of a plant to help prevent *wind-rock*, to *blanch* the *stems*, or to encourage stem rooting.

Epicormic shoots. Shoots that develop from latent or *adventitious* buds on or from the *trunk* of a tree or shrub. (See also *Water shoots*.)

Epigeal. Type of seed *germination* in which the seed is pushed above soil level by elongation of the *hypocotyl*. (Cf *Hypogeal*.)

Epiphyte. A plant that grows on another plant without being parasitic, and obtains moisture and nutrients from the atmosphere without rooting into the soil.

Ericaceous. 1) Term describing plants of the *family* Ericaceae, usually *lime*-hating and requiring soils of pH6.5 or less (see also *Calcifuge*). 2) Of compost, with an appropriate *pH* or acidity for growing ericaceous plants.

Espalier. A plant trained with the main stem vertical and (usually) three or more tiers of branches horizontally placed on either side in a single plane; often applied to fruit trees.

Evergreen. Of plants that retain their foliage for more than one growing season; **semi-evergreen** plants retain only a small proportion of their leaves for more than one season.

Eye. 1) A dormant or latent growth *bud*, such as the eye of a potato or dahlia tuber. 2) The centre of a flower, especially if different in colour from the petals.

F1 hybrids. First-generation plants obtained from crossing two selected pure-breeding parents to produce uniform, vigorous, and high-yielding offspring. Seed from F1 hybrids does not come *true*. **F2 hybrids**: plants that result from *self-* or *cross-fertilization* of F1 hybrids; they are less uniform than their parents.

Falls. The pendent or horizontally placed *tepals* or *petals* of irises and some related plants.

Family. A category in plant classification, a grouping together of related *genera*, for example the family Rosaceae includes the genera *Rosa*, *Sorbus*, *Rubus*, *Prunus*, and *Pyracantha*.

Fastigiate. With the branches (usually of trees and shrubs) growing vertically and almost parallel with the main stem.

Feathered. Of *maiden* trees that have several *lateral* branches ("feathers").

Fertile (of plants). Producing viable seed; shoots bearing flowers are also said to be fertile shoots as opposed to non-flowering (sterile) shoots.

Fertilization. The fusion of a *pollen* grain nucleus (male) with an *ovule* (female) to form a fertile seed.

Fibrous. 1) Of roots, fine and often branching and dense. 2) Of loam, containing fibre derived from (dead) grass roots.

Filament. The *stalk* of the *stamen* which bears the *anther*.

Fimbriate. Of part of a plant that has a fringed margin. Plant organs with a fringe of hairs are said to be ciliate.

Flat. An American term for a shallow seed-box or container.

Flat grafting. See *Grafting*.

Floating cloche. Lightweight sheet, usually of woven polypropylene (fibre fleece), placed over a crop, which is lifted up by the plants as they grow. It provides some frost protection while allowing water and light penetration. Also known as floating mulch. (See also *Cloche*.)

Floret. A (generally) small flower in a *flowerhead* consisting of many flowers.

Flower. The part of the plant containing the reproductive organs usually surrounded by *sepals* and *petals*. The basic flower forms are: **single**, with one row of usually four to six petals; **semi-double**, with two or three times the normal number of petals usually in two or three rows; **double**, with more than the normal number of petals in several rows with few or no *stamens* produced; **fully double**, flowers usually rounded in shape, with densely packed petals and with the stamens obscured or absent. (Cf *Flowerhead*.)

Flowerhead. A mass of small *flowers* or *florets* that together appear to form a single flower as in members of the family Compositae.

Force. To induce plant growth, usually of flowers or fruit by control of the environment, normally by increasing the temperature.

Forma (f.). A variant within a *species* usually distinguished only by minor characteristics. *Clematis montana* f. *grandiflora* is a larger-flowered, more vigorous form of *C. montana*; also loosely used for any variant of a species.

Formative pruning. A method of pruning that is carried out on young trees and shrubs to develop the basic branch structure of the desired form or shape.

Foundation planting. The basic, and usually permanent, structural and shelter planting of trees and shrubs in a garden.

Frame. See *Cold frame*.

Framework. The permanent branch structure of a tree or shrub; the main branches that determine its ultimate shape. **Framework plants**: the plants in a garden that form the basis or structure of the design. (Cf *Foundation planting*.)

Frame-working (of fruit trees). Pruning back all side growths to the main framework and grafting *scions* of a different *cultivar* onto each main framework branch.

French layering. See *Layering*.

Friable (of soil). Of a good, crumbly texture; capable of forming a *tilth* that can be worked easily.

Frond. 1) The *leaf*-like organ of a fern. Some ferns produce both barren and *fertile* fronds, the latter bearing *spores*. 2) Loosely applied to large, usually *compound* leaves such as those of palms.

Frost hardy. See *Hardy*.

Frost pocket. A site, often a hollow, where cold air gathers, that is subject to severe and often prolonged frosts.

Frost tender. See *Tender*.

Fruit. The fertilized, ripe *ovary* of a plant containing one to many seeds, for example, berries, hips, capsules, and nuts; the term is also used of edible fruits.

Fruit bud. See *Bud*.

Fruit set. The successful development of fruits after *pollination* and *fertilization*.

Fully double. See *Flower*.

Fully reflexed. See *Reflexed*.

Fungicide. A chemical that kills fungi, especially those responsible for various plant diseases.

Genus (pl. **genera**). A category in plant classification ranked between *family* and *species*. A group of related species linked by a range of common characters; for example, all species of horse chestnut are grouped under the genus *Aesculus*. (See also *Cultivar*, *Family*, *Forma*, *Hybrid*, *Subspecies*, and *Variety*.)

Germination. The physical and chemical changes that take place as a seed starts to grow and develop into a plant.

Girdling. 1) The removal of bark all round a stem or branch caused by animal or physical damage or by a constricting tie that prevents the flow of water and *nutrients* to the upper part of the plant, eventually causing the death of all the tissue above the girdled trunk or branch. 2) See *Bark-ringing*.

Glaucous. With a blue-green, blue-grey, grey, or white bloom.

Graft. To join artificially one or more plant parts to another.

Graft union. The point at which *scion* and *rootstock* are joined.

Grafting. A method of *propagation* by which an artificial union is made between the *scion* of one plant and the *rootstock* of another so that they eventually function as one plant. Methods include apical-wedge grafting; bud-grafting (including chip-budding and T-budding); flat grafting; saddle grafting; side grafting (see Cacti and other Succulents, "Side grafting", p.351); side-wedge grafting; spliced side grafting; spliced side-veneer grafting; whip (or splice) grafting; and whip-and-tongue grafting. (For details see Principles of Propagation, "Grafting and budding", pp.635–636.)

Grafting tape. Tape used to protect a *graft union* during healing.

Green manure. A quick-maturing, leafy crop such as mustard that is grown specifically to be dug back into, and thereby enrich, the soil.

Greenwood cutting. See *Cutting*.

Ground colour. Main (background)

colour of petals.

Ground cover. Usually low-growing plants that quickly cover the soil surface and suppress weeds.

Growth bud. See *Bud*.

Half hardy. Used of a plant not tolerating frost in a given climatic zone. The term generally implies an ability to withstand lower temperatures than *tender*.

Half standard. A tree or shrub that has a clear stem of 1–1.5m (3–5ft) between ground level and the lowest branches.

Hardening off. Gradually acclimatizing plants that have been raised under cover to cooler, outdoor conditions.

Hardpan. See *Pan*.

Hardwood cutting. See *Cutting*.

Hardy. Able to withstand year-round climatic conditions, including frost, without protection.

Haulm. The top-growth of plants such as potatoes and legumes.

Head. 1) The part of a tree above a clear *trunk*. 2) A dense *inflorescence*.

Head back. To prune back the main branches of trees or shrubs by half or more.

Heading. See *Heart up*.

Heart up. The stage at which vegetables such as lettuces or cabbages begin to produce tight "hearts" or "heads" of inner leaves.

Heavy (of soil). Having a high proportion of clay.

Heel. A small piece or strip of bark or wood that is retained at the base of a *cutting* when it is pulled away from a main stem.

Heel cutting. See *Cutting*.

Heeling in. Temporary planting until a plant can be placed in its permanent position.

Herb. 1) A plant grown for its medicinal or flavouring properties or for its scented foliage. 2) Botanically, a *herbaceous* plant.

Herbaceous. A non-*woody* plant in which the upper parts die down to a rootstock at the end of the growing season. It is chiefly applied to *perennials*, although botanically it also applies to *annuals* and *biennials*.

Herbicide. A chemical used to control or kill weeds.

Humus. The chemically complex, organic residue of decayed vegetable matter in soil. Also often used to describe partly decayed matter such as *leaf mould* or *compost*.

Hybrid. The offspring of genetically different parents usually of distinct taxa (see *Taxon*). Hybrids between species of the same *genus* are known as interspecific hybrids. Those between different but usually closely related *genera* are known as intergeneric hybrids. (See also *F1 hybrids* and *F2 hybrids*.)

Hybrid vigour. An improvement in growth and yield shown by some hybrids.

Hybridization. The process by which *hybrids* are formed.

Hydroculture. The cultivation of plants in nutrient-rich water, sometimes with sterile aggregates. (See also *Hydroponics*.)

Hydroponics. Growing plants in dilute solutions of nutrients. Applied loosely to any form of soilless culture.

Hypocotyl. The portion of a *seed* or *seedling* just below the *cotyledons*.

Hypogeal. Type of seed *germination* in which the *seed* and *cotyledons* remain below the soil surface while the young shoot (plumule) emerges above soil level.

Incurved. Applied to petals of flowers and *florets* that curve inwards to form a compact, rounded shape. **Incurving** flowerheads are less compact with more loosely arranged but still incurved florets.

Indehiscent. Of a *fruit* that does not split open to release its seeds. (Cf *Dehiscent*.)

Indeterminate. 1) Used of an *inflorescence* not terminated by a single flower, in which the primary axis (stem) continues to develop as the lower flowers open (e.g. a *raceme* as in delphiniums). 2) Used of tall or *cordon* tomatoes, which, in a suitable climate, can grow to an indefinite length. (Cf *Determinate*; *Semi-determinate*.)

Inflorescence. A group of flowers borne on a single axis (stem); for example, *racemes*, *panicles*, and *cymes*.

Informal. Applied to some cultivars of chrysanthemums, dahlias, and other flowers with irregular flower formation.

Inorganic. Of a chemical compound, one that does not contain carbon. Inorganic fertilizers are refined from naturally occurring chemicals or produced artificially. (Cf *Organic*.)

Insecticide. A *pesticide* used to control or kill insects.

Intercropping. The growing of quick-maturing vegetable crops between slower-growing crops to make maximum use of the available space.

Intergeneric hybrid. See *Hybrid*.

Intermediate. 1) A term applied to chrysanthemums with flowerheads intermediate in shape between *reflexed* and *incurved*. 2) A hybrid with characters intermediate between its two parents.

Internodal cutting. See *Cutting*.

Internode. The portion of stem between two *nodes*.

Interplanting. 1) The planting of fast-maturing plants between slower-growing plants to provide a display while they mature. 2) The planting of two or more types of plants together to provide a display of different colours or textures (e.g. tulips among wallflowers). Often used in relation to bedding.

Interspecific hybrid. See *Hybrid*.

Irrigation. 1) General term for watering. 2) The use of a system of basins, channels, or sprinkler systems to provide a controlled supply of water to plants.

John Innes compost. *Loam*-based *composts* devised by the John Innes Horticultural Institute in Norwich, UK, and made to a standard formula.

Knot garden. Beds laid out in a formal, often complex, pattern, formed from dwarf hedges or clipped herbs.

Lateral. A side growth that arises from a shoot or root.

Layer planting. A form of *interplanting* in which groups of plants flower in succession having been planted closely together.

Layering. A method of *propagation* by which a *shoot* is induced to *root* while still attached to the parent plant. The basic form is self layering, which occurs naturally in some plants. Methods include: air layering (also known as Chinese layering or marcottage), French layering, mound layering (see THE HERB GARDEN, "Mound layering", p.414), serpentine layering, simple layering, stooling, tip layering, and trench layering. (For details, see PRINCIPLES OF PROPAGATION, "Layering", p.631.)

Leaching. The loss from the topsoil of soluble *nutrients* by downward drainage.

Leader. 1) The main, usually central, stem of a plant. 2) The *terminal* shoot of a main branch.

Leaf. A plant organ, variable in shape and colour but often flattened and green, borne on the stem, that performs the functions of *photosynthesis*, *respiration*, and *transpiration*.

Leaf cutting. See *Cutting*.

Leaf mould. Fibrous, flaky material derived from decomposed leaves, used as an ingredient in potting media and as a soil improver.

Leaf-bud cutting. See *Cutting*.

Leaflet. One of the subdivisions of a *compound* leaf.

Legume. A one-celled, *dehiscent fruit* splitting at maturity into two, belonging to the *family* Leguminosae.

Light. 1) The movable cover of a *cold frame*. 2) Of soil, with a high proportion of sand and little clay.

Lime. Loosely, a number of compounds of calcium; the amount of lime in soil determines whether it is *alkaline*, *acid*, or *neutral*.

Line out. To plant out young plants or insert cuttings in lines in a nursery bed or frame.

Lithophyte. A plant naturally growing on rocks (or in very stony soil) and usually obtaining most of its nutrients and water from the atmosphere.

Loam. A term used for soil of medium texture, often easily worked, that contains more or less equal parts of sand, silt, and clay, and is usually rich in humus. If the proportion of one ingredient is high, the term may be qualified as silt-loam, clay-loam, or sandy loam.

Lute. A piece of equipment used for working (luting) top-dressings into lawns.

Maiden. A *grafted* tree in its first year. (See also *Whip*.)

Maincrop (of vegetables). Those cultivars that produce crops throughout the main growing season, doing so over a longer period than either early or late cultivars.

Marcottage. An alternative name for air layering; see *Layering*.

Marginal water plant. A plant that grows partially submerged in shallow water or in constantly moist soil at the edge of a pond or stream.

Medium. 1) A *compost*, growing mixture, or other material in which plants may be propagated or grown. 2) Applied to those soils that are intermediate in character between *heavy* and *light*. (See also *Loam*.)

Meristem. Plant tissue that is able to divide to produce new cells. Shoot or root tips contain meristematic tissue and may be used for *micropropagation*.

Micronutrients. Chemical elements essential to plants but needed only in very small quantities, also known as trace elements. (See also *Nutrients*.)

Micropropagation. Propagation of plants by *tissue culture*.

Midrib. The primary, usually central vein of a leaf or leaflet.

Module. Applied to various types of container, particularly those used in multiples for sowing seed and pricking out seedlings.

Monocarpic. Flowering and fruiting only once before dying; such plants may take several years to reach flowering size.

Monocotyledon. A flowering plant that has only one *cotyledon* or seed leaf in the seed; it is also characterized by narrow, parallel-veined *leaves*, and parts of the flower in threes or multiples of three.

Monoecious. Bearing separate male and female reproductive organs on the same plant.

Monopodial. Growing indefinitely from an apical or *terminal bud* on a stem. (Cf *Sympodial*.)

Moss peat. See *Peat*.

Mound layering. See *Layering*.

Mulch. A material applied in a layer to the soil surface to suppress weeds, conserve moisture, and maintain a preferably cool, even root temperature.

Multiple cordon. See *Cordon*.

Mutation. An induced or spontaneous genetic change, often resulting in shoots with variegated foliage or flowers of a different colour from the parent plant. A mutation is also known as a sport.

Mycorrhizae. Soil fungi that live in beneficial association with plant roots.

Naturalize. To establish and grow as if in the wild.

Neck. See *Collar*.

Nectar. Sugary liquid secreted from a *nectary*; often attractive to pollinating insects.

Nectary. Glandular tissue usually found in the flower, but sometimes found on the leaves or stems, that secretes *nectar*.

Neutral (of soil). With a *pH* value of 7, i.e. neither *acid* nor *alkaline*.

Nodal cutting. See *Cutting*.

Node. The point on a stem from which one or more leaves, shoots, branches, or flowers arise.

Non-remontant. Flowering or fruiting only once in a single flush. (Cf *Remontant*.)

Nursery bed. An area used for germinating seeds or growing on young plants before planting them out in their permanent positions.

Nut. A one-seeded, *indehiscent fruit* with a tough or woody coat, for example an acorn. Less specifically, all fruits and seeds with woody or leathery coats.

Nutrients. Minerals (mineral ions) used to develop proteins and other compounds required for plant growth.

Offset. A young plant that arises by natural, vegetative reproduction, usually at the base of the parent plant; in bulbs, offsets are initially formed within the bulb *tunic* but later separate out. Also known as offshoots.

Offshoot. See *Offset*.

Open-pollination. Natural pollination. (See also *Pollination*.)

Opposite. Term describing two leaves or other plant organs, at the same level on opposite sides of a stem or other axis. (Cf *Alternate*.)

Organic. 1) Chemically, referring to compounds containing carbon derived from decomposed plant or animal organisms. 2) Loosely, applied to mulches, composts, or similar materials derived from plant materials. 3) Also applied to crop production and gardening without the use of synthetic or non-organic materials.

Ovary. The basal part of the pistil of a flower, containing one or more *ovules*; it may develop into a *fruit* after *fertilization*. (See also *Carpel*.)

Ovule. The part of the *ovary* that develops into the *seed* after *pollination* and *fertilization*.

Oxygenator. Submerged aquatic plant that releases oxygen into the water.

Packs. Compartmented trays in which individual seeds or seedlings are grown.

Pan. 1) A shallow, earthenware or plastic pot that is much wider than it is deep. 2) A layer of soil that is impermeable to water and oxygen and impedes root growth and drainage. Some pans (hardpans) occur naturally on clay or iron-rich soils. Soils capped (see *Capping*) by heavy rain or excess watering, or by continuous use of cultivation machinery, are also known as pans or hardpans.

Panicle. An *indeterminate*, branched *inflorescence* often consisting of several racemose branches (see *Raceme*). Also loosely used to describe any branching inflorescence.

Parterre. A level area containing ornamental beds, often with low-growing plants and enclosed in dwarf hedges. (Cf *Knot garden*.)

Parthenocarpic. The production of fruit without *fertilization* having taken place.

Pathogens. Micro-organisms that cause disease.

Pathovar (pvar.). A subdivision of several bacterial species.

Peat. Partially decayed, humus-rich vegetation formed on the surface of waterlogged soils. **Moss** or **sphagnum peat** is largely derived from partially decayed sphagnum moss and is used in potting composts. **Sedge peat** is derived from sedges, mosses, and heathers; it is coarser than moss peat and less suitable for potting composts.

Peat bed. Beds usually built from *peat* blocks and filled with very peaty soil; used to grow acid-loving plants, particularly in soils with a high *pH*.

Peat blocks. Blocks of peat cut from natural peat deposits.

Peat substitute. A term applied to a number of different organic materials – such as coconut fibre – used in place of peat for potting composts and soil improvers.

Peduncle. The *stalk* of a *flower*.

Peltate (of leaves). A leaf with the stalk usually attached centrally beneath the leaf blade; sometimes the stalk may be off-centre within the leaf margin.

Perennial. Strictly, any plant living for at least three seasons; commonly applied to *herbaceous* plants and *woody* perennials (i.e. trees and shrubs).

Perianth. The collective term for the *calyx* and the *corolla*, particularly when they are very similar in form, as in many bulb flowers.

Perianth segment. One portion of a *perianth*, usually resembling a *petal* and sometimes known as a *tepal*.

Perlite. Small granules of expanded, volcanic minerals added to growing media to improve aeration.

Perpetual. Of plants that bloom more or less continuously throughout the growing season or over long periods of time.

Pesticide. A chemical substance, usually manufactured, that is used to kill pests including insects (*insecticide*), mites (*acaricide*), and nematodes (*nematicide*).

Petal. A modified leaf, often brightly coloured; one part of the *corolla* usually of a *dicotyledonous* flower. (Cf *Tepal*.)

Petiole. The *stalk* of a *leaf*.

pH. A measure of alkalinity or acidity, used horticulturally to refer to soils. The scale measures from 1 to 14; pH7 is neutral, above 7 is alkaline, and below 7 acid. (See also *Acid*, *Alkaline*, and *Neutral*.)

Photosynthesis. The production of organic compounds required for growth in plants by a complex process involving *chlorophyll*, light energy, carbon dioxide, and water.

Picotee. A term describing *petals* with a narrow margin of a contrasting colour.

Pinching out. The removal of the growing tip of a plant (by finger and thumb) to induce the production of *sideshoots* or the formation of flower buds. Also known as "stopping".

Pistil. See *Carpel*.

Pith (of stems). The soft plant tissue in the central part of a stem.

Pleaching. A technique whereby branches from a row of trees are woven together and trained to form a wall or canopy of foliage.

Plumule. See *Hypogeal*.

Plunge. To sink a pot up to its rim in a bed of ashes, peat, sand, or soil to protect the roots of the plant or plants in the pot from extremes of temperature.

Pod. An ill-defined term generally applied to any dry, *dehiscent fruit*; it is particularly used for peas and beans.

Pollarding. The regular pruning back of the main branches of a tree to the main stem or trunk, or to a short branch framework, usually to a height of about 2m (6ft). (Cf *Coppicing*.)

Pollen. The male cells of a plant, formed in the *anther*.

Pollination. The transfer of *pollen* from *anthers* to *stigmas*. (See also *Cross-pollination*, *Open-pollination*, and *Self-pollination*.)

Pollinator. 1) The agent or means by which *pollination* is carried out (e.g. insects, wind). 2) Used in fruit growing to describe a *cultivar* required to ensure fruit set on another self- or partially *self-sterile* cultivar.

Polyembryonic. Containing more than one embryo in an *ovule* or *seed*.

Pome fruit. A firm, fleshy *fruit* formed by the fusion of the *ovary* and the hypanthium (the fused base of *calyx* and *corolla*); for example an apple or pear.

Pompon. Usually small, almost globular *flowerheads* made up of numerous *florets*.

Potting compost (also potting mix or potting mix). A mixture of *loam*, *peat substitute* (or *peat*), sand, and *nutrients* in varying proportions. Soilless *composts* contain no loam and mainly comprise peat with nutrients added.

Potting on. Transferring a plant from one pot to a larger one.

Potting up. Transferring seedlings into individual pots of compost.

Pricking out. The transferring of young seedlings from where they have germinated in beds or containers to positions where they have room to grow on.

Propagation. The increase of plants by *seed* (usually sexual) or *vegetative* (asexual) means.

Propagator. A structure that provides a humid atmosphere for raising seedlings, rooting cuttings, or other plants being propagated.

Proximal end (of *cuttings*). The end that was originally nearest to the *crown* of the parent plant. (Cf *Distal end*.)

Pseudobulb. The thickened, *bulb*-like *stem* of a *sympodial* orchid arising from a (sometimes very short) *rhizome*.

Quartered rosette. A rosetted flower with the petals arranged in four, more or less equal, sections.

Raceme. An *indeterminate*, unbranched *inflorescence* with usually many stalked flowers borne on an elongated axis (stem).

Radicle. A young root.

Rain shadow. An area of ground next to a wall or fence that is sheltered from prevailing winds and therefore receives less rain than open ground.

Rambler. A trailing *climber*.

Ray flower (or floret). Small flower with a tubular *corolla*, as borne in the outermost ring of a *Compositae* flowerhead.

Recurved. Applied to petals of flowers and florets that curve backwards.

Reflexed. Applied to petals of flowers and florets that bend sharply backwards at an angle of more than 90°. They are sometimes called fully reflexed. Also loosely applied to any flower in which the petals or *perianth segments* are *recurved*.

Remontant. Of a plant that flowers more than once during the growing season (often applied to roses and strawberries). (Cf *Non-remontant*.)

Renewal pruning. A system in which the *laterals* are constantly cut back to be replaced by young laterals stimulated by pruning.

Respiration. The release of energy from complex *organic* molecules as a result of chemical changes.

Revert. To return to an original state, for example when a variegated plant produces a plain green leaf.

Rhizome. A specialized, usually horizontally creeping, swollen or slender, underground *stem* that acts as a storage organ and produces aerial shoots at its apex and along its length.

Rib. Radiating branch on a fan-trained tree.

Rind. The outer bark of a shrub or tree outside the *cambium* layer.

Ripewood cutting. See *Cutting*.

Root. The part of a plant, normally underground, that anchors it and through which water and *nutrients* are absorbed. (See also *Aerial root*.)

Root ball. The roots and accompanying soil or *compost* visible when a plant is removed from a container or lifted from the open ground.

Root cutting. See *Cutting*.

Root run. The area of soil into which a plant's roots may extend.

Rooting. The production of roots, usually from cuttings.

Rooting hormone. A chemical compound synthesized in powder or liquid form and used at low concentrations to encourage root production.

Rootstock. A plant used to provide the root system for a *grafted* plant.

Rose (of a watering can). A perforated nozzle that diffuses and regulates the flow of water.

Rosette. 1) A cluster of leaves radiating from approximately the same point, often borne at ground level at the base of a very short stem. 2) A more or less circular arrangement of petals.

Rotation. See *Crop rotation*.

Rounded. Regularly curved, as in a circle.

Runner. A horizontally spreading, usually slender, stem that runs above ground and roots at the *nodes* to form new plants. Often confused with *stolon*.

Saddle grafting. See *Grafting*.

Sap. The juice of a plant contained in the cells and vascular tissue.

Sapling. A young tree; a seedling or any young tree before the wood hardens.

Scandent. Ascending or loosely climbing. (See also *Climber*.)

Scarification. 1) Abrasion or chemical treatment of a seed coat in order to speed up water intake and induce *germination*. 2) Removing moss and thatch from a lawn using a scarifier or rake.

Scion. A *shoot* or *bud* cut from one plant to *graft* onto a *rootstock* (stock) of another.

Scrambling climber. See *Climber*.

Scree. A slope comprising rock fragments formed by the weathering of rock faces: simulated in gardens as

scree beds, in which high-altitude *alpines* that need excellent *drainage* may be grown.

Sedge peat. See *Peat*.

Seed. The ripened, fertilized *ovule* containing a dormant embryo capable of developing into an adult plant.

Seed dormancy. See *Dormancy*.

Seed leaf. See *Cotyledon*.

Seedhead. Any *fruit* that contains ripe seeds.

Seedling. A young plant that has developed from a seed.

Selection. A plant selected for particular characteristics and usually propagated to retain the same characteristics.

Self layering. See *Layering*.

Self-clinging climber. See *Climber*.

Self-fertile. Of a plant that produces viable *seed* when fertilized with its own *pollen*. (See also *Fertilization*, *Pollination*, *Self-pollination*, and *Self-sterile*.)

Self-incompatible. See *Self-sterile*.

Self-pollination. The transfer of *pollen* from the *anthers* to the *stigma* of the same *flower*, or alternatively to another flower on the same plant. (Cf *Cross-pollination*.)

Self-seed. To shed fertile seeds that produce *seedlings* around the parent plant.

Self-sterile. A plant unable to produce viable *seed* after self-fertilization, and requiring a different *pollinator* in order for fertilization to occur. Also known as "self-incompatible" – incapable of self-fertilization.

Semi-deciduous. See *Deciduous*.

Semi-determinate. Used of tall or *cordon* tomatoes that will only grow to 1–1.2m (3–4ft) long. (Cf *Determinate*; *Indeterminate*.)

Semi-double. See *Flower*.

Semi-evergreen. See *Evergreen*.

Semi-ripe cutting. See *Cutting*.

Sepal. The outer *whorl* of the *perianth* of a flower, usually small and green, but sometimes coloured and *petal*-like.

Serpentine layering. See *Layering*.

Set. 1) A small onion, shallot bulb, or potato *tuber*, selected for planting. 2) A term describing flowers that have been successfully fertilized and have produced small *fruits*.

Sexual reproduction. A form of reproduction involving *fertilization*, giving rise to *seed* or *spores*.

Sheet mulch. A *mulch* using an artificially produced material (e.g. plastic).

Shoot. A branch, stem, or twig.

Shrub. A woody-stemmed plant, usually branched from or near the base, lacking a single *trunk*.

Side grafting. See *Grafting*.

Sideshoot. A stem that arises from the side of a main *shoot*.

Side-wedge grafting. See *Grafting*.

Simple (mainly of leaves). Undivided. (Cf *Compound*.)

Simple layering. See *Layering*.

Single. See *Flower*.

Single cordon. See *Cordon*.

Single digging. A method of digging in which only the topsoil is turned over to a depth of one *spit*.

Snag. A short stub or frayed end left

after incorrect pruning.

Softwood cutting. See *Cutting.*

Soil mark. The usually noticeable point on a plant's stem that shows the original soil level before the plant was lifted.

Species. A category in plant classification, the lowest principal rank below *genus* containing closely related, very similar individuals.

Specimen plant. A striking plant, usually a tree or shrub in prime condition, grown where it can be seen clearly.

Spent (of flowers). Dying or dead.

Spike. A racemose (see *Raceme*) and hence *indeterminate inflorescence* that bears unstalked flowers along a common axis (stem).

Spikelet. A small spike, forming part of a compound *inflorescence*; often applied to grasses where the flower-head consists of several flowers with basal *bracts*.

Spit. The depth of a spade's blade, usually 25–30cm (10–12in).

Splice grafting. An alternative name for whip grafting, see *Grafting.*

Spliced side grafting. See *Grafting.*

Spliced side-veneer grafting. See *Grafting.*

Sporangium. A body that produces *spores* on a fern.

Spore. The minute, reproductive structure of flowerless plants, such as ferns, fungi, and mosses.

Sport. See *Mutation.*

Spray. A group of *flowers* or *flowerheads* on a single, branching stem, such as occurs on many chrysanthemums and carnations.

Spur. 1) A hollow projection from a petal, often producing *nectar*. 2) A short branch or branchlet bearing flower buds, as on fruit trees.

Stalk. A general term describing the stem of a leaf or flower (e.g. petiole, peduncle).

Stamen. The male reproductive organ in a plant, comprising the pollen-producing *anther* and usually its supporting *filament* or *stalk*.

Standard. 1) A tree with at least 2m (6ft) of stem below the first branches (see also *Half-standard*). 2) A shrub trained so that it has a clear length of stem below the branches (1–1.2m/3–4ft for roses). 3) One of the three inner and more erect *perianth segments* of the iris flower. 4) The largest, usually uppermost petal of a flower in the *subfamily* Papilionoideae (peas and beans) of the *family* Leguminosae.

Station sow. To sow seed individually or in small groups at fixed intervals along a row or *drill*.

Stem. The main axis of a plant, usually above ground and supporting leaves, flowers, and fruits.

Stem cutting. See *Cutting.*

Stem tip cutting. See *Cutting.*

Sterile. 1) Not producing flowers or viable seed. (Cf *Fertile*.) 2) Of flowers without functional *anthers* and pistils (see *Carpel*).

Stigma. The apical portion of a *carpel*, usually borne at the tip of a *style*, which receives *pollen* prior to *fertilization*.

Stock. See *Rootstock.*

Stock plant. A plant used to obtain propagating material, whether seed or

vegetative material.

Stolon. A horizontally spreading or arching stem, usually above ground, which roots at its tip to produce a new plant. Often confused with *runner*.

Stone fruits. Fruits, also known as "drupes", with one or more seeds ("stones") surrounded by fleshy, usually edible tissue. They are common in the genus *Prunus* (e.g. apricots, plums, cherries) and some other plants, such as mangos, that produce *indehiscent*, woody fruits.

Stool. A number of shoots arising, more or less uniformly, from the base of an individual plant, for example some shrubs cut back regularly to produce propagating material and also chrysanthemums.

Stooling. 1) See *Layering.* 2) The routine pruning back of woody plants by *coppicing.*

Stopping. See *Pinching out.*

Strain. A loose, undefined term sometimes applied to races of seed-raised plants; not a term accepted under the International Code for the Nomenclature of Cultivated Plants because of its imprecise definition.

Stratification. Storage of seed in warm or cold conditions to overcome *dormancy* and aid *germination.*

Stylar column. *Styles* fused together.

Style. The usually elongated part of a *carpel* between the *ovary* and *stigma*, not always present.

Subfamily. A category in plant classification, a division within the *family*.

Sub-lateral. A sideshoot originating from a *lateral* shoot or branch.

Subshrub. 1) A low-growing plant that is entirely *woody*. 2) A plant that is woody at the base but has soft, usually *herbaceous*, growth above.

Subsoil. The layers of soil beneath the *topsoil*; these are usually less fertile and of poorer texture and structure than the topsoil.

Subspecies. A subdivision of a *species*, higher in rank than varietas (see *Variety*) or *forma*.

Succulent (of plants). A plant with thick, fleshy leaves and/or stems adapted to store water. All cacti are succulents.

Sucker. 1) A shoot that arises below ground from a plant's roots or underground stem. 2) On *grafted* plants, a sucker is any shoot that arises below the *graft union*.

Sympodial. Definite growth of a *shoot* terminating in an *inflorescence* or dying; growth is continued by *lateral* buds. (Cf *Monopodial*.)

Systemic. Term describing a *pesticide* or *fungicide* that is absorbed and distributed through a plant when applied to the soil or foliage.

Tap root. The primary, downward-growing *root* of a plant (especially a tree); also applied loosely to any strong, downward-growing root.

Taxon (pl. **taxa**). A group of living organisms at any rank; applied to groups of plants or entities that share distinct, defined characters.

T-budding. See *Grafting.*

Tender. Of a plant that is vulnerable to frost damage.

Tendril. A modified leaf, branch, or stem, usually filiform (long and slender) and capable of attaching itself to a support. (See also *Climber*.)

Tepal. A single segment of a perianth that cannot be distinguished either as a sepal or petal, as in *Crocus* or *Lilium*. (See also *Perianth segment*.)

Terminal. At the tip of a stem or branch; usually refers to a bud or flower.

Terminal bud. See *Bud.*

Terrarium. An enclosed container made of glass or plastic in which plants are grown.

Terrestrial. Growing in the soil; a land plant. (Cf *Epiphyte* and *Aquatic*.)

Thatch. A layer of dead, *organic* matter intermingled with living stems that accumulates on the soil surface in lawns.

Thin (of soil). Used loosely of poor soil, prone to *capping* and drought.

Thinning. The removal of seedlings, shoots, flowers, or fruit buds to improve the growth and quality of the remainder.

Tilth. A fine, crumbly, surface layer of soil produced by cultivation.

Tip layering. See *Layering.*

Tip prune. To cut back the growing tip of a shoot to encourage sideshoots or to remove damaged growth.

Tissue culture (of plants). The growing of plant tissue under sterile conditions in artificial media.

Top-dressing. 1) An application of soluble fertilizers, fresh soil, or *compost* to the soil surface around a plant or to lawns to replenish nutrients. 2) A decorative dressing applied to the soil surface around a plant.

Topiary. The art of clipping and training trees and shrubs into various, usually intricate, geometric or free shapes.

Topsoil. The uppermost, normally fertile, layer of soil.

Trace element. See *Micronutrients.*

Trailing climber. See *Climber.*

Translocated (of dissolved nutrients or weedkillers). Moving within the vascular system (conducting tissues) of a plant.

Transpiration. The loss of water by evaporation from the leaves and stems of plants.

Transplanting. Moving a plant from one position to another.

Tree. A *woody*, perennial plant usually with a well-defined *trunk* or stem with a *head* or *crown* of branches above.

Trench digging. See *Double digging.*

Trench layering. See *Layering.*

True (True-breeding). Of plants that when self-pollinated (see *Self-pollination*) give rise to offspring similar to their parents.

Trunk. The thickened, woody, main stem of a tree.

Truss. A compact cluster of flowers or fruits.

Tuber. A swollen, usually underground, organ derived from a stem or root, used for food storage.

Tufa. Porous limestone rock that absorbs and retains moisture; used for cultivating alpine plants difficult to grow in garden soil.

Tunic. The fibrous membranes or papery outer skin of *bulbs* or *corms*.

Tunicate. Enclosed in a *tunic*.

Turion. 1) A detached, overwintering, usually fleshy, *bud* produced by certain water plants. 2) A term sometimes applied to an *adventitious* shoot or *sucker.*

Twining climber. See *Climber.*

"U" cordon. A double *cordon*.

Underplanting. Low-growing plants planted beneath larger plants.

Union. See *Graft union.*

Upright. Term describing the habit of a plant with vertical or semi-vertical, main branches. (Cf *Fastigiate*.)

Urn-shaped (of flowers). Globose to cylindrical in shape with a somewhat constricted mouth; "U"-shaped.

Variable. Varying in character from the type; particularly of seed-raised plants that vary in character from the parent.

Variegated. Marked with various colours in an irregular pattern; particularly used for leaves patterned with white and yellow markings but not confined to these colours.

Variety. 1) Botanically, a naturally occurring variant (varietas - var.) of a wild *species*, between the rank of *subspecies* and *forma*. 2) Also commonly but imprecisely used to describe any variant of a plant. (Cf *Cultivar*.)

Vegetative growth. Non-flowering, usually leafy growth.

Vegetative propagation. The increase of plants by asexual methods normally resulting in genetically identical individuals.

Vermiculite. A lightweight, mica-like mineral allowing good water retention and aeration when used in cutting compost and other potting media.

Water shoots. Applied usually to *epicormic shoots* that frequently arise close to pruning wounds on tree trunks or branches.

Whip. A young seedling or grafted tree without *lateral* branches.

Whip grafting. See *Grafting.*

Whip-and-tongue grafting. See *Grafting.*

Whorl. The arrangement of three or more organs arising from the same point.

Widger. A spatula-shaped tool used for transplanting or *pricking out* seedlings.

Windbreak. Any structure but often a hedge, fence, or wall that shelters plants and filters strong winds.

Wind-rock. The destabilizing of a plant's roots by strong wind.

Winter wet. Excessive amounts of water that accumulate in the soil during the winter months.

Woody. Ligneous, a term describing stems or trunks that are hard and thickened rather than soft and pliable. (Cf *Herbaceous*.)

Wound. A cut or broken area in a plant.

Wound paint. A specialized paint that used to be applied to a cut surface of a plant after pruning.

INDEX

O

U

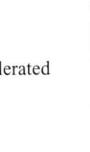

ACKNOWLEDGEMENTS

Photography credits

The position on the page is given from top to bottom and across the page from left to right. The photographs in plant portrait boxes are numbered sequentially from left to right across the rows and from the top row to the bottom row. Where the picture is in a step-by-step sequence it is given the number of its caption.

ADAS Crown ©: 621 bottom 1–6, 660 centre left
Ted Andrews: 214 centre left
Heather Angel: 641 bottom left
Jane Aspden: 92 bottom, 338, 339 top left
A–Z Collection: 484 centre left, 488 centre left
Harry Baker: 420 bottom, 488 bottom left and right
B & B Photographs: 652 bottom centre above, 660 bottom right, 662 bottom left
Gillian Beckett: 232 portrait box 1 and 8
Birmingham Botanical Gardens: 482 left
Boys Syndication: 125 top left, 497 bottom left
Christopher Brickell: 77 top right, 269 top sequence 4
W. Atlee Burpee & Co.: 532 bottom right
Prof. Chin: 522 bottom right, 523 top left, 530 centre left, bottom right, and inset, 479 centre right, inset, and bottom left, 486 bottom, 487 top left, centre, and bottom left
Trevor Cole: 261 top
Eric Crichton:, 85 top, 93 bottom left and right, 126 bottom right, 151 bottom right, 152 top and bottom right, 172, 173 top right, 175 top left, 194 bottom left, 210 bottom, 226, 227 box 3, 228 bottom left, 232 top left and right, 233 top left and right, 234 portrait box 2, 254, 258 top, 387 top right, 388 bottom, 389 top and bottom, 404, 497 top, 498, 598 top right
Geoff Dann: 258 bottom
Jack Elliott: 229 bottom left, 255 top
Raymond Evison: 127 top, 138 portrait box 7, 139 bottom left
Forestry Commission: 653 bottom left, 655 centre right
John Galbally: 196 centre centre, 197 top centre, 197 top right. 197 bottom left above and bottom far right
Garden Picture Library: 152 bottom left, 210 top right, 211 top, 226 box 4, 257 top, 283 top right and bottom, 340 bottom left, 359 top right; Linda Burgess 146; Christopher Fairweather 206; John Ferro Sims 27 bottom right; Nigel Francis 24 bottom left; John Glover 35 bottom left, 47 bottom left, 175 bottom, 208; Georgia Glynn-Smith 46 right, 615 top centre; Gil Hanly 34 bottom left; Sunniva Harte 16 top; Carole Hellman 209 bottom; Michael Howes 17 top; Lamontagne 173 bottom; Zara McCallmont 35 bottom right; Clive Nichols 42 bottom left; Lorraine Pullin 23 centre left; Howard Rice 20 bottom left, 28 bottom left, 47 bottom right, 180 top right; J.S. Sira 256, 336, 46l; Ron Sutherland 28 bottom right; Brigitte Thomas 23 centre, 34 top; Juliette Wade 21 bottom centre; Mel Watson 615 top right; Steve Wooster 43 top right
Will Giles: 60 bottom left, 61 top left, 61 top right, 61 bottom centre, 356 top right, 357 bottom right
John Glover: 94 bottom left, 282, 566, 567 top

Jerry Harpur: 21 top right, 25 top left, 26 top, 34 bottom left, 55 top left, 58 top and bottom left, 124, 126 top, 151 bottom left, 178 top, 182 bottom, 196 centre right, 256 bottom, 280, 307 top, 309 bottom, 312 bottom left and bottom right, 313 top right and bottom, 354, 386, 401 top right, 420 top, 422 bottom, 423 bottom, 492, 493 top, 593 top; Jon Calderwood 22 bottom right; Beth Chatto 178 bottom; Sir Terence Conran 356 top centre; Simon Fraser 28 top; Marcus Harper Gorse Hill Abbey Farm 47 top right, 122; Helmingham Hall 15 bottom left; Arabella Lennox 26 bottom left; HMP Leyhill/The Garden of Eden 490; Valerie Murray 92 top; Old Rectory, Billingford 48 left; Piet Oudolf 47 centre left, 174; Park Farm 177 top; Pettifers, Oxon 172; Roford Manor, Oxford 17 bottom; Diana Ross 23 centre right; Xa Tollemache 25 bottom left; Terry Welch 27 top left; Gordon White 176 top; Wollerton Hall, Shropshire 25 top right
Holt Studios International: 648 bottom right, 650 centre, centre left, centre right above, centre right below, and bottom right, 656 bottom right, 658 top left, 662 bottom centre, 664 top centre and bottom centre, 665 top right, 666 centre left above, 667 bottom centre right and bottom left, 671 bottom left, 672 top centre left
Horticulture Research International, Kirton: 250 top sequence 3, 650 bottom centre, 654 right, 661 bottom left
ICI Agrochemicals: 649 top right
Clive Innes: 340 top
Andrew Lawson: 15 top, 16 top, 21 top left, centre left, bottom right, and centre centre, 22 bottom left, 23 bottom, 24 top, 29 bottom, 41 top centre, 47 top left, 49 centre, bottom left, bottom centre, and right, 50 top left, 51 top left, top right, bottom left, and bottom right, 55 top right, 77 top left and top right, 125 bottom, 151 top, 153 top left and bottom, 174 top left, 210 top left, 226 bottom, 229 top left and bottom right, 284 bottom right, 306, 307 bottom, 308 bottom and top, 310 top left, 311 bottom, 312 top, 314, 315 top, 316 top, 352, 360 top, 402, 415, 493 bottom; Bosvigo House, Cornwall 40 top; Cothay Manor, Somerset 47 bottom right; Ann and Charles Fraser 18; The Garden House, Devon 20 bottom right; Lady Farm, Somerset 49 bottom right; Dan Pearson 26 bottom right; Pettifers, Oxon 14; The Priory, Kemerton 49 top centre; G. Robb/Hampton Court Show 1999 27 top left; Roford Manor, Oxford 16 bottom; Whichford Pottery 304; Wollerton Hall, Shropshire 49 top left
Elvin McDonald: 340 bottom right, 458 bottom, 531 centre left and inset, 538 centre right
MAFF Crown ©: 657 centre, 664 centre
Ray Main/Mainstream: Jacket main pic
Marston & Langinger Ltd: 356 bottom centre and bottom left, 357 top right; Halpern Associates 357

Silvia Martin: 591 bottom
John Mattock: Mr and Mrs J.S. Mattock 166 centre right
Tania Midgley: 421 top
Graeme Moore: 387 top left
J. Nicholas: 638 bottom
Clive Nichols: 50 bottom, 88; Architectural Plants, Sussex 29 top right; Jill Billington 19 top right; Eastgrove Cottage 170; Lady Farm, Somerset 177 bottom; Mr and Mrs D. Terry 23 top, 36
Oxford Scientific Films: 126 bottom left, 665 bottom left, 668 left
Park Seeds: 532 bottom left and right
Photos Horticultural: 423 top, 660 top left, 665 top centre and centre right
Michael Pollock: RHS Wisley 614 top left
Royal Botanic Gardens, Kew: 483 centre
Royal Horticultural Society, Wisley: 496 bottom, 645 top right, 649 bottom left and right, 652 bottom and centre, 653 top right and bottom centre, 654 centre and centre left below, 655 bottom left, 656 centre and bottom centre, 659 top right, centre left above, centre right, and bottom right, 661 top right, 662 top left and centre right above, 663 centre, centre right, and bottom right, 666 top left, top right, centre left bottom, bottom centre, and bottom right
Harry Smith Horticultural Photographic Collection: 58 bottom right, 85 bottom right, 209 top left, 341, 360 bottom, 480 top, 483 top left, 484 centre right, 489 centre, 523 centre left, 667 centre left
Sports Turf Research Institute: 667 centre right above
Lauren Springer: 55 portrait box 1
Prof. H.D. Tindall: 467 bottom, 480 bottom, 481 top, 483 top right and bottom, 486 top left and right, 515 centre left and bottom right, 543 bottom, 545 centre
Elizabeth Whiting Associates: 54, 57 bottom, 91 top, 255 bottom, 283 top left, 290 top, 406 bottom left
Steve Wooster: 90, 128 bottom left, 148, 175 top right, 194 top, 584, 593 bottom left, 595 bottom left, 606
Tom Wright: 127 bottom, 211 bottom

Additional photography by:
Jane Burton, Peter Chadwick, Eric Crichton, Geoff Dann, John Glover, Jerry Harpur, Neil Holmes, Jacqui Hurst, Dave King, Andrew McRobb, Andrew Lawson, Andrew de Lory, Tim Ridley, Karl Shone, and Gerry Young

Dorling Kindersley would like to thank the following for:

Specialist advice
Mr Ted Andrews (sweet peas); Peter and Fiona Bainbridge (landscape design and construction); Harry Baker (fruit); Graham Davis (Water Regulations Advisory Scheme); Dr Bob Ellis (vegetable cultivar lists); Dennis Gobbee (rose hybridizing); Patrick Goldsworthy, British Agrochemical Association (chemical controls); Ken Grapes, Royal National Rose Society; Tony Hender (Seedlings); Peter Orme (rock garden design and construction); Terence and Judy Read (grape cultivar lists); Prof. S. Sansavini (fruit cultivar lists); Pham van Tha (fruit cultivar lists); and in particular the many staff at the RHS Garden, Wisley, who so patiently and freely gave of their time to advise on horticultural techniques throughout this project.

Providing plants or locations for photographs
Mrs Joy Bishop; Brickwall House School, Northiam; Brinkman Brothers Ltd, Walton Farm Nurseries, Bosham; Denbies Wine Estate, Dorking; Mrs Donnithorne; Martin Double; J.W. Elliott & Sons (West End) Limited, Fenns Lane Nursery, Woking; Elsoms Seeds Ltd, Spalding; Mrs Randi Evans; Adrian Hall Ltd, Putney Garden Centre, London; Mr & Mrs R.D. Hendriksen, Hill Park Nurseries, Surbiton; The Herb and Heather Centre, West Haddlesey; Hilliers Nurseries (Winchester) Ltd, Romsey; Holly Gate International Ltd, Ashington; John Humphries, Sutton Place Foundation, Guildford; Iden Croft Herbs, Staplehurst; Mr de Jager; Nicolette John; David Knuckey, Burncoose Nursery; Mr & Mrs John Land; Sarah Martin; Frank P. Matthews Ltd, Tenbury Wells; Mr & Mrs Mead; Anthony Noel, Fulham Park Gardens, London; Andrew Norfield; Notcutts Garden Centre, Bagshot; Bridget Quest-Ritson; Royal Botanic Gardens, Kew; Royal Horticultural Society Enterprises; Lynn and Danny Reynolds, Surrey Water Gardens, West Clandon; Rolawn, Elvington; Mrs Rudd; Miss Skilton; Carole Starr; Mr & Mrs Wagstaff; Mrs Wye.

Tools for demonstration photographs
Spear and Jackson Products Ltd, Wednesbury, West Midlands; Felco secateurs supplied by Burton McCall Group, Leicester.

Supplying equipment
Agralan, Ashton Keynes; Bob Andrews Ltd, Bracknell; Black and Decker Europe, Slough; Blagdon Water Garden Products PLC, Highbridge; Bloomingdales Garden Centre, Laleham; Bulldog Tools Ltd, Wigan; Butterley Brick Ltd, London; CEKA Works Ltd, Pwllheli; Challenge Fencing, Cobham; J. B. Corrie & Co Ltd, Petersfield; Dalfords (London) Ltd, Staines; Diplex Ltd, Watford; Direct Wire Ties Ltd, Hull; Robert Dyas (Ltd), Guildford; Fishtique, Sunbury-on-Thames; Fluid Drilling Ltd, Stratford-upon-Avon; Gardena UK Ltd, Letchworth Garden City; Gloucesters Wholesales Ltd, Woking; Harcros, Walton-on-Thames; Haws Elliott Ltd, Warley; Honda UK Ltd, London; Hozelock Ltd, Birmingham; ICI Garden Products, Haslemere; LBS Polythene, Colne; Merck Ltd, Poole; Neal Street East, London; Parkers, Worcester Park; Pinks Hill Landscape Merchants Ltd, Guildford; Qualcast Garden Products, Stowmarket; Rapitest, Corwen; Seymours, Ewell; Shoosmith & Lee Ltd, Cobham; SISIS Equipment Ltd, Macclesfield; Thermoforce Ltd, Maldon.

Additional assistance
Sarah Ashun, Jennifer Bagg, Kathryn Bradley-Hole, Lynn Bresler, Diana Brinton, Kim Bryan, Susan Conder, Jeannette Cossar, Diana Craig, Penny David, Paul Docherty, Howard Farrell, Roseanne Hooper, David Joyce, Steve Knowlden, Mary Lambert, Claire Lebas, Margaret Little, Louise McConnell, Caroline Macy, Eunice Martins, Ruth Midgley, Peter Moloney, Sarah Moule, Fergus Muir, Chez Picthall, Sandra Schneider, Janet Smy, Mary Staples, Tina Tiffin, Roger Tritton, Anne de Verteuil, John Walker.

Abbreviations

C	centigrade	ml	millilitre(s)
cf	compare	mm	millimetre(s)
cm	centimetre(s)	oz	ounce(s)
cv(s)	cultivar(s)	p(p).	page(s)
F	fahrenheit	pl.	plural
f.	forma	pvar.	pathovar
fl oz	fluid ounce(s)	sp.	species
ft	foot, feet	spp.	species (pl.)
g	gram(s)	sq	square
in	inch(es)	subsp.	subspecies
kg	kilogram(s)	syn.	synonym(s)
lb	pound(s)	var.	varietas
m	metre(s)	yd	yard(s)

Note: The generic and species names of plants are abbreviated to their initial letters after their first full mention in a sentence or a list.